Frommer's

W9-ARQ-392

England
from $75 a Day

25th Edition

by Darwin Porter, Danforth Prince
& Donald Olson

Here's what the critics say about Frommer's:

"Amazingly easy to use. Very portable, very complete."
—*Booklist*

"Detailed, accurate, and easy-to-read information for all price ranges."
—*Glamour Magazine*

"Hotel information is close to encyclopedic."
—*Des Moines Sunday Register*

"Frommer's Guides have a way of giving you a real feel for a place."
—*Knight Ridder Newspapers*

WILEY
Wiley Publishing, Inc.

Wiley Publishing, Inc.

111 River St.
Hoboken, NJ 07030-5744

ISBN 0-7645-4108-0

Editor: Christine Ryan
Production Editor: Heather Wilcox
Cartographer: Elizabeth Puhl
Photo Editor: Richard Fox
Production by Wiley Indianapolis Composition Services

Front cover photo: Culpepper Garden, Grounds of Leeds Castle, Kent.

For information on our other products and services or to obtain technical support, please contact our Customer Care Department within the U.S. at 800/762-2974, outside the U.S. at 317/72-3993 or fax 317/572-4002.

Wiley also publishes its books in a variety of electronic formats. Some content that appears in print may not be available in electronic formats.

Manufactured in the United States of America

5 4 3 2 1

Contents

List of Maps

About the Authors

Veteran travel writers **Darwin Porter** and **Danforth Prince** have written numerous best-selling Frommer's guides, notably to Germany, France, Italy, England, and Spain. Porter, who was bureau chief for the *Miami Herald* when he was 21, wrote the first Frommer's guide to Germany and has traveled extensively in the country. Prince, who began writing with Porter in 1982, worked for the Paris bureau of the *New York Times*.

Donald Olson (London chapters) is a novelist, playwright, and travel writer. His sixth novel, *My Three Husbands* (written under the nom de plume Swan Adamson), was published in 2003. *Oregon Ghosts*, his play based on Oregon's legendary spirits, premiered in Portland in 2003. His plays have also been produced in London, New York, Amsterdam, and Rotterdam. Donald Olson's travel stories have appeared in the *New York Times, Travel & Leisure, Sunset, National Geographic* guides, and many other national publications. He is the author of *Frommer's London from $90 a Day, London For Dummies, Germany For Dummies,* and *England For Dummies,* which won the 2002 Lowell Thomas Travel Writing Award for "Best Guidebook."

An Invitation to the Reader

In researching this book, we discovered many wonderful places—hotels, restaurants, shops, and more. We're sure you'll find others. Please tell us about them, so we can share the information with your fellow travelers in upcoming editions. If you were disappointed with a recommendation, we'd love to know that, too. Please write to:

Frommer's England from $75 a Day, 25th Edition
Wiley Publishing, Inc. • 111 River St. • Hoboken, NJ 07030-5744

An Additional Note

Please be advised that travel information is subject to change at any time—and this is especially true of prices. We therefore suggest that you write or call ahead for confirmation when making your travel plans. The authors, editors, and publisher cannot be held responsible for the experiences of readers while traveling. Your safety is important to us, however, so we encourage you to stay alert and be aware of your surroundings. Keep a close eye on cameras, purses, and wallets, all favorite targets of thieves and pickpockets.

Other Great Guides for Your Trip:

Frommer's London from $90 a Day
Frommer's Portable London from $90 a Day
Frommer's England
Frommer's Great Britain
England For Dummies

Frommer's Star Ratings, Icons & Abbreviations

Every hotel, restaurant, and attraction listing in this guide has been ranked for quality, value, service, amenities, and special features using a **star-rating system.** In country, state, and regional guides, we also rate towns and regions to help you narrow down your choices and budget your time accordingly. Hotels and restaurants are rated on a scale of zero (recommended) to three stars (exceptional). Attractions, shopping, nightlife, towns, and regions are rated according to the following scale: zero stars (recommended), one star (highly recommended), two stars (very highly recommended), and three stars (must-see).

In addition to the star-rating system, we also use **seven feature icons** that point you to the great deals, in-the-know advice, and unique experiences that separate travelers from tourists. Throughout the book, look for:

Finds	Special finds—those places only insiders know about
Fun Fact	Fun facts—details that make travelers more informed and their trips more fun
Kids	Best bets for kids and advice for the whole family
Moments	Special moments—those experiences that memories are made of
Overrated	Places or experiences not worth your time or money
Tips	Insider tips—great ways to save time and money
Value	Great values—where to get the best deals

The following **abbreviations** are used for credit cards:

AE	American Express	DISC	Discover	V	Visa
DC	Diners Club	MC	MasterCard		

Frommers.com

Now that you have the guidebook to a great trip, visit our website at **www.frommers.com** for travel information on more than 3,000 destinations. With features updated regularly, we give you instant access to the most current trip-planning information available. At Frommers.com, you'll also find the best prices on airfares, accommodations, and car rentals—and you can even book travel online through our travel booking partners. At Frommers.com, you'll also find the following:

- Online updates to our most popular guidebooks
- Vacation sweepstakes and contest giveaways
- Newsletter highlighting the hottest travel trends
- Online travel message boards with featured travel discussions

What's New in England

There will always be an England, or so the saying goes, and that may be true, but it won't always be the same country. The landscape is constantly shifting and being redefined at all times. Here are some of the latest developments.

PLANNING YOUR TRIP One new development that you might want to take note of is that the U.K.'s national tourism agency has changed its name from the stern and rather forbidding British Tourist Authority to the snazzier and more forthright **VisitBritain (www.visitbritain.com).** Not only that, it's closed its walk-in offices in Chicago and Canada, so in North America everything now gets filtered through the New York office (see "Visitor Information" in chapter 2 for contact information). You can still get all kinds of useful information from them, and the website is far more user-friendly.

LONDON Getting Around Mayor Ken has set up a new **Riverside RV1 bus service** that travels between Waterloo Bridge and Tower Bridge and stops at all the new attractions on the South Bank. It's the same fare as all London buses (£1/$1.60), or you can use your Visitor Travelcard. For more information, call London travel information at © **020/7222-1234** or surf over to **www.transportforlondon.gov.uk.**

Thanks to the mayor, all bus and Underground travel cards get you a third off the price of Thames boat trips. That will include the river hoppa between the two Tate galleries once the arty new Millbank pier is completed, hopefully by the time you read this. See chapter 3 for more information on navigating London.

Where to Stay In hopes of filling empty bedrooms, hotels and B&Bs held their prices steady between 2002 and 2003. Some even *lowered* their rates. Almost every London hotel we visited while researching this edition of *England from $75 a Day* was willing to negotiate prices. And nearly every hotel manager urged us to tell readers to check the hotel's website for special promotions.

One of the nicest surprises for budget travelers who want to stay in the Victoria and Westminster area is the complete makeover of the **Luna & Simone Hotel** (p. 100), 47–49 Belgrave Rd., SW1 (© **020/7834-5987;** www.lunasimonehotel.com). It now has a smooth contemporary look that makes it a real standout in an area of mostly frumpy or dumpy B&Bs.

There's now a **Comfort Inn** (p. 95) at 6–14 Pembridge Gardens, W2 (© **020/7229-6666**), in Notting Hill Gate. Happily for budget travelers, this well-placed place offers much better rates if you deal directly with them rather than central reservations. See chapter 3 for more places to lay your head without straining your wallet.

Exploring London All of London's national museums—world-class institutions like the British Museum, the Victoria & Albert, the Natural History Museum, the Science Museum, the Museum of London, the Tate Modern, and the Tate Britain—are now free. Some of these places used to charge £8 ($13) admission.

Contemporary art watchers no longer have to trek miles to see the often creepy and self-publicizing works championed by art dealer Charles Saatchi. The **Saatchi Gallery** (p. 154) moved to County Hall, Southbank, SE1 (© **020/7823-2363**), of all places, in April 2003. There, in the former offices of the London City Council right next to the London Eye observation wheel, you can now see the works that created such a sensation at the "Sensation" show (you might have heard about it when it came to the Brooklyn Museum).

Architecturally, in addition to historic stars like the Tower of London, Westminster Abbey, and Buckingham Palace, London has a host of new glamour-puss buildings and structures, including Norman Foster's (everyone's current darling) environmentally "green" **City Hall,** his "glass gherkin" skyscraper in the City, and his sleek **Millennium Bridge** linking St. Paul's to the Tate Modern. Graceful new pedestrian walkways on **Hungerford Bridge** make walking from Embankment to the South Bank a real pleasure, day or night. And though it's now over 3 years old, let's not forget the **British Airways London Eye** (p. 131), Jubilee Gardens, Southbank SE1 (© **0870/500-0600**). This giant observation wheel, which offers stunning views over London, has been so popular that the London Council is thinking of keeping it revolving after its original 5-year lifespan is up.

Americans will be interested to hear that the house where **Benjamin Franklin** lived between 1757 and 1775 is due to open to the public in early 2004 after a lengthy and ongoing restoration. To find out more, call (© **020/7930-9121**). See chapter 4 for details on all of London's museums and attractions.

THE THAMES VALLEY At Windsor, site of the castle that is the favorite home of Queen Elizabeth II, the **Jubilee Garden** (p. 190) is drawing thousands of visitors. These new 2-acre gardens inside the castle's main entrance were created to honor the Queen's Jubilee. On another front, her Majesty is selling her homemade jams and even her specially brewed beer at the **Windsor Farm Shop** (p. 191), Datchet Road, Old Windsor (© **01753/62300**). The queen also sells pheasants and partridges bagged in royal shoots.

KENT, SURREY & SUSSEX In Brighton, called "London by the Sea," the **Brighton Museum & Art Gallery,** Royal Pavilion Gardens (© **01273/290900**), has opened across from the Royal Pavilion. Immediately, this has become one of the great cultural attractions of southeast England, with an eclectic collection of world art and artifacts. See p. 265.

WILTSHIRE & SOMERSET A great new way to explore ancient Stonehenge, one of the great attractions of the West Country, is to rent a bike from **Hayball's Cycle Shop** (p. 316) and set out. It's also a great way to see the countryside as you bike through the mysterious Salisbury Plain.

Bath is bursting forth with more attractions, including the **Holburne Museum of Art** (p. 326), Great Pulteney Street (© **01225/466669**), which has been hailed as "one of the most perfect small museums of Europe." It was created to display a collector's treasure trove, including masterpieces by Gainsborough.

Operated by the National Trust, **The Museum of Costume and Assembly Rooms** (p. 326), Bennett Street (© **01225/47785**), includes not only a grand ballroom but also one of the best museums devoted to fashion and costume in Europe. In addition, the **Victoria Art Gallery** (p. 328), Bridge Street (© **01225/ 477233**), is being hailed as one of the country's best collections of British and European art from the 15th century to the present.

Generating the most excitement among the attractions of Bath, the **Thermae Bath Spa** (p. 327), The Hetling Pump Room, Hot Bath St. (© **01225/780308**), is the only place in the U.K. where you can bathe in natural spring water. Health, leisure, architecture, history, and culture are combined at this new spa with its bubbling, mineral-rich waters.

In the neighboring city of Bristol, **At-Bristol** (p. 336), Anchor Road, Harbourside (© **0117/909-2002**), is turning into another formidable West Country attraction. Hailed as an "awesome extravaganza," it combines science and technology in a way that's both accessible and fun. The attraction also features a giant screen IMAX theatre.

DEVON   In the resort of Lynmouth, **Shelley's Hotel** (© **01598/53219**) has been established. It was the former "Mrs. Hooper's Lodgings," where the romantic poet, Shelley, brought his child bride, Harriet Westbrook, in 1812. See p. 378.

CORNWALL   Britain's largest garden restoration project, the **Lost Gardens of Heligan** (© **01726/845100**), lies on 80 acres of land near the fishing village of Mevagissey on the rugged Cornish coast, southwest of St. Austell. These gardens virtually "slept" for 7 decades before they were rediscovered and restored. Once they had been part of the 1,000-acre estate of the Tremayne family, in residence here since the 16th century. See p. 384.

STRATFORD-UPON-AVON   Harvard House, High Street (© **01789/ 204507**), was the home of Katherine Rogers, mother of John Harvard, founder of Harvard University. Today the house has been turned into a Museum of British Pewter, tracing the use of pewter from the Roman era until modern times. See p. 443.

YORKSHIRE   There's been a change in the sleepy little market town of Thirsk made famous by former resident James Herriot, author of *All Creatures Great and Small*. Waiting to receive guests is **Oswalds Restaurant with Rooms,** Front Street, Sowerby (© **01845/523655**). This was the site where Herriot treated his last horse. Today you can sleep comfortably on the restored site or enjoy some of the finest dining in the area. See p. 642.

The Best of England from $75 a Day

With this guide, you can see the best of England—even the best of pricey London—without spending a fortune. We'll show you how to save money on lodgings, food, transportation, sightseeing, after-dark diversions, and the like.

Because we steer clear of tourist traps and expensive diversions, you'll come closer to experiencing the real England and enjoy a truer slice of life. There's great joy in discovering a bargain while you meet people and learn a lot while traveling. With that in mind, we've scoured the country in search of the best places and experiences, and in this chapter we'll share our very personal and opinionated choices. We hope they'll give you some ideas and get you started.

1 The Best Destinations for Low-Cost Vacations

- **The Dorset Coast:** In summer, many vacationers flock to high-priced Devon and Cornwall; hoteliers often double their prices. The Dorset coast, stamping ground of Thomas Hardy and Jane Austen, is an equally enchanting, much less expensive, alternative. The coast is riddled with coves and inlets; rural inland areas brim with scenic villages. See chapter 7.

- **Dartmoor National Park:** In the spirit of *Hound of the Baskervilles,* be prepared for a haunting but thrilling tour of this great park southwest of London. You could explore from Exeter and Plymouth, but it's more fun to stay at an area youth hostel or campground. The best villages from which to visit these eerie moors are Princeton, Okehampton, or Postbridge. Public transportation is severely limited, so rent a bike and head off for adventure. See chapter 9.

- **East Anglia:** There's a lot more here than just Cambridge. After you've toured the colleges, explore the cathedral town of Ely or the little market towns of Thaxted and Saffron Walden. Stay at B&Bs and eat in pubs. See chapter 13.

- **Central England:** Stratford-upon-Avon is the main draw, but you should also explore lesser-known Midlands towns such as Hereford, Worcester, and Shrewsbury. Each is filled with B&Bs and affordable restaurants, and you'll get a lot closer to the true heart of England than at the more tourist-trodden joints. See chapter 12.

- **Northeast England:** Everybody seemingly heads for the south coast of Devon and Cornwall. Equally alluring is a trek through some of the highlands of Northeastern England, including Haworth, home of the Brontë sisters, as well as the Yorkshire Dales National Park and the North York Moors National Park. Throughout this area are a lot of affordable and

England

comfortable B&Bs, and plenty of local pubs and small dining rooms

where the eating is good and moderate in price. See chapter 17.

2 The Best Things to See & Do for Free (or Almost)

For details on England's money-saving sightseeing passes, see chapter 2, "Planning an Affordable Trip to England."

- **Seeing the Art Treasures of England:** The British Museum and the Tate Britain in London offer some of the greatest treasures the world has known, from Old Masters to the Rosetta stone. Admission is free thanks to government subsidies. See p. 134 for the British Museum, p. 141 for the Tate Britain.

- **Touring England's Cathedrals:** Many people go to England just to tour the cathedral circuit. Nearly all are free; some request a donation. Begin, of course, at London's Westminster Abbey (p. 145). From the capital, head in virtually any direction in your cathedral search—we suggest Winchester (p. 278), Salisbury (p. 316), Canterbury (p. 228), Lincoln (p. 552), Ely (p. 503), and Liverpool (p. 576).

- **Pub-crawling:** A pub-crawl is one of the most hallowed of British social and cultural traditions. Ornate taps fill tankards and mugs in pubs found in every village, hamlet, and town. Quaint signs bearing such names as the EAGLE ARMS, the RED LION, the WHITE SWAN, the BULL, and the ROYAL OAK dot the landscape. Go not only for drink but also for conviviality and, at times, for entertainment or food. Log fires roar in winter; in summer, drinkers stand outside in the bracing air. See "The Best Pubs" category later in this chapter for our favorites.

- **Visiting Stonehenge:** One of the world's most celebrated prehistoric monuments, Stonehenge, near Salisbury in Wiltshire, is some 5,000 years old. Its construction and original purpose remain a mystery. Pay a small admission fee or see it from Amesbury Hill, 2.4km (1½ miles) up the road on the A303. See p. 321.

- **Biking Through the Cotswolds:** There's no better place to cycle than the Cotswolds, less than 160km (100 miles) west of London. Its green rolling hills and rain-nurtured pasturelands are peppered with ivy-covered inns, stone walls, and honey-colored stone cottages. Village names evoke an England of long ago—Bourton-on-the-Water, Upper Slaughter, Chipping Campden, Moreton-in-Marsh, Cirencester, or Wotton-under-Edge. See chapter 11.

- **Punting on the Cam:** Gliding along in a flat-bottom boat (or "punt"), pushing a long pole into the River Cam's shallow bed, you bypass the weeping willows along the banks, watch students stroll along the graveled walkways, and take in the picture-postcard vistas. Go on a summer's day; pack a lunch and picnic on the riverbank. You can share the reasonable cost with a few fellow passengers. See "Punting on the Cam," p. 495.

- **Walking the Yorkshire Moors:** A trekker's delight, these purple-heathered moors of *Wuthering Heights* fame cover more than 1,424 sq. km (550 sq. miles) and encompass some 2,140km (1,130 miles) of public footpaths. To the east, you'll find a cliff-studded coastline; inland, only the odd sheep, dramatic scenery, and mist will keep you company. See chapter 17.

3 The Best Museums

- **The British Museum** (London; ℂ 020/7323-8299): When Sir Hans Sloane died in 1753, he bequeathed to England his vast collection of art and antiquities. This formed the nucleus of a huge collection that came to include such remarkable objects as the Rosetta stone and the Parthenon sculptures (which Greece wants back). See p. 134.
- The **National Gallery** (London; ℂ 020/7747-2885): One of the world's greatest collections of Western art—from Leonardo da Vinci to Rembrandt to Picasso—dazzles the eye at this museum. The gallery is especially rich in Renaissance works. See p. 138.
- **Tate Britain** (London; ℂ 020/7887-8000): Sir Henry Tate, a sugar producer, started it all with 70 or so paintings. The collection grew considerably when artist J. M. W. Turner bequeathed some 300 paintings and 19,000 watercolors to England upon his death. Having handed International Modernism over to the new Tate Modern, Tate Britain now concentrates on British work dating back to 1500. See p. 141.
- **The American Museum** (Claverton, 3.2km/2 miles east of Bath; ℂ 01225/460503): Housed in a neoclassical country house, this museum presents 2 centuries of American life and styles—including George Washington's mother's gingerbread recipe. See p. 326.
- **The Fitzwilliam Museum** (Cambridge; ℂ 01223/332900): Although London museums dominate this list, there are outstanding regional collections, including this gem down the road from King's College. Exhibits range from paintings by Titian and Renoir to Chinese, Egyptian, and Greek antiquities. See p. 493.
- **Walker Art Gallery** (Liverpool; ℂ 01514/784199): This gallery deserves to be better known. It owns one of the finest collections of European paintings, a nearly complete overview of British painting (from Tudor days to the present), and an outstanding collection of Pre-Raphaelites. See p. 575.

4 The Best Cathedrals

Entrance to cathedrals is usually free, although there may be charges to enter the crypts and other areas. Donations are welcomed, however.

- **Westminster Abbey** (London; ℂ 020/7222-7110): One of the world's greatest Anglo-French Gothic buildings, this minster (large church) has witnessed a parade of English history—from the crowning of William the Conqueror on Christmas Day 1066 to the funeral of Diana, Princess of Wales, in 1997. Most of the kings and queens of England have been crowned here; many are buried here as well. See p. 145.
- **Canterbury Cathedral** (Kent; ℂ 01227/762862): Object of countless pilgrimages of the kind described in Chaucer's *Canterbury Tales,* the original cathedral was destroyed by fire (1067). A new cathedral was also destroyed by fire (1174); thereafter the present structure was built. Thomas à Becket, archbishop of Canterbury, was murdered here; his shrine was an important site for pilgrims until the Reformation. See p. 228.
- **Winchester Cathedral** (Hampshire; ℂ 01962/857225): Construction of the Winchester Cathedral, which dominates the

ancient capital of old Wessex, began in 1079. It is England's longest medieval cathedral, noted for its 12-bay nave. Many famous people are buried here, including novelist Jane Austen. See p. 278.

- **Salisbury Cathedral** (Wiltshire; ℂ 01722/555120): The most stylistically unified of English cathedrals, this edifice was built between 1220 and 1265. Its landmark spire was constructed from 1285 to 1320. Salisbury Cathedral epitomizes the early English style of architecture. See p. 316.

- **Lincoln Cathedral** (Lincoln; ℂ 01522/544544): This is one of the Great Gothic edifices of England, rich in the architectural styles of the early English and decorated periods, with a nave dating back to the 12th century. Its central tower is the second tallest in England. See p. 552.

- **York Minster** (York; ℂ 01904/557216): The largest Gothic cathedral north of the Alps is among the grandest, with the largest single surviving collection of medieval stained glass in England. Its unusual octagonal Chapter House has a late-15th-century choir screen and a wooden vaulted ceiling. See p. 620.

5 The Best Castles, Palaces & Historic Homes

Most of these places charge an entrance fee (sometimes steep), but if that's what's needed to see these elegantly appointed mansions, country houses, and palaces, we think it's worth the money! Passes are available from English Heritage and the National Trust to help you save on the admission fees (see tips 17 and 24 under "50 Money-Saving Tips" in chapter 2 for details).

- **Woburn Abbey** (Woburn; ℂ 01525/290666): A Cistercian abbey for 4 centuries, Woburn Abbey, the seat of the dukes of Bedford, features Queen Victoria's Bedroom and the Canaletto Room, with 21 perspectives of Venice. The popular grounds house a Wild Animal Kingdom, the best collection in England after the London Zoo. See p. 223.

- **Hatfield House** (Hertfordshire; ℂ 01707/262823): Hatfield was the childhood home of Elizabeth I; she was under an oak tree there when she learned she had become queen of England. Hatfield remains one of England's largest and finest country houses, complete with antiques, tapestries, paintings, and even Elizabeth's red silk stockings. See p. 222.

- **Windsor Castle** (Windsor; ℂ 020/7321-2233): The world's largest inhabited stronghold and England's largest castle, Windsor Castle has been a royal abode since William the Conqueror constructed a "motte and bailey" here in 1070. Severely damaged by fire in 1992, the castle now welcomes visitors to help defray restoration costs. Its major attraction is the great Perpendicular Chapel of St. George's, begun by Edward IV. The chancel's three-tiered stalls abound with misericords and ornate carvings. See p. 189.

- **Blenheim Palace** (Woodstock; ℂ 01993/811091): England's answer to Versailles, this extravagant baroque palace designed by Sir John Vanbrugh was the home of the 11th duke of Marlborough and the birthplace of Sir Winston Churchill. Sarah, the duchess of Marlborough, battled the architects and builders from the beginning, wanting "a clean sweet house and garden be it ever so small." The structure measures

850 feet from end to end. Capability Brown designed the gardens. See p. 215.

- **Knole** (Kent; ✆ **01732/462100**): Begun in 1456 by the archbishop of Canterbury, Knole is celebrated for its 365 rooms, 52 staircases, and 7 courts. One of England's largest private houses, Knole is a splendid Tudor edifice set in a 404-hectare (1,000-acre) deer park. See p. 251.
- **Penshurst Place** (Kent; ✆ **01892/870307**): This outstanding country mansion (built 1346) has been expanded by Tudor, Jacobean, and neo-Gothic wings. It was home to poet Sir Philip Sidney (1554–86); in its day, the house attracted literati, including Ben Jonson. See p. 254.
- **Hever Castle & Gardens** (Kent; ✆ **01732/865224**): This was the childhood home of the ill-fated Anne Boleyn. In 1903, William Waldorf Astor bought the castle, restored it, and landscaped the grounds. From the outside, it still looks like it did in Tudor times; a moat and drawbridge protect the castle. See p. 254.
- **Beaulieu Abbey & Palace House** (Beaulieu, in New Forest; ✆ **01590/612345**): The home of the first Lord Montagu, Palace House blends monastic Gothic architecture with Victorian trappings. Many visitors consider the National Motor Museum, which is on the premises and displays more than 250 antique automobiles, more interesting than the house. See p. 292.
- **Harewood House & Bird Garden** (West Yorkshire; ✆ **01132/886331**): Edwin Lascelles began constructing this "essay in Palladian architecture" in 1759. Its grand design was planned by Robert Adam, Thomas Chippendale, and Capability Brown, who developed the grounds. A 1.8-hectare (4½-acre) bird garden features exotic species from the world over. See p. 638.
- **Castle Howard** (North Yorkshire; ✆ **01653/648333**): This was the first building designed by Sir John Vanbrugh, and, as it turned out, his masterpiece. It was the principal setting for the popular TV series *Brideshead Revisited*. A gilt-and-painted dome tops the striking entrance, and the surrounding park is one of the most grandiose in Europe. See p. 637.

6 The Best Gardens

- **Royal Botanic (Kew) Gardens** (outside London; ✆ **020/8940-1171**): Everything from delicate exotics to everyday flowers and shrubs blooms in profusion here in this 120-hectare (300-acre) garden; it also houses the largest herbarium on earth. The gardens are part of a vast lab that identifies plants from throughout the globe. Fabled landscape architect Capability Brown laid out some of the grounds. A delight in any season. See p. 166.
- **Sissinghurst Castle Garden** (Kent; ✆ **01580/15330**): These gardens were created by Vita Sackville-West and Harold Nicholson. They were landscaped between the surviving parts of an Elizabethan mansion. Although overrun in summer, this garden is the most intriguing on the doorstep of London, some 33km (21 miles) northeast of Cranbrook. We prefer the garden in autumn because of its stunning colors then. See p. 254.
- **Stourhead** (near Shaftesbury; ✆ **01747/841152**): You'll find the most famous garden in England here, where English landscape gardening was born. Stourhead

is the best-executed example of the "natural landscaping" that swept England in the 1700s. The grounds have been described as a painting by Constable in three dimensions, with its wealth of flowering shrubs, trees, and numerous beds of multi-hued blooms. Grottoes, bridges, and temples add to the allure. See p. 346.

- **Hidcote Manor Garden** (near Chipping Campden; © **01386/438333**): Near one of the most charming Cotswold towns, this stunning garden is laid out around a stone-built manor house. It's the largest garden in the Cotswolds and one of the most intriguing in all of Britain. Major Lawrence Johnstone, an American horticulturist, traveled the world and brought back specimens to plant in the garden he created in 1907. See p. 436.

7 The Best B&Bs

- **Vicarage Private Hotel** (London; © **020/7229-4030**): Eileen and Martin Diviney share their London home and its traditionally furnished rooms. It's well located near Kensington High Street. Sewing kits, hair dryers, and other amenities are provided, all for £76 ($122) in a double without bathroom, a bargain in high-priced London. See p. 92.
- **Tilbury Lodge** (Oxford; © **01865/862138**): On a quiet country lane in the village of Botley, this is a warm and inviting guesthouse. Well-furnished, comfortable bedrooms are rented, often to families. Opt for the romantic four-poster if available. Rates are £60 ($96) in a double. See p. 211.
- **Alexandra House** (Canterbury; © **01227/767011**): This house is a 10-minute walk from Canterbury Cathedral. Nothing fancy, but the clean and comfortable rooms come at the right price: from £52 ($83) in a double without bathroom. See p. 233.
- **Jeake's House** (Rye; © **01797/222828**): This is the premier B&B in high-and-dry Rye, the former seaport. Built in 1689, the guesthouse welcomes guests into its Laura Ashley–style bedrooms, which rent for £78 ($125) in a double without bathroom. See p. 242.
- **Dudley House** (Brighton; © **01273/676794**): Located in England's premier seaside resort, this cream-colored Victorian town house features well-decorated bedrooms. A double without bathroom begins at £40 to £45 ($64–$72). See p. 268.
- **Ennys** (St. Hilary, near Penzance; © **01736/740262**): A former flower farm, Ennys has good and comfortable rooms; another reason to stay here is the home-style cookery, sometimes of surprising sophistication. Add a heated swimming pool and prices beginning at £50 to £55 ($80–$88) a night. See p. 389.
- **The Marlyn Hotel** (Stratford-upon-Avon; © **01789/293752**): This place (built in 1890) welcomes guests who come to pay their respects to the Bard. Each modernized bedroom comes with a complete collection of Shakespeare's works. The cost is £52 ($83) for a double without bathroom. See p. 449.
- **Hambutts Mynd** (Painswick; © **01452/812352**): Two blocks from the center of this pretty Cotswolds village, you'll find this

17th-century windmill converted into a home of warmth and charm, with views of the nearby fields and hills—all for a price of £55 to £60 ($88–$96) for a double, including an English breakfast. See p. 417.

8 The Best Moderately Priced Hotels

- The **Rushmore Hotel** (London; ℂ **020/7370-3839**): Interior-design buffs in particular will love this gracious town-house hotel. The interior is an extravaganza of muraled ceilings and stage-set bedrooms. The price for all this glamour: £79 ($126) double. Not bad for pricey London. See p. 91.
- **Red Lion** (Clovelly; ℂ **01237/ 431237**): This inn lies at the bottom of the country's steepest cobblestone main street. Once you reach it, at just £87.50 ($140) for the night, you'll be amply rewarded. Bask near the stone seawall of a little harbor; have a drink in the pub and a meal in the seaview dining room before retiring to your cozy lair. See p. 376.
- **The Cott Inn** (Dartington; ℂ **01803/863777**): This inn, possibly the second oldest in England, was built in 1320. Although much has changed over the years, it remains a low, rambling two-story building of stone, cob, and plaster, with a thatch roof and thick walls. Your low-ceilinged double room will be quaint but a good deal at £70 ($112). The Cott's pub is a gathering place for the locals and a good place for a drink on a windy night, as log fires keep the lounge and bar snug. See p. 368.

- **Brompton House** (Bath; ℂ **01225/420972**): In this city on the Avon, you can follow the trails of many leading literary and political figures and enjoy England's most celebrated spa. Prices tend to run high here, but this elegant Georgian rectory with excellent doubles for £65 to £95 ($104–$152) offers good value. It's set on tranquil grounds within an easy commute of the city. See p. 330.
- **The Beadles** (Middleton, near Salisbury; ℂ **01980/862922**): Located in an enchanting setting, this Georgian house lies in .4-hectare (1-acre) gardens with a view of the much-painted Salisbury Cathedral. A warm welcome and good beds await at a cost of £60 ($96) for two people. From here, visit Stonehenge and the New Forest. See p. 320.
- **Rothay Garth Hotel** (Ambleside; ℂ **01539/32217**): In one of the most beautiful areas of the Lake District, stay in an elegant century-old country house set in beautiful gardens—all at a fair price, £88 ($141) for a double. In warm weather, enjoy a sunny garden room; when autumn winds blow, retreat to the lounge with its log fires. See p. 606.

9 The Best Dining Bargains

- **North Sea Fish Restaurant,** 7–8 Leigh St., WC1 (ℂ **020/7387-5892**): Cabbies know everything, and they're always right, as you'll find out if you travel by taxi. Their vote goes to the restaurant, for the national dish, fish-and-chips. Fish platters run £8.30 to £16.95 ($13–$27). See p. 112.
- **Brown's Restaurant and Bar** (Brighton; ℂ **01273/323501**): The very popular Brown's serves

bistro-style continental food and British traditional fare. Prices begin at £7.50 ($12). See p. 269.

- **Mulberry House** (Torquay; ② **01803/213639**): The Mulberry's Lesley Cooper is an inspired cook. Prices for a lunch of solid English fare start at £10.50 ($17). See p. 365.
- **Harper's Restaurant** (Salisbury; ② **01722/333118**): The chef-owner takes pride in making everything homemade, uncomplicated, and wholesome. A fixed-price lunch of £7.20 ($12) is one of the best values in town. See p. 320.
- **Evans Fish Restaurant** (Bath; ② **01225/463981**): Since 1908,

this family-run enterprise has served only the freshest of fish. It offers meals costing from £4.50 ($7.20). See p. 332.

- **Arundel House Restaurant** (Cambridge; ② **01223/367701**): Overlooking the River Cam, this acclaimed restaurant's hearty fixed-price dinner, costing £19 ($30), is one of the best values in town. See p. 498.
- **Don Pepe Restaurant and Tapas Bar** (Liverpool; ② **0151/231-1909**): This drinking and dining emporium's Spanish cuisine, including delectable tapas, breaks "ye olde English" dining monopoly. Meals cost from £6.95 ($11). See p. 582.

10 The Best Pubs

Pubs come in all styles, but atmosphere is the key. Some are extravagant Victorian gin palaces; others occupy long-gone monasteries or abandoned factories. Some are sleek and modern; others are in the country and open onto riverbanks with weeping willows and white swans floating gracefully by. Cornwall may have the largest concentration of good pubs in England, say 30 for every 100,000 in population. Not far behind, with about 25 per every 100,000, are Devon, Cumbria (embracing the Lake District), Gloucestershire, Oxfordshire, Somerset, and North Yorkshire.

- **The Lamb & Flag** (London; ② **020/7497-9504**): There are plenty of outstanding pubs in London, but it's hard to beat this one for history. It hasn't changed much from when Dickens prowled this neighborhood and described the clientele. See p. 186.
- **Ye Olde Starre Inne** (York; ② **01904/623063**): Dating from 1644, this is said to be the oldest licensed pub in this ancient cathedral city. Settle down on a Victorian

settle before the open fireplace and enjoy a pint. See p. 628.

- **The Ship Inn** (Exeter; ② **01392/272040**): Once frequented by Sir Francis Drake, Sir Walter Raleigh, and Sir John Hawkins, this pub is the most celebrated in Devon. It still provides tankards of real ale and food in large portions, as in Elizabethan times. See p. 358.
- **Mermaid Inn** (Rye; ② **01797/223065**): This ancient Sussex seaport boasts the most charming pub in southeast England. Elizabeth I came to the Mermaid in 1573, when it was already 150 years old. It welcomes visitors for a pint or some freshly caught local fish. See p. 244.
- **The Turk's Head** (Penzance; ② **01736/363093**): The oldest pub in Penzance (1233) is filled with artifacts and timeworn beams. Take your lager into the summer garden or retreat to the snug inner chambers when the wind blows cold. See p. 392.
- **Lamb Inn** (Burford; ② **01993/823155**): This is our favorite

place for a lager in all the Cotswolds. In a mellow old house from 1430, it's a good place to spend the night, have a traditional English meal, or just a beer. Snacks are served. See p. 425.

- **The Black Swan** (Stratford-upon-Avon; © **01789/297312**): This has been a popular hangout for Stratford players since the 18th century. Locals affectionately call it "The Dirty Duck." In cool weather an open fireplace blazes; stick around and order the chef's specialty: honey-roasted duck. See p. 452.

2

Planning an Affordable Trip to England

It's possible to have a rich and rewarding travel experience without spending a fortune or sacrificing fun or comfort. That goal has been foremost ever since this guide first appeared in 1964, when you could tour England for $5 a day.

Over the years we've made countless trips through the countryside and learned affordable England inside and out. In this chapter, we'll outline the various regions of England, tell you what you need to know in advance, and show you how to set up your trip so you can find the best bargains.

1 The $75-a-Day Premise

This guide to inexpensive travel differs from some of its competitors. For example, we believe in paying a little more from time to time in order to secure reasonably priced accommodations that are clean, decent, and welcoming. Likewise, we don't limit ourselves to "bangers and mash" or cheap fast food. We've picked places to dine that are simple but good, serving well-prepared British, continental, and foreign fare. We also know that you'll want to splurge sometimes, so we've offered slightly more expensive choices for those occasions—memorable places that still offer great value.

Budget travel isn't just about cutting expenses on the road. It's about bringing you into contact with the locals—the folks who run the B&Bs and pour the pints in the pubs. Arthur Frommer, the pioneering publisher of this guide, writes that over the years Frommer's readers have discovered a major principle of travel: "The less you spend, the more you enjoy; the less you spend, the better you encounter the realities of the countries you visit, and thus receive the most lasting rewards of the travel experience."

The best value for money is found outside London and away from other tourist meccas such as Stratford-upon-Avon, Oxford, Cambridge, or Canterbury. We suggest spending less time in London (perhaps 3 days), then heading out to explore the beautiful English countryside. Spend a few days or more exploring East Anglia or the Lake District, so beloved by the Romantic poets. Walk the country lanes of Devon and discover hidden hamlets ripe for an Agatha Christie murder mystery. Shopping for bric-a-brac can unearth affordable treasures, and you'll also find more budget-friendly B&B prices. Pub lunches are the way to go, followed by dinner in a small tavern, perhaps one once patronized by Johnson and Boswell.

The daily budget of $75 a day promised in this book's title is meant to cover your basic living costs on the road: three meals a day and half the price of a straightforward double room. The costs of sightseeing, transportation, shopping, and entertainment are extra, but we'll tell you how to keep those costs down, too. The minimum $75-a-day budget roughly breaks down to $45 per person for a double room, which includes a hearty breakfast; $10 for lunch; and $20 for dinner.

But what about the word "from" in the title? We've phrased it that way so we can include establishments that are slightly more expensive than the $75-a-day budget but are still terrific buys. We can thereby offer you places with unique historical, cultural, or architectural features, and let you decide when to splurge. Every place included in this book offers value, even if it's slightly higher than the breakdown given above. (Conversely, we'll tell you about many bargains that could let you manage for even less than $75 a day.) We've assumed that you demand more comfort than in your student days, so we don't send you to any marginal properties. We promise to bring you comfortable lodgings, great food, and loads of fun for a reasonable price!

2 50 Money-Saving Tips

The cost of travel to and within England has risen in recent years, so you'll need to know general money-saving guidelines to keep costs trimmed before you go and while you are there.

AIRFARES

The bucks you save can begin even before you leave home. Shop around before you fly, and consider the following strategies:

1. Never accept the first airline deal offered. Keep calling and questioning until all reasonable options have been exhausted and you've priced all the airlines that fly to your destination.

2. Be flexible about your intended dates of departure and return. Ask about the cutoff dates for low, shoulder, and high season flights, and adjust your schedule if you can.

3. Try to arrange transport midweek, when rates are usually less expensive than during weekends.

4. Keep calling the airlines—availability of cheap seats changes daily. As the departure date nears, additional low-cost seats might become available, although this is less likely during peak travel seasons.

5. Check "bucket shops" or consolidators for last-minute discount fares that are even cheaper than their advertised and already discounted fares.

6. Ask about air/land packages. The savings that packages can afford might suddenly transform what had been expensive lodgings—or an expensive car rental—into a more affordable vacation option.

ACCOMMODATIONS

7. Always consider staying in a room without private bathroom. This can save you anywhere from £5 to £25 ($8–$40) on the price of a comparable room with facilities en suite.

8. Patronize bed-and-breakfasts; this is one of the best ways to tour England and pay only a modest sum for lodgings. Throughout the country, B&B signs are posted. Usually this is a way small property owners earn extra money. Most of them serve a decent, filling English breakfast that will fortify you for the day.

9. There are more than 350 youth hostels in England, and they're a terrific deal for those who don't mind shared facilities. Many of them have private rooms—usually double or family rooms—but the cheapest accommodations are in shared dormitory facilities. No age restriction is imposed.

10. Stay in university housing, often available at Easter and from mid-June to September 1, in major towns and cities. It's a bit of

a hassle, and individual universities have to be contacted. You can also contact **Venuemasters,** The Workstation, Patermoster Row, Sheffield S1 2BX (© **0114/249-3090;** www.venuesmasters.co.uk), for a list of rates and possibilities.

11. Some of the cheapest B&B deals in Britain are "scouted out" by *Bed and Breakfast* (GB), P.O. Box 66, Henley-on-Thames, Oxfordshire, England RG9 1XS (© **01491/578803;** fax 01491/410806). They blanket not only England, but also Scotland and Wales, and their offerings begin at only £17 ($27) per person nightly.

DINING

12. Choose the set menu. The French call it table d'hôte, the English set menu or fixed-price menu, but the result is the same: a major savings to you. It's estimated that in some restaurants if you order a set menu it will cost 30% less than if you'd ordered the same dishes a la carte. Many of the best deals are available at lunch, although countless restaurants offer set dinners as well.

13. Patronize the pubs, especially at lunch. Pub lunches throughout England are the dining bargains of the country—everything washed down with some lager, if you wish. But it's also possible to enjoy pub meals in the evening, when you'll get some dishes that are served in the dining room, for a fraction of the price.

14. Consider picnicking whenever the weather cooperates. Some foodstuffs from a local grocer or a simple sandwich from a deli will taste delicious with one of England's beautiful city parks or spectacular country vista as a backdrop.

15. Don't overtip. Service (10%–15% plus 17.5% VAT) is usually included in the price of your food item. Where the service has been

included, it's customary to leave only some small change.

16. Watch the booze. Wine and liquor are expensive in England.

SIGHTSEEING

17. Join English Heritage, the public organization responsible for the preservation, conservation, and maintenance of historic buildings and monuments in England. Membership entitles you to free entry to all their properties, including Stonehenge, Dover Castle, and Osborne House (Queen Victoria's Isle of Wight retreat), and half-price entrance to selected properties in Scotland, Wales, and the Isle of Man. You'll also receive a guide to the properties, a map and events diary, and the quarterly *English Heritage Magazine.* Annual costs are £31 ($50) adults or £55 ($88) for families. You can join at any property or contact English heritage, 429 Oxford St., London W1R 2HD (© **020/7973-3434**).

18. Patronize the many museums that charge no admission, including the world-famous British Museum.

19. Students and seniors should take advantage of special discounts granted with proof of age and/or identity. Domestic train fares in England are also reduced for students.

20. Families can take advantage of special discounts that can cut admission costs considerably. Ask about a "family ticket."

21. The open-air entertainment of the churches and parks of England is free. Take advantage of their richness.

22. In Stratford-upon-Avon, don't pay individual prices for admission to all the famous properties associated with the Bard. Begin at Shakespeare's birthplace on Henley Street and purchase just one ticket, costing £13 ($21) for adults

and £6 ($10) for children, which will let you visit five of the other important sights, in addition to Shakespeare's Birthplace. Seniors and students pay only £12 ($19).

23. In York, the cathedral city of northeast England, one of the best deals is a free 1½-hour walking tour conducted by a volunteer guide. Filled with legend and lore, it encapsulates as "living theater" the tumultuous history of that city.

24. The Royal Oak Foundation, the U.S. affiliate of the National Trust, offers members free entry to some 240 National Trust sites in Britain and some 100 properties in Scotland. The membership of $50 per person or $75 per household can be earned back in admission prices to just a few of these properties. For more data write Royal Oak Foundation, 26 W. Broadway, Suite 950, New York, NY 10004 (℄ **800/913-6565** or 212/480-2889).

SHOPPING

25. The best buys in England are local crafts, woolen products (including tweeds, scarves, skirts, sweaters, and tartans), and traditional Celtic jewelry; such world-renowned pottery and china as Royal Doulton, Wedgwood, and Royal Worcester are also a relative bargain. You can also find excellent and high-quality posters, along with art prints, crafts, and art books, in many of England's museums.

26. Price items that you think you might want to look for before you leave home, so that you'll know a bargain when you see one.

27. Patronize factory outlets. At these you can save as much as 50%, although the really prestigious names in china, such as Wedgwood and Royal Doulton, don't discount merchandise at their factory outlets.

28. Go for the London department store sales during 2 weeks in January and 1 week in July. Many Europeans cross the English Channel just to take advantage of these sales. Look for the advertisements in local newspapers.

29. Check out flea markets, or "street markets," which you'll find all over England, but especially in London. You may have to wade through a lot of junk, but you might find an attractive, reasonably priced souvenir. Try haggling—it works.

30. Reclaim the 17.5% Value Added Tax (VAT).

TRANSPORTATION

31. Purchase a BritRail Classic Pass, allowing unlimited rail travel in the British Isles during a set time period. In first class, adult fares range from $285 for 4 days to $915 for 1 month. In second class, fares range from $189 for 4 days to $609 for 1 month.

32. BritRail also sells a number of "Rover Passes," which are great for exploring southwest England. The most helpful is the Freedom of the Southwest Rover, offering unlimited travel on trains on and to the southwest, including Cornwall and Devon. You're allowed to travel any 8 days in a consecutive 15-day period for £61 to £71.50 ($98–$114).

33. To explore East Anglia, including Cambridge, avail yourself of an Anglia Rover Ticket, costing from £30 ($48). This ticket is sold only at rail stations in East Anglia, and entitles you to a week's unlimited travel on all rail lines in this district northeast of London.

34. To explore the northeast of England, you can purchase the North East Rover from rail ticket offices for £73 ($117). This pass allows unlimited train travel for 7 days, which represents huge discounts

off regular fares if you plan to do a lot of traveling.

35. **Stray Travel,** 171 Earls Court Rd., London, SW5 (② **020/ 7373-7737;** www.straytravel. com), offers one of the best deals in Britain, targeted at rambling hostelers. For only £159 ($254) you can make a clockwise circuit of such places as Windsor, Stratford-upon-Avon, Bath, York, Cambridge, the Lake District, and even Edinburgh, ending up back in London (the starting point). Trips are generally by bus. Other itineraries and destinations are available as well. Tickets are valid for up to 6 months.

36. Nearly all visitors to the West Country head for Salisbury and nearby Stonehenge. Without a car, it's difficult and expensive to get around. Wilshire & Dorset, the local bus company in Salisbury, solves the problem by offering a 1-day Explorer ticket costing £5.75 ($9) or a 7-day Busabout ticket for £25 ($40). It's the best transportation deal in the area.

37. The Cotswolds may be one of the major sightseeing regions of England, but there's no way you can get around to all the scenic villages by public transportation. What to do? The best deal is to get a group together and rent a car for about £34 ($54) a day. Try **Apex Self Drive,** Marshall House, Wymans Lane, Cheltenham (② **01242/ 233084**). Trains frequently link London with Cheltenham.

38. Hitchhiking is too dangerous these days to be recommended by us. However, ride sharing is a viable alternative. Contact **Freewheelers,** 21 Low Friar St., Newcastle-upon-Thyne, NE1 5UE; www.freewheelers.co.uk, which matches passengers and drivers for tours of England.

39. Buy a Diamond Rover Ticket for £7 ($11) and visit many of the major attractions of Greater London, including Windsor Castle and Hampton Court. It's good for a day and is a remarkable transportation value.

40. If you decide to rent a car for your trip, do some careful research before you leave. Price all competing rates, and ask your airline if they have fly/drive packages. Remember also that gasoline—called "petrol"—is expensive in Britain, so be sure to factor that cost into your transportation budget.

ENTERTAINMENT

41. In Stratford-upon-Avon, standby tickets for students and seniors range in price from £8 to £13 ($13–$21), a huge reduction off the cost of regular seats, and are available immediately before shows at the **Royal Shakespeare Theatre Box Office,** Waterside (② **01789/403404**).

42. Can't afford the high price of a London West End theater seat? Patronize "fringe theaters" in cellars, pubs, back rooms, and other creative venues. Some of the best include **King's Head,** 115 Upper St. (② **020/7226-1916;** Tube: Angel); the **Young Vic,** 66 The Cut (② **020/7928-6363;** Tube: Waterloo); and **Almeida Theatre,** Almeida Street (② **020/7359-4404;** Tube: Angel).

43. In London, go to the **Leicester Square Ticket Booth** where tickets for many London shows are available at half price—but not for the hits, of course. Tickets are sold only on the day of performance. There's a £2.50 ($4) booking fee.

44. Patronize nightclubs early or very late to get a discount; go to matinees instead of evening performances; hunt down free concerts

such as those staged in churches at lunch or at colleges by students; in jazz clubs or other venues sit at a bar instead of a table; and join the fun at happy hours at bars (usually between 5:30 and 7:30pm) when tabs are slashed 30% to 50%.

SERVICES & OTHER TRANSACTIONS

45. Always change your money at a bank, not at a hotel or store. If you use a credit or charge card, remember that you'll be billed at a later date, and the rate of exchange from the date of transaction to the billing date may have changed, adversely or favorably.

46. Ask at your hotel if there is a surcharge on local or long-distance calls. Often there is—anywhere from 40% to an astonishing 200%! Make your calls at the nearest post office. The most convenient way to call the U.S. from England is USA Direct, which bypasses the foreign operator and automatically links you with an AT&T operator in America. In England, the access number is **0800/890011.**

FOR STUDENTS

47. Get an **International Student Identity Card (ISIC)** before even arriving in Britain. It can save you big bucks on hotels, attractions, and transportation. This card is better than a specific university identification because the ISIC is recognized worldwide. For more details on this card and other tips, refer to "Student Travel" under "Specialized Travel Resources" below.

48. Students get discounts on everything from travel to theaters and museums. Check in at **STA Travel,** 11 Goodge St., London W1T 2PF (© **020/7436-7779**). Here you can learn what discounts are available, including inexpensive flights. You'll need an International Student ID Card (ISIC).

49. **Youth Hostels Association (YHA)** runs hostels in both the UK and in Ireland. If you plan to tour Britain on the cheap, a membership of £13 ($21) gets you England and Wales. If you're under 18, a membership costs only £6.50 ($10). For more information, contact **Trevelyvan House,** Dimple Road, Matlock, Devon DE4 3YH (© **01629/ 592-600;** www.yha.org.uk).

FOR SENIORS

50. The best transit deal for those 60 or over is a Senior Railcard, costing £18 ($29). It entitles its holder to up to 33% off most rail fares in Britain. This card can be purchased at any major British Rail Travel Centre.

3 The Regions in Brief

England is a part of the United Kingdom, which is made up of England, Wales, Scotland, and Northern Ireland. Only 130,346 sq. km (50,327 sq. miles)—about the same size as New York State—England has an amazing amount of rural land and natural wilderness and an astonishing regional, physical, and cultural diversity.

LONDON Seven million people live in this mammoth metropolis, covering more than 1,577 sq. km (609 sq. miles). The **City of London** proper is merely 2.5 sq. km (1 sq. mile); the rest of the city is made up of separate villages, boroughs, and corporations. See chapters 3 and 4.

THE THAMES VALLEY England's most famous river runs from its source in the Cotswolds eastward to Kew and beyond. This western stretch—a land of meadows, woodlands, attractive villages, small market towns, and rolling hillsides—is one of England's most scenic areas. Highlights include **Windsor Castle** (Elizabeth II's favorite residence) and nearby **Eton College,** founded by a young Henry VI in 1440. **Henley-on-Thames,** site of the Royal Regatta, remains our favorite Thames-side town; at the city of **Oxford,** you can tour the university colleges. See chapter 5.

THE SOUTHEAST (KENT, SURREY & SUSSEX) This is the land of Charles Lamb, Virginia Woolf, Sir Winston Churchill, and Henry James. Some of England's biggest attractions are here: **Brighton,** with its extravagant folly, the **Royal Pavilion; Canterbury Cathedral;** the **White Cliffs of Dover;** and dozens of country homes and castles such as **Hever, Leeds,** and **Chartwell** (Churchill's modest abode). The Southeast's real charm lies in towns such as Rye and Winchelsea (Sussex) and Haslemere (Surrey). Most of the Sussex shoreline is built up; seaside towns are often tacky. Tearooms, antiques shops, pubs, and small inns abound in the area. Surrey is a commuter suburb of London, easily reached for day trips. See chapter 6.

HAMPSHIRE & WILTSHIRE Southwest of London, these two counties possess two of England's greatest cathedrals (**Winchester** and **Salisbury**) and one of Europe's most powerful prehistoric monuments, **Stonehenge.** But there are other reasons to visit. Hampshire is bordered on its western side by the woodlands and heaths of **New Forest. Portsmouth** and **Southampton** loom large in naval heritage. You might ferry over to the **Isle of Wight,** where Victoria preferred to vacation. In Wiltshire, you first encounter the **West Country,** with its scenic beauty and monuments—**Wilton House,** the 17th-century home of the earls of Pembroke, and **Old Sarum,** the remains of what may have been an Iron Age fortification. For Hampshire, see chapter 7. For Wiltshire, see chapter 8.

DORSET & SOMERSET These counties, along with Devon & Cornwall (see next entry), are England's great vacation centers and retirement havens. Dorset, associated with Thomas Hardy, features rolling downs, rocky headlands, well-kept villages, and rich farmlands. Somerset, of King Arthur and Camelot fame, offers the magical town of **Glastonbury.** Cities worth a visit include **Bath,** with impressive Roman baths and Georgian architecture, and **Wells,** with its great cathedral. For Dorset, see chapter 7. For Somerset, see chapter 8.

THE SOUTHWEST (DEVON & CORNWALL) Devon has both **Exmoor** and **Dartmoor,** and northern and southern coastlines peppered with famous resorts (**Lyme Regis**) and such villages as **Clovelly.** In Cornwall, you're never more than 32km (20 miles) from the rugged coastline, which terminates at **Land's End.** Don't miss **Plymouth,** departure point of the *Mayflower.* For Devon, see chapter 9. For Cornwall, see chapter 10.

THE COTSWOLDS This bucolic land of honey-colored limestone villages, where rural England unfolds before you like a storybook, is wonderful to tour. Wool made medieval Cotswolders prosperous, but now they welcome visitors with lovely inns and pubs. Start at **Burford,** traditional gateway to the region, then continue on to **Bourton-on-the-Water, Lower and Upper Slaughter, Stow-on-the-Wold, Moreton-in-Marsh, Chipping Campden,** and **Broadway. Cirencester** is the unofficial capital of the south Cotswolds, **Cheltenham** a still-elegant Regency spa. Our favorite villages are **Painswick,** with its minute cottages, and **Bibury,** with its cluster of weavers' cottages, **Arlington Row.** See chapter 11.

STRATFORD & WARWICK The Central Midlands is both Shakespeare Country and the birthplace of the

Industrial Revolution, which made Britain the world's first industrialized country. The foremost tourist magnet is **Stratford-upon-Avon,** but visitors also come for the great **Warwick Castle** and the ruins of **Kenilworth Castle. Coventry,** heavily bombed in World War II, is renowned for its outstanding modern cathedral. See chapter 12.

BIRMINGHAM & THE WEST MIDLANDS

This area embraces the "Black Country" of the industrial age. **Birmingham,** nicknamed "Brum," is Britain's second largest city. The sprawling metropolis is still dominated by its overpass jungles, tacky suburbs, and a plethora of Victorian architecture, but urban renewal is underway. The English marshes cut through the former counties of **Shropshire** and **Herefordshire. Ironbridge Gorge** was at the heart of the Industrial Revolution, and the famous **Potteries** are in Staffordshire. See chapter 12.

EAST ANGLIA

East Anglia is a very flat, semicircular geographic bulge northeast of London. **Cambridge,** with its colleges and river, is the chief attraction; its most important museum is the **Fitzwilliam.** But visitors also flock here for the scenery and its solitary beauty—the landscapes that John Constable painted are still here, as are the thatched cottages. The Fens—a broad expanse of fertile, black soil lying north of Cambridge—remains our favorite district; visit **Ely Cathedral** there. See chapter 13.

THE EAST MIDLANDS

Although this area encompasses some of the worst of industrial England, there is great natural beauty as well as stately homes here. The latter include **Chatsworth,** seat of the dukes of Devonshire; **Sulgrave Manor,** ancestral home of George Washington; and **Althorp House,** childhood home of the late Princess of Wales. **Lincoln Cathedral,** one of England's greatest, was rebuilt in the late Middle Ages.

Bostonians like to visit their namesake, the seaport town of **Boston. Nottingham** evokes Robin Hood, although the deforested **Sherwood Forest** isn't what it was in the outlaw's heyday. See chapter 14.

THE NORTHWEST

Stretching from Liverpool to the Scottish border, northwestern England can be a bucolic delight if you avoid its industrial pockets and explore the unspoiled countryside. But four cities merit stopovers along the way. The Roman city of **Chester** is a well-preserved medieval town, known for its encircling wall. **Manchester,** another Roman town, is focusing its renewal on **Castlefield,** its historic core and urban heritage park. **Liverpool,** where the Beatles got started, is culturally alive and intriguing; it now has a branch of London's Tate Gallery. The resort of **Blackpool** is big, brash, and a bit tawdry, drawing the Midlands working class for Coney Island–style fun by the sea. See chapter 15.

THE LAKE DISTRICT

This literary lakeland and national park resonates with echoes of the Wordsworths, Samuel Taylor Coleridge, John Ruskin, and Beatrix Potter, among many. **Windermere** makes the best touring base, but there are other good ones, including **Grasmere** and **Ambleside.** See chapter 16.

YORKSHIRE & NORTHUMBRIA

Yorkshire is familiar to fans of the Brontës and James Herriot. **York,** with its immense cathedral and medieval streets, attracts the most attention, although more visitors are calling on **Leeds** and **Bradford.** Northumbria comprises Northumberland, Cleveland, Durham, and Tyne and Wear. **Hadrian's Wall,** built by the Romans, is a highlight. The great cathedral castle at **Durham** served as an English fortress during the border battles with the Scots; it's one of Britain's finest Norman churches. **Fountains Abbey** is the country's largest monastic ruin. Country homes abound, among them **Harewood House** and **Castle Howard.** See chapter 17.

4 Visitor Information

Before you go, you can obtain general information from the offices of Visit-Britain (formerly called the British Tourist Authority, or BTA):

- **In the United States:** 551 Fifth Ave., Suite 701, New York, NY 10176-0799 (© **800/462-2748** or 212/986-2200).
- **In Canada:** 5915 Airport Rd., Mississagua, Toronto, ON L4V 1T1 (© **888/VISIT-UK** in Canada, or 905/405-1840).
- **In Australia:** Level 16, Gateway, 1 Macquarie Place, Sydney NSW 2000 (© **02/9377-4400**).
- **In New Zealand:** Level 17, NZI House, 151 Queen St., Auckland 1 (© **09/303-1446;** fax 09/377-6965).

At **www.visitbritain.com**, you'll find information about special interests, attractions, trip-planning tips, festivals, accommodations, and more.

For a full information pack on London, write to the **London Tourist Board,** Glenn House, Stag Place, London SW1E 6LT (© **020/7932-2000**). You can also call the recorded-message service, **Visitorcall** (© **01891/ 505490**), 24 hours a day. Various topics are listed; calls cost 50p (80¢) per minute.

You can usually pick up a copy of *Time Out,* the most up-to-date source for what's happening in London, at any international newsstand. You can also check it out on the Net at **www. timeout.co.uk**.

To book accommodations with a credit card (MasterCard or Visa), call the **London Tourist Board Booking Office** at © **020/76042890.** They're available Monday through Friday from 9am to 6pm (London time). There is a £5 ($8) fee for booking.

WHAT'S ON THE WEB? As we mentioned above, there's a wealth of information tapped at **www.visit britain.com**. The site lets you order brochures online, provides trip-planning hints, and even allows e-mail questions for prompt answers. All of Great Britain is covered.

Go to **www.baa.com** for a guide and terminal maps for Heathrow, Gatwick, Stansted, and other lesser airports, including flight arrival times, duty-free shops, airport restaurants, and info on getting from the airports to downtown London. Getting around London can be confusing, so you may want to visit **www.tfl.gov.uk** for up-to-the-minute info. For the latest on London's theater scene, consult **www.officiallondontheatre.co.uk**. At **www.multimap.com**, you can access detailed street maps of the whole United Kingdom—just key in the location or even just its postal code, and a map of the area will appear. For directions to specific places in London, consult **www.streetmap.co.uk**.

You may also wish to check out one of the following websites. **AOL members** can type in the keyword "Britain" and find a vibrant guide to the U.K. that gives you the skinny on arts, dining, nightlife, and more. To access the AOL London guide, type in the keyword "London." **A2B Travel** (www. a2btravel.com) is a site focusing on helping travelers plan and book their trips. It has lots of nifty tools such as bus, rail, and ferry guides; a point-to-point mileage calculator; and a guide to more than two dozen U.K. airports. At **www.britannia.com** you'll find much more than a travel guide—it's chock-full of lively features, history, and regional profiles, including sections on Wales and King Arthur. **UK**

for Visitors, from About.com (http:// gouk.about.com/travel/gouk), is a useful gateway that links to local information sites all over the country.

It also offers a limited guide to hotels and restaurants, but you're better off going to a specialist for both.

5 Entry Requirements & Customs

ENTRY REQUIREMENTS

All U.S. citizens, Canadians, Australians, New Zealanders, and South Africans must have a passport with at least 2 months validity remaining. No visa is required. The immigration officer will also want proof of your intention to return to your point of origin (usually a round-trip ticket) and visible means of support while you're in Britain. If you're planning to fly from the United States or Canada to the United Kingdom and then on to a country that requires a visa (India, for example), you should secure that visa before you arrive in Britain.

Your valid driver's license and at least 1 year of driving experience is required to drive personal or rented cars.

For information on how to get a passport, go to the Fast Facts section of this chapter—the websites listed provide downloadable passport applications as well as the current fees for processing passport applications. For an up-to-date country-by-country listing of passport requirements around the world, go the "Foreign Entry Requirements" Web page of the U.S. State Department at **http://travel.state.gov/foreignentryreqs.html**.

CUSTOMS
WHAT YOU CAN BRING INTO ENGLAND

Non-EU Nationals can bring in, duty-free, 200 cigarettes, 100 cigarillos, 50 cigars, or 250 grams of smoking tobacco. This amount is doubled if you live outside Europe. You can also bring in 2 liters of wine and either 1 liter of alcohol over 22 proof or 2 liters of wine under 22 proof. In addition, you can bring in 60cc (2.03 oz.) of perfume, a quarter liter (250ml) of eau de toilette, 500 grams (1 lb.) of coffee, and 200 grams (½ lb.) of tea. Visitors 15 and over may also bring in other goods totaling £145 ($232); the allowance for those 14 and under is £72.50 ($116). (Customs officials tend to be lenient about general merchandise, realizing the limits are unrealistically low.)

Citizens of the U.K. who are **returning from a European Union (EU) country** will go through a separate Customs Exit (called the "Blue Exit") especially for EU travelers. In essence, there is no limit on what you can bring back from an EU country, as long as the items are for personal use (this includes gifts), and you have

---

Tips Passport Savvy

Allow plenty of time before your trip to apply for a passport; processing normally takes 3 weeks but can take longer during busy periods (especially spring). And keep in mind that if you need a passport in a hurry, you'll pay a higher processing fee. When traveling, safeguard your passport in an inconspicuous, inaccessible place like a money belt and keep a copy of the critical pages with your passport number in a separate place. If you lose your passport, visit the nearest consulate of your native country as soon as possible for a replacement.

already paid the necessary duty and tax. However, customs law sets out guidance levels. If you bring in more than these levels, you may be asked to prove that the goods are for your own use. Guidance levels on goods bought in the EU for your own use are 3,200 cigarettes, 200 cigars, 400 cigarillos, 3 kilograms of smoking tobacco, 10 liters of spirits, 90 liters of wine, 20 liters of fortified wine (such as port or sherry), and 110 liters of beer.

U.K. citizens returning from **a non-EU country** have a customs allowance of: 200 cigarettes; 50 cigars; 250 grams of smoking tobacco; 2 liters of still table wine; 1 liter of spirits or strong liqueurs (over 22% volume); 2 liters of fortified wine, sparkling wine, or other liqueurs; 60cc (ml) perfume; 250cc (ml) of toilet water; and £145 worth of all other goods, including gifts and souvenirs. People under 17 cannot have the tobacco or alcohol allowance. For more information, contact HM Customs & Excise at © **0845/010-9000** (from outside the U.K., 020/8929-0152), or consult their website at www.hmce.gov.uk.

WHAT YOU CAN TAKE HOME FROM ENGLAND

Returning **U.S. citizens** who have been away for at least 48 hours are allowed to bring back, once every 30 days, $800 worth of merchandise duty-free. You'll be charged a flat rate of 4% duty on the next $1,000 worth of purchases. Be sure to have your receipts handy. On mailed gifts, the duty-free limit is $200. With some exceptions, you cannot bring fresh fruits and vegetables into the United States. For specifics on what you can bring back, download the invaluable free pamphlet *Know Before You Go* online at **www.customs.gov**. (Click on "Travel" and "Know Before You Go Online Brochure.") Or contact the **U.S. Customs Service,** 1300 Pennsylvania Ave. NW, Washington, DC 20229 (© **877/287-8867**), and request the pamphlet.

For a clear summary of **Canadian** rules, write for the booklet *I Declare,* issued by the **Canada Customs and Revenue Agency** (© **800/461-9999** in Canada, or 204/983-3500; www.ccra-adrc.gc.ca). Canada allows its citizens a C$750 exemption, and you're allowed to bring back duty-free one carton of cigarettes, 1 can of tobacco, 40 imperial ounces of liquor, and 50 cigars. In addition, you're allowed to mail gifts to Canada valued at less than C$60 a day, provided they're unsolicited and don't contain alcohol or tobacco (write on the package "Unsolicited gift, under $60 value"). All valuables should be declared on the Y-38 form before departure from Canada, including serial numbers of valuables you already own, such as expensive foreign cameras. *Note:* The $750 exemption can only be used once a year and only after an absence of 7 days.

The duty-free allowance in **Australia** is A$400 or, for those under 18, A$200. Citizens can bring in 250 cigarettes or 250 grams of loose tobacco, and 1,125 milliliters of alcohol. If you're returning with valuables you already own, such as foreign-made cameras, you should file form B263. A helpful brochure available from Australian consulates or Customs offices is *Know Before You Go.* For more information, call the **Australian Customs Service** at © **1300/363-263,** or log on to www.customs.gov.au.

The duty-free allowance for **New Zealand** is NZ$700. Citizens over 17 can bring in 200 cigarettes, 50 cigars, or 250 grams of tobacco (or a mixture of all three if their combined weight doesn't exceed 250g); plus 4.5 liters of wine and beer, or 1.125 liters of liquor. New Zealand currency does not carry import or export restrictions. Fill out a certificate of export, listing the valuables you are taking out of the country; that way, you can bring them back without paying duty. Most questions are answered in a free pamphlet available at

New Zealand consulates and Customs offices: *New Zealand Customs Guide for Travellers, Notice no. 4.* For more information, contact **New Zealand** **Customs,** The Customhouse, 17–21 Whitmore St., Box 2218, Wellington (© **04/473-6099** or 0800/428-786; www.customs.govt.nz).

6 Money

It's a good idea to exchange at least some money—just enough to cover airport incidentals and transportation to your hotel—before you leave home, so you can avoid lines at airport ATMs (automated teller machines). You can exchange money at your local American Express or Thomas Cook office or your bank. If you don't live near a bank with currency-exchange services, you can contact American Express for traveler's checks and foreign currency (they charge a $15 order fee and additional shipping costs) at www.american express.com or © **800/807-6233.**

POUNDS & PENCE

Britain's decimal monetary system is based on the pound (£), which is made up of 100 pence (written as "p"). Pounds are also called "quid" by Britons. There are £1 and £2 coins, as well as coins of 50p, 20p, 10p, 5p, 2p, and 1p. Banknotes come in denominations of £5, £10, £20, and £50.

As a general guideline, the price conversions in this book have been computed at the rate of £1 = $1.60 (U.S.). Bear in mind, however, that exchange rates fluctuate daily.

ATMS

The easiest and best way to get cash away from home is from an ATM (automated teller machine). The **Cirrus** (© **800/424-7787;** www. mastercard.com) and **PLUS** (© **800/ 843-7587;** www.visa.com) networks span the globe; look at the back of your bank card to see which network you're on, then call or check online for ATM locations at your destination. Be sure you know your personal identification number (PIN) and your daily withdrawal limit before you leave home.

Also keep in mind that many banks impose a fee every time a card is used at a different bank's ATM, and that fee can be higher for international transactions (up to $5 or more) than for domestic ones (where they're rarely more than $1.50). On top of this, the bank from which you withdraw cash may charge its own fee.

You can also get cash advances on your credit card at an ATM. Keep in mind that credit card companies try to protect themselves from theft by limiting the funds someone can withdraw outside their home country, so call your credit card company before you leave home. Also keep in mind that most credit cards start charging you interest on a cash advance the moment you withdraw it.

TRAVELER'S CHECKS

Traveler's checks are something of an anachronism from the days before the ATM made cash accessible at any time. Traveler's checks used to be the only sound alternative to traveling with dangerously large amounts of cash. They were as reliable as currency, but, unlike cash, could be replaced if lost or stolen.

These days, traveler's checks are less necessary because most cities have 24-hour ATMs that allow you to withdraw small amounts of cash as needed. However, keep in mind that you will likely be charged an ATM withdrawal fee if the bank is not your own, so if you're withdrawing money every day, you might be better off with traveler's checks—provided that you don't mind showing identification every time you want to cash one.

You can get traveler's checks at almost any bank. **American Express**

The British Pound & the U.S. Dollar

At the time of writing, $1 = approximately 70p (or $1.60 = £1), and this was the rate used to calculate the dollar values in this book (rounded to the nearest dime if the amount is under $5, rounded to the nearest dollar if the amount is over $5). Exchange rates are volatile. If you have access to the Web, you can get the current equivalents at **www.xe.net/currency**.

U.K.£	U.S.$	U.K.£	U.S.$
.05	.08	6.00	9.60
.10	.16	7.00	11.20
.25	.40	8.00	12.80
.50	.80	9.00	14.40
.75	1.20	10.00	16.00
1.00	1.60	15.00	24.00
2.00	3.20	20.00	32.00
3.00	4.80	25.00	40.00
4.00	6.40	30.00	48.00
5.00	8.00	35.00	56.00

offers denominations of $20, $50, $100, $500, and (for cardholders only) $1,000. You'll pay a service charge ranging from 1% to 4%. You can also get American Express traveler's checks over the phone by calling © **800/221-7282;** Amex gold and platinum cardholders who use this number are exempt from the 1% fee.

Visa offers traveler's checks at Citibank locations nationwide, as well as at several other banks. The service charge ranges between 1.5% and 2%; checks come in denominations of $20, $50, $100, $500, and $1,000. Call © **800/732-1322** for information. AAA members can obtain Visa checks without a fee at most AAA offices or by calling © **866/339-3378. Master-Card** also offers traveler's checks. Call © **800/223-9920** for a location near you.

Foreign currency traveler's checks are useful if you're traveling to one country, or to the Euro zone; they're accepted at locations such as bed-and-breakfasts where dollar checks may not be, and they minimize the amount of math you have to do at your destination. The downside is that you may have to pay conversion fees twice: once when buying the checks and again to change any unused checks back to your home currency after your trip. **American Express, Visa,** and **MasterCard** all offer checks in British pounds and Euros, among other currencies.

If you choose to carry traveler's checks, be sure to keep a record of their serial numbers separate from your checks in the event that they are stolen or lost. You'll get a refund faster if you know the numbers.

CREDIT CARDS

Credit cards are a safe way to carry money, they provide a convenient record of all your expenses, and they generally offer good exchange rates. You can also withdraw cash advances from your credit cards at banks or ATMs, provided you know your PIN. If you've forgotten yours, or didn't even know you had one, call the number on the back of your credit card and ask the bank to send it to you. It usually takes

5 to 7 business days, though some banks will provide the number over the phone if you tell them your mother's maiden name or some other personal information. Your credit card company will likely charge a commission (1% or 2%) on every foreign purchase you make, but don't sweat this small stuff; for most purchases, you'll still get the best deal with credit cards when you factor in things like ATM fees and higher traveler's check exchange rates.

For tips and telephone numbers to call if your wallet is stolen or lost, go to "Lost & Found" in the Fast Facts section of this chapter.

Places in England that accept credit cards take MasterCard and Visa and, to a much lesser extent, American Express. Diners Club trails in a poor fourth position.

7 When to Go

WHEN YOU'LL FIND BARGAINS
The cheapest time to travel to England is the off season: November 1 to December 12 and December 25 to March 14. Weekday flights are cheaper than weekend fares, often by 10% or more.

Rates generally increase March 14 to June 5 and in October. They hit their peak in the high seasons, from June 6 to September 30 and December 13 to 24. Most Britons take their holidays in July and August, so you'll have to deal with crowds and limited availability of accommodations during those months.

You can avoid crowds by planning trips for November and January through March. Sure, it may be rainy and cold, but England doesn't shut down when the tourists leave! The winter season includes some of London's best theater, opera, ballet, and classical music offerings. Additionally, many hotel prices drop by 20% and cheaper accommodations offer weekly rates, unheard of during peak seasons. By arriving after the winter holidays, you can also take advantage of post-Christmas sales to buy woolens, china, crystal, silver, clothing, handcrafts, and curios.

In short, spring offers the countryside at its greenest, autumn brings the bright colors of the northern moorlands, and summer's warmer weather gives rise to many outdoor music and theater festivals. But winter offers savings across the board and a chance to see Britons going about their everyday lives largely unhindered by tourist invasions.

THE CLIMATE   Yes, it rains, but you'll rarely get a true downpour. Pack an umbrella and prepare yourself for a short daily drizzle. It's heaviest in November (2½ in. on average).

Temperatures rarely drop below 35°F (2°C) or go above 78°F (26°C). Evenings are cool, even in summer. Note that the British, who consider chilliness wholesome, like to keep thermostats several degrees below the American comfort level. Hotels have central heating but are usually kept just above the goose bump (here, "goose pimple") margin.

London's Average Daytime Temperature & Monthly Rainfall

	Jan	Feb	Mar	Apr	May	June	July	Aug	Sept	Oct	Nov	Dec
Temp. (°F)	40	40	44	49	55	61	64	64	59	52	46	42
Temp. (°C)	4	4	7	9	13	16	16	18	15	11	8	6
Rainfall (in.)	2.1	1.6	1.5	1.5	1.8	1.8	2.2	2.3	1.9	2.2	2.5	1.9

HOLIDAYS England observes New Year's Day, Good Friday, Easter Monday, May Day (1st Mon in May), spring and summer bank holidays (last Mon in May and Aug, respectively), Christmas Day, and Boxing Day (Dec 26).

CALENDAR OF EVENTS

January

Schroders London Boat Show. Europe's largest boat show, held at the ExCel Docklands, E16 XL. Call © 01784/223627; www.boatshows. co.uk for details. January 8 to January 18.

Charles I Commemoration, London. To mark the anniversary of the execution of King Charles I "in the name of freedom and democracy," hundreds of cavaliers march through central London in 17th-century dress, and prayers are said at Whitehall's Banqueting House. Last Sunday in January. Call © 020/8781-9500.

Chinese New Year, London. The famous Lion Dancers in Soho perform free on the nearest Sunday to Chinese New Year. Either in late January or early February (based on the lunar calendar).

February

Jorvik Festival, York. This 2-week festival celebrates this historic cathedral city's role as a Viking outpost. For more information, call © 01904/621756.

March

Crufts Dog Show, Birmingham. The English, they say, love pets more than offspring. Crufts offers an opportunity to observe the nation's pet lovers doting on 8,000 dogs, representing 150 breeds. It's held at the National Exhibition Centre, Birmingham, West Midlands. Tickets can be purchased at the door. For more information, call © 0121/780-4141. Early March.

April

Easter Parade, London. A memorable parade of brightly colored floats and marching bands around Battersea Park.

Martell Grand National Meeting, outside Liverpool. England's premier steeplechase event takes place over a 4-mile course at **Aintree Racecourse,** Aintree (© 0151/5232600). Early April.

Flora London Marathon. More than 30,000 competitors run from Greenwich Park to Buckingham Palace; call © 020/790-201-89, or go to www.london-marathon.co.uk for information. If you'd like to take the challenge, call from May to June a year prior for an application. Mid-April.

The Shakespeare Season, Stratford-upon-Avon. The Royal Shakespeare Company begins its annual season, presenting works by the Bard in his hometown, at the **Royal Shakespeare Theatre,** Waterside (© 01789/403403; www.rsc.org. uk). Tickets are available online, at the box office, or through such agents as **Keith Prowse** (© 800/669-8687; www.keithprowse.com). April to January.

May

Brighton Festival. England's largest arts festival, with some 400 different cultural events. For information, write the **Brighton Tourist Information Centre** (© 0906/711-2255; www.visitbrighton.co. uk; 10 Bartholomew Sq., Brighton BN1 1JS). Most of May.

Royal Windsor Horse Show. The country's major show-jumping presentation, held at the Home Park, Windsor, Berkshire, is attended by the queen herself. For more information, call ✆ **01753/ 860-633,** or visit www.royal-windsor-horse-show.co.uk. Mid-May.

Glyndebourne Festival. One of England's major cultural events, this festival is centered at the 1,200-seat Glyndebourne Opera House in Sussex, some 54 miles south of London. Tickets, costing anywhere from £15 to £150 ($24–$240), are available from **Glyndebourne Festival Opera Box Office,** Lewes, East Sussex BN8 5UU (✆ **01273/ 812-321;** www.glyndebourne.com). Mid-April to late August.

Bath International Music Festival. One of Europe's most prestigious festivals of music and the arts features as many as 1,000 performers at various venues in Bath. For information, contact the **Bath Festivals Trust,** 5–6 Broad St., Bath, Somerset BA1 5LJ (✆ **01225/462231;** www.bathfestivals.org.uk). Late May to early June.

Chelsea Flower Show, London. The best of British gardening, with plants and flowers of the season, is displayed at the Chelsea Royal Hospital. Contact your local **VisitBritain Office** (see "Visitor Information," earlier in this chapter) to find out which overseas reservations agency is handling ticket sales, or contact the **Chelsea Show Ticket Office,** Shows Department, Royal Horticultural Society, Vincent Square, London SW1P 2PE (✆ **020/7649-7422**). Tickets are also available through **London Ticketmaster** (✆ **020/7344-4444**). Late May.

Royal Academy's Summer Exhibition, London. This institution, founded in 1768, has for some 2 centuries held Summer Exhibitions of living painters at Burlington House, Piccadilly Circus. Call ✆ **020/ 7439-7438** for more information, or visit www.royalacademy.org.uk. Early June to August.

Chichester Festival Theatre. Some great classic and modern plays are presented at this West Sussex theater. For tickets and information, contact the **Festival Theatre,** Oaklands Park, West Sussex P019 4AP (✆ **01243/781312;** www.cft.org. uk). The season runs May to October.

June

Vodafone Derby Stakes. This famous horse-racing event (the "Darby," as it's called here) is held at Epsom Downs, Epsom, Surrey. Men wear top hats and women, including the queen, put on silly millinery creations. For more details, call ✆ **01372/470-047;** www.epsomderby.co.uk. First week of June.

Trooping the Colour. This is the queen's official birthday parade, a quintessential British event, with exquisite pageantry as she inspects her regiments and takes their salute as they parade their colors before her at the Horse Guards Parade, Whitehall. Tickets for the parade and two reviews, held on preceding Saturdays, are allocated by ballot. Applicants must write between January 1 and the end of February, enclosing a self-addressed stamped envelope or International Reply Coupon to the **Ticket Office,** HQ Household Division, Horse Guards, Whitehall, London SW1A 2AX. Exact dates and ticket prices will be supplied later. The ballot is held in mid-March, and only successful applicants are informed in April. Call ✆ **020/7414-2271** for information. Held on a day designated in June (not necessarily the queen's actual birthday).

Grosvenor House Art and Antiques Fair, London. This very prestigious antiques fair is held at Grosvenor House, Park Lane. For information, contact Grosvenor House Art and Antiques Fair, Grosvenor House, 86–90 Park Lane, London W1A 3AA (℅ **020/7495-8743;** www.grosvenor-antiques fair.co.uk). Ten days in mid-June.

Aldeburgh Festival of Music and the Arts. The composer Benjamin Britten launched this festival in 1948. For more details on the events, and for the year-round program, write to **Aldeburgh Foundation,** High Street, Aldeburgh, Suffolk IP15 5AX (℅ **01728/687-110;** www.aldeburgh.co.uk). Two weeks from mid- to late June.

Royal Ascot Week. Although Ascot Racecourse is open year-round for guided tours, events, exhibitions, and conferences, there are 25 race days throughout the year, with the feature races being Royal Ascot Week (also called the Royal Meeting) for 4 days in June, Diamond Day in late July, and the Festival at Ascot in late September. For information, contact **Ascot Racecourse,** Ascot, Berkshire SL5 7JN (℅ **01344/622211;** www. ascot.co.uk).

The Exeter Festival. The town of Exeter hosts more than 150 events celebrating classical music, ranging from concerts and opera to lectures. Festival dates and offerings vary each year, and more information is available by contacting the **Exeter Festival Office** at ℅ **01392/265200;** www.exeter.gov.uk. Late June to mid-July.

Lawn Tennis Championships, Wimbledon. Ever since players took to the grass courts at Wimbledon in 1877, this tournament has attracted quite a crowd. Acquiring tickets and overnight lodgings during the annual tennis competitions at Wimbledon can be difficult to arrange independently. Two outfits

that can book both hotel accommodations and tickets to the event include **Steve Furgal's International Tennis Tours,** 11828 Rancho Bernardo Rd., San Diego, CA 92128 (℅ **800/258-3664** or 858/675-3555; www.tours4tennis.com), and **Championship Tennis Tours,** 15221 N. Clubgate Dr., Suite 1058, Scottsdale, AZ 85254 (℅ **800/468-3664** or 480/429-7700; www.tennistours.com). Early bookings are strongly advised. Tickets for Centre and Number One courts are obtainable through a lottery. Write in from August to December to **A.E.L.T.C.,** P.O. Box 98, Church Road, Wimbledon, London SW19 5AE (℅ **020/8944-1066**). Outside court tickets are available daily, but be prepared to wait in line. Late June through early July.

City of London Festival. This annual art festival is held in venues throughout the city. Call ℅ **020/7377-0540;** www.colf.org for information. June and July.

Ludlow Festival. This is one of England's major arts festivals, complete with an open-air Shakespeare performance within the Inner Bailey of Ludlow Castle. Concerts, lectures, readings, exhibitions, and workshops round out the offerings. From March onward, a schedule can be obtained from the box office. Contact **The Ludlow Festival Box Office,** Castle Square, Ludlow, Shropshire SY8 1AY, enclosing a self-addressed stamped envelope (℅ **01584/872150;** www. ludlowfestival.co.uk). The box office is open daily beginning in early May. Late June to early July.

Shakespeare Under the Stars. The Bard's works are performed at the **Open Air Theatre,** Inner Circle, Regent's Park, NW1, in London. Take the Tube to Baker Street.

Performances are Monday to Saturday at 8pm; Wednesday, Thursday, and Saturday also at 2:30pm. Call © **020/7935-5756** (http://open airtheatre.org) for more information. Previews begin in early June and last throughout the summer.

July

Henley Royal Regatta, Henley, in Oxfordshire. This international rowing competition is the premier event on the English social calendar. For more information, call © **01491/572-153** (or visit www.hrr.co.uk). Early July.

Kenwood Lakeside Concerts. These annual concerts on the north side of Hampstead Heath have continued a British tradition of outdoor performances for nearly 50 years. Fireworks displays and laser shows enliven the premier musical performances. The audience catches the music as it drifts across the lake from the performance shell. Concerts are held every Saturday. For more information, call © **020/8348-1286.** Early July to late August.

The Proms, London. A night at "The Proms"—the annual Henry Wood promenade concerts at Royal Albert Hall—attracts music aficionados from around the world. Staged almost daily (except for a few Sun), these concerts were launched in 1895, and are the principal summer engagements for the BBC Symphony Orchestra. Cheering and clapping, Union Jacks on parade, banners and balloons—it's great summer fun. For more information, call © **020/7589-8212;** www.bbc.co.uk/proms. Mid-July through mid-September.

August

Cowes Week, off the Isle of Wight. This yachting festival takes place in early August. For more information,

call © **01983/295744;** www.cowesweek.co.uk.

Notting Hill Carnival, Ladbroke Grove, London. One of the largest annual street festivals in Europe, attracting more than half a million people. There's live reggae and soul music plus great Caribbean food. Call © **020/8964-0544;** www.portowebbo.co.uk for information. Two days in late August.

International Beatles Week, Liverpool. Tens of thousands of fans gather in Liverpool to celebrate the music of the Fab Four. There's a whole series of concerts from international cover bands, plus tributes, auctions, and tours. **Cavern City Tours,** a local company, offers hotel and festival packages that include accommodations and tickets to tours and events, starting around £99 ($158) for 2 nights. For information, contact **Cavern City Tours** at © **0871/222-1963;** www.cavern-liverpool.co.uk or the **Tourist Information Centre** in Liverpool at © **0151/7095111.** Late August.

September

Burghley Horse Trials, Lincolnshire. This annual event is staged on the grounds of the largest Elizabethan house in England, Burghley House, Stamford, Lincolnshire (© **01780/752131;** www.burghley-horse.co.uk). Early September.

Horse of the Year Show, Wembley Arena, Wembley. Riders fly from every continent to join in this festive display of horsemanship (much appreciated by the queen). The British press calls it an "equine extravaganza." It's held at Wembley Arena, outside London. For more information, call © **020/8900-9282;** www.hoys.co.uk. Late September to early October.

October

Cheltenham Festival of Literature. This Cotswold event features readings, book exhibitions, and theatrical performances—all in the spa town of Gloucestershire. Call ✆ **01242/263-494** for more details, or 01242/237377 to receive mailings about the event (www. cheltenhamfestivals.co.uk). Early to mid-October. A smaller spring weekend festival takes place in early April (same contact information as for the main festival).

Opening of Parliament, London. Ever since the 17th century, when the English beheaded Charles I, British monarchs have been denied the right to enter the House of Commons. Instead, the monarch opens Parliament in the House of Lords, reading an official speech that is written by the government. Queen Elizabeth II rides from Buckingham Palace to Westminster in a royal coach accompanied by the Yeoman of the Guard and the Household Cavalry. The public galleries are open on a first-come, first-served basis. Call ✆ **020/7219-4272**; www.parliament.uk. Late October to mid-November.

Quit Rents Ceremony, London. At the Royal Courts of Justice, the Queen's Remembrancer receives token rents on behalf of the queen. The ceremony includes splitting sticks and counting horseshoes.

Call ✆ **020/7947-6000** for more information. Early October.

November

London-Brighton Veteran Car Run. This race begins in London's Hyde Park and ends in the seaside resort of Brighton, in East Sussex. Call ✆ **01753/765-000**; www. vccofgb.co.uk for more details. First Sunday in November.

Guy Fawkes Night, throughout England. This British celebration commemorates the anniversary of the "Gunpowder Plot," an attempt to blow up King James I and parliament. Huge organized bonfires are lit throughout London, and Guy Fawkes, the plot's most famous conspirator, is burned in effigy. Check *Time Out* for locations. Early November.

Lord Mayor's Procession and Show, The City, London. The queen has to ask permission to enter the square mile in London called the City—and the right of refusal has been jealously guarded by London merchants since the 17th century. Suffice to say that the lord mayor is a powerful character, and the procession from the Guildhall to the Royal Courts is appropriately impressive. You can watch the procession from the street; the banquet is by invitation only. Call ✆ **020/ 7606-3030**; www.lordmayorshow. org. Second Saturday in November.

8 Health & Safety

STAYING HEALTHY

You'll encounter few health risks while traveling in England. The tap water is safe to drink, the milk is pasteurized, and health services are good. The crisis over mad cow disease appears to be over, as do the effects of the epidemic of foot-and-mouth disease, which began in the spring of 2001 (and which is rarely passed to humans).

Other than that, traveling to England doesn't pose any health risk.

WHAT TO DO IF YOU GET SICK AWAY FROM HOME

If you need a doctor, your hotel can recommend one, or you can contact your embassy or consulate. Outside London, dial ✆ **100** and ask the operator for the local police, who will give you the name, address, and telephone number of a doctor in your area. *Note:* U.S. visitors who become ill while they're in England are eligible only for free *emergency* care. For other treatment, including follow-up care, you'll be asked to pay.

In most cases, your existing health plan will provide the coverage you need. But double-check; you may want to buy **travel medical insurance** instead. (See the section on insurance, below.) Bring your insurance ID card with you when you travel.

If you suffer from a chronic illness, consult your doctor before your departure. For conditions like epilepsy, diabetes, or heart problems, wear a **Medic Alert Identification Tag** (② 800/ 825-3785; www.medicalert.org), which will immediately alert doctors to your condition and give them access to your records through Medic Alert's 24-hour hotline.

Pack **prescription medications** in your carry-on luggage, and carry prescription medications in their original containers, with pharmacy labels—otherwise, they won't make it through airport security. Also bring along copies of your prescriptions in case you lose your pills or run out. Don't forget an extra pair of contact lenses or prescription glasses. Carry the generic name of prescription medicines, in case a local pharmacist is unfamiliar with the brand name.

Contact the **International Association for Medical Assistance to Travelers (IAMAT;** ② 716/754-4883 or 416/652-0137; www.iamat.org) for

tips on travel and health concerns in the countries you're visiting, and lists of local, English-speaking doctors. The United States **Centers for Disease Control and Prevention** (② 800/311-3435; www.cdc.gov) provides up-to-date information on necessary vaccines and health hazards by region or country. Any foreign consulate can provide a list of area doctors who speak English. If you get sick, consider asking your hotel concierge to recommend a local doctor—even his or her own. You can also try the emergency room at a local hospital; many have walk-in clinics for emergency cases that are not life threatening. You may not get immediate attention, but you won't pay the high price of an emergency room visit.

STAYING SAFE

Like all big cities, London has its share of crime, but in general it is one of the safer destinations of Europe. Pickpockets are a major concern, but violent crime is relatively rare, especially in the heart of London. Even so, it is not wise to go walking in parks at night. King's Cross at night is a dangerous area, frequented by prostitutes. In London, take all the precautions a prudent traveler would in any large city. Conceal your wallet or else hold onto your purse, and don't flaunt your wealth, be it jewelry or cash. The same precautions prevail in larger cities such as Birmingham, Leeds, and Manchester. In these uncertain times, it is always prudent to check the U.S. State Department's travel advisories at http://travel.state.gov.

9 Travel Insurance

Check your existing insurance policies and credit card coverage before you buy travel insurance. You may already be covered for lost luggage, canceled tickets, or medical expenses. The cost of travel insurance varies widely, depending on the cost and length of

your trip, your age, health, and the type of trip you're taking.

TRIP-CANCELLATION INSURANCE Trip-cancellation insurance helps you get your money back if you have to back out of a trip, if you have to go home early, or if your travel supplier goes bankrupt. Allowed reasons for cancellation can range from sickness to natural disasters to the State Department declaring your destination unsafe for travel. (Insurers usually won't cover vague fears, though, as many travelers discovered who tried to cancel their trips in Oct 2001 because they were wary of flying.) In this unstable world, trip-cancellation insurance is a good buy if you're getting tickets well in advance—who knows what the state of the world, or of your airline, will be in 9 months? Insurance policy details vary, so read the fine print—and especially make sure that your airline or cruise line is on the list of carriers covered in case of bankruptcy. For information, contact one of the following insurers: **Access America** (© 866/807-3982; www.accessamerica.com); **Travel Guard International** (© 800/826-4919; www.travelguard.com); **Travel Insured International** (© 800/243-3174; www.travelinsured.com); and **Travelex Insurance Services** (© 888/457-4602; www.travelex-insurance.com).

MEDICAL INSURANCE Most health insurance policies cover you if you get sick away from home—but check, particularly if you're insured by an HMO. With the exception of certain HMOs and Medicare/Medicaid, your medical insurance should cover medical treatment—even hospital care—overseas. However, most out-of-country hospitals make you pay your bills up front, and send you a refund after you've returned home and filed the necessary paperwork. And in a worst-case scenario, there's the high cost of emergency evacuation. If you require additional medical insurance, try **MEDEX International** (© 800/527-0218 or 410/453-6300; www.medexassist.com) or **Travel Assistance International** (© 800/821-2828; www.travelassistance.com; for general information on services, call the company's Worldwide Assistance Services, Inc., at © 800/777-8710).

LOST-LUGGAGE INSURANCE On domestic flights, checked baggage is covered up to $2,500 per ticketed passenger. On international flights (including U.S. portions of international trips), baggage is limited to approximately $9.10 per pound, up to approximately $635 per checked bag. If you plan to check items more valuable than the standard liability, see if your valuables are covered by your homeowner's policy, get baggage insurance as part of your comprehensive travel-insurance package, or buy Travel Guard's "BagTrak" product. Don't buy insurance at the airport, where it's usually overpriced. Be sure to take any valuables or irreplaceable items with you in your carry-on luggage; many valuables (including books, money, and electronics) aren't covered by airline policies.

If your luggage is lost, immediately file a lost-luggage claim at the airport, detailing the luggage contents. For most airlines, you must report delayed, damaged, or lost baggage within 4 hours of arrival. The airlines are required to deliver luggage, once found, directly to your house or destination free.

10 Specialized Travel Resources

TRAVELERS WITH DISABILITIES

Many London hotels, museums, restaurants, and sightseeing attractions have wheelchair ramps; this is less true in rural England. Persons with disabilities are often granted special discounts at attractions and, in some cases, nightclubs. These are called "concessions" in Britain. It always pays to ask. Free information and advice is available from **Holiday Care,** Imperial Building, 2nd floor, Victoria Road, Horley, Surrey RH6 7PZ (© **01293/774-535;** fax 01293/784-647; www.holidaycare. org.uk).

Bookstores in London often carry *Access in London* (£7.95/$13), a publication listing facilities for persons with disabilities, among other things.

The transport system, cinemas, and theaters are still pretty much off-limits, but **Transport for London** does publish a leaflet called *Access to the Underground,* which gives details of elevators and ramps at individual Underground stations; call © **020/ 79183312.** And the **London black cab** is perfectly suited for those in wheelchairs; the roomy interiors have plenty of room for maneuvering.

London's most visible organization for information about access to theaters, cinemas, galleries, museums, and restaurants is **Artsline,** 54 Chalton St., London NW1 1HS (© **020/ 73882227;** fax 020/73832653; www. artsline.org.uk). It offers free information about wheelchair access, theaters with hearing aids, tourist attractions, and cinemas. Artsline will mail information to North America, but it's more helpful to contact Artsline once you arrive in London; the line is staffed Monday through Friday from 9:30am to 5:30pm.

An organization that cooperates closely with Artsline is **Tripscope,** The Courtyard, 4 Evelyn Rd., London W4 5JL (© **020/85807021;** www.just mobility.co.uk), which offers advice on travel in Britain and elsewhere for persons with disabilities.

Many travel agencies offer customized tours and itineraries for travelers with disabilities. **Flying Wheels Travel** (© **507/451-5005;** www.flying wheelstravel.com) offers escorted tours and cruises that emphasize sports and private tours in minivans with lifts. **Accessible Journeys** (© **800/846-4537** or 610/521-0339; www.disability travel.com) caters specifically to slow

walkers and wheelchair travelers and their families and friends.

Organizations that offer assistance to travelers with disabilities include the **MossRehab Hospital** (www.moss resourcenet.org), which provides a library of accessible-travel resources online; the **Society for Accessible Travel and Hospitality** (© **212/447-7284;** www.sath.org; annual membership fees: $45 adults, $30 seniors and students), which offers a wealth of travel resources for all types of disabilities and informed recommendations on destinations, access guides, travel agents, tour operators, vehicle rentals, and companion services; and the **American Foundation for the Blind** (© **800/232-5463;** www.afb.org), which provides information on traveling with Seeing Eye dogs.

For more information specifically targeted to travelers with disabilities, the community website **iCan** (www. icanonline.net/channels/travel/index. cfm) has destination guides and several regular columns on accessible travel. Also check out the quarterly magazine *Emerging Horizons* ($14.95 per year, $19.95 outside the U.S.; www.emerginghorizons.com); **Twin Peaks Press** (© **360/694-2462;** http://disabilitybookshop.virtualave. net/blist84.htm), offering travel-related books for travelers with special needs; and *Open World Magazine,* published by the Society for Accessible Travel and Hospitality (see above; subscription: $18 per year, $35 outside the U.S.).

GAY & LESBIAN TRAVELERS

England has one of the most active gay and lesbian scenes in the world, centered mainly around London. Gay bars, restaurants, and centers are also found in all large English cities, notably Bath, Birmingham, Manchester, and especially Brighton.

Lesbian and Gay Switchboard (© **020/78377324**) is open 24 hours a day, providing information about gay-related activities in London or advice in general. The **Bisexual Helpline** (© 020/85697500) offers useful information, but only on Tuesday and Wednesday from 7:30 to 9:30pm, and Saturday between 9:30am and noon. London's best gay-oriented bookstore is **Gay's the Word,** 66 Marchmont St., WC1 (© 020/72787654; www.gaystheword.co.uk; Tube: Russell Square), the largest such store in Britain. The staff is friendly and helpful and will offer advice about the ever-changing scene in London. It's open Monday through Saturday from 10am to 6:30pm, and Sunday from 2 to 6pm. At Gay's the Word as well as other gay-friendly venues, you can find a number of publications, many free—including *Boyz, Pink Paper* (with a good lesbian section), and *9X,* filled with data about new clubs and whatever else is hot on the scene.

The **International Gay & Lesbian Travel Association** (IGLTA; © 800/448-8550 or 954/776-2626; www.iglta.org) is the trade association for the gay and lesbian travel industry, and offers an online directory of gay- and lesbian-friendly travel businesses; go to their website and click on "Members."

Many agencies offer tours and travel itineraries specifically for gay and lesbian travelers. **Above and Beyond Tours** (© 800/397-2681; www.abovebeyondtours.com) is the exclusive gay and lesbian tour operator for United Airlines. **Now, Voyager** (© 800/255-6951; www.nowvoyager.com) is a well-known San Francisco–based gay-owned and operated travel service.

The following travel guides are available at most travel bookstores and gay and lesbian bookstores, or you can order them from **Giovanni's Room** bookstore, 1145 Pine St., Philadelphia, PA 19107 (© 215/923-2960; www.giovannisroom.com): *Frommer's Gay*

& Lesbian Europe (Wiley Publishing, Inc.), an excellent travel resource; *Out and About* (© 800/929-2268 or 415-644-8044; www.outandabout.com), which offers guidebooks and a newsletter 10 times a year packed with solid information on the global gay and lesbian scene; *Spartacus International Gay Guide* and *Odysseus,* both good, annual English-language guidebooks focused on gay men; the *Damron* guides, with separate, annual books for gay men and lesbians; and *Gay Travel A to Z: The World of Gay & Lesbian Travel Options at Your Fingertips,* by Marianne Ferrari (Ferrari Publications; Box 35575, Phoenix, AZ 85069), a very good gay and lesbian guidebook series.

SENIOR TRAVEL

Many discounts are available to seniors. Be advised that in England you often have to be a member of an association to get discounts. Public-transportation reductions, for example, are available only to holders of British Pension books. However, many attractions do offer discounts for seniors (women 60 or over and men 65 or over). Even if discounts aren't posted, ask if they're available.

If you're over 60, you're eligible for special 10% discounts on **British Airways** through its Privileged Traveler program. You also qualify for reduced restrictions on APEX cancellations. Discounts are also granted for BA tours and for intra-Britain air tickets booked in North America. **British Rail** offers seniors discounted rates on first-class rail passes around Britain. See "By Train from Continental Europe" in the "Getting There" section, later in this chapter.

Don't be shy about asking for discounts, but carry some kind of identification that shows your date of birth. Also, mention you're a senior when you make your reservations. Many hotels offer seniors discounts.

Members of **AARP** (formerly known as the American Association of Retired Persons), 601 E St. NW, Washington, DC 20049 (© **800/424-3410** or 202/434-2277; www.aarp.org), get discounts on hotels, airfares, and car rentals. AARP offers members a wide range of benefits, including *AARP: The Magazine* and a monthly newsletter. Anyone over 50 can join.

Many reliable agencies and organizations target the 50-plus market. **Elderhostel** (© **877/426-8056;** www.elderhostel.org) arranges study programs for those aged 55 and over (and a spouse or companion of any age) in the U.S. and in more than 80 countries around the world. Most courses last 5 to 7 days in the U.S. (2–4 weeks abroad), and many include airfare, accommodations in university dormitories or modest inns, meals, and tuition. **ElderTreks** (© **800/741-7956;** www.eldertreks.com) offers small-group tours to off-the-beaten-path or adventure-travel locations, restricted to travelers 50 and older.

Recommended publications offering travel resources and discounts for seniors include: the quarterly magazine *Travel 50 & Beyond* (www.travel50andbeyond.com); *Travel Unlimited: Uncommon Adventures for the Mature Traveler* (Avalon); *101 Tips for Mature Travelers,* available from Grand Circle Travel (© **800/221-2610** or 617/350-7500; www.gct.com); *The 50+ Traveler's Guidebook* (St. Martin's Press); and *Unbelievably Good Deals and Great Adventures That You Absolutely Can't Get Unless You're Over 50* (McGraw Hill).

FAMILY TRAVEL

If you have enough trouble getting your kids out of the house in the morning, dragging them thousands of miles away may seem like an insurmountable challenge. But family travel can be immensely rewarding, giving you new ways of seeing the world through smaller pairs of eyes.

On airlines, you must request a special menu for children at least 24 hours in advance. If baby food is required, however, bring your own and ask a flight attendant to warm it to the right temperature.

Arrange ahead of time for such necessities as a crib, bottle warmer, and a car seat (in England, small children aren't allowed to ride in the front seat).

Chelsea Baby Hire, 108 Dorset Rd., SW19 3HD (© **020/85408830;** www.chelseababyhire.co.uk), offers baby equipment for rent. The **London black cab** (© **020/7432-1432;** www.londonblackcab.com) is a lifesaver for families; the roomy interior allows a stroller to be lifted right into the cab without unstrapping baby.

A recommendable London babysitting service is **Childminders** (© **020/74875040;** www.babysitter.co.uk). Babysitters can also be found for you at most hotels.

To find out what's on for kids while you're in London, pick up the leaflet *Where to Take Children,* published by the London Tourist Board. If you have specific questions, ring **Kidsline** (© **020/7487-5040;** www.kidsline.co.uk) Monday through Friday from 4 to 6pm and summer holidays from 9am to 4pm, or the **London Tourist Board**'s special children's information lines (© **0891/505-490**) for listings of special events and places to visit for children. The number is accessible in London at 50p (80¢) per minute.

The University of New Hampshire runs **Familyhostel** (© **800/733-9753** or 603/862-1147; fax 603/862-1113; www.learnunh.edu), an intergenerational alternative to standard guided tours. You live on a European college campus for the 2- or 3-week program, attend lectures and seminars, go on lots of field trips, and do all the sightseeing—all of it guided by a team of experts and academics. It's designed for children (ages 8–15), parents, and grandparents.

Look also for our "Kids" icon, indicating attractions, restaurants, or hotels and resorts that are especially family friendly.

Remember that for people 15 and under, a passport is valid for only 5 years, costing $40, whereas for those 16 and up, a passport is valid for 10 years, costing $60.

Familyhostel (© **800/733-9753;** www.learn.unh.edu/familyhostel) takes the whole family, including kids ages 8 to 15, on moderately priced domestic and international learning vacations. Lectures, field trips, and sightseeing are guided by a team of academics.

You can find good family-oriented vacation advice on the Internet from sites like the **Family Travel Network** (www.familytravelnetwork.com); **Traveling Internationally with Your Kids** (www.travelwithyourkids.com), a comprehensive site offering sound advice for long-distance and international travel with children; and **Family Travel Files** (www.thefamilytravelfiles.com), which offers an online magazine and a directory of off-the-beaten-path tours and tour operators for families.

Finally, look for the soon-to-be-published *Frommer's London with Kids* (Wiley Publishing, Inc.).

STUDENT TRAVEL

The **American Institute for Foreign Study,** River Plaza, 9 W. Broad St., Stamford, CT 06902 (© **800/727-2437;** www.aifsabroad.com), offers 3- and 6-month academic programs in London, costing from $11,245 to $21,990, including meals and housing. The **Institute for International Education,** 809 United Nations Plaza, New York, NY 10017 (© **212/883-8200;** www.iie.org), also administers student grants and applications for

study-abroad programs in England and other European countries. The **Council on International Educational Exchange (CIEE),** International Study Programs, 603 Third Ave., 20th floor, New York, NY 10017 (© **212/822-2755;** www.ciee.org), can offer a term or a whole year at its London study center, which combines Goldsmith College and Imperial College, both parts of the University of London, and the University of Westminster. It is also possible to enroll in summer courses at **Oxford University** (© **01865/270000;** www.ox.ac.uk), and **Cambridge** (© **01223/337733;** www.cam.ac.uk).

The **International Student Identity Card (ISIC)** is the only officially acceptable form of student identification, good for discounts on rail passes, plane tickets, theaters, museums, and so on. It has a partnership with eKit to offer a "communications solution" called ISIConnect for cheap phone calls and free e-mail. You also get basic health and life insurance and a 24-hour help line. If you're no longer a student but are still under 26, you can buy an **International Youth Travel Card,** which will get you the insurance and some of the discounts (but not student admission prices in museums). Both passes cost $22 and are available from **STA Travel** (© **800/781-4040;** www.statravel.com). Ask for a list of offices in major cities so that you can keep the discounts flowing (and aid lines open) as you travel. (*Note:* In 2002, STA Travel bought competitors **Council Travel** and **USIT Campus** after they went bankrupt. It's still operating some offices under the Council name, but it's owned by STA.)

The **International Student Travel Confederation** website (www.istc.org) is a useful source of advice and directions to member organizations all over the world.

The International Student House, 229 Great Portland St., W1W 5PN (℃ **020/76318310;** www.ish.org.uk), lies at the foot of Regent's Park across from the Tube stop for Great Portland Street. It's a beehive of activity, such as discos and film showings, and rents blandly furnished, institutional rooms for £33 ($53) single, £25 to £26.50 ($40–$42) per person double, £20 ($32) per person triple, and £18 ($29) per person in a dorm. Laundry facilities are available; a £10 ($16) key deposit is charged. Reserve way in advance.

The **University of London Student Union (ULU),** Malet Street, WC1 (℃ **020/7664-2000;** www.ulu.lon.ac.uk), caters to more than 70,000 students and may be the largest of its kind in the world. In addition to a gym and fitness center with squash and badminton courts, the Malet Street building houses several shops, bars, restaurants, a bank, a ticket-booking agency, and an STA travel office. And there's an action-packed schedule of gigs and club nights. Stop by or phone for information on university activities. The student union building is open Monday to Thursday from 8:30am to 11pm, Friday 8:30am to 1am, Saturday 9am to 1am, and Sunday 9am to 10:30pm. It is sometimes closed on weekends in August. Take the Tube to Goodge Street.

London's youth hostels are not only some of the cheapest sleeps—they're also great spots to meet other student travelers and pick up discounts to local attractions. You have to be a member of **Hostelling International (International Youth Hostel Federation),** which you can join at any hostel for $28 adults, $18 for seniors (55-plus), or free if you're under 18. To apply in the United States and make advance international bookings, contact **Hostelling International (AYH),** 8401 Colesville Rd., Silver Spring, MD 20910 (℃ **301/495-1240;** www.hiayh.org). You can also book dorm-beds online and e-mail hostels about other options through the English website (www.yha.org.uk).

The Hanging Out Guides (www.frommers.com/hangingout), published by Frommer's, is the top student travel series for today's students, covering everything from adrenaline sports to the hottest club and music scenes.

SINGLE TRAVELERS

Many people prefer traveling alone, and for independent travelers, solo journeys offer infinite opportunities to make friends and meet locals. Unfortunately, if you like resorts, tours, or cruises, you're likely to get hit with a "single supplement" to the base price. Single travelers can avoid these supplements, of course, by agreeing to room with other single travelers on the trip. An even better idea is to find a compatible roommate before you go from one of the many roommate locator agencies.

Travel Companion Exchange (TCE; ℃ 631/454-0880; www.travelcompanions.com) is one of the nation's oldest roommate finders for single travelers. Register with them and find a travel mate who will split the cost of the room with you and be around as little, or as often, as you like during the day. **Travel Buddies Singles Travel Club** (℃ **800/998-9099;** www.travelbuddiesworldwide.com), based in Canada, runs small, intimate, single-friendly group trips and will match you with a roommate free of charge and save you the cost of single supplements. **TravelChums** (℃ **212/787-2621;** www.travelchums.com) is an Internet-only travel-companion matching service with elements of an online personals-type site, hosted by the respected New York–based Shaw Guides travel service. **The Single Gourmet Club** (www.singlegourmet.com/chapters.html) is an international social, dining, and travel club for singles of all ages, with offices in 21 cities in the U.S. and Canada. Membership costs $75 for the first year, $50 to renew.

Many reputable tour companies offer singles-only trips. **Singles Travel International** (© 877/765-6874; www.singlestravelintl.com) offers singles-only trips to places like London, Fiji, and the Greek Islands. **Backroads** (© 800/462-2848; www.backroads.com) offers more than 160 active trips to 30 destinations worldwide, including Bali, Morocco, and Costa Rica.

For more information, check out Eleanor Berman's *Traveling Solo: Advice and Ideas for More Than 250 Great Vacations* (Globe Pequot), a guide with advice on traveling alone, whether on your own or on a group tour. (It's been updated for 2003.) Or turn to the **Travel Alone and Love It** website (www.travelaloneandloveit.com), designed by former flight attendant Sharon Wingler, the author of the book of the same name. Her site is full of tips for single travelers.

11 Planning Your Trip Online

SURFING FOR AIRFARES

The "big three" online travel agencies, **Expedia.com, Travelocity.com,** and **Orbitz.com** sell most of the air tickets bought on the Internet. (Canadian travelers should try expedia.ca and Travelocity.ca; U.K. residents can go for expedia.co.uk and opodo.co.uk.) Each has different business deals with the airlines, and may offer different fares on the same flights, so it's wise to shop around. Expedia and Travelocity will also send you **e-mail notification** when a cheap fare becomes available to your favorite destination. Of the smaller travel agency websites, **SideStep** (www.sidestep.com) has gotten the best reviews from Frommer's authors. It's a browser add-on that purports to "search 140 sites at once," but in reality only beats competitors' fares as often as other sites do.

Also remember to check **airline websites,** especially those for low-fare carriers whose fares are often misreported or simply missing from travel agency websites. Even with major airlines, you can often shave a few bucks from a fare by booking directly through the airline and avoiding a travel agency's transaction fee. But you'll get these discounts only by **booking online:** Most airlines now offer online-only fares that even their phone agents know nothing about. For the websites of airlines that fly to and from your destination, go to "Getting There," later in this chapter.

Great **last-minute deals** are available through free weekly e-mail services provided directly by the airlines. Most of these are announced on Tuesday or Wednesday and must be purchased online. Sign up for weekly e-mail alerts at airline websites or check mega-sites that compile comprehensive lists of last-minute specials, such as **Smarter Living** (smarterliving.com). For last-minute trips, **lastminute.com** in Europe often has better deals than the major-label sites.

If you're willing to give up some control over your flight details, use an **opaque fare service** like **Priceline** (www.priceline.com; www.priceline.co.uk for Europeans) or **Hotwire** (www.hotwire.com). Both offer rock-bottom prices in exchange for travel on a "mystery airline" at a mysterious time of day, often with a mysterious change of planes enroute. The mystery airlines are all major, well-known carriers. But your chances of getting a 6am or 11pm flight are pretty high. Hotwire tells you flight prices before you buy; Priceline usually has better deals than Hotwire, but you have to play their "name our price" game. If you're new at this, the helpful folks at **BiddingForTravel** (www.biddingfortravel.com) do a good job of demystifying Priceline's prices. Priceline and Hotwire are great

Frommers.com: The Complete Travel Resource

For an excellent travel-planning resource, we highly recommend Frommers.com (www.frommers.com). We're a little biased, of course, but we guarantee that you'll find the travel tips, reviews, monthly vacation giveaways, and online-booking capabilities thoroughly indispensable. Among the special features are our popular **Message Boards,** where Frommer's readers post queries and share advice (sometimes even our authors show up to answer questions); **Frommers.com Newsletter,** for the latest travel bargains and insider travel secrets; and **Frommer's Destinations Section,** where you'll get expert travel tips, hotel and dining recommendations, and advice on the sights to see for more than 3,000 destinations around the globe. When your research is done, the **Online Reservations System** (www.frommers.com/book_a_trip) takes you to Frommer's preferred online partners for booking your vacation at affordable prices.

for flights between the U.S. and Europe, including England.

For much more about airfares and savvy air-travel tips and advice, pick up a copy of *Frommer's Fly Safe, Fly Smart* (Wiley Publishing, Inc.).

SURFING FOR HOTELS

Of the "big three" sites, **Expedia** may be the best choice, thanks to its long list of special deals. **Travelocity** runs a close second. Hotel specialist sites **hotels.com** and **hoteldiscounts.com** are also reliable. An excellent free program, **TravelAxe** (www.travelaxe.net), can help you search multiple hotel sites at once, even ones you may never have heard of.

Priceline and Hotwire are even better for hotels than for airfares; with both, you're allowed to pick the neighborhood and quality level of your hotel before offering up your money. Priceline's hotel product even covers Europe and Asia, though it's much better at getting five-star lodging for three-star prices than at finding anything at the bottom of the scale. *Note:* Hotwire overrates its hotels by one star—what Hotwire calls a four-star is a three-star anywhere else.

SURFING FOR RENTAL CARS

For booking rental cars online, the best deals are usually found at rental-car company websites, although all the major online travel agencies also offer rental-car reservations services. Priceline and Hotwire work well for rental cars, too; the only "mystery" is which major rental company you get, and for most travelers the difference between Hertz, Avis, and Budget is negligible.

12 The 21st-Century Traveler

INTERNET ACCESS AWAY FROM HOME

Travelers have any number of ways to check their e-mail and access the Internet on the road. Of course, using your own laptop—or even a PDA (personal digital assistant) or electronic organizer with a modem—gives you the most flexibility. But even if you don't have a computer, you can still access your e-mail and even your office computer from cybercafes.

WITHOUT YOUR OWN COMPUTER

It's hard nowadays to find a city that *doesn't* have a few cybercafes. Although there's no definitive directory for cybercafes—these are independent businesses, after all—three places to start looking are at **www.cybercaptive.com**, **www.netcafeguide.com**, and **www.cybercafe.com**.

Aside from formal cybercafes, most **youth hostels** nowadays have at least one computer you can get to the Internet on. And most **public libraries** across the world offer Internet access free or for a small charge. Avoid **hotel business centers**, which often charge exorbitant rates.

Most major airports now have **Internet kiosks** scattered throughout their gates. These kiosks, which you'll also see in shopping malls, hotel lobbies, and tourist information offices around the world, give you basic Web access for a per-minute fee that's usually higher than cybercafe prices. The kiosks' clunkiness and high price means they should be avoided whenever possible.

To retrieve your e-mail, ask your **Internet Service Provider (ISP)** if it has a Web-based interface tied to your existing e-mail account. If your ISP doesn't have such an interface, you can use the free **mail2web** service (www.mail2web.com) to view and reply to your home e-mail. For more flexibility, you may want to open a free, Web-based e-mail account with **Yahoo! Mail** (http://mail.yahoo.com). (Microsoft's Hotmail is another popular option, but Hotmail has severe spam problems.) Your home ISP may be able to forward your e-mail to the Web-based account automatically.

If you need to access files on your office computer, look into a service called **GoToMyPC** (www.gotomypc.com). The service provides a Web-based interface for you to access and manipulate a distant PC from anywhere—even a cybercafe—provided your "target" PC is on and has an always-on connection to the Internet (such as with Road Runner cable). The service offers top-quality security, but if you're worried about hackers, use your own laptop rather than a cybercafe to access the GoToMyPC system.

WITH YOUR OWN COMPUTER

Major Internet Service Providers (ISP) have **local access numbers** around the world, allowing you to go online by simply placing a local call. Check your ISP's website or call its toll-free number and ask how you can use your current account away from home, and how much it will cost.

If you're traveling outside the reach of your ISP, the **iPass** network has dial-up numbers in most of the world's countries. You'll have to sign up with an iPass provider, who will then tell you how to set up your computer for your destination(s). For a list of iPass providers, go to www.ipass.com and click on "Reseller Locator." Under "Select a Country" pick the country that you're coming from, and under "Who is this service for?" pick "Individual." One solid provider is **i2roam** (www.i2roam.com; ✆ **866/811-6209** or 920/235-0475).

Wherever you go, bring a **connection kit** of the right power and phone adapters, a spare phone cord, and a spare Ethernet network cable.

Most business-class hotels throughout the world offer dataports for laptop modems, and a few thousand hotels in the U.S. and Europe now offer high-speed Internet access using an Ethernet network cable. You'll have to bring your own cables either way, so **call your hotel in advance** to find out what the options are.

Many business-class hotels in the U.S. also offer a form of computer-free Web browsing through the room

TV set. We've successfully checked Yahoo! Mail and Hotmail on these systems.

If you have an 802.11b/**Wi-fi** card for your computer, several commercial companies have made wireless service available in airports, hotel lobbies, and coffee shops, primarily in the U.S. **T-Mobile Hotspot** (www.t-mobile. com/hotspot) serves up wireless connections at more than 1,000 Starbucks coffee shops nationwide. **Boingo** (www.boingo.com) and **Wayport** (www.wayport.com) have set up networks in airports and high-class hotel lobbies. IPass providers (see above) also give you access to a few hundred wireless hotel lobby setups. Best of all, you don't need to be staying at the Four Seasons to use the hotel's network; just set yourself up on a nice couch in the lobby. Unfortunately, the companies' pricing policies are byzantine, with a variety of monthly, per-connection, and per-minute plans.

Community-minded individuals have also set up **free wireless networks** in major cities around the world. These networks are spotty, but you get what you (don't) pay for. Each network has a home page explaining how to set up your computer for their particular system; start your explorations at www.personaltelco.net/index.cgi/WirelessCommunities.

USING A CELLPHONE

The three letters that define much of the world's **wireless capabilities** are GSM (Global System for Mobiles), a big, seamless network that makes for easy cross-border cellphone use throughout Europe and dozens of other countries worldwide. In the U.S., T-Mobile, AT&T Wireless, and Cingular use this quasi-universal system; in Canada, Microcell and some Rogers customers are GSM, and all Europeans and most Australians use GSM.

If your cellphone is on a GSM system, and you have a world-capable phone such as many (but not all) Sony Ericsson, Motorola, or Samsung models, you can make and receive calls across civilized areas on much of the globe, from Andorra to Uganda. Just call your wireless operator and ask for "international roaming" to be activated on your account. Unfortunately, per-minute charges can be high—usually $1 to $1.50 in Western Europe and up to $5 in places like Russia and Indonesia.

World-phone owners can bring down their per-minute charges with a bit of trickery. Call up your cellular operator and say you'll be going abroad for several months and want to "unlock" your phone to use it with a local provider. Usually, they'll oblige. Then, in your destination country, pick up a cheap, prepaid phone chip at a mobile phone store and slip it into your phone. (Show your phone to the salesperson, as not all phones work on all networks.) You'll get a local phone number in your destination country—and much, much lower calling rates.

Otherwise, **renting** a phone is a good idea. (Even worldphone owners will have to rent new phones if they're traveling to non-GSM regions, such as Japan or Korea.) While you can rent a phone from any number of overseas sites, including kiosks at airports and at car-rental agencies, we suggest renting the phone before you leave home. That way you can give loved ones your new number, make sure the phone works, and take the phone wherever you go—especially helpful when you rent overseas, where phone-rental agencies bill in local currency and may not let you take the phone to another country.

Phone rental isn't cheap. You'll usually pay $40 to $50 per week, plus airtime fees of at least a dollar a minute. If you're traveling to Europe, though, local rental companies often offer free incoming calls within their home country, which can save you big bucks. The bottom line: Shop around.

Two good wireless rental companies are **InTouch USA** (© 800/872-7626; www.intouchglobal.com) and **Road-Post** (© 888/290-1606 or 905/272-5665; www.roadpost.com). Give them your itinerary, and they'll tell you what wireless products you need. InTouch will also, for free, advise you on whether your existing phone will work overseas; simply call © **703/222-7161** between 9am and 4pm EST, or go to http://intouchglobal.com/travel.htm.

For trips of more than a few weeks spent in one country, **buying a phone** becomes economically attractive, as many nations have cheap, no-questions-asked prepaid phone systems.

Stop by a local cellphone shop and get the cheapest package; you'll probably pay less than $100 for a phone and a starter calling card. Local calls may be as low as 10¢ per minute, and in many countries incoming calls are free.

True wilderness adventurers, or those heading to less-developed countries, should consider renting a **satellite phone** (see above). Per-minute call charges can be even cheaper than roaming charges with a regular cellphone, but the phone itself is more expensive (up to $150 a week), and depending on the service you choose, people calling you may incur high long-distance charges.

13 Getting There

BY PLANE

The best strategy for securing the lowest fare is to shop around and remain as flexible as you can about dates. Fares are generally lower mid-day Monday through Thursday. There are also seasonal fare differences, with peak season during the summer, basic during winter, and shoulder in between. Travel during Christmas and Easter weeks is usually more expensive.

The following airlines fly the enormously popular routes from North America to Great Britain.

British Airways (© 800/AIRWAYS; www.britishairways.com) offers flights from 18 U.S. cities to Heathrow and Gatwick airports as well as many others to Manchester, Birmingham, and Glasgow. Nearly every flight is nonstop. With more add-on options than any other airline, British Airways can make a visit to Britain cheaper than you might have expected. The 1993 union of some of BA's functions and routings with US Airways opened additional North American gateways to BA, improved its services, and reduced some of its fares. Ask about packages that include both airfare and discounted accommodations in Britain.

Known for its consistently excellent fares, **Virgin Atlantic Airways** (© 800/862-8621; www.virgin-atlantic.com) flies daily to either Heathrow or Gatwick from Boston, Newark, New York's JFK, Los Angeles, San Francisco, Washington's Dulles, Miami, Orlando, and Chicago.

American Airlines (© 800/433-7300; www.aa.com) offers daily flights to London's Heathrow from half a dozen U.S. gateways—New York's JFK (six times daily), Chicago's O'Hare and Boston (twice daily), and Miami, Newark, and Los Angeles (once daily).

Depending on day and season, **Delta Air Lines** (© 800/241-4141; www.delta.com) runs one or two daily nonstop flights between Atlanta and Gatwick. Delta also offers nonstop daily service from Cincinnati.

Northwest Airlines (© 800/225-2525; www.nwa.com) flies nonstop from Minneapolis and Detroit to Gatwick or makes connections via other cities, such as Boston or New York.

Continental Airlines (© 800/525-0280; www.continental.com) has daily flights to London Gatwick from Houston and Newark, as well as daily service to Birmingham and Manchester from Newark.

United Airlines (© 800/241-6522; www.united.com) flies nonstop from New York's JFK and Chicago's O'Hare to Heathrow two or three times daily, depending on the season. United also offers nonstop service twice a day from Washington's Dulles plus once-a-day service from Newark, Los Angeles, San Francisco, and Boston to Heathrow.

For travelers departing from Canada, **Air Canada** (© 888/247-2262 in U.S., or 800/268-7240 in Canada; www.aircanada.ca) flies daily to London's Heathrow nonstop from Vancouver, Montreal, and Toronto. There are also frequent direct services from Calgary and Ottawa. **British Airways** (© 800/247-9297) has direct flights from Toronto, Montreal, and Vancouver.

For travelers departing from Australia, **British Airways** (© 800/247-9297) has flights to London from Sydney, Melbourne, Perth, and Brisbane. **Qantas** (© 131313; www.qantas.com) offers flights from Australia to London's Heathrow. Direct flights depart from Sydney and Melbourne. Some include free stopovers in Bangkok or Singapore.

Air New Zealand (© 800/262-1234) has direct flights to London from Auckland, departing Wednesday, Saturday, and Sunday.

Short flights from Dublin to London are available through **British Airways** (© 800/AIRWAYS), with four flights daily into Gatwick. **Aer Lingus**

Flying with Film & Video

Never pack film—developed or undeveloped—in checked bags, as the new, more powerful scanners in U.S. airports can fog film. The film you carry with you can be damaged by scanners as well. X-ray damage is cumulative; the faster the film, and the more times you put it through a scanner, the more likely the damage. Film under 800 ASA is usually safe for up to five scans. If you're taking your film through additional scans, U.S. regulations permit you to demand hand inspections. In international airports, you're at the mercy of airport officials. On international flights, store your film in transparent baggies, so you can remove it easily before you go through scanners. Keep in mind that airports are not the only places where your camera may be scanned: Highly trafficked attractions are X-raying visitors' bags with increasing frequency.

Most photo supply stores sell protective pouches designed to block damaging X-rays. The pouches fit both film and loaded cameras. They should protect your film in checked baggage, but they also may raise alarms and result in a hand inspection.

An organization called **Film Safety for Traveling on Planes (FSTOP;** © 888/301-2665; www.f-stop.org) can provide additional tips for traveling with film and equipment.

Carry-on scanners will not damage **videotape** in video cameras, but the magnetic fields emitted by the walk-through security gateways and handheld inspection wands will. Always place your loaded camcorder on the screening conveyor belt or have it hand-inspected. Be sure your batteries are charged, as you will probably be required to turn the device on to ensure that it's what it appears to be.

(© **800/FLY-IRISH;** www.aerlingus.ie) flies into Heathrow. Flights from Dublin to London are also available through **Ryan Air** (© **0870/156-9569;** www.ryanair.com) and **British Midland** (© **0870/607-0555;** www. flybmi.com).

GETTING THROUGH THE AIRPORT

With the federalization of airport security, security procedures at U.S. airports are more stable and consistent than ever. Generally, you'll be fine if you arrive at the airport **1 hour** before a domestic flight and **2 hours** before an international flight; if you show up late, tell an airline employee and he or she will probably whisk you to the front of the line.

Bring a **current, government-issued photo ID** such as a driver's license or passport, and if you've got an E-ticket, print out the **official confirmation page;** you may need to show your confirmation at the security checkpoint, and your ID at the ticket counter or the gate. (Children under 18 do not need photo IDs for domestic flights, but the adults checking in with them need them.)

Security lines are getting shorter than they were during 2001 and 2002, but some doozies remain. If you have trouble standing for long periods of time, tell an airline employee; the airline will provide a wheelchair. Speed up security by **not wearing metal objects** such as big belt buckles or clanky earrings. If you've got metallic body parts, a note from your doctor can prevent a long chat with the security screeners. Keep in mind that only **ticketed passengers** are allowed past security, except for folks escorting passengers with disabilities or children.

Federalization has stabilized **what you can carry on** and **what you can't.** The general rule is that sharp things are out, nail clippers are okay, and food and beverages must be passed through the X-ray machine—but that security screeners can't make you drink from your coffee cup. Bring food in your carry-on rather than checking it, as explosive-detection machines used on checked luggage have been known to mistake food (especially chocolate, for some reason) for bombs. Travelers in the U.S. are allowed one carry-on bag, plus a "personal item" such as a purse, briefcase, or laptop bag. Carry-on hoarders can stuff all sorts of things into a laptop bag; as long as it has a laptop in it, it's still considered a personal item. The Transportation Security Administration (TSA) has issued a list of restricted items; check its website (www.tsa.gov) for details.

At press time the TSA had started phasing out **gate check-in** at all U.S. airports. Passengers with E-tickets and without checked bags can still beat the ticket-counter lines by using **electronic kiosks** or even **online check-in.** Ask your airline which alternatives are available, and if you're using a kiosk, bring the credit card you used to book the ticket. If you're checking bags, you will still be able to use most airlines' kiosks; again call your airline for up-to-date information. **Curbside check-in** is also a good way to avoid lines, although a few airlines still ban curbside check-in entirely; call before you go.

FLYING FOR LESS: TIPS FOR GETTING THE BEST AIRFARE

Passengers sharing the same airplane cabin rarely pay the same fare. Travelers who need to purchase tickets at the last minute, change their itinerary at a moment's notice, or fly one-way often get stuck paying the premium rate. Here are some ways to keep your airfare costs down.

- Passengers who can book their tickets **long in advance,** who can **stay over Saturday night,** or who

fly midweek or **at less-trafficked hours** will pay a fraction of the full fare. If your schedule is flexible, say so, and ask if you can secure a cheaper fare by changing your flight plans.

- You can also save on airfares by keeping an eye out in local newspapers for **promotional specials** or **fare wars,** when airlines lower prices on their most popular routes. You rarely see fare wars offered for peak travel times, but if you can travel in the off-months, you may snag a bargain.
- Search **the Internet** for cheap fares (see "Planning Your Trip Online").
- **Consolidators,** also known as bucket shops, are great sources for international tickets, although they usually can't beat the Internet on fares within North America. Start by looking in Sunday newspaper travel sections; U.S. travelers should focus on the *New York Times, Los Angeles Times,* and *Miami Herald. Beware:* Bucket shop tickets are usually nonrefundable or rigged with stiff cancellation penalties, often as high as 50% to 75% of the ticket price, and some put you on charter airlines with questionable safety records. Several reliable consolidators are available on the Net. **STA Travel** is now the world's leader in student travel, thanks to their purchase of Council Travel. It also offers good fares for travelers of all ages. **Flights.com** (© **800/TRAV-800;** www.flights.com) started in Europe and has excellent fares worldwide, but particularly to that continent. It also has "local" websites in 12 countries. **FlyCheap** (© **800/FLY-CHEAP;** www.flycheap.com) is owned by packageholiday megalith MyTravel and so has especially good access to fares for sunny destinations. **Air Tickets**

Direct (© **800/778-3447;** www.airticketsdirect.com) is based in Montreal and leverages the currently weak Canadian dollar for low fares.

- Join **frequent-flier clubs.** Accrue enough miles, and you'll be rewarded with free flights and elite status. It's free, and you'll get the best choice of seats, faster response to phone inquiries, and prompter service if your luggage is stolen, your flight is canceled or delayed, or if you want to change your seat. You don't need to fly to build frequent-flier miles—**frequent-flier credit cards** can provide thousands of miles for doing your everyday shopping.
- For many more tips about air travel, including a rundown of the major frequent-flier credit cards, pick up a copy of *Frommer's Fly Safe, Fly Smart* (Wiley Publishing, Inc.).

LONG-HAUL FLIGHTS: HOW TO STAY COMFORTABLE

Long flights can be trying; stuffy air and cramped seats can make you feel as if you're being sent parcel post in a small box. But with a little advance planning, you can make an otherwise unpleasant experience almost bearable.

- Your choice of airline and airplane will definitely affect your legroom. Among U.S. airlines, American Airlines has the best average seat pitch (the distance between a seat and the row in front of it). Find more details at www.seatguru.com, which has extensive details about almost every seat on six major U.S. airlines. For international airlines, research firm Skytrax has posted a list of average seat pitches at www.airlinequality.com.
- Emergency exit seats and bulkhead seats typically have the most legroom. Emergency exit seats are usually held back to be assigned

the day of a flight (to ensure that the seat is filled by someone able-bodied); it's worth getting to the ticket counter early to snag one of these spots for a long flight. Keep in mind that bulkheads are where airlines often put baby bassinets, so you may be sitting next to an infant.

- To have two seats for yourself, try for an aisle seat in a center section toward the back of coach. If you're traveling with a companion, book an aisle and a window seat. Middle seats are usually booked last, so chances are good you'll end up with three seats to yourselves. And in the event that a third passenger is assigned the middle seat, he or she will probably be more than happy to trade for a window or an aisle.

- Ask about entertainment options. Many airlines offer seatback video systems where you get to choose your movies or play video games—but only on some of their planes. (Boeing 777s are your best bet.)

- To sleep, avoid the last row of any section or a row in front of an emergency exit, as these seats are the least likely to recline. Avoid seats near highly trafficked toilet areas. You also may want to reserve a window seat so that you can rest your head and avoid being bumped in the aisle.

- Get up, walk around, and stretch every 60 to 90 minutes to keep your blood flowing. This helps avoid deep vein thrombosis, or "economy-class syndrome," a rare and deadly condition that can be caused by sitting in cramped conditions for too long.

- Drink water before, during, and after your flight to combat the lack of humidity in airplane cabins—which can be drier than the Sahara. Bring a bottle of water on board. Avoid alcohol, which will dehydrate you.

- If you're flying with kids, don't forget to carry on toys, books, pacifiers, and chewing gum to help them relieve ear pressure buildup during ascent and descent. Let each child pack his or her own backpack with favorite toys.

BY CAR FROM CONTINENTAL EUROPE

If you plan to transport a rented car between England and France, check in advance with the car-rental company about license and insurance requirements and additional drop-off charges before you begin.

The English Channel is crisscrossed with "drive-on, drive-off" car-ferry services, with many operating from Boulogne and Calais in France. From either of those ports, Sealink ferries will carry you, your luggage, and, if you like, your car. The most popular point of arrival along the English coast is Folkestone.

Taking a car beneath the Channel is more complicated and more expensive. Since the Channel Tunnel's opening, most passengers have opted to ride the train alone, without being accompanied by their car. The Eurostar trains, discussed below, carry passengers only; Le Shuttle trains carry freight cars, trucks, and passenger cars.

Count on at least £227 ($363) for a return ticket, but know that the cost of moving a car on *Le Shuttle* varies according to the season and day of the week. Frankly, it's a lot cheaper to transport your car across by conventional ferryboat, but if you insist, here's what you'll need to know: You'll negotiate both English and French customs as part of one combined process, usually on the English side of the Channel. You can remain within your vehicle even after you drive it onto a flatbed railway car during the 35-minute crossing. (For 19 min. of this crossing, you'll actually be underwater;

if you want, you can leave the confines of your car and ride within a brightly lit, air-conditioned passenger car.) When the trip is over, you simply drive off the flatbed railway car and toward your destination. Total travel time between the French and English highway system is about 1 hour. As a means of speeding the flow of perishable goods across the Channel, the car and truck service usually operates 24 hours a day, at intervals that vary from 15 minutes to once an hour, depending on the time of day. Neither BritRail nor any of the agencies dealing with reservations for passenger trains through the Chunnel will reserve space for your car in advance, and considering the frequency of the traffic on the Chunnel, they're usually not necessary. For information about *Le Shuttle* car-rail service after you reach England, call © **0870/535-3535;** www.eurotunnel.com).

Duty-free stores, restaurants, and service stations are available to travelers on both sides of the Channel. A bilingual staff is on hand to assist travelers at both the British and French terminals.

BY TRAIN FROM CONTINENTAL EUROPE

Britain's isolation from the rest of Europe led to the development of an independent railway network with different rules and regulations from those observed on the Continent. That's all changing now, but one big difference that may affect you still remains: If you're traveling to Britain from the Continent, *your Eurailpass will not be valid when you get there.*

In 1994, Queen Elizabeth and President François Mitterand officially opened the Channel Tunnel, or Chunnel, and the Eurostar express passenger train began twice-daily service between London and both Paris and Brussels— a 3-hour trip. The $15 billion tunnel, one of the great engineering feats of all time, is the first link between Britain and the Continent since the Ice Age.

So if you're coming to London from say, Rome, your Eurailpass will get you as far as the Chunnel. At that point you can cross the English Channel aboard the Eurostar, and you'll receive a discount on your ticket. Once in England, you must use a separate BritRail pass or purchase a direct ticket to continue on to your destination.

Rail Europe (© **800/848-7245** in U.S., or 800/361-RAIL in Canada; fax 800/432-1329; www.raileurope. com) sells direct-service tickets on the Eurostar between Paris or Brussels and London. A one-way fare between Paris and London costs $279 in first class and $199 in second class.

In London, make reservations for **Eurostar** by calling © **0870/530-0003;** in Paris, call © **01/44-51-06-02;** and in the United States, it's © **800/EUROSTAR** (www.eurostar. com). Eurostar trains arrive and depart from London's Waterloo Station, Paris's Gare du Nord, and Brussels's Central Station.

BY FERRY/HOVERCRAFT FROM CONTINENTAL EUROPE

P & O Ferries (© **800/677-8585** or 08705/20-20-20; www.posl.com) operates car and passenger ferries between Dover and Calais, France (25 sailings a day; 75 min. each way).

By far the most popular route across the English Channel is between Calais and Dover. **HoverSpeed** (© **0870/5240241;** www.hoverspeed.com) operates at least 12 hovercraft crossings daily; the trip takes 35 minutes. They also run a SeaCat (a catamaran propelled by jet engines) that takes slightly longer to make the crossing between Boulogne and Folkestone. The SeaCats depart about four times a day on the 55-minute voyage.

Traveling by hovercraft or SeaCat cuts the time of your surface journey from the Continent to the United Kingdom. A hovercraft trip is definitely a fun adventure, because the vessel is technically "flying" over the water. A SeaCat crossing from Folkestone to Boulogne is longer in miles, but it is covered faster than conventional ferryboats making the Calais–Dover crossing. For reservations and information, call HoverSpeed (see above). For foot passengers, a typical adult fare, with a 5-day return policy, is £24 ($36) or half fare for children.

BY BUS

If you're traveling to London from elsewhere in the United Kingdom, consider purchasing a **Britexpress Card,** which entitles you to a 30% discount on National Express (England and Wales) and Caledonian Express (Scotland) buses. Contact a travel agent for details.

Bus connections to Britain from the continent are generally not very comfortable, though some lines are more convenient than others. One line with a relatively good reputation is **Eurolines,** 52 Grosvenor Gardens, London SW1W 0AU (© **020/77308235;** www.eurolines.com). They book passage on buses traveling twice a day between London and Paris (9 hr.); three times a day from Amsterdam (12 hr.); three times a week from Munich (24 hr.); and three times a week from Stockholm (44 hr.). On the longer routes, which employ two alternating drivers, the bus proceeds almost without interruption, taking occasional breaks for meals.

14 Packages for the Independent Traveler

Before you start your search for the lowest airfare, you may want to consider booking your flight as part of a travel package. Package tours are not the same thing as escorted tours. Package tours are simply a way to buy the airfare, accommodations, and other elements of your trip (such as car rentals, airport transfers, and sometimes even activities) at the same time and often at discounted prices—kind of like one-stop shopping. Packages are sold in bulk to tour operators—who resell them to the public at a cost that usually undercuts standard rates.

One good source of package deals is the airlines themselves. Most major airlines offer air/land packages, including **American Airlines Vacations** (© 800/321-2121; www.aavacations.com), **Delta Vacations** (© 800/221-6666; www.deltavacations.com), **Continental Airlines Vacations** (© 800/301-3800; www.coolvacations.com), and **United Vacations** (© 888/854-3899; www.unitedvacations.com). Great deals can often be found by booking a package tour through **Virgin Atlantic Airways** (© **800/862-8621;** www.virgin.com).

Far and away, the most options are with **British Airways Holidays** (© **877/428-2228;** www.britishairways.com). Its offerings within the British Isles are more comprehensive than those of its competitors and can be tailored to your specific interests and budget. Many tours, such as the 9-day, all-inclusive tour through the great houses and gardens of England, include the ongoing services of a guide and lecturer. But if you prefer to travel independently, without following an organized tour, a sales representative can tailor an itinerary specifically for you, with discounted rates in a wide assortment of big-city hotels. If you opt for this, you can rent a car or choose to take the train. For a free catalog and additional information, call British Airways before you book; some of the company's available options are contingent upon the purchase of a round-trip transatlantic air ticket.

Several big **online travel agencies**—Expedia, Travelocity, Orbitz, Site59, and Lastminute.com—also do a brisk business in packages. If you're unsure about the pedigree of a smaller packager, check with the Better Business Bureau in the city where the company is based, or go online at www.bbb.org. If a packager won't tell you where it's based, don't fly with them.

Liberty Travel (© **888/271-1584,** or 201/934-3888 to be connected with the agent closest to you; www.libertytravel.com), one of the biggest packagers in the Northeast, often runs a full-page ad in the Sunday papers. **American Express Travel** (© **800/ 941-2639;** www.travelimpressions.com.com) is another option. Check out its **Last Minute Travel Bargains** site (www.lastminute.com), offered in conjunction with **American Express,** with deeply discounted vacation packages and reduced airline fares that differ from the E-savers bargains that Continental e-mails weekly to subscribers. **Northwest Airlines** offers a similar service. Posted on Northwest's website (www.nwa.com) every Wednesday, its **Cyber Saver Bargain Alerts** offer special hotel rates, package deals, and discounted airline fares.

Travel packages are also listed in the travel section of your local Sunday newspaper. Or check ads in the national travel magazines such as *Arthur Frommer's Budget Travel Magazine, Travel &* *Leisure, National Geographic Traveler,* and *Condé Nast Traveler.*

Package tours can vary by leaps and bounds. Some offer a better class of hotels than others. Some offer the same hotels for lower prices. Some offer flights on scheduled airlines, while others book charters. Some limit your choice of accommodations and travel days. You are often required to make a large payment up front. On the plus side, packages can save you money, offering group prices but allowing for independent travel. Some even let you add on a few guided excursions or escorted day trips (also at prices lower than if you booked them yourself) without booking an entirely escorted tour.

Before you invest in a package tour, get some answers. Ask about the **accommodations choices** and prices for each. Then look up the hotels' reviews in a Frommer's guide and check their rates for your specific dates of travel online. You'll also want to find out what **type of room** you get. If you need a certain type of room, ask for it; don't take whatever is thrown your way. Request a nonsmoking room, a quiet room, a room with a view, or whatever you fancy.

Finally, look for **hidden expenses.** Ask whether airport departure fees and taxes, for example, are included in the total cost.

15 Getting Around England

BY CAR
The British car-rental market is among the most competitive in Europe. Nevertheless, car rentals are relatively expensive, unless you avail yourself of one of the promotional deals frequently offered by British Airways and others.

Because cars in Britain travel on the left side of the road, their steering wheels are positioned on the "wrong" side of the vehicle. This means that if your rental car has a manual transmission (most do), you'll be shifting with your left hand. You'll pay more for an automatic—and make sure to request one when you reserve. Most car-rental companies accept your U.S. driver's license, provided you're 23 years old (21 in rare instances) and have had the license for more than a year.

TIPS FOR SAVING MONEY   Car-rental rates vary even more than airline fares. The price will depend on

Money-Saving Car-Rental Tip

Many rental companies grant discounts to those who reserve their cars in advance (usually 48 hr.) through toll-free reservations offices in the renter's home country. Rentals of a week or more are almost always less expensive per day than day rentals.

the size of the car, where and when you pick it up and drop it off, the length of the rental period, where and how far you drive it, whether you purchase insurance, and a host of other factors. A few key questions could save you hundreds of dollars:

Are weekend rates lower than weekday rates? For instance, ask if the rate is the same for Friday morning pickup as it is for Thursday night.

Is a weekly rate cheaper than the daily rate? If you need to keep the car for 4 days, it may be cheaper to keep it for 5, even if you don't need it that long.

Does the agency assess a drop-off charge if you do not return the car to the same location where you picked it up? Is it cheaper to pick up the car at the airport rather than a downtown location?

Are special promotional rates available? If you see an advertised price in your local newspaper, be sure to ask for that specific rate; otherwise, you may be charged the standard cost. Terms change constantly, and phone operators may not volunteer information.

Are discounts available for members of AARP, AAA, frequent-flyer programs, or trade unions? If you belong to any of these organizations, you may well be entitled to discounts of up to 30%.

What is the cost of adding an additional driver's name to the contract?

How many free miles are included in the price? This may well be negotiable, depending on the length of your rental.

How much does the rental company charge to refill your gas tank if you return with the tank less than full? Though most rental companies claim these prices are "competitive," fuel is almost always cheaper in town. Allow enough time to refuel the car yourself before returning it.

THE MAJOR COMPANIES Rentals are available through **Avis** (© **800/331-1084;** www.avis.com), **British Airways** (© **800/AIRWAYS;** www.britishairways.com), **Budget** (© **800/472-3325;** www.budget. com), and **Hertz** (© **800/654-3001;** www.hertz.com). **Kemwel Holiday Auto** (© **800/678-0678;** www. kemwel.com) is among the cheapest and most reliable of the local rental agencies. **AutoEurope** (© **800/223-5555** in the U.S., or 0800/899893 in London; www.autoeurope.com) acts as a wholesale company for rental agencies in Europe.

When you reserve a car, be sure to ask if the price includes the 17.5% VAT.

RENTAL INSURANCE Before you drive off in a rental car, check that you're insured. Hasty assumptions about your personal auto insurance or a rental agency's additional coverage could end up costing you tens of thousands of dollars—even if an accident you're involved in was clearly the fault of another driver.

The basic insurance coverage offered by most car-rental companies, the Loss/Damage Waiver (LDW) or Collision Damage Waiver (CDW), can cost as much as $20 a day.

U.S. drivers who have their own car insurance are usually covered in the United States for loss of or damage to a rental car and for liability in case of injury to any other party involved in an accident. But coverage usually doesn't extend outside the United States. Find out whether you are covered in England, whether your policy extends to all persons driving the rental car, how much liability is covered in case an outside party is injured in an accident, and whether the type of vehicle you are renting is included under your contract (rental trucks, sports utility vehicles, and luxury vehicles such as a Jaguar may not be covered).

Most major credit cards provide some coverage—provided they were used to pay for the rental. No matter whether they cover damage to or theft of your rental, credit cards will not cover liability, the cost of injury to an outside party, or damage to an outside party's vehicle. When you are driving outside the U.S., you may seriously want to consider purchasing additional liability insurance from your rental company. Be sure to check the terms, however; some rental agencies only cover liability if the renter is not at fault.

Be aware that each credit card company has its own peculiarities. Most American Express Optima cards, for instance, do not provide any insurance. American Express does not cover vehicles valued at over $50,000 when new, luxury vehicles (such as a Porsche), or vehicles built on a truck chassis. MasterCard does not provide coverage for loss, theft, or fire damage, and only covers collision damage if the rental period does not exceed 15 days. Obviously, terms vary widely, so call your credit card company directly before you rent.

DRIVING RULES & REQUIREMENTS   In England, you drive on the left and pass on the right. Road signs are clear, and the international symbols are unmistakable.

You must present your passport and driver's license when you rent a car in Britain. No special British license is needed. It's a good idea to get a copy of the British Highway Code, available from almost any gas station or newsstand ("news stall" in British).

Warning: Pedestrian crossings are marked by striped lines ("zebra stripes") on the road. Flashing lights near the curb indicate that drivers must stop and yield the right of way if a pedestrian has stepped out into the "zebra crossing" zone to cross the street.

ROAD MAPS   The best road map is *The Ordinance Survey Motor Atlas of Great Britain,* whether you want the fastest route to Manchester or need to locate some obscure village. Revised annually, it's published by Temple Press and is available at most bookstores, including **Foyle, Ltd.,** 113 and 119 Charing Cross Rd., London, WC2 H0EB (© **020/7440-3225**).

BREAKDOWNS   If you are a member of AAA in the United States, you are automatically eligible for the same roadside services you receive at home. Be sure to bring your membership card with you on your trip. In an emergency, call the **Automobile Association of Great Britain**'s emergency road service (© **0800/887-766**). If you are not a member of AAA, you may want to join one of England's two major auto clubs—the Automobile Association (AA) and the Royal Automobile Club (RAC). Membership, available through your car-rental agent, entitles you to free legal and technical advice on motoring matters plus a whole range of discounts on automobile products and services.

The **AA** is located at Carr Ellison House, William Armstrong Drive, New Castle-upon-Tyne NE4 7YA (© **0870/550-0600**). The **RAC** can be contacted at P.O. Box 700, Bristol, Somerset BS99 1RB (© **0800/828282**).

If your car breaks down on the highway, you can call for 24-hour breakdown service from a roadside phone. The 24-hour number to call for **AA** is ✆ **0800/262-050;** for **RAC** it is ✆ **0800/828282.** All superhighways (motorways in Britain) are provided with special emergency phones connected to police traffic units; the police can contact either auto club on your behalf.

GASOLINE   Petrol, as it's called here, is sold by the liter (4.2l to a U.S. gal.). Prices are much higher than in the United States, and most stations are self-serve. In some remote areas, stations are few and far between; many are closed on Sunday.

BY PLANE

British Airways (✆ **800/AIRWAYS;** www.britishairways.com) flies to more than 20 cities outside London, including Manchester, Glasgow, and Edinburgh. Ask about BA's Super Shuttle Saver fares, which can save you up to 50% on travel to certain key British cities. If seats are available on the flight of your choice, no advance reservations are necessary—although to benefit from the lowest prices, passengers must spend a Saturday night away from their point of origin and fly during specified off-peak times. Flights are usually restricted to weekdays 10am to 3:30pm.

For passengers planning on visiting widely scattered destinations within the United Kingdom, perhaps with a side trip to a city on Europe's mainland, British Airways' **Europe Airpass** allows discounted travel in a continuous loop involving between 3 and 12 cities. Passengers must end their journey where they began it and fly exclusively on BA flights. Such a ticket (for example, London to Paris to Manchester, returning to London) will cut the cost of each segment of the itinerary by about 40% to 50% over individually booked tickets. The pass allows travel to about a dozen of the U.K.'s most-visited cities and regions, with discounted add-ons to most of

BA's European destinations as well. While the Airpass is a good bargain for round-trip travel between London and Rome, it's not very practical for travel from, say, Rome to Madrid. You'd be better off traveling between points on the Continent by full-fare airline ticket, train, bus, or car.

The Europe Airpass must be booked and paid for at least 7 days before a passenger's departure from North America. All segments of the itinerary, including transatlantic passage, must be booked at the same time. Some changes are permitted in flight dates (but not destinations) after the ticket is issued. Check with British Airways for full details and restrictions.

BY TRAIN

A Eurailpass is not valid in Great Britain, but there are several special passes for train travel outside London. For railroad information, go to Rail Travel centers in the main London railway stations (Waterloo, King's Cross, Euston, and Paddington).

You can download faxable order forms or order online using a BritRail Pass Shopping Cart feature (www. britainontrack.com).

BRITRAIL TRAVEL PASSES

If you're traveling beyond London anywhere in the United Kingdom, consider purchasing a **BritRail Consecutive Pass.** These passes allow you to travel for a consecutive number of days for a flat rate. In first class adults pay $285 for 4 days, $405 for 8 days, $609 for 15 days, $769 for 22 days, and $915 for 1 month. In second class, fares are $189 for 4 days, $269 for 8 days, $405 for 15 days, $515 for 22 days, and $609 for 1 month. Seniors (60 and over) qualify for discounts in first class travel: It's $245 for 4 days, $345 for 8 days, $519 for 15 days, $659 for 22 days, and $779 for 1 month. Passengers under 26 quality for a **Youth Pass:** $155 for 4 days, $219 for 8 days, $285 for 15 days,

Train Travel from London to Principal Cities

To	From (London Stations)	Typical No. of Trains Per Day	Miles	Travel Time
Bath	Paddington	25	107	1 hr. 11 min.
Birmingham	Euston/Paddington	35	113	1 hr. 37 min.
Bristol	Paddington	46	119	1 hr. 26 min.
Carlisle	Euston	10	299	3 hr. 40 min.
Chester	Euston	16	179	2 hr. 36 min.
Exeter	Paddington	17	174	1 hr. 55 min.
Leeds	King's Cross	19	185	2 hr. 12 min.
Liverpool	Euston	14	193	2 hr. 34 min.
Manchester	Euston	16	180	2 hr. 27 min.
Newcastle	King's Cross	26	268	2 hr. 50 min.
Penzance	Paddington	29	305	5 hr.
Plymouth	Paddington	14	226	2 hr. 35 min.
York	King's Cross	27	188	1 hr. 57 min.

$359 for 22 days, and $429 for 1 month.

BritRail Passes allow unlimited travel in England, Scotland, and Wales on any British Rail scheduled train over the whole of the network during the validity of the pass without restrictions. The more versatile pass is **BritRail FlexiPass,** allowing you to travel a specific number of days within a 2-month time period. It costs $519 for 8 days of travel in first class or $349 in standard class. Discounts are granted to seniors, and children (ages 5–15) pay half the adult fare. For the **BritRail Family Pass,** you can purchase any adult or senior BritRail Pass, which allows one child (ages 5–15) to travel for free according to the same limitations as the adult fare.

The **BritRail Days Out from London Pass** is best suited for visitors wishing to make day trips to places like Oxford and Cambridge. There's no need to hassle with line-ups to purchase tickets; you can go directly to your train and board. The cost for 2 days within an 8-day period is $89 for adults and $31 for children in first class or $59 for adults and $21 for children in second class.

To call BritRail in the United States, dial © **866/BRITAIL** or 877/677-1066; fax 877/477-1066; www.britrail.net.

Travelers who arrive from France by boat and pick up a British Rail train at Dover arrive at **Victoria Station,** in the center of London. Those journeying south by rail from Edinburgh arrive at **King's Cross Station.**

BY BUS

In Britain, a long-distance touring bus is called a "coach"; "buses" are taken for local transportation. There's an efficient and frequent express motorcoach network—run by National Express and other independent operators—that links most of Britain's towns and cities. Destinations off primary routes are easily reached by stopping and transferring to a local bus. Tickets are relatively cheap, often half the price of rail fare. It's usually cheaper to purchase a round-trip ("return") ticket than two one-way fares separately.

Victoria Coach Station, on Buckingham Palace Road (© **020/7730-3466**), is the departure point for most large coach operators. The coach station is located just 2 blocks from Victoria Rail Station. For credit card sales (MasterCard and VISA only), call ☎ **020/7730-3499** Monday to Saturday 9am to 7pm. For cash purchases, get there at least 30 minutes before departure.

National Express runs luxurious long-distance coaches with hostesses, light refreshments, reclining seats, toilets, and nonsmoking areas. Details about all coach services can be obtained by phoning ☎ **020/7529-2000** daily 8am to 10pm (or visit www.national expressgroup.com). The National Express ticket office at Victoria Station opens 6am to 11pm.

If you plan to focus on England and Wales, you might want to consider **National Express's Tourist Trail Pass,** offering unlimited travel on their network. A 3-day pass costs £49 ($78); a 5-day pass, £85 ($136); an 8-day pass, £135 ($216); and a 14-day pass, £190 ($304).

For journeys within a 56km (35-mile) radius of London, try the **Green Line Coach Service,** Endsleigh Road, Merstham Redhill, Surrey RH1 3LX (☎ **0870/608-7261;** www.greenline. co.uk). With a 1-day Diamond Rover Ticket, costing £8 ($13) for adults and £5 ($8) for children, you can visit many of the attractions of Greater London and the surrounding region, including Windsor Castle and Hampton Court. The pass is valid on almost all Green Line routes Monday to Friday after 9am and all day Saturday and Sunday.

Green Line has bus routes called Country Bus Lines that circle through the periphery of London. Although they do not usually go directly into the center of the capital, they do hook up with the Green Line coaches and red buses that do.

16 Tips on Accommodations

Reserve your accommodations as far in advance as possible, even in the so-called slow months from November to April. Tourist travel to London peaks from May to October; during that period, it's hard to come by a moderate or inexpensive hotel room.

CLASSIFICATIONS Unlike some countries, England doesn't have a rigid hotel-classification system; its Tourist Board rates accommodations in two ways: Crowns (zero to five) indicate the presence or absence of amenities, without further comment. In addition, the board judges hostelries on their standards, quality, and hospitality; they are rated "listed," "approved,"

"commended," "highly commended," and "deluxe" (the highest). "Listed" accommodations are for the most part very modest. However, the system is voluntary, and many hotels do not participate. Crown ratings are posted outside the buildings.

Many hotels, especially older ones, have added modern wings, with all the amenities, to their less up-to-date sections. When making reservations, always ask what section of the hotel you'll be staying in, if it has extensions.

All hotels once included an English breakfast of bacon and eggs in the room price, but that is no longer the case. In some hotels, a continental

---

Bathroom Tips

The designation of a private shower (or bathtub) in a room description doesn't necessarily mean that the room also has a toilet. Similarly, a room that's described as not having a private bathroom may have an in-room sink.

Value Tips for Saving on Your Hotel Room

The rack rate is the maximum rate that a hotel charges for a room—usually the price that's officially posted somewhere in the room. Hardly anybody pays this price, however, and there are many ways to save a bundle.

1. **Don't be afraid to bargain.** Get in the habit of asking for a lower price than the first one quoted. Always ask politely if a less expensive room is available, or whether any special rates apply to you. You may qualify for corporate, student, military, senior, or other discounts.

2. **Dial direct.** When booking a room in a chain hotel, call the hotel's local line, as well as the toll-free number, and see where you get the best deal. A hotel makes nothing on a room that stays empty. The front desk clerk is aware of vacancies and will often grant deep discounts in order to fill up.

3. **Remember the law of supply and demand.** Resort hotels are most crowded (*read:* most expensive) on weekends; discounts are usually available for midweek stays. On the flip side, business hotels in downtown locations are busiest during the week; expect discounts over the weekend.

4. **Look into group or long-stay discounts.** If you come as part of a group, you should be able to negotiate a bargain. Likewise, when you're planning a long stay in town—usually from 5 days to 1 week—you may qualify for a discount. Generally, you receive 1 night free after a 7-night stay.

5. **Avoid excess charges.** When you book a room, ask whether the hotel charges for parking. Most hotels have free, available space, but many urban or beachfront hotels don't. Find out before you use your room phone whether the hotel imposes a surcharge on local or long-distance calls. A pay phone, however inconvenient, may save you money.

6. **Book an efficiency.** A room with a kitchenette allows you to shop and eat meals in. Families especially will save money on food this way.

7. **Investigate reservation services.** These outfits usually work as consolidators, buying up or reserving rooms in bulk and then selling them to customers at a discount. *But remember:* These discounts apply to rack rates, so you may get a better deal directly through the hotel. Some of the more reputable providers: **Accommodations Express** (☎ 800/950-4685; www.accommodationsexpress.com); **hoteldiscount.com** (☎ 800/96HOTEL; www.180096HOTEL.com); and **Quikbook** (☎ 800/789-9887, includes fax on demand service; www.quikbook.com). On the inexpensive side, **Hostelling International USA**, 8401 Colesville Rd., Silver Springs, MD 20910 (☎ 202/783-6161; fax 202/783-6171; www.hiausa.org), has a directory of low-cost lodging around the country.

breakfast is offered, but that usually means just tea or coffee and toast.

BED-&-BREAKFASTS   In towns, cities, and villages throughout England, homeowners take in paying guests. Watch for the familiar bed-and-breakfast (B&B) signs. Generally, these are modest family homes, although they are sometimes like small hotels, with as many as 15 rooms. If they're that big, they are more properly classified as guesthouses. B&Bs are the cheapest places you can stay in England and still be comfortable.

Hometours International, P.O. Box 11503, Knoxville, TN 37939 (© **800/367-4668** or 865/690-8484; www.hometours.com), will make bed-and-breakfast reservations in England, Scotland, and Wales. This is the only company that guarantees reservations for more than 400 locations in Britain. Accommodations are paid for in the United States in dollars. Prices start as low as $50 per person per night, although they can go as high as $100 per person in London. Hometours can arrange for apartments in London or cottages in Britain beginning at $800 per week. It also offers walking tours of Britain, with prices starting as low as $850 for 7 days, including meals, tour guide, and accommodations.

Reservations for bed-and-breakfast accommodations in London can also be made by writing (not calling) the **British Travel Centre,** Rex House, 1 Lower Regent St., London SW1 4PQ. Once in London, you can visit their office (Tube: Piccadilly Circus).

In addition, Susan Opperman and Rosemary Lumb run **Bed and Breakfast Nationwide,** P.O. Box 2100, Clacton-on-Sea, Essex CO16 9BW, an agency specializing in privately owned bed-and-breakfasts all over Great Britain. Homes range from small cottages to large manor houses, as well as working farms, and prices vary

accordingly. You may be sure that owners have been specially selected for their sincere interest in overseas visitors. Remember that these are private homes, so hotel-type services are not available. You will, however, be assured of a warm welcome, a comfortable bed, a hearty breakfast, and a glimpse of British life. Write for a free brochure. To book accommodations outside London, call © **01255/ 831235** or fax 01255/831437; www.bedandbreakfastnationwide.com, daily 9am to 6pm.

FARMHOUSES

In many parts of the country, farmhouses have a few rooms set aside for paying guests, who usually arrive in the summer months. Farmhouses don't have the facilities of most guesthouses, but they have a rustic appeal and charm, especially for motorists, as they tend to lie off the beaten path. Prices are generally lower than bed-and-breakfasts or guesthouses, and sometimes you're offered some good country home cooking (at an extra charge) if you make arrangements in advance.

Farm Stay UK, National Agricultural Centre, Stoneleigh Park, Warwickshire CV8 2LZ (© **024/7669-6909;** www.farmstayuk.co.uk), publishes an annual directory in early December that includes 1,000 farms and bed-and-breakfasts throughout the United Kingdom. The directory, called *Stay on a Farm,* costs £3.95 ($6) for postage and may be purchased by credit card. The listings include quality ratings, the number of bedrooms, nearby attractions and activities, prices, and line drawings of each property. Also listed are any special details, such as rooms with four-poster beds or activities on the grounds (fishing, for example). Many farms are geared toward children, who can participate in light chores—gathering eggs or just tagging along—for an authentic farm experience. The prices range from £21 to £53 ($34–$85) a night and include an English breakfast and usually private facilities. (The higher prices are for stays at mansions and manor houses.)

Another option is self-catering accommodations, which are usually cottages or converted barns that cost from £165 to £510 ($264–$816) per week and include dishwashers and central heating. Each property is inspected annually not only by the Farm Holiday Bureau but also by the English Tourist Board. The majority of the properties, with the exception of those located in the mountains, are open year-round.

NATIONAL TRUST PROPERTIES The **National Trust of England,** Wales, and Northern Ireland, 36 Queen Anne's Gate, London SW1H 9AS (✆ **020/7222-9251;** www.nationaltrust.org.uk), is Britain's leading conservation organization. In addition to the many castles, forests, and gardens it maintains, the National Trust owns 300 houses and cottages in some of the most beautiful parts of the United Kingdom. Some of these properties are in remote and rural locations, some have incomparable views of the coastline, and others stand in the heart of villages and ancient cities.

Most of these comfortable self-catering holiday accommodations are available for rental year-round. Possibilities include a former coast guard cottage in Northumbria, a gaslit hideaway on the Isle of Wight, a country house above the Old Brewhouse at Chastleton, a 15th-century manor house hidden in the Cotswolds, and superb cottages in Devon and Cornwall. Houses can be booked for a week or more; many can be booked for midweek or weekend breaks on short notice, particularly in autumn and winter. National Trust properties can sleep from 2 to 12 guests, and range in price from £170 ($272) per week for a small winter rental to £1,705 ($2,728) per week for a larger property in peak season. Prices include VAT. Call ✆ **01225/791-199** for reservations.

Although anyone can book rentals through the National Trust, the trust's U.S. affiliate, the **Royal Oak Foundation,** 26 W. Broadway, Suite 950, New York, NY 10004 (✆ **800/913-6565** or 212/480-2889; www.royal-oak.org), publishes a full-color 120-page booklet that describes all National Trust holiday rental properties, their facilities, and prices. Copies cost $10 for nonmembers. Individual annual memberships are $50, and family memberships are $75. Benefits include free admission to all National Trust sites and properties open to the public, plus discounts on reservations at their cottages and houses as well as air and train travel.

HOLIDAY COTTAGES & VILLAGES Throughout England, there are fully furnished studios, houses, cottages, "flats" (apartments), and even trailers suitable for families or groups that can be rented by the month. From October to March, rents are sometimes reduced by 50%.

VisitBritain and most tourist offices have lists available. One recommended rental agency is **At Home Abroad, Inc.,** 405 E. 56th St., Suite 6H, New York, NY 10022 (✆ **212/421-9165;** fax 212/752-1591; www.athomeabroadinc.com). Interested parties should write or fax a description of their needs, and At Home Abroad will send listings at no charge.

British Travel International, P.O. Box 299, Elkton, VA 22827 (✆ **800/327-6097** or 540/298-2232; fax 540/298-2347; www.britishtravel.com), represents 8,000 to 10,000 rental properties in the United Kingdom, with rentals by the week (Sat–Sat). It requires a 50% payment at the time of booking. A catalog with pictures of its offerings is available for a $5 fee that is counted toward the deposit. It has everything from honey-colored, thatch-roofed Cotswold cottages to apartments in a university city. The company represents about 100 hotels in London whose rates are discounted by 5% to 50%, depending on the season and market conditions. It also has listings of some 4,000 bed-and-breakfast establishments. British Travel International serves as North American representative of the United Kingdom's largest bus company, National Express.

Barclay International Group (BIG), 3 School St., Glen Cove, NY 11542 (© **800/845-6636** or 516/759-5100; fax 516/609-0000; www.barclay web.com), specializes in short-term apartment rentals in London and English countryside cottages. These rentals may be appropriate for families, groups of friends, or businesspeople traveling together, and are sometimes less expensive than equivalent stays in hotels. Apartments available for overnight stays are usually more luxurious than you'd imagine. (The company prefers that you stay a minimum of 3 nights and charges a premium if your stay is shorter.) Furnished with a kitchen, they offer a low-cost alternative to restaurant

---

Tips   How to Get Your VAT Refund

To receive back a portion of the value-added tax paid on purchases made in Britain, first ask the store personnel if they do VAT refunds and what their minimum purchase for this is. Once you've achieved this minimum, ask for the paperwork; the retailer has to fill out a portion themselves. Several readers have reported that merchants have told them that they can get refund forms at the airport on their way out of the country. This is not true! You must get a refund form from the retailer, and it must be completed by the retailer on the spot.

Fill out your portion of the form and then present it, along with the goods, at the Customs office in the airport. Allow a half-hour to stand in line. *Remember:* You're required to show the goods at your time of departure, so don't pack them in your luggage and check it; put them in your carry-on instead.

Once you have the paperwork stamped by the officials, you have two choices: You can mail the papers and receive your refund in either a British check (no!) or a credit card refund (yes!); or you can go directly to the Cash VAT Refund desk at the airport and get your refund in cash. *The bad news:* If you accept cash other than sterling, you'll lose money on the conversion rate. (If you plan to mail your paperwork, remember to bring a stamp with you to the airport; if you forget, you can usually get stamps from stamp machines or convenience stores in the terminal.)

Be advised that many stores charge a flat fee for processing your refund, so £3 to £5 ($5–$8) may be automatically deducted from your total refund. But because the VAT in Britain is 17.5%, getting back 15% is doing just fine.

Note: If you're traveling to other countries within the European Union, you don't need to go through this process in Britain. Prior to departure from your final EU destination, you file for all your VAT refunds at one time.

meals. Apartments suitable for one or two occupants begin, during off-peak season, at around $500 a week (including VAT) and can go much higher for deluxe accommodations with hotel-like features and amenities. For extended stays in the English countryside, BIG has country cottages in the Cotswolds, the Lake District, Oxford, and farther afield in Scotland and Wales. The company can arrange for tickets for sightseeing attractions, BritRail passes, and various other "extras."

At the lower-priced end of the spectrum, there's **Hoseasons Holidays,** Sunway House, Raglan Road, Lowestoft, NR32 2LW (✆ **01502/502-588;** fax 01502/514-298; www.hoseasons.co.uk), a reservations agent based in Suffolk (East Anglia). They arrange stopovers in at least 300 vacation villages throughout Britain. Although many are isolated in bucolic regions far from cities and towns covered in this guidebook, others lie within an hour's drive of Stratford-upon-Avon or Oxford. Don't expect luxury or convenience: Vacation villages in England usually consist of a motley assortment of trailers, uninsulated bungalows, and/or mobile homes perched on cement blocks. They're intended as frugal escapes for claustrophobic urbanites with children. Such a place might not meet your expectations for an English countryside vacation (and a minimum booking of 3 nights is usually required), but it's hard to beat the rate. A 3-day stay begins at £87 ($139) per person, double occupancy.

YOUTH HOSTELS

Youth Hostels Association (England and Wales) operates a network of 230 youth hostels in major cities, in the countryside, and along the coast. They can be contacted at Customer Services Department, YHA, Trevelyan House, Dimple Road, Matlock, Derbyshire DE4 3YH (✆ **0870/870-8808;** www.yha.org.uk), for a free map with locations of each youth hostel and full details, including prices. For a full list of British YMCAs, call the **National Council of YMCAs** (✆ **020/8520-5599;** www.ymca.org.uk).

17 Discount Sightseeing Passes

Several passes are available that can cut down considerably on entrance costs to the country's stately homes and gardens. If you plan to do extensive touring, you'll save a lot of pounds by using one of these passes instead of paying the relatively steep entrance fees on an attraction-by-attraction basis.

COUNTRY-WIDE PASSES

Listed below are three organizations that offer passes waiving admission charges to hundreds of historical properties located throughout the United Kingdom. Each is a good deal; the money you save on visitation to just a few of the sites pays for the price of the pass.

The British National Trust offers members free entry to some 240 National Trust sites in England and more than 100 properties in Scotland. With an emphasis on gardens, castles, historic parks, abbeys, and ruins, National Trust sites include Chartwell, St. Michael's Mount, and Beatrix Potter's House. Individual memberships cost £32.50 ($52) annually, family memberships (for up to seven people) cost £60 ($96); so savings on admission charges, combined with discounts on holiday cottage reservations and British Air or BritRail travel, make this especially appealing. Members receive a listing of all properties, maps, and essential information for independent tours, and listings and reservations for holiday cottages located on the protected properties. Visa and MasterCard are accepted.

Contact **The British National Trust,** 36 Queen Anne's Gate, London

SW1H 9AS (© 020/7222-9251; www.nationaltrust.org.uk); or **The Royal Oak Foundation,** 26 Broadway, Suite 950, New York, NY 10004 (© **800/913-6565** or 212/480-2889; www.royal-oak.org).

English Heritage (www.englishheritage.org.uk) sells 7- and 14-day **Overseas Visitor Passes** as well as annual memberships that offer free admission to more than 300 historical sites in England and half-price admission to more than 100 additional sites in Scotland, Wales, and the Isle of Man. (Admission to these sites outside England becomes free for anyone who renews an annual membership after the 1st year.) Sites include Hadrian's Wall, Stonehenge, and Kenilworth Castle. Free or reduced admission to 450 historic reenactments and openair summer concerts, a handbook detailing all properties, and a map are also included. Those with annual memberships also receive events and concerts diaries and *Heritage Today,* a quarterly magazine.

A 7-day Overseas Visitor Pass runs £13.50 ($22) for an adult, free for a child 15 and under, and £30 ($48) for a family of six or less. Annual memberships cost £31 ($50) for an adult, £20 ($32) for youths ages 16 to 21, free for youths under 16, and £55 ($88) for a family. MasterCard and Visa are accepted. For visitor passes and membership, contact **Customer Services, English Heritage,** 429 Oxford St., London W1R 2HD (© **020/7973-3434**), or join directly at the site.

The **Great British Heritage Pass,** available through BritRail, allows entry to more than 500 public and privately owned historic properties, including Shakespeare's birthplace, Stonehenge, Windsor Castle, and Edinburgh Castle. This pass gains you entrance into many private properties not otherwise accessible. Passholders receive *The Great British Heritage*

Gazetteer, a list of the properties with maps and essential information.

A 7-day pass costs $54, a 15-day pass is available for $75, and a 1-month pass is $102. Passes are nonrefundable, and there is no discounted children's rate. A $10 handling fee is charged additionally for each pass issued. To order passes, contact **BritRail Travel International, Inc.,** 500 Mamaroneck Ave., Suite 314, Harrison, NY 10528; visit BritRail's **British Travel Shop** at 551 Fifth Ave. (at 45th St.), New York, NY 10176; call © **800/677-8585;** or check them out on the Web at www.britrail.com.

LONDON DISCOUNT PASSES

In addition to the discount transportation passes offered in London (See "Getting Around," in chapter 3), budget-minded tourists can take advantage of a sightseeing pass that offers discounts on dining, lodging, and attractions.

A **London for Less Card and Guidebook** costs $19.95 and gets you a 20% to 30% discount for various attractions, theater and concert tickets, restaurants and shops, tours, car rental, hotels, fees at Travelex foreign currency exchanges, and telephone calls. You may have neither time nor inclination to use a lot of the coupons; but with money off at the Royal Shakespeare Company, Royal Opera, Royal Ballet, and Royal Philharmonic, plus savings on admissions or tours at Buckingham Palace, the Tower of London, Westminster Abbey, Hampton Court Palace, Kensington Palace, and Kew Gardens, you're sure to cover the signon cost. Any extra shopping and dining discounts will be a bonus. The card and book are available in London at any tourist info center. To buy it before you leave home, call © **888/GO-FOR-LESS** (www.for-less.com), or visit the **BritRail Travel Office,** 551 Fifth Ave., 7th floor, New York, NY.

The **London Pass** ★★ provides admission to 60 attractions in and around London, £5 ($8) worth of phone calls, "timed" admission at some attractions, which allows you to bypass the queues, plus free travel on public transport (buses, tubes, and trains), and a pocket guidebook. It costs £32 ($51) for 1 day, £55 ($88) for 2 days, £71 ($114) for 3 days, or £110 ($176) for 6 days for adults. Children pay £20 ($32), £34 ($54), £45 ($72), or £61 ($98). The pass includes admission to St. Paul's Cathedral, HMS *Belfast,* the Jewish Museum, and the Thames Barrier Visitor Centre, and many more. Visit the website at www.londonpass.com or call © **01664/500-107.** *Tip:* Purchase the pass before you go because passes purchased in London do not include free transportation.

18 Recommended Reading

GENERAL & HISTORY

Anthony Sampson's *The Changing Anatomy of Britain* (Random House) still gives great insight into the idiosyncrasies of English society, Winston Churchill's *History of the English-Speaking Peoples* (Dodd Mead) is a tour de force in four volumes, while *The Gathering Storm* (Houghton-Mifflin) captures Europe on the brink of World War II.

My Love Affair with England (Ballantine), by Susan Allan Toth, tells of England's "many-layered past," and includes such tidbits as why English marmalade tastes good only when consumed as part of a real (make that greasy) English breakfast.

Britons: Forging the Nation (1707–1837) (Yale University Press), by Linda Colley, took more than a decade to finish. Ms. Colley takes the reader from the date of the Act of Union (formally joining Scotland and Wales to England) to the succession of the adolescent Victoria to the British throne. *Children of the Sun* (Basics Books), by Martin Green, portrays the "decadent" Twenties and the lives of such people as Randolph Churchill, Rupert Brooke, the Prince of Wales, and Christopher Isherwood.

In *A Writer's Britain* (Knopf), contemporary English author Margaret Drabble takes readers on a tour of the sacred and haunted literary landscapes of England, places that inspired Hardy, Woolf, Spenser, and Marvell.

Outsiders often paint more penetrating portraits than residents of any culture ever can. In England's case, many have expressed their views of the country at different periods. An early-18th-century portrait is provided by K. P. Moritz in *Journeys of a German in England in 1782* (Holt, Rinehart & Winston), about his travels from London to the Midlands. Nathaniel Hawthorne recorded his impressions in *Our Old Home* (1863), as did Ralph Waldo Emerson in *English Traits* (1856). For an ironic portrait of mid-19th-century Victorian British morals, manners, and society, seek out *Taine's Notes on England* (1872). Henry James comments on England at the turn of the 20th century in *English Hours.* In *A Passage to England* (St. Martins Press), Nirad Chaudhuri analyzes Britain and the British in a delightful, humorous book—a process continued today by such authors as Salman Rushdie, V. S. Naipaul, and Paul Theroux. Among the interesting portraits written by natives are Cobbet's *Rural Rides* (1830), depicting early-19th-century England; *In Search of England* (Methuen) by H. V. Morton; and *English Journey* (Harper) by J. B. Priestley. For what's really going on behind that serene Suffolk village scene, read Ronald Blythe's *Akenfield: Portrait of an English Village* (Random House).

ART & ARCHITECTURE

For general reference, there's the huge multivolume *Oxford History of English*

Art (Oxford University Press), and also the *Encyclopedia of British Art* (Thames Hudson), by David Bindman. *Painting in Britain 1530–1790* (Penguin), by Ellis Waterhouse, covers British art from the Tudor miniaturists to Gainsborough, Reynolds, and Hogarth, while *English Art, 1870–1940* (Oxford University Press), by Dennis Farr, covers the modern period. David Piper's *The Artist's London* (Oxford University Press) does what the title suggests—captures the city that artists have portrayed.

On architecture, for sheer amusing, opinionated entertainment try John Betjeman's *Ghastly Good Taste—the Rise and Fall of English Architecture* (St. Martin's Press). *A History of English Architecture* (Penguin), by Peter Kidson, Peter Murray, and Paul Thompson, covers the subject from Anglo-Saxon to modern times. Nikolaus Pevsner's *The Best Buildings of England: An Anthology* (Viking) and his *Outline of European Architecture* (Penguin) concentrate on the great periods of Tudor, Georgian, and Regency architecture. Mark Girouard has written several books on British architecture including *The Victorian Country House* (Country Life) and *Life in the English Country House* (Yale University Press), a fascinating social/architectural history from the Middle Ages to the 20th century, with handsome illustrations. *Looking Up in London* (Wiley Publishing, Inc.), by Jane Peyton, takes a fresh look at some of London's many architectural gems. *The Architect's Guide to London* (Reed International), by Renzo Salvadori, documents 100 landmark buildings with photographs and maps. *Nairn's London* (Penguin), by Ian Nairn, is a stimulating discourse on London's buildings. *London One: The Cities of London and Westminster* and *London Two: South* (Penguin) are works of love by well-known architectural writers Bridget Cherry and Nikolaus Pevsner.

ABOUT LONDON

London Perceived (Hogarth), by novelist and literary critic V. S. Pritchett, is a witty portrait of the city's history, art, literature, and life. Virginia Woolf's *The London Scene: Five Essays* (Random House) brilliantly depicts the London of the 1930s. *In Search of London* (Methuen), by H. V. Morton, is filled with anecdotal history and well worth reading, though written in the 1950s.

In *London: The Biography of a City* (Penguin), popular historian Christopher Hibbert paints a lively portrait. For some real 17th-century history, you can't beat the *Diary of Samuel Pepys* (written 1660–69), and for the flavor of the 18th century, try Daniel Defoe's *Tour Thro' London About the Year 1725* (Ayer).

Americans in London (William Morrow), by Brian N. Morton, is a street-by-street guide to clubs, homes, and favorite pubs of over 250 illustrious Americans who made London a temporary home. The *Guide to Literary London* (Batsford), by George Williams, charts literary tours through London from Chelsea to Bloomsbury. Donald Olsen's *The City as a Work of Art: London, Paris, and Vienna* (Yale University Press) is a well-illustrated text tracing the evolution of these great cities.

FICTION & BIOGRAPHY

Among English writers are found some of the greatest exponents of mystery and suspense novels from which a reader can get a good feel for English life both urban and rural. Agatha Christie, P. D. James, and Dorothy Sayers are a few of the familiar names, but the great London character is, of course, Sherlock Holmes of Baker Street, created by Arthur Conan Doyle. Any of these writers will give pleasure and insight into your London experience.

England's literary heritage is so vast, it's hard to select particular titles, but here are a few favorites. Master story-teller Charles Dickens re-creates Victorian London in such books as *Oliver Twist, David Copperfield,* and his earlier satirical *Sketches by Boz.*

Edwardian London and the '20s and '30s is captured wonderfully in any of Evelyn Waugh's social satires and comedies; any work from the Bloomsbury group will also prove enlightening, like Virginia Woolf's *Mrs. Dalloway,* which peers beneath the surface of the London scene. For a portrait of wartime London there's Elizabeth Bowen's *The Heat of the Day;* for an American slant on England and London there's Henry James's *The Awkward Age.*

Among 18th-century figures, there's a great biography of Samuel Johnson by his friend James Boswell, whose *Life of Samuel Johnson* (Modern Library College Editions) was first published in 1791. Antonia Fraser has written several biographies of English monarchs and political figures, including Charles II and Oliver Cromwell. Her most recent is *The Wives of Henry VIII* (Knopf), telling the sad story of the six women foolish enough to marry the Tudor monarch.

Another great Tudor monarch, Elizabeth I, emerges in a fully rounded portrait: *The Virgin Queen, Elizabeth I, Genius of the Golden Age* (Addison-Wesley), by Christopher Hibbert.

Another historian, Anne Somerset, wrote *Elizabeth I* (St. Martin's Press), which was hailed by some critics as the most "readable and reliable" portrait of England's most revered monarch to have emerged since 1934.

No woman—or man, for that matter—had greater influence on London than did Queen Victoria during her long reign (1837–1901). The Duchess of York (Prince Andrew's former wife, "Fergie") along with Benita Stoney, a professional researcher, captures the era in *Victoria and Albert: A Family Life at Osborne House* (Prentice Hall).

One reviewer said that HRH writes about "England's 19th-century rulers not as historical figures but as a loving couple and caring parents."

Another point of view is projected in *Victoria: The Young Queen* (Black-well), by Monica Charlot. This book has been praised for its "fresh information"; it traces the life of Victoria until the death of her husband, Prince Albert, in 1861. Queen Elizabeth II granted Charlot access to the Royal Archives.

In *Elizabeth II, Portrait of a Monarch* (St. Martin's Press), Douglas Keay drew on interviews with Prince Philip and Prince Charles.

Richard Ellman's *Oscar Wilde* (Knopf) also reveals such Victorian-era personalities as Lillie Langtry, Gilbert and Sullivan, and Henry James along the way. Quintessential English playwright Noël Coward and the London he inhabited, along with the likes of Nancy Mitford, Cecil Beaton, John Gielgud, Laurence Olivier, Vivien Leigh, Evelyn Waugh, and Rebecca West, are captured in Cole Lesley's *Remembered Laughter* (Knopf). *The Lives of John Lennon* (William Morrow), by Albert Goldman, traces the life of this most famous of all '60s musicians.

Dickens (Harper Perennial), by Peter Ackroyd, is a study of the painful childhood of the novelist. It's a massive volume, tracing everything from the reception of his first novel, *The Pickwick Papers,* to his scandalous desertion of his wife.

Other good reads include *Wild Spirit: The Story of Percy Bysshe Shelley* (Hodder & Stoughton), by Margaret Morley, a fictionalized biography of the poet. *Gertrude Jekyll* (Viking), by Sally Festing, paints a portrait of the woman called "the greatest artist in horticulture." *Anthony Trollope* (Knopf), by Victoria Glendinning, is a provocative portrait of the English novelist. *Lawrence and the Women: The*

Intimate Life of D. H. Lawrence (HarperCollins), by Elaine Feinstein, examines involvements with female friends and lovers of this passionately sensitive novelist.

FAST FACTS: England

For information on London, refer to "Fast Facts: London," in chapter 3.

Area Codes The country code for England is **44**. The area code for London is **020**.

Business Hours With many, many exceptions, business hours are Monday through Friday from 9am to 5pm. In general, stores are open Monday through Saturday from 9am to 5:30pm. In country towns, there is usually an early closing day (often on Wed or Thurs), when the shops close at 1pm.

Car Rentals See "Getting Around England," earlier in this chapter.

Climate See "When to Go," earlier in this chapter.

Currency See "Money," earlier in this chapter.

Customs See "Entry Requirements & Customs," earlier in this chapter.

Documents Required See "Entry Requirements & Customs," earlier in this chapter.

Drugstores In Britain, they're called "chemists." Every police station in the country has a list of emergency chemists. Dial "0" (zero) and ask the operator for the local police, who will give you the name of one nearest you.

Electricity British electricity is 240 volts AC (50 cycles), roughly twice the voltage in North America, which is 115 to 120 volts AC (60 cycles). American plugs don't fit British wall outlets. Always bring suitable transformers and/or adapters—if you plug an American appliance directly into a European electrical outlet without a transformer, you'll destroy your appliance and possibly start a fire. Tape recorders, VCRs, and other devices with motors intended to revolve at a fixed number of revolutions per minute probably won't work properly even with transformers.

Embassies & High Commissions See chapter 3, "Fast Facts: London."

Emergencies Dial **999** for police, fire, or ambulance. Give your name, address, and telephone number and state the nature of the emergency.

Holidays See "When to Go," earlier in this chapter.

Information See "Visitor Information," earlier in this chapter, and the individual city/regional chapters that follow.

Legal Aid The American Services section of the U.S. Consulate (see "Embassies & High Commissions," under "Fast Facts: London," in chapter 3) will give you advice if you run into trouble abroad. They can advise you of your rights and will even provide a list of attorneys (for which you'll have to pay if services are used). But they cannot interfere on your behalf in the legal processes of Great Britain. For questions about American citizens who are arrested abroad, including ways of getting money to them, telephone the **Citizens Emergency Center** of the Office of Special Consulate Services in Washington, D.C. (© **202/647-5225**).

Liquor Laws The legal drinking age is 18. Children under 16 aren't allowed in pubs, except in certain rooms, and then only when accompanied by a parent or guardian. Don't drink and drive. Penalties are stiff.

In England, pubs can legally be open Monday through Saturday from 11am to 11pm, and on Sunday from noon to 10:30pm. Restaurants are also allowed to serve liquor during these hours, but only to people who are dining on the premises. The law allows 30 minutes for "drinking-up time" at the end of the evening. In hotels, liquor may be served from 11am to 11pm to both residents and nonresidents; after 11pm, only residents, according to the law, may be served.

Lost & Found Be sure to tell all of your credit card companies the minute you discover your wallet has been lost or stolen and file a report at the nearest police precinct. Your credit card company or insurer may require a police report number or record of the loss. Most credit card companies have an emergency toll-free number to call if your card is lost or stolen; they may be able to wire you a cash advance immediately or deliver an emergency credit card in a day or two. Visa's U.S. emergency number is ℂ **800/847-2911** or 410/581-9994; from the U.K. call 0800/89-1725. American Express cardholders and traveler's check holders should call ℂ **800/221-7282** in the U.S.; outside the U.S. you can call the Global Assist Hotline collect at 715/343-7977. MasterCard holders should call ℂ **800/307-7309** or 636/722-7111 in the U.S., 0800/96-4767 in the U.K.

If you need emergency cash over the weekend when all banks and American Express offices are closed, you can have money wired to you via **Western Union** (ℂ **800/325-6000**; www.westernunion.com).

Identity theft or fraud are potential complications of losing your wallet, especially if you've lost your driver's license along with your cash and credit cards. Notify the major credit-reporting bureaus immediately; placing a fraud alert on your records may protect you against liability for criminal activity. The three major U.S. credit-reporting agencies are **Equifax** (ℂ **800/766-0008**; www.equifax.com), **Experian** (ℂ **888/397-3742**; www.experian.com), and **TransUnion** (ℂ **800/680-7289**; www.transunion.com). Finally, if you've lost all forms of photo ID call your airline and explain the situation; they might allow you to board the plane if you have a copy of your passport or birth certificate and a copy of the police report you've filed.

Mail Post offices and sub-post offices are open Monday through Friday from 9am to 5:30pm and Saturday from 9:30am to noon.

Sending an airmail letter to North America costs 45p (70¢) for 10 grams (.35 oz.), and postcards require a 40p (65¢) stamp. British mailboxes are painted red and carry a royal coat of arms. All post offices accept parcels for mailing, provided they are properly and securely wrapped.

Passports **For Residents of the United States:** Whether you're applying in person or by mail, you can download passport applications from the U.S. State Department website at **http://travel.state.gov**. For general information, call the **National Passport Agency** (ℂ **202/647-0518**). To find your regional passport office, either check the U.S. State Department website or call the **National Passport Information Center** (© **900/225-5674**); the fee is 55¢ per minute for automated information and $1.50 per minute for operator-assisted calls.

For Residents of Canada: Passport applications are available at travel agencies throughout Canada or from the central **Passport Office,** Department of Foreign Affairs and International Trade, Ottawa, ON K1A 0G3 (© **800/567-6868;** www.dfait-maeci.gc.ca/passport).

Police Dial **999** if the matter is serious. Losses, thefts, and other criminal matters should be reported to the police immediately.

Safety Stay in well-lit areas and out of questionable neighborhoods, especially at night. In Britain, most of the crime perpetrated against tourists is pickpocketing and mugging. These attacks usually occur in such cities as London, Birmingham, or Manchester. Most villages are safe.

Taxes To encourage energy conservation, the British government levies a 25% tax on gasoline (petrol). There is also a 17.5% national value-added tax (VAT) that is added to all hotel and restaurant bills and is included in the price of many items you purchase. This can be refunded if you shop at stores that participate in the Retail Export Scheme (signs are posted in the window). See the "How to Get Your VAT Refund" box earlier in this chapter.

In October 1994, Britain imposed a departure tax. Currently it is £22 ($35), but it is included in the price of your ticket.

Telephone To call England from North America, dial **011** (international code), **44** (Britain's country code), the local area codes (usually three or four digits and found in every phone number we've given in this book), and the seven-digit local phone number. The local area codes found throughout this book all begin with "0" (zero); you drop the "0" if you're calling from outside Britain, but you need to dial it along with the area code if you're calling from another city or town within Britain. For calls within the same city or town, the local number is all you need.

For **directory assistance** in London, dial **142;** for the rest of Britain, **192.**

There are three types of public pay phones: those taking only coins, those accepting only phone cards (called Cardphones), and those taking both phone cards and credit cards. At coin-operated phones, insert your coins before dialing. The minimum charge is 10p (15¢).

Phone cards are available in four values—£2 ($3.20), £4 ($6), £10 ($16), and £20 ($32)—and are reusable until the total value has expired. Cards can be purchased from newsstands and post offices. Finally, the credit-call pay phone operates on credit cards—Access (MasterCard), Visa, American Express, and Diners Club—and is most common at airports and large railway stations.

To make an international call from Britain, dial the international access code (**00**), then the country code, then the area code, and finally the local number. Or call through one of the following long-distance access codes: **AT&T USA Direct** (© **1800/CALLATT**), **Canada Direct** (© **0800/890016**), **Australia** (© **0800/890061**), and **New Zealand** (© **0800/890064**). Common country codes are: USA and Canada, **1;** Australia, **61;** New Zealand, **64;** and South Africa, **27.**

For calling **collect** or if you need an international operator, dial **155.**

Caller beware: Some hotels routinely add outrageous surcharges onto phone calls made from your room. Inquire before you call! It'll be a lot cheaper to use your own calling-card number or to find a pay phone.

Time England follows Greenwich mean time (5 hr. ahead of Eastern Standard Time), with British summertime lasting (roughly) from the end of March to the end of October. For most of the year, including summer, Britain is 5 hours ahead of the time observed in the eastern United States. Because of different daylight-savings-time practices in the two nations, there's a brief period (about a week) in autumn when Britain is only 4 hours ahead of New York, and a brief period in spring when it's 6 hours ahead of New York.

Tipping For cab drivers, add about 10% to 15% to the fare on the meter. However, if the driver loads or unloads your luggage, add something extra.

In hotels, porters receive 75p ($1.20) per bag, even if you have only one small suitcase. Hall porters are tipped only for special services. Maids receive £1 ($1.60) per day. In top-ranking hotels, the concierge will often submit a separate bill showing charges for newspapers and other items; if he or she has been particularly helpful, tip extra.

Hotels often add a service charge of 10% to 15% to most bills. In smaller bed-and-breakfasts, the tip is not likely to be included. Therefore, tip for special services such as the waiter who serves you breakfast. If several people have served you in a bed-and-breakfast, you may ask that 10% to 15% be added to the bill and divided among the staff.

In both restaurants and nightclubs, a 15% service charge is added to the bill, which is distributed among all the help. To that, add another 3% to 5%, depending on the service. Waiters in deluxe restaurants and nightclubs are accustomed to the extra 5%. Sommeliers (wine stewards) get about £1 ($1.60) per bottle of wine served. Tipping in pubs isn't common, but in wine bars, the server usually gets about 75p ($1.20) per round of drinks.

Barbers and hairdressers expect 10% to 15%. Tour guides expect £2 ($3.20), though it's not mandatory. Gas station attendants are rarely tipped, and theater ushers don't expect tips.

3

Settling into London

Europe's largest city is like a great wheel with Piccadilly Circus at the hub and dozens of communities branching out from it. Since London is such a conglomeration of neighborhoods, each with its own personality, first-time visitors may get confused. You'll probably spend most of your time in the West End, where many attractions are located, and the historic and financial part of London known as "the City," which includes the Tower of London and St. Paul's Cathedral. South Kensington, with its bevy of world-class museums, is another tourist beat. And so, increasingly, is the south bank of the Thames. This chapter helps you get your bearings, with neighborhood descriptions and a compilation of affordable hotels and restaurants found in London's most popular areas.

1 Orientation

ARRIVING
BY PLANE

Four airports serve London (plus Luton, a small charter airport). The one you'll fly into depends on your flight's point of departure. Chances are you'll be landing at either Heathrow or Gatwick.

LONDON HEATHROW AIRPORT Located about 21km (13 miles) west of London, Heathrow (© **0870/000-0123** for flight information; www.baa.co.uk) is one of the world's busiest airports. It has four terminals, each relatively self-contained. Terminal 4, the most modern, handles the long haul and transatlantic operations of British Airways. Most transatlantic flights on U.S. based airlines arrive at Terminal 3. Terminals 1 and 2 receive the intra-European flights of several European airlines.

The cheapest way to get into Central London from Heathrow is by **Underground** (Piccadilly Line), which takes about 45 minutes and costs £3.70 ($6). The fastest way to get in is by **Heathrow Express** (© **0845/600-1515;** www.heathrowexpress.co.uk), a train service that runs every 15 minutes (5:07am–12:08am) between the airport and Paddington Station in Central London; it costs £11.70 ($19) one-way and takes 15 minutes (23 min. from Terminal 4). You can buy tickets on the train or at self-service machines at Heathrow Airport. **National Express** (© **08705/747777;** www.nationalexpress.com) runs the **Airbus,** a bus service that leaves from outside every terminal and goes to over 20 stops in Central London for £8 ($13). A **taxi** into Central London costs about £45 ($72) and can take up to 5 passengers. For more information about train or bus connections, call © **020/7222-1234.**

GATWICK AIRPORT Although Heathrow still dominates, more and more scheduled flights land at Gatwick (© **08700/002-468;** www.baa.co.uk), located 40km (25 miles) south of London. From Gatwick, the fastest way to get to

London is via the **Gatwick Express** trains (℃ **08705/301-530;** www.gatwick express.com), which leave for Victoria Station in London every 15 minutes during the day and every hour at night. The one-way fare for the 30-minute journey is £11 ($18), half price for children 5 to 15, free for children under 5. **Checker Cars** (℃ **08700/000303**) provide 24-hour taxi service between Gatwick to Central London; the trip usually costs about £65 ($104).

LONDON STANSTED AIRPORT   Located 81km (50 miles) northeast of London, Stansted (℃ **0870/000303**), mostly handles flights to and from the European continent. From Stansted, your best bet to central London is the **Stansted Express** train (℃ **01332/387601;** www.stanstedexpress.com) to Liverpool Street Station which runs every 15 minutes from 8am to 5pm, and every 30 minutes in the early mornings, evening weekdays and weekends; it costs £13 ($28) for a standard ticket and takes 42 minutes. The A6 **Airbus** (www.national express.com) runs 24 hours a day to both Victoria rail and coach stations, and costs £8 ($13); trip time is about 1 hour, 30 minutes.

LONDON CITY AIRPORT   Located just 10km (6 miles) east of the City, London City Airport (℃ **020/7646-0088**) is served by airlines that fly to and from several European destinations. A blue-and-white **bus** charges £5 ($8) to take you from the airport to the Liverpool Street Station, where you can connect with rail or Underground transportation. The bus runs daily every 10 minutes during the hours the airport is open (approximately 6:50am–9:20pm, except Sat when it closes at 1pm).

BY TRAIN

Eurostar trains originating in Paris or Brussels and traveling through the Chunnel arrive at Waterloo Station. Visitors from Amsterdam arrive at the Liverpool Street Station, and those journeying south by rail from Edinburgh pull in at King's Cross Station. Each of these stations is connected to London's vast bus and Underground network. All have phones, restaurants, pubs, luggage-storage areas, and London Regional Transport Information centers.

BY CAR

If you're taking a car ferry across the Channel, you can quickly connect with a motorway into London. Remember to drive on the left! London is encircled by a ring road (M25). Determine where you want to go and follow the signs there.

Once you're in London, we don't recommend driving. Parking is scarce and expensive and the streets impossibly confusing for any but long-time drivers. Before you arrive in London, call your hotel and ask for advice on where to park your car. Better still, don't bring one at all.

VISITOR INFORMATION

The **British Visitor Centre,** 1 Regent St., SW1 (no phone; www.visitbritain. com; Tube: Piccadilly Circus), caters to walk-in visitors and carries information on all parts of Britain. On the premises are a travel agency, a theater-ticket agency, a hotel-booking service, a bookshop, and a souvenir shop. Open Monday from 9:30am to 6pm, Tuesday through Friday from 9am to 6:30pm, Saturday and Sunday from 10am to 4pm (Sat to 5pm June–Sept).

Equally useful is the **London Tourist Board's Tourist Information Centre,** forecourt of Victoria Station, SW1 (Tube: Victoria). The center deals with accommodations in all size and price categories. It can arrange for travel, tour-ticket sales, and theater reservations; open Monday through Saturday from 8am to 8pm (to 6pm in winter, to 9pm June–Sept), Sunday from 8am to 6pm. The

London at a Glance

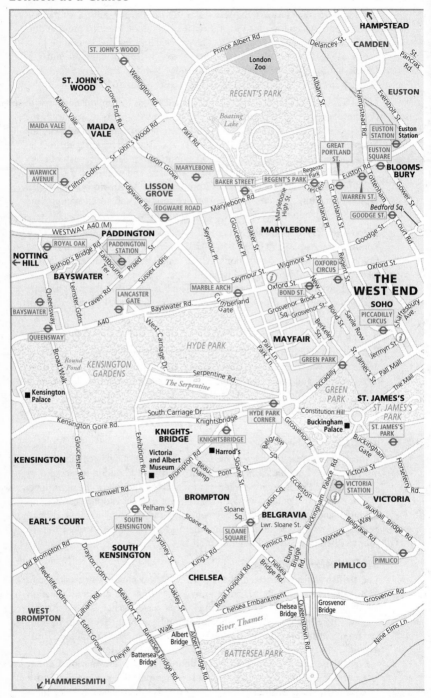

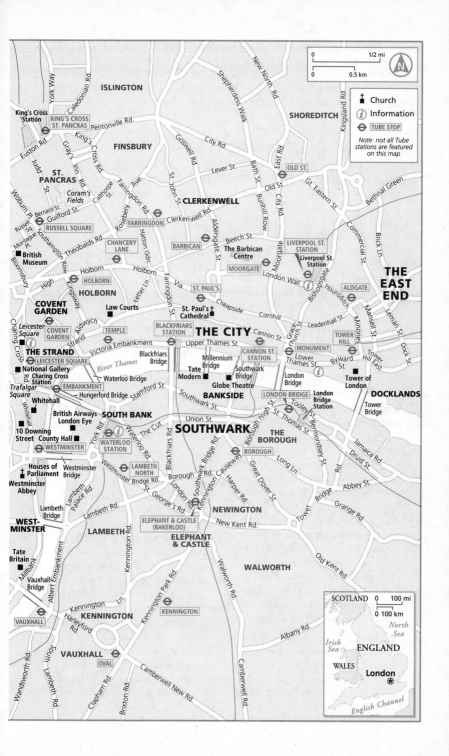

tourist board also maintains offices at Heathrow Airport's Terminals 1, 2, and 3 (Underground Concourse), at the Liverpool Street Tube station, and Waterloo International train station. The tourist board has a 24-hour recorded information service, **Visitorcall** (✆ **01839/123456**), which, for a fee of 60p (95¢) per minute, will play updated recorded messages about tourist attractions; their website is www.londontown.com.

LONDON'S NEIGHBORHOODS IN BRIEF

The West End Neighborhoods

Mayfair Bounded by Piccadilly, Hyde Park, and Oxford and Regent streets, this is the most elegant, fashionable section of London, filled with luxury hotels, Georgian town houses, and swank shops. Grosvenor Square (pronounced *Grove*-nor) is nicknamed "Little America" because it's home to the American embassy and a statue of Franklin D. Roosevelt; Shepherd Market, sandwiched within Mayfair, is a tiny village of pubs, two-story inns, book and food stalls, and restaurants. You'll want to dip into this exclusive section at least once.

Marylebone First-time visitors head here to explore Madame Tussaud's or walk along Baker Street in the footsteps of the fictional Sherlock Holmes. The streets form a near-perfect grid, with the major ones running north-south from Regent's Park toward Oxford Street. Marylebone (*Mar*-lee-bone) Lane and High Street retain some of their former village atmosphere, otherwise this is now a rather anonymous area. At Regent's Park, you can visit the London Zoo, Queen Mary's Gardens, or, in summer, see Shakespeare performed in an open-air theater.

St. James's Often called "Royal London," this is home to Elizabeth II, who lives at its most famous address, Buckingham Palace. The neighborhood begins at Piccadilly Circus and moves southwest, incorporating Pall Mall, The Mall, St. James's Park, and Green Park; it's "frightfully convenient," as the English say, encompassing American Express on Haymarket and many of London's leading department stores. Stop in at Fortnum & Mason (181 Piccadilly), the world's most luxurious grocery store.

Piccadilly Circus & Leicester Square Piccadilly Circus is the very heart and soul of London, its gaudy living room, with the same kind of traffic, neon, and jostling crowds you'd find in New York's Times Square. For a little more grandeur, retreat to the Regency promenade of exclusive shops, the Burlington Arcade. Leicester Square is a center of theaters, restaurants, movie palaces, and nightlife; it's where you'll find **tkts,** the half-price booth for theater tickets.

Soho The densely packed streets in the heart of the West End are famous for their cosmopolitan mix of people and trades. A decade ago, Soho was in decline, with the thriving sex industry threatening to engulf it. That process has now been reversed: respectable businesses, fashionable restaurants, and fine shops prosper here, and it's become the heart of London's gay population. Soho starts at Piccadilly Circus and is bordered by Regent Street, Oxford Street, Charing Cross Road, and the Shaftesbury Avenue theaters. London's Chinatown, centered on Gerrard Street, is small, authentic, and packed with excellent restaurants. But Soho's heart—with marvelous delicatessens, butchers, fish stores, wine merchants, and an open-air fresh-food market—is farther north, on Brewer, Old Compton, and Berwick streets. North of Old Compton are Dean, Frith, and Greek streets, with fine restaurants, pubs, and clubs, like Ronnie Scott's for jazz.

Bloomsbury This district, a world unto itself, lies northeast of Piccadilly Circus. It is London's academic heart, home of the University of London, colleges, and bookstores. Despite its student population, this neighborhood is fairly staid. The writer Virginia Woolf lived here and was a leader of a group of artists and writers known as "the Bloomsbury Group." The heart of Bloomsbury is Russell Square, its adjacent streets lined with hotels and B&Bs. Most visitors come to visit the British Museum, one of the world's greatest repositories of treasures.

Nearby is Fitzrovia, bounded by Great Portland, Oxford, and Gower streets. Goodge Street, with its many shops and pubs, forms the heart of the "village," once a haunt of artists and writers such as Ezra Pound, Wyndham Lewis, and George Orwell. The bottom end of Fitzrovia is a virtual extension of Soho, with a cluster of Greek restaurants.

Holborn This old borough, which abuts the City to the west, is the heart of legal London—its barristers, solicitors, and law clerks call it home. As a 14-year-old, Charles Dickens was employed as a solicitor's clerk at Lincoln's Inn Fields. "Old Bailey" (Central Criminal Court) has symbolized English justice through the years (Fagin went to the gallows from this site in *Oliver Twist*). The area, centrally located but too business-oriented to be of much interest to visitors, was named after Holborn Viaduct, the world's first overpass.

Covent Garden & The Strand The flower, fruit, and "veg" market is long gone, but memories of Professor Henry Higgins and Eliza Doolittle linger on. Covent Garden contains the city's liveliest group of restaurants, pubs, and cafes outside of Soho, and some of the city's hippest shops—including the world's only Dr. Marten's Super Store, at 12 Regent St. The marketplace, with its glass and iron roofs, has been magnificently restored. This is traditionally London's theater area; Charles II's mistress Nell Gwynne made her debut at the Theatre Royal Drury Lane in 1665. The Royal Opera House recently reopened after a major renovation.

Beginning at Trafalgar Square, The Strand runs east into Fleet Street and borders Covent Garden to the south. It's flanked with theaters, shops, hotels, and restaurants. The Strand runs parallel to the River Thames.

Westminster Westminster has been the British seat of government since the days of Edward the Confessor. Dominated by the Houses of Parliament and Westminster Abbey, the area runs along the Thames to the east of St. James's Park. Trafalgar Square, at the northern end, remains a testament to England's victory over Napoleon in 1805. The famous square is now joined to the adjacent National Gallery, London's greatest painting gallery. Whitehall, the main thoroughfare, links Trafalgar Square with Parliament Square, where you'll find the Houses of Parliament with their famous clock tower. You can see the inside of Churchill's Cabinet War Rooms or the outside of no. 10 Downing Street, home to the prime minister (although the large Blair family actually lives in no. 11). No visit is complete without a call at Westminster Abbey, one of the greatest Gothic churches in the world. Westminster also encompasses Victoria, named unofficially for bustling

Victoria Station, "gateway to the Continent."

The City & Environs

The City When Londoners speak of "the City," they don't mean all of London, only the original square mile (called Londinium by the Romans) that's now Britain's version of Wall Street. The buildings here include the Bank of England, the London Stock Exchange, and Lloyd's of London. Despite its age, the City doesn't readily reveal its past; much of it has been swept away by the Great Fire of 1666, the World War II Blitz, the IRA bombs of the early 1990s, and the zeal of modern developers. Yet it retains a medieval character; landmarks include St. Paul's Cathedral, which stood virtually alone among the rubble after the Blitz and remains one of London's most enduring landmarks.

The City still prefers to function independently of the rest of London and is presided over by the Lord Mayor of London. It even has its own **Information Centre** at St. Paul's Churchyard, EC4 (✆ **020/ 7332-1456**).

South Bank This intriguing area lies on the south bank of the Thames across from the Houses of Parliament and is easily accessed by several bridges, including the new twin footbridges on Hungerford Bridge. You can't miss the South Bank because it's the site of the gigantic British Airways London Eye observation wheel. Although not an official district, South Bank is home to the South Bank Arts Centre, one of the largest arts centers in Europe. Culture buffs flock to its many galleries and halls, including the Royal National Theatre, Royal Festival Hall, Hayward Gallery, and the National Film Theatre; County Hall, beside the observation wheel, is also attracting visitors to new

attractions. A riverside promenade runs from the observation wheel all the way east to Tower Bridge and beyond, past newly revitalized areas. The stunning new Tate Modern is connected to St. Paul's across the river by the new Millennium Bridge. Along the riverside promenade you'll also pass Shakespeare's Globe Theatre and Exhibit, a reconstruction of an Elizabethan playhouse, the new London City Hall, and Southwark Cathedral.

Central London Beyond the West End

Knightsbridge One of London's most fashionable neighborhoods, Knightsbridge is a top residential and shopping district, just south of Hyde Park. Harrods, on Brompton Road, is its chief attraction. Nearby Beauchamp Place (pronounced *Beech*-am) is a Regency-era boutique-lined little street with a scattering of fashionable restaurants.

Belgravia South of Knightsbridge, this area has long been the aristocratic quarter of London, rivaling Mayfair in grandeur. Although it reached the pinnacle of its prestige during Victoria's reign, it's still a chic address; the duke and duchess of Westminster, one of England's richest families, live at Eaton Square. Its centerpiece is Belgrave Square. When town houses were built around 1830, the aristocrats followed—even Victoria's mother, the duchess of Kent.

Chelsea This stylish Thames-side district lies south of Belgravia. It is an elegant village filled with town houses and little mews dwellings that only successful stockbrokers, solicitors, and celebrities can afford. It begins at Sloane Square, made famous by the late Princess Diana and her "Sloane Rangers" of the 1980s. Chelsea has always been a favorite of writers and artists, including Oscar Wilde (who was arrested here at the Cadogan Hotel), George Eliot, James Whistler, J. M. W. Turner, Henry James, and Thomas Carlyle. Mick Jagger and Margaret Thatcher have been more recent residents. Its major boulevard is King's Road, where Mary Quant launched the miniskirt and the English punk look was born. The lively hip-hop of King's Road is atypical of otherwise upmarket Chelsea. Every year the Chelsea Flower Show, one of the big events of the London social calendar, is held on the grounds of the Chelsea Hospital.

Kensington This Royal Borough lies west of Kensington Gardens and Hyde Park and is traversed by two of London's major shopping streets, Kensington High Street and Kensington Church Street. From the time asthmatic William III fled Whitehall Palace for the fresher air of Nottingham House, the district has enjoyed royal associations. Nottingham House became Kensington Palace, where Queen Victoria was born, and where the late Princess Diana and her two young princes lived for a time. Kensington Palace is open to the public, and Kensington Gardens is one of London's greatest parks.

South Kensington, southeast of Kensington Gardens and Earl's Court, is often called "Museum-land" because of its complex of museums on land bought with proceeds from Prince Albert's 1851 Great Exhibition, held in Hyde Park. You'll find the Natural History Museum, Victoria and Albert Museum, and Science Museum, all of which are now free; nearby is Royal Albert Hall, a famous circular concert hall. One of the district's chief curiosities is the Albert Memorial, which Queen Victoria had erected in memory of her Prince Consort. South Kensington is also

home to plenty of restaurants and B&Bs.

Earl's Court This residential district, which lies below Kensington and borders the western half of Chelsea, attracts a young crowd at night to its pubs, wine bars, and coffeehouses. It's long been a base for budget travelers (particularly Australians), thanks to a wealth of B&Bs and budget hotels and its easy access to central London: 15 minutes by Tube.

Once regarded as the boondocks, West Brompton is now considered an extension of central London. It lies directly south of Earl's Court and southeast of West Kensington. It has many good restaurants, pubs, and taverns, as well as some budget hotels.

Notting Hill Increasingly fashionable Notting Hill is bounded on the north by Bayswater Road and on the east by Kensington. It has many turn-of-the-20th-century mansions and small houses sitting on quiet, leafy streets, plus a growing number of hot restaurants and clubs. On the north end, west of Bayswater Road, is the increasingly hip neighborhood of Notting Hill Gate. Portobello Road is home to London's most famous street market. Nearby, lovely Holland Park lends its name to the chichi residential neighborhood that surrounds it.

Paddington & Bayswater Paddington Station anchors the neighborhood of Paddington, north of Kensington Gardens and Hyde Park. It attracts budget travelers who fill up the B&Bs in Sussex Gardens and Norfolk Square. South of Paddington, north of Hyde Park, and abutting more fashionable Notting Hill to the west is Bayswater, a sort of unofficial area also filled with a large number of B&Bs attracting budget travelers. There aren't any major or even minor tourist attractions in either area.

Farther Afield

The East End Traditionally, this was one of London's poorest districts, and was nearly bombed out of existence by the Nazis. The East End extends east from the City, encompassing Stepney, Bow, Poplar, West Ham, Canning Town, and other districts. The East End has always been filled with legend and lore. It's the home of the Cockney, London's most colorful character. To be a true Cockney, it's said that you must have been born "within the sound of Bow Bells," a reference to a church, St. Mary-le-Bow. Many immigrants to London have found a home here.

Docklands In the last two decades, this area—bordered roughly by Tower Bridge to the west and London City Airport and the Royal Docks to the east—has undergone an ambitious redevelopment. It has attracted many businesses, including most of the London newspapers; warehouses have been converted to Manhattan-style lofts; and museums, entertainment complexes, shops, and an ever-growing list of restaurants have popped up. Canary Wharf, on the Isle of Dogs, is the heart of Docklands; it is dominated by the 800-foot-high "Canary Wharf Tower," London's tallest commercial building. On the south side of the river the Victorian warehouses of Butler's Wharf have been converted into offices, workshops, houses, shops, and restaurants.

Butler's Wharf is also home to the Design Museum.

To get to Docklands, take the Underground to Tower Hill and pick up the **Docklands Light Railway** (© **020/7363-9696**), an elevated train system that will take you as far as Greenwich.

Greenwich Some 6km (4 miles) to the north of the city, Greenwich enjoyed its heyday under the Tudors. Henry VIII and his daughters, Mary I and Elizabeth I, were born here; Greenwich Palace, Henry's favorite, is long gone, but the cluster of historic buildings that remain led to UNESCO's naming of Greenwich as a World Heritage Site. Today's visitors come to this lovely Thameside village to visit the 1869 tea clipper *Cutty Sark,* the Old Royal Observatory (ground zero in the reckoning of terrestrial longitudes), the 17th-century Queen's House, the National Maritime Museum, and the Old Royal Naval College.

Hampstead This desirable residential suburb of north London, beloved by Keats and Hogarth, is a weekend favorite of Londoners. Everybody from Sigmund Freud to John Le Carré has lived here. Its centerpiece is Hampstead Heath, nearly 160 hectares (800 acres) of rolling meadow and woodland with panoramic views; it has maintained its rural atmosphere even though engulfed by cityscapes on all sides. The hilltop village is filled with cafes, tearooms, and restaurants; some of the pubs have historic pedigrees.

2 Getting Around

Remember that cars drive on the left, and vehicles have the right-of-way in London over pedestrians, except in striped "zebra crossings." Wherever you walk, always look both ways before stepping off a curb.

BY PUBLIC TRANSPORTATION

Transportation within London is easy and fairly inexpensive if you buy one of the many discount passes that are offered (see below). The main problem is that the streets are very congested, so that buses often move slowly, and the Underground has become less reliable and in need of major work. Both the **Underground** (Tube) and bus systems are operated by Transport for London (www.tfl.gov.uk/tfl), which operate Travel Information Centres in the Underground stations at King's Cross/St. Pancras, Oxford Circus, St. James's Park, Liverpool Street, and Piccadilly Circus; the main line stations at Euston, Paddington, and Victoria; the bus stations at Hammersmith and West Croydon; the Waterloo International Railway Station; and all four terminals at Heathrow Airport. They take reservations for London Transport's guided tours and have free Underground and bus maps and other information. A **24-hour telephone information service** is available by calling ℂ **020/7222-1234.**

DISCOUNT PASSES   Travelcards for unlimited travel on the bus and Underground system within Greater London can be purchased for 1-day, 2-day, and 7-day periods, and even longer. A Travelcard also gets you a third off all river service tickets and is good for the Docklands Light Rail. A **One-Day Travelcard** allowing travel in zones 1 and 2 (all of Central London, but after 9:30am) costs £4.10 ($6) for adults and £2 ($3.20) for children 5 to 16. A **Weekend Travelcard,** valid for one weekend or any two consecutive days, is £6.10 ($10) for adults and £3 ($4.80) for children. A **One-Week Travelcard** costs £16.50 ($26) for adults, £6.80 ($11) for children.

The **Family Travelcard** is good for groups that include up to 2 adults traveling with one to four children. It's a 1-day go-as-you-please card that allows for as many journeys as you wish on the Tube, buses (excluding night buses), and the Docklands Light Railway. The family card is valid after 9:30am Monday through Friday, all day on weekends, and public holidays. The cost is £2.70 ($4.30) for adults, or 60p ($1) for children.

All the passes listed above are available at any London Underground ticket window. You can purchase One-Day and Weekend Travelcards from the automated ticket machines at London Underground stations. Any pass of 7 days duration or more requires a Photocard. If you're 16 years old or older, bring along a passport-type picture of yourself and the Photocard will be issued free. Children must obtain a Photocard to use child-rate Travelcards; in addition to a passport-type photograph, proof of age is required (passport or birth certificate). Teenagers (14 or 15) are charged adult fares on all services unless they have this card.

The **Visitor Travelcard,** available only in North America, is worthwhile if you plan to travel a lot within Greater London. There are two versions of this card: one allows for unlimited transport within all six zones of Greater London's Underground and the entire bus network, the other is good for zones 1 and 2. Visitor Travelcards do not require Photocards. A pass good for 3 consecutive days of all-zone travel costs $31 for adults and $14 for children ages 5 to 15; a pass good for 4 consecutive days of travel costs $41 for adults, $17 for children; and a pass good for 7 consecutive days costs $62 for adults, $26 for children.

Tips **Transit Info**

For information on the Underground or for bus schedules and fares, call the **24-hour hot line** at ℂ **020/7222-1234,** but expect long delays before an actual person comes to the phone. See the full-color London Underground map on the inside back cover of this guide.

Zone 1 and 2 passes cost $21, $27, and $33 for adults, $9, $11, and $13 for kids. For more information, contact **Rail Europe** (© **888/382-7245** in U.S. and Canada; www.raileurope.com) or **BritRail** (© **866/BRITRAIL** or 877/677-1066; www.britrail.net).

BY UNDERGROUND

The "Tube," as it's known locally, is the fastest, easiest way to get around (at least, when it's working properly). All Underground stations are clearly marked with a red circle and blue crossbar. You descend by stairways, escalators, or huge elevators, depending on the depth. The escalators sometimes stop working, requiring long treks down to the platforms.

If you have British coins, you can get your ticket at a vending machine. Otherwise, buy it at the ticket office. You can transfer as many times as you like as long as you stay within the Underground. The flat fare for one trip within the Central zone is £1.60 ($2.60). Your ticket must be presented when you get off (either fed into a turnstile or handed to a inspector). If you're caught without a valid ticket, you'll be fined £10 ($16) on the spot. If you owe extra money, you'll be asked to pay the difference by the attendant. Keep in mind that most trains stop running at midnight (11:30pm on Sun).

BY BUS

The first thing you learn about London buses is that nobody just gets on them. You queue up (that is, form a single-file line) at the bus stop. You can pick up a free bus map at one of London Regional Transport's Travel Information Centres listed above.

The zone system for buses was recently overhauled so that all of Central London is now Zone 1, and the fare anywhere within it is £1 ($1.60). Outside the central zone, the fare is 70p ($1.10); night buses cost £1.50 ($2.40). London still has some of the old-style Routemaster buses, with both a driver and a conductor who issues tickets. Newer buses have only a driver, and you pay as you enter.

BY TAXI

You can get a cab from a cab station or hail one on the street if the yellow light on the roof is on. For a radio cab, call © **020/7272-0272** or 020/7253-5000.

The minimum fare is £1.40 ($2.20) with increments of 20p (30¢) based on distance or time. Each additional passenger is charged 40p (60¢). Passengers pay 10p (15¢) for each piece of luggage in the driver's compartment and any other item more than 2 feet long. Surcharges are imposed after 8pm and on weekends and public holidays. All these tariffs include value-added tax (VAT). We recommend tipping 10% to 15% of the fare. Taxis take all major credit cards. Steer clear of minicabs, which do not have meters and require negotiating fees, and ride only in a licensed black cab.

If you call for a cab, the meter starts running when the taxi receives instructions from the dispatcher, so you could find £1.50 ($2.40) or more already on the meter when you step inside.

Cab sharing is permitted in London, and allows cabbies to offer rides for two to five people. The taxis accepting such riders display a sign on yellow plastic with the words "shared taxi." Each of two sharing riders is charged 65% of the fare a lone passenger would be charged. Three people pay 55%, four pay 45%, and five (the seating capacity of all new London cabs) pay 40% of the single-passenger fare.

FAST FACTS: London

American Express The main office is at 30–31 Haymarket, SW1 (© 020/ **7484-9610;** www.americanexpress.com; Tube: Piccadilly Circus). Full services are available Monday through Friday from 8:30am to 7pm; currency-exchange only on Saturday 9am to 6:30pm, and Sunday from 10am to 5pm.

Babysitters If your hotel can't recommend a sitter, call **Universal Aunts** (© **020/7386-5900**), which has been in business for nearly 20 years. The rates are £6.50 ($10) per hour during the day and £5 ($8) per hour after 6pm. There is a 4-hour minimum, an agency fee of £3.50 ($6), and you'll pay the sitter's travel both ways.

Currency Exchange Generally, London's banks provide the best exchange rates. You're likely to get a better rate for traveler's checks than for cash. At the airports, there are branch offices of the main banks, but these charge a small fee. There are also bureaux de change at the airports, with offices around London; they charge a fee for cashing traveler's checks and personal U.K. checks and for changing foreign currency into pounds sterling. Some travel agencies, such as American Express and Thomas Cook, offer currency-exchange services (see "Money," in chapter 2). One of the easiest and least expensive ways to obtain currency is by using your bankcard at an ATM.

Dentists Try the **Dental Emergency Care Service,** Guy's Hospital, St. Thomas's Street, SE1 (© 020/7955-5000), a first-come, first-served clinic on the 23rd floor, Monday to Friday 8:45am to 3pm. On Saturday and Sunday, emergency dental service is available from 9am to 4pm at **Kings College,** Denmark Hill, Camberwell SE5 (© 020/7345-3591).

Doctors The National Health Service now runs a telephone help line, **NHS Direct** (© **0845/4647**), which is a useful first port of call for noncritical illnesses. Otherwise, London has five private walk-in **Medicentres,** offering the same services as a GP; those at Victoria Station and the Plaza mall at Bond Street Tube station are open every day (© **0870/600-0870**). **Medcall,** 2 Harley St., W1 (© **0800/136106**), operates a late-night practice and 24-hour call-out.

Embassies & High Commissions The U.S. Embassy is at 24 Grosvenor Sq., W1 (© 020/7499-9000; Tube: Bond St.). For passport and visa information, however, go to the U.S. Passport and Citizenship Unit, 55–56 Upper Brook St., London, W1 (© 020/7499-9000, ext. 2563 or 2564; Tube: Marble Arch or Bond St.). Hours are Monday through Friday from 8:30am to 5:30pm.

The Canadian High Commission, MacDonald House, 38 Grosvenor Sq., W1 (© **020/7258-6600;** Tube: Bond St.), handles visas for Canada. Hours are Monday through Friday from 8am to 4pm.

The Australian High Commission is at Australia House, The Strand, WC2 (© **020/7379-4334;** Tube: Charing Cross or Aldwych). Hours are Monday through Friday from 10am to 4pm.

The New Zealand High Commission is at New Zealand House, 80 Haymarket at Pall Mall, SW1 (© **020/7930-8422;** Tube: Charing Cross or Piccadilly Circus). Hours are Monday through Friday from 9am to 5pm.

The Irish Embassy is at 17 Grosvenor Place, SW1 (© **020/7235-2171;** Tube: Hyde Park Corner). Hours are Monday through Friday from 9:30am to 1pm and 2:15pm to 5pm.

Emergencies In London, for police, fire, or an ambulance, dial 🕾 **999.**

Hospitals Around a dozen city hospitals offer 24-hour walk-in emergency care. The most central is **University College Hospital,** Grafton Way, WC1 (🕾 **020/7387-9300**). The two best alternatives are **Chelsea & Westminster Hospital,** 369 Fulham Rd., SW10 (🕾 **020/8746-8000**), on the Chelsea/Fulham border; and **St. Mary's Hospital,** Praed Street, W2 (🕾 **020/7886-6666**), in Paddington.

Hot Lines The **Rape Crisis Line** (🕾 **020/7837-1600**) accepts calls after 6pm. **Samaritans,** 46 Marshall St. (🕾 **020/7734-2800**), maintains a crisis hot line that helps with all kinds of trouble from 9am to 9pm daily when a live attendant's on duty to handle emergencies; at other times, a series of recorded messages suggests other phones and addresses that callers can turn to for help. **Alcoholics Anonymous** (🕾 **020/7833-0022**) answers its hot line daily from 10am to 10pm. The **Lesbian & Gay Switchboard** (🕾 **020/ 7837-7324**) is open 24 hours for help or advice on just about anything.

Information See "Visitor Information" earlier in this chapter.

Maps If you plan on exploring London in any depth, you'll need a detailed street map with an index. *London A to Z,* the ultimate street-by-street reference, is available at bookstores and newsstands everywhere.

Police In an emergency, dial 🕾 **999** (no coins are needed).

Telephone For directory assistance in London and throughout the U.K. dial 🕾 **192;** for international inquiries, dial 🕾 **153.** (For more information, see "Telephone" under "Fast Facts," in chapter 2.)

Travel Information Call 🕾 **020/7222-1234,** 24 hours daily.

Taxes Unless otherwise specified, rates quoted in this chapter already include the value-added tax (VAT) of 17.5%.

3 Accommodations You Can Afford

London is a challenge for budget travelers. It's difficult to find a halfway decent double room for less than £60 ($96) a night. More often than not you'll have to pay a lot more than that, and even at a higher price you may not like what you get.

Don't be discouraged, though. We've scoured this expensive city to find a wide assortment of affordable hotels and B&Bs where you can stay comfortably. Some are real gems. None of them are dumps.

But here's the lowdown about London budget accommodations: Most budget hotels aren't hotels at all, in the sense of having elevators, porters, and private bathrooms. Rather, they are family-type guesthouses where you carry your own luggage up steep narrow stairs. Hundreds of these four- and five-story hotels dot the city. They may all appear the same, but once inside you'll find varying degrees of cleanliness, service, and friendliness. Inevitably, the ones that are well maintained and have the friendliest hosts are the ones with the most repeat business. A truly welcoming host makes all the difference.

Most bed-and-breakfast hotels (B&Bs) were once private and often quite grand residences. Some are Georgian—that is, around 200 years old—and many more are Victorian. Usually the houses are part of a long terrace of nearly identical buildings. B&Bs usually serve an English or continental breakfast; few serve any other meal. Usually the rooms are fairly small; the rooms on the top floors, where servants once lived, tend to be the smallest. Rooms in B&Bs almost always have sinks, closet and dresser space, a desk, and maybe an armchair. The bathroom may be a half flight down, two flights down, or on the same floor. Increasingly, B&Bs are upgrading to include private bathrooms in as many rooms as possible. These bathrooms, however, are usually tiny, pre-fab, all-in-one units with showers only. In some cases, you'll find rooms with private showers but toilets down the hall.

Always ask what is included in the room rate. In the case of a B&B, ask to see your room before accepting it.

RESERVATIONS BY MAIL   Most hotels and B&Bs require at least a day's deposit before reserving a room for you. This can be accomplished by an international money order or a personal check, or it can often be done with a credit card. Usually you can cancel a room reservation 1 week ahead of time and get a full refund. But if you cancel at the last minute, the hotel may keep your deposit, and there is very little you can do to get it back. At more and more hotels and B&Bs you can reserve rooms online. Not only is it convenient, there are often special lower rates for online booking.

MONEY-SAVING STRATEGIES

NEGOTIATE   Hotel occupancy rates in London are down, mainly because Americans have not been traveling there in the numbers they used to. What this means is that you can often negotiate a better price for a room than the listed rate.

SURF THE WEB   To help fill up empty rooms, nearly all hotels now offer special promotional offers on their websites. Whenever possible, look up a hotel on its website to see what special deals are being offered. Generally you will save by booking online.

B&BS IN PRIVATE HOMES   For a real insight into London life, consider booking into a private home. You'll save money, too; prices range from approximately £30 to £50 ($48–$80) per person, according to the quality of the home and its location. Many agencies specialize in this type of rental. To get you going, check with the following: **Uptown Reservations** (© 020/7351; www.uptownres. co.uk); **Host and Guest Service** (© 020/7385-9922; www.host-guest.co.uk); and **At Home in London** (© 020/8748-1943; www.athomeinlondon.co.uk). They all book B&B accommodations in selected private homes in Greater London. Host families are selected for their friendliness and hospitality as well as the appeal of their homes.

Properties in Central London are more expensive because they're closer to the center. You can save by booking in a London suburb such as Camden Town, Hammersmith, or Southgate, then commuting into town by train.

SELF-CATERING ACCOMMODATIONS   It's possible to find a small Central London flat that sleeps two or three people for £400 to £500 ($640–$800) per week. Agencies to try include **The Independent Traveller** (© 01392/860807;

(*Value* **More Money-Saving Tips**

For additional suggestions on reducing the cost of your hotel room in London, see "Fifty Money-Saving Tips" and "Tips on Accommodations" in chapter 2.

Where to Stay in Central London

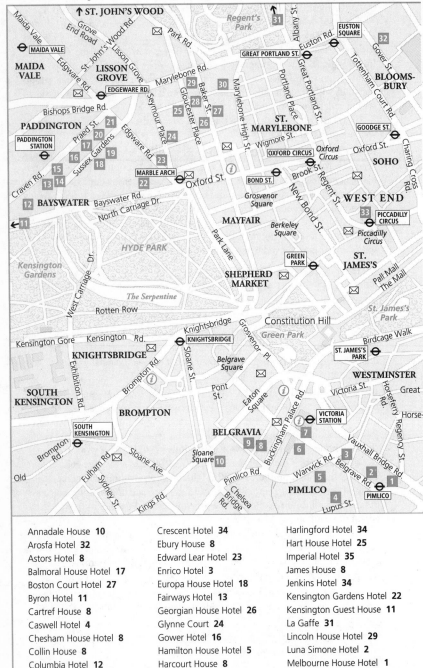

Annadale House **10**
Arosfa Hotel **32**
Astors Hotel **8**
Balmoral House Hotel **17**
Boston Court Hotel **27**
Byron Hotel **11**
Cartref House **8**
Caswell Hotel **4**
Chesham House Hotel **8**
Collin House **8**
Columbia Hotel **12**

Crescent Hotel **34**
Ebury House **8**
Edward Lear Hotel **23**
Enrico Hotel **3**
Europa House Hotel **18**
Fairways Hotel **13**
Georgian House Hotel **26**
Glynne Court **24**
Gower Hotel **16**
Hamilton House Hotel **5**
Harcourt House **8**

Harlingford Hotel **34**
Hart House Hotel **25**
Imperial Hotel **35**
James House **8**
Jenkins Hotel **34**
Kensington Gardens Hotel **22**
Kensington Guest House **11**
La Gaffe **31**
Lincoln House Hotel **29**
Luna Simone Hotel **2**
Melbourne House Hotel **1**

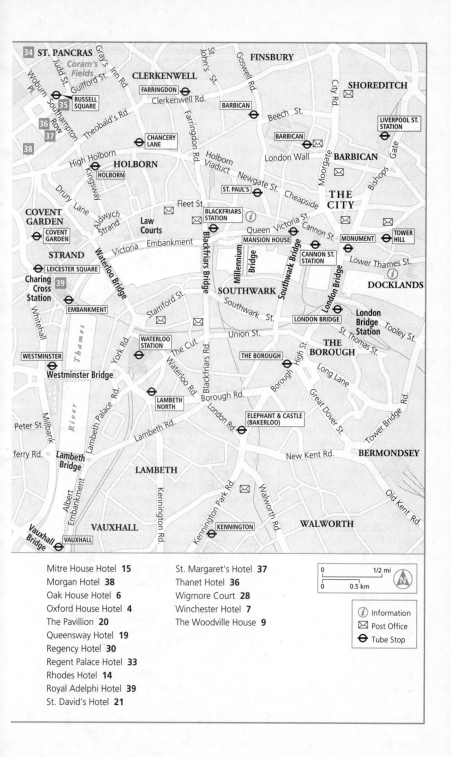

Mitre House Hotel **15**
Morgan Hotel **38**
Oak House Hotel **6**
Oxford House Hotel **4**
The Pavillion **20**
Queensway Hotel **19**
Regency Hotel **30**
Regent Palace Hotel **33**
Rhodes Hotel **14**
Royal Adelphi Hotel **39**
St. David's Hotel **21**

St. Margaret's Hotel **37**
Thanet Hotel **36**
Wigmore Court **28**
Winchester Hotel **7**
The Woodville House **9**

| 0 | | 1/2 mi |
| 0 | 0.5 km | |

ⓘ Information
✉ Post Office
⊖ Tube Stop

www.gowithit.co.uk), run by the very friendly and experienced Mary and Simon Ette; **Emperors Gate Short Stay Apartments** (© 020/7244-8409; www.apartment-hotels.com); **Residence Apartments** (© 020/7727-0352; www.residence-apartments.com); and the super-budget **Acorn Management Services** (© 020/8202-3311; www.acorn-london.co.uk). All of these agencies charge a commission fee.

STUDENT DORMS   During the summer and sometimes at Easter, you can find accommodations starting at around £22 ($35) per person at the dozens of university dorms in London. For details of what's available, try **Venuemasters** (© 0114/249-3090; www.venuemasters.co.uk), which promotes academic conference and vacation facilities all over the U.K. Or contact the three central London universities directly: **University of London** (© 020/7862-8880; www.lon.ac.uk/accom); **University of Westminster** (© 020/7911-5796; www.westminster.ac.uk/comserv/halls.htm); or **City University** (© 020/7477-8037; www.city.ac.uk/ems/accomm1.htm).

BLOOMSBURY

The heart of Bloomsbury is Russell Square, and the streets jutting off from the square are lined with hotels and B&Bs. If you're searching for a hotel on foot, try the following itinerary: From the Russell Square Underground station, walk first along Bernard Street. Then, 1 long block north of Bernard Street, try Coram Street, another hotel-lined block; after that, go to Tavistock Place, running 1 block north of Coram and parallel to it. North of Tavistock Place is Cartwright Gardens, which has a number of converted town houses catering to overnight guests. On the other side of Russell Square (opposite Bernard St.) there are relatively high-priced hotels on Bloomsbury Street and the less-expensive B&Bs of Gower Street. Always ask to see the room before you accept it and pay.

Arosfa Hotel   This brick-fronted town house was the home of Pre-Raphaelite painter Sir John Everett Millais, a fact noted on a plaque displayed in front. In 2003 the Arosfa was closed for a complete refurbishment and was scheduled to reopen in September. Work wasn't complete as of press time, so it's impossible to describe what the final outcome will be, but the Arosfa has always been a simple, unpretentious, cost-effective hotel with small to midsize rooms. Prefab bathroom units are now being installed in all of the rooms, and walls and ceilings are being stripped and redone with an apricot-and-white color scheme. The hotel's polite, hardworking owners, the Dortas, formerly worked at the Ridgemount, just down the street. The improvements can only add to the Arosfa's low-key appeal.

83 Gower Street, WC 1. © and fax **020/7636-2115**. 17 units. £45 ($72) single; £66 ($106) double; £79 ($126) triple; £92 ($147) quad. Rates include English breakfast. MC, V. Tube: Goodge St. **Amenities:** Breakfast room; lounge. *In room:* TV, hair dryer, coffeemaker.

Crescent Hotel   The Crescent, built in 1810 as a private residence on Cartwright Gardens, has managed to keep its comfortably elegant Georgian surroundings intact. Mrs. Cockle, the manager, is one of the kindest hosts on the street. Guests have been returning for 4 decades to enjoy the comfortable, homey atmosphere. Traditional furnishings and a cozy sitting room add to the charm. Bedrooms range from small singles with shared bathrooms to more spacious twin and double rooms with private (but very tiny) bathrooms. Guests have access to the gardens and private tennis courts.

49–50 Cartwright Gardens, London WC1H 9EL. © **020/7387-1515**. Fax 020/7383-2054. www.crescenthoteloflondon.com. 27 units, 18 with bathroom (some with shower only, some with shower and toilet). £73

($117) single with bathroom, £46 ($74) single without bathroom, £51 ($82) single with shower; £89 ($1142) double with bathroom; £99 ($158) triple with bathroom. Rates include English breakfast. MC, V. Tube: Russell Sq., King's Cross, or Euston. **Amenities:** Lounge; tennis courts; babysitting. *In room:* TV, hair dryer.

Harlingford Hotel ⭐⭐ Andrew Davies is the third generation of his family to run this B&B, a dignified, dove-gray, Georgian-era building on the corner of Marchmont Street and Cartwright Gardens. A perfectionist by nature, he recently oversaw the smart, designer-aided overhaul of the hotel interiors, which are neutral with bright splashes of color. The bathrooms are small but adequate. With their gracious arched windows and high ceilings, the lounge and breakfast rooms on either side of the white, airy entrance hall are a real asset. The breakfast room is modern and cheery. As a guest, you can get a key and enjoy the communal gardens opposite the hotel. The only downside: no elevator.

61–63 Cartwright Gardens, London WC1H 9EL. ℂ **020/7387-1551.** Fax 020/7387-4616. www.harlingford hotel.com. 44 units, all with bathroom (shower only). £72 ($115) single; £90 ($144) double/twin; £100 ($160) triple; £108 ($173) quad. Rates include full English breakfast. AE, DC, MC, V. Tube: Euston or Russell Sq. **Amenities:** Lounge. *In room:* TV, coffeemaker.

Jenkins Hotel ⭐ *(Value)* Jenkins has been a hotel since the 1920s and appeared in the PBS mystery series *Poirot.* Today the style is trad-lite: very English but relaxed about it. Sam Bellingham and his partner Felicity Langley-Hunt recently refurbished the entire hotel, putting bathrooms in all but one of the rooms. A double with private bathroom is still a few pounds cheaper here than elsewhere in Cartwright Gardens. Rivals score points for having lounges, but Jenkins offers better in-room amenities. There's one nice double room (no. 10) on the fourth floor (no elevator), but the top choice is the second-floor room no. 5, where two rooms on the front, with floor-to-ceiling windows, have been knocked into one. The room to avoid is the pretty but cavelike basement double. Sam's two friendly Labradors, Tiggy and George, hang out in the kitchen which, with its huge pine table, doubles as reception. There are rackets and balls to borrow if you want to play tennis in communal gardens opposite. Jenkins is completely nonsmoking.

45 Cartwright Gardens, London WC1H 9EH. ℂ **020/7387-2067.** Fax 020/7383-3139. www.jenkinshotel. demon.co.uk. 13 units, 12 with bathroom (most with shower only). £52–£72 ($83–$115) single; £85 ($136) double/twin; £105 ($168) triple. Rates include full English breakfast. MC, V. Tube: Euston or Russell Sq. **Amenities:** Nonsmoking rooms; garden. *In room:* TV, fridge, coffeemaker, hair dryer, safe.

St. Margaret's Hotel ⭐⭐ The welcome here inspires devoted loyalty. One guest stayed for 28 years, then asked to have her ashes buried in the back garden! Mrs. Marazzi is the second generation of her family to run this nonsmoking B&B, which rambles over four houses. The rooms are simple, and no two are alike. Budget travelers should go for the cheap double, which has the toilet just outside. The Marazzis recently created some beautiful extra public bathrooms, so it's easy to survive the sharing experience. If you can afford it, room no. 53 is a marvelous first-floor triple, which normally costs £125 ($200) but which two people can take for £100 ($160). It has a king-size bed, a single bed, and a gray-tiled, private bathroom with a corner tub. And off it is a small private conservatory, looking onto the quiet communal garden that all the guests can use. St. Margaret's has two lounges, one with a TV and the other for guests who prefer peace and quiet. Newspapers are delivered. You'll pay an extra £1 ($1.60) if you stay only 1 night.

26 Bedford Place, London WC1B 5JL. ℂ **020/7636-4277.** Fax 020/7323-3066. www.stmargaretshotel.co.uk. 64 units, 10 with bathroom (most with shower only). £50.50 ($81) single without bathroom; £64.50 ($103) double without bathroom, £78–£95 ($125–$152) double with bathroom. Rates include full English breakfast.

MC, V. Tube: Russell Sq. or Holborn. **Amenities:** Lounge; babysitting arranged; nonsmoking rooms; garden. *In room:* TV.

Thanet Hotel   This quiet, 200-year-old Georgian terrace links busy Russell Square with the more peaceful Bloomsbury Square and is very close to Covent Garden and the rest of the West End. The Orchard family, the third-generation hoteliers that run the Thanet, began to refurbish the hotel last year. The bedrooms have been repainted and have new carpet, curtains and bedcovers. Room no. 5 has French doors and its own balcony. The Orchards have also redone the bathrooms with bright white tiles. This guesthouse, with its blue awning, exuberant window boxes, and lovely blue-toned breakfast room, has long won plaudits as a good budget bet.

The Orchards recently took over the former University of Iowa student hostel next door and began to tidy it up. **Pickwick Hall** (✆ **020/7323-4958;** pickwickhall@aol.com) is a friendly place, with no age restrictions and space for 35 weary heads. It costs £25 ($40) for a single, £40 ($64) for a twin, and £15 to £18 ($24–$29) per person in a dorm.

8 Bedford Place, London WC1B 5JA. ✆ **020/7636-2869.** Fax 020/7323-6676. www.thanethotel.co.uk. 16 units, all with bathroom (shower only). £69 ($110) single; £94 ($150) double/twin; £102 ($164) triple; £112 ($179) quad. Rates include full English breakfast. AE, MC, V. Tube: Russell Sq. or Holborn. *In room:* TV, coffeemaker, hair dryer, radio.

WORTH A SPLURGE

Imperial Hotel ★ *Value*   A few pounds more expensive than Bloomsbury's toniest B&Bs, the Imperial is both a splurge and a good deal. The decor isn't particularly plush. In fact, it's rather dated. What you do get, though, is an affordable, full-service hotel just a stone's throw from Covent Garden and Soho. It's a complete monstrosity from the outside—a huge, corrugated, concrete box taking up half the eastern side of Russell Square with a row of shops at street level. There are nine floors of bedrooms, and the third is nonsmoking. The hotel does a lot of tour-group business, but the rooms have stood up well to the traffic. They're all a decent size, have unusual triangular-shaped bay windows, and excellent storage space. In most of the doubles and twins, the en suite toilet and tub/shower are handily separate. The Imperial has a vineyard to make its Bordeaux house wine and a farm just outside London, which delivers produce every day to be served up in the rather grim Elizabethan Restaurant. Otherwise, the Day & Night Bar, an oasis of up-to-the-minute style with Internet sites, is open for light food and drinks until 2am. If you'd rather forego the amenities and pay a few pounds less, check out the website because the company owns five other Bloomsbury hotels, all a few pounds cheaper than the Imperial.

Russell Sq., London WC1B 5BB. ✆ **020/7278-7871.** Fax 020/7837-4653. www.imperialhotels.co.uk. 448 units. £73 ($117) single; £98 ($157) double/twin. Rates include full English breakfast. AE, DC, DISC, MC, V. Tube: Russell Sq. **Amenities:** Restaurant; cafe/bar; access to nearby health club; concierge; limited room service; babysitting; laundry service; dry cleaning; nonsmoking rooms. *In room:* TV, coffeemaker, trouser press, radio.

Morgan Hotel ★★   It's a real treat to find a B&B with air-conditioning and double-glazing, particularly in an elegant 18th-century terrace house. It makes staying at the Morgan Hotel a pleasure. It's more expensive than other local B&Bs (still cheaper than Cartwright Gardens), but then, period-style decoration does tend to bump the price up. There are pretty floral bedspreads and decorative borders on the walls, and every room is different. If there are two of you, go for the first-floor room that opens onto the garden at the back, which no one else gets to use. The basic single room is tiny, and there are much better single rooms elsewhere. Otherwise, it's almost worth staying here just to see the oak-paneled breakfast room with its wooden booths. A few doors away, the Morgan has four wonderful one-bedroom apartments, which go for £125 ($200) a night including breakfast, or £175 ($280) if you want to have a foldaway bed and sleep three.

24 Bloomsbury St., London WC1B 3QJ. ℭ **020/7636-3735.** Fax 020/7636-3045. 15 units, all with bathroom (most with shower only). £65–£80 ($104–$128) single; £95 ($152) double/twin; £125 ($200) triple. Rates include full English breakfast. MC, V. Tube: Goodge St. or Tottenham Court Rd. *In room:* A/C, TV, hair dryer.

CHELSEA
This fashionable district begins at Sloane Square and runs south to the Thames and westward toward Earl's Court and West Brompton. Its commercial spinal cord is King's Road. The visitor seeking budget accommodations won't find anything too easy on the pocketbook here, but those who can afford a splurge may want to settle in to savor Chelsea's charm.

WORTH A SPLURGE
Annadale House   The five floors of this late Victorian brick-fronted town house on a safe, quiet street close to Sloane Square are decorated with an eclectic mix of English antiques and modern furniture. Resident manager Pat O'Keeffe monitors her guests during check-in and checkout, but otherwise maintains a laissez-faire attitude. Bedrooms are cozy and comfy rather than grand and have small shower-only bathrooms. No. 14 is a large pleasant double or quad, and no. 15 looks into the back garden and has a soft, romantic feel. There's no bar or public area but guests can use the small kitchen and are welcome to enjoy the charming back garden. Continental breakfast costs £5 ($8) and is served in your room. Single women will feel comfortable here.

39 Sloane Gardens, London SW1W 8EB. ℭ **020/7730-6291.** Fax 020/7730-2727. info@annadale-hotel.co. uk. 15 units. £60–£70 ($96–$112) single; £95–£110 ($144–$176) double; £120 ($192) triple; £130 ($208) quad. AE, DC, MC, V. Tube: Sloane Sq. **Amenities:** Garden; use of kitchen. *In room:* TV, hair dryer.

COVENT GARDEN & PICCADILLY CIRCUS
If you stay in Covent Garden—due east of both the West End and Soho—you'll be right in the thick of things. It's the site of London's liveliest group of restaurants, pubs, and cafes outside Soho, and the restored marketplace and surrounding streets teem with trendy shops. Although there are few budget accommodations choices here, it's a great place to hang out. Nearby Piccadilly Circus is the heart of London.

Regent Palace Hotel ✯ *Value*   This London behemoth, located smack dab in the center of the West End just off Piccadilly Circus, was built in 1915, long before travelers expected private bathrooms in their rooms. In recent years it's been gradually upgrading by installing pre-fab shower/toilet/basin units in some of the rooms and sprucing up room decor. The rooms without "en suite facilities" are actually preferable (and cheaper, of course) because they have a bit more space. The public bathrooms are kept locked to make sure they're spotless; if you need to use a shower, the housekeeper will ride the elevator up at any time with the key and fresh towels. That's quite a deal at a weekday price that knocks socks off many B&Bs. The decor is comfortable if plain, and some of the beds aren't as firm as Americans like them; the spruced-up lobby looks like an air terminal, right down to the weekend check-in queues. Breakfast is extra, so skip it and find a charming cafe in nearby Soho instead. That's really the selling point of the Regent Palace—its fabulous location right in the heart of everything. This hotel has a history of offering cheap rates through a host of accommodations sites, so plug the name into a search engine and see what you come up with.

Glasshouse St., Piccadilly Circus, London W1A 4BZ. ℂ 020/7734-0716. Fax 020/7734-6435. 887 units, 383 with bathroom (shower only). £64–£75 ($102–$120) single without bathroom; £69–£89 ($110–$142) double/twin without bathroom, £119–£129 ($190–$206) double/twin with bathroom; £95–£105 ($152–$168) triple without bathroom; £119–£138 ($190–$221) quad without bathroom. 32 units adapted for travelers with disabilities. Lower rates apply Sun–Thurs. Discount available for long stays. AE, DC, MC, V. Tube: Piccadilly Circus. **Amenities:** Pub and coffee bar; concierge; limited room service; laundry service; dry cleaning; nonsmoking rooms. *In room:* TV; coffeemaker, radio.

Royal Adelphi Hotel *(Finds* It's by no means grand, but you'll like this unassuming hotel for its in-the-thick-of-it location, behind Trafalgar Square on the lively pedestrian walk that leads from the Strand to Embankment and Hungerford Bridge, and for the friendliness of the management. It's a favorite with London Marathon runners, so you'll have to book early if you want to stay here in April. The Royal Adelphi is almost a splurge, especially because breakfast is not included (full English is £8/$13 and continental £4/$6). The rooms are modest and can get hot in summer because there's no air-conditioning. The decor is respectable rather than plush, and the lounge and hotel bar (open 24 hr.) show signs of wear and tear. But refurbishment is in the works. Room no. 504 is a cozy triple with a good-size white-tiled bathroom with a tub and shower. There's double-glazing on the windows, but ask for a room in back if you're particularly noise-sensitive.

21 Villiers St., London WC2N 6ND. ℂ 020/7930-8764. Fax 020/7930-8735. www.royaladelphi.co.uk. 47 units, 34 with bathroom (some with shower only). £50 ($80) single without bathroom; £68 ($109) single with bathroom or double/twin without bathroom; £90 ($144) double/twin with bathroom; £120 ($192) triple with bathroom. AE, DC, MC, V. Tube: Embankment or Charing Cross. **Amenities:** Bar. *In room:* TV, coffeemaker, hair dryer, radio.

EARL'S COURT

Another popular hotel and B&B district is this area below Kensington, bordering the western half of Chelsea. A 15-minute Tube ride from the Earl's Court Tube station takes you into the heart of Piccadilly. A young crowd comes at night for the pubs, wine bars, and coffeehouses.

Beaver Hotel *⚲* On a quiet, tree-lined crescent of Victorian terrace houses dating from 1887, this four-story hotel offers a nice choice of rooms and even has an elevator (something of a rarity in this price range). The newly refurbished rooms with small private bathrooms are the most spacious; some have been painted in quite vibrant colors. There are adequate hallway facilities for those rooms without a private bathroom. Free coffee and tea are available all day and there's a nonsmoking TV lounge.

57–59 Philbeach Gardens, London SW5 9ED. ℂ 020/7373-4553. Fax 020/7373-4555. www.beaverhotel. co.uk. 38 units, 24 with bathroom. £40 ($64) single without bathroom, £60 ($96) single with bathroom; £85 ($136) double with bathroom; £99 ($158) triple with bathroom. Rates include English breakfast. AE, DC, MC, V. Tube: Earl's Court. **Amenities:** Breakfast room; bar; lounge; babysitting. *In room:* TV, hair dryer, safe.

Hotel Plaza Continental It sounds like a big fancy chain hotel, but the Hotel Plaza Continental is actually a B&B that occupies a white-fronted Victorian row house built in the 1870s. It's about a 2-minute walk from the Tube stop and a few minutes walk from the Earl's Court Exhibition Centre. The compact rooms are accessible by elevator and have decent-size private bathrooms, most of them with tub/shower combinations. The bedroom decor is better than in many B&Bs, but overall it's a bit faded and the new management was planning to completely refurbish the place starting sometime in 2003. Rooms have double-glazing to minimize street noise but they vary in quality, so ask to look at one before you settle in. There's a pleasant breakfast room.

9 Knaresborough Place, London SW5 0TP. ℂ **020/7370-3246.** Fax 020/7373-9571. www.hotelplaza continental.co.uk. 20 units. £40–£65 ($64–$104) single; £70–£85 ($112–$136) double; £105 ($168) triple. Rates include continental breakfast. AE, MC, V. Tube: Earl's Court. **Amenities:** Breakfast room. *In room:* TV, hair dryer, coffeemaker.

Philbeach Hotel   The Philbeach is a one-stop entertainment bonanza for gay travelers and somehow manages to do it at budget rates. It's a really friendly place and attractive, too. The whole building was recarpeted and most of the rooms got new beds in 2000. Some of the rooms are small so go for one of the little mezzanine doubles. They share a terrace overlooking a pretty garden. One is en suite, and the other shares a bathroom. It's about four bedrooms to every public facility. The Princess Restaurant, with its conservatory setting, serves Thai cuisine and residents get a 20% discount. The hotel has a cozy basement bar, and the Monday party nights are a blast. This isn't the place to come if you're looking for a quiet hidey-hole.

30–31 Philbeach Gardens, London SW5 9EB. ℂ **020/7373-1244.** Fax 020/7244-0149. 40 units, 15 with bathroom (most with shower only). £35–£50 ($52–$80) single without bathroom, £60 ($96) single with bathroom; £65 ($104) double without bathroom, £90 ($144) double with bathroom; £75 ($120) triple without bathroom, £100 ($160) triple with bathroom. Rates include continental breakfast. Discount available for 1-week stays. No 1-night stays on Sat. AE, DC, MC, V. Tube: Earl's Court. **Amenities:** Restaurant; bar; garden, nonsmoking rooms. *In room:* TV, coffeemaker, hair dryer, iron, safe.

Rushmore Hotel ★★   This gracious town-house hotel has Italianate classical scenes decorating the hallway and ceilings. The breakfast room is in a limestone-paved conservatory with wrought-iron furniture and potted orchids. Every bedroom is a different exuberant stage set. One has gothic looping curtains and a canopy over the bed. In another, you'll find a chandelier and Louis XIV pale-blue walls, with panels sketched out in gold. There's a great family room under the eaves, and a porter will carry up your bags. The Rushmore will take bookings for specific rooms and you can preview some of them on the website (which features seasonal specials). All the rooms had new carpet a couple of years ago, and the bathrooms were given a tiled makeover in 2003. The welcoming staff will let you send a fax and pick up e-mail. There are irons at reception and safety deposit boxes. If the Rushmore were anyplace other than in Earl's Court, it would certainly bust the budget.

11 Trebovir Rd., London SW5 9LS. ℂ **020/7370-3839.** Fax 020/7370-0274. www.rushmore-hotel.co.uk. 22 units, all with bathroom (most with shower only). £59 ($94) single; £79 ($126) double/twin; £89 ($142) triple; £99 ($158) family room. Rates include continental breakfast. Discount available for 1-week stays. 10% discount for seniors. Under-12s stay free in parent's room. AE, DC, MC, V. Tube: Earl's Court. **Amenities:** Laundry services; dry cleaning; nonsmoking rooms. *In room:* TV, coffeemaker, hair dryer.

WORTH A SPLURGE
Barkston Gardens Hotel   Established in 1905, this hotel occupies six adjoining town houses. In 1993, the hotel was bought by a British chain and given a complete overhaul. There's a gleaming marble lobby with a big bar-lounge next to it. Bedrooms, larger than you'll find in B&Bs, are comfortably up to date, with wheat-colored walls and contemporary furniture. All rooms have good-size bathrooms equipped with shower-tub combinations.

34–44 Barkston Gardens, London SW5 0EW. ℂ **020/7373-7851.** Fax 020/7370-6570. www.cairnhotel group.co.uk. 93 units. £89 ($142) single; £115 ($184) double; £125 ($200) triple. AE, DC, MC, V. Tube: Earl's Court. **Amenities:** Restaurant; bar; room service; babysitting; laundry/dry cleaning. *In room:* TV, hair dryer.

Henley House ★ This newly refurbished B&B stands out from the pack and exudes a warm, welcoming charm. The redbrick Victorian row house sits on a communal fenced-in garden that guests can use. A ground-floor sitting room overlooks a rear courtyard. The decor throughout is bright and contemporary; a typical room has warmly patterned wallpaper, chintz fabrics, and granite-topped desks and credenzas. Each room comes with a small, white-tiled, shower-only bathroom. Breakfast is served in a lovely glass-roofed room filled with orchids.

30 Barkston Gardens, London SW5 0EN. ✆ 020/7370-4111. Fax 020/7370-0026. www.henleyhousehotel. com. 20 units. £69–£85 ($110–$136) single; £89–£112 ($142–$179) double. Rates include continental breakfast. AE, DC, MC, V. Tube: Earl's Court. **Amenities:** Breakfast room; lounge; babysitting. *In room:* TV, hair dryer.

Kensington International Inn ★ *(Finds)* This polished and professionally run establishment on an elegant 1860s street just reopened after a half-million-pound overhaul. It's high in style and low in price. The rooms are small to medium in size but the contemporary decor is surprisingly chic, utilizing pale wheat colors and sleek wooden headboards and furnishings. Bathrooms are also small, with glass-walled showers. There's a hip little bar, a conservatory lounge, and a high standard of service. You may find a lower price on their website than the rack rates listed below.

4 Templeton Place, London SW5 9LZ. ✆ 020/7370-4333. Fax 020/7244-7873. www.kensingtoninternational inn.com. 60 units. £100 ($160) single; £120 ($192) twin/double; £140 ($224) triple. Rates include continental breakfast. AE, DC, MC, V. Tube: Earl's Court. **Amenities:** Bar; nonsmoking rooms. *In room:* TV, coffeemaker, hair dryer, safe, trouser press.

KENSINGTON & HOLLAND PARK

Kensington is an upscale neighborhood west of Knightsbridge and north of Earl's Court. Throughout the area you'll find a number of fine B&Bs. This district, close to Kensington Palace, is a convenient place to stay. Holland Park is an equally upscale mostly residential neighborhood that adjoins Kensington on the west side.

Abbey House ★ There are no private bathrooms at Abbey House, which is why it can charge these rates in such a posh part of town. It's only a short walk up to Notting Hill, or downhill to Kensington High Street. Abbey House, owned by Albert and Carol Nayach, is a gem set in a gracious Victorian square. The bright hallway has a checkerboard floor and wrought-iron staircase lined with lithographs of glum-faced royals. The bedrooms are simple, attractive, and big for London. The second-floor room at the front gets the balcony above the front door. The bathrooms are Laura Ashley style and impeccable; there's one for every three bedrooms. And there's a kitchenette, where you can make tea and coffee for free. The staff treat you terribly well here, whether you need a hair dryer, babysitting, or restaurant advice.

11 Vicarage Gate, London W8 4AG. ✆ 020/7727-2594. Fax 020/7727-1873. www.abbeyhousekensington. com. 16 units, none with bathroom. £45 ($72) single; £74 ($118) double/twin; £90 ($144) triple; £100 ($160) quad. Rates include full English breakfast. Discount available off season. No credit cards. Tube: High St. Kensington or Notting Hill Gate. **Amenities:** Babysitting arranged. *In room:* TV, no phone.

Vicarage Private Hotel ★ Eileen Diviney, who runs Vicarage Private Hotel, just added en suite bathrooms to the first and second floors and redecorated the rooms. An en suite ground-floor twin at the back, no. 3, is a splurge but marvelous—high-ceilinged and furnished with pretty painted tables and old-fashioned metal bedsteads. But you really don't have to splash out here. Most of the rooms are big, the ceilings are high up to the fourth floor, and all are done in a Victorian country style. Four bedrooms share each public bathroom, and there are separate toilets. If you're trying to weigh this B&B up against Abbey House right next door, then there are other things to consider apart from the fancier decor here and marginally higher price. Instead of putting TV sets in the rooms, Vicarage Private Hotel has a TV lounge. Hair dryers are standard, instead of at the reception desk. And you don't have to leave your room to make tea or coffee. Oh, and there are kippers (smoked herring) and porridge on a breakfast menu fit for warriors.

10 Vicarage Gate, London W8 4AG. (℗ **020/7229-4030.** Fax 020/7792-5989. www.londonvicaragehotel.com. 17 units, 2 with bathroom. £46 ($74) single without bathroom; £76–£78 ($122–$125) double/twin without bathroom, £102 ($163) double/twin with bathroom; £93–95 ($149–$152) triple without bathroom; £102 ($163) family room without bathroom. Rates include full English breakfast. No credit cards. Personal checks from U.S. banks accepted if received at least 2 months ahead of visit. Tube: High St. Kensington or Notting Hill Gate. **Amenities:** Babysitting arranged. *In room:* Coffeemaker, hair dryer, no phone.

SUPER-CHEAP SLEEPS

Kensington Guest House *Kids* *Value*   This neat and well-kept family-run B&B, on a tree-lined but busy street just a few meters from the Holland Park Tube station, is a more appealing choice than the Ravna Gora across the street. The building, over 150 years old, has always been a hostelry. Bea and Bill McElhill, the friendly and hardworking owners, offer pleasant twin bedrooms, two of which are large enough to be made into family units. All of the rooms have full kitchens, including fridge, stove, sink, and dishes. A full English breakfast is brought to your room in the morning. Don't expect fancy decor, but do expect a warm welcome and extremely reasonable prices.

712 Holland Park Ave., London W11 3QZ. (℗ **020/7460-7080.** Fax 020/7221-1077. www.hotellondon.co.uk. 6 units, 3 with private bathroom. £40 ($64) single without bathroom; £60 ($96) double without bathroom, £70 ($112) double with bathroom; £80 ($128) family room without bathroom, £90 ($144) family room with bathroom. AE, MC, V. Tube: Holland Park. *In room:* TV, fridge, kitchenette, no phone.

Ravna Gora Hotel *Value*   Backpackers and students often use this super-budget hotel as a one-night crash pad, even though the comfort level is minimal. This once very grand house was built in 1829 and lived in by Queen Victoria's barrister. For nearly 50 years it's been operated as a hotel by a Yugoslav family, the Jovanovics, who don't bother with frills and bows but offer basic rooms in rather spartan surroundings. The beds are clean and the place is decent, especially since some of the rooms have been repainted and new hallway showers have been installed. The location is a bit out of the way, but the Tube stop is just across the street. Lower prices below are for rooms without private bathrooms.

29 Holland Park Ave., London W11 3RW. (℗ **020/7727-7725.** Fax 020/7221-4282. 23 units, 3 with bathroom. £32–£45 ($51–$72) single; £54–£64 ($86–$102) double; £66–£86 ($106–$138) triple; £88–£96 ($141–$154) quad. Rates include English breakfast. AE, MC, V. Tube: Holland Park. **Amenities:** Breakfast; lounge. *In room:* TV.

SOUTH KENSINGTON

South Kensington has long been one of the most popular areas to stay in London. Prices have steadily crept up but there are still some fine lower-cost B&Bs and hotels to be found. There are a number of colleges and institutes that draw large numbers of students from around the world.

Astons Apartments ★★   Behind the redbrick facades of three Victorian town houses you'll find the very model of a modern apartment hotel. Maids swoop through every day. You can see your face in the polished, wood handrail on the stairs. The reception desk, where you can send a fax or drop off your dry cleaning or have someone order a theater or tour ticket, is manned until 9pm.

Prices verge on being a splurge for budget travelers, but you get good value for your money and the website often has hot deals. If money is tight, forget the singles and the great family room in the basement with its open-plan kitchen and sofa bed for the kids. You can do better elsewhere. But the rest of the studios should impress even the most exacting guests. A dozen were recently refurbed, with more in the works. The Executive doubles and quads are larger and have some extra amenities, including larger bathrooms. Bathrooms throughout are tiled and have showers. All the studios have fully equipped kitchenettes, hidden behind foldaway doors, and there's a big supermarket nearby.

31 Rosary Gardens, London SW7 4NH. © 800/525-2810 or 020/7590-6000. Fax 020/7590-6060. www. astons-apartments.com. 54 units. Standard studios: £65 ($104) single; £90 ($144) double; £125 ($200) triple. Executive studios: £125 ($200) double; £165 ($264) quad. Children stay free in parent's room. AE, DISC, MC, V. Tube: Gloucester Rd. **Amenities:** Business center; nonsmoking rooms. *In room:* TV, dataport, kitchenette, coffeemaker, hair dryer.

Swiss House Hotel ⚝ If you've just gotta have your space, man, then Swiss House could be the answer to your prayers. If they're available, Peter Vincenti lets out his huge quads to two people for £99 ($158). But you don't have to splurge because the standard doubles are a good size, too, and this is a lovely place. Guests walk past a curtain of greenery—plants hang from every window ledge, railing, and balcony—and under an old-fashioned canopy to the front door. Inside, chintz, dried flowers, and original fireplaces create a homey, country-style atmosphere. Traffic noise can be a problem on Old Brompton Road, so try to get a room at the back looking over the peaceful communal garden (you'll have to be content with looking, though; it's not open to guests). The proprietor is an extremely welcoming and helpful host, providing room service of soups and "monster" sandwiches from midday until 9pm. You can also pay a £6 ($10) supplement for a full English breakfast. Someone will carry your bags up and buy your favorite newspaper.

171 Old Brompton Rd., London SW5 0AN. © 020/7373-2769. Fax 020/7373-4983. www.swiss-hh.demon. co.uk. 16 units, 15 with bathroom (most with shower only). £51 ($82) single without bathroom, £71 ($114) single with bathroom; £89–£104 ($142–$166) double/twin with bathroom; £120 ($192) triple with bathroom; £134 ($214) quad with bathroom. Rates include continental breakfast. Discount of 5% for 1-week stay and cash payment (US$ accepted). AE, DC, MC, V. Tube: Gloucester Rd. **Amenities:** Secretarial services; limited room service; babysitting arranged; laundry service; nonsmoking rooms. *In room:* TV, hair dryer.

SUPER-CHEAP SLEEPS

Clearlake Hotel *(Kids)* *(Value)* This splendidly unglamorous hotel, owned and managed for 45 years by Andrew Asherskovic, offers a range of fantastic-value, self-catering options in an upscale, unbeatable location. It's located on a quiet street opposite Kensington Gardens at the eastern end of Kensington High Street. What really sells the Clearlake is the huge amount of space you get, except where modern partitions cut into the gracious proportions to make single rooms or toe-to-toe twins. Despite some recent redecoration, many of the apartments resemble student digs—a jumble of fancy gilt mirrors next to a host of 1970s horrors, and even theater props left over from plays the owner puts on. Idiosyncratic is the best word to describe the place. It's ideal for families. Staff can lend you cribs, strollers, and high chairs, as well as arrange babysitting. For maximum space, stay in the building next door, where every floor is a huge, old-fashioned flat. For an extra £4 ($6) you can have continental breakfast served in your room.

18–19 Prince of Wales Terrace, London W8 5PQ. © 020/7937-3274. Fax 020/7376-0604. www.clearlake hotel.co.uk. 25 units, all with bathroom (some with shower only). £53 ($85) double; £65 ($104) double/twin studio; £80 ($128) triple studio; £98–£110 ($157–$176) 1-bedroom apt; £115–£125 ($184–$200) 2-bedroom apt; £197 ($315) 3-bedroom apt. Weekly rates and long-stay discounts available. AE, DC, MC, V. Tube: High St. Kensington or Gloucester Rd. **Amenities:** Babysitting arranged; laundry and dry cleaning service; nonsmoking rooms. *In room:* TV, kitchen, coffeemaker, hair dryer.

NOTTING HILL

Notting Hill, above the northeastern tip of Kensington Gardens, is bounded on the south by Bayswater Road, on the east by Gloucester Terrace, on the north by Westway, and on the west by Shepherd's Bush. It has many turn-of-the-20th-century mansions and small houses on quiet, leafy streets. This once scruffy area has become trendy and expensive but visitors still flock to Portobello Road to visit the famous Portobello Market.

Comfort Inn Notting Hill ★ *Value*   The owners of this Comfort Inn franchise actively urge you to book direct with them and not through central reservations. By doing so, you'll get a rate at least 10% lower than the official one, and often lower still (their lower "direct booking" rates are the ones listed below). The hotel will make deals based on occupancy levels, so the quoted offer can change every week. Located on a quiet, pretty street off Notting Hill Gate, the Comfort Inn stretches across five terrace houses. The rooms are on the three upper floors (there's an elevator) and are a fair size for London. Rear windows look across fire escapes and rooftops, while second-floor rooms on the front have access to an east-facing balcony. Rooms have been redecorated with a nice business feel and equipped with firm new beds. The bathrooms are also newly renovated. There are a few newly redone and fairly charming rooms on a little internal courtyard. The Comfort Inn is a practical choice in a superb location. Breakfast is a self-service buffet, or you can pay £5.95 ($10) for full English.

6–14 Pembridge Gardens, London W2 4DU. ✆ 020/7229-6666. Fax 020/7229-3333. www.lth-hotels.com. 64 units, all with bathroom. £49–£72 ($78–$115) single; £58–£94 ($93–$150) double/twin; £75–£115 ($120–$184) triple; £92–£129 ($147–$206) quad. Rates include continental breakfast. Lower rates apply mid-July to Aug and Dec–Feb. Discount available for 1-week stays. AE, DC, MC, V. Tube: Notting Hill Gate. **Amenities:** Bar; babysitting arranged; laundry service; dry cleaning; Internet access; nonsmoking rooms. *In room:* TV, dataport, coffeemaker, hair dryer, radio, safe.

The Gate Hotel ★   Portobello Road is a hot tourist spot because of its market and antiques shops. Which makes The Gate a fun place to stay, if you don't mind crowds of people marching past. The hotel has been in existence since 1932, and the present owners have run it for over 20 years. Look for a tiny, brick, curved-front, late Georgian house with hanging baskets and a parrot (named Sergeant Bilko) living in a caged-in area in front. Guests eat breakfast in their rooms, which have all been refurbished. The look is attractive, with paneled furniture and blue carpet and linen, and ceiling fans. The bigger rooms each have a small sofa bed for an extra person. There are hair dryers at reception.

6 Portobello Rd., London W11 3DG. ✆ 020/7221-0707. Fax 020/7221-9128. www.gatehotel.com. 6 units, 5 with private bathroom (most with shower only). £45–65 ($72–$104) single; £65–£100 ($104–$160) double. Rates include continental breakfast. MC, V. Tube: Notting Hill Gate. *In room:* TV, fridge, radio.

Portobello Gold *Finds*   Portobello Gold's conservatory restaurant is a local institution and a great deal: Two courses could cost you as little as £14.50 ($23). The bar menu is almost as long as the regular one, and dishes rarely top £6.50 ($10). Guests have unlimited Web access in the second-floor cybercafe or can pay £5 ($8) for a wireless set-up in their room. The rooms are almost unbelievably tiny but freshly decorated. All have a shower but only three have a toilet; the rest share the facility in the hallway. If you have long legs, ask for the 7-foot-long Captain's bed. For a very special treat, rent the two-story apartment with private roof terrace, then make like a movie star and tour London in Portobello Gold's 1952 Buick convertible (£60/$96 for up to five people).

97 Portobello Rd., London W11 2QB. ℭ **020/7460-4910.** Fax 020/7460-4911. www.portobellogold.com. 6 units, 3 with bathroom; 1 apt. £60 ($96) single without bathroom, £75 ($120) single with bathroom; £70 ($112) double without bathroom, £85 ($136) double with bathroom; £180 ($288) apt. Rates include continental breakfast. Lower price Sun–Thurs. Discount for 1-week stays. MC V. Tube: Notting Hill Gate. **Amenities:** Restaurant; bar; free Internet access. *In room:* TV, wireless Internet access.

MARYLEBONE

The principally Georgian district of Marylebone (pronounced *Mar*-li-bone) is below Regent's Park, northwest of Piccadilly Circus, facing Mayfair to the south and extending north of Marble Arch at Hyde Park. A number of simple but gracious town houses in this residential section have been converted into private hotels, and discreet bed-and-breakfast signs appear in the windows. If you don't have a reservation, start at Edgware Road and walk past Seymour and Great Cumberland Place.

Edward Lear Hotel   Previous reviews of this hotel always mentioned the pretty Georgian houses with their gold-tipped railings and luxuriant window boxes; the excellent location, just behind Marble Arch; the nice people working there; and the charming lounge and big-windowed breakfast room. Then came the "but . . .," because the standards upstairs—up five narrow flights in one house and four in the other—never matched up to the rest. Long-time owner Peter Evans finally began a renovation program in 2001 and some of the bedrooms have now been redecorated. The new look is drab but clean and the rooms aren't a bad size for London, with decent storage provided by the quirky built-in furniture. Try for room no. 18, a double overlooking a mews in back with its bathroom down a little flight of stairs. There's no double-glazing at the Edward Lear so rooms in the front bear the brunt of traffic noise along busy Seymour Street. Some rooms have a cupboard-size shower but no toilet and the rest share bathrooms that are adequate but dated. So there are good deals here, depending how laid-back you are about shared plumbing.

28–30 Seymour St., London W1H 5WD. ℭ **020/7402-5401.** Fax 020/7706-3766. www.edlear.com. 31 units, 4 with bathroom (8 with shower only). £47.50 ($76) single without bathroom, £60 ($96) single with bathroom; £66.50 ($106) double without bathroom; £74–£89 ($118–$142) double/twin with bathroom; £89–£99 ($142–$158) triple without bathroom; £99–105 ($158–$168) family room with bathroom. Rates include full English breakfast. Children under 2 stay free in parent's room; £9.50 ($15) for extra child's bed. Discount of 10% for 1-week stays (not July–Aug) and for Internet bookings. MC, V. Tube: Marble Arch. **Amenities:** Lounge; Internet access. *In room:* TV, coffeemaker, hair dryer, radio.

Lincoln House Hotel   Behind a brown-brick facade originally built as a private house during the Georgian era, this much-refurbished guesthouse offers dependable accommodations in a desirable neighborhood, a 5-minute walk from Marble Arch. Each of the small but pleasant bedrooms contains a tiny bathroom with a tiny shower. The standard of service is high here and the overall atmosphere is welcoming and inviting. Many European consumer associations have endorsed the hotel for its good value.

33 Gloucester Place, London W1H 3PD. ℭ **020/7486-7630.** Fax 020/7486-0166. www.lincoln-house-hotel.co.uk. 24 units. £69 ($110) single; £79 ($126) double; £115 ($184) triple. Rates include English breakfast. AE, DC, MC, V. Tube: Marble Arch or Baker Street. **Amenities:** Breakfast room; lounge. *In room:* TV, coffeemaker, fridge, hair dryer.

Regency Hotel   This is a centrally located hotel that was built, along with most of its neighbors, in the late 1800s. Although it was gutted and renovated in 1991, it's now looking a bit worn, even threadbare, but it remains one of the better hotels on the street. The simple, conservatively decorated bedrooms are scattered over four floors. The breakfast room is in what used to be the cellar. The small, well-kept bathrooms come with a shower. The neighborhood is protected as a historic district, and Marble Arch, Regent's Park, and Baker Street all lie within a 12-minute walk.

19 Nottingham Place, London W1M 3FF. © 020/7486-5347. Fax 020/7224-6057. www.regencyhotelwest end.co.uk. 20 units. £68 ($109) single; £85–£89 ($136–$142) double; £125 ($200) family room. Rates include English breakfast. AE, DC, MC, V. Tube: Baker St. **Amenities:** Breakfast room; lounge; room service. *In room:* TV, minibar, coffeemaker, hair dryer, trouser press.

Wigmore Court Hotel ⭐   The owner of this rather appealing Georgian-era B&B, Najma Jinnah, knows the long climb to the fifth floor is a turn-off for a lot of guests, even though they get help with their bags, so she has introduced a reward system. Anyone who does make it to the top can sink into a four-poster bed to recover. There are two more, one each on the second and third floors. Budget travelers can get a very good deal here. There's a small fourth-floor double which shares a bathroom, one floor up, with a single and costs £13 ($21) less than the others. Though it faces the front, there is double-glazing throughout. The rooms at the back look over a mews. The decor is a pleasant mix of traditional styles. Guests can use the kitchen and laundry facilities.

23 Gloucester Place, London W1H 3PB. © 020/7935-0928. Fax 020/7487-4254. www.wigmore-hotel.co.uk. 18 units, 16 with bathroom (some with shower only). £62–£75 ($99) single; £89 ($96) double; £120 ($192) triple; £130 ($208) quad. Rates include full English breakfast. Discount of 10% for 1-week stays. MC, V. Tube: Marble Arch. **Amenities:** Laundry facilities; use of kitchen. *In room:* TV, coffeemaker, hair dryer.

SUPER-CHEAP SLEEPS

Boston Court Hotel   This simple hotel offers good, affordable accommodations in a centrally located Victorian-era building within walking distance of Oxford Street shopping and Hyde Park. The rooms have been refurbished and redecorated with a no-nonsense decor. Larger-than-average bathrooms are a selling point. Room no. 6, a double with a big bathroom with a tub, is one of the better rooms. Several rooms have private showers but you share a toilet down the hall.

26 Upper Berkeley St., Marble Arch, London W1H 7PF. © 020/7723-1445. Fax 020/7262-8823. www.boston courthotel.co.uk. 15 units, 8 with private bathroom. £45–£49 ($72–$78) single with shower only; £55–£59 ($88–$94) single with bathroom; £69 ($110) double with shower only; £75–£79 ($120–$126) double with bathroom; £85–£89 ($136–$142) triple with bathroom. Rates include continental breakfast. MC, V. Tube: Marble Arch. **Amenities:** Laundry. *In room:* TV/VCR, fridge, fan, coffeemaker, hair dryer.

Glynne Court Hotel ⭐   In the Marble Arch area of Marylebone, this clean and comfortable B&B is in one of the more desirable places to live. Hyde Park and Oxford Street are close at hand. The guesthouse is white with carriage lamps on each side of the front door, and is run with a low-key flair. The rooms were nicely redone in 2002 and have a kind of Italianate style. Bathrooms are well kept and contain showers. A continental breakfast is served in your room.

41 Great Cumberland Place, London W1H 7LG. © 020/7258-1010. Fax 020/7258-0055. www.glynne-court-hotel.com. 13 units. £39 ($62) single without bathroom; £45 ($72) single with shower only; £69 ($110) double with bathroom; £75 ($120) triple with bathroom. Rates include continental breakfast. AE, DC, MC, V. Tube: Marble Arch. *In room:* TV, coffeemaker.

WORTH A SPLURGE

Georgian Hotel ⭐   Central London is stuffed with luxury hotels and suffers from an acute lack of small, personally run, mid-price hotels. This hotel, near Baker Street and within walking distance of Oxford Street and Regents Park, fills that gap. Run by the same family since 1973, the Georgian House has a dedicated staff and management intent on improving the hotel. Rooms have decent-size private bathrooms or showers. There's an elevator to all floors. Most of the bedrooms are decorated with a pleasant blue and gold color scheme. The ground-floor accommodations are the least preferred. Don't expect views from some of the back rooms, which open onto a wall.

87 Gloucester Place, London W1H 3PG. ℭ 020/7935-2211. Fax 020/7486-7535. www.londoncentralhotel.com. 19 units. £75 ($120) single; £90 ($144) double; £100 ($160) triple; £130 ($208) family room. Rates include continental breakfast. AE, MC, V. Tube: Baker St. **Amenities:** Breakfast room; lounge. *In room:* TV, coffeemaker.

Hart House Hotel ★★   Andrew Bowden, who took over the management of Hart House from his parents, has one of the most welcoming and professionally run B&Bs in London. A Georgian town house built in 1782 and used by members of the French nobility during the French Revolution, it has retained its dignified entrance hall (with a huge fragrant bouquet of flowers) and polished paneling that gives way to pretty floral wallpaper. The rooms (all nonsmoking) are attractive and comfortable with small but immaculate bathrooms. Double-glazing screens out the traffic roar on Gloucester Place, the busy road from Oxford Street to Baker Street. The top floor double is a peaceful high-up hideaway, but there's no elevator to reach it. Room no. 6, a huge twin at the back with a marvelous leaded-glass bay window and a bathroom up a little flight of stairs, is another sought-after room. Reception has cots to lend out.

51 Gloucester Place, London W1H 3PE. ℭ 020/7935-2288. Fax 020/7935-8516. www.harthouse.co.uk. 15 units, all with bathroom (some with shower only). £65 ($104) single; £95 ($152) double/twin; £120 ($192) triple; £150 ($240) quad. Rates include full English breakfast. Discounts for 6 nights or more. AE, MC, V. Tube: Marble Arch or Baker St. **Amenities:** Babysitting arranged; laundry service; dry cleaning; nonsmoking rooms. *In room:* TV, coffeemaker, hair dryer.

VICTORIA & WESTMINSTER

Directly south of Green Park and Buckingham Palace, wedged in between Westminster to the east, Pimlico to the south, and Belgravia to the west, is an area called Victoria, after sprawling Victoria Station. Known as "Gateway to the Continent," Victoria Station is where you get buses or trains to Dover and Folkestone for the trip across the Channel to France. The British Airways Terminal, the Green Line Coach Station, and the Victoria Coach Station are all just 5 minutes from Victoria Station. If you're looking for hotels and B&Bs in this area, your best bet is Ebury Street, directly east of Victoria Station and Buckingham Palace Road, where you'll find some of the best moderately priced lodgings in central London (Ebury St. actually considers itself Belgravia). Westminster, the government quarter of London, is where you find the Houses of Parliament and Westminster Abbey.

Astors Hotel   This hotel is just a stone's throw from Buckingham Palace and a 5-minute walk from Victoria's mainline and Tube stations. A brick-fronted Victorian building with a bright yellow door, it's clean, functional, and a bit cramped. The rooms are satisfactory if undistinguished; some have small tiled bathrooms with showers. Because space and furnishings vary greatly, ask to see a room before you take it. There's a cheery breakfast room.

110–112 Ebury St., London SW1W 9QD. ℭ 020/7730-3811. Fax 020/7823-6728. 22 units, 10 with bathroom. £60 ($96) single or double without bathroom, £75 ($120) single or double with bathroom; from £140 ($224) family room with bathroom. Rates include English breakfast. MC, V. Tube: Victoria. **Amenities:** Breakfast room. *In room:* TV, coffeemaker, fan, no phone.

Caswell Hotel   This Westminster hotel has four floors of clean but fairly personality-free bedrooms. Private bathrooms are very small with a shower stall; corridor bathrooms are adequate and well maintained. This is a place to stay if you're not concerned about interior decor and are looking for a low-priced room in Central London.

25 Gloucester St., London SW1V 2DB. © 020/7834-6345. Fax 020/7834-4900. 19 units, 8 with bathroom. £42 ($67) single without bathroom; £54 ($86) double without bathroom, 74 ($118) double with bathroom. Rates include English breakfast. MC, V. Tube: Victoria. **Amenities:** Breakfast room; lounge. *In room:* TV, minibar, hair dryer.

Chesham House Hotel   Just 5 minutes from Victoria Station, this hotel is often cited in roundups of the best B&Bs in London. That's because it's well run and has a kind of low-key charm that many places lack. Chesham House consists of two brick Georgian buildings connected on the top floor and in the basement breakfast area. The facade, with its old-fashioned carriage lamps and pretty window boxes, has won prizes in local competitions. The bedrooms are unfussy and comfortable. In 2003 a major refurbishment was set to begin to install bathrooms in all of the rooms, so the "without bathroom" rates below will change when work is completed.

64–66 Ebury St., London SW1W 9QD. © 020/7730-8513. Fax 020/7730-1845. www.chesham-house-hotel.com. 23 units. £35 ($56) single without bathroom; £55 ($88) double without bathroom; £70 ($112) double with bathroom or triple without bathroom. Rates include English breakfast. AE, DC, MC, V. Tube: Victoria. **Amenities:** Breakfast room; lounge. *In room:* TV, hair dryer, trouser press, no phone.

Collin House ⭐   You could easily walk straight past the discreet slate nameplate announcing Collin House. That would be a shame because it's one of the best B&Bs on Ebury Street. For a start, it's well worth foregoing a private bathroom, even though all the showers are new, because there are never more than two bedrooms sharing each public facility. You'll also get a room at the back, which is blissfully quiet. All the rooms with private bathrooms look out onto Ebury Street, and there is no soundproofing. Most of the rooms have been redecorated over the past couple of years and there is new carpeting on the stairs and an attractive lounge. None of the other Ebury Street B&Bs listed here have one because the buildings are so small. The small basement breakfast room with bench seating and a skylight is like a cross between a canteen and a chapel. Collin House is nonsmoking throughout.

104 Ebury St., London SW1W 9QD. ©/fax 020/7730-8031. www.collinhouse.co.uk. 12 units, 8 with bathroom (shower only). £55 ($88) single with bathroom; £68 ($109) double/twin without bathroom, £82 ($131) double/twin with bathroom; £95 ($152) triple without bathroom. Rates include full English breakfast. MC, V. Tube: Victoria. **Amenities:** Lounge, nonsmoking. *In room:* TV, no phone.

Ebury House Hotel ⭐⭐   On highly competitive Ebury Street, this comfortable B&B stands out, thanks to the welcome you get from its owner-manager, Peter Evans. The bedrooms, while no pacesetters for style, are well maintained and decorated with a mishmash of colors and fabrics. In some rooms new bathrooms have been installed, but they're tiny. Shared bathrooms with showers are on each floor. There's thick new carpeting in the hallway. Breakfast, including a cooked vegetarian option, is served in the pine-paneled breakfast room. Guests are welcome to enjoy the small back garden. Lower prices below are for rooms without bathrooms.

102 Ebury St., London SW1W 9QD. © 020/7730-1350. Fax 020/7259-0400. www.ebury-house-hotel.com. 13 units, 6 with bathroom. £40–65 ($64–$104) single; £55–£75 ($88–$120) double; £70–£95 ($112–$152) triple; £105 ($168) quad with bathroom. Rates include English breakfast. MC, V. Tube: Victoria. **Amenities:** Breakfast room. *In room:* TV, coffeemaker, hair dryer, no phone.

Hamilton House Hotel   This hotel just off Warwick Square has low prices and not much personality, but it's clean and will serve if you just want an inexpensive room for a night or two. Its renovated bedrooms are small, but all have had bathroom units installed. The front rooms can be noisy; the more tranquil rooms are located in the rear.

60 Warwick Way, London SW1V 1SA. ℂ 020/7821-7113. Fax 020/7630-0806. www.hamiltonhousehotel. com. 45 units. £69 ($110) single; £85 ($136) double. Rates include English breakfast. AE, DC, MC, V. Tube: Victoria. **Amenities:** Restaurant; bar; lounge. *In room:* TV, hair dryer.

Harcourt House ★ *(Value*   This early Victorian town house served as a gentleman's lodgings in the late 1880s and the proprietors, David and Glesni Wood, spent years lovingly redecorating the whole place to recapture the original style and atmosphere. Heritage junkies will love it so long as they're not too finicky about details, but other guests may find the preponderance of winey colors rather dark. The two-tone maroon and rich yellow rooms have reproduction brass bedsteads; all have bright tiled bathrooms with showers. The Woods are clearly avid antiques hunters. The hall and stairs are lit with crystal chandeliers and decorated with junk-shop finds like the framed montage of Titanic memorabilia. The breakfast room has a real-flame fire and a restored wood-and-slate floor.

50 Ebury St., London SW1W 0LU. ℂ 020/7730-2722. Fax 020/7730-3998. www.harcourthousehotel.co.uk. 10 units. £50 ($80) single; £70 ($112) double/twin; £90 ($144) triple. Rates include full English breakfast. Discount available off season. AE, MC, V. Tube: Victoria. *In room:* TV, coffeemaker, hair dryer, no phone.

James House/Cartref House ★ *(Kids*   Ebury Street calls itself Belgravia, but this is no hushed tycoon's enclave. There are dozens of places to stay on either side of the junction with Elizabeth Street. James House and Cartref House are separate B&Bs on opposite sides of the road, both run by the very welcoming Derek and Sharon James. The main difference between the two B&Bs is in the number of private bathrooms. All 10 rooms in James House have one, but they're very small. At Cartref House, only three rooms share each immaculately kept bathroom. All the bedrooms are nicely decorated; nothing fancy, but comfortable. Fans have been installed in all the rooms, a boon during summer heat waves. There's a delightful conservatory dining room. Two things to note: Breakfast stops at 8:30am, and kids have to be over 12 to stay in the top bunk in the James House family room. Both houses are totally nonsmoking. Lower rates below are for rooms that share bathrooms.

108–129 Ebury St., London SW1W 9DU. ℂ 020/7730-7338 or 020/7730-6176. Fax 020/7730-7338. www. jamesandcartref.co.uk. 19 units, 13 with bathroom (shower only). £52–£62 ($83–$99) single; £70–£85 ($112–$136) double/twin; £95–£110 ($152–$176) triple; £135 ($216) family room with bathroom. Rates include full English breakfast. AE, MC, V. Tube: Victoria. **Amenities:** Nonsmoking rooms. *In room:* TV, coffeemaker, hair dryer, fan, no phone.

Luna & Simone Hotel ★★   This family-run hotel stands out by a mile on this scruffy terrace. The outside of the big stucco-fronted house gleams bright white and has glass panels etched with the hotel name around the entrance porch. The Desiras have worked wonders on the inside, too. They've renovated all the bedrooms and put private bathrooms in all but two singles. The rooms vary widely in size, but with their blue carpeting and cream-colored walls and newly tiled bathrooms (all with showers), they beat all the dowdy, badly designed hotels and B&Bs for miles around. The beechwood and marble-clad reception area is all new, too, as is the smart-looking breakfast room, now totally nonsmoking. The look throughout is light, simple, and modern, a refreshing change from the interiors of so many Victorian buildings.

47–49 Belgrave Rd., London SW1V 2BB. © 020/7834-5897. Fax 020/7828-2474. www.lunasimonehotel.
com. 36 units. £40 ($64) single; £60–£80 ($96–$128) double/twin; £80–£100 ($128–$160) triple. Rates
include full English breakfast. MC, V. Tube: Victoria or Pimlico. **Amenities:** Internet access; lounge. *In room:*
TV, coffeemaker, hair dryer, safe.

Melbourne House Hotel   Hotel bathrooms are expensive and hard work to
maintain, so many small budget hotels really let guests down. Not so Melbourne
House, where the tiles gleam and the shower units were all replaced in 1999.
John Desira (cousin of Peter Desira, who owns Luna Simone up the road) and
his wife have run this spotless, nonsmoking B&B for 30 years. The rooms are a
decent size for central London, with ample storage space, but the decor is very
simple with a pinky-corally color scheme that won't be everyone's cup of tea.
Carpets, beds, and furniture were recently replaced, and the lounge given a facelift. There's a family room that combines a double, a twin, and a private bathroom, good for parents traveling with two older children.

79 Belgrave Rd., London SW1V 2BG. © 020/7828-3516. Fax 020/7828-7120. www.melbournehousehotel.
co.uk. 17 units, 15 with bathroom (most with shower only). £30 ($48) single without bathroom; £60 ($96)
single with bathroom; £85 ($136) double/twin; £100 ($160) triple; £120 ($192) family room. Rates include
continental breakfast. MC, V. Tube: Pimlico or Victoria. **Amenities:** Nonsmoking rooms. *In room:* TV, coffeemaker, hair dryer.

Oxford House Hotel   This 1840s Victorian town house a few blocks from
Victoria Station is a very homey place owned and operated by an Indian-born
interior designer, Y. A. Kader, and his Irish wife, Terry. The house has some nice
features but looks a bit worn—maybe "lived in" is a better description, since it
also serves as the Kaders' home. The flowery wallpaper is a nice touch, All of the
rooms have washbasins but none has a private bathroom; bathrooms with tubs
are located on every landing and are shared by three rooms. Single rooms up on
the fourth floor are rather small and cramped. The copious breakfast is served in
a cozy cellar-level room.

92–94 Cambridge St., London SW1V 4QG. © 020/7834-6467. Fax 020/7834-0225. 15 units, none with
bathroom. £40 ($64) single; £50–£54 ($80–$86) double; £63–£66 ($101–$106) triple; £84–£88 ($134–$140)
quad. Rates include English breakfast. MC, V. Tube: Victoria. **Amenities:** Breakfast room; lounge. *In room:* No
phone.

Winchester Hotel ★★ *Finds*   One of the best choices along Belgrave Road,
this hotel is owned and managed by Jimmy McGoldrick, an unforgettable host
who goes out of his way to make his customers happy. Guests have been returning for 20 years, and if you stay here you'll understand why. Jimmy's staff maintains an extremely high level of service and cleanliness. The recently refurbed
bedrooms are comfy and well decorated. Every room has a small private bathroom with a good shower. Guests are served a big English breakfast in a lovely
and inviting room. There's a sleek modernity throughout that's rare in small
London hotels.

17 Belgrave Rd., London SW1 1RB. © 020/7828-2972. Fax 020/7828-5191. 18 units. £85 ($136) single or
double; £110 ($176) triple; £140 ($224) quad. Rates include English breakfast. No credit cards. Tube: Victoria.
Amenities: Breakfast room; lounge. *In room:* TV, hair dryer, radio, intercom.

The Woodville House ★★ *Finds*   In terms of furnishings and overall decor,
this small, attractive hotel is better than all the other B&Bs on Ebury Street.
Rooms are individually designed, with tasteful touches such as canopied beds
and William Morris Arts-and-Crafts wallpaper. Rare for London, most of the
accommodations are air-conditioned. So what's the drawback? There are no private bathrooms, so every three rooms share one (there's a bathtub in one of

them, all the rest have showers). A hearty English breakfast is served in the attractive dining room, and guests are welcome to use the small back garden.

107 Ebury St., SW1W 9QU. ☎ **020/7730-1048**. Fax 020/7730-2547. 12 units, none with bathroom. £46 ($74) single; £66 ($106) double; £96 ($154) quad. Rates include continental breakfast. MC, V. Tube: Victoria. **Amenities:** Breakfast room; garden. *In room:* TV, A/C (in some rooms). Phone only for receiving calls.

SUPER-CHEAP SLEEPS

Enrico Hotel *Value*   The hotels along Warwick Way fill up every night because of their proximity to Victoria Station, but standards are often low along this street. Happily, the Enrico has consistently worked to maintain high standards while charging some of the lowest rates along this well-trodden street. Bedrooms are simply furnished, nothing special. There are no views to speak of, and rooms can be noisy because of traffic. But it's a decent, money-saving option. Book a room without bathroom; hallway facilities are adequate and spacious, while those cramped showers are not worth the extra pounds.

77–79 Warwick Way, London SW1V 1QP. ☎ **020/7834-9538**. Fax 020/7233-9995. 26 units (8 with shower only). £40 ($64) single without bathroom; £45 ($72) double without bathroom; £55 ($88) double with shower. Rates include continental breakfast. MC, V. Tube: Victoria. **Amenities:** Lounge; room service. *In room:* Hair dryer.

Oak House Hotel *Value*   Mr. and Mrs. Symington, the owners of this tiny hotel, would like to retire. But their repeat customers won't let them. Thanks to its owners, this place has lots of homespun Scottish charm. When Mr. Symington isn't putting on his kilt for Scottish festivities, he's out driving a taxi. Mrs. Symington welcomes guests to her small, quiet, immaculately maintained bedrooms with white vinyl wall covering and rather spartan air. Half of the rooms have double beds; the others are twins. Bathrooms are spotless and equipped with showers. Rooms may be reserved only for 5 or more consecutive days.

29 Hugh St., London SW1V 1QJ. ☎ **020/7834-7151**. 6 units, none with bathroom. £46 ($74) single or double. No credit cards. Tube: Victoria. **Amenities:** Breakfast room. *In room:* TV, hair dryer, no phone.

PADDINGTON & BAYSWATER

The area around Paddington Station, northwest of Kensington Gardens and Hyde Park, is another popular hotel area jammed with budget accommodations. As always, you'd be well advised to telephone ahead to see if rooms are available. If you don't have a reservation, begin your trek by taking the Underground to either Paddington or Edgware Road and walking to Sussex Gardens, which is a long avenue flanked by bed-and-breakfast houses. Many of these places are very run down—in fact, some of the budget hotels in this area now deal with homeless people sent from the local authorities. If you're unable to find a room on Sussex Gardens, then try Norfolk Square, which lies near Sussex Gardens (even closer to Paddington Station).

Bayswater, slightly to the west of Hyde Park and to the north of Kensington Gardens, is an unofficial district with a number of decently priced lodgings and inexpensive restaurants. Once this area of London had a strong Russian influence, a characteristic that lives on in St. Petersburg Place, the most charming street of Bayswater. As in Paddington, you need to pick and choose carefully among the B&Bs in Bayswater because some are quite scruffy.

Balmoral House Hotel   The Balmoral, named after the famous Scottish retreat of Prince Albert and Queen Victoria, is a converted Victorian row house overlooking Sussex Gardens. Pretty flower boxes decorate the windows in the summer. The comfortable rooms are simple but well kept; about 15 bedrooms are in a Victorian-era annex across the street. Bedrooms in both sections were renovated in the early 1990s. All units contain small, well-maintained bathrooms with showers.

156 Sussex Gardens, London W2 1UD. ℂ **020/7723-7445**. Fax 020/7402-0118. www.balmoralhousehotel. co.uk. 32 units. £40 ($64) single; £65 ($104) double; £80 ($128) triple. Rates include English breakfast. MC, V. Tube: Paddington or Lancaster Gate. **Amenities:** Breakfast room; lounge. *In room:* TV, coffeemaker, hair dryer.

Columbia Hotel ✸ *Kids*   On the north side of Hyde Park, less than a mile from Marble Arch, five Victorian houses are linked together to form the Columbia Hotel. It's been renovated frequently over the years, but still manages to retain elements of its Victorian style. A spacious, elegant lounge, bar, and breakfast room are part of the facilities. Bedrooms are generally spacious, with high ceilings; all have private bathrooms. The hotel offers several connecting rooms, which make it suitable for families. Many of the bedrooms open onto Hyde Park.

95–99 Lancaster Gate, London, W2 3NS. ℂ **020/7402-0021**. Fax 020/7706-4691. www.columbiahotel.co. uk. 100 units. £65 ($104) single; £83 ($133) double; £108 ($173) triple; £125 ($200) quad. Rates include English breakfast. AE, MC, V. Tube: Lancaster Gate. **Amenities:** Lounge; bar; breakfast room; room service; laundry. *In room:* TV, coffeemaker, hair dryer.

Europa House Hotel   Another budget option along Sussex Gardens, this family-run hotel offers rooms that have private bathrooms with showers. The bedrooms are well maintained but a bit cramped and not particularly memorable. Most of the rooms were recently refurbished. Some of the multiple-bed rooms have thin mattresses, but most are firm and comfortable. Rooms in back are quieter.

151 Sussex Gardens, London W2 2RY. ℂ **020/7402-1923** or 020/7723-7343. Fax 020/7224-9331. www. europahousehotel.com. 20 units. £45 ($72) single; £56–£65 ($90–$104) double; £20 ($32) per person family room. Rates include English breakfast. AE, DC, MC, V. Tube: Paddington. **Amenities:** Breakfast room; lounge. *In room:* TV, hair dryer.

Fairways Hotel ✸   This is a large, late Georgian house designed in the 1820s in the style of John Nash. The inside exudes a truly charming English ambience. Stephen James Adams, who took over the management from his parents (they ran the hotel for 25 years), made several improvements in 2002, laying new carpeting and redoing all the communal toilets and showers. The strong personal touch throughout Fairways makes it a home away from home. All the rooms are different, the ones in back much quieter. There's a lovely first-floor double at the back, which has perhaps the biggest closet in London, brass fittings in the bathroom, and two boudoir chairs flanking a small table. The basic twin is a good deal. The decor is a bit more mix 'n' match, but it's a nice-size room and only shares the bathroom with a single. Guests with a car can park for free.

186 Sussex Gardens, London W2 1TU. ℂ **020/7723-4871**. Fax 020/7723-4871. www.fairways-hotel.co.uk. 17 units, 10 with bathroom (some with shower only). £52 ($83) single without bathroom, £70 ($112) single with bathroom; £72 ($115) twin without bathroom; £80 ($128) double/twin with bathroom; £110 ($176) triple with bathroom; £125 ($200) family room with bathroom. Rates include full English breakfast. MC, V. Tube: Paddington. **Amenities:** Nonsmoking rooms. *In room:* TV, coffeemaker, hair dryer, safe, no phone.

Garden Court Hotel ✸   There are cheaper B&Bs in Bayswater but what you won't find elsewhere is such out-and-out appeal, such high standards, or such a genuinely warm welcome. Edward Connolly's grandfather opened Garden Court in 1954 in a pair of pretty Victorian town houses. Inside, it's not luxe—except for the swanky new entrance hall, it's more like a much-loved home. The main lounge has some fine old furniture, ancestral portraits, fat novels to borrow, and free hot drinks. The best value are the rooms without private bathrooms (they all have washbasins), because only two rooms share each public facility. Otherwise, the prices are a little high for Queensway. The rooms are all different: One has pretty yellow wallpaper and white painted furniture, another broad blue stripes. Second-floor front bedrooms lead out onto balconies. The hotel has a small private terrace at the back and access to the public garden square opposite. Breakfast is called "continental" but you can get eggs and bacon if you want. The lower prices below are for rooms without private bathrooms.

30–31 Kensington Gardens Sq., London W2 4BG. ℭ **020/7229-2553.** Fax 020/7727-2749. www.garden courthotel.co.uk. 32 units, 16 with bathroom (some with shower only). £39–£58 ($62–$93) single; £58–£88 ($93–$141) double/twin; £72–£99 ($115–$158) triple; £82–£120 ($131–$192) family room. Rates include continental breakfast. MC, V. Tube: Bayswater or Queensway. **Amenities:** Garden. *In room:* TV, hair dryer.

Gower Hotel *Value*   A real bargain in the Paddington area, this is a small family-run B&B operated by the Stavrous, who provide personalized service to their guests. The property received an overhaul in 1999 and the bedrooms still look pretty good, but there are threadbare spots in the hallway carpets and the breakfast room could use a refurb. The rooms are medium in size and all but a couple of singles have a new shower in the small bathroom. Many rooms are suitable for three guests, though space is a bit cramped for these.

129 Sussex Gardens, W2 2RX. ℭ 020/7262-2262. Fax 020/7262-2006. 21 units, 19 with bathroom (shower only). £45 ($72) single without bathroom, £55 ($86) single with bathroom; £72 ($115) double; £90 ($144) triple. Rates include English breakfast. MC, V. Tube: Paddington. **Amenities:** Breakfast room; lounge. *In room:* TV, coffeemaker, hair dryer.

Kensington Gardens Hotel   A renovation vastly improved this hotel, giving it a pleasant entrance hall and some overall personality. Rooms are warm and inviting, but most of them are pretty small. If you don't mind trudging up the narrow stairs, you'll be rewarded with good views from some of the top bedrooms. Some of the bathrooms have tubs, others have showers only.

9 Kensington Gardens Sq., London W2 4QN. ℭ 0207/221-7790. Fax 020/7792-8612. www.kensington gardenshotel.co.uk. 17 units, 15 with bathroom. £65 ($104) single; £85 ($136) double; £105 ($166) triple. Rates include continental breakfast. AE, DC, MC, V. Tube: Bayswater. **Amenities:** Breakfast room; lounge. *In room:* TV, coffeemaker, hair dryer.

Mitre House Hotel ★★ *Kids*   This fine hotel stretches across four Georgian town houses and is kept in tiptop shape by the Chris brothers, who recently took over management from their parents. It's a great family hotel because of the assortment of accommodations. There are rooms with a double bed and two singles, 2-bedroom family suites with a private bathroom, and superior family suites that face quiet, leafy Talbot Square and have a toilet and tub-shower off a little private corridor. Junior suites, with lots of extra amenities and a Jacuzzi in the bathroom, make a good splurge choice. All the rooms are above average size for London; those at the back are quieter, though the view north across back alleys to Paddington isn't very inspiring. Mitre House may not be the cheapest deal around, but it's a good value. Hair dryers and tea/coffeemakers are available at the reception desk. There's a big and very pleasant lounge and bar, and even an elevator.

178–184 Sussex Gardens, London W2 1TU. ℭ 020/7723-8040. Fax 020/7402-0990. www.mitrehouse hotel.com. 69 rooms, all with bathroom (some with shower only). £60–£70 ($96–$112) single; £80 ($128) double/twin; £90 ($144) triple; £100 ($160) family room; £110 ($176) junior suite. Rates include full English breakfast. AE, DC, MC, V. Tube: Paddington. **Amenities:** Bar; babysitting arranged; laundry service; dry cleaning. *In room:* TV, radio.

Queensway Hotel   On a tree-lined road close to Hyde Park and Marble Arch, this hotel is ideal for shopping along Oxford Street and Bond Street. Personal service and hospitality have long characterized this place, which received much refurbishment during the mid-1990s. The hotel is one of the most immaculate along the gardens. Bedrooms are moderately spacious and comfortably furnished, with small bathrooms (most with shower, some with tub). Rooms vary in size; some of the more expensive doubles have a Jacuzzi. The hotel is actually two Victorian houses joined together and the reception room still has the original mantelpiece and deep-cove moldings. A cooked English breakfast is available for £3.50 ($6).

147–149 Sussex Gardens, London W2 2RY. ✆ 020/7723-7749. Fax 020/7262-5707. 43 units. £55 ($88) single; £78 ($125) double; £93 ($149) triple. Rates include continental breakfast. AE, DC, MC, V. Tube: Paddington. **Amenities:** Breakfast room; lounge. *In room:* TV, hair dryer.

Rhodes Hotel ✷ *Kids*   Chris Crias, the owner of the Rhodes since 1978, recently spruced up the entire hotel in an £80,000 ($116,000) decorating extravaganza. The velvet-curtained lounge and the downstairs dining room now boast hand-painted Greek-inspired murals, and painted angels gaze down from the ceiling on the way to the second floor. Other recent improvements include air-conditioning in the main part of the hotel (though not in the annex, which is why the rooms are cheaper there) and dataports for Internet access (free except for phone charges) in all the rooms. The bedroom decor is quite simple and comfortable. Number 220 has its own little private roof terrace, complete with table and chairs. The bunks in the family room are the nicest I've seen, dark wood and 3 feet wide. The continental breakfast includes ham and cheese; you can order an English breakfast for £3 ($4.80).

195 Sussex Gardens, London W2 2RJ. ✆ 020/7262-0537. Fax 020/7723-4054. www.rhodeshotel.com. 18 units, all with bathroom (most with shower only). £50–£60 ($80–$96) single; £75–£85 ($120–$136) double/ twin; £85–£90 ($136–$144) triple; £100–£110 ($160–$176) quad. Discount available for weekday and 3-day stays. Rates include continental breakfast. MC, V. Tube: Paddington. *In room:* TV, dataport, hair dryer, coffeemaker, fridge.

St. David's Hotel ✷   In early 2002, George and Foulla Neokleos finished the mammoth job of refurbishing all four of their buildings. The new look is unusual but appealing, with vanilla-colored walls and moldings and original fireplaces highlighted with yellow. St. David's is a treasure trove of architectural details. One room has a domed ceiling, and there's a lovely, stained-glass window on the stairs of no. 20. These Victorian houses have balconies across the front from which guests on the second floor can admire the pretty communal gardens. In the basement, there's a truly enormous and a very good value family room that can fit five people and has a proper built-in shower. The others are drop-in units that vary in size depending on what each bedroom can cope with. Irons and hair dryers are available at reception. When they say "full English breakfast" here, it really does mean full, with mushrooms, tomatoes, and baked beans on top of all the rest. All in all, this is a very good good-value choice. Lower prices listed below are for rooms without bathrooms.

14–20 Norfolk Sq., London W2 1RS. ✆ 020/7723-4963. Fax 020/7402-9061. www.stdavidshotels.com. 70 units, 60 with bathroom (most with shower only). £39–£49 ($62–$78) single; £59–£69 ($94–$110) double; £70–£80 ($112–$128) triple; £80–£90 ($128–$144) quad. All rates include full English breakfast. AE, DC, MC, V. Tube: Paddington. *In room:* TV, coffeemaker.

WORTH A SPLURGE

Byron Hotel ✷   A well-kept and comfortably old-fashioned English country house aura permeates this town-house hotel. The hotel has recently had its interior redesigned and refurbished. The immaculately kept bedrooms are on the small side but they're comfortable and nicely done. Each room is named after a stately manor house of England. Most rooms have an en suite bathroom with tub and shower; singles have showers only, so you share a toilet. Nothing to worry about with housekeeping standards this high.

36–38 Queensborough Terrace, London W2 3SH. ☎ 020/7243-0987. Fax 020/7792-1957. www.capricorn hotels.co.uk. 45 units. £78 ($125) single with shower; £105–£120 ($168–$192) double with bathroom; £135 ($216) triple with bathroom; £150 ($240) quad. Rates include English breakfast. AE, DC, MC, V. Tube: Queensway or Bayswater. **Amenities:** Breakfast room; 2 lounges; limited room service; dry cleaning. *In room:* A/C, coffeemaker, hair dryer, trouser press.

The Pavilion *(Finds)* Splurging here won't get you room service except when someone brings your continental breakfast (there's no dining room). It won't get you a grand-size bedroom, or even a luxurious bathroom (the showers are small and rather dated, though they are well maintained). What you're paying for is the glam factor, whether it's real or not. Ex-model Danny Karne and his sister Noshi took over the Pavilion a decade ago and turned it into London's groovi-est affordable town-house hotel. Every room is decorated with billowing fabrics, antiques, and recycled junkshop finds, sometimes with more dash than polish. The only downside is the general scarcity of closet space. A new sitting room, with doors out to a little courtyard, is called the Purple Parlour. The Pavilion is for people who want something memorable, something more than a place to sleep, wash, and change clothes between adventures. It's an adventure. You might even bump into a future rock star on the stairs, as this is a favorite music business sleep—which is probably why it can smell kind of smoky.

34–36 Sussex Gardens, London W2 1UL. ☎ 020/7262-0905. Fax 020/7262-1324. www.eol.net.mt/pavilion. 27 units, all with bathroom (most with shower only, 2 with tub only). £60–85 ($96–$136) single; £100 ($160) double/twin; £120 ($192) triple. Rates include continental breakfast. AE, DC, MC, V (4% surcharge for paying by credit card). Tube: Edgware Rd. *In room:* TV, coffeemaker.

HAMPSTEAD

La Gaffe *(★)(Finds)* A 15-minute Tube ride from central London, this little gem is nestled in exclusive Hampstead Heath. It dates from 1734 and was a shepherd's cottage before being turned into a residential inn with a well-known restaurant. Although relatively small, it offers many of the amenities its larger competitors do. The well-furnished rooms are cozy with firm beds and have small bathrooms with shower stalls. Special rooms include a honeymoon room with a four-poster and a Jacuzzi, plus a studio with kitchen and washing machine.

111 Heath St., Hampstead, London NW3 6SS. ☎ 020/7435-8965. Fax 020/7794-7592. www.lagaffe.co.uk. 18 units. £80 ($128) single; £90 ($144) double; £125 ($200) studio. Rates include continental breakfast. AE, DISC, MC, V. Tube: Hampstead Heath. **Amenities:** Restaurant; bar. *In room:* TV, hairdryer, coffeemaker.

AIRPORT HOTELS

Most regularly scheduled planes land at Heathrow or Gatwick. If you need to be near either airport, consider the following suggestions instead of the well-adver-tised and more-expensive chain hotels.

NEAR HEATHROW

The Swan The Swan is on the south bank of the Thames, beside Staines Bridge and 15 minutes by car from Heathrow. This attractive old inn has a repu-tation hospitality. The traditionally furnished rooms come in a variety of sizes, but all have private bathrooms. Breakfast and home-cooked meals are served in a gazebo-style dining room. The hotel was scheduled to undergo a complete ren-ovation starting in 2003. The lower rates below are for weekends.

The Hythe, Staines, Middlesex TW18 3JB. ☎ **0178/445-2494.** Fax 0178/446-1593. 11 units. £60–£84 ($96–$134) single; £80–£94 ($128–$150) double; £100–£125 ($160–$200) suite. Rates include English breakfast. AE, DC, MC, V. Tube: Heathrow; then taxi. **Amenities:** Restaurant; bar; lounge. *In room:* TV, coffeemaker.

Upton Park Guest House   The cab ride from Heathrow to this hotel is about 15 minutes and the owners can arrange for a cheaper local cab to meet you. Or you can take the train and walk, because the hotel is only 5 minutes from Slough station. This is a Victorian building on a private estate with a tranquil park just opposite. A major refurbishment has just been completed on the 15 bedrooms, giving them all private bathrooms. The rooms are comfortably furnished in a modern style and larger than most London hotel rooms. The next stage of this project will involve redoing the building next door and adding 15 more bedrooms by 2004. Lower rates are for weekends.

41 Upton Park, Slough, Berkshire SL1 2DA. ☎ **01753/528797.** Fax 01753/550208. www.uptonparkguest house.co.uk. 15 units. £40–£65 ($64–$104) single; £55–£75 ($88–$120) double. Rates include English breakfast. AE, MC, V. Train to Slough Station. **Amenities:** Restaurant; bar; lounge; breakfast room. *In room:* TV, dataport, coffeemaker.

NEAR GATWICK

The Manor House   The owners of Manor House, Steve and Joanne Jeffries, include transportation from Gatwick Airport as part of the price of their lodgings. Their home is a sprawling neo-Tudor affair set on 1 hectare (2 acres) of land, amid fields that surround it on all sides. It was originally built in 1894 as a supplemental home for the Lord of Ifield, who never actually moved in. Two of the rooms share a bathroom, whereas the others have private bathrooms with shower-tub combinations. Each room has flowered wallpaper, and simple, traditional accessories. Breakfast is the only meal served.

Bonnetts Lane, Ifield, Crawley, Sussex RH11 0NY. ☎ **01293/512298.** Fax 01293/518046. www.manorhousegatwick.co.uk. 6 units, 4 with private bathroom. £30 ($48) single without bathroom, £37 ($59) single with bathroom; £45 ($72) double with bathroom; £55 ($88) triple with bathroom. Rates include English breakfast. MC, V. Parking £2 ($3.20) per day. **Amenities:** Breakfast room; lounge. *In room:* TV.

4 Great Deals on Dining

London wasn't known as a dining capital until quite recently. In the past decade there's been a dramatic turnaround in culinary offerings, and London is now considered one of the food capitals of Europe. Eating out can be an extremely expensive proposition in London, so be on the lookout for fixed-price lunches and dinners and special pre- and post-theater menus. You'll find these at some of London's top restaurants.

Bland, overcooked meat and soggy vegetables still abound in many of London's "caffs" (cafes) and other low-cost eateries. But don't despair—across the board, food quality is improving, and even those on tight budgets will find many acceptable options. Don't overlook the all-you-can-eat carvery restaurants in central London; these serve up England's famous roasts, especially roast beef and its classic accompaniment, Yorkshire pudding. Roast chicken, pork, and English lamb are also served at these good-value places.

The once-ubiquitous fish-and-chips shops, or "chippies," have become harder to find in London; those that remain are of such varying quality that it's difficult for a visitor to find really good English fish and chips. Proper shops offer a selection of battered, deep-fried fish, including plaice, cod, haddock, skate, and rockfish. The fish is served with french fries (called "chips"), vinegar, and salt. The vinegar is meant to offset the grease in which the fish and potatoes have

Where to Dine in Central London

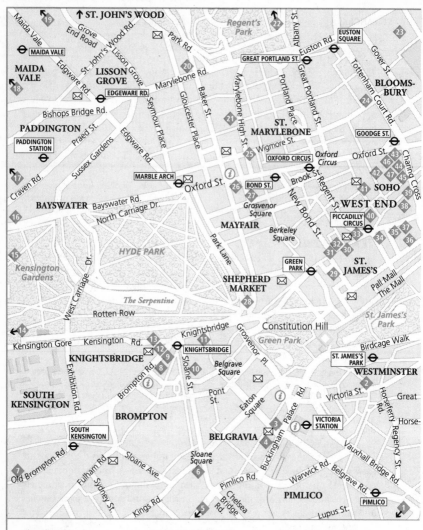

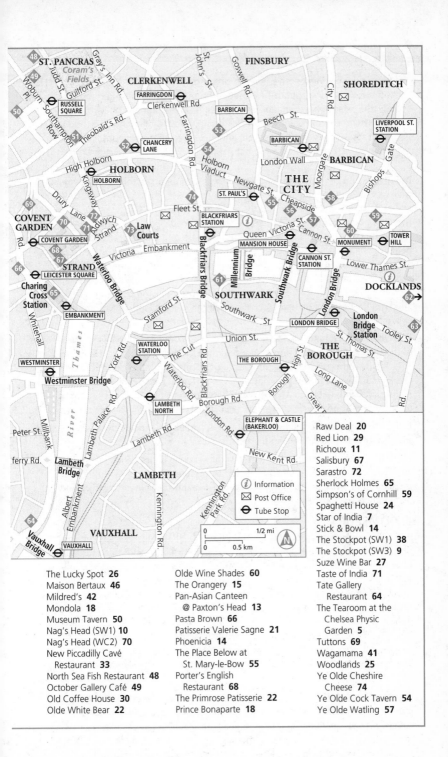

ST. PANCRAS
Coram's Fields
Grays Inn Rd.
St. John's St.
Goswell Rd.
FINSBURY
SHOREDITCH
City Rd.
Judd St.
Guilford St.
CLERKENWELL
FARRINGDON
Clerkenwell Rd.
Woburn Pl.
Southampton Row
RUSSELL SQUARE
Theobald's Rd.
BARBICAN
Beech St.
LIVERPOOL ST. STATION
CHANCERY LANE
BARBICAN
London Wall
BARBICAN
Bishops Gate
Moorgate
HOLBORN
High Holborn
Kingsway
HOLBORN
Holborn Viaduct
Newgate St.
ST. PAUL'S
THE CITY
Cheapside
Drury Lane
Aldwych
COVENT GARDEN
Fleet St.
BLACKFRIARS STATION
CANNON ST.
COVENT GARDEN
Law Courts
Strand
Victoria Embankment
Queen Victoria St.
MANSION HOUSE
CANNON ST. STATION
MONUMENT
TOWER HILL
STRAND
LEICESTER SQUARE
Waterloo Bridge
Blackfriars Bridge
Millennium Bridge
Southwark Bridge
London Bridge
Lower Thames St.
Charing Cross Station
EMBANKMENT
SOUTHWARK
DOCKLANDS
Stamford St.
Southwark St.
LONDON BRIDGE
London Bridge Station
Tooley St.
River Thames
WATERLOO STATION
The Cut
Union St.
THE BOROUGH
St. Thomas St.
THE BOROUGH
WESTMINSTER
York Rd.
Waterloo Rd.
Blackfriars Rd.
THE BOROUGH
Borough High St.
Long Lane
Westminster Bridge
LAMBETH NORTH
Borough Rd.
London Rd.
ELEPHANT & CASTLE (BAKERLOO)
Lambeth Palace Rd.
Lambeth Bridge
Peter St.
Millbank
ferry Rd.
Lambeth Bridge
Lambeth Rd.
New Kent Rd.
LAMBETH
Kennington Rd.
Kennington Park Rd.

Information
Post Office
Tube Stop

Albert Embankment
VAUXHALL
VAUXHALL
Vauxhall Bridge

0   1/2 mi
0   0.5 km

Raw Deal **20**
Red Lion **29**
Richoux **11**
Salisbury **67**
Sarastro **72**
Sherlock Holmes **65**
Simpson's of Cornhill **59**
Spaghetti House **24**
Star of India **7**
Stick & Bowl **14**
The Stockpot (SW1) **38**
The Stockpot (SW3) **9**
Suze Wine Bar **27**
Taste of India **71**
Tate Gallery
  Restaurant **64**
The Tearoom at the
  Chelsea Physic
  Garden **5**
Tuttons **69**
Wagamama **41**
Woodlands **25**
Ye Olde Cheshire
  Cheese **74**
Ye Olde Cock Tavern **54**
Ye Olde Watling **57**

The Lucky Spot **26**
Maison Bertaux **46**
Mildred's **42**
Mondola **18**
Museum Tavern **50**
Nag's Head (SW1) **10**
Nag's Head (WC2) **70**
New Piccadilly Cavé
  Restaurant **33**
North Sea Fish Restaurant **48**
October Gallery Café **49**
Old Coffee House **30**
Olde White Bear **22**

Olde Wine Shades **60**
The Orangery **15**
Pan-Asian Canteen
  @ Paxton's Head **13**
Pasta Brown **66**
Patisserie Valerie Sagne **21**
Phoenicia **14**
The Place Below at
  St. Mary-le-Bow **55**
Porter's English
  Restaurant **68**
The Primrose Patisserie **22**
Prince Bonaparte **18**

Value Ethnic Dining Is the Spice of Life

If you find most inexpensive London offerings too bland for your palate, head for one of the zillions of ethnic restaurants in the West End, especially the ever-popular Indian dining rooms. These appear on virtually every street corner. Chinese, Greek, Italian, West Indian, African, and Cypriot restaurants abound as well, and most are quite reasonable.

---

been fried. You can eat in the shop, usually at a communal table, or take your food outside in a container.

This chapter includes many pubs. The pub represents far, far more than merely a place for drinking. Millions of English people grab "pub grub" at the regular lunchtime hour. Lately, many pubs have been upgrading their food; the better ones are now called "gastropubs." The pub, or neighborhood "local," can also function as a club, front parlor, betting office, debating chamber, or television lounge. Smoking is still permitted in many London restaurants, but an increasing number of places have at least a nonsmoking section (not always effective). Vegetarian restaurants are almost always nonsmoking. If you can't bear cigarette smoke, it's probably best to steer clear of pubs at peak hours.

PRICES   All restaurants and cafes in Britain are required to display the prices of the food and drink they offer in a place where customers can see them before entering the eating area. Charges for service and any minimum charge or cover charge must also be made clear. The prices shown must include the 17½% VAT. Most places add a 10% to 15% service charge to your bill; look at your check to make sure. If no service charge has been added, leave a 12% to 15% tip.

RESERVATIONS   In the listings below, reservation policies are noted. If not specifically mentioned, reservations aren't needed.

HOURS   Restaurants in London keep widely varying hours, depending on the establishment. In general, lunch is offered from noon to 2 or 3pm, and dinner is served from 6 or 7pm to 9:30pm. Many restaurants open an hour earlier, and many others stay open later.

BLOOMSBURY

British Museum Restaurant TRADITIONAL BRITISH   This is the best place for lunch if you're exploring the wonders of the world-renowned museum. Located on the lobby level of the West Wing, it is decorated with a dozen full-size copies of bas-reliefs from an ancient Greek temple. The format is self-service. A few hot specials (including a vegetarian selection) and crisp salads are made fresh every day, and there's always a good selection of fish and cold meat dishes. Try the soup and baguette special, which changes daily. Desserts include pastries and cakes. A separate cafe offers coffee, sandwiches, pastries, and soup.

Great Russell St., WC1. ✆ 020/7323-8256. Main courses £6.45–£8.45 ($10–$14); £5.75 ($9) soup and baguette special. MC, V. Mon–Sun cold food 10am–5pm; hot food daily 11:30am–2:30pm. Tube: Holborn or Tottenham Court Rd.

Museum Tavern BRITISH   Across the street from the British Museum, this pub (ca. 1703) retains most of its antique trappings: velvet, oak paneling, and cut glass. Traditional English food is served with shepherd's pie, sausages cooked in English hard cider, and chef's specials on the hot-food menu. Cold fare includes turkey-and-ham pie, ploughman's lunch (a pub staple of bread, cheese, and pickled onions), and salads. Several English ales, cold lagers, cider, Guinness, wines, and spirits are available.

49 Great Russell St., WC1. ✆ **020/7242-8987**. Bar snacks £2–£6 ($3.20–$10). AE, MC, V. Mon–Sat 11am–11pm; Sun noon–10:30pm. Tube: Holborn or Tottenham Court Rd.

Spaghetti House ITALIAN   Located in the vicinity of Russell Square, this is the leader of a chain of spaghetti-and-pizza houses. Chianti bottles enhance the inviting atmosphere on the four floors of this restaurant. The menu, designed with healthy eating in mind, features delicious, freshly made pasta dishes and much-loved regional Italian dishes—a cornucopia of olive oil, grilled meats and fish, grilled vegetables, and salads. There are at least 10 different pasta varieties and 10 different meat dishes based on veal, beef, or chicken. Saltimbocca, the classic veal-and-ham dish from Rome, is popular.

15–17 Goodge St., W1P. ✆ **020/7636-6582**. Main courses £6.75–£14.80 ($11–$24). AE, DC, MC, V. Mon–Thurs noon–11pm; Fri–Sat noon–11:30pm; Sun 12:30–10pm. Tube: Goodge St.

COVENT GARDEN & THE STRAND

Food for Thought VEGETARIAN   Here you'll find some of the best and least expensive vegetarian food in Covent Garden. During peak dining hours it's usually jam-packed, so come after the rush. Food selections change twice a day; they include excellent soups with whole-meal bread, freshly made salads, quiches, curries, and casseroles, with daily hot specials. All food is prepared from fresh, quality produce. The nonsmoking restaurant is ideally situated for the Covent Garden shopper or the pre-theater diner.

31 Neal St., WC2. ✆ **020/7836-0239**. Main courses £3.75–£6.50 ($6–$10). No credit cards. Mon–Sat 9:30am–8:30pm; Sun noon–4pm. Tube: Covent Garden.

The George TRADITIONAL BRITISH   This pub with its half-timbered facade was built as a coffeehouse in 1723 and still retains much of the original architecture. Hot and cold platters, including bangers and mash, fish and chips, steak-and-kidney pie, and lasagna, are served from a food counter at the back of the pub. Additional seating is available in the basement, where a headless cavalier is said to haunt the same premises where he enjoyed his liquor in an earlier day.

213 The Strand, WC2. ✆ **020/7427-0941**. Main courses £5.50–£7.95 ($9–$13). AE, MC, V. Mon–Fri 11am–11pm; Sat noon–3pm. Tube: Temple.

Nag's Head BRITISH   The Nag's Head is one of London's most famous Edwardian pubs. Today, the pub is popular with young people. The draft Guinness is very good. Lunch is typical pub grub: sandwiches, salads, pork cooked in cider, and garlic prawns. The sandwich platters mentioned above are served only at lunch (noon–3pm); snacks are available in the afternoon.

10 James St., WC2. ✆ **020/7836-4678**. Reservations not accepted. Sandwiches £4.25 ($7); salads £6.50 ($10). AE, DC, MC, V. Mon–Fri 11am–11pm; Sat noon–11pm; Sun noon–10:30pm. Tube: Covent Garden.

Porter's English Restaurant ✪ *Value* TRADITIONAL BRITISH   A comfortable, two-storied restaurant with a friendly, informal, and lively atmosphere, Porter's specializes in classic English pies, including Old English fish pie, lamb and apricot, ham, leek, and cheese. They also serve grilled English fare, including pork chops and sirloin and lamb steaks. Main courses are generous and accompanied by vegetables and side dishes—you hardly need appetizers. The desserts include classic spotted dick (suet pudding with raisins) in custard. A traditional English tea is also served from 2:30 to 5:30pm for £3.50 ($6) per person.

17 Henrietta St., WC2. ⓒ **020/7836-6466.** Reservations recommended. Main courses £8.95–£12.95 ($14–$21); fixed-price menu £19.95 ($32). AE, DC, MC, V. Mon–Sat noon–11:30pm; Sun noon–10:30pm. Tube: Covent Garden or Charing Cross.

Sarastro ⭐ TURKISH/CYPRIOT   The setting makes you feel like you're in a prop room of an opera house—and, in fact, you can hear live opera on Sunday and Monday evenings and at Sunday lunchtime. This is a fun place, especially after a show. The decor is sort of neo-Ottoman, and the cuisine celebrates the bounty of the Mediterranean, especially Turkey and Cyprus. Launch yourself with such delights as asparagus in red-wine sauce or fresh grilled sardines. Market-fresh fish is usually the way to go, especially fresh river trout or the grilled halibut. A zesty favorite is lamb Anatolian style (that is, with eggplant and zucchini); they also serve well-seasoned lamb meatballs. Chicken Sarastro with walnuts and raisins is the house specialty.

126 Drury Lane, WC2. ⓒ **020/7836-0101.** Reservations required. Main courses £7.50–£15 ($12–$21); fixed-price lunch £17.50 ($28), fixed-price dinner £22.50 ($35); pre-theater menu £21 ($34). AE, MC, DC, V. Daily noon–midnight. Tube: Covent Garden.

Taste of India INDIAN   This is one of the most respected Indian restaurants in London, with a regular clientele of theatergoers, members of Parliament, and businesspeople. In a busy but intimate setting dotted with Indian artwork, you can enjoy the sometimes fiery, sometimes subtle cuisine of northern and southern India. Specialties include a range of Tandoori dishes (prawns, chicken, lamb, or vegetarian dishes slow-cooked in a clay pot), elegant preparations of lamb (including one cooked with cream and yogurt), and some of the best vegetarian dishes available anywhere.

25 Catherine St., Covent Garden, WC2. ⓒ **020/7836-6591.** Reservations recommended. Main courses £6.50–£12 ($10–$19); fixed-price buffet lunch £8.95 ($14); fixed-price 2-course dinner £13.50 ($22); fixed-price pre-theater meal (served 5:30–7:30pm only) £9.95 ($16). AE, DC, MC, V. Daily noon–2:30pm and 5:30pm–midnight. Tube: Covent Garden.

Tuttons INTERNATIONAL   This bustling brasserie at the corner of Russell Street and the Piazza, with tables out on the pavement, is a good place to people-watch. The interior color scheme is bullfight-red and bright lemon-yellow. The food's not bad, and the fixed-price menus are a good value for pricey Covent Garden. Begin with an appetizer such as goat cheese, and then follow with grilled lambsteak or poached salmon with spinach and lemon sauce. Spicy fish cakes with tomatoes and coriander are another offering, as is the baked cod or the Thai chicken and mint salad with ginger. For dessert, since you're in Covent Garden, why not take on the Eliza Doolittle favorite: sticky toffee pudding with hot caramel.

11–12 Russell St., WC2. ⓒ **020/7836-4141.** Main courses £12.90–£15.50 ($21–$25); fixed-price lunch and pre-theater supper £12.90 ($21). AE, MC, V. Daily 9:30am–11:30pmt. Tube: Covent Garden.

HOLBORN

North Sea Fish Restaurant (Finds SEAFOOD   The fish served in this famous fish-and-chips restaurant is purchased fresh every day; the quality is high, the prices low. In the view of London's most diehard chippie devotees, it's the best in town. The fish is usually served battered and deep-fried, but you can also order it grilled. The menu is wisely limited. Students from the Bloomsbury area flock to the place. Really good chips, too.

7–8 Leigh St., WC1. ⓒ **020/7387-5892.** Reservations recommended. Fish platters £8.30–£16.95 ($13–$27). AE, DC, MC, V. Mon–Sat noon–2:30pm and 5:30–10:30pm. Tube: King's Cross or Russell Sq.

October Gallery Café *Finds* *Kids* INTERNATIONAL   Located in a former Victorian school building near the British Museum, this is both a gallery and an eatery. The menu, which changes daily, offers eclectic seasonal dishes as varied as the cross-cultural exhibits and performances that take place here. Portions are generous, and half-plates are available for children. Menu items include meat or vegetarian chili, Thai green curry, and spinach and feta in phyllo pastry. There are homemade cakes and fruit salad for dessert. Outdoor dining is available in the lush, plant-filled courtyard during warm weather. You can bring your own wine; corkage is £1 ($1.60).

24 Old Gloucester St., WC1. ✆ 020/7831-1618. Reservations recommended. Main courses £5 ($8). No credit cards. Tues–Fri 12:30–2:30pm (gallery open until 5:30pm). Closed 1st week of Aug to 2nd week of Sept and 2 weeks at Christmas. Tube: Holborn.

SUPER-CHEAP EATS

The Fryer's Delight SEAFOOD/BRITISH   This restaurant enjoys a reputa-tion as one of the better fast-food eateries in London. The generous main courses include fried chicken, fish and chips (including rock cod, plaice, and haddock), steak-and-kidney or beef-and-onion pies, and sausages accompanied by pickled cucumber and onions, peas, or baked beans. Takeout comes wrapped in plain white paper, or you can eat at one of the five tables on the premises.

19 Theobalds Rd., WC1. ✆ 020/7405-4114. Reservations not accepted. Fish and chips £3 ($4.80); pies and chips £2.30 ($3.70). No credit cards. Mon–Sat noon–10pm; takeout noon–11pm. Tube: Holborn.

THE CITY

Bow Wine Vaults *Finds* BRITISH/MODERN EUROPEAN   This is one of London's most famous wine bars, in existence long before the wine-bar craze began in the 1970s. It attracts cost-conscious diners and drinkers to its vaulted cellars for sandwiches and Welsh rarebit. More elegant meals, served in the street-level din-ing room, include calves' liver and bacon with onion gravy, ricotta and spinach ravioli, sirloin with fries, and pan-fried scallops served on black-eyed bean puree.

10 Bow Churchyard, EC4. ✆ 020/7248-1121. Reservations recommended. Cover 50p (80¢). Bar food £5 ($8). Main courses £9–£17 ($14–$27). AE, DC, MC, V. Mon–Fri Bar 11am–11pm; restaurant 11:45am–3pm. Tube: Mansion House, Bank, or St. Paul's.

Fox and Anchor ✦ *Finds* TRADITIONAL BRITISH   For British breakfast at its best, try this place, which has been serving traders from the nearby Smith-field meat market since the pub was built in 1898. Breakfasts are gargantuan, especially if you order the "Full House"—a plate that includes sausage, bacon, kidneys, eggs, beans, black pudding, and a fried slice of bread, along with unlim-ited tea or coffee, toast, and jam. You'll also find typical pub grub on the menu for lunch and dinner. The Fox and Anchor is noted for its range of fine English ales, all available at breakfast.

115 Charterhouse St., EC1. ✆ 020/7253-5075. Reservations recommended. "Full house" breakfast £7.50 ($12); main courses £6.50–£12 ($10–$19). AE, MC, V. Mon–Fri from 7am. Closing time varies from 8–11pm. Tube: Barbican or Farringdon.

The George & Vulture TRADITIONAL BRITISH   Dickens enthusiasts seek out this Pickwickian place founded in 1660. English lunches are served on the tavern's three floors. Besides daily specials, the menu includes a mixed grill, a loin chop, and fried Dover sole filets with tartar sauce. Potatoes and buttered cabbage are the standard vegetables, and the apple tart is always reliable. The Pickwick Club, headed by Cedric Dickens, a great-great-grandson of Charles Dickens, meets in this pub about six times a year for reunion dinners.

3 Castle Court, Cornhill, EC3. © **020/7626-9710.** Reservations accepted if you agree to arrive by 12:45pm. Main courses £8–£15 ($12–$24). AE, DC, MC, V. Mon–Fri noon–2:45pm. Tube: Bank.

Olde Wine Shades ENGLISH

This is the oldest wine house in The City (dating from 1663), and the only City tavern to survive the Great Fire in 1666 and Hitler's bombings of 1940. Only 90m (300 ft.) from the famous monument designed by Sir Christopher Wren to commemorate the Great Fire, it's decorated with oil paintings and 19th-century political cartoons; it's also one of the many London bars that Dickens frequented. There's a restaurant downstairs, but you can also eat light meals upstairs, including Breton pâté and French bread with ham. You can order jacket (baked) potatoes filled with cheese, venison pie with a salad garnish, or ham and mozzarella.

6 Martin Lane, Cannon St., EC4. © **020/7626-6876.** Main courses £7–£14 ($11–$24). AE, MC, V. Mon–Fri 8:30am–10pm. Closed bank holidays. Tube: Cannon St.

The Place Below at St. Mary-le-Bow ⊛ (Finds) VEGETARIAN

St. Mary-le-Bow is a beautiful Christopher Wren church built on the site of a much earlier one. Today, the arched Norman vaults are home to one of the most atmospheric and delicious cheap eateries in the City. The menu changes daily but you'll always find a hot dish of the day, two salads (one dairy-free), and a quiche. Because The Place Below gets so busy at lunchtime, it offers £2 ($3.20) off all main course prices between 11:30am and noon. You'll save about the same amount on most dishes if you take out rather than eat in. Soup is a dynamite deal at £3.10 ($5). The Place Below has just introduced a new espresso and sandwich bar, and extended its hours to 3:30pm. So you could just come for a rich chocolate brownie and a cappuccino. There is seating for 50 outside in Bow Churchyard.

St. Mary-le-Bow, Cheapside, EC2. © **020/7329-0789.** Main courses £5.50–£7.50 ($9–$12). MC, V. Mon–Fri 7:30am–3:30pm. Tube: St. Paul's, Bank.

Simpson's of Cornhill BRITISH

This is the latest manifestation of what was a gentlemen only "eating club," established back in 1759. This restaurant (not to be confused with Simpson's on the Strand) finally allowed women through its doors in 1916. There are two levels; the upstairs houses a traditional bar, the downstairs is a wine bar. The traditional English fare includes chops, steaks, rabbit, steak-and-kidney pie, and cold Scotch salmon. The house specialty is stewed cheese, a mixture of melted cheddar with Worcestershire sauce and spices, spread on toast. Meals are heavy, but their quality makes this a popular lunch destination.

38½ Ball St., EC3. © **020/7626-9985.** 3-course meal and drink £12–£13 ($19–$21). AE, DC, MC, V. Mon–Fri 11:30am–3pm. Closed holidays. Tube: Bank.

Ye Olde Cheshire Cheese ⊛ (Kids) BRITISH

Set within a recently remodeled, carefully preserved building whose foundation was laid in the 13th century, this is the most famous of the old City chophouses and pubs. It claims to be the spot where Dr. Samuel Johnson (who lived nearby) entertained admirers with his acerbic wit. Today it has six bars and two dining rooms. The house specialties include "ye famous pudding" (steak, kidney, mushrooms, and game) and Scottish roast beef with Yorkshire pudding and horseradish sauce. Sandwiches, salads, and standby favorites like steak-and-kidney pie are also available, as are dishes like Dover sole. Many American families select this pub as the restaurant in which to introduce their kids to English cooking.

Wine Office Court, 145 Fleet St., EC4. © **020/7353-6170.** Main courses £7.95–£12.95 ($13–$21). AE, DC, MC, V. Mon–Fri noon–9:30pm; Sat noon–2:30pm and 6–11pm; Sun noon–3pm. Drinks and bar snacks daily 6–9:30pm. Tube: St. Paul's or Blackfriars.

Ye Olde Cock Tavern BRITISH   Dating back to 1549, this tavern boasts a long line of literary patrons: Samuel Pepys mentioned it in his diaries, Dickens frequented it, and Tennyson referred to it in one of his poems, a framed copy of which is proudly displayed near the front entrance. It's one of the few buildings in London to have survived the Great Fire of 1666. At street level, you can order a pint and bar snack food, steak-and-kidney pie, or a cold chicken-and-beef plate with salad. Upstairs you can order a variety of meals including an all-day breakfast, chicken coriander, lasagna, chicken masala, or chicken and chips.

22 Fleet St., EC4. ℭ 020/7353-8570. Main courses £5–£7 ($8–$11); 2-meal deal £6.99 ($11); all-day breakfast £3.95 ($6). AE, DC, MC, V. Mon–Fri noon–2:30pm; pub Mon–Fri 11am–11pm. Tube: Temple or Chancery Lane.

Ye Olde Watling BRITISH   One of London's oldest and most venerated pubs, Ye Olde Watling was rebuilt after the Great Fire of 1666. On the ground level is a mellow pub; upstairs is an intimate restaurant where, under oak beams and at trestle tables, you can dine on simple English main dishes for lunch. The menu varies daily, with such reliable standbys as fish and chips, lamb satay, lasagna, fish cakes, and (usually) a vegetarian dish. All are served with two vegetables or salad, plus rice or potatoes.

29 Watling St., EC4. ℭ 020/7653-9971. Main courses £6–£7 ($10–$11); bar snacks from £2 ($3.20). AE, MC, V. Mon–Fri 11am–11pm. Tube: Mansion House.

TRAFALGAR SQUARE

Café in the Crypt BRITISH DINER   Right on Trafalgar Square, this is a great place to grab a bite to eat before or after a visit to the National Gallery. Simple healthy food costs a lot less here than at more commercial places. It's a self-service cafeteria, where diners choose from a big salad bar and a choice of two traditional main courses—one might be shepherd's pie. The other light-lunch options include filled rolls and delicious cups of soup. The menu changes daily, but one fixture is that most traditional of British desserts, bread-and-butter pudding (bread soaked in eggs and milk with currants and then oven-baked). The door to the crypt is on the right-hand side of the church.

St. Martin-in-the-Fields, Duncannon St., WC2. ℭ 020/7839-4342. Rolls and sandwiches £2.50–£3.10 ($4–$5); main courses £5.95–£6.50 ($9–$10). No credit cards. Mon–Wed 10am–8pm; Thurs–Sat 10am–11pm. Tube: Charing Cross.

Crivelli's ITALIAN   In addition to its more obvious allure as a repository for art, the National Gallery contains this well-liked Italian restaurant in the Sainsbury Wing with a view over Trafalgar Square, and a stylish continental ambience. The menu includes homemade soup, pizzas cooked in a wood oven, fishcakes, and homemade pasta. This is not "institutional" food: only fresh produce is used and all dishes are cooked on the premises. There is also an Italian bar where you can get home-baked organic panini and croissants with various fillings.

In National Gallery, Trafalgar Sq., WC2. ℭ 020/7839-3321. Main courses £7.50–£13.50 ($12–$24). Bar snacks £5–£7 ($8–$11). AE, MC, V. Daily 10am–4pm; Wed 10am–9pm. Tube: Charing Cross.

Sherlock Holmes BRITISH   The Sherlock Holmes was the old gathering spot for the Baker Street Irregulars, a once-mighty clan of mystery lovers who met here to honor the genius of Sir Arthur Conan Doyle's most famous fictional character. Upstairs, you'll find a re-creation of the living room at 221B Baker Street and such "Holmesiana" as the serpent of *The Speckled Band* and the head of *The Hound of the Baskervilles*. In the upstairs dining room, you can order complete meals with wine; try "Copper Beeches" (grilled butterfly chicken breasts with lemon and herbs), then select dessert from the trolley. Downstairs is mainly for drinking, but there's a good snack bar with cold meats, salads, cheeses, and wine and ales sold by the glass.

10 Northumberland St., WC1. ℂ 020/7930-2644. Main courses £7.95–£12.95 ($13–$21); snacks £2.25–£6.95 ($3.60–$11). MC, V. Restaurant Mon–Thurs noon–3pm and 5–10pm; Fri–Sun noon–10pm; pub Mon–Sat 11am–11pm; Sun noon–10:30pm. Tube: Charing Cross or Embankment.

PICCADILLY CIRCUS

New Piccadilly Café Restaurant CONTINENTAL   Just around the corner from the Tube station, this no-frills eatery is recognizable by the red neon EATS sign in the window. The restaurant, which opened in 1951, is popular with tourists and show people from the Piccadilly Theatre next door. Omelets, pizza, salads, and dessert are served along with generous portions of sausage or bacon and chips, steak, veal, fresh fish, chicken, pasta, and vegetable dishes. Takeout service is available, and customers can bring their own beverages.

8 Denman St., W1. ℂ 020/7437-8530. Reservations not accepted. Main courses £5–£6.50 ($8–$11). No credit cards. Daily 11am–9:30pm. Closed Christmas, Boxing Day, and Easter Sunday. Tube: Piccadilly Circus.

Red Lion BRITISH   With its early-1900s decorations and 150-year-old mirrors, this little Victorian pub has lots of atmosphere. You can order pre-made sandwiches, but once they're gone you're out of luck. On Saturday, homemade fish and chips are also served. Wash down your meal with Ind Coope's fine ales or the house's special beer, Burton's, an unusual brew made of spring water from the Midlands town of Bourton-on-Trent.

2 Duke of York St. (off Jermyn St.), SW1. ℂ 020/7321-0782. Sandwiches £2.80 ($4.50); fish and chips £7.50 ($12). No credit cards. Mon–Fri 11:30am–11pm; Sat noon–11pm. Tube: Piccadilly Circus.

WORTH A SPLURGE

Criterion Brasserie ⋆ MODERN FRENCH   This used to be the only place where diners could sample the cooking of Michelin three-star bad boy Marco Pierre White without remortgaging their homes. It's still well worth coming to the Criterion because of the fixed-price meals, but it's going to be a splurge. Right on Piccadilly Circus, the inside is like a Byzantine palace with its fantastic gold vaulted ceiling. The staff is often pressed for time. But the cuisine is superb. Don't try the three-course early dinner, unless you eat at the speed of lightning. Save the Criterion for a lunchtime blowout. Big favorites are ballottine of salmon with herbs and *fromage blanc,* and risottos are always real star performers.

224 Piccadilly, W1. ℂ 020/7930-0488. Reservations essential. Main courses £12–£15 ($19–$22); fixed-price lunch £14.95–£17.95 ($22–$29); fixed-price dinner £14.95 ($22), order before 6:30pm. AE, DC, MC, V. Mon–Sat noon–2:30pm; 5:30–11:30pm. Tube: Piccadilly Circus.

LEICESTER SQUARE

Balans MODERN BRITISH   On Old Compton Street in Soho, Balans is the best known gay restaurant in London and stays open almost 'round the clock. Although the food is British, it is an eclectic cuisine, borrowing freely from whatever kitchen it chooses, from the Far East to America. You can fill up on one of the succulent pastas—try the black-ink tortellini sprinkled with scallops. Grills are popular, especially the tuna teriyaki or the charred roast chicken. Balans has a party pub atmosphere and is a good place to meet people.

60 Old Compton St., W1. ℂ 020/7437-5212. Main courses £7–£16 ($11–$26). AE, MC, V. Tues–Thurs 8am–4am; Fri–Sat 8am–6am; Sun 8am–2am. Tube: Piccadilly Circus or Leicester Sq.

Cork & Bottle Wine Bar ★ *Value* INTERNATIONAL   Don Hewitson, a connoisseur of fine wines for more than 30 years, presides over a treasure trove of vintages. The most successful dish is a raised cheese-and-ham pie, with a cream cheese–like filling and crisp well-buttered pastry—not your typical quiche. There's also chicken and apple salad, Lancashire hotpot, Mediterranean prawns with garlic and asparagus, lamb in ale, and tandoori chicken.

44–46 Cranbourn St., WC2. ☏ 020/7734-7807. Reservations not accepted after 6:30pm. Main courses £6.50–£11.95 ($10–$19); glass of wine from £3.75 ($6). AE, DC, MC, V. Mon–Sat 11am–11:30pm; Sun noon–10:30pm. Tube: Leicester Sq.

Ed's Easy Diner AMERICAN   This is one of four branches of the popular diner, steeped in retro Americana, with 1950s and 1960s rock 'n' roll on the jukebox, a horseshoe-shaped counter with the kitchen in the middle, and a staff that fits the theme. The restaurant offers good diner staples such as burgers, fried onion rings, and waffles, and some lighter fare such as Caesar salads and tuna salad. For dessert you can have pecan or apple pie.

12 Moor St., W1. ☏ 020/7439-1955. Reservations not accepted. Main courses £3.95–£5.50 ($6–$9). MC, V. Sun–Thurs 11:30am–11pm; Fri–Sat 11:30am–1am. Tube: Leicester Sq. or Tottenham Court Rd.

Mildred's ★ *Finds* VEGETARIAN   Mildred's is one of London's most enduring vegetarian and vegan dining spots. It's a busy, bustling diner with casual, friendly service. Sometimes it's a bit crowded and tables are shared. The menu changes daily, but features an array of homemade soups, casseroles, and salads. The stir-fries are delectable. Save room for dessert, especially the nutmeg-and-mascarpone ice cream or the chocolate rum and amaretto pudding.

58 Greek St., W1. ☏ 020/7494-1634. Reservations not accepted. Main courses £5.30–£6.50 ($8–$10). No credit cards. Mon–Sat noon–11pm. Tube: Tottenham Court Rd.

Pasta Brown EGG DISHES/SANDWICHES/PASTA   This family-owned restaurant is brimming over with old photos, copper pots, herbs, breads, and hanging sausages. Pasta Brown dishes up breakfasts using homemade sausage, high-quality bacon, and the same maize-fed eggs the queen eats. Gears shift at lunch, with a variety of sandwiches piled high with layers of meat (the specialty is corned beef), cheese, and vegetables. In the evening, Pasta Brown's menu gives way to 29 varieties of pasta and sauces, from penne to tortellini, Neapolitan to carbonara. Meals include salad and garlic bread, and desserts feature carrot cake and homemade tiramisu.

24 Bedford St., WC2. ☏ 020/7240-0230. Reservations not accepted. Breakfast and lunch £4–£6 ($6–$10); main courses £4–£5.95 ($6–$10). No credit cards. Mon–Fri 7:30am–9pm; Sat 7:30am–midnight; Sun 11am–8:15pm. Closed Christmas. Tube: Leicester Sq.

SUPER-CHEAP EATS

Salisbury BRITISH   Salisbury's glittering cut-glass mirrors reflect the faces of English stage stars (and hopefuls) sitting around the curved buffet-style bar. A less prominent place to dine is the old-fashioned wall banquette with its copper-topped tables and Art Nouveau decor. The pub serves inexpensive fish and chips and sausage and mash. A buffet with both hot and cold food is available at all times.

90 St. Martin's Lane, WC2. ☏ 020/7836-5863. Main courses £4–£7 ($6–$11). AE, DC, MC, V. Mon–Sat 11am–11pm; Sun noon–10pm. Tube: Leicester Sq.

The Stockpot *Value* TRADITIONAL BRITISH/CONTINENTAL   This cozy little restaurant offers one of the best dining bargains in London. Meals include a bowl of minestrone, spaghetti Bolognese (the eternal favorite), a plate of braised lamb, and the apple crumble (or other desserts). At these prices, the food is hardly refined, but filling and satisfying nonetheless. With two levels of dining in a modern room, The Stockpot has a share-the-table policy during peak dining hours.

38 Panton St. (off Haymarket, opposite the Comedy Theatre), SW1. ⓒ 020/7839-5142. Reservations accepted for dinner. Main courses £2.50–£5.90 ($4.20–$9); fixed-price 2-course lunch £3.90 ($6); fixed-price 3-course dinner £6.40 ($10). No credit cards. Mon–Sat 7am–11pm; Sun 7am–9:30pm. Tube: Piccadilly Circus or Leicester Sq.

SOHO

Amalfi Ristorante NEAPOLITAN   Established in the 1950s when many of its patrons were unfamiliar with fare such as pizza, this place continues to thrive as many competitors come and go. Crowded and bargain-priced, its crew of Italian chefs prepares dishes such as spaghetti, pizzas, veal in white-wine sauce, minestrone, and lasagna. Fresh salads are served with many of the main courses. If you have room for dessert, an in-house patisserie makes good Italian pastries.

29–31 Old Compton St., W1. ⓒ 020/7437-7284. Reservations recommended. Main courses £5–£12 ($8–$19). AE, DC, MC, V. Mon–Sat noon–midnight; Sun noon–10pm. Tube: Leicester Sq.

Café Pasta ITALIAN   There are seven Café Pasta restaurants in London, all offering a relaxed dining atmosphere, but this location has the edge with an exhibition kitchen and outdoor dining in warm weather. The chain offers large, filling Italian meals made with fresh ingredients. The food isn't innovative, but it's good, inexpensive, and served by a helpful staff. Sample menu items include spaghetti with bacon and Gorgonzola cheese, rosemary-buttered garlic egg tagliatelle, and penne with cauliflower in a chile, cream, and tomato sauce. In the morning and afternoons, French bread sandwiches and pastries are available.

184 Shaftesbury Ave., W1. ⓒ 020/7379-0198. Main courses £4.95–£11.75 ($8–$19). AE, DC, MC, V. Mon–Sat noon–11:30pm; Sun noon–11pm. Tube: Tottenham Court Rd.

Chiang Mai *Kids* THAI   This restaurant in the center of Soho is named after the ancient northern capital of Thailand, a region known for its rich, spicy foods. Try their hot and sour dishes or vegetarian meals. It's located next door to Ronnie Scott's, the most famous jazz club in England (see "London After Dark," in chapter 4), so it's a good stop for an early dinner before a night on the town. Children's specials are available.

48 Frith St., W1. ⓒ 020/7437-7444. Main courses £6.95 ($11); 2-course set lunch £9.90 ($16). AE, MC, V. Mon–Sat noon–3pm and 6–11pm; Sun 6–10:30pm. Tube: Leicester Sq. or Tottenham Court Rd.

Old Coffee House ✦ BRITISH   The Old Coffee House takes its name from the coffeehouse heyday of 1700s London, when the drink was labeled "the devil's brew." The pub still serves pots of filtered coffee. It is heavily decorated with bric-a-brac, including old musical instruments and World War I recruiting posters. In the upstairs restaurant you can enjoy good lunches of such typical English fare as steak-and-kidney pie and scampi and chips. Vegetarian dishes and burgers and fries are also popular.

49 Beak St., W1. ⓒ 020/7437-2197. Main courses £3.75–£5 ($6–$8). MC, V. Mon–Sat noon–3pm. Pub Mon–Sat 11am–11pm; Sun noon–3pm and 7–10:30pm. Tube: Oxford Circus or Piccadilly Circus.

Wagamama ✦ *Value* *Kids* JAPANESE   Try this trendsetting noodle bar modeled after the ramen shops of Japan if you're exploring Soho and want a delicious, nutritious meal in a smoke-free environment. You enter along a stark, glowing hall with a busy open kitchen and descend to a large open room with communal tables. The specialties are ramen, Chinese-style thread noodles served in soups with various toppings, and the fat white noodles called *udon*. You can also order various rice dishes, vegetarian dishes, dumplings, vegetable and chicken skewers, and tempura. Your order is sent via radio signal to the kitchen and arrives the moment it's ready, which means that not everyone in a group will be served at the same time. You may have to stand in line to get in, but it's worth the wait. There are nine other Wagamamas scattered throughout the city.

10A Lexington St., W1. ✆ 020-7292-0990. Tube: Piccadilly Circus (then a 5-min. walk north on Shaftesbury Ave. and Windmill St., which becomes Lexington St.). Reservations are not accepted. Main courses: £5.35–7.50 ($9–$12). MC, V. Mon–Thurs noon–11pm; Fri–Sat noon–midnight; Sun 12:30–10pm.

WORTH A SPLURGE

Dumpling Inn ⊛ CHINESE   Despite its incongruous name, this is a rather elegant restaurant serving a delectable brand of Peking Mandarin cuisine. Its special piquancy comes from the inclusion of Mongolian ingredients, best represented in a savory stew called "hot pot." Regulars come here for the beef in oyster sauce, the seaweed and sesame-seed prawns on toast, duck with chile and black-bean sauce, and the fried sliced fish with sauce. Naturally, the specialty is dumplings; you can make a meal from the dim sum list. Chinese tea is extra. Service is leisurely, so don't dine here before a theater date.

15a Gerrard St., W1. ✆ 020/7437-2567. Reservations recommended. Main courses £5.10–£14 ($8–$22); fixed-price lunch or dinner £14–£25 ($22–$40). AE, MC, V. Sun–Thurs 11:30am–11:30pm; Fri–Sat 11:30am–1am. Tube: Piccadilly Circus.

WESTMINSTER & VICTORIA

The Albert ⊛ ENGLISH   The Albert is a real bit of Victorian England, visited for its sumptuous roasts traditionally prepared and sliced for you at its Carvery. The pub, which opened in 1852, is one of a handful of pubs with bells controlled from the floor of the houses of Parliament, used to notify patrons when an important vote is coming up. At the Carvery you can get turkey, pork, and beef. Fish lovers and vegetarians can also find something to their liking here. Desserts are served from the trolley.

52 Victoria St., SW1. ✆ 020/7222-5577. Reservations recommended. Fixed-price Carvery meals £3–£5.95 ($4.80–$10); fixed-price 3-course meal £16.95 ($27). AE, DC, MC, V. Carvery, daily noon–9:30pm. Pub, Mon–Sat 11am–11pm; Sun noon–10:30pm. Tube: St. James's Park.

Jenny Lo's Teahouse ⊛ CANTONESE/SZECHUAN   Jenny Lo's father was Britain's best-known Chinese chef, and this is where he had his cookery school. His restaurant, Ken Lo's Memories of China, is still going strong in nearby Ebury Street but it's very pricey. This teahouse, however, is quite affordable. The decor is simple but stylish, utilizing long shared tables, wooden chairs, and bright splashes of color. There's a short menu, mainly rice, soup noodles, and wok noodles, including ones with a southeast Asian twist (hot coconut). Try the luxurious black-bean seafood noodles. Side dishes include such street-food classics as onion cakes. The staff is extremely friendly and helpful, which soothes any irritation if you have to wait for a table. Jenny Lo has also commissioned her own tonic teas from Chinese herbalist Dr. Xu. Long life and happiness are on the menu here.

14 Eccleston St., SW1. ✆ 020/7259-0399. Reservations not accepted. Main courses £5–£7.50 ($8–$12). No credit cards. Mon–Fri 11:30am–3pm; Sat noon–3pm; Mon–Sat 6–10pm. Tube: Victoria.

SUPER-CHEAP EATS

The Green Café CONTINENTAL   This 26-seat cafe, run by the Fiori family since 1955, counts neighborhood workers, cabbies, and professionals in suits among its regular customers. There is a different daily special, and everything, including bread and pastas, is homemade. Menu items include English breakfast, sandwiches, fresh fish and chips, pastas, and roast beef, lamb, chicken, or pork with vegetables.

16 Eccleston St., SW1. ⓒ 020/7730-5304. Reservations not accepted. Main courses £3–£5 ($4.80–$8). No credit cards. Mon–Fri 6am–6:30pm; Sat 6:30am–noon. Closed holidays. Tube: Victoria.

WORTH A SPLURGE

Tate Gallery Restaurant ⚑ MODERN BRITISH   This attractive restaurant draws many wine fanciers because it offers what may be the best bargains for superior wines anywhere in Britain. The restaurant's English menu, which changes monthly, might include pheasant casserole, pan-fried skate with black butter and capers, pasta primavera with broccoli pesto sauce, and a selection of other vegetarian dishes. Access to the restaurant is through the museum's main entrance on Millbank.

Millbank, SW1. ⓒ 020/7887-8877. Reservations recommended. Main courses £9.95–£18.50 ($16–$30); fixed-price 2-course lunch £16.75 ($27); fixed-price 3-course lunch £19.50 ($32). Minimum charge £16.75 ($27). AE, DC, MC, V. Mon–Sat noon–3pm; Sun noon–4pm. Tube: Pimlico.

MAYFAIR

The Granary TRADITIONAL BRITISH   This family-operated country-style restaurant has served a simple but flavorful array of home-cooked dishes since 1974. The daily specials might include beef bourguignon, chicken and mushroom risotto, smoked salmon, chicken pie, and steak-and-kidney pie, with vegetarian options such as spicy Moroccan vegetables. Tempting desserts are bread-and-butter pudding and Brown Betty (both served hot). The large portions guarantee that you won't go hungry. Cookery is standard, even routine, but still quite good for the price.

39 Albemarle St., W1. ⓒ 020/7493-2978. Main courses £8.60–£9.60 ($14–$15). MC, V. Mon–Fri 11:30am–7:30pm; Sat 11:30am–3:30pm. Tube: Green Park.

Hard Rock Cafe 𝘒𝘪𝘥𝘴 AMERICAN   This is the original Hard Rock, now a worldwide chain of rock 'n' roll–themed diners. The portions on the beef-laden menu are generous, and the price of a main dish includes a salad and fries or baked potato. The fajitas are always a good choice. The dessert menu offers homemade apple pie and thick, cold shakes. Of course there's a merchandise store.

150 Old Park Lane, W1. ⓒ 020/7629-0382. Main courses £7.75–£15 ($12–$24). AE, DC, MC, V. Sun–Thurs 11:30am–12:30am; Fri–Sat 11:30am–1am. Closed Christmas. Tube: Green Park or Hyde Park Corner.

Suze Wine Bar PACIFIC RIM   Café Suze at 11 Glentworth St., NW1 (ⓒ **020/ 7486-8216**), in Marylebone, was so successful that the New Zealand owners opened this charming wine bar in Mayfair. There's a comfortable bistro-like ambience; the walls are maroon and hung with modern art. The food is Australasian with some international crossovers and always simply and well prepared. Try the succulent New Zealand green-tipped mussels, a house specialty, or the New Zealand scallops. You can also get New Zealand rack of lamb. There are several sharing platters to choose from: Italian antipasti, vegetarian, Greek, seafood, and cheese. A favorite dessert is Pavlova: a light meringue cover with kiwi fruit, strawberries, passion fruit, and mangoes. And, of course, you can get a fine glass of wine.

41 North Audley St., W1. ⓒ 020/7491-3237. Reservations recommended. Main courses £5.95–£13.50 ($10–$22); platters to share £5.95–£10.95 ($10–$18). AE, DC, MC, V. Mon–Sat 11am–11pm. Tube: Green Park.

KNIGHTSBRIDGE & BELGRAVIA

Le Metro ⭐ INTERNATIONAL   Located just around the corner from Harrods, Le Metro draws a fashionable crowd to its basement precincts. The place serves good, solid, reliable food prepared with flair. The menu changes frequently, but recent offerings included pan-fried snapper, shepherd's pie, and spiced couscous with roast vegetables. You can order special wines by the glass.

28 Basil St., SW3. ℂ **020/7589-6286.** Main courses £8.50–£10.50 ($12.75–$15.75). AE, DC, MC, V. Mon–Sat 7:30am–10:30pm. Tube: Knightsbridge.

Pan-Asian Canteen @ Paxton's Head ⭐ *(Finds* GASTROPUB/PAN-ASIAN There's been a pub on this spot since 1632 but the present one dates from the turn of the last century. Every inch of it, inside and out, is paneled in polished mahogany. So the new Pan-Asian Canteen upstairs comes as a bit of a surprise. The cool, modern, Bangkok-green dining room has three big teak tables, which can seat 12 people each, eating communal style. Depending on the day and time, you could have one to yourself or be elbow-to-elbow with businessmen, backpackers, and shoppers on a break. The fixed-price dinners are a great value, and the regular prices make this a perfect light meal break. The menu is very strong on seafood, from the fishcake starter to clams, red snapper, and deliciously juicy king prawns revved up with chile. But there's lots to tempt vegetarians and carnivores, too. The pork ribs sprinkled with sesame seeds made a very tasty starter and there's always a chicken curry. The pub has several real ales on tap.

153 Knightsbridge, SW1. ℂ **020/7589-6627.** Reservations not accepted. Main courses £5.50–£7.25 ($9–$12); fixed-price dinners £16–£20 ($26–$32). AE, MC, V. Mon–Sat noon–10:30pm; Sun 12:30–9pm. Tube: Knightsbridge.

SUPER-CHEAP EATS

Stockpot *(Value* ENGLISH/CONTINENTAL/VEGETARIAN   Serving predominantly English fare with just a few continental dishes scattered throughout the menu, Stockpot is one of the best dining deals to be found in London. The menu changes twice daily. Starters might include chicken-liver pâté or a mushroom tartlet; featured main courses are Lancashire hot pot, steak-and-kidney pie, filet of chicken with Normandy sauce, or lamb cutlets with red-wine and mushroom sauce. The selection always includes three or four vegetarian meals, with offerings such as lasagna, moussaka, or tagliatelle with broccoli. To finish, try the orange sponge pudding with cream or apple crumble.

6 Basil St., SW3. ℂ **020/7589-8627.** Main courses £2.60–£6.50 ($4–$10); fixed-price lunch £3.70 ($6) lunch, fixed-price dinner £6.40 ($10). No credit cards. Mon–Sat 7am–11pm; Sun 7am–10pm. Tube: Knightsbridge.

CHELSEA

Henry J. Beans (But All His Friends Call Him Hank) Bar & Grill *(Kids* AMERICAN   Popular, uninhibited, and deafeningly loud, this is a no-holds-barred American-style saloon. The clientele tends to be youthful, though on weekends the place fills up with young families. The decor was inspired by the pop-surrealistic 1960s and 1970s, with art and accessories by Andy Warhol wannabes. Check the chalkboard for daily specials; menu items tend to include fried chicken, nachos, taco salads, and many kinds of burgers and sandwiches. An array of health-conscious salads is also available for vegetarians and meat eaters alike, low on fat and high in health value.

195–197 King's Rd., SW3. ℂ **020/7352-9255.** Main courses £6–£7.50 ($10–$12). AE, MC, V. Mon–Sat 10am–11pm; Sun noon–10:30pm. Tube: Sloane Sq.

King's Head & Eight Bells BRITISH   The menu at this nice Chelsea pub features homemade specials of the day, such as fish and chips or sausage with chips, and includes at least one vegetable main dish. On Sunday, a roast of the day is served. It's good, solid pub grub; nothing more, nothing less.

50 Cheyne Walk, SW3. ℰ 020/7352-1820. Main courses £5.95–£10.35 ($11–$17). MC, V. Mon–Sat 11am–11pm; Sun noon–10:30pm. Tube: Sloane Sq.

Le Shop *Kids* CREPES   Offering salads, galettes (buckwheat crepes), and Breton-style crepes, this was the first crepe shop to open in London, and it remains among the best. Diners can choose from the menu or build their own crepes from a large selection of meat, vegetable, and sweet fillings. Half portions are available for children. Front window tables make for entertaining dining, as this stretch of King's Road offers a pedestrian parade of fashionistas.

329 King's Rd., SW3. ℰ 020/7352-3891. Crepes £5–£9 ($8–$14). MC, V. Daily 10:30am–midnight. Closed Christmas. Tube: Sloane Sq.; then bus 11 or 19.

Oriel FRENCH BRASSERIE *Kids*   Oriel is in a fantastic location, right on the corner of Sloane Square, and everyone knows it. It's always hopping, so if you're planning to eat rather than grab a coffee or a quick drink (wine by the glass is very reasonably priced), try to arrive a little ahead of normal mealtimes. The upstairs is classic brasserie, with big mirrors, square-topped tables, and high ceilings. There are a few pavement tables for people-watching. Downstairs, marshmallow-soft sofas make you never want to leave. The food is a good value, from *moules marinières* (mussels) to salads or sausage and mash. Oriel has vegetarian dishes and will provide reduced-price portions for the kids.

50–51 Sloane Sq., SW1. ℰ 020/7730-2804. Main courses £8.45–£13.95 ($14–$22). AE, DC, MC, V. Mon–Sat 8:30am–10:45pm; Sun 9am–10pm. Tube: Sloane Sq.

SUPER-CHEAP EATS

Chelsea Kitchen *Value* INTERNATIONAL   This is a sister to the Stockpot chain, which also has a diner on King's Road. The Chelsea Kitchen is a lot more convenient, and the food is a little better. The cuisine is not remotely haute by any stretch, but it's a fantastically good deal. The menu never changes. It runs from omelets and burgers to salads and more substantial hot dishes, such as goulash, spaghetti Bolognese, and braised lamb chops. Chelsea Kitchen is no-frills on the decor side, too, with polished wooden tables and bum-numbing booths. The service sometimes sorely lacks a smile. But the prices are so "Old World" that it gets screamingly busy, particularly in the evening.

98 King's Rd., SW3. ℰ 020/7589-1330. Main courses £3–£6.10 ($4.80–$10); fixed-priced meal £6–£6.70 ($10–$11). No credit cards. Mon–Sat 7:30am–11:45pm. Tube: Sloane Sq.

KENSINGTON

Benedicts IRISH/INTERNATIONAL   In a district filled with high-priced restaurants, Benedicts keeps its tabs reasonable, with Irish and international meals. Along with a good selection of wines, you can order country pâté, perhaps wild Irish smoked salmon, then follow with steak-and-ale pie or hot Gaelic pepper steak laced with Irish whiskey. Don't expect a scene from the Emerald Isle, though: the waitstaff seems to be more Albanian than Irish.

106 Kensington High St., W8. ℰ 020/7937-7580. Main courses £6.55–£10.95 ($11–$18). AE, MC, V. Mon–Fri noon–3pm and 5–10:30pm; Sat noon–10:30pm; Sun 4–9pm. Tube: Kensington High St.

Stick & Bowl *Value* CHINESE   With only 30 seats, Stick & Bowl is not a place to linger over dinner, but the fast-paced dining is offset by more than 50 inexpensive menu selections, including soups, meat and fish dishes, and pork and seafood main courses served with rice and vegetables. Shoppers on Kensington High Street consider this both a quick meal and a good bargain.

31 Kensington High St., W8. ✆ 020/7937-2778. Reservations not accepted. Main courses £4–£5.50 ($6–$9). No credit cards. Daily 11:30am–11pm. Closed Christmas and Boxing Day. Tube: High St. Kensington.

SOUTH KENSINGTON

Daquise POLISH/EASTERN EUROPEAN   This old favorite, established during World War II, is still going strong. It immediately became a focal point of Polish culture in London, attracting a network of refugees who used it as a center to locate missing persons and organize a tattered but heroic resistance to Hitler. Today, almost all the staff speaks Polish and nationalistic memories are kept alive amid an old-fashioned decor with framed oil paintings decorating the walls. You might begin with borscht or marinated herring with potato salad, then follow with stuffed cabbage or beef stroganoff, perhaps blinis with smoked salmon. Everything is cooked old-country style.

20 Thurloe St., SW7. ✆ 020/7589-6117. Reservations recommended. Main courses £5–£10.50 ($8–$17); fixed-price lunch £7 ($11). MC, V. Daily 11:30am–11pm. Tube: South Kensington.

Noor Jahan ✯ *Finds* INDIAN   The chef at this well-established restaurant prepares an interesting selection of Indian food, mostly from the north with its more delicate mix of fruit and spices and less fatty cooking. The appetizers and soups are exotic, and you can have a wide array of fresh vegetables that follow old-time recipes. The tandoori dishes (cooked in a clay oven) are always good. The chicken Tikka (marinated and barbecued) or the tandoori fish (usually fresh trout in a spicy sauce) are standouts. The lamb dishes are also worth the long walk from the Tube stop, especially Rogan Josh, cooked with glazed tomatoes, green herbs, and spices—fairly hot, but not tear-producing. Vegetarians will find good choices as well.

2A Bina Gardens, SW5. ✆ 020/7373-6522. Main courses £6.50–£11.50 ($10–$18); fixed-price menu £18.50 ($30). AE, DC, MC, V. Daily noon–2:45pm and 6–11:45pm. Tube: Gloucester Rd. or South Kensington.

The Oratory *Finds* MODERN BRITISH   Named for the nearby Brompton Oratory, and close to the V&A and Knightsbridge shopping, this funky bistro serves up some of the best and least expensive food in tony South Ken. The high-ceilinged room is decorated in what might be called Modern Rococo, with enormous glass chandeliers, patterned walls and ceiling, and wooden tables with wrought-iron chairs. Take note of the daily specials on the blackboard, especially any pasta dishes. The homemade fishcakes, seared tuna, and kiev of chicken stuffed with risotto, spinach and a tomato and basil sauce are all noteworthy. For dessert, the sticky toffee pudding with ice cream is a melt-in-the-mouth delight.

232 Brompton Rd., SW3. ✆ 020/7584-3493. Main courses £8.50–£14.50 ($14–$23); set menu lunch £8.50 ($14). MC, V. Daily noon–11pm. Tube: Knightsbridge or South Kensington.

Star of India INDIAN   This is one of the oldest Indian restaurants in London, dating back to the 1950s, but it has a cuisine kept fresh and alive by its cosmopolitan owner, Reza Muhammed. Menu items derive from throughout India, evoking the subcontinent in all its varied culinary exoticism. Examples include baked eggplant slices stuffed with sesame seeds and cottage cheese, served with mustard seeds, fresh tomatoes, and a garlic dip. Also look for roasted leg of lamb in rich tomato-and-onion gravy, or chicken and lentil kebabs. There's also a sophisticated roster of dishes slow-cooked in the tandoori oven, including a succulent dessert of fresh pineapple chunks flavored with saffron and fennel seed, caramelized in the tandoori, and served with freshly-made vanilla ice cream.

154 Old Brompton Rd., South Kensington, SW5. ℭ **020/7373-2901.** Main courses £9.75–£19.75 ($16–$32). AE, DC, MC, V. Daily noon–2:45pm; Mon–Sat 6pm–midnight; Sun 7–11:15pm. Tube: Gloucester Rd.

WORTH A SPLURGE

Phoenicia ✯ LEBANESE   Phoenicia is highly regarded for the quality of its Lebanese cuisine—outstanding in presentation and freshness—and for its moderate prices. For the best value, go for lunch, when you can enjoy a buffet of more than two dozen meze (appetizers), presented in little pottery dishes. Each day at lunch, the chef prepares two or three home-cooked dishes, including chicken in garlic sauce or stuffed lamb with vegetables. To start, you can select from such classic Middle Eastern dishes as hummus or stuffed vine leaves. The chefs bake fresh bread and two types of pizza daily in a clay oven. Minced lamb, spicy and well flavored, is an eternal favorite. Various charcoal-grilled dishes are also offered.

11–13 Abingdon Rd., W8. ℭ **020/7937-0120.** Reservations recommended on weekends. Main courses £10–£15 ($16–$24); buffet lunch £12.95–£14.95 ($19.40–$22.40); fixed-price dinner £16.80–£30.90 ($29–$49). AE, DC, MC, V. Daily 12:15pm–midnight; buffet lunch Sat–Sun 12:15–3:30pm. Tube: High St. Kensington.

NOTTING HILL GATE

Books for Cooks ✯ *Value* *Finds* INTERNATIONAL   Housed in the back room of a shop stocking 12,000 cookbook titles, this restaurant makes good use of its proximity to Portobello Road Market, where a daily rotation of visiting chefs go to buy seasonal ingredients and then return to the kitchen to experiment with new recipes. The delectably varied menu changes radically from day to day, but diners can always expect a two- and three-course meal consisting of soup, a vegetable dish, and cake. Light lunches are a steal at £5 ($8)—hot soup and bread in the winter, a salad or homemade savory tart in the summer. Seating is limited to just 15, and reservations aren't accepted; so arrive early for a table.

4 Blenheim Crescent, W11. ℭ **020/7221-1992.** Reservations not accepted. Fixed-price menus £5–£7 ($8–$11). AE, DC, MC, V. Tues–Sat 10am–6pm. Tube: Notting Hill Gate or Ladbroke Grove.

Mondola SUDANESE   Very small and intimate, on the fringe of trendy Notting Hill, this bohemian hangout specializes in the spicy cuisine of the Sudan. The food is a blend of cuisines, borrowing from the traditions of North Africa, Ethiopia, and even the Middle East. Although the menu is limited, the dishes are well prepared from fresh ingredients. Begin with the classic soup of the region, made with meat and peanuts. Then opt for lamb, especially the tasty chops marinated in African spices. Ground red chiles add zest to many of the dishes. Lentils with caramelized garlic are another treat, and there's a generous salad bar costing £11 ($18) for two persons. Bring your own wine or beer, as the restaurant does not have a liquor license.

139 Westbourne Grove, W11. ℭ **020/7229-4734.** Reservations recommended. Fixed-price meals £17 ($28). MC, V. Daily 1–11pm. Tube: Notting Hill Gate.

Prince Bonaparte ✯ *Finds* INTERNATIONAL   This offbeat restaurant serves great pub grub in what was a grungy boozer in the days before Notting Hill Gate became fashionable. The pub is filled with mismatched furniture from schools and churches; mellow jazz and lazy blues fill the air except on Friday and Saturday when DJs spin house and hip-hop. The menu roams the world for inspiration: Moroccan chicken with couscous is good, and seafood risotto is delicious, as is the vegetarian salad of beet root, new potatoes, walnuts, and egg-plant. Roast lamb, tender and juicy, appears on the traditional Sunday menu.

80 Chepstow Rd., W2. ✆ 020/7313-9491. Reservations required. Main courses £7–£14 ($11–$22). MC, V. Mon–Sat noon–11pm; Sun noon–10:30pm. Tube: Notting Hill Gate or Westbourne Park.

MARYLEBONE

The Lucky Spot ITALIAN   Located near the American Embassy, this small Italian restaurant is so popular with the office crowd that it is best avoided between noon and 1pm. English breakfast is served in the morning, and freshly made sandwiches, a number of pasta dishes, pizza, salads, fresh fish, and steaks are available for lunch or dinner. Afternoon tea is served with scones and cakes. There is take-out service, and although the restaurant does not feature a bar, din-ers are allowed to bring their own wine.

14 North Audley St., W1. ✆ 020/7493-0277. Reservations not accepted. Main courses £6.90–£13.50 ($11–$22). No credit cards. Mon–Sat 7am–6pm. Closed holidays. Tube: Marble Arch or Bond St.

Raw Deal *(Value* VEGETARIAN   The cook draws her inspiration from Italy, central Europe, and England at this homelike and unpretentious self-service veg-etarian restaurant. The menu includes at least two freshly made vegetarian spe-cials of the day, perhaps zucchini and eggplant with mozzarella, tomatoes, and hazelnuts, or mushroom tarts, plus an array of salads. Everything is completely fresh for the day. Raw Deal is especially popular at lunchtime because of the many office workers who cram in here; in the evening, however, the atmosphere is more relaxed. A full line of beer, wine, and spirits is available.

65 York St., W1. ✆ 020/7262-4841. Main courses £5.50–£6 ($9–$10). No credit cards. Mon–Fri 8am–9:30pm (last order); Sat 8am–8:30pm. Tube: Baker St.

Woodlands *(Value* INDIAN/VEGETARIAN   The vegetarian cuisine of south India is served at this cost-conscious restaurant. In a pastel-colored dining room lined with Indian paintings and filled with Indian music, diners choose from an unusual selection of *thalis* (variety plates) or *dosas* (spicy vegetarian pancakes). Lentils and rice liberally flavored with herbs are staples. Most of the staff are from south India, and are happy to advise patrons about how and what to order.

77 Marylebone Lane, W1. ✆ 020/7486-3862. Reservations recommended. Main courses £4.50–£5.95 ($7–$10); fixed-price meal £12–£14 ($20–$22). AE, DC, MC, V. Daily noon–3pm and 6–11pm. Tube: Bond St.

PADDINGTON & BAYSWATER
WORTH A SPLURGE

Halepi ✦ GREEK/CYPRIOT   Run by the Kazolides family since 1966, this establishment is one of the best Greek restaurants in London. Despite its presti-gious reputation, the dining atmosphere is informal, with long rows of brightly clothed tables and bouzouki background music. Menu items rely heavily on lamb and include kebabs, *klefticon* (baby lamb prepared with aromatic spices), moussaka (minced lamb and eggplant with bechamel sauce), and *dolmades* (vine leaves stuffed with lamb and rice). *Afelia* is a filet of pork cooked with wine and spices and served with potatoes and rice. Fish and seafood lovers can choose from scallops, sea bass, Scotch halibut, and Indonesian shrimp (prepared with lemon juice, olive oil, garlic, and spring onion sauce). The homemade baklava is recommended for dessert, and the wine list features numerous selections imported from Greece and Cyprus.

18 Leinster Terrace, W2. ✆ 020/7262-1070. Reservations required. Main courses £9–£28.50 ($14–$46). AE, DC, MC, V. Daily noon–midnight. Closed Dec 25–26. Tube: Queensway.

AWAY FROM THE CENTER
GOLDERS GREEN

Bloom's KOSHER   This is London's most famous kosher restaurant, dating back to 1920. The cooking is strictly *fleishig* (non-dairy) kosher at this large, bustling place. Members of London's Jewish community flock here on Saturday night when the restaurant opens "when the sun goes down," and Bloom's keeps bustling and busy until the wee hours of the morning. It remains the best place in London for things like chopped herring, calves'-foot jelly, liverwurst, hot tongue, boiled fowl leg, and kishke stuffing, as well as potato latkes, *lokschen* (noodle) pudding, cold beetroot borscht by the glass, and, of course Israeli wines (red or white). And they still do an egg-and-onion sandwich.

130 Golders Green Rd., NW11. ℭ 020/8455-1338. Main courses £12–£22 ($19–$34). AE, DC, MC, V. Sun–Thurs 11am–1am; Fri 11am–3pm (to 2pm Dec–Feb). Closed Sat. Tube: Golders Green.

ALONG THE THAMES

The Bengal Clipper ✦ INDIAN   Set within the dining and entertainment complex of Butler's Wharf, this likable restaurant in a former spice warehouse is decorated with modern Indian artwork and has large windows that look out over its Thameside neighborhood. You can enjoy a cuisine that includes many vegetarian choices derived from the formerly Portuguese colony of Goa and the once-English land of Bengal. There is a zestfulness and spice to the cuisine, but it is never overpowering. The chefs keep the menu fairly short so that all the ingredients can be purchased fresh daily. A tantalizing and tasty specialty is stuffed *murgh masala,* a tender breast of chicken with potato, onion, apricots, and almonds cooked with yogurt and served with a delectable curry sauce. The perfectly cooked duckling comes in a tangy sauce with a citrus bite. One of the finest dishes is marinated lamb simmered in cream with cashew nuts and seasoned with fresh ginger. The karkra chop, a spicy patty of minced crab blended with mashed potatoes and peppered with Goan spices, is also recommended. The papadums and homemade chutneys add to the experience.

Shad Thames, Butler's Wharf, SE1. ℭ 020/7357-9001. Reservations recommended. Main courses £8–£15 ($12–$24); fixed menu from £10 ($16); Sunday buffet £8 ($12). AE, DC, MC, V. Mon–Sat noon–3pm and 6–11:30pm; Sun noon–4pm and 6–11pm. Tube: London Bridge.

The Carvery *Kids Value* TRADITIONAL BRITISH   If you're down visiting the Tower of London, you can partake of one of London's best dining deals. You can have all the fabulous roasts you can eat at this renowned establishment, located on the Thames. There's a wide range of appetizers, and the buffet carving-table boasts a roast leg of Southdown lamb with mint sauce and a roast leg of English pork with applesauce. The chef will carve your choice of roast for you; you'll then serve yourself buttered peas, roast potatoes, new carrots, and gravy. You'll also find cold food and assorted salads. Desserts might include chocolate fudge cake or a sherry trifle.

Tower Thistle Hotel, St. Katharine's Wharf, E1. ℭ 020/7481-2575. All-you-can-eat meals £19.95 ($32). Half price for children 5–14; free for those 4 and under. Mon–Sat noon–2:30pm; Sun–Thurs 5:30–10:30pm; Fri–Sat 5–11:30pm; Sun 6–10:30pm. Tube: Tower Hill.

Dickens Inn by the Tower *Kids* TRADITIONAL BRITISH   This three-floor restaurant is in an 1830 brick warehouse that once housed spices imported from afar. Large windows provide sweeping views of the Thames and Tower Bridge. On the ground level, you'll find the Tavern Bar, serving sandwiches, lasagna, steaming bowls of soup and chili, bar snacks, and other foods kids love.

On the floor above is Pizza on the Dock, offering four sizes of pizzas that should also make the kids happy. Above that, you'll find a relatively formal and expensive dining room, Grill on the Dock, specializing in fish dishes.

St. Katharine's Way, E1. ℂ 020/7488-2208. Reservations recommended. Tavern Bar, snacks and meals £4.95–£6.50 ($8–$10); pizzas £7.30–£16.50 ($12–$26). Grill on the Dock, main courses £12.95–£19 ($21–$30). AE, DC, MC, V. Grill on the Dock daily noon–3pm and 6:30–10:30pm; Tavern Bar daily 11am–3pm; Pizza on the Dock daily noon–10pm. Tube: Tower Hill.

Founders Arms (Finds) MODERN BRITISH   This modern pub-restaurant sits right on the Thames on the South Bank, a few minutes walk east from the South Bank Centre or west from the new Tate Modern and Shakespeare's Globe. You can sit inside or out beside the river. Though there are some pub favorites, like Lincolnshire sausages with mash, meat pies, and Lancashire hotpot, there are other dishes that are more ambitious. Pasta, fresh fish, and other daily specials are listed on a blackboard.

52 Hopton St., SE1. ℂ 020/7928-1899. Main courses £3.75–£11.50 ($6–$18). AE, MC, V. Open: Mon–Sat noon–8:30pm; Sun noon–7pm. Tube: Waterloo or London Bridge.

HAMPSTEAD HEATH

Byron's ✸ MODERN EUROPEAN   Named in honor of Lord Byron, this is a pleasant restaurant with innovative food served in understated dining rooms illuminated by candles. Menu items are creative and flavorful. Examples include seared scallops with herb purée and caramelized carrots; steamed smoked haddock mousse with a spicy curry sauce and fresh horseradish cream; baked spring chicken with Savoy cabbage and prune sauce; and roast venison filet in brioche crust with squash purée. For dessert, look for the dark- and white-chocolate mousse.

3A Downshire Hill, Hampstead, NW3. ℂ 020/7435-3544. Reservations recommended. Main courses £9.75–£17.75 ($16–$28); fixed-price 3-course lunch £12.50 ($20; Mon–Sat only). AE, MC, V. Mon–Sat noon–3pm and 7–11pm; Sun noon–4pm and 7–10pm. Tube: Hampstead.

Olde White Bear ENGLISH   A Hampstead Heath landmark, this pub attracts villagers and visitors alike to its relaxed Victorian-style precincts. The bar menu is seasonally adjusted but is likely to include charcoal-grilled tuna steak with a spicy lentil salsa, baked eggplant slices, or well-stuffed sandwiches. The food is above average, although most visitors come here just to pub it up.

Well Rd., NW3. ℂ 020/7435-3758. Main courses £5–£10 ($8–$16). MC, V. Mon–Sat 11am–11pm; Sun noon–10:30pm. Tube: Hampstead.

AFTERNOON TEA

Tea is serious business in England. In a nation where per-capita consumption of tea rests at a whopping five cups a day, the tea-taking ritual forms an integral part of the national psyche. Arguments rage about the proper way to prepare a pot of tea, accompanied by lofty debate about how to warm, stir, and flavor it, and what blend of leaves is either the most flavorful, most prestigious, or both.

Viewed as a civilized pause in the day's activities, taking afternoon tea is particularly appealing to people who don't have time for lunch or who plan an early theater engagement. Afternoon tea usually lasts from 3:30 to 6:30pm. If you do it properly, this relaxing, drawn-out affair usually consists of three courses: first, dainty finger sandwiches, then scones with jam and clotted cream, and finally an arrangement of bite-size sweets.

A formal afternoon tea can be very pricey for the traveler on a budget, but many visitors regard it as essential as sightseeing. You could always drop in to a local tea shop for a "cuppa"; but if you want to splurge English-style, consider making a reservation at one of the following: **Brown's Hotel** (© 020/7493-6020), **Claridges,** Brook Street (© 020/7629-8860), **Palm Court Lounge,** in the Park Lane Hotel (© 020/7499-6321), or the **Ritz Palm Court,** in the Ritz Hotel (© 020/7493-8181). The cost of an afternoon tea at any of them will begin at about £20 ($32).

Burgh House   An outstanding example of Queen Anne architecture, historic Burgh House hosts concerts, lectures, exhibitions, and a local history museum. Tea is served throughout business hours, and a variety of fresh baked cakes and pastries is available.

New End Sq., NW3. © 020/7431-0144. Reservations required on Sun. Tea from 70p ($1.10); cakes from £1.40 ($2.25). No credit cards. Wed–Sun 11am–5:30pm. Tube: Hampstead.

Café in the Crypt   St. Martin-in-the-Fields church was built in 1726, and its crypt is the burial place of such notables as Nell Gwynne and Thomas Chippendale. Tea is available throughout the day from the pastry counter, but tea service is from 3:15 to 5pm. Pastries, croissants, cakes, and scones are baked on the premises. This is also a good spot for lunch or dinner (see listing above).

St. Martin-in-the-Fields Church, Trafalgar Sq., WC2. © 020/7839-4342. Tea from 95p ($1.50); cakes from £1.50 ($2.40). No credit cards. Mon–Wed 10am–8pm; Thurs–Sat 10am–10pm; Sun noon–8pm. Tube: Charing Cross.

The Georgian Restaurant ⭑   As long as anyone can remember, teatime at Harrods has been one of the most distinctive features of Europe's most famous department store. A flood of visitors is somehow gracefully herded into a high-volume but nevertheless elegant room. Many come here expressly for the tea ritual, where the staff hauls silver pots and trolleys laden with pastries and sandwiches through the cavernous dining hall. Most exotic is Betigala tea, a rare blend from China, similar to Lapsang Souchong.

On the 4th floor of Harrods, 87–135 Brompton Rd., SW1. © 020/7225-6800. High tea £18.50 ($30) or £25.50 ($41) with Harrods champagne, per person. AE, DC, MC, V. Teatime Mon–Sat 3:45–5:30pm. Tube: Knightsbridge.

Maison Bertaux   Soho's best-loved tea shop, Maison Bertaux was established in 1871. There are eight or nine teas to choose from, and freshly baked croissants and pastries are available.

28 Greek St., W1. © 020/7437-6007. Reservations not accepted. Tea from £1.80 ($2.90). No credit cards. Daily 9am–8pm. Tube: Piccadilly Circus or Leicester Sq.

The Orangery ⭑   Set about 45m (150 ft.) north of Kensington Palace, The Orangery occupies a long and narrow garden pavilion built in 1704 by Queen Anne as a site for her tea parties. The cakes here are homemade English treats, from the Victoria sponge on the cheapest set menu to the Belgian chocolate on the priciest. There are three tea-time blowouts to choose from: level one gets you sandwich, shortbread, and the aforementioned cake; add £1 ($1.60) to swap the sandwich for a scone with cream and jam; and the top treat assembles all of the above, plus a glass of bubbly. The atmosphere is lovely in this elegant conservatory, yet the prices make most tea spots look like a real rip-off.

Kensington Palace, Kensington Gardens, W8. © 020/7376-0239. Fixed-price teas £6.95–£13.95 ($11–$22). MC, V. Daily 10am–6pm (5pm Oct–Easter); tea served from 3pm. Tube: Kensington High St. or Queensway. Nonsmoking.

Patisserie Valerie Sagne   Located near Madame Tussaud's and Regent's Park, this tearoom, established in 1926, remains unchanged in the face of High

Street renovations. Croissants, pastries, and scones, baked on the premises, and handmade chocolates are available for takeout as well as tea service.

105 Marylebone High St., W1. ℂ 020/7935-6240. Reservations not accepted. Tea from £1.80 ($2.90). AE, MC, V. Mon–Fri 7:30am–7pm; Sat 8:30am–7pm; Sun 9am–6pm. Tube: Baker St. or Marble Arch.

The Primrose Patisserie   Built in Victorian times, this tearoom retains the essence of that era. Tea is served throughout the day, and a variety of cakes are available, including their most popular, apple crumblet. Salads and sandwiches are served as well. This is a convenient place to rejuvenate yourself before or after a visit to nearby Regent's Park.

136 Regent's Park Rd., NW1. ℂ 020/7722-7848. Reservations not accepted. Tea from 80p ($1.30). No credit cards. Daily 8am–9pm. Tube: Chalk Farm.

Richoux   Try the old-fashioned atmosphere of Richoux, established in the 1920s. You can order hot scones with strawberry jam and whipped cream or choose from a selection of pastries behind a display case. A full menu, with fresh salads, sandwiches, burgers, and more is served all day. There are three other locations: a branch at the bottom of Bond Street, 172 Piccadilly (ℂ 020/7493-2204; Tube: Piccadilly Circus or Green Park); one at 41A S. Audley St. (ℂ 020/7629-5228; Tube: Green Park or Hyde Park Corner); and one at 3 Circus Rd. (ℂ 020/7483-4001; Tube: St. John's Wood).

86 Brompton Rd. (opposite Harrods), Knightsbridge, SW3. ℂ 020/7584-8300. Full tea £13.25 ($21); £23.50 ($38) for 2. AE, DC, MC, V. Mon–Sat 8am–7pm; Sun 10am–6:30pm. Tube: Knightsbridge.

The Tearoom at the Chelsea Physic Garden   The Chelsea Physic Garden, founded in 1675, encompasses only 1.5 hectares (3½ acres) crisscrossed with gravel paths and ringed with a high brick wall that shuts out the roaring traffic of Royal Hospital Road. On the 2 days a week it's open, the tearoom is likely to be filled with botanical enthusiasts sipping cups of tea as fortification for their garden treks. The setting is a rather banal-looking Edwardian building. Since the tearoom is only an adjunct to the glories of the garden itself, don't expect the lavish rituals of dedicated teatime establishments. But you can carry your cakes and cups of tea outside into a garden that, despite meticulous care, always looks a bit unkempt; plants are left untrimmed to encourage bird life and seed production.

66 Royal Hospital Rd., SW3. ℂ 020/7352-5646. Tea with cake £4 ($6). No credit cards. Wed noon–5pm; Sun 2–6pm. Closed Nov–Mar. Tube: Sloane Sq.

4

Exploring London

London is more eclectic and electric than ever, with a sheer energy, outrageous fashion sense, trendy dining scene, and a nightlife that's second to none. What makes the city so fascinating is its cultural diversity. It seems that half the world is flocking here, not just from the far-flung former colonies of the British Empire but also from Algeria, Argentina, China, and Senegal. These recent transplants are transforming a city once considered drab and stuffy through their talents and new ideas.

In this chapter, we can explore only a fraction of London's excitement.

We've sought out the hottest buzzes in shopping and nightlife, but we also provide plenty on time-tested treasures: ancient monuments, literary shrines, walking tours, Parliament debates, royal castles, waxworks, palaces, cathedrals, and royal parks.

Note: As a rule (unless indicated below), children's prices at London attractions apply to those ages 16 and under, you must be 60 or older to obtain available senior discounts, and for students to get available discounted admissions they must have a valid student ID card.

SIGHTSEEING SUGGESTIONS FOR FIRST-TIME VISITORS

For the first-time visitor, the question is never what to do, but what to do first.

If You Have 1 Day

Make sure to see Westminster Abbey, with its Poets' Corner and historic tombs. After you've visited the abbey, walk over to see Big Ben and the Houses of Parliament. Right across the river is the British Airways London Eye, an enormous observation wheel that takes you high above London for spectacular views. Before you do that, head over to Buckingham Palace to witness the Changing of the Guard (if it's being held), then walk over to Downing Street for a glimpse (through a high-security fence) at no. 10, home of the Prime Minister. For dinner, try a Covent Garden restaurant such as Porter's English Restaurant. For a nightcap, head over to the Red Lion in Mayfair,

where you can enjoy a lager in the ultimate Victorian pub.

If You Have 2 Days

Spend your first day as above. Devote a good part of the second day to exploring the British Museum, one of the world's biggest and best. Spend the afternoon at the Tower of London, where you can see the collection of crown jewels (expect slow-moving lines). For dinner, go to one of London's landmark restaurants such as Simpson's-in-the-Strand, where your roast will be carved at your table. The city is full of cultural delights, so choose a play, a musical, or a concert to enjoy.

If You Have 3 Days

Spend days 1 and 2 as above. On the third day, go to the National Gallery,

Value Money-Saving Passes

Now that so many of London's major museums offer free admission, sight-seeing passes aren't necessarily a great way to save money. Before you buy one, always check to see what attractions the pass actually covers. Depending on the pass you choose, you can get discounts on major attractions (such as the Tower of London), shopping, restaurants, and in some cases free public transportation. Keep in mind that some passes must be purchased before arriving in the London in order to take full advantage of their benefits. Among the passes we recommend are the **London for Less Card** (© 888/GO-FOR-LESS in the U.S.; www.for-less.com), and the **London Pass** (www.londonpass.com). For details on these passes, see "Discount Sightseeing Passes," in chapter 2.

facing Trafalgar Square, in the morning. Then visit the National Portrait Gallery right behind the National Gallery, and spend the afternoon strolling and shopping at the bookstores along Charing Cross Road or the endless boutiques in Covent Garden. Have dinner in Covent Garden or neighboring Soho.

If You Have 4 Days

Spend the first 3 days as above. On the morning of the fourth day, head for the City, the financial district of London, and explore St. Paul's Cathedral. Spend a few hours strolling the City and visit a few of its many attractions, or take the new Millennium Bridge from St. Paul's over to the new Tate Modern. In the late afternoon, head down

King's Road in Chelsea to check out the boutiques, followed by dinner at a Chelsea restaurant.

If You Have 5 Days

After spending the first 4 days as above, spend your fifth morning exploring the Victoria and Albert Museum, or the Tate Britain (have lunch at either of the museums). Spend the rest of the afternoon strolling along the South Bank and Bankside, London's hottest new area, from the British Airways London Eye observation wheel to the Tate Modern and on to the stunning new London City Hall. If you haven't already crammed in as many West End shows as you can on the first 4 nights, attend the theater this final evening.

1 The Top Attractions

British Airways London Eye ★★ *Kids* "Passengers" on the Eye can see straight into the Buckingham Palace garden, much to the queen's chagrin. At 133m (443 ft.) high, this is the world's tallest observation wheel. Located on the south bank, next to County Hall, the Eye gives you a ½-hour "flight" with stunning 40km (25-mile) views over the capital. It's better when the sun isn't shining, as the glare makes it difficult to see out. And the passenger pods should have maps of the landmarks you're seeing (instead you have to pay £4.50/$7 for a guidebook). Book in advance to avoid too much hanging about. The Eye will keep spinning at least through December 2003, and probably longer because it's such a popular attraction, but they've jacked the prices up in a kind of "last call."

Jubilee Gardens, SE1. © 0870/500-0600. www.ba-londoneye.com. Admission £11 ($18) adults, £10 ($16) seniors, £5.50 ($9) children 5-15. Open daily 9:30am; last admission varies seasonally (8–10pm). Tube: Waterloo or Westminster. River services: Festival Pier.

Central London Attractions

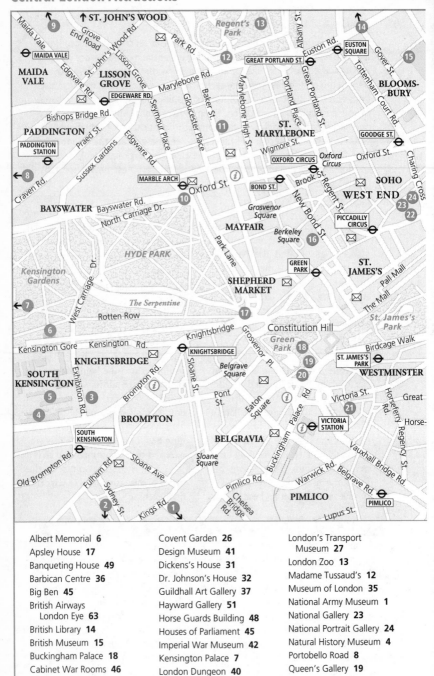

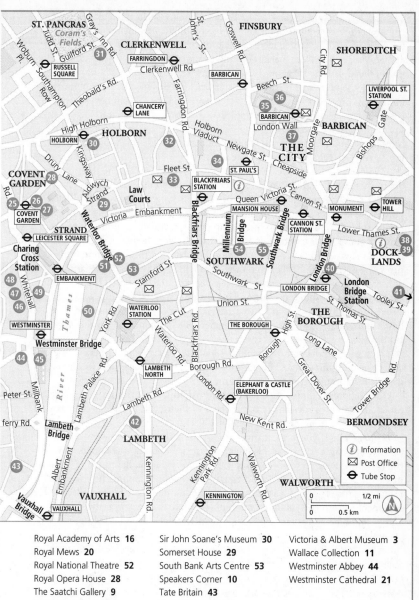

The British Museum ✮✮✮   The British Museum shelters one of the most comprehensive collections of art and artifacts in the world, including countless treasures of ancient and modern civilizations. The museum is so vast (with 4km/2½ miles of galleries) that you might want to take one of the 1½-hour tours offered daily at 10:30am, 1, and 3pm for £8 ($13).

During the year 2000, the "Great Court" project designed by Lord Norman Foster was completed, realigning the access to the galleries. The inner courtyard is now canopied by a transparent roof that transforms the area into a covered square housing a bookshop and restaurants. The center of the Great Court features the Round Reading Room restored to its original Victorian splendor. (For information on the British Library, see p. 150.)

As you enter the front hall, head first to the **Assyrian Transept** on the ground floor, where you'll find the winged and human-headed bulls and lions that once guarded the gateways to the palaces of Assyrian kings. Nearby is the **Black Obelisk of Shalmaneser III** ✮ (858–824 B.C.) depicting Jehu, king of Israel, paying tribute. Continue into the angular hall of Egyptian sculpture to see the **Rosetta stone** ✮✮✮, whose discovery led to the deciphering of hieroglyphs. Also on the ground floor is the Duveen Gallery, housing the **Parthenon sculptures** ✮✮✮ from the Parthenon on the Acropolis in Athens. The Department of Medieval and Later Antiquities has its galleries on the first floor (2nd floor to Americans). One exhibit, the **Sutton Hoo Anglo-Saxon burial ship** ✮✮✮ discovered in Suffolk, is a treasure trove of gold jewelry, armor, weapons, bronze bowls and cauldrons, silverware, and the inevitable drinking horn of the Norse culture.

The featured attractions of the upper floor are the Egyptian Galleries, especially the **mummies** ✮✮. The galleries of the City of Rome and its empire include exhibits of art before the Romans.

One section is devoted to the **Sainsbury African Galleries** ✮, one of the finest collections of African art and artifacts in the world. It features changing displays selected from more than 200,000 objects.

Insider's tip: If you're a first-time visitor, you will, of course, want to concentrate on some of the fabled treasures previewed above. But why not duck into the British Museum several times on your visit, even if you have only an hour or two to see the less heralded but equally fascinating exhibits. These include rooms covering Taoism, Confucianism, and Buddhism. The Chinese collection is particularly strong. Sculpture from India is as fine as anything at the Victoria and Albert. The ethnography collection is increasingly being beefed up, especially the Mexican Gallery, which traces that country's art from the 2nd millennium B.C. to the 16th century A.D. A new gallery nearby for the North American collection has just opened. Finally, the museum has opened a new money Gallery in room no. 68, tracing the story of money.

Great Russell St., WC1. ✆ 020/7323-8000. www.thebritishmuseum.ac.uk. Free admission. Galleries: Sat–Wed 10am-5:30pm, Thurs–Fri 10am–8:30pm. Great Court: Sun–Wed 9am–6pm, Thurs–Sat 9am–11pm. Closed Jan 1, Good Friday, and Dec 24–26. Tube: Holborn, Tottenham Court Rd., or Goodge St.

Buckingham Palace ✮ *(Overrated*   This massive building is the Queen's official residence and one of the most famous buildings in the capital. You can tell that Her Maj is at home when the Royal Standard flies at the masthead.

The palace was built as a country house for the duke of Buckingham. In 1762 George III bought it because he needed room for his 15 children. Since then, the building has been expanded, remodeled, faced with Portland limestone, and

The British Museum

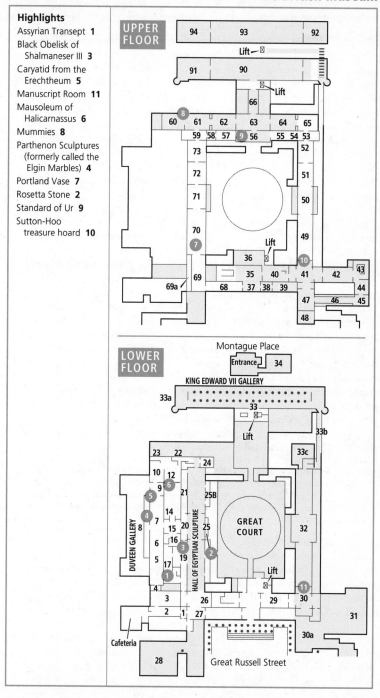

Highlights

Assyrian Transept **1**

Black Obelisk of Shalmaneser III **3**

Caryatid from the Erechtheum **5**

Manuscript Room **11**

Mausoleum of Halicarnassus **6**

Mummies **8**

Parthenon Sculptures (formerly called the Elgin Marbles) **4**

Portland Vase **7**

Rosetta Stone **2**

Standard of Ur **9**

Sutton-Hoo treasure hoard **10**

bombed twice during the Blitz. Today, contained within a 17-hectare (42-acre) garden, it stands 108m (360 ft.) long and has 600 rooms. The queen's family occupies 12 of them; the rest are used as offices and reception rooms.

The palace is open to the public for 8 weeks in August and September, when the royal family is away on vacation in Scotland. Nothing that you actually see on the self-guided tour justifies the exorbitant admission price, although you do get to wander in the famous gardens and see Queen Victoria's enormous ballroom. Keep in mind that the 19 staterooms on view are not the rooms where the Royals live, only where they entertain and carry out official duties. The timed-entry tickets are available in advance or on the day of at the ticket kiosk near the palace.

Insider's tip: You can avoid the long queues (sometimes up to an hour) by purchasing tickets in advance by credit card (© **020/7321-2233**), although a £1 ($1.60) service charge is added. Visitors with disabilities can reserve tickets directly through the palace by calling © **020/7930-5526.**

Buckingham Palace's most famous spectacle is the **Changing of the Guard.** The ceremony begins at 11:15am and lasts for half an hour. It's one of the finest examples of military pageantry you'll ever see. The new guard, marching behind a band, comes from either the Wellington or Chelsea barracks and takes over from the old guard in the forecourt of the palace. The guard changes daily from April through July, every other day for the rest of the year. The ceremony may be abruptly canceled during "uncertain" weather conditions. Always consult tourist information offices or local publications for schedules before arriving.

The Royal Mews ✈, also on Buckingham Palace Road, is one of the finest working stables in the world today. Gilded and polished state carriages, such as the gold state coach used at every coronation since 1831, are housed here, along with the horses that draw them.

In 2002, as part of her Golden Jubilee celebrations (generally regarded as a public-relations dud), Queen Elizabeth reopened the **Queen's Gallery** ✈. In the newly redesigned galleries you can see paintings and precious objects from the enormous Royal art collection. Items on display change throughout the year.

The Mall, SW1. © **020/7389-1377.** 020/7799-2331 recorded info, 020/7321-2233 credit-card bookings, or 020/7839-1377 for visitors with disabilities. www.royalresidences.com. State Rooms £12 ($19) adults, £10 ($16) seniors, £6 ($10) under-17s, £30 ($48) family ticket. Aug 1–Sept 28 daily 9:30am–4:15pm (last admission 3:15pm). Royal Mews £5 ($8) adults, £4 ($6) seniors, £2.50 ($4) under-17s, £12.50 ($20) family ticket. Mar–July 11am–4pm (last admission 3:15pm); Aug–Sept 10am–5pm (last admission 4:15pm). Queen's Gallery £6.50 ($10), £5 ($8) over 60 and student, £3 ($4.80) under 17. Daily 10am–5:30pm (last admission 4:30pm). Changing of the Guard free (call © **020/7799-2331** for recorded information). Tube: St. James's Park, Green Park, or Victoria.

Houses of Parliament ✈✈   The Houses of Parliament, along with their trademark clock tower, are quintessential symbols of London. They're the strongholds of Britain's democracy, the assemblies that effectively trimmed the sails of royal power. Both the House of Commons and the House of Lords are in the former royal Palace of Westminster, the king's residence until Henry VIII moved to Whitehall. The current Gothic Revival buildings date from 1840 and were designed by Charles Barry. (The earlier buildings were destroyed by fire in 1834.) Assisting Barry was A. W. N. Pugin, who designed the paneled ceilings, tiled floors, stained glass, clocks, fireplaces, umbrella stands, and even the inkwells. There are more than 1,000 rooms and 3km (2 miles) of corridors.

The clock tower at the eastern end houses the world's most famous timepiece. **"Big Ben"** refers not to the clock tower itself, but to the largest bell in the chime, which weighs close to 14 tons.

You may observe parliamentary debates from the Stranger's Galleries in both houses. Sessions usually begin in mid-October and run to the end of July, with recesses at Christmas and Easter. The debates in the House of Commons are often lively and controversial (seats are at a premium during crises). The chances of getting into the House of Lords when it's in session are generally better than for the more popular House of Commons, where even the queen isn't allowed. Under Tony Blair's New Labour government, the 600 peers in the House of Lords lost their hereditary posts and were replaced by "people's peers" (considered by many Londoners to be as useless as the old peers). If you want to attend a session, line up at Stephen's Gate, heading to your left for the entrance into the Commons or to the right for the Lords. The London daily newspapers announce sessions of Parliament.

Both houses are open to the general public for 75-minute **guided tours** only during a limited period each year (July 26–Aug 30 and Sept 19–Oct 5). Tickets can be booked through Firstcall (© **0870/906-3773;** www.firstcalltickets.com), and cost £7 ($11). You must be there 10 minutes before your tour begins.

Westminster Palace, Old Palace Yard, SW1. House of Commons © 020/7219-3000. House of Lords © 020/7219-3107. www.parliament.uk. Free admission, subject to recess and sitting times. House of Commons: Mon 1:30–8:30pm, Tues–Wed 11:30am–7:30pm, Thurs–Fri 9:30am–3pm. House of Lords: Mon–Wed from 2:30pm, Thurs and occasionally Fri from 11am. Queue at St. Stephen's entrance, near the statue of Oliver Cromwell. Tube: Westminster.

Kensington Palace Located at the western edge of Kensington Gardens, Kensington Palace was acquired by William and Mary in 1689 and remodeled by Sir Christopher Wren. George II, who died in 1760, was the last king to use it as a royal residence. Princess Diana lived here when in London; the area in front of the palace drew tens of thousands of mourners after her death.

You can tour the main **State Apartments** of the palace, but many rooms are private and still lived in by lesser Royals. One of the more interesting chambers to visit is Queen Victoria's bedroom, where, on the morning of June 20, 1837, she was aroused from her sleep with the news that she had succeeded to the throne, following the death of her uncle, William IV. She was 18 years old. As you wander through the apartments, you'll see many fine paintings from the Royal Collection. A special attraction is the **Royal Ceremonial Dress Collection,** which shows restored rooms from the 19th century, including Victoria's birth room and a series of settings with the appropriate court dress of the day. Several of Diana's famous frocks are on display, as are the dowdier frocks worn by Queen Elizabeth II.

Kensington Gardens adjoins Hyde Park. On the southern edge stands the recently restored **Albert Memorial,** honoring Queen Victoria's consort.

Fun Fact **The Lowdown on Big Ben**

Just as the Eiffel Tower is the symbol of Paris, Big Ben is the international icon of London. Completed in 1858 and 1859, the 95m (316-ft.) clock reputedly takes its name from Sir Benjamin Hall, the first commissioner of public works and evidently a gentleman of considerable proportions. The clock mechanism in this tower alone weighs 5 tons. Big Ben kept time for 117 years before succumbing to "metal fatigue" in 1976, at which time major repairs were needed to keep it running. When the House of Commons is in session, the light above the clock is lit.

(*Value* **Cheap Thrills: What to See & Do for Free (or Almost) in London**

Visit museums. London's greatest museums are now free. The world-class treasure troves where you can now roam for free include the British Museum, National Gallery, National Portrait Gallery, Tate Britain, Tate Modern, Natural History Museum, Science Museum, Victoria & Albert Museum, Museum of London, and Sir John Soane's Museum. And don't forget the British Library, with its marvelous collection of literary gems.

Watch the changing of the guard. This Buckingham Palace event has more pomp and circumstance than any other royal ceremony on earth.

Explore Hampstead Heath. Take the Tube north to Hampstead for the most delightful ramble in London, following in the footsteps of Keats and other luminaries. The heath's near-wilderness feel is a delicious contrast to London's other manicured parks. Drop in later for a pint at a local pub.

Take in a spectacular city view. Take the Tube to Tower Hill or Tower Gateway, then cross Tower Bridge. Wander along the south bank of the mighty Thames at night and gaze upon London's historic landmarks and skyscrapers, floodlit in all their evening spectacle and finery.

Soak up the scene in Regent's Park. Once the exclusive hunting grounds of royalty, it's now used by everybody from footballers to barefoot couples in summer. Regent's Park is home to the London Zoo, the Open Air Theatre's Shakespeare in the Park, the Prince Regent's original grand terraces, and Queen Mary's rose gardens.

Go to Court at the Old Bailey Public Gallery, Warwick Passage. Britain's Central Criminal Court, or the "Old Bailey," was built on the foundations of the infamous Newgate Gaol. These courtrooms have seen it all, from Oscar Wilde to the Yorkshire Ripper (but never Jack). Robed and bewigged barristers and judges still administer justice with much formality and theatricality.

Attend a poetry reading at Royal Festival Hall. Part of the creatively fertile London Arts Centre Project, The Voice Box (① **020/7921-0906**; Tube: Waterloo) stages poetry and prose readings, usually by celebrated writers. Admission is £2.50 ($4) for adults and from £2 ($3.20) for students. For a schedule, check a free copy of the "Literature Quarterly" brochure. Next door is the Poetry Library (① **020/7921-0943**), Britain's largest collection of 20th-century poetry. Membership is free, but you must bring a current ID. It's open Tuesday through Sunday from 11am to 8pm.

The Broad Walk, Kensington Gardens, W8. ① **020/7937-9561**. www.hrp.org.uk. Admission £10 ($16) adults, £7.50 ($12) seniors and students, £6.50 ($10) children 5-16, £28 ($45) family. Mar–Oct daily 10am–5pm; Nov–Feb daily 10am–4pm. Tube: Queensway or Bayswater on the north side of the gardens; High St. Kensington on the south side; then you'll have a long walk.

National Gallery ★★★   In an impressive neoclassical building, the National Gallery houses one of the most comprehensive collections of Western paintings, representing all the major schools from the late 13th to the early 20th centuries. The largest part of the collection is devoted to the Italians, including the Sienese, Venetian, and Florentine masters, housed in the Sainsbury (West) Wing.

A Florentine gem by Masaccio is displayed, as well as notable works by Piero della Francesca, Leonardo da Vinci, Michelangelo, and Raphael. Among the 16th-century Venetian masters, the most notable works include a rare *Adoration of the Kings* by Giorgione, *Bacchus and Ariadne* by Titian, *The Origin of the Milky Way* by Tintoretto, and *The Family of Darius Before Alexander* by Veronese. Adjoining rooms are filled with works by major Italian masters of the 15th century, such as Giovanni Bellini, Mantegna, and Botticelli.

The painters of northern Europe are well represented. Of the early Gothic works, the Wilton Diptych (French or English school, late 14th c.) is the rarest treasure; it depicts Richard II being introduced to the Madonna and Child by John the Baptist and Edward the Confessor. Jan van Eyck's portrait of G. Arnolfini and bride and Brueghel the Elder's Bosch-like *Adoration* are shown. The National has a fine collection of Rembrandts; his *Self-Portrait at the Age of 34* shows him in the prime of his life, while his *Self-Portrait at the Age of 63* is deeply moving and revealing.

Five of the greatest homegrown artists—Constable, Turner, Reynolds, Gainsborough, and Hogarth—have masterpieces here, as do three Spanish giants. Velázquez's portrait of the sunken-faced Philip IV, El Greco's *Christ Driving the Traders from the Temple,* and Goya's portraits of the duke of Wellington and the mantilla-wearing *Doña Isabel de Porcel* are all masterworks.

Other rooms offer early-19th-century French painters (Delacroix and Ingres), later 19th-century Impressionists (Manet, Monet, Renoir, and Degas), and post-Impressionists (Cézanne, Seurat, and van Gogh).

Insider's tip: The National Gallery has a computer information center, located in the Micro Gallery in the Sainsbury Wing, where visitors can design a free personal tour map. You can eat at the upscale **Crivelli's Garden Restaurant and Italian Bar** (✆ **020/7747-2869**) in the Sainsbury Wing or in the self-service Gallery Café in the basement of the main building.

Trafalgar Sq., WC2. ✆ 020/7747-2885. www.nationalgallery.org.uk. Free admission. Daily 10am–6pm; Wed 10am–9pm. Free guided tours daily 11:30am and 2:30pm. Closed Jan 1 and Dec 24–26. Tube: Charing Cross, Embankment, or Leicester Sq.

Natural History Museum ⭐⭐ *Kids*   It roars. It opens its jaws and moves its head. And it's the biggest hit the museum has ever had: a **robotic Tyrannosaurus Rex** hovering over a fresh dino-kill. It's worth a trip just to watch the 4m- (12-ft.-) tall toothy beast, driven by motion sensors, react to the appearance of each new human meal (not suitable for young kids). Before you see "T" you'll encounter two cunning-looking animatronic raptors eyeing you from atop a perch. All this takes place in a Victorian hall full of **dinosaur skeletons** and exhibitions about the life of the 'saurs. Head to the **Earth Galleries** for the earthquake and volcano simulations that hint at the terror of the real thing. Kids also love the slithery and slimy critters in the **Creepie-Crawlies** exhibit.

Sir Hans Sloane was such a prolific collector that his treasures overflowed the British Museum. Hence the decision to build this palatial building (1881) fit "for housing the works of the Creator." Yet it, too, can display only a fraction of its animal, vegetable, and mineral specimens. An exciting project is set to revolutionize all that, opening both the storerooms and the science labs, with their 300 white-coated experts, to public view. The £28 million first phase of the Darwin Centre opened in summer 2002.

Moments **St. Paul's in the Spring**

If you visit London in the spring, take a stroll through St. Paul's free gardens when the roses are in bloom.

Cromwell Rd., S. Kensington, SW7. © 020/7938-9123. www.nhm.ac.uk. Admission free. Mon–Sat 10am–5:50pm; Sun 11am–5:50pm. Closed Dec 23–26. Guided 45-min. tours daily £3 ($5) adults, [b]1.50 ($2.40) children. Tube: South Kensington.

St. Paul's Cathedral ✿ During World War II, newsreel footage showed the dome of St. Paul's Cathedral lit by fires caused by German bombings. That it survived at all is a miracle: It was badly hit twice during the early years of the Blitz. Then again, St. Paul's is accustomed to calamity, having been burned down three times and destroyed once by invading Norsemen. After the Great Fire of 1666, the old St. Paul's was razed, making way for a new Renaissance structure designed (after many mishaps and rejections) by Sir Christopher Wren and built between 1675 and 1710. It is an Anglican cathedral, and was the site of Princess Diana's wedding to Prince Charles in 1981.

The classical dome of St. Paul's dominates the City's square mile. Inside, the cathedral is laid out like a Greek cross; it houses few art treasures (Grinling Gibbons's choir stalls excepted) but many monuments, including one to the duke of Wellington and a memorial chapel to American service personnel who lost their lives in World War II while stationed in the United Kingdom. Encircling the dome is the Whispering Gallery, so be careful what you say. You can climb to the very top of the dome for a spectacular 360-degree view of London. In the crypt lie not only Wren but also Wellington and Lord Nelson. A fascinating Diocesan Treasury was opened in 1981.

Guided "Supertours" last 1½ hours and include parts of the cathedral not open to the general public. They take place Monday through Saturday at 11am, 11:30am, 1:30pm, and 2pm and cost £2.50 ($4) adults, £2 ($3.20) seniors and students, and £1 ($1.60) children, plus the regular admission fee. Audio tours lasting 45 minutes are available until 3pm; they cost £3.50 ($6) for adults, £3 ($4.80) seniors and students.

St. Paul's Churchyard, EC4. © 020/7236-4128. www.stpauls.co.uk. Cathedral £6 ($10) adults, £5 ($8) seniors and students, £3 ($4.80) children 6–16, free for children 5 and under. Sightseeing Mon–Sat 8:30am–4pm. No sightseeing Sun (services only). Tube: St. Paul's.

Science Museum ✿✿✿ *Kids* This is one of the best science museums in the world. The striking new £45 million ($28 million) **Wellcome Wing** houses six new exhibitions presenting the latest developments in science, medicine, and technology. Find out what the kids might look like in 30 years in the *Who am I?* gallery. For a more intimate portrait, check out the gory digital cross-sections in *The Visible Human Project.* This is fantasyland for gadget geeks, who'll love all the interactivity. There's a 450-seat IMAX cinema on the first floor and another huge new gallery, **Making the Modern World,** links the Wellcome Wing to the old museum. Using some of the most iconic treasures of the permanent collection—the Apollo 10 space capsule, an early train known as Stephenson's Rocket, and a fleece from famous Scottish clone, Dolly the Sheep—it charts 250 years of technological discoveries and their effects on our culture.

The new galleries are stunning, but don't let them dazzle you into forgetting the rest of this marvelous museum. It is home to many pioneering machines:

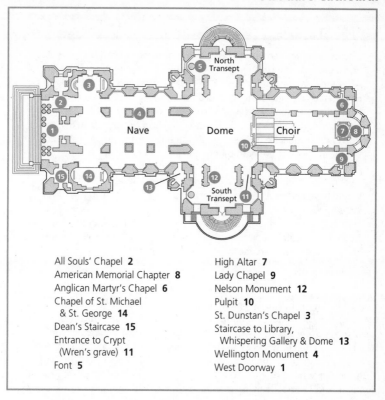

All Souls' Chapel **2**
American Memorial Chapter **8**
Anglican Martyr's Chapel **6**
Chapel of St. Michael
  & St. George **14**
Dean's Staircase **15**
Entrance to Crypt
  (Wren's grave) **11**
Font **5**

High Altar **7**
Lady Chapel **9**
Nelson Monument **12**
Pulpit **10**
St. Dunstan's Chapel **3**
Staircase to Library,
  Whispering Gallery & Dome **13**
Wellington Monument **4**
West Doorway **1**

Arkwright's spinning machine, for instance, and the Vickers "Vimy" aircraft, which made the first Atlantic crossing in 1919. The basement is dedicated to children, with water, construction, sound and light shows, and games. Although the museum introduced free admission in December 2001, it does still charge for shows at the IMAX and rides on its two simulators.

Exhibition Rd., SW7. © 020/7938-8000. www.sciencemuseum.org.uk. Free admission. Daily 10am–6pm. Tube: S. Kensington.

Tate Britain ⭐⭐⭐ The new Tate Modern at Bankside hogs most of the limelight, but the shifting around of the Tate collections has also seen a huge overhaul at the original gallery, founded in 1897. The refurbished Tate Britain reopened in November 2001 with more exhibition space and a suite of airy new galleries. Having handed International Modernism over to Bankside, Tate Britain now concentrates on British work dating back to 1500. It ditched the chronological displays for a thematic approach. **Art Now** focuses on new media and experimental work by foreign artists living in London and Brits based here and abroad; **Private and Public** includes portraits and scenes of daily life; **Artists and Models** explores nudes and self-portraiture; **Literature and Fantasy** is for visionary artists such as William Blake and Stanley Spencer; and **Home and Abroad** looks at the landscape artist at home and abroad. Juxtaposing very different kinds of work isn't always successful, but the vibrancy of the place can't help but give you a rush. Important artists, like Gainsborough,

The Wren Style

One of the great geniuses of his age, Sir Christopher Wren (1632–1723) was a professor of astronomy at Oxford before becoming an architect. After the Great Fire of London in 1666, Wren was chosen to rebuild the devastated city and its many churches, including St. Paul's, on which work began in 1675. His designs had great originality and he became known for groundbreaking spatial effects in his visionary fusion of classical and baroque. He believed in classical stability and repose, yet liked to enliven his churches with baroque whimsy and fantasy.

In our view his crowning glory is his dome over St. Paul's, which is celebrated for the beauty of its proportions. Surely Michelangelo would have patted Wren on the back. If during his stay in France Wren stole an idea or two from the Invalides in Paris, well, we'll never tell. Nothing better represents the Wren style than the facade of St. Paul's, in which he combined classical columns, looking almost like Greek temples, with baroque decorations and adornments.

Constable, Hogarth, and Hockney, get their own rooms, which should pacify the traditionalists. The illustrations of mystical poet-artist William Blake for such works as *The Book of Job, The Divine Comedy,* and *Paradise Lost* are here, too. The collection of works by J. M. W. Turner is its largest collection of works by a single artist; Turner himself willed most of the paintings here to the nation.

In the modern collections are works by Matisse, Dalí, Modigliani, Munch, Bonnard, and Picasso. Truly remarkable are the several enormous abstract canvases by Mark Rothko, the group of paintings and sculptures by Giacometti, and the paintings of one of England's best-known modern artists, Francis Bacon. Sculptures by Henry Moore and Barbara Hepworth are also displayed.

Insider's tip: After you've seen all the grand art, don't hasten away so quickly. Drop in to the Tate Britain Shop for some of the best art books and the most high-quality printed postcards in London. Or take tea at the Coffee Shop with its excellent cakes and pastries, or lunch at the Tate Gallery Restaurant (see p. 120 in "Where to Dine," in chapter 3), where you get to enjoy good food, Rex Whistler art, and the best and most reasonably priced wine list in London.

Millbank, SW1. © 020/7887-8000. www.tate.org.uk. Free admission; special exhibitions sometimes incur a charge varying from £6.50–£8.50 ($10–$14). Daily 10:30am–5:50pm. Closed Dec 24–26. Tube: Vauxhall. River service: Millbank Pier.

Tate Modern ★★★ The Tate Modern, London's new and wildly popular cathedral of modern art, occupies the defunct Bankside Power Station on the South Bank of the Thames opposite St. Paul's Cathedral. You enter the huge old turbine hall, left empty, and three floors of galleries where the work is arranged thematically rather than chronologically: **Landscape/Matter/Environment, Still Life/Object/Real Life, History/Memory/Society,** and **Nude/Action/Body.** In some rooms, paintings are next to sculptures next to installations. Others are devoted to a single artist—like the marvelous Joseph Beuys sculptures. The display concept is certainly challenging, but the themes often seem spurious, lacking the quirky spirit of a mixed private collection where one person's taste is the guide.

There's no such thing as a flash visit to Tate Modern. Set aside half a day if you can. Free guided tours start daily at 10:30am, 11:30am, 2:30pm, and 3:30pm, each focusing on one of the four themes. Be sure to go up to the glass-roofed level seven to see the spectacular views across the Thames. The cafe there is often mobbed so time your visit for early mealtimes. It is also open for dinner until 9:30pm on Friday and Saturday but doesn't take bookings.

25 Sumner St., SE1. © 020/7887-8000. www.tate.org.uk. Free admission. Temporary exhibitions £5.50–£8.50 ($9–$14). Sun–Thurs 10am–6pm; Fri–Sat 10am–8pm. Tube: Southwark, Mansion House, or St. Paul's. River services: Bankside Pier.

The Tower of London ★★★   This is the most perfectly preserved medieval fortress in Britain and you'll need at least 2 or 3 hours for your visit. Over the centuries, the Tower has served as a palace and royal refuge; a prison, military base, and supplies depot; home to the Royal Mint and the Royal Observatory; and finally a national monument. The oldest part is the massive **White Tower,** built in 1078 by the Norman king, William the Conqueror, to protect London and discourage rebellion among his new Saxon subjects. Every king after him added to the main structure, so that when Edward I completed the outer walls in the late 13th century, they enclosed a 7-hectare (18-acre) square. Walk round the top of them for a bird's-eye view of how the Tower of London would have looked when it was in use.

The **Crown Jewels,** glittering in the Jewel House in Waterloo Barracks, are the real must-see. Here you'll see the Imperial State Crown, encrusted with 3,200 precious stones, including a 317-carat diamond. **The Chapel Royal of St. Peter ad Vincula** contains the graves of all the unfortunates executed at the Tower. The Scaffold Site, where the axeman dispatched seven of the highest-ranking victims, including Henry VIII's wives Anne Boleyn and Catherine Howard, is just outside. Everyone else met their end on **Tower Green** after arriving by boat at **Traitors' Gate.** The **Bloody Tower** was where Richard of Gloucester locked up his young nephews while he usurped his crusading brother Edward IV. The princes' bodies were later mysteriously found by the White Tower. Today, an exhibit recreates how Sir Walter Raleigh might have lived during his 13-year imprisonment after the Gunpowder Plot against James I.

The royal menagerie moved out in 1834 to form the new London Zoo—all except the **ravens.** Legend has it Charles II was told that if they ever left the Tower the monarchy would fall. Ever since, a few birds with clipped wings have been kept in a lodging next to Wakefield Tower, looked after by a yeoman warder. The **yeoman warders,** or Beefeaters, have guarded the Tower for centuries. Now usually retired soldiers, they lead tours every half-hour from 9:30am to 3:30pm and give vivid talks at 9:30, 10:15, 11:30am, 2:15, 4:30, and 5:15pm (the 1st one on Sun is at 10:30am). Costumed guides also recreate historic happenings.

Insider's tip: The Tower of London has an evening ritual called the **Ceremony of the Keys,** the locking up of the Tower. The Yeoman Warder will explain to

---

⟨ Tips Time-Saving Tower Tips

A few ways to avoid the notoriously long lines at the Tower of London: Purchase your admission ticket in a kiosk at any Tube station before emerging above ground. Also, it's best to go early; the hordes descend in the afternoon. Arrive the moment the gates open—and try to avoid Sundays, when crowds are awful.

guests the ceremony's significance. For free tickets, write to the Ceremony of the Keys, Waterloo Block, Tower of London, London EC3N 4AB, and request a specific date (but also list alternative dates). At least 6 weeks' notice is required. All requests must be accompanied by a self-addressed stamped envelope (British stamps only) or two International Reply Coupons. With ticket in hand, you'll be admitted by a Yeoman Warder at 9:35pm.

Tower Hill, EC3. (℃) **0870/756-6060**, or 0870/756-7070 (box office). www.hrp.org.uk. Admission £11.50 ($18) adults, £8.75 ($14) seniors and students, £7.50 ($12) children, free for children under 5, £34 ($54) family. Mar–Oct Tues–Sat 9am–6pm, Sun–Mon 10am–6pm; Nov–Feb Tues–Sat 9am–5pm, Sun–Mon 10am–5pm. Last tickets sold 1 hr. before closing. Closed Dec 24–26 and Jan 1. Tube: Tower Hill. Boats: From Westminster Pier.

Trafalgar Square ⭐   One of London's greatest landmarks, Trafalgar Square honors England's great military hero Horatio, Viscount Nelson (1758–1805). Lord Nelson was a hero of the Battle of Calvi, where he lost an eye; the Battle of Santa Cruz, where he lost an arm; and the Battle of Trafalgar, where he lost his life. A statue of Nelson stands atop a 44m (145-ft.) granite column, created by E. H. Baily in 1843, in the center of the square. The column looks down Whitehall toward the Old Admiralty, where Nelson's body lay in state. The figure of the naval hero towers 5m (17 ft.) high—not bad for a man who stood 5 feet 4 inches. Queen Victoria's favorite animal painter, Sir Edward Landseer, added the four lions at the column base in 1868. The pools and fountains, Sir Edwin Lutyens' last work, were added in 1939.

Sir Charles Barry, designer of the Houses of Parliament, created the present square in the 1830s. It has just received a much-welcomed makeover that connects it to the National Gallery so that visitors no longer have to cross a street roaring with traffic to reach it. Still a favorite spot for political demonstrations, it's also the site of two London traditions: the giant Christmas tree installed every December (an annual gift from Norway to the British people, as thanks for sheltering its royal family during World War II) and the raucous celebrations on New Year's Eve.

To the southeast of the square, at 36 Craven St., stands a house Benjamin Franklin occupied when he was a general of the Philadelphia Academy (1757–74). To the north rises the National Gallery, built in the 1830s; in front of the building is a copy of a J. A. Houdon statue of George Washington. To the left of St. Martin's Place is the National Portrait Gallery, a collection of British greats (and not-so-greats). Also on the square is the landmark St. Martin-in-the-Fields by James Gibbs, with its towering steeple—the resting place of Sir Joshua Reynolds, William Hogarth, and Thomas Chippendale.

At the intersection of Pall Mall and Charing Cross Rd. Tube: Charing Cross.

Victoria and Albert Museum ⭐⭐⭐ *(Moments)*   The Victoria and Albert is the greatest museum in the world devoted to the decorative arts. It's also one of the liveliest and most imaginative museums in London—where else would you find the quintessential "little black dress" in the permanent collection?

The medieval holdings include such treasures as the early-English Gloucester Candlestick; the Byzantine Veroli Casket, with its ivory panels based on Greek plays; and the Syon Cope, a highly valued embroidery made in England in the early 14th century. An area devoted to Islamic art houses the Ardabil Carpet from 16th-century Persia.

The V&A houses the largest collection of Renaissance sculpture outside Italy. A highlight of the 16th-century collection is the marble group Neptune with Triton by Bernini. The cartoons by Raphael, which were conceived as designs

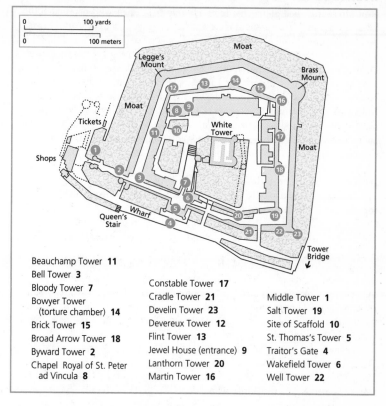

0 | 100 yards
0 | 100 meters

Moat

Legge's Mount

Brass Mount

Moat

Tickets

White Tower

Moat

Shops

Wharf

Queen's Stair

Tower Bridge ↓

Beauchamp Tower **11**
Bell Tower **3**
Bloody Tower **7**
Bowyer Tower
  (torture chamber) **14**
Brick Tower **15**
Broad Arrow Tower **18**
Byward Tower **2**
Chapel Royal of St. Peter
  ad Vincula **8**

Constable Tower **17**
Cradle Tower **21**
Develin Tower **23**
Devereux Tower **12**
Flint Tower **13**
Jewel House (entrance) **9**
Lanthorn Tower **20**
Martin Tower **16**

Middle Tower **1**
Salt Tower **19**
Site of Scaffold **10**
St. Thomas's Tower **5**
Traitor's Gate **4**
Wakefield Tower **6**
Well Tower **22**

for tapestries for the Sistine Chapel, are owned by the queen and on display here. A most unusual, huge, and impressive exhibit is the Cast Courts, life-size plaster models of ancient and medieval statuary and architecture.

The museum has the greatest collection of Indian art outside India, plus Chinese and Japanese galleries as well. In complete contrast are suites of English furniture, metalwork, and ceramics, and a superb collection of portrait miniatures, including the one Hans Holbein the Younger made of Anne of Cleves for the benefit of Henry VIII, who was again casting around for a suitable wife. The Dress Collection includes a collection of corsetry through the ages that's sure to make you wince. There's also a remarkable collection of musical instruments.

In 2001, the V&A opened 15 new galleries—called The British Galleries—unfolding the story of British design from 1500 to 1900. From Chippendale to Morris, all of the top British designers are featured in some 3,000 exhibits ranging from 19th-century furniture by Charles Rennie Mackintosh to the "Great Bed of Ware," mentioned in Shakespeare's *Twelfth Night.*

Cromwell Rd., SW7. ℂ 020/7942-2000. www.vam.ac.uk. Free admission. Thurs–Tues 10am–5:45pm; Wed and last Fri each month 10am–10pm. Closed Dec 24–26. Tube: S. Kensington.

Westminster Abbey ★★★ Nearly every figure in English history has left his or her mark on Westminster Abbey. The Saxon king Edward the Confessor took over a Benedictine abbey and rebuilt the old minster church on this spot, overlooking Parliament Square. The first king crowned here was Harold (1066), who soon afterwards died at the Battle of Hastings; the man who defeated him, Edward's cousin William, was also crowned at the abbey. The coronation tradition has continued to the present day, broken only twice (Edward V and Edward VIII). In September 1997, the abbey served as the setting for the funeral of Diana, Princess of Wales and, in 2002, for that of the Queen Mother.

Built on the site of the ancient Lady Chapel in the early 16th century, the **Henry VII Chapel** 🟊🟊🟊 is one of the loveliest in Europe, with its fan vaulting, Knights of Bath banners, and tomb of the king. His feuding granddaughters, half-sisters Mary I and Elizabeth I, are, ironically, buried in the same tomb. Elizabeth's archrival, Mary Queen of Scots, is entombed on the other side of the chapel. In one end of the chapel, you can stand on Cromwell's memorial stone and view the Royal Air Force chapel and its Battle of Britain memorial stained-glass window, unveiled in 1947 to honor the RAF.

The most hallowed spot in the abbey is the **Chapel of Edward the Confessor** 🟊🟊, who was canonized in the 12th century. In the saint's chapel sits the Coronation Chair, made at Edward I's behest in 1300 to display the Stone of Scone, upon which Scottish kings were formerly crowned. Seized by the English in 1296, the stone was returned to Scotland in 1998.

The crowded **Poets' Corner** 🟊, in the back of the South Transept, has monuments to everybody—Chaucer, Shakespeare, Ben Jonson, Milton, Samuel Johnson, Austen, Coleridge, Wordsworth, the Brontës, Thackeray, Dickens, Tennyson, Kipling, Dylan Thomas, and even an American—Longfellow. The most stylized monument is Sir Jacob Epstein's bust of William Blake. Chaucer and Jonson are among the few actually buried here.

Statesmen and men of science such as Disraeli, Newton, Watt, Faraday, and Darwin are interred or honored by monuments here. Near the west door are the **1965 Sir Winston Churchill Memorial** and the **Tomb of the Unknown Warrior,** commemorating the British who died in World War I. Totally obscure personages are buried here too, including one of the abbey's plumbers.

Off the Cloisters, the **College Garden** (open Tues–Thurs) is the oldest garden in England, under cultivation for more than 900 years. Surrounded by high walls that dull the roar of passing traffic, its flowering trees dot the lawns while its park benches provide comfort.

Up to six 90-minute tours of the abbey are conducted by the vergers Monday through Saturday, beginning at 10am and costing £3 ($4.80) per person.

Insider's tip: Far removed from the pomp and glory of this edifice is the **Abbey Museum** and its bag of oddities. It's located in the undercroft (or crypt), part of the monastic buildings erected between 1066 and 1100. Here are the effigies used instead of the real corpses for lying-in-state ceremonies. You'll see the almost lifelike effigies of Admiral Nelson (his mistress arranged his hair) and Edward III, his lip warped by the stroke that felled him. Other treats include a Middle English lease to Chaucer, the much-used sword of Henry VI, and the Essex Ring Elizabeth I gave to her favorite earl (before she changed her mind about him). *Note:* Both the Pyx Chamber (where samples of coins were kept while they awaited tests for purity) and Abbey Museum were closed as of press time, but will hopefully reopen in 2004.

Broad Sanctuary, SW1. ☎ 020/7222-5152. www.westminster-abbey.org. Admission £6 ($10) adults, £3 ($4.80) seniors, students, and children 11–18, free for children under 11. Mon–Fri 9am–4:45pm; Sat 9:30am–2:45pm; last admission 1 hr. before closing. Open Sun for worship only. Chapter House, Pyx Chamber, and Abbey Museum [b]2.50 ($4) adults, £1.90 ($3) seniors and students, £1.30 ($2) children under 16; reduced with Abbey admission, free with guided and audio tour. Chapter House, Apr–Sept 9:30am–5:30pm;

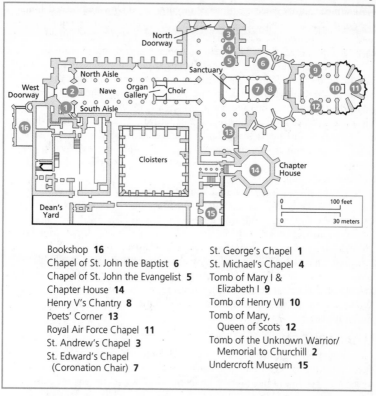

Bookshop **16**
Chapel of St. John the Baptist **6**
Chapel of St. John the Evangelist **5**
Chapter House **14**
Henry V's Chantry **8**
Poets' Corner **13**
Royal Air Force Chapel **11**
St. Andrew's Chapel **3**
St. Edward's Chapel
 (Coronation Chair) **7**

St. George's Chapel **1**
St. Michael's Chapel **4**
Tomb of Mary I &
 Elizabeth I **9**
Tomb of Henry VII **10**
Tomb of Mary,
 Queen of Scots **12**
Tomb of the Unknown Warrior/
 Memorial to Churchill **2**
Undercroft Museum **15**

Oct 10am–5pm; Nov–Mar 10am–4pm. Pyx Chamber and Abbey Museum daily 10:30am–4pm. Cloister 8am–6pm. College Garden Apr–Sept Tues–Thurs 10am–6pm; Oct–Mar 10am–4pm. St. Margaret's Church Mon–Fri 9:30am–3:45pm; Sat 9:30am–1:45pm; Sun 2–5pm. Tube: Westminster or St. James's Park.

2 More Attractions

OFFICIAL LONDON

Whitehall, seat of the British government, grew up on the grounds of White-hall Palace, which was turned into a royal residence by Henry VIII after he snatched it from Cardinal Wolsey. Whitehall extends south from Trafalgar Square to Parliament Square. Along it you'll find the Home Office, the Old Admiralty Building, and the Ministry of Defence.

Visit the fascinating **Cabinet War Rooms,** a bombproof bunker suite of rooms left as they were when abandoned by Winston Churchill and the British government at the end of World War II. Visitors receive a step-by-step personal sound guide, providing a detailed account of each room's function and history.

The entrance to the War Rooms is by Clive Steps at the end of King Charles Street, SW1 (© **020/7766-0121**), off Whitehall near Big Ben. Admission is £5.80 ($9) for adults, £4.20 ($7) for seniors and students, and free for children 16 and under. Open from April to September daily 9:30am to 6pm, October through March daily 10am to 5:30pm, last admission 5:15pm; closed during Christmas holidays. Tube: Westminster, St. James's.

An armed security gate now protects the entrance to **Downing Street,** so all you can do is peek through the railings to get a glimpse of the modest little town house at no. 10. Walpole was the first prime minister to live here, Churchill the most famous, but Margaret Thatcher was around longer than any of them.

Nearby, north of Downing Street, is the **Horse Guards Building** ✮, Whitehall (© **020/7414-2396;** Tube: Westminster), now headquarters of the horse guards of the Household Division and London District. There has been a guard changing here since 1649, when the site was the entrance to old Whitehall Palace. You can watch the Queen's Life Guards ceremony at 11am Monday through Saturday (10:30am Sun), or see the hourly smaller change of the guard, when mounted troopers are changed. At 4pm you can watch the evening inspection, when 10 unmounted troopers and two mounted troopers assemble in the courtyard.

Across the street is Inigo Jones's **Banqueting House** ✮✮, Palace of Whitehall, Horse Guards Avenue (© **020/7930-4179;** Tube: Westminster, Charing Cross, or Embankment). Admission is £4 ($6) for adults, £3 ($4.80) for seniors and students, and £2.60 ($4) for children (ages 5–16). Open Monday through Saturday from 10am to 5pm (last admission 4:30pm). Site of the execution of Charles I, William and Mary also accepted the crown of England here, but preferred to live at Kensington Palace. The Banqueting House is all that's left of Whitehall Palace, which burned to the ground in 1698. The most notable feature of this ceremonial hall is an allegorical ceiling painted by Peter Paul Rubens.

LEGAL LONDON

The smallest borough in London, bustling Holborn (pronounced *Ho*-burn), is often referred to as Legal London, home of the city's barristers, solicitors, and law clerks; it also embraces Bloomsbury. Holborn, which houses the ancient **Inns of Courts**—Gray's Inn, Lincoln's Inn, Middle Temple, and Inner Temple—was severely damaged during the Blitz. The razed buildings were replaced with modern offices, but the borough retains pockets of its former days.

Some 60 or more Law Courts are found at **The Strand** (Tube: Holborn, Temple), presently in use, where all civil and some criminal cases are heard. Admission is free. The courts are open during sessions Monday to Friday from 10am to 4:30pm. No cameras, tape recorders, video cameras, or cellular phones are allowed during sessions. Designed by G. E. Street, the neo-Gothic buildings (1874–82) contain more than 1,000 rooms and 6km (3½ miles) of corridors. Sculptures of Christ, King Solomon, and King Alfred grace the front door; Moses stands at the back entrance.

The court known as the **Old Bailey,** on Newgate Street, EC4 (© **020/7248-3277**), replaced the infamous Newgate Prison, site for public hangings and other "public entertainments." Take the Tube to Temple, Chancery Lane, or St. Paul's. Travel east on Fleet Street, which becomes Ludgate Hill. Cross Ludgate Circus and turn left to the Old Bailey, a domed structure with the figure of Justice standing atop it. Admission is free; children under 14 are not admitted; ages 14 to 16 must be accompanied by an adult. No cameras or tape recorders are allowed. Hours are Monday to Friday 10:30am to 1pm and 2 to 4:30pm.

It's fascinating to watch the bewigged barristers presenting their cases to the high court judges. Entry is strictly on a first-come basis. Guests queue up outside. Courts 1 to 4, 17, and 18 are entered from Newgate Street, the balance from Old Bailey (the street).

Banqueting House **7**

Buckingham Palace **13**

Cabinet War Rooms **8**

Horse Guards Building **6**

Houses of Parliament **10**

National Gallery **3**

National Portrait Gallery **2**

Nelson's Column **4**

St. Martin-in-the-Fields **1**

Tate Britain **11**

Westminster Abbey **9**

Westminster Cathedral **12**

Whitehall **7**

MORE MUSEUMS & GALLERIES

Apsley House ⭐ This was the town house of the "Iron Duke," Wellington, the British general who defeated Napoleon at Waterloo and later became prime minister. The building was designed by Robert Adam and constructed in the late 18th century. In the vestibule, you'll find a colossal marble statue of Napoleon by Canova presented to the duke by George IV. In addition to the famous *Waterseller of Seville* by Velázquez, the collection includes works by Correggio, Jan Steen, and Pieter de Hooch.

Insider's tip: Apsley House seems an unlikely place for it, but here you'll find some of the finest silver and porcelain in Europe. Grateful to Wellington for saving their thrones, European monarchs endowed him with treasures. Head for the Plate and China Room on the ground floor first. The Sèvres Egyptian service was intended as a divorce present from Napoleon to Josephine, but she refused it; eventually, Louis XVIII of France presented it to the duke. The Portuguese Silver Service in the dining room, created between 1812 and 1816, has been called the single greatest artifact of Portuguese neoclassical silver.

149 Piccadilly, Hyde Park Corner, SW1. (€ 020/7499-5676. www.apsleyhouse.org.uk. Admission £4.50 ($7) adults, £3 ($4.80) seniors, free for children under 18. Tues–Sun 11am-5pm. Closed Jan 1, Good Friday, May 1, and Dec 24–26. Tube: Hyde Park Corner.

British Library ⭐⭐ One of the world's greatest libraries moved its 12 million books, manuscripts, and other rare printed items from the British Museum to a new building at St. Pancras in 1998. The library's fascinating collection of rare books is on display in three special exhibition rooms open free to the public. Here you'll find two of the four surviving copies of King John's Magna Carta, the Gutenberg Bible, the journals of Captain Cook, and Nelson's last letter to Lady Hamilton. You can also see the Diamond Sutra, dating from A.D. 868 and said to be the oldest surviving printed book. Almost every major author—Dickens, Austen, Charlotte Brontë, Keats, and hundreds of others—is represented in the English literature section. Shakespeare documents include a mortgage bearing his signature and a copy of the First Folio of 1623. Using headphones set up around the room, you can listen to thrilling audio snippets, even James Joyce reading a passage from *Finnegan's Wake.* In a fascinating interactive display called "Turning the Pages," you can read a complete Leonardo da Vinci notebook electronically by putting your hands on a computer screen that flips from one page to another. In the Historical Documents section are letters written by everybody from Henry VIII and Elizabeth I to Napoleon and Churchill. In the music displays, you can see scores by Beethoven, Handel, and Stravinsky, and lyric drafts by Lennon and McCartney.

96 Euston Rd., NW1. (€ 020/7412-7332. www.bl.uk. Free admission. Wed–Fri 9:30am–6pm; Tues 9:30am-8pm; Sat 9:30am–5pm; Sun 11am–5pm. Tube: King's Cross/St. Pancras.

Courtauld Gallery See Somerset House, below.

Design Museum Part of the Docklands development, this museum displays manufactured products that have won acclaim, even affection, for their design. The museum's changing exhibitions explain why and how mass-produced objects work and look the way they do, and the importance of design in everyday life. Depending on what's on display, you may see cars (the Volkswagen Bug), furniture (the anglepoise lamp), appliances, graphics, and ceramics. The museum shop has everything from designer socks to sleek alarm clocks.

Butlers Wharf, Shad Thames, South Bank, SE1. (€ 20/7403-6933. www.designmuseum.org. Admission £8 ($13) adults, £4 ($6) seniors and students, £16 ($26) family ticket. Daily 10am–5:45pm. Tube: Tower Hill or London Bridge.

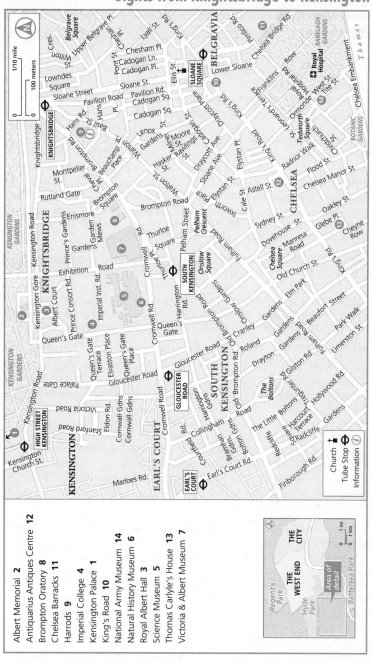

Albert Memorial **2**
Antiquarius Antiques Centre **12**
Brompton Oratory **8**
Chelsea Barracks **11**
Harrods **9**
Imperial College **4**
Kensington Palace **1**
King's Road **10**
National Army Museum **14**
Natural History Museum **6**
Royal Albert Hall **3**
Science Museum **5**
Thomas Carlyle's House **13**
Victoria & Albert Museum **7**

Guildhall Art Gallery ⚡   In 1999 Queen Elizabeth opened a new £70 million gallery in the City, a continuation of the original gallery launched in 1886 that was burned down in a severe air raid in May 1941. Many famous and much-loved pictures that for years were known only through temporary exhibitions and reproductions are once again available for the public to see in a permanent setting. The new gallery can display only 250 of the 4,000 treasures it owns. A curiosity is the huge double-height wall built to accommodate Britain's largest independent oil painting, John Singleton Copley's *The Defeat of the Floating Batteries at Gibraltar, September 1782.* The Corporation of London in the City owns these works, and has been collecting them since the 17th century. The most popular section is the Victorian collection, including such well-known favorites as Millais's *My First Sermon* and *My Second Sermon,* and Landseer's *The First Leap.* There is also a large landscape of Salisbury Cathedral by John Constable. Since World War II, all paintings acquired by the gallery concentrate on London subjects.

Guildhall Yard, EC2 ⓒ 020/7332-3700. www.guildhall-art-gallery.org.uk. Admission £2.50 ($4) adults, £1 ($1.60) seniors and students, free for children 16 and under; free on Fri and daily from 3:30pm. Mon–Sat 10am–5pm; Sun noon–4pm. Tube: Bank, St. Paul's, Mansion House or Moorgate.

Hayward Gallery   This gallery, part of the South Bank Centre, presents a changing program of major contemporary and historical exhibitions. The gallery closes between exhibitions, so check before crossing the Thames.

Belvedere Rd., South Bank, SE1. ⓒ **020/7960-4242,** or 020/7261-0127 for recorded information. www. hayward.org.uk. Admission fees vary but are usually £8 ($13) adults, £5.50 ($9) seniors and students, free for children under 16. Mon and Thurs–Sun 10am–6pm; Tues–Wed 10am–8pm. Tube: Waterloo or Embankment.

Hermitage Rooms   See Somerset House, below.

Imperial War Museum ⚡   At one time this large domed building built in 1815 housed the Bethlehem Royal Hospital for the Insane, or Bedlam. It now houses collections relating to the madness of two world wars and other conflicts since 1914. There are four floors of exhibitions, including the Large Exhibits Gallery (a vast area of historical displays), two floors of art galleries, and a dramatic re-creation of London at war during the Blitz. You can see a Battle of Britain Spitfire, the rifle carried by Lawrence of Arabia, and Hitler's political testament, as well as models, decorations, uniforms, photographs, and paintings. A Holocaust Exhibition detailing Nazi persecution in Europe opened in 2000.

Lambeth Rd., SE1. ⓒ **020/7416-5321.** www.iwm.org.uk. Free admission. Daily 10am–6pm. Closed Dec 24–26. Tube: Lambeth North or Waterloo.

London's Transport Museum ⚡ *Kids*   Once home to the flower market, this splendidly restored Victorian building now houses horse buses, motor buses, trams, trolley buses, railway vehicles, models, maps, posters, photographs, and audiovisual displays—all tracing 200 years of London transport history. The story is enlivened by interactive video exhibits—put yourself in the driver's seat of a bus or Tube train. The fabulous gift shop sells a variety of London Transport souvenirs. The museum has "kidzones"—interactive programs for children so parents can enjoy the museum without having to entertain their brood. The range of historic vehicles on display is fascinating.

The Piazza, Covent Garden, WC2. ⓒ **020/7379-6344.** Admission £5.95 ($10) adults, £3.95 ($6) seniors, £15 ($24) family ticket, free for children under 16. Sat–Thurs 10am–6pm; Fri 11am–6pm. Closed Dec 24–26. Tube: Covent Garden or Charing Cross.

Madame Tussaud's *Overrated* *Kids*   In 1770, an exhibition of life-size wax figures was opened in Paris by J. C. Curtius. His niece, Strasbourg-born Marie Tussaud, who learned the secret of making lifelike replicas, joined him. During the French Revolution, the head of almost every distinguished victim of the guillotine was molded by Madame Tussaud or her uncle. She immigrated to London in 1802 and soon opened her "exhibition."

While some of the figures on display today come from Madame Tussaud's own molds (she worked until she was 81), the exhibition has kept up with the times in producing new images. An enlarged Grand Hall houses years of royalty, many heads of state and political leaders, and old favorites. In the "Chamber of Horrors" (not appropriate for young children), you can experience the vicarious thrill of walking through a Victorian London street haunted by the shadowy terror of Jack the Ripper. The instruments and victims of death penalties are juxtaposed with present-day murderers in prison. You can also mingle with current pop, sports, and movie stars.

Stars of a more celestial variety are the showstoppers in the **London Planetarium** ✿, next door. It's the largest planetarium in Europe and features a simulated space journey through exploding nebulae to the very edge of the universe.

Marylebone Rd., NW1. ✆ 020/7935-6861. www.madame-tussauds.co.uk. Admission £14.95 ($24) adults, £11.80 ($19) seniors, £10.50 ($17) children under 16. Combination tickets, including the planetarium, £16.95 ($27) adults, £13.50 ($22) seniors, and £12 ($19) children 5–16, free for children under 5. Madame Tussaud's: opening times vary by season and weekday or weekend (9, 9:30, and 10am), closing at 5:30pm. Planetarium: daily 10am–5:30pm; shows every 40 min. 12:20–5pm, weekends/holidays from 10:20am. Closed Dec 25. Tube: Baker St.

Museum of London ✿✿   Located in the Barbican district, the Museum of London traces the city's history from prehistoric times to the postmodern era, through relics, costumes, household effects, maps, and models. Anglo-Saxons, Vikings, Normans—they're all here, displayed on two floors around a central courtyard and in new galleries that are part of an ongoing redevelopment plan.

Among the sights: the death mask of Oliver Cromwell; the Great Fire of London in living color and sound; reconstructed Roman dining rooms with kitchen and utensils; cell doors from Newgate Prison, made famous by Dickens; and a shop counter with pre–World War II prices on the items. But the pièce de résistance is the lord mayor's coach, built in 1757 and weighing 3 tons. Still used each November in the Lord Mayor's Procession, this gilded horse-drawn vehicle is like a fairy-tale coach.

150 London Wall, EC2. ✆ 020/7600-3699. Free admission. Tues–Sat 10am–5:50pm; Sun noon–5:50pm; last entry 5:30. Tube: St. Paul's, Barbican, or Moorgate. To get to the museum, which overlooks London's Roman and medieval walls, go up to the elevated pedestrian precinct at the corner of London Wall and Aldersgate, 5 min. from St. Paul's.

National Army Museum ✿   Located in Chelsea, this museum traces the history of the British land forces, the Indian army, and colonial land forces. The collection starts with 1485, when the Yeomen of the Guard was formed. The saga of the forces of the East India Company is traced, from its beginnings in 1602 to Indian independence in 1947. The gory and glory are all here—from Florence Nightingale's lamp to the cloak wrapped around the dying General James Wolfe at Quebec in 1759. There are also "cases of the heroes," mementos of men such as the dukes of Marlborough and Wellington. But the field soldiers aren't forgotten; the Nation in Arms Gallery tells their story in two world wars, including an exhibit of the British Army in the Far East from 1941 to 1945.

Royal Hospital Rd., SW3. ✆ 020/7730-0717. www.national-army-museum.ac.uk. Free admission. Daily 10am–5:30pm. Closed Jan 1, Good Friday, May bank holiday, and Dec 24–26. Tube: Sloane Sq.

National Portrait Gallery ★★   In a gallery of remarkable and unremarkable pictures (they're here for their notable subjects rather than their artistic quality), a few paintings tower over the rest, including Sir Joshua Reynolds's first portrait of Samuel Johnson ("a man of most dreadful appearance"). Among the best are Nicholas Hilliard's miniature of a handsome Sir Walter Raleigh and a full-length Elizabeth I, along with the Holbein cartoon of Henry VIII. There's also a portrait of William Shakespeare that bears the claim of being the "most authentic contemporary likeness" of its subject. One of the most famous pictures in the gallery is the group portrait of the Brontë sisters (Charlotte, Emily, and Anne) painted by their brother, Bramwell. An idealized portrait of Lord Byron by Thomas Phillips is also on display.

The recently redesigned galleries of Victorian and early-20th-century portraits occupy the whole of the first floor and display portraits from 1837 (when Victoria took the throne) to present day; later 20th-century portraiture includes major works by such artists as Warhol and Hambling. Some of the more notable personalities of the past two centuries are on show: T. S. Eliot, Disraeli, Macmillan, Sir Richard Burton, Elizabeth Taylor, and our two favorites: G. F. Watts's famous portrait of his great actress wife, Ellen Terry, and Vanessa Bell's portrait of her sister, Virginia Woolf. The late Princess Diana's portrait on the Royal Landing seems to attract the most viewers. The Gallery has recently opened a new cafe and art bookshop.

In 2000 Queen Elizabeth opened the Ondaatje Wing of the gallery, granting the gallery more than 50% more exhibition space. The most intriguing of the new space is the splendid Tudor Gallery, opening with portraits of Richard III and Henry II, his conqueror in the Battle of Bosworth in 1485. There's also a portrait of Shakespeare that the gallery first acquired in 1856. Rooms lead through centuries of English monarchs, with some literary and artistic figures thrown in. A Balcony Gallery displays more recent figures whose fame has lasted longer than Warhol's predicted 15 minutes. These include everybody from Mick Jagger to Joan Collins, and certainly the Baroness Thatcher. This new wing certainly taps into the cult of the celebrity.

St. Martin's Place, WC2. ✆ 020/7306-0055. www.npg.org.uk. Free admission. Fee charged for some special exhibits. Sat–Wed 10am–6pm; Thurs–Fri 10am–9pm. Tube: Charing Cross or Leicester Sq.

Royal Academy of Arts   Established in 1768, the academy was cofounded by Sir Joshua Reynolds, Thomas Gainsborough, and Benjamin West, among others. Since its beginning, each member has had to donate an artwork; over the years the academy has built up a sizable collection. The annual summer exhibition has been held for over 2 centuries and is one of the events of the London year; you can attend and purchase work by young artists from throughout Britain. Major traveling exhibitions are usually on view in the main galleries.

Burlington House, Piccadilly, W1. ✆ 020/7300-8000. www.royalacademy.org.uk. Admission £10 ($16) adults, £8 ($13) seniors, £1.50–£2.50 ($3.20–$4) children. Sat–Thurs 10am–6pm; Fri 10am–10pm. Closed Dec 24–25. Tube: Piccadilly Circus or Green Park.

Saatchi Gallery   Charles Saatchi is one of Britain's greatest and most controversial private collectors, and his new gallery on the south bank features rotating displays from his vast holdings plus exhibitions from other international collections and museums. Saatchi's aim is to introduce new and unfamiliar art to a wider audience. Some of it, frankly, is little more than self-publicity with little or no intellectual content. Some of it is deliberately meant to be shocking. Saatchi, after all, was the man behind the "Sensation" show that caused so much ruckus when it opened at the Brooklyn Museum. Damien Hirst's 4m (14-ft.) tiger shark preserved in a formaldehyde-filled tank and Marc Quinn's frozen "head," cast from nine pints of plasma taken from the artist over several months, are among the Saatchi holdings. Regardless of the exhibition on display at the time of your visit, it's almost guaranteed to be fascinating, and possibly repulsive.

County Hall, Southbank, SE1. © 020/7825-2363. www.saatchi-gallery.co.uk. Admission £8.50 ($14), £6.50 ($11) seniors and students. Sun–Thurs 10am–6pm; Fri–Sat 10am–10pm. Tube: Waterloo or Westminster.

Sir John Soane's Museum ✿   This was the former home of Sir John Soane (1753–1837), an architect who rebuilt the Bank of England (not the present structure). With his multiple levels, fool-the-eye mirrors, flying arches, and domes, Soane was a master of perspective and a genius of interior space—his picture gallery displays three times the number of paintings a room of similar dimensions would be expected to hold. Hogarth's satirical series, The Rake's Progress, includes his much-reproduced *Orgy and The Election,* a satire on mid-18th-century politics. Soane also filled his house with classical sculpture. On display is the sarcophagus of Pharaoh Seti I, found in a burial chamber in the Valley of the Kings. Also exhibited are architectural drawings from the 30,000 kept in the Soane Gallery. On the first Tuesday of each month the house is open late and is lit by candles to magical effect.

13 Lincoln's Inn Fields, WC2. © 020/7405-2107. Free admission. Tues–Sat 10am–5pm; 1st Tues of each month also 6–9pm. Tours given Sat at 2:30pm £3 ($4.80). Closed bank holidays. Tube: Chancery Lane or Holborn.

Somerset House ✿✿   The late Queen Mother once remarked how sad it was that the courtyard at Somerset House had become an Inland Revenue car park. It was just the spur needed by the long-running campaign to open up the 1,000-room civil service palace, designed by Sir William Chambers (1724–96), to the public. The government moved its workers out and the Heritage Lottery Fund coughed up the millions needed to restore the buildings, the courtyard with its new fountains, and the river terrace, where there's now a summer cafe, cheaper than the new restaurant indoors. A heady mix of high culture and street enter-tainment, the "new" Somerset House houses three major museums and hosts a program of open-air performances, talks, and workshops (© **020/7845-4670** box office). The restoration is proceeding in phases and you can already visit the **Seamen's Waiting Hall,** where naval officers came to collect their commissions. The 45-minute tours at 11am and 3:15pm on Tuesday, Thursday, and Saturday cost £2.75 ($4.40).

The **Courtauld Gallery** ✿ (© **020/7848-2526**; www.courtauld.ac.uk) has been in Somerset House since 1989. Its chief benefactor, textile mogul Samuel Courtauld, collected Impressionist and post-Impressionist paintings, which are still the gallery's main strength—Manet's *Bar at the Folies Bergères;* Monet's *Banks of the Seine at Argenteuil; Lady with Parasol* by Degas; *La Loge* by Renoir; van Gogh's *Self-Portrait with Bandaged Ear;* and several Cézannes, including *The Card Players.* But you'll find work by most great names (lots of Rubens), right up to modern greats Ben Nicholson, Graham Sutherland, and Larry Rivers. At noon on Tuesday, Thursday, and Saturday, 1-hour tours cost £7.50 adults ($12), £7 ($11) concessions.

The **Gilbert Collection** ✿✿ (© **020/7420-9400**; www.gilbert-collection.org. uk) is also in the South Building, as well as in the vaults beneath the river terrace. The glittering gold, silver, and mosaics were valued at £75 million when Arthur

City Sights

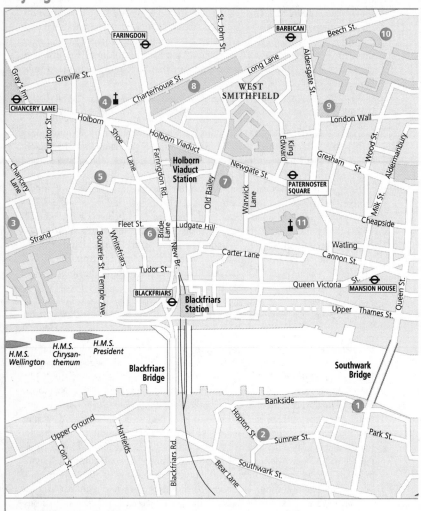

FARINGDON

CHANCERY LANE

BARBICAN

Beech St.

St. John St.

Long Lane

Greville St.

Charterhouse St.

WEST
SMITHFIELD

Aldersgate St.

Gray's Inn

Holborn

Shoe Lane

Holborn Viaduct

Cursitor St.

Farringdon Rd.

Holborn
Viaduct
Station

Newgate St.

London Wall

King Edward

Gresham St.

Wood St.

Aldermanbury

Chancery Lane

Old Bailey

Warwick Lane

PATERNOSTER
SQUARE

Milk St.

Cheapside

Strand

Fleet St.

Bride Lane

Ludgate Hill

New Br.

Carter Lane

Watling

Cannon St.

Bouverie St.

Whitefriars

Tudor St.

Queen Victoria St.

MANSION HOUSE

Queen St.

Temple Ave.

BLACKFRIARS

Blackfriars
Station

Upper Thames St.

H.M.S.
Wellington

H.M.S.
Chrysan-
themum

H.M.S.
President

Blackfriars
Bridge

Southwark
Bridge

Bankside

Upper Ground

Hatfields

Blackfriars Rd.

Hopton St.

Sumner St.

Park St.

Coin St.

Bear Lane

Southwark St.

Regent's
Park

THE
WEST END

THE
CITY

Hyde
Park

Area of
detail

Battersea Park

0   1 mi
0   1 km

Barbican Centre **10**
Design Museum **18**
Docklands **19**
Dr. Johnson's House **5**
Fishmonger's Hall **23**
Guildhall Art Gallery **12**
London Bridge **22**
London Dungeon **20**
Museum of London **9**

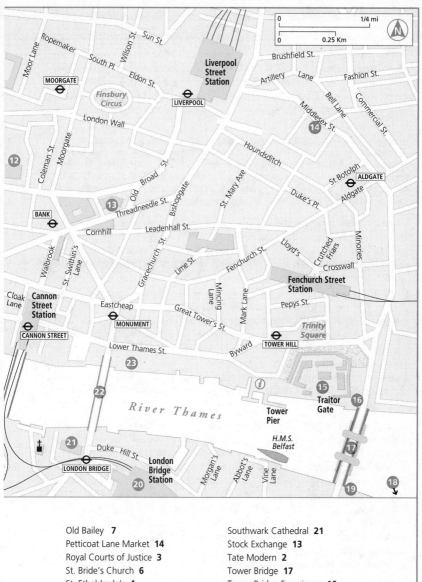

Old Bailey **7**

Petticoat Lane Market **14**

Royal Courts of Justice **3**

St. Bride's Church **6**

St. Etheldreda's **4**

St. Paul's Cathedral **11**

Shakespeare's Globe Theatre
& Exhibition **1**

Smithfield Market **8**

Southwark Cathedral **21**

Stock Exchange **13**

Tate Modern **2**

Tower Bridge **17**

Tower Bridge Experience **16**

Tower of London **15**

✝ Church

ⓘ Information

⊖ Tube Stop

Gilbert donated the 800-piece collection to the nation in 1996. There are objects here from Princess Diana's old home, Althorp. The 1-hour tour on Tuesday, Thursday, and Saturday costs £5.50 ($9) adults, £5 ($8) concessions.

The last and most extraordinary of the treasures of Somerset House are the **Hermitage Rooms** ⭐ (© **020/7845-4630;** www.hermitagerooms.com). This offshoot of the State Hermitage Museum in St. Petersburg exhibits pieces from the Russian Imperial collections in changing shows. Half the tickets are sold in advance (© **020/7413-3398;** www.ticketmaster.co.uk), half at the door, for half-hourly timed entry.

Strand, WC2. © 020/7845-4600. www.somerset-house.org.uk. Free admission to Somerset House. Courtauld Gallery £5 ($8) adults, £4 ($6) seniors, free for youth under 18; free Mon 10am–2pm. Gilbert Collection £5 ($8) adults, £4 ($6) seniors, free for youth under 18. Hermitage Rooms £6 ($10) adults, £4 ($6) concessions, free for children under 5. Same-day admission to 2 collections, save £1 ($1.60), all 3, save £2 ($3.20). Courtyard 7:30am–11pm (7pm in winter). Galleries and exhibitions daily 10am–6pm (last admission 45 min.–1 hr. earlier). Closed Jan 1 and Dec 24–26. Tube: Temple, Covent Garden or Charing Cross.

Tower Bridge Experience ⭐   Tower Bridge, built in 1894, is one of the world's most celebrated landmarks and possibly the most photographed and painted bridge on earth. In 1993 an exhibition opened inside the bridge to commemorate its century-old history. Visitors can now go up the north tower to high-level walkways between the two towers with spectacular views of St. Paul's, the Tower of London, and the Houses of Parliament—a photographer's dream. You're then led down the south tower and on to the bridge's original engine room, with its Victorian boilers and steam-pumping engines that used to raise and lower the bridge for ships to pass. Exhibits housed in the towers use advanced technology, including animatronic characters, video, and computers to illustrate the history of the bridge.

London SE1. © 020/7403-3761. www.towerbridge.org.uk. Admission £4.50 ($7) adults, £4 ($4.80) seniors, students, and children under 16. Daily 9:30am–6pm (last entry 5pm). Closed Dec 25–26. Tube: Tower Hill or London Bridge. River services: Tower Pier.

Wallace Collection ⭐⭐   This outstanding collection of artworks, bequeathed to the nation by Lady Wallace in 1897, is still displayed in its founders' house. The mostly French works of art include important pictures by artists of all European schools. There's sculpture, furniture, goldsmiths' work, Sèvres porcelain, and valuable collections of majolica and European and Asian arms and armor. Frans Hals' *Laughing Cavalier* is the most celebrated painting in the collection, but Pieter de Hooch's *A Boy Bringing Pomegranates* and Watteau's *The Music Party* are also well known. There's a marvelous new sculpture garden and cafe under a glass roof covering the courtyard.

Hertford House, Manchester Sq., off Wigmore St., W1. © 020/7963-9500. www.wallacecollection.org. Free admission. Mon–Sat 10am–5pm; Sun noon–5pm. Closed Jan 1, Dec 24–26, Good Friday, and May Day. Tube: Bond St.

LITERARY LANDMARKS

See the discussion of Hampstead Village in section 4, "Sights on the Outskirts," for details on Keats House. See section 1, "The Top Attractions," for details on Poets' Corner in Westminster Abbey.

Dickens's House   In Bloomsbury stands the simple abode in which Charles Dickens wrote *Oliver Twist* and finished *The Pickwick Papers*. Dickens only lived here a couple of years, but the place is a virtual Dickensian shrine; it contains his study, manuscripts, and personal relics, as well as reconstructed interiors.

Virginia Woolf: A Neighborhood of Her Own

Born in London in 1882, author Virginia Woolf lived in London for most of her life, and set many of her works there. She spent her formative years at 22 Hyde Park Gate, off Kensington High Street. After her father's death (1905), Virginia moved to Bloomsbury and settled near the British Museum. She lived first at 46 Gordon Sq., east of Gower Street and University College; here, the nucleus of the soon-to-be celebrated Bloomsbury Group was formed. Virginia then moved to 29 Fitzroy Sq., west of Tottenham Court Road, in a house once occupied by Shaw. During the next 2 decades, she resided at several more Bloomsbury addresses, including Brunswick Square, Tavistock Square, and Mecklenburg Square. (These homes have either disappeared or have been altered beyond recognition.) At Tavistock Square (1924–39) and at Mecklenburg Square (1939–40) she operated Hogarth Press with her husband Leonard. She published her own work as well as T. S. Eliot's *The Waste Land*. To escape from urban life, the Woolfs purchased Monk's House in the village of Rodmell in Sussex. They lived here until 1941, when Virginia drowned herself in the nearby River Ouse. Her ashes were buried in the Monk's House garden.

48 Doughty St., WC1. ℭ 020/7405-2127. www.dickensmuseum.com. Admission £4 ($6) adults, £3 ($4.80) students, £2 ($3.20) children, £9 ($16) family ticket. Mon–Sat 10am–5pm; Sun 11am–5pm. Closed Dec 25. Tube: Russell Sq.

Dr. Johnson's House   Samuel Johnson and his copyists compiled his famous dictionary in this Queen Anne house, where the lexicographer, poet, essayist, and fiction writer lived from 1748 to 1759. Although he also lived elsewhere, the Gough Square house is the only one of his London residences remaining. The 17th-century building has been painstakingly restored, and it's well worth a visit.

17 Gough Sq., EC4. ℭ 020/7353-3745. Admission £4 ($6) adults, £3 ($4.80) seniors and students, £1 ($1.60) children 11–16, free for children under 10, £9 ($14) family ticket. May–Sept Mon–Sat 11am–5:30pm; Oct–Apr Mon–Sat 11am–5pm. Tube: Blackfriars or Temple. Walk up New Bridge St. and turn left onto Fleet. Gough Sq. is tiny and hidden, north of Fleet.

Shakespeare's Globe Theatre & Exhibition ✸   This is a re-creation on the exact site of the stage where many of Shakespeare's plays were first performed at the turn of the 17th century. The late American producer, Sam Wanamaker, spent some 20 years raising funds for this project to re-create this Elizabethan theater. A fascinating exhibit tells the story of the new Globe's construction, using the material (including goat's hair in the plaster), techniques, and craftsmanship of 400 years ago. This isn't quite an exact replica: It seats 1,500 patrons, not the 3,000 that regularly squeezed in during Shakespeare's tenure; and the thatched roof has been specially treated with a fire retardant. In May 1997, the Globe's company staged its first slate of plays. Guided tours of the facility are offered throughout the day. See "London After Dark," later in this chapter, for details on attending a play here.

New Globe Walk, Bankside, SE1. ℭ 020/7902-1500. www.shakespeares-globe.com. Exhibition and tour admission £8 ($13) adults, £6.50 ($10) seniors and students, £5.50 ($9) children under 15, £24 ($38) family.

Oct–Apr daily 10am–5pm; May–Sept daily 9am–noon and 12:30–4pm. Guided tours every 30 min. or so. Closed Dec 24–25. Tube: Mansion House or London Bridge.

Thomas Carlyle's House ☆   From 1834 to 1881, Thomas Carlyle, author of *The French Revolution,* and Jane Baillie Welsh Carlyle, his wife and noted epistolarian, resided in this modest 1708 terraced house. Jane Carlyle described it as being "of most antique physiognomy, quite to our humour; all wainscoted, carved and queer-looking, roomy, substantial, commodious, with closets to satisfy any Bluebeard." It is furnished essentially as it was in their day. The most interesting room is the (not-so-soundproof) soundproof study in the skylit attic, filled with Carlyle memorabilia—his books, a letter from Disraeli, personal effects, a writing chair, even his death mask.

24 Cheyne Row, SW3. ☎ 020/7352-7087. Admission £3.60 ($6) adults, £1.80 ($2.90) children. Apr–Oct Wed–Fri 2–5pm; Sat–Sun 11am–4pm. Closed Nov–Mar. Tube: Sloane Sq. Bus: no. 11, 19, 22, or 239. Located ¾ of a block from the Thames, near the Chelsea Embankment along King's Rd.

LANDMARK CHURCHES

Many of the churches listed below offer free lunchtime concerts—it's customary to leave a small donation. A full list of churches offering lunchtime concerts is available from the London Tourist Board.

Brompton Oratory, Brompton Road (☎ **020/7808-0908;** www.bromptonoratory.org.uk; Tube: S. Kensington), done in the Italian Renaissance style, is famous for its musical services. Its organ has nearly 4,000 pipes. After Westminster Cathedral and York Minster, this has the widest nave in England.

St. Bride's Church ☆, on Fleet Street (☎ **020/7427-0133;** Tube: Blackfriars), known as the church of the press, is also a remarkable landmark. The current church is the eighth one that's stood here. Its spire has four octagonal tiers capped by an obelisk topped off with a ball and vane. It's said this soaring confection (234 ft. tall) inspired the wedding cakes of a pastry cook who lived in Fleet Street in the late 17th century. The crypts are now a museum. There are concerts every Tuesday and Friday.

St. Etheldreda's, Britain's oldest Roman Catholic church, lies on Ely Place, Holborn Circus, EC1 (☎ **020/7405-1061;** Tube: Farringdon, Chancery Lane), leading off Charterhouse Street at Holborn Circus. Built in 1251, it was mentioned by the Bard in both *Richard II* and *Richard III.* The church was built by and was the property of the diocese of Ely in Cambridgeshire; it survived the Great Fire. Until this century, the landlord of Ye Olde Mitre public house near Ely Place had to obtain his license from the Justices of Cambridgeshire rather than in London. Ely Place is still a private road, with impressive iron gates and a lodge for the gatekeeper. The church has a distinguished musical tradition, with an 11am Latin Mass on Sunday.

St. Martin-in-the-Fields ☆, overlooking Trafalgar Square, WC2 (☎ **020/ 7766-1100;** Tube: Charing Cross), is the Royal Parish Church. The first known church on the site was built in the 13th century; the present classically inspired church, with its famous steeple, dates from 1726. Because of its vantage point in the theater district, it has drawn many actors to its door, none more notable than Nell Gwynne, mistress of Charles II. She is buried in the crypt. Throughout World War II, many Londoners rode out uneasy nights there, while Blitz bombs rained down overhead; one blasted out all the windows. Today the crypt has a pleasant restaurant, a bookshop, and a gallery. It is home to London's original **Brass Rubbing Centre** (☎ 020/7930-9306). St. Martin-in-the-Fields is famous for its roster of mostly Baroque concerts, some of them lit by candlelight. There are free lunchtime concerts on Monday, Tuesday and Friday at 1:05pm, and evening recitals Thursday to Saturday.

The spectacular brick-and-stone **Westminster Cathedral** ★, Ashley Place (**℟ 020/7798-9055;** Tube: Victoria), is the headquarters of the Roman Catholic church in Britain. Done in high Byzantine style, it's massive. One hundred different marbles fill the richly decorated interior. Mosaics emblazon the chapels and the vaulting of the sanctuary. Climb to the top of the 273-foot-tall campanile, and you'll be rewarded with a sweeping view over Victoria and Westminster. There are sung masses and free organ concerts on Sunday.

ALONG THE THAMES

All of London's history and development is linked to this winding river, which connects the city with the North Sea. For centuries the Thames was London's highway and main street, the source of its wealth and its power. Even now, there is a row of fascinating attractions lying on, across, and alongside the River Thames.

After years of neglect, the areas next to the river, on the south bank, have undergone an amazing renaissance. To see it all, walk along the riverside promenade that stretches from Westminster Bridge (the area called South Bank) to Tower Bridge and the newly gentrified area east of it, called Butler's Wharf.

Rising beside Westminster Bridge, across from the Houses of Parliament, is the world's largest observation wheel, the **British Airways London Eye** (see "The Top Attractions," earlier in this chapter). Strolling east from the wheel, you'll pass a whole series of riverside landmarks, including the **South Bank Centre,** a cultural mecca that's the site of Royal Festival Hall and the National Theatre; Shakespeare's Globe Theatre & Exhibition (see "Literary Landmarks," above, for more information); the new Tate Modern (described under "The Top Attractions," earlier in this chapter), and the stunning new **London City Hall,** which opened in 2003.

London Bridge, contrary to popular belief, has never "fallen down"; but it was dismantled and shipped to Arizona in 1971 and immediately replaced by a new London Bridge. It still spans the river from the Monument (a tall pillar commemorating the Great Fire) to Southwark Cathedral, parts of which date from 1207. The newest span over the mighty Thames is the sleek new Millennium Bridge, a footbridge designed by Lord Norman Foster to connect the Tate Modern to the area around St. Paul's Cathedral.

3 London's Parks & Gardens

London has the greatest system of parklands of any large city on the globe. The largest green space is **Hyde Park** ★★, once a favorite deer-hunting ground of Henry VIII. Including the adjoining Kensington Gardens, it covers 254 hectares (636 acres) of central London with velvety lawn interspersed with ponds, flowerbeds, and trees. Running through the width is a 16-hectare (41-acre) lake called the **Serpentine. Rotten Row,** a 2km (1½-mile) sand track, is reserved for horseback riding.

At the northeastern corner of Hyde Park, near Marble Arch, is **Speaker's Corner,** where anyone can get up and speak. The only rules: no blasphemy, obscenity, or incitement to riot. The tradition began in 1855, 17 years before the right to assembly was guaranteed, when a mob of 150,000 gathered to attack a proposed Sunday Trading Bill (it took about 150 years before stores could open on Sun). Orators from all over Britain have been taking advantage of this spot ever since.

The lovely **Kensington Gardens** 🏛🏛 blends with Hyde Park to the west and borders on the grounds of Kensington Palace. Here you'll find the celebrated statue of Peter Pan, with the bronze rabbits. The **Albert Memorial** is here, and so is Kensington Palace (described under "The Top Attractions," earlier in this chapter), the post-divorce home of Diana, Princess of Wales.

East of Hyde Park, across Piccadilly, stretch **Green Park** and **St. James's Park,** completing an almost unbroken chain of landscaped beauty. This area is ideal for picnics; a romantic lake supports a variety of ducks and pelicans that descend from a pair the Russian ambassador presented to Charles II in 1662.

Regent's Park 🏛🏛🏛 covers most of the district north of Baker Street and Marylebone Road. Designed by the 18th-century genius John Nash for a palace of the prince regent that never materialized, this is the most classically beautiful of London's parks. Its heart is a Queen Mary's Rose Garden planted around a small lake that's alive with waterfowl and spanned by Japanese bridges; the open-air theater and London Zoo are also here. As in all the local parks, there are hundreds of deck chairs on the lawns in which to sunbathe (for a small fee).

The 14-hectare (36-acre) **London Zoo** 🏛 (© 020/7722-3333) is more than 150 years old and houses some 8,000 animals, including some of the rarest endangered species on earth. Perennial favorites include the elephants, penguins, lions, hippos, and monkeys. You can watch the penguins or the denizens of the aquarium being fed their lunch daily at 2:30pm. Admission is £11 ($18) for adults, £9 ($14) seniors and students, £8 ($3) for children 4 to 14, and free for children under 4. Open daily from 10am to 5:30pm (4pm Nov–Feb). Tube: Camden Town. Bus: no. 274 or Z2 (summer only).

See "Sights on the Outskirts," below, for details on Hampstead Heath and Kew Gardens.

4 Sights on the Outskirts

HAMPSTEAD HEATH & VILLAGE

Hampstead Heath 🏛🏛 is 320 hectares (800 acres) of continuous high heath, park, wood, and grassland, located about 6km (4 miles) north of the center of London. On a clear day you can see St. Paul's and even the hills of Kent south of the Thames from here. For years, Londoners have come here to fly kites, sun worship, fish the ponds, swim, picnic, or jog. At the shore of Kenwood Lake, in the northern section, is a concert platform devoted to symphony performances on summer evenings. In Waterlow Park in the northeast corner, ballets, operas, and comedies are staged at the Grass Theatre in June and July.

When the Underground came to **Hampstead Village** 🏛 (Tube: Hampstead) in 1907, its attraction as a place to live became widely known. Writers, artists, architects, musicians, and scientists came to join earlier residents; D. H. Lawrence, P. B. Shelley, R. L. Stevenson, and Kingsley Amis all lived here, and John Le Carré and Glenda Jackson still do. The Regency and Georgian houses in this village are just 20 minutes by Tube from Piccadilly Circus. Flask Walk, a pedestrian mall, contains a mix of historic pubs, toyshops, and chic boutiques. The original village, on the side of a hill, has old roads, alleys, steps, courts, and groves to be strolled through.

Keats House John Keats lived here for only 2 years; he died in Rome of tuberculosis in 1821, at age 25. In Hampstead, Keats wrote some of his most celebrated poems, including "Ode on a Grecian Urn" and "Ode to a Nightingale." His Regency house possesses the manuscripts of his last sonnet ("Bright star, would I were steadfast as thou art") and a portrait of him on his deathbed in a house on Rome's Spanish Steps.

Wentworth Place, Keats Grove, Hampstead, NW3. ✆ 020/7435-2062. Admission £3 ($4.80) adults, £1.50 ($2.40) seniors and students, free for children under 16. Apr–Oct Tues–Sun noon–5pm; Nov–Mar Tues–Sun noon–4pm. Call to check times and winter closure. Tube: Belsize Park or Hampstead. Bus: no. 24 from Trafalgar Sq.

Kenwood House ⭐ Built as a gentleman's country home, Kenwood was later enlarged and decorated in neoclassical style by Robert Adam, starting in 1764. The house contains period furniture and a treasure trove of paintings by Rembrandt, Turner, Hals, Gainsborough, Reynolds, and others.

Hampstead Lane, NW3. ✆ 020/8348-1286. Free admission. Apr–Sept daily 10am–6pm; Oct daily 10am–5pm; Nov–Mar daily 10am–4pm (10:30am Wed and Fri). Closed Dec 24–25. Tube: Hampstead, Archway, or Golders Green. Bus: no. 210.

Fenton House ⭐ This National Trust property is on the west side of Hampstead Grove, just north of Hampstead Village. Built in 1693, it's one of the earliest, largest, and finest houses here. You pass through beautiful wrought-iron gates to reach the redbrick house in a walled garden. It houses the outstanding Benton-Fletcher collection of early keyboard musical instruments, dating from 1540 to 1805. Occasional concerts are given.

Hampstead Grove, NW3. ✆ 020/7435-3471. Admission £4.40 ($7) adults, £2.20 ($3.50) children 16 and under, £11 ($18) family ticket. Apr–Oct Wed–Fri 2–5pm, Sat–Sun 11am–5pm; Mar Sat–Sun 2–5pm. Closed Nov–Feb. Tube: Hampstead.

Freud Museum After he and his family left Nazi-occupied Vienna as refugees, Sigmund Freud lived, worked, and died in this spacious three-story redbrick house in north London. Rooms on view contain original furniture, letters, photographs, paintings, and personal effects of Freud and his daughter, Anna. In the study and library, you can see the famous couch and his large collection of Egyptian, Roman, and Asian antiquities.

20 Maresfield Gardens, NW3. ✆ 020/7435-2002. www.freud.org.uk. Admission £5 ($8) adults, £2 ($3.20) students, free for children under 12. Wed–Sun noon–5pm. Tube: Finchley Rd.

Highgate Cemetery ⭐ A stone's throw east from Hampstead Heath, Highgate Village has 16th- and 17th-century mansions, as well as small cottages, lining three sides of the now pondless Pond Square. Its most outstanding feature, however, is this beautiful cemetery, laid out around a huge, 300-year-old cedar tree and laced with serpentine pathways. The cemetery was so popular and fashionable in the Victorian era that it was extended on the other side of Swain's Lane in 1857. The most famous grave is that of Karl Marx, who died in Hampstead in 1883; his grave, marked by a gargantuan bust, is in the eastern cemetery. In the old western cemetery—accessible only by guided tour, given hourly in summer—lie Michael Faraday and Christina Rossetti. Tours are given at noon, 2pm, and 4pm weekdays, and every hour on Saturday and Sunday; call ahead to make an appointment before trekking out here.

Swain's Lane, N6. ✆ 020/8340-1834. East Cemetery £2 ($3.20); West Cemetery £3 ($4.80); £1 ($1.60) to bring a small camera. East Cemetery Apr–Oct Mon–Fri 10am–5pm, Sat–Sun 11am–5pm; Nov–Mar closes at 4pm. West Cemetery tours Apr–Oct Mon–Fri 2pm, Sat–Sun 11am, 1, and 3pm; Nov–Mar Sat–Sun at noon, 1, 2, and 3pm. Tube: Archway. No children under 8 in the West Cemetery.

A TRIP OUT TO HAMPTON COURT

Hampton Court Palace ⭐⭐⭐ Cardinal Wolsey's 16th-century palace, located 21km (13 miles) west of London, teaches us a lesson: Don't try to outdo the boss, particularly if his name is Henry VIII. The rich cardinal did just that; he eventually lost his fortune, power, prestige, and his lavish palace to Henry, who took over and even outdid Wolsey. Among the Tudor additions were the Anne Boleyn gateway, with its 16th-century astronomical clock; the aptly named Great Hall, with its hammer-beam ceiling; and a tiltyard, tennis court, and kitchen.

Hampton Court had quite a retinue to feed; cooking was done in the Great Kitchen. Henry cavorted through the various apartments with his wife of the moment—from Anne Boleyn to Catherine Parr (who lived to bury her spouse). Charles I was imprisoned here at one time and managed to escape—temporarily.

Although the palace enjoyed prestige and pomp in Elizabethan days, it owes much of its present look to William and Mary—or rather to Sir Christopher Wren, who designed the Northern or Lion Gates, intended as the main entrance to the new parts of the palace. Jean Tijou made the fine wrought-iron screen at one end of the south gardens around 1694. You can parade through the apartments, filled with porcelain, furniture, paintings, and tapestries. The King's Dressing Room has some of the best art, mainly old master paintings on loan from Queen Elizabeth II. Be sure to inspect the royal chapel. Then, to confound yourself totally, you might want to get lost in the **Maze,** also designed by Wren.

The famed gardens are open daily year-round. A garden cafe and restaurant are in the Tiltyard Gardens.

You can get to Hampton Court by train, bus, boat, or car. Twice-hourly trains from Waterloo Station make the half-hour trip to Hampton Court Station. Boat service (© **020/7930-2062;** www.wpsa.co.uk) is offered to and from Westminster Pier in London. If you're driving from London, take A308 to the junction with A309 on the north side of Kingston Bridge.

East Molesey, Surrey. © **0870/752-7777,** or 0870/753-7777 (tickets by phone). www.hrp.org.uk. Admission £11 ($18) adults, £8.25 ($13) seniors and students, £7.25 ($12) children 5–15, free for children under5, £33 ($53) family ticket. Apr–Oct Mon 10:15am–6pm, Tues–Sun 9:30am–6pm (last admission 5:15pm); Nov–Mar Mon 10:15am–4:30pm, Tues–Sun 9:30am–4:30pm (last admission 3:45pm). Park 7am–dusk. Closed Dec 24–26.

GREENWICH ★★★

When London overwhelms you, and you'd like to escape for a beautiful, sunny afternoon on the city's outskirts, make it Greenwich.

Greenwich mean time is the basis of standard time throughout most of the world, and Greenwich has been the zero point used in the reckoning of terrestrial longitudes since 1884. But this lovely village—the center of British seafaring when Britain ruled the seas—is also home of the Royal Naval College, the National Maritime Museum, the Queen's House, and the Old Royal Observatory. Recognizing this outstanding assemblage of historic buildings, UNESCO named Maritime Greenwich a World Heritage Site. You can also visit the famous clipper ship *Cutty Sark,* docked at Greenwich Pier.

GETTING THERE By Underground, take the **Jubilee Line** to Greenwich North. The Tube is quick—only 15 minutes from Green Park. You can also take **Docklands Light Rail** from Tower Gateway near the Tower of London to Island Gardens, the last stop, and then walk through the Victorian foot tunnel beneath the Thames. You'll come out next to the *Cutty Sark.* Or you can reach Greenwich by boat. Vessels operated by **Thames River Services,** Westminster Pier, Victoria Embankment (© **020/7930-1616;** www.riverthames.co.uk; Tube: Westminster), depart from Westminster Pier throughout the year for the 1-hour trip to Greenwich. A return (round-trip) fare is £7.80 ($12) for adults, £6.30 ($10) for seniors, £3.90 ($5) for children, and £20.25 ($32) for a family ticket.

VISITOR INFORMATION The **Greenwich Tourist Information Centre,** Pepys House, Cutty Sark Gardens (© **0870/608-2000**), open daily 10am to 5pm, conducts walking tours of Greenwich's major sights. The tours, which cost £4 ($6), depart daily at 12:15 and 2:15pm and last 1½ to 2 hours. Advance reservations aren't required, but it's a good idea to phone in advance to verify times.

SEEING THE SIGHTS

The National Maritime Museum, the Old Royal Observatory, and **Queen's House** stand together in a beautiful royal park, high on a hill overlooking the Thames. All three attractions are free and open daily from 10am to 5pm (to 6pm in summer). For more information about any of them, call © **020/8858-4422** or visit www.nmm.ac.uk. Together with the baroque buildings of the Old Royal Naval College they form a UNESCO World Heritage Site.

From the days of early seafarers to 20th-century sea power, the **National Maritime Museum** illustrates the glory that was Britain at sea. The cannon, relics, ship models, and paintings tell the story of British naval battles. Look for some oddities here—everything from the dreaded cat-o'-nine-tails used to flog sailors until 1879 to Nelson's Trafalgar coat, with the fatal bullet hole in the left shoulder clearly visible. As part of a millennium makeover, the museum spent £20 million in a massive expansion that added 16 new galleries devoted to British maritime history and current maritime issues.

Old Royal Observatory is the original home of Greenwich Mean Time. It has the largest refracting telescope in the United Kingdom and a collection of historic timekeepers and astronomical instruments. You can stand astride the meridian and set your watch precisely by the falling time-ball. Sir Christopher Wren designed the Octagon Room. Here the first royal astronomer, Flamsteed, made his 30,000 observations that formed the basis of his *Historia Coelestis Britannica.* Edmond Halley, he of the eponymous Halley's Comet, succeeded him. In 1833, the ball on the tower was hung to enable shipmasters to set their chronometers accurately.

Designed by Inigo Jones, **Queen's House** (1616) is a fine example of this architect's innovative style. It's most famous for the cantilevered tulip staircase, the first of its kind. Carefully restored, the house contains a collection of royal and marine paintings and other objets d'art.

The Last of the Great Clipper Ships

Six kilometers (4 miles) east of London, berthed at Greenwich Pier, lies the last and ultimate word in sail power: the *Cutty Sark*, King William Walk, Greenwich, SE10 (© 020/8858-3445; www.cuttysark.org.uk). Named after the witch in Robert Burns's poem "Tam O'Shanter," it was the greatest of the breed of clipper ships that carried tea from China and wool from Australia in the most exciting ocean races ever sailed. The *Cutty Sark*'s record stood at a then-unsurpassed 584km (363 miles) in 24 hours. Launched in Scotland in 1869, the sleek three-master represented the final fighting run of canvas against steam. Although the age of the clippers was brief, they did outpace the steamers as long as there was wind to fill their billowing mountain of sails. On board the *Cutty Sark* you'll find a museum devoted to clipper lore. Admission is £3.95 ($6) for adults and £2.95 ($4.70) for seniors, students, and children over 5. A family ticket costs £9.80 ($16). It's open daily from 10am to 5pm, closed December 24 to December 26.

Nearby is the **Royal Naval College** ⭐⭐, King William Walk, off Romney Road (© **020/8269-4747**). Designed by Sir Christopher Wren in 1696, it occupies 4 blocks named after King Charles, Queen Anne, King William, and Queen Mary. Formerly, from 1422 to 1640, Greenwich Palace stood here. It's worth stopping in to see the magnificent Painted Hall by Thornhill, where the body of Nelson lay in state in 1805, and the Georgian Chapel of St. Peter and St. Paul. Open daily 10am to 5pm; admission is free.

A VISIT TO KEW ⭐⭐

Fourteen kilometers (9 miles) southwest of central London near Richmond, Kew is home to the **Royal Botanic Gardens,** the best-known botanic gardens in Europe, and **Kew Palace** ⭐⭐, former residence of George III and Queen Charlotte. The easiest way to get to Kew is by taking the **District Line Tube** to the Kew Gardens stop; the journey takes about 30 minutes. You can also take a boat from Westminster Pier (© **020/7939-2062;** www.wpsa.co.uk).

Royal Botanic (Kew) Gardens ⭐⭐⭐   These world-famous gardens offer thousands of varieties of plants. But Kew is no mere pleasure garden—it's essentially a vast scientific research center that happens to be beautiful. The gardens, on a 120-hectare (300-acre) site, encompass lakes, greenhouses, walks, pavilions, and museums, along with fine examples of the architecture of Sir William Chambers. Among the 50,000 plant species are notable collections of ferns, orchids, aquatic plants, cacti, mountain plants, palms, and tropical water lilies.

No matter what season you visit Kew, there's always something to see, from the first spring flowers through winter. Gigantic hothouses grow species of shrubs, blooms, and trees from every part of the globe, from the Arctic Circle to tropical rainforests. Attractions include a newly restored Japanese gateway in traditional landscaping, as well as exhibitions that vary with the season. The newest greenhouse, the **Princess of Wales Conservatory** (beyond the rock garden), encompasses 10 climatic zones, from arid to tropical; it has London's finest collection of miniature orchids. The **Marianne North Gallery** (1882) is an absolute gem, paneled with 246 different types of wood that the intrepid Victorian artist collected on her world journeys; she also collected 832 paintings of exotic and tropical flora, all of which are displayed on the walls. Afternoon tea is offered at the **Orangery;** there's no better place in the gardens. The **Visitor Centre** at Victoria Gate houses an exhibit telling the story of Kew, as well as a bookshop.

Kew Palace and **Queen Charlotte's Cottage** are set within the Royal Botanic Gardens. The palace, a dark red brick structure with Dutch gables, was constructed in 1631; at its rear is the very formal Queen's Garden, filled with plants thought to have grown here in the 17th century. The palace, used as a home by George III (the king who went mad), is reminiscent of an elegant country house. You can wander through the dining room, the breakfast room, and go upstairs to the Queen's drawing room where musical evenings were staged. The rooms are wallpapered with designs used at the time. Perhaps the most intriguing exhibits are little possessions once owned by royal occupants—everything from snuffboxes to Prince Frederick's gambling debts. Queen Charlotte's Cottage was used by the royal family as a summer house.

Richmond, Surrey. © **020/8332-5622.** www.rbgkew.org.uk. Admission £7.50 ($12) adults, £5.50 ($9) concessions and late entry 45 min. before buildings close, free for children 16 and under with adult. Daily from 9:30am; closing times vary seasonally (3:45, 5, 5:30, and 6pm), buildings close 1 hr. earlier. Queen Charlotte's Cottage open summer weekends only. Kew Palace currently closed for renovations. Tube: District Line to Kew Gardens. By boat: ferry from Westminster Pier (© **020/7930-2062;** www.wpsa.co.uk).

Moments **Have Tea at Kew**

Across the street from the Royal Botanic Gardens is the **Original Maids of Honour Tearooms,** 288 Kew Rd. (℘ **020/8940-2752**), one of the finest tearooms in the area. Its oak paneling and old leaded-glass windows give the place a cozy warmth. The homemade cakes are delectable, as are the scones. The Maids of Honour is their pastry specialty, originally baked for Henry VIII. Afternoon tea is £4.50 to £9 ($7–$14). The tearoom is open Monday 9:30am to 1pm and Tuesday to Saturday 9:30am to 6pm; tea is served from 2:30 to 5:30pm.

5 Especially for Kids

Kids of all ages will enjoy the attractions listed below. For current information about what to do with children in London, you can call **Kidsline** (℘ **09068/ 663344**), a computerized service that costs 60p (95¢) a minute. Or pick up a copy of the monthly listings magazine *Kids Out,* available at newsstands.

London Dungeon   Situated under the arches of London Bridge Station, the dungeon is a series of tableaux, more grisly than Madame Tussaud's, that reproduce horrible scenes from British life through the ages. The rumble of trains overhead adds to the horror of the place, and although kids love the gory ghoulishness of it all, it's not appropriate for really young children. Dripping water and caged rats enhance the atmosphere. The heads of executed criminals were stuck on spikes for onlookers to observe through glasses hired for the occasion. There's a burning at the stake and a torture chamber with racking, branding, and fingernail extraction. The Great Fire of London is brought to crackling life by a computer-controlled spectacular that re-creates Pudding Lane, where the fire started. And, of course, you get to spend time with Jack the Ripper.

28–34 Tooley St., SE1. ℘ **0900/600-0666**. Admission £10.95 ($18) adults, £9.50 ($15) seniors and students, £6.95 ($11) children under 15 (must be accompanied by an adult). Apr–Sept daily 10am–6:30pm; Oct–Mar daily 10am–5:30pm; late openings July–Aug. Closed Dec 25. Tube: London Bridge.

Bethnal Green Museum of Childhood   Here you'll find displays of toys past and present; the variety of dolls alone is staggering. The dollhouses range from simple cottages to miniature mansions, complete with fireplaces, grand pianos, carriages, furniture, kitchen utensils, and pets. The museum displays optical toys, toy theaters, marionettes, puppets, and soldiers and battle toys of both world wars. There is also a display of children's clothing and furniture.

Cambridge Heath Rd., E2. ℘ **020/8980-2415**. www.museumofchildhood.org.uk. Free admission. Sat–Thurs and Sun 10am–5:50pm. Tube: Bethnal Green.

6 Organized Tours

BUS TOURS

If your time is more limited than your budget, then bagging all the big sites from the top of a double-decker bus may be the best bet. **The Big Bus Company** (℘ **020/7233-9533;** www.bigbus.co.uk) leaves from Green Park, Victoria, and Marble Arch daily, from 8:30am to 7pm (4:30pm in winter) on three different routes that take anything from 1½ to 2½ hours. Tickets include a river cruise and walking tours, and cost £16 ($26) for adults and £6 ($10) children. Valid for 24 hours, they let you hop on and off at 54 locations. Big Bus often has special offers, too, throwing in cheap theater tickets, fast-entry to popular attractions, and so on. The **Original London Sightseeing Tour** (© 020/8877-1722; www.theoriginaltour.com) has been going since the Festival of Britain in 1951. The 2-hour tour leaves from Piccadilly Circus, Victoria, Baker Street, or Marble Arch, every 15 to 20 minutes, from 8:30am to 7pm. This one has 90 stops to hop on and off at during the day. It costs £15 ($24) for adults, £7.50 ($12) for under-16s, and £45 ($72) for a family. You'll save a bit by booking online, but you can buy your tickets on board.

BOAT TRIPS

The fabulously loopy **London Duck Tours** ★★ (© 020/7928-3132; www.londonducktours.com) has adapted several World War II amphibious troop carriers, known as DUKWs, to civilian comfort levels, painted them screaming yellow, and now runs 80-minute road and river trips. Tours start behind County Hall (site of the British Airways London Eye giant observation wheel). You're picked up on Chicheley Street, then rumble through Westminster and up to Piccadilly, gathering bemused stares as you pass many of London's major tourist sites. Then the vehicle splashes into the Thames at Vauxhall for a 30-minute cruise up as far as the Houses of Parliament. The high ticket price of £16.50 ($26) for adults, £13 ($21) seniors, £11 ($18) children, and £49 ($78) for families is worth it in vacation-snap value alone. The ongoing commentary is very funny.

Thanks to Mayor Ken Livingston, you can now use your Travelcard to get a third off most boat trip tickets. The Thames has always served as the city's highway, and there are 23 piers along its London stretch, from Hampton Court to Gravesend in the estuary. The funky Millbank Pier, by Tate Britain, is the newest (2002) and fanciest. At last count, more than 10 companies were running cruises and rush-hour-only ferries. There's a full schedule on the London Transport website (www.tfl.gov.uk/river), or pick up its **Thames River Services** booklet at Tube stations and tourist information offices.

The best value (even before the Travelcard discount) is the **Crown River Cruises** service (© 020/7936-2033) from Westminster to St. Katherine's Dock, stopping by the South Bank Centre and London Bridge, from 11am to 6:30pm in summer (until 3pm in winter). A return ticket costs £6.30 ($10) for adults, £5.30 ($8) seniors, and £3.15 ($5) under-16s. The round-trip takes 1 hour but the ticket is valid all day, so you can hop on and off to sightsee.

Don't forget: You can go to Hampton Court and the Royal Botanic Gardens Kew by boat. Those trips are more expensive, and there are fewer headline sights on the way, but they do make for a great day out.

You can also take a boat along the Regent's Canal. From April to October, **Jason's Trip** (© 020/7286-3428; www.jasons.co.uk; Tube: Warwick Ave.) operates a 90-minute tour from the wharf opposite 60 Blomfield Rd. in Little Venice. The painted narrow boat leaves at 10:30am (except in Oct), 12:30pm, and 2:30pm and takes you past Brownings Island (so called because Robert Browning lived there), through the Maida Hill Tunnel and Regent's Park, to Camden Lock. The round-trip price is £6.95 ($11) for adults, £5.50 ($9) for children, £20 ($32) for a family ticket; £5.95 ($10) and £4.75 ($7), respectively, one-way. **London Waterbus Company** (© 020/7482-2660; Tube: Warwick Ave., Camden Town) travels the same stretch of canal, leaving every hour from 10am to 5pm. The fares are as follows: one-way £4.80 ($8) adult, £3.10 ($5) children; round-trip £6.20 and £4 ($10 and $6). Their all-in-one ticket including admission to London Zoo costs £12.90 ($21) adults and 9.40 ($15) children. This is a real bargain.

WALKING TOURS

Original London Walks (© 020/7624-3978; www.walks.com) offers the best regularly scheduled public walks, covering a variety of routes and using superb guides. More than 100 walks a week are offered year-round on themes ranging from royalty to rock stars (and, of course, Jack the Ripper). Walks cover 1½km to 3km (1 mile–2 miles) and cost £5 ($8) for adults or £4 ($6) for seniors and students. Children 16 and under go free. No reservations are needed. Call or visit the website to find out what walks are offered when, then show up at the appropriate Tube station to meet the guide.

7 Shopping

London is very expensive, but there are a few bargains to be had. The trick is to shop the sales. Your best bet is to ignore anything American and to concentrate on all things British. You can, surprisingly, find good value in French goods, almost the equivalent of what you find in Paris.

London keeps fairly uniform store hours. The norm is 10am opening and 5:30pm closing, usually staying open later on Wednesday or Thursday night, until 7 or 8pm. Stores may stay open 6 hours on Sunday; usually they choose 11am to 5pm. Stores in designated tourist areas and flea markets are exempt from this law, and may be open all day on Sunday. Thus, Covent Garden, Greenwich, and Hampstead are big Sunday venues for shoppers.

THE SECRET OF THE SALES

Traditionally, stores in Britain have two major sale periods: January and July. Discounts can range from 25% to 50% at leading department stores, such as Harrods and Selfridges. The best buys are on Harrods logo souvenirs, English china (seconds are trucked in from factories in Stoke-on-Trent), and English designer brands like Jaeger. Beware, though: There's a huge difference in the quality of the finds bought in genuine sales, where stores are actually clearing the shelves, and the goods bought at "produced" sales, where special merchandise has been hauled in just for the sale.

THE TOP SHOPPING STREETS & NEIGHBORHOODS

There are several key streets where you'll find London's best retail stores.

THE WEST END   The West End includes the posh Mayfair district and is home to the core of London's big-name shopping. Most of the department stores, designer shops, and multiples (chain stores) have their flagships in this area. The key streets are **Oxford Street** for affordable shopping (start at Marble Arch Tube station if you're ambitious, or Bond St. station if you just want to see

---

Tips **Tax-Free Shopping**

Global Refund (www.taxfree.se) is your best bet for getting VAT refunds at the airport. In London you can shop where you see the GLOBAL REFUND TAX-FREE SHOPPING sign. When leaving Britain, simply show your purchases, receipts, and passport to customs, and have your Global Refund checks stamped. You have several choices—immediate cash at one of Global Refund's offices, crediting to a chosen credit card or bank account, or a bank check sent to a chosen address. Refunds offices are conveniently situated at all major exit points such as Gatwick and Heathrow airports.

some of it) and **Regent Street,** which intersects it at Oxford Circus (Tube: Oxford Circus). While there are several branches of the private label department store Marks & Spencer, their Marble Arch store (on Oxford St.; Tube: Marble Arch) is the flagship. Regent Street, which runs to Piccadilly, has more upscale department stores, including the famed Liberty of London.

In between the two, parallel to Regent Street, is **Bond Street** (Tube: Bond St.), which connects Piccadilly with Oxford Street. Divided into New and Old, Bond Street is synonymous with the luxury trade and the hot address for international designers from Chanel and Ferragamo to Versace and Donna Karan.

Burlington Arcade (Tube: Piccadilly Circus), the famous glass-roofed, Regency-era passage leading off Piccadilly, looks like a period exhibition and is lined with intriguing shops and boutiques. The small, smart stores specialize in fashion, jewelry, Irish linen, cashmere, and more. If you linger in the arcade until 5:30pm, you can watch the beadles, those ever-present attendants in their black-and-yellow livery and top hats, ceremoniously put in place the iron grills that block off the arcade until 9 the next morning, at which time they remove them to mark the start of a new business day. At 5:30pm, a hand bell called the Burlington Bell is sounded, signaling the end of business.

Jermyn Street, on the far side of Piccadilly, is a 2-block-long street devoted to high-end men's haberdashers and toiletries shops, many in business for centuries. Several hold royal warrants, including Turnbull & Asser, where Prince Charles has his pj's made.

The West End leads to the theater district, so there are two more shopping areas: the still-not-ready-for-prime-time **Soho,** where the sex shops are slowly being turned into cutting-edge designer shops, and **Covent Garden,** a shopping world unto itself. The original marketplace has overflowed its boundaries and taken over the surrounding neighborhood so that you can enjoy wandering in the maze of streets as you shop. Covent Garden is especially mobbed on weekends.

KNIGHTSBRIDGE & CHELSEA   This is the second-most famous of London's retail districts and the home of Harrods (see below). Nearby **Sloane Street** is chockablock with designer shops, as is another street in the opposite direction, **Cheval Place.** Walk toward Museum Row and you'll soon find **Beauchamp Place** (pronounced Bee-cham; Tube: Knightsbridge). The street is 1 block long, but it features the shops where young British aristos buy clothing.

King's Road (Tube: Sloane Sq.), the main street of Chelsea, will always be a symbol of London in the swinging sixties. Today, the street is still frequented by young people but has become a lineup of markets and "multistores," large or small conglomerations of indoor stands, stalls, and booths within one building or enclosure.

Chelsea doesn't begin and end with King's Road. If you choose to walk the other direction from Harrods, you connect to a part of Chelsea called **Brompton Cross,** another hip and hot area for designer shops. Also seek out **Walton Street,** a little snake of a street running from Brompton Cross back toward the museums. Two of its 3 blocks are devoted to luxury shops where you can buy aromatherapy, needlepoint, or costume jewelry.

Finally, don't forget all those museums right there in the corner of the shopping streets. They all have great gift shops.

KENSINGTON & NOTTING HILL   **Kensington High Street** (Tube: High St. Kensington) is the new hangout of the hipper teens, who have graduated from Carnaby Street and are ready for street chic. While there are a few staples of basic British fashion on this strip, most of the stores feature items that stretch; are very, very short; or are very, very tight.

From Kensington High Street, you can walk up **Kensington Church Street,** which, like Portobello Road, is one of the city's main shopping avenues for antiques. Kensington Church Street ends at the Notting Hill Gate Tube station, where you go for shopping in **Portobello Road;** the dealers and the weekend market are 2 blocks beyond.

TO MARKET, TO MARKET

THE WEST END   The most famous market in all of England, **Covent Garden Market** (© **020/7836-9136;** Tube: Covent Garden), offers several different markets daily from 9am to 6:30pm (it's most fun to come on Sun, when the number of vendors and the level of entertainment hits a peak). Covent Garden Market itself (in the restored hall) offers one of the best shopping opportunities in London with specialty shops that sell fashions and herbs, gifts and toys. Apple Market is the fun, bustling market in the courtyard, where traders sell just about everything. Many items are handmade, with some craftspeople selling their own wares, except on Mondays, when antiques dealers replace the craftspeople. Out back is **Jubilee Market** (© **020/7836-2139**), with cheap clothes and books; antiques dealers take over on Mondays.

St. Martin-in-the-Fields Market (Tube: Charing Cross) is good for teens and hipsters who don't want to trek all the way to Camden Market (see below) and can make do with imports from India and South America, crafts, and some local football souvenirs. It's located beside St. Martin-in-the-Fields, the famous church facing Trafalgar Square; hours are Monday through Saturday from 11am to 5pm, and Sundays noon to 5pm.

NOTTING HILL   Whatever you collect, you'll find it at the **Portobello Road Market** (Tube: Notting Hill Gate). It's mainly a Saturday happening, from 6am to 5pm. You needn't be here at the crack of dawn—9am is fine—you just want to beat the motor-coach crowd. Portobello has become synonymous with antiques, but don't take the stall-holder's word for it that the fiddle he's holding is a genuine Stradivarius; it might be from an East End pawnshop.

The market is divided into three major sections. The most crowded is the antiques section, running between Colville Road and Chepstow Villas to the south. (*Warning:* Beware of pickpockets in this area.) The second section (and the oldest part) is the "fruit and veg" market, lying between Westway and Colville Road. In the third section there's a flea market, where Londoners sell bric-a-brac and secondhand goods.

NORTH LONDON   If it's Wednesday, it's time for **Camden Passage** (© **020/7359-9969;** Tube: Angel) in Islington, where each Wednesday (8am–4pm) and Saturday (9am–5pm) there's a very upscale antiques market.

Don't confuse Camden Passage with **Camden Market** (Tube: Camden Town), which is for teens and others into body piercing, blue hair, and vintage clothing. Serious collectors of vintage may want to explore Camden market during the

Shopping Tip
Some 90 antique and art shops along Portobello Road are open during the week when the street market is closed. This is a better time for the serious collector to shop because you'll get more attention from dealers.

week, when the teen scene isn't quite so overwhelming. Market hours are 9:30am to 5:30pm daily.

THE DEPARTMENT STORES

Fortnum & Mason, Ltd., 181 Piccadilly, W1 (© 020/7734-8040; Tube: Piccadilly Circus), the world's most elegant grocery store, is a British tradition dating from 1707. Enter the doors and be transported to another world of deep-red carpets, crystal chandeliers, wooden staircases, and tailcoated assistants. The grocery department is renowned for its impressive selection of the finest foods from around the world. You can wander through the four floors and inspect the bone china and crystal-cut glass, find the perfect present in the leather or stationery departments, or browse the furniture, paintings, and ornaments in the antiques department. There are also beauty and fashion items for men and women.

Harrods, 87–135 Brompton Rd., Knightsbridge, SW1 (© 020/7730-1234; Tube: Knightsbridge), remains an institution, but in the last decade or so it has grown increasingly dowdy. If you're looking for the latest trends, shop elsewhere. With some 300 departments, the range, variety, and quality of merchandise still dazzles the visiting out-of-towner.

The whole fifth floor is devoted to sports and leisure, with a wide range of equipment and attire. Toy Kingdom is on the fourth floor, along with children's wear. The Egyptian Hall, on the ground floor, sells crystal from Lalique and Baccarat, plus porcelain. There's also a men's grooming room, a jewelry department, and a fashion department for younger customers. When you're ready for a break, you have a choice of 18 restaurants, cafes, and bars. Best of all are the Food Halls, stocked with a huge variety of foods. Harrods began as a grocer in 1849, and that's still the heart of the business. The motto remains, "If you can eat or drink it, you'll find it at Harrods."

Harvey Nichols, 109–125 Knightsbridge, SW1 (© 020/7235-5000; Tube: Knightsbridge), known locally as Harvey Nicks, has its own gourmet-food hall and fancy restaurant on the fifth floor. Women's clothing is the largest segment of its business, but the huge store is crammed with the best designer home furnishings and gifts.

Liberty, 214–220 Regent St. (© 020/7734-1234; Tube: Oxford Circus), restored to its original neo-Tudor splendor with a whitewashed and half-timbered exterior and wooden-paneled galleries within, has six floors of fashion, china, and home furnishings, as well as the famous Liberty Print fashion fabrics, upholstery fabrics, scarves, ties, luggage, and gifts.

Tips Shipping It Home

Many shoppers opt to have their goods shipped straight from London to their homes (no schlepping!). **Mail + Pack,** 343–453 Latimer Rd., London W10 6RA (© 020/8964-2410; Tube: Latimer Rd.), specializes in packing small to medium-size consignments, although they can also arrange for the shipment of antiques and a wide range of collectibles. Their rates include all packing charges, Customs documentation, and home delivery; excluding duties and taxes. It's less expensive if you carry the goods directly to the company's headquarters, but they will also arrange to pick up your goods, for a fee, at your London hotel or at the place where you made the original purchase.

Marks & Spencer, 458 Oxford St., W1 (© **020/7935-7954;** Tube: Marble Arch), England's most popular chain store, is called M & S or Marks & Sparks. Their fortune has been made in selling high quality, private label (St. Michael) clothing for all, plus home furnishings and groceries at slightly less-than-regular retail prices. The store offers good value. M & S is famous for its cotton-knit underwear, which 7 out of every 10 women in London wear.

SOME CLASSIC LONDON FAVORITES

ANTIQUES   At the **Antiquarius,** 131–141 King's Rd., SW3 (© **020/7351-5353;** Tube: Sloane Sq.), more than 120 dealers offer specialized merchandise, such as antique and period jewelry, silver, first-edition books, boxes, clocks, prints, and paintings, a lot of items from the 1950s. Closed Sunday. **Alfie's Antique Market,** 13–25 Church St., NW8 (© **020/7723-6066;** Tube: Marylebone, Edgware Rd.), is the biggest and one of the best-stocked conglomerates of antique dealers in London, all crammed into the premises of what was once a department store (before 1880). It contains more than 370 stalls, showrooms, and workshops scattered over 3,252 sq. m (35,000 sq. ft.) of floor space. Closed Sunday and Monday. A whole antique district has grown up around Alfie's along Church Street. *Note:* See also "To Market, To Market" above. Portobello Road is really the prime hunting ground.

BATH & BODY   There are branches of **The Body Shop** everywhere, and prices are much lower than they are in the United States. Check out the branch at 374 Oxford St., W1 (© **020/7409-7868;** Tube: Bond St.). **Boots The Chemist** has branches everywhere too, including one across the street from Harrods, at 72 Brompton Rd., SW3 (© **020/7589-6557;** Tube: Knightsbridge). The best values here are the house brands of beauty products, including versions of The Body Shop (two lines, Global and Naturalistic), and Chanel makeup (called No. 7). **Culpepper the Herbalist,** 8 The Market, Covent Garden, WC2 (© **020/7379-6698**), is where you can stock up on essential oils or dream pillows, candles, sachets, and aromatherapy fans. There's another branch in Mayfair at 21 Bruton St., W1 (© **020/7629-4559**). **Floris,** 89 Jermyn St., SW1 (© **020/7930-2885;** Tube: Piccadilly Circus), stocks a variety of toilet articles and fragrances in floor-to-ceiling mahogany cabinets dating from the Great Exhibition of 1851. **Czech & Speake,** 39C Jermyn St. SW1 (© **020/7439-0216;** Tube: Piccadilly Circus), has seven fragrance lines, including their best-selling perfume, 88, an elixir of sandalwood, vetiver, and cassie. **Neal's Yard Remedies,** 15 Neal's Yard, WC2 (© **020/7379-7222;** Tube: Covent Garden), is known everywhere for its homemade bath, beauty, and aromatherapy products packaged in cobalt-blue bottles. The Victorian perfumery called **Penhaligon's,** 41 Wellington St., WC2 (© **020/7836-2150;** Tube: Covent Garden), offers a large selection of perfumes, aftershaves, soaps, and bath oils for women and men.

FASHION: TRUE BRIT   Every internationally known designer worth his or her weight in shantung has a boutique in London, but the best buys are on sturdy English styles that last forever. **Next,** 20 Long Acre, WC2 (© **020/7836-1516;** Tube: Covent Garden), is a chain of "affordable fashion" stores for men, women, and kids. **Westaway & Westaway,** 62–65 and 92–93 Great Russell St., WC1 (© **020/7405-4479;** Tube: Tottenham Court Rd.), opposite the British Museum, is a substitute for a shopping trip to Scotland. Here you'll find kilts, scarves, waistcoats, capes, dressing gowns, and rugs in authentic clan tartans. They also sell cashmere, camel's hair, and Shetland knitwear, along with Harris tweed jackets, Burberry raincoats, and cashmere overcoats for men.

Moments Where London's Top Designers Go for Inspiration

Just for fun head for **Brick Lane** in E1 in London's East End, taking the Tube to Liverpool Street, then bus no. 8 heading toward the emerging district of Shoreditch. Here along Brick Lane beginning at 7am (winding down around noon), vendors from the far corners of the long-gone British Empire sell "any and everything." The street is lined with inexpensive Indian restaurants, the best of which is **Beigel Bake,** 159 Brick Lane, E1 (© **020/7729-0616**), if you want to hang out until lunch.

Another tip: If you like to see African-Caribbean life as uniquely lived in London, head for the **Brixton Market** along Electric Avenue, SW9. Take the Tube to Brixton. To the sound of Jamaica reggae, with lots of Bob Marley, you can munch down on jerk pork and other West Indian eats and search for bargains, including the cheapest clothing sold in London.

Electric Avenue is the virtual main street of London's African-Caribbean life; it was immortalized in the 1980s by Eddie Grant, the Jamaican singer. As you stroll the avenue with mostly fruit and vegetable stalls, duck into **Granville Arcade** for Britain's widest selection of African fabrics, reggae disks, and shopping surprise upon surprise. The market is best visited Monday, Tuesday, Thursday, and Saturday 8am to 6pm; Wednesday 8am to 1pm, and Friday 8am to 7pm.

FASHION: VINTAGE & SECONDHAND CLOTHING   A London institution since the 1940s, **Pandora,** 16–22 Cheval Place, SW7 (© **020/7589-5289;** Tube: Knightsbridge), stands in fashionable Knightsbridge, a stone's throw from Harrods. Outfits are usually no more than 2 seasons old and prices are generally one-third to one-half the retail value. For the best in original streetwear from the 1950s, 1960s, and 1970s, **Pop Boutique,** 6 Monmouth St., WC2 (© **020/7497-5262;** Tube: Covent Garden), is tops. Right next to the chic Covent Garden Hotel, it has great vintage wear at affordable prices.

Note: There's no VAT refund on used clothing.

FILOFAX   All major department stores sell Filofax supplies, but the full range is carried in their own stores. Go to the main West End branch, **The Filofax Centre,** at 21 Conduit St., W1 (© **020/7499-0457;** Tube: Oxford Circus); it's larger and fancier than the Covent Garden branch at 69 Neal St. (© **020/7836-1977**), with the entire range of inserts and books at about half the U.S. price. They also have good sales; calendars for the next year go on sale very early (about 10 months in advance).

HOME DESIGN & HOUSEWARES   At the **Conran Shop,** Michelin House, 81 Fulham Rd., SW3 (© **020/7589-7401;** Tube: S. Kensington), you'll find high style at reasonable prices from the man who invented it all for Britain: Sir Terence Conran. It's great for gifts and home furnishings.

MUSEUM SHOPS   Most shoppable is the **London Transport Museum Shop,** adjacent to Covent Garden Marketplace, WC2 (© **020/7379-6344;** Tube: Covent Garden), which carries reasonably priced retro and antique travel posters as well as tons-of-fun gifts and souvenirs. The London Underground maps in their original size as seen at every Tube station can be purchased here. The best museum shop in London is the **Victoria and Albert Gift Shop,** Cromwell Road, SW7 (© **020/7938-8500;** Tube: S. Kensington), selling cards, books, and the usual items, along with reproductions from the museum archives.

MUSIC   The biggies in town are **Tower Records,** 1 Piccadilly Circus, W1 (© **020/7439-2500;** Tube: Piccadilly Circus), one of the largest tape, record, and CD stores in Europe, and its major rival, the **Virgin Megastore,** 14–16 Oxford St., W1 (© **020/7631-1234;** Tube: Tottenham Court Rd.). You'll find whatever you're looking for at either one.

SHOES   Dr. Martens makes a brand of shoe so popular that there's an entire department store selling accessories, gifts, and even clothes: **Dr. Martens' Department Store,** 1–4 King St., WC2 (© **020/7497-1460;** Tube: Covent Garden). Teens come to worship here because ugly is beautiful—and because the prices are far better than they are in the United States or elsewhere in Europe. **Shelly's,** 266 Regent St., W1 (© **020/7287-0939;** Tube: Oxford Circus), the flagship of the mother of all London shoe shops, sells hip shoes and boots for everyone from tots to grown-ups.

TEAS   **The Tea House,** 15A Neal St., WC2 (© **020/7240-7539;** Tube: Covent Garden), sells everything associated with tea, tea drinking, and teatime. It boasts more than 70 quality teas and tisanes, including the best of China, India, Japan, and Sri Lanka, plus such longtime favorite English blended teas as Earl Grey. The shop also offers novelty teapots and mugs, among other items.

TOYS   **Hamleys,** 188–196 Regent St., W1 (© **020/7494-2000;** Tube: Oxford Circus), is the finest toyshop in the world—more than 35,000 toys and games on 7 floors of fun and magic. A huge selection is offered, including soft, cuddly stuffed animals, as well as dolls, radio-controlled cars, train sets, model kits, board games, outdoor toys, and computer games. There's also a small branch at Covent Garden and another at Heathrow Airport.

8 London After Dark

Weekly publications such as *Time Out* and *Where* carry full entertainment listings, including information on restaurants and nightclubs. You'll also find listings in daily newspapers, notably the *Times* and the *Telegraph.*

THE THEATER

In London, you'll have a chance to see the world-renowned English theater on its home ground. Matinees are on Wednesday (Thurs at some theaters) and on Saturday. Most theaters are closed on Sunday. It's impossible to describe all of London's theaters in this space, so below are listed just a few.

GETTING TICKETS

If you want to see specific shows, especially hit ones, purchase your tickets in advance. The best way is to buy your ticket from the theater's box office, which you can do over the phone using a credit card. You'll pay the theater price and pick up the tickets the day of the show. You can also go to a reliable ticket agent (the greatest cluster is in Covent Garden), but remember, you'll pay a hefty fee of at least 25% when you're dealing with any ticket agency in London or in the U.S.

   With offices in London and the United States, **Keith Prowse** can reserve tickets for hit shows weeks or even months in advance. In the United States, contact

(*Value* **Purchase Discount Tickets Wisely**

The Society of London Theatre operates **tkts** (no phone), a half-price ticket booth in Leicester Square, where tickets for many shows are available at half price, plus a £2 ($3.20) service charge. Tickets are sold only on the day of performance, and there is a limit of four per person. You cannot return tickets; MasterCard and Visa are accepted. Hours are daily from noon to 6:30pm.

Warning: Beware of scalpers ("touts") who hang out in front of theaters with hit shows. There are many reports of scalpers selling forged tickets, and their prices are outrageous.

them at (© **800/669-7469;** www.keithprowse.com). In London, their number is © 020/7836-9001. **First Call** (© **0129/453-744;** www.firstcalltickets.com) is the U.K.'s largest independent ticket agency; you can purchase many tickets online from them.

For tickets and information to just about any show and entertainment in London, **Global Tickets** (www.globaltickets.com) has a U.S. number (© **800/223-6108** or 914/328-2150). They also have offices in London at the Britain Visitor Centre, 1 Regent St., SW1 (© **020/7734-4555**). They'll mail tickets to your home, fax confirmation, or leave tickets at the box office. Another option is the London-based **Albemarle of London** (© **020/7637-9041;** www.albemarle-london.com); their website has one of the best London theatre listings.

London theater tickets are priced quite reasonably when compared with those in New York. Prices span £18 to £60 ($13–$96), depending on the seat and the show. Sometimes **gallery seats** (the cheapest) are sold on the day of the performance, so you'll have to head to the box office early in the day to buy and return an hour before the performance to queue up, since they're not reserved seats. Many of the major theaters offer reduced-price tickets to students with a valid student ID on a standby basis. When available, these tickets are sold 30 minutes prior to curtain. Line up early for popular shows, as standby tickets go fast and furious.

THE MAJOR COMPANIES & THEATERS

Old Vic   The Old Vic is a 180-year-old repertory theater whose facade and much of the interior have been restored to their original early-19th-century style. This fabled theater was where Sir John Gielgud made his debut in 1921 and where Lord Laurence Olivier directed the first National Theatre. The Cut, Waterloo Rd., SE1. © **020/7928-7616,** or 020/7928-1722 (box office). Plays £15–£30 ($24–$48). AE, MC, V. Tube: Waterloo.

Royal National Theatre   This is the flagship of British theater. Home to one of the world's greatest stage companies, the National houses not one but three theaters. Across its three stages the National presents a repertoire of the finest theater in the world, from classic drama to award-winning new plays, from comedy to musicals to shows for young people. Box office open Monday through Saturday from 10am to 11pm. South Bank, SE1. © **020/7452-3000.** www.nationaltheatre.org.uk. Tickets £9–£35 ($14–$56); midweek matinees, Sat matinees, and previews cost less. MC, V. Tube: Waterloo, Embankment, or Charing Cross.

The Royal Opera House—The Royal Ballet & the Royal Opera   The Royal Ballet and the Royal Opera are at home in a magnificently restored theater

Central London Theaters

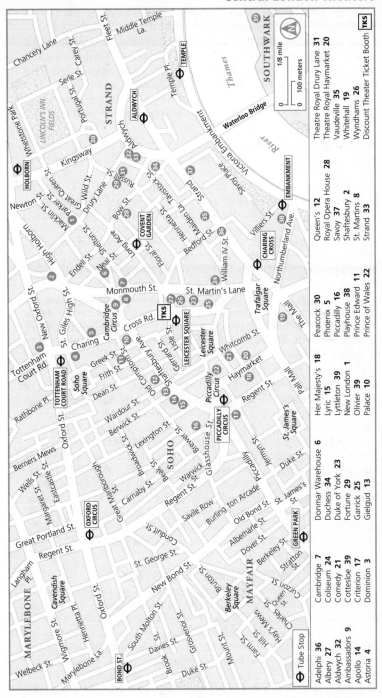

Theatre Royal Drury Lane **31**
Theatre Royal Haymarket **20**
Vaudeville **35**
Whitehall **19**
Wyndhams **26**
Discount Theater Ticket Booth **TKS**

Queen's **12**
Royal Opera House **28**
Savoy **37**
Shaftesbury **2**
St. Martins **8**
Strand **33**

Peacock **30**
Phoenix **5**
Piccadilly **16**
Playhouse **38**
Prince Edward **11**
Prince of Wales **22**

Her Majesty's **18**
Lyric **15**
Lyttleton **39**
New London **1**
Olivier **39**
Palace **10**

Donmar Warehouse **6**
Duchess **34**
Duke of York **23**
Fortune **29**
Garrick **25**
Gielgud **13**

Cambridge **7**
Coliseum **24**
Comedy **21**
Cottesloe **39**
Criterion **17**
Dominion **3**

Adelphi **36**
Albery **27**
Aldwych **32**
Ambassadors **9**
Apollo **14**
Astoria **4**

Φ Tube Stop

1/8 mile
100 meters

with spectacular new public spaces, including a rooftop restaurant, and bars and shops. Backstage tours are given daily at 10:30am, 12:30pm, and 2:30pm (not on Sun or matinee days). Performances of the Royal Opera are sung in the original language with supertitles. The Royal Ballet, which ranks with top companies such as the Kirov and the Paris Opera Ballet, performs a repertory with a tilt toward the classics. You can queue for specially priced day-of-show tickets starting at 10am. The box office is open Monday through Saturday from 10am to 8pm. Bow St., Covent Garden, WC2. ⓒ 020/7304-4000. www.royalopera.org. Tickets £10–£150 ($16–$240). MC, V. Tube: Covent Garden.

Royal Shakespeare Company (RSC)   Although the Barbican Theatre is still one of its performance venues, the company now uses various theaters in the West End, such as The Gielgud and the Theatre Royal Haymarket, and has expanded its season. To see this illustrious company perform you'll need to peruse the various theatre listings when you arrive in London, or, better yet, surf the RSC website **www.rsc.org.uk**. The ticket situation has been decentralized, so you'll have to get tickets at the various theaters, just as you would for any other West End show; ticket prices vary according to the show, the theater, and the stars performing. For more information you can call the Ticket Hotline in Stratford (ⓒ **0870/609-1110**), but remember: It's a long-distance call. Barbican Centre, Silk St., EC2; ⓒ 020/7638-8891 for box office; Tube: Barbican, Moorgate; tickets £15–£32.50 ($24–$52). Gielgud Theatre, Shaftesbury Ave, W1; ⓒ 020/7494-5065 for box office; Tube: Leicester Sq.; tickets £15–£37.50 ($24–$60), same-day tickets £15 ($24), standby ½ hr before performance £15 ($24) seniors and students. Theatre Royal Haymarket, Haymarket, W1; ⓒ 0870/609-1110 (Stratford box office) or go in person to theatre box office; Tube: Piccadilly Circus; tickets £12–£40 ($19–$64).

Shakespeare's Globe Theatre   In May 1997, the new Globe Theatre—a replica of the Elizabethan original, thatched roof and all—staged its first slate of plays on the exact site of the 16th-century theater where the Bard originally staged his work. Productions vary in style and setting; but the theatergoer's experience is otherwise kept as authentic as possible, with no focused stage lighting and seating on wooden benches in thatch-roofed galleries. About 500 "groundlings" can stand in the uncovered yard around the stage, just as they did when the bard himself was here. From May through September, the company holds performances Tuesday through Saturday at 3 and 7pm, and Sunday at 4pm; the schedule may be affected by the weather, since this is an outdoor theater. For details on the exhibition that tells the story of the re-creation of the Globe, as well as guided tours of the theater, see section 2, earlier in this chapter. New Globe Walk, Bankside, SE1. ⓒ 020/7401-9919. www.shakespeares-globe.com. Tickets £5 ($8) for groundlings, £8–£30 ($13–$48) for gallery seats. AE, MC, V. Tube: Mansion House.

THE REST OF THE PERFORMING ARTS SCENE

Barbican Centre   Like the South Bank Centre, this large arts complex is home to music and theater. The Barbican Theatre is one of the London venues for the Royal Shakespeare Company (see above), while the Barbican Hall is the permanent home of the **London Symphony Orchestra** (www.lso.co.uk) and host to visiting orchestras and performers, from classical to jazz, folk, and world music. An hour before performances of classical music concerts, unsold tickets go on sale for £6 ($10). You'll find restaurants, cafes, and bars in the various venues. The box office is open daily from 10am to 8pm. Silk St., The Barbican, EC2. ⓒ 020/7638-8891, or 020/7382-7297 (24-hr recorded into). Tickets £9–£45 ($14–$72). AE, MC, V. Tube: Barbican, Moorgate, St. Paul's, Liverpool St., or Bank.

English National Opera   The London Coliseum, built in 1904 as a variety theater and converted into an opera house in 1968, is London's largest theater. The English National Opera is one of the two national opera companies and performs a wide range of works, from great classics to Gilbert and Sullivan to new and experimental operas. A repertory of 18 to 20 productions, all performed in English, is presented 5 or 6 nights a week. The English National Ballet also performs here. About 200 discounted balcony tickets go on sale the day of performance at 10am. London Coliseum, St. Martin's Lane, WC2. ℂ 020/7632-8300. www.eno.org. Tickets £8–£160 ($13–$96). MC, V. Tube: Charing Cross or Leicester Sq.

Kenwood Lakeside Concerts   Presented on the north side of Hampstead Heath, these band and orchestral concerts have been a British summer tradition for over 50 years. In recent years, laser shows and fireworks have added to a repertoire that includes everything from rousing versions of the 1812 Overture to jazz and opera. The final concert of the season always features some of the Pomp and Circumstance Marches of Sir Edward Elgar, everyone's favorite imperial composer. Music drifts across the lake from the performance amphitheater above a verdant scene that encourages wine-and-cheese parties on the grass. Concerts take place from July to early September, every Saturday at 7:30pm. Kenwood, Hampstead Lane, Hampstead Heath, London NW3 7JR. ℂ 020/7413-1443. Tickets for adults £9 ($13.50) for seats on the grass lawn, £11–£16 ($16.50–$24) for reserved deck chairs. Reductions of 25% for seniors and students. AE, MC, V. Tube: Golders Green or Archway, then bus no. 210.

Open Air Theatre   This outdoor theater is in an idyllic setting in the center of Regent's Park. Presentations are mainly Shakespeare, usually in period costume, and both seating and acoustics are excellent. If it rains, you're given tickets for another performance. The season runs from the end of May through mid-September, Monday through Saturday at 8pm, plus Wednesday, Thursday, and Saturday matinees at 2:30pm. The box office is open daily from 10am to 8pm. Inner Circle, Regent's Park, NW1. ℂ 020/7486-2431. http://openairtheatre.org. Tickets £8.50–£25 ($14–$40). AE, MC, V. Tube: Baker St.

Royal Albert Hall   Opened in 1871 and dedicated to the memory of Queen Victoria's consort, Prince Albert, this round building encircles one of the world's most famous auditoriums with a seating capacity of 5,200. Since 1941, the hall has been the setting for the BBC Henry Wood Promenade Concerts ("The Proms"), a concert series that lasts for 8 weeks between mid-July and mid-September. Although most of the audience occupies reserved seats, true aficionados usually opt for standing room in the orchestra pit for close-up views of the musicians performing on stage. The programs are outstanding and often present newly commissioned works for the first time. The box office is open daily from 10am to 8pm. Kensington Gore, SW7. ℂ 020/7589-2141. Tickets £6–£130 ($10–$208) depending on the event. AE, MC, V. 8pm. Tube: S. Kensington, High St. Kensington, or Knightsbridge.

Sadler's Wells Theatre   This is one of London's most famous contemporary dance venues and also hosts theater and music productions and solo performances. In the early 1990s, the turn-of-the-century theater was demolished, and a new building of innovative design was completed in 1998. The original facade has been restored, but the interior has been completely revamped to create a stylish, cutting-edge theater dedicated to audience comfort. The box office is open daily from 10am to 8pm. Rosebery Ave., Islington, EC1. ℂ 020/7863-6000. www.sadlers wells.com. Tickets £9–£60 ($14–$96). MC, V. Tube: Angel.

South Bank Arts Centre   The South Bank Centre is comprised of three concert halls on the south side of the Thames near Waterloo Bridge: Royal Festival Hall, Queen Elizabeth Hall, and the Purcell Room. Classical music, ballet, jazz, popular classics, pop, and contemporary dance performances are presented in a year-round performance schedule. The center also accommodates the internationally famous Hayward Gallery (see earlier in this chapter) whose exhibitions include both contemporary and historical art. The Royal Festival Hall offers free lunchtime music from 12:30pm and free commuter jazz in the foyer from 5:15pm to 6:45pm on Fridays. The box office is open daily from 9am to 9pm. South Bank, SE1. ℂ 020/7960-4242. www.sbc.org.uk. Tickets £6–£40 ($10–$64). AE, MC, V. Tube: Waterloo or Embankment.

THE CLUB & MUSIC SCENE
CABARET & COMEDY

The Comedy Store   This is a London showcase for established and emerging comic talent. Many big TV personalities got their start here. You must be over 18 to see a show. The club opens 1½ hours before each show. Go on Tuesday when the humor is more cutting-edge and the riffs right out of the headlines. Shows start at 8pm nightly; there's also a late show Saturday nights at 11:30pm. 1A Oxendon St., off Piccadilly Circus, SW1. ℂ 020/7344-0234. www.thecomedystore.co.uk. Cover £12–£18 ($19–$29). Tube: Leicester Sq. or Piccadilly Circus.

ROCK

Barfly Club   In a dingy residential neighborhood in north London, this traditional-looking pub is distinguished by the roster of rock 'n' roll bands who come in from throughout the U.K. for bouts of beer and high-energy music. You can get virtually anything here, which adds to the sense of fun and adventure. The roster of world-class groups who were "discovered" here includes Oasis. You'll usually hear three different bands a night. It's open nightly from 7pm to 2 or 3am, with most musical acts beginning at 8:15pm. The Monarch, 49 Chalk Farm Rd., NW1. ℂ 020/7482-4884. www.barflyclub.com. Cover £5–£10 ($8–$16). Tube: Northern Line to Camden Town or Chalk Farm Station.

The Bull & Gate   Smaller, cheaper, and less touristy than many of its competitors, the Bull & Gate is the unofficial headquarters of London's pub-rock scene. Usually relatively unknown rock bands are served up back-to-back within a woodsy, somewhat battered Victorian pub setting where everyone seems to spill beer on the floor and no one cares. This is off-the-beaten-track London at its most authentic. Blur, Madness, and Pulp all played here before they hit the big time, and may drop in again from time to time. It's open daily from 11am to midnight, with music nightly starting at 9pm. 389 Kentish Town Rd., NW5. ℂ 020/7485-5358. www.bullandgate.co.uk. Cover £5 ($8). Tube: Kentish Town.

The Rock Garden   The Rock Garden has a restaurant at street level, and a bar and stage in the cellar known as The Gardening Club. Dire Straits, the Police, and U2 all played here in the early days. You may see tomorrow's Oasis here, or just a bunch of birds or blokes you'll never hear from again. Open Monday through Thursday from 5pm to 3am, Friday and Saturday from 5pm to 5am, and Sunday from 7pm to midnight. 6–7 The Piazza, Covent Garden, WC2. ℂ 020/7836-4052. Cover for The Gardening Club £5–£12 ($8–$19); diners enter free. Tube: Covent Garden.

TRADITIONAL ENGLISH MUSIC

Cecil Sharp House   This was the focal point of the folk revival in the 1960s and as headquarters of the English Folk Dance and Song Society, it continues to treasure, document, and nurture this music. Here you'll find a whole range of traditional English music and dancing performed. Call for hours (which vary) and to see what's on. 2 Regent's Park Rd., NW1. © 020/7485-2206. www.efdss.org. Tube: Camden Town.

JAZZ & BLUES

100 Club   The less plush and less expensive 100 Club is a serious rival of the city's many jazz clubs. Its cavalcade of bands includes the best British jazz musicians as well as many touring Americans. Rock, R&B, and blues are also on tap. Open Monday through Thursday from 7:30 to 11:30pm; Friday from noon to 3pm and 8:30pm to 2am; Saturday from 7:30pm to 1am; and Sunday from 7:30 to 11:30pm. 100 Oxford St., W1. © 020/7636-0933. www.the100club.co.uk. Cover £9–£10 ($14–$16). Tube: Tottenham Court Rd. or Oxford Circus.

Ain't Nothing But Blues Bar   Featuring mostly local acts, the club also books American bands on tour, and bills itself as the only true blues place in town. On weekends, prepare to queue. From the Oxford Circus Tube exit, walk south on Regent Street, turn left on Great Marlborough Street, and then take a quick right on Kingly Street. Open Monday through Wednesday from 6pm to 1am, Thursday from 6pm to 2am, and Friday and Saturday from 6pm to 3am. 20 Kingly St., W1. © 020/7287-0514. Cover Fri–Sat £5–£18 ($8–$29) free before 8:30pm. Tube: Oxford Circus.

Pizza Express Jazz Club   Yes, it's a restaurant, but it also serves up some of the best jazz in London presented by mainstream artists. This darkly lit club offers jazz that's cool and pies that are hot (you must order food). Make reservations, as this place fills up quickly. Open daily from noon to 1am. 10 Dean St., W1. © 020/7437-9595. Cover £10–£20 ($16–$32). Tube: Tottenham Court Rd.

Ronnie Scott's   Mention jazz in London and people immediately think of Ronnie Scott's, long the European citadel of modern jazz. Featured on almost every bill is an American band, often with a top-notch singer. The club's in the heart of Soho, a 10-minute walk from Piccadilly Circus via Shaftesbury Avenue. There are three separate areas: the Main Room, the Upstairs@Ronnie's disco club (separate entrance and admission £3–£7/$4.80–$11; included with admission to the Main Room), and the Downstairs Bar. If you have a student ID, your cover from Monday through Wednesday costs £10 ($16). In the Main Room you can either stand at the bar to watch the show or sit at a table and order dinner. The more intimate Downstairs Bar is a quiet rendezvous. Upstairs@Ronnie's has a separate entrance and spins different sounds nightly, with salsa-inspired Club Latino taking over Fridays and Saturdays. Open Monday through Saturday from 8:30pm to 3am. 47 Frith St., W1. © 020/7439-0747. Cover Mon–Thurs £15 ($24); Fri–Sat £25 ($40). Tube: Tottenham Court Rd., Leicester Sq., or Piccadilly Circus.

DANCE CLUBS

Bagley's Studios   The premises are vast, echoing, a bit grimy, and set in the bleak industrial landscape behind King's Cross Station. But on Friday, Saturday and Sunday, Bagley's morphs into one of London's most animated raves. It's scattered over two floors, each the size of an American football field and divided into a trio of individual rooms, each with its own ambience and sound system. You'll be happiest here if you wander from room to room, searching out the site that best corresponds to your energy level at the moment. The choices include rooms devoted to garage, club classics, "banging" (hard house) music, and "bubbly" upbeat dance music. Non-weekend nights are given over to whatever promoter has booked the space. Open Friday to Sunday from 10pm to 7am. King's Cross Freight Depot, off York Way, N1. ✆ **020/7278-2777**. Cover £14–£25 ($6–$40). Tube: King's Cross.

Bar Rumba   A secret address among Latinophiles, Bar Rumba leans toward radical jazz fusion on some nights, "phat" funk on other occasions. Boasting two full bars, it has a different musical theme every night, and Tuesday and Wednesday are the only nights you probably won't have to line up at the door. Monday showcases jazz, hip-hop, and drum & bass; Fridays feature soul, R&B, and swing. Saturday is the most popular night, featuring a mix of house and garage. Open Monday through Thursday from 5pm to 3:30 am, Friday from 5pm to 4am, Saturday from 9pm to 6am, and Sunday from 8pm to 1:30 am. 36 Shaftesbury Ave., W1. ✆ **020/7287-2715**. http://barrumba.co.uk. Cover £3–£12 ($4.80–$22). Tube: Piccadilly Circus.

The Cross   In the backwaters of King's Cross, this club collects a hip crowd that comes to dance. The building's warm brick-lined vaults create a stylish interior with a good vibe. Call to find out who's performing. Open Friday and Saturday from 10pm to 6am. The Arches, King's Cross Goods Yard, York Way, N1. ✆ **020/7837-0828**. Cover £8–£15 ($13–$24). Tube: King's Cross.

Equinox   The Equinox has nine bars, the city's largest dance floor, and a restaurant styled after a 1950s American diner. Virtually every kind of dance music is featured here. The setting is lavishly illuminated with one of Europe's largest lighting rigs, and the crowd is as varied as London itself. Summer visitors can enjoy theme nights, geared to entertaining a worldwide audience. Open Monday through Saturday from 9pm to 3am. Leicester Sq., WC2. ✆ **020/7437-1446**. Cover £2–£12 ($3.20–$19). Tube: Leicester Sq.

Hanover Grand   Thursdays are funky, attracting dancers in whatever they happened to have at the front of their closets; on Friday and Saturday the crowd gets more stylish. Dance floors are always busy here, as crowds surge up and down the stairs interconnecting the two levels. Open Wednesday through Thursday from 10pm to 4am, Friday from 11pm to 4am, and Saturday from 10:30pm to 4:30am. 6 Hanover St., W1. ✆ **020/7499-7977**. Cover £5–£15 ($8–$24). Tube: Oxford Circus.

Hippodrome   Here is one of London's greatest discos, an enormous place where light and sound beam in from all directions. Revolving speakers descend from the roof to deafen you, and you can watch yourself on closed-circuit video. The place is the most touristy nightclub in London, but also attracts a lot of locals who come here to meet foreigners. Open Monday through Saturday from 9am to 3am. Leicester Sq., WC2. ✆ **020/7499-7977**. Cover £3–£12 ($4.80–$19). Tube: Leicester Sq.

Sound   Right in the very heart of London, this massive venue books some of the biggest acts in popular music. Everybody from Puff Daddy/P. Diddy to Robbie Williams. The club offers a cafe at ground level, a restaurant in the basement, and a top-floor nightclub with dancing. Almost every night of the week a different experience is featured, from live salsa to '70s theme nights where the patrons dress the role. Swiss Centre at 10 Wardour St., Leicester Square, W1. ✆ **020/7287-1010**. Cover £10 ($16) on weekends. Tube: Leicester Sq.

Subterania   This unpretentious, informal club changes its style during the week to reflect the live bands it books. You'll have to call to find out who's playing and what the vibe will be like. The place contains a busy dance floor on its street level and a mezzanine-style bar upstairs. Energy levels are perked up by a collection of orange, purple, and blue sofas upholstered in faux leopard skin. Friday night features soul, funk, hip-hop, and swing; Saturday night, house and garage. Open Monday, Tuesday, and Thursday from 8pm to 2am; Wednesday from 9:30pm to 2am; and Friday and Saturday from 9:30pm to 3am. 12 Acklam Rd., W10. © 020/8960-4590. Cover £5–£10 ($8–$16) Tube: Ladbroke Grove.

Velvet Room   Classy vibrancy is the catch phrase, as DJs spin favorite dance hits into the wee hours. Open Monday and Thursday from 10pm to 3am, Wednesday from 10pm to 2:30am, and Friday and Saturday from 10pm to 4am. 143 Charing Cross Rd., WC2. © 020/7739-4655. Cover £6–£10 ($10–$16). Tube: Tottenham Court Rd.

The Zoo Bar   Its developers spent millions of pounds to create the slickest, glossiest, flashiest, and most psychedelic decor in London. The decor of the hyper-trendy upstairs bar focuses on a menagerie of real and mythical animals, meticulously depicted in mosaics beneath a glassed-in ceiling dome. Downstairs, no one will care if you can't think of anything witty to say, because you can't be heard over the music anyway. The crowd is over 18, under 35-ish, and beyond gender designation. Open Monday through Saturday from 4pm to 3:30am and Sunday from 4 to 10:30pm. 13–18 Bear St., WC2. © 020/7839-4188. Entrance venues free before 11pm, cover £4–£5 ($6–$8) thereafter. Tube: Leicester Sq.

LATIN RHYTHMS

Cuba   This is a Spanish/Cuban-style bar-restaurant upstairs and a music club downstairs. The crowd is an odd mix of diners, after-work drinkers, Latinophile music aficionados, and dancers, here to eat, drink, and check out live musical acts from Cuba, Brazil, Spain, and other Latin countries. Open Monday through Saturday from noon to 3am and Sunday from 2 to 10:30pm. 11 Kensington High St., W8. © 020/7938-4137. Cover £3–£8 ($4.50–$12). Tube: High St. Kensington.

Salsa   This lively bar-restaurant and music club for Latinophiles features musical acts from Central and South America. Dance lessons are available nightly starting at 6:30pm; live music starts at 9pm. Some of the best Latin dancers in London show up here. Open Monday through Saturday from 5:30pm to 2am and Sunday from 6pm to midnight. 96 Charing Cross Rd., WC2. © 020/7379-3277. Cover £2–£8 ($3–$12). Tube: Leicester Sq.

THE GAY & LESBIAN SCENE

The most reliable source of information on gay clubs and activities is the **Gay Switchboard** (© **020/7837-7324;** www.llgs.org.uk). The staff runs a 24-hour service for information on places and activities.

The Box   This popular rendezvous spot is adjacent to Seven Dials, one of Covent Garden's best-known traffic junctions. Daily, from noon on, the place does most of its business as a restaurant, serving meal-size salads, club sandwiches, and soups. Food service ends abruptly at 5:30pm when it becomes more of a cafe-bar hangout. Open Monday through Saturday from 11am to 11pm and Sunday from 6:30 to 10:30pm. 32–34 Monmouth St. (at Seven Dials), WC2. © 020/7240-5828. Tube: Covent Garden.

Candy Bar   This is the most popular lesbian bar in London at the moment. It has a wonderfully mixed clientele from butch to femme and young to old. There are a bar and a club downstairs. Design is simple, with bright colors and lots of mirrors upstairs and darker and more flirtatious downstairs. Men are welcome as long as a woman escorts them. Open Monday through Thursday from noon to 1am, Friday and Saturday from noon to 3am, and Sunday from noon to 11pm. 23–24 Bateman St., W1 © 020/7437-1977. Cover Fri–Sat £5 ($8). Tube: Tottenham Court Rd.

The Champion This large Victorian-era pub features a courtyard and a low-key but definitely cruisy crowd of men in their prime. Open Monday through Saturday from 11am to 11pm and Sunday from 1am to 10:30pm. 1 Wellington Terrace, Gayswater Rd., W2 ⓒ 020/7229-5056. Tube: Notting Hill Gate.

Coleherne One of London's landmark gay pubs, the Coleherne has for years and years been the hangout for denim and leathermen; it's just reopened with a redesigned interior and it's busier than ever. Open Monday through Saturday from 11am to 11pm and Sunday from 11am to 10:30pm. 261 Old Brompton Rd., SW5 ⓒ 020/7244-5951. Tube: Earl's Court.

The Edge When the late-night dance music is playing, the two lower floors tend to be the most high-energy, animated, and crowded. If you want quiet conversation, keep climbing for the upper floors. During the day, come and have a bite to eat or a light afternoon snack and wait for the transformation as the sun goes down. Open Monday through Saturday from 11am to 11pm and Sunday from noon to 10:30pm. 11 Soho Sq., W1. ⓒ 020/7439-1313. Tube: Tottenham Court Rd.

G-A-Y The biggest gay dance venue in Europe opens its doors every Saturday from 10:30pm to 5am. A smaller version, not strictly gay, is held Monday, Thursday, and Friday in Astoria's basement, same hours. London Astoria, 157 Charing Cross Rd., Soho, WC2. ⓒ 020/7734-6963. www.g-a-y.co.uk. Cover £3 ($4.80) Mon, Thurs, and Fri; £10 ($16) Sat. Tube: Tottenham Court Rd.

Heaven This landmark club in the vaulted cellars of Charing Cross Railway Station is reminiscent of a huge air-raid shelter. One of England's biggest gay clubs (it holds 2,000), it's divided into four different areas, each connected by a labyrinth of catwalks, stairs, and hallways. Heaven features big-name DJs spinning all kinds of vibes, and different theme nights; you can print flyers from the website that will reduce the price of admission. Open Monday and Wednesday from 10:30pm to 3am, Friday from 10:30pm to 6am, and Saturday from 10:30pm to 5:30pm. The Arches, Craven St., WC2. ⓒ 020/7930-2020. www.heaven-london.com. Cover £5–£12 ($8–$19). Tube: Charing Cross, Embankment.

Kudos The bar crowd is mostly gay men, including well-dressed "suits" on their way home from the office. The cafe in the back serves snacks: baked potatoes with toppings, small pizzas, and smoked salmon on a bagel. You can also get main courses like grilled chicken, pasta, and burgers. There are daily specials as well. Kudos offers customers free or reduced-price entry tickets to nearby clubs like G-A-Y and Heaven. 10 Adelaide St., WC2. ⓒ 020/7379-4573. Main courses £4–£7 ($6–$11). MC, V. Tube: Charing Cross.

Madame Jo Jo's This was London's poshest, most popular, and professional drag show until it changed hands and became a mostly straight dance club. Expensive drag shows are now presented on Saturday nights only. Call to see what's up Sunday through Friday. Open Wednesday from 10am to 2am, Thursday from 9:30pm to 3am, Friday from 10pm to 5am, Saturday from 10:30pm to 3am, and Sunday from 9am to 3pm and 9:30pm to 2:30am. 8 Brewer St., W1. ⓒ 020/7734-2473. Cover £5–£10 ($8–$16); £37 ($59) Sat cabaret only. Tube: Piccadilly Circus.

The Yard You enter through a secretive arch into a paved courtyard set back from the teeming Soho streets. In warm weather, as darkness falls over London, the courtyard becomes one of the favorite gay gathering spots in Soho. The bar faces the courtyard and has an upstairs lounge that allows double-decker cruising. Open Monday through Saturday from 11am to 11pm and Sunday from 11am to 10:30pm. 57 Rupert St., W1. ⓒ 020/77437-2652. Tube: Leicester Sq.

THE BAR & PUB SCENE

For additional pub listings, see "Great Deals on Dining," in chapter 3.

OUR FAVORITE BARS

Bad Bobs Bar & Restaurant   Established long ago in Dublin, this lively venue washes Ireland up on the shores of London. Featuring live music, four bars and "Lillie's Bordello" form the ultimate party place and a setting for live music. 66 Chandos Place, W1. ✆ 020/7836-8000. Tube: Leicester Sq.

Barty Club   Set in a dingy residential neighborhood in north London, this is a traditional-looking pub that's distinguished by the rock 'n' roll bands that come in from throughout the U.K. for bouts of beer and high-energy music. You'll usually hear three different bands a night. Open nightly from 7:30pm to 2 or 3am. At the Falcon Pub, 234 Royal College St. NW1. ✆ 020/7482-4884. Cover £7–£11 ($11–$18). Tube: Camden Town.

Beach Blanket Babylon   Go here if you're looking for a hot singles bar that attracts a crowd in their 20s and 30s. This Portobello joint—named after a kitschy musical revue in San Francisco—is very cruisy. The decor is like a Gothic grotto (or a medieval dungeon?). Saturday and Sunday nights are the hot, crowded times to show up for bacchanalian revelry. 45 Ledbury Rd., W11. ✆ 020/7229-2907. Tube: Notting Hill Gate.

Downstairs at the Phoenix   This is where Laurence Olivier made his stage debut in 1930, although he couldn't stop giggling even though the play was drama. Live music is featured, but it's the hearty welcome, the good beer, and friendly patrons that make this "rediscovered" theater bar worth a detour. 1 Phoenix St., WC2. ✆ 020/7836-1077. Tube: Tottencourt Court Rd.

The Latest Rumours   This has emerged as the number-one wine bar in the Covent Garden area. Whether it's a Bloody Mary you seek, perhaps a plate of English cuisine, or a reasonably priced bottle of wine, this is one of the most fun joints in town. There's a wide range of drinks, coffees, champagnes, and wines. 33–35 Wellington St., WC2. ✆ 020/7836-0038. Tube: Covent Garden.

OUR FAVORITE PUBS

There's no better way to determine the character of the different villages that make up London than to drop into the local for a pint. Eavesdrop to hear the accents, slang, and topics that differentiate upper-crust Kensington from blue-collar Wapping. Identify the local lush, catch up on gossip, and, while you're at it, enjoy some of the finest ciders, ales, stouts, and malt whiskies in the world.

⌒Finds Drinks a la Americana

Everybody's heard of the Hard Rock Cafe and Planet Hollywood, but the real news coming out of London is the opening of so many American-theme bars. **Navajo Joe,** 34 King St., WC2 (✆ 020/7240-4008), offers the largest tequila selection outside of Mexico, and some pretty hot southwestern cuisine. For the atmosphere of a different part of the American South, head for **Old Orleans,** corner of Wellington and Tavistock Streets, WC2 (✆ 020/7497-2433), with its colorful cocktail bar and its rich decor from the old American South in its restaurant featuring Creole cuisine. Both are reached by taking the Tube to Covent Garden.

The Heart of the City

Central London is chock-full of wonderful old pubs with histories almost as rich and varied as the city itself. **The Black Friar,** 174 Queen Victoria St., EC4 (© **020/7236-5474;** Tube: Blackfriars), will shift you into the Edwardian era, with its fabulous marble and bronze Art Nouveau decor, featuring bas-reliefs of mad monks, a low-vaulted mosaic ceiling, and seating built into golden marble recesses. It's especially popular with an after-work crowd, and offers Adams, Wadworth 6X, Tetleys, and Brakspears on tap. **The Cittie of Yorke,** 22 High Holborn, WC1 (© **020/7242-7670;** Tube: Holborn, Chancery Lane), boasts the longest bar in all of Britain, rafters ascending to the heavens, and a row of immense wine vats, giving it the air of a medieval Great Hall—which seems appropriate for a pub in service at this location since 1430. Samuel Smiths OB is on tap, and the bar also offers such novelties as chocolate-orange flavored vodka. **The Lamb & Flag,** 33 Rose St., off Garrick Street, WC2 (© **020/7497-9504;** Tube: Leicester Sq.), is little changed from when Dickens prowled this neighborhood and described the clientele. The pub has a scandalous history: Dryden was almost killed by a band of thugs outside its doors in December 1679, and it was nicknamed the "Bucket of Blood" during the Regency period (1811–20) after the bare-knuckled prizefights it hosted. Courage Best and Directors, Morlands Old Speckled Hen, John Smiths, and Wadworth 6X are on tap. **Olde Mitre,** Ely Place, EC1 (© **020/7405-4751;** Tube: Chancery Lane), is the namesake of a working-class inn built here in 1547, when the Bishops of Ely controlled the district. It's a small pub with an odd mix of customers. Friary Meux, Ind Coope Burton, and Tetleys are on tap. **Seven Stars,** 53 Carey St., WC2 (© **020/7242-8521;** Tube: Holborn), is tiny and plain except for its collection of Toby mugs and law-related art. The art pays obvious tribute to the pub's location at the back of the Law Courts and its large clientele of barristers, who fill the place. A great place to listen and learn some British legal slang. Courage Best and Directors are on tap, as well as a selection of malt whiskies.

West London

The Churchill Arms, 119 Kensington Church St., W8 (© **020/7727-4242;** Tube: Notting Hill Gate, High St. Kensington), is loaded with Churchill memorabilia. This place offers a week of celebration leading up to his birthday on November 30. Show up then and you may get recruited to help decorate the place, as visitors are often welcomed like old regulars here. Decorations and festivities surround Halloween, Christmas, and St. Patrick's Day as well, helping to create as much of a homey, village feel as you're likely to find. **The Dove,** 19 Upper Mall, W6 (© **020/8748-5405;** Tube: Ravenscourt Park), is the Thamesside pub where James Thomson composed "Rule Britannia." For toasting the old empire, you can hoist a Fullers London Pride or ESB, among the offerings on tap. **Ladbroke Arms,** 54 Ladbroke Rd., W11 (© **020/7727-6648;** Tube: Holland Park), is known for its food and has been honored as London's "Dining Pub of the Year." A changing menu includes such dishes as chicken breast stuffed with avocado or garlic steak in pink peppercorn sauce. With its art prints and background jazz, the place doesn't look or sound like a traditional pub feel, but it's a pleasant stop and a good meal. Eldridge Pope Royal Oak, John Smiths, and Courage Best and Directors are among the offerings on tap, and there are several malt whiskies as well.

5

The Thames Valley

The historic Thames Valley and Chiltern Hills are close enough to London to easily be reached by car, train, or Green Line coach. You can explore this area during the day and get back to London in time for a West End show.

The most visited historic site in England is **Windsor Castle,** 34km (21 miles) west of London. Going to Windsor Castle is the most popular day trip for those venturing outside London for the first time. If you base yourself in Windsor, you can spend another day exploring some of the sights on its periphery, including Eton, Runnymede, and Savill Garden.

If your visit coincides with the spring social sporting season, you can head to **Ascot** or **Henley-on-Thames** for two famous events, Ascot and the Royal Regatta. Be sure to wear a hat! There are great historic homes and gardens in the area, including Woburn Abbey, Hatfield House, Hughenden Manor, Mapledurham House, and the Wellington Ducal Estate. If your time is severely limited, **Woburn Abbey** and **Hatfield House** are the most important to see. Woburn Abbey could take an entire day, whereas Hatfield requires only a morning or afternoon.

The Home Counties, land of river valleys and gentle hills, make for wonderful drives. The beech-clad **Chilterns** are at their most beautiful in spring and autumn. This 64km (40-mile) chalk ridge extends from the Thames Valley to the old Roman city of **St. Albans** in Hertfordshire. Boating holidays on the region's 322km (200-mile) network of canals are popular.

The main reason for visiting Oxfordshire is to explore the university city of **Oxford,** an hour's ride from London by car or train. There's too much to see and do for a day trip, however. Plan to spend the night; the next morning you can visit **Blenheim Palace,** England's answer to Versailles. Oxfordshire is a land of great mansions, old churches, and rolling farmland.

1 Windsor ⍟ & Eton ⍟⍟

33km (21 miles) W of London

If it didn't have the castle, Windsor would still be a charming Thames town to visit. But because it is home to the royal family's best-known asset, it is virtually overrun in summer by tourists who all but obscure the town's charm. Windsor Castle remains Britain's second-most-visited historic building, after the Tower of London, attracting 1.2 million visitors a year.

The good news is that, after the disastrous fire of 1992, Windsor Castle has been restored, even though some of the new designs for it have been labeled "Gothic shocker" or "ghastly." Despite such media criticism, a remarkable exercise in restoration went on. Wood-carvers used ancient drawknives to smooth 1,200-pound unseasoned oak beams, following the same techniques as their medieval predecessors. Gilders applied gold leaf while plasterers formed little

> ## Value   Cheap Thrills: What to See & Do for Free (or Almost) in the Thames Valley
>
> **Watch the changing of the guard at Windsor.** It's the biggest tourist show in town—and it's free. Devotees think it's more enjoyable than the version at London's Buckingham Palace. You'll hear a full regimental band.
>
> **Watch the sun set over Oxford.** If you're a bit of a romantic, watch the sun go down over Oxford; you'll understand why it's called "The City of Dreaming Spires." The sun jumps and dances its way across everything from University College to Magdalen College.
>
> **Enjoy the sound of music in Oxford.** All the colleges have chapels, many of architectural interest; most present classical concerts and recitals. The best music is in three college chapels with their own choir schools: New College, Magdalen College, and Christ Church.
>
> **See a performance by the Olivier of tomorrow.** For low ticket prices, university drama groups regularly stage plays at various Oxford colleges. The actors often stun you with their performances; theatrical agents from London may be in the audience looking for the next big star.
>
> **Tour the Thames.** One of the most beautiful stretches of the Thames lies between Eton and Pangbourne, where Kenneth Grahame, author of *The Wind in the Willows,* lived. It is the most romantic part of the Thames Valley and is best toured by boat; but a drive between the two towns offers an intimate glimpse of the river's bank. Swans glide gracefully below ancient bridges, towering beech trees overhang the banks, and carefully cultivated private gardens slope down to the water.
>
> **Stroll through romantic gardens.** The University Botanical Gardens, England's oldest of this kind (founded 1621), is on Rose Lane, Oxford. One ancient yew tree from that period still survives. Enter a 17th-century gate and find yourself in a delightful secret garden, ideal for a stroll.

flowers by hand—like the work done 9 centuries ago when William the Conqueror began building the castle.

In November 1997, Queen Elizabeth II reopened the state apartments, following a £37 million ($56 million) project that returned most ruined parts to their original condition (work ended in late 1999). Completed in time for the queen's 50th wedding anniversary, the restoration was the subject of a British television program, *Windsor Restored,* produced by Edward Windsor, the queen's youngest son. Even Prince Charles came on camera to discuss everything from fabricating the new roof to reinstalling the stained-glass windows. This documentary has been shown around the world.

ESSENTIALS

GETTING THERE   The train from Waterloo or Paddington Station in London makes the trip in 30 minutes (you'll have to transfer at Slough to the Slough–Windsor shuttle train). More than a dozen trains make the trip every day; the cost is £6.50 ($10) round-trip. Call **Thames Trains, Ltd.,** at ✆ 08457/484950 for more information.

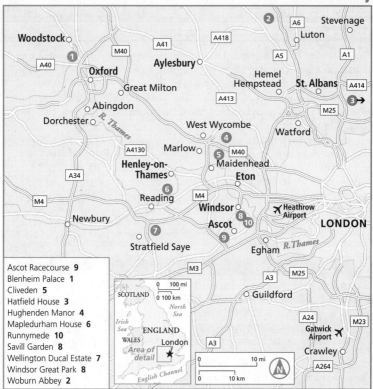

Ascot Racecourse **9**
Blenheim Palace **1**
Cliveden **5**
Hatfield House **3**
Hughenden Manor **4**
Mapledurham House **6**
Runnymede **10**
Savill Garden **8**
Wellington Ducal Estate **7**
Windsor Great Park **8**
Woburn Abbey **2**

Green Line coaches (© **0870/7261**) nos. 700 and 702 from Hyde Park Corner in London take about 1½ hours, depending on the day of the week. A same-day round-trip costs £8 ($13). The bus drops you near the parish church, across the street from the castle.

If you're driving from London, take the M4 west.

VISITOR INFORMATION   A **Tourist Information Centre** is located across from Windsor Castle on High Street (© **01753/743900** or visit www.windsor. gov.uk). An information booth is also in the Tourist Centre at Windsor Coach Park. Both are open Monday through Friday from 10am to 4pm, Saturday from 10am to 5pm. They also book walking tours for the Oxford guild of guides.

CASTLE HILL SIGHTS

Windsor Castle ★★★   William the Conqueror first ordered a castle built here. Since his day, it's been a fateful spot for English sovereigns: John cooled his heels at Windsor while waiting to sign the Magna Carta at nearby Runnymede; Charles I was imprisoned here before losing his head; Elizabeth I renovated; Victoria mourned her Albert, who died here in 1861; and the royal family rode out much of World War II behind its sheltering walls. When Queen Elizabeth II is in residence, the royal standard flies.

With 1,000 rooms, Windsor is the world's largest inhabited castle. In November 1992, a fire swept through and severely damaged part of it. The castle has since reopened; the damaged rooms have been completely restored over a 5-year period by some of Britain's finest craftspeople. The apartments display artworks, porcelain, armor, furniture, three Verrio ceilings, and several 17th-century Gibbons carvings. Works by Rubens adorn the King's Drawing Room; the smaller King's Dressing Room displays a Dürer, Rembrandt's portrait of his mother, and Van Dyck's triple portrait of Charles I. The grand reception room, with its Gobelin tapestries, is the most spectacular apartment.

We think that Windsor's Changing of the Guard is much more exciting and moving than London's exercises. Here, the guard marches through town when the queen is in residence, stopping traffic as it wheels into the castle to the tune of a full regimental band; when the queen is not here, a drum-and-pipe band is mustered. From April to June, the ceremony takes place daily at 11am; otherwise, the guard is changed every 48 hours, weather permitting. Call © **01753/868286** to find out when the ceremony will take place.

Castle Hill. © **020/7321-2233**. www.royalresidences.com. Admission £11.50 ($18) adults, £6 ($10) children 16 and under, £29 ($46) family of 4. Mar–Oct daily 9:45am–5:15pm; Nov–Feb daily 9:45am–4:15pm. Last admission 1 hr. before closing. Closed for periods in Apr, June, and Dec when the royal family is in residence.

Queen Mary's Doll's House

A palace in perfect miniature, the Doll's House was given to Queen Mary in 1923 as a symbol of national goodwill. The house, designed by Sir Edwin Lutyens, was created on a scale of 1 to 12. It took 3 years to complete and involved the work of 1,500 tradesmen and artists. Each room is exquisitely furnished, every item a miniature masterpiece. Working elevators stop on every floor, and all five bathrooms have running water.

Castle Hill. © **01753/868286**, or 01753/831118 for recorded information. Admission is included in entrance to Windsor Castle. Mar–Oct daily 10am–4pm; Nov–Feb daily 10am–3pm. Call ahead to confirm opening times.

St. George's Chapel ★★★

A gem of the Perpendicular style, this chapel shares the distinction with Westminster Abbey of being a pantheon of English monarchs. The present St. George's was founded in the late 15th century by Edward IV on the former site of the Chapel of the Order of the Garter (Edward III, 1348). The nave has remarkable fan vaulting and holds the tomb of George V and Queen Mary, designed by Sir William Reid Dick. Off the nave in the Urswick Chapel, the Princess Charlotte memorial reminds us that, if she had survived childbirth in 1817, Charlotte, not her cousin Victoria, would have ruled the Empire. In the aisle are tombs of George VI and Edward IV. The Edward IV "Quire," with its imaginatively carved 15th-century choir stalls (crowned by lacy canopies and Knights of the Garter banners), evokes the pomp and pageantry of the Middle Ages. In the center, a flat tomb contains the vault of the beheaded Charles I, along with Henry VIII and his third wife, Jane Seymour. Finally, you may inspect the Prince Albert Memorial Chapel for a taste of Victorian opulence.

Castle Hill. © **01753/868286**. Admission is included in entrance to Windsor Castle. Mon–Sat 10am–4pm. Closed Sun and briefly in mid-June.

Jubilee Garden

To celebrate Queen Elizabeth's Jubilee, the 1-hectare (2-acre) Jubilee Garden was created inside the castle's main entrance. Filled with trees, roses, and flowering shrubs, it was created by Tom Stuart-Smith, a Chelsea Flower show gold medalist. The garden is the first established at Windsor Castle since the days of George IV in the 1820s. It is the setting for band concerts throughout the year. The garden extends from the main gates of Windsor to St. George's Gate on Castle Hill. Color is provided by broad swaths of woodland perennials. White rambling roses clothing the old stone walls are particularly romantic.

Same hours and admission as for castle.

Windsor Farm Shop Had any of the queen's jars of jam lately, maybe her homemade pork pie, or a bottle of her special brew? If not, head for this outlet, selling produce from her estates outside Windsor, including pheasants and partridges bagged at royal shoots. This retail outlet is found in converted Victorian potting sheds on the edge of the royal estate. Much of the produce bears the seal of the Royal Farms. The cream, yogurt, ice cream, and milk come from the two Royal Dairy farms. This latest make-a-pound scheme was devised in the brain of Prince Philip. The meat counter is especially awesome, with its cooked hams and massive ribs of beef. The steak-and-ale pies are especially tasty. You can stock up on the Queen's vittles and head for a picnic in the area. You can also purchase 15-year-old whisky from Balmoral Castle in Scotland.

Datchet Rd., Old Windsor. © 0153/623800. Free admission. Mon–Fri 9am–5pm; Sat 9–6pm; Sun 10am–4pm.

NEARBY ETON COLLEGE ★★

Eton is home of what is arguably the most famous public school (private school, to Americans) in the world. From Windsor Castle's ramparts, you look down on the river and Eton's famous playing fields.

You can take a train from Paddington Station, go by car, or take the Green Line bus to Windsor. By car, take the M4 motorway to Exit 5 to go straight to Eton. *Insider's tip:* Parking is likely to be a problem, so we advise turning off M4 at Exit 6 to Windsor; you can park here and take an easy stroll past Windsor Castle and across the Thames bridge. Follow Eton High Street to the college.

Eton College was founded by 18-year-old Henry VI in 1440. Some of England's greatest, including the duke of Wellington, have played on these fields. Twenty prime ministers were educated here, as well as writers such as George Orwell, Aldous Huxley, Ian Fleming, and Percy Bysshe Shelley, who, during his years at Eton (1804–10), was dubbed "Mad Shelley" or "Shelley the Atheist" by his fellows. Princes William and Harry, second and third in line to the throne, both studied here. If it's open, take a look at the Perpendicular chapel, with its 15th-century paintings and reconstructed fan vaulting.

The history of Eton College since its inception is depicted in the Museum of Eton Life, Eton College, located in vaulted wine cellars under College Hall, originally used by the college's masters. The displays, ranging from formal to extremely informal, include a turn-of-the-century boy's room, schoolbooks, canes used by senior boys to punish their juniors, and birch sticks used by masters for the same purpose.

Admission to the school and museum is £3.70 ($6) for adults and £2 ($3.20) for children under 15. You can also take guided tours for £4.70 ($8). Eton College is open from late March to late April and late June to early September, daily from 10:30am to 4:30pm; from late April to late June and early September to early October, daily from 2 to 4:30pm. Call in advance; Eton may close for special occasions. Open dates vary every year depending on term and holiday dates. It's best to call. For information, call © **01753/671177.**

MORE TO SEE & DO IN & AROUND WINDSOR

The town of Windsor is largely Victorian, with lots of brick buildings and a few remnants of Georgian architecture. In and around the castle are two cobblestone streets, Church and Market, which have antiques shops, silversmiths, and pubs. Nell Gwynne, who needed to be on call for Charles II, supposedly occupied one shop on Church Street. After lunch or tea, you may want to stroll along the 3-mile, aptly named, Long Walk.

Moments Royalty Watchers

On Sunday, there are often polo matches in Windsor Great Park and at Ham Common; you may see Prince Charles playing and Prince Philip serving as umpire while the queen watches. The park is the site of the queen's occasional equestrian jaunts. On Sunday she attends a little church near the Royal Lodge; she prefers to drive herself there, later returning to the castle for Sunday lunch. For more information, call the Tourist Information Centre (see above).

Savill Garden, in Windsor Great Park, Wick Lane, Englefield Green, Egham, Surrey (② **01753/860222**). Open daily year-round (except Christmas) 10am to 6pm (4pm in winter); admission is £4 ($6) for adults, £3.50 ($5) seniors, and free for children 16 and under. Five miles from Windsor along A30, turn off at Wick Road and follow the signs to the gardens; also signposted from Egham and Ascot. The nearest rail station is at Egham; from here, take a taxi for 3 miles.

Established in 1932, the 14-hectare (35-acre) garden is one of the finest of its type in the Northern Hemisphere. The display starts in spring with rhododendrons, camellias, and daffodils beneath the trees; throughout the summer there are spectacular displays of flowers and shrubs presented in a natural state. There's a licensed, self-service restaurant and gift shop on the premises. Adjoining the Savill Garden are the Valley Gardens, full of shrubs and trees in a series of wooded natural valleys running down to the water. It's open daily year-round. Entrance to the gardens is free, although parking costs £1.50 ($2.25) per vehicle.

On the B3022 Bracknell/Ascot Road, outside Windsor, you'll find **Legoland** (② **08705/040404;** www.lego.com/legoland), a 60-hectare (150-acre) theme park that opened in 1996. Although a bit corny, it's fun for the entire family. Attractions, spread across five main activity centers, include Duplo Gardens, offering a boat ride, puppet theater, and water works, plus a Miniland, showing European cities or villages re-created in minute detail from millions of Lego bricks. Enchanted Forest has treasure trails, a castle, and animals created from Lego bricks. The latest attraction is Dragon Knight's Castle, taking you back to the days of knights and dragons and including a blazing dragon roller coaster. The park is open daily from 10am to 6pm from mid-March to October. Admission varies through the season, starting at £18.95 to £22.95 ($30–$37) for adults, £12.95 to £16.95 ($21–$27) for seniors, and £15.95 to £19.95 ($26–$32) for children 3 to 15 (free for children 2 and under).

Only 5km (3 miles) south of Windsor is **Runnymede,** the 75-hectare (188-acre) meadow on the south side of the Thames, in Surrey, where it's believed that King John put his seal on the Great Charter after intense pressure from his feudal barons and lords. Today, Runnymede is also the site of the John F. Kennedy Memorial, an acre of English ground given to the United States by the people of Britain. The memorial, a large block of white stone, is hard to see from the road, but is clearly signposted and reached after a short walk. The pagoda that shelters it was placed here by the American Bar Association to acknowledge the fact that American law stems from the English system.

The historic site, to which there is free access all year, lies beside the Thames, 1km (½ mile) west of the hamlet of Old Windsor on the south side of the A308. If you're driving on the M25, exit at Junction 13. The nearest rail connection is at Egham, 1km (½ mile) away. Trains depart from London's Waterloo Station and take about 25 minutes.

BOAT TOURS, HORSE RIDES & GUIDED WALKS OF WINDSOR

French Brothers, Ltd., Clewer Boathouse, Clewer Court Road, Windsor (© **01753/851900**), offers a multitude of boat tours. One tour departs from Windsor Promenade, Barry Avenue, for a 35-minute round-trip to Boveney Lock. The cost is £4.20 ($7) for adults, half price for children 16 and under. You can also take a 2-hour tour through the Boveney Lock and past stately private riverside homes, the Bray Film Studios, Queens Eyot, and Monkey Island, for £6.60 ($11) for adults, half price for children. The *Lucy Fisher,* a replica of a Victorian paddle steamer, departs Runnymede on a 45-minute tour, passing Magna Carta Island, among other sights. This tour costs £4.20 ($7) for adults, half price for children. Longer tours between Maidenhead and Hampton Court are also offered. The boats offer light refreshments and have a well-stocked bar, plus the decks are covered in case of an unexpected shower.

The tourist office can put you in touch with a Blue Badge (official) guide to lead you on a walking tour of town. These guided tours cost £45 ($72) per hour, so form a group to split the cost. Advance booking is essential.

SHOPPING

A colorful traditional English perfumery, **Woods of Windsor,** Queen Charlotte Street (© **01753/868125**), dates from 1770. It offers soaps, shampoos, scented drawer liners, and hand and body lotions, all prettily packaged in pastel-flower and bright old-fashioned wraps. **The Token House,** High Street (© **01753/863263**), is the largest gathering of china and crystal. Place settings in Wedgwood, Royal Albert, Minton, and Spode, plus Portmeirion bowls, Royal Dalton figurines, Waterford crystal stemware and collector plates, bowls, and vases are stacked throughout the airy, bright shop, along with silver-plated and stainless-steel cutlery. **The Reject China Shop** (© **01753/850870** or 855272) across the street has less-expensive items, but it has no connection to The Token House. **Billings & Edmonds,** 132 High St., Eton (© **01753/861348**), is a distinctive clothing store offering excellent traditional tailoring, suits made to order, and a complete line of cufflinks, shirts, ties, and accessories. **Asquith's Teddy Bear Shop,** 33 High St., Eton (© **01753/831200**), appeals to your inner child with every bear imaginable, including Winnie the Pooh and Paddington. Clothes from jeans to Eton College uniforms mix with tinware and hatboxes, all covered in teddy-bear prints.

WHERE TO STAY IN THE WINDSOR AREA

Note: During the Ascot races and Windsor Horse Show, reservations are necessary far in advance.

Langton House   Located a 5-minute walk northeast from Windsor Castle, this large double-fronted Victorian house is built of dark red brick and dates

---

Moments Windsor from a Queen Victoria Carriage

You can also take a 30-minute carriage ride up the sycamore-lined length of Windsor Castle's Long Walk. Horses with their carriages and drivers line up beside the castle waiting for fares, charging from about £20 ($32) for up to four passengers.

from the 1860s. Emerging from its earlier role as a nursing home, it offers a trio of well-scrubbed bedrooms on the building's upstairs, interconnected via a hallway sitting area and a small communal kitchen with tea-making facilities. The nonsmoking bedrooms are simply but cozily furnished, with a private bathroom equipped with shower stalls. The hotel has one room available for those with limited mobility.

46 Alma Rd., Windsor, Berkshire SL4 3HA. (C) **01753/858299.** www.langtonhouse.co.uk. 3 units. £60 ($96) single; £70 ($112) double. All rates include breakfast. No credit cards. **Amenities:** Breakfast room; lounge. *In room:* TV, hair dryer.

Mrs. Bronwen Hughes *Value*   Built of brick in 1898, a 10-minute walk from Windsor Castle, this hotel boasts a well-accessorized layout that's among the most comfortable of any B&B within its price category. Mrs. Hughes, hostess of this sprawling Victorian home, is a former British Airways cabin attendant who knows how to make newcomers feel comfortable in her well-furnished, nonsmoking bedrooms, which have private shower-only or shower/tub combo bathrooms. No meals are served other than breakfast, but guests are allowed to use the kitchen.

62 Queen Rd., Windsor, Berkshire SL4 3BH. (C) and fax **01753/866036.** 2 units. £35 ($56) single; £55 ($88) double; family unit suitable for up to 3 adults and 3 children, £25 ($40) per adult plus £15 ($24) per child. All rates include breakfast. No credit cards. **Amenities:** Breakfast room. *In room:* TV, coffeemaker, hair dryer.

WORTH A SPLURGE

Royal Adelaide Hotel   This interesting Georgian building is opposite the famous Long Walk leading to Windsor Castle, 5 minutes away. Named for Queen Adelaide, who visited the premises during her reign, thereby dubbing it "royal," all its well-furnished rooms have recently been refurbished. Though small, bathrooms have sufficient shelf space and have shower-tub combinations.

46 King's Rd., Windsor, Berkshire SL4 2AG. (C) **01753/863916.** Fax 01753/830682. www.meridianleisure. com. 42 units. £99–£115 ($158–$184) double. Rates include English breakfast. AE, DC, MC, V. **Amenities:** Restaurant; bar; room service; babysitting. *In room:* TV, coffeemaker, trouser press, safe.

Ye Harte & Garter Hotel   On Castle Hill opposite Windsor Castle is the old Garter Inn. Named for the Knights of the Garter, and used as the setting for scenes in Shakespeare's *The Merry Wives of Windsor,* the Garter burned down in the 1800s and was rebuilt as part of one hostelry that included the Harte. From the front rooms, you can watch the guards marching up High Street every morning on their way to change the guard at the castle. The recently renovated rooms are comfortable and rather functionally furnished, though they vary greatly in size. More expensive are the Windsor rooms, which have front views and Jacuzzis. Regardless of size or location, each has a small but well-maintained bathroom with a shower-tub combination.

31 High St., Windsor, Berkshire SL4 1PH. (C) **01753/863426.** Fax 01753/830527. harteandgarter@windsor. com. 39 units. £125 ($200) double; £180 ($288) suite. AE, DC, MC, V. **Amenities:** 2 restaurants; bar; laundry service. *In room:* TV, coffeemaker, hair dryer, trouser press.

WHERE TO DINE

Clairmont Coffee DELI   Returning after touring Windsor Castle, you might stop here for a light lunch or a gourmet coffee. Rest your feet and enjoy a "toastie," a choice of toppings on white or wheat bread, toasted and served open-faced. The Clairmont serves a variety of sandwiches, including vegetarian choices such as avocado and cress on a French baguette. In addition to the many coffees and teas to choose from, croissants, danishes, and cakes will satisfy your sweet tooth.

5 High St. (C) **01753/621082.** Main courses £2.25–£4.50 ($3.60–$7). No credit cards. Daily 8:30am–5:30pm.

Drury House Restaurant ENGLISH   A meal here can be included in a tour of Windsor Castle, only a stone's throw away. Owner Mr. Nicholson states with pride that all luncheons served in this wood-paneled 17th-century restaurant are home-cooked "and very English." A refreshing tea is also served, with home-made scones with jam and freshly whipped cream or freshly made cakes.

4 Church St. ✆ **01753/863734.** Reservations required. Fixed-price menus £6–£9 ($10–$14). No credit cards. Daily 9:30am–5:30pm.

Gilbey's ⭐ MODERN BRITISH/CONTINENTAL   Just across the bridge from Windsor, this charming place is on Eton's main street, among the antiques shops. It's furnished with modern furniture, and there's a glassed-in conservatory out back. A brigade of seven chefs turns out good modern British dishes. Begin with one of the well-prepared soups or a smoked salmon and artichoke tart. Main dishes include pan-fried skate wing with a champagne, chile, and caper risotto, or roasted pigeon with a mushroom and venison stuffing and braised red cabbage. For dessert try the delicious white and dark mousse with amaretto cream.

82–83 High St., Eton. ✆ **01753/854921.** Reservations recommended. Main courses £9.95–£15.95 ($16–$26). Set menu 2 course lunch £10.95 ($18); 2 course dinner £13.50 ($22). AE, DC, MC, V. Daily noon–2:30pm and 6–10pm.

Slug and Lettuce Pub ENGLISH   Had this pub existed during the Middle Ages, soldiers from Windsor Castle directly across the street could have tossed spears down from their battlements at the drinkers inside. It's now part of a nationwide chain. The decor is appropriately dark, antique-looking, and rustic, with a busy bar adjacent to a dining area that serves breakfast from 10am to noon, followed by lunches and dinners offered without interruption from noon until closing. Fare is staunchly British—bangers and mash, steak-and-kidney pie, and steaks—and more esoteric fare such as grilled swordfish, steamed mussels in white-wine sauce, and supreme of chicken. You'll find a baffling array of English ales on tap, but you can't go wrong with either a Spitfire or a Master Brew.

5 Thames St. ✆ **01753/864405.** Reservations not accepted. Main courses £6.95–£8.25 ($11–$13). AE, MC, V. Mon–Sat 11am–11pm; Sun noon-10:30pm.

Thai Castle Restaurant THAI   Close to the castle, on Windsor's main street near Eton Bridge, this welcome change from a bit too much British grub offers food prepared by a Bangkok-born staff who understand the subtle and fiery nuances of their native dishes. Amid a decor of exposed brick and Thai art, enjoy *satay* (marinated chicken or beef grilled on bamboo skewers), minced pork in flaky pastry served with sweet-and-sour sauce, Thai-style fisherman's soup loaded with spices, stir-fried beef with oysters and red and green peppers, or a wide selection of flavorful prawn, noodle, and seafood dishes. The menu considers vegetarian palates as well, with a hot-and-sour Thai salad with peanuts and tomatoes or fresh seasonal vegetables stir-fried in a curry sauce. Dessert might be a banana fritter or coconut ice cream.

12 Thames St. ✆ **01753/842186.** Reservations recommended. Main courses £5.25–£7.45 ($8–$12). Set price 2 course lunch £6.95 ($11); 2 course dinner £16 ($26). AE, MC, V. Daily noon–2:30pm and 6:30–10:45pm.

Uncle Sam's American Steak House AMERICAN   Despite its location near Windsor Castle on one of the most English streets in Britain, this steak-house pursues a resolutely American concept of dining out. The bar is adorned with posters of Hollywood legends (Monroe, De Niro); the consciously rustic dining area sometimes gets boisterous. The bill of fare features 10 kinds of juicy burgers, American drugstore–style milkshakes, pastas such as spaghetti, and thick, juicy steaks. If you feel guilty afterwards, have fish and chips for breakfast!

10 High St. ℂ **01753/866655.** Reservations recommended. Main courses £6–£14 ($10–$22). DC, MC, V. Daily noon–11pm.

SIDE TRIPS FROM WINDSOR

If you have time to spare, you can take any number of fascinating excursions. If you have time for only one, make it Hughenden Manor (see below).

HIGH WYCOMBE: HUGHENDEN MANOR

Hughenden Manor ★★   This Victorian country manor acquaints us with a remarkable man, Benjamin Disraeli, one of the most enigmatic figures of 19th-century England. At age 21, Dizzy published anonymously his five-volume novel *Vivian Grey*. He entered politics in 1837 while continuing to write novels that met with greater acclaim. In 1839, he married an older widow for her money; they apparently developed a most harmonious relationship. In 1848, Disraeli acquired Hughenden Manor, which suited his fast-rising political and social position. His political fame rests on his term as prime minister from 1874 to 1880. He became Queen Victoria's friend; she paid him a rare honor by visiting Hughenden (1877). In 1876, Disraeli became the earl of Beaconsfield, and he died in 1881. Instead of being buried at Westminster Abbey, he chose the simple graveyard of Hughenden Church. Today, Hughenden houses an odd assortment of memorabilia, including a lock of Disraeli's hair, letters from Victoria, autographed books, and a portrait of Lord Byron.

High Wycombe. ℂ **01494/755573.** Admission £4.50 ($7) adults, £2.25 ($3.60) children, £11.50 ($18) family ticket. Garden only £1.60 ($2.55) adults, 80p ($1.30) children. Apr–Oct Wed–Sun 1–4:30pm; Mar Sat–Sun only 1–4:30pm. Closed Nov–Feb and Good Friday. From Windsor take M4 (toward Reading), then A404 to A40. Continue north of High Wycombe on A4128 for about 2.5km (1½ miles). From London, catch coach no. 711 to High Wycombe, then board a Beeline bus (High Wycombe–Aylesbury no. 323 or 324).

WEST WYCOMBE ★

Snuggled in the Chiltern Hills 48km (30 miles) west of London and 24km (15 miles) northwest of Windsor, the village of West Wycombe retains an early-18th-century atmosphere, even if the thatched roofs have been replaced by tiles, and some buildings have been replaced altogether.

A visit to West Wycombe wouldn't be complete without a tour of **West Wycombe Park,** seat of the Dashwood family. Now owned by the National Trust, it's of historical and architectural interest. The house is an excellent example of Palladian-style English architecture. The interior is lavishly decorated with 18th-century paintings and antiques. In the mid–18th century, Sir Francis Dashwood began an ambitious building program at West Wycombe. His strong interest in architecture and design led him to undertake a series of monuments and parks that are still among the finest in the country. For information on the estate, call the West Wycombe Estate Office at West Wycombe, ℂ **01494/524411.** The house and grounds are open daily March through August from 11am to 5pm. Admission is £4.20 ($7) adults, £2 ($3.20) children 16 and under. For just the grounds, it's £3 ($4.80).

Sir Francis commissioned the excavation of a cave on the estate, to serve as a meeting place for "The Knights of St. Francis of Wycombe," later called the notorious Hellfire Club, dedicated to partying, drinking, and ravishing innocent virgins. Some satanic rites also took place here, primarily to inspire further debauchery. The half-mile-long cave is filled with stalactites and stalagmites and dotted with statues of Sir Francis, his friend Lord Sandwich, and even Ben

Franklin. For information call ☎ **01494/533739.** The caves are open daily March through September from 11am to 5pm; off season on Saturday and Sunday only from 11am to 5pm. Admission is £3.50 ($6) adults, £2 ($3.20) seniors and children 16 and under. The cave tour includes stops for talks about former Hellfire members; it lasts 30 minutes.

Other sights include the **Church of St. Lawrence,** perched on West Wycombe Hill and topped by a huge golden ball. Parts of the church date from the 13th century; its richly decorated interior was copied from a 3rd-century Syrian sun temple. The view from the hill is worth the trek up. Near the church stands the Dashwood mausoleum, modeled after Constantine's Arch in Rome.

After your tour of the park, head for **George & Dragon,** High Street (☎ **01494/464414**), for a pint or a good, inexpensive lunch. This 1720 building, a former coaching inn, has a cheerful log fire, a comfortably sized bar (crowded on weekends), and an impressive oak staircase with its own ghost. There is a separate nonsmoking room open to children, a children's play area, and a garden for dining outside. You can even spend the night here if you wish; the pub has eight cozily furnished rooms with private bathroom, phone, and TV, costing £75 ($120) for a double, including breakfast.

To get to West Wycombe from Windsor, take the M4 (toward Reading), then A404 to A40. Signs to follow en route include Maidenhead, Marlow, and Oxford. West Wycombe lies immediately to the west of Hughenden Manor.

CLIVEDEN: FORMER HOME OF LADY ASTOR

Cliveden House ★★   Now a National Trust property, Cliveden House, once home of Lady Astor, stands on a constructed terrace of mature gardens high above the Thames. William Winde created the estate's original mansion and the vast sweep of the lawns in 1666 for the second duke of Buckingham. The father of King George III reared his sons here. After a fire in 1795, Sir Charles Barry, the architect of the Houses of Parliament, redesigned the house into its present gracefully symmetrical form. A soaring clock tower was added to one side as a later Victorian folly. When the duke of Southerland sold the house to the Astors in 1893, Queen Victoria lamented the act. The house remained part of the Astor legacy until 1966. It holds a notable collection of paintings and antiques. Three rooms are open to the public, as is the Octagon Temple, with its rich mosaic interior. The surrounding gardens are distinguished in their variety, ranging from Renaissance-style topiary to meandering forest paths with vistas of statuary and flowering shrubs. There is a rose garden, a magnificent parterre, and an amphitheater where "Rule Britannia" was played for the first time. There are 150 hectares (375 acres) of garden and woodland to explore.

The house is also used as a hotel, but we haven't reviewed it as a place to stay in this guide because rooms are among the most expensive in England.

16km (10 miles) northwest of Windsor. ☎ 01628/605069. Admission to grounds £6 ($10) adults, £3 ($4.80) children, £15 ($24) family ticket. Admission to house £1 ($1.60) extra. Grounds open mid-Mar to Oct daily 11am–6pm; Nov–Dec 11am–4pm. House open Apr–Oct Thurs and Sun 3–6pm (3 rooms of the mansion are open to the public, as is the Octagon Temple, with its rich mosaic interior). From Windsor, follow M4 toward Reading to the junction at no. 7 (direction Slough West). At the roundabout, turn left onto A4 signposted MAIDENHEAD. At the next roundabout, turn right signposted BURNHAM. Follow the road for 4km (2½ miles) to a T junction with B476. The main gates to Cliveden are directly opposite.

THE COTTAGE WHERE MILTON WROTE *PARADISE LOST*

The modern residential town of **Gerrards Cross** is often called the Beverly Hills of England, as it attracts wealthy Londoners. To the north is **Chalfont St. Giles.** To reach it, take the A355 north from Windsor bypassing Beaconsfield until you come to the signposted cutoff for Chalfont St. Giles to the east. Chalfont St. Giles is a typical English village, though its history goes back to Roman times. Activity is clustered around the village green and pond, with shops, pubs, and cafes.

The poet John Milton lived here during the Great Plague of 1665. It was in the 16th-century **John Milton's Cottage,** Chalfont St. Giles (© **01494/872313**), that he completed *Paradise Lost* and started *Paradise Regained.* Its four rooms contain many relics and exhibits devoted to Milton. It is open March through October Tuesday through Sunday 10am to 1pm and 2 to 6pm. Admission is £2.50 ($4) adults, £1 ($1.60) children 16 and under.

2 Henley-on-Thames ⟨ ⟩ & the Royal Regatta ⟨ ⟩⟨ ⟩

56km (35 miles) W of London

At the eastern edge of Oxfordshire stands Henley-on-Thames, a small town and resort at the Chilterns foothills. It is home to the annual Royal Regatta, held in late June and early July. Henley lies on a stretch of the Thames known for calm waters, unobstructed bottom, and predictable currents; it is a rower's mecca. The regatta, inaugurated in 1839, is the competition for international oarspersons.

The Elizabethan buildings, the tearooms, and the inns along the town's High Street will fulfill your fantasy of an English country town. Henley is an excellent stopover en route to Oxford; its fashionable inns are far from cheap, however.

ESSENTIALS

GETTING THERE   Trains depart from London's Paddington Station but require a change at the junction in Twyford. More than 20 trains make the journey daily; the trip takes about 40 minutes. For rail information, call © **0845/ 7484950.**

About 10 buses depart every day from London's Victoria Coach Station for Reading. From Reading, take local bus no. 421 to Henley. These buses depart every hour. Call **0870/5808080** for more information.

If you're driving from London, take the M4 toward Reading to Junction 819; then head northwest on the A4130.

VISITOR INFORMATION   The **Tourist Information Centre** is at King's Arms Barn, King's Road (© **01491/578034**). Winter hours are Monday to Saturday 9:30am to 5pm, and Sunday 11am to 4pm. Summer hours are Monday to Saturday 9:30am to 6pm, and Sunday 10am to 5pm.

THE HENLEY ROYAL REGATTA

The Henley Royal Regatta, held the first week in July, is one of the country's premier racing events. Admission to the Regatta Enclosure is open to all. If you want a close-up view from the Stewards' Enclosure, however, you'll need a guest badge, obtainable only through a member. Information is available from the Secretary, Henley Royal Regatta, Henley-on-Thames, Oxfordshire RG9 2LY (© **01491/572153**).

During the annual 5-day event, up to 100 races are run each day, with starts scheduled as frequently as every 5 minutes. This event is open only to all-male crews of up to nine at a time. In late June, rowing events for women are held at the 3-day Henley Women's Regatta.

If you want to float on the waters of the Thames yourself, stop by the town's largest and oldest outfitter, **Hobbs & Sons, Ltd.,** Station Road Boathouse (© **01491/572035**), established in 1870. Open daily from April to October from

8:30am to 5:30pm, their armada of watercraft includes rowboats that rent for between £8 to £10 ($13–$16) per hour. Motorboats can be rented for £20 to £40 ($32–$64) per hour. On the premises, a chandlery shop sells virtually anything a boat crew could need, as well as souvenir items such as straw boater's hats and commemorative T-shirts.

A MUSEUM

The **River and Rowing Museum,** Mill Meadows (✆ **01491/415610;** www. rrm.co.uk), celebrates the Thames and those oarsmen and -women who row upon it. Opened by Queen Elizabeth in 1998, the £17.5 million ($28 million) museum, designed by English architect David Chipperfield, is the finest of its kind in Britain. It opens onto the banks of the Thames just south of Henley Bridge. The Rowing Gallery follows the saga of rowing from the days of the Greeks, including models of Arctic whaleboats in the 1700s, elaborate Venetian gondolas, and coastal lifeboats that pulled many a victim from the cold waters of the North Sea. In a more modern exhibit, you'll find the boat in which British oarsmen captured the gold medal in the Olympic games at Atlanta in 1996. The museum reaches out to embrace the saga of the Thames itself and the history of the regatta in Henley in particular. It's open Monday to Friday from 10am to 5pm, Saturday and Sunday from 10:30am to 5pm. Admission is £4.95 ($8) for adults, £3.75 ($6) for seniors and children, and £13.95 ($22) for a family ticket.

WHERE TO STAY IN THE AREA

Lenwade Guest House ✦   Built in the early 1900s, this semidetached Victorian guesthouse is owned and operated by Jacquie and John Williams. Entering from the small courtyard filled with flowering vines and lush foliage, you'll see a 5-foot stained-glass window thought to depict Joan of Arc. Another detail that makes this place memorable is the large winding staircase with its original pine spindles and handrails. The individually decorated rooms contain hot and cold running water; some have private shower-only bathrooms.

3 Western Rd., Henley-on-Thames, Oxfordshire RG9 IJL. ✆ and fax **01491/573468.** www.w3b-ink. com/lenwade. 3 units, 2 with bathroom. £45 ($72) single; £60 ($96) double. All rates include English breakfast. No credit cards. **Amenities:** Breakfast room; lounge. *In room:* TV, dataport, coffeemaker, hair dryer.

Shepherds   Constructed in the mid-1600s, this building's recorded history begins in 1726 when it was acquired and enlarged by the ancestors of its present owner, Susan Fulford-Dobson. Set amid 3.2 hectares (8 acres) of parklands (2.4 hectares/6 acres of which are devoted to horses), Shepherds is a creeper-covered country home facing a village green about 5km (3 miles) northwest of Henley. A reception area is furnished with antiques and English country accessories. The small bedrooms have chintz curtains and private shower-only bathrooms.

Rotherfield Greys, Henley-on-Thames, Oxfordshire RG9 4QL. ✆ and fax **01491/628413.** 2 units. £58 ($93) double. Rates include English breakfast. No credit cards. Closed Sept–Apr and 1 week at Christmas. **Amenities:** Breakfast room; lounge. *In room:* TV, coffeemaker, hair dryer, no phone.

WHERE TO DINE

Argyll BRITISH   This very Scottish pub, complete with tartan carpeting and framed prints of Scottish soldiers, is a popular lunch spot with locals. The homemade meals are the main attraction. They serve hearty portions of steak-and-kidney pie, shepherd's pie, and other favorites.

15 Market Place. ✆ **01491/573400.** Main courses and platters £2.95–£10 ($4.70–$16). AE, MC, V. Daily 11am–11pm.

The Flower Pot ENGLISH/INTERNATIONAL   Built around 1870, the Flower Pot retains much of its original Victorian atmosphere despite many renovations (most recently in 1993). The place rents out four upstairs bedrooms with TVs; two have private bathrooms. Including an English breakfast, a single without bathroom costs £45 ($72). A double rents for £60 ($96) with a bathroom. But this place is more famous for its pub and food than for accommodations. The pub grub is far above standard, including poultry, poached salmon with dill sauce, fish pie, and pan-fried trout. Come here to eat or stay for earthy, unpretentious, and straightforward atmosphere—and honest value.

Aston, near Henley-on-Thames, Oxfordshire RG9 3DG. ℭ **01491/574721.** Reservations recommended for dinner. Main courses £3–£15 ($4.80–$24). MC, V. Mon–Sat noon–2pm and 6:30–9pm; Sun noon–2pm. Pub Mon–Sat 11am–11pm; Sun noon–3pm and 7–10:30pm. Located 3km (2 miles) southeast of Henley, just off the A423 Henley-Maidenhead road.

SIDE TRIPS FROM HENLEY
A ROMANTIC BOAT TRIP TO A HISTORIC HOME

Mapledurham House 🖈 *Finds*   The Blount family mansion lies beside the Thames in the unspoiled village of Mapledurham. The house has Elizabethan ceilings and a great oak staircase, as well as the portraits of the two beautiful sisters with whom the poet Alexander Pope, a frequent visitor here, fell in love. The family chapel, built in 1789, is a fine example of modern Gothic architecture. Cream teas with homemade cakes are available at the house. On the grounds, the last working water mill on the Thames still produces flour.

The most romantic way to reach this lovely old house is to take the boat that leaves the promenade next to Caversham Bridge at 2pm on Saturday, Sunday, and bank holidays from Easter to September. The journey upstream takes about 45 minutes; the boat leaves Mapledurham again at 5pm for the return, leaving plenty of time to walk through the house. The round-trip boat ride from Caversham costs £4.50 ($7) for adults and £3 ($4.80) for children 16 and under. Further details can be obtained from **Thames Rivercruises Ltd.,** Pipers Island, Bridge Street, Caversham Bridge, Reading (ℭ **01189/481088**).

Mapledurham. ℭ **01189/723350.** Admission to house and mill £6 ($10) adults, £3 ($4.80) children 5–14, free for children 4 and under. Easter–Sept Sat–Sun and bank holidays 2–5pm. Closed Oct–Easter. From Henley-on-Thames, head south along A4155 toward Reading. At the junction with A329 head west. Mapledurham is signposted from this road. Or take the boat trip described above.

THE WELLINGTON DUCAL ESTATE

Stratfield Saye House 🖈   The extent of the fortune acquired by the duke of Wellington and his descendants is obvious in this combined house and country park. The complex's centerpiece is the 17th-century Stratfield Saye House, the home of the dukes of Wellington since 1817, when a grateful Parliament bought it to thank the "Iron Duke" for his victory over Napoleon at the Battle of Waterloo. Memorabilia of the first duke is on view, including his billiard table, battle spoils, and pictures. The funeral carriage that once rested in St. Paul's Cathedral's crypt is on display. In the gardens is the grave of Copenhagen, Wellington's charger at Waterloo. There are extensive landscaped grounds, a tearoom, and a gift shop.

Although extensive parks and gardens surround Stratfield Saye, only those adjacent to the house are open to the public. If you're looking for greenery and lovely landscaping, try Wellington Country Park (see below).

1.5km (1 mile) west of Reading, beside A33 to Basingstoke. ℭ **01256/882882.** www.stratfield-saye.co.uk. Admission £6 ($10) adults, £3 ($4.80) children 5–15, free for children under 5. Combined ticket for Stratford Saye and Wellington Country Park £7 ($11) adults, £4 ($6) children. July 7–Aug 3 daily 11:30am–5pm. From Henley, head south along A1455.

Wellington Country Park *Finds*   This is a favorite place for the locals to picnic and stroll; it has a nice lake filled with waterfowl and miles of well-maintained walking paths. But there are attractions inside as well: a riding school; a miniature steam railway; a deer park; and the Thames Valley Time Trail, a walk-through series of exhibits related to the region's geology and the dinosaurs that once inhabited it.

Riseley, Reading, Berkshire RG7 1SP. © 01189/326444. www.wellington-country-park.co.uk. Admission £4.50 ($7) adults, £2.25 ($3.60) children 5–16, free for children under 5. Combined ticket for Stratford Saye and Wellington Country Park £6.75 ($11) adults, £3.75 ($6) children. Park and exhibits open Mar 1–Oct 31 daily 10am–5:30pm.

3 Oxford: The City of Dreaming Spires

86km (54 miles) NW of London; 86km (54 miles) SE of Coventry

A walk down the long sweep of The High, one of the most striking streets in England; a mug of cider in one of the old student pubs; the sound of May Day dawn when choristers sing in Latin from Magdalen Tower; students in traditional gowns whizzing past on rickety bikes; towers and spires rising majestically; nude swimming at Parson's Pleasure; the roar of a cannon launching the bumping races; a tiny, dusty bookstall where you can pick up a valuable first edition—all this belongs to Oxford, home of one of the greatest universities in the world.

Romantic Oxford is still here, but to get to it, you'll also have to experience the bustling and crowded city that is also Oxford. The never-ending stream of polluting buses and the fast-flowing pedestrian traffic may surprise you—the city core now feels more like London than the sleepy town Oxford once was. Surrounding the perimeter, suburban sprawl keeps spreading in a not particularly attractive manner.

At any time of the year, you can enjoy a tour of the colleges; many of these represent a peak in England's architectural history, while others epitomize a valley of Victorian contributions. The Oxford Tourist Information Centre (see below) offers guided walking tours daily throughout the year. Just don't mention the "other place" (Cambridge) and you shouldn't have any trouble. Comparisons between the two universities are inevitable: Oxford is better known for the arts, Cambridge more for the sciences.

The city predates the university—it was a Saxon town in the early part of the 10th century. By the 12th century, Oxford was growing in reputation as a seat of learning, at the expense of Paris. The first colleges were founded in the 13th century. The story of Oxford is filled with conflicts too complex to elaborate here; let's say that the relationship between town and gown hasn't always been as peaceful as it is today—riots have flared, and both sides share guilt. The young people of Oxford now work out their aggressiveness in sporting competitions.

Ultimately, the test of a great university lies in the caliber of the people it turns out. Oxford can name-drop a mouthful: Roger Bacon, Sir Walter Raleigh, John Donne, Sir Christopher Wren, Samuel Johnson, Edward Gibbon, William Penn, John Wesley, Matthew Arnold, Lewis Carroll, Arnold Toynbee, Graham Greene, A. E. Housman, and T. E. Lawrence—just to name a few.

ESSENTIALS

GETTING THERE   Trains from Paddington Station reach Oxford in 1½ hours. Five trains run every hour. A cheap, same-day round-trip ticket costs £16 ($26); a 5-day round-trip ticket is £18.50 ($30). For more information, call © 0845/7484950.

Oxford CityLink provides coach service from London's Victoria Station (𝒞 **08705/808080**) to the Oxford Bus Station. Coaches usually depart about every 30 minutes during the day; the trip takes approximately 1¾ hours. A same-day round-trip ticket costs £10 ($16) for adults, £8 ($13) for children 3 to 15.

If you're driving, take the M40 west from London and just follow the signs. Traffic and parking are a disaster in Oxford, and not just during rush hours. However, there are four large park-and-ride parking lots on the north, south, east, and west of the city's ring road, all well marked. Parking is free at all times. The lots are on the Woodstock road near the Peartree traffic circle, on the Botley road toward Farringdon, on the Abingdon road in the southeast, and on the A40 toward London.

VISITOR INFORMATION The **Oxford Tourist Information Centre** is at 15–16 Broad St. (𝒞 **01865/726871**). The center sells a comprehensive range of maps, brochures, and souvenir items, as well as the famous Oxford University T-shirt. It provides hotel-booking services for £3 ($4.80). Guided walking tours leave from the center daily (see below). Open Monday through Saturday from 9:30am to 5pm and Sunday and bank holidays in summer from 10am to 3:30pm.

GETTING AROUND Competition thrives in Oxford transportation, and the public benefits with swift, clean service by two companies. The **Oxford Bus Company,** 395 Cowley Rd. (𝒞 **01865/785400**), has green Park and Ride buses that leave from four parking lots in the city using the north-south or east-west routes. A round-trip ticket costs £1.80 ($2.90). Their CityLink buses are blue and travel to London, Heathrow, and Gatwick. The company's red CityLink buses cover 15 routes in all suburbs, with a day pass allowing unlimited travel for £2.70 ($4.30). Weekly and monthly passes are available. The competition, **Stagecoach,** Unit 4, Horsepath, Cowley (𝒞 **01865/772250**), uses blue-and-cream minibuses and red-blue-and-orange coaches. City buses leave from Queen Street in Oxford's city center. Explorer passes cost £5.50 ($9). Abington Road buses are marked "wantage," and Iffley Road buses are labeled "Rose Hill."

TOURS OF OXFORD

The best way to get a running commentary on the important sights is to take a 2-hour **walking tour** through the city and the major colleges. The tours leave daily from the Oxford Information Centre at 11am and 2pm. Tours costs £6.50 ($10) for adults and £3 ($4.80) for children; the tours do not include New College or Christ Church.

The **Oxford Story,** 6 Broad St. (𝒞 **01865/790055**), is a concise and entertaining audiovisual ride through the campus. It explains the structure of the colleges and highlights architectural and historical features. Visitors are also filled in on the general background of the colleges and the antics of some of the famous people who have passed through the University's portals. In July and August the audiovisual presentation is daily from 9:30am to 5pm. From September to December Monday to Saturday 10am to 4:30pm, Sunday 11am to 4:30pm, and

Moments **A Nostalgic Walk**

Our favorite pastime here is to take Addison's Walk through the water meadows. The stroll is named after a former Oxford alumnus, Joseph Addison, the 18th-century essayist and playwright noted for his contributions to *The Spectator* and *The Tatler*.

Oxford

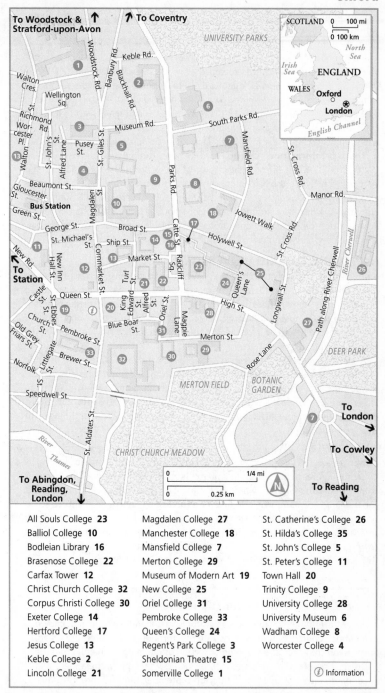

SCOTLAND
North Sea
Irish Sea
ENGLAND
WALES
Oxford
London
English Channel

0 100 mi
0 100 km

To Woodstock & Stratford-upon-Avon
To Coventry

UNIVERSITY PARKS

Keble Rd.
Woodstock Rd.
Banbury Rd.
Blackhall Rd.
Walton Cres.
Wellington Sq.
Walton St.
Richmond Rd.
Worcester Pl.
Walton St.
St. John's St.
Alfred Lane
Pusey St.
St. Giles St.
Museum Rd.
South Parks Rd.
Mansfield Rd.
St. Cross Rd.
Manor Rd.
Beaumont St.
Gloucester St.
Green St.
Magdalen St.
Parks Rd.
Catte St.
Jowett Walk
Bus Station
George St.
Broad St.
Holywell St.
St. Michael's St.
Ship St.
Cornmarket St.
Market St.
Radcliff Sq.
New Rd.
To Station
New Inn Hall St.
Turl St.
King Edward St.
Alfred St.
Oriel St.
Queen's Lane
High St.
Longwall St.
Castle St.
St. Ebbes St.
Church St.
Queen St.
Blue Boar St.
Magpie Lane
Merton St.
Old Grey Friars St.
Pembroke St.
Littlegate St.
Brewer St.
Rose Lane
Norfolk St.
Speedwell St.
St. Aldates St.

River Cherwell
Path along River Cherwell
DEER PARK
To London
To Cowley

MERTON FIELD
BOTANIC GARDEN

River Thames
CHRIST CHURCH MEADOW

To Abingdon, Reading, London
To Reading

0   1/4 mi
0   0.25 km

N

All Souls College **23**	Magdalen College **27**	St. Catherine's College **26**
Balliol College **10**	Manchester College **18**	St. Hilda's College **35**
Bodleian Library **16**	Mansfield College **7**	St. John's College **5**
Brasenose College **22**	Merton College **29**	St. Peter's College **11**
Carfax Tower **12**	Museum of Modern Art **19**	Town Hall **20**
Christ Church College **32**	New College **25**	Trinity College **9**
Corpus Christi College **30**	Oriel College **31**	University College **28**
Exeter College **14**	Pembroke College **33**	University Museum **6**
Hertford College **17**	Queen's College **24**	Wadham College **8**
Jesus College **13**	Regent's Park College **3**	Worcester College **4**
Keble College **2**	Sheldonian Theatre **15**	
Lincoln College **21**	Somerville College **1**	*i* Information

January to June Monday to Saturday 10am to 4:30pm, Sunday 11am to 4:30pm. Admission is £7 ($11) for adults and £5.50 ($9) for seniors, students, and children. A family ticket for two adults and two children is £20.50 ($33).

For a good orientation, hour-long, open-top bus tours around Oxford are available from **Guide Friday,** whose office is at the railway station (② **01865/ 790522**). Buses leave every 20 minutes daily; in summer, buses leave every 5 to 10 minutes. Tickets are good for the day. Tours begin daily at 9:30am year-round. The cost is £9 ($14) for adults, £7 ($11) for students and seniors, £3 ($4.80) for children 5 to 14 years old, and children under 5 ride free; a family ticket for two adults and two children is £19 ($30). Tickets can be purchased from the driver.

Tourist Information Centre, Old School Building, Gloucester Green (② **01865/726871**), offers a ghost tour, which explores Oxford's ghoulish and gory past. The office also has a number of walking tours, with the ghost tour available Friday and Saturday evenings July through October from 7 to 8:30pm, covering the dark alleyways around the ancient schools. The cost is £5.85 ($9.35) for adults and £3 ($4.80) for children; tickets are available at the office during the day. Day tours begin at 10am daily, including Christmas.

EXPLORING OXFORD UNIVERSITY

Some visitors arriving at Oxford ask, "Where's the campus?" Locals may look bemused in reply, for Oxford University consists of 35 colleges sprinkled throughout the town. (The distinction between American and British colleges is that the latter do not grant degrees; only their affiliated university can do so.) To tour all of these would be a formidable task; it's best to focus on a handful of the better-known colleges.

A word of warning: A university's main business is to educate—and this role at Oxford has been severely hampered by the stream of visitors who disturb academic pursuits. Visiting is now restricted to certain hours; groups may be no larger than six. There are areas where visitors are not allowed at all. The tourist office will be happy to advise you when and where you may take in the sights of this great institution.

AN OVERVIEW   For a bird's-eye view of the city and colleges, climb **Carfax Tower** ⋆, located in the center of the city. This structure is distinguished by its clock and figures that strike on the quarter hour. Carfax Tower is all that remains from St. Martin's Church, where William Shakespeare once stood as godfather for William Davenant, who also became a successful playwright. A church stood on this site from 1032 until 1896. The tower used to be higher, but after 1340 it was lowered, following complaints from the university to Edward III that townspeople threw stones and fired arrows at students during town-and-gown disputes. Admission is £1.50 ($2.40) for adults, £1 ($1.60) for children. The

---

⟨Finds A Pokey Home for Old Masters

Almost overlooked by the average visitor is an unheralded little gem known as **Christ Church Picture Gallery,** entered through the Canterbury Quad. Here you come across a stunning collection of old masters, mainly from the Dutch, Flemish, and Italian school, including works by Michelangelo and Leonardo da Vinci. Open April through September, Monday through Saturday from 10:30am to 1pm and 2 to 5:30pm (closes at 4:30pm Oct–Mar). Admission is £2 ($3.20) for adults and £1 ($1.60) for seniors and students.

Tips A Quiet Oasis

Though ignored by the average visitor, the **Botanic Gardens** opposite Magdalen were first planted in 1621 on the site of a Jewish graveyard from the early Middle Ages. Bounded by a curve of the Cherwell, they still stand today and are the best place in Oxford to escape the invading hordes. Open daily from noon to 4pm; admission is £2 ($3.20).

---

tower is open year-round, except for Christmas Eve to January 1. April through October, hours are from 10am to 5pm daily. Off-season hours are Monday through Saturday 10am to 3:30pm. Children under 5 are not admitted. For information, call ℂ **01865/792653.**

CHRIST CHURCH ★★   Begun by Cardinal Wolsey as Cardinal College in 1525, Christ Church (ℂ **01865/276150;** www.chch.ox.ac.uk), known as the House, was founded by Henry VIII in 1546. Facing St. Aldate's Street, Christ Church has the largest quadrangle of any college in Oxford. Tom Tower houses Great Tom, an 18,000-pound bell. It rings at 9:05pm nightly, signaling the closing of the college gates. The 101 times it peals originally signified the number of students in residence at the time the college was founded. Although the student body has grown significantly, Oxford traditions live forever. There are some interesting portraits in the 16th-century Great Hall, including works by Gainsborough and Reynolds. There's also a separate portrait gallery.

The college chapel was constructed over a period of centuries, beginning in the 12th century. (Incidentally, it's not only the college chapel but also the cathedral of the diocese of Oxford.) The cathedral's most distinguishing features are its Norman pillars and the vaulting of the choir, dating from the 15th century. In the center of the great quadrangle is a statue of Mercury mounted in the center of a fishpond. The college and cathedral can be visited between 9am and 5:30pm, though times vary. It's best to call before you visit. The entrance fee is £3 ($4.80) for adults and £2 ($3.20) for children.

MAGDALEN COLLEGE   Magdalen (pronounced *Maud*-lin) College, High Street (ℂ **01865/276000;** www.magd.ox.ac.uk), was founded in 1458 by William of Waynflete, bishop of Winchester and later chancellor of England. Its alumni range from Wolsey to Wilde. Opposite the botanic garden, the oldest in England, is the bell tower, where the choristers sing in Latin at dawn on May Day. Charles I, his days numbered, watched the oncoming Roundheads from this tower. Visit the 15th-century chapel, in spite of many of its latter-day trappings. Ask when the hall and other places of special interest are open. The grounds of Magdalen are the most extensive of any Oxford college; there's even a deer park. You can visit year-round between 1pm and dusk daily. Admission is £3 ($4.80).

MERTON COLLEGE ★★   Founded in 1264, Merton College, Merton Street (ℂ **01865/276310;** www.merton.ox.ac.uk), is among the three oldest colleges at the university. It stands near Corpus Christi College on Merton Street, the sole survivor of Oxford's medieval cobbled streets. Merton College is noted for its library (which is closed at press time), built between 1371 and 1379 and said to be the oldest college library in England. Though a tradition once kept some of its most valuable books chained, now only one book is secured in that manner to illustrate that historical custom. One of the library's treasures is an astrolabe (an astronomical instrument used for measuring the altitude of the

---

Tips Oxford or Cambridge—Which to Choose?

Not all of us can go to both Oxford and Cambridge, so which to choose if you're pressed for time and can spare only a day out of London? We'd opt for Cambridge over Oxford because Cambridge more closely lives up to the image of what an English university town is like.

Although the university dominates central Oxford, it is also an industrial city known for its motor industry. Its 120,000 permanent residents seem to keep to themselves and go about their lives trying to evade the thousands of tourists descending on their inner core. Oxford has some of England's greatest architecture, some excellent museums, and better student pubs than restaurants. On an ideal itinerary, it should not be crossed off the list.

Cambridge, on the other hand, is really an agricultural market town, a more tranquil and secluded place. It's set just at the doorstep of the Fens, a vast area just north of the city that's a strange but fascinating terrain of reclaimed marshland and quaking bogs. In addition to its architecture and university, Cambridge allows you to preview life in East Anglia, chock full of the kind of bucolic landscapes once painted by John Constable. (For more on Cambridge, see chapter 13.)

Unlike Oxford, Cambridge is more compact and can be easily walked and explored on a rushed day trip. You can go "punting" on the River Cam; explore "the Backs," that green swathe of land straddling the river; and walk the half-mile parade of colleges from Magdalene to Peterhouse. Not bad for a day's outing. And you may fall so in love with English university towns that you'll decide to stay in England an extra day to take in Oxford after all.

---

sun and stars) thought to have belonged to Chaucer. You pay £1 ($1.60) to visit the ancient library as well as the Max Beerbohm Room (the satirical English caricaturist who died in 1956). The library and college are open Monday through Friday from 2 to 4pm, and Saturday and Sunday from 10am to 4pm. It's closed for 1 week at Easter and Christmas and on weekends during the winter.

NEW COLLEGE New College, New College Lane, off Queen's Lane (© **01865/279555**), was founded in 1379 by William of Wykeham, bishop of Winchester and later lord chancellor of England. His college (preparatory school) at Winchester supplied a constant stream of students. The first quadrangle, dating from before the end of the 14th century, was the first built in Oxford and the model for the other colleges. The antechapel contains Sir Jacob Epstein's remarkable modern sculpture of Lazarus and a fine St. James by El Greco. Another college treasure is a crosier (pastoral staff of a bishop) once owned by the founding father. In the garden, you can stroll among the remains of the old city wall and the mound. Open daily Easter to October 11am to 5pm; off season 2 to 4pm. Admission is £2 ($3.20) in season only.

Insider's tip: New College is known for its "notorious gargoyles." Check them out at the bell tower, decorated with Seven Virtues on one side and Seven Deadly Sins on the other. The Virtues are just as grotesque as the Deadly Sins.

THE OLD BODLEIAN LIBRARY ★★   This famed library on Catte Street (© **01865/277224;** www.bodley.ox.ac.uk) was launched in 1602, initially funded by Sir Thomas Bodley. It is home to some 50,000 manuscripts and more than five million books. Over the years the library has expanded from the Old Library complex to other buildings, including the Radcliffe Camera next door. The easiest way to visit the library is by taking a guided tour, leaving from the Divinity School across the street from the main entrance. In summer there are four tours Monday through Friday, and two on Saturday; in winter, two tours leave per day. Call for specific times.

SHOPPING

Golden Cross, an arcade of first-class shops and boutiques, lies between Cornmarket Street and the Covered Market (or between High St. and Market St.). Parts of the colorful gallery date from the 12th century. Many buildings remain from the medieval era, along with some 15th- and 17th-century structures. The market has a reputation as the Covent Garden of Oxford, where live entertainment takes place on Saturday mornings in summer, ranging from dancing in Radcliffe Square to performances by the Magdalen College Choir from high atop Magdalen Tower. In the arcade shops you'll find a diverse selection of merchandise, including handmade Belgian chocolates, specialty gifts, clothing for both women and men, and luxury leather goods. In its way, **Alice's Shop,** 83 St. Aldate's (© **01865/723793**), played an important role in English literature. Set within a 15th-century building that has housed some kind of shop since 1820, it was a general store (selling brooms, hardware, and the like) during the time that Lewis Carroll, then a don (professor) of mathematics at Christ Church College, was composing *Alice in Wonderland.* It is believed to have been the model for settings within the book. Today, the place is a favorite stopover of Lewis Carroll fans from as far away as Japan, who gobble up commemorative pencils, chess sets, party favors, bookmarks, and in rare cases original editions of some of Carroll's works. The **Bodleian Library Shop,** Old School's Quadrangle, Radcliffe Square, Broad Street (© **01865/277216**), specializes in Oxford souvenirs: books, paperweights, Oxford banners, coffee mugs, and more. **Castell & Son (The Varsity Shop),** 13 Broad St. (© **01865/244000**), is the best outlet in Oxford for clothing emblazoned with the Oxford logo or heraldic symbol. Choices include whimsical and dead-serious neckties, hats, T-shirts, sweatshirts, pens, bookmarks, beer and coffee mugs, and cuff links. It's commercialized Oxford with a lingering sense of dignity and style.

Moments Punting

Punting on the River Cherwell remains Oxford's favorite outdoor pastime. At **Punt Station,** Cherwell Boathouse, Bardwell Road (© **01865/515978**), you can rent a punt (a flat-bottom boat maneuvered by a long pole) for £10 to £12 ($16–$19) per hour, plus a £50 to £60 ($80–$96) deposit. Similar charges apply to punt rentals at **Magdalen Bridge Boathouse** (© **01865/ 202643**). Punts are rented from mid-March to mid-October, daily from 10am until dusk. Hours of operation seem to be rather informal; you're not always guaranteed that someone will be there to rent you a boat, even if it's sitting there.

WHERE TO STAY IN & AROUND OXFORD

Accommodations in Oxford are limited. Recently, motels have sprouted on the outskirts—good for those who want modern amenities. In addition, if you've got a car, you may want to consider country houses or small B&Bs on the outskirts of town; they're the best choices in the area if you don't mind commuting.

The **Oxford Tourist Information Centre,** Gloucester Green, behind the bus bays (*© 01865/726871*), operates a year-round room-booking service for a £3 ($4.80) fee, plus a 10% refundable deposit. If you want to seek lodgings yourself, the center has a list of accommodations, maps, and guidebooks.

Adams Guest House   This nonsmoking guesthouse, operated by John Strange, is in Summertown, 2km (1¼ miles) from Oxford opposite Radio Oxford. The very basic rooms have private showers-only bathrooms. Don't expect anything fancy here; the price is good for the area. Breakfast is served in a dining room decorated in an old-world style. Mr. Strange will provide touring tips. A bus runs every few minutes to the city center. The neighborhood offers the Midland Bank (opposite the Adams), seven restaurants, shops, a post office, a swimming pool, a bicycle-rental shop, and a launderette.

302 Banbury Rd., Summertown, Oxford OX2 7ED. *© 01865/556118.* 6 units, all with shower. £40 ($64) single; £55 ($88) double. Rates include English breakfast. No credit cards. Bus: no. 2 or 7 from Cornmarket. **Amenities:** Breakfast room; lounge. *In room:* TV, coffeemaker, hair dryer, no phone.

Brown's Guest House   This year-round guesthouse, a redbrick Victorian, is one of the better bets along Iffley Road, about a mile from the city center. The pleasantly furnished, recently refurbished bedrooms have hot and cold running water and central heating; some rooms are small. There are adequate showers outside the rooms. Families are catered to, with special breakfasts if requested. Nearby extras include a post office, launderette, grocery store, drugstore, and bike-rental shop. This is a nonsmoking guesthouse.

281 Iffley Rd., Oxford, Oxfordshire OX4 4AQ. *© 01865/246822.* 8 units, 4 with bathroom. £35 ($56) single without bathroom; £58 ($93) double without bathroom, £70 ($112) double with bathroom. Rates include English breakfast. MC, V. Bus: no. 3, 4, or 4A. **Amenities:** Breakfast room; lounge. *In room:* TV, coffeemaker, hair dryer.

The Burlington House ★★ *Value*   In the choice residential section of Summertown, just a 5-minute bus ride from the center, this is a B&B that has won awards from the Automobile Association and the English Tourism Council. Built in the closing months of 1889, the Burlington was a former Victorian businessman's house before its successful conversion into a luxury first-rate B&B. Totally renovated, it is a stylish choice either for an overnight or a longer stay in Oxford. The nonsmoking bedrooms are attractively furnished and comfortably inviting. As one reader put it, "bottled water, water pressure, air-freshener, shoe shine kit, security," it's all here. Bedrooms are light, and there are such small but thoughtful extras as homemade cookies waiting for you. Breakfast is excellent with freshly squeezed orange juice and free-range eggs along with such delights as freshly ground Lavazza coffee and Greek yogurt. From April to October there is a 2-night minimum stay. Children over 12 are welcomed.

374 Banbury Rd., Summertown, Oxford OX2 7PP. *© 01865/513513.* Fax 01865/311785. stay@burlington-house.co.uk. 11 units, 10 with bathroom. £58 ($93) single; £75–£85 ($120–$136) double. Rates include breakfast. AE, MC, V. Bus: no. 2 or 7. **Amenities:** Breakfast room; lounge. *In room:* TV, dataport, coffee-/tea-maker, hair dryer, iron.

Cotswold House ★   This stone house is one of the better B&Bs in the area. The nonsmoking bedrooms vary in size, with one on the ground floor. All are comfortable and meet a high standard. All rooms are neatly furnished with clean shower-only bathrooms. Two rooms are available for those with limited mobility. Traditional and vegetarian breakfasts and fresh fruit are always available, all with generous Irish helpings. There is ample off-street parking. The Walkers help with maps and give good touring advice. Buses pass by about every 5 minutes.

363 Banbury Rd., Oxford, Oxfordshire OX2 7PL. ℭ **01865/310558.** www.cotswoldhouse.co.uk. 7 units. £50–£55 ($80–$88) single; £75 ($120) double. Rates include English breakfast. MC, V. Bus: no. 2 or 7. Located 2.5km (1½ miles) from the city center; use the ring road. **Amenities:** Breakfast room; lounge. *In room:* TV, coffeemaker, hair dryer.

Courtfield Private Hotel

This meticulously maintained B&B is suitable for motorists who don't want to face the congested city center; it stands on a tree-lined street near the center of Iffley Village. If you're not driving, there's adequate public transportation. The nonsmoking house has been modernized with triple-glazed windows in the bright, spacious bedrooms, most of which contain private shower-only bathrooms, one in Art Deco marble.

367 Iffley Rd., Oxford, Oxfordshire OX4 4DP. ℭ and fax **01865/242991** (but call before faxing). 6 units. £41 ($66) single; £58 ($93) double; £70 ($112) triple. Rates include English breakfast. MC, V. Bus: no. 4A, 4B, or 4C. **Amenities:** Breakfast room; lounge. *In room:* TV, coffeemaker, hair dryer, no phone.

Galaxie Private Hotel

When it was built about a century ago, this red brick hotel served as a plush private mansion for a prosperous local family. This little nonsmoking hotel is better than ever following a recent refurbishment and upgrade, with a conservatory lounge added. Today, although most of its garden has been paved over as a parking lot, it still stands in a neighborhood of similar large houses in the suburb of Summertown. Each of the well-maintained bedrooms is equipped with reading lights, electric shaver outlets, hot and cold running water, and central heating. One room is available for those with limited mobility. Furnishings are of a high standard. Most units come with tidily kept, shower-only bathrooms. Although no meals other than breakfast are served, the hotel is within a short walk of at least five restaurants and two pubs. A public leisure center, with two indoor pools, is located just behind the hotel. A public bus runs down Banbury Road to the center of Oxford.

180 Banbury Rd., Oxford, Oxfordshire OX2 7BT. ℭ **01865/515688.** Fax 01865/556824. www.galaxie.co.uk. 34 units, 30 with bathroom. £49 ($78) single without bathroom, £60 ($96) single with bathroom; £76 ($122) double without bathroom, £88 ($141) double with bathroom. All rates include English breakfast. MC, V. Bus: no. 7, 20, 21, or 22. 1.6km (1 mile) north of Oxford center. **Amenities:** Breakfast room; lounge. *In room:* TV, dataport, coffeemaker, hair dryer.

Green Gables Guest House

This hotel lies about 1.5km (1 mile) south of the city on A4144. It was originally a large Edwardian private residence of a local toy manufacturer. Mr. & Mrs. Bhella, among the best hosts in the Oxford area, continue to make improvements to this property. Many of their nonsmoking bedrooms are quite large; all are in spic-and-span condition, each with a private shower-only bathroom. One ground-floor bedroom is suitable for persons with limited mobility. The nonsmoking breakfast room is bright and inviting. Trees screen the house from the main road, and parking for eight cars is available. If you walk 135m (450 ft.) to the traffic lights by the Fox & Hounds pub, then turn left, you will come to the River Thames. For a ramble, follow the signposts to the Longbridge Nature Park. Even prettier is the walk to Iffley Lock, past the Isis riverside pub. You can cross the river at the lock and climb to Iffley Village, dating from Saxon times and still known for its remarkable Norman church, one of England's finest.

326 Abingdon Rd., Oxford, Oxfordshire OX1 4TE. ℭ **01865/725870.** Fax 01865/723115. www.greengables. uk.com. 11 units. £52–£70 ($83–$112) single or double. Rates include English breakfast. AE, MC, V. **Amenities:** Breakfast room; lounge. *In room:* TV, dataport, coffeemaker.

Highfield West   Three miles from the heart of Oxford, Highfield West is on a residential road within easy access of the ring road surrounding Oxford. The little village of Cumnor, with its two country inns serving food and drink, is within walking distance. Blenheim Palace is a few miles away, and a pleasant day can be spent in some of the Cotswold villages. Richard and Diana Mitchell offer nonsmoking accommodations in single, double, or family rooms, most with private shower-only bathrooms. They have recently completed some major improvements, making the bedrooms more inviting than ever, with new carpets and new bathroom fittings. One room is available for those with limited mobility. A bus into Oxford stops just outside their front garden, and there's also a good local taxi service. All meals are vegetarian.

188 Cumnor Hill, Oxford, Oxfordshire OX2 9PJ. ℭ **01865/863007.** highfieldwest@email.msn.com. 6 units, 4 with bathroom. £29–£35 ($46–$48) single without bathroom; £52–£62 ($83–$99) double with bathroom. Rates include English breakfast. No credit cards. Bus: no. 4 or 4B. **Amenities:** Breakfast room; lounge; pool. *In room:* TV.

Marlborough House Hotel   About 2.5km (1½ miles) north of Oxford, this traditionally designed, three-story structure was built in 1990, unlike most of its Victorian neighbors. The comfortably furnished rooms contain private bathrooms with shower-tub combinations, and continental breakfast trays. There's a nonsmoking policy.

321 Woodstock Rd., Oxford, Oxfordshire OX2 7NY. ℭ **01865/311321.** Fax 01865/515329. www.oxfordcity. co.uk/hotels/marlborough. 17 units. £65–£70 ($104–$112) single; £80–£84 ($128–$134) double; £99 ($158) triple; £120 ($192) family. Rates include continental breakfast. Midweek and weekend discounts arranged Sept–June. AE, DC, MC, V. Children under 5 years of age are not accepted. **Amenities:** Breakfast room; lounge; laundry/dry cleaning. *In room:* TV, dataport, coffeemaker, hair dryer.

Nanford Guest House   The Nanford's 65 rooms make it (by far) the largest B&B in Oxford; its aura is that of a cost-conscious hotel, not a home that lets out rooms. Built in 1910, it has housed everyone from rock band members to academics on sabbatical from all over the world. In the mid-1990s, new carpeting and beds were added to every room. The small rooms are simple and unpretentious, each in many cases with a small refrigerator and all with a private shower-only bathroom. There's no bar or cocktail lounge here, and the English breakfasts served every morning are the only meals provided.

137 Iffley Rd., Oxford OX4 1EJ. ℭ **01865/244743.** Fax 01865/249596. www.allworld-vacation.com/uk/ eng10.htm. 50 units. £30 ($48) single; £40 ($64) double. AE, DC, MC, V. **Amenities:** 2 breakfast rooms. *In room:* TV, fridge (some units), coffeemaker.

The Oxford Lodge   Located about 5km (3 miles) north of Oxford, near the beginning of the A34 highway leading away from town, this large commercial hotel is suitable if you have a car. The hotel is easy to spot because of the international flags fluttering in the breezes. Lower-level rooms open onto private terraces. Furnishings are of the motel type, with built-in necessities. Each well-maintained room has a picture window and individually controlled heating. Bathrooms, although small, have adequate shelf space and showers and tubs.

Peartree Roundabout, Woodstock Rd., Oxford, Oxfordshire OX2 8JZ. ℭ **01865/554301.** Fax 01865/513474. www.travelodge.co.uk. 150 units. £49.95 ($80) single or double. AE, MC, V. Park and Ride bus, with frequent trips from downtown Oxford to a public parking lot nearby. **Amenities:** Restaurant; dining room. *In room:* TV, coffeemaker.

Pine Castle Hotel   Set about 2.5km (1½ miles) southeast of the city center, the building housing this hotel is from 1901. The Pine Castle doubled its size in 1994 when its owners, Peter and Marilyn Morris, bought the building's other half. The hotel retains the stained-glass windows and fireplaces of its original construction. The small bedrooms are furnished with simple pine furniture and accessories, including a private shower-only bathroom. Rooms are all quiet and comfortable.

292 Iffley Rd., Oxford, Oxfordshire OX4 4AE. ℭ 01865/241497. Fax 01865/727230. 7 units. £55–£59 ($88–$94) single; £65–£71 ($104–$114) double. Rates include English breakfast. MC, V. Bus: no. 3, 4A, 4B, or 4C. **Amenities:** Restaurant; bar; room service. *In room:* TV, coffeemaker, hair dryer, no phone.

River Hotel   This hotel lies just west of Oxford's commercial core, and charges less than many of its slightly more central competitors. A respected local crafts-man, whose casement windows and flower boxes are still in place, built it around 1900. About a quarter of the accommodations lie across the street, within a com-fortable stone-sided annex, whose architectural details resemble those of the main house. The cozy bedrooms offer comfortable beds and clock radio alarms. Bath-rooms are small but well equipped and contain showers and tubs.

17 Botley Rd., Oxford OX2 OAA. ℭ 01865/243475. Fax 01865/724306. www.riverhotel.co.uk. 20 units. £65 ($104) single; £76 ($122) double; £100 ($160) family room. Rates include breakfast. MC, V. Bus: no. 4C or 52. **Amenities:** Breakfast room; bar. *In room:* TV, dataport, coffeemaker, hair dryer.

Tilbury Lodge   On a quiet country lane about 3km (2 miles) west of the cen-ter of Oxford, this small nonsmoking hotel is a short distance from the railway station, where hotel staff will pick you up to save you the walk. Eddie and Eileen Trafford accommodate guests in their well-furnished and comfortable rooms, and welcome children. The most expensive room has a four-poster bed. Rooms vary in size but all are cozily comfortable; most have adequate space. Bathrooms, although tiny, are well kept, usually with a shower stall.

5 Tilbury Lane, Eynsham Rd., Botley, Oxford, Oxfordshire OX2 9NB. ℭ 01865/862138. Fax 01865/863700. www.oxfordcity.co.uk/hotels/tilbury. 9 units. £45–£50 ($72–$80) single; £60–£72 ($96–$115) double; £75–£85 ($120–$136) double with 4-poster bed. Rates include English breakfast. MC, V. Bus: no. 42, 45, 45A, 45B, or 109. **Amenities:** Breakfast room; lounge; Jacuzzi. *In room:* TV, coffeemaker, hair dryer.

SUPER-CHEAP SLEEPS: A HOSTEL

The **YHA Youth Hostel,** 2A Botley Road, Oxford (ℭ **01865/727275;** national office ℭ **01727/845047;** www.yha.org.uk), is the cheapest place to stay in the area. The hostel costs £14 to £19 ($22–$30), including breakfast, with 112 bunk beds in dorms of 6 to 12, with showers, basins, TV in the lounge, and commu-nal kitchens. Dinner is £5.95 ($10) and picnic lunches £4 ($6). Three rooms are available for those with limited mobility. American Express, MasterCard, and Visa are accepted. The hostel is very close to the Oxford train station, and buses run every 5 minutes until 11pm, and less frequently in the overnight hours. Book at least a week ahead in summer.

WHERE TO DINE

If you just want to have a picnic, or don't mind your food on the run, Oxford abounds in places where you can pick up delicious, low-cost items. A supermar-ket is an especially good choice if you are using self-catering facilities in a hostel. Even better, head for the Covered Market on Market Street, a half block east of Cornmarket Street. Here bakers tempt you with their delicious goods, and you'll enjoy the greengrocer's bounty from the heart of England. On Wednesday, head for the "Wednesday Market" on Gloucester Green by the bus station. Here you can pick up pies, produce, or whatever.

As a college town, Oxford also has plenty of fast-food and ethnic joints, and is known for its "kebab vans" that park around town at night, feeding hungry students with their skewers of spicy meats. They're found at St. Aldate's, High Street, Queen Street, and Broad Street.

Al-Shami LEBANESE   Ideal for meals all afternoon and late into the evening, this Lebanese restaurant has awakened the sleepy taste buds of Oxford. Before it opened, the only ethnic restaurants open after the theaters got out were Chinese and Indian. Many diners don't go beyond the appetizers, of which there are more than 35 delectable hot and cold selections—from falafel to lamb's brains salad. Charcoal-grilled chopped lamb, chicken, or beef constitute most of the entrees, but vegetarian meals are also available. In between, guests nibble on raw vegetables. Desserts are chosen from the trolley.

25 Walton Crescent. ✆ **01865/310066.** Reservations recommended. Main courses £5.75–£12 ($9–$19); fixed-price menu £15 ($24). MC, V. Daily noon–midnight.

Browns ⍟ ENGLISH/CONTINENTAL   Oxford's busiest and most bustling English brasserie suits all groups, from babies to undergraduates to grandmas. A 10-minute walk north of the town center, it occupies the premises of five Victorian shops whose walls were removed to create one large, echoing, and very popular space. Bare wood floors, plaster walls, and a thriving bar (where lots of people seem to order Pimms) make the place an evening destination in its own right. A young, enthusiastic staff serves traditional English cuisine. Your meal might include meat pies, hot salads, burgers, pastas, steaks, and poultry. Afternoon tea here is a justly celebrated Oxford institution. Reservations are not accepted, so if you want to avoid a delay, come during off-peak dining hours.

5–11 Woodstock Rd. ✆ **01865/319600.** Main courses £6–£15 ($10–$24); afternoon tea £4 ($6). MC, V. Mon–Sat 11am–11:30pm; Sun noon–11:30pm.

Chiang Mai Kitchen THAI   Housed in a 17th-century Tudor building with wooden floors and paneling, this restaurant offers a wide array of Thai dishes. Soups may include hot-and-sour chicken or a prawn-and-seafood concoction. The main courses range from various salads to Thai curries, including chicken, beef, and game. An extensive vegetarian menu is also offered featuring several noodle dishes.

130A High St. ✆ **01865/202233.** Reservations recommended. Main courses £5–£10.50 ($8–$17). AE, DC, MC, V. Mon–Sat noon–2:30pm and 6–10:30pm.

Nosebag ⟨Value⟩ ENGLISH/CONTINENTAL   This self-service upstairs cafeteria on a side street off Cornmarket, opposite St. Michael's Church, is very popular with students. At mealtimes there's usually a line down the stairs. At lunch, you can get homemade soup, followed by the dish of the day, perhaps moussaka. Baked potato with a variety of fillings is a good accompaniment, as is the hot garlic bread. The menu leans to vegetarian dishes. Wine is available by the glass.

6–8 St. Michael's St. ✆ **01865/721033.** Lunch main courses £3.50–£6.50 ($6–$10); dinner main courses £3.50–£8.25 ($6–$13). AE, MC, V. Mon–Thurs 9:30am–10pm; Fri–Sat 9:30am–10:30pm; Sun 9:30am–9pm.

Rosie Lee's ENGLISH   The casual environment of this restaurant makes it a favorite of the Oxford crowd. Enjoy a variety of cream or lemon teas with a selection of cakes and scones that changes daily. You could also follow the lead of the many students who come here to have a sandwich as they pore over piles of books. *Be warned:* The scholarly patrons tend to crowd the place at afternoon tea; stop by earlier or later in the day if you want to have a more relaxing meal.

Finds Pubs with a Pedigree

Every college town the world over has a fair number of bars, but few can boast local watering holes with such atmosphere and history as Oxford. A short block from The High, overlooking the north side of Christ Church College, **The Bear Inn,** Alfred Street (© **01865/728164**), is a landmark, built in the 13th century and mentioned time and again in English literature. Around the lounge bar you'll see the remains of thousands of ties, clipped throughout history and labeled with the names of their (former) owners.

Even older than the Bear is **The Turf Tavern,** 7 Bath Place (off Holywell St.; © **01865/243235**), on a very narrow passageway near the Bodleian Library. The pub is reached via St. Helen's Passage, which stretches between Holywell Street and New College Lane. (You'll probably get lost, but any student worth his beer can direct you.) Thomas Hardy used the place as the setting for *Jude the Obscure.* During his student days at Oxford, future U.S. president Bill Clinton frequented the place. At night, the nearby old tower of New College and part of the old city wall are floodlit, and during warm weather you can choose a table in any of the three separate gardens that radiate outward from the pub's central core.

The King's Arms, 40 Holywell St. (© **01865/242369**), attracts a mix of students, gays, and professors. One of the best places in town for conversation, the pub, owned by Young's Brewery, features six of the company's ales as well as lagers and bitters that change periodically.

Just outside of town, about 4km (2½ miles) north of Oxford, the **Trout Inn,** 195 Godstow Rd., Wolvercote (© **01865/302071**), is a private world where you can get ale, beer, and standard fare. Drink in one of the historic rooms, or go out in sunny weather to sit on a stone wall. On the grounds are peacocks, ducks, swans, and herons. On your way there and back, look for the view of Oxford from the bridge. Take bus 520 or 521 to Wolvercote, then walk half a mile; it's also fun to bike here from Oxford.

51 High St. © **01865/244429**. Afternoon tea £4–£6 ($6–$10); sandwiches £2.85–£5 ($4.55–$8). No credit cards. Tues–Sun 9am–6pm.

MORE CHEAP EATS

If you're in the mood for ethnic food, you'll find the best hunting grounds to be the first quartet of blocks along Cowley Road. Among the most popular eateries here are **Hi-Lo Jamaican Eating House,** 70 Cowley Rd. (© **01865/725984**), which serves a goat, chicken, pork, fish, or vegetarian main course with vegetables, rice, and peas for £8 to £12 ($13–$19) at lunch, or £7.50 to £18.50 ($12–$30) at dinner. Snacks such as plantain patties and soups go for £3.50 to £4.50 ($6–$7). Still hungry? Check out **Georgina's Coffee Shop,** Covered Market, above Beaton's Deli (© **01865/249527**), and stop to admire the Toulouse-Lautrec posters as you choose from sandwiches and daily specials or bagels and pastries, all of which are reasonably priced. **Heroes,** 8 Ship St. (© **01865/723459**), makes the best Italian-style subs, ranging from about £1.95 to £2.50 ($3.10–$4) for a curried chicken sandwich. There's always a happening scene at **Café Moma,** 30 Pembroke St. (© **01865/722733**), tucked away under the Museum of Modern Art. It attracts the local young artsy crowd who like its freshly made salads as well as vegan main courses like the "nutroast," made from ground nuts, onions, and spices. A vegetarian main course and two salads will run you £5 ($8); soup starts at £2 ($3.20). Where to go for the cheapest but most well-stuffed sandwiches in town? It's **Harvey's of Oxford,** 58 High St. (© **01865/723152**). Near Magdalen College, it always seems to have a line at the door. Their sandwiches, each one a meal unto itself, start at just £1.85 ($2.95). If a sandwich really isn't enough, their rich carrot cake will finish you off. Students laud their cherry flapjacks, too.

OXFORD AFTER DARK
THE PERFORMING ARTS
Highly acclaimed orchestras playing in truly lovely settings mark the Music at Oxford series at the **Oxford Playhouse,** Beaumont Street (© **01865/305305;** www.oxfordplayhouse.com). The autumn season runs from mid-September to December, the winter season from January to April, the spring-summer season from May to early July. Tickets range from £9 to £24 ($14–$38). Classical music is performed by outstanding groups such as the European Union Chamber Orchestra, the Canterbury Musical Society, the Bournemouth Symphony, and the Guild Hall String Ensemble of London. All performances are held in the Sheldonian Theatre, a particularly attractive site designed by Sir Christopher Wren, with paintings on the ceiling.

The Apollo, George Street (© **01865/243041** for ticket reservations), is Oxford's primary theater. Tickets are £6.50 to £49.50 ($10–$79). A continuous run of comedy, ballet, drama, opera, and even rock contributes to the variety. The Welsh National Opera often performs, and The Glyndebourne Touring Opera appears regularly. Advance booking is recommended, though some shows may have tickets the week of the performance. Don't try for tickets for popular shows on the same day.

At the **Oxford Playhouse,** performances range from Shakespeare to modern comedy and drama. Tickets are £9 to £24 ($14–$38). They are open most nights year-round, except some Sundays and the week after Christmas.

THE CLUBS: BLUES, JAZZ & CELTIC ROCK
Freud, Walton Street at Great Clarendon Street (© **01865/311171**), cover £4.50 ($7) Friday and Saturday after 10pm, has turned a 19th-century church, stained-glass windows and all, into a jazz and folk club with an expansive array of drink choices. **The Zodiac,** 190 Crowley Rd. (© **01865/726336**), cover £4 to £11 ($6–$18), presents everything from easy listening to Celtic rock. It's open usually from about 7:30pm to 2am Monday through Friday, 9pm to 2am Saturday (closed

---

Tips Outdoor Bargains

For some of the best productions in England, with some of the most talented actors, ask the tourist office about summer performances in the college gardens. Student productions have traditionally been held there, but increasingly, professional companies have been taking over the space. Two Shakespeare troupes perform here, as well as other groups. Ticket costs are significantly less than you'd find for a comparable experience elsewhere.

Sun). Some major English bands share club ownership. Local and big-name bands are featured along with DJs, so call ahead to know what you're getting.

THE PUB SCENE

The Head of the River, Abingdon Road at Folly Bridge, near the Westgate Centre Mall (𝒞 **01865/721600**), is operated by the family brewery Fuller Smith and Turner. It's a lively place where they offer true traditional ales and lagers, along with very good sturdy fare. In summer, guests sit by the river and can rent a punt or a boat with an engine. Five rooms, all with bathroom and overlooking the river, are available for £78 to £95 ($125–$152) in summer, including breakfast, newspaper, and parking.

See the box "Pubs with a Pedigree," above, for more great pub options.

4 Woodstock & Blenheim Palace ⟨★⟨★⟨★

100km (62 miles) NW of London; 13km (8 miles) NW of Oxford

The small country town of Woodstock, the birthplace in 1330 of the Black Prince, ill-fated son of King Edward III, lies on the edge of the Cotswolds. Some of the stone houses here were constructed when Woodstock was the site of a royal palace. This palace had so suffered the ravages of time that its remains were demolished when Blenheim Palace was built. Woodstock itself was once the seat of a flourishing glove industry.

ESSENTIALS

GETTING THERE   Take the train to Oxford (see "Essentials," under Oxford, earlier in this chapter). The **Gloucester Green** bus (no. 20) leaves Oxford about every 30 minutes during the day. The trip takes just over a half-hour. Call **Stagecoach** at 𝒞 **01865/772250** for details. If you're driving, take A44 from Oxford.

VISITOR INFORMATION   The **Tourist Information Centre** is on Hensington Road (𝒞 **01993/813276**). Open March through October Monday through Saturday 9:30am to 5:30pm, November through February 10am to 5pm; year round Sunday 1 to 5pm.

ONE OF ENGLAND'S MOST MAGNIFICENT PALACES

Blenheim Palace   The extravagantly baroque Blenheim Palace is England's answer to Versailles. Blenheim is the home of the 11th duke of Marlborough, a descendant of John Churchill, the first duke, an on-again, off-again favorite of Queen Anne's. In his day, the duke was the supreme military figure in Europe; he defeated the forces of Louis XIV near a village named Blenheim on the Danube. The lavish palace was built for him as a gift from the queen. It was designed by Sir John Vanbrugh, also the architect of Castle Howard; the landscaping was created by Capability Brown. The palace is loaded with antiques, porcelain, oil paintings, tapestries, and chinoiserie.

North Americans know Blenheim as the birthplace of Sir Winston Churchill. The room in which he was born is included in the palace tour, as is the Churchill exhibition, four rooms of letters, books, photographs, and other relics. Today the former prime minister lies buried in Bladon Churchyard, near the palace. If the palace exterior looks familiar, that's because actor Kenneth Branagh's 1996 version of *Hamlet* was filmed here.

Insider's tip: The Marlborough Maze, 54m (177 ft.) from the palace, is the second largest symbolic hedge maze on earth, with an herb and lavender garden, a butterfly house, and inflatable castles for children. Be sure to look for the castle's gift shops, tucked away in an old palace dairy. Here you can purchase a wide range of souvenirs and handicrafts, even locally made preserves.

C **01993/811091.** www.blenheimpalace.com. Admission £10 ($16) adults, £8 ($13) seniors and students, £5 ($8) children 5–15, free for children under 5, family ticket £26 ($42). Open daily 9am–5pm. Last admission 4:45pm. Closed Nov to mid-Mar.

WHERE TO STAY

The Laurels The Laurels is just off the town center, but within a few minutes' walk of the heart of town and the Blenheim Palace grounds. Built in 1890 for the manager of a then-flourishing glove factory, this guesthouse has undergone considerable renovation. The decor is traditional, and Malcolm and Nikki Lloyd have furnished the house with Victorian and Edwardian pieces in keeping with its origins. The nonsmoking rooms are attractively decorated and well maintained, two with a private shower-only bathroom and one with shower/tub combo.

40 Hensington Rd., Woodstock, Oxfordshire OX20 1JL. *C* and fax **01993/812583.** www.laurelsguest house.co.uk. 3 units. £50–£60 ($80–$96) single or double. Rates include English breakfast. MC, V. At the Punch Bowl Public House, turn onto Hensington Rd.; it's .5km (¼ mile) ahead on the right. **Amenities:** Breakfast room; lounge. *In room:* TV, hair dryer.

WHERE TO DINE

Brotherons Brasserie ENGLISH   Brotherons, in the heart of town, is your best bet for a meal. Carefully chosen fresh ingredients are one reason for its success. Potted plants, pine chairs and tables, and gas mantels make for a simple but effective decor. Meals usually feature a selection of crudités, smoked salmon, or game pie, and there's always a vegetarian dish. Families with small children are welcomed.

1 High St. *C* **01993/811114.** Main courses £8–£12.50 ($13–$20). AE, DC, MC, V. Daily noon–2:30pm and 6:30–10:30pm. Bus: no. 206.

TWO FAVORITE LOCAL PUBS

The Star Inn (*C* **01993/811373**) serves three locally brewed real ales: Tetleys, Wadworth 6X, and Marston's Pedigree. Enjoy the requisite bar munchies as well as full dinners. The management boasts that its half shoulder of lamb is the most tender around because of the slow cooking process. You can also pick and choose from a hot and cold buffet that features salads and sandwich fixings. **The King's Head** is tucked away at 11 Park Lane (*C* **01993/812164**) in Woodstock. Tourists seem to like this place, though it's a bit hard to find. Its local moniker, the "potato pub," comes from the wide variety of stuffed potato jackets (skins) that it serves. Enjoy these with real ale; the owners serve a different specialty ale every month. If you come for dinner, a three-course meal, which may include fish, ribs, or homemade lasagna, costs about £6 to £10 ($10–$16).

5 Aylesbury

74km (46 miles) NW of London; 35km (22 miles) E of Oxford

Aylesbury has retained much of its ancient charm and character, especially along the narrow Tudor alleyways and in the 17th-century architecture of the houses in the town center. Among the more interesting structures is St. Mary's Church, which dates from the 13th century and features an unusual spirelet. The 15th-century King's Head Public House, a National Trust property, has seen many famous faces in its time, including Henry VIII, a frequent guest while he was courting Anne Boleyn.

The market, which has been an integral part of the town since the 13th century, is still a thriving force in Aylesbury life. Markets are held on Wednesday, Friday, and Saturday, and a flea market on Tuesday. During the 18th and 19th centuries, ducks were the most famous commodities of the Aylesbury market. The pure white birds, a delicacy for the rich and famous of London, were much sought after for their dinner tables. The demand for Aylesbury duck declined in the 20th century, although not before the breed became threatened with extinction. But today most ducks served at restaurants are raised elsewhere, lessening the threat to the Aylesbury duck, now enjoyed more for its beauty than flavor.

ESSENTIALS

GETTING THERE   Aylesbury is 1 hour by train from London's Marylebone Station, or 25 minutes off the M25 via A41. For rail information, call ℂ **0845/ 7484950.**

VISITOR INFORMATION   The **Aylesbury Tourist Information Centre** is at 8 Bourbon St. (ℂ **01296/330559**). Open April through October Monday through Saturday 9:30am to 5pm, November through March 10am to 4:30pm.

SEEING THE SIGHTS

Aylesbury is blessed with an abundance of interesting architecture. If you aren't busy spending money at the market, you may want to stroll through the town to see the houses and buildings that line the streets. Hickman's Almshouses and the Prebendal Houses date from the 17th century; you can walk by after enjoying tea at St. Mary's Church just down the road.

Buckinghamshire County Museum   This museum is located in two buildings, a house and grammar school both dating from the 18th century. The newest addition to the recently refurbished museum is the Roald Dahl Children's Gallery. Dahl's children's books, especially *Charlie and the Chocolate Factory* and *James and the Giant Peach,* come to life as visitors ride in the Great Glass Elevator or crawl inside the Giant Peach. The hands-on exhibits don't stop upon entering the main museum, however. Innovative displays focusing on the cultural heritage of Buckinghamshire are interactive and touchable. Advance arrangements are necessary for the Children's Gallery because of the large number of school groups that visit.

Church St. ℂ **01296/331441.** www.buckscc.gov.uk/museum/index.stm. Admission to main museum is free. Children's Gallery £3.50 ($6) adults, £2.75 ($4.40) children. Mon–Sat 10am–5pm; Sun 2–5pm.

Oak Farms Rare Breeds Park   While you're in the area, you'll want to see those famous Aylesbury ducks. This is the best place to catch sight of the once-threatened species. This traditional working farm is home to a variety of animals, from sheep to pigs, many of which are rare breeds. Guests can hand-feed special food to the animals and take a picnic to enjoy. There's also a nature trail.

Off A41 on the way to Broughton. ℂ **01296/415709.** Admission £3 ($4.80) adults, £2 ($3.20) ages 16 and under. Daily 10am–5pm. Closed Nov to mid-Feb.

Waddesdon Manor ✯   Built by Baron Ferdinand de Rothschild in the 1870s, the manor features French Renaissance architecture and a variety of French furniture, carpets, and porcelain. Eighteenth-century artwork by several famous English and Dutch painters is exhibited, and there are, not surprisingly, wine cellars. In the surrounding gardens, an aviary houses exotic birds. On the premises is a restaurant and gift shop, both featuring a vast assortment of Rothschild wines.

Bicester Rd. © **01296/653226.** www.waddesdon.org.uk. Admission to house and grounds £10 ($16) adults, £7.50 ($12) children; grounds only £3 ($4.80) adults, £1.50 ($2.40) children. House open Apr–Oct Wed–Sun and bank holidays 11am–4pm. Grounds and aviary late Feb to late Dec Wed–Sun and bank holidays 10am–5pm.

WHERE TO STAY

West Lodge Hotel   Close to Aylesbury, this Victorian hotel on the A41 outdoes all others in the area with its facilities, the best of which must be its own hot-air balloon. The comfortable nonsmoking rooms are furnished with nice extras and private shower-only or tub bathrooms. One room is available for those with limited mobility. For dinner, Montgolfier is a French restaurant located across the street named after the brothers who made the first successful hot-air balloon flight in 1783. A three-star Michelin-trained French chef presides over a guests-only daily table d'hôte dinner.

45 London Rd., Aston Clinton, Aylesbury HP22 5HL. © **01296/630362.** Fax 01296/630151. www.west lodge.co.uk. 10 units. £45–£65 ($72–$104) single; £75–£85 ($120–$136) double. All rates include breakfast. AE, DC, MC, V. **Amenities:** Breakfast room; bar; Jacuzzi; sauna; room service (8am–8:30pm). *In room:* TV, dataport, coffeemaker, hair dryer.

WHERE TO DINE

Bottle & Glass *Finds* ⚐ ENGLISH   Because of its lavish sense of charm and nostalgia, no one seems to mind the short trek to this bucolic reminder of Olde England. The setting is a 1660s thatch-roofed cottage that functioned as a rough-and-tumble village pub until the mid-1990s. Around 1995, members of the Southwood family upgraded the food and service rituals to the point where most of its business today derives from a restaurant trade that draws visitors in from throughout the nearby region. No one will mind if you drop in just for a pint, but if you're hungry, menu items focus on old-fashioned but flavorful dishes that helped fortify the Empire builders of the early 20th century. Examples include bangers and mash; smoked salmon with horseradish sauce; garlic mushrooms; rib-eye steaks; and grilled Dover sole.

In the hamlet of Gibraltar, 8km (5 miles) southeast of Aylesbury beside route A418. © **01296/748488.** Reservations recommended. Main courses £15–£32 ($24–$51). AE, DC, MC. V. Daily noon–3pm; Mon–Sat 5–10pm. From Aylesbury, follow the signs to Oxford, following Route A418 for 8km (5 miles) southwest of Aylesbury.

AYLESBURY AFTER DARK

The Hobgoblin, Kingsbury Square (© **01296/415100**), was built in 1742, but has been in service as a pub for only a few years. Among the on-tap offerings are house ales Hobgoblin and Wychwood, as well as John Smith's, and there is also a full bar. Snack food is available, as are such distractions as pool tables, TVs, and video games. Sunday nights there's live jazz (no cover). On weekends, the second floor opens as a dance club called Merlin's, open Wednesday, Friday, and Saturday 10pm to 2:30am, cover £5 ($8) Friday and Saturday.

6 St. Albans ⚐

41km (27 miles) NW of London; 66km (41 miles) SW of Cambridge

Dating back 2,000 years, today's cathedral city of St. Albans was named after a Roman soldier who was the first Christian martyr in England. Medieval pilgrims made the trek to visit the shrine of St. Alban, and visitors today still find the ancient cathedral city and the surrounding countryside inspiring.

Beatrix Potter created *Peter Rabbit* in this borough, and George Bernard Shaw found inspiration in the view from his countryside home near Ayot St.

Lawrence. As you explore, you'll be treading in the footsteps of Elizabeth I and Henry VIII.

Although today industry has crept in and Greater London keeps getting ever greater, St. Albans is situated at the center of what was once "the market basket of England." The 1,000-year-old tradition of the street market continues as merchants of every kind set up colorful stalls to display their goods. The market, one of the largest in the southeast, is held on Wednesday and Saturday.

Tourism has become very important to the town, being near the M25 and the M1 and on the way to many historic homes and attractions. St. Albans itself is home to several museums, well-preserved Roman ruins, and beautiful gardens.

ESSENTIALS

GETTING THERE   St. Albans is easily reached from London. North London Railways leaves from London's Kings Cross Station every 40 minutes. The rail connection, ThamesLink, takes you from London to St. Albans in just 20 minutes. From London, Green Line coach no. 724 also runs to St. Albans frequently. For rail information, call © **0845/7484950.** For bus information, dial © **0870/608-1608.**

If you're driving, take the M25 Junction 21A or 22; M1 Junctions 6, 7, or 9; and A1 (M) Junction 3.

VISITOR INFORMATION   The **Tourist Information Centre** is at the Town Hall, Market Place (© **01727/864511**). From Easter to October, its hours are Monday through Saturday from 9:30am to 5:30pm; off-season hours are Monday through Saturday from 10am to 4pm. From the end of July until mid-September, the office is also open most Sundays from 10am to 4pm.

EXPLORING THE TOWN

The Association of Honorary Guides, a trained group of local volunteers, provides guided walks. These include a tour of the **Roman Verulamium** and the **Medieval Town,** a ghost walk, and a coaching-inn walking tour. In addition to pre-booked tours, free public guided walks are available on Sunday; the tour begins at 3pm at the clock tower. Guides are also available on Sunday at the Verulamium Museum and Roman Theatre to give short talks on a number of topics concerning the Romans and their time in the area. Full details can be obtained from the Tourist Information Centre (see above) or from the Tours Secretary (© **01727/833001**).

The **Cathedral of St. Albans** ♠, Holywell Hill and High Street (© **01727/ 860780;** www.stalbanscathedral.org.uk), is still known as "the Abbey" to the locals, even though Henry VIII dissolved it as such in 1539. Construction was launched in 1077, making it one of the early Norman churches of England. The bricks, especially visible in the tower, came from the old Roman city of Verulamium, located at the foot of the hill. The nave and west front of the cathedral date from 1235.

The queen opened the new chapter house, the first modern building beside a great medieval cathedral in the country, in 1982. The structure houses an information desk, gift shop, and restaurant. There is also a free (donations accepted) video detailing the history of the cathedral that you can view.

St. Albans Cathedral and the chapter house are generally open daily from 7:30am to 5:45pm. In addition to church services, there are often organ recitals that are open to the public. The church's choir can sometimes be heard rehearsing, if they're not on tour.

Verulamium Museum at St. Michael's ⭐ (© **01727/751810;** www.stalbans museums.org.uk) stands on the site of the ancient Roman city of the same name. Here you'll view some of the finest Roman mosaics in Britain as well as re-created Roman rooms. Part of the Roman town hall, a hypocaust (an ancient design for heating rooms), and the outline of houses and shops are still visible in the park that surrounds the museum. Open year-round Monday through Saturday from 10am to 5:30pm and Sunday from 2 to 5:30pm, admission is £3.30 ($5) for adults, £2 ($3.20) for seniors and children, and £8 ($13) for a family ticket. By car, Verulamium is 15 to 20 minutes from Junction 21A on the M25; it is also accessible from Junctions 9 or 6 on the M1; follow the signs for St. Albans and the Roman Verulamium. A train to St. Albans City Station will put you within 3km (2 miles) of the museum.

Just a short distance from Verulamium is the **Roman Theatre** (© **01727/ 835035**). The structure is the only theater of the period that is open to visitors in Britain. You can tour the site daily between 10am and 5pm (4pm in winter). Admission is £1.60 ($2.55) for adults, £1.10 ($1.75) for seniors and students, and 50p (80¢) for children.

Museum of St. Albans, Hatfield Road (© **01727/819340**), is open Monday to Saturday 10am to 5pm, Sunday 2 to 5pm. Admission is free. The museum details the history of St. Albans from the departure of the Romans to the present day. It is located in the city center on A1057 Hatfield Road and is a 5-minute walk from St. Albans City Station.

From St. Albans you can visit **Gorhambury** (© **01727/855000**), a classic mansion built in 1777. The private home, owned by the earl and countess of Verulam, contains 16th-century enameled glass and historic portraits. It's open May to September from 2 to 5pm on Thursday only. Admission is £6 ($10) for adults, £4 ($6) for seniors, and £3 ($4.80) for children. Gorhambury is located 4km (2½ miles) west of St. Albans near the A5. From the Verulamium Museum, cross Bluehouse Hill Road; the house is about a mile up a private drive.

The **Batchwood Indoor Tennis Centre,** which has four indoor courts plus outdoor courts, has professional coaches available for all play levels. In addition, Batchwood's 18-hole golf course is one of the finest public courses in the country. Both are located on the grounds of the Batchwood Hall mansion on Batchwood Drive (© **01727/844250**).

SHOPPING

Its frantic pace defines the twice-weekly street market, held every Wednesday and Saturday on St. Peters Street. By contrast, modern off-street precincts and small specialty shops in St. Albans combine to create a unique, laid-back atmosphere the rest of the week. **Whittard's of Chelsea,** 25 Market Place (© **01727/ 867092**), carries teas and coffees as well as mugs, teapots, biscuits, and chocolates. The **Past Times Shop,** 33 Market St. (© **01727/812817**), sells items that cover 12 historic eras. Here you'll find books on historic places, jewelry, clothes such as Victorian-style nightdresses, and CDs featuring music from a variety of time periods. For antiques, visit **By George,** 23 George St. (© **01727/853032**). St. Albans' largest antique center, the building also houses a tearoom and crafts arcade. **Forget-Me-Not Antiques,** 27 High St. (© **01727/848907**), specializes in jewelry, especially Victorian name brooches. At **St. Albans Antique Centre,** 9 George St. (© **01727/844233**), up to 20 dealers gather to sell their goods. Browse through the furniture and collectibles, then have a light snack in the tearoom or tour the gardens.

WHERE TO STAY

Ardmore House Hotel ⭐ *Finds*   This charming Edwardian residence with a Victorian annex is on a residential road close to town and recreational activities, including golf, swimming, and fitness centers. The hotel is privately owned and family run. All rooms are comfortably modern and have private shower-only bathrooms; the most desirable room of the house has a four-poster bed for "special occasions." Bedrooms have limed wood fitting and a color-coordinated decor. Ten nonsmoking bedrooms are available for guests. An elegant lounge provides a soothing atmosphere to read or talk to fellow guests. Breakfast is offered in an airy, sunny room overlooking the rear garden.

54 Lemsford Rd., St. Albans AL1 3PR. ℂ and fax **01727/859313.** www.ardmorehousehotel.com. 40 units. £58 ($93) single; £70–£95 ($112–$152) double; £35 ($56) per person family rate (minimum of 3); £20 ($32) children under 12. All rates include breakfast. AE, MC, V. **Amenities:** Breakfast room; bar; lounge. *In room:* TV, dataport, coffeemaker, hair dryer.

The Black Lion Inn *Value*   This is the finest pub hotel in the area, and one of the best bargains. A former bakery built in 1837, it lies in the most colorful part of town, St. Michael's Village, where bustling coaches from London once arrived. Bedrooms are utterly simple and plain and, although a bit cramped, are well maintained, each with a small bathroom. One room is available for those with limited mobility.

St. Michael's Village, Fishpool St., St. Albans, Hertfordshire AL3 4SB. ℂ **01727/851786.** Fax 01727/859243. www.theblacklioninn.com. 16 units, 14 with bathroom. £48–£55 ($77–$88) single or double without bathroom; £54–£60 ($86–$96) single or double with bathroom. AE, MC, V. **Amenities:** Restaurant (pub food); bar; babysitting; laundry service. *In room:* TV, dataport, coffeemaker, hair dryer, iron/ironing board, trouser press.

WHERE TO DINE

The best budget dining in St. Albans is in the pubs.

Garibaldi ENGLISH/SEAFOOD/THAI   One of the most mellow pubs in town, it's known for its "hidey-holes" around the small island bar; there is also a cafe-style dining area off the main room. At the front is a patio terrace. The pub serves up ESB, London Pride, and Admans beers; you're sure to find one to suit your taste. A variety of dishes, from simple sandwiches to large seafood platters, is served.

62 Albert St. ℂ **01727/855046.** Main dishes £3–£8.50 ($4.80–$14). MC, V. Thurs–Sat 6–10pm.

Kingsbury Mill Waffle House ENGLISH   This restaurant, along with an upstairs museum, is housed inside a working mill. Visit the museum before eating to view milling and farming artifacts. The meals themselves revolve around plain or whole-wheat Belgian waffles served with a variety of sweet and savory toppings. As a meal you may enjoy the ham, cheese, and mushroom concoction. Ice cream favorites include the pecan-and-butterscotch and chocolate flavors. The restaurant boasts that about half of all ingredients used are organically produced.

St. Michael's St. ℂ **01727/853502.** Main courses £2.50–£7 ($4–$11). MC, V. Daily 10am–6pm.

Rose & Crown ENGLISH   In a 300-year-old building near Verulamium Park, this pub is often uncrowded and tranquil because of its out-of-the-way location. There are two open fireplaces that are warm and inviting in winter. A variety of beers is served, including Tetley and Stella Artois.

St. Michael's St. ℂ **01727/851903.** Main courses £2.70–£7.25 ($4.30–$12). MC, V. Mon–Fri 11:30am–3pm; Mon–Fri 5:30–11pm; Sat 11am–11pm.

Ye Olde Fighting Cocks *(Finds)* ★ ENGLISH   The Guinness Book of World Records lists this as the oldest licensed house in England; the original foundation was laid in A.D. 700. William the Conqueror is said to have been a guest here. The name recalls when cockfights were a regular event; today you can drink in what used to be the pit. Eight real ales are served, along with five guest ales. This is a real budget eatery; lunch includes ploughman's lunch (bread and cheese), steak-and-kidney pie, chili, and other hot meals. Dinners are a tad fancier; favorites are the stuffed prawns and the salmon steak.

Abby Mill Lane. © 01727/869152. Lunch £3.95–£7.50 ($6–$12); dinner £5.95–£7.50 ($10–$12). AE, MC, V. Mon–Sat noon–11:30pm; Sun noon–10:30pm.

THEATER PERFORMANCES

St. Albans' nightlife centers around theater. The Company of Ten, with its base at the **Abbey Theatre,** Westminster Lodge, Holywell Hill (© **01727/857861**), is one of the leading amateur dramatic companies in Britain. The troupe presents 10 productions each season in either the well-equipped main auditorium or a smaller studio. Performances begin at 8pm; tickets cost from £6 to £8 ($10–$13). The **Maltings Arts Theatre,** in the Maltings Shopping Centre (© **01727/844222**), presents performances based on literature—from Shakespeare to modern novels. Plays are generally presented only once and begin at 8pm on Thursday, Friday, and Saturday (there is a children's show at 3pm). Tickets are £7.50 to £9 ($12–$14).

SIDE TRIPS FROM ST. ALBANS

Hatfield House ★★★   Hatfield was much a part of the lives of both Henry VIII and his daughter Elizabeth I. In the old palace, built in the 15th century, Elizabeth played as a child. Although Henry was married to her mother, Anne Boleyn, at the time of Elizabeth's birth, the marriage was later nullified (Anne lost her head and Elizabeth her legitimacy). Henry liked stashing away his other daughter, Mary Tudor, at Hatfield. When Mary became queen of England and set about becoming "Bloody Mary," she found Elizabeth troublesome. For a while she kept her in the Tower of London, but eventually let her return to Hatfield, where Elizabeth learned of her succession to the throne in 1558.

Only the banqueting hall of the original Tudor palace remains; the rest is Jacobean. The hall has much antique furniture and many tapestries and paintings, as well as three often-reproduced portraits, including the ermine and rainbow portraits of Elizabeth I. The Great Hall is suitably medieval, complete with a minstrel's gallery. One of the rarest exhibits is a pair of silk stockings said to have been worn by Elizabeth herself, the first woman in England to don such apparel. The park and the gardens are worth exploring. Luncheons and teas are available from 11am to 5pm in the converted coach house in the Old Palace yard.

Elizabethan banquets are staged in the banqueting hall of the Old Palace on Tuesday and Thursday through Saturday, with much gaiety and music. Guests are invited to drink in an anteroom, then join the long tables for a feast of five courses with continuous entertainment from a group of Elizabethan players, minstrels, and jesters. Wine is included in the cost of the meal, but your before-dinner drinks are not. The cost is £34.50 ($55) on Tuesday and Thursday, £36 ($58) on Friday, and £39 ($62) on Saturday. For reservations, call © **01707/ 262055.**

9.5km (6 miles) east of St. Albans on A414. © 01707/262823 for information. www.hatfield-house.co.uk. Admission £7.50 ($12) adults, £4 ($6) for persons under 16. Easter Saturday–Sept 30, house is open daily noon–4pm; park and gardens open daily 11am–5:30pm. From St. Albans, take A414 east and follow the brown signs that lead you directly to the estate. By bus, take the University bus from St. Albans City Station. Hatfield House is directly across from Hatfield Station.

Shaw's Corner *Finds* ★   George Bernard Shaw lived here from 1906 to 1950. The utilitarian house, with its harsh brickwork and rather comfortless interior, is practically as he left it at his death. In the hall, his hats still hang, as if ready for him to don one. Shaw wrote 6 to 8 hours a day, even when he'd reached his 90s—he is said to have muttered, "This damned energy will not let me stop." Evidence of his longtime relationship with the written word is obvious throughout the house; even one of his old typewriters is still in position. Shaw was famous for his eccentricities, vegetarianism, longevity, and, of course, vast literary output, the most famous of which is probably *Pygmalion,* on which the musical *My Fair Lady* was based.

Off Hill Farm Lane, in the village of Ayot St. Lawrence. ℂ **01438/820307.** Admission £3.60 ($6) adults, £2 ($3.20) children. Apr–Oct Wed–Sun and bank holidays 1–5pm. From St. Albans, take B651 to Wheathampstead. Pass through the village, go right at the roundabout, and take the first left turn. A mile up on the left is Brides Hall Lane, which leads to the house.

Mosquito Aircraft Museum   This is the oldest aircraft museum in Britain. The hall where the de Havilland Aircraft Company developed the "Mosquito," the most versatile aircraft of World War II, is no longer open to the public. However, the museum displays more than 20 types of aircraft, including modern military and civil jets, along with aircraft engines and other memorabilia. Several of the displays are hands-on exhibits. There is also an active restoration program; visitors are encouraged to get a close look at the refurbishment process.

On the grounds of Salisbury Hall, just off the main M25 London–St. Albans Rd. ℂ **01727/822051.** Admission £5 ($8) adults; £3 ($4.80) children 5–16, seniors, and students with identification; free for children under 5; £13 ($21) family ticket. Mar–Oct Tues, Thurs, and Sat 2–5:30pm; Sun and bank holidays 10:30am–5:30pm. Take M25 Junction 22 at London Colney about 8km (5 miles) south of St. Albans. The museum is on B556.

7 Woburn Abbey: England's Great Georgian Manor ★★★

70km (44 miles) N of London

Aside from Windsor Castle, the most visited attraction in the Home Counties is spectacular Woburn Abbey; try to visit it even if you have to miss all the other historic homes in this chapter. This great 18th-century Georgian mansion has been the traditional seat of the dukes of Bedford for more than 3 centuries.

TOURING THE ESTATE

Woburn Abbey   In the 1950s the duke of Bedford opened Woburn Abbey to the public to pay off his debt of millions of pounds in inheritance taxes. In 1974, he turned the estate over to his son and daughter-in-law, the marquess and marchioness of Tavistock, who reluctantly took on the business of running the 75-room mansion, which draws hundreds of thousands of visitors a year and employs more than 300 people as staff.

The state apartments are rich in furniture, porcelain, tapestries, silver, and a valuable art collection, including paintings by Van Dyck, Holbein, Rembrandt, Gainsborough, and Reynolds. A series of paintings by Canaletto, all views of Venice, grace the walls of the Venetian Room, an intimate dining room. One of the most notable paintings is the Armada Portrait of Elizabeth I, where her hand rests on a globe as Philip's "invincible" armada perishes in the background.

Queen Victoria and Prince Albert visited Woburn Abbey in 1841; Victoria's Dressing Room displays a fine collection of 17th-century Dutch paintings. Among the oddities and treasures are the Grotto of Shells, a Sèvres dinner service (gift of Louis XV), and a chamber devoted to memorabilia of "The Flying Duchess," wife of the 11th duke of Bedford, a remarkable woman who disappeared at age 72 on a solo flight in 1937, the same year Amelia Earhart did.

Today, Woburn Abbey is surrounded by a 3,000-acre deer park, home to the famous Père David deer herd, originally from China and saved from extinction at Woburn. The **Woburn Safari Park** has lions, tigers, giraffes, camels, monkeys, Przewalski's horses, bongos, elephants, and other animals.

1km (½ mile) from the village of Woburn, which is 21km (13 miles) southwest of Bedford. © 01525/ 290666. www.woburnabbey.co.uk. Admission £8.50 ($14) adults, £7.50 ($12) seniors, £4 ($6) children. House open late Mar to late Sept Mon–Sat 11am–4pm, Sun 11am–5pm; Oct and Jan to late Mar Sat–Sun and bank holidays 11am–4pm. In summer, travel agents can book you on organized coach tours out of London. Otherwise, if driving, take M1 north to Junction 12 or 13, where directions are signposted.

NEARBY SHOPPING

In a wonderful old building, **Town Hall Antiques,** Market Place (© 01525/ 290950), is a treasure trove of collectibles and antiques, including early English porcelain and pieces from the 1940s. An unusual array of Victorian, Georgian, and Edwardian commemoratives are also sold. There's something here for everyone—clocks, Victorian jewelry, brass, copper, and "kitchenalia."

WHERE TO STAY & EAT

Few visitors stop over here for the night. However, Copperfields and Magpie (see below) rent simple rooms at affordable prices.

The Black Horse INTERNATIONAL   One of a half dozen pubs and restaurants in Woburn, most visitors call it their favorite. Originally opened in 1824 as a coaching inn, it retains a dark, woodsy interior reminiscent of the era of its construction. It sits behind a stucco-sheathed Georgian facade on the town's main street. Simple platters, sometimes designed to accompany the ales and lagers served in the pub, include "filled baguettes" (sandwiches on French bread), steaks, lasagna, ploughman's lunch, and spicy soups inspired by Thai cuisine. The restaurant occupies a separate room, and features steaks and fish, such as Dover sole grilled with lemon butter or salmon with dill and white-wine sauce.

1 Bedford St. © 01525/290210. Pub platters £5.95–£12.95 ($10–$21); main courses £8.95–£24 ($14–$38). AE, DC, MC, V. Mon–Sat noon–2:30 and 6–9:30pm; Sun noon–8:30pm.

Copperfields TEA   Situated on a cobblestone street, near the abbey and an array of interesting shops, this tearoom overflows with old-world charm. Lace-covered tables and windows enhance the low-beamed ceilings and original fireplace. Homemade cakes are a favorite here; don't count calories, just enjoy a piece of chocolate-rum or Victoria's sponge cake. Copperfields is also a B&B, with four rooms that rent for between £17 and £42 ($27–$67) per person. The large, simply decorated rooms are in a 1700s Georgian building.

15–16 Marketplace, Woburn MK17 9PZ. © 01525/290464. Cream teas £4.25 ($7); sandwiches and soups £2.60–£3.40 ($4.15–$5). AE, MC, V. Daily 10am–5pm.

Magpie ENGLISH   After your tour of the abbey, head here for food and drink. This is a very small, family-run pub in a 16th-century former coaching inn located near the Woburn Golf Club. The beers of choice are Ruddles Best, Webster's, and Marston's Pedigree. The food is simple but filling fare, including well-stuffed sandwiches or a ploughman's lunch. There's also a separate restaurant. At the side of the pub is a courtyard with tables when the weather's nice. If you'd like to stay over, the pub rents nine basic but quite decent bedrooms, costing £50 ($80) for a double without bathroom or £65 ($104) with bathroom. Singles are also available for £40 ($64) without a bathroom and £50 ($80) with a bathroom.

Bedford St., Woburn MK17 9QB. ⓒ 01525/290219. Bar lunches and sandwiches £3–£10 ($4.80–$16). MC, V. Mon–Sat noon–2pm and 7–9pm; Fri–Sun noon–4pm.

6

Kent, Surrey & Sussex

Lying to the south and southeast of London are the shires (counties) of Kent, Surrey, and Sussex, fascinating areas within easy commuting distance of the capital.

In Kent, **Canterbury** is the major highlight and makes the best base for exploring the area. **Dover,** Britain's historic gateway to the Continent, is famed for its white cliffs. This county is on the fringes of London, yet far removed in spirit and scenery. Cherry blossoms, orchards, and hop fields dot the fertile landscape, earning **Kent** the title of "the garden of England"—and in England, that's saying something.

But despite the devastation suffered during World War II (the Luftwaffe flew over Kent during the Blitz), the area remains a collection of interesting old towns and castles, and it boasts some of Europe's grandest mansions. If time is limited, seek out the big four: **Knole,** one of England's largest private houses, a great example of Tudor architecture; **Hever Castle,** from the end of the 13th century, a gift from Henry VIII to Anne of Cleves; **Penshurst Place,** a magnificent English Gothic mansion; and lovely **Leeds Castle,** near Maidstone, dating from A.D. 857. Although it doesn't compare with these mansions, **Chartwell House** merits a visit as the home of Sir Winston Churchill.

With the outward expansion of London's borders, it's a wonder that the tiny county of Surrey hasn't been gobbled up. Yet its countryside remains unspoiled, even though many people commute to jobs in London (45 min. to an hour away).

King Harold's love for Sussex changed the course of English history. Had the brave Saxon waited longer in the north in 1066, he could have marshaled adequate reinforcements before heading south to meet the Normans at Hastings. But Duke William's soldiers were ravaging the countryside he knew so well, and Harold rushed to counter them.

The old towns and villages of Sussex, particularly **Rye** and **Winchelsea,** are far more intriguing than, say, the larger seaside resort of **Brighton.** No Sussex village is lovelier than **Alfriston** (and the innkeepers know it, too); **Arundel** is noted for its castle; and the cathedral city of **Chichester** is a mecca for theater buffs. The old market town of **Battle** was the actual setting for the Battle of Hastings.

Where to base yourself in Sussex? The best option is Brighton, with its wide choice of hotels, restaurants, and nightclubs; it's more exciting here than at Hastings. But if you seek old-English charm and village life, head to Alfriston or Rye.

1 Canterbury ★★★

90km (56 miles) SE of London

In *The Canterbury Tales,* Chaucer's knight, solicitor, nun, squire, parson, merchant, miller, and others spin tales as they make the pilgrimage to the shrine of Thomas à Becket, archbishop of Canterbury, who was slain by four knights of

Kent, Surrey & Sussex

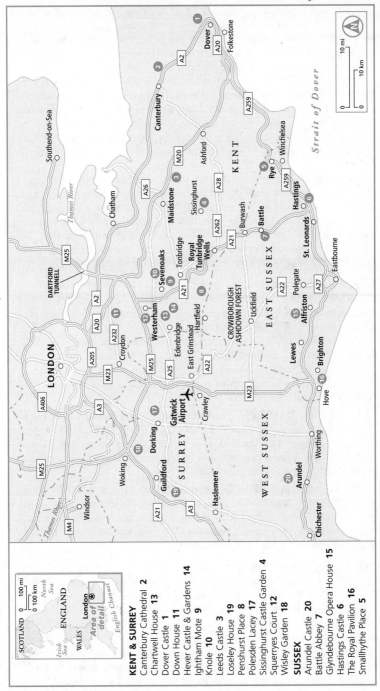

KENT & SURREY

Canterbury Cathedral **2**
Chartwell House **13**
Dover Castle **1**
Down House **11**
Hever Castle & Gardens **14**
Ightham Mote **9**
Knole **10**
Leeds Castle **3**
Loseley House **19**
Penshurst Place **8**
Polesden Lacey **17**
Sissinghurst Castle Garden **4**
Squerryes Court **12**
Wisley Garden **18**

SUSSEX

Arundel Castle **20**
Battle Abbey **7**
Glyndebourne Opera House **15**
Hastings Castle **6**
The Royal Pavilion **16**
Smallhythe Place **5**

Henry II on the evening of December 29, 1170. (Henry later walked barefoot from Harbledown to the tomb of his former friend, where he allowed himself to be flogged in penance.) Henry VIII finally tore down the shrine in 1538, as part of his campaign to destroy monasteries and graven images. But by then, Canterbury had become a self-sufficient attraction.

This medieval Kentish city on the River Stour is the ecclesiastical capital of England. The city was once completely walled, and many traces of its old fortifications remain. Canterbury was inhabited centuries before the birth of Jesus Christ. Although its most famous incident was Becket's murder, the city witnessed other major events, including Bloody Mary's order to burn nearly 40 victims at the stake. Richard I (The Lionheart) returned this way from crusading, and Charles II passed through on the way to claim his crown.

Canterbury pilgrims continue to arrive today—these days they're called "daytrippers"—as they overrun the city and its monuments. It's amazing that the city's central core is as interesting and picture-perfect as it is, considering the enormous damage caused by the 1941 Blitz. The city has an active university life—mainly students from the University of Kent—and an enormous number of pubs. Its High Street is filled with shoppers in from the country. Try to explore Canterbury in the early morning or the early evening, after the busloads have departed.

ESSENTIALS

GETTING THERE   There is frequent train service from Victoria, Charing Cross, Waterloo, and London Bridge stations. The journey takes 1½ hours. For rail information, call ✆ **0845/7484950.**

The bus from Victoria Coach Station takes 2 to 3 hours and leaves every halfhour. For schedules, call ✆ **0870/243-3711.**

If you're driving from London, take A2, then M2. Canterbury is signposted all the way. The city center is closed to cars, but it's only a short walk from several parking areas to the cathedral.

VISITOR INFORMATION   The **Canterbury Tourist Information Centre** is at 34 St. Margaret's St., Canterbury CT1 2TG (✆ **01227/378100**). Open daily April through October 9:30am to 5:30pm, November through March 9:30am to 5pm. A few doors away from St. Margaret's Church, the Centre sells a useful guidebook, *National Travelguide.*

GETTING AROUND BY BIKE   **Byways Bicycle Hire,** 2 Admiralty Walk (✆ **01227/277397**), will deliver a bike to your hotel, but you must make a £50 ($80) deposit. Rentals are £10 ($16) per day. For the same deposit, you can also arrange rentals at **Downland Cycle Hire,** West Railway Station (✆ **01227/479643**), which charges £11 ($18) per day.

SEEING THE CATHEDRAL

Canterbury Cathedral ✪✪✪   The foundation of this splendid cathedral dates from A.D. 597, but the earliest part of the present building is the great Romanesque crypt from around A.D. 1100. The monastic "quire" erected on top of this was destroyed by fire in 1174, only 4 years after the murder of Becket in the northwest transept, still one of Europe's most famous places of pilgrimage. The destroyed "quire" was immediately replaced by a magnificent early Gothic one, which was the first major expression of that architectural style in England.

The cathedral is noteworthy for its medieval tombs of royal personages, such as Henry IV and Edward the Black Prince, as well as numerous archbishops. The great 14th-century nave and the famous central "Bell Harry Tower" date from

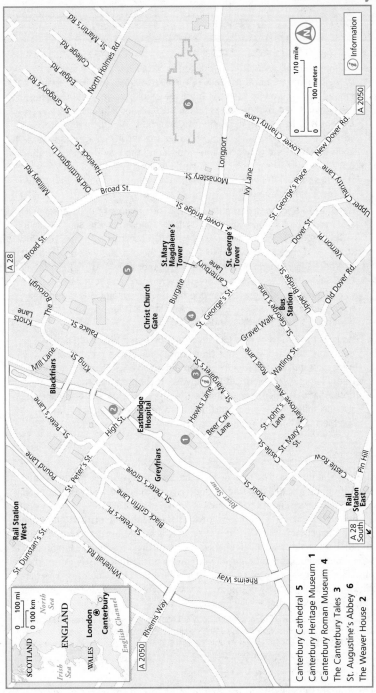

Canterbury

St. Martin's Rd.
College Rd.
Edgar Rd.
St. Gregory's Rd.
North Holmes Rd.
Military Rd.
Old Ruttington Ln.
Havelock St.
Broad St.
Broad St.
A 28
The Borough
Knots Lane
Palace St.
King St.
Mill Lane
Blackfriars
St. Peter's Lane
Pound Lane
St. Peter's St.
Whitehall Rd.
St. Dunstan's St.

Rail Station West

St. Peter's Pl.
Black Griffin Lane
St. Peter's Grove

Greyfriars

High St.

Eastbridge Hospital

Hawks Lane
Beer Cart Lane
Castle St.
St. Mary's St.
St. John's Lane
Marlowe Ave.
Stour St.
Castle Row
Pin Hill
Rheims Way
Rheims Way

Rail Station East

A 28 South

River Stour

St. Margaret's St.
Watling St.
Ross Lane
Gravel Walk
St. George's Ln.
Upper Bridge St.

Bus Station

St. George's St.
Burgate

Christ Church Gate

Canterbury Cathedral

St. Mary Magdalene's Tower

St. George's Tower

St. George's St.
Lower Bridge St.
Broad St.
Monastery St.
Longport
Ivy Lane
St. George's Place
Dover St.
Vernon Pl.
Old Dover Rd.
Upper Chantry Lane
Lower Chantry Lane
New Dover Rd.

A 2050

ⓘ Information

A 2050

N

0 — 1/10 mile
0 — 100 meters

① ② ③ ④ ⑤ ⑥

Canterbury Cathedral **5**
Canterbury Heritage Museum **1**
Canterbury Roman Museum **4**
The Canterbury Tales **3**
St. Augustine's Abbey **6**
The Weaver House **2**

SCOTLAND
ENGLAND
WALES
London ⊛
Canterbury
North Sea
Irish Sea
English Channel
0 — 100 mi
0 — 100 km
A 2050

the late Middle Ages. The present cathedral stands on spacious precincts amid
the ruins of monasterial buildings—cloisters, chapter house, and Norman water
tower—that have survived to the present.

Although Henry VIII destroyed Becket's shrine, the site of that tomb is in
Trinity Chapel, near the high altar. The saint is said to have worked miracles,
and the cathedral has some rare stained glass depicting those feats. The windows
were removed as a precaution at the beginning of the Blitz, wisely as it turned
out: The replacement windows were blown in. Much of Canterbury was flat-
tened, but the main body of the church was unharmed except for the cathedral
library, damaged during a 1942 air raid.

11 The Precincts. (℃ 01227/762862. www.canterbury-cathedral.org. Admission £4 ($6) adults, £3 ($4.80)
students, seniors, and children. Guided tours £3.50 ($5) adults, £2.50 ($4) students and seniors, £1.50 ($2.40)
children, £6.50 ($10) family. Easter–Sept 30 Mon–Sat 9am–6:30pm; Oct 1–Easter Mon–Sat 9am–4:30pm;
year-round Sun 12:30–2:30pm and 4:30–5:30pm.

OTHER ATTRACTIONS

The Canterbury Tales   One of the most visited museums in town re-
creates the pilgrimages of Chaucerian England through a series of medieval

Explore the field of Saxon blood. The decisive battle between Saxon King Harold of England and William of Normandy took place in 1066. To honor victory in the Battle of Hastings, William the Conqueror ordered the construction of Battle Abbey at Battle in 1094. The high altar of the abbey was created on the exact spot where Harold was killed by an arrow in his eye. Today, you can wander through the ruins. Pick up a map at the tourist bureau and walk the "Battlefield Trail," a mile-long hike along a green hillside that once overflowed with Saxon blood.

View a major center of Christianity. Embracing all styles of medieval architecture, Canterbury Cathedral was reconstructed several times. Miraculously spared from Nazi bombs, it stands today, regal as ever, and to visit is to walk through English history. The first great English poet, Geoffrey Chaucer (1345–1400), details in his rambunctious *Canterbury Tales* the journey of pilgrims to the shrine of St. Thomas à Becket, slain in the cathedral. The medieval stained glass alone is worth the visit.

See the White Cliffs of Dover. Subject of song, film, and legend, the White Cliffs of Dover extend southwest some 11km (7 miles) from Dover toward Folkestone. Evoking memories of the Blitz of World War II, these cliffs are the first view of England that cross-Channel passengers see. To drive along this coast is to get a stunning view. Remains of fortifications erected against Hitler in 1940 are still visible. From Dover, follow A20 southwest along the coast for 13km (8 miles). At Folkestone, stroll on the Leas, a broad, mile-long walkway that skirts the cliff edge. You can see France in the distance.

tableaux. Visitors are handed headsets with earphones, which give oral recitations of five of the Canterbury Tales and the murder of Thomas à Becket. Audiovisual aids bring famous characters to life; a complete tour takes about 45 minutes.

23 St. Margaret's St. (off High St., near the cathedral). ☎ **01227/454888.** Admission £6.50 ($10) adults, £5.50 ($9) seniors and students, £5 ($8) children 5–16, free for children 4 and under, family ticket £20 ($32). Mar–Aug daily 10am–4:30pm; Sept–Oct daily 10am–5:30pm; Nov–Feb daily 10am–5pm .

Canterbury Heritage Museum   Set in the ancient Poor Priests' Hospital with its medieval interiors and soaring oak roofs, this museum features award-winning displays that showcase the best of the city's treasures and lead the visitor through crucial moments that have shaped Canterbury's history. State-of-the-art video, computer, and hologram technology transports the visitor back to the Viking raids and the Blitz. Collections include a huge display of pilgrim badges from medieval souvenir shops and the Rupert Bear Gallery.

Stour St. ☎ **01227/452747.** Admission £3 ($4.80) adults; £2 ($3.20) seniors, students, and children 5–18; free for children under 5. Year-round Mon–Sat 10:30am–5pm; June–Oct Sun 1:30–5pm. Last entry time 4pm. Closed Christmas week and Good Friday.

Finds A Stroll Down Medieval Lane

The most charming street in Canterbury is Mercery Lane, a bustling little street that still evokes the charm of Canterbury as it existed in the Middle Ages. A walk along this street also gives you the best views of the western towers of Canterbury Cathedral. You'll also have an equally good view of Christchurch Gate.

Canterbury Roman Museum   Located beneath street level, this museum is constructed around actual archaeological excavations. Interactive computer shows and actual handling of Roman artifacts bring the past to life for all ages. The Roman town of Durovernum Cantiacorum was established shortly after Emperor Claudius' invasion of the area in A.D. 43, and continued to flourish for nearly 400 years. Visitors can follow the archaeologists' detective work through an excavated Roman house site with patterned mosaics, discovered after the wartime bombing.

Butchery Lane. ℂ 01227/785575. Admission £2.60 ($4.15) adults; £1.65 ($2.65) students, seniors, and children; £6.80 ($11) family ticket. Year-round Mon–Sat 10am–5pm; June–Oct Sun 1:30–5pm. Last entry time 4pm. Closed Christmas week and Good Friday.

St. Augustine's Abbey ⭐⭐   Mostly ground-level ruins remain of one of the most historic religious centers in the country. In an attempt to convert the Saxons, Pope Gregory I sent Augustine to England in 597. Ethelbert, the Saxon King, allowed Augustine and his followers to build a church outside the city walls. Augustine was buried here, along with other archbishops and Anglo-Saxon kings; it lasted until Henry VIII tore it down. Adjacent to the remains are the abbey buildings that Henry converted into a royal palace; it was used briefly by Elizabeth I and Charles I, among others. In its day, the abbey church rivaled the cathedral in size; enough of the ruins remain to conjure the whole of the cloister, church, and refectory.

Corner of Lower Chantry Lane and Longport Rd. ℂ 01227/767345. Admission £3 ($4.80) adults, £3.30 ($5) students and seniors, £1.50 ($2.40) children. Apr–Sept daily 10am–6pm; Oct–Mar daily 10am–4pm.

WALKING & BOAT TOURS

From Easter to early November, daily guided tours of Canterbury are organized by the **Guild of Guides** (ℂ **01227/459779**), costing £3.20 ($5) for adults, £2.70 ($4.30) for students and children over 14, and £20 ($32) for a family ticket. Meet at the Tourist Information Centre at 34 St. Margaret's St., in a pedestrian area opposite of the cathedral, daily (including Sun) at 10am and 4:30pm. From the beginning of July to the end of August, a second tour leaves at 11:30am Monday through Saturday.

From just below the Weavers House, boats leave for half-hour **trips on the river** with a commentary on the history of the buildings you pass.

SHOPPING

Canterbury Pottery, 38 Burgate, just before Mercury Lane (ℂ **01227/452608**), sells handmade pottery: vases, mugs, and teapots in earth colors of blues, greens, and browns. This sturdy fare wears well, including house-number plates that take 2 weeks to complete, but can be mailed to your home. Put on your tweed jacket and grab your pipe for a trip to the secondhand **Chaucer Bookshop,** 6–7 Beer Cart Lane (ℂ **01227/453912**), with first editions (old and modern), out-of-print books, leather-bound editions, and a good selection of local history books. **The**

Albion Bookstop, 13 Mercery Lane ((©) **01227/768631**), can sell you good local folding maps. At the **Chaucer Centre,** 22 St. Peter's St. ((©) **01227/470379**), *The Canterbury Tales* in book and tape formats joins all things Chaucerian, including T-shirts, St. Justin jewelry from Cornwall, Ellesmere cards, and balls and plates for juggling.

WHERE TO STAY

Alexandra House ⊛ On a quiet road off St. Dunstan's Street, this guesthouse, built around 1901, is a 10-minute walk from the cathedral. Shirley and Terry Barber welcome you to their family-run establishment, consistently rated an outstanding B&B. The bedrooms are on three different floors and contain a simple but clean decor—not the patched carpets and shrunken bedspreads found in many Canterbury B&Bs at this price. Almost all units also come equipped with neatly kept shower-only bathrooms. In back is a garden with a patio and chairs.

1 Roper Rd., Canterbury, Kent CT2 7EH. (©) 01227/767011. Fax 01227/786617. www.alexandrahouse.net. 8 units, 5 with bathroom (tub or shower). £30 ($48) single without bathroom; £44–£46 ($70–$74) double without bathroom; £52–£55 ($83–$88) double with bathroom. Rates include English breakfast. No credit cards. Free parking. **Amenities:** Breakfast room; residents' bar. *In room:* TV, coffeemaker, hair dryer, no phone.

Ann's Hotel ⊛ This family-owned B&B stands on an artery leading out of town, a 10-minute walk from the town center (follow the signs to M2 to London). Given the rates, the place is surprisingly luxurious, an imposing Victorian house restored to its original grandeur. Ann Dellaway rents well-furnished, comfortable, midsize bedrooms, some with four-poster beds. Each bedroom is individually designed, with all the touches of a fine English country house. Fifteen rooms have private bathrooms with showers. An English breakfast is served in a bright, spacious dining room along with a selection of fine teas, marmalades, and jams. Guests convene in an elegant lounge with a Victorian fireplace.

63 London Rd., Canterbury, Kent CT2 8JZ. (©) 01227/768767. Fax 01227/768172. 20 units. £24 ($38) single without bathroom, £30 ($48) single with bathroom; £38–£50 ($61–$80) double. Rates include English breakfast. MC, V. **Amenities:** Breakfast room; lounge. *In room:* TV, hair dryer.

Cathedral Gate Hotel For those who want to stay close to the cathedral, there is no better choice: The hotel is a 10-minute walk from the train station. Built in 1438, adjoining Christchurch Gate and overlooking the Buttermarket, this former hospice became one of the earliest of the fashionable coffeehouses and teahouses of England in the early 1600s, and the interior reveals many little architectural details of that era. The rooms are comfortably furnished, with sloping floors and massive oak beams. You'll sleep better than the pilgrims who often stopped over here, sometimes crowding in as many as six and eight in a bed. Rooms with a bathroom have a shower stall; otherwise, corridor baths are adequate and you rarely have to line up for one. Lunchtime bar snacks and dinner are served. The menu is a deliciously sinful throwback to the 1960s Lancashire. A courtyard garden with cathedral views is available for guests.

36 Burgate, Canterbury, Kent CT1 2HA. (©) 01227/464381. Fax 01227/462800. www.cathgate.co.uk. 27 units, 12 with bathroom. £25–£33.50 ($40–$54) single without bathroom, £58 ($93) single with bathroom; £48–£58 ($77–$93) double without bathroom, £88 ($141) double with bathroom. Rates include continental breakfast. AE, DC, MC, V. **Amenities:** Dining room; bar; lounge. *In room:* TV, coffeemaker, hair dryer.

Ersham Lodge Hotel This long-established lodge is a 5-minute walk from the cathedral, central to major places of interest, entertainment, and shopping. It's an attractive, twin-galleried Victorian house set back from the road to Dover in the midst of many shade trees. There's a private parking lot. The French family welcomes guests to Canterbury, and expresses genuine concern about their guests' well-being and comfort. There are a few ground-floor rooms and several especially reserved for nonsmokers. Bedrooms are well appointed, with nice extras, and a private shower-only bathroom. The public areas include a bright patio and garden, and a ground-floor sitting room.

12 New Dover Rd., Canterbury, Kent CT1 3AP. © **01227/463174.** Fax 01227/455482. www.ersham-lodge. co.uk. 11 units. £45–£59.50 ($72–$95) double. Rates include English breakfast. MC, V. Closed Dec–Jan. **Amenities:** Breakfast room; bar; lounge. *In room:* TV, coffeemaker, hair dryer.

Kingsbridge Villa *(Value)* Located in the historic heart of town, this is a bright, inviting guesthouse built in the 1750s on Roman foundations. During its lifetime, it has served as a weaving factory and later as a pub. Today it has the remains of an ancient Roman well in its cellar. Bedrooms, ranging from small to medium, are comfortably furnished, well maintained, and most have private shower-and-tub bathrooms.

15 Best Lane, Canterbury, Kent CT1 2JB. © **01227/766415.** 13 units, 9 with bathroom. £25 ($40) single without bathroom, £30–£35 ($48–$56) single with bathroom; £36–£40 ($58–$64) double without bathroom; £50–£55 double with bathroom. Rates include English breakfast. No credit cards. **Amenities:** Restaurant; bar; lounge. *In room:* TV, dataport, coffeemaker, hair dryer.

Kingsmead House *(★)* Jan and John Clark, one of the most hospitable couples in the region, welcome you to their 17th-century home. Their timbered house is located about 6 to 8 minutes from the heart of Canterbury off Kingsmead Road. Although you'll pay more here than in a typical peas-in-the-pod B&B, the taste and comfort level justifies the price. A stay here is truly like visiting a well-kept and attractive private home. Since there are only three well-furnished rooms, each guest gets personal attention. The rooms are fresh and bright, and the whole atmosphere is state-of-the-art, enough to please the most demanding guest. All have neatly kept private bathrooms with shower-tub combinations.

68 St. Stephens Rd., Canterbury, Kent CT2 7JF. © **01227/760132.** 3 units. £50–£55 ($80–$88) double. Rates include English breakfast. No credit cards. Free parking. **Amenities:** Breakfast room; lounge. *In room:* TV, coffeemaker, no phone.

Peregrine House *(★)* In the center of Canterbury, yet on a quiet lane and only a 2-minute walk from the Cathedral, this B&B is a restored Regency-styled building. Bedrooms are midsize and comfortably furnished, most with a small private bathroom with shower. The hosts are ingratiating and welcoming and will help ease your adjustment into Canterbury. The house has been fully refurbished, yet the prices are still reasonable. For those who don't like to climb stairs, some rooms are available on the ground floor. Early breakfast is provided if needed, and special diets are catered.

18 Hawks Lane, Canterbury CT1 2NU. © **01227/472153.** Fax 01227/455233. 8 units, 6 with bathroom. £20 ($32) single without bathroom, £30 ($48) single with bathroom; £90 ($144) double without bathroom, £110 ($176) double with bathroom; £75 ($120) family room with bathroom. Rates include English breakfast. Free parking. **Amenities:** Breakfast room. *In room:* TV, coffeemaker, hair dryer.

St. Stephens Guest House This is in a quiet part of the city, yet close to the main attractions. Set in well-kept gardens and lawns, St. Stephens is one of the most attractive buildings in Canterbury. It is owned and managed by Jack and Hazel Johnson. While the character of the house has been retained, modern accommodations include central heating, shaver outlets, and a private shower-only bathroom in almost every room.

100 St. Stephens Rd., Canterbury, Kent CT2 7JL. 📞 and fax **01227/767644**. 12 units, 11 with bathroom. £49 ($78) double without bathroom, £60 ($96) double with bathroom. Rates include English breakfast. No credit cards. From Westgate Tower, head down North Lane. **Amenities:** Breakfast room; lounge. *In room:* TV, coffeemaker, hair dryer, no phone.

The White House   You'll find this Regency town house on a lane inside the old city walls, off St. Peter's Street next to the Marlowe Theatre. The new owners, Frances and Alan MacDonald, are informed hosts who add a personal touch to everything. Most of the rooms are good size; all are comfortably well equipped with private shower-only or bathtub-only bathrooms. A superb English breakfast is served at a communal table in an elegant dining and sitting room.

6 St. Peters Lane, Canterbury, Kent CT1 2BP. 📞 **01227/761836**. 9 units. £35–£40 ($56–$64) single; £55–£60 ($88–$96) double; £75–£80 ($120–$128) triple or family unit for 4. Rates include English breakfast. No credit cards. **Amenities:** Breakfast room; lounge. *In room:* TV, coffeemaker, hair dryer, no phone.

Yorke Lodge   This spacious, elegant Victorian guesthouse, close to the city center and the cathedral, is much improved and made even more inviting with new decorations, new beds, and better plumbing in all of the private bathrooms, which contain shower-tub combinations. Off-street parking is available. Proprietor Victoria O'Shey aims to pamper her guests. All the midsize bedrooms contain comfortable beds. Two rooms have four-poster beds. There's a conservatory opening onto a walled garden, plus a library stocked with information about the area. Breakfasts are large and offer variety.

50 London Rd., Canterbury, Kent CT2 8LF. 📞 **01227/451243**. Fax 01227/462006. www.yorkelodge.com. 8 units. £35–£45 ($56–$72) single; £60–£80 ($96–$128) double; £75–£85 ($120–$136) family unit for 3–4. Rates include English breakfast. MC, V. Follow the signs to the M2/London Rd. **Amenities:** Breakfast room; lounge. *In room:* TV, coffeemaker, no phone.

A NEARBY PLACE TO STAY

The Old Coach House *(Finds)* ⭐   The inn stands halfway between Canterbury and Dover on the A2 (southbound), which makes it ideal for exploring, shopping, country walking, or horse riding. A coaching inn in the 19th century, it is now run as a relaxed French country *auberge* by chef-patron Jean-Claude Rozard and his English wife, Julie. Rooms are a bit small, like a pub hotel, but each has a small bath with a shower stall.

Dover Rd., Barham, Kent. 📞 **01227/831218**. Fax 01227/831932. 10 units. £48 ($77) single; £55 ($88) double. MC, V. **Amenities:** Restaurant; bar; lounge; babysitting. *In room:* TV, coffeemaker, hair dryer, safe.

WHERE TO DINE

Alberrys Wine and Food Bar ⭐ INTERNATIONAL   This fun place is located in the center of town near the bus station. You eat in the same area where slaves of the Romans once toiled; some of the exposed foundation belonged to a Roman amphitheater. Alberrys offers an inexpensive and frequently changing repertoire of well-prepared food. A meal might include soup of the day and charcoal-grilled rump steak with pepper sauce, followed by homemade sticky chocolate pudding with vanilla ice cream. The Victorian cartoon on Alberrys' wine list claims that "tomorrow morning you'll be able to perform great feats of strength if you drink plenty of wine tonight." Beer and mixed drinks are served, and wine is available by the glass.

38 St. Margaret's St. 📞 **01227/452378**. Main courses £5–£10.50 ($8–$17). AE, DC, MC, V. Mon–Sat noon–3pm and 6–9pm (restaurant); 10am–2am (bar).

Augustine's Restaurant ENGLISH/FRENCH   Located in a Georgian structure 90m (300 ft.) from St. Augustine's Abbey, this bistro offers English fare in a casual and relaxed atmosphere. Sidney and Branka Agg own the establishment, comprising two dining rooms with an uncomplicated decor of wooden floors and tables. To begin, try the mushrooms in cheese and garlic or one of the daily soups, such as leek, mushroom, and tomato; then go on to pan-fried filet of sea bass in a potato crust and tomato fondue with lemon sauce or lamb with gratin dauphiniose. Desserts are traditionally English, including such favorites as spotted dick (no smirking, please) and apple crumb.

1–2 Longport. ✆ **01227/453063.** Main courses £9.50–£16.90 ($15–$27). Set-price lunch £10.95 ($18). AE, MC, V. Tues–Sun noon–1:45pm; Tues–Sat 6:30–9:15pm. Closed first 2 weeks in Jan.

Dove ★ *(Finds*   In this little hamlet directly north of Canterbury and signposted along A299, this pub is well worth the trek out of town. We'd be there every night if we lived nearby. Order a Shepherd Neame ale from the lavishly decorated bar, and settle back to peruse the choices on the chalkboard menu. The pub grub is the best we've found in the greater Canterbury area. Fresh local ingredients, which are changed daily, might feature grilled sardines with virgin olive oil and garlic, sautéed locally caught shrimp with pickled ginger and fresh herbs, even a whole grilled black bream with herbs. We'd also recommend the roast duck breast flavored with ginger and cinnamon, or the baked cod with a tomato-and-basil sauce. For dessert, the lemon tart is a classic. In fair weather head for the sheltered garden, or in the winter find a place in front of the log fire.

Plum Pudding Lane, Dargate. ✆ **01227/751360.** Reservations not needed. Main courses £4.25–£13 ($7–$21). No credit cards. Pub: Tues–Sun 11:30am–11pm; restaurant: Tues–Sun noon–1:30pm; Wed 7–9pm.

Il Vaticano ITALIAN   The best-known pasta parlor in Canterbury is housed in this 14th-century building, which lies off High Street in the commercial center of the city. The trattoria-style decor features bentwood chairs, small marble-top tables, and exposed brick. All pasta is made on the premises, and you get a choice of sauces. Some of the best include baby clams in a tomato, garlic, and herb sauce, or black olives and mushrooms in a tomato sauce. Baked lasagna and tortellini filled with spinach and ricotta cheese are also served.

35 St. Margaret's St. ✆ 01227/765333. Main courses £8.75–£10 ($14–$16). AE, DC, MC, V. Daily 10am–10pm.

CANTERBURY AFTER DARK

Gulbenkian Theatre, University of Kent, Giles Lane (✆ **01227/769075**), is open from 11am to 5pm during school terms (except Cricket Week, the 1st week in Aug) and offers a potpourri of jazz and classical productions, dance, drama, comedy, and a mix of new and student productions. Check newspapers for schedules; tickets cost £3 to £16 ($4.80–$26).

Marlowe, The Friars (✆ **01227/787787**), is Canterbury's only commercial playhouse. It's open year-round and offers drama, jazz and classical concerts, and contemporary and classical ballet. Tickets cost from £14 to £35 ($22–$56).

A favorite local pub, **Alberrys Wine & Food Bar,** 38 St. Margaret's St. (✆ **01227/452378**), offers live music, mostly jazz, played by local and student groups. Cover charges range from £3 ($4.80). The menu offers affordable daily specials and light snacks at lunch and dinner.

A laid-back student hangout, **The Cherry Tree,** 10 White Horse Lane (✆ **01227/451266**), offers a wide selection of beers, including Bass Ale on draft, Cherry Tree ale, three traditional lagers, and four bitters. The atmosphere is clubby, filled with casual conversation. If you visit for lunch, you'll find a 32-item menu—the best pub menu in town—plus three types of ploughman's lunch. On Sundays they offer a traditional English roast for £5 ($8).

Another good choice on your Canterbury pub-crawl is **The Flying Horse,** 1 Dover St. (© **01227/463803**), which attracts a garrulous mix of young and old. This 16th-century pub bridges generations from oldsters to the hip student crowd.

2 The White Cliffs of Dover

122km (76 miles) SE of London; 134km (84 miles) NE of Brighton

In Queen Victoria's day, Dover basked in popularity as a seaside resort, but now it's known mostly as a port for cross-Channel car and passenger traffic between England and France (notably Calais). Dover was one of England's most vulnerable targets during World War II; repeated bombings destroyed much of its harbor. Dover has regained some importance since the Channel Tunnel (Chunnel) opened in 1994.

Unless you're on your way to France or want to use Dover as a base for exploring its surroundings, skip a visit here. Dover has always been rather dull except for those white cliffs. Even its hotels are second-rate; many prefer to stay in Folkestone, about 10 miles to the southwest.

ESSENTIALS

GETTING THERE   Frequent trains run between Victoria Station or Charing Cross Station in London and Dover daily from 5am to 10pm. You arrive in Dover at Priory Station, off Folkestone Road. During the day, two trains per hour depart Canterbury East Station heading for Dover. For rail information, call © **0845/7484950.**

Frequent buses leave throughout the day—daily 7:30am to 11pm—from London's Victoria Coach Station bound for Dover. Call © **08705/808080** for schedules. The local bus station is on Pencester Road (© **01304/240024**). Stagecoach East Kent provides daily bus service between Canterbury and Dover.

If you're driving from London, head first to Canterbury (see above), then continue along A2 southeast until you reach Dover, on the coast.

VISITOR INFORMATION   The **Tourist Information Centre** is on Old Town Gaol Street (© **01304/205108**). It's open Monday to Friday from 9am to 5:30pm, Saturday 10am to 4pm, July and August daily from 9am to 5pm.

EXPLORING DOVER

You'll get your best view of the **white cliffs** ★★ as you arrive at Dover by ferry or hovercraft from Calais. Otherwise, walk out to the end of the town's Prince of Wales pier, the largest of its western docks; the cliffs loom above you. Or, you could drive 5 miles east of Dover to the pebble-covered beaches of Deal, a fishing hamlet. Here, a local fisherman might take you on an informal boat ride.

Deal Castle ★   Deal Castle is .5km (¼ mile) south of the Deal town center, 8km (5 miles) from Dover. A defensive fort built around 1540, it's the most spectacular example of the low, squat forts constructed by Henry VIII. Its 119 gun positions made it the most powerful of his defense forts. Centered around a circular keep surrounded by two rings of semicircle bastions, the castle was protected by an outer moat. The entrance was approached by a drawbridge with an iron gate. The castle was damaged by bombs during World War II but has been restored to its earlier form. A free videotape of the castle is included in the admission charge.

On the seafront. © 01304/372762. Admission £3.20 ($5) adults, £2.60 ($4.15) seniors, £1.60 ($2.55) children. Apr–Sept daily 10am–6pm; Oct–Mar Wed–Sun 10am–4pm. Closed Dec 24–26.

Dover Castle ★★★   Rising nearly 120m (400 ft.) above the port is one of the oldest and best-known castles in England. Its keep was built at the command of Becket's fair-weather friend, Henry II, in the 12th century. The ancient castle was called back to active duty as late as World War II. The "Pharos" on the grounds is a lighthouse built by the Romans in the first half of the 1st century. The Romans first landed at nearby Deal in 54 B.C., but after 6 months they departed and didn't return until nearly 100 years later, in A.D. 43, when they stayed and occupied the country for 400 years. The castle houses a military museum and a film center, plus "Live and Let's Spy," an exhibition of World War II spying equipment.

Castle Hill. ℭ **01304/211067**. Fax 0130/214739. Admission £8 ($13) adults, £4 ($6) children under 15, £6 ($10) seniors and students, £20 ($32) family. Apr–Sept daily 10am–6pm (last tour at 5pm); Oct daily 10am–6pm (last tour at 4pm); Nov–Mar daily 10am–4pm (last tour at 3pm). Bus: 90 bound for Deal.

Secret War Time Tunnels   These secret tunnels, used during the early years of World War II, were originally excavated to house cannons to be used (if needed) against an invasion by Napoleon. Some 200 feet below ground, they were the headquarters of Operation Dynamo, when more than 300,000 troops from Dunkirk were evacuated in 1940. Once off-limits to all but those with the strongest security clearance, the networks of tunnels can now be toured. Stand in the very room where Sir Bertram Ramsey issued orders; experience the trauma of life in an underground operating theater; and look out over the English Channel from the hidden cliff-top balcony, just as Churchill did during the Battle of Britain.

Dover Castle, Castle Hill. ℭ **01304/211067** or 01304/201628. Free admission with castle admission. Open same days and hours as the castle. Last tour leaves 1 hr. before castle closing time. Bus: 90 bound for Deal.

Roman Painted House   This 1,800-year-old Roman structure, called Britain's "buried Pompeii" and located in the town center near Market Square, has exceptionally well-preserved walls and an under-floor heating system. It's famous for its unique bacchic murals and has won four national awards for presentation. Brass-rubbing is also offered.

New St. ℭ **01304/203279**. Admission £2 ($3.20) adults, 80p ($1.30) seniors and children 16 and under. Apr–Sept Tues–Sun 10am–5pm.

WHERE TO STAY

Ardmore Private Hotel   Adjacent to Dover Castle, the Ardmore enjoys popularity with the channel-crossing crowd for its convenient location near the port and hovercraft terminal, within easy reach of the town center. Carmen and Len Morriss, among the more accommodating hosts in the area (they also run St. Martin's Guest House; see below), have done much to modernize this house (ca. 1796), but have retained some of its original architectural style, with many Victorian touches. They keep their nonsmoking bedrooms shipshape; each unit is suitable for a double or twin, even a family room. Some rooms have a harbor view. Units have private bathrooms or showers and double-glazed windows. At the rear is a modern leisure center.

18 Castle Hill Rd., Dover, Kent CT16 1QW. ℭ **01304/205895**. Fax 01304/208229. www.ardmoreph.co.uk. 4 units. £40–£50 ($64–$80) single or double; £58–£68 ($93–$109) family unit. Rates include English breakfast. MC, V. **Amenities:** Breakfast room; lounge. *In room:* TV, coffeemaker, hair dryer, no phone.

Beulah House ★   This elegant late Victorian house, presided over by Anita Owens, is convenient to the western docks and the center of Dover. As the couple makes improvements, they respect their home's original character, highlighted by the gardens in back, with sculptured yews and roses. The bedrooms (all nonsmoking) are handsomely furnished and equipped with neatly kept bathrooms containing showers. The ideal room is on the ground floor, with a four-poster bed and exclusive use of an adjoining bathroom. Children are welcome here, with some rooms being most suitable for families. An international crowd of guests is served breakfast. There's also a small conservatory overlooking the gardens in the rear.

94 Crabble Hill, London Rd., Dover, Kent CT17 0SA. *©* **01304/824615**. www.beulahguesthouse.co.uk. £40 ($64) single; £56 ($90) double. Rates include English breakfast. MC, V. Free parking outside; £4 ($6) in the garage. **Amenities:** Breakfast room; lounge. *In room:* TV, coffeemaker, no phone.

Number One Guest House   The castle overlooks this quaint Georgian town house, built in 1800 and one of Dover's oldest remaining homes, located near town, port, and the Channel Tunnel and Cruise Terminal. John and Adeline Reidy offer a smart atmosphere of a bygone age, with old-fashioned hospitality and service, and comfortable single, double, and family rooms, where you'll find courtesy coffee and where you are served breakfast. All units contain neatly kept bathrooms with shower. This cozy, well-maintained house (decorated with Victorian furnishings) has a pretty-in-pink lounge that opens out back to a secret walled garden where you can relax on summer evenings.

1 Castle St., Dover, Kent CT16 1QH. *©* **01304/202007**. Fax 01304/214078. www.number1guesthouse.co.uk. 5 units. £30 ($48) single; £44–£54 ($70–$86) double; £60–£65 ($96–$104) triple; £65–£70 ($104–$112) family unit for 4. Rates include English breakfast. No credit cards. Free parking outside; £2 ($3.20) in the garage. **Amenities:** Breakfast room; lounge; room service (7:15–8:30am). *In room:* TV, coffeemaker, hair dryer, no phone.

St. Martins Guest House   A few blocks from the cross-Channel ferries and the hoverport, resting on the castle hillside, this 1840s house is maintained and furnished to high standards, with full central heating. Ample parking is available. The good-size bedrooms, with color-coordinated decor, have double-glazed windows and private showers. Guests meet in an attractive pine-furnished breakfast room. The house has a great lounge and residents-only liquor license.

17 Castle Hill Rd., Dover, Kent CT16 1QW. *©* **01304/205938**. Fax 01304/208229. www.stmartinsgh.co.uk. 6 units. £25–£35 ($40–$56) single; £40–£48 ($64–$77) double; £58–£68 ($87–$102) family unit. Rates include English breakfast. MC, V. **Amenities:** Breakfast room; lounge. *In room:* TV, hair dryer, no phone.

Westbank Guesthouse *★* *Kids*   One of the best B&Bs in the area, Westbank is convenient to the train station and town center, and a 5-minute ride to the docks and hoverport. Mr. and Mrs. Michael have modernized this attractive semi-detached Victorian house without losing its character. Bedrooms are well appointed and very comfortable, ranging from a spacious family unit to a single. Shared and private shower-only baths are both adequate and spick-and-span. It's a family favorite; cots and cribs are available and high chairs are offered in the dining room, where a generous English breakfast is served beginning at 6am for those early Channel crossings.

239–241 Folkestone Rd., Dover, Kent CT17 9LL. *©* **01304/201061**. www.westbankguesthouse.co.uk. 13 units, 7 with shower only. £32–£40 ($51–$64) double without bathroom; £37–£45 ($59–$72) double with shower only. Rates include English breakfast. MC, V. Free parking. **Amenities:** Breakfast room. *In room:* TV, coffeemaker, hair dryer, no phone.

WHERE TO DINE

Finding a good place to eat in Dover isn't easy; France may be just across the Channel, but French cuisine often seems light years away. Our recommendations are all in the town center. For food on the run, your best bet is **Tower Kebab,** 12 Towerhamlets Rd. (*©* **01304/242170**), which makes great takeout.

King of the kebab, it offers many varieties, each with pita bread and a salad. Prices range from £3 to £7 ($4.80–$11). Sandwiches, freshly made salads, and tempting desserts round out the menu. This is also one of the best places in town to get the ingredients for a picnic.

Britannia INTERNATIONAL   If you want a typically English, pub-style meal, try this restaurant, whose windows overlook the ferry terminal and the ships arriving from Calais and Boulogne. Its lovely facade has a bow window with lots of gilt and brass nautical accents. The popular pub is on the ground floor, the restaurant on the upper level. The fare is typical of what you'd find to eat along a motorway in England. Try a prawn cocktail or a pâté to start, followed by rump steak or a mixed grill. There's a selection of vegetarian dishes. Dover sole is a specialty, available at market prices. Three TVs in the pub will keep sports fans happy.

41 Townwall St. ✆ 01304/203248. Main courses £5.95–£12 ($10–$19). MC, V. Restaurant daily noon–2pm and 6–9pm. Pub Mon–Sat 11am–11pm, Sun noon–10:30pm.

Chaplin's Restaurant and Coffee Bar BRITISH   This restaurant offers a bit of whimsy, with Charlie Chaplin mementos scattered throughout the dining room. The menu is typically English: steak-and-kidney pie, roast lamb, Lancashire hot pot, and cottage pie. Sandwiches, salads, and burgers are also featured. A breakfast special of two sausages, two slices of bacon, beans or tomatoes, an egg, and bread is offered throughout the day.

2 Church St. ✆ 01304/204870. Main courses £3.50–£7.95 ($5–$13). MC, V. Mon–Sat 8:30am–8pm; Sun 9:30am–8pm.

3 The Ancient Seaport of Rye ★★

100km (62 miles) SE of London

Rye, originally an island, flourished in the 13th century. In its halcyon days, it was a smuggling center, its residents sneaking in contraband from the marshes to stash away in little nooks. But the sea receded from Rye, leaving it perched like a giant whale out of water, 2 miles from the Channel. Attacked several times by French fleets, Rye was practically razed in 1377. But it rebuilt itself successfully, in full Elizabethan panoply. When Elizabeth I visited in 1573, she was so impressed that she bestowed upon the town the distinction of Royal Rye. Long considered a special place, it has over the years attracted famous people, such as novelist Henry James.

Rye's narrow cobblestone streets twist and turn like a labyrinth, and jumbled along them are buildings whose sagging roofs and crooked chimneys indicate the town's medieval origins. The town overflows with sites of architectural interest.

Neighboring Winchelsea has also witnessed the waters' ebb. It traces its history from Edward I and has enjoyed many dramatic moments, such as its sacking by the French. In the words of one 19th-century writer, Winchelsea is "a sunny dream of centuries ago." The finest sight in this dignified residential town is a badly damaged 14th-century church with a number of remarkable tombs.

ESSENTIALS

GETTING THERE   From London, the **Southern Region Line** offers trains south from Charing Cross or Cannon Street Station, with a change at Ashford, before continuing on to Rye. You can also go via Tunbridge Wells with a change in Hastings. Trains run every hour during the day, arriving at the Rye Train Station off Cinque Ports Street. The trip takes 1½ to 2 hours. Call ✆ 0845/ 7484950 for schedules and information.

The train, not the bus, is the best public transport way to get to Rye, but once you're there you'll find buses departing every hour on the hour for many regional destinations, including Hastings. Schedules are posted on signs in the parking lot. For bus information on connections in the surrounding area, call © **0870/608-2608.**

If you're driving from London, take M25, M26, and M20 east to Maidstone, going southeast along A20 to Ashford. At Ashford, continue south on A2070.

VISITOR INFORMATION   The **Rye Tourist Office** is in the Heritage Centre on the Strand Quay (© **01797/226696**). It's open daily from March to the end of October from 9am to 5:30pm, and November through February from 10am to 4pm and Sunday 10am to 2pm. The Heritage Centre houses a free exhibition and is also home to **Story of Rye,** a sound-and-light show depicting more than 700 years of Rye's history. Adults pay £2.50 ($4), seniors and students £1.50 ($2.40), and children £1 ($1.60).

EXPLORING THE AREA

In Rye, the old town's entrance is **Land Gate,** where a single lane of traffic passes between massive, 12m- (40-ft.-) high stone towers. The parapet of the gate has holes through which boiling oil used to be poured on unwelcome visitors, such as French raiding parties.

Rye has had potteries for centuries, and today is no exception, with a number of outlets in town. The best potteries include the **Rye Pottery,** Ferry Road (© **01797/223038**); **Rye Tiles,** Wishward Street (© **01797/223038**); **David Sharp Ceramics,** The Mint (© **01797/222620**); and the **Cinque Ports Pottery,** Conduit Hill (© **01797/222033**), where you can see the potters at work during the week. The town also abounds in antiques and collectibles shops and new and used bookstores.

St. Mary's Parish Church   This notable mid-12th-century church has a 16th-century clock flanked by two gilded cherubs (known as "Quarter Boys" because they strike the bells on the quarter-hour). St. Mary's is often referred to as "the cathedral of East Sussex" because of its expansive size and ornate beauty. If you're brave, you can climb a set of wooden stairs and ladders to the bell tower for an impressive view.

Church Square. © **01797/224935.** Admission to tower £2 ($3.20) adults, £1 ($1.60) children. Contributions appreciated to enter the church. June–Aug daily 9am–7pm; off season daily 9am–5:30pm.

Lamb House   Henry James lived at Lamb House from 1898 to 1916. Many James mementos are scattered throughout the house, which is set in a walled garden. Its previous owner joined the gold rush in North America but perished in the Klondike, and James was able to buy the freehold for a modest £2,000 ($3,200). Some of his well-known books were written here. In *English Hours,* James wrote: "There is not much room in the pavilion, but there is room for the hard-pressed table and tilted chair—there is room for a novelist and his friends."

West St. (at the top of Mermaid St.). © **01892/890651.** Admission £2.60 ($4.15) adults, £1.30 ($2.10) children. Wed and Sat 2–6pm. Closed Nov–Mar.

Rye Castle Museum   This stone fortification was constructed around 1250 by Henry III to defend the coast against the French. For 300 years it was the town jail but has long since been converted into a museum. In 1996, the Medieval Tower was restored.

Gungarden. ℂ **01797/226728.** Admission £2.90 ($4.65) adults, £2 ($3.20) students and seniors, £1.50 ($2.40) children, £5.95 ($10) family ticket. Apr–Oct daily 10:30am–1pm and 2:30–5pm; Nov–Mar Sat–Sun 10:30am–1pm and 2–3:30pm.

Smallhythe Place ⭐ *Finds*   On the outskirts of Winchelsea, this was for 30 years the country house of Dame Ellen Terry, the English actress acclaimed for her Shakespearean roles, who had a long theatrical association with Sir Henry Irving; she died here in 1928. This timber-framed structure, of the "continuous-jetty" type, dates from the first half of the 16th century and is filled with Terry memorabilia—playbills, props, makeup, and a striking display of costumes. An Elizabethan barn, converted into a theater in 1929, is open to view on most days.

Smallhythe (on B2082 near Tenterden, about 9.5km/6 miles north of Rye). ℂ **01580/762334.** Admission £3.40 ($5) adults, £1.70 ($2.70) children, £8.54 ($14) family ticket. Apr–Oct Sat–Wed 11am–5pm. Closed Good Friday. Bus: 312 from Tenterden or Rye.

WHERE TO STAY IN THE AREA

Cliff Farm   Jeff and Pat Sullivin receive guests on their nearly 2 hectares (4½ acres) of property, located 3km (2 miles) east of Rye toward Iden Lock. Because of the farm's elevated position, you'll have good views of the area, particularly over Romney Marsh, well known for its fishing. Guest rooms in the 200-year-old farmhouse approximate the interior of a comfortable working farm of that era, with antiquated wooden furnishings, hardwood floors, and decorative floral wallpaper. Rooms are tastefully decorated. There's a sitting room where a log fire blazes during cool weather. Farm produce means a generous country breakfast, and you can see the farm animals as you stroll around.

Military Rd., Iden Lock, Rye, East Sussex TN31 7NY. ℂ and fax **01797/280331.** www.s-h-systems. co.uk/hotels/clifffarm.html. 3 units, none with private bathroom. £17 ($27) per person double. Rates include English breakfast. No credit cards. Closed Dec–Feb. **Amenities:** Breakfast room; lounge. *In room:* No phone.

Jeake's House ⭐⭐   Rye's premier B&B is a hidden treasure on the same street as the famous Mermaid Inn (see "Worth a Splurge," below). The five-floor house near the rail station was built in 1689 as a wool storehouse for Samuel Jeake II; it was later joined with a Quaker meetinghouse next door. American writer Conrad Aiken, who wrote for *The New Yorker* as "Samuel Jeake Jr.," lived here for nearly 25 years and was visited by T. S. Eliot, Henry James, Paul Nash, and Radclyffe Hall (author of *The Well of Loneliness*). The owner, Jenny Hadfield, takes loving care of this house and eagerly shares Aiken's collected letters and poems. The bedrooms have been handsomely styled with Laura Ashley prints. Those units with private bathrooms have hand-painted tiles made at a Sussex factory; each has a shower. Breakfast, traditional or vegetarian, is taken in a former galleried chapel, now elegantly converted.

Mermaid St., Rye, East Sussex TN32 7ET. ℂ **01797/222828.** Fax 07197/222623. www.jeakeshouse.com. 11 units, 10 with bathroom; 2 suites. £35 ($56) single without bathroom, £40 ($64) single with bathroom; £78 ($125) double without bathroom, £88 ($141) double with bathroom; £100 ($160) suite. Rates include English breakfast. MC, V. **Amenities:** Breakfast room; bar; lounge. *In room:* TV, coffeemaker, hair dryer.

Little Orchard House ⭐⭐   This hotel, located in the town center at the western end of High Street, is among Rye's most elegant and moderately priced accommodations. The 1720 Georgian town house was originally the home of Rye's mayor, Thomas Proctor; other prominent politicians have lived nearby, including Prime Minister David Lloyd George in the 1920s. The house is tastefully furnished with antiques and Georgian paneling. A large open fireplace in the lounge-study has a blazing fire when needed, a big bouquet of dried flowers otherwise.

The good-size bedrooms have private bathrooms with shower-tub combinations. Two units contain a four-poster bed. From the lounge-study and the intimate breakfast room, you see the old-style walled garden with espaliered fruit trees.

3 West St., Rye, East Sussex TN31 7ES. © 01797/223831. www.littleorchardhouse.com. 2 units. £50–£70 ($80–$112) single; £70–£100 ($112–$160) double. Rates include English breakfast. MC, V. Parking £3 ($4.80). **Amenities:** Breakfast room; lounge. *In room:* TV/VCR, coffeemaker, mini-fridge, hair dryer, no phone.

Little Saltcote *Finds*　This attractive guesthouse is a 5-minute walk east of the town center, in a peaceful rural setting. The house was built in 1901 on land that, until 1400, had been beneath the sea. Perhaps this has inspired the fertility of the rear garden, a riot of color in springtime. The well-appointed rooms—all doubles—have central heating, razor outlets, hot and cold running water, and some contain showers. A vegetarian breakfast can be provided for those who want it. Forecourt parking is available.

22 Military Rd., Rye, East Sussex TN31 7NY. © 01797/223210. Fax 01797/224474. www.smoothhound. co.uk/hotels/littlesaltcote.html. 5 units, 3 with shower. £25 ($40) single without bathroom, £30 ($48) single with bathroom; £42 ($67) double without bathroom, £50 ($80) double with bathroom. Rates include English breakfast. MC, V. **Amenities:** Breakfast room; laundry; babysitting. *In room:* TV, coffeemaker, hair dryer, no phone.

Playden Oasts Hotel　This hotel, sitting on three-quarters of an acre of land and surrounded by other residential buildings, consists of three adjacent towers called oasts, each round at the base and capped with a conical roof that tapers to a narrow air vent at the top. The towers were built between 1850 and 1890 to dry the hops (a key ingredient in beer and ale) local farmers once produced in abundance. The three oasts remained in working use until 1965, when a local entrepreneur made them into a coherent whole. After a disastrous fire, the oasts were repaired and upgraded again in 1986, and the hotel now provides comfortable (and unusual) accommodations. Only two of the eight accommodations are within the walls of the original kilns; the other six, rectangular in form, are cozy, with tea-making facilities and rustic furniture. All have well-kept bathrooms with showers. Robert Press, your host, offers directions to the agrarian hamlet of Playden, about a mile northeast of Rye. Don't overlook this unusual inn as a place to grab lunch, dinner, or afternoon tea. British cuisine is served at lunch and dinner every day. Advance reservations are required.

Peasmarsh Rd., Playden, Rye, East Sussex TN3 7UL. © 01797/223502. www.playdenoasts.co.uk. 8 units. £45–£55 ($72–$88) single; £65–£75 ($104–$120) double. Rates include English breakfast. AE, DC, MC, V. **Amenities:** Restaurant; bar; lounge; health club; babysitting. *In room:* TV, coffeemaker, hair dryer, no phone.

The Strand House ★★　Set in a garden at a foothill, this weathered historic house and cottage catches the eye, along with the sheep that graze in the meadows separating the hotel from the sea. The house dates from the 1490s and has irregular oak floors; the low, heavy oak ceiling beams came from ships. It is thought that a tunnel near the house leads up to Winchelsea, a relic of the days when smuggling was a primary industry here. There's ample parking on the hotel grounds. All bedrooms have recently been redecorated, and include wall-to-wall carpeting, central heating, and private bathrooms containing showers. One of the rooms includes a four-poster bed. A private breakfast room with a huge inglenook fireplace is reserved for the guests.

Just off A259, Winchelsea, East Sussex TN36 4JT. © 01797/226276. Fax 01797/224806. www.smooth hound.co.uk/hotels/strand.html. 10 units. £38–£42 ($61–$67) single; £58–£78 ($93–$125) double. Rates include English breakfast. MC, V. **Amenities:** Breakfast room; bar; garden; lounge; free parking. *In room:* TV, coffeemaker, hair dryer, no phone.

WHERE TO DINE

In addition to the places recommended below, consider **The Olde Bell,** 33 The Mint (© **01797/223323**), where you get some of the best pub grub in town. If you're sightseeing on the run, check out **Anatolian's Kebabs,** 16A Landgate (© **01797/226868**), which has Rye's best sandwiches, costing from £3 ($4.80). You can get a filling lunch at **Fletcher's House,** Lion Street (© **01797/222227**), open daily 10am to 5:30pm, where dramatist John Fletcher was born in 1579. Upstairs is an antiques-filled, oak-paneled room from the 1400s. Lunches cost from £3.50 ($5); a good cream tea goes for £3.65 ($6).

Swan Cottage Tea Rooms ENGLISH TEA   Dating from 1420, this black-and-white half-timbered cottage lies in one of the most historic buildings in town. Located on the main street, surrounded by antiques shops and pottery outlets, it is one of the preferred places for afternoon tea. We prefer the room in the rear, especially on a windy day, because it has a big brick-built fireplace. Delectable pastries and cakes await you, along with a selection of Darjeeling, Earl Grey, Pure Assam, and other teas.

41 The Mint, High St. © 01797/222423. Afternoon tea £5 ($8); cakes and pastries £1–£2 ($1.60–$3.20). MC. Mon–Wed 10:30am–5pm.

WORTH A SPLURGE

Mermaid Inn ⭐ ENGLISH   Located between West Street and the Strand, the Mermaid had been open for 150 years when Elizabeth I visited Rye in 1573. This most famous of old smugglers' inns of England was well known to the Hawkhurst Gang. In addition to serving good food, the most charming tavern in Rye has 28 comfortable bedrooms to rent, but they are budget bursting. Even if you don't dine or stay at the Mermaid, drop in at the old Tudor pub, with its 16-foot-wide fireplace (look for a priest's hiding hole).

Mermaid St. © 01797/223065. Reservations recommended. Fixed-price 3-course lunch £19.50 ($31); fixed-price 2-course lunch £16 ($26); fixed-price 4-course dinner £35 ($56). AE, MC, V. Daily noon–2:30pm and 7–9:30pm.

4 1066 & All That: Hastings ⭐ & Battle

Hastings: 63km (45 miles) SW of Dover; 101km (63 miles) SE of London. Battle: 54km (34 miles) NE of Brighton; 88km (55 miles) SE of London

The world has seen bigger skirmishes, but few are as well remembered as the Battle of Hastings in 1066. William, duke of Normandy, landed on the Sussex coast and lured King Harold (already fighting Vikings in Yorkshire) southward to defeat, and the destiny of the English-speaking people was changed forever.

The actual battle occurred at what is now Battle Abbey (8 miles away), but the Norman duke used Hastings as his base of operations. You can visit the abbey, have a cup of tea in Battle's main square, and then be off, as the rich countryside of Sussex is much more intriguing than this sleepy market town.

Hastings itself is a little seedy and run-down. If you're seeking an English seaside resort, head for Brighton instead (see section 10, later in this chapter).

ESSENTIALS

GETTING THERE   Daily trains run hourly from London's Victoria Station or Charing Cross to Hastings. The trip takes 1½ to 2 hours. The train station at Battle is a stop on the London-Hastings rail link. For rail information, call © **0845/7484950.**

Hastings is linked by bus to Maidstone, Folkestone, and Eastbourne, which has direct service with scheduled departures. **National Express** operates regular daily service from London's Victoria Coach Station. If you're in Rye or Hastings in summer, several frequent buses run to Battle. For information and schedules, call © **020/7529-2000.**

If you're driving from the M25 ring road around London, head southeast to the coast and Hastings on A21. To get to Battle, cut south to Sevenoaks and continue along A21 to Battle via A2100.

VISITOR INFORMATION   In Hastings, the **Hastings Information Centre** is at Queen's Square, Priory Meadow (© **01424/781111**). It's open daily 8:30am to 6:15pm.

In Battle, the **Tourist Information Centre** at 88 High St. (© **01424/773721**) is open April through September daily from 10am to 6pm; off season Monday through Saturday from 10am to 4pm and Sunday from 11am to 3pm.

EXPLORING THE HISTORIC SITES

Battle Abbey   Harold, last of the Saxon kings, fought bravely here for his kingdom and his life. As legend has it, an arrow through the eye killed him, and his body was dismembered. To commemorate the victory, William the Conqueror founded Battle Abbey; some of the construction stone was shipped from his own lands at Caen in northern France.

During the Dissolution of the Monasteries by Henry VIII (1538–39), the church of the abbey was largely destroyed. Some buildings and ruins, however, remain in what Tennyson called "O Garden, blossoming out of English blood." The main building still standing is the Abbot's House, which is leased to a school for boys and girls and is open to the general public only during summer holidays. Of architectural interest is the gatehouse, whose octagonal towers stand at the top of Market Square. The entire north Precinct Mall is still standing; the ancient Dorter Range, where the monks once slept, is an interesting sight.

The town of Battle flourished around the abbey. While it has remained a medieval market town, many of the old half-timbered buildings have regrettably lost much of their original character because of stucco plastering carried out by more recent generations.

At the south end of Battle High St. (a 5-min. walk from the train station). © **01424/773792.** Admission £5 ($8) adults, £3.50 ($5) seniors and students, £2.50 ($4) children, £11.30 ($18) family ticket. Apr–Sept daily 10am–6pm; Oct daily 10am–5pm; Nov–Mar daily 10am–4pm.

Hastings Castle   In ruins now, the first Norman castle built in England sprouted on a western hill overlooking Hastings around 1067. The fortress was demilitarized by John in 1216 and was later used as a church. Owned by the Pelham dynasty from the latter 16th century to modern times, the ruins have been turned over to Hastings. Precious little is left from the time when proud knights, imbued with a spirit of pomp and spectacle, wore bonnets and girdles. An

---

Kids **Especially for Kids**

Battle Abbey is a great place for the kids. There's not only a themed play area here, but a daily activity sheet is distributed at the gate. You can relax with a picnic or stroll in the parkland that once formed the monastery grounds.

audiovisual presentation details the castle's history, including the famous battle of 1066. From the mount, you'll have a good view of the coast and promenade.

Castle Hill Rd., West Hill. ⓒ 01424/781112. Admission £3.20 ($5) adults, £2.60 ($4.15) seniors and students, £2.10 ($3.35) children. Easter–Sept daily 10am–5pm; Oct–Easter daily 11am–3pm. Take the West Hill Cliff Railway from George St. to the castle for 80p ($1.30), 40p (65¢) children.

SEASIDE AMUSEMENTS

Linked by a 5km (3-mile) promenade along the sea, Hastings and St. Leonards were given a considerable boost in the 19th century by Victoria, who visited several times. Neither town enjoys such royal patronage today; rather, they do a thriving business with English families on vacation, who frequent the usual shops and English resort amusements.

Smugglers Adventure *Kids*   Descend into the once-secret underground haunts of the smugglers of Hastings. In these chambers, where the smugglers stashed their booty away from customs authorities, you can see an exhibition and museum, watch a video in a theater, and take a subterranean adventure walk with 50 life-size figures, along with dramatic sound and lighting effects.

St. Clements Caves, West Hill. ⓒ 01424/422964. Admission £5.50 ($9) adults, £3.65 ($6) children, £15.75 ($25) family. Apr–Sept daily 10am–5:30pm; Oct–Mar daily 11am–4:30pm. Take the West Cliff Railway from George St. to West Hill for 70p ($1.10) adults, 40p (65¢) children.

WHERE TO STAY IN & AROUND HASTINGS

Eagle House Hotel   One of the best hotels in the area, this three-story mansion, originally built in 1860 as a palatial private home, lies in a residential section about a 10-minute walk from the beaches (it's adjacent to St. Leonards Shopping Centre). The well-furnished bedrooms come in various shapes and sizes; all have central heating and private bathrooms with a shower or bathtub.

12 Pevensey Rd., St. Leonards, East Sussex TN38 0JZ. ⓒ 01424/430535. Fax 01424/437771. www.eagle househotel.com. 18 units. £38 ($61) single; £57 ($91) double. Rates include English breakfast. AE, DC, MC, V. **Amenities:** Restaurant; bar; lounge; room service (8am–10:30pm). *In room:* TV, hair dryer.

Parkside House   A 15-minute walk north of Hastings's center, in a neighborhood of legally protected architecture and wildlife, this bed-and-breakfast hotel dates from 1880, when it was built of brick and slate. Views from many of the windows overlook a private garden and a duck pond in Alexander Park, a greenbelt that's said to be the largest municipal park in southeast England. Brian Kent, the owner, offers comfortable and well-maintained small- to medium-size bedrooms, each with a private shower-only bathroom. Guests have access to the hotel's modest inventory of recorded films.

59 Lower Park Rd., Hastings, East Sussex TN34 2LD. ⓒ 01424/433096. Fax 01424/421431. 5 units. £30–£40 ($48–$64) single; £60 ($96) double. Rates include English breakfast. MC, V. **Amenities:** Breakfast room; lounge; laundry. *In room:* TV w/VCR, coffeemaker, hair dryer, no phone.

WHERE TO STAY NEAR BATTLE

Netherfield Hall ⭐   Opposite the village church this charming choice lies in the hamlet of Netherfield, 4km (2½ miles) west of Battle. This house was built with architectural remnants salvaged from older buildings throughout Sussex. With the ample use of very old oaken beams and antique stained-glass windows, the house appears older than its 1983 construction. Jean and Tony Hawes offer well-furnished, English country-style bedrooms, each recently redecorated. All units contain neatly kept bathrooms equipped with shower-tub combinations. The Hawes can direct guests to nearby pubs and restaurants. A tearoom is open daily (except Tues), where coffee is served in the morning and cream teas are served in the afternoon. English-made gifts are available in the tearoom. There is also a beautiful golf course a half-mile away; clubs can be rented there if necessary.

Netherfield, near Battle, East Sussex TN33 9PQ. ☎ 01424/774450. 3 units. £60 ($96) double. Rates include English breakfast. No credit cards. Closed Feb. Take A2100; Netherfield is signposted 4km (2½ miles) west of Battle. **Amenities:** Breakfast room; lounge; laundry. *In room:* TV, coffeemaker, hair dryer, no phone.

WORTH A SPLURGE

Little Hemingfold Hotel ⭐ *Finds*   Little Hemingfold lies 2.5km (1½ miles) from Battle off A2100 and is reached by going down a steep road. It's a rustic white building that's part 17th-century and part early Victorian. Each small bedroom is individually decorated in a cozy, homelike way. Guests often enjoy aperitifs on the lawn, and a grass tennis court is available. French and English meals are served.

Telham, Battle, East Sussex TN33 0TT. ☎ 01424/774338. Fax 01424/775351. 12 units. £46 ($74) single; £92 ($147) double. Rates include English breakfast. AE, MC, V. Take A2100 from Battle for 2.5km (1½ miles) and turn at the sign. **Amenities:** Restaurant; bar; lounge; tennis court. *In room:* TV, coffeemaker.

WHERE TO DINE
IN HASTINGS

Because Hastings is a fishing center, it has a multitude of competing small seafood restaurants along the street fronting the beach at the east side of the city (on the way to the older part of town).

Victoria's Tea Room (D-Day's)   Courthouse Street in Hasting's Old Town is antiques row. The hub and centerpiece is this combination tearoom and antique store. The owners, D-Day (born on the day of the Normandy invasion) and Beverly White, have transformed their oak-beamed 18th-century premises into the coziest tearoom in town and have filled its nether regions with an intriguing collection of period furniture and "collectible junk" including everything from Victorian sideboards to World War I gas masks. The place is especially appealing when the wind and rain blow in from the Channel.

19 Courthouse St., Hastings Old Town. ☎ 01424/465-205. Cream teas £2.50 ($4); sandwiches £2–£3 ($3.20–$4.80). No credit cards. Mon–Thurs and Sat 10am–4:30 or 5pm; Sun noon–4:30pm.

IN BATTLE

The Blacksmith Restaurant ⭐ CONTINENTAL/HUNGARIAN   On the upper (northwestern) edge of Battle, this restaurant occupies a 15th-century stone-sided cottage that for many years housed the village blacksmith. Inside, beneath medieval timbers rescued from old galleons, you can appreciate the European cuisine of Martin and Christine Howe. Many dishes are inspired by the cuisine of Hungary, such as grilled avocados stuffed with Hungarian Liptoi cheese, chilled wild-cherry soup, calves' liver prepared Dutch style with smoked ham and onions, and a signature version of roast duck finished with honey and a wild-cherry sauce. The dessert trolley will probably contain an Eszterházy torte or a Shomloi Délice, a concoction of pulverized walnuts, sultanas, sponge cake, rum, and chocolate sauce.

43 High St. ☎ 01424/773200. Reservations recommended. Main courses £8–£16.50 ($13–$26); 2- to 3-course fixed-price lunch £11.50–£13.95 ($18–$22); 3-course fixed-price supper £14.75–£18 ($24–$29). MC, V. Tues–Sun noon–2:30pm and 7–10:30pm.

The Gateway Restaurant ENGLISH   A few paces from the entrance to Battle Abbey, this low-beamed 17th-century building is no longer a blacksmith's forge. The Gateway is the best place in town for afternoon tea and a good and reasonably priced restaurant. A wide variety of homemade pastries, including chocolate profiteroles, is offered. Afternoon clotted-cream teas are a delight.

Lunches include such classic English dishes as cottage pie, steak-and-kidney pie, chicken-and-leek pie, and beer-and-mushroom casserole.

78 High St. *C* 01424/772856. Reservations required only for Sat dinner. Main courses £4.50–£6.50 ($7–$10) at lunch; clotted-cream tea £3.95 ($6). AE, MC, V. Daily 9am–5:30pm.

5 Royal Tunbridge Wells

58km (36 miles) SE of London; 53km (33 miles) NE of Brighton

Dudley Lord North, courtier to James I, is credited with the accidental discovery in 1606 of the mineral spring that led to the creation of a fashionable resort. Over the years, the "Chalybeate Spring" became known for its curative properties, the answer for everything from too many days of wine and roses to failing sexual prowess. It's still possible to take the waters today.

The spa resort reached its peak in the mid–18th century under the foppish patronage of Beau Nash (1674–1761), dandy and self-anointed final arbiter on how to act, what to say, and even what to wear (he got men to remove their boots in favor of stockings). Tunbridge Wells continued to enjoy a prime spa reputation up through the reign of Victoria, who vacationed here as a child, and in 1909 Tunbridge Wells received its Royal status.

Today, the spa is long past its zenith. But the town is a pleasant place to stay and can serve as a base for exploring the many historic homes in Kent (see below). It's very easy, for example, to tour Sissinghurst and Chartwell from here.

The most remarkable feature of the town itself is The Pantiles, a colonnaded walkway for shoppers, tea drinkers, and diners, built near the wells. If you walk around town, you'll see many other interesting and charming spots. Entertainment is presented at the Assembly Hall and Trinity Arts Centre.

ESSENTIALS

GETTING THERE Two to three trains per hour leave London's Charing Cross Station during the day bound for Hastings, but going via the town center of Royal Tunbridge Wells. The trip takes 50 minutes. For rail information, call *C* 0845/7484950.

There are no direct bus links with Gatwick Airport or London. However, there is hourly service during the day between Brighton and Royal Tunbridge Wells (call *C* 0870/6082608 for the bus schedule). Purchase tickets aboard the bus.

If you're driving from London, after reaching the ring road around London, continue east along M25, cutting southeast at the exit for A21 to Hastings.

VISITOR INFORMATION The **Tourist Information Centre,** Old Fish Market, The Pantiles (*C* 01892/515675), provides a full accommodations list and offers a room-reservations service. It is open Monday through Saturday 9am to 5pm (9am–6pm in summer) and Sunday 10am to 4pm.

WHERE TO STAY

Bankside *Value* For a real taste of English hospitality, try this guesthouse located in a quiet neighborhood within walking distance of restaurants, attractions, and the train station. Mrs. Anne Kibbey offers pleasant, comfortable rooms, either double or twin (no singles). Each nonsmoking room has recently been redecorated, and private bathrooms containing showers have been installed. Her English breakfast will fortify you for the day.

6 Scotts Way, Royal Tunbridge Wells, Kent TN2 5RG. *C* 01892/531776. 3 units. £25 ($40) single; £40 ($64) double. Rates include English breakfast. No credit cards. **Amenities:** Breakfast room. *In room:* TV, coffeemaker, hair dryer, no phone.

Clarken Guest House   This spacious, comfortable, 19th-century home is on the principal road between Eastbourne and Hastings. It's a 10-minute walk from the main train station, where rail connections are made into London, and it's almost the same distance to the Pantiles. Two bedrooms are suitable for families. Some accommodations come with a private bathroom equipped with a shower. One room is available for those with limited mobility. The place is kept immaculate, and has a warm, hospitable atmosphere.

61 Frant Rd., Royal Tunbridge Wells, Kent TN2 5LH. ℭ **01892/533397.** 9 units, 4 with bathroom. £23.50 ($38) single without bathroom, £28.20 ($45) single with bathroom; £45 ($72) double without bathroom, £55.60 ($89) double with bathroom. Rates include English breakfast. No credit cards. **Amenities:** Breakfast room. *In room:* TV, coffeemaker, hair dryer, no phone.

Danehurst House ★ *(Finds*   Set in Rusthall, a residential satellite hamlet about 2.5km (1½ miles) west of the center of Tunbridge Wells, this mock-Tudor house is from 1920 and built of stone and partially exposed exterior beams. It sits within a small garden adjacent to similar houses on either side. The nonsmoking bedrooms are decorated with fresh pastel colors, recently upgraded upholstery, and a scattering of old furniture. All have tidy bathrooms with shower-tub combinations. Public rooms include a conservatory and a library. Although someone might whip you up a simple evening meal if you prefer to dine in-house, only breakfast is served on a regular basis.

41 Lower Green Rd., Rusthall, near Tunbridge Wells, Kent TN4 8TW. ℭ **01892/527739.** Fax 01892/514804. www.danehurst.net. 5 units. £45–£65 ($72–$104) single; £65–£89 ($104–$142) double. AE, DC, MC, V. **Amenities:** Breakfast room; bar; lounge. *In room:* TV, coffeemaker, hair dryer, no phone.

WHERE TO DINE

Downstairs at Thackeray's ★ FRENCH/ENGLISH   This restaurant is the less-expensive counterpart to a famous upstairs gastronomical enclave, whose prices are higher than a budget traveler can afford. Downstairs, however, is a fun, likable, reasonably priced, and bustling place. Set on the street level of Tunbridge Wells's second-oldest house (built around 1660 and home to novelist William Thackeray), it offers fewer than 30 seats for good but cost-conscious dining. You're welcome to drop in just for a drink at the stand-up bar, where recorded jazz plays softly. Most visitors, however, opt for full meals, which might include filet of salmon with asparagus sauce, eggplant with tomatoes and mozzarella, or roast duck with prunes and port sauce.

85 London Rd. ℭ **01892/511921.** Reservations recommended. Main courses £16–£22.50 ($26–$36); fixed-price lunch £11.50–£12.50 ($18–$20). AE, MC, V. Tues–Sun noon–2:30pm; Tues–Sat 6:30–10:30pm.

6 Kent's Country Houses, Castles & Gardens

Many of England's finest country houses, castles, and gardens are in Kent. Located here are the palace of **Knole,** one of England's largest private houses, with a vast complex of courtyards and buildings; **Hever Castle,** the childhood home of Anne Boleyn, later the home of William Waldorf Astor; **Leeds Castle,** a spectacular castle with American ties; and **Penshurst Place,** a stately Elizabethan home and early-17th-century literary salon. Kent has a bevy of homes that once belonged to famous men but have been turned into intriguing museums, such as **Chartwell,** where Sir Winston Churchill lived for many years, and **Down House,** where Charles Darwin wrote *On the Origin of Species.*

At least a week is needed to see all these historic properties—more time than most visitors have. When you make your choices, keep in mind that Knole, Hever, Penshurst, Leeds, and Chartwell deserve your attention most. If you have

---

Tips **Planning Your Visit**

Note that Leeds Castle allows morning visits; most Kentish castles and country homes are open to visitors only in the afternoon.

---

only a day, you might confine your time to Chartwell and Knole. An entire second day is needed to visit Leeds Castle and Hever Castle.

If you have more time for castle-hopping, visit **Canterbury Cathedral** in the morning of your third day (when most castles are closed), then tour Penshurst Place in the afternoon. (See section 1 of this chapter for details on Canterbury.) Two other notable attractions are **Sissinghurst Castle Garden** and **Ightham Mote,** a National Trust property dating from 1340 and open afternoons during the week and mornings Saturday and Sunday.

We find the guided tours to some of Kent's more popular stately homes too rushed and too expensive to recommend; you can tour each attraction far more reasonably on your own. Because public transportation into and around Kent can be awkward, we advise driving from London, especially if you plan to visit more than one place in a day. Accordingly, this section is organized as you might drive it from London; however, if it's possible to get to an attraction via public transportation, that information is given below.

Chartwell ✦   This was Churchill's home from 1922 until his death. While not as grand as his birthplace (Blenheim Palace), Chartwell has preserved its rooms as the Conservative politician left them—maps, documents, photographs, pictures, personal mementos, and all. Two rooms display gifts that the prime minister received from people the world over. There is a selection of many of his well-known uniforms, including his famous "siren-suits" and hats. Terraced gardens descend toward the lake, where you'll find black swans swimming. Many of Churchill's paintings are displayed in a garden studio. You can see the garden walls that the prime minister built with his own hands and the pond where he sat to feed the Golden Orfe (Golden Carp). A restaurant on the grounds is open 10:30am to 5pm on days when the house is open.

Near the town of Edenbridge. ✆ **01732/868381**. Admission to house, garden, and studio £6.50 ($10) adults, £3.25 ($5) children, £16.25 ($26) family. Late Mar to early Nov Wed–Sun 11am–5pm; July–Aug Tues–Sun 11am–5pm. If driving from London, head east on M25, taking the exit to Westerham. Dr. 3km (2 miles) south of Westerham on B2026 and follow the signs.

Quebec House   This square, redbrick gabled house was the boyhood home of Gen. James Wolfe, who led the victorious English over the French in the battle for Quebec. Wolfe was born in Westerham in 1727 and lived here until he was 11 years old. A National Trust property, Quebec House contains an exhibition about the capture of Quebec and memorabilia associated with the military hero, such as his traveling canteen, complete with a griddle, frying pans, and decanters, evoking the life of an 18th-century officer on a campaign. At the rear of the walled garden are the former stables, dating from Tudor times.

At the junction of Edenbridge and Sevenoaks Rd. (A25 and B2026). ✆ **01959/562206**. Admission £3 ($4.80) adults, £1.50 ($2.40) children. Apr–Oct Sun and Tues 2–6pm.

Squerryes Court   Built in 1681 and owned by the Warde family for 250 years, this still-inhabited manor house has a fine collection of old-master paintings from the Italian, 17th-century Dutch, and 18th-century English schools, along with antiques, porcelain, and tapestries, all acquired or commissioned by the Wardes in the 18th century. There are pictures and relics of General Wolfe's family; he received his commission on the grounds of the house, and a cenotaph marks the spot. The de Squerie family lived in a house on this site from the 13th to the 15th centuries; they restored the formal gardens that dot the banks surrounding the lake with spring bulbs, azaleas, herbaceous borders, and old roses to maintain a year-round beauty.

1km (½ mile) west of the center of Westerham (10 min. from Exit 6 or Exit 5 on M25). (*C*) **01959/562345.** www.squerryes.co.uk. Admission to house and garden £4.80 ($8) adults, £4.10 ($7) seniors and students, £2.60 ($4.15) children under 14. Garden only £3.20 ($5) adults, £2.70 ($4.30) seniors, £1.60 ($2.55) children under 14. Apr 1–Sept 30 Wed and Sat–Sun grounds open noon–5:30pm, house 1:30–5:30pm. Take A25 just west of Westerham and follow the signs.

Down House   This was the final residence of the famous naturalist Charles Darwin. When he moved here in 1842, he wrote, "House ugly, looks neither old nor new." Nevertheless, he lived there "in happy contentment" until his death in 1882. The drawing room, dining room, billiard room, and old study have been restored as they were when Darwin was working on his famous, still controversial book *On the Origin of Species,* first published in 1859. The museum also includes collections and memorabilia from Darwin's voyage on the HMS *Beagle.* The garden retains its original landscaping and a glass house, beyond which lies the Sand Walk or "Thinking Path," where Darwin took his daily solitary walk.

On Luxted Rd., in Downe. (*C*) **01689/859119.** Admission £6.30 ($10) adults, £4.50 ($7) students and seniors, £3 ($4.80) children. Apr–Oct daily 10am–6pm; Nov–Mar Wed–Sun 10am–4pm. Closed Dec 24–26. From Westerham, get on A233 and drive 9km (5½ miles) south of Bromley to the village of Downe. Down House is .5km (¼ mile) southeast of the village. From London's Victoria Station, take a train (available daily) to Bromley South, then go by bus no. 146 (Mon–Sat only) to Downe or to Orpington by bus no. R2.

Knole ★★   Begun in the mid–15th century by Thomas Bourchier, archbishop of Canterbury, and set in a 1,000-acre deer park, Knole is one of the largest private houses in England and one of the finest examples of pure English Tudor-style architecture. Henry VIII liberated the former archbishop's palace from the reluctant Archbishop Cranmer in 1537. Henry spent considerable sums of money on Knole, but he didn't spend much time here; history records one visit in 1541. It served as a royal palace until Elizabeth I granted it to Thomas Sackville, first earl of Dorset, whose descendants have lived here ever since. Virginia Woolf, often a guest of the Sackvilles, used Knole as the setting for her novel *Orlando.* The building was given to the National Trust in 1946.

The house covers 3 hectares (7 acres) and has 365 rooms, 52 staircases, and 7 courts. The elaborate paneling and plasterwork provide a background for the 17th- and 18th-century tapestries and rugs, Elizabethan and Jacobean furniture, and the collection of family portraits.

8km (5 miles) north of Tonbridge, at the Tonbridge end of the town of Sevenoaks. (*C*) **01732/462100.** www.nationaltrust.org.uk. Admission to house £5.60 ($9) adults, £2.75 ($4.40) children, £13.75 ($22) family.

(*Tips*   **The Inside Scoop on Visiting Knole**

If you want to see a bed that's to die for, check out the state bed of James II in the King's Bedroom. And, although most people don't know this, you can take afternoon tea at Knole. From the early 17th century, the tearooms were used as a brewery. Today, you can enjoy a pot of tea with scones, jam, and cream, or devour a gâteau such as carrot-and-walnut sponge topped with a cream cheese–and–lemon juice icing.

Moments Touring Leeds Castle

Once described by Lord Conway as the loveliest castle in the world, **Leeds Castle** ★★★ (© **01622/765400**) dates from A.D. 857. Originally constructed of wood, it was rebuilt in 1119 into its present stone structure on two small islands in the middle of a lake; it was an almost impregnable fortress before the importation of gunpowder. Henry VIII converted it to a royal palace.

The castle has strong links with America through the sixth Lord Fairfax, who while owning the castle also held 2 million hectares (5 million acres) in Virginia and was a close friend and mentor of the young George Washington. The last private owner, the Hon. Lady Baillie, restored the castle with a superb collection of fine art, furniture, and tapestries, then bequeathed it to the Leeds Castle Foundation. The royal apartments, Les Chambres de la Reine (the queen's chambers), located in the Gloriette, are now open to the public. The Gloriette, the oldest part of the castle and the last stronghold against attack, dates from Norman and Plantagenet times, with additions by Henry VIII.

Within the surrounding parkland is a wildwood garden and landscape where rare swans, geese, and ducks abound. Dog lovers will enjoy the **Dog Collar Museum** at the gatehouse, with a unique collection of collars dating from the Middle Ages. A 9-hole **golf course** is open to the public. The **Culpepper Garden** is a delightful English-country flower garden. Beyond are the castle greenhouses, with a **maze** centered on a beautiful underground grotto. The **vineyard,** recorded in the *Domesday Book,* is again producing Leeds Castle English white wine.

Insider's tip: Hurried visitors overlook the Aviary, but it's really special. Opened by Princess Alexandra in 1988, it houses a collection of more than 100 rare species of birds, including parakeets and cockatoos. In addition to conservation, the Aviary aims at successful breeding and reintroduction of endangered species into their original habitats.

Snacks, salads, cream teas, and hot meals are offered daily at several places on the estate, including **Fairfax Hall,** a restored 17th-century tithe barn, and the **Terrace Restaurant,** with a full range of hot and cold meals.

March through October, the grounds are open daily from 10am to 5pm, and the castle daily from 11am to 5:30pm; November through

Admission to gardens £2 ($3.20) adults, £1 ($1.60) children. House open late Mar to early Nov Wed–Sun 11am–4pm; Good Friday and bank holiday Mon 11am–4pm. Gardens open only 1st Wed of the month May–Sept 11am–4pm; last admission at 3pm. Park is open daily to pedestrians and open to cars only when the house is. To reach Knole from Chartwell, drive north to Westerham, pick up A25, and head east for 13km (8 miles). Frequent train service is available from London (about every 30 min.) to Sevenoaks, and then you can take the connecting hourly bus service, a taxi, or walk the remaining 2.5km (1½ miles) to Knole.

Ightham Mote ★   Dating from 1340, Ightham Mote was extensively remodeled in the early 16th century. You'll cross a stone bridge over a moat to its central courtyard. From the Great Hall, known for its magnificent windows, a Jacobean staircase leads to the old chapel on the first floor, where you go through

February, the grounds are open daily from 10am to 3pm, the castle daily from 10:15am to 3:30pm. Closed last Saturday in June and first Saturday in July before open-air concerts. **Admission** to the castle and grounds is £11 ($18) for adults and £7.50 ($12) for children (ages 4–15). Seniors and students pay £9.50 ($15). Car parking is free; a free, fully accessible minibus is available for those who cannot manage the ½-mile walk from the parking area to the castle.

Trains run frequently from London's Victoria Station to Maidstone. Buses run weekdays from London's Victoria Coach Station to Maidstone, 36 miles to the southeast. If you're driving, from London's ring road, continue east along M26 and M20. The castle is 6km (4 miles) east of Maidstone at the junction of the A20 and the M20 London-Folkestone roads.

Kentish Evenings are presented in Fairfax Hall on the first Saturday of the month throughout the year (except Aug). A cocktail reception starts at 7pm, followed by a private guided tour of the castle. Guests feast on a five-course banquet, starting with smoked salmon mousse, followed by broth and roast beef carved at the table, plus seasonal vegetables. A half bottle of wine is included in the overall price of £42 ($63) per person. During the meal, musicians play appropriate music for the surroundings and the occasion. Advance reservations are required, made by calling the castle. Kentish Evenings finish at 12:30am, so it's best to stay overnight nearby rather than drive back late at night.

Accommodations may be found at Grangemoor/Grange Park, 4–8 St. Michael's Rd. (off Tunbridge Rd.), Maidstone, Kent ME16 8B5 (✆ 01622/677623; fax 01622/678246), comprising two buildings across the street from one another, located in a tranquil residential area close to the center of Maidstone. **Grangemoor,** the main accommodation, has 38 well-furnished rooms, each with a private shower-only bathroom, phone, and TV. The cost is £55 ($88) for a double Monday to Thursday; £52 ($78) Friday to Sunday. Rates include English breakfast. Across the street, **Grange Park** has 12 similarly furnished rooms, renting for £52 ($78) a night, including English breakfast. There is also a Tudor-style bar and restaurant, offering a three-course meal for £16.50 ($26). Children are welcome in both the bar and restaurant area.

the solarium, with its oriel window, to the Tudor chapel, with its painted ceiling, timbered outer wall, and ornate chimneys.

Unlike many other ancient houses in England that have housed the same family for centuries, Ightham Mote passed from owner to owner, each family leaving its mark on the place. When the last private owner, an American who made much of the restoration feasible, died, he bequeathed the house to the National Trust, which chose to keep the Robinson Library laid out as it looked in a 1960 issue of *Homes & Gardens*.

✆ **01732/810378.** Admission £6 ($10) adults, £3 ($4.80) children, £15 ($24) family. Sun–Mon and Wed–Fri 10am–5:30pm. Closed Nov–Mar. Drive 9.5km (6 miles) east of Sevenoaks on A25 to the small village of Ivy Hatch; the estate is 4km (2½ miles) south of Ightham; it's also signposted from A227.

Penshurst Place ★★   This stately home is one of England's greatest defended manor houses, standing in a peaceful rural setting little changed over the centuries. In 1338, Sir John de Pulteney, four times lord mayor of London, built the manor house whose Great Hall still forms the heart of Penshurst after more than 600 years. The young Edward VI presented the house to Sir William Sidney, in whose family it has remained. Sir Philip Sidney, the soldier-poet, was born here in 1554. At the beginning of the 17th century, Penshurst was known as a center of literature. Former guest Ben Jonson, the first of many famous visiting poets, praised the architecture of Penshurst and the hospitality of its hosts.

The Long Gallery has a suite of ebony-and-ivory furniture from Goa. Beneath that, the Nether Gallery houses the Sidney family collection of armor. You can also see the splendid state dining room. The Stable Wing has an interesting toy museum, with dolls, toy soldiers, dollhouses, and many other playthings from past generations. The Baron's Hall possesses one of the greatest surviving medieval interiors. On the grounds are nature and farm trails plus an adventure playground for children.

10km (6 miles) west of Tunbridge. ☎ **01892/870307.** Admission to house and grounds £6.50 ($10) adults, £4.50 ($7) children 5–16. Grounds only £5 ($8) adults, £4 ($6) children 5–16. Free for children 4 and under. Apr–Oct daily house noon–5:30pm, grounds 10:30am–6pm; Nov Sat–Sun only house noon–5:30pm, grounds 11am–6pm. Closed Nov–Feb. From M25 Junction follow A21 to Tunbridge, leaving at the Hildenborough exit; then follow the brown tourist signs. The nearest mainline station is Tunbridge.

Hever Castle & Gardens ★   Hever Castle dates from 1270, when the massive gatehouse, the outer walls, and the moat were first constructed. Some 200 years later, the Bullen (or Boleyn) family added a comfortable Tudor dwelling house inside the walls. Anne Boleyn, second wife of Henry VIII and mother of Elizabeth I, grew up here.

In 1903, William Waldorf Astor acquired the estate and invested time, money, and imagination in restoring the castle, building the "Tudor Village," and creating gardens and lakes. The Astor family's contribution to Hever's rich history can be appreciated through its collections of furniture, paintings, and objets d'art, as well as the quality of its workmanship, particularly in the woodcarving and plasterwork. The gardens were created between 1904 and 1908. They have now reached their maturity and are ablaze with color throughout most of the year. The spectacular Italian Garden contains statuary and sculpture, dating from Roman to Renaissance times, acquired by Astor in Italy. The formal gardens include a walled Rose Garden, fine topiary work, and a maze. There's a 14-hectare (35-acre) lake and streams, cascades, and fountains.

5km (3 miles) southeast of Edenbridge, on the road to Hever. ☎ **01732/865224.** Admission to castle and gardens £8.40 ($13) adults, £7.10 ($11) seniors and students, £4.60 ($7) children 5–16, £21.40 ($34) family ticket (2 adults, 2 children). Garden only £6.70 ($11) adults, £5.70 ($9) seniors and students, £4.40 ($7) children 5–16, £17.80 ($28) family ticket. Free for children 4 and under. Gardens daily 11am–6pm; castle daily noon–6pm. Closed Dec–Feb. To get here, follow the signs northwest of Royal Tunbridge Wells; it's 5km (3 miles) southeast of Edenbridge, midway between Sevenoaks and East Grinstead, and 30 min. from Exit 6 of M25.

Sissinghurst Castle Garden ★   These spectacular gardens, situated between surviving parts of an Elizabethan mansion, were created by one of England's most famous and dedicated gardeners, Bloomsbury writer Vita Sackville-West, and her husband, Harold Nicolson. In spring, the garden is resplendent with flowering bulbs and daffodils in the orchard. The white garden reaches its peak in June. The large herb garden, a skillful montage that reflects Sackville-West's profound plant knowledge, has something to show all summer long, and the cottage garden, with its flowering bulbs, is at its finest in the fall. Meals are available in the Granary Restaurant. The garden area is flat, so it's wheelchair accessible; however, only two wheelchairs are allowed at a time.

© **01580/715330.** Admission £6.50 ($10) adults, £2 ($3.20) children, family ticket £16 ($26). Apr–Oct Mon–Tues and Fri 11am–6:30pm, Sat–Sun 10am–6:30pm. The garden is 85km (53 miles) southeast of London and 24km (15 miles) south of Maidstone. It's most often approached from Leeds Castle, which is 6.5km (4 miles) east of Maidstone at the junction of A20 and M20 London–Folkestone roads. From this junction, head south on B2163 and A274 through Headcorn. Follow the signposts to Sissinghurst.

7 Historic Mansions & Gardens in Dorking & Guildford

Dorking, birthplace of Lord Laurence Olivier, lies on the Mole River at the foot of the North Downs. Some of the most scenic spots in the shire are close by, including Silent Pool, Box Hill, and Leith Hill.

The guildhall in Guildford, a country town on the Wey River, has an ornamental projecting clock that dates from 1683. Charles Dickens thought that High Street, which slopes to the river, was one of the most beautiful in England.

ESSENTIALS

GETTING THERE   Frequent daily train service to Dorking takes 35 minutes from London's Victoria Station. The train to Guildford departs London's Waterloo Station and takes 40 minutes. For information, call © **0845/7484950.**

Green Line buses (no. 714) leave from London's Victoria Coach Station daily, heading for Kingston with a stop at Dorking. The trip takes 1 hour. National Express operates buses from London's Victoria Coach Station daily, with a stopover at Guildford on its runs from London to Portsmouth. For schedules, call © **0870/5808080.** It's usually more convenient to take the train.

If you're driving to Dorking, take the A24 south from London. If you're driving to Guildford from London, head south along the A3.

VISITOR INFORMATION   The **Guildford Tourist Information Centre** is at 14 Tunsgate (© **01483/444333**). It's open October through April, Monday through Saturday from 9:30am to 5pm, and May through September, Monday through Saturday from 9am to 5:30pm and Sunday from 10am to 4:30pm.

THE TOP SIGHTS

Loseley House ⭐   This beautiful and historic Elizabethan mansion visited by Elizabeth I, James I, and Mary II has been featured in TV and film. Artworks include paneling from Henry VIII's Nonesuch Palace, period furniture, a carved chalk chimney piece, magnificent ceilings, and cushions made by Elizabeth I. Lunch and tea are served in the Courtyard Restaurant from 11am to 5pm.

Loseley Park (4km/2½ miles southwest of Guildford). © **01483/304440.** Admission £6 ($10) adults, £5 ($8) students and seniors, £3 ($4.80) children. May–Sept Wed–Sun 11am–5pm.

Polesden Lacey   This Regency villa, built in 1824, houses the Greville collection of antiques, paintings, and tapestries. In the early part of this century it was enlarged to become a comfortable Edwardian country house and home to a celebrated hostess, Mrs. Ronald Greville, who frequently entertained royalty from 1906 to 1939. The estate consists of 560 hectares (1,400 acres). Stroll the 18th-century garden, lined with herbaceous borders and featuring a rose garden and beech trees.

A few miles from Great Bookham, off A246 Leatherhead–Guildford Rd. © **01372/452048.** Admission to grounds £4 ($6), £10 ($16) family. Admission to house £7 ($11), £17.50 ($28) family. Grounds daily 11am–6pm. House Mar 22–Oct Wed–Sun and bank holidays 11am–5pm.

Wisley Garden ★★   This is one of the great gardens of England. In every season, this 100-hectare (250-acre) garden has a profusion of flowers and shrubs—the alpine meadow carpeted with wild daffodils in spring, Battleston Hill brilliant with rhododendrons in early summer, the heather garden's colorful foliage in the fall, or a riot of exotic plants in the greenhouses in winter. Recent additions include model gardens and a landscaped orchid house. This garden has a laboratory where botanists, plant pathologists, and entomologists experiment and assist amateur gardeners. A large gift shop stocks a wide range of gardening books.

Wisley (near Ripley, just off M25, Junction 10, on A3 London–Portsmouth Rd.). ✆ **01483/224234.** Admission £6 ($10) adults, £2 ($3.20) children 6–16, free for children under 6. Mon–Fri 10am–dusk; Sat–Sun 9am–dusk.

WHERE TO STAY & EAT
IN DORKING
Lincoln Arms Hotel   The Lincoln Arms is adjacent to the Dorking railway station and receives a lot of after-work business from workers commuting from London's Victoria Station, a 35-minute train ride away. Most of the income is generated at its popular pub, where half the town seems to congregate to drink and munch bar snacks. This trend has become particularly pronounced since its sale to a brewery, Friary Meux (makers of Carlsberg and Tetley beer), in the early 1990s. The brewery considers it a vital part of their chain. The pub has pool tables and offers platters of food ordered at the bar. An American-themed dinner menu includes steaks and sandwiches. Overnight guests will appreciate the large, self-styled "old-worldy" bedrooms upstairs. Equipped with private shower-only bathrooms and well-used furniture, they're tidy, cozy, and comfortable. There is one room available for those with limited mobility.

Station Approach, Dorking, Surrey RH4 1TF. ✆ **01306/882820.** www.lincolnarms-dorking.co.uk. 21 units. £55 ($88) single; £75 ($120) double; £95 ($152) triple. MC, V. **Amenities:** Restaurant; 2 bars; lounge. *In room:* TV, coffeemaker, no phone.

IN GUILDFORD
Atkinsons Guesthouse *Value*   This nonsmoking guesthouse is a 10-minute walk to the town center, opposite a scenic park with tennis courts and swimming. This most reasonable B&B benefits from the warmth of Alex Ridley's welcome and the quality of her rooms, redecorated in 1997. Three good-size rooms have central heating, and private bathrooms contain showers. You can also use ironing facilities. Her breakfasts are plentiful and well prepared.

129 Stoke Rd., Guildford, Surrey GU1 1ET. ✆ **01483/538260.** 4 units, 2 with bathroom. £35 ($56) single without bathroom; £47 ($75) double without bathroom; £50–£60 ($80–$96) double with bathroom. Rates include English breakfast. AE, DC, MC, V. **Amenities:** Breakfast room. *In room:* TV, coffeemaker, hair dryer, no phone.

NEAR GATWICK AIRPORT
The King's Arms Inn   This 14th-century inn stands on an old Roman road, and is one of the region's most reliable pubs and stopovers. The comfortable nonsmoking bedrooms upstairs are well kept and cozy, with private shower-only baths. Much of the business comes from the on-site restaurant, decorated in a country rustic style. Its culinary inspiration comes from its resident chef, who traveled widely before returning to put down roots in Ockley; the result is an unusual combination of English, Malay, Burmese, and Thai.

Stanc St., Ockley, near Guildford, Surrey RH5 5TP. ✆ and fax **01306/711224.** 6 units. £50 ($80) single; £70 ($112) double. Rates include English breakfast. AE, MC, V. **Amenities:** Restaurant; bar. *In room:* TV, dataport, coffeemaker, hair dryer.

Lynwood Guest House   This good B&B lies only 15 minutes from the airport either by car or train, about .5km (¼ mile) from Redhill Railway Station, or a 35-minute train ride from London. The small nonsmoking accommodations are immaculately maintained, all with showers. Breakfast is generous and well prepared. The guesthouse is a 6-minute walk from a park with tennis courts, a large shopping center, and a leisure center with swimming.

50 London Rd., Redhill, Surrey RH1 1LN. ℂ 01737/766894. Fax 01737/778253. www.lynwoodguest house.co.uk. 9 units. £32–£35 ($51–$56) single; £50–£55 ($80–$88) double. Rates include English breakfast. MC, V. **Amenities:** Breakfast room; lounge. *In room:* TV, coffeemaker, hair dryer, no phone.

The Red Lion Pub ✯ ENGLISH   One of the region's most charming pubs lies 5km (3 miles) north of Haslemere. Originally built of sandstone and Sussex stone in the 1690s, it offers outdoor seating during warm weather in front of the pub (with a view of the village green) or in back, amid shrubs and flowers chosen for their scent. The staff and regular clients share in a jovial esprit de corps. Snacks can be ordered across the bar top. More elaborate fare, with table service, is available in a separate area, where you can order pepper chicken in a Dijon-flavored cream sauce, steak-and-kidney pie, Armenian lamb with rice pilaf, game pie, and traditional homemade desserts.

The Green, Fernhurst. ℂ 01428/643112. Main courses £4–£14.95 ($6–$24); pub snacks £3.75–£10 ($6–$16). MC, V. Daily noon–2:30pm and 6:30–9:30pm. Pub Mon–Sat noon–3pm and 5–11pm, Sun noon–3pm and 7–10:30pm.

WHERE TO SHARE A PINT IN GUILDFORD

The **White House,** 8 High St. (ℂ 01483/302006), is another riverside pub, with a conservatory overlooking a lovely waterside garden. Pub grub is available at lunch and dinner; sandwiches are offered all day. They serve traditional London ales aged in barrels.

8 Chichester

50km (31 miles) W of Brighton; 110km (69 miles) SW of London

Chichester might have remained a market town were it not for the Chichester Festival Theatre. One of the oldest Roman cities in England, Chichester draws a crowd from all over the world for its theater presentations. Other than the theater, there's not much else to see. But the town does make a good base for exploring a history-rich part of southern England.

Finds Bosham: A Hidden Discovery

In addition to the sights listed in this chapter, you might want to stop in nearby Bosham, a sailing resort and one of the most charming villages in West Sussex. It's 6.5km (4 miles) west of Chichester on A259, and there's good bus service between the two towns. Bosham was where Christianity was first established on the Sussex coast. The Danish King Canute made it a seat of his North Sea empire; it was the location of a manor (now gone) of the last Saxon king, Harold, who sailed from here to France on a journey that led to the Norman invasion in 1066. Bosham's little church, which stands near the harbor and is reached by a narrow lane, is even depicted in the Bayeux Tapestry. The graveyard overlooks the boats, and the church is filled with ship models and relics.

ESSENTIALS

GETTING THERE   Trains depart for Chichester from London's Victoria Station once every hour during the day. The trip takes 1½ hours. However, if you visit Chichester to attend the theater, plan to stay over—the last train back to London is at 9pm. For rail information, call ℂ **0845/7484950.**

Buses leave from London's Victoria Coach Station once a day. For schedules call ℂ **08705/808080.**

If you're driving from London's ring road, head south on A3, turning onto A286 for Chichester.

VISITOR INFORMATION   The **Tourist Information Centre,** 29A South St. (ℂ **01243/775888**), is open Monday through Saturday 9:15am to 5:15pm, April through September Sunday 10am to 4pm.

THE CHICHESTER FESTIVAL THEATRE

Only a 5-minute walk from Chichester Cathedral and the old Market Cross, the 1,400-seat theater, with its apron stage, stands on the edge of Oaklands Park. It opened in 1962 under its first director, Lord Laurence Olivier. Its reputation has grown steadily, pumping new vigor and life into the former walled city, appeasing many irate locals who felt the city's money would have been better spent on a swimming pool.

The **Chichester Festival Theatre** ✮, built in the 1960s, offers plays and musicals during the summer season, from May to September; in the winter and spring months, it offers orchestras, jazz, opera, theater, ballet, and a Christmas "panto" for the entire family. **The Minerva,** built in the late 1980s, is a multifunctional cultural center with a theater plus dining and drinking facilities. The Minerva Studio Theatre and the Chichester Festival Theatre are managed by the same board of governors, but present different programs and plays.

Theater reservations made over the telephone will be held for a maximum of 4 days (call ℂ **01243/781312**). It's better to mail inquiries and checks to the Box Office, Chichester Festival Theatre, Oaklands Park, Chichester, West Sussex P019 6AP. MasterCard, Visa, and American Express are accepted. Season ticket prices range from £9 to £32 ($14–$51).

Roman Palace   This is what remains of the largest Roman residence yet discovered in Britain. Built around A.D. 75 in villa style, it has many mosaic-floored rooms and even an under-floor heating system. The gardens have been restored to their original 1st-century plan. You can see what an archaeological dig from July 1996 unearthed. The story of the site is told in an audiovisual program or by text in the museum. Guided tours are offered twice a day.

North of A259, off Salthill Rd. (signposted from Fishbourne; 2.5km/1½ miles from Chichester). ℂ **01243/ 785859.** Admission £5 ($8) adults, £2.50 ($4) children, £12.50 ($20) family ticket. Mar–Oct daily 10am–5pm (6pm in Aug); late Feb and Nov to mid-Dec daily 10am–4pm; mid-Dec to mid-Feb Sat–Sun 10am–4pm. Buses stop regularly at the bottom of Salthill Rd.; located within a 5-min. walk of British Rail's Fishbourne station.

Weald & the Downland Open Air Museum   In the beautiful Sussex countryside, historic buildings have been reconstructed on a 16-hectare (40-acre) downland site. The structures show the development of traditional building from medieval times to the 19th century, in the weald and downland area of southeast England.

Reconstructions include a Tudor market hall, a medieval farmstead and other houses from the 14th to the 17th centuries, a working water mill producing stone-ground flour, a blacksmith's forge, plumbers' and carpenters' workshops, a

> **Tips   Staying in a Private Home**
>
> Because Chichester draws a fashionable crowd from London and else-
> where to attend theater, its inns are pricey. So, for cheap digs, we suggest
> booking into one of the little private B&Bs. These are really family homes
> where rooms are now rented because the children are gone. The best of
> them are listed below.

toll cottage, a 17th-century tread wheel, agricultural buildings including thatched
barns and an 18th-century granary, a charcoal burner's camp, and a 19th-century
village school. A "new" reception area with shops and offices is set in Longport
House, a 16th-century building rescued from the site of the Chunnel.

At Singleton, 6 miles north of Chichester on A286 (the London Rd.). ✆ **01243/811348.** Admission £7 ($11)
adults, £4 ($6) children, £19 ($30) family ticket. Mar–Oct daily 10:30am–6pm; Nov–Feb Wed and Sat–Sun
10:30am–4pm. Bus: 60 from Chichester.

WHERE TO STAY

The Bedford Hotel ✦   This is one of the best all-around moderately priced
accommodations in Chichester; the 18th-century building is located in the town
center. The comfortable and quiet rooms contain neatly kept bathrooms
equipped with showers. In summer, advance reservations are strongly advised
(see also "Where to Dine," below).

Southgate, Chichester, West Sussex PO19 1DP. ✆ **01243/785766.** Fax 01243/533175. 20 units. £65 ($104)
single; £90 ($144) double. Rates include English breakfast. AE, DC, MC, V. **Amenities:** Restaurant; lounge;
room service; massage. In room: TV, coffeemaker, hair dryer.

Hatpins ✦✦ *Finds*   The owner of this B&B was once a wedding dress designer
and milliner. Tucked away at the northern end of the creeks of Chichester Harbour, Hatpins lies in the charming old village of Old Bosham, 5km (3 miles)
west of the center of Chichester. A charming home run by Mrs. Mary Waller, it
offers an inviting, cozy interior filled with antiques, including half-tester or Victorian brass beds. The spacious comfortable bedrooms are beautifully furnished
with well-selected draperies and decorations along with old-fashioned bathrooms with claw-foot tubs.

Bosham Lane, Old Bosham, Chichester PO18 8HG. ✆ and fax **01243/572644.** www.hatpins.co.uk. 6 units.
£50–£70 ($80–$112) single; £80–£100 ($128–$160) double; £120 ($192) suite. No credit cards. Rates include
breakfast. **Amenities:** Breakfast room. In room: TV, coffeemaker, hair dryer, no phone.

Litten House ✦ *Value*   In the city center this 18th-century Georgian house
offers a warm welcome and a cozy atmosphere. The domain of Mrs. Victoria
Steward, it is set behind a landscaped area, convenient to all the attractions. The
rooms are very spacious, and two bunk beds can be added for a family room if
needed. Try for one of the bedchambers overlooking the well-tended garden.
Each room is furnished with hot and cold running water, and the shared facilities in the hallway are more than adequate and well kept. Breakfast features the
likes of homemade jams and freshly made breads; it can be served in the garden
if weather permits.

148 St. Pancras, Chichester, West Sussex PO19 1SH. ✆ **01243/774503.** Fax 01243/539187. www.smooth
hound.co.uk/hotels/littenho.html. 3 units. £27–£30 ($43–$48) single; £44–£50 ($70–$80) double; £64–£70
($102–$112) family. Rates include English breakfast. AE, MC, V. **Amenities:** Garden; conservatory. In room:
TV, coffeemaker, hair dryer (on request), iron.

WHERE TO DINE

The Bedford Hotel Restaurant ENGLISH   One of the best places for a formal dinner is this long-established private hotel dating back to the 1700s. The food is well prepared, the ingredients fresh, and the service relaxed but efficient. Start with mussels in a white-wine, onion, and cream sauce, or Highland smokies (smoked haddock) served with a whiskey cream sauce. Then proceed with sirloin steak with a Drambuie sauce or trout Véronique with a white-wine and grape sauce. Vegetarian dishes are also available. Top your meal off with one of the freshly made desserts of the day. See "Where to Stay," above, for hotel review.

Southgate. ℂ **01243/785766.** Reservations recommended. Main courses £8–£12 ($13–$19); fixed-price Sun menu £17.50 ($28). AE, DC, MC, V. Daily 7–8:30pm.

Shepherd's Tea Rooms TEA/PASTRIES   Located in a white building with blue trim in the center of town, the tearoom is casual, with a mix of locals and tourists. The interior is simple but nice, with fine china on lace-covered tables. You'll find croissants, scones, and a variety of cakes, plus chocolate éclairs and meringues. Earl Grey, Darjeeling, English Breakfast, and other teas are served.

35 Little London. ℂ **01243/774761.** Afternoon tea £6 ($10); cakes, scones, and pastries 50p–£1.95 ($.80–$3.10). MC, V. Mon–Fri 9:15am–5pm; Sat 9am–5pm; Sun 10am–4pm.

9 Arundel: One of England's Great Castles

34km (21 miles) W of Brighton; 93km (58 miles) SW of London

The small town of Arundel in West Sussex nestles at the foot of one of England's most spectacular castles. Without the castle, it would be just another English market town. The town was once an Arun River port, and its residents enjoyed the prosperity of considerable trade and commerce. However, today the harbor traffic has been replaced with tourist buses.

ESSENTIALS

GETTING THERE   Trains leave hourly during the day from London's Victoria Station. The trip takes 1¼ hours. For rail information, call ℂ **0845/7484950.**

Most bus connections are through Littlehampton, opening onto the English Channel west of Brighton. From Littlehampton, you can leave the coastal road by taking bus no. 11, which runs between Littlehampton and Arundel hourly during the day. If you're dependent on public transportation, the tourist office (see below) keeps an update on the possibilities.

If you're driving from London, follow the signs to Gatwick Airport. From there, head south toward the coast along A29.

VISITOR INFORMATION   The **Tourist Information Centre,** 61 High St. (ℂ **01903/882268**), is open from April to October, Monday through Friday from 9am to 5pm and on weekends from 10am to 5pm; off season Monday through Friday from 10am to 2:30pm and on weekends from 10am to 2:30pm.

SEEING THE SIGHTS

Arundel Castle 🤍🤍   The ancestral home of the dukes of Norfolk, Arundel Castle is a much-restored mansion of considerable importance. Its history is associated with two of the great families of England—the Fitzalans and the powerful Howards. This castle received worldwide exposure when it was chosen to "play" Windsor Castle in the film *The Madness of King George,* in which Nigel Hawthorne, as George III, ran around the Arundel courtyard in a mad frenzy, chased by Helen Mirren.

Arundel Castle has suffered destruction over the years, particularly during the Civil War, when Cromwell's troops stormed its walls, perhaps in retaliation for the sizable contribution Thomas Howard, the 14th earl of Arundel, made to Charles I. In the early 18th century, the castle was virtually rebuilt; in late Victorian times, it was remodeled and extensively restored again. Today, it's filled with a valuable collection of antiques, along with paintings by old masters such as Van Dyck and Gainsborough. Surrounding the castle, in the center off High Street, is a 440-hectare (1,100-acre) park whose scenic highlight is Swanbourne Lake.

On Mill Rd. ℂ **01903/883136.** www.arundelcastle.org. Admission £9 ($14) adults, £7 ($11) seniors, £5.50 ($9) children 5–16, free for children 4 and under, £24.50 ($39) family ticket. Apr–Oct Sun–Fri noon–5pm. Closed Nov–Mar.

Arundel Cathedral   A Roman Catholic cathedral, the Cathedral of Our Lady and St. Philip Howard stands at the highest point in town. It was constructed for the 15th duke of Norfolk by A. J. Hansom (who invented the Hansom cab), but not consecrated as a cathedral until 1965. The interior includes the shrine of St. Philip Howard, featuring Sussex wrought-iron work. On the street level, adjacent to the tourist information office, is the Heritage of Arundel Museum. It displays postcards, memorabilia, antique costumes, and historic documents relating to the history of Arundel and its famous castle.

London Rd. ℂ **01903/882297.** www.arundelcathedral.org. Free admission, but donations appreciated. Daily 9:30am–dusk. From the town center, continue west from High St.

WHERE TO STAY

Arden Guest House   Jeff and Carol Short run this pleasant and uncomplicated bed-and-breakfast hotel consisting of two connected houses a short walk from Arundel Castle. Fronted with dark-colored flint and painted stone, the older of the two houses was originally built in 1804. Each of the comfortable but simple accommodations has hot-and-cold running water and hot-beverage facilities. Rooms with bathrooms have neatly kept accommodations containing showers.

4 Queens Lane, Arundel, West Sussex BN18 9JN. ℂ **01903/882544.** 8 units, 3 with shower only. £44 ($70) single or double without bathroom; £48 ($77) single or double with bathroom. Rates include English breakfast. No credit cards. **Amenities:** Breakfast room; lounge. *In room:* TV, coffeemaker, no phone.

Arundel House   Leslie Wigman is the resident owner of this 16th-century guesthouse and licensed restaurant, a 6-minute walk from the rail station and only seconds away from the castle entrance. It offers snug, comfortable rooms with private shower-only bathrooms. The house is open for morning coffee, hot meals, afternoon teas, and Sussex cream teas.

11 High St., Arundel, West Sussex BN18 9AD. ℂ **01903/882136.** 6 units. £30 ($48) single; £50 ($80) double. Rates include English breakfast. MC, V. Bus: 212. **Amenities:** Restaurant; lounge. *In room:* TV, no phone.

Portreeves Acre   This modern two-story house built by a local architect lies within a stone's throw of the ancient castle and rail station. Today, the glass-and-brick building is the property of Charles and Pat Rogers. The good-size double guest rooms are on the ground floor and have views of the flowering acre in back. All rooms are well organized and include a small bath with a shower stall. The River Arun borders the property on one side.

2 Causeway, Arundel, West Sussex BN18 9JJ. ℂ **01903/883277.** 3 units. £50 ($80) single or double. Rates include English breakfast. No credit cards. Bus: 212. **Amenities:** Breakfast room. *In room:* TV, coffeemaker, no phone.

St. Mary's Gate Inn   At the foot of Arundel's famous castle, this unpretentious two-story building derives most of its income from the busy pub (see also "Where to Dine," below) that fills its street level. Indeed, its management refuses to call itself a hotel at all, stressing its purveying of food and drink since 1520. The small bedrooms upstairs are simple, much renovated, and decent, with modest furnishings and a kind of cozy charm. All units come with neatly kept small bathrooms containing showers and tubs. To check in, you register at the bar—certainly a convenience if you've had a few pints.

London Rd., Arundel, West Sussex BN18 7BA. ℭ **01903/883145.** Fax 01903/882256. www.stmarysgate.co. uk. 10 units. £55 ($88) double. Rates include English breakfast. AE, DC, MC, V. **Amenities:** Restaurant; bar; room service (7am–10pm); laundry. *In room:* TV, coffeemaker, hair dryer, iron/board.

The Swan Hotel   You'll recognize the building on the town's main street by its white-stucco facade and the flowering plants that hang, garden style, from its window boxes. Already well established as a pub with simple bedrooms, this hotel received a boost in business after it was radically renovated and upgraded in 1994. The owners took a Georgian inn, originally built in 1839, and injected it with new life. The rooms are decorated in the style of an English country cottage, and are cozy and comfortable, with private shower-only baths. On the hotel's ground floor next to the pub, there's a restaurant illuminated with a pair of skylights and filled with potted plants.

High St., Arundel, West Sussex BN18 9AG. ℭ **01903/882314.** Fax 01903/883759. www.swan-hotel.co.uk. 15 units. £60 ($96) single; £65 ($104) double. Rates include English breakfast. AE, MC, V. Bus: 212. **Amenities:** Restaurant; bar; lounge; room service (7am–10pm). *In room:* TV, coffeemaker, hair dryer.

The Town House ✦   The best of the town's small hotels stands across a busy street from the crenellated fortifications surrounding the castle. Mac McElwee is the guiding light behind this little gem, which has elegantly decorated rooms with modern baths equipped with showers. A few rooms retain their original Regency detailing and ornate plasterwork (see also "Where to Dine," below).

High St., Arundel, West Sussex BN18 9AJ. ℭ **01903/883847.** info@thetownhouse.co.uk. 5 units. £40 ($64) single; £80 ($128) double. Rates include English breakfast. MC, V. Bus: 212. **Amenities:** Restaurant; bar. *In room:* TV, coffeemaker, hair dryer, no phone.

WHERE TO DINE
IN TOWN

Butler's Wine Bar and Restaurant INTERNATIONAL   Located near the castle, the building that houses this establishment goes back to the 18th century. It was converted from a chemist's shop (pharmacy) in the 1960s, and it offers hearty fare at reasonable prices, featuring fresh meats, fish, pastas, and a few other Italian specialties.

25 Tarrant St. ℭ **01903/882222.** Reservations recommended. Main courses £2.95–£9.95 ($4.70–$16) lunch, £9.95–£16.95 ($16–$27) dinner. AE, DC, MC, V. Mon–Sat 11am–3pm and 7–11pm.

The Country Life VEGETARIAN/ENGLISH   Housed in an 18th-century candle factory, the building itself dates to 1609, although no one seems to know what its initial function was. Today, however, it's known as a place to get a good, creative, reasonably priced meal. There are several vegetarian choices daily, but carnivores can opt for shepherd's pie.

1 Tarrant Sq. ℭ **01903/883456.** Main courses £4–£6 ($6–$10). No credit cards. Fri–Wed 10:30am–5pm.

St. Mary's Gate Inn ENGLISH   Recommended for its overnight accommodations (see above), this is a stone-fronted two-story building. It was built in the

1520s as an inn. Place your food order at the counter top; someone then carries the plates to a seat in one of four small drinking and dining areas, some of which are paneled. Food items range from simple pub-style snacks (salads, bowls of chili, and sandwiches) to more substantial fare such as pastas, fish dishes, and steaks. There's usually a vegetarian dish of the day. An outdoor patio in back provides additional seating during clement weather.

London Rd. (℃) **01903/883145.** Main courses £6.25–£15.50 ($10–$25). AE, MC, V. Daily noon–2:30pm and 6–9:30pm. Pub daily 10am–11:30pm.

Town House Hotel Restaurant ENGLISH   Recommended as a hotel (see above), this is also one of the town's leading restaurant choices. The owners invite guests into their elegant dining room, located on the street level. The restaurant is noted for its 17th-century gilt-carved walnut ceiling, originally from a baroque Italian palace; part of this ceiling was once installed in the home of Douglas Fairbanks Jr. Typical dishes include English trout with almonds and fresh sole; though familiar, the fare is quite good.

65 High St. (℃) **01903/883847.** Reservations required. Main courses £6–£12 ($10–$19). MC, V. Daily 10am–5:30pm.

ON THE OUTSKIRTS

George & Dragon ★ *Finds* BRITISH   About 5km (3 miles) north of Arundel, the most visible building in the agrarian hamlet of Houghton is one of the neighborhood's most popular pubs. Its most prestigious client was Charles II, who stopped for food and drink after his coronation at Scone, in Scotland, with the enemy troops of Cromwell in hot pursuit. (Charles escaped to sanctuary in France, returning in triumph to London in 1660 after the death of Cromwell.) Originally a farmhouse, the George & Dragon is built around a 13th-century core containing two timber-and-flint cottages. The inglenook fireplaces were designed for spit-roasting the huge joints that formed the centerpiece of many an English meal. In winter, fires blaze; in summer, diners and drinkers migrate to a garden and terrace in back. Menu items include fresh fish, homemade soups, pâtés, English cheese, and such traditional dishes as a roast half duckling in a client's choice of orange, apple, port, or gooseberry sauce.

Houghton. (℃) **01798/831559.** Main courses £6.95–£12.95 ($11–$21). MC, V. Mon–Fri noon–3pm and 6–11pm; Sat–Sun 11am–11pm. Bus: 31. From Arundel, turn off A284 at Bury Hill onto B2139.

10 Brighton: London by the Sea ★★

83km (52 miles) S of London

Brighton was one of the first of the great seaside resorts of Europe. The Prince of Wales (the future George IV), the original swinger who was to shape so much of Brighton's destiny, arrived in 1783; his presence and patronage gave immediate status to the seaside town. Fashionable dandies from London, including Beau Brummell, turned up. The construction business boomed as Brighton blossomed with charming and attractive town houses and well-planned squares and crescents. From the prince regent's title came the voguish word Regency, which came to characterize an era, especially between 1811 and 1820. Under Victoria, and despite her avoidance of the place, Brighton continued to flourish.

But early in the 20th century, as the English began to discover more glamorous spots on the Continent, Brighton lost much of its old joie de vivre. People considered it "tatty," and it began to feature the usual run of fun-fair-type English seaside amusements. However, that state of affairs changed some time ago, thanks to the huge numbers of Londoners who moved in and became commuters. The invasion has made Brighton increasingly lighthearted and sophisticated; it now attracts a fair number of gay vacationers, and a beach east of town has been set aside for nude bathers (Britain's first such venture).

ESSENTIALS

GETTING THERE   Fast trains (41 a day) leave from Victoria or London Bridge Station and make the trip from London in 55 minutes. For rail information, call ✆ **0845/7484950.**

Buses from London's Victoria Coach Station take around 2 hours.

If you're driving, M23 (signposted from central London) leads to A23, which takes you into Brighton.

VISITOR INFORMATION   At the **Tourist Information Centre,** 10 Bartholomew Sq. (✆ **0906/7112255;** www.tourism.brighton.co.uk), opposite the town hall, you can make hotel reservations, reserve tickets for National Express coaches, and pick up a list of current events. It's open Monday through Friday 9am to 5pm and Saturday 10am to 4pm; March through October Sunday 10am to 4pm.

GETTING AROUND   The **Brighton Borough Transport** serves both Brighton and Hove with frequent and efficient service. Local fares are only £1 ($1.60). Free maps giving the company's routes are available at the Tourist Information Centre (see above). You can also call the company directly at ✆ **01273/ 886200.**

SPECIAL EVENTS   If you're here in May, the international **Brighton Festival,** the largest arts festival in England, features drama, literature, visual art, dance, and concerts ranging from classical to rock. A festival program is available annually in February for those who want to plan ahead.

THE ROYAL PAVILION

The Royal Pavilion at Brighton ★★★   Among the royal residences of Europe, the Royal Pavilion at Brighton, a John Nash version of an Indian Mogul's palace, is unique. Ornate and exotic, it has been subjected over the years to the most devastating wit of English satirists and pundits, but today we can examine it more objectively as one of the most outstanding examples of the Orientalist elements of the English Romantic Movement.

A neoclassical villa had been built on the site in 1787 by Henry Holland, replacing a farmhouse; but it no more resembled its present appearance than a caterpillar does a butterfly. By the time Nash had transformed it from simple villa into oriental fantasy, the prince regent had become King George IV, who, with one of his mistresses, Lady Conyngham, lived in the palace until 1827.

A decade passed before Victoria, a newly crowned queen, arrived in Brighton. Although she brought Albert and the children on occasion, the monarch and Brighton just didn't mix; the very air of the resort seemed too flippant for her. By 1845, Victoria began packing, and the royal furniture was carted off. Its royal owners gone, the Pavilion was in danger of being torn down, but by a narrow vote Brightonians agreed to purchase it. Gradually, it was restored to its former splendor, enhanced in no small part by the return of much of its original furniture, including many items loaned by the queen.

Of exceptional interest is the domed Banqueting Room, with a chandelier of bronze dragons supporting lily-like glass globes. The Great Kitchen, with its old

Brighton

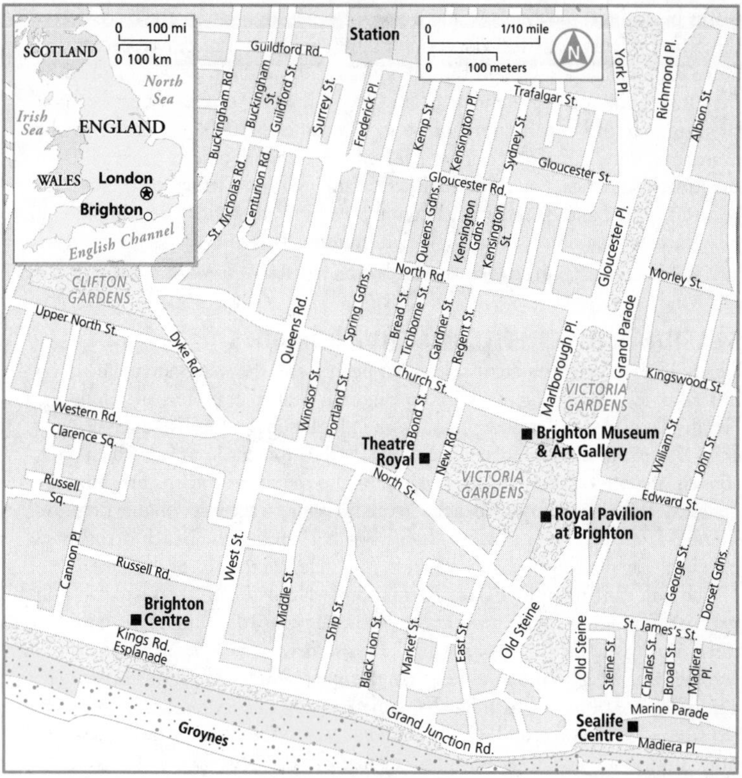

revolving spits, keeps a collection of Wellington's pots and pans from his London town house at Hyde Park Corner. In the State Apartments, particularly the domed salon, dragons wink at you, serpents entwine, lacquered doors shine. The Music Room, with its scalloped ceiling, is a fantasy of water lilies, flying dragons, reptilian paintings, bamboo, silk, and satin.

In the first-floor gallery, look for Nash's views of the Pavilion in its elegant heyday. Other beautifully restored attractions include Queen Victoria's Apartments and the South Galleries, once breakfast rooms for George IV's guests. Refreshments are available in the Queen Adelaide Tea Room, with a balcony overlooking the Royal Pavilion Gardens. A new exhibit explores the gardens.

© **01273/290900.** www.royalpavilion.org.uk. Admission £5.80 ($9) adults, £4 ($6) seniors and students, £3.40 ($5) children 5–15, free for children 5 and under, £15 ($24) family ticket. Apr–Sept daily 9:30am–5:45pm; Oct–Mar daily 10am–5:15pm. Closed Dec 25–26.

Brighton Museum & Art Gallery ★ After a £10 million pound redevelopment, one of the great cultural attractions in the southeast of England has opened. In Victorian buildings opposite the Royal Pavilion, the museum is devoted to an eclectic collection of world art and artifacts, ranging from Salvador Dalí's "Mae West's Lips Sofa" to costumes worn at King George IV's coronation in 1821. Employing all the latest museum interpretative techniques, the museum is one of the most user-friendly outside London. The central gallery displays 20th-century decorative art, including furniture by Philippe Starck, works by Lalique and Bugatti, and a host of other luminaries. You'll see everything from Henry Willett's collection of 2,000 pieces of innovative porcelain to Shiro Kuramata's "How High the Moon Chair" from 1986 (it was inspired by the Duke Ellington jazz standard). The "Fashion & Style" Gallery draws upon Brighton's extensive collections of period costumes over the centuries. In the museum's World Art Collection, you'll find some 15,000 objects collected from the Americas, Africa, Asia, and the Pacific, ranging from Vietnamese water puppets to a black basalt George Washington bust by Wedgwood. The ethnological case features such objects as an Egyptian mummy case.

Royal Pavilion Gardens. ℭ 01273/290900. Free admission. Tues 10am–7pm; Wed–Sat 10am–5pm; Sun 2–5pm.

SEASIDE AMUSEMENTS & ACTIVE PURSUITS

The beaches at Brighton aren't sandy, but pebbly, and the waters are polluted. So instead of swimming, most visitors to Brighton sunbathe, promenade along the boardwalk, play video arcade games, drink in local pubs and "caffs," and generally enjoy the sea air. Beachfront areas are more for the promenade crowd, which often consists of gay men and lesbians. Brighton is also the site of Britain's first officially designed **clothing-optional beach,** located a short walk west of the Brighton Marina. Local signs refer to it as "Nudist Beach." **Telescombe Beach,** frequented mostly by gay men and lesbians, lies 7km (4½ miles) to the east of the Palace Pier.

And you can't miss the **Palace Pier,** a somewhat battered late-Victorian iron structure jutting seaward toward France. Built between 1889 and 1899 and renovated during the early 1990s, it's lined with somewhat tacky concessions and a late-night crowd a bit more sinister than the one that frequents it during the day. The older West Pier is a rusting, abandoned hulk, a solitary reminder of forgotten steam-age pleasures and seafront holidays, with a beach in front that's sometimes used as a rendezvous point for gay men.

One of the best and most challenging 18-hole golf courses around is the **East Brighton Golf Club,** Roedean Road (ℭ 01273/604838). A less challenging 18-hole course is the **Hollingbury Park Golf Club,** Ditching Road (ℭ 01273/552010). Buses from the Old Steine are available to both courses.

An indoor pool, diving pool, learner's pool, solarium, and water slide are available daily at the **Prince Regent Swimming Complex,** Church Street (ℭ 01273/685692).

If you enjoy wagering on the horses, visit the **Brighton Races,** held frequently between April and October at the Brighton Racecourse, Race Hill (ℭ 01273/603580). An admission fee is charged.

SHOPPING

Mall rats head for Churchill Square, Brighton's spacious shopping center, with major chain stores such as Habitat. The shopping center runs from Western Road to North Street (about 3km/2 miles long) and offers many inexpensive shops and stalls with great buys on everything from antiques to woolens. On Saturdays, there are many more antique exhibits and sidewalk stalls. Regent Arcade, located between East Street, Bartholomew Square, and Market Street, sells artwork, jewelry, and other gift items, as well as high-fashion clothing. Everyone raves about the shopping on The Lanes, although some may find it too quaint. The Lanes is a closely knit section of alleyways off North Street in Brighton's Old Town; many of the present shops were once fishers' cottages. The shopping is mostly for tourists, and, while you may fall for a few photo ops, you'll find that the nearby North Lains—between The Lanes and the train station—is the area for up-and-coming talent and alternative retail. Just wander along a street called Kensington Gardens to get the whole effect. There are innumerable shops in The Lanes with antique books and jewelry; many boutiques are found in converted backyards on Duke Lane just off Ship Street. In the center of The Lanes is Brighton Square, ideal for relaxing or for people-watching near the fountain on one of the benches or from a cafe-bar.

On Sunday, Brighton has a good flea market in the parking lot of the train station. On the first Tuesday of each month, there's the **Brighton Racecourse Antiques and Collectors Fair** (9am–3pm) with about 300 stalls.

While browsing around the Brighton Marina, bargain hunters can find brand-name goods at discount prices at **Merchants Quay Factory Outlet Shopping** (𝄢 01273/693636), with everything from pottery to books to designer clothes to perfumes. There are many stores to visit at the Brighton Marina. One is **Leave It to Jeeves** (𝄢 01273/818585), which sells old photographs of the local area, illustrations, prints, and a complete framing service.

In addition to malls and shopping complexes, Brighton abounds in specialty shops. These caught our eye: **Bears and Friends of Brighton,** 41 Meeting House Lane (𝄢 01273/208940), attracts teddy-bear buffs; **Culpepper,** 12D Meeting House Lane (𝄢 01273/327939), is the place for bath salts, fine English soap, herbal medicines, herbs, natural plant oils, potpourri, and spices; **Le Jazz Hot,** 14 Prince Albert St. (𝄢 01273/206091), offers a fine selection of Art Deco and Art Nouveau ceramics, plus collections of Bakelite jewelry, deco chrome, and period furniture. **Pecksniff's Bespoke Perfumery,** 45–46 Meeting House Lane (𝄢 01273/723292), will create a fragrance just for you. They hand-blend flowers, herbs, and natural oils to make traditional English scents, and will keep your formula on file for when you need a refill. **The Pavilion Shop,** The Royal Pavilion, East Street, Brighton (𝄢 01273/292798), is the finest gift shop in Brighton. Here you can purchase many gift and home-furnishing items in the style of the design schools that created the look (from Regency to Victorian) at The Royal Pavilion. Also available are books, jams, needlepoint kits, notebooks, pencils, stencil kits, and other souvenirs.

WHERE TO STAY

The Adelaide Hotel   This small hostelry is in the center of Brighton, just behind the West Pier. It occupies a restored Regency building that has been modernized and decorated without losing its early-19th-century ambience. The small- to midsize units have neatly kept shower-only bathrooms. The higher prices quoted below are for rooms with a four-poster bed.

51 Regency Sq., Brighton, East Sussex BN1 2FF. 𝄢 01273/205286. Fax 01273/220904. 12 units. £39–£45 ($62–$72) single; £68–£95 ($109–$152) double. Rates include English breakfast. AE, MC. V. Bus: 6. **Amenities:** Breakfast room; bar; lounge; laundry. *In room:* TV, coffeemaker, hair dryer.

Alvia Hotel   This Victorian structure (renovated in 1994) offers a bit of old-world charm. The midsize rooms are decorated in an English country-house motif; two have four-poster beds. Each small tiled bathroom comes with a shower. The only meal offered here is breakfast, but there are plenty of dining establishments nearby.

36 Upper Rock Gardens, Brighton, East Sussex BN2 1QF. 𝄢 01273/682939. www.alviahotel.co.uk. 10 units, 8 with bathroom (tub or shower). £15–£25 ($24–$40) single without bathroom; £35–£60 ($56–$96) single with bathroom; £40–£60 ($64–$96) double without bathroom, £60–£120 ($96–$192) double with bathroom. Rates include English breakfast. MC, V. **Amenities:** Breakfast room; lounge. *In room:* TV, coffeemaker, hair dryer, no phone.

Ambassador Hotel A family-run hotel on a waterfront square, the recently expanded Ambassador overlooks the Palace Pier. Many guest rooms were renovated in 1996 and 1997. The rooms are comfortably furnished and have neatly maintained private bathrooms with showers. The front bedrooms have a sea view, and there's also an attractive residents' lounge.

22–23 New Steine, Marine Parade, Brighton, East Sussex BN2 1PD. © **01273/676869.** Fax 01273/689988. www.ambassadorhotelbrighton.com. 24 units. £28–£38 ($45–$61) single; £68–£80 ($109–$128) double. Children 11 and under share a room with 2 adults for half price. Rates include English breakfast. AE, DC, MC, V. Bus: 27. **Amenities:** Breakfast room; bar; lounge. *In room:* TV, coffeemaker, hair dryer.

Ascott House Hotel Michael and Avril Strong's establishment is just a short walk from the Royal Pavilion and near the pier and the famous Lanes with its shops and boutiques. This popular licensed hotel has a reputation for comfort, cleanliness, and good breakfasts. The neatly kept, comfortable rooms have individually furnished accommodations; most provide full private bathrooms with showers. The front bedrooms have a sea view.

21 New Steine, Marine Parade, Brighton, East Sussex BN2 1PD. © **01273/688085.** Fax 01273/623733. www.ascotthousehotel.com. 15 units. £30–£40 ($48–$64) single; £65–£120 ($104–$192) double. Rates include English breakfast. MC, V. Bus: 27. **Amenities:** Breakfast room; bar; lounge. *In room:* TV, hair dryer.

Brighton Marina House Hotel ★ One of the best accommodations in its price range at Brighton, this white, Regency-style town house sits about a block from the sea near an interesting collection of antiques shops. Many accommodations have high ceilings and elaborate plasterwork. The rooms that are mid-size come with small bathrooms fitted with showers. Visitors have use of the elegant front parlor, and evening meals are available upon request.

8 Charlotte St., Marine Parade, Brighton, East Sussex BN2 1AG. © or fax **01273/605349.** www.brighton-mh-hotel.co.uk. 10 units, 7 with shower. £19–£45 ($30–$72) single without bathroom; £39–£79 ($62–$126) double with bathroom. Rates include English breakfast. AE, DC, MC, V. Bus: 7 or 27. **Amenities:** Breakfast room; lounge. *In room:* TV, coffeemaker, hair dryer,.

Cowards Guest House Built in 1807, this five-story Regency-era house sits, like many of its neighbors, behind a cream-colored stucco facade; inside, it has been extremely well preserved in nearly mint condition. The charming owners, Gerry Breen and his partner Cyril Coward (a cousin of the late playwright and bon vivant, Noël Coward), maintain an all-male enclave that appeals to gay men. It is located near a wide roster of gay bars.

The bedrooms resemble standard rooms in modern British hotels, all equipped with private shower facilities.

12 Upper Rock Gardens, Brighton BN2 1QE. © **01273/692677.** www.surf.to/cowards. 6 units. £30 ($48) single; £60–£70 ($96–$112) double. Rates include breakfast. MC, V. **Amenities:** Breakfast room. *In room:* TV, coffeemaker, fans, fridge, no phone.

Dudley House A few steps from the sea stands a cream-colored Victorian town house. This hotel was upgraded from a run-down boarding house when the former owners tore down some walls and cut the number of rooms by half in 1987, making the remaining rooms that much larger. The result is a spick-and-span, well-decorated hotel. The rooms are unusually large, each with room for a separate seating area. Some have bay windows; some are equipped with private shower-only bathrooms.

10 Madeira Place, Brighton, East Sussex BN2 1TN. © **01273/676794.** 6 units, 3 with bathroom. £40–£45 ($64–$72) single or double without bathroom; £50–£65 ($80–$104) single or double with bathroom. Rates include English breakfast. MC, V. Bus: 1, 3, or 7. **Amenities:** Breakfast room; lounge. *In room:* TV, hair dryer, no phone.

Harvey's   Leonard Harvey runs this nonsmoking bed-and-breakfast in the center of Brighton, close to the seafront. The building dates from the 17th century; its rooms have recently been renovated and increased in number. The clean, bright rooms have new furniture and central heating; some have views of the sea and private shower-only bathrooms. For breakfast, there is a choice of English, Continental, or vegetarian.

1 Broad St., Brighton, East Sussex BN2 1TJ. 𝄞 and fax **01273/699227.** 8 units. £35–£50 ($56–$80) single without bathroom; £50–£70 ($80–$112) single or double with bathroom. Rates include breakfast. No credit cards. Bus: 25. **Amenities:** Breakfast room. *In room:* TV, no phone.

Malvern Hotel   Only a stone's throw from the seafront, this 1820 Regency building is on an attractive square. What makes this a winning choice over other similar B&Bs nearby is the personal service offered by the resident owners and staff. The small- to midsize rooms are well maintained and brightly furnished, each with a shower-only bathroom.

33 Regency Sq., Brighton, East Sussex BN1 2GG. 𝄞 **01273/324302.** Fax 01273/324285. 12 units. £35–£45 ($56–$72) single; £70–£90 ($112–$144) double. Rates include continental breakfast. MC, V. Bus: 6. **Amenities:** Breakfast room; lounge. *In room:* TV, coffeemaker, hair dryer, no phone.

New Europe Hotel   This postwar hotel is Brighton's largest, best-accessorized, busiest, and most fun gay hotel. Unlike many of its competitors, it welcomes women, even though they might be uncomfortable at a hotel with two mostly male bars on its premises. Bedrooms can sometimes be noisy (from the bars below), but are comfortable, clean, and unadorned. All units contain well-maintained, shower-only bathrooms. If you want the staff to camp it up for you before your arrival (adding balloons, champagne, flowers, and streamers), someone on the staff will, for a fee, be happy to comply.

31–32 Marine Parade, Brighton BN2 1TR. 𝄞 **01273/624462.** Fax 01273/624575. www.legendsbar.co.uk. 30 units. £20–£30 ($32–$48) single; £50–£70 ($80–$112) double. Rates include breakfast. AE, DC, MC, V. Bus: 27. **Amenities:** Breakfast room; 2 bars. *In room:* TV, coffeemaker, no phone.

WHERE TO DINE

Mock Turtle Tea Shop, 4 Pool Valley (𝄞 **01273/327380**), is a small, busy tearoom where many locals stop by to gossip and take their tea. While it offers only a few sandwiches, the varieties of cakes, flapjacks, tea breads, and fluffy scones with homemade preserves (most popular: strawberry) or whipped cream are spot-on. Everything is made fresh daily. It also serves a variety of good teas.

Brown's Restaurant and Bar ENGLISH/CONTINENTAL   Bustling and popular, Brown's was established in the 1970s in a location off a narrow alleyway that intersects with one of Brighton's main shopping streets, The Lanes. It contains two distinct areas: a bar (its entrance is technically at 34 Ship St. nearby) and a large brasserie-style restaurant, where varnished hardwoods contrast pleasantly with white plaster walls. In the bar, "filled baguettes" (sandwiches) are served throughout the day. English breakfasts are a morning staple every day until noon. Most customers view the bar, however, as a place for drinking and conversation. Diners usually head directly for the restaurant, where a bistro-style menu, with frequent adjustments for seasonal ingredients, is featured. Menu items include Dijon-laced chicken, salads, club sandwiches, Brown's rack of lamb, and a filet steak.

3–4 Duke St. 𝄞 **01273/323501.** Main courses £7.50–£14.75 ($12–$24). AE, MC, V. Daily noon–10:30pm. Bar Mon–Fri 9am–11pm; Sat 10am–11pm; Sun noon–10:30pm. Bus: 7 or 52.

Donatello Pizzeria Ristorante ITALIAN   A cousin to Pinocchio Pizzeria Ristorante (see below), Donatello brings savory Italian cuisine to the heart of the Lanes, a district especially popular with American visitors. Diners come here to sample the wide variety of pizza, including the delectable pescatora, with tomato, mussels, peppers, tuna, and garlic. A good selection of fish dishes is offered, along with popular meat and poultry dishes of Italy. The chef also prepares a wide range of antipasti and pasta dishes.

3 Brighton Place, The Lanes. ℂ **01273/775477.** Main courses £9–£17.65 ($14–$28); pizza £4.65–£9.50 ($7–$15); fixed-price menu £9.40–£13.50 ($15–$22). AE, DC, MC, V. Daily 11:30am–11:30pm. Bus: 7.

Food for Friends ✦ Value VEGETARIAN   A standout on "Restaurant Row" in Brighton, this self-service restaurant offers the freshest food and best value. There may be a wait, but most patrons don't mind. While in a vegetarian restaurant you expect homemade soups, fresh salads, and the like, here you get many exotic varieties of vegetarian cookery, including dishes from India, Bali, or Mexico, depending on the night. The owners say they never use artificial additives. They make their dishes with organic produce and farmhouse cheeses, homemade yogurts, and unrefined oils. Cakes and breads are baked daily.

17A Prince Albert St., The Lanes. ℂ **01273/202310.** Main courses £7–£8.95 ($11–$14). AE, MC, V. Daily 11:30am–11:30pm. Bus: 7 or 52.

Pinocchio Pizzeria Ristorante ITALIAN   This popular restaurant is near the Theatre Royal and opposite the Royal Pavilion gardens. A cousin to Donatello Pizzeria Ristorante (see above), Pinocchio has a light, airy atmosphere together with a bright, efficient Italian staff. It offers a large selection of pastas and pizzas, with specialty desserts. Try breast of chicken with garlic, mushrooms, and a white-wine sauce, or fresh monkfish filet in a green peppercorn, brandy, and cream sauce.

22 New Rd. ℂ **01273/677676.** Reservations recommended. Main courses £5.35–£11.45 ($9–$18); fixed-price meal £7.30–£9.40 ($12–$15). AE, DC, MC, V. Mon–Sat 11:30am–11:30pm; Sun noon–9:30pm.

BRIGHTON AFTER DARK

Brighton offers lots of entertainment options. You can find out what's happening by picking up the local entertainment monthly, the *Punter,* and by looking for *What's On,* a single sheet of weekly events posted throughout the city.

THEATER   There are two theaters that offer drama throughout the year: the **Theatre Royal,** New Road (ℂ **01273/328488**), which has pre-London shows, and the **Gardner Arts Center** (ℂ **01273/685861**), a modern theater-in-the-round, located on the campus of Sussex University, a few miles northeast of town in Falmer. Bigger concerts in all genres are held at **Brighton Centre,** Russell Road (ℂ **08709/009100**), a 5,000-seat facility featuring mainly pop-music shows.

CLUBBING IT   Nightclubs also abound. Cover charges range from free admission (usually on early or midweek nights) to £10 ($16), so call the clubs about admission fees and updates in their nightly schedules, which can vary from week to week or season to season. The smartly dressed can find their groove at **Steamers,** King's Road (ℂ **01273/775432**), located in the Metropole Hotel, which insists on smart casual attire. **Creation,** West Street (ℂ **01273/321628**), is a popular club that features Gay Night on Sunday. **The Escape Club,** 10 Marine Parade (ℂ **01273/606906**), home to both gay and straight dancers, has two floors for dancing, and offers different musical styles on different nights of the week. One of the most popular dancing clubs in Brighton is **Event 2** at **Kingswest,** on West

Street (© **01273/732627**). Big, bold and brash, the club sports millions of dollars in lighting and dance-floor gadgetry. Tucked away around the back of Event II is **Orianas,** Kingswest, on West Street (© **01273/325899**), rather similar in ambience to the parent club. **Gloucester,** Gloucester Plaza (© **01273/699068**), has a variety of music throughout the week, from 1970s and 1980s music to alternative and groove. For a change of pace, visit **Casablanca,** Middle Street (© **01273/321817**), which features jazz with an international flavor.

THE PUB SCENE Pubs are a good place to kick off the evening, especially the **Colonnade Bar,** New Road (© **01273/328728**), which has been serving drinks for more than 100 years. It gets a lot of theater business because of its proximity to the Theatre Royal. **Cricketers,** Black Lion Street (© **01273/ 329472**), is worth a stop: It's Brighton's oldest pub, parts dating from 1549. **The Squid and Starfish,** 77 Middle St. (© **01273/727114**), is a good place to meet fellow travelers from the neighboring Backpacker's Hostel. Beachside drinking lures them to **Fortune of War,** 157 King's Rd. (© **01273/205065**). **H. J. O'Neils,** 27 Ship St. (© **01273/827621**), is an authentic Irish pub located at the top of The Lanes. Stop here to be fortified by traditional Irish pub grub (they make the best Irish stew in town), a creamy pint of Guinness, and a soundtrack of folk music.

GAY NIGHTLIFE

A complete, up-to-date roster of the local gay bars is available in any copy of *G-Scene* magazine (© **01273/749947**), distributed for free in gay hotels and bars throughout the south of England. See also "Brighton After Dark," above, for a few popular dance clubs.

Doctor Brighton's Bar, 16 Kings Rd., The Seafront (© **01273/328765**), open Monday to Saturday noon to 11pm, Sunday noon to 10:30pm, is the largest and most consistently reliable choice. Built around 1750, with a checkered past including stints as a smuggler's haven and abortion clinic, it has more history, and more of the feel of an old-time Victorian pub, than any of its competitors. The staff energetically welcomes the entire gay community: "We get everyone from 18-year-old designer queens to 50-year-old leather queens, and they, along with all their friends and relatives, are welcome." As there's no real lesbian bar in town, gay women tend to congregate here.

Two of the town's busiest and most flamboyant gay bars lie within the **New Europe Hotel** (see "Where to Stay," above). **Legends,** a pubby, clubby, woodsy-looking bar with a view of the sea, is open to the public daily from noon to 11pm, and to New Europe Hotel residents and their guests till 5am. Legends features cross-dressing cabarets three times a week (Tues and Thurs at 9pm, Sun afternoons at 2:30pm), when tweedy-looking English matrons and diaphanous Edwardian vamps are portrayed with bucketloads of tongue-in-cheek satire and humor. **Schwarz** is a cellar-level denim-and-leather joint that does everything it can to encourage its patrons to wear some kind of uniform. Schwarz is open Friday and Saturday 10:30pm to 2am only; cover £3 ($4.80). For more information on both Legends and Schwarz, call © **01273/624462.**

The Marlborough, 4 Princes St. (© **01273/570028**), has been a scene staple for years. Set across from the Royal Pavilion, this woodsy-looking Victorian-style pub has a second-floor cabaret theater. It remains popular with the gay and, to a lesser degree, straight community. A changing roster of lesbian performance art and both gay and straight cabaret within the second-floor theater is offered.

Wanna go dancing? The largest and most frenetic gay disco in the south of England is **Club Revenge,** 32–34 Old Steine (☏ **01273/606064**), a combination of architectural elements from the Victorian, Art Deco, and post-disco eras, with a sweeping view over the amusement arcades of the Palace Pier. It has two floors, multiple bars, an interior color scheme of turquoise, blue, and red, and a clientele representing every conceivable subculture within the gay world. Open Monday to Saturday 9pm to 2am; cover £5 to £8 ($8–$13).

11 Alfriston ★★ & Lewes ★

100km (60 miles) S of London

Nestled on the Cuckmere River, Alfriston is one of England's most beautiful villages. It lies northeast of Seaford on the English Channel, near the resort of Eastbourne and the modern port of Newhaven. During the day, Alfriston is overrun by coach tours (it's very popular). The High Street, with its old market cross, looks just like what you'd always imagined a traditional English village to be. Some of the old houses still have hidden chambers where smugglers stored their loot (alas, the loot is gone); there are also several old inns.

Only about a dozen miles away, along A27 toward Brighton, is the rather somber market town of Lewes. Thomas Paine lived at Bull House on High Street, in what is now a restaurant. Since the home of the Glyndebourne Opera is only 2.5km (1½ miles) to the east, it's hard to find a place to stay in Lewes during the renowned annual opera festival.

ESSENTIALS

GETTING THERE   Trains leave from London's Victoria Station and London Bridge Station for Lewes. One train per hour makes the 1¼-hour trip daily. Trains are more frequent during rush hours. For rail information, call ☏ **08457/ 484950.** There is no rail service to Alfriston.

Buses run daily to Lewes from London's Victoria Coach Station, although the 3-hour trip has so many stops that it's better to take the train. Call ☏ **08705/ 808080** for schedules.

A bus runs from Lewes to Alfriston every 30 minutes. It's operated by **The East Sussex County Busline** and is called Local Rider no. 125. For bus information and schedules in the area, call ☏ **0870/6082608.** The bus station at Lewes is on East Gate Street in the center of town.

If you're driving, head east along M25 (the London ring road), cutting south on A26 via East Grinstead to Lewes. Once at Lewes, follow A27 east to the signposted turnoff for the village of Alfriston.

VISITOR INFORMATION   The **Tourist Information Centre** is in Lewes at 187 High St. (☏ **01273/483448**). Open Easter through October Monday through Friday from 9am to 5pm, Saturday from 10am to 5pm, Sunday from 10am to 2pm. Off season: Monday through Friday from 9am to 5pm, Saturday from 10am to 2pm.

THE GLYNDEBOURNE OPERA FESTIVAL ★

From Lewes, take the A26 to the B2192, following the signs to Glynde and Glyndebourne. From Alfriston, follow the hamlet's main street north of town in the direction of highway A27, then turn left following signs first to Glynde, then to Glyndebourne.

In 1934, a group of local opera enthusiasts established an opera company based in the hamlet of Glyndebourne, 2.5km (1½ miles) east of Lewes and 8km

(5 miles) northwest of Alfriston. The festival has been running ever since, and remains one of the best regional opera companies in Britain.

In 1994, the original auditorium was demolished; a dramatic modern glass, brick, and steel structure, designed by noted English architect Michael Hopkins, was built adjacent to some (mostly ornamental) vestiges of the original building. The new auditorium is known for its acoustics. Operas are presented here only between mid-May and late August; the productions tend to be of unusual works.

For information, contact the **Glyndebourne Festival,** P.O. Box 2624, Glyndebourne (Lewes), E. Sussex BN8 5UW, ⓒ **01273/815000;** www.glyndebourne.co. uk). You can call the box office at ⓒ **01273/813813.** Tickets range from £10 to £145 ($16–$232). You usually can get last-minute tickets because of cancellations by season-ticket holders, but if you want to see a specific performance, buy a ticket several months in advance. It's fun to pack your own picnic to enjoy before the performance; stock up in Lewes.

EXPLORING THE TWO TOWNS

Towering above the valley of the Ouse River in Lewes lie the splendid remains of **Lewes Castle,** begun in 1066 and completed 3 centuries later. For the most sweeping view of the area, you can climb the castle keep. The castle was constructed after the Norman Conquest; today the castle houses the Barbican House Museum revealing "The Story of Lewes Town" with a sound-and-light show based on a scale model of the town. The museum also shelters the Sussex Archaeological Society's collection (see below) plus changing temporary exhibitions. Admission to the castle is £4.20 ($7) or £2.10 ($3.35) for children 16 and under. Students and seniors pay £3.70 ($6). Hours are Tuesday to Saturday 10am to 5:30pm and Sunday, Monday, and Bank Holidays 11am to 5:30pm.

Anne of Cleves House   This half-timbered house was part of Anne of Cleves's divorce settlement from Henry VIII, but Anne never lived in it—there's no proof that she even visited Lewes. Today, it's a museum of local history, cared for by the Sussex Archaeological Society. The museum has a furnished bedroom and kitchen alongside displays of furniture, the local history of the Wealden iron industry, and other crafts.

52 Southover High St., Lewes. ⓒ **01273/474610.** Admission £2.85 ($4.55) adults, £2.50 ($4) students, £1.40 ($2.25) children. Apr–Nov Mon–Sat 10am–5:30pm, Sun noon–5pm; Dec–Mar Tues, Thurs, and Sat 10am–5:30pm. Bus: 123.

Drusillas Park *Kids*   This fascinating, medium-size park has a flamingo lake, Japanese garden, and unusual breeds of domestic animals, among other attractions. The park is perfect for families with children. Check out the newly converted £85,000 ($136,000) bat house, where a family of 20 Rodrigues fruit bats has taken up residence. With a wingspan of about 1m (3 ft.) and rich golden-brown fur, they are one of the most beautiful and rare bat species in the world.

About 1 mile outside Alfriston, off A27. ⓒ **01323/874100.** www.drusillas.co.uk. Admission £9.50 ($15) adults, £8.50 ($14) seniors and children. Daily 10am–5pm (4pm in winter). Closed Dec 24–26. Bus: 126.

Museum of Sussex Archaeology   Adjacent to the castle is this museum, where a 20-minute audiovisual show is available by advance request. Audio tours of the castle are also available.

169 High St., Lewes. ⓒ **01273/486290.** Joint admission ticket to both castle and museum £4.20 ($7) adults, £3.70 ($6) seniors and students, £2.10 ($3.35) children, £11.40 ($18) family ticket. Mon–Sat 10am–5:30pm; Sun 11am–5:30pm. Closed Dec 25–26. Bus: 27, 28, 121, 122, 166, 728, or 729.

WHERE TO STAY
IN ALFRISTON

Frog Firle   To beat the high prices of Alfriston, frugal travelers escape to the hostel-like accommodations at this well-preserved 16th-century farmhouse just south of town in the Cuckmere Valley. The stone structure still retains some of its original character, with its exposed beams, oak timbering, and a room from the early 16th century. On cold nights when the winds blow in from the Channel, there's a wood-burning fire glowing. Dinner can be ordered, and there's also a self-catering kitchen. Bathroom facilities offer a shower only, and there are no storage lockers or laundry rooms. An 11pm curfew is imposed.

Alfriston, near Polegate, East Sussex BN26 5TT. *©* **01323/870423.** Fax 01323/870615. 68 beds. £13 ($21) adults; £7 ($11) children under 18. MC, V. Bus: 727. **Amenities:** Breakfast room; lounge. *In room:* No phone.

George Inn   The George dates from 1397, making it one of the oldest inns in the country. It was once a rendezvous for smugglers. The midsize bedrooms are inviting and comfortable; two of them have four-poster beds. All rooms have neatly kept bathrooms equipped with a tub. The George, however, is better known for good food. A garden is in back, but most guests head for the restaurant with its Windsor chairs and beamed ceiling.

High St., Alfriston, Polegate, East Sussex BN26 5SY. *©* **01323/870319.** Fax 01323/871384. george-inn@ hotmail.com. 8 units. £40 ($64) single; £60–£80 ($96–$128) double. Rates include English breakfast. MC, V. Bus: 727. **Amenities:** Restaurant; bar; laundry. *In room:* TV, coffeemaker, no phone.

Riverdale House *Value*   Set on a hill overlooking the town, this small B&B is one of the finest in the area. A restored Victorian home, it offers handsomely furnished bedrooms in various sizes. Each comes with a small but well-kept private bathroom with shower. Most rooms open onto lovely countryside views including a well-kept garden in front. Riverdale also has a large conservatory where guests socialize or else enjoy the reading material.

Seaford Rd., Alfriston, East Sussex BN26 5TR. *©* **01323/871038.** 5 units. £60–£65 ($96–$104) double. Rates include breakfast. MC, V. **Amenities:** Breakfast room; guest lounge. *In room:* TV, coffeemaker.

IN LEWES

Accommodations are difficult to find during the Glyndebourne Opera Festival (see above), but are adequate at other times.

Crown Inn   Built around 1760, this is one of the oldest inns in Lewes, a 30-minute ride from Gatwick and 60 minutes from London. Located opposite the town's war memorial, it stands at a traffic circle on the main street. The hotel, run by Brian and Gillian Tolton, is considerably refurbished, though still a bit creaky. Pub lunches are served daily in a Victorian conservatory.

191 High St., Lewes, East Sussex BN7 2NA. *©* **01273/480670.** Fax 01273/480679. www.crowninn-lewes. co.uk. 9 units, 7 with bathroom. £38 ($61) single without bathroom, £47–£50 ($75–$80) single with bathroom; £55 ($88) double without bathroom, £60–£65 ($96–$104) double with bathroom. Rates include English breakfast. MC, V. **Amenities:** Breakfast room; bar. *In room:* TV, coffeemaker.

WHERE TO DINE
IN ALFRISTON

The **George Inn** (see "Where to Stay," above) is known for its good food. A full a la carte menu is offered in this candlelit restaurant; the chefs specialize in fresh local fish and home cooking.

The Starr Inn ENGLISH   Serving a diverse daily menu, this restaurant inhabits a 13th-century building, and the bar still features wooden posts from that time. Although there's a contemporary British theme, food choices are eclectic and well prepared.

High St. *C* **01323/870495.** 2-course meal £21 ($34); 3-course meal £24.50 ($39). AE, MC, V. Daily 7–11pm.

The Tudor House TEA/PASTRIES   The Tudor, located in a 14th-century building, offers two well-lit tearooms with oak paneling and brass, providing a calm setting for afternoon tea. Cheese, ham-and-cheese, and egg salad sandwiches, and muffins, danish, scones, and a variety of cakes are served.

High St. *C* **01323/870891.** Afternoon tea £3.25 ($5); sandwiches £2.75 ($4.40); cakes and pastries £1.50 ($2.40). AE, DC, MC, V. Daily 10:30am–5pm.

Ye Olde Smugglers ENGLISH   This restaurant is housed in a 1358 building that once served as headquarters for the infamous Stanton Collins and his band of smugglers. Owing to its checkered past, the place sits atop a series of escape tunnels, since filled in with concrete. The restaurant itself, including the main dining room, is still riddled with secret passages, so cleverly concealed that you might never notice. Locals joke that if you aren't careful, you'll get lost and never be found; the chef boasts that once you taste his steaks and roasts, you won't want to leave anyway. The place serves main courses including rump roast, trout, and a vegetable plate.

Market Cross. *C* **01323/870241.** Main courses £8.50 ($14). MC, V. Daily 11am–2:30pm and 6:30–11pm.

IN LEWES

Pailin THAI   Spicy-hot Thai food has come to Lewes, though some fiery-hot dishes have been toned down for English taste buds. Begin with the lemon chicken soup with lemon grass, followed by a crab-and-prawn "hot pot." A special favorite with locals is the barbecued marinated chicken, served with a spicy but delectable sweet-and-sour plum sauce. Vegetarian meals are served; children are welcome and given small portions at reduced prices.

20 Station St. *C* **01273/473906.** Main courses £5–£9 ($8–$14); fixed-price lunch or dinner £14–£16 ($22–$26). AE, DC, MC, V. Mon–Sat noon–2:30pm and 6:30–10:30pm. Closed Nov 5 and Dec 25–26.

7

Hampshire & Dorset:
Austen & Hardy Country

The English jealously guard the shires of Hampshire and Dorset as special rural treasures. Everybody knows Southampton and Bournemouth, but less known is the hilly countryside farther inland. Scenes from *Burke's Landed Gentry*, from fireplaces where stacks slowly deplete as logs burn, to wicker baskets of apples freshly picked from a nearby orchard, come to mind. Beyond the pear trees, on the crest of a hill, you'll find the ruins of a Roman camp. You can travel through endless lanes and discover tiny villages and thatched cottages untouched by the industrial invasion. Old village houses, now hotels, have a charming quality. A village pub, with two rows of kegs filled with varieties of cider, is where the hunt gathers.

Jane Austen wrote of Hampshire's firmly middle-class inhabitants, all doggedly convinced that Hampshire was the greatest place on earth. Her six novels, including *Pride and Prejudice* and *Sense and Sensibility*, have earned her a place among the pantheon of 19th-century writers and unexpected popularity among latter-day film directors and producers. Her books provide an insight into the manners and mores of the English during her time. Although the details of this life have now largely faded, the general mood and spirit of the Hampshire she depicted remain intact. You can visit her grave in Winchester Cathedral and the house where she lived, Chawton Cottage.

Hampshire encompasses the South Downs, the Isle of Wight (Victoria's favorite retreat), and the naval city of Portsmouth. We've concentrated this chapter on two major areas: Southampton, for its central location, and Winchester, for its history.

Dorset is Thomas Hardy country. Some of its towns and villages, although altered considerably, are still recognizable from his descriptions. "The last of the great Victorians," as he was called, died in 1928 at age 88. His tomb occupies a position of honor in Westminster Abbey.

One of England's smallest shires, Dorset encompasses the old seaport of Poole in the east and Lyme Regis in the west. Dorset borders the English Channel. This is a land of farms and pastures—Dorset butter is served at many an afternoon tea—with plenty of sandy heaths and chalky downs.

Where to stay? You'll find the most hotels, but not the greatest charm, at the seaside resort of Bournemouth. More intriguing than Bournemouth is the much smaller Lyme Regis, with its famed seaside promenade, the Cobb, favored by Jane Austen and a setting for John Fowles's *The French Lieutenant's Woman*. If you're interested in things maritime, opt for Portsmouth, the premier port of the south and the home of HMS *Victory*, Nelson's flagship. For the history buff and Austen fans, it's Winchester, the ancient capital of England, with a cathedral built by William the Conqueror. Winchester

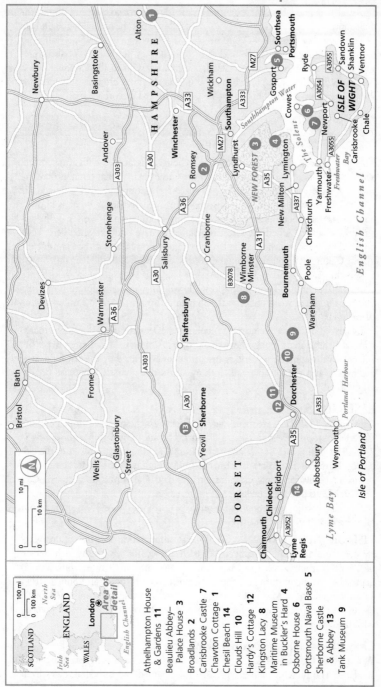

Alton **1**
Southsea **Portsmouth**
Gosport **5** Ryde
Wickham
M27
Southampton
A33
Winchester
Newbury
Basingstoke
H A M P S H I R E
A33
Andover
A30
A30
A303
Romsey **2**
M27
Lyndhurst
A333
Cowes
Southampton Water
A3055 Sandown
Shanklin
Ventnor
A3054
ISLE OF
WIGHT
6 A3055
Newport **7**
Carisbrooke
Chale
NEW FOREST **3** **4**
The Solent
Yarmouth
Freshwater
Freshwater
Bay

Stonehenge
Cranborne
A36
Salisbury
A30
B3078
Wimborne
Minster **8**
Bournemouth
New Milton
Lymington
A35
A337
Christchurch
Poole
English Channel

Devizes
Warminster
A36
A303
Shaftesbury
A303
9 Wareham

Bath
Bristol
Frome
A303
Sherborne **13**
Yeovil
A30
Dorchester **11** **12**
10
A353
A35

Wells
Glastonbury
Street
D O R S E T
Bridport
Chideock
Charmouth **14**
Abbotsbury
Weymouth
Isle of Portland
A3052
Lyme Regis
Lyme Bay
Portland Harbour
A352

N

10 mi
0
10 km
0

Athelhampton House & Gardens **11**
Beaulieu Abbey–Palace House **3**
Broadlands **2**
Carisbrooke Castle **7**
Chawton Cottage **1**
Chesil Beach **14**
Clouds Hill **10**
Hardy's Cottage **12**
Kingston Lacy **8**
Maritime Museum in Buckler's Hard **4**
Osborne House **6**
Portsmouth Naval Base **5**
Sherborne Castle & Abbey **13**
Tank Museum **9**

also makes a good base for exploring the countryside.

The best beaches are at Bournemouth, set among pines, sandy beaches, and fine coastal views, and at Chesil Beach, a 32km- (20-mile-) long bank of shingle running from Abbottsbury to the Isle of Portland, and great for beach-combing. But the natural highlight here is the New Forest, 233.5 sq. km (145 sq. miles) of heath and woodland preserved by William the Conqueror as a private hunting ground, still ideal for walking and exploring.

1 Winchester ★★

115km (72 miles) SW of London; 20km (12 miles) N of Southampton

The most historic city in Hampshire, Winchester is associated with King Arthur and the Knights of the Round Table. In the Great Hall, all that remains of Winchester Castle, a round oak table with space for Arthur and his 24 knights, is attached to the wall—but all that is undocumented romance. What is known, however, is that when the Saxons ruled the ancient kingdom of Wessex, Winchester was its capital. Alfred the Great is believed to have been crowned here; he is honored by a statue. Ethelred the Unready came this way, as did the Danish conqueror Canute, who ousted him (and got his wife, Emma, in the bargain).

Winchester is a mecca for Jane Austen fans. Visit her grave in Winchester Cathedral (as Emma Thompson did while working on her adaptation of *Sense and Sensibility*), as well as her house, Chawton Cottage, 24km (15 miles) east of Winchester.

Its past glory but a memory, Winchester is essentially a market town today, lying on the downs along the Itchen River. Although Winchester hypes its ancient past, the modern world is ensconced, as evidenced by the fast food, reggae music, and the cheap retail clothing stores that mar its otherwise perfect High Street.

ESSENTIALS

GETTING THERE   Frequent daily trains to Winchester leave from London's Waterloo Station. The trip takes 1½ hours. For rail information, call ℂ **0845/ 748-4950.** Trains arrive at Winchester Station, Station Hill, northwest of the city center. **National Express** buses leaving from London's Victoria Coach Station depart regularly for Winchester during the day. The trip takes 2 hours. Call ℂ **020/7529-2000** for schedules and information.

If you're driving, from Southampton drive north on the A335; from London, take the M3 motorway southwest.

VISITOR INFORMATION   The **Tourist Information Centre,** at the Winchester Guildhall, The Broadway (ℂ **01962/840500;** www.visitwinchester.co. uk), is open from October to May, Monday to Saturday, 10am to 5pm; June to September, Monday through Saturday from 9:30am to 6pm, and Sunday from 11am to 4pm. From May to October, guided walking tours are conducted for £3 ($4.80) per person, departing from this tourist center. Departure times vary; check with the center once you're there.

EXPLORING IN & AROUND WINCHESTER

Winchester Cathedral ★★★   This has long been one of the great churches of England. The present building, Britain's longest medieval cathedral, dates from 1079; its Norman heritage is still in evidence. When a Saxon church stood on this spot, St. Swithun, bishop of Winchester and tutor to young King Alfred, suggested

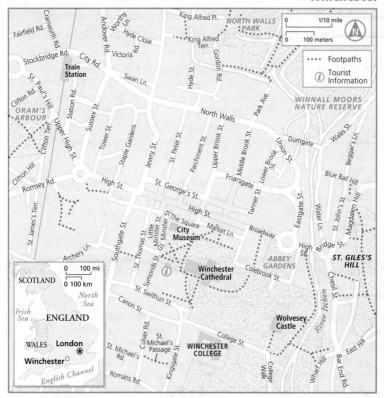

modestly that he be buried outside. Following his subsequent indoor burial, it rained for 40 days. To this day, if you ask a Winchesterian what will happen if it rains on St. Swithun's Day, July 15, you'll get a forecast of 40 days of rain.

In the present building, the nave, with its two aisles, is most impressive, as are the chantries, the reredos (late 15th c.), and the elaborately carved choir stalls. Jane Austen is buried here; her grave is marked with a commemorative plaque. There are chests containing the bones of Saxon kings and the remains of the Viking conqueror Canute and his wife, Emma, in the presbytery. The son of William the Conqueror, William II (Rufus), is also buried at the cathedral.

The library houses Bishop Morley's 17th-century book collection, and an exhibition room contains the 12th-century Winchester Bible. The Triforium shows sculpture, woodwork, and metalwork from 11 centuries and affords magnificent views over the rest of the cathedral.

The Close. ✆ **01962/857200.** www.winchester-cathedral.org.uk. Free admission to the cathedral, but £3.50 ($6) donation requested. Admission to library and Triforium Gallery £1 ($1.60) adults, 50p (80¢) children. Free guided tours year-round 10am–3pm hourly. Crypt is often flooded during winter, but part may be seen from a viewing platform. Library and Triforium Gallery Easter–Oct Mon 2–4:30pm, Tues–Sat 11am–4:30pm; Nov–Dec Wed and Sat 11am–3:30pm; Jan–Easter Sat 11am–3:30pm.

The Hospital of St. Cross ★★   The hospital was founded in 1132 and is the oldest charitable institution in the country. It was established by Henri du Blois, the grandson of William the Conqueror, as a link for social care and to supply life's

Spend a day in Old Portsmouth. Long a bastion of the British fleet, Old Portsmouth survived heavy Nazi bombardment during the Blitz. You can wander among its pubs, gray-painted warships, and fortifications. Start by seeing what's left of the medieval ramparts. Walk down Broad Street (once filled with brothels) and board Nelson's flagship *Victory* a mile away. Finish with a visit to *Mary Rose,* the pride of Henry VIII until it sank in 1545.

Follow in the footsteps of Hardy. Thomas Hardy immortalized the town of Dorchester in his novel *The Mayor of Casterbridge.* You can wander its High Street, where many 17th-century homes remain. Head out for the Wessex countryside where he set many of his novels, including *Tess of the D'Urbervilles.*

Hike across the Isle of Wight. This piece of England was cast adrift long ago in the English Channel. Pastoral and nautical at the same time, it offers some of southern England's best hiking opportunities. The best hiking is in the south, filled with steep cliffs overlooking the Channel.

Call on Jane Austen. Films and the BBC's miniseries *Pride and Prejudice* have given the novelist a new legion of fans. Her world lives on in a former bailiff's cottage in the village of Chawton. Learn here about other locales associated with her novels and immortal heroines like Emma Woodhouse.

Explore the New Forest. It's neither new nor totally a forest, but the former royal hunting grounds of William the Conqueror forms one of England's great nature reserves. Once commoners could have their eyes put out if they so much as startled a deer here, but the wildlife preserve is more hospitable today. You might catch a glimpse of a few of the 2,000 wild horses and ponies that roam the area.

Hang out at Cobb Beach. If the novel *The French Lieutenant's Woman* (or the movie of the same name) is one of your favorites, you can re-enact the famous scene at the old seaport of Lyme Regis. It is here that author John Fowles placed his heroine, Sarah. Pleasure craft and lobster boats tie up here; join the old salts for a pint in one of the whitewashed little pubs along the seafront.

necessities to the local poor and famished travelers. It continues the tradition of providing refreshments to visitors; simply stop at the Porter's Lodge for a Wayfarer's Dole, and you'll receive some bread and ale. St. Cross is set amid the beautiful scenery that inspired Keats and Trollope, and is still the home of 25 brothers, whose residence is on one side of the historic landmark.

Cross Rd. ✆ **01962/851-375.** Admission £2 ($3.20). May–Sept daily 9:30am–5pm; off season daily 10:30am–3:30pm.

Winchester College ✮   Winchester College was founded by William of Wykeham, Bishop of Winchester and Chancellor to Richard II; students first attended in 1394. Its buildings have been in continuous use for 600 years. The structures vary from Victorian Tudor Gothic to the more modern trimmings of the New Hall designed in 1961. The Chapel Hall, kitchens, and the Founder's Cloister all date back to the 14th century. In the 17th century buildings were added on the south side, including a schoolroom constructed between 1683 and 1687.

73 Kings Gate. 🕐 **01962/621209.** www.winchestercollege.org. Admission £2.50 ($4). Mon–Sat 10:45am–noon; Mon, Wed, Fri, and Sun 2–3:15pm.

SHOPPING   Fill up your empty suitcases over at **Cadogan,** 30–31 The Square (🕐 **01962/877399**). They've got an upscale and stylish selection of British clothing for both men and women. For a unique piece of jewelry by one of the most acclaimed designers of today, stroll into **Carol Darby Jewellery,** 23 Little Minster St. (🕐 **01962/867671**).

WHERE TO STAY

Farrells Bed & Breakfast   On St. Cross Road, less than a kilometer south of the city center, this Victorian house is furnished in period fashion but has modern comforts. The small- to midsize guest rooms, all doubles, have adequate hallway bathrooms or else private facilities with shower. Over the years, the rooms and comforts here have drawn favorable responses from readers, who constantly cite the owners' hospitality.

5 Ranelagh Rd., St. Cross, Winchester, Hampshire SO23 9TA. 🕐 **01962/869555.** 3 units, 1 with bathroom. £44 ($70) double without bathroom, £50 ($80) double with bathroom. Rates include English breakfast. No credit cards. Bus: no. 1, 1A, 2, 2A, 29, 47, or 69. **Amenities:** Breakfast room. *In room:* TV, coffeemaker.

Shawlands ✸   In an upscale residential neighborhood about a mile south of Winchester's center, Shawlands, built in 1960, lies across the road from the open fields of a large private estate. Intended for use by the extended family of Kathy Pollock (a retired nutritionist) and her husband, William, the non-smoking house is comfortable, spacious, and cozy. Made of brick, it has casement windows with leaded inserts and small- to midsize bedrooms. (One of these was converted from a garage.) Bedrooms are comfortably furnished and hallway bathrooms are well maintained, and one room is set aside for those with limited mobility. Breakfasts are enhanced by Mrs. Pollock's homemade brown bread and homemade marmalade, served every morning as part of a time-tested ritual.

46 Kilham Lane, Winchester, Hampshire SO22 5QD. 🕐 and fax **01962/861166.** kathy@pollshaw.u-neet.com. 5 units, 1 with bathroom. £32–£40 ($51–$64) single without bathroom; £42–£45 ($67–$72) double without bathroom, £52 ($83) double with bathroom. Rates include English breakfast. MC, V. From Winchester's center follow Romsey Rd. south for a mile. **Amenities:** Breakfast room. *In room:* TV, coffeemaker, hair dryer, no phone.

(Moments **Rambling the South Downs Way**

For a day of rambling through the countryside, try strolling part of South Downs Way, a 159km (99-mile) trail from Winchester to Eastbourne; Clarendon Way, a 39km (24-mile) path from Winchester to Salisbury; or Itchen Way, a beautiful riverside trail from near Cheriton to Southampton.

Winchester and the surrounding area is by far one of the best places to fish in England, especially for trout. Try your hand at any of the many nearby rivers including the Rivers Itchen, Test, Meon, Dever, and Avon. The Tourist Information Centre (see above) will provide complete details on the best spots.

Moments   Jane Austen, from Hampshire to Hollywood

Jane Austen is enjoying unprecedented stardom on the silver screen. Cinematic versions of her works first appeared in the 1940s; the most famous of the early films was Laurence Olivier's and Greer Garson's *Pride and Prejudice,* the first of at least four cinematic adaptations. Film versions have been made (and remade) of all six major Austen novels. But 1995 was definitely Austen's cinematic heyday: a BBC production of *Persuasion,* a BBC/A&E remake of *Pride and Prejudice,* and a Columbia Tri-Star production of *Sense and Sensibility. Clueless* was a modern-day version of *Emma;* followed in quick succession by a lush cinematic version of *Persuasion.* A year later, a film of the original *Emma* came along, and 1999 saw the first film staging of *Mansfield Park.*

Why this surge of passion for a long-deceased author? Savvy Hollywood types realized long ago that Ms. Austen's novels provide the stylish and socially acceptable skeletons for stories that focus on salons from the most spectacular country houses in England. Warehouses of historically accurate costumes are designed with taste and materials much better than their originals. This, coupled with psychologically intriguing characters who never dip into the profane, gives Austen's works box office clout.

Austen's posthumous catapult to fame has brought a flood of visitors to her house, **Chawton Cottage,** in Chawton, 1 mile southwest of Alton off A31 and B3006, 24km (15 miles) east of Winchester (© **01420/83262**). Daughter of a rector with lots of charm but little money, Ms. Austen, her sisters, and their mother lived in this house by permission of a brother, Edward, who through a complicated arrangement became heir to it. You can see where the author spent the very productive last 7½ years of her life, and where she became ill in 1816 with what would later be called Addison's disease; she died in July 1817. This unpretentious but pleasant cottage has the table on which she rewrote three novels and wrote three new ones, including *Emma.* There's an attractive garden where you can picnic and an old bake house with Austen's donkey cart. A bookshop stocks new and secondhand books. Open March to November daily 11am to 4pm, December, and January to February, Saturday and Sunday 11am to 4pm. Admission is £4 ($6) for adults, £3 ($4.80) seniors and students, 50p (80¢) for children 8 to 18. Closed December 25 and 26.

Across the road from Austen's house is an idyllic place for tea. **Cassandra's Cup,** Chawton (© **01420/83144**), is known for its home baking, especially its delectable scones. You can also buy freshly made sandwiches and tasty cakes and pastries. Take your tea in a traditional setting decorated in green and white, with lace curtains and tablecloths. Later you can browse in their shops for souvenirs, perhaps old porcelain. Open daily 10:30am to 4:30pm.

WHERE TO DINE

The Eclipse Inn ENGLISH   This is one of the venerated old inns of town. Lady Alicia Lisle was hung in The Square after being declared a traitor for harboring

Cromwell's army at the inn. Her ghost is said to roam through the building, but regulars don't seem intimidated by her. In fact, they spent so much time here that they leave their mugs hanging on hooks from the ceiling, ready for the next pint. Stop in for a salad, sandwich, or one of their daily specials, including vegetarian and meat pies. Wash it down with one of their cask ales and a lively tale from said regulars.

25 The Square, Winchester. ☎ **01962/865676**. Daily specials, soups, salads, and sandwiches £2.50–£6.50 ($4–$10). AE, MC, V. Daily 11am–11pm.

Royal Oak Pub ★ *Finds* ENGLISH   The Royal Oak is located in a passageway next to the God Begot House on the High Street. A busy pub with plenty of atmosphere, it reputedly has the oldest bar in England. The cellar of this establishment was originally built in 944 to dispense drink to Winchester's pilgrims; the present building was constructed in 1630 atop the much older foundation. Various hot dishes and snacks are available, and a traditional Sunday lunch is also served. But Royal Oak isn't going to win any culinary awards; it's a place for drinking, a traditional cask alehouse known as a hogshead.

Royal Oak Passage. ☎ **01962/842701**. Bar snacks and platters £3–£8 ($4.80–$13); cask ale from £2.10 ($3.35). MC, V. Daily 11am–11pm. Bus: no. 25.

William Walkers Restaurant ENGLISH/CONTINENTAL   A few steps from the cathedral, this well-known hotel contains two eateries. A bright, informal section, with a separate entrance from the street, offers a big spread for lunch. A typical meal includes soup, breaded plaice with fried potatoes, apple pie and cream, plus coffee. They also offer a traditional afternoon tea. More formal meals are served in the other eatery, where a collection of English antiques and a view of the cathedral create one of the city's most elegant dining spots.

In the Wessex Hotel. Paternoster Row. ☎ **01962/861611**. Reservations recommended. Fixed-price lunch from £8.50–£10 ($14–$16), dinner from £16.95 ($25). AE, DC, MC, V. Daily lunch buffet 12:30–2pm. Wessex Restaurant daily 12:30–2pm and 7–9:45pm. Bus: no. 25.

WINCHESTER AFTER DARK

The place to go is The Porthouse, Upper Brook Street (☎ **01962/869397**), a pub-cum-nightclub, sprawling across three floors. Different nights have different themes, from karaoke to retro music, from the 1960s through the 1980s. On Friday the 25-plus crowd takes over. There's a ground-floor pub where lunch is served. Cover £7 ($11), Thursday to Saturday nights after 9pm only.

2 Portsmouth & Southsea ★

120km (75 miles) SW of London; 30km (19 miles) SE of Southampton

Four American states may have a Portsmouth, but their forerunner is the old port and naval base on the Hampshire coast, seat of the British navy for 500 years. German bombers in World War II leveled the city, hitting about ninetenths of its buildings. But the seaport was rebuilt admirably and now aggressively promotes its military attractions. It draws visitors interested in the nautical history of England as well as World War II buffs.

Portsmouth's maritime associations are known around the world. From Sally Port, the most interesting district in the Old Town, countless naval heroes have embarked to fight England's battles—never more than on June 6, 1944, when Allied troops set sail to invade occupied France.

Southsea, adjoining Portsmouth, is a popular seaside resort with fine sands, lush gardens, bright lights, and a host of vacation attractions. Many historic monuments stand along the stretches of open space, where you can walk on the Clarence Esplanade, look out on the Solent channel, and view the busy shipping activities of the harbor.

ESSENTIALS

GETTING THERE Trains from London's Waterloo Station stop at Portsmouth and Southsea Station frequently throughout the day. The trip takes 2½ hours. Call © **0845/7484950.**

National Express coaches out of London's Victoria Coach Station make the run to Portsmouth and Southsea every 2 hours during the day. The trip takes 2 hours and 45 minutes. Call © **020/7529-2000** for information and schedules.

If you're driving from London's ring road, drive south on the A3.

VISITOR INFORMATION The **Tourist Information Centre,** at The Hard in Portsmouth (© **023/9282-6722**), is open daily April through September from 9:30am to 5:15pm, and October through March daily from 9:30am to 5:15pm.

EXPLORING PORTSMOUTH & SOUTHSEA

You might want to begin your tour in Southsea, where there are a number of naval monuments. These include the big anchor from Nelson's ship *Victory;* a commemoration of the officers and men of HMS *Shannon* for heroism in the Indian Mutiny; an obelisk with a naval crown, honoring the memory of the crew of HMS *Chesapeake;* a massive column, the Royal Naval Memorial, honoring those lost at sea in the two world wars; a shaft dedicated to men killed in the Crimean War; and commemorations of those who fell victim to yellow fever while in Queen Victoria's service in Sierra Leone and Jamaica.

MARITIME ATTRACTIONS IN PORTSMOUTH

You can buy a ticket that admits you to all three attractions: HMS *Victory,* the *Mary Rose,* the HMS *Warrior 1860,* and the Royal Naval Museum. It costs £13.75 ($22) for adults, £11 ($18) for seniors, and £8.90 ($14) for children.

The *Mary Rose* Ship Hall and Museum ✦ The *Mary Rose,* flagship of the fleet of Henry VIII's wooden men-of-war, sank in the Solent channel in 1545 in full view of the king. In 1982, Prince Charles watched the *Mary Rose* break the water's surface after more than 4 centuries on the ocean floor, not exactly ship-shape but surprisingly well preserved. The remains are now on view, although the hull must be kept permanently wet.

The hull and more than 20,000 items brought up by divers constitute one of England's major archaeological discoveries. You'll see the nearly complete equipment of the ship's barber-surgeon, with cabin saws, knives, ointments, and plaster ready for use; long bows and arrows, some in shooting order; carpenters' tools; leather jackets; and fine lace and silk. Close to the Ship Hall is the *Mary Rose* Exhibition, where artifacts recovered from the ship are stored. It features an audiovisual theater and a spectacular two-deck reconstruction of a segment of the ship, with the original guns. A display with sound effects recalls the sinking of the vessel.

College Rd., Portsmouth Naval Base. © 023/9275-0521. www.flagship.org.uk. See above for admission prices. Apr–Oct daily 10am–5:30pm; Nov–Mar daily 10am–5pm. Closed Dec 25. Use the entrance to the Portsmouth Naval Base through Victory Gate and follow the signs.

HMS *Victory* ✦✦✦ Of major interest is Lord Nelson's flagship, a 104-gun, first-rate ship that is the oldest commissioned warship in the world, launched May 7, 1765. It earned its fame on October 21, 1805, in the Battle of Trafalgar,

HM NAVAL BASE

Victory Gate

The Hard St.

Ferry to Gosport

Ferry to Ryde

Queen St.

Kent St.

Park Rd.

RN Sports Centre

Ferry Terminal

Gunwharf Rd.

George Rd.

Burnaby Rd.

Cambridge Rd.

Anglesey Rd.

University of Portsmouth

Alfred Rd.

Market Way

Winston

Churchill Ave.

Hants Terr

St. Paul's Rd.

St. James Rd.

Somers Rd.

St. Andrew's Rd.

Broad St.

St. Thomas St.

High St.

Museum Rd.

King's Rd.

Cottage Grove

Round Tower

Square Tower

Penny St.

Pembroke Rd.

Castle Rd.

Southsea Terr.

Ferry to Fishbourne

Amusement Park

Pier Rd.

Duisburg Way

Hovercraft Terminal

0 1/4 mi
0 0.25 km

SCOTLAND

North Sea

Irish Sea

ENGLAND

WALES   London

Portsmouth

English Channel

0 100 mi
0 100 km

HMS *Victory* 2
HMS *Warrior* 5
Lord Nelson Statue 7
Mary Rose 1
Mary Rose Ship Hall
  & Museum 4
Portsmouth City Museum 6
Royal Naval Museum 3
Victory's Anchor 8

when the English scored a victory over the combined Spanish and French fleets. It was in this battle that Lord Nelson lost his life. The flagship, after being taken to Gibraltar for repairs, returned to Portsmouth with Nelson's body on board (he was later buried at St. Paul's in London).

1–7 College Rd., in Portsmouth Naval Base. ✆ 023/9286-1533. www.flagship.org.uk. See above for admission prices. Apr–Oct daily 10am–5:30pm; Nov–Mar daily 10am–5pm. Closed Dec 25. Use the entrance to the Portsmouth Naval Base through Victory Gate and follow the signs.

Royal Naval Museum ★   The museum is next to Nelson's flagship, HMS *Victory,* and the *Mary Rose,* in the heart of Portsmouth's historic naval dockyard. The only museum in Britain devoted exclusively to the general history of the Royal Navy, it houses relics of Nelson and his associates, together with unique collections of ship models, naval ceramics, figureheads, medals, uniforms, weapons, and other memorabilia. Special displays feature "The Rise of the Royal Navy" and "HMS *Victory* and the Campaign of Trafalgar."

In the dockyard, Portsmouth Naval Base. ✆ 023/9272-7562. See above for admission prices. Apr–Oct daily 10am–5:30pm; Nov–Mar daily 10am–5pm.

Royal Navy Submarine Museum   Cross Portsmouth Harbour by one of the ferries that bustles back and forth all day to Gosport. Some departures go directly from the station pontoon to HMS *Alliance* for a visit to the submarine museum, which traces the history of underwater warfare and life from the earliest days to the present nuclear age. Within the refurbished historical and nuclear galleries, the principal exhibit is HMS *Alliance,* and after a brief audiovisual presentation, visitors are guided through the boat by ex-submariners. Midget submarines, not all of them English, including an X-craft, can be seen outside the museum.

Haslar Jetty Rd., Gosport. ℂ 023/9252-9217. www.rnsubmus.co.uk. Admission £4 ($6) adults, £2.75 ($4.40) children and seniors, £11 ($18) family. Apr–Oct daily 10am–5:30pm; Nov–Mar daily 10am–4:30pm. Last tour 1 hr. before closing. Closed Dec 25. Bus: 19. Ferry: From The Hard in Portsmouth to Gosport.

MORE ATTRACTIONS

Charles Dickens's Birthplace Museum   The 1804 small terrace house, in which the famous novelist was born in 1812 and lived for a short time, has been restored and furnished to illustrate the middle-class taste of the southwestern counties of the early 19th century.

393 Old Commercial Rd. (near the center of Portsmouth, off Mile End Rd./M275 and off Kingston Rd.). ℂ 023/9282-7261. Admission £2.50 ($4) adults, £1.80 ($2.90) seniors, £1.50 ($2.40) students, free for children 12 and under. Daily 10am–5:30pm. Closed Nov–Mar.

Southsea Castle   A fortress built of stones from Beaulieu Abbey in 1545 as part of King Henry VIII's coastal defense plan, the castle is now a museum. Exhibits trace the development of Portsmouth as a military stronghold, as well as the naval history and the archaeology of the area. The castle is in the center of Southsea near the D-Day Museum.

Clarence Esplanade, Southsea. ℂ 023/9282-7261. www.southseacastle.co.uk. Admission £2.50 ($4) adults, £1.80 ($2.90) seniors, £1.50 ($2.40) students and children 13–18, £6.50 ($10) family, free for children 12 and under. Apr–Sept daily 10am–5:30pm. Closed Nov–Mar.

D-Day Museum   Next door to Southsea Castle, this museum, devoted to the Normandy landings, displays the Overlord Embroidery, which shows the complete story of Operation Overlord. The appliquéd embroidery, believed to be the largest of its kind (82m/272 ft. long and 1m/3 ft. high), was designed by Sandra Lawrence and took 20 women of the Royal School of Needlework 5 years to complete. A special audiovisual program includes displays such as reconstructions of various stages of the mission. You'll see a Sherman tank in working order, jeeps, field guns, and even a DUKW (popularly called a Duck), an incredibly useful amphibious truck that operates on land and sea.

Clarence Esplanade (on the seafront), Southsea. ℂ 023/9282-7261. www.ddaymuseum.co.uk. Admission £5 ($8) adults, £3.75 ($6) seniors, £3 ($4.80) children and students, £13 ($21) family, free for children under 5. Apr–Sept 10am–5:30pm; Oct–Mar 10am–5pm. Closed Dec 24–26.

Portsmouth City Museum   This museum explains the history of Portsmouth; some areas are audiovisual, and two exhibitions (galleries) change throughout the year. Permanent displays are devoted to the history of Portsmouth through the ages. An example would be a dining room set up in the 1950s with the furnishings and atmosphere of the time.

Museum Rd. ℂ 023/9282-7261. www.portsmouthrecordsoffice.co.uk. Free admission. Apr–Sept 10am–5:30pm; Oct–Mar 10am–5pm. Closed Dec 24–26.

Portsmouth Natural History Museum *Kids*   This museum is mainly for children; it documents the history of Portsmouth and how it has developed from the age of the dinosaurs and changed over the years.

Cumberland House, Eastern Parade, in Southsea. ℂ 023/9282-7261. www.portsmouthnaturalhistory.co.uk. Admission £2.50 ($4) adults, £1.80 ($2.90) seniors, £1.50 ($2.40) students, free for children under 12 (with adult). Daily 10am–5:30pm.

Finds   The Best Walks, the Best Picnics

Southsea Common, between the coast and houses of the area, known in the 13th century as Froddington Heath and used for army bivouacs, is a picnic and play area today. Walks can be taken along Ladies' Mile if you tend to shy away from the common's tennis courts, skateboard and roller-skating rinks, and other activities.

Portchester Castle   On a spit of land on the northern side of Portsmouth Harbour are the remains of this castle, plus a Norman church. Built in the late 12th century by King Henry II, the castle is set inside the impressive walls of a 3rd-century Roman fort built as a defense against Saxon pirates when this was the northwestern frontier of the declining Roman Empire. By the end of the 14th century, Richard II had modernized the castle and had made it a secure small palace. Among the ruins are the hall, kitchen, and great chamber of this palace.

On the south side of Portchester off A27 (between Portsmouth and Southampton, near Fareham). © 023/ 9237-8291. Admission £3 ($4.80) adults, £2.30 ($3.70) seniors, £1.50 ($2.40) children 5–15, free for children 4 and under. Apr–Oct daily 10am–6pm; Nov–Mar daily 10am–4pm.

WHERE TO STAY

The Birchwood Guest House   This nonsmoking Victorian terraced house is just a few minutes walk from the seafront. The owners create a friendly and informal atmosphere and provide nicely furnished bedrooms with tidily kept bathrooms with showers. A well-appointed lounge is also available to residents.

44 Waverly Rd., Southsea, Hants P05 2PP. © 02392/811337. ged@birchwood.uk.com. 7 units. £20–£25 ($32–$40) single; £45–£65 ($72–$104) double. Rates include breakfast. MC, V. With South Parade Pier on left, take 1st right onto roundabout; at 3rd exit turn into Waverly Rd. **Amenities:** Bar; lounge. In room: TV, cof-feemaker, hair dryer.

Fortitude Cottage   Maggie Hall owns this charming waterside cottage over-looking the fishing quay at Portsmouth's harbor. There are three well-maintained, simple, but comfortably furnished bedrooms, one double and two twin-bedded rooms. All rooms have private shower-only bathrooms. Breakfast is served in a bow-windowed dining room with a harbor view.

51 Broad St., Old Portsmouth, Hampshire P01 2JD. © and fax **02392/823748.** www.fortitudecottage.co.uk. 43 units. £55–£60 ($88–$96) double. Rates include English breakfast. MC, V. Bus: Old Portsmouth. **Amenities:** Breakfast room. In room: TV, coffeemaker, hair dryer, iron, safe, no phone.

WHERE TO DINE

The Southsea area has a number of cheap eateries. The best deal is offered at the **Shirin Kebab House,** 58 Kingston Rd. (© 02392/699421), open Wednesday to Sunday 2:30pm to 2am. Their pita sandwiches are the best in town, and their spicy kebabs begin at £3 ($4.80); takeout is done here. If you'd like to pick up a pizza or order a plate of pasta, your best deal is at **Fabio's,** 108 Palmerston Rd. (© **02392/811139**), open daily noon to 3pm and 5pm to midnight, with prices beginning at £6 ($10). Takeout prices are 25% less. For some English pub grub, head for that longtime sailor favorite, **The Ship & Castle,** 1 The Hard (© **02392/ 832009**), where prices begin at £5 ($8) and there's a large daily selection made with fresh ingredients. If you'd like to go on a pub-crawl later, there are many beer and alehouses nearby that have quenched the thirst of sailors for years. Although Churchill denounced British naval tradition as "nothing but rum, sodomy, and lash," here it's more like a bottle of gin or a pint of ale.

Country Kitchen VEGETARIAN   This self-service establishment is housed in a building from the 1840s; its main dining area is at street level, with an overflow upstairs. All meals are freshly prepared on the premises daily, with only natural and organic products used. The place is known locally for its wide range of homemade cakes and varieties of tea. Some dishes are vegan (without dairy, eggs, or meat). Many non-vegetarian customers come to enjoy the special atmosphere of this well-run establishment. Children are welcome, and there's a nonsmoking policy. Takeout service is also available.

59 Marmion Rd., Southsea. (✆ **02392/811425**. Soups and salads £1.35–£3.95 ($2.15–$6); main courses £3.95 ($6). No credit cards. Mon–Sat 9am–4:45pm. Bus: no. 3 or 23.

Rosie's Vineyard CONTINENTAL   This eatery is patterned after a brasserie in France. This wine bar and bistro was originally a Victorian greengrocer, and its understated decor still includes some 19th-century stained-glass accents. In summer, guests prefer tables in the pergola garden. The cookery is accomplished and often imaginative, and the menu changes with the season. Dishes include grilled goat-cheese salad, Scottish salmon in puff pastry with white sauce, grilled halibut with ginger and spring onions, and sautéed escalloped pork in a creamy walnut sauce. Live jazz is heard on Friday at 8pm and Sunday lunch at 12:30pm.

87 Elm Grove, Southsea. (✆ **02392/755944**. Reservations recommended. Main courses £8–£11.50 ($13–$18). AE, MC, V. Mon–Sat 7–11pm; Sun noon–3pm and 7–10:30pm. Bus: no. 3 or 23.

3 Southampton

139km (87 miles) SW of London; 258km (161 miles) E of Plymouth

To many North Americans, England's number-one passenger port, home base for the *Queen Elizabeth 2,* is the gateway to Britain. Alas, Southampton has become a city of sterile wide boulevards, parks, and dreary shopping centers. During World War II, as some 31.5 million soldiers set out from here (more than twice that number in World War I), Southampton was repeatedly bombed, destroying its old character. Today, the rather shoddy downtown section represents what happens when the architectural focus is timeliness rather than grace.

While there's not much to see in the city, there's a lot on its outskirts. If you're in Southampton between ships, you may want to explore some of the major sights of Hampshire nearby (New Forest, Winchester, the Isle of Wight, and Bournemouth, in neighboring Dorset).

Southampton's supremacy as a port dates from Saxon times, when Canute the Great was proclaimed king here in 1017. The city was especially important to the Normans, helping them keep in touch with their homeland. Its denizens were responsible for bringing in the bubonic plague, which wiped out a quarter of the English population in the mid–14th century. On the Western Esplanade is a memorial tower to the Pilgrims, who set out on their voyage to the New World from Southampton on August 15, 1620. Both the *Mayflower* and the *Speedwell* sailed from here but were forced by storm damage to put in at Plymouth, where the *Speedwell* was abandoned.

In the spring of 1912, the "unsinkable" White Star liner, the 46,000-ton *Titanic,* sailed from Southampton on its maiden voyage. Shortly before midnight on April 14, while steaming at 22 knots, the great ship collided with an iceberg and sank to the bottom of the icy Atlantic. The sinking of the *Titanic* was one of the greatest maritime disasters in history—1,513 people perished.

ESSENTIALS

GETTING THERE   Trains depart from London's Waterloo Station several times daily. The trip takes just over an hour. Call ☎ **0845/7484950.**

National Express operates hourly departures from London's Victoria Coach Station. The trip takes 2½ hours. Call ☎ **020/7529-2000** for information and schedules.

If you're driving, take the M3 southwest from London.

VISITOR INFORMATION   The **Tourist Information Centre,** 9 Civic Centre Rd. (☎ **023/8022-1106**), is open Monday through Wednesday and Friday and Saturday from 9am to 5pm, Thursday from 10am to 5pm; closed Good Friday, Easter Monday, Christmas, December 26, and New Year's Day.

EXPLORING SOUTHAMPTON

Ocean Village and the town quay on Southampton's waterfront are bustling with activity and are filled with shops, restaurants, and entertainment possibilities.

West Quay Retail Park, the first phase of Southampton's £250 million ($402.5 million) Esplanade development, has become a major hub for shoppers. The central shopping area is pedestrian-only, and tree- and shrub-filled planters provide a backdrop for summer flowers and hanging baskets. You can sit and listen to the buskers (street entertainers) or perhaps watch the world parade from one of the nearby restaurants or pavement cafes. For a vast array of shops, try the **Town Quay** (☎ **023/8023-4397**), the **Canutes Pavilion** at Ocean Village (☎ **023/8022-8353**), or **Southampton Market** (☎ **023/8061-6181**).

The most intriguing shopping on the outskirts is at the **Whitchurch Silk Mill,** 28 Winchester St., Whitchurch (☎ **01256/892065**). Admission is £3.75 ($6) for adults, £3.25 ($5) for seniors, £1.75 ($2.80) for children, and £9 ($14) for a family ticket. Visitors flock to this working mill, located in colorful surroundings on the River Test. Historic looms weave silk here as in the olden days, and visitors can observe water-wheel-powered machinery, warping, and winding. The gift shop sells silk on the roll, ties, scarves, handkerchiefs, jewelry, and souvenirs. Hours are Tuesday through Sunday from 10:30am to 5pm.

Southampton Maritime Museum   This museum is housed in an impressive 14th-century stone warehouse with a magnificent timber ceiling. Its exhibits trace the history of Southampton, including a model of the docks as they looked at their peak in the 1930s. Also displayed are artifacts from some of the great ocean liners whose home port was Southampton.

The most famous of these liners was the fabled *Titanic,* which was partially built in Southampton and sailed from this port on its fateful, fatal voyage. James Cameron's box office smash has increased traffic to the relatively small *Titanic* exhibit at the museum. It features photographs of the crew (many of whom were from Southampton) and passengers, as well as letters from passengers, Capt.

Finds Those Shoes Are Made for Walking

City tour guides offer a wide range of free guided walks and regular city bus tours. Free guided walks of the town are offered throughout the year on Sunday and Monday at 10:30am and June to September twice daily at 10:30am and 2:30pm. Tours start at Bargate. For details of various boat or bus trips that might be offered at the time of your visit, check with the tourist office.

Edward Smith's sword, and a video with an interview with the fallen captain plus modern interviews with survivors.

The Wool House, Town Quay. © 023/8022-3941. Free admission. Apr–Sept Tues–Fri 10am–1pm, Sat 10am–1pm and 2–4pm, Sun 2–5pm; Oct–Mar Tues–Sat 10am–4pm, Sun 2–4pm. Closed bank holiday Mon, Christmas, and Boxing Day.

WHERE TO STAY

Finding accommodations right in Southampton isn't as important as it used to be. Few ships now arrive, and the places to stay just outside the city are just as good, if not better. For other accommodations in the area, refer to the "New Forest" section, below. However, we'll provide some budget accommodations for those who may want to stay in the city proper.

Banister House Hotel *Value*   This private hotel lies in a residential area close to the city center, convenient to a number of restaurants, pubs, and shops; it is one of your best bets if you're seeking affordable rates. Alain and Sue Ridley will be pleased to house you in one of their well-maintained bedrooms; among the amenities is hot and cold running water (even in those without full plumbing fixtures).

11 Brighton Rd., Southampton, Hampshire SO15 2JJ. © 02380/221279. Fax 02380/226551. 22 units, 15 with shower only. £26 ($42) single without bathroom; £32 ($51) single with bathroom; £46 ($74) double without bathroom; £49 ($78) double with shower and toilet. Rates include English breakfast. MC, V. Bus: no. 5, 11, 15, or 20. Free parking. **Amenities:** Dining room; bar; laundry. *In room:* TV, coffeemaker.

Hunters Lodge Hotel 🛱   This white-fronted Victorian villa lies in the suburb of Shirley, easily accessible from the M3 or M27, just south of the town center amid similar buildings and lots of restaurants and shops. It is convenient to the city center (just a 5-min. taxi ride from the piers), has front and side gardens, a parking area, and a reputation as one of Southampton's best small hotels. The rooms are tastefully decorated and comfortable, each with a small bathroom with shower stall. In the cozy lounge bar an open fire burns in the winter months, creating a convivial atmosphere.

25 Landguard Rd., Shirley, Southampton, Hampshire SO15 5DL. © 02380/227919. Fax 023/230913. www. hunterslodgehotel.net. 14 units. £45 ($72) single; £60 ($96) double. Rates include English breakfast. AE, MC, V. Bus: no. 25 or 29. **Amenities:** Dining room; bar; lounge. *In room:* TV, coffeemaker, hair dryer.

The Star Hotel 🛱   One of the better moderately priced inns in the town center, the Star may date from 1601. It was a fashionable meeting place in Georgian times. The public Victoria Room commemorates the visit of little Princess Victoria in 1831 at age 12. Many passengers spent the night here before embarking upon the ill-fated voyage of the *Titanic*. The Star has kept abreast of the times; it rents centrally heated midsize bedrooms, mainly with private bathrooms with shower.

26 High St., Southampton, Hampshire SO14 2NA. © 02380/339939. Fax 023/335291. www.thestarhotel.com. 45 units, 39 with bathroom. £45 ($72) single without bathroom, £60 ($96) single with bathroom; £85 ($136) double with bathroom. Rates include English breakfast. MC, V. Closed Dec 23–Jan 5. Bus: no. 2, 6, 8, or 13. **Amenities:** Restaurant; bar; laundry. *In room:* TV, coffeemaker.

WHERE TO DINE

La Margherita ITALIAN   Popular with families, this restaurant offers pizza and pasta, as well as veal, poultry, beef, and fish dishes—nothing special, but not bad, either. It has one of the most extensive menus in town, beginning with a wide choice of appetizers, ranging from antipasti to Parma ham and melon. Look for the catch of the day, possibly shark steak prepared Sicilian style or red mullet. Several vegetarian dishes are offered, even veggie burgers. You can order wine by the glass and end your meal with a strong espresso.

1 Town Quay. © **023/8033-3390.** Main courses £10.95–£14.95 ($18–$24); pastas and pizzas £6.95–£8.50 ($11–$14). AE, MC, V. Mon–Sat noon–3pm and 6pm–midnight.

Pearl Harbour CANTONESE   Meals here are far superior to those in many other Chinese restaurants on England's southern coast. Set on the second floor of a building in the heart of town, the place serves a tempting array of fish specialties, including fried prawns in nine different versions along with steamed fish and stewed crab with ginger and spring onion. Half as many chicken dishes are featured, including a favorite—fried chicken flavored with chili and black-bean sauce. Duck, such as boned roast duck with sliced pineapple and ginger, is a specialty, and an assortment of typical Asian beef and pork dishes is also offered.

86A Above Bar St. © **023/8022-5248.** Main courses £7–£10 ($11–$16). AE, DC, MC, V. Daily noon–11pm. Bus: no. 5.

The Red Lion ✦ ENGLISH   One of the few architectural jewels to have survived World War II, this pub is still going strong. It began as a Norman cellar in the 13th century, but its high-ceilinged and raftered Henry V Court Room is of Tudor vintage. The trial of the earl of Cambridge and his accomplices, Thomas Grey and Lord Scrope, condemned to death for plotting against the life of the king in 1415, took place here. Today the Court Room is adorned with coats-of-arms of noble peers of the condemned trio. The Red Lion is a fascinating place for a drink and a chat. Typical pub snacks are served in the bar, whereas in the somewhat more formal restaurant section the well-seasoned specialties include an array of steaks, roasts, and fish platters.

55 High St. © **023/8033-3595.** Main courses £6.50–£13 ($10–$21); pub snacks £3–£4.95 ($4.80–$8). MC, V. Daily noon–2:30pm and 7–9:30pm. Pub Mon–Sat 11am–11pm; Sun noon–10:30pm. Bus: no. 1, 2, 6, or 8.

A SIDE TRIP TO BROADLANDS: HOME OF THE LATE EARL OF MOUNTBATTEN

Broadlands ✦   Broadlands was the home of Louis, first earl of Mountbatten of Burma, who was assassinated in 1979. Lord Mountbatten, called "the last war hero," lent the house to his nephew, Prince Philip, and Princess Elizabeth as a honeymoon haven in 1947; in 1981, Prince Charles and Princess Diana began their honeymoon here. Broadlands is now owned by Lord Romsey, Lord Mountbatten's eldest grandson, who has created a fine exhibition and audiovisual show depicting the highlights of his grandfather's brilliant career as a sailor and statesman. The house, originally linked to Romsey Abbey, was transformed into an elegant Palladian mansion by Capability Brown (who landscaped the parkland and grounds) and Henry Holland.

13km (8 miles) northwest of Southampton in Romsey, on A31. © **01794/505010.** www.broadlands.net. Admission £5.95 ($10) adults, £4.95 ($8) students and seniors, £3.95 ($6) children 12–16, free for children under 12. June 10–Sept 1 daily noon–5:30pm.

4 The New Forest ✦✦

152km (95 miles) SW of London; 16km (10 miles) W of Southampton

Encompassing about 37,000 hectares (92,000 acres), the New Forest is a large tract created by William the Conqueror, who laid out the limits of this then-private hunting preserve. Successful poachers faced the executioner if they were caught, and those who hunted but missed had their hands severed. Henry VIII loved to hunt deer in the New Forest, but he also saw an opportunity to build up the British naval fleet by supplying oak and other hard timbers to the boat-yards at Buckler's Hard on the Beaulieu River.

Today, you can visit the old shipyards and the museum, with its fine models of men-of-war, pictures of the old yard, and dioramas showing the building of these ships, their construction, and their launching. It took 2,000 trees to construct one man-of-war. A motorway cuts through the area, and the once-thick forest has groves of oak trees separated by wide tracts of common land that's grazed by ponies and cows, hummocky with heather and gorse, and frequented by rabbits. Away from the main roads, where signs warn of wild ponies and deer, you'll find a private world of peace and quiet.

ESSENTIALS

GETTING THERE   By train, go to Southampton, where rail connections can be made to a few centers in the New Forest. Where the train leaves off, bus connections can be made to all towns and many villages. Southampton and Lymington have the best bus connections to New Forest villages.

If you're driving, head west from Southampton on the A35.

VISITOR INFORMATION   The **New Forest Visitor Centre,** Main Car Park, Lyndhurst (✆ **023/8028-2269**), is open daily from 10am to 6pm April through September, and daily from 10am to 5pm October through March.

SEEING THE SIGHTS

Beaulieu Abbey & Palace House ★★   The abbey, the house, and the National Motor Museum stand on the property of Lord Montagu of Beaulieu (pronounced *Bew*-ley). A Cistercian abbey was founded on this spot in 1204, and its ruins can be explored today. The Palace House was the great gatehouse of the abbey before being converted into a private residence in 1538. It is surrounded by gardens. **The National Motor Museum,** one of the best and most comprehensive automotive museums in the world (with more than 250 vehicles) is on the grounds and open to the public. The collection was built around Lord Montagu's family collection of vintage cars. Famous autos include four land-speed record holders, including Donald Campbell's Bluebird. A remarkable exhibit is called "Wheels"; in a darkened environment, visitors travel in specially designed "pods" that carry up to two adults and one child along a silent electric track. The pods move at predetermined but variable speeds and can rotate almost 360 degrees. Seated in these, you'll view displays (with audiovisual effects) spanning 100 years of motor development without the fatigue of standing in line. For further information, contact the visitor reception manager at the John Montagu Building (✆ **01590/612345**).

Beaulieu, on B3056 in the New Forest (8km/5 miles southeast of Lyndhurst and 23km/14 miles west of Southampton). ✆ 01590/612345. www.beaulieu.co.uk. Admission £11.95 ($19) adults, £9.95 ($16) seniors and students, £6.95 ($11) children 4–16, free for children 3 and under, £33.95 ($54) family (2 adults and up to 3 children). May–Sept daily 10am–6pm; Oct–Apr daily 10am–5pm. Closed Dec 25. Buses run from the Lymington bus station Mon–Sat; Sun you'll need a taxi or car.

Maritime Museum ★   Buckler's Hard, a historic 18th-century village 4km (2½ miles) from Beaulieu on the banks of the River Beaulieu, is where ships for Nelson's fleet were built, including the admiral's favorite, *Agamemnon,* as well as *Eurylus* and *Swiftsure.* The Maritime Museum highlights the village's shipbuilding history as well as Henry Adams, master shipbuilder; Nelson's favorite ship; Buckler's Hard and Trafalgar; and models of Sir Francis Chichester's yachts and items of his equipment. The cottage exhibits re-create 18th-century life in Buckler's

Hard—stroll through the New Inn of 1793 and a shipwright's cottage of the same period or look in on the family of a poor laborer.

The walk back to Beaulieu, 4km (2½ miles) on the riverbank, is well marked through the woodlands. During the summer, you can take a 20-minute cruise on the River Beaulieu in the present *Swiftsure*, an all-weather catamaran cruiser.

Buckler's Hard. (*C*) 01590/616203. Admission £5 ($8) adults, £4.50 ($7) students, seniors, and children. Easter–Sept daily 10am–5pm; Oct–Easter daily 11am–4pm.

WHERE TO STAY

Bay Tree House   A well-furnished single and a double room are available for rent in this family home. Guests share the one bathroom. For families with children, a cot or a small bed can be added to a room. It's best to write ahead to Annette Allen to reserve your room.

1 Clough Lane, Burley, near Ringwood, Hampshire BH24 4AE. (*C*) and fax 01425/403215. 2 units, none with bathroom. £24–£26 ($38–$42) single; £44 ($70) double. Rates include English breakfast. No credit cards. Closed Dec. From the center of the village green at Burley, follow the signs toward Ringwood. **Amenities:** Breakfast room; babysitting; laundry. *In room:* TV, coffeemaker, hair dryer.

Ormonde House Hotel   Set back from the main road, this is a reasonably priced and well-run hotel with a tasteful decor and spacious bedrooms. Guests check in here to relax, and they are well provided for as they do so. Rooms are nonsmoking and equipped with both tub and showers; the luxury units contain king-size beds and a whirlpool bath. The location is just a 5-minute walk from the center of the village. On-site is a popular licensed restaurant, offering freshly prepared English dishes.

Southampton Rd., Lyndhurst, Hampshire S043 7BT. (*C*) 02380/282806. Fax 02380/282004. www.ormonde house.co.uk. 19 units. £35 ($56) per person Mon–Fri; £40 ($64) per person Sat–Sun. Rates include breakfast. AE, MC, V. **Amenities:** Restaurant; bar; lounge. *In room:* TV, dataport, coffeemaker, hair dryer.

Whitemoor House Hotel ★ *(Value)*   The most desirable of Lyndhurst's inexpensively priced lodgings is located on A35 leaving Lyndhurst on the road to Southampton. The house was built in the 1930s, and although the public rooms are comfortable, the social center revolves around an outdoor patio within sight of a pleasant garden and an ornamental fishpond. The Whitemoor is small, so reservations are strongly recommended. Each midsize accommodation is immaculately kept and has plenty of room; many overlook New Forest moors. Each unit is equipped with a small bathroom with shower. Breakfast and dinner are served.

Southampton Rd., Lyndhurst, Hampshire S043 7BU. (*C*) and fax 023/8028-2186. www.smoothhound.co.uk/ hotels/whitemoo.html. 8 units. £45 ($72) single; £65 ($104) double. Rates include English breakfast. MC, V. **Amenities:** Dining room; lounge; babysitting. *In room:* TV, coffeemaker.

WHERE TO DINE

The Forester's Arms *(Value)* ENGLISH   This pub dates back hundreds of years—so far back that even locals don't know how old it is. The place features a television, a jukebox, and a much quieter separate eating area seating 42. The original beamed ceiling runs throughout, but carpeting and updated wooden furnishings have been added. The menu, the same at lunch and dinner, features traditional pub items such as homemade pies, curries, and burgers with chips.

Brookley Rd., Brockenhurst. (*C*) 01590/623397. Main courses £4.25–£10.50 ($7–$17). MC, V. Mon–Fri 11am–2:30pm and 6–9pm.

Hunters Wine Bar ENGLISH   This small, 250-year-old pub seats 30 in a room featuring original hardwood floors, beamed ceilings, and an inglenook fireplace. The menu is seasonal, based on the local market's produce. The lunch menu features sandwiches, seafood platters, and pies; dinner includes salmon cakes, grilled pesto lamb cutlets, and seafood, including fresh crab. Ringwood English bitter is featured on hand pump.

24 High St., Lyndhurst. ✆ 023/8028-2217. Main courses £4–£11 ($60–$18). MC, V. Daily 11am–11pm.

Mailman's Arms ENGLISH/SEAFOOD   This 200-year-old pub features the original fireplace; it has been updated with wall-to-wall carpeting and a country decor of lacy curtains and wooden furnishings, with plates and old photographs adorning the walls. The daily lunch menu consists of sandwiches, specials, and vegetarian dishes. The dinner menu is primarily seafood. There's a beer garden in the back, and Marston's beers are featured on tap.

71 High St., Lyndhurst. ✆ 023/8028-4196. Main courses £3.75–£9 ($6–$14). MC, V accepted for bills over £10 ($16). Daily noon–2:30pm and 6:30–9pm.

WORTH THE SPLURGE

Simply Poussin ✿ FRENCH/ENGLISH   Serving the best food in the area, Le Poussin is located in what was originally a 19th-century stable and workshop. To reach it, pass beneath the arched alleyway (located midway between 49 and 55 Brookley Rd.) and enter the stylishly simple premises directed by English-born chef Alexander Aitken and his wife, Caroline.

Amid a decor accented with framed 19th-century poems and illustrations celebrating the pleasures of poultry, the staff will offer fish and game dishes whose ingredients usually come fresh from the nearby New Forest. Try the "Fruits of the New Forest"—individually cooked portions of pigeon, wild rabbit, hare, and venison, encased in puff pastry and served with game sauce. Dessert choices change seasonally but usually include a lemon tart with lime sorbet, or a passion-fruit soufflé.

The Courtyard, 55 Brookley Rd., Brockenhurst. ✆ 01590/623063. Reservations recommended 1 month in advance on weekends. 2-course lunch £10 ($16), 3-course lunch £15 ($24); 2-course dinner £15 ($24), 3-course dinner £20 ($32). MC, V. Tues–Sat noon–2pm and 7–10pm.

5 The Isle of Wight ★★

146km (91 miles) SW of London; 6km (4 miles) S of Southampton

The Isle of Wight is known for its sandy beaches and its ports, long favored by the yachting set. The island has attracted such literary figures as Alfred Lord Tennyson and Charles Dickens. Tennyson wrote his beloved poem "Crossing the Bar" en route across the Solent from Lymington to Yarmouth. A vacation on the island sounds a bit dated, though many British families come to relax and enjoy the natural beauty. You may want to come just for the day. Some parts are rather tacky, especially Sandown and Shanklin, though other areas out on the island are still tranquil and quite beautiful.

The Isle of Wight is compact, measuring 37km (23 miles) from east to west, 21km (13 miles) north to south. **Ryde** is the railhead for the island's transportation system. **Yarmouth** is something else—a busy little harbor providing a mooring for yachts and also for one of the lifeboats in the Solent area.

Cowes is the premier port for yachting in Britain. Henry VIII ordered the castle built here, but it's now the headquarters of the Royal Yacht Squadron. The seafront, the Prince's Green, and the high cliff road are worth exploring. Hovercraft are built in the town, which is also the home and birthplace of the well-known maritime photographer Beken of Cowes. In winter, everyone wears oilskins and wellies, leaving a wet trail behind them.

Newport, a bustling market town in the heart of the island, is the capital and has long been a favorite of British royalty. Along the southeast coast are the twin resorts of **Sandown,** with its new pier complex and theater, and **Shanklin,** at the southern end of Sandown Bay, which has held the British annual sunshine record more times than any other resort. Keats once lived in Shanklin's Old Village. Farther along the coast, **Ventnor** is called the "Madeira of England" because it rises from the sea in a series of steep hills.

On the west coast are the many-colored sand cliffs of **Alum Bay.** The Needles, three giant chalk rocks, and the Needles Lighthouse, are the farther features of interest at this end of the island. If you want to stay at the western end of Wight, consider **Freshwater Bay.**

ESSENTIALS

GETTING THERE   A direct train from London's Waterloo Station to Portsmouth deposits travelers directly at the pier for a ferry crossing to the Isle of Wight; ferries are timed to meet train arrivals. Travel time from London to the arrival point of Ryde on the Isle of Wight (including ferry-crossing time) is 2 hours. One train per hour departs during the day from London to Portsmouth. For rail information, call ✆ **0845/7484950.**

Drive to Southampton and take the ferry, or leave Southampton and head west along the A35, cutting south on the A337 toward Lymington on the coast, where the ferry crossing to Yarmouth (Isle of Wight) is shorter than the trip from Southampton.

Red Funnel operates a vehicle ferry service from Terminal 1 in Southampton to East Cowes; the trip takes 55 minutes. An inclusive round-trip fare (valid for 5 days) costs from £49.50 to £60 ($79–$96) for four persons, depending on the season. More popular with train travelers from Waterloo Station in London is a Hi-Speed passenger-only catamaran operating from the Town Quay Terminal 2 in Southampton, going to West Cowes; the trip takes 22 minutes. A day return fare costs £11.80 ($19) for adults and £5.90 ($9) for children. For ferry departure times, call ✆ **02380/334010.**

The **White Link ferry** (✆ **0870/582-7744**) operates between Portsmouth and Ryde, taking 20 minutes and costing £12.80 ($20) for adults and £6.40 ($10) for children, day return. Daytime departures are every 30 minutes in summer and every 60 minutes in winter. A final option involves a Hovercraft that travels from Southsea (Portsmouth's neighbor) to Ryde, charging £9.70 ($16) for adults and £4.80 ($8) for children for day return. For information on departure times and schedules, call ✆ **01983/811000.**

GETTING AROUND   Visitors can explore the Isle of Wight just for the day on the Island Explorer bus service. Tickets may be purchased on the bus, and you can board or leave the bus at any stop on the island. The price of a Day Rover is £7 ($11) for adults and £4 ($60) for children. It also entitles you to passage on the island's only railway, which runs from the dock at Ryde to the center of Shanklin, a distance of 13km (8 miles). For further information, call **Southern Vectis** at ✆ **01983/532373.**

VISITOR INFORMATION   The **information office** is at 67 High St., Shanklin (✆ **01983/862942**). It's open Monday through Saturday from March to mid-July and September through October from 9am to 6pm, from mid-July to August from 9am to 8:45pm, and November through March from 10am to 4pm. It's best to call first, as these hours are subject to change.

SEEING THE SIGHTS
QUEEN VICTORIA'S FAVORITE RESIDENCE & A MEDIEVAL CASTLE

Osborne House ★★   Queen Victoria's most cherished residence was built at her own expense. Prince Albert contributed to many aspects of the design of the Italian-inspired mansion, which stands amid lush gardens right outside the village of Whippingham. The rooms remain as Victoria knew them, down to the French piano she used to play and all the cozy clutter of her sitting room. Grief-stricken at the death of Albert in 1861, she asked that Osborne House be kept as it was, and so it has been. Even the turquoise scent bottles he gave her, decorated with cupids and cherubs, are still in place. The queen died here on January 22, 1901.

1.5km (1 mile) southeast of East Cowes. ℂ 01983/200022. House and grounds £7.50 ($12) adults, £5.60 ($9) seniors, £3.80 ($6) children, £18.80 ($30) family ticket. Admission to grounds only £4 ($60) adults, £3 ($4.80) seniors, £2 ($3.20) children. Apr–Sept daily 10am–6pm (house closes at 5pm); Oct daily 10am–5pm; Nov to mid-Dec and Feb–Mar, Sun–Thurs 10am–2:30pm (guided tours only). Closed mid-Dec to Jan. Bus: 4 or 5.

Carisbrooke Castle ★★   This fine medieval castle lies in the center of the Isle of Wight. In 1647, during one of the most turbulent periods of English history, Charles I was imprisoned here, far from his former seat of power in London, by Cromwell's Roundheads. On the castle premises is the 16th-century Well House, where, during periods of siege, donkeys took turns treading a large wooden wheel connected to a rope that hauled up buckets of water from a well. Accessible from the castle's courtyard is a museum (ℂ 01983/523112) with exhibits pertaining to the social history of the Isle of Wight and the history of Charles I's imprisonment.

Carisbrooke, 2km (1¼ miles) southwest of Newport. ℂ 01983/522107. Castle and museum £4.60 ($7) adults, £3.80 ($6) seniors and students, £2.50 ($4) children, £12.50 ($20) family ticket. Apr–Sept daily 10am–6pm; Oct daily 10am–5pm; Nov–Mar daily 10am–4pm. Bus: 91A.

WHERE TO STAY
IN RYDE

Ryde makes a good base camp for a visit to the Isle of Wight: Many tour buses leave from Ryde, the ferry and hovercraft dock here, and the train station is here.

Dorset Hotel   Built in the late 19th century to accommodate government officials who accompanied Victoria on her summer visits to the Isle of Wight, this hotel is a 10-minute walk west of the ferryboat terminal in Ryde. Painted cream with beige trim, the stone-sided hotel offers a heated outdoor swimming pool that remains open throughout the year. The rooms are modernized and comfortable, 20 with private shower-only or tub bathrooms or else access to an adequate hallway bathroom. A dining room on the premises serves traditional English fare.

31 Dover St., Ryde, Isle of Wight P033 2BW. ℂ and fax 01983/564327. www.thedorsethotel.co.uk. 23 units, 20 with bathroom. £22 ($35) single without bathroom; £30 ($48) single with bathroom; £37 ($59) double without bathroom; £42 ($67) double with bathroom. Rates include English breakfast. MC, V. Free parking. Amenities: Dining room; outdoor pool. In room: TV, coffeemaker, hair dryer, no phone.

Seaward Guest House   Dave Wood receives guests in the century-old Seaward. Everything is well kept in the comfortably furnished bedrooms, including hot and cold running water. The public bathrooms are tidily kept for those who must share facilities. Breakfast is four courses. Even if they can't accommodate you in their busy season, they'll have suggestions as to where you can find a room.

14–16 George St., Ryde, Isle of Wight P033 2EW. ⓒ and fax **01983/563168**. 7 units, 2 with bathroom. £20 ($32) single without bathroom; £36 ($58) double without bathroom, £44 ($70) double with bathroom. Rates include English breakfast. MC, V. **Amenities:** Breakfast room. *In room:* TV, coffeemaker, iron.

IN SHANKLIN

Brambles   This vegan B&B, run by John and Mary Anderson, extends a friendly welcome to its international coterie of nonsmoking guests. The individually decorated bedrooms have comfortable furnishings. For relaxation, there is a conservatory-style bar and an invitingly furnished lounge. An evening meal can be arranged if requested in advance.

Clarence Rd., New Shanklin, Isle of Wight P037 7BH. ⓒ **01983/862507**. Fax 01983/862326. 3 units, all with shower. £25 ($40) single; £44 ($70) double. Rates include breakfast. No credit cards. From Ryde on A3055, take 3rd turn on right after Texaco garage. **Amenities:** Breakfast room. *In room:* Coffeemaker, hair dryer.

Culham Lodge ⋆   This small, friendly, family-run hotel rests on the border of Shanklin. The compact bedrooms are attractively decorated and come with efficiently organized private bathrooms with shower. Home-cooked breakfasts and dinners are served in the nonsmoking dining room. The nonsmoking lounge provides books and games for the guests; a small conservatory leads to a beautiful garden.

Landguard Manor Rd., Shanklin, Isle of Wight P037 7HZ. ⓒ and fax **01983/862880**. metcalf@culham99. freeserve.co.uk. 10 units, all with shower. £25 ($40) single; £50 ($80) double. Rates include breakfast. V. Follow A3055 from Ryde through the traffic signals, go right into Green Lane, then right again into Landguard Manor Rd. **Amenities:** Dining room; lounge; outdoor pool. *In room:* TV, coffeemaker, hair dryer, no phone.

IN TOTLAND BAY

Littledene Lodge Hotel   In this small hotel, you receive plenty of personal attention. The standards are high here, and the owner frequently makes changes in the decor and keeps everything invitingly spick-and-span for her international array of visitors. Each midsize room comes with a small bathroom with shower. Good English food is served in the spacious bar/dining room.

Granville Rd., Totland Bay, Isle of Wight P039 0AX. ⓒ and fax **01983/752411**. 7 units. £26–£52 ($42–$83) single or double. Rates include English breakfast. MC, V. Closed Nov–Feb. **Amenities:** Restaurant; bar; TV lounge; room service (8am–10pm). *In room:* TV, coffeemaker, hair dryer (on request), no phone.

Sentry Mead Hotel ⋆   Mike and Julie Hodgson run this year-round establishment in West Wight, 4km (2½ miles) west of the ferry terminal at Yarmouth. The hotel is only a short walk from Alum Bay and Needles; it stands on spacious grounds at the edge of Totland's Turf Walk and offers a view of the Solent. It was built in 1891 as the summer home of a Londoner, a Mr. Fox, who disembarked *en famille* with a rather large staff and entourage annually. The midsize bedrooms have private showers and bathrooms. The breakfast consists of four courses. Mrs. Hodgson, a master chef, prepares international as well as British food served in both the dining room and the bar, where lunches are offered.

Madeira Rd., Totland Bay, Isle of Wight P039 0BJ. ⓒ **01983/753212**. www.sentry-mead.co.uk. 14 units. £50 ($80) single; £100 ($160) double. Rates include English breakfast. MC, V. **Amenities:** Restaurant; bar; room service (8am–10pm); laundry/dry cleaning. *In room:* TV, coffeemaker, hair dryer.

WHERE TO DINE: WORTH A SPLURGE

The Cottage ⋆⋆ ENGLISH/FRENCH   This restaurant is in a 200-year-old stone-sided cottage set among thatch-covered buildings in the center of Shanklin. Inside, two floors of pink-and-blue dining rooms are accented by lace tablecloths and heavy oak beams. For starters try the prawns pecorino or the delicious avocado Ritz. Sample main courses may include braised guinea fowl smothered in a port-and-apricot sauce or Dover sole pan-fried with lemon butter. For the more adventurous, try the ostrich, pan-fried and served with a green peppercorn sauce. Two lounges accommodate smokers; the garden and courtyard are open in summer for drinks.

8 Eastcliff Rd., Shanklin Old Village. ⓒ **01983/862504.** Reservations recommended. Main courses £11–£17.50 ($18–$28). AE, DC, MC, V. Tues and Thurs–Sun 7–9:30pm. Closed Feb to mid-Mar and Oct to mid-Nov.

6 In & Around Bournemouth ⟨★

166km (104 miles) SW of London; 24km (15 miles) W of the Isle of Wight

This south-coast resort at the doorstep of the New Forest didn't just happen—it was carefully planned and executed as a true city in a garden. Bournemouth was "discovered" back in Victoria's day, when sea bathing became an institution. Its most distinguished physical feature is its "chines" (narrow, shrub-filled, steep-sided ravines) along the coastline. Today, flower-filled, park-dotted Bournemouth is filled with an abundance of architecture inherited from those arbiters of taste, Victoria and her son, Edward.

Bournemouth, along with neighboring Poole and Christchurch, forms the largest urban area in the south of England. It makes a good base for exploring a historically rich part of England; on its outskirts are the New Forest, Salisbury, Winchester, and the Isle of Wight.

ESSENTIALS

GETTING THERE   An express train from London's Waterloo Station takes 2½ hours, with frequent service throughout the day. For schedules and information, call ⓒ **0845/7484950.** Arrivals are at the Bournemouth Rail Station, on Holden Surst Road.

Buses leave London's Waterloo Station every 2 hours during the day, heading for Bournemouth. The trip takes 2½ hours. Call ⓒ **0870/5808080** for information and schedules.

If you're driving, take the M3 southwest from London to Winchester, then the A31 and the A338 south to Bournemouth.

VISITOR INFORMATION   The **information office** is at Westover Road (ⓒ **01202/451731**). From May to September, it's open Monday through Saturday from 9am to 5:30pm, Sunday from 10am to 5:30pm; from September to May, hours are Monday through Saturday from 9:30am to 5:30pm.

EXPLORING THE AREA

The resort's amusements are varied. At the **Pavilion Theatre,** you can see West End–type productions from London. The **Bournemouth Symphony Orchestra** is justly famous in Europe. And there's the usual run of golf courses, band concerts, variety shows, and dancing.

⟨*Moments* The "Green Lungs" of Bournemouth

About a sixth of Bournemouth's nearly 4,800 hectares (12,000 acres) consists of green parks and flowerbeds such as the **Pavilion Rock Garden,** which is perfect for a stroll. The total effect, especially in spring, is striking and helps explain Bournemouth's continuing popularity with the garden-loving English.

Finds **Exploring Nearby Wareham**

This historic little town on the Frome River 3km (2 miles) west of Bournemouth is an excellent center for touring the South Dorset coast and the Purbeck Hills. See the remains of early Anglo-Saxon and Roman town walls. The Saxon church of St. Martin has an effigy of T. E. Lawrence (Lawrence of Arabia), who died in a motorcycle crash in 1935. His former home, **Clouds Hill** (✆ **01929/405616**), lies 11km (7 miles) west of Wareham (1.5km/1 mile north of Bovington Camp) and is extremely small. Open April to October, Wednesday to Friday and on Sunday noon to 5pm; bank holiday Mondays noon to 5pm. Admission is £2.60 ($4.15); free for children 4 and under.

And of course, this seaside resort has a spectacular **beach** ⋆⋆—11km (7 miles) of uninterrupted sand stretching from Hengistbury Head to Alum Chine. Most of it is known simply as **Bournemouth Beach,** although its western edge, when it crosses over into the municipality of Poole, is called **Sandbanks Beach.** Beach access is free, and a pair of blue flags will indicate where the water's fine for swimming. The flags also signify the highest standards of cleanliness, management, and facilities. A health-conscious, nonsmoking zone now exists at Durley Chine, East Beach, and Fisherman's Walk. Fourteen full-time lifeguards patrol the shore and the water; they are helped by three volunteer corps during the busiest summer months. The promenade is traffic-free during the summer. There are two piers, one at Boscombe and the other at Bournemouth.

Amenities at the beach include beach bungalows, freshwater showers, seafront bistros and cafes, boat trips, rowboats, jet skis, and Windsurfers. Cruises run in the summer from Bournemouth Pier to the Isle of Wight.

The traffic-free town center, with its wide avenues, is elegant but by no means stuffy. Entertainers perform on the corners of streets that are lined with boutiques, cafes, street furniture, and plenty of meeting places. Specialized shopping is found mainly in the suburbs—Pokesdown for antiques and collectibles, Westbourne for individual designer fashion and home accessories. Victorian shopping arcades can be found in both Westbourne and Boscombe.

Russell-Cotes Art Gallery and Museum   This museum recently reopened after a major overhaul. Based in a remarkable Victorian house (1897), the Russell-Cotes boasts an outstanding collection of Victorian fine art and sculpture, ethnography, and modern British art. A new museum extension and re-landscaped gardens will house an extension program of contemporary crafts and sculpture commissions.

East Cliff. ✆ **01202/451800.** Free admission. Tues–Sun 10am–5pm.

The Shelley Rooms *Finds*   True romantics and die-hard fans of Percy Bysshe Shelley should visit this small museum and study room, housed in Boscombe Manor, the one-time home of his son, Sir Percy Florence Shelley. The rooms are devoted to the works of the great poet and his circle, primarily those written during the last few months of Shelley's life in San Terenzo, Italy.

Beechwood Ave., Boscombe. ✆ **01202/303571.** Free admission. Tues–Sun 2–5pm.

Tank Museum   Aficionados of military history should head to this installation maintained by the British military. Among the dozens of rare and historic armed vehicles are exhibitions and memorabilia on the life of T. E. Lawrence (Lawrence of Arabia).

In the village and army base of Bovington Camp. ☎ **01929/405096.** www.tankmuseum.co.uk. Admission £7.50 ($12) adults, £6.50 ($10) seniors, £5 ($8) children 5–16, £21 ($34) family. Daily 10am–5pm.

Waterfront Museum   This museum celebrates the nautical influences that made the region great, with exhibits about the effects of seafaring commerce since the days of the ancient Romans.

High St., Poole. ☎ **01202/262600.** Free admission. Apr–Oct Mon–Sat 10am–5pm, Sun noon–5pm; Nov–Mar Mon–Sat 10am–3pm, Sun noon–3pm.

Christchurch Priory Church   The present monastic church was begun in 1094 on a site where a church has been since A.D. 700. It is famous for its Norman nave and turret, monks' quire with its Jesse reredos and misericords, Lady Chapel, chantries, 15th-century bell tower, and St. Michael's loft, once a school but now a museum.

Quay Rd., Christchurch. ☎ **01202/485804.** Admission £1.50 ($2.40) adults, £1 ($1.60) children. Year-round Mon–Sat 9:30am–5pm; Sun 2:15–5pm.

Red House Museum   This museum occupies a redbrick building originally constructed in 1764 as a workhouse. In 1951, a civic-minded resident donated his extensive collection of archaeological and cultural artifacts to form the basis of the town's most visible public monument. An art gallery on the premises sells paintings, and exhibits showcase the region's cultural and social history.

Quay Rd., Christchurch. ☎ **01202/482860.** Admission £1.50 ($2.40) adults, 80p ($1.30) seniors and children. Tues–Sat 10am–5pm; Sun 2–5pm.

WHERE TO STAY

Mayfield Private Hotel   In a residential neighborhood about a 15-minute walk east of Bournemouth's center, this hotel dates from around 1900, when it was built as a private home. A brick house with a garden, and painted white, it's the domain of the Barling family, whose midsize rooms are attractive and uncomplicated, with shower-only bathrooms. Residents can request an evening meal.

46 Frances Rd., Bournemouth, Dorset BH1 3SA. ☎ and fax **01202/551839.** www.mayfieldhotel.com. 8 units. £25 ($40) single; £40–£44 ($60–$66) double. Rates include English breakfast. No credit cards. Closed Dec. **Amenities:** Dining room. *In room:* TV, coffeemaker, hair dryer, trouser press.

Sea-Dene House   Set about a mile west of Bournemouth's center, a short walk uphill from the sea, this house is a successful conversion from a former private home built in 1906 by an Edwardian industrialist for his mistress. As you climb the building's stairs, notice the hearts carved into the balustrade, symbols attributed by the genteel owner, Liz Jones, to the building's original love motif. The hotel has attractively furnished, well-maintained rooms; two of the top-floor bedrooms offer views of the sea. Bedrooms, all doubles, come in various shapes and sizes, each with a small, efficiently organized bathroom. Breakfast is served in a dining room; evening meals can be prepared if advance notice is given.

10 Burnaby Rd., Bournemouth, Dorset BH4 8JF. ☎ **01202/761372.** 3 units. £55 ($88) double. Rate includes English breakfast. No credit cards. Bus: no. 17. **Amenities:** Breakfast room. *In room:* TV, coffeemaker, hair dryer, no phone.

Sunnydene ✦   This Victorian private hotel is in a substantial gabled house on a tree-lined road between the Central Station and Bournemouth Bay. The fairly simple but very comfortable rooms are carpeted and centrally heated, with hot and cold running water; seven have individual small bathrooms with a shower

---

(Finds   Exploring Poole & Christchurch

True history buffs usually head 6.5km (5 miles) west to Poole, or 6.5km (5 miles) east to Christchurch; both predate Bournemouth by thousands of years. Both have large, shallow harbors, the type favored by ancient Romans.

---

stall. The corridor bathrooms are adequate and frequently refreshed. The hotel is licensed, and drinks and other refreshments are served in the sun lounge.

11 Spencer Rd., Bournemouth, Dorset BH1 3TE. © 01202/552281. 10 units, 8 with bathroom. £46 ($74) double without bathroom, £52 ($83) double with bathroom. Rates include breakfast. No credit cards. Bus: no. 121 or 124. **Amenities:** Bar; sun lounge. *In room:* TV, coffeemaker, no phone.

Westcliff Hotel ★★   Near Durley Chine, this hotel lies a 5-minute walk from the town center. This was once the luxurious south-coast home (1876) of the duke of Westminster. Now run by the Blissert family, the hotel draws lots of repeat business. As befits a former private home, bedrooms come in various shapes and sizes, but all are comfortably furnished and well maintained, with a small bathroom with a shower and adequate shelf space. You can order bar snacks or complete dinners at the hotel's Art Deco restaurant. There's a large garden and a parking area.

27 Chine Crescent, W. Cliff, Bournemouth, Dorset BH2 5LB. © 01202/551062. Fax 01202/315377. www. newwestcliffhotel.co.uk. 53 units. £58–£84 ($93–$134) double. Rates include English breakfast. Half board (breakfast and dinner) £34–£49 ($54–$78) per person. MC, V. **Amenities:** Restaurant; bar; pool; Jacuzzi; sauna; solarium; theater area with cinema. *In room:* TV, coffeemaker, hair dryer, trouser press.

WHERE TO DINE

Coriander MEXICAN   This restaurant, located in a pedestrian-only zone, brings south-of-the-Yankee-border flair to staid Bournemouth. All menu items are prepared with fresh ingredients. The coriander (cilantro) soup is a favorite you are unlikely to find anywhere else; it's green, spicy, and creamy. The varied menu includes standard Mexican specialties—enchiladas, burritos, and fajitas—plus some interesting vegetarian dishes; you can also order a crab dinner or a steak Mexicana.

22 Richmond Hill. © 01202/552202. Reservations required on weekends. Main courses £7–£13 ($11–$21); fixed-price meals £9.95–£11.50 ($16–$18). AE, MC, V. Daily noon–10:30pm.

Saint Michel ★ BRITISH/FRENCH   This is a smart brasserie-style restaurant and bar that offers some of the best Anglo-French cookery at the resort. With a traditional decor, it is warm and inviting. Its chefs don't muck up the ingredients with a lot of fancy sauces. Food is relatively straightforward, but the preparation is right on target. You might order, for example, grilled calves' liver with bacon or something more imaginative—a twice-baked Finnan haddock soufflé. They also prepare an excellent roast duck here with glazed apples, and the sea bass with pesto sauce is another worthy choice. It's family friendly, and service is gracious. You can also dine inexpensively at the bar.

In the Swallow Highcliff Hotel, 105 St. Michael's Rd. W. Cliff. © 01202/315716. Reservations recommended. Main courses £15–£17 ($24–$27); fixed-price lunch £16 ($26). DC, MC, V. Sun–Fri noon–2pm; Mon–Sat 7–9:30pm.

BOURNEMOUTH AFTER DARK

A choice of major art venues offers great performances throughout the year. International Centre's Windsor Hall hosts leading performers from London; the

Pavilion puts on West End musicals as well as dancing with live music; and the Winter Gardens, the original home and favorite performance space of the world-famous Bournemouth Symphony Orchestra, offers regular concerts. Program and ticket information for all three of these venues is available by calling © **01202/456456.**

EN ROUTE TO DORCHESTER: A 17TH-CENTURY MANSION

Kingston Lacy   An imposing 17th-century mansion set on 100 hectares (250 acres) of wooded park, Kingston Lacy was the home of the Bankes family for more than 300 years. They entertained such distinguished guests as Edward VII, George V, Kaiser Wilhelm II, and Thomas Hardy. The house displays artworks by Rubens, Titian, and Van Dyck, along with Egyptian artifacts.

The present structure replaced Corfe Castle, the Bankes home destroyed in the Civil War. While her absent husband served as Charles I's chief justice, Lady Bankes led the defense of the castle, withstanding two sieges before having to surrender to Cromwell's forces in 1646 because of a treacherous follower. The keys of Corfe Castle hang in the library at Kingston Lacy.

At Wimborne Minster, on B3082 (Wimborne–Blandford Rd.), 2.5km (1½ miles) west of Wimborne. © **01202/ 883402.** Admission to the house, garden, and park £6.80 ($11) adults, £3.40 ($5) children, £18 ($29) family ticket. Garden only £3.50 ($6) adults, £1.75 ($2.80) children. Sat–Wed noon–5:30pm; park daily 11am–6pm. Closed Nov–Mar.

7 Dorchester: Hardy's Home

192km (120 miles) SW of London; 43km (27 miles) W of Bournemouth

In his 1886 novel *The Mayor of Casterbridge,* Thomas Hardy gave Dorchester literary fame. Actually, Dorchester was notable even in Roman times, when Maumbury Rings, the best Roman amphitheater in Britain, was filled with the sounds of 12,000 spectators screaming for the blood of the gladiators. Today it's a sleepy market town that seems to go to bed right after dinner.

ESSENTIALS

GETTING THERE   Trains run from London's Waterloo Station each hour during the day. The trip takes 2½ hours. For rail information, call © **0845/7484950.** Dorchester has two train stations, the South Station at Station Approach and the West Station on Great Western Road. For information about both, call © **0845/ 7484950.**

Several **National Express** coaches a day depart from London's Victoria Coach Station heading for Dorchester. The trip takes 3¾ hours. Call © **020/7529-2000** for information and schedules.

If driving from London, take the M3 southwest, then the A30 toward Salisbury to connect with the A354 for the final approach to Dorchester.

VISITOR INFORMATION   The **Tourist Information Centre** is at Unit 11, Antelope Walk (© **01305/267992**). It's open from April to October, Monday through Saturday from 9am to 5pm; from May to September, Sunday from 10am to 3pm; and from November to March, Monday through Saturday from 9am to 4pm.

EXPLORING IN & AROUND DORCHESTER

About 1.5km (1 mile) east of Dorchester is **Stinsford Church,** where Hardy's heart is buried, as are his two wives. To get to the church, officially the Church of St. Michael, follow the signs from Dorchester for the Kingston Maurward

---

Finds Don't Forget the Gardens

Although many visitors come to Dorchester to see **Athelhampton House,** the gardens are even more inspiring; Hardy visited them often. Dating from 1891, they are full of vistas, and their beauty is enhanced by the River Piddle flowing through and by the fountains. These walled gardens contain the famous topiary pyramids and two pavilions designed by Inigo Jones. You'll see fine collections of tulips, magnolias, roses, clematis, and lilies, as well as a 15th-century dovecote.

Agricultural College, then just before the entrance gates to the college, turn right, following the signs toward the Stinsford Church.

The best place for tea in this bustling market town is the **Potter Inn,** 19 Durngate St. (© **01305/260312**), with a blue-and-white interior and a small herb-and-flower garden out back with several tables. Many guests stop in for some of the delectable ice creams such as butter pecan, but a proper sit-down tea is served for £3.50 ($6). You can also order freshly made sandwiches, cakes, scones, and pastries.

Athelhampton House & Gardens ★★ This is one of England's great medieval houses, the most beautiful and historic in the south, lying a mile east of Puddletown. Thomas Hardy mentioned it in some of his writings but called it Athelhall. It was begun during the reign of Edward IV on the legendary site of King Athelstan's palace. A family home for over 500 years, it's noted for its 15th-century Great Hall, Tudor great chamber, state bedroom, and King's Room.

In 1992, a dozen of the house's rooms were damaged by an accidental fire caused by faulty wiring in the attic. However, skilled craftspeople restored all the magnificent interiors.

Insider's tip: Though many visitors come to see the house, the gardens are even more inspiring, and were often visited by Thomas Hardy. See the box "Don't Forget the Gardens," above.

On A35, 8km (5 miles) east of Dorchester. © 01305/848363. www.athelhampton.co.uk. Admission £7 ($11) adults, £6.30 ($10) seniors, £4.95 ($8) students. Mar–Oct Sun–Fri 10:30am–5pm; Nov–Feb Sun 10:30am–5pm. Take the Dorchester–Bournemouth Rd. (A35) east of Dorchester for 8km (5 miles).

Dorset County Museum ★ This museum has a gallery devoted to memorabilia of Thomas Hardy's life. In addition, you'll find an archaeological gallery with displays and finds from Maiden Castle, Britain's largest Iron Age hill fort, plus galleries on the geology, local history, and natural history of Dorset.

High West St. (next to St. Peter's Church). © 01305/262735. Admission £3.90 ($6) adults, £2.60 ($4.15) seniors, £2.35 ($3.75) children 5–16, free for children under 5, £8.70 ($14) family. May–Oct daily 10am–5pm; Nov–Apr Mon–Sat 10am–5pm. Closed Good Friday, Christmas Day.

Hardy's Cottage ★ Thomas Hardy was born in 1840 at Higher Bockhampton. His home, now a National Trust property, may be visited by appointment. Approach the cottage on foot—it's a 10-minute walk—after parking your vehicle in the space provided in the woods. Write in advance to Hardy's Cottage, Higher Bockhampton, Dorchester, Dorset DT2 8QJ, England, or call the number below.

Higher Bockhampton (5km/3 miles northeast of Dorchester and 1km/½ mile south of Blandford Road/A35). © 01305/262366. Admission £2.80 ($4.50). Sun–Thurs 11am–5pm. Closed Nov–Mar.

WHERE TO STAY

The Casterbridge Hotel 🏆 This stone-fronted Georgian house in the heart of town was originally built around 1780 with stones taken from a demolished prison nearby. Owned by several generations of the Turner family since the 1930s, this hotel offers clean and well-maintained midsize rooms with a private bathroom with shower. The cheaper rooms are rather small, but all are quintessentially English in their tastes, fabrics, and furniture. Breakfast is the only meal served, but the hotel keeps copies of menus from most of the town's restaurants in its parlor/sitting room.

49 High East St., Dorchester, Dorset DT1 1HU. ✆ **01305/264043.** Fax 01305/260884. www.casterbridge hotel.co.uk. 15 units. £48–£64 ($77–$102) single; £80–£100 ($128–$160) double. Rates include English breakfast. AE, DC, MC, V. Closed Dec 25–26. **Amenities:** Bar for residents; laundry/dry cleaning. *In room:* TV, coffeemaker, hair dryer.

Wessex Royale Hotel 🏆 Located in the town center and built on medieval foundations, the Wessex is a Georgian structure that once belonged to the earl of Ilchester. The public rooms contain much of the original wooden paneling, along with fireplaces and decorative work. The hotel has been modernized and considerably upgraded, each bedroom containing a private bathroom with tub-shower combination. All bathrooms have been refurbished. It has a busy restaurant, Durberville, and a good wine list.

32 High West St., Dorchester, Dorset DT1 1UP. ✆ **01305/262660.** Fax 01305/251941. www.wessex-royale-hotel.com. 29 units. £65 ($104) single; £85 ($136) double. Rates include English breakfast. AE, DC, MC, V. **Amenities:** Restaurant (English); bar; 24-hr. room service. *In room:* TV, coffeemaker, hair dryer.

Westwood House Hotel This Georgian town house in central Dorchester, may have been a coaching house for Lord Ilchester. The hotel was recently taken over by Sylvia Bucknall and restored. The comfortably furnished midsize rooms are equipped with private bathrooms with showers. Guests are directed to The Mock Turtle Restaurant, a short walk away (see "Where to Dine," below).

29 High West St., Dorchester, Dorset DT1 1UP. ✆ **01305/268018.** Fax 01305/250282. www.westwood house.co.uk. 6 units. £45–£85 ($72–$136) single or double. Rates include English breakfast. AE, MC, V. **Amenities:** Breakfast room. *In room:* TV, coffeemaker, hair dryer.

WHERE TO DINE

The Horse with the Red Umbrella ENGLISH/CONTINENTAL The window of this 300-year-old shop/coffeehouse on the main street is filled with home-baked goods. Inside you'll find tables and chairs where you can people-watch and enjoy quiche and various toasted snacks. They offer such standard fare as stuffed baked potatoes, pizzas, omelets, and baked macaroni.

10 High West St. ✆ **01305/262019.** Sandwiches £2–£4 ($3.20–$6); snacks £1.50–£5 ($2.40–$8). No credit cards. Mon–Sat 8:30am–4:30pm.

The Mock Turtle 🏆 MODERN BRITISH/CONTINENTAL This restaurant, in a Georgian-style building whose stone facade and bow window date to the early 1700s, is one of the best in town. Inside in the dining rooms, exposed stone and brick mingle with strong, dark colors and antiques to create the effect of a private town house. The menu changes about every 6 weeks, according to the availability of ingredients. Depending on the season of your visit, you may find Cajun-blackened chicken steak; medallions of pork with a green-pepper-and-lime sauce; roast duckling with black currants, mango, and crème de cassis; or black pudding with onion-and-apple relish. Fresh fish, prepared in stylish and unusual combinations, is usually available.

34 High West St. ℂ **01305/264011.** Reservations recommended. Main courses £9–£14 ($14–$22). AE, MC, V. Mon–Sat 7–9:30pm; Tues–Fri noon–2pm.

Webster's Number 6 Wine Bar & Bistro CONTINENTAL   Located off High Street and adjacent to the town's prison, this is the second in a chain of wine bars that stretches across the south of England. Contained in what was a Victorian forge, Webster's offers an atmospheric interior with racks of wine bottles, plants, and artwork, and a wide selection of wines from virtually everywhere. Good-tasting menu items include burgers, king prawns, shark steak, and roast pork.

6 North Sq. ℂ **01305/267679.** Lunch main courses £3.50–£6.95 ($6–$11); dinner main courses £5.50–£14 ($9–$22). MC, V. Daily 6:30–9:30pm.

8 Dorset's Coastal Towns: Chideock ⊛⊛, Charmouth & Lyme Regis ⊛⊛

Chideock & Charmouth: 251km (157 miles) SW of London; 1.5km (1 mile) W of Bridport. Lyme Regis: 256km (160 miles) SW of London; 40km (25 miles) W of Dorchester

Chideock is a charming village hamlet of thatched houses with a dairy farm in its center. A mile from the coast, it's a gem of a place for overnight stopovers and even better for longer stays. You may be tempted to explore the countryside and the rolling hills.

On Lyme Bay, Charmouth, like Chideock, is another winner. A village of Georgian houses and thatched cottages, Charmouth provides some of the most dramatic coastal scenery in West Dorset. The village is west of Golden Cap, the highest cliff along southern England's coast, according to adventurers who measure such things.

Also on Lyme Bay near the Devonshire border, Lyme Regis is one of the most attractive resorts along the south coast. For those who shun big, commercial resorts, Lyme Regis is ideal—it's a true English coastal town with a mild climate. Seagulls fly overhead, the streets are steep and winding, and walks along Cobb Beach are brisk. The views, particularly of the craft in the harbor, are so photogenic that John Fowles, a longtime resident of the town, selected it as the setting for the 1980 film of his novel *The French Lieutenant's Woman*.

During its heyday, Lyme Regis was a major seaport; it later developed into a small spa. Among its visitors were Jane Austen, who wrote her final novel, *Persuasion* (based partly on the town's life), after staying here in 1803 and 1804.

ESSENTIALS
GETTING THERE   The nearest train connection to Chideock and Charmouth is Dorchester (see "Essentials," in the Dorchester section, above). Buses run frequently through the day, west from both Dorchester and Bridport.

To get to Lyme Regis, take the London-Exeter train, getting off at Axminster and continuing the rest of the way by bus. For rail information, call ℂ **0845/ 7484950.** Bus no. 31 runs from Axminster to Lyme Regis (one bus per hour during the day). There's also **National Express** bus service (no. 705) that runs daily in summer at 9:50am from Exeter to Lyme Regis, taking 1¾ hours. Call ℂ **0870/ 5808080** for schedules and information.

If you're driving to Chideock and Charmouth from Bridport, continue west along the A35. To get to Lyme Regis from Bridport, continue west along the A35, cutting south to the coast at the junction with the A3070.

VISITOR INFORMATION   In Lyme Regis, the **Tourist Information Centre,** at Guildhall Cottage, Church Street (ℂ **01297/442138**), is open November through March, Monday through Friday from 10am to 4pm and Saturday from 10am to 2pm; in April, daily from 10am to 5pm; May through September, Monday through Friday from 10am to 4pm and Saturday and Sunday from 10am to 5pm; and October, daily from 10am to 5pm.

EXPLORING THE TOWNS

Chideock and Charmouth are the most beautiful villages in Dorset. It's fun to stroll though them to see the well-kept cottages, well-manicured gardens, and an occasional 18th- or 19th-century church. Charmouth, more than Chideock, boasts a small-scale collection of unusual antiques shops. Both villages are less than a mile from the western edge of Chesil Beach, one of the Hampshire coast's most famous (and longest) beaches. Although it's covered with shingle (sharp rocks), and hard on your feet if you go sunbathing, the beach nonetheless provides 8km (5 miles) of sweeping views toward France.

Another famous building is **The Guildhall,** Bridge Street (call the tourist office for information), whose Mary and John Wing (built in 1620) houses the completed sections of an enormous tapestry woven by local women. Depicting Britain's colonization of North America, it's composed of a series of 3.5m-by-1m (11-ft.-by-4-ft.) sections, each of which took a team of local women 2 years to weave. Admission is free, but the charge to add a stitch to the final tapestry as a kind of charitable donation is £1.50 ($2.40). It's open Monday through Friday from 10am to 4pm, but only if someone is working on the tapestry.

The surrounding area is a fascinating place for botanists and zoologists because of the predominance of blue Lias, a sedimentary rock well suited to the formation of fossils. In 1810, Mary Anning (at the age of 11) discovered one of the first articulated ichthyosaur skeletons. She went on to become one of the first professional fossilists in England. Books outlining walks in the area and the regions where fossils can be studied are available at the local information bureau.

WHERE TO STAY
IN CHIDEOCK

Betchworth House   At the edge of the village is a 17th-century guesthouse on the main road; there's a large parking area just opposite the house. The homey (homely in British) accommodations are always immaculate and have recently been redecorated and furnished to a high standard. A walled garden lies in back of the building.

Moments   Following the Town Crier Around

Today in Lyme Regis, one of the town's most visible characters is **Richard J. Fox,** three-time world champion Town Crier who, though retired, still does **guided walks.** Famed for his declamatory delivery of official (and sometimes irreverent) proclamations, he follows a 1,000-year-old tradition of newscasting. Dressed as Thomas Payne, a dragoon who died in Lyme Regis in 1644 during the Civil War, Mr. Fox leads visitors on a 1½-hour walk around the town every Tuesday and Thursday at 2:30pm, beginning at The Guildhall (mentioned below). No reservations are necessary, and the price is £3 ($4.80) for adults and £2 ($3.20) for children. He can be reached on the premises of **Mister Fox,** 17 Haye St. (© **01297/443568** or 01297/445097). This shop sells such wares as woodcrafts and shells and is open daily from 10am to 5pm (until 6:30pm in summer).

Main St., Chideock, Dorset DT6 6JW. ℂ **01297/489478.** www.lymeregis.com/betchworth-house/. 5 units. £35 ($56) single; £50 ($80) double. Rates include English breakfast. MC, V. Bus: no. 31 from Dorchester. **Amenities:** Breakfast room. *In room:* TV, coffeemaker, hair dryer, no phone.

Chideock House Hotel ★★ In a village of winners, this 16th-century thatched house is the prettiest. Roundheads used the house in 1645; the ghosts of the local martyrs still haunt the site in which their trial was held. Located near the road, it's protected by a stone wall; a driveway leads to a large parking area. The beamed lounge, recently face-lifted, has two fireplaces, one an Adam fireplace with a wood-burning blaze on cool days. All bedrooms, in a variety of sizes, come with bathrooms with showers. The superior rooms add hair dryers, dressing gowns, and toiletries. There is a garden in back. The restaurant, serving both French and English cuisine, offers dinner nightly; lunch is also served in season. There's even homemade ice cream.

Main St., Chideock, Dorset DT6 6JN. ℂ **01297/489242.** Fax 01297/489184. www.chideockhousehotel.com. 8 units. £60–£80 ($96–$128) double. Rates include English breakfast. £105–£125 ($168–$200) double with half-board. AE, MC, V. Bus no. 31 from Bridport. **Amenities:** Restaurant; bar. *In room:* TV, coffeemaker, hair dryer.

IN CHARMOUTH

Queen's Armes Hotel ★★ For those who like a bit of history with their hotel: Catherine of Aragon, daughter of Ferdinand and Isabella of Spain and soon to be the first of Henry VIII's wives, stayed at this small medieval house near the sea in 1501, having arrived at nearby Plymouth. It also figured in the flight of the defeated King Charles I with the Roundheads in hot pursuit. The Queen's Armes' hidden virtues include a rear flower garden, oak-beamed interiors, a dining room with dark-oak tables and Windsor chairs, and a living room with Regency armchairs and antiques. The nonsmoking bedrooms come in a variety of shapes and sizes, each equipped with a tidy bathroom with shower. You can also order dinner here. The hotel specializes in well-prepared English and French fare; there's also a vegetarian menu.

The Street, Charmouth, Dorset DT6 6QF. ℂ and fax **01297/560339.** carole@cmapstone.freeserve.co.uk. 11 units. £37 ($59) single; £74 ($118) double. Rates include English breakfast. V. Closed last 2 weeks in Dec. **Amenities:** Restaurant; lounge; bar. *In room:* TV, coffeemaker, no phone.

IN LYME REGIS

Coverdale Guesthouse This house, built in the 1920s, is set in a residential neighborhood about 5 minutes from the center of town and the waterfront. This B&B is a pretty and inviting home; its front large bay windows provide a view of the sea, and there's a small garden out back. The comfortable midsize rooms are all nonsmoking; eight have shower-only bathrooms, and one has a combination shower/tub bathroom.

Woodmead Rd., Lyme Regis, Dorset DT7 3AB. ℂ **01297/442882.** Fax 01297/444673. coverdale@tinyworld.co.uk. 9 units. £25 ($40) single; £44–£56 ($70–$90) double. Rates include breakfast. No credit cards. Closed Nov–Jan. **Amenities:** Breakfast room. *In room:* TV, coffeemaker, hair dryer (on request), no phone.

The Red House ★ *Finds* Opening onto a dramatic view of the coastline, this is a stately 1920s house, once the private home of a well-known mariner. It has been successfully converted to receive paying guests. Set on well-groomed grounds, it offers a sweep of Lyme Bay and some 30 miles of the Dorset coastline, yet is within walking distance of the harbor and the center of town. Rooms, all doubles, are good-size and attractively and comfortably furnished, each with a private bathroom with shower. Breakfast can be taken on a private balcony overlooking the coast.

Sidmouth Rd., Lyme Regis, Dorset DT7 3ES. ⓒ and fax **01297/442055.** 3 units. £33–£40 ($53–$64) single; £44–£58 ($70–$93) double. MC, V. Closed mid-Nov to Easter. **Amenities:** Breakfast room; lounge. *In room:* TV, fridge, coffeemaker, hair dryer (on request), iron (on request), no phone.

WHERE TO DINE
IN CHIDEOCK

George Inn ENGLISH Dating from 1685, this is the oldest hostelry in Chideock, 22 miles west of Dorchester. The George has two large bars, a comfortable family room, and a 60-seat restaurant. The owner, Paul Crisp, serves food in the bar, including stuffed omelets, stuffed chicken breast, succulent Dorset steaks, stuffed trout, chicken chasseur, daily specials, and a range of homemade desserts. Many vegetarian meals are offered.

On A35, in Chideock. ⓒ **01297/489419.** Reservations required. Main courses £3.80–£12.95 ($6–$20); fixed-price Sun lunch £8.95 ($13). MC, V. Daily noon–2pm and 6:30–9:30pm.

IN LYME REGIS

Pilot Boat Inn ENGLISH   Built in 1844, and once a hangout for some of the region's most notorious smugglers, this is the best pub in Lyme Regis. Its lounge bar, accented with the somber local stone known as blue Lias, has a nautical decor and views of the River Lyme. Pub fare consists of fresh sandwiches made of locally caught crab and the hot soup of the day. Hot main dishes might include the ubiquitous steak-and-kidney pie and a sea grill; the catch of the day is usually written on a chalkboard menu. The restaurant also features a special children's menu and a vegetarian menu with at least eight offerings. Desserts are typically English.

Bridge St. ⓒ **01297/443157.** Reservations recommended. Main courses £7.50–£11.75 ($12–$19). DC, MC, V. Daily 11am–10pm. Pub Mon–Sat 10am–11pm; Sun noon–10:30pm.

9 Sherborne

205km (128 miles) SW of London; 30km (19 miles) NW of Dorchester

A little gem of a town with well-preserved medieval, Tudor, Stuart, and Georgian buildings still standing, Sherborne is in the heart of Dorset, surrounded by wooded hills, valleys, and chalk downs. Sir Walter Raleigh lived here before his fall from grace.

ESSENTIALS
GETTING THERE   Frequent trains depart from London's Waterloo Station through the day. The trip takes 2 hours. For information, call ⓒ **0845/7484950.**

One **National Express** coach departs daily from London's Victoria Coach Station. Call ⓒ **0870/5808080** for information and schedules.

If you're driving, take the M3 west from London, continuing southwest on the A303 and the B3145.

VISITOR INFORMATION   The **Tourist Information Centre,** on Digby Road (ⓒ **01935/815341**), is open April through October, Monday through Saturday from 9:30am to 5:30pm, and November through March, Monday through Saturday from 10am to 3pm.

EXPLORING SHERBORNE
In addition to the attractions listed below, you can go to Cerne Abbas, a village south of Sherborne, to see the Pitchmarket, where Thomas and Maria Washington, uncle and aunt of American president George Washington, once lived.

Sherborne Old Castle ⚔ The castle was built by the powerful Bishop Roger de Caen in the early 12th century, but it was seized by the crown at about the time of King Henry I's death in 1135 and Stephen's troubled accession to the throne. The castle was given to Sir Walter Raleigh by Queen Elizabeth I. The gallant knight built Sherborne Lodge in the deer park close by (now privately owned). The buildings were mostly destroyed in the Civil War, but you can still see a gatehouse, some graceful arcades, and decorative windows.

Castleton, off A30, 1km (½ mile) east of Sherborne. ℂ **01935/812730.** Admission £1.80 ($2.90) adults, £1.40 ($2.25) seniors and students, 90p ($1.45) children 5–16, free for children 4 and under. Apr–Oct daily 10am–6pm; Nov–Mar Wed–Sun 10am–4pm. Follow the signs 1.5km (1 mile) east from the town center.

Sherborne Castle ⚔ Sir Walter Raleigh built this castle in 1594, when he decided that it would not be feasible to restore the old castle to suit his needs. This Elizabethan residence was a square mansion, to which later owners added four Jacobean wings to make it more palatial. After King James I had Raleigh imprisoned in the Tower of London, the monarch gave the castle to a favorite Scot, Robert Carr, banishing the Raleighs from their home. In 1617, it became the property of Sir John Digby, first earl of Bristol, and has been the Digby family home ever since. The mansion was enlarged by Sir John in 1625, and in the 18th century, the formal Elizabethan gardens and fountains of the Raleighs were altered by Capability Brown, who created a serpentine lake between the two castles. The 8 hectares (20 acres) of lawns and pleasure grounds around the 20-hectare (50-acre) lake are open to the public. In the house are fine furniture, china, and paintings by Gainsborough, Lely, Reynolds, Kneller, and Van Dyck, among others.

Cheap St. (off New Rd. 1.5km/1 mile east of the center). ℂ **01935/813182.** www.sherbornecastle.com. Castle and grounds £6 ($10) adults, £5.50 ($9) seniors, free for ages 15 and under. Grounds only £3.25 ($5) adults, free for children under 15. Apr 1–Oct 31 Tues–Thurs, Sat–Sun, and bank holidays 11am–5pm. Last admission 4:30pm.

Sherborne Abbey ⚔⚔ One of the great churches of England, this abbey was founded in A.D. 705 as the Cathedral of the Saxon Bishops of Wessex. In the late 10th century, it became a Benedictine monastery, and since the Reformation it has been a parish church. Famous for its fan-vaulted roof added by Abbot Ramsam at the end of the 15th century, it was the first of its kind erected in England. Inside are many fine monuments, including Purbeck marble effigies of medieval abbots as well as Elizabethan "four-poster" and canopied tombs. The baroque statue of the earl of Bristol stands between his two wives and dates from 1698. A public school occupies the abbey's surviving medieval monastic buildings and was the setting for the classic film *Good-bye, Mr. Chips.*

Abbey Close. ℂ **01935/812452.** Free admission but donations for upkeep welcomed. Apr–Sept daily 8:30am–6pm; Oct–Mar daily 8:30am–4pm.

WHERE TO STAY

The Alders ⚔ *Finds* The Alders offers the peace and quiet of the picture-postcard village of Sanford Orcas, only a few minutes from Sherborne. The attractively furnished, good-size, nonsmoking bedrooms offer modern bathrooms with shower units. A lounge for guests overlooks the garden. A traditional breakfast is served family style at one large table.

Sanford Orcas, near Sherborne, Dorset DT9 4SB. ℂ **01963/220666.** Fax 01963/220106. www.thealdersbb.com. 3 units. £50 ($80) single or double. Rate includes breakfast. No credit cards. From town take A3148 toward Marston Magna; after 4km (2½ miles) take signposted turn to Sanford Orcas. At T-junction in village turn left toward Manor House. **Amenities:** Breakfast room; guest lounge. *In room:* TV, coffeemaker, hair dryer, no phone.

The Antelope Hotel This family-type hotel is in the Sherborne historic district on A30. The inn dates from the 18th century. It's a good base for touring the area and has comfortably furnished, good-size bedrooms equipped with tidily kept bathrooms with private showers. The hotel operates an Italian restaurant where continental meals are served.

Greenhill, Sherborne, Dorset DT9 4EP. © **01935/812077.** Fax 01935/816473. 19 units. £49.50 ($79) single; £69.50 ($111) double; £74.50 ($119) family. Rates include English breakfast. AE, MC, V. **Amenities:** Restaurant; bar; laundry. *In room:* TV, coffeemaker, hair dryer, trouser press.

Sherborne Hotel ★ *Kids* Built of red brick in 1969, this two-story hotel lies near a school and a scattering of factories and houses. Although popular with business travelers, it's more elegant than a typical roadside hotel, with more amenities than might be expected and easy access to Sherborne's historic center. Attracting both business travelers and visitors, the hotel gets high marks for quality. Its bedrooms, small to medium in size, are too functional to be the most glamorous in the area. Eleven of the rooms are spacious enough for small families. The small baths are tidily kept, each with a shower.

Horsecastles Lane (near the A30 Rd. and about 1.5km/1 mile west of Sherborne's center), Sherborne, Dorset DT9 6BB. © **01935/813191.** Fax 01935/816493. 58 units. Sun–Thurs £65.50 ($105) single or double; Fri–Sun £95.50 ($153) single or double. AE, DC, MC, V. **Amenities:** Restaurant; bar; room service. *In room:* TV, coffeemaker, hair dryer, trouser press.

10 Shaftesbury

160km (100 miles) SW of London; 46km (29 miles) NE of Dorchester

This typical Dorsetshire market town dates from the 9th century, when Alfred the Great founded an abbey and made his daughter its first abbess. King Edward the Martyr (d. 978) was buried here. Canute died in the abbey (d. 1035) but was buried in Winchester. Little now remains of the abbey, but the ruins are beautifully laid out. The museum adjoining St. Peter's Church at the top of Gold Hill provides a good idea of what the ancient Saxon hilltop town was like.

Today, ancient cottages with thatched roofs and tiny paned windows line the steep cobbled streets, and modern stores compete with the outdoor market on High Street and the cattle market off Christy's Lane. The town is an excellent center from which to visit Hardy Country (it appears as Shaston in *Jude the Obscure*), Stourhead Gardens, and Longleat House. (The gardens and house are covered in chapter 8.)

ESSENTIALS

GETTING THERE With no direct train access, you have to take the Exeter train leaving from London's Waterloo Station to Gillingham in Dorset, where a 6.5km (4-mile) bus or taxi ride to Shaftesbury awaits you. Trains from London run every 2 hours. For rail information, call © **0845/7484950.**

Bus connections are possible from London's Victoria Coach Station once a day, with two or three daily connections from Bristol, Bath, Bournemouth, and Salisbury. The Tourist Information Centre (see below) keeps up-to-date transportation hookups in the area.

If you're driving, head west from London on the M3, continuing along the A303 until the final approach by the A350.

VISITOR INFORMATION The **Tourist Information Centre,** 8 Bell St. (© **01747/853514**), is open daily April through October from 10am to 5pm;

November through March hours are from 10am to 1pm Monday through Wednesday, and from 10am to 5pm Thursday through Saturday.

EXPLORING SHAFTESBURY

The ruins of **Shaftesbury Abbey** ✪, Park Walk (✆ **01747/852910**), flank one edge of Gold Hill. It was founded in A.D. 888 by King Alfred—who appointed his daughter, Ethelgiva, as its first abbess—and closed by Henry VIII during the Dissolution of the Monasteries in 1539, then later fell into ruin. Over the centuries, its stones were used widely for other building projects in town, including those houses on Gold Hill. Excavations of the site continue, but during warm weather; from March 29 to October 31 you can visit the abbey daily from 10am to 5pm. Admission is £1.50 ($2.40) for adults, £1 ($1.60) for students and seniors, and 60p (95¢) for children under 14.

A TEATIME BREAK   Near Shaftesbury in Dorset, on the A350 Blandford road, 20 miles from Warminster, is the **Milestones Tea Room,** Compton Abbas (✆ **01747/812197**). This 17th-century thatched cottage is the ideal English tearoom, with a summer garden and a splashing fountain. It stands right next to the church and has views over the Dorset hills. The spotless little place is presided over by Ann and Roy Smith, who serve real farmhouse teas or a ploughman's lunch, as well as fresh sandwiches. Open April through October, Friday through Wednesday.

WHERE TO STAY

Because rooms, especially inexpensive ones, are limited around Shaftesbury in summer, it's wise to make reservations ahead of time.

The Knoll   This red brick Victorian family house has a large garden with lovely views and a gallery of watercolors painted by owner Bryan Pickard. This nonsmoking facility has been restored by Bryan and his wife Kate, who have charmingly decorated the bedrooms and added many special touches, including hair dryers and beverage makers. Breakfast is served in a room overlooking the garden. The house is only a 3-minute walk from the town center and a choice of restaurants.

Bleke St., Shaftesbury, Dorset, SP7 8AH. ✆ **01747/855243.** www.pick-art.org.uk. 1 unit with shower. £54 ($86) single or double. Rates include breakfast. AE, MC, V. Closed Dec 25. **Amenities:** Breakfast room. *In room:* TV, coffeemaker, hair dryer, no phone.

Vale Mount   About 2 minutes from the heart of town and open all year, this comfortable, pleasantly furnished house is a good bargain. A free parking area is nearby. Rooms, although small, are quite comfortable; several rooms were recently redecorated.

17A Salisbury St., Shaftesbury, Dorset SP7 8EL. ✆ **01747/852991.** 5 units, none with bathroom. £18 ($29) single; £36 ($58) double. Rates include English breakfast. No credit cards. Free parking nearby. **Amenities:** Breakfast room.

WHERE TO DINE

Half Moon BRITISH/INDIAN   Located a half-mile from the center of town, this local pub features a good restaurant that's popular with townspeople, although many come only to drink during regular pub hours. Your best bet is to opt for one of the daily specials prepared fresh, based on whatever looked good at the market. The regular menu features the usual homemade meat pies, some good steaks, a selection of vegetarian dishes, and some Indian specialties.

Salisbury Rd. ✆ **01747/852456.** Main courses £6.50–£11.50 ($10–$18). MC, V. Daily noon–2:30pm and 6–9:30pm.

King's Arms BRITISH   In the center of town, only 2 blocks from the town hall, this pub serves traditional grub and does so quite well. Its daily specials attract a lively lunchtime business of locals who consider the fare "dependable." Although the King's Arms doesn't attract gourmets, its dishes are substantial, made with fresh ingredients, and quite tasty. There is also a selection of vegetarian dishes, plus what the publicans call "light bites"—sandwiches and the like.

Bleke St. © 01747/852746. Main courses £5–£10 ($8–$16). MC, V. Daily 11am–11pm.

Two Brewers BRITISH/CONTINENTAL   Located on one of the main streets of town, this is not only one of Shaftesbury's most venerated pubs, but it does a substantial restaurant business as well. Many local B&B owners send their clients here for dinner—and sometimes even join them. For those accustomed to English dining, the fare here is familiar, including the usual pastas, especially a tasty lasagna. You can also order a decent chili, the inevitable and seemingly ubiquitous scampi, seafood dishes, and an assortment of British steaks, some from the Black Angus cattle of Scotland. Service is good, and there's a convivial atmosphere.

St. James's St. © 01747/854211. Main courses £5.50–£11.50 ($9–$18). AE, DC, MC, V. Mon–Sat 11am–3pm and 6–11pm; Sun noon–3pm and 6–10:30pm.

8

Wiltshire & Somerset

For a look at the "West Countree," we move now into Wiltshire and Somerset, two of the most historic shires of England. Once you reach this area of pastoral woodland, London seems far removed.

Most people agree that the West Country begins in Wiltshire at Salisbury, with its early English cathedral. Nearby is Stonehenge, England's oldest prehistoric monument. As you cross Wiltshire, you'll be entering a country of chalky, grassy uplands and rolling plains. Much of the shire is agricultural, and a large part is pastureland.

Somerset has some of the most beautiful scenery in England. The undulating limestone hills of Mendip and the irresistible Quantocks are especially lovely in spring and fall. Somerset opens onto the Bristol Channel, with Minehead serving as its chief resort. Somerset also encompasses the territory around the old port of Bristol and the Roman city of Bath, known for its abbey and spa water, lying beside the river Avon. The shire is rich in legend, history, and fanciful associations with King Arthur and Queen Guinevere, Camelot, and Alfred the Great. Its villages are noted for the tall towers of their parish churches.

The two best places to base yourself while you explore the area are Bath and Salisbury. From Salisbury you can visit Stonehenge and Old Sarum, the two most fabled ancient monuments in the West Country, as well as visit the stones at Avebury. Glastonbury, its once-great abbey now a ruined sanctuary, may be one of Britain's oldest inhabited sites. The greatest natural spectacle in the area is Exmoor National Park, stretching for 686 sq. km (265 sq. miles) on the north coast of Devon and Somerset. Two other major attractions, Longleat House and the fabled gardens at Stourhead, can be visited in a busy day while you're based at Bath.

1 Salisbury ★★

144km (90 miles) SW of London; 85km (53 miles) SE of Bristol

Long before you've entered Salisbury, the spire of its cathedral comes into view—just as John Constable captured it on canvas. The 404-foot pinnacle of the early English and Gothic cathedral is the tallest in England.

Salisbury, or New Sarum, lies in the valley of the Avon River. Filled with Tudor inns and tearooms, it is the only true city in Wiltshire. It's an excellent base for visitors to Stonehenge or Avebury, most of whom rush on their way after visiting the cathedral. But this old market town is interesting in its own right; choose to linger, and you'll find a pub-to-citizen ratio as high as anywhere in England.

ESSENTIALS
GETTING THERE **Network Express** trains depart for Salisbury hourly from Waterloo Station in London; the trip takes 2 hours. **Sprinter** trains offer fast, efficient service every hour from Portsmouth, Bristol, and South Wales.

Value Cheap Thrills: What to See & Do for Free
(or Almost) in Wiltshire & Somerset

Contemplate the mystery of Stonehenge. Europe's most famous prehistoric monument is a puzzle of the ages. Constructed in stages from around 3000 B.C., it looms in lonely isolation over the Salisbury Plain. It's amazing how these early builders attained such a complicated understanding of astronomy and mathematics. For many visitors, watching the sun go down at Stonehenge is one of England's most evocative sights.

Attend a summer "festival" in Bath. Set in the green hills of the Avon Valley, this spa town regains its old joie de vivre in summer. The traffic-free city center is lively day and night, with bric-a-brac shops, museums, Roman baths, street musicians, and fashionable people. Or take in the honey-colored Georgian houses, among England's finest architecture.

Explore Exmoor National Park. One of the greatest places for walks is this unspoiled land of bucolic farms and lonely, windswept moors. Much of it encompasses beautiful river valleys, with the moors sometimes extending to the edge of the cliffs. There are some 700 miles of walking paths, but the most dramatic is the coastal trail.

View Salisbury Cathedral. Few sights in the West Country are as enthralling as the Salisbury Cathedral spire, the tallest in England. The cathedral dates from 1220, the spire from 1285. Later you can explore this dreamy town nestled among the water meadows where the rivers Nadder, Bourne, and Avon meet.

Spend a day at Glastonbury. Join the mystics, spiritualists, doomsayers, counter-culture people, and ordinary folk and wander around a place that claims to be the seat of the Arthurian myth; the birthplace of Christianity in England; the resting place of the Holy Grail; the burial site for Arthur and Guinevere (beneath Glastonbury Abbey); a rest stop for Jesus, Joseph of Arimathea, Patrick, and Augustine; and a passage to the underworld. Whew. How could you stay away?

Bike in the Mendip Hills. Rent a bike at **Bike City,** 31 Broad St., Wells (© **01749/671711**), arm yourself with a map from the tourist office, and set out to explore the Mendip Hills, a limestone chain stretching 40km (25 miles) from Frome in the southeast to the resort of Weston-super-Mare. Known for their caves, gorges, and "swallow-holes," the hills can be viewed at various scenic places, even on a 5km (3-mile) ride. To see one of the most scenic parts, go from Wells on a side road 3km (2 miles) northwest to Wookey Hole, where the River Axe gushes to the surface.

There is also direct rail service from Exeter, Plymouth, Brighton, and Reading. For rail information, call © **0845/7484950** in the United Kingdom.

Five **National Express** buses per day run from London, Monday through Friday. On Saturday and Sunday, four buses depart Victoria Coach Station for Salisbury. The trip takes 2½ hours. Call © **08705/808080** for schedules and information.

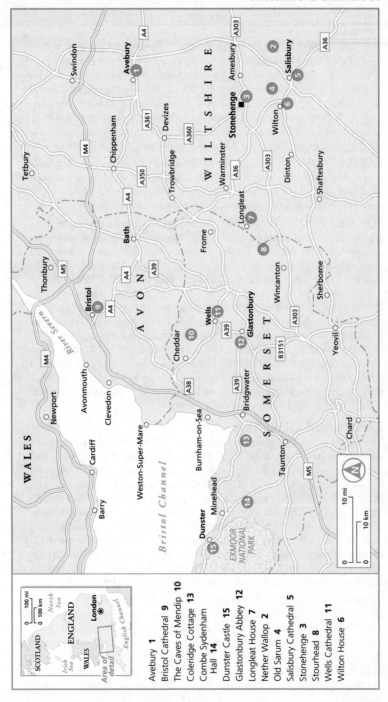

WALES

SCOTLAND
ENGLAND
WALES
London
Area of
detail
North
Sea
Irish
Sea
English Channel
100 mi
100 km

Avebury **1**
Bristol Cathedral **9**
The Caves of Mendip **10**
Coleridge Cottage **13**
Combe Sydenham
Hall **14**
Dunster Castle **15**
Glastonbury Abbey **12**
Longleat House **7**
Nether Wallop **2**
Old Sarum **4**
Salisbury Cathedral **5**
Stonehenge **3**
Stourhead **8**
Wells Cathedral **11**
Wilton House **6**

If you're driving from London, head west on M3 to the end of the run, continuing the rest of the way on A30.

VISITOR INFORMATION The **Tourist Information Centre** is at Fish Row (℡ **01722/334956**), open October through April Monday through Saturday 9:30am to 5pm; May Monday through Saturday 9:30am to 5pm, Sunday 10:30am to 4:30pm; June and September Monday through Saturday 9:30am to 6pm, Sunday 10:30am to 4:30pm; July through August, Monday through Saturday 9:30am to 7pm, Sunday 10:30am to 5pm. You can easily see Salisbury by foot, either on your own or by taking a guided daytime or evening walk sponsored by the Centre. Tickets are £2.50 ($4) adults and £1 ($1.60) children.

GETTING AROUND If you'd like to bike out to Stonehenge, go to **Hayball's Cycle Shop,** 26–30 Winchester St. (℡ **01722/411378**), which rents mountain bikes for £10 ($16) per day. For an extra £5 ($8) you can keep the bike overnight. A £25 ($40) cash deposit is required. A 7-day rental is £60 ($96).

SPECIAL EVENTS The **Salisbury St. George's Spring Festival** in April is a traditional medieval celebration of the city's patron saint. You can witness St. George slaying the dragon in the Wiltshire mummers play and see acrobats and fireworks.

With spring comes the annual **Salisbury Festival** (℡ **01772/332241,** or 01722/320333 for the box office). The city drapes itself in banners, and street theater—traditional and unexpected—is offered everywhere. There are also symphony and chamber music concerts in Salisbury Cathedral, children's events, and much more. It takes place from mid-May through the beginning of June.

At the end of July, you can see The **Salisbury Garden and Flower Show,** Hudson's Field (℡ **0118/9478996**). This features a floral marquee packed with Chelsea exhibits and display gardens created especially for the event. But there's plenty more for the rest of the family, including specialty food tastings, antiques and crafts sales, and a vintage and classic car show.

EXPLORING SALISBURY

Many shops in Salisbury are set in beautiful medieval timber-framed buildings. As you wander through the colorful market or walk the ancient streets, you'll find everything from touristy gift shops to unique specialty stores. Hard-core shoppers and locals alike gravitate to The **Old George Mall Shopping Centre,** 23B High St. (℡ **01722/333500**), a short walk from the cathedral. In its more than 40 individual shops and High Street stores you can find the latest fashions in knitwear, sportswear, and baby wear, household appliances, CDs, toiletries, and greeting cards. Another place of note, inside a 14th-century building with hammered beams and some original windows, is **Watsons,** 8–9 Queen St. (℡ **01722/ 320311**). This elegant store carries bone china from Wedgwood, Royal Doulton, and Aynsley, Dartington glassware, and a fine line of paperweights.

Salisbury Cathedral ★★★ You can search all of England, but you'll find no better example of the early English, or pointed, architectural style than Salisbury Cathedral. Construction on this magnificent building was begun as early as 1220 and took 38 years to complete—rather fast as cathedrals go. (Most of Europe's grandest cathedrals took 3 c. to build.) Salisbury Cathedral is thus one of the most homogenous of the great European cathedrals.

The cathedral's especially attractive 13th-century octagonal chapter house (with its fine sculpture) possesses one of four surviving original texts of the Magna Carta, along with treasures from the diocese of Salisbury and manuscripts and artifacts

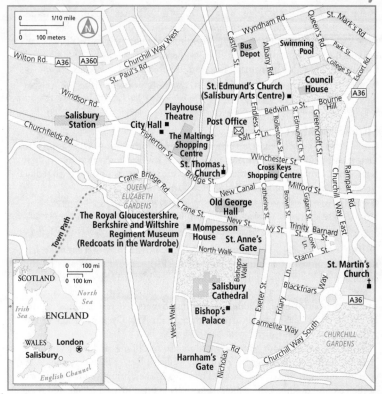

Salisbury

belonging to the cathedral. The cloisters enhance the cathedral's beauty, along with an exceptionally large close. There are at least 75 buildings in the compound, some from the early 18th century, others from much earlier.

That 123m (404-ft.) spire was one of the world's tallest structures when it was constructed toward the end of the 13th century. The construction process required extremely advanced technology for its time. The spire was not part of the original design, being conceived and superimposed some 30 years after the rest. In 1668 Sir Christopher Wren expressed alarm at the tilt of the spire, but no further shift has since been measured. The whole ensemble is still standing and can actually be visited on guided tours, Monday to Saturday 11am to 2pm (extra tours in summer depending on demand). The cost of the tour is £3 ($4.80).

© 01722/555120. www.salisburycathedral.org.uk. Suggested donation £3.50 ($6) adults, £2.50 ($4) students and seniors, £2 ($3.20) children, £8 ($13) family ticket. Jan–May and Sept–Dec Mon–Sat 7:15am–6:15pm; June–Aug Mon–Sat 7:15am–8:15pm. Sun year-round 7:15am–6:15pm.

Mompesson House ⋆ Built in 1701 by Charles Mompesson, then a member of Parliament for Old Sarum, this is a beautiful example of the Queen Anne style and is well known for its fine plasterwork ceilings and paneling. There is also a collection of 18th-century drinking glasses. Visitors can wander through a garden and then order a snack in the garden tearoom.

Cathedral Close. © 01722/335659. Admission £3.90 ($6) adults, £1.95 ($3.10) children under 18. Apr–Oct Sat–Wed 11am–5pm.

The Royal Gloucestershire, Berkshire, and Wiltshire Regiment (Salisbury) Museum The elegant house that is home to this museum dates from 1254 and contains exhibits covering 3 centuries of military history. Visitors can relax in the garden leading to the River Somerset (with views made famous by Constable) and enjoy homemade fare from the Redcoats Tea Rooms.

The Wardrobe, 58 The Close, Salisbury, Wiltshire. ✆ **01722/414536.** www.thewardrobe.org.uk. Admission £2.50 ($4) adults, £2 ($3.20) seniors, 75p ($1.20) children. Feb–Mar and Nov Tues–Sun 10am–5pm; Apr–Oct daily 10am–5pm.

SIGHTS NEARBY

Old Sarum 🏛 Believed to have been an Iron Age fortification, Old Sarum was then used by the Saxons and later flourished as a walled town into the Middle Ages. The Normans built a cathedral and a castle here; parts of the old cathedral were taken down to build the city of New Sarum (Salisbury).

3km (2 miles) north of Salisbury off A345 on Castle Rd. ✆ **01722/335398.** Admission £2 ($3.20) adults, £1.50 ($2.40) seniors, £1 ($1.60) children. Apr–Sept daily 10am–5pm; Oct daily 10am–5pm; Nov–Mar daily 10am–5pm. Bus nos. 3, 5, 6, 7, 8, and 9 run every 20 min. during the day from the Salisbury bus station.

Wilton House 🏛🏛 The 16th-century home of the earls of Pembroke has undergone numerous alterations, notably the 17th-century staterooms by the celebrated architect Inigo Jones, most recently in Victoria's day. Many famous people have either lived at or visited Wilton; it is believed that Shakespeare's troupe entertained here. Eisenhower and his advisers laid preparations for the D-day landings at Normandy here, with only the Van Dyck paintings in the Double Cube room as silent witnesses.

The house is filled with beautifully maintained furnishings and displays world-class art, including paintings by Van Dyck, Rubens, Brueghel, and Reynolds. A dynamic film, introduced and narrated by Anna Massey, brings to life the history of the Pembrokes since 1544, when Henry VIII granted them the land. You then visit a reconstructed Tudor kitchen and Victorian laundry plus "The Wareham Bears," a unique collection of some 200 miniature dressed teddy bears.

Giant Cedars of Lebanon trees grow on the 8-hectare (21-acre) estate; the oldest were planted in 1630. The Palladian Bridge was built in 1737 by the ninth earl and Roger Morris. There are rose and water gardens, riverside and woodland walks, and a huge adventure playground for children.

5km (3 miles) west of Salisbury on A36. ✆ **01722/746720.** www.wiltonhouse.co.uk. Admission £9.25 ($15) adults, £7.50 ($12) seniors, £5 ($8) children 5–15, £22 ($35) family ticket, free for children under 5. Price inclusive of grounds. Easter–Oct daily 10:30am–5:30pm (last entrance at 4:30pm).

WHERE TO STAY

Castlewood Guest House This cozy and unpretentious guesthouse lies a 15-minute walk north of Salisbury Cathedral, on the opposite side of the six-lane peripheral road (A345) that encircles the city. The most pleasant way to get there is to take the riverside walkway along the banks of the Avon. Built in the early 1900s, with flowerbeds and hanging flower baskets in front, the house stands in a neighborhood filled with other B&Bs and a scattering of restaurants. The midsize bedrooms retain many original architectural features, and contain either private, shower-only bathrooms or offer easy access to hallway facilities.

45 Castle Rd., Salisbury, Wiltshire SP1 3RH. ✆ **01722/324809.** Fax 01722/503105. 5 units, 3 with bathroom. £27.50 ($44) single without bathroom; £45 ($72) double without bathroom, £50 ($80) double with bathroom. Rates include English breakfast. No credit cards. Take any bus marked Stonehenge. **Amenities:** Breakfast lounge. *In room:* TV, coffeemaker, no phone.

Glen Lyn Guest House   The owners offer a warm welcome to their Victorian home and garden, located on a tree-lined lane just a 5-minute walk from the city's center. The comfortably furnished midsize rooms are centrally heated; some en suite bathrooms are shower-only. Shared hallway facilities are adequate. The house is nonsmoking.

6 Bellamy Lane, Milford Hill, Salisbury, Wiltshire SP1 2SP. ☎ and fax **01722/327880**. www.glenlynbandbat salisbury.co.uk. 7 units, 4 with bathroom. £35 ($56) single without bathroom; £47.50 ($76) double without bathroom, £53–£64 ($85–$102) double with bathroom. Rates include English breakfast. AE, DC, MC, V. Children under 12 aren't accepted. **Amenities:** Breakfast room; lounge. *In room:* TV, coffeemaker, hair dryer, no phone.

Hayburn Wyke Guest House   This Victorian house is on A345, next to Victoria Park and less than a kilometer from the city center, the cathedral, and Old Sarum. Dawn and Alan Curnow will warmly welcome you and your family. They offer completely redecorated small bedrooms, most often with shower-only bathrooms. Ironing facilities are available. The English breakfast is hearty and fortifying for the day.

72 Castle Rd., Salisbury, Wiltshire SP1 3RL. ☎ and fax **01722/412627**. www.hayburnwykeguesthouse.co.uk. 7 units, 4 with bathroom. £35 ($56) single without bathroom, £40 ($64) single with bathroom; £44–£48 ($70–$77) double without bathroom, £54–£58 ($86–$93) double with bathroom. Rates include English breakfast. MC, V. Bus: 3. **Amenities:** Breakfast room; babysitting. *In room:* TV, coffeemaker, hair dryer, no phone.

Malvern Guest House ⊛   In a solidly comfortable Edwardian house built in 1934, whose rear garden abuts the River Avon, this family-run nonsmoking inn sits on a quiet cul-de-sac 7 minutes north of the town center by foot. The owners, Jack and Freda Elkins, are former publicans who offer newly decorated bedrooms with shower-and-tub bathrooms. Their breakfasts even incorporate freshly grown grilled tomatoes from their garden and homemade strawberry jam. There's a guest lounge available for the use of residents.

31 Hulse Rd., Salisbury, Wiltshire SP1 3LU. ☎ **01722/327995**. www.malvernguesthouse.com. 3 units. £38–£42 ($61–$67) single; £50 ($80) double. Rates include English breakfast. No credit cards. **Amenities:** Breakfast room; lounge. *In room:* A/C, coffeemaker, hair dryer, iron.

Rokeby Guest House ⊛   This well-managed guesthouse stands just east of the town center, beside a busy residential street that eventually becomes the A30 highway. It was built in 1901 as a private home and vaguely recalls the redbrick chalets of central Europe. It's owned and managed by Karen and Mark Rogers, whom readers of this guide have praised lavishly. The bedrooms are high ceilinged, often large, and filled with the original high wainscoting. Most of them come with shower-only bathrooms. Breakfasts are served family style in the couple's dining room. Set on half-acre grounds, the Rokeby's rear garden has an enclosed gazebo, providing a refuge for midsummer glasses of wine.

3 Wain-a-Long Rd., Salisbury, Wiltshire SP1 1LJ. ☎ and fax **01722/329800**. www.rokebyguesthouse.co.uk. 9 units, 7 with bathroom. £45 ($72) single with bathroom; £55 ($88) double with bathroom. Rates include English breakfast. No credit cards. Free parking. **Amenities:** Breakfast room; gym; bar; lounge. *In room:* TV, coffeemaker, hair dryer, iron (on request), safe (on request).

White Lodge   This attractive, brick-gabled private residence is located at the edge of the city on A30 coming in from London, opposite St. Mark's Church. The entrance is a glassed-in porch filled with flowers and trailing vines. The midsize bedrooms are pleasant and comfortably furnished. Hallway bathrooms are tidily kept, and there's rarely a wait in line. The breakfast is personalized.

68 London Rd., Salisbury, Wiltshire SP1 3EX. ☎ **01722/327991**. 6 units, none with bathroom. £25 ($40) single; £50 ($80) double. Rates include English breakfast. No credit cards. Bus: 32 or 57. **Amenities:** Breakfast room; lounge. *In room:* TV, coffeemaker, hair dryer, iron, no phone.

Fun Fact **On the Trail of Miss Marple**

The little village of Nether Wallop (not to be confused with Over Wallop or Middle Wallop) lies 13km (8 miles) east of Salisbury, 19km (12 miles) from Stonehenge, and 16km (10 miles) from Winchester, on a country road between A343 and A30. Agatha Christie fans should note that, in PBS's Miss Marple mysteries, it serves as the fictitious town of St. Mary Mead, Miss Marple's home.

Wyndham Park Lodge   This appealing Victorian 1881 house is an easy walk to the heart of Salisbury and its cathedral and about a 5-minute walk to a swimming pool and the bus station. The small- to midsize bedrooms come with a double bed or twin beds, and are comfortably furnished with Victorian and Edwardian antiques and matching floral curtains and wallpaper; they also have private, shower-only bathrooms or in one case a tub-and-shower combination.

51 Wyndham Rd., Salisbury, Wiltshire SP1 3AB. ℂ 01722/416517. Fax 01722/328851. www.wyndhampark lodge.co.uk. 4 units. £32–£36 ($51–$58) single; £42–£46 ($67–$74) double; £60–£66 ($96–$106) family room for 3. Rates include English breakfast. MC, V. **Amenities:** Breakfast room. *In room:* TV, hair dryer, no phone.

A NEARBY PLACE TO STAY

The Beadles *Finds*   This traditional Georgian house with antique furnishings is situated in a small, unspoiled English village, 11km (7 miles) east of Salisbury, with excellent access to Stonehenge, Wilton House, the New Forest, and Hardy's rambling moors. Owners David and Anne Yuille-Baddeley delight in providing information on the area. The Beadles has a view of the cathedral and unobstructed views of the beautiful Wiltshire countryside from its 1-acre gardens. This nonsmoking household contains rooms with twins or doubles, each with a small private bathroom with shower. Children are welcome in the 12-seat dining room. Writing materials and picnic hampers (including vegetarian and special menus) are provided upon request. Warm-weather meals are served on the patio or in the conservatory, and a pre-dinner drink is free.

Middleton, Middle Winterslow, near Salisbury, Wiltshire SP5 1QS. ℂ 01980/862922. Fax 01980/863565. www. guestaccom.co.uk/754.htm. 3 units. £45 ($72) single; £60 ($96) double. Rates include English breakfast. MC, V. Turn off A30 at Pheasant Inn to Middle Winterslow. Enter the village, make the 1st right then turn right again, and it's the 1st right after "Trevano." **Amenities:** Breakfast room; lounge. *In room:* TV, hair dryer, coffeemaker, iron.

WHERE TO DINE

Foodies should stop in at **David Brown Food Hall & Tea Rooms,** 31 Catherine St. (ℂ **01722/329363**). They carry the finest fresh foods—meats, cheeses, breads, and other baked goods—making it a terrific place to put together a picnic.

Charcoal Grill TURKISH   The cooks here follow recipes handed down for generations in their family, and their Turkish treats have awakened the taste buds of Salisbury. Kebabs, available for takeout, are the most reliable fare, although they also prepare a Turkish moussaka, made with the traditional lamb, potatoes, and eggplant (although our latest sampling of this dish tasted suspiciously like shepherd's pie). Large portions and a staff that seems slightly ill at ease characterize this still recommendable place.

18 Fisherton St. ℂ 01722/322134. Reservations recommended. Main courses £4–£8.50 ($6–$14). No credit cards. Daily noon–midnight.

Harper's Restaurant ENGLISH/INTERNATIONAL   The chef-owner of this place prides himself on preparing homemade, uncomplicated, and wholesome "real food," and generally the kitchen succeeds in that goal. The pleasantly decorated restaurant is on the second floor of a redbrick building at the back side of Salisbury's largest parking lot, in the center of town. You can order from two different menus, one featuring cost-conscious bistro-style platters, including beefsteak casserole with "herbey dumplings." A longer menu listing items requiring a bit more preparation includes all-vegetarian pasta diavolo or spareribs with french fries and rice.

6–9 Ox Row, Market Sq. © 01722/333118. Reservations recommended. Main courses £6.50–£13.50 ($10–$22); 2-course fixed-price meals £7.20–£11 ($12–$18) at lunch and dinner. AE, DC, MC, V. Daily noon–2pm and 6–9:30pm (closed at 10pm on Sat). Closed Sun Oct–May.

Michael Snell TEA/PASTRIES/MEALS The best all-around tearoom and patisserie in Salisbury, this place specializes in tea, coffee, and handmade chocolates. The place is an offshoot of a family-run chocolate company that opened here before World War II. In fair weather, umbrella-shaded tables are set out on the square where you can enjoy a Wiltshire clotted-cream tea with scones. There are also tables overlooking the river. Among the desserts, try the Forêt Noire gâteau, a Black Forest cake. A reasonable luncheon menu, ranging from local smoked trout to turkey-and-ham pie, is offered from 11:30am to 2:30pm. Coffee is roasted on the premises, and children's portions are also available.

8 St. Thomas's Sq. © 01722/336037. Main courses £5.65–£9.25 ($9–$15); cream teas £4.25 ($7). MC, V. Mon–Sat 8:30am–6pm.

SALISBURY AFTER DARK

The **Salisbury Playhouse,** Malthouse Lane (© **01722/320117,** or 01722/320333 for the box office), produces some of the finest theater in the region. Food and drink are available from the bar and restaurant to complete your evening's entertainment.

The **City Hall,** Malthouse Lane (© **01722/334332,** or 01722/327676 for the box office), has a program of events to suit most tastes and ages in comfortable surroundings. A thriving entertainment center, it attracts many of the national touring shows in addition to local amateur events, exhibitions, and sales—a place to enjoy yourself at a reasonable price.

The **Salisbury Arts Center,** Bedwin Street (© **01722/321744**), housed within the former St. Edmund's Church, offers a wide range of performing and visual arts. A typical season has a broad mix of music, contemporary and classic theater, and dance performances, plus cabaret, comedy, and family shows. Regular workshops are available for all ages in arts, crafts, theater, and dance. The lively cafe-bar is a pleasant meeting place.

A good pub is **The Pheasant** on Salt Lane (© **01722/320675**), near the bus station, which attracts locals as well as visitors on their way to Stonehenge. Snacks, ploughman's lunches, and hot pub grub, including meat pies, are served all day. Wash them down with an assortment of ales. The **Avon Brewery Inn,** 75 Castle St. (© **01722/327280**), decorated like a Victorian saloon from the 1890s, has an idyllic garden setting overlooking the River Avon. It offers some of the tastiest and most affordable food in town.

2 Prehistoric Britain: Stonehenge ✶✶✶ & Avebury ✶✶

Stonehenge ✶✶✶ This huge circle of lintels and megalithic pillars, believed to be anywhere from 3,500 to 5,000 years old, is the most important prehistoric monument in Britain. Some visitors may be disappointed when they see that

Stonehenge is nothing more than concentric circles of stones. But Stonehenge represents an amazing engineering feat, since many of the boulders, the bluestones in particular, were moved many miles (perhaps from southern Wales) to this site.

The widely held view of 18th- and 19th-century romantics—that Stonehenge was the work of the druids—is without foundation. The construction, using boulders that weigh several tons, is believed to have predated the arrival in Britain of the Celtic cult. Recent excavations continue to bring new evidence to bear on questions of origin and purpose. But controversy swirls, especially since the publication of *Stonehenge Decoded,* by Gerald S. Hawkins and John B. White, which maintains that Stonehenge was an astronomical observatory—that is, a Neolithic "computing machine" capable of predicting eclipses.

Your ticket permits you to go inside the fence surrounding the site that protects the stones from vandals and souvenir hunters. You can go all the way up to a short rope barrier, about 50 feet from the stones. In spring 1996, a full circular tour around Stonehenge was started. A modular walkway has been introduced to cross the archaeologically important avenue, the area that runs between the Heel Stone and the main stone circle. This enables visitors to complete a full circuit of the stones and to see one of the best views of a completed section of Stonehenge as they pass by. This is an excellent addition to the informative audio tour.

Wilts & Dorset (© **01722/336855**) runs several buses daily (depending on demand) from Salisbury to Stonehenge, as well as buses from the Salisbury train station to Stonehenge. The bus trip to Stonehenge takes 40 minutes, and a round-trip ticket costs £5.50 ($9) for adults and £2.75 ($4.40) for children ages 5 to 14 (4 and under ride free).

At the junction of A303 and A344/A360. © **01980/623108** for information. Admission £4.40 ($7) adults, £3.30 ($5) seniors and students, £2.30 ($3.70) children, £11 ($18) family ticket. June–Aug daily 9:30am–7pm; Mar 16–May and Sept–Oct 15 daily 9am–5pm; Oct 16–Mar 15 daily 9:30am–4pm. If you're driving, head north on Castle Rd. from the center of Salisbury. At the first roundabout (traffic circle), take the exit toward Amesbury (A345) and Old Sarum. Continue along this road for 13km (8 miles) and then turn left onto A303 in the direction of Exeter. You'll see signs for Stonehenge, leading up A344 to the right. It's 3km (2 miles) west of Amesbury.

Avebury 👀   One of the largest prehistoric sites in Europe, Avebury lies on the Kennet River, 11km (7 miles) west of Marlborough and 32km (20 miles) north of Stonehenge. Some visitors say visiting Avebury, in contrast to Stonehenge, is a more organic experience—you can walk right up and around the stones, as no fence keeps you away. Also, the site isn't mobbed with tour buses.

Visitors can walk around the 11-hectare (28-acre) site at Avebury, winding in and out of the circle of more than 100 stones, some weighing up to 50 tons. The stones are made of *sarsen,* a sandstone found in Wiltshire. Inside this large circle are two smaller ones, each with about 30 stones standing upright. Native Neolithic tribes are believed to have built these circles.

Wilts & Dorset (© **01722/336855**) has two buses (nos. 5 and 6) that run between the Salisbury bus station and Avebury three times a day Monday

---

(Finds Biking to Stonehenge

If you'd like to bike out to Stonehenge, go to **Hayball's Cycle Shop,** 26–30 Winchester St. (© **01722/411378**), which rents mountain bikes for £9 ($14) per day. For an extra £2.50 ($4), you can keep the bike overnight. A £25 ($40) deposit is required. A 7-day rental is £65 ($104). Hours are daily from 9am to 5pm.

through Saturday and twice a day on Sunday. The one-way trip takes 1 hour and 40 minutes. Round-trip tickets are £5.50 ($9) for adults and £2.75 ($4.40) for children ages 5 to 14 (kids 4 and under ride free).

Also here is the **Alexander Keiller Museum** (© **01672/539250**), which houses one of Britain's most important archaeological collections, including material from excavations at Windmill Hill and Avebury, and artifacts from other prehistoric digs at West Kennet, Long Barrow, Silbury Hill, West Kennet Avenue, and the Sanctuary. The museum is open April through October daily from 10am to 6pm, November through March daily from 10am to 4pm. Admission is £4 ($6) for adults and £2 ($3.20) for children.

On A361 between Swindon and Devizes (1.5km/1 mile from the A4 London–Bath Rd.). The closest rail station is at Swindon, 19km (12 miles) away, which is served by the main rail line from London to Bath. For rail information call © 0845/7484950. A limited bus service (no. 49) runs from Swindon to Devizes through Avebury.

3 Bath ★★★: Britain's Most Historic Spa Town

184km (115 miles) W of London; 21km (13 miles) SE of Bristol

Long before its modern popularity, the Romans knew Bath as Aquae Sulis. The foreign legions founded their baths here (which you can visit today) to ease their rheumatism in the curative mineral springs. In 1702, Queen Anne made the trek from London to the mineral springs of Bath, on a bend of the River Avon, thereby launching a fad that would make the city the most celebrated spa in England.

The most famous name connected with Bath was the 18th-century dandy Beau Nash, who cut a striking figure as he crossed the city, carted around in a sedan chair, with all the plumage of a bird of paradise. While dispensing (at a price) trinkets to the courtiers and aspirant gentlemen of his day, this polished arbiter of taste and manners made dueling déclassé.

The 18th-century architects John Wood the Elder and his son provided a proper backdrop for Nash's considerable social talents. Using stone from the nearby hills, the Woods designed a city so substantial and lasting that Bath remains the most harmoniously laid-out city in England. During Georgian and Victorian times, this city attracted leading political and literary figures such as Dickens, Thackeray, Nelson, and Pitt. Canadians may know that General Wolfe lived on Trim Street, and Australians may want to visit 19 Bennett St., where their founding father, Admiral Phillip, lived. Even Henry Fielding came this way, observing in *Tom Jones* that the ladies of Bath "endeavour to appear as ugly as possible in the morning, in order to set off that beauty which they intend to show you in the evening."

The city suffered devastating destruction from the infamous Baedeker air raids of 1942, but remarkable restoration and careful planning have ensured that Bath retains its handsome look today. Its parks, museums, and architecture draw hordes of visitors, so prices remain high. Nonetheless, Bath is one of the high points of the West Country and a good base for exploring Avebury.

ESSENTIALS

GETTING THERE   Trains leave London's Paddington Station bound for Bath once every hour during the day. The trip takes about 1½ hours. For rail information, call © **0845/7484950.**

One **National Express** coach leaves London's Victoria Coach Station every 2 hours during the day. The trip takes 2½ hours. Coaches also leave Bristol bound

for Bath, and make the trip in 50 minutes. For schedules and information, call
© **08705/808080.**

Drive west on M4 to the junction with A4, on which you continue west to
Bath.

VISITOR INFORMATION   The **Bath Tourist Information Centre** is at
Abbey Chambers, Abbey Church Yard (© **01225/477101;** www.visitbath.co.uk),
next to Bath Abbey. It's open June through September, Monday through Saturday
from 9:30am to 6pm, Sunday from 10am to 4pm; off season, Monday through
Saturday from 9:30am to 5pm and Sunday from 10am to 4pm.

SPECIAL EVENTS   Bath's graceful Georgian architecture provides the setting
for one of Europe's most prestigious international festivals of music and the arts,
the annual Bath International Music Festival. For 17 days in late May and early
June, the city is filled with more than 1,000 performers. The festival focuses on
classical music, jazz, new music, and the contemporary visual arts, with orchestras, soloists, and artists from all over the world. In addition to the main music
and art program, there are walks, tours, talks, free street entertainment, a free
Festival Club, and opening night celebrations with fireworks. For detailed information, contact the **Bath Festivals Box Office,** 2 Church St., Abbey Green,
Bath BA1 1NL (© **01225/463362**).

SEEING THE SIGHTS

You'll want to stroll around to see some of the buildings, crescents, and squares
in town. The **North Parade** (where Goldsmith lived) and the **South Parade**
(where English novelist and diarist Frances Burney once resided) represent the
harmonious work of John Wood the Elder. He also designed beautiful **Queen
Square,** where both Austen and Wordsworth once lived. Also of interest is **The
Circus** ★★★, built in 1754, as well as the shop-lined Pulteney Bridge, designed
by Robert Adam and often compared to the Ponte Vecchio of Florence.

The younger John Wood designed the **Royal Crescent** ★★★, an elegant
half-moon row of town houses (copied by Astor architects for their colonnade
in New York City in the 1830s). At **No. 1 Royal Crescent** (© **01225/428126**),
the interior has been redecorated and furnished by the Bath Preservation Trust
to look as it might have toward the end of the 18th century. The house is located
at one end of Bath's most magnificent crescents, west of the Circus. Admission
is £4 ($6) for adults and £3.50 ($6) for children, seniors, and students; a family
ticket is £10 ($16). Open from mid-February to October, Tuesday through Sun-
day from 10:30am to 5pm, and November, Tuesday through Sunday from
10:30am to 4pm (last admission 30 min. before closing); closed Good Friday.

Free 1¾-hour walking tours are conducted throughout the year by the
Mayor's Honorary Society (© **01225/477786**). Tours depart from outside the
Roman Baths Sunday through Friday at 10:30am and 2pm, Saturday at
10:30am; May through September, another tour is added on Tuesday, Friday,
and Saturday at 7pm. To tour Bath by bus, you can choose among several tour
companies. Among the best is **Patrick Driscoll,** Elmsleigh, Bathampton
(© **01225/462010**), with tours that are more personalized than most.

The **Jane Austen Centre,** 40 Gay St. (© **01225/443000**), is located in a Georgian town house on an elegant street where Miss Austen once lived. Exhibits and
a video convey a sense of what life was like in Bath during the Regency period.
The center is open Monday through Saturday from 10am to 5pm and Sunday
from 10:30am to 5:30pm. Admission is £4.45 ($7) for adults, £3.65 ($6) students, and £2.45 ($3.90) children.

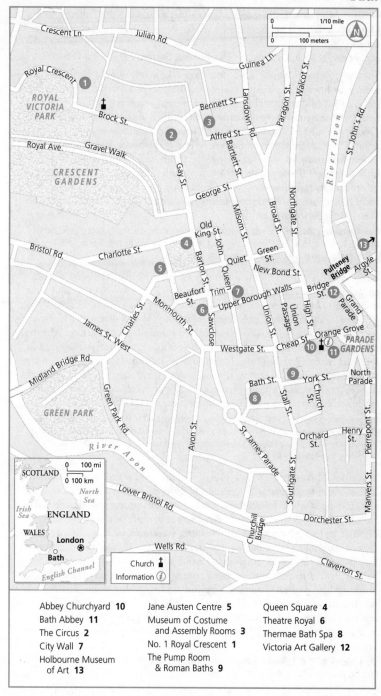

Abbey Churchyard **10**

Bath Abbey **11**

The Circus **2**

City Wall **7**

Holbourne Museum
of Art **13**

Jane Austen Centre **5**

Museum of Costume
and Assembly Rooms **3**

No. 1 Royal Crescent **1**

The Pump Room
& Roman Baths **9**

Queen Square **4**

Theatre Royal **6**

Thermae Bath Spa **8**

Victoria Art Gallery **12**

River Avon boat cruises depart from a pier adjacent to the Pulteney Bridge (directly across the water from the Parade Gardens). Cruises last 50 minutes and are £5 ($8) for adults, £2.50 ($4) for children. They run from Easter to October via two boats maintained by **The Boating Station** (© **01225/466407**).

The American Museum 🎔🎔 Just 4km (2½ miles) outside Bath, you can sense what life was like in America prior to the mid-1800s in the first American museum established outside the United States. Located in a Greek Revival house, the museum sits on extensive grounds high above the Somerset Valley. Among the authentic exhibits shipped over the Atlantic are a New Mexico room, a Conestoga wagon, an Early American beehive oven, the dining room of a New York town house of the early 19th century, and (on the grounds) a copy of Washington's flower garden at Mount Vernon. Throughout the summer, the museum hosts various special events, from displays of Native American dancing and 1700s military drills to very realistic reenactments of the French and Indian War and the American Civil War.

Claverton Manor, Bathwick Hill. © **01225/460503**. Admission £6 ($10) adults, £5.50 ($9) seniors and students, £3.50 ($6) children 5–16, free for children 4 and under. Late Mar to early Nov museum Tues–Sun 2–5pm; garden Tues–Fri 1–6pm, Sat–Sun noon–6pm. Bus: 18.

Bath Abbey 🎔 Built on the site of a much larger Norman cathedral, the present abbey is a fine example of the late Perpendicular style. When Elizabeth I came to Bath in 1574, she ordered a national fund to be set up to restore the abbey. The west front is the sculptural embodiment of a Jacob's Ladder dream of a 15th-century bishop. When you go inside and view its many windows, you'll see why the abbey is called the "Lantern of the West." Note the superb fan vaulting, with its scalloped effect. Beau Nash was buried in the nave and is honored by a simple monument totally out of keeping with his flamboyant character. In 1994, the Bath Abbey Heritage Vaults opened on the south side of the abbey. This subterranean exhibition traces the history of Christianity at the site since Saxon times.

Orange Grove and High St. © **01225/422462**. www.bathabbey.org. £2.50 ($4) donation requested. Admission to the Heritage Vaults, £2.50 ($4) adults, £1.50 ($2.40) seniors, students, and children. Abbey, Apr–Oct Mon–Sat 9am–6pm; Nov–Mar Mon–Sat 9am–4:30pm; year-round Sun 1–2:30pm and 4:30–5:30pm. The Heritage Vaults, Mon–Sat 10am–4pm.

Holburne Museum of Art 🎔 *Finds* This has been called, quite accurately, "one of the most perfect small museums of Europe." It was constructed in 1796 as a building in which to entertain guests to Sydney Gardens, one of whom was Jane Austen. It was converted into a museum at the turn of the 20th century to display a collection of Sir William Holburne's treasures, such as a bronze nude favored by Louis XIV, along with some of the finest Renaissance majolica in England. Also on display are works illuminating the glittering society of 18th-century Bath at its pinnacle, including masterpieces by Thomas Gainsborough, including his *The Byam Family* (on indefinite loan). Other choice tidbits from this treasure trove include the lovely portrait of *The Reverend Carter Thelwall and His Family* by Stubbs, and such surprising exhibits as a Steinway piano used for rehearsals of his music by Rachmaninoff. The museum is also the temporary venue of traveling exhibits.

Great Pulteney St. © **01225/466669**. www.bath.ac.uk/Holburne. Admission £3.50 ($6). Mid-Feb to mid-Dec Tues–Sat 10am–5pm, Sun 2:30–5:30pm.

Museum of Costume and Assembly Rooms 🎔🎔 Operated by the National Trust and housed in an 18th-century building, the grand **Assembly**

Rooms played host to dances, music recitals, and tea parties. Although damaged in World War II, the elegant rooms have been gloriously restored and look much as they did when Jane Austen and Thomas Gainsborough attended events here.

Housed in the same building, the **Museum of Costume** sports one of the best collections of fashion and costume in Europe. A fascinating audio tour escorts visitors through the history of fashion—including accessories, lingerie, and shoes—from the 16th century to the present day. Highlights include a 17th-century "silver tissue" dress; an ultra-restricting whalebone corset; an original suit, once owned by Dame Margot Fonteyn, from Christian Dior's legendary "New Look" collection; and the ultra-sheer Versace dress made famous—or infamous—by actress Jennifer Lopez. The museum is also famous for its "Dress of the Year" collection, which highlights notable ideas in contemporary style. Some selections have been notably prescient; its choice for the 1987 dress of the year was by then-unknown designer John Galliano. Only 2,000 of the museum's 30,000 items are on display at any one time, but exhibits change frequently and special themed collections are often presented. Plan on at least an hour or two.

Bennett St. ℂ 01225/477785. www.museumofcostume.co.uk. Admission £5.50 ($9) adults, £4.50 ($7) seniors and students, £3.75 ($6) children 6 and over, £15 ($24) family ticket. Admission includes free audio tour. Daily 10am–5pm. Last admission 4:30pm. Closed December 25–26.

The Pump Room ★ **& Roman Baths** ★★   Founded in A.D. 75 by the Romans, the baths were dedicated to the goddess Sulis Minerva; in their day, they were an engineering feat. They're among the finest Roman remains in the country, and are still fed by Britain's most famous hot-spring water. After centuries of decay, the original baths were rediscovered during Victoria's reign. The site of the Temple of Sulis Minerva has been excavated and is now open. The museum displays many interesting objects from Victorian and recent digs (including Minerva's head).

Coffee, lunch, and tea, usually with music from the Pump Room Trio, can be enjoyed in the 18th-century pump room, overlooking the hot springs. There's also a drinking fountain with hot mineral water (it tastes horrible).

In the Bath Abbey churchyard. ℂ 01225/477785. www.romanbaths.co.uk. Admission £8.50 ($14) adults, £4.50 ($7) children, £22 ($35) family ticket. Apr–Sept daily 9am–6pm; Oct–Mar Mon–Sat 9am–5pm.

Theatre Royal Bath   Theatre Royal, located next to the new Seven Dials development, was restored in 1982 and refurbished with plush seats, red carpets, and a painted proscenium arch and ceiling; it is now the most beautiful theater in Britain. It has 940 seats, with a small pit and grand tiers rising to the upper circle. Despite all the work, Theatre Royal has no company, depending upon touring shows to fill the house during the 8-week theater season each summer. Beneath the theater, reached from the back of the stalls or by a side door, are the theater vaults. One contains a bar, another a restaurant (reviewed on p. 333).

A studio theater at the rear of the main building opened in 1996. The theater publishes a list of forthcoming events; its repertoire includes West End shows, among other offerings.

Sawclose. ℂ 01225/448844. www.theatreroyal.org.uk. Tickets £10–£25 ($15–$37.50). Box office Mon–Sat 10am–8pm, Sun noon–8pm. Shows Mon–Wed at 7:30pm; Thurs–Sat at 8pm; Wed and Sat matinees at 2:30pm.

Thermae Bath Spa ★★   This is the only place in the U.K. where you can bathe in natural, hot spring water. Used for thousands of years, the restored baths are in operation for the first time since 1978. Health, leisure, architecture, history, and culture are all combined here. Five impressive heritage buildings, including the sacred Cross Bath, have been restored to create one of Europe's most remarkable spas (a stunning new glass-and-stone building was also constructed). Facilities include indoor and outdoor thermal spa bathing, steam rooms, massage and treatment rooms, a restaurant, and a visitor center.

One of the most eye-catching parts of the new spa is an open-air, rooftop pool, from which bathers can gaze out over the skyline of the city. Because of its naturally hot water, the rooftop pool is open all year. The location is set in the center of the city, just 31m (100 ft.) from the Roman Baths. The steam rooms are particularly impressive, with four circular glass pods, a "waterfall" shower, footbaths, an open-air terrace, and a solarium. A dozen wet treatment rooms feature such luxuries as hydrotherapy, hay and herbal wraps, a Vichy shower, mud treatments, and shiatsu/watsu.

The Hetling Pump Room, Hot Bath St. *C* **01225/780308.** Admission: £17 ($27) for 2-hr. session, £23 ($37) for 4-hr. session, £35 ($56) for all-day ticket. Daily 9am–10pm.

Victoria Art Gallery   This relatively unknown gallery showcases the area's best collection of British and European art from the 15th century to the present. Most of the works are on display in the sumptuous Victorian Upper Gallery. The collection includes paintings by artists who have lived and worked in the Bath area, including Gainsborough. Singled out these days for special attention is the art of Walter Richard Sickert (1860–1942) since Patricia Cornwell's best-seller, *Portrait of a Killer: Jack the Ripper—Case Closed,* named him the real Jack the Ripper in 2002 (though many critics and historians don't think Cornwell proved that claim conclusively). In the two large modern galleries downstairs, special exhibitions are shown. These exhibitions change every 6 to 8 weeks, and are likely to feature displays ranging from cartoons to boat sculpture.

Bridge St. *C* 01225/477233. Free admission. Tues–Fri 10am–5:30pm; Sat 10am–5pm.

SHOPPING

Bath is loaded with markets and fairs, antiques centers, and small shops. There are literally hundreds of opportunities to buy (and ship) anything you want, including the famous spa waters, for sale by the bottle. Prices are usually less than in London but more than in the British boonies. The whole city is basically one long, slightly uphill shopping area. It's not defined by one High Street, as are other British towns. If you arrive by train, don't be misled by a lack of scenery—within 2 blocks there are several shopping streets. If you are a serious shopper intent on hitting the flea markets, the best day to visit is Wednesday.

The **Bartlett Street Antiques Centre,** Bartlett Street (*C* **01225/466689**), encompasses 60 dealers and 160 showcases displaying furniture, silver, antique jewelry, paintings, clocks, toys, military items, and collectibles. Another option is the **Great Western Antiques Centre,** Bartlett Street (*C* **01225/424243**), with 30 dealers, where you'll find costumes, costume jewelry, trains and other railway items, lace and linens, porcelain and glass, silver, music boxes, canes, and much more. **Walcot Reclamation,** 108 Walcot St. (*C* **01225/444404**), a sprawling and appealingly dusty storeroom of 19th-century architectural remnants, stands .5km (¼ mile) northeast of the town center. Its 1,858-sq.-m (20,000-sq.-ft.) warehouse offers pieces from demolished homes, schools, hospitals, and factories throughout southern England. Mantelpieces, panels, columns, and ornaments are organized historically. Items range from a complete 1937 Georgian library of Honduran mahogany to objects costing around £10 ($16). Anything can be altered by a battery of artisans who skillfully adapt antique fittings for modern homes. **The**

⌐Fun Fact Mmmm . . . Monkey Tea!

Whittard of Chelsea, 10 Union Passage (✆ **01225/483529**), is the most charming and unusual tea emporium in Bath. Inside, you'll find strainers, traditional tea services (with a large selection of offbeat teapot designs), biscuits, cozies, caddies, and teas from all parts of the former Empire. Looking for a fabulously exotic tea to wow your friends with back home? Try monkey-picked oolong—a Chinese tea whose leaves are so inaccessible they must be gathered by trained monkeys.

Bath Stamp & Coin Shop, 12–13 Pulteney Bridge (✆ **01225/463073**), the largest purveyor of antique coins and stamps in Bath, offers hundreds of odd and unusual numismatics. The inventory includes Roman coins, some of which were unearthed in archaeological excavations near Bath. **The Beaux Arts Gallery,** 13 York St. (✆ **01225/464850**), near the abbey, is the largest, most important gallery of contemporary art in Bath, specializing in well-known British artists. Closely linked to the London art scene, the gallery occupies a pair of interconnected, stone-fronted Georgian houses. Its half dozen showrooms exhibit objects beginning at £30 ($48).

WHERE TO STAY

Aquae Sulis Hotel ★   This small, family-run hotel is known for its cleanliness, personal service, and excellent English breakfasts with welcoming hosts David and Jane Carnegie. This south-facing Edwardian property lies close to the major attractions. Its midsize bedrooms are warmly inviting and comfortable, all with well-maintained private bathrooms and all nonsmoking. All the tidy bathrooms contain a private shower, except one, which has a tub-and-shower combo. Snacks and evening meals are tasty, well prepared, and most affordable, and guests can mingle in a lovely old oak bar and lounge.

174–176 Newbridge Rd., Bath BA1 3LE. ✆ 01225/420061. Fax 01225/339064. 14 units. £49–£69 ($78–$110) single; £59–£89 ($94–$142) double. Rates include English breakfast. AE, DC, MC, V. **Amenities:** Dining room; laundry. *In room:* TV, dataport, coffeemaker, hair dryer, trouser press.

Badminton Villa   Located about half a mile south of the city center, this house dates from 1883 when it was built as part of a now extremely desirable suburban development. Constructed of honey-colored blocks of Bath stone, it lies on a hillside with sweeping views over Bath. When acquired in 1992 by John and Sue Burton, the villa had fallen into derelict disrepair; the couple has gracefully transformed it into one of the most charming small hotels in Bath, furnished with an eclectic mix of objects gathered by the Burtons during their travels. The small- to midsize bedrooms have been considerably improved, with double-glazed windows, upgraded showers, and new carpeting throughout. Bathrooms have either tub or shower. There's a three-tiered garden with patio.

10 Upper Oldfield Park, Bath, Somerset BA2 3JZ. ✆ 01225/426347. Fax 01225/420393. www.smooth hound.co.uk/hotels/badminton.html. 5 units. £48–£55 ($77–$88) single; £62–£70 ($99–$112) double; £70–£75 ($112–$120) triple. Rates include English breakfast. MC, V. Bus: 14. **Amenities:** Breakfast room; guest lounge. *In room:* TV, coffeemaker, hair dryer.

Bailbrook Lodge Hotel *Kids*   This restored Georgian town house, which adjoins A4 3km (2 miles) east of Bath, offers outstanding views of the Avon Valley. The four most expensive rooms contain four-poster beds; the double-room suites bear such names as the Jane Austen, the Beau Nash, and the Queen Charlotte. Eight units open onto garden and lawns, and the remaining rooms overlook the grounds of Bailbrook House, a Georgian mansion designed by John Everleigh, a famous architect of his day. Eight of the units come with a private shower-only bathroom, the rest with tub and shower combination. The hosts welcome children, providing such extras as a kiddie menu, cribs, and high chairs.

35–37 London Rd. W., Bath, Somerset BA1 7HZ. ✆ 01225/859090. Fax 01225/852299. www.bailbrook lodge.co.uk. 12 units. £42 ($67) single; £70–£75 ($112–$120) double. Rates include English breakfast. AE, DC, MC, V. Bus: 3, 13, or 23. **Amenities:** Breakfast room; bar; limited room service. *In room:* TV, coffeemaker, hair dryer, iron, safe, no phone.

Brompton House This elegant Georgian building (1777) is set in tranquil grounds within an easy commute of the heart of the city. When Bathwick was still a village, the old rectory of St. Mary's Church was built on the site of a 16-century manor farm; a Victorian wing was added in 1835. The hotel is well run by its helpful owners, David and Susan Selby. The good-size rooms are tastefully furnished and decorated and are equipped with private, shower-only bathrooms. In the elegant dining room, a traditional English, continental, vegetarian, or whole food breakfast is served.

St. Johns Rd., Bathwick, Bath, Somerset BA2 6PT. ✆ 01225/420972. Fax 01225/420505. www.brompton house.co.uk. 18 units. £48–£55 ($77–$88) single; £65–£95 ($104–$152) double. Rates include English breakfast. AE, MC, V. From the M4 motorway, take Exit 18 and proceed along A46 to Bath; at the approach to the city, turn left at the traffic light (signposted to A36 Warminster) and over the Cleveland Bridge take an immediate right onto St. Johns Rd. **Amenities:** Breakfast room; lounge; room service (7:30–9:30am). *In room:* TV, coffeemaker, hair dryer.

Cedar Lodge This nonsmoking B&B lies in a residential suburb about 1.5km (1 mile) east of the town center. This home was built in 1778 by a Cotswold wool merchant with ties to the Fairfax family of Virginia. Your hosts are Derek and Maria Beckett, an engaging Anglo-Hungarian couple who spend part of their time conducting research in criminal psychology for the British government. They offer comfortable small- to medium-size bedrooms, each with a private shower-only bathroom.

13 Lambridge, London Rd., Bath, Somerset BA1 6BJ. ✆ 01225/423468. 3 units. £50 ($80) single; £60–£75 ($96–$120) double. Rates include English breakfast. No credit cards. Bus: 13. **Amenities:** Breakfast room. *In room:* TV, coffeemaker (on request), hair dryer (on request), iron (on request), no phone.

Cheriton House This elegant 1870s home still offers many of its original architectural adornments, including fireplaces. The owners work hard to make guests comfortable in this nonsmoking home, and the large house is spotlessly clean. Each unit comes with an efficiently organized and tidily kept bathroom with shower or tub. There is ongoing refurbishment in the bedrooms. This is really a house for adults, not young children. Only breakfast is served.

9 Upper Oldfield Park, Bath, Somerset BA2 3JX. ✆ 01225/429862. Fax 01225/428403. www.cheriton house.co.uk. 13 units. £48–£60 ($77–$96) single; £58–£95 ($93–$152) double. Rates include English breakfast. Children under 12 not accepted. AE, DC, MC, V. Bus: 14, 14A, or 14B. **Amenities:** Breakfast room; lounge. *In room:* TV, dataport, coffeemaker, hair dryer, iron.

Grove Lodge Guest House This typical Georgian home (1787) is located near the city center and is serviced by frequent buses at the front gate. A warm welcome and personal attention are guaranteed by the owners, Peter Richards and Isabel Miles. The nonsmoking lodge has well-furnished and spacious rooms, most with large windows overlooking a stone terrace, a garden, and the surrounding wooded hills. There are large family rooms available, sleeping three or four people; all units are equipped with hot and cold running water, and one room is set aside for those with limited mobility.

11 Lambridge, London Rd., Bath, Somerset BA1 6BJ. ℂ **01225/310860.** Fax 01225/429630. 5 units. £36–£43 ($58–$69) single without bathroom; £65–£72 ($104–$115) single with bathroom; £75–£85 ($120–$136) double without bathroom. Rates include English breakfast. Discounts available for 3 or more people. MC, V. Bus: 13 or 231. **Amenities:** Breakfast room; lounge. *In room:* TV, coffeemaker, hair dryer, no phone.

Haydon House ★★ *Finds*   Built of honey-colored stone early in the Edwardian Age, this house is peacefully situated about a mile from the bustling center of Bath; many guests use Haydon House as a base for an extended visit. The midsize nonsmoking rooms, named for and decorated in a native berry theme, include a generous hospitality tray with complimentary sherry and homemade shortbread. Each unit comes with a private bathroom with shower and tub. The owners—Gordon Marr, a former commander in the Royal Navy, and his wife Magdalene Ashman-Marr—provide a very sustaining Bloomfield Breakfast each morning. As most guests prefer to sample the restaurants and pubs in the area, they do not provide an evening meal. The owners can arrange guided tours by car at very affordable rates, and are most helpful with route planning, recommendations, and reservations, including booking seats at the Theatre Royal.

9 Bloomfield Park, Bath, Somerset BA2 2BY. ℂ and fax **01225/444919.** www.haydonhouse.co.uk. 5 units. £45–£65 ($72–$104) single; £75–£108 ($120–$173) double. Rates include English breakfast. AE, MC, V. Bus: 14 or 14B. **Amenities:** Breakfast room; lounge; laundry/dry cleaning. *In room:* TV, dataport, coffeemaker, hair dryer.

Leighton House ★★ *Value*   At the southern side of the city on the A367 road to Exeter (Devon), this Victorian residence from the 1870s is a 10-minute walk from the center of Bath, and minibuses pass by frequently. Rhona Sampson offers one of the best-value accommodations in the area. A nonsmoking facility, the hotel rents elegant and spacious bedrooms, individually furnished and decorated.

139 Wells Rd., Bath, Somerset BA2 3AL. ℂ 01225/314769. Fax 01225/443079. www.leighton-house.co.uk. 8 units. £55 ($88) single; £70–£95 ($112–$152) double; £75–£115 ($120–$184) family unit. Rates include English breakfast. AE, MC, V. On approaching Bath, follow A367 Exeter signs but ignore the light vehicles only sign; turn left onto A37/A367 (the Wells Rd.) and follow the black railings uphill (450m/1,500 ft.); when the railings end, turn left into Hayesfield Park and Leighton House will be on the right. **Amenities:** Breakfast room; lounge. *In room:* TV, coffeemaker, hair dryer.

Number Ninety Three   This well-run, elegant Victorian guesthouse is within easy walking distance of the city center and the rail and National Bus stations. It is a traditional B&B, British style: small, but immaculately kept and well maintained. The owner, a mine of local information, undertakes an ongoing program of maintenance and redecoration in the slower winter months. Bedrooms, small to medium in size, are beautifully maintained and comfortably furnished. Bathrooms are small with a shower stall. The house is nonsmoking.

93 Wells Rd., Bath, Somerset BA2 3AN. ℂ 01225/317977. 4 units. £35–£55 ($56–$88) single; £45–£65 ($72–$104) double; £65–£85 ($104–$136) triple. Rates include English breakfast. No credit cards. Bus: 3, 13, 14, 17, or 231; ask for Lower Wells Rd. stop. **Amenities:** Breakfast room; lounge. *In room:* TV, hair dryer, coffeemaker, no phone.

WORTH A SPLURGE

Bath Paradise House Hotel ★ *Finds*   In a tranquil location a 7-minute walk from the city, this is a small and personally run establishment operated by Claire and Nick Potts, who made many fans among Frommer's readers when they operated a B&B in another location. Paradise House is in a 17th-century manse that has been considerably upgraded and stands on a half-acre of well-landscaped grounds. This is a 1735 house constructed from the classic, honey-colored Bath stone. All of the individually decorated bedrooms are good-size and welcoming. The two delightful four-poster garden rooms open onto panoramic views of Bath. All units have private bathrooms, two with showers only.

86–88 Holloway, Bath BA2 4PX. ℭ **01225/317723.** Fax 01225/482005. www.paradise-house.co.uk. 11 units. Mon–Thurs £87–£115 ($139–$184) double; £125–£150 ($200–$240) suite. AE, DC, MC, V. **Amenities:** Licensed for alcohol in lounge; limited room service; babysitting; laundry. *In room:* TV, coffeemaker, hair dryer, iron.

Wentworth House In the prosperous residential neighborhood of Bloom-field, this hotel lies a mile south of the city center. This four-story house was built in 1887 for the region's wealthiest coal merchant. Many original features remain, including a staircase some consider a decorative wonder, and many of the ceiling's cove moldings. Set in three-quarters of an acre of gardens, behind a facade of chiseled Bath stone, the house is the property of the Boyle family. The midsize bedrooms contain comfortable furnishings, and 16 of them have a private shower-only bathroom. The hotel offers five nonsmoking rooms. Snacks and light suppers are served by prior arrangement.

106 Bloomfield Rd., Bath, Somerset BA2 2AP. ℭ **01225/339193.** Fax 01225/310460. www.wentworth house.co.uk. 18 units. £55–£60 ($88–$96) single; £75–£105 ($120–$168) double. Rates include English breakfast. MC, V. Bus: 14. **Amenities:** Restaurant; bar; lounge; outdoor heated pool. *In room:* TV, coffeemaker, hair dryer.

WHERE TO DINE

Café Retro INTERNATIONAL This popular locale operates as a breakfast and lunchtime cafe on the ground floor and an evening restaurant on the second floor. A hip, eclectic ambience with wood floors and church pews supports a style of food that is affordable without sacrificing quality. Simple but filling lunch dishes include burgers, sandwiches, and salads. Dinner might feature roast belly of pork stuffed with Stilton and walnuts covered with a wild mushroom sauce, or twice-baked cheese soufflé with celeriac sauce. A three-course dinner menu is offered daily.

18 York St. ℭ **01225/339347.** Cafe dishes £4–£6 ($6–$10); 3-course menu £17.95 ($29). AE, MC, V. Cafe: daily 9am–6pm; restaurant: daily 6:30–11pm.

Demuth's Vegetarian Restaurant ★★ *Finds* VEGETARIAN Many British guides for vegetarians rank this restaurant among the top six vegetarian restaurants in Britain. This bright, cheery nonsmoking place prepares everything in-house, using only fresh produce and organic items. Patrons with special diets or food allergies receive special attention here. Main courses include pan-fried vegetables with rice noodles, seared tofu, and ginger and tamari apple marinade. Fresh salads and puddings for dessert round out the menu.

2 North Parade Passage. ℭ **01225/446059.** Main courses £6–£11 ($10–$18). AE, MC, V. Sun–Fri 10am–10pm; Sat 9am–11pm.

Evans Fish Restaurant ★ *Value* SEAFOOD Only a 3-minute walk from the abbey and train station, this is a family restaurant that was started by Mrs. Harriet Evans in 1908. It features fish dinners at moderate prices; a meal might include the soup of the day, fried filet of fish with chips, and a choice of desserts. Only the freshest of fish is served, although some readers find the fish overcooked. The lower floor has a self-service section; on the second floor an Abbey Room caters to families. The nicest dining spot is the Georgian Room, named for its arched windows and fireplace. From the take-out section, you can order a number of crisply fried specialties, such as deep-fried scampi with chips.

7–8 Abbeygate St. ⓒ **01225/463981.** Main courses £4.50–£7 ($7–$11). MC, V. Mon–Fri 11:30am–3pm; Sat 11:30am–6pm.

The Moon and Sixpence ★★ INTERNATIONAL   One of the leading restaurants and wine bars of Bath, The Moon and Sixpence occupies a stone structure east of Queen Square. At lunch, a large cold buffet with a selection of hot dishes is featured in the wine bar section. In the upstairs restaurant overlooking the bar, full service is offered. Main courses are likely to include filet of lamb with caramelized garlic or roast breast of duck with Chinese vegetables. Look for the daily specials on the continental menu.

6A Broad St. ⓒ **01225/460962.** Reservations recommended. Main courses £13.75–£14.50 ($22–$23); fixed-price lunch £7.50 ($12); fixed-price dinner £20.75–£24.75 ($33–$40). AE, MC, V. Daily noon–2:30pm; Mon–Thurs 5:30–10:30pm; Fri–Sat 5:30–11pm; Sun 6–10:30pm.

The Pump Room Restaurant ★ ENGLISH   Run by Milburns Restaurants, this place is a tradition in Bath; its latest incarnation opened in 1988. Guests often enjoy music from the Pump Room Trio or the resident pianist while they drink or eat. Typically served during coffee are Bath Buns or plain scones served with clotted cream and strawberry jam. Hot dishes include minute steak and poached salmon filet. The famous Pump Room tea is a favorite, even among locals who enjoy their Earl Grey, Darjeeling, or whatever, along with sandwiches, scones, cakes, and pastries. The food sticks to such tried-and-true favorites that it rarely goes wrong.

In the Roman Baths, Stall St. ⓒ **01225/444477.** Main courses £9–£13.50 ($14–$22). AE, MC, V. Daily 9:30am–4:30pm (5:30pm during summer).

Sally Lunn's House ENGLISH   Sally Lunn, who may have been fictional, is a legend in Bath. She was a baker who supposedly came from France during the 1680s. Today the cellar bakery where she supposedly worked and recent excavations showing the earlier buildings constitute a museum (open Mon–Sat 10am–6pm and Sun 11am–6pm). Her namesake establishment is a tiny gabled licensed coffeehouse and restaurant, a 1-minute walk from the abbey and Roman baths. The house is a Bath landmark—the wooden frame building, oldest in the city, dates from about 1482; a Georgian bow window is set in the "new" stone facade put up around 1720. On the ground and first floors, the buns that made Sally Lunn famous are served sweet or savory, fresh from the modern bakery on the third floor. Excellent coffee and toasted buns with "lashings" of butter, whole-fruit strawberry jam, and real clotted cream are everybody's favorite. Buns are also served with various salads, chili, traditional Welsh rarebit, or other items. Candlelit dinners, served after 6pm, might include a whole poached trout cooked with a soft stuffing or a quarter of a young roast duck in a rich orange sauce.

4 North Parade Passage. ⓒ **01225/461634.** Reservations recommended for dinner. Main courses £7.48–£9.48 ($12–$15); lunch plates £3.38–£6.88 ($5–$11). MC, V (for dinner only). Mon–Sat 10am–10pm; Sun 11am–6pm.

Theatre Vaults Restaurant INTERNATIONAL   An imaginative entrepreneur converted the stone vaults beneath the Theatre Royal into an engaging brasserie. Its late closing makes it a favorite of the after-theater crowd. Menu specialties include homemade game terrines and soups, fresh fish of the day, juicy steaks, and regional dishes prepared by the French chef. The fare isn't too imaginative, but it's good.

Sawclose at Barton St. ⓒ **01225/442265.** Reservations required. 2-course fixed-price lunch and dinner £14.20 ($23); 3-course lunch and dinner £16.45 ($26). AE, DC, MC, V. Mon–Sat 5:30–7:30pm; Wed and Sat noon–2pm.

The Walrus and the Carpenter ANGLO-AMERICAN/VEGETARIAN
Named after Lewis Carroll's poem, and decorated like a whimsically hip version
of a French bistro, this poster-plastered place defines itself as Bath's "bohemian
hangout for everybody." It resides in a Georgian building of historical interest,
located near the Theatre Royal. Specialties include steaks, burgers, and such vegetarian dishes as mushroom moussaka with pita bread and salad, spinach
lasagna, and an array of salads that are virtually meals in themselves. The food is
filling and competently prepared.

28 Barton St. (C) **01225/314864.** Reservations required Fri–Sun. Main courses £6.95–£14.95 ($11–$24);
lunch £3.95–£7 ($6–$11). AE, MC, V. Mon–Sat noon–2:30pm and 6–11pm; Sun noon–11pm.

BATH AFTER DARK
To gain a very different perspective of Bath, you may want to take the **Bizarre
Bath Walking Tour** ((C) **01225/335124**), a 1½-hour improvisational tour of the
streets during which the tour guides pull pranks, tell jokes, and behave in a
humorously annoying manner toward tour-goers and unsuspecting residents.
Running nightly at 8pm from Easter to September, no reservations are neces-
sary; just show up, ready for anything, at the Huntsman Inn at North Parade
Passage. Cost is £5 ($8) for adults, £4 ($6) for students and children.

After your walk, you may need a drink, or may want to check out the local
club and music scene. At **The Bell,** 103 Walcot St. ((C) **01225/460426**), music
ranges from jazz and country to reggae and blues on Monday and Wednesday
nights and Sunday at lunch. On music nights, the band performs in the center
of the long, narrow 400-year-old room.

The two-story **Hat and Feather,** 14 London St. ((C) **01225/425672**), has live
musicians or DJs playing funk, reggae, or dance music nightly.

SIDE TRIPS FROM BATH
LACOCK ✿: AN 18TH-CENTURY VILLAGE
From Bath, take the A4 about 12 miles to the A350, then head south to
Lacock, a village showcasing English architecture from the 13th through the
18th centuries. Unlike many villages that disappeared or were absorbed into
bigger communities, Lacock remained largely unchanged because of a single
family, the Talbots, who owned most of it and preferred to keep their traditional village traditional. Turned over to the National Trust in 1944, it's now
one of the best-preserved villages in England, with many 16th-century homes,
gardens, and churches. Notable is the Perpendicular-style St. Cyriac Church,
Church Street, built by wealthy wool merchants between the 14th and 17th
centuries.

Lacock Abbey, High Street ((C) **01249/730227**), founded in 1232 for Augustinian canonesses, was updated and turned into a private home in the 16th century. It fell victim to Henry VIII's Dissolution, when, upon establishing the
Church of England, he seized existing church properties to bolster his own
wealth. Admission for all church properties is £6.50 ($10) for adults and £3.60
($6) for children; a family ticket costs £17.60 ($28). Open from Easter to October, daily from 11am to 5pm.

While on the grounds, stop by the medieval barn, home to the **Fox Talbot
Museum** ((C) **01249/730459**). Here, William Henry Fox Talbot carried out his
early experiments with photography, making the first known photographic
prints in 1833. In his honor, the barn is now a photography museum featuring
some of those early prints. Open daily, March through October from 11am to
5:30pm. Admission is £4.20 ($7) for adults and £2.50 ($4) for children.

Where to Stay

The George Inn (see "Where to Dine," below) offers rooms at a nearby farm-house.

The Old Rectory ★ *Finds*   Mrs. Sexton owns this nonsmoking Victorian home which she had turned it into a great little B&B. She offers comfortably furnished double rooms, two with four-poster beds, that are accessible for those with limited mobility. Guests have free access to 3 hectares (7 acres), and can even play croquet if they wish.

Cantax Hill, Lacock, Wiltshire SN15 2JZ. (✆ **01249/730335.** www.oldrectorylacock.co.uk. 6 units. £32.45 ($52) single; £50–£65 ($80–$104) double; £65–£90 ($104–$144) family room. Rates include English breakfast. No credit cards. **Amenities:** Breakfast room; lounge. *In room:* TV, hair dryer, iron.

Where to Dine

The Carpenter's Arms ENGLISH   This 16th-century public house's charm derives partly from its many small rooms, nooks, and crannies; the locals know the food is good, also. Lunch is typical bar food—steak-and-kidney pie, salads, jacket potatoes, and the like. An a la carte menu offers patrons more substantial fare at dinner, including homemade soups and a selection of fresh meat, fish, and vegetarian dishes.

22 Church St. (✆ **01249/730203.** Reservations recommended on weekends. Lunch and dinner £7–£11.95 ($11–$19). AE, MC, V. Daily 11am–3pm and 6–11pm.

The George Inn ENGLISH   In a building that has housed a pub since 1361, the George retains vestiges of the past, notably the uneven floors and a large open fireplace once used for spit roasting. Now run by John Glass, it has been equipped with modern conveniences, and has an extensive garden used for dining in summer; there's even a children's playground. About 30 daily specials are written on a chalkboard in addition to a regular menu of fish, meat, and vegetarian dishes; these may include kangaroo, wild boar, and beef steaks. Two popular desserts are bread-and-butter pudding and sticky toffee pudding.

4 West St., Lacock, Wiltshire SN15 2LH. (✆ **01249/730263.** Main courses £7.95–£14.95 ($13–$24). MC, V. Mon–Fri 10am–2:30pm and 5–11pm; Sat–Sun 10am–11pm.

4 Bristol ★★

192km (120 miles) W of London; 21km (13 miles) NW of Bath

Bristol, the largest city in the West Country, is just across the Bristol Channel from Wales and is a good place to base yourself for touring western Britain. This historic inland port is linked to the sea by 11km (7 miles) of the navigable River Avon. Bristol has long been rich in seafaring traditions and has many links with the early colonization of America. In fact, some claim that the new continent was named after a Bristol town clerk, Richard Ameryke. In 1497, John Cabot sailed from Bristol and pioneered the discovery of the northern half of the New World.

Although Bath is much more famous, Bristol does have some attractions, such as a colorful harbor life, that makes it at least a good overnight stop in your exploration of the West Country.

ESSENTIALS

GETTING THERE   Bristol Airport (✆ **0870/1212747**) is conveniently situated beside the main A38 road, just over 11km (7 miles) from the city center.

Rail services to and from the area are among the fastest and most efficient in Britain. **British Rail** runs very frequent services from London's Paddington

Station to each of Bristol's two main stations: Temple Meads in the center of Bristol, and Parkway on the city's northern outskirts. The trip takes 1¼ hours. For rail information, call © **0845/7484950.**

National Express buses depart every hour during the day from London's Victoria Coach Station, making the trip in 2½ hours. For more information and schedules, call © **020/7529-2000.**

If you're driving, head west from London on the M4.

VISITOR INFORMATION The **Tourist Information Centre** is in The Annex, Wildscreen Walk, Harbourside, Bristol (© **0117/9260767**). In winter, it's open Monday through Saturday from 10am to 5pm and Sunday from 11am to 4pm; from 9:30am to 5:30pm daily in summer.

EXPLORING THE TOWN

Guided **walking tours** are conducted in summer and last about 1½ hours. They depart from Neptune's Statue on Saturday at 2:30pm and on Thursday at 7pm. Guided tours are also conducted through Clifton, a suburb of Bristol with more Georgian houses than Bath. Consult the tourist office (see above) for more information.

Clifton Suspension Bridge, spanning the beautiful Avon Gorge, has become the symbol of the city of Bristol. Originally conceived in 1754, it was completed more than 100 years later, in 1864. The architect, Isambard Kingdom Brunel, died 5 years before its completion. His fellow engineers continued his vision, completing the bridge as a memorial to him. A visitor center is in a former Victorian hotel just 200m (656 ft.) from the bridge. There you can see a superbly intricate scale model of Brunel's bridge, as well as an exhibition outlining the story of its construction. The visitor center is open daily from Easter to September from 10am to 5:50pm and from October to Easter Monday through Friday from 11am to 4pm and on Saturday and Sunday from 11am to 5pm. Admission is £1.90 ($3.05) for adults, £1.70 ($2.70) for seniors, and £1.30 ($2.10) for children under 16 years.

At-Bristol ★★   At this museum, science, nature, and art are brought to life. This unique West Country attraction is found at the harborside, a section sculpted around public open spaces. The physicist Paul Davies has hailed the "awesome extravaganza for setting new standards for making science and technology both accessible and fun." The area's only giant-screen **IMAX Theatre** features files that take you on a journey to an International Space Station, through the workings of the human body, or on a voyage from snow-capped peaks to the kaleidoscopic reefs of color and life in the ocean off the Baja California peninsula. The West Country's first true 21st-century science center, **Explore,** features a "hands-on, minds-on" experience of science. At this world-of-tomorrow attraction, you can do everything from enter the eye of a tornado to be the star of your own TV sitcom. At **Wildwalk** you can journey from the origins of life itself to the ends of the earth, come face to face with scorpions, and walk through a tropical forest with free-flying birds and butterflies. Between the exhibits are shops and cafes, set among sculptures and beautiful landscaping.

Anchor Rd., Harbourside. © 0117/909-2000. Single attraction tickets: £7.50 ($12) adults, £4.95 ($8) children to Explore; £6.50 ($10) adults, £4.50 ($7) children to Wildwalk; £6.50 ($10) adults, £4.50 ($7) children to IMAX. Two attractions on same day: £12 ($19) adults or £8.20 ($13) children for Explore and Wildwalk; £12 ($19) for adults, £8.20 ($13) children for Explore and IMAX, and £11 ($18) for adults or £7.75 ($12) for children for Wildwalk and IMAX. Daily 10am–6pm.

Bristol Cathedral ⭐   This former Augustinian abbey was begun in the 12th century; the central tower was added in 1466. The chapter house and gatehouse are good examples of late Norman architecture. In 1539, the abbey was closed and the incomplete nave demolished; three years later, it became the Cathedral Church of the Holy and Undivided Trinity. In 1868, plans were drawn up to complete the nave according to its medieval design; architect G. E. Street found the original pillar bases, ensuring that the cathedral would end up looking as it was intended to. J. L. Pearson added the two towers at the western end and further reordered the interior.

The eastern end of the cathedral, especially the choir, gives the structure a unique place in the development of British and European architecture. The nave, choir, and aisles are all of the same height, creating a large hall. Bristol Cathedral is the best example of a "hall church" in Great Britain and one of the finest in the world. Its interior was even praised by Sir John Betjeman, the poet laureate.

College Green. ✆ 0117/9264879. Free admission; £2.50 ($4) donation requested. Daily 8am–6pm. Bus: 8 or 9.

St. Mary Redcliffe Church ⭐⭐   The parish church of St. Mary Redcliffe is one of England's finest examples of Gothic architecture. During her 1574 visit, Elizabeth I is reported to have described it as "the fairest, goodliest, and most famous parish church in England." Thomas Chatterton called it "the pride of Bristol and the western land." Its American Chapel houses the tomb and armor of Adm. Sir William Penn, father of Pennsylvania's founder.

12 Colston Parade. ✆ 01179/291487. Free admission. Donations are welcome. Daily 8:30am–5pm.

SS *Great Britain*   In Bristol, the world's first iron steamship and luxury liner has been partially restored to its 1843 appearance, although it's still a long way from regaining its title as a "floating palace." This vessel, weighing 3,443 tons, was designed by Isambard Brunel, the Victorian engineer-architect.

City Docks, Great Western Dock. ✆ 01179/260680. www.ss-great-britain.com. Admission £6.25 ($10) adults, £5.25 ($8) seniors, £3.75 ($6) children, £16.50 ($26) family. Apr–Oct daily 10am–5:30pm; Nov–Mar daily 10am–4:30pm. Bus: 511 from city center, a long haul.

Theatre Royal   Built in 1766, this is now the oldest working playhouse in the United Kingdom. It is the home of the Bristol Old Vic. Backstage tours leave from the foyer. Tours are run Friday and Saturday at noon and cost £3 ($4.80) for adults and £2 ($3.20) for children and students under 19. Call the box office for the current schedule.

King St. ✆ 01179/493993. Box office ✆ 01179/877877. Tickets £8.50–£25 ($14–$40). Bus: Any City Centre bus.

SHOPPING

Many major shops are now open on Sunday. The biggest shopping complex is the mainly pedestrian-only Broadmead, with High Street store branches, cafes, and restaurants. Many specialty shops are found at **Clifton Village,** a Georgian setting where houses intermingle with parks and gardens. Here you'll find a wide array of shops selling antiques, arts and crafts, and designer clothing. The Galleries (opened 1991) is a totally enclosed mall, providing three levels of shopping and restaurants. The **St. Nicholas Markets,** opened in 1745, are still going strong, selling antiques, memorabilia, handcrafted gifts, jewelry, and haberdashery. The **West End** is another major shopping area, taking in Park Street, Queen's Road, and Whiteladies Road—streets known for their clothing outlets, bookstores, and unusual gift items from around the world, as well as wine bars and restaurants. The best antiques markets are The **Bristol Antique Centre,** Brunel Rooms, Broad Plain; **Clifton Antiques Market** and **New Antiques Centre,** the Mall in Clifton; and **Clifton Arcade,** Boyces Avenue, Clifton. Both Clifton outlets are closed Monday but the Bristol Antique Centre is open daily, including Sunday.

WHERE TO STAY

Downlands House   This well-appointed nonsmoking Victorian home is on a tree-lined road on the periphery of the Durdham Downs. About 3km (2 miles) from the center of Bristol, it lies on a bus route in a residential suburb. The recently redecorated bedrooms have private, shower-only bathrooms or adequate hallway facilities, and one room on the ground floor is available for those with limited mobility. It's basic, but inviting.

33 Henleaze Gardens, Henleaze, Bristol, Somerset BS9 4HH. © 0117/9621639. Fax 0117/9621639. www.downlandshouse.com. 10 units, 7 with bathroom. £36 ($58) single without bathroom, £47 ($75) single with bathroom; £50 ($80) double without bathroom, £65 ($104) double with bathroom. Rates include English breakfast. AE, MC, V. Bus: 1, 2, 3, or 501. **Amenities:** Breakfast room. *In room:* TV, coffeemaker, hair dryer.

Oakfield Hotel   Instead of lodging in central Bristol, many visitors head for the leafy Georgian suburb of Clifton, 1 mile north, near the famous Suspension Bridge. With an Italianate facade, this impressive guesthouse from the 1840s resembles a New York town house on a quiet street. Furnishings are modest, but it is still comfortable here; new bedding and curtains have recently been added. Hallway bathrooms, though small, are adequate for the job. Maintenance is high, under the watchful eye of Mrs. P. Hurley.

52–54 Oakfield Rd., Clifton, Bristol, Somerset BS8 2BG. © 0117/9733643. Fax 0117/9744141. 27 units, none with private bathroom. £35 ($56) single; £45 ($72) double. Rates include English breakfast. No credit cards. Bus: 8 or 9. **Amenities:** Breakfast room. *In room:* TV.

Tyndall's Park Hotel   This elegant early Victorian house retains many of its original features, including a marble fireplace and ornate plasterwork. Note the fine staircase in the imposing entrance hall. The nonsmoking hotel still observes the old traditions of personal service. There is a Victorian aura in the bedrooms, which range from small to medium, and each is clean and comfortable. One room on the ground floor is set aside for those with limited mobility. Bathrooms are small but adequate, each with a shower.

4 Tyndall's Park Rd., Clifton, Bristol, Somerset BS8 1PG. © 0117/9735407. Fax 0117/9237965. www. tyndallsparkhotel.co.uk. 15 units. £40–£48 ($64–$77) single; £50–£58 ($80–$93) double. Rates include English breakfast. MC, V. Bus: 8 or 9. **Amenities:** Dining room; bar; guest lounge. *In room:* TV, dataport, coffeemaker, hair dryer.

WHERE TO DINE

The Flipper ★ *Finds* FISH AND CHIPS   Close to the bus station, amid the city's biggest cluster of stores, the Flipper serves the best fish and chips in Bristol. Good-tasting cod (and slightly costlier plaice and halibut) is dished out from a fast-food countertop on the street level. Breakfast is served all day, and an upstairs wood-paneled dining room offers wait service.

6 St. James Barton. © 0117/9290260. Main courses £3.50–£5.95 ($6–$10). No credit cards. Mon–Sat 7:30am–6pm. Bus: 20, 22, or 75.

Pizza on the Hill PIZZA   This popular and informal pizza joint does a thriving business in leafy Clifton, 2.5km (1½ miles) northeast of Bristol's center, near the university. It's a fun place with a jigsaw collage on the walls and trick mirrors in the hallway. The place serves the best pizzas in Bristol, offering 13 varieties. You'll also find good-tasting crepes, tender steaks, and freshly made salads on the menu.

122 St. Michael's Hill, Clifton. ℂ **0117/9293675.** Main courses £2.95–£4.95 ($4.70–$8) at lunch, £6.95–£9.95 ($11–$16) at dinner. MC, V. Daily noon–2pm and 6pm–midnight. Bus: 8 or 9.

Quartier Vert ★ MEDITERRANEAN   Here's a great place for a drink, tapas, or a full meal; it's very popular with locals. Choose from a varied and hearty selection of tapas or, if you prefer, a great Mediterranean meal such as grilled tuna steak, vegetable pasta, or everyone's favorite, shellfish risotto. In the summer, eating on the patio is *très* chic.

85 Whiteladies Rd. ℂ **0117/9734482.** Reservations recommended. Main courses £9.95–£16.50 ($16–$26). AE, MC, V. Mon–Sat 9am–11pm; Sun 10am–10:30pm.

BRISTOL AFTER DARK

While Bath seems more stiff and formal, Bristol clubs and pubs are more laid-back, drawing more working-class Brits than yuppies. Some of the best pubs are along King Street, especially **Llandoger Trow,** 5 King St. (ℂ **0117/9260783**), with its mellow West Country ambience. **Lakota,** 6 Upper York St. (ℂ **0117/ 9426208**), off Stokes Croft, is known for its all-night "groove parties," with a funk soundtrack. However, the cover is a bit steep, ranging from £3 to £25 ($4.80– $40), depending on what's featured that night.

In a converted freight steamer moored on the Grove, **Thelka** (ℂ **0117/ 9293301**) is where acid jazz rains down. The other leading venue for jazz is the **Bebop Club** at The Bear, Hotwell Road (ℂ **0117/9877796**). The leading comedy club is **Jester's,** Cherdeham Road (ℂ **0117/9096655**). Cover charges for the clubs range from £8 to £11.50 ($13–$18), but can vary depending on the entertainment offered.

5 Wells ★★ & the Caves of Mendip ★

197km (123 miles) SW of London; 34km (21 miles) SW of Bath

To the south of the Mendip Hills, the cathedral town of Wells is a medieval gem. Wells was a vital link in the Saxon kingdom of Wessex, long before the arrival of William the Conqueror. Once the seat of a bishopric, it was toppled from its ecclesiastical hegemony by its rival city Bath. But the subsequent loss of prestige has paid off handsomely for Wells today; having reached the pinnacle, it fell into a slumber, and much of its old look was preserved.

Many visitors come only for the afternoon or morning, look at the cathedral, then press on to Bath for the evening. But you might consider making a tranquil stopover in one of the town's old inns.

ESSENTIALS

GETTING THERE   Wells has good bus connections with its surrounding towns and cities. Take the train to Bath (see section 3 of this chapter) and continue the rest of the way by **Badgerline** bus no. 175. Departures are every hour Monday through Saturday and every 2 hours on Sunday. Both no. 376 and 378 buses run between Bristol and Glastonbury every hour Monday through Saturday and every 2 hours on Sunday. Call ℂ **01179/553231** for bus schedules and information.

If you're driving, take M4 west from London, cutting south on A4 toward Bath and continuing along A39 into Wells.

VISITOR INFORMATION   The **Tourist Information Centre** is at the Town Hall, Market Place (© **01749/672552**), open daily November through March 10am to 4pm and April through October 9:30am to 5:30pm.

SEEING THE SIGHTS

Wells Cathedral ✦✦✦   Begun in the 12th century, this is a well-preserved example of early English architecture. The medieval sculpture of its west front—six tiers of hundreds of recently restored statues—is without equal. The western facade was completed in the mid–13th century. The landmark central tower was erected in the 14th century, its fan-vaulting attached later. The inverted arches were added to strengthen the top-heavy structure. Much of the stained glass dates from the 14th century, as does the fan-vaulted Lady Chapel in the decorated style. To the north is the recently restored 13th-century vaulted chapter house. Look for a medieval astronomical clock in the north transept.

After a visit to the cathedral, walk along its cloisters to the moat-surrounded Bishop's Palace. The Great Hall, built in the 13th century, is in ruins. Finally, the street known as Vicars' Close is one of the most beautifully preserved in Europe.

In the center of town, Chain Gate. © **01749/674483**. www.wellscathedral.org.uk. Free admission but donations appreciated: £4.50 ($7) adults, £3 ($4.80) seniors, £1.50 ($2.40) students and children. Apr–Oct daily 7am–7pm; Nov–Mar daily 7am–6:15pm.

Wookey Hole Caves & Paper Mill ✦   Just 2 miles from Wells, you'll first come to the source of the Axe River. The Witch of Wookey was turned to stone in the first chamber of the caves, according to legend. It is believed that these caves were inhabited by prehistoric people at least 60,000 years ago. A tunnel, opened in 1975, leads to chambers unknown in early times and previously accessible only to divers.

Leaving the caves, you follow a canal path to the mill. Here, the best-quality handmade paper has been made by skilled workers since the 17th century. There are "hands-on vats," where visitors try their hand at making a sheet of paper, and an Edwardian Penny Pier Arcade where new pennies can be exchanged for old ones with which to play the original machines. Other attractions include the Magical Mirror Maze, an enclosed passage of multiple-image mirrors.

Wookey Hole, near Wells. © **01749/672243**. www.wookey.co.uk. 2-hr. tour £8.80 ($14) adults, £5.50 ($9) children 16 and under. Apr–Oct daily 10am–5:30pm; Nov–Mar daily 10:30am–4:30pm. Closed Dec 17–25. Follow the signs from the center of Wells for 3km (2 miles). Bus: 172 from Wells.

Cheddar Showcaves & Gorge ✦✦   The village of Cheddar, birthplace of the cheese, lies a short distance from Bath, Bristol, and Wells, at the foot of Cheddar Gorge. Within this gorge are the Cheddar Caves, underground caverns with impressive formations. The caves, more than a million years old, include Gough's Cave, with its cathedral-like caverns, and Cox's Cave, with its calcite sculptures and brilliant colors. In the Cheddar Gorge Heritage Centre a 9,000-year-old skeleton is displayed. You can climb Jacob's Ladder for cliff-top walks and Pavey's Lookout Tower for views over Somerset.

Adults and children over 12 years of age can book an Adventure Caving expedition for £12.50 ($20), which includes overalls, helmets, and lamps. Other attractions include local craftspeople at work, ranging from the glass blower to the sweets maker, plus the Cheddar Cheese & Cider Depot.

Cheddar, Somerset. © **01934/742343**. www.cheddarcaves.co.uk. Admission £8.90 ($14) adults, £5.90 ($9) children 5–15, free for 4 and under. Easter–Sept daily 10am–5pm; Oct–Easter daily 10:30am–4:30pm. Closed Dec 24–25. From A38 or M5, cut onto A371 to Cheddar.

WHERE TO STAY

Budget accommodations in Wells are more reasonably priced than equivalent lodgings at Bath. Parking can be scarce in town, but the hotels listed below all offer free parking to guests.

IN WELLS

Ancient Gate House Hotel ★★ The back of this 14th-century hotel, run by Francesco Rossi, opens onto views of the cathedral and the lawn in front of the cathedral's west door. Each midsize room is comfortable and well furnished (six have four-poster beds). Franco also runs the Rugantino Restaurant attached to the hotel, where pastas and Italian dishes are a specialty.

20 Sadler St., Wells, Somerset BA5 2RR. ℂ 01749/672029. www.ancientgatehouse.co.uk. 9 units. £63 ($101) single without bathroom; £78.50 ($126) double without bathroom, £70 ($112) double with bathroom. Rates include English breakfast. AE, MC, V. **Amenities:** Restaurant; bar. *In room:* TV, coffeemaker, hair dryer (on request).

Bekynton House Built in the 1700s to house clergymen of the nearby cathedral, this stone house is named after the region's most famous ecclesiastic (a 12th-c. bishop named Bekynton). It is owned and managed by Rosaleen and Desmond Gripper, escapees from the financial district in London. The house contains small but comfortable bedrooms, each with a private, shower-only bathroom. If you pay with a credit card, expect your total bill to increase by 3%. This hotel is nonsmoking.

7 Saint Thomas St. (B3139 to Radstock), Wells, Somerset BA5 2UU. ℂ 01749/672222. www.bekynton-house.co.uk. 4 units. £40 ($64) single; £48–£55 ($77–$88) double; £72 ($115) triple. Rates include English breakfast. MC, V. **Amenities:** Breakfast room; lounge. *In room:* TV, coffeemaker, hair dryer.

Sherston Inn This pub, on the edge of town on the road to Glastonbury (A39), boasts a beer garden. It's a 10-minute walk from the cathedral, Bishop's Palace, and Wells Museum. Part of the building is from the 17th century. The owner rents very modest, small but clean bedrooms. Bar meals are served in the cozy Moat Bar or the more spacious restaurant.

Priory Rd., Wells, Somerset BA5 1SU. ℂ 01749/673743. 6 units, none with bathroom. £27 ($43) single; £55 ($88) double. Rates include English breakfast. MC, V. **Amenities:** Pub. *In room:* TV, coffeemaker.

ON THE OUTSKIRTS

Burcott Mill This hotel, built in the 18th century as a stone-sided flour mill, lies on the outskirts of the village of Wookey (on B3139), beside the River Axe about 3km (2 miles) from Wells. The midsize bedrooms are country comfortable and plain. There are three pubs within walking distance of the accommodations, each serving meals. The mill was restored by its owners, Ian and Leslie Burt, to become a fully working flour mill; if requested, they will show you the electricity-gathering process.

Burcott, Wookey, near Wells, Somerset BA5 1NJ. ℂ 01749/673118. www.burcottmill.com. 6 units. £24 ($38) single; £64 ($102) double; £24 ($38) per person family unit. Rates include English breakfast. MC, V. **Amenities:** Breakfast room; lounge; tearoom. *In room:* TV, dataport, coffeemaker, hair dryer.

Crapnell Farm About 5km (3 miles) from Wells and 1.5km (1 mile) from the local golf club, this 300-year-old farmhouse offers a bucolic respite from city bustle. The 104-hectare (260-acre) working dairy farm is situated on the south side of Mendip Hills. All the small rooms are comfortably and cozily furnished. Dinner is available by arrangement.

Dinder, near Wells, Somerset BA5 3HG. © 01749/342683. 3 units. £30 ($48) single; £50 ($80) double. Rates include English breakfast. No credit cards. **Amenities:** Breakfast room; snooker room; TV lounge. *In room:* TV, coffeemaker.

WHERE TO DINE

The City Arms ENGLISH   The former city jail, 2 blocks from the bus station, is now a pub with an open courtyard furnished with tables, chairs, and umbrellas. In summer it's a mass of flowers, and there's an old vine growing in the corner. Full meals may include homemade soup of the day followed by fresh salmon, lamb in burgundy sauce, or stuffed quail in Cointreau sauce. From the charcoal grill you can order rump steak or chicken with Stilton cheese, and long-time favorites include beef Wellington or steak-kidney-and-ale pie. Vegetarian dishes are also offered. Upstairs is an Elizabethan timbered restaurant. The food is a notch above the typical pub grub.

69 High St. © 01749/673916. Reservations recommended. Main courses £4.95–£14 ($8–$22). MC, V. Daily 9am–10pm (closes at 9pm on Sun).

Ritcher's ⊛ FRENCH   This eatery occupies a 16th-century stone cottage whose entrance lies behind a wrought-iron gate and a tile-covered passageway running beneath another building near the cathedral. One of the best restaurants in town, Ritcher's contains a likable bistro on the ground floor and a more formal restaurant one floor above street level. Menu items in the bistro include turkey and venison pies, platters of fresh asparagus, and a modernized version of salade niçoise served with a raspberry vinaigrette. The cuisine in the upstairs restaurant is more ambitious, including saddle of lamb roasted with garlic-and-herb crust and Beaujolais sauce, or slices of Scottish salmon glazed with fresh-water prawns in a Chablis-flavored cream sauce. The chefs don't always pull off every dish, but there is care and concern with the cuisine.

5 Sadler St. © 01749/679085. Reservations required for the restaurant only. 2-course fixed-price lunch £8.95 ($14), 3-course fixed-price lunch £10.95 ($18); 2-course fixed-price dinner £19.50 ($31), 3-course fixed-price dinner £23 ($37). MC, V. Bistro: Sun–Thurs noon–2pm and 7–9:30pm, Fri–Sat noon–2pm and 7–10pm. Restaurant: lunch by appointment only; dinner Tues–Sat 6:30–9:15pm.

6 Glastonbury Abbey ⊛ ⊛

218km (136 miles) SW of London; 42km (26 miles) S of Bristol; 6 miles SW of Wells

Glastonbury may be one of the oldest inhabited sites in Britain. Excavations have revealed Iron Age lakeside villages on its periphery (some of the items discovered can be seen in a little museum on High St.). After the destruction of its once-great abbey, the town lost prestige; now it is just a market town with a rich history. The ancient gatehouse entry to the abbey is a museum, and its principal exhibit is a scale model of the abbey and its community buildings as they stood in 1539, at the time of the Dissolution.

Where Arthurian myth once held sway, there's now a subculture of mystics, spiritualists, and hippies, all drawn to the kooky legends whirling around the town. Glastonbury is England's New Age center, where Christian spirituality blends with druidic beliefs. The average visitor comes just to see the ruins and the monuments, but the streets are often filled with people trying to track down Jesus, Arthur, and Lancelot.

ESSENTIALS

GETTING THERE   Go to Taunton, which is on the London–Penzance line that leaves frequently from London's Paddington Station. For rail information, call (℃) **0845/7484950.** From Taunton, you'll have to take a bus the rest of the way. Take the Southern National bus (no. 17) to Glastonbury between Monday and Saturday. There are six departures per day, and the trip takes 1 hour. Call **Southern National** at (℃) **01823/272033** for details.

You can also leave London's Paddington Station for Bristol Temple Meads and go the rest of the way by Badgerline bus no. 376. It runs from Bristol via Wells to Glastonbury every hour Monday through Saturday; on Sunday, the schedule is reduced to every 3 hours. The trip takes 2 hours. For information about Badgerline bus service, call (℃) **01179/553231.**

One **National Express** bus a day (no. 403) leaves London's Victoria Coach Station at 6:30pm and arrives in Glastonbury at 10pm. For more information and schedules, call (℃) **020/7529-2000.**

If you're driving, take the M4 west from London, then cut south on the A4 via Bath to Glastonbury.

VISITOR INFORMATION   The **Tourist Information Centre** is at The Tribunal, 9 High St. ((℃) **01458/832954**). It's open year-round Sunday through Thursday from 10am to 4pm, and Friday and Saturday from 10am to 4:30pm.

SEEING THE SIGHTS

Glastonbury Abbey   Though it's no more than a ruined sanctuary today, Glastonbury Abbey was once one of the wealthiest and most prestigious monasteries in England. It provides Glastonbury's claim to historical greatness, an assertion augmented by legendary links to St. Joseph of Arimathea, King Arthur, Queen Guinevere, and St. Patrick.

It is said that Joseph of Arimathea journeyed to what was then the Isle of Avalon, with the Holy Grail in his possession. According to tradition, he buried the chalice at the foot of the conical Glastonbury Tor, and a stream of blood burst forth. You can scale this more than 150m- (500-ft.-) high hill today, on which rests a 15th-century tower.

Joseph, so it goes, erected a church of wattle in Glastonbury. (In fact, excavations have shown that the town may have had the oldest church in England.) The saint is said to have leaned against his staff, which immediately changed into a fully blossoming tree; a cutting alleged to have survived from the Holy Thorn can be seen on the abbey grounds today—it blooms at Christmastime. Some historians have traced this particular story back to Tudor times.

Another famous chapter, popularized by Tennyson in the Victorian era, holds that Arthur and Guinevere were buried on the abbey grounds. In 1191, monks dug up the skeletons of two bodies on the south side of the Lady Chapel, said to be those of the king and queen. In 1278, in the presence of Edward I, the bodies were removed and transferred to a black marble tomb in the choir. Both the burial spot and the shrine are marked today.

A large Benedictine Abbey of St. Mary grew out of the early wattle church. St. Dunstan, who was born nearby, was the abbot in the 10th century and later became archbishop of Canterbury. Edmund, Edgar, and Edmund "Ironside," three pre-Norman English kings, were buried at the abbey.

In 1184, a fire destroyed most of the abbey and its vast treasures. It was eventually rebuilt with great difficulty, only to be dissolved by Henry VIII. Its last abbot, Richard Whiting, was hanged at Glastonbury Tor. Like the town's Roman forum, the abbey was long used as a stone quarry.

Today you can visit the ruins of the chapel, linked by an early English galilee to the nave of the abbey. The best-preserved building is a 14th-century octagonal Abbot's Kitchen, where oxen were once roasted whole to feed wealthier pilgrims.

Magdalene St. ✆ **01458/832267** for information. www.glastonburyabbey.com. Admission £3.50 ($6) adults, £3 ($4.80) students and seniors, £1.50 ($2.40) children 5–16 years, £8 ($13) family ticket. Daily 10am–5pm.

Somerset Rural Life Museum   The history of the Somerset countryside since the early 19th century is chronicled here. Its centerpiece is the abbey barn, built around 1370. The magnificent timbered room, stone tiles, and sculptural details (including the head of Edward III) make it special. There is also a Victorian farmhouse containing exhibits that illustrate Somerset farming during the "horse age" as well as domestic and social life in Victorian times. In summer, there are demonstrations of butter making, weaving, basketwork, and many other traditional, rapidly disappearing craft and farming activities.

Abbey Farm, Chilkwell St. ✆ **01458/831197**. www.somerset.gov.uk/museums. Free admission. Mon–Sat 10am–5pm.

WHERE TO STAY

The George & Pilgrims ★★   One of the few pre-Reformation hostelries still left in England, this inn stands in the center of town and once offered hospitality to Glastonbury pilgrims. Its facade looks like a medieval castle, with stone-mullioned windows with leaded glass. Some of the rooms were formerly monks' cells; others have four-poster beds, veritable carved monuments of oak. You may be given the Henry VIII Room, from which the king watched the burning of the abbey in 1539. Units are doubles and come in a variety of shapes and sizes, as befits a hotel of this vintage. Some of the bedrooms have recently been refurbished. Some of the rooms have just a shower, others a tub and shower combined.

1 High St., Glastonbury, Somerset BA6 9DP. ✆ **01458/831146**. Fax 01458/832252. 13 units. £55–£95 ($88–$152) double. Rates include English breakfast. AE, DC, MC, V. **Amenities:** Restaurant; bar. In room: TV, coffeemaker, hair dryer, trouser press.

Little Orchard   On the A361 Glastonbury-Shepton Mallet road, 1.6km (1 mile) from the town center, is a Tyrolean-type brick structure at the foot of Glastonbury Tor, with its striking views of the Vale of Avalon. Rodney and Dinah Gifford rent comfortably furnished midsize bedrooms, three of which are in the garden house. There is a color TV in the lounge. In summer, guests can enjoy the sun patio and large garden.

Ashwell Lane, Glastonbury, Somerset BA6 8BG. ✆ **01458/831620**. www.smoothhound.co.uk/hotels/orchard.html. 5 units. £22 ($35) single; £44 ($70) double. Rates include English breakfast. No credit cards. **Amenities:** Breakfast room; TV lounge. In room: Coffeemaker, hair dryer, no phone.

Number Three Hotel ★   This small property, adjoining the Glastonbury ruins, is housed in a Georgian structure. The nonsmoking rooms, all doubles, are tastefully and individually decorated. The bathrooms are small, but well organized with adequate shelf space.

3 Magdalene St., Glastonbury, Somerset BA6 9EW. ✆ **01458/832129**. Fax 01458/834227. www.number three.co.uk. 5 units (with tub or shower). £65 ($104) single; £90–£100 ($144–$160) double. Rates include continental breakfast. AE, MC, V. Closed Dec–Jan. **Amenities:** Breakfast room. In room: TV, dataport, coffeemaker, hair dryer.

WHERE TO DINE

The Brasserie ENGLISH/CONTINENTAL   This is a solid, reliable choice in a town not known for its dining. There's a reasonably priced a la carte menu with the chef's special of the day posted on chalkboards. Dishes may include peppered soup, warm avocado and walnuts in a light Stilton sauce, and vegetarian choices such as broccoli-and-cream-cheese bake or vegetable stroganoff with a timbale of saffron and wild rice.

In the George & Pilgrims Hotel, 1 High St. © **01458/831146.** Reservations recommended. Set price lunch and dinner, 2-course £11.95 ($19), 3-course £15 ($24). AE, DC, MC, V. Daily noon–2:30pm and 7–9:30pm.

Rainbow's End Café VEGETARIAN   Much appreciated for its all-vegetarian cuisine, this restaurant occupies the street level of a very old white-fronted building. There's a garden terrace in back for outdoor dining during warm weather and an interior where pine-wood tables are accented with tablecloths and fresh flowers. Daily specials are posted on a chalkboard; menu items include quiche, pizza, stuffed baked potatoes, salads, hot vegetarian platters, and cakes. The food is rather bland—as the locals like it.

17A High St. © **01458/833896.** All items 75p–£5 ($1.20–$8). No credit cards. Mon–Tues and Thurs 10am–4pm; Fri–Sat noon–4pm and 6:30–9:30pm; Sun 11am–4pm. Bus: 158 or 358.

7 Longleat House ⟨★⟩⟨★⟩⟨★⟩ & Stourhead Gardens ⟨★⟩⟨★⟩⟨★⟩

Longleat House is 31km (19 miles) S of Bath and 43km (27 miles) NW of Salisbury. Stourhead is 14km (9 miles) NW of Shaftesbury.

If you're driving, you can visit both Longleat and Stourhead in one busy day. Follow the directions to Longleat given below, then drive 10km (6 miles) down B3092 to Stourton, a village just off the highway, 5km (3 miles) northwest of Mere (A303), to reach Stourhead.

Longleat House and Safari Park ⟨★★★⟩   A magnificent Elizabethan house built in early Renaissance style, **Longleat House** was owned by the seventh marquess of Bath. On first glimpse it's romantic enough, but once you've been inside, it's hard not to be dazzled by the lofty rooms and their exquisite paintings and furnishings. From the Elizabethan Great Hall and the Library to the State Rooms and the grand staircase, the house is filled with all manner of beautiful things. The walls of the State Dining Room are adorned with fine tapestries and paintings, and the lower dining room has displays of silver and porcelain. The library represents the finest private collection in the country. The Victorian kitchens are open, offering a glimpse of life "below the stairs" in a well-ordered country home. Various exhibitions are mounted in the stable yard.

Adjoining Longleat House is **Longleat Safari Park.** The park hosts several species of magnificent and endangered wild animals, including rhinoceros and elephants, free to roam these bucolic surroundings. Here you can walk among giraffes, zebras, camels, and llamas, and view lions and tigers, including England's only white tiger, from your car. You can also ride on a safari boat around the park's lake to see gorillas and feed sea lions. You can see the park by train for a railway adventure, or visit the tropical butterfly garden.

The park provides plenty of theme-park-like thrills as well, including an Adventure Castle, a Doctor Who exhibition, and the world's longest maze, The Maze of Love. Commissioned by the marquess of Bath and designed by Graham Burgess, the maze was inspired by the Garden of Love in Villandry, France, and Botticelli's Primavera. Lying between Longleat House and the Orangery, it first appears to be a traditional parterre with gravel paths and small leafed box hedging; on closer examination, its amorous shapes become apparent. Most obvious are four giant hearts and a pair of women's lips, but there are many more. Love's flower, the rose, has been planted in the beds, and climbing roses trail over the heart-shaped arches. More than 1,300 rose bushes have been planted with names that enhance the symbolic story: First Kiss, Eve, Seduction, and more. The Maze of Love opened to the public on Valentine's Day, 2000, and now visitors can enjoy the scent of its roses in summer while finding their way through the maze.

In Longleat, near Warminster. © **01985/844400.** www.longleat.co.uk. Admission to Longleat House £9 ($14) adults, £6 ($10) children; Safari Park £9 ($14) adults, £6 ($10) children. Special exhibitions and rides require separate admission tickets. Passport tickets for all attractions £16 ($26) adults, £13 ($21) seniors and children 4–14. House open daily 10am–5:30pm. Park open Apr–Nov 2 daily 10am–6pm (last cars admitted at 5pm or sunset). From Bath or Salisbury, take the train to Warminster; then take a taxi to Longleat (about 10 min.). Driving from Bath, take A36 south to Warminster; then follow the signposts to Longleat House. From Salisbury, take A36 north to Warminster, following the signposts to Longleat House.

Stourhead ★★★   In a country of superlative gardens and gardeners, Stourhead is the most fabled of all, the most celebrated example of 18th-century English landscape gardening. But more than that, it's a delightful place to wander, discovering the bridges, grottoes, and temples tucked away among its trees, flowers, and colorful shrubs. Stourhead is a garden for all seasons, but it is at its most idyllic in summer when the rhododendrons are in full bloom.

The house at Stourhead, designed by Colin Campbell, was built for Henry Hoare I (a banker) between 1721 and 1725. It closely resembles the villas Palladio built for wealthy Venetians. The magnificent interior hosts an outstanding library and a wealth of paintings, art treasures, and Chippendale furniture. But the glory of Stourhead is its 40 hectares (100 acres) of prime landscaped gardens, replete with neoclassical follies, lakes, and grottoes. Henry Hoare II, known as "Henry the Magnificent," contributed greatly to the development of the landscape of this magnificent estate.

The garden began with the Grotto (1740) lined with tufa, a water-worn limestone deposit. The springs of the Stour were redirected into the cold bath where a lead copy of the sleeping Ariadne lies. Henry Flitcroft designed the first building, the Tuscan Temple of Flora, in 1744. The wooden seats copy those placed near the original altar where images of pagan gods were laid. Marble busts of Marcus Aurelius and Alexander the Great stand in niches on the wall. In a cave beyond her, the white lead statue of the River God is seen dispensing justice to the waves and to the nymphs who inhabit his stream. The Pantheon (Temple of Hercules) was built in 1754 to house Rysbrack's statues of Hercules and Flora and other classical figures. The temple was originally heated through brass grilles. The nearby Iron Bridge replaced a wooden one in 1860.

In 1765, Flitcroft built the Temple of Apollo (or the Sun); to get there, the visitor goes over the public road via a rock-work bridge. This temple is based on a round temple excavated at Baalbek (modern Lebanon); the statues that were in its niches are now on the roof of Stourhead House. The Turf Bridge was copied from Palladio's bridge in Vicenza. The early-15th-century Bristol High Cross commemorates the monarchs who benefited the city of Bristol; it was moved and set up by Henry Hoare II at Stourhead in 1765. His redbrick folly, Alfred's Tower (1765–72), is a remarkable Stourhead feature. It sits 48m (160 ft.) above the borders of Wiltshire, Somerset, and Dorset, and has 221 steps.

The Obelisk was built in 1840 of Bath stone, replacing the original of Chilmark stone constructed by William Privet in 1746. The three fine redbrick walled terraces were built in the early 19th century to supply cut flowers, fresh fruit, salads, and vegetables to the mansion house. They were in use up to the deaths of Sir Henry and Lady Alda Hoare in 1947. The lower was an herbaceous garden together with a peach and vine house. The pool was part of an irrigation system fed by rainwater from the greenhouses and stable yard.

The plant center is situated near the entrance to the main parking lot in part of the Old Glebe Farm, a small estate dairy farm. This was a working farm until the early 1970s; today visitors can buy plants here that they've seen in the garden.

Lunches and suppers are served at the Spread Eagle Inn, near the entrance to the garden. Boxes are available to order for picnics in the grounds and garden. The Spread Eagle is noted for dinner in the evening and for its Sunday lunches in the autumn, winter, and spring. A self-service buffet is available in the Village Hall tearoom.

High St., Stourhead. (©) **01747/841152.** Admission for garden or house Mar–Oct £5.10 ($8) adults, £2.90 ($4.65) children; off season garden only £3.95 ($6) adults, £1.90 ($3.05) children. Fri–Tues 9am–7pm (or until dusk). Last admission is at 4:30pm. Getting to Stourhead by public transportation is very difficult. You can take the train from Bath to Frome, a 30-min. trip. From here it's still 10 miles away. Most visitors take a taxi from Frome to Stourhead. A direct bus from Bath runs only on the 1st Sat of each month.

8 Dunster ⭐⭐ & Exmoor National Park ⭐⭐

294km (184 miles) W of London; 5km (3 miles) SE of Minehead

The village of Dunster, in Somerset, lies near the eastern edge of Exmoor National Park. It grew up around the original Dunster Castle, constructed as a fortress for the de Mohun family, whose progenitor came to England with William the Conqueror. The village, about 4 miles from the Cistercian monastery at Cleeve, has an ancient priory church and dovecote, a 17th-century gabled yarn market, and little cobbled streets dotted with whitewashed cottages.

ESSENTIALS

GETTING THERE   The best rail link is to travel to Minehead via Taunton, which is easily reached on the main London–Penzance line from Paddington Station in London. For rail information, call (©) **0845/7484950.** From Minehead, you have to take a taxi or bus to reach Dunster.

At Taunton, you can take one of the seven **Southern National** coaches (no. 28; (©) **01823/272033**) leaving hourly Monday through Saturday, with only one bus on Sunday. Trip time is 1 hour and 10 minutes. Buses (no. 38 or 39) from Minehead stop in Dunster Village at the rate of one per hour, but only from June to September. Off-season visitors must take a taxi.

If driving from London, head west along the M4, cutting south at the junction with the M5 until you reach the junction with the A39, going west to Minehead. Before your final approach to Minehead, cut south to Dunster along the A396.

VISITOR INFORMATION   Dunster doesn't have an official tourist office, but **Exmoor National Park Visitor Centre** ((©) **01643/821835**) is at Dunster Steep, 3km (2 miles) east of Minehead. It's open from Easter to October daily from 10am to 5pm, plus limited hours in winter (call ahead).

EXPLORING THE AREA

Dunster Castle ⭐⭐   Dunster Castle is on a tor, from which you can see Bristol Channel. It stands on the site of a Norman castle granted to William de Mohun of Normandy by William the Conqueror shortly after the conquest of England. The 13th-century gateway, built by the de Mohuns, is all that remains of the original fortress. In 1376, Lady Elizabeth Luttrell bought the castle and its lands; her family owned it until it was given to the National Trust in 1976, together with 12 hectares (30 acres) of surrounding parkland.

The first castle was largely demolished during the Civil War. The present Dunster Castle is a Jacobean house constructed in the lower ward of the original fortifications in 1620, then rebuilt in 1870 to look like a castle. From the terraced walks and gardens, you'll have good views of Exmoor and the Quantock Hills.

Some of its outstanding artifacts are the 17th-century panels of embossed painted and gilded leather depicting the story of Antony and Cleopatra. There's also a remarkable allegorical 16th-century portrait of Sir John Luttrell (shown wading naked through the sea with a female figure of peace and a wrecked ship in the background). The 17th-century plasterwork ceilings of the dining room and the finely carved staircase balustrade of cavorting huntsmen, hounds, and stags are also noteworthy.

On A396 (just off A39). ℂ 01643/821314. Admission to castle and grounds £6.40 ($10) adults, £3.20 ($5) children, £16 ($26) family ticket; to grounds only £3.50 ($6) adults, £1.50 ($2.40) children, £8 ($13) family ticket. Castle Apr–Sept Sat–Wed 11am–5pm; Oct Sat–Wed 11am–4pm. Grounds Jan–Mar and Oct–Dec daily 11am–4pm; Apr–Sept daily 10am–5pm. Take bus no. 28 or 39 from Minehead.

EXMOOR NATIONAL PARK ★★

Between Somerset and Devon, along the northern coast of England's southwest peninsula, is Exmoor National Park, an unspoiled plateau of lonely moors. One of the most cherished national parks in Britain, it includes the wooded valleys of the rivers Exe and Barle, the Brendon Hills (a sweeping stretch of rocky coastline), and such sleepy but charming villages as Culbone, Selworthy, Parracombe, and Allerford. Bisected by a network of heavily eroded channels for brooks and streams, the park is distinctive for its lichen-covered trees, gray-green grasses, gorse, and heather. The moors reach their highest point at Dunkery Beacon, 512m (1,707 ft.) above sea level.

Although it's one of the smallest national parks in Britain, it contains one of the most beautiful coastlines in England. Softly contoured, without the dramatic peaks and valleys of other national parks, the terrain is composed mostly of primeval layering of sandstone slate. Although noteworthy for a scarcity of trees, the terrain sustains a limited handful of very old oak groves that forestry experts study for their growth patterns. On clear days, the coast of South Wales, 32km (20 miles) away, can be seen across the Bristol Channel estuary. The wildlife that thrives on the park's rain-soaked terrain includes the wild Exmoor pony, whose bloodlines can be traced from ancient species.

Although there are more than 1,127km (700 miles) of walking paths in the park, most visitors stay either on the coastal trail that winds around the bays and inlets of England's southwestern peninsula or along some of the shorter riverside trails.

The park's administrative headquarters is located within a 19th-century workhouse in the village of Dulverton, in Somerset, near the park's southern edge. A program of walking tours is offered at least five times a week; themes include Woodland Walks, Moorland Walks, Bird Watching Excursions, and Deer Spottings. Most of the tours last from 4 to 6 hours; all are free, with an invitation to donate. Wear sturdy shoes and rain gear.

For the "Exmoor Visitor" brochure, which lists events, guided walks, and visitor information, contact the **Exmoor National Park Visitor Centre,** Dulverton, Somerset TA22 9EX (ℂ **01398/323841**), open daily Easter to October 10am to 5pm; winter 10:30am to 2:30pm.

NEARBY SIGHTS

Combe Sydenham Hall ★   This hall was the home of Elizabeth Sydenham, wife of Sir Francis Drake; it stands on the ruins of monastic buildings associated with nearby Cleeve Abbey. Here you can see a cannonball that supposedly halted the wedding of Lady Elizabeth to a rival suitor in 1585. The gardens include Lady Elizabeth's Walk, which circles ponds originally laid out when the knight was courting his bride-to-be. The valley ponds, fed by springs, are full of rainbow trout (ask about fly-fishing lessons). You can also take a woodland walk to Long Meadow, with its host of wildflowers; see a deserted hamlet, whose population reputedly was wiped out by the Black Death; and visit a historic corn mill. In the hall's tearoom, smoked trout and pâté are produced on oak chips, as in days of yore, and there is a shop, working bakery, and car park.

Monksilver. (℃) **01984/656284**. Admission £5.50 ($9) adults, £2.30 ($3.70) children. Country Park, Easter–Sept Sun–Fri 9am–5pm; courtroom and gardens, May–Sept at 1:30pm for guided tours only, Mon and Wed–Thurs. From Dunster, drive on A39, following signs pointing to Watchet and/or Bridgwater. On the right, you'll see a minor zoo, Tropiquaria, at which you turn right and follow the signs pointing to Combe Sydenham.

Coleridge Cottage This is where Samuel Taylor Coleridge was living when he penned "The Rime of the Ancient Mariner." During his 1797 to 1800 residence here, he and his friends, William Wordsworth and sister Dorothy, enjoyed exploring the Quantock woods. The parlor and reading room of his National Trust property are open to visitors.

The hamlet of Nether Stowey is on A39, north of Taunton, across the Quantock Hills to the east of Exmoor. The cottage is at the west end of Nether Stowey on the south side of A39.

35 Lime St., Nether Stowey, near Bridgwater. (℃) **01278/732662**. Admission £3 ($4.80) adults, £1.50 ($2.40) children. Apr 1–Oct 1 Tues–Thurs and Sun 2–5pm. From Minehead, follow A39 east about 48km (30 miles), following the signs to Bridgwater. About 13km (8 miles) from Bridgwater, turn right, following signs to Nether Stowey.

WHERE TO STAY & DINE IN THE AREA

Dollons House ★ *Value* Named after former occupants who lived here during the early 1700s, and set close to the foundation of Dunster Castle, this nonsmoking house provides the most charming and convenient cost-conscious lodging in town. For many generations the building was used as a pharmacy, and at one time it was a site where some of the most famous orange marmalade in Britain was mass-produced for consumption by members of Parliament in London. In the early Victorian era, a cream-colored stucco facade, accented with egg and dart patterns, was added, making the building look newer than it actually is. The nonsmoking bedrooms are inspired by the decor of an old-fashioned country cottage, "less frilly than Laura Ashley," and very comfortable. There's a gift shop on the premises specializing in pottery from local craftspeople.

10–12 Church St., Dunster TA24 6SH. (℃) **01643/821880**. Fax 01643/822016. 3 units. £37.50 ($60) single; £55 ($88) double. Rates include English breakfast. MC, V. **Amenities:** Breakfast room; TV lounge. *In room:* TV, coffeemaker, hair dryer.

Tea Shoppe ENGLISH Parts of this ancient cottage date to 1495, and it's been a popular tearoom and eatery since the 1930s. The well-prepared menu features Exmoor venison trencher prepared in red wine and port, savory rabbit pie, chicken-and-bacon salad, and a pan-fried chicken filet in tarragon cream sauce with vegetables. There are daily vegetarian specials. For starters, we recommend a sampler platter of local cheese. Desserts include a wide variety of freshly made tarts.

3 High St. (℃) **01643/821304**. Main courses £6–£11 ($10–$18). MC, V. Mar–Oct daily 11am–4pm, Tues–Sat 7–9pm (last order 9pm); Nov–Dec Fri–Sun 11am–4pm, Fri–Sat 7–9pm (last order 9pm). Closed Jan.

9

Devon

Devon, the great patchwork-quilt area of southwest England, another part of the "West Countree," abounds in cliff-side farms, rolling hills, foreboding moors, semitropical plants, and fishing villages that provide some of the finest scenery in England. You can pony trek across moor and woodland, past streams and sheep-dotted fields, or relax at a local pub to soak up atmosphere and ale.

The British approach sunny Devon with the excitement they normally reserve for hopping across the channel. Along the "English Riviera" lie seaports, villages, and resorts synonymous with holidays in the sun, such as Torquay, Clovelly, and Lynton–Lynmouth. In South Devon, where Drake and Raleigh set sail from, tranquillity prevails; on the bay-studded coastline of North Devon, pirates and smugglers once found haven.

Almost every village is geared to accommodate visitors, but many small towns and fishing villages don't allow cars to enter. These towns have parking areas on the outskirts, with a long walk to reach the center of the harbor. From mid-July to mid-September the most popular villages are quite crowded, so make reservations for a place to stay well in advance.

Along the southern coast, the best bases to explore the region from are Exeter, Plymouth, and Torquay. Along the north coast, we suggest Lynton–Lynmouth. The area's most charming village (with very limited accommodations) is Clovelly. The greatest natural spectacle is the Dartmoor National Park, northeast of Plymouth, a landscape of gorges and moors filled with gorse and purple heather, and home of the Dartmoor pony.

If you're taking the bus around Devon, Stagecoach Devon and Western National bus lines combine to offer a discounted **"Explorer Ticket."** Adults can enjoy unlimited use of the lines at these rates: £5 ($8) adults, £3.50 ($6) children for 1 day, or £20 ($32) adults, £10 ($16) children for 7 days. You can plan your journeys from the maps and timetables available at any **Western National** office when you purchase your ticket (© **01209/719988**) or **Devon General Office** (© **01752/495250**). For further information, contact **Stagecoach Devon Ltd.,** Paris Street, Exeter, Devon FX1 2JP (© **01392/427711**).

1 Exeter ★★

322km (201 miles) SW of London; 74km (46 miles) NE of Plymouth

The Romans founded Exeter in the 1st century A.D. on the banks of the River Exe. Two centuries later it was encircled by a mighty stone wall, traces of which remain today. Conquerors and would-be conquerors stormed the fortress in later centuries; one of these, William the Conqueror, brought Exeter to its knees on short notice.

Under the Tudors, the city grew and prospered. Sir Walter Raleigh and Sir Francis Drake were two of the striking figures who strolled through Exeter's

Devon

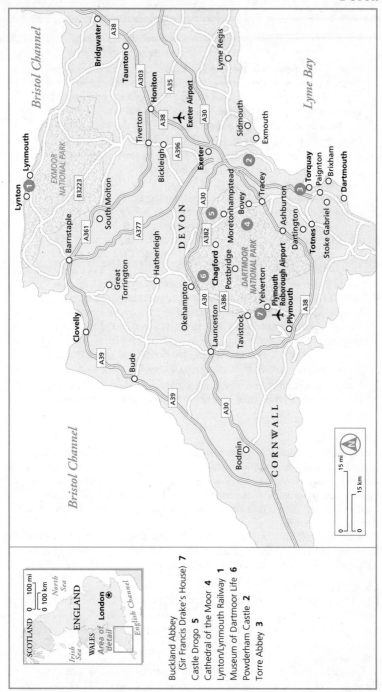

Bristol Channel

Lyme Bay

EXMOOR NATIONAL PARK

DEVON

DARTMOOR NATIONAL PARK

CORNWALL

Bristol Channel

Bridgwater ○ A38

Taunton ○

Honiton ○ A35

A303

Tiverton ○

A38

Exeter Airport ✈

Lyme Regis ○

Sidmouth ○

Exmouth ○

A396

Bickleigh ○

Exeter ○

Moretonhampstead

A30

Tracey ○

Torquay ○

Brixham ○

Paignton ○

Dartmouth

Bovey ○

Ashburton ○

A382

Chagford

Postbridge

Dartington ○

Totnes ○

Stoke Gabriel ○

Lynmouth ○

Lynton ○

Barnstaple ○

A361

South Molton ○

A377

Hatherleigh ○

Great Torrington ○

Okehampton ○

A30

A386

Launceston ○

Tavistock ○

Plymouth Roborough Airport ✈

Yelverton ○

Plymouth ✈

A38

Clovelly

Bude ○

A39

A39

A30

Bodmin ○

15 mi

15 km

N

SCOTLAND

ENGLAND

WALES

Area of detail

London ✹

North Sea

Irish Sea

English Channel

0 — 100 mi
0 — 100 km

Buckland Abbey
(Sir Francis Drake's House) **7**

Castle Drogo **5**

Cathedral of the Moor **4**

Lynton/Lynmouth Railway **1**

Museum of Dartmoor Life **6**

Powderham Castle **2**

Torre Abbey **3**

351

Value Cheap Thrills: What to See & Do for Free (or Almost) in Devon

Head to the beach on the English Riviera. Three seaside towns—Torquay, Brixham, and Paignton—form the longest sweep of beachfront in Britain. This almost continuous sweep of sandy beach opening onto calm waters has earned the title "the English Riviera." The Gulf Stream climate supports subtropical vegetation, and the palm trees imported from Australia in the 19th century still make for a beachy backdrop.

Go in search of the traditional Devonshire cream tea. On faraway granges long ago, traditional Devonshire farmers' wives perfected the medieval process of simmering a batch of whole cow's milk, sometimes for a day or two, at very low temperatures, to create the region's famous Devonshire clotted cream. Silken-textured and rich, with just enough acidity to perk up the taste buds, it isn't "clotted" at all; it's a very English version of the French crème fraîche. In every town and village of Devon you can wander into a tea shop and partake of this specialty.

Spend a morning in Devon's most enchanting village. At one time people read about Clovelly, especially in Charles Kingsley's novel on the Spanish Armada, published as *Westward Ho!* The entire village is privately owned, and its cobbled High Street is Devon's most beautiful. It's also England's steepest, rising up from a cliff at the harbor. Along the tortuous path you'll pass brightly painted houses and gardens in this toylike setting. No, it wasn't designed by Disney; this place is real.

Escape to Dartmoor. The very name evokes an Agatha Christie murder mystery. Covered with heather and gorse, this treeless area is

---

streets. In May 1942, the Germans bombed Exeter, destroying many of its architectural treasures. The town was rebuilt, but the new, impersonal-looking shops and offices can't replace the lost Georgian crescents and the black-and-white-timbered buildings with their plastered walls. Fortunately, much was spared; Exeter still has its Gothic cathedral, a renowned university, some museums, and several historic houses.

Exeter is a good base for exploring both Dartmoor and Exmoor National Parks, two of England's finest. (Exmoor National Park is covered in chapter 8.) It's also a good place to spend a day—there's lots to do in the city's old core.

ESSENTIALS

GETTING THERE   **Exeter Airport** (© 01392/367433) serves the southwest, offering both chartered and scheduled flights. Lying 8km (5 miles) east of the historic center of Exeter, it has scheduled flights to and from Belfast (only in summer), Jersey, Dublin (Mar–Oct), and the Isles of Scilly, but no direct flights from London.

Trains from London's Paddington Station depart every hour during the day. The trip takes 2½ hours. For rail information, call © 0845/7484950 in the United Kingdom. Trains also run every 20 minutes during the day between pockmarked with boggy pits, ideal for depositing a corpse. Severe and inhospitable, Dartmoor is also mysterious and fascinating. Legend says that the "black hounds of hell" roam across the moors collecting the souls of the damned. If you're driving, one of the most scenic roads is the B3212 running southwest from Exeter to Plymouth. Allow about an hour or so to travel this wild landscape, which stretches for more than 72km (45 miles). Make your base the village of Chagford, long a retreat for artists and writers.

Wander around Old Dartmouth. The very name reeks of British naval tradition. This was an important port as early as 1147, when 164 ships sailed from here on the Second Crusade. Even by 1944 Dartmouth was still a major port, as 485 American warships embarked from here to launch the D-day landings. On an estuary of the Dart, the town is filled with crooked half-timbered buildings and looks much as it did in Sir Walter Raleigh's day. The Britannia Royal Naval College has been turning out Britain's finest seamen since 1905.

Call on Plymouth and its *Mayflower* memories. Few Americans in this part of England would want to miss the seaport from which the *Mayflower* sailed. Although launched in Southampton, Plymouth was the last port the vessel saw before reaching the New World. Much is left that is old and fascinating, especially the Barbican, where wealthy Elizabethan merchants constructed homes. Spend a morning or afternoon here exploring its pubs, restaurants, art galleries, and antiques stores.

Exeter and Plymouth; the trip takes 1 hour. Trains often arrive at Exeter St. David's Station at St. David's Hill.

A **National Express** coach departs from London's Victoria Coach Station every 2 hours during the day; the trip takes 4 hours. You can also take bus no. 38 or 39 between Plymouth and Exeter. During the day, two coaches depart per hour for the 1-hour trip. For information and schedules call © **020/7529-2000.**

If you're driving from London, take the M4 west, cutting south to Exeter on the M5 (junction near Bristol).

VISITOR INFORMATION   The **Tourist Information Centre** is at the Civic Centre, Paris Street (© **01392/265700;** fax 01392/265260). It's open Monday through Saturday from 9am to 5pm, and from July to August Monday to Saturday 9am to 5pm and Sunday 10am to 4pm.

SPECIAL EVENTS   A classical music lover's dream, the **Exeter Festival,** held the first 2 weeks in July, includes more than 150 events, ranging from concerts and opera to lectures. Festival dates and offerings vary from year to year, and more information is available by contacting the **Exeter Festival Office,** Civic Center (© **01392/265200;** www.exeter.gov.uk).

EXPLORING EXETER

Exeter Cathedral ★★   The Roman II Augusta Legion made its camp on the site where the Cathedral Church of Saint Peter now stands in Exeter. It has been occupied by Britons, Saxons, Danes, and Normans. The English Saint Boniface, who converted northern Germany to Christianity, was trained here in A.D. 690. The present cathedral structure was begun around 1112, and the twin Norman towers still stand. Between the towers runs the longest uninterrupted true Gothic vault in the world, at a height of 20m (66 ft.) and a length of 90m (300 ft.). It was completed in 1369 and is the finest existing example of Decorated Gothic architecture. The Puritans destroyed the cathedral cloisters in 1655, and a German bomb finished off the twin Chapels of St. James and St. Thomas in May 1942. Now restored, it's one of the prettiest churches anywhere. Its famous choir sings evensong every day except Wednesday during school term. On school holidays, visiting choirs perform.

1 The Cloisters. ℂ **01392/255573.** www.exeter-cathedral.org.uk. Free admission; a donation of £3 ($4.50) is requested of adults. Mon–Fri 7:30am–5:15pm; Sat 7:30am–5:15pm; Sun 7:30am–7:30pm.

Exeter Guildhall   This colonnaded building is the oldest municipal building in the kingdom—the earliest reference to it is in a deed from 1160. The Tudor front that straddles the pavement was added in 1593. Inside you'll find a fine display of silver and a number of paintings. The ancient hall is paneled in oak.

High St. ℂ **01392/665500.** Free admission. Mon–Fri 10am–1pm and 2–4pm. It's best to call before visiting.

St. Nicholas Priory   This is the guest wing of a Benedictine priory founded in 1070. You'll see fine plaster ceilings and period furniture. A recent summer exhibit featured Russian ceramics and crafts.

The Mint, off Fore St. ℂ **01392/265858.** Free admission. Call for opening arrangements.

Underground Passages   These tunnels, accessible from High Street, were built to carry the medieval water supply into the city. By entering the new underground interpretation center, visitors can view a video and exhibition before taking a guided tour.

Boots Corner, off High St. ℂ **01392/665887.** Admission £3.75 ($6) adults, £2.75 ($4.40) children, £11 ($18) family ticket. June–Sept Mon–Sat 10am–5pm; Oct–May Tues–Fri noon–5pm, Sat 10am–5pm.

Powderham Castle ★   This private house is occupied by the countess and earl of Devon, who let Ismail Merchant and James Ivory use their home as a setting for *Remains of the Day,* starring Anthony Hopkins and Emma Thompson. It was built in the late 14th century by Sir Philip Courtenay, sixth son of the second earl of Devon, and his wife, Margaret, granddaughter of Edward I. Their magnificent tomb is in the south transept of Exeter Cathedral.

⌒*Moments*   **A Relic from William the Conqueror**

Just off "The High," at the top of Castle Street, stands an impressive **Norman Gatehouse** from William the Conqueror's castle. Although only the house and walls survive, the view from here and the surrounding gardens is panoramic. Stand here for a moment and contemplate all the invasions that have assaulted Exeter, from the Romans to the Nazi bombers of World War II.

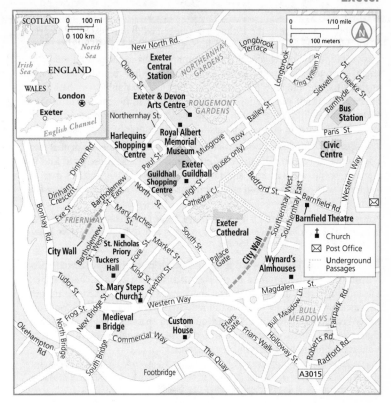

The castle has many family portraits and fine furniture, including a remarkable clock that plays full tunes at 4pm, 8pm, and midnight; some 17th-century tapestries; and a chair used by William III for his first council of state at Newton Abbot. The chapel dates from the 15th century, with hand-hewn roof timbers and carved pew ends.

In Powderham, Kenton. ☎ **01626/890243**. www.powderham.co.uk. Admission £6.90 ($11) adults, £6.40 ($10) seniors, £3.90 ($6) children 5–17, free for children 4 and under, £17.70 family ticket. ($28). Easter–Oct Sun–Fri 10am–5:30pm. Take the A379 Dawlish Rd. 13km (8 miles) south of Exeter; the castle is signposted.

SHOPPING

Exeter has long been famous for its silver. If you seek, ye shall find old Exeter silver, especially spoons, sold in local stores. **Burfords,** 17 Guildhall, Queen Street (☎ **01392/254901**), sells modern silver and jewelry.

You can find a number of antiques dealers in Exeter. At least six are on the Quay off Western Way. **The Quay Gallery Antiques Emporium** (☎ **01392/213283**) houses 10 dealers who sell furniture, porcelain, metalware, and other collectibles. **The Antique Centre** on the Quay (☎ **01392/493501**) has 20 dealers.

The Edinburgh Woolen Mill, 23 Cathedral Yard (☎ **01392/412318**), carries a large selection of woolen goods, including kilts, Aran jumpers, tartan travel rugs, and quality wool suits for women and trousers for men.

A daily market on Sidwell Street is Exeter's version of an American flea market.

WHERE TO STAY

Established as a college in the 19th century, upgraded to university status in the 1950s, **University of Exeter,** Birks Hall, New North Road (✆ **01392/211500;** www.exeter.ac.uk), offers economical accommodations to the general public in several dormitories during Easter break and from mid-July to mid-September. A single with bathroom rents for £25.95 ($42) per night; a double with bathroom costs £22.50 ($36) per person, including breakfast. You're entitled to use the sports facilities, including tennis, squash, badminton, and a heated pool, or roam the 300 acres of grounds and gardens of the campus.

Claremont   This Regency-style 1840 town house is in a quiet residential area close to the city center. The nonsmoking rooms, much like those you'd find in a private home, are well kept and tastefully decorated. Each unit has a small bathroom with a shower. Geoff and Jacqueline Self, who run the property, assist visitors in many ways.

36 Wonford Rd., Exeter, Devon EX2 4LD. ✆ **01392/274699.** 3 units. £38 ($61) single; £48–£52 ($77–$83) double; £85 ($136) suite for 4. Rates include English breakfast. No credit cards. Bus: H. **Amenities:** Restaurant. *In room:* TV, dataport, coffeemaker, hair dryer, no phone.

The Edwardian ★★   This is one of the most elegant Edwardian town houses in Exeter, tastefully converted to receive guests with its antique charm intact. The location is near the center of town and Exeter Cathedral. Bedrooms are well furnished and beautifully decorated to reflect the period; a number have four-poster beds. Bathrooms come with adequate shelf space and are shower or tub units. Exonian Michael Rattenbury, who runs the guesthouse with his wife, Kay, is always willing to help guests plan excursions.

30–32 Heavitree Rd., Exeter, Devon EX1 2LQ. ✆ **01392/276102.** Fax 01392/253393. www.edwardianexeter. co.uk. 12 units. £40 ($64) single; £56–£62 ($90–$99) double. Rates include breakfast. AE, MC, V. **Amenities:** Breakfast room; lounge. *In room:* TV, dataport, coffeemaker, hair dryer.

Park View Hotel   This landmark Georgian house, near the heart of town and the train station, offers comfortable accommodations; most have been redecorated and refurnished as part of an ongoing refurbishment. Rooms with private bathroom have a shower; only two have a tub-and-shower combination. The hotel offers five nonsmoking rooms. Guests take their breakfast in a cozy room opening onto the hotel's garden. Breakfast is the only meal served, but the staff will pack lunch for touring.

8 Howell Rd., Exeter, Devon EX4 4LG. ✆ **01392/271772.** Fax 01392/253047. www.parkviewexeter.co.uk. 13 units, 11 with bathroom. £24 ($38) single without bathroom, £32 ($51) single with bathroom; £45 ($72) double without bathroom, £50–£60 ($80–$96) double with bathroom. Rates include English breakfast. AE, MC, V. **Amenities:** Breakfast room; lounge. *In room:* TV, dataport, coffeemaker, hair dryer.

Raffles ★★   A rival of The Edwardian (see above), this restored Victorian town house is furnished with antiques and set in a walled garden. Only minutes from the town center, it offers well-furnished and tastefully decorated bedrooms, each with small private bathrooms with shower. Four nonsmoking rooms are available for guests. Maintenance is of a high level, and the welcome is warm. Owners Richard and Sue Hyde are also antiques dealers, and some of the items in their house can be purchased. Raffles has a license to serve alcohol to guests, and evening meals are available if requested. Much of the fare is cooked with organic ingredients.

11 Blackall Rd., Exeter, Devon EX 4 4HD. ✆ and fax **01392/270200.** www.raffles-exeter.co.uk. 7 units. £36 ($58) single; £56 ($90) double; £66 ($106) family unit. Rates include breakfast. AE, MC, V. **Amenities:** Dining room; lounge. *In room:* TV, coffeemaker, hair dryer, no phone.

Trees Mini Hotel This redbrick hostelry is a 5-minute walk from the city center, on a quiet street near a small park and the bus station. Designed as a private home around the turn of the century, it contains recently refurbished, cozy bedrooms, each with easy access to corridor facilities. Guests can be housed in the main building or else at Town Barton, which was originally the manor house of Sir Ralph de Doddiscomb in 1241. Town Barton lies only 180m (600 ft.) away and is reached by private footpath

2 Queens Crescent, York Rd., Exeter, Devon EX4 6AY. ℭ **01392/259531.** Fax 01392/214673. www.smooth hound.co.uk/hotels/treesmin.html. 12 units, 1 with bathroom. £22 ($35) single; £44 ($70) double without bathroom. Rates include English breakfast. No credit cards. **Amenities:** Breakfast room. *In room:* TV, coffeemaker, hair dryer, no phone.

NEARBY PLACES TO STAY

Lord Haldon Hotel ★★ If you're driving, your best bet might be this hotel, 6.5km (4 miles) southwest of Exeter. Constructed in 1737 as a smaller version of Buckingham Palace, this was the seat of the lords of Haldon. A major part of the original structure burned in the 20th century, but the remaining wing has been made into a country-house hotel, incorporating an archway created by 18th-century architect Sir Robert Adam. Rooms are of good size and most have countryside views; all contain bathrooms with shower. Three of the units have four-poster beds and 19 rooms are nonsmoking. Fresh local produce is used for the traditional British dishes served in the elegant Chandelier Restaurant.

Kings Dr., Dunchideock, near Exeter, Devon EX6 7YF. ℭ **01392/832483.** Fax 01392/833765. www.lord haldonhotel.co.uk. 23 units. £55 ($88) single; £85 ($136) double. Rates include English breakfast. MC, V. **Amenities:** Restaurant; bar; room service (7:30am–9pm). *In room:* TV, dataport, coffeemaker, hair dryer.

The Nobody Inn ★ *Finds* Ignore the punny name; someone is always waiting to welcome you to the inn. In a village west of Exeter, this hotel is housed in two buildings. The manor house, where five rooms are located, has a rich history—it was given to Ralph de Doddiscomb by Richard I (the Lionheart) during the Holy Wars. There are two rooms in the main building, along with a restaurant and bar. Most accommodations come with a private shower, and one room that is wheelchair accessible is available for those with limited mobility.

Doddiscombsleigh, near Exeter, Devon EX6 7PS. ℭ **01647/252394.** Fax 01647/252978. www.thenobody inn.com. 7 units, 5 with bathroom. £23–£33 ($37–$53) single without bathroom, £38 ($61) single with bathroom; £33 ($53) double without bathroom, £70 ($112) double with bathroom. Rates include breakfast. AE, MC, V. The inn does not accommodate children under 14. **Amenities:** Restaurant; bar. *In room:* TV, dataport, minibar, coffeemaker, hair dryer.

WHERE TO DINE

Coolings Wine Bar ENGLISH Set in a Victorian building on a short cobblestone street that intersects the High Street near the center of Exeter, this welcoming place offers beams, checkered tablecloths, and tables that spill over into the cellar. The food, prepared on the premises, includes a plentiful selection of meats, pies, and quiches, as well as such changing specialties as chicken Waldorf and sugar-baked ham, each served with freshly prepared salads. There's nothing experimental here, just hearty Devonshire cookery. Wine by the glass includes many dozens of vintages from throughout Europe. The full menu is available only at lunch, noon to 3:30pm.

11 Gandy St. ℭ **01392/434184.** Soups £2.85 ($4.55); main courses £5–£6.70 ($8–$11). MC, V. Mon–Sat 10am–11pm; Sun 10am–10:30pm. Bus: N.

Herbie's Whole Food Restaurant *Value* VEGETARIAN Known by its trademark sign in front, Herbie's is your best bet for generous portions of vegetarian fare at the lowest prices. This is where to meet counter-cultural Exeter, especially those attached to the lively Exeter and Devon Arts Centre. Homemade meals are the feature here, along with the town's largest variety of vegetarian dishes.

15 North St. ℂ 0139/258473. Meals £2.50–£6.95 ($4–$11). MC, V. Mon–Fri 10:30am–2:30pm; Sat 10:30am–4pm; Tues–Sat 6–9:30pm.

Port Royal Inn ENGLISH   With a flowering patio at the edge of the Exe, this antique pub lies a 10-minute walk northeast of the town center. It was built in the 1790s as a boat-repair shop. During warm weather, drinkers and diners congregate on the outdoor patio, where a landing stage extends out into the river. The owners proudly stock 10 types of real ale. Salads are tempting, or you can order a pâté and toast. Sandwiches made from granary bread are filled with meat or cheese. Two or three hot specials are served on Sundays and may include seafood, roast chicken, or roast lamb. There are desserts and a good selection of ports and sherries. All food is ordered at the pub but delivered to your table.

The Quay at Larkbeare Rd. ℂ 01392/272360. Main courses £4.95–£10.50 ($8–$17). AE, DC, MC, V. Mon–Sat 11am–11pm; Sun noon–10:30pm. Blue minibus: R, K, or S.

The Ship Inn ★★ ENGLISH   This inn lies in the town center and was often visited by Sir Francis Drake, Sir Walter Raleigh, and Sir John Hawkins. Of it Drake wrote: "Next to mine own shippe, I do most love that old 'Shippe' in Exon, a tavern in Fyssh Street, as the people call it, or as the clergie will have it, St. Martin's Lane." The pub still provides tankards of real ales, lager, and stout, and is still loved by locals. A large selection of snacks is offered in the bar daily; the restaurant upstairs provides more substantial, if uninspired, English fare. At lunch or dinner, you can order from a wide selection including French onion soup, grilled lemon sole, and five different steaks. Portions are large.

St. Martin's Lane. ℂ 01392/272040. Reservations recommended. Main courses £3.50–£8 ($6–$13). MC, V. Restaurant: Mon–Fri noon–3pm and 6–9:30pm; Sat 11am–11pm. Pub: Mon–Sat 11am–11pm; Sun noon–10:30pm. Bus: N.

EXETER AFTER DARK

Exeter is a lively university town offering an abundance of classical concerts and theater productions as well as clubs and pubs. If you need information concerning cultural events and theaters, the **Exeter Arts Booking and Information Centre,** Princesshay (ℂ **01392/211080**), open daily 9:30am to 5pm, provides a monthly brochure of upcoming events and sells tickets.

An abundance of concerts, opera, dance, and film can be found year-round at the **Exeter & Devon Arts Centre,** Bradninch Place, Gandy Street (ℂ **01392/ 667080**), and Exeter University's **Northcott Theatre,** Stocker Road (ℂ **01392/ 493493**), home to a professional theater company.

On the club scene, head to **Volts,** The Quay (ℂ **01392/211347,** or 01392/ 435820 info line), a two-story club featuring funk, soul, dance, and alternative on the first floor and The Hot House, playing classic pop, on the second floor. The crowd here is young, and there's a full bar and fast food available. The cover charge varies from free to £3 ($4.80). Attracting a more diverse crowd, **The Warehouse/Boxes Disco,** Commercial Road (ℂ **01392/259292**), is another split club, with different music styles featured throughout the week. The cover charge varies from free to £5 ($8) before 11pm, and £6 ($10) afterward; this gets you into both clubs.

Pubs vary from the ancient and haunted to the traditional and modern. The **Turks Head,** High Street (ℂ **01392/256680**), is housed in a 600-year-old dungeon allegedly haunted by the Turks who were tortured and killed here. The first two floors are unchanged from that bygone era, but the top three floors were turned into the existing pub more than 450 years ago. It was a favorite hangout and scribbling spot for Charles Dickens, whose favorite chair is on display. Today, it's a lively pub with a computerized jukebox and a fast-food menu. The **Well House Tavern,** Cathedral Close (© **01392/223611**), is part of the Royal Clarence Hotel. It's housed in a building believed to date from the 14th century, although the Roman well in the basement predates that estimate. It, too, is allegedly haunted—only the ghost here, affectionately called Alice, is said to be good-spirited; she appears in a flowing white dress. Join Alice and the other regulars for a pint or a light meal. Featuring a great view of the canal, **Double Locks,** Canal Banks (© **01392/256947**), welcomes a varied crowd, largely students. It features live music with no cover charge two or three evenings a week, and you can get traditional pub grub to go with your pint. Although spaciously spread through a Georgian mansion, the **Imperial Pub,** New North Road (© **01392/434050**), is friendly to frugal travelers, with the cheapest brand-name beer in town, starting at £1.45 ($2.30), and a fast-food menu.

2 Dartmoor National Park ★★

341km (213 miles) SW of London; 21km (13 miles) W of Exeter

This national park lies northeast of Plymouth, stretching from Tavistock and Okehampton on the west to near Exeter in the east, a granite mass that sometimes rises to a height of 600m (2,000 ft.) above sea level. The landscape offers vistas of gorges with rushing water, spiny shrubs, and purple heather ranged over by Dartmoor ponies—a foreboding landscape for the experienced walker only.

In Dartmoor, you'll find 805km (500 miles) of foot and bridle paths and more than 90,000 acres of common land with public access. The country is rough, and on the high moor you should always make sure you have good maps, a compass, and suitable clothing and shoes.

ESSENTIALS

GETTING THERE   Take the train from London to Exeter, then use local buses to connect you with the various villages of Dartmoor.

Transmoor Link, a public transport bus service, usually operates throughout the summer, and is an ideal way to get onto the moor. Information on the Transmoor Link and on the bus link between various towns and villages on Dartmoor is available from the **Transport Coordination Centre** (© **01392/382800**).

If you're driving, Exeter is the most easily reached gateway. From here, continue west on the B3212 to such centers of Dartmoor as Easton, Chagford, Moretonhampstead, and North Bovey. From these smaller towns, tiny roads—often not really big enough for two cars—cut deeper into the moor.

VISITOR INFORMATION   The main source of information is the **Dartmoor National Park Tourist Information Centre,** Town Hall, Bedford Square, Tavistock (© **01822/612938**). It will book accommodations within a 24km (15-mile) radius for free. It's open April through October daily 9:30am to 5pm. From November to March, it's open on Monday, Tuesday, Friday, and Saturday from 10am to 4:30pm.

EXPLORING THE MOORS

The **Dartmoor National Park Authority (DNPA)** runs **guided walks** of varying difficulty, ranging from 1½ to 6 hours for a trek of some 14km to 19km

(9 miles–12 miles). All you have to do is turn up suitably clad at your selected starting point. Details are available from DNP information centers or from the **Dartmoor National Park Authority,** High Moorland Visitor Centre, Tavistock Road, Princetown (near Yelverton) PL20 6QF (✆ **01822/890414**). Guided tours cost £3 ($4.80) for a 2-hour walk, £4 ($6) for a 3-hour walk, £4.50 ($7) for a 4-hour walk, and £5 ($8) for a 6-hour walk. These prices are subsidized by the national park services.

For **horseback riding** on Dartmoor, there are too many establishments to list. All are licensed, and you are accompanied by an experienced rider/guide. The moor becomes dangerous when fogs descend on treacherous marshlands without warning. Prices are around £10 ($16) per hour, £16 ($26) for a half-day, and £27 ($43) for a full day. Most riding stables are listed in a useful free publication, *The Dartmoor Visitor,* which also provides details on guided walks, places to go, accommodations, local events, and articles about the national park. *The Dartmoor Visitor* is obtainable from DNPA information centers and tourist information centers or by mail. Send an International Reply Coupon to the DNPA headquarters (address above).

CAMPING IN THE PARK

A few official campsites exist, but many campers prefer the open moor for the night. Since the moor is privately owned, seek permission before camping. Only 1 night in a single spot is permitted. Campsites include **Ashburton Caravan Park,** Waterleat, Ashburton (✆ **01364/652552**); **River Dart Country Park,** Holne Park, Ashburton (✆ **01364/652511**); and **Yertiz Caravan and Camping Park,** Exeter Road, Okehampton (✆ **01837/52281**). Most sites are open April through September; charges begin at £5.95 ($10) per person per night.

CHAGFORD 🐾: A GOOD BASE FOR EXPLORING THE PARK

349km (218 miles) SW of London; 21km (13 miles) W of Exeter; 32km (20 miles) NW of Torquay

Six hundred feet above sea level, Chagford is an ancient town; surrounded by moors, it's a good base from which to explore the often forlorn but romantic north Dartmoor. It's also Sir Francis Drake country. Chagford overlooks the River Teign in its deep valley and is overshadowed by the high granite tors. There's good fishing in the Teign. From Chagford, the most popular excursion is to Postbridge, a village with a prehistoric clapper bridge.

To get here, take a train to Exeter (see earlier in this chapter), and then catch a local bus to Chagford (Transmoor Link National Express bus no. 82). If you're driving from Exeter, drive west on A30, then south on A382 to Chagford.

EXPLORING THE TOWN

Sir Francis Drake's House 🎖 Constructed in 1278, Sir Francis Drake's House was originally a Cistercian monastery. After dissolution in 1539, it became the countryseat of sailors Sir Richard Grenville and then Sir Francis Drake. The house remained in the Drake family until 1946, when the abbey and grounds were given to the National Trust. The abbey is now a museum and houses exhibits including Drake's drum, banners, and other artifacts.

Buckland Abbey, Yelverton. ✆ **01822/853607**. Admission £5 ($8) adults, £2.50 ($4) children. Apr–Oct Fri–Wed 10:30am–5:30pm; Nov–Mar Sat–Sun 2–5pm. Last admission 45 min. before closing. Go 5km (3 miles) west of Yelverton off A386.

Castle Drogo 🎖 This massive granite castle, in the hamlet of Drewsteignton some 27km (17 miles) west of Exeter, was designed and built between 1910 and

1930 by Sir Edwin Lutyens, then at his height, for his client Julius Drewe. It was the last large-scale private country house built in the United Kingdom. Although castellated and turreted like a medieval castle, it was never intended for military use. The castle occupies a bleak but dramatic position high above the Teign, with views sweeping out over the moors.

The tour covers an elegant series of formal rooms designed in the best Edwardian tradition, including drawing rooms, dining rooms, salons, and a gun room. There are two restaurants on the premises, both with waiting service, and a tearoom where tea, pastries, and snacks are served buffet-style.

Insider's tip: The castle is so overpowering it's easy to forget the secluded gardens. But they are wonderful: a sunken lawn enclosed by raised walkways, a circular croquet lawn (sets are available for rent), geometrically shaped yew hedges, and a kiddies' playroom based on a 1930s residence.

6.5km (4 miles) northeast of Chagford and 9.5km (6 miles) south of the Exeter–Okehampton Rd. (A30). *C* **01647/433306**. Admission (castle and grounds) £5.90 ($9) adults, £2.95 ($4.70) children. Grounds only £2.90 ($4.65) adults, £1.45 ($2.30) children. Apr–Oct Wed–Sun 11am–5:30pm; grounds daily 10:30am–dusk. Take A30 and follow the signs.

WHERE TO STAY

Glendarah House   Located at the edge of town, this comfortable nonsmoking Victorian house, owned by John and Sylvia Croxen, makes a good base for exploring Dartmoor National Park. In 1994, the house was refurbished to a high standard, adding TVs and shower-only bathrooms to all rooms. Ample breakfasts are provided, and many leisure pursuits are close at hand, including golf, fishing, horseback riding, swimming, walking, and bird-watching. One room is available for those with limited mobility.

Lower St., Chagford, Devon TQ13 8BZ. *C* **01647/433270**. Fax 01647/433483. www.glendarah-house.co.uk. 3 units. £25 ($40) single; £50 ($80) double. Rates include English breakfast. No credit cards. Bus: 359. **Amenities:** Breakfast room. *In room:* TV, dataport, coffeemaker, hair dryer, no phone.

WHERE TO DINE

Ring o' Bells BRITISH   Food and wine are still dispensed from this site, a tradition since the 12th century, although the historic building you'll see today dates from around Shakespeare's time. Its antiquity is enhanced with exposed oak, slate floors, and photographs of old Chagford and the weather-beaten folk who used to work on its surrounding farms. You'll be welcome to hoist a glass of Butcombe Ale. If you're hungry, look for different versions of "fish on the bone" (a manner of preparation that adds to the flavor), venison in red-wine sauce, crab from local waters, roast beef with mashed potatoes, or a limited selection of vegetarian dishes. The inn also rents out four comfortably furnished, nonsmoking bedrooms, two equipped with private bathroom. A double without bathroom costs £40 ($64); with bathroom it's £45 ($72). Rates include breakfast; each unit comes with TV and beverage maker.

44 The Square. © 01647/432466. Reservations recommended for dinner. Main courses £6.25–£13.50 ($10–$22). MC, V. Daily 8:30am–2pm; 5–6pm (tea); 6–9pm.

OTHER TOWNS IN & AROUND DARTMOOR

Some 21km (13 miles) west of Exeter, the peaceful little town of **Moreton-hampstead** is perched on the edge of Dartmoor. It contains an old market cross and several 17th-century colonnaded almshouses.

The much-visited Dartmoor village of **Widecombe-in-the-Moor** is only 11km (7 miles) from Moretonhampstead. The fame of this village stems from an old folk song about Tom Pearce and his gray mare, listing the men on their way to Widecombe Fair when they met with disaster. Widecombe has a parish church worth visiting, the so-called **Cathedral of the Moor;** with a roster of vicars beginning in 1253, this house of worship, nestled in a green valley, is surrounded by legends. When the building was restored, a wall plate was found bearing the badge of Richard II (who reigned 1377–99), the figure of a white hart. Despite its fame, the town itself is disappointing, tacky, and unkempt.

The market town of **Okehampton** owes its existence to the Norman castle built by Baldwin de Bryonis, sheriff of Devon, under orders from his uncle, William the Conqueror, in 1068. The Courtenay family lived here for many generations until Henry VIII beheaded one of them and dismantled the castle in 1538.

Museum of Dartmoor Life, at the Dartmoor Centre, 3 West St., Okehampton (© **01837/52295**), is housed in an old mill with a water wheel and is part of the Dartmoor Centre, a group of attractions around an old courtyard. Also here are working craft studios, a Victorian Cottage Tearoom, and a tourist information center. Museum displays cover all aspects of Dartmoor's history from prehistoric times, including some old vehicles—a Devon box wagon of 1875 and a 1922 Bull-nose Morris motorcar—and a reconstructed cider press and a blacksmith. The museum is open from October to Easter, Monday through Friday from 10am to 4pm, and from Easter to October, Monday through Saturday from 11am to 4:30pm. It also opens on Sunday June through September from 10am to 5pm. Admission is £2 ($3.20) for adults, £1.80 ($2.90) for seniors, £1 ($1.60) for children, and £5.60 ($9) for a family ticket (two adults, two children).

Many traditional artisans still work throughout the area, including basket weavers, wood turners, and potters. Indulge yourself with genuine Devon pieces of craftsmanship. In the Dartmoor National Park in West Devon, **The Yelverton Paperweight Centre,** Leg O'Mutton (© **01822/854250**), presents an impressive display of more than 800 glass paperweights for sale along with paintings of Dartmoor scenes. **The Kountry Kit,** 22–23 West St., Tavistock (© **01822/613089**), carries all the best names in gear and outerwear. It is also a clearinghouse of name-brand seconds.

WHERE TO STAY & DINE

The Castle Inn ⭑ A 16th-century structure next to Lydford Castle, this inn lies midway between Okehampton and Tavistock. With its pink facade and row of rose trellises, it is the hub of the village. The owners have maintained the character of the commodious old rustic lounge. One room, called the "Snug," has a group of high-backed oak settles arranged in a circle. The bedrooms are not large but are attractively furnished, often with mahogany and marble Victorian pieces. There's an equal split between bathrooms with a shower only and those with a tub-and-shower combination.

Lydford, near Okehampton (1 mile off A386), Devon EX20 4BH. © **01822/820241.** Fax 01822/820454. castle11yd@aol.com. 9 units. £45–£55 ($72–$88) single; £65–£90 ($104–$144) double. MC, V. **Amenities:** Restaurant; bar; limited room service (8am–9pm). *In room:* TV, coffeemaker, hair dryer.

Lydford House Hotel ★ *Finds*   This family-run, country-house hotel is 11km (7 miles) south of Okehampton, just off A386, and it's on your right as you approach the hamlet of Lydford, just on the edge of Dartmoor. Standing amid 3.2 hectares (8 acres) of gardens and pastureland, it was built in 1880 for Dartmoor artist William Widgery; his paintings hang in the residents' lounge. All the midsize rooms have private, shower-only or shower-and-tub bathrooms, and 10 rooms are nonsmoking. The owners offer varied and interesting menus, all home-cooked using local produce. The property includes a tearoom (open for light snacks) and riding stables. The hotel offers two rooms for those with limited mobility.

Lydford, near Okehampton, Devon EX20 4AU. © **01822/820347.** Fax 01822/820442. 12 units. £37.50 ($60) per person. Rates include English breakfast. MC, V. **Amenities:** Restaurant; bar; tearoom; gift shop; riding stables. *In room:* TV, dataport, coffeemaker, hair dryer.

Old Walls Farm ★   This nonsmoking country home is set on a 1930s working farm in the heart of the moors. The owners will draw handmade maps and pinpoint places of interest within driving distance. Relax around a stone fireplace in the drawing room or, on a sunny day, enjoy the all-glass sunroom with its exceptional view of the moorland. The midsize bedrooms are comfortably furnished and most inviting, each with a shower or shower-and-tub combination. Breakfast is a special event in the dining room, and you can eat as much as you want.

Ponsworthy, near Widecombe-in-the-Moor and Newton Abbot, Devon TQ13 7PN. © **01364/631222.** 2 units. £22 ($35) single; £44 ($70) double. Rates include English breakfast. No credit cards. Closed Christmas week. Take the A38 divided highway between Exeter and Plymouth. Turn right past Ashburton onto B3357, then right at Poundsgate onto the Ponsworthy-Widecombe road. Go through the hamlet of Ponsworthy, crossing the narrow bridge with a phone kiosk on the right, and look for the B&B sign on the left about 540m (1,800 ft.) on. **Amenities:** Breakfast room. *In room:* Coffeemaker, no phone.

Ring of Bells   Located beside the village green of a hamlet full of thatched cottages, this is a nonsmoking family-run inn, restaurant, and pub, which was originally built during the 13th century. Today it retains its thatched roof and cottage garden, though part of the space in back has been transformed into an outdoor pool. The building's walls are almost a meter (3 ft.) thick. Some of the bedrooms—all doubles—contain four-poster beds; all are comfortable and well furnished, and include a private, shower-only bathroom. Beneath time-blackened beams, you can have meals in the pub. Bolero Leisure also offers meals in the somewhat more formal restaurant. Golfers can head over to the Manor House Hotel's 18-hole course, about 1.5km (1 mile) away.

North Bovey, near Newton Abbott, Devon TQ13 8RB. © **01647/440375.** www.ringofbellsinn.com. 5 units. £30 ($48) single; £60 ($96) double. Rates include English breakfast. MC, V. To reach Ring of Bells by public transit, take the bus to Moretonhampstead from either Torquay or Exeter, then a taxi the final 2.5km (1½ miles). **Amenities:** Restaurant; bar. *In room:* Coffeemaker, hair dryer, no phone.

3 Torquay: The English Riviera ★

357km (223 miles) SW of London; 37km (23 miles) SE of Exeter

In 1968, Torquay, Paignton, and Brixham joined to form "The English Riviera" as part of a plan to turn the area into one of the super three-in-one resorts of Europe. The area today—the birthplace of mystery writer Agatha Christie—opens onto 35km (22 miles) of coastline and 18 beaches.

Torquay is set against a backdrop of the red cliffs of Devon, with many sheltered pebbly coves. With its parks and gardens, including numerous subtropical plants, it's often compared to the Mediterranean. At night, concerts, productions from the West End, vaudeville shows, and ballroom dancing keep the vacationers and many honeymooners entertained.

ESSENTIALS

GETTING THERE   The nearest connection is Exeter Airport, 40 minutes away. Frequent trains run throughout the day from London's Paddington Station to Torquay, whose station is at the town center on the seafront. The trip takes 2½ hours. For rail information, call © **0845/7484950.**

National Express coach links from London's Victoria Coach Station leave every 2 hours during the day for Torquay. For information and schedules, call © **020/7529-2000.**

If you're driving from Exeter, head west on the A38, veering south at the junction with the A380.

VISITOR INFORMATION   The **Tourist Information Centre** is at Vaughan Parade (© **01803/297428**), open Monday to Thursday 8:40am to 5:15pm and Friday 8:40am to 4:15pm.

PALM TREES & AGATHA CHRISTIE

This resort town offers one of the balmiest climates in Britain, thanks to the Gulf Stream. It's so temperate that subtropical plants such as palm trees and succulents thrive.

Torre Abbey   Originally built as a monastery in 1196, converted into a private home in the 16th century, Torre Abbey has long been associated with Torquay's leading citizens. Today the Town Council maintains it as a museum. The museum features a room that closely approximates Agatha Christie's private study. After the mystery writer's death, her family donated for display her Remington typewriter, many of her original manuscripts, an oil portrait of Ms. Christie as a young woman, family photographs, and more.

Kings Dr. (just east of Torquay's center). © 01803/293593. Admission £3.25 ($5) adults, £1.70 ($2.70) children. Easter or Apr (whichever is earlier)–Oct daily 9:30am–6pm.

Oldway Mansion   The conspicuous consumption of England's Gilded Age is on display here. The mansion was built in 1874 by Isaac Merritt Singer, founder of the sewing machine empire; his son Paris later enhanced its decor, massive Ionic portico, and 17 acres of Italianate gardens. The mansion's eclectic decor includes a scaled-down version of the Hall of Mirrors in the Palace of Versailles. During its Jazz Age heyday, Oldway served as a rehearsal and performance space for Isadora Duncan, who was having an affair with Paris.

Torbay Rd., in Preston, near Paignton (a short drive south of the center of Torquay on the main Paignton-Torquay road). © 01803/207933. Tours available Easter–Oct between 10am and 1pm for £1 ($1.60). Admission free without guided tour. Year-round Mon–Fri 9am–5pm; Apr–Oct Sat 9am–5pm, Sun 2–5pm.

WHERE TO STAY

In addition to the following, the Mulberry House (see "Where to Dine," below) also rents rooms.

Colindale   The Colindale is a good choice, and about as central as you'd want—it opens onto King's Garden, within a 5-minute walk of Corbyn Beach and a 3-minute walk from the railway station. One of a row of attached brick Victorian houses, with gables and chimneys, it's set back from the road, with a parking lot in front. Rooms come in a range of sizes and shapes and are cozily furnished in a Victorian style; each has a private shower and all are nonsmoking.

20 Rathmore Rd., Chelston, Torquay, Devon TQ2 6NY. ℂ **01803/293947.** www.colindalehotel.co.uk. 8 units, 6 with bathroom. £25 ($40) single; £50 ($80) double. Rates include English breakfast. AE, DC, MC, V. Free parking. **Amenities:** Breakfast room; bar. *In room:* TV, coffeemaker, hair dryer, iron, no phone.

Craig Court Hotel (Value)   This nonsmoking hotel is in a large Victorian mansion with southern exposure, a short walk from the heart of town. Owner Ann Box offers excellent value in its modernized rooms. Bedrooms tend to be small and cozy, with a compact, well-organized private bathroom plus a shower. In addition to the good, wholesome food served here, there is a well-appointed lounge and an intimate bar.

10 Ash Hill Rd., Castle Circus, Torquay, Devon TQ1 3HZ. ℂ **01803/294400.** Fax 01803/212525. 10 units, 9 with bathroom. £25 ($40) single; £50 ($80) double. Rates include English breakfast. No credit cards. Take St. Marychurch Rd. (signposted St. Marychurch, Babbacombe) from Castle Circus (the town hall), and make the first right onto Ash Hill Rd.; the hotel is on the right. **Amenities:** Restaurant; bar. *In room:* TV, coffeemaker, hair dryer.

Fairmount House Hotel ★ (Finds)   This well-preserved Victorian building retains the stained glass, marble fireplaces, and other adornments of that age; it stands in a tranquil residential area about a mile from the harbor. The good-size guest rooms are comfortable and well furnished, and come with private, shower-only bathrooms. Sound British cooking can be ordered.

Herbert Rd., Chelston, Torquay, Devon TQ2 6RW. ℂ and fax **01803/605446.** www.fairmounthousehotel.co.uk. 8 units. £30–£33 ($48–$53) per person. Rates include breakfast. MC, V. Closed early Nov to early Mar. Follow the signs to Cockington Village and turn right onto Herbert Rd. Bus: 24 or 25. **Amenities:** Restaurant; bar. *In room:* TV, coffeemaker, hair dryer, no phone.

Glenorleigh ★★   Many consider this Victorian villa the best B&B in Torquay. Every season they seem to try a bit harder here. The good-size nonsmoking bedrooms have been tastefully modernized, each with a private, shower-only bathroom. One room is available for those with limited mobility. In summer, many guests book for the week, so you'll have to call to see if they have space.

26 Cleveland Rd., Torquay, Devon TQ2 5BE. ℂ and fax **01803/292135.** 16 units. £26–£36 ($42–$58) single; £52–£72 ($83–$115) double. Rates include English breakfast. MC, V. Closed Nov–Dec. When you reach the traffic lights at Torre Station, bear right into Avenue Rd. (A379); Cleveland Rd. is the first left. **Amenities:** Dining room; bar; outdoor pool; game room; solarium. *In room:* TV, coffeemaker, hair dryer (on request), iron (on request), no phone.

Norcliff Hotel   This Italianate Victorian villa is set on a high plateau overlooking Lyme Bay, in the residential suburb of Babbacombe Downs, about 2.5km (1½ miles) west of the center of Torquay. The midsize bedrooms are conservative, simple, clean, and modest, sometimes with sea views. About 10 rooms are in an uninspired modern extension (1992), along with an indoor heated swimming pool. Each comes with a tidily maintained private bathroom with shower.

Sea Front, Babbacombe Downs, Torquay, Devon TQ1 3LF. ℂ **01803/328456.** Fax 01803/328023. 27 units. £25 ($40) single; £50 ($80) double. Rates include English breakfast. MC, V. **Amenities:** Dining room; bar; pool; sauna; game room. *In room:* TV, dataport, coffeemaker, hair dryer (on request).

WHERE TO DINE

Mulberry House ★★ (Value) ENGLISH   This restaurant is situated in one of Torquay's Victorian villas, facing a patio of plants and flowers, with outside tables for summer lunches and afternoon teas. Lesley Cooper is an inspired cook; she'll feed you well in her little dining room, seating two dozen diners at midday. The vegetarian will find comfort here, and others can feast on Lesley's smoked ham rissoles, honey-roasted chicken, or grilled or sautéed filets of sole with tartar sauce. Traditional roasts draw the Sunday crowds. The choice is wisely limited so that everything will be fresh. You can stay here in one of three bedrooms, each comfortably furnished and well kept, with private bathroom. B&B charges range from £35 ($56) per person daily, making it one of the area's best bargains.

1 Scarborough Rd., Torquay, Devon TQ2 5UJ. ℂ 01803/213639. Reservations required. Main courses £10.50–£15.50 ($17–$25). No credit cards. Wed–Sun noon–2pm and 7:30–9:30pm. Bus: 32. From the Sea Front, turn up Belgrave Rd.; Scarborough Rd. is the first right.

No. 7 SEAFOOD   A 2-minute walk from Torquay's center, located within a stone-sided building at least a century old, this restaurant recaptures the late Victorian and Edwardian era, when fish was served to holiday-making factory workers with a minimum of fuss and bother. Dining here means bare pinewood floors, plastic tablecloths, and deliberately simple table settings of a napkin, a cup, and a glass. Menu items include carefully prepared versions of fish and chips (cod in winter, plaice in summer); scallops with vermouth and butter sauce; Devon cobbler (a local form of fish pie); and a medley of sole with crabmeat with a cheese sauce.

The Beacon Terrace, Outer Harbour. ℂ 01803/295055. Reservations recommended. Main courses £8.95–£25 ($14–$40). AE, MC, V. Wed–Sat 12:45–1:45pm and 7–9:45pm.

Remy's ⭐⭐ FRENCH   The finest nonhotel restaurant in Torquay, Remy's serves good food at reasonable prices, offering a fixed-price three-course menu that changes daily. French owner and chef Remy Bopp sets great store by his ingredients, whether they be fresh fish from a local fishmonger or vegetables from the market. Everything is homemade, including the bread, ice cream, sorbet, and pastries. Guests can also enjoy his carefully selected group of French wines. The food is straightforward and rarely overdone, beginning with the pâté of the chef (garlic, herbs, and pork), and moving on to such main dishes as roast chicken in an orange sauce or lamb's kidneys in a mustard sauce.

3 Croft Rd. ℂ 01803/292359. Reservations required. Fixed-price menu £19.50 ($31). MC, V. Tues–Sat 7:30–9:30pm. From the Sea Front, head north on Shedden Hill. Bus: 32.

TORQUAY AFTER DARK

There are seven theaters in town open year-round, offering everything from Gilbert and Sullivan and tributes to Sinatra and Nat King Cole to Marine Band concerts and comedy shows. Among the most active are the **Palace Avenue Theatre,** Palace Avenue, Paignton (ℂ **01803/665800**), and the **Princess Theatre,** Torbay Road (ℂ **01803/414120**).

Fifteen area nightclubs cater to everyone from teeny-boppers to the gay scene, but dancing rules here, and there's virtually nowhere to catch live club acts. Among the better dance clubs are **Claires,** Torwood Street (ℂ **01803/211097**), for house music Thursday to Saturday nights, with a cover charge from £3 to £7 ($4.80–$11), depending on the DJ; and the **Monastery,** Torwood Gardens Road (ℂ **01803/292929**), Saturday only, where you'll get your fill of hip-hop and electronica—the dancing lasts from midnight until 7am.

4 Totnes ⭐

358km (224 miles) SW of London; 20km (12 miles) NW of Dartmouth

One of the oldest towns in the West Country, the borough of Totnes rests quietly in the past, content to let the Torquay area remain in the vanguard of the building boom. On the River Dart, upstream from Dartmouth, Totnes is so totally removed in character from Torquay that the two towns could be in different countries. Totnes has several historic buildings, notably the ruins of a Norman castle, an ancient guildhall, and the 15th-century red sandstone Church of St. Mary. In the Middle Ages the town was encircled by walls; the North Gate serves as a reminder of that era.

ESSENTIALS

GETTING THERE   Totnes is on the main London–Plymouth line. Trains leave London's Paddington Station frequently throughout the day. For rail information, call © **0845/7484950.**

Totnes is served locally by the Western National and Devon General bus companies (© **01752/402060** in Plymouth for information about routings).

If you're driving from Torquay, head west on the A385.

Many visitors approach Totnes by river steamer from Dartmouth. Contact **Dart Pleasure Craft,** River Link (© **01803/834488**), for information.

VISITOR INFORMATION   The **Tourist Information Centre** is at the Town Mill, Coronation Road (© **01803/863168**). It's open in winter Monday to Friday 9:30am to 5pm and Saturday 10am to 4pm. Summer hours are Monday to Friday 9:30am to 5pm and Saturday 9:30am to 5pm.

EXPLORING TOTNES

The Elizabethan Museum   This 16th-century home of a wealthy merchant houses furniture, costumes, documents, and farm implements of the Elizabethan Age. One room is devoted to local resident Charles Babbage (1792–1871), a mathematician and inventor who invented a calculating machine that used cards perforated with a coded series of holes; the machine's capacity for memory made it a prototypical computer. Babbage also invented the ophthalmoscope, speedometer, and cowcatchers.

70 Fore St. © 01803/863821. Admission £1.50 ($2.40) adults, £1 ($1.60) seniors, 25p (40¢) children. Easter–Oct Mon–Fri 10:30am–5pm.

Totnes Castle   Crowning the hilltop at the northern end of High Street, this castle was built by the Normans shortly after they conquered England. It's one of the best examples of motte and bailey construction remaining in the United Kingdom. Although the outer walls survived, the interior is mostly in ruins.

Castle St. © 01803/864406. www.castleexplorer.co.uk. Admission £1.80 ($2.90) adults, 90p ($1.45) children. Mar 29–Sept 30 daily 10am–6pm; Oct daily 10am–5pm.

Totnes Guildhall   This is the symbol of Totnes. Originally built as a priory in 1553, it contains an old gaol, a collection of civic memorabilia, and the table Oliver Cromwell used to sign documents during his 1646 visit here.

Ramparts Walk. © 01803/862147. Admission £1 ($1.60) adults, 50p (80¢) seniors, 25p (40¢) children. Easter–Oct Mon–Fri 10:30am–1pm and 2–4pm.

〔*Moments* To Market with "the Elizabethans"

Totnes is known for its colorful markets staged in the center of town at Civic Square on Friday from 8am to 3pm year-round and on Tuesday from 8am to 3pm from May through September. Many vendors wear Elizabethan costumes. You may want to wander throughout the town enjoying its old bookstores, antiques shops, and retailers hawking handcrafted goods, lace, clothes, knits, and handmade shoes and toys, plus myriad other gifts.

WHERE TO STAY IN THE AREA

The Cott Inn ★★ Built in 1320, this hotel is the second-oldest hostelry in England. It's a low, rambling two-story building of stone, cob, and plaster, with a thatched roof and thick walls. Upstairs, the owners rent low-ceilinged double rooms in all shapes and sizes. Carpets, curtains, and beds have recently been refurbished; somehow, private bathrooms with shower stalls have been squeezed in. Two rooms are set aside for nonsmokers. The inn is a gathering place for Dartingtonians, and you'll feel the pulse of English country life here. Log fires keep the lounge and bar snug in winter. Whether a guest of the hotel or not, you'll want to visit the tavern (five beers are on draft), where you can also order a meal.

Dartington, near Totnes (on the old Ashburton-Totnes turnpike), S. Devon TQ9 6HE. ℂ 01803/863777. Fax 01803/866629. www.thecottinn.co.uk. 5 units. £50 ($80) single; £70 ($112) double. Rates 10% lower Oct–Easter. DC, MC, V. Free Parking. Bus: no. X80 travels from Totnes to Dartington, but most people take a taxi for the 2.5km (1½-mile) journey. **Amenities:** Restaurant; bar. *In room:* TV, dataport, coffeemaker, hair dryer.

The Old Forge ★ This is a restored former blacksmith's and wheelwright's workshop dating back 6 centuries. Christine Hillier and David Miller run the hotel, which boasts a walled garden. Near the Dart, B&B accommodations are provided in attractively decorated midsize bedrooms, four of which suit families. No smoking is allowed inside, and each unit comes with a small, shower-only private bathroom. Recent improvements include a Jacuzzi, spa, and a conservatory. There is also a 2-bedroom Wheelwright's Cottage with a sofa bed; the unit sleeps six comfortably.

Seymour Place, Totnes, Devon TQ9 5AY. ℂ 01803/862174. www.oldforgetotnes.com. 10 units. £44–£52 ($70–$83) single; £54–£74 ($86–$118) double. Rates include English breakfast. MC, V. From the monument at the foot of Shopping St., cross the bridge over the river and take the second right. **Amenities:** Breakfast room; lounge; spa; Jacuzzi; conservatory. *In room:* TV, dataport, coffeemaker, hair dryer.

Orchard House ★ *Finds* Lying between Totnes and Kingsbridge, this is a delightful little choice. It takes its name from the location, which is within an old cider orchard. It's a real find for those who appreciate the charms of bucolic Devon. The house enjoys a tranquil location among mature gardens. The bedrooms are beautifully furnished, and each has a private bathroom with shower. Bathrooms are large and airy with elegant toiletries provided. Local produce is used in the English cooked breakfasts. The house is nonsmoking.

Horner, Halwell, near Totnes, Devon TQ9 7LB. ℂ 01548/821448. www.orchard-house-halwell.co.uk. 3 units. £40–£46 ($64–$74) double. Rates include breakfast. No credit cards. Closed Nov–Feb. Get off the A38 at the Buckfastleigh Totnes junction and follow the road into Totnes. Upon entering the town, turn right for Kingsbridge (A381) and drive to Harbertonford. After passing a garage, take the second right for 2.5km (1½ miles), turning right at the sign marked HORNER. Take the next right. Orchard House is the second house on the left. **Amenities:** Breakfast room. *In room:* TV, coffeemaker, no phone.

WHERE TO DINE IN THE AREA

When it's teatime, **Greys Dining Room,** 96 High St. (ℂ 01803/866369), sets out its fine silver and china to welcome you in an atmosphere of wood paneling and antiques. About 40 kinds of teas and homemade cakes and scones invite you to extend the afternoon.

Crank's Health Food Restaurant ★ VEGETARIAN Affiliated with the London-based Crank's restaurant chain, this is the region's leading health-food restaurant. Contained in Dartington's farmstead-turned-crafts-center 2.5km (1½ miles) northwest of Totnes, it serves only compost-grown vegetables, live-culture yogurts, and freshly extracted fruit juices. The Devonshire cream teas served include whole-meal scones, whole-fruit jams, and freshly clotted local cream. For our tastes most dishes are underseasoned, although this is what local diners seem to prefer.

Dartington Cider Press Centre, Shinners Bridge. © **01803/862388**. Soups £2.75–£2.90 ($4.40–$4.65); main courses £4.75–£5.95 ($8–$10). MC, V. Daily 9:30am–5pm. Closed Sun in winter. Bus: X80 travels through Dartington from Plymouth to Torquay.

Willow Vegetarian Restaurant VEGETARIAN   At the top of Totnes' main street, this vegetarian whole-food restaurant offers an Indian menu on Wednesday and live music on Friday. Otherwise, it serves both exotic and traditional food, including main courses, cakes, and salads made on the premises from fresh, high-quality, often organic ingredients. Seasoning is not the kitchen's strong point, but most diners leave satisfied. It's self-service during the day, table service in the evening. There's even a list of organic wines.

87 High St. © **01803/862605**. Reservations recommended at night. Main courses £9.50–£15 ($15–$24). No credit cards. Mon–Sat 10am–5pm; Wed, Fri, and Sat 7–10:30pm; additional evenings in July and Aug.

5 Dartmouth ★★

378km (236 miles) SW of London; 56km (35 miles) SE of Exeter

At the mouth of the Dart, this ancient seaport is the home of the Britannia Royal Naval College. Traditionally linked to England's maritime greatness, Dartmouth sent out the young midshipmen who made sure that "Britannia ruled the waves." You can take a river steamer up the Dart to Totnes (book at the kiosk at the harbor); the scenery along Devon's most beautiful river is panoramic. Dartmouth's 15th-century castle was built during the reign of Edward IV. The town's most noted architectural feature is the Butter Walk, which lies below Tudor houses. The Flemish influence in some of the houses is pronounced.

ESSENTIALS
GETTING THERE   Dartmouth is not easily reached by public transport. Trains run to Totnes and Paignton. One bus a day runs from Totnes to Dartmouth. Call © **0870/6082608** for schedules.

If you're driving from Exeter, take the A38 southwest, cutting southeast to Totnes on the A381; then follow the A381 to the junction with the B3207.

Riverboats make the 16km (10-mile) run from Totnes to Dartmouth, but these trips depend on the tide and operate only from Easter to the end of October. See "Essentials," in the Totnes section above for details on obtaining boat schedules.

VISITOR INFORMATION   The **Tourist Information Centre** is at the Engine House, Mayors Avenue (© **01803/834224**), and is open April through October, Monday through Saturday from 9:30am to 5pm and Sunday from 10am to 4pm (off season Mon–Sat 9:30am–4:30pm).

EXPLORING DARTMOUTH
Many visitors come to Dartmouth for the bracing salt air and a chance to explore the surrounding marshlands, rich in bird life and natural beauty. The historic monuments here are steeped in much of the legend and lore of Channel life and historic Devon.

The town's most historic and interesting church is **St. Petrox,** on Castle Road, a 17th-century Anglican monument with an ivy-draped graveyard whose tombstones evoke the sorrows of Dartmouth's maritime past. The church is open daily 7am to dusk.

It's worth walking through **Bayard's Cove,** a cobbled, half-timbered water-front area that's quite charming. Set near the end of Lower Street, it prospered during the 1600s thanks to its ship-repair services. In 1620, its quays were the site for repairs of the Pilgrims' historic ships, the *Speedwell* and the *Mayflower,* just after their departure from Plymouth.

Dartmouth Castle   Built during the 15th century, the castle was later outfit-ted with artillery and employed by the Victorians as a coastal defense station. A tour of its bulky ramparts and somber interiors provides insight into the ever-changing nature of warfare, and you'll see sweeping views of the surrounding coast and flatlands.

Castle Rd. (1km/½ mile south of the town center). ℂ **01803/833588.** Admission £3.30 ($5) adults, £1.70 ($2.70) children. Apr–Sept daily 10am–6pm; Oct daily 10am–5pm; Nov–Mar Wed–Sun 10am–4pm.

Dartmouth Museum   This is the region's most interesting maritime museum, focusing on the British Empire's military might of the 18th century. Built between 1635 and 1640, it's set amid an interconnected row of 17th-century buildings—**The Butter Walk**—whose overhanging, stilt-supported facade was designed to provide shade for the butter, milk, and cream sold there by local milkmaids. Today the complex houses the museum as well as shops selling wines, baked goods, and more.

In the Butter Walk. ℂ **01803/832923.** Admission £1.50 ($2.40) adults, £1 ($1.60) seniors, 50p (80¢) chil-dren. Mar–Oct Mon–Sat 11am–5pm; Nov–Feb Mon–Sat noon–3pm.

WHERE TO STAY

Ford House ⭐   Originally a town house created for a rich shipyard owner, this renovated building is today an elegant guesthouse within easy walking distance of the center of town. Jayne and Richard Turner run a topnotch B&B, one of Dart-mouth's finest, welcoming guests to their Regency home, convenient to the shops and pubs of Dartmouth. The nonsmoking bedrooms are tastefully and individu-ally decorated and furnished with king- or queen-size beds in double rooms (twin beds in singles). All have private bathrooms with shower except for one double with its own private shower across the hall (a £10/$16 discount for that one). Breakfast is one of the finest of the Dartmouth B&Bs, with free-range eggs, even such English delights as deviled kidneys, kippers, and smoked haddock.

44 Victoria Rd., Dartmouth, Devon TQ6 9DX. ℂ and fax **01803/834047.** 4 units. £65 ($104) single; £85 ($136) double. MC, V. Closed Nov–Feb. **Amenities:** Breakfast room; lounge. *In room:* TV, fridge, coffeemaker, hair dryer, iron, no phone.

Sunnybanks   This is a centrally located 1880s house that was built as a local doctor's home and office. Each individually decorated bedroom contains com-fortably upholstered furniture and discreet floral motifs. The hotel offers six rooms for nonsmokers. A patio in the rear garden offers warm-weather seating amid flowering shrubs and trees.

1 Vicarage Hill, Dartmouth, Devon TQ6 9EW. ℂ and fax **01803/832766.** www.sunnybanks.com. 10 units, 1 with full bathroom (8 with shower only). £22–£30 ($35–$48) single; £50–£55 ($80–$88) double. Rates include English breakfast. No credit cards. Buses marked Plymouth or Kings Bridge all stop nearby. **Ameni-ties:** Breakfast room. *In room:* TV, coffeemaker, hair dryer, no phone.

WHERE TO DINE

Carved Angel Café ⭐⭐ *(Finds* ENGLISH   This low-budget cafe and brasserie is connected with a very upscale, elegant, and pricey local dining rooms, the Carved Angel Restaurant. By carefully entering the brasserie and not the restaurant, you'll be guaranteed a well-prepared, fairly priced meal presented in a setting reeking of bucolic charm and traditional English wholesomeness. Menu items are listed on a blackboard and change daily, according to season and the chef's inspiration. Examples include tagliatelle with broccoli and blue cheese, stir-fried chicken with snow peas, warm goat cheese salad with honey-mustard dressing, grilled filet of mullet, and lemon-flavored cheesecake. Soups are rich and nutritious, and there are always at least three traditional "puddings." The restaurant is fully licensed.

7 Foss St. ⓒ **01803/834842**. Reservations not necessary. Main courses at lunch £3–£7 ($4.80–$11), at dinner £10–£15 ($16–$24). MC, V. Mon–Fri noon–3pm; Thurs–Sat 7–9pm.

A FAVORITE LOCAL PUB

Just a 2-minute walk from Bayard's Cove is one of our favorite pubs, **The Cherub,** 13 Higher St. (ⓒ **01803/832571**). It was built in 1380 as the harbormaster's house. Today this charming pub is a great place to drink and dine on simple traditional British platters and bar snacks. There's a more formal dining room upstairs that serves a number of fish dishes, steaks, lamb, and duck.

6 Plymouth ★★

387km (242 miles) SW of London; 258km (161 miles) SW of Southampton

The historic seaport of Plymouth is more romantic in legend than in reality. But this was not always so—during World War II, greater Plymouth lost at least 75,000 buildings to Nazi bombs. The heart of present-day Plymouth, including the municipal civic center on the Royal Parade, has been entirely rebuilt; the way it was rebuilt remains highly controversial.

For the old part of town, you must go to the Elizabethan section, known as the **Barbican,** and walk along the quay where Sir Francis Drake (once the mayor of Plymouth) did. In 1577, Drake set sail from here on his round-the-world voyage. The Barbican also holds special interest for visitors from the United States: It was the final departure point of the Pilgrims in 1620. Their ships, the *Mayflower* and the *Speedwell,* had sailed from Southampton in August of that year, but put into Plymouth after they suffered storm damage. Here, the *Speedwell* was abandoned as unseaworthy; the *Mayflower* made the trip to the New World alone.

ESSENTIALS

GETTING THERE   Plymouth Airport lies 6.5km (4 miles) from the center of the city. **Brymon Airways** (ⓒ **01752/204090**) has direct service from the London airports, Heathrow and Gatwick, to Plymouth.

Frequent trains run from London's Paddington Station to Plymouth in 3¼ to 4 hours. For rail information, call ⓒ **0845/7484950** in the U.K. The **Plymouth Train Station** lies on North Road, north of the Plymouth Center. Western National Bus no. 83/84 runs from the station to the heart of Plymouth.

National Express has frequent daily bus service between London's Victoria Coach Station and Plymouth. The trip takes 4½ hours. Call ⓒ **020/7529-2000** for schedules and information.

If you're driving from London, take the M4 west to the junction with the M5 going south to Exeter. From Exeter, head southwest on the A38 to Plymouth.

VISITOR INFORMATION   The **Tourist Information Centre** is at the Island House, The Barbican (ⓒ **01752/304849**). A second information center, **Plymouth Discovery Centre,** is at Crabtree Marsh Mills, Plymouth (ⓒ **01752/ 266030**). Both are open from Easter to October Monday through Saturday from 9am to 5pm and Sunday from 10am to 4pm; and from November to Easter Monday through Friday from 10am to 5pm and Saturday from 9am to 4pm.

SEEING THE SIGHTS

To commemorate the spot from which the *Mayflower* sailed for the New World, a white archway was erected in 1934 and capped with the flags of Great Britain and the United States; it stands at the base of Plymouth's West Pier, on the Barbican. Incorporating a granite monument erected in 1891, the site is known as the **Mayflower Steps** or **Memorial Gateway.**

The **Barbican** is a mass of narrow streets, old houses, and quayside shops selling antiques, brass work, old prints, and books. It's a perfect place for strolling and browsing through shops at your leisure.

Fishing boats still unload their catch at the wharves, and passenger-carrying ferryboats run short harbor cruises. A trip includes views from the water of Drake's Island in the sound, the dockyards, naval vessels, and The Hoe—a greenbelt in the center of the city that opens onto Plymouth Harbour. A cruise of Plymouth Harbour costs £5 ($8) for adults and £2.50 ($4) for children. A family ticket costs £11 ($18). Departures are February through November, with cruises leaving every half-hour from 10am to 4pm daily. These **Plymouth Boat Cruises** are booked at 8 Anderton Rise, Millbrook, Torpoint (© **01752/822797**).

New Street Gallery   This gallery is a 5-minute walk from the town center in Plymouth's historic Barbican, near the Mayflower Steps. It specializes in contemporary arts and crafts, with changing exhibitions of paintings and ceramics.

38 New St., The Barbican. © **01752/221450.** Free admission. Mon noon–4pm; Tues–Sat 10am–4pm. Bus: 39.

Plymouth Gin Distillery   The Pilgrims met here before sailing for the New World; this is one of Plymouth's oldest surviving buildings. Plymouth Gin has been produced here for 200 years on a historic site that dates from a Dominican monastery built in 1425. There are public guided tours. A Plymouth Gin Shop is on the premises.

Black Friars Distillery, 60 Southside St. © **01752/665292.** www.plymouthgin.com. Admission £2.75 ($4.40) adults, £2.25 ($3.60) children 10–18, free for children 9 and under. Jan–Feb Mon–Sat 10am–5pm; Mar–Dec daily 10am–4pm. Closed Christmas–Easter. Bus: 54.

Prysten House   Reconstructed in the 1930s with American help, Prysten House displays a model of Plymouth in 1620 and tapestries depicting the colonization of America. At the entrance is the gravestone of the captain of the U.S. brig *Argus,* who died in 1813 after a battle in the English Channel.

Finewell St. © **01752/661414.** Admission £1 ($1.60) adults, 50p (80¢) children. Mon–Sat 9:30am–6:30pm.

WHERE TO STAY

Present-day pilgrims from the New World looking for affordable lodging are advised to head for the Hoe, where there are a number of inexpensive B&Bs on a peaceful street near the water.

Astor Hotel   The Astor is situated on a street lined with 19th-century buildings. Built during the Victorian era for a prosperous sea captain, the building underwent a major restoration in 1987. Today the hotel has comfortable bedrooms, ranging from small to spacious, each well appointed with a compact bathroom with shower stall. Thirty-one rooms are nonsmoking rooms, and the ground floor rooms are available for those with limited mobility. The Astor has well-decorated public lounges and a cozy and accommodating bar.

14–22 Elliott St., The Hoe, Plymouth, Devon PL1 2PS. © **01752/225511.** Fax 01752/251994. www.astorhotel. co.uk. 62 units. £40–£65 ($64–$104) single; £80–£120 ($128–$192) double. Rates include English breakfast. AE, MC, V. Parking £3.50 ($6). **Amenities:** Restaurant; 2 bars; 24-hr. room service; laundry. *In room:* TV, dataport, coffeemaker, hair dryer, trouser press.

Camelot Hotel   This neat, tall hotel stands on a small road just off the grassy expanse of the Hoe. There's a lounge with color TV and VCR; you can also watch in a comfortably furnished midsize bedroom, some with a private shower-only bathroom and some with shower-tub combination bathrooms. Guests frequent the pleasant small bar and restaurant. The hotel offers four nonsmoking rooms.

5 Elliot St., The Hoe, Plymouth, Devon PL1 2PP. © **01752/221255.** Fax 01752/603660. 18 units. £43 ($69) single; £55 ($88) double; £65 ($104) family room. Rates include English breakfast. AE, DC, MC, V. Bus: 54. **Amenities:** Restaurant; bar; lounge. *In room:* TV, dataport, coffeemaker, hair dryer (on request).

Georgian House ✿   Located on the Hoe, about 5 minutes from the ferry terminal, this is one of the finest guesthouses in Plymouth. Each nonsmoking bedroom is comfortably furnished with private shower-only bathrooms in eight units, the rest with tub-and-shower combination. British and international meals are served.

51 Citadel Rd., The Hoe, Plymouth, Devon PL1 3AU. © **01752/663237.** Fax 01752/253953. 11 units. £26 ($42) single; £39 ($62) double. Rates include English breakfast. AE, DC, MC, V. Closed Dec 23–Jan 10. Parking £2 ($3.20). Bus: 54. **Amenities:** Breakfast room; lounge. *In room:* TV, dataport, coffeemaker, hair dryer, iron.

Lamplighter Hotel   Occupying a house whose stucco-covered 1850 exterior resembles that of its neighbors, this comfortable and unpretentious address is close to the Hoe and the Barbican. The modernized, nonsmoking, midsize rooms are clean, simple, and uncluttered. The most desirable are the seven rooms with private bathrooms with both shower and toilet. The other units contain a private shower, but the toilet for each room is outside in the hall.

103 Citadel Rd., The Hoe, Plymouth, Devon PL1 2RN. © **01752/663855.** Fax 01752/228139. lamplighter hotel@ukonline.co.uk. 9 units. £25 ($40) single without full bathroom; £30 ($48) single with full bathroom; £38 ($61) double without full bathroom, £44 ($70) double with full bathroom. Rates include English breakfast. MC, V. **Amenities:** Breakfast room; lounge. *In room:* TV, coffeemaker, no phone.

Osmond Guest House   A bay-fronted, three-story house built in 1898, this hotel is well known and popular. The owner, Mrs. Carol Richards, will pick guests up at the bus or train station if they arrange it in advance. The original high plaster ceilings have been carefully preserved. Each basic, simply furnished room is comfortable and well maintained.

42 Pier St., Plymouth, Devon PL1 3BT. © **01752/229705.** Fax 01752/269655. 6 units, 4 with bathroom. £20 ($32) single without bathroom; £40 ($64) double without bathroom, £45 ($72) double with bathroom. Rates include English breakfast. MC, V. Bus: 25 or 39. **Amenities:** Breakfast room. *In room:* TV, coffeemaker, hair dryer, iron, no phone.

St. Rita Hotel   The St. Rita is close to the train station, in a row of blue Victorian houses along the main bus route to the city center, approximately a mile away. The small rooms are clean and comfortable, with adequate hallway facilities, and one ground-floor room is available for those with limited mobility. Accommodations at the back are quieter.

76 Alma Rd., Plymouth, Devon PL3 4HD. © **01752/667024.** Fax 01752/262161. strita@btconnect.com. 14 units, 4 with bathroom. £17.50 ($28) single without bathroom, £22.50 ($36) single with bathroom; £40 ($64) double without bathroom, £45 ($72) double with bathroom; £22.50 ($36) per person suite. Rates include English breakfast. V. Bus: 28B or 43A. **Amenities:** Dining room; lounge. *In room:* TV, coffeemaker, no phone.

Wiltun Hotel   The Wiltun overlooks Drake's Island and Plymouth Sound. This Victorian house has many modern facilities but retains several of the architectural features of the 1850s. The nonsmoking midsize rooms have recently been refurbished; some rooms are suitable for families. Each unit comes with a small but tidily maintained private bathroom with shower. There's a private lawn

---

Moments Your "Catch," the Seagulls & the Barbican

On a fair day head down by the Barbican side of the Plymouth Harbour. Here you'll see a hungry line of locals queuing up at a little kiosk called **Cap'n Jaspars**, dispensing fresh fish from the local catch. Enjoy a fish sandwich at one of the wooden picnic tables while seagulls fly overhead. This is such a fine little moment, you will wonder why the Pilgrims ever set sail from here.

---

to relax on and watch the ships go by. Guests have free access to the Warleigh House Estate and Woodlands on the River Tavy, where there are fishing and shooting opportunities. The estate lies 9.5km (6 miles) away.

39 Grand Parade, West Hoe, Plymouth, Devon PL1 3DQ. (C) and fax **01752/667072.** www.wiltunhotel.co.uk. 11 units. £35–£70 ($56–$112) single; £60–£150 ($96–$240) double. Rates include English breakfast. MC, V. Bus: 25. Follow the signs to the Hoe, at the western end of the city. **Amenities:** Breakfast room; bar. *In room:* TV, dataport, coffeemaker, hair dryer, no phone.

WHERE TO DINE

The Ganges INDIAN   This Indian tandoori restaurant, part of a chain with other West Country branches, provides a good change of pace from traditional English cookery. You can dine in air-conditioned, candlelit comfort while enjoying an array of spicy dishes. The chef's specialty, a whole tandoori chicken, is superbly spiced and flavored. There's the usual array of curries and biryanis. Vegetarians will find sustenance here, too.

36 Brettonside. (C) **01752/220907.** Main courses £6–£12 ($10–$19). 3-course fixed price meal £15 ($24). AE, MC, V. Daily 5:30pm–midnight. Bus: 54.

The Plymouth Arts Centre Restaurant VEGETARIAN   This eatery offers one of the most filling and down-home vegetarian meals in town; it's also ideal for a snack. Quiche, veggie burgers, curries, nutloafs, and fresh salads are among the specialties. You can even see a movie downstairs if you'd like.

38 Looe St. (C) **01752/202616.** Main courses £3–£8.50 ($4.80–$14). MC, V. Mon 10am–5pm; Tues–Wed 10am–8pm; Thurs–Sat 10am–8:30pm. Bus: The restaurant is a 2-min. walk from the Plymouth bus station.

The Ship ★ ENGLISH   This stone building faces the marina, and its tables offer a view over the harbor. Pass through a pub and go up one flight of stairs, where a well-stocked salad bar and a carvery await you. The carvery presents at least three roast joints, and you eat as much as you want; the first course is a help-yourself buffet, and a chef carves your meat selection for your second. Desserts cost extra. This is one of the best food values in Plymouth, but it's best to go for lunch; the place becomes mainly a drinking establishment in the evening. The food is more bountiful than gourmet.

The Barbican. (C) **01752/667604.** Reservations recommended. Carvery £8 ($13) per adult for 2 courses, £11.75 ($19) for 3 courses; £3.45 ($6) children's meal. AE, MC, V. Daily 11am–10:30pm. Bus: 54.

7 Clovelly ★★★

384km (240 miles) SW of London; 18km (11 miles) SW of Bideford

This is the most charming of all Devon villages and one of the West Country's main attractions. Starting at a great height, the village cascades down the mountainside. Its narrow, cobblestone High Street makes driving impossible;

you park your car at the top and make the trip on foot; supplies are carried down by donkeys. Every step of the way provides views of tiny cottages, with their terraces of flowers lining the main street. The village fleet is sheltered at the stone quay at the bottom.

The major sight of Clovelly is Clovelly itself. Charles Kingsley once wrote " . . . it is as if the place had stood still while all the world had been rushing and rumbling past it." The price of entry to the village (see below) includes a guided tour of a fisherman's cottage as it would have been at the end of the 1800s. Also included in the entry fee is the Kingsley Exhibition, which traces the life of the author of *Westward Ho!* and *Water Babies*. Kingsley lived in Clovelly while his father was the church curate.

Just below the Kingsley Exhibition is a crafts gallery, where you have a chance to see and buy a wide variety of works by local artists and craftspeople. Once you've reached the end, you can sit and relax on the quay, taking in the views and absorbing Clovelly's unique atmosphere from this tiny, beautifully restored 14th-century quay.

Once you're at the bottom, how do you get back up? Those in good shape can climb back up these impossibly steep cobbled streets to the top and the parking lot. Those who can't make the climb up the slippery incline go to the rear of the Red Lion Inn and queue up for a Land Rover. In summer, the line can be long; considering the alternative, it's worth the wait.

To avoid the tourist crowd, stay out of Clovelly from around 11am until teatime. When the midday congestion is at its height, visit nearby villages such as Bucks Mills (5km/3 miles to the east) and Hartland Quay (6.5km/4 miles to the west).

ESSENTIALS

GETTING THERE   From London's Paddington Station, trains depart for Exeter frequently. At Exeter, passengers transfer to a train headed for the end destination of Barnstaple. Travel time from Exeter to Barnstaple is 1¼ hours. From Barnstaple, passengers transfer to Clovelly by bus.

From Barnstaple, about one bus per hour, operated by either the Red Bus Company or the Filers Bus Company, goes to Bideford. The trip takes 40 minutes. At Bideford, connecting buses (with no more than a 10-min. wait between arrival and departure) continue on for the 30-minute drive to Clovelly. Two Land Rovers make continuous round-trips to the Red Lion Inn from the top of the hill. The Clovelly Visitor Centre (see below) maintains up-to-the-minute transportation information about getting to Clovelly, depending on your location.

If driving from London, head west on the M4, cutting south at the junction with the M5. At the junction near Bridgewater, continue west along the A39 toward Lynton. The A39 runs all the way to the signposted turnoff for Clovelly.

VISITOR INFORMATION   Go to the **Clovelly Visitor Centre** (✆ **01237/ 431781**), where you'll pay £3.50 ($6) adults, £2.50 ($4) for kids under 7, for the cost of parking, use of facilities, entrance to the village, and an audiovisual theater admission, offering a multiprojector show tracing the story of Clovelly back to 2000 B.C. Also included in the price is a tour of a fisherman's cottage and admission to the **Kingsley Exhibition** (see above). It's open Monday through Saturday from 9am to 5:30pm April through October, daily from 10am to 4pm November through March, and daily from 9am to 6pm July through September.

WHERE TO STAY & DINE

New Inn ★★   About halfway down High Street is the village pub, a good meeting place at sundown. It offers the best lodgings in the village, in two buildings on opposite sides of the steep street (but only a 3.5m/12-ft. leap between their balconies). Each bedroom is relatively small but comfortable; two are large enough for a family. Eight rooms have TVs and phones. Only a few have a small private bathroom with a shower stall, but the corridor bathrooms are adequate and you rarely have to wait for one. If you're driving, you park in the lot at the entrance to the town. It's advisable to pack a smaller overnight bag, since your luggage will be carried down (but returned to the top by donkey). This little country inn is also recommended for meals in the oak-beamed dining room.

High St., Clovelly, N. Devon EX39 5TQ. ✆ **01237/431303.** Fax 01237/431636. 18 units, 8 with bathroom. £22.50 ($36) single without bathroom, £44.25 ($71) single with bathroom; £45 ($72) double without bathroom, £88.50 ($142) double with bathroom. Rates include English breakfast. AE, MC, V. **Amenities:** Restaurant; bar; tour desk. *In room:* TV, dataport, coffeemaker, hair dryer, trouser press.

Red Lion ★   At the bottom of the steep cobbled street, set on the stone seawall of the harbor, Red Lion occupies the prime position in the village. Rising three stories with gables and a courtyard, it's a truly unspoiled country inn, where life centers around an antique pub and the villagers come to satisfy their thirsts over pints of ale. Most rooms have spectacular sea views and have recently been refurbished. Many are small, but two are spacious enough for a family. All have hot and cold running water, adequate furnishings, and a tub-and-shower combination. Dinner is available in the sea-view dining room.

The Quay, Clovelly, Devon EX39 5TF. ✆ **01237/431237.** Fax 01237/431044. www.redlion-clovelly.co.uk. 11 units. £87.50 ($140) single or double. Rates include English breakfast. AE, MC, V. **Amenities:** Restaurant; bar. *In room:* TV, coffeemaker, hair dryer.

8 Lynton–Lynmouth ★

330km (206 miles) W of London; 94km (59 miles) NW of Exeter

The north coast of Devon is particularly dramatic in Lynton, a village some 150m (500 ft.) high, which is a good center for exploring the Doone Valley and the part of Exmoor that overflows into the shire from neighboring Somerset. The Valley of the Rocks, west of Lynton, offers the most panoramic scenery.

ESSENTIALS

GETTING THERE   The town is rather remote, and the local tourist office recommends that you rent a car to get here. However, local daily trains from Exeter arrive at Barnstaple. For rail information, call ✆ **0845/7484950.**

From Barnstaple, bus service is provided to Lynton at a frequency of about one every hour. Call ✆ **01598/752225** for schedules.

If you're driving, take the M4 west from London to the junction with the M5, then head south to the junction with the A39. Continue west on the A39 to Lynton–Lynmouth.

VISITOR INFORMATION   The **Tourist Information Centre** is at the Town Hall, Lee Road (✆ **01598/752225**), and is open from Easter to October daily from 8:30am to 6pm and from November to Easter from 10am to 4pm Monday through Saturday.

SEEING THE SIGHTS

Lynton is linked to its twin, Lynmouth—located about 150m (500 ft.) below, near the edge of the sea—by one of the most celebrated **railways** in Devon. The century-old train uses no electricity and no power. Instead, the railway covers the differences in distance and altitude by means of a complicated network of cables and pulleys, allowing cars to travel up and down the face of the rocky cliff. The length of the track is 259m (862 ft.) with a gradient of 1 inch, which gives it a vertical height of approximately 150m (500 ft.). The two passenger cars are linked together with two steel cables, and the operation of the lift is on the counterbalance system, which is simply explained as a pair of scales where one side, when weighted by a water ballast, pulls the other up. The train carries about 40 passengers at a time for 50p (80¢) adults, 30p (50¢) children. Trains depart daily from February to October, at 2- to 5-minute intervals, from 9am to 7pm. From November to March, the train is shut down.

The East Lyn and West Lyn rivers meet in Lynmouth, a popular resort with the British. For a **panoramic view** of the rugged coastline, you can walk on a path that runs along the cliff halfway between the towns. From Lynton, or rather from Hollerday Hill, you can look out onto Lynmouth Bay, Countisbury Foreland, and Woody Bays in the west. From Hollerday Hill, the view encompasses the Valley of Rocks, formed during the Ice Age by towering rock formations with names such as "The Devil's Cheesewring." The Valley of Rocks' centerpiece, Castle Rock, is renowned for its resident herd of wild goats.

From Lynmouth harbor, regular boat trips go along what the English have dubbed "The Heritage Coast" of North Devon. You can cruise past nesting colonies of razorbills, guillemots, dunlin, and kittiwakes, with the gulls soaring in the thermals by the highest sea cliffs in England.

Other activities in the locale include fishing, putting, bowls, tennis, pony trekking, and golf courses lying within a 32km (20-mile) radius. The Tourist Information Centre (see above) also keeps abreast of the various outdoor pursuits (which change seasonally) available at the time of your visit.

WHERE TO STAY

Bonnicott House Hotel ★★   Built as a rectory in 1820 and listed as a building of historical interest, the Bonnicott is owned by Brenda and Barry Parker Smith. Since acquiring this licensed hotel, the owners have embarked on an extensive refurbishing program, updating decor and furnishings and installing central heating. All bedrooms and public rooms have views over Lynmouth Bay or the Lyn Valley. The most expensive room is a new Bishop's Suite, featuring a "Gothic"-style bed. The terraced patio garden overlooks the sea; on a clear day Wales's coast can be seen. On cooler days, pick up a book from the small library and relax by the log fire. The food is home-style. No smoking is permitted.

10 Watersmeet Rd., Lynmouth, North Devon EX35 6EP. ℂ 01598/753346. 8 units. £23 ($37) single; £46–£80 ($74–$128) double. Rates include English breakfast. MC, V. Closed Nov to mid-Mar. **Amenities:** Breakfast room; bar. *In room:* TV, coffeemaker, hair dryer, iron, safe, no phone.

The Denes Guesthouse ★   Built during the 1920s, this neo-Victorian, slate-roofed gabled guesthouse sits at the end of a small terrace on a quiet residential street at Lynton's western edge; it also sits at the edge of the Valley of the Rocks (see "Seeing the Sights," above). The accommodations are tastefully decorated and completely nonsmoking. The bedrooms are spacious, all with hot and cold running water. Tasty and filling meals are served in a cheerful dining room.

Longmead, Lynton, Devon EX35 6DQ. ℂ 01598/753573. www.thedenes.com. 5 units, 3 with bathroom. £18 ($29) single without bathroom, £19.50 ($31) single with bathroom; £36 ($58) double without bathroom, £48 ($77) double with bathroom. Rates include English breakfast. MC, V. **Amenities:** Breakfast room; babysitting. *In room:* TV, coffeemaker, iron, no phone.

Highcliffe House Hotel   Situated in an 1870s Victorian house, Highcliffe House offers a relaxing getaway. Located on the side of Sinai Hill above Lynton and Lynmouth, it offers panoramic views of the River Lyn and the coastline. Although the house has been restored and modern amenities have been added, none of its old-world charm has been sacrificed. The nonsmoking bedrooms are comfortably furnished, and each comes with a private bathroom, mainly with tub-and-shower combination. In the dining room, meals made from fresh ingredients are served. The candlelit dining room adjoins a conservatory where guests can watch the night fall on the cliffs of Devon and Wales.

Sinai Hill, Lynton, Devon EX35 6AR. © **01598/752235.** www.highcliffehouse.co.uk. 6 units. £60–£90 ($96–$144) double. Rates include English breakfast. MC, V. **Amenities:** Dining room; lounge. *In room:* TV, coffeemaker, hair dryer, no phone.

Sandrock   This substantial three-story house stands on the road that leads from Lynton to the Valley of the Rocks. The house is on the lower part of a hill beside the road, and most of its bedrooms open onto views of the beginning peaks of the Valley of the Rocks. Owners Mr. and Mrs. Harrison take a personal interest in the welfare of their guests. The bedrooms, generally quite large and sunny, have interesting layouts and water basins. The third floor has dormer windows, making its rooms even cozier. Most of the bedrooms contain small bathrooms with a tub-and-shower combination. In the Sandrock Bar, visitors meet the Lynton locals after a routine dinner, which costs £14.50 ($23) and up.

Longmead, Lynton, Devon EX35 6DH. © **01598/753307.** Fax 015989/752665. 8 units, 7 with bathroom. £24.50 ($39) single; £49 ($78) double. Rates include English breakfast. AE, MC, V. Closed Dec–Jan. **Amenities:** Restaurant; bar. *In room:* TV, coffeemaker, hair dryer.

Shelley's Hotel ★★ *(Finds)*   Established more than 2 centuries ago, "Mrs. Hooper's Lodgings" was where the romantic poet brought his child bride, Harriet Westbrook, in 1812. Today it's been transformed into a remarkable little hotel of charm and grace. Shelley left without paying his bill, incidentally. In the center of the village, the hotel, opening onto views of Lynmouth Bay, has been tastefully restored and individually decorated, some of its handsomely furnished bedrooms with their own private conservatory and balcony. All accommodations come with private bathrooms—some with shower, some with combined shower and tub. Big windows make the rooms bright when the sun is shining, and the staff is most helpful and welcoming. Readers have praised the full English breakfast with such delights as smoked salmon, waffles with maple syrup, kedgeree, and kippers.

8 Watersmeet Rd., Lynmouth EX35 6EP. © **01598/53219.** Fax 01598/753751. www.shelleyshotel.freeuk. com/lynmouth.html. 11 units. £59–£99 ($94–$158) double. MC, V. **Amenities:** Restaurant; bar. *In room:* TV, coffeemaker, hair dryer.

Victoria Lodge ★   This elegant hotel, west of Church Hill, is imbued with a Victorian theme throughout following a complete refurbishing and redecorating. A nonsmoking hotel, it's known locally for its comfort and cuisine. Each centrally heated bedroom is decorated in a Victorian motif; some deluxe units have four-poster beds. Six rooms have private, shower-only bathrooms, and three rooms have shower-tub combination bathrooms. The cuisine is a fairly standard blend of English and Continental; vegetarian and special diets can be honored.

Lee Rd., Lynton, Devon EX35 6BS. © and fax **01598/753203.** www.victorialodge.co.uk. 9 units. £40–£67 ($64–$107) single; £54–£84 ($86–$134) double. Rates include English breakfast. MC, V. **Amenities:** Breakfast room; lounge; bar. *In room:* TV, coffeemaker, hair dryer, no phone.

Woodlands Woodlands is a small private hotel located in Exmoor National Park, a few minutes walk from Lynton's city center. Many stay here to relax in the peaceful, quiet atmosphere, particularly the large garden that extends down to the river. Most of the nonsmoking, midsize rooms have pleasant views of the wooded valley opposite. All meals are homemade with local ingredients when possible and served in hearty portions. Children under age 12 are discouraged from staying here.

Lynbridge Rd., Lynton, North Devon EX35 6AX. (C) **01598/752324.** Fax 01598/753828. www.woodlands guesthouse.co.uk. 7 units, all with bathroom. £25 ($40) single; £50 ($80) double. Rates include breakfast. MC, V. **Amenities:** Breakfast room; bar. *In room:* TV, coffeemaker, hair dryer, iron, no phone.

WHERE TO DINE

The Greenhouse Restaurant INTERNATIONAL Established in 1890 as a tearoom, this pink-and-gray Victorian restaurant perched atop a 152m (500-ft.) cliff offers a panoramic view of the Bristol Channel through its all-glass front. A nautical theme permeates the restaurant; the bar even has a water wheel built into it. Owners Chris and Anjali Peters serve a large menu as varied as you're likely to find anywhere—a result, they say, of his being part Indian and her being part Chinese. Whatever the reason, offerings range from British to American, Chinese, Indian, Italian, and beyond. Locals and tourists flock in to dine on the popular prawn *jalfrezi* (succulent shrimp in a spicy, medium-hot curry sauce); fresh local trout with almonds and herbs; or a 12-ounce chicken breast in cheese-and-ham sauce. Many dishes are made with fresh local seafood, and there are more than a dozen vegetarian choices. For something lighter, choose from among several salads, soups, and sandwiches.

6 Lee Rd., Lynton. (C) **01598/753358.** Reservations required. Main courses £12.95–£14.95 ($21–$24). AE, MC, V. Sat–Thurs 11:30am–3pm and 6–10pm. Closed Jan.

10

Cornwall

The ancient duchy of Cornwall is in the extreme southwestern part of England, known as "the toe." This peninsula is a virtual island, culturally if not geographically. Encircled by coastline, it abounds in rugged cliffs, hidden bays, fishing villages, sandy beaches, and sheltered coves where smuggling was once rampant. Although many of the little seaports with hillside cottages resemble towns along the Mediterranean, Cornwall retains its own distinctive flavor.

Cornwall had its own language until about 250 years ago, and some of the old words (*pol* for pool, *tre* for house) still survive. The Cornish dialect is better understood by the Welsh than by those who speak the queen's English.

We suggest that you base yourself at one of the smaller fishing villages, such as East or West Looe, Polperro, Mousehole, or Portloe, to experience the duchy's true charm. Many of the villages, such as St. Ives, are artists' colonies. Except for St. Ives and Port Isaac, the most interesting places lie on the southern coast, the so-called Cornish Riviera; but the northern coast has its peculiar charm, too. The majestic coastline is studded with fishing villages and hidden coves for swimming, with Penzance and St. Ives serving as major meccas. A little farther west is Land's End, where England actually does end. There are the Isles of Scilly, 43km (27 miles) off the Cornish coast, with five inhabited islands out of more than 100. Here you'll find the Abbey Gardens of Tresco, with 5,000 species of plants.

1 The Fishing Villages of Looe & Polperro ⍟

Looe: 422km (264 miles) SW of London; 32km (20 miles) W of Plymouth; Polperro: 434km (271 miles) SW of London; 10km (6 miles) SW of Looe; 42km (26 miles) W of Plymouth

A seven-arched stone bridge that spans the river connects the ancient twin towns of East and West Looe. Houses on the hills are stacked one on top of the other in terrace fashion. In either village, you can find good accommodations.

Fishing and sailing are popular in the area; Looe is noted for shark fishing. The sandy coves, as well as East Looe Beach, are spots for swimming. Cliff paths and chalky downs beyond the towns are worth a ramble. But you may prefer walking the narrow, crooked medieval streets of East Looe, with its old harbor and 17th-century guildhall.

Cliffs surround the old fishing village of Polperro. It is reached by a steep descent from the top of a hill via the main road leading to Polperro. You can take the 7km (4.5-mile) cliff walk from Looe to Polperro, but the less adventurous will want to drive. However, to avoid summer gridlock, you're not allowed to take cars into town in July and August unless you have a hotel reservation. There's a large parking area, which charges according to the length of stay. For those unable to walk, a horse-drawn bus will take visitors to the town center.

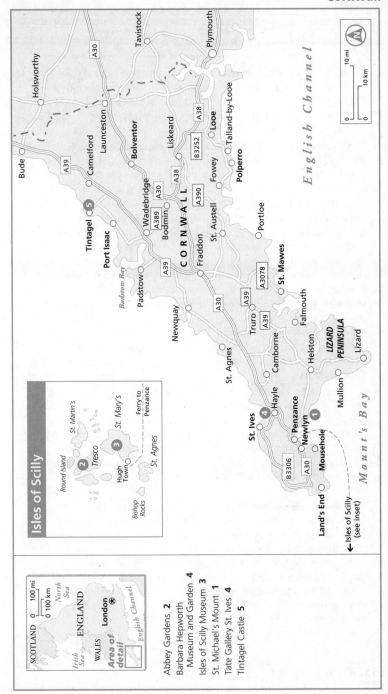

Cornwall

Isles of Scilly

Round Island
St. Martin's
Tresco
St. Mary's
Hugh Town
Bishop Rocks
St. Agnes
Ferry to Penzance

English Channel

Plymouth
Tavistock
A30
Holsworthy
Launceston
Bude
A39
Camelford
Bolventor
Liskeard
A38
Looe
Talland-by-Looe
Fowey
Polperro
B3252
A38
A30
Wadebridge
A389
Bodmin
A390
St. Austell
Portloe
Tintagel **5**
Port Isaac
Badstow Bay
Padstow
A39
Fraddon
St. Mawes
A3078
Newquay
A30
Truro
A39
Falmouth
St. Agnes
Camborne
Helston
LIZARD PENINSULA
Lizard
Hayle
Mullion
St. Ives **4**
Penzance
Newlyn
Mousehole
B3306
A30
Land's End
Isles of Scilly (see inset)
Mount's Bay

C O R N W A L L

SCOTLAND
ENGLAND
WALES
London
Irish Sea
North Sea
English Channel
Area of detail
0   100 mi
0   100 km

Abbey Gardens **2**
Barbara Hepworth Museum and Garden **4**
Isles of Scilly Museum **3**
St. Michael's Mount **1**
Tate Gallery St. Ives **4**
Tintagel Castle **5**

10 mi
10 km

Value   Cheap Thrills: What to See & Do for Free (or Almost) in Cornwall

Relive the days of King Arthur. Cliff-top Tintagel Castle (now in ruins) is said to be the birthplace of King Arthur. No matter that archaeologists say the castle dates as late as the mid-13th century. Lovers of chivalry and romance can still summon images of Galahad, Lancelot, and the rest of the Knights of the Round Table riding out to seek the Holy Grail.

Hang out with the artists in St. Ives. Already renowned as home to the Barbara Hepworth Museum and the Tate Gallery, the coastal fishing village of St. Ives has been a major artists' colony since the days of Hepworth and Ben Nicholson—a great place to pick up amazing art for very little money.

Drive through Daphne du Maurier country. Nothing captures the wild Cornish landscape more than the novels of Daphne du Maurier (1907–89), author of *Rebecca*. Head for the village of Bolventor; du Maurier used the Jamaica Inn here (© 01566/86250) as the setting for her novel of the same name. Opposite the inn a small road leads to Dozmary Pool, into which Sir Bedivere threw Excalibur at Arthur's behest.

Visit Britain's subtropical haven. The Isles of Scilly archipelago evokes the Mediterranean with its mild climate and subtropical vegetation. Head for Tresco to explore more than 5,000 species of plants in the abbey gardens, planted in 1830. The collection of figureheads from ships wrecked off the rugged coast puts you in eerie touch with Cornish seafaring tradition.

Drive across Bodmin Moor. Dartmoor in Devon is better known, but the moor north and east of Bodmin almost equals it in legends. With brown, barren hills, broken only by tors, it was a land of smugglers and pirates. The best route is to head for the village of Camelford; there you'll find signposts leading to Rough Tor and Brown Willy, highest points of the moor. Drive to the parking lot at the foot of Rough Tor and hike on to Brown Willy, a mile away; this is one of the most scenic hikes in Cornwall.

Become enthralled with the Cornish coast. The jagged coastline of Cornwall invites exploration. One 32km (20-mile) stretch of the coast north of the Camel River is peppered with wild beaches ideal for surfing, lonely sand dunes, historic spots, dramatic cliffs, and small seafaring villages with quaint pubs. Go to the town of Wadebridge, 13km (8 miles) east of Padstow. From there follow the B3314 for 4km (2½ miles) to the signposted turnoff for the quaintly named "Rock." Go another 4.5km (3 miles) to the car park at Daymer Bay, where you can hike along the cliffs. It's a memory likely to linger.

ESSENTIALS

GETTING THERE   Daily trains run from Plymouth to Looe, and rail connections can also be made from Exeter (Devon) and Bristol (Avon). Most visitors drive to Polperro, but the nearest main-line station is at Liskeard, less than

4 hours from London's Paddington Station, with a branch line to Looe. Taxis meet incoming trains to take visitors to the various little villages in the area. For rail information in the area, call *C* **0845/7484950.**

Local bus companies have various routings from Plymouth into Looe. Ask at the tourist office in Plymouth for a schedule (see chapter 9). You can take a local bus to Polperro from Liskeard or Looe.

If you're driving to Looe from Plymouth, take A38 west, then B3253. To get to Polperro, follow A387 southwest from Looe.

VISITOR INFORMATION The **Tourist Information Centre** is at the Guildhall, Fore Street (*C* **01503/262072**), open in summer daily 10am to 2pm, in winter Saturday only 10am to 2pm.

EXPLORING POLPERRO

Polperro is one of Cornwall's handsomest villages; parts still have a 17th-century appearance. Cliffs surround it, and a stream called the Pol runs through it. The heart of the village is its frequently photographed and painted fishing harbor, where pilchard boats, loaded to the gunwales, used to dock. At one time nearly every man, woman, and child in the village spent time salting down pilchards for the winter—or smuggling. Today tourism has replaced contraband.

WHERE TO STAY
IN & AROUND LOOE

Coombe Farm *Finds* This country house is surrounded by 4 hectares (10½ acres) of lawns, meadows, woods, streams, and ponds, with views down a wooded valley to the sea. Martin and Sylvia Eades have furnished the centrally heated house with antiques and paintings. The snug and cozy rooms, all doubles, come in various shapes and sizes, each with an efficiently organized private bathroom with shower. Open log fires blaze in the dining room and lounge in cool weather. Dinner, served in the candlelit dining room with views of the sea, includes traditional English and Cornish dishes.

Widegates, near Looe, Cornwall PL13 1QN. *C* 01503/240223. Fax 01503/240895. www.coombefarmhotel. co.uk. 3 units. £32 ($51) single; £74 ($118) double. Rates include English breakfast. AE, MC, V. Closed Nov–Feb. Located on the B3253 road just south of the village of Widegates between Hessenford (1.6km/1 mile) and Looe (5.5km/3½). **Amenities:** Outdoor pool; room service (8am-9:30pm). *In room:* TV, dataport, coffeemaker, hair dryer.

Fieldhead Hotel The Fieldhead, built in 1896 as a private home, is now one of the area's best hotels. Commanding a view of the sea, it is situated on 1 hectare (2 acres) of gardens. The rooms have a high standard of traditional furnishings and are well maintained. Rooms are warm and inviting, most of them opening onto panoramic views of St. George's Island and the bay. Each has a compact private bathroom, and there are two rooms for those with limited mobility. Three rooms are large enough for families.

Portuan Rd., Hannafore, W. Looe, Cornwall PL13 2DR. *C* 01503/262689. Fax 01503/264114. www. fieldheadhotel.co.uk. 16 units. £28–£47 ($45–$75) single; £56–£94 ($90–$150) double. Rates include English breakfast. AE, MC, V. **Amenities:** Restaurant; bar; outdoor heated pool; room service (8am-10:30pm); laundry service. *In room:* TV, dataport, coffeemaker, hair dryer, trouser press.

Klymiarven Hotel Best approached from Barbican Road from the village of St. Martin, the Klymiarven is one of the best hotels in the area. Set on 1 hectare (2 acres) of woodland and terraced gardens with views of the harbor, the hotel has an elegant lounge, sunny lounge bar, and terrace overlooking a heated swimming pool. The 1590s cellars have a smugglers' passage, flagstone floors,

The Lost Gardens of Heligan

Visiting the **Lost Gardens of Heligan** ✦✦✦ is like taking a time capsule back to Victoria's day. Europe's largest garden restoration project sprawls over 32 hectares (80 acres) of pure enchantment, with award-winning gardens. Near the fishing village of Mevagissey, these gardens "slept" for nearly 7 decades before they were rediscovered and restored.

On the gardens were part of the 400 hectare (1,000-acre) Victorian estate of the Tremayne family, in residence here since the 16th century. As family fortunes declined after World War I, the gardens were allowed to decay, and the grand estate itself was converted to apartments.

As Cornwall enjoys a subtropical climate, it didn't take long for rampant weeds, brambles, and other unchecked growth to blanket the gardens, even "burying" the tall palm trees in time.

In 1990, composer Tim Smit, with his friend, builder John Nelson, rediscovered the garden along with heir to the estate, John Willis. The estate had by then been reduced to 32 hectares (80 acres). The men became so enchanted with this secret garden that restoration was launched shortly thereafter.

Both professionals and volunteers began the gargantuan project of reclaiming the gardens. Greenhouses were rebuilt, ornamental pools cleaned and put into working order, pineapple pits redug, orchards replanted, and new plants put into the earth as they were in the 19th century. Part of the gardens encompasses a "Jungle," an extraordinary dell evocative of a Garden of Eden. Giant tree ferns, palms, bamboo, and other vegetation rise from the earth. All that is missing is a swinging appearance by Tarzan.

Beyond the jungle rises the "Lost Valley," with its woodland, flowers, and lakes. The location near the fishing village of Mevagissey is southwest of St. Austell, near Pentewan, off the Mevagissey Road or B3273. In summer the gardens are open from 10:30am to 6pm (they close at 5pm off season). Admission is £6 ($10) for adults, £5.50 ($9) for seniors, £3 ($4.80) for ages 5 to 15 (free for 4 and under). A family ticket sells for £17 ($27). For more information, call © **01726/845100; www.heligan.com.**

and old timber beams. It's run by the Russell family, who offer a relaxed atmosphere. The tastefully furnished midsize nonsmoking double bedrooms contain efficiently organized private bathrooms with shower. British and international cuisine is served in a candlelit restaurant.

Barbican Hill, East Looe, Cornwall PL13 1BH. © and fax **01503/262333.** www.klymiarven.co.uk. 14 units. £28–£55 ($45–$88) per person. Single supplement £5–£10 ($8–$16). Rates include English breakfast. MC, V. Closed Dec–Jan. **Amenities:** Restaurant; bar; pool. *In room:* TV, dataport, coffeemaker.

Osborne House Licensed Restaurant With Bed & Breakfast Rooms This 17th-century building stands on a tiny street in this village, a few minutes' walk to the sea and the main shopping area. The small rooms are comfortably if plainly furnished, with shower-only bathrooms. The dining room has Old-World charm, with bright brasses and copper kettles adorning a large hearth. The owners offer a varied menu of fresh fish, Cornish beef, lamb, and game.

Lower Chapel St., East Looe, Cornwall PL13 1AT. (C) **01503/262970.** 4 units. £35 ($56) single; £50 ($80) double. Rates include English breakfast. AE, MC, V. Closed Jan and Nov. **Amenities:** Restaurant; bar. *In room:* TV, dataport, coffeemaker.

Panorama Hotel   This immaculate nonsmoking hotel in the center of town lets you enjoy views of the harbor and rugged coastline. You always get a polite welcome and personal service at this Cornish outpost. The recently decorated midsize bedrooms are comfortable, each with a small, shower-only bathroom. Front bedrooms have balconies overlooking the bay. Fresh produce, fish from the quay, and vegetarian options are always featured.

Hannafore Rd., West Looe, Cornwall PL13 2DE. (C) **01503/262123.** Fax 01503/265654. www.looe.co.uk. 9 units. £48–£58 ($77–$93) double. Single supplement £3 ($4.80). Rates include English breakfast. MC, V. **Amenities:** Dining room; bar. *In room:* TV, coffeemaker. No phone.

Trenderway Farm ★★ *Finds*   Dating from the late 16th century, this is a real discovery, an old farmstead lying in lovely countryside at the top of the Valley of Polperro, only a 5-minute drive from either Polperro or the fishing port of Looe. Still a working farm, it is one of the finest and most tranquil little retreats in Cornwall. You can stay in a twin- or king-size double bed in the main farmhouse or in a converted barn adjacent to the house (one of these accommodations is a four-poster unit). All the rooms are beautifully furnished with a bath and shower and are all nonsmoking. Lynne Tuckett, the owner, brings the flair of a professional decorator to the bedrooms.

Pelynt, near Polperro, Cornwall PL13 2LY. (C) **01503/272214.** Fax 01503/272991. 4 units. www.trenderwayfarm. co.uk. £80 ($128) double. Rates include English breakfast. MC, V. Lies between the Pelynt and Polperro forks of the western road from Looe; .5km (¼ mile) west of the A387, .75km (½ mile) before Pelynt. **Amenities:** Breakfast room. *In room:* TV, coffeemaker, hair dryer (on request), iron. No phone.

IN POLPERRO

Penryn House Hotel   This country-style hotel reflects the peace of its Cornish fishing village heritage. The good-size nonsmoking bedrooms have private, shower-only bathrooms. A fireside lounge bar offers local produce and fresh seafood. The house often stages murder mystery weekends, with 1920s costumes optional.

The Coombs, Main St., Polperro, Cornwall PL13 2RG. (C) **01503/272157.** Fax 01503/273055. www.hotels cornwall.org. 10 units. £24 ($38) single; £48–£62 ($77–$99) double. Single supplement £8 ($13). Rates include English breakfast. AE, MC, V. **Amenities:** Restaurant; bar. *In room:* TV, dataport, coffeemaker, hair dryer.

WHERE TO DINE
IN LOOE

The Water Rail SEAFOOD   This restaurant, housed in a 14th-century structure near the quay, sits a 2-minute walk from the river and the beach. Its specialty is freshly caught fish, sometimes even sardines. Daily offerings are based on seasonal availability, and the menu is an interesting mix of dishes. The Water Rail has won the praise of many a diner, although some have found the seafood overcooked. Wine is available by the glass.

Lower Market St., East Looe. (C) **01503/262314.** Reservations required in summer only. Fixed-price 3-course menu £14.95 ($24). AE, V. Wed–Mon 7–10pm.

IN POLPERRO

The Kitchen ★ *Finds* SEAFOOD   This pink cottage, halfway down to the harbor from the parking area, was a wagon-builder's shop; it's now a restaurant run by Vanessa and Ian Bateson (Vanessa makes the desserts and bread). It offers good English cooking, with everything homemade and fresh. The seasonal menu features local fresh fish. Typical dishes include Fowey sea trout with lemon-and-herb butter and breast of duckling with blueberry-and-Drambuie sauce. Many vegetarian dishes are offered as main courses.

Fish na Bridge. ℂ 01503/272780. Reservations required. Main courses £13–£18 ($21–$29). MC, V. Tues–Sun 7–9:30pm. Closed Oct.

The Three Pilchards ENGLISH   Locals and visitors come to this harborside pub. It's a large L-shaped room with a black oak interior and a fireplace that burns brightly at night. Sit in the window seat and listen to the talk of the villagers, even if you do not understand a word of their dialect. Food ranges from sandwiches and jacket potatoes to curry, steaks, and salads.

The Quay. ℂ 01503/272233. Pub snacks £2.50–£11.95 ($4–$19). MC, V. Daily 11am-11pm.

2 The Lizard Peninsula ⭑

517km (323 miles) SW of London; 34km (21 miles) S of Falmouth

The southernmost point in England is the Lizard, a remarkable spot with jagged rocks reaching out into the sea where cormorants and gulls fish. The lesser known of Cornwall's two peninsulas (Land's End is the other), the Lizard is characterized by beaches, small villages, coastal walks, and crafts studios. Some of the best beaches are at the coves at Poldhu and Kynance. Its seagoing people have long known the often-furious nature of the coastline, giving certain places epithets like "the Devil's Frying Pan." Many shipwreck victims are buried in the cemetery at the Church of St. Keverne. Rare flora and fauna can be found at Goonhilly Downs. British Telecom's Goonhilly Satellite Earth Station can be seen from most parts of the Lizard; it's the country's largest radio-receiving and space-tracking station.

There are no big resorts here, just scattered small hotels and B&B houses; some close in the winter, as this is essentially a summer place. Most accommodations and eating places are in the village of Mullion.

ESSENTIALS

GETTING THERE   The nearest railway station is 37km (23 miles) from the Lizard Peninsula in the town of Redruth, which is on the direct London–Penzance line. Trains leave London from Paddington Station. Call ℂ 0845/7484950 for schedules and information. No bus service is available. From Falmouth, take A394 west to the junction with A3083, which you can take south to Lizard Point.

VISITOR INFORMATION   Go to the **Tourist Information Centre** at 28 Killigrew St. in Falmouth (ℂ 01326/312300), open Easter through September Monday through Friday 9am to 5pm and Saturday 9am to 5pm; July through August Sunday 10am to 5pm; October through Easter Monday through Friday 9am to 1pm and 2 to 5pm.

⌒ *Fun Fact* **Lizard Tongues**

Some observers claim that the Lizard is "the most Cornish place" in Cornwall; it was the last place where the Cornish language was spoken before linguistic "modernization."

Moments Trekking the Cornish Coast

Much of Cornwall is an evocatively barren landscape, composed of gray rocks, weathered headlands jutting seaward, and very few trees. The weather alternates between bright sunshine and the impenetrable fogs for which the English Channel is famous.

The land and seascapes provide a scenic backdrop for hiking around the Cornish peninsula's coastline. The government maintains a clearly signposted coastal path more than 966km (600 miles) long that skirts the edge of the sea, following the tortured coastline from Minehead (in Somerset, near Dunster) to Poole (in Dorset, near Bournemouth). En route, the path crosses some of the least developed regions of southern England, including hundreds of acres of privately owned land as well as the northern border of the Exmoor National Park.

Throughout is a sense of ancient Celtic mysticism and existential loneliness. Low-lying gorse, lichens, and heathers characterize the vegetation. In marked contrast to the windblown uplands, verdant subtropical vegetation grows in the tidal estuaries of the Fowey, Fal, Helford, and Tamar rivers.

Your options for exploring the coasts of Cornwall, Devon, and Dorset are numerous. It's a full 4 to 6 weeks of hard trekking to do the whole thing, though most people just pick a short section for a day hike. Although the route is sometimes arduous, no special equipment other than sturdy shoes, good stamina, and waterproof clothing is required.

You may also want to pick up a locally researched and annually revised book: The South West Way Association's *The Complete Guide to the South West Coast Path—Great Britain's Longest Trail*. This book divides the 966km (600-mile) coast path into manageable segments, rates them for degrees of difficulty, and contains a comprehensive accommodations section with addresses of pubs, bed-and-breakfasts, inns, hotels, and campsites en route. The book can be ordered from the **South West Coast Path Association,** 1 Orchard Dr., Kingskerswell, Newton Abbot, Devon, England TQ12 5DG (✆ and fax **01752/896237;** www.swcp.org.uk), at a cost of £8 ($13) including postage.

The loneliness of the Cornish moors could be marred by hundreds of other people with exactly the same idea during Britain's school holidays. If possible, schedule your visit for relatively quiet periods, and remember that the weather between late October and early May is rainy, foggy, and windy—romantic, but no fun for hiking.

WHERE TO STAY & DINE

Landewednack House ✦   A landmark building in the area, this elegant Georgian country home has been sensitively restored. It overlooks the water from its panoramic and tranquil setting. In its long history it has seen many owners come and go; once it was a rectory. Peter and Marion Stanley now offer well-furnished nonsmoking bedrooms with various types of beds ranging from a twin or double to a queen four-poster. Each comes with a private shower bathroom (one with a

Jacuzzi). In cool weather, guests relax in front of a log-burning fire; in summer they find a place in the walled garden by the heated swimming pool.

Landewednack House, Church Cove, The Lizard, Cornwall TR12 7PQ. ℂ **01326/290909.** Fax 01326/290192. 3 units. £39–£44 ($62–$70) per person. Rates include English breakfast. MC, V. **Amenities:** Breakfast room; pool; dinner by arrangement. *In room:* TV, coffeemaker, hair dryer, no phone.

Penmenner House Hotel ⭐   Behind a simple facade is one of the area's most appealing guesthouses. The house opens onto views of the Lizard lighthouse and coastal scenery. Guests receive Cornish hospitality and cozy, comfortable non-smoking accommodations with mostly private, shower-only bathrooms. Previous guests have included Virginia Woolf, Lytton Strachey, and Desmond MacCarthy. We strongly recommend that you reserve your room ahead of time.

Penmenner Rd., Lizard, Cornwall TR12 7NR. ℂ **01326/290370.** 6 units, 5 with bathroom. £23–£26.50 ($37–$42) per person. Rates include English breakfast. MC, V. Take A30 to Redruth, then follow the signs to Helston and Lizard. **Amenities:** Breakfast room; lounge; bar. *In room:* TV, coffeemaker, hair dryer, no phone.

3 Penzance ⭐⭐

448km (280 miles) SW of London; 123km (77 miles) SW of Plymouth

This little harbor town, made famous by Gilbert and Sullivan, sits at the end of the Cornish Riviera. It's noted for a moderate climate—it's one of the first English towns to see spring flowers—and for the summer throngs that descend for fishing, sailing, and swimming. Overlooking Mount's Bay, Penzance is graced in places with subtropical plants.

The buccaneers in *The Pirates of Penzance* were not entirely fictional. The town was raided by Barbary pirates; partly destroyed by Cromwell's troops; ransacked and burned by the Spaniards; and bombed by the Germans. In spite of all this, Penzance offers tranquil resort living today.

The westernmost town in England, Penzance makes a good base for exploring Land's End, the Lizard, St. Michael's Mount, St. Ives, Newlyn, Mousehole, and even the Isles of Scilly.

ESSENTIALS
GETTING THERE   Ten express trains depart daily from Paddington Station in London for Penzance. The trip takes 5½ hours. Call ℂ **0845/7484950.**

The **Rapide,** run by National Express from Victoria Coach Station in London (ℂ **020/7529-2000**), costs £30.50 ($49) for the one-way trip from London, which takes about 8½ hours. The buses have toilets and reclining seats.

Drive southwest across Cornwall on the A30 all the way to Penzance.

VISITOR INFORMATION   The **Tourist Information Centre** is on Station Road (ℂ **01736/362207**). It's open from the end of May to September, Monday through Friday from 9am to 5:30pm, Saturday from 10am to 5pm, and Sunday from 10am to 1pm; from October to May, hours are Monday through Friday from 9am to 5pm and Saturday from 10am to 1pm.

SEEING THE SIGHTS AROUND PENZANCE
Castle on St. Michael's Mount ⭐   Rising about 75m (250 ft.) from the sea, St. Michael's Mount is topped by a part medieval, part 17th-century castle. It's 5km (3 miles) east of Penzance and is reached at low tide by a causeway. At high tide, the mount becomes an island, reached only by motor launch from Marazion. In winter, you can go over only when the causeway is dry.

A Benedictine monastery, the gift of Edward the Confessor, stood on this spot in the 11th century. The castle now has a collection of armor and antique furniture. A tea garden is on the island, as well as a National Trust restaurant, both open in summer. The steps up to the castle are steep and rough, so wear sturdy shoes. To avoid disappointment, call the number listed below to check on the tides, especially during winter.

On St. Michael's Mount, Mount's Bay. © **01736/710507.** Admission £4.80 ($8) adults, £2.40 ($3.85) children, £13 ($21) family ticket. Apr–Oct Mon–Fri 10:30am–5:30pm (open weekends in summer); Nov–Mar Mon, Wed, and Fri by conducted tour only, which leaves at 11am, noon, 2, and 3pm, weather and tide permitting. Bus no. 2 or 2A from Penzance to Marazion, the town opposite St. Michael's Mount. Parking £1.50 ($2.40).

Minack Theatre   One of the most unusual theaters in southern England, this open-air amphitheater was cut from the side of a rocky Cornish hill near the village of Porthcurno, 14km (9 miles) southwest of Penzance. Its legendary creator was Rowena Cade, an arts enthusiast and noted eccentric, who began the theater after World War I by physically carting off much of the granite from her chosen hillside. On the premises, an exhibition hall showcases her life and accomplishments. She died a very old woman in the 1980s, confident of the enduring appeal of her theater to visitors from around the world.

Up to 750 visitors at a time can sit directly on grass- or rock-covered ledges, sometimes on cushions if they're available, within sight lines of both the actors and a sweeping view out over the ocean. Experienced theatergoers sometimes bring raincoats for protection against the occasional drizzle. Theatrical events are staged by repertory theater companies that travel throughout Britain and are likely to include everything from Shakespeare to musical comedy.

Porthcurno. © **01736/810694.** www.minack.com. Theater tickets £7 ($11) adults, £3.50 ($6) children; tour tickets £2.50 ($4) adults, £1.80 ($2.90) seniors, £1 ($1.60) children. Exhibition hall, Oct–Mar daily 10am–4pm; Apr–Sept 9:30am–6pm. Performances end of May to mid-Sept, matinees Wed and Fri at 2pm, evening shows Mon–Fri at 8pm. Leave Penzance on A30 heading toward Land's End; after 5km (3 miles), bear left onto B3283 and follow the signs to Porthcurno.

WHERE TO STAY

Camilla House Hotel ⭐   This comfortable, nicely furnished, nonsmoking house is located near the town promenade, within walking distance of shops and restaurants. A local mariner built this house for his family in 1836. The small to midsize bedrooms will give you the feeling of being "at home." Susan and Simon Chapman are most helpful in providing tourist information for attractions in Penzance and surrounding areas. They're also agents for the Skybus (airplane) and Scillonian III (ferry) and book day trips to the Isles of Scilly. A delicious English breakfast is served in a charming dining room.

12 Regent Terrace, Penzance, Cornwall. © and fax **01736/363771.** www.camillahouse-hotel.co.uk. 8 units. £26 ($42) single; £50–£70 ($80–$112) double. Rates include English breakfast. AE, MC, V. **Amenities:** Breakfast room; bar; lounge. *In room:* TV, coffeemaker, hair dryer, no phone.

Ennys ⭐ *Finds*   Once a flower farm, Ennys produces mainly vegetables today. Owned by Jill Charlton, this Cornish granite farmhouse has a slate roof; its front section dates back to the 17th century, and other portions are thought to be much older. The nonsmoking bedrooms are furnished in an old-fashioned farmhouse style with patchwork quilts and four-poster beds; two have shower-only bathrooms and three have shower/tub combination bathrooms. The hostess prepares an afternoon Cornish-style cream tea. Guests can enjoy a large flower garden, a heated swimming pool, and a grass tennis court.

St. Hilary, Penzance, Cornwall TR20 9B2. ☎ **01736/740262**. www.ennys.co.uk. 5 units. £50–£55 ($80–$88) single; £75–£90 ($120–$144) double; £110–£130 ($176–$208) family suite. Rates include English breakfast. MC, V. Closed Nov–Jan. **Amenities:** Dining room; pool; tennis court. *In room:* TV, coffeemaker, hair dryer, no phone.

The Georgian House

Once the home of the mayors of Penzance, reputedly haunted by the ghost of a Mrs. Baines (a previous owner), the Georgian is a completely renovated, intimate hotel. The bright, cozy nonsmoking rooms are small to medium in size and have basins. Most units also have a small private bathroom with a shower stall; otherwise, the corridor bathrooms are adequate. The house has a comfortable reading lounge, a licensed nautical-themed bar, and an intimate dining room, where good Cornish meals are served April through October.

20 Chapel St., Penzance, Cornwall TR18 4AW. ☎ and fax **01736/365664**. 11 units. £28–£32 ($45–$51) single; £46–£54 ($74–$86) double. Rates include English breakfast. MC, V. **Amenities:** Dining room; lounge; bar. *In room:* TV, coffeemaker, hair dryer, iron, no phone.

Kimberley House ✦

This nonsmoking B&B is in a Victorian house between the promenade and the town center, opposite Penlee Park and near the Morrab Gardens. The owners provide their guests good food, somewhat basic accommodations, and tips about what to see in the area. As befits a Victorian house, accommodations come in various shapes and sizes. A rather large dinner of home-cooked English food can be arranged.

10 Morrab Rd., Penzance, Cornwall TR18 4EZ. ☎ and fax **01736/362727**. 8 units, 2 with shower. £16–£18 ($26–$29) single; £36–£42 ($58–$67) double. Rates include English breakfast. No credit cards. Closed Jan. **Amenities:** Dining room; lounge. *In room:* TV, coffeemaker, no phone.

Lynwood Guest House

Roy and Teresa Stacey own this bed-and-breakfast located a few hundred meters from the town center. The Victorian house is constructed of granite blocks and is appointed appropriately. The comfortable nonsmoking accommodations are well furnished and maintained. Breakfast is the only meal served, but there are many restaurants and pubs nearby.

41 Morrab Rd., Penzance, Cornwall TR18 4EX. ☎ and fax **01736/365871**. www.penzance.co.uk/lynwood-guesthouse. 7 units, 4 with bathroom. £16.50 ($26) single without bathroom, £19.50 ($31) single with bathroom; £33 ($53) double without bathroom, £39 ($62) double with bathroom. Rates include English breakfast. AE, DC, MC, V. **Amenities:** Breakfast room. *In room:* TV, coffeemaker, hair dryer, no phone.

Richmond Lodge

This early Victorian house with a nautical flavor is a few steps from Market Jew Street (the main street) and within an easy walk of the Promenade along the seawall; the Morrab Gardens are across the street. Mr. and Mrs. Webb, the owners, provide helpful service in this homelike place. The best rooms have a bathroom and a four-poster bed. The Lodge is nonsmoking and provides one room for those with limited mobility.

61 Morrab Rd., Penzance, Cornwall TR18 4EP. ☎ **01736/365560**. 7 units, 4 with bathroom. £20 ($32) single without bathroom; £38 ($61) double without bathroom, £42 ($67) double with bathroom. Rates include English breakfast. V, MC. **Amenities:** Breakfast room; lounge. *In room:* TV, coffeemaker, hair dryer, no phone.

The Summer House

This nonsmoking hotel is situated 50m (164 ft.) from the Promenade and the sea. The 150-year-old Regency house was built by a seafaring captain. With its wide sweeping staircase, it's quite different from the usual Victorian bed-and-breakfast. Two of the rooms have shower/tub combination bathrooms and three have shower only bathrooms. Owners Linda and Ciro Zaino extend warm hospitality and serve a delicious breakfast in their elegant dining room.

Cornwall Terrace, Penzance, Cornwall, TR18 4HL. ℂ **01736/363744.** Fax 01736/360959. www.summer house-cornwall.com. 5 units. £70 ($112) single; £75–£95 ($120–$152) double. Rates include English breakfast. MC, V. **Amenities:** Restaurant; lounge. *In room:* TV, coffeemaker, hair dryer, no phone.

Tarbert Hotel This dignified granite-and-stucco house, built in 1830, is a 2-minute walk northwest of the town center. Bedrooms range from small to medium, with pleasantly coordinated colors and comfortable furniture. Some rooms retain the original high ceilings and elaborate cove moldings. Each unit has a small, compact bathroom, efficiently organized, with a tub-and-shower combination. Recent improvements include a new reception area, completely refurbished lounge, and sun patio. An on-site restaurant specializes in fresh local seafood.

11–12 Clarence St., Penzance, Cornwall TR18 2NU. ℂ **01736/363758.** Fax 01736/331336. www.tarbert-hotel.co.uk. 12 units. £32–£38 ($51–$61) single; £60–£84 ($96–$134) double. Rates include English breakfast. AE, MC, V. Closed Dec 23–Jan 26. **Amenities:** Restaurant; bar; lounge. *In room:* TV, dataport, coffeemaker, hair dryer.

Tremont Hotel This turn-of-the-century house is on a tree-lined street just up from Mount's Bay, off the Promenade and seafront. The owners, Alvin and Jackie Williams, run this nonsmoking guesthouse with a welcoming style, offering well-maintained midsize bedrooms that are tastefully and comfortably furnished. One room is large enough to accommodate families.

Alexandra Rd., Penzance, Cornwall TR18 4LZ. ℂ **01736/362614.** 12 units. £20–£25 ($32–$40) single; £40–£50 ($64–$80) double. Rates include English breakfast. No credit cards. **Amenities:** Breakfast room; lounge. *In room:* TV, coffeemaker, hair dryer, no phone.

Woodstock Guest House ⭐ This nonsmoking B&B in the center of Penzance fronts the sea, in a Victorian town house that once housed a private family. John and Cherry Hopkins are among the most helpful B&B owners in Penzance, and their location is ideal, as their property opens onto Morrab Gardens. Most of their midsize bedrooms contain a shower-only private bathroom, and some units can accommodate three beds. A special room on the ground floor has a four-poster bed among other extras.

29 Morrab Road, Penzance, Cornwall TR18 4EZ. ℂ and fax **01736/369049.** 8 units, 5 with private bathroom. £17–£26 ($27–$42) per person. Rates include breakfast. MC, V. **Amenities:** Breakfast room. *In room:* TV, coffeemaker, hair dryer, no phone.

WHERE TO DINE

The **Nelson Bar,** in the Union Hotel on Chapel Street in Penzance (ℂ **01736/ 362319**), is known for its robust pub grub and collection of Nelsoniana. It's the place where the admiral's death at Trafalgar was first revealed to the English. Lunch and dinner are served daily. Other possibilities for very casual eating include **Snatch-a-Bite,** 45 New St. (ℂ **01736/366866**), near Lloyds Bank off Market Jew Street. This place is known for its well-stuffed sandwiches costing £3 ($4.80) and freshly made salads, a meal unto themselves, going for £4 ($6) and up. Open Monday through Saturday, 9am–4pm.

Bakewell Restaurant ⭐ INTERNATIONAL Just off Chapel Street, this family-run restaurant offers its own flower- and palm-filled courtyard as well as two dining rooms. For Penzance, it is imbued with a rather continental atmosphere. We are impressed with the skill of the cooks and the choice of their first-rate ingredients. The favorite starter—and justifiably so—is a coarse French country terrine with pork, pistachios, and cognac. The local sirloin steak is a delight when served with a pepper sauce along with pecan-stuffed mushrooms, or else you might opt for the freshly roasted turbot with an herb purée with a mustard *beurre blanc* sauce. For something more traditional, try the Cornish lamb with Irish cabbage and new potatoes. The menu is more limited at lunch but equally tasty.

Old Bake House Lane, off Chapel St. ℂ **01736/331-331.** Reservations recommended. Dinner main courses £10.50–£17 ($17–$27). Lunch main courses £4.50–£6 ($7–$10). MC, V. Mon–Sat 6:30–11pm; July–Aug Mon–Sat also noon–2:30pm.

Dolphin Tavern ENGLISH   Head here for some of the best and most afford-able pub grub in town. This large, friendly pub attracts a young crowd in sum-mer with its menu variety. The Dolphin not only pulls a tasty pint, but serves a hearty breakfast or cream tea at almost any time. Their tasty Cornish pasties are well known. The identical lunch and dinner menus carry items such as meat pies, grilled steaks, a roast of the day, and seafood, usually among the daily specials.

22 Quay St. ℂ **01736/364106.** Main courses £4.10–£10.50 ($7–$17). Mon–Sat 11am–11pm; Sun noon–10:30pm.

The Turk's Head ENGLISH/INTERNATIONAL   Dating from 1233, this inn claims to be the oldest in Penzance. It serves the finest food of any pub in town, far superior to its chief rival, the nearby Admiral Benbow. In summer, drinkers overflow into the garden. Inside, the inn is decorated in a mellow style befitting its age, with flatirons and other artifacts hanging from timeworn beams. Meals include fishermen's pie, local seafood, chicken curry, and prime steaks including rib eye. See the chalkboards for the daily specials.

49 Chapel St. ℂ **01736/363093.** Main courses £5–£12 ($8–$19); bar snacks £2.95 ($4.70). AE, MC, V. Daily 11am–3pm and 5:30–11pm. From the rail station, turn left just past Lloyd's Bank.

4 The Isles of Scilly ✱

43km (27 miles) WSW of Land's End

Several miles off the Cornish coast, the **Isles of Scilly** are warmed by the Gulf Stream enough to have thriving semitropical plants; they have no signs of frost in some winters. They're the first landfall most oceangoing passengers see when coming from North America.

There are five inhabited and more than 100 uninhabited islands in the group. Some are only a few square kilometers, whereas the largest, St. Mary's, encom-passes some 78 sq. km (30 sq. miles). Three of these islands—**Tresco, St. Mary's,** and **St. Agnes**—attract mainland visitors. Early flowers are the main export, and tourism is the main industry.

The Isles of Scilly figured prominently in the myths and legends of the ancient Greeks and Romans; in Celtic legend, they were inhabited entirely by holy men. There are more ancient burial mounds here than anywhere else in southern England; artifacts have established that people lived here more than 4,000 years ago. Today there's little left of this history to see.

St. Mary's is the capital, with about seven-eighths of the total population of all the islands; the ship from the mainland docks here, at Hugh Town. However, if you'd like to make a day visit, we recommend the helicopter flight from Penzance to Tresco, the neighboring island, where you can enjoy a day's walk through 294 hectares (735 acres), mostly occupied by the Abbey Gardens.

ESSENTIALS

GETTING THERE   You can fly by plane or helicopter. **Isles of Scilly Sky-bus Ltd.** (℃ **01736/785220**) operates 2 to 20 flights per day, depending on the season, between Penzance's Land's End Airport and Hugh Town on St. Mary's Island. Flight time on the eight-passenger fixed-wing planes is 15 minutes each way. The round-trip fare is £68 to £91 ($109–$146) for same-day return, and £58 to £91 ($93–$146) if you plan to stay overnight.

A helicopter service run by **British International Helicopters,** Penzance Heliport Eastern Green (© **01736/363871** for recorded information), operates, weather permitting, up to 26 helicopter flights, Monday through Saturday, between Penzance, St. Mary's, and Tresco. Flight time is 20 minutes from Penzance to either island. A same-day round-trip fare is £81 to £117 ($130–$187). A bus, whose timing coincides with the departure of each flight, runs to the heliport from the railway station in Penzance for £1 ($1.60) per person each way.

The rail line ends in Penzance (see "Getting There," in section 3, above).

Slower, but more cadenced and contemplative, is a ship leaving from the **Isles of Scilly Travel Centre,** on Quay Street in Penzance (© **08457/105555** toll-free from anywhere in the U.K., or 01736/362009). It departs at least 6 days a week between April and October, requiring 2 hours and 40 minutes for the segment between Penzance and Hugh Town, with an additional 20 or so minutes for the second leg of the trip, which is from Hugh Town to Tresco. It departs Monday through Friday at 9:15am, returning from St. Mary's at 4:30pm. Saturday departures usually follow the Monday through Friday timing, but not always, as the managers sometimes add a second Saturday sailing to accommodate weekend holidaymakers, depending on the season. Between November and March, service is extremely limited, sometimes nonexistent. Depending on the time of year, a same-day round-trip ticket from Penzance to St. Mary's costs £30 ($48) for adults and £15 ($24) for children 15 and under.

VISITOR INFORMATION St. Mary's Tourist Information Office, at High Street, St. Mary's (© **01720/422536**), is open April through October, Monday through Saturday from 8:30am to 5:30pm, Sunday from 9am to noon; November through March, it's open Monday through Friday from 8:30am to 5pm, and Saturday from 8:30am to noon.

TRESCO

No cars or motorbikes are allowed on Tresco, but bikes can be rented by the day; the hotels use a special wagon towed by farm tractor to transport guests and luggage from the harbor.

For the best selections of island crafts, visit Phoenix, Portomellon Industrial Estate, St. Mary's (© **01720/422900**). At this studio, you can watch original artifacts being made into stained glass. The shops also sell a wide assortment of gifts, including jewelry and leaded weights. The Isles of Scilly Perfumery, Porthloo Studios, St. Mary's (© **01720/423304**), a 10-minute walk from the center of Hugh Town, is packed with intriguing gifts made from plants grown on the Isles—from a delicate shell-shaped soap to fine fragrances, cosmetics, potpourri, and other accessories.

Abbey Gardens ⓐ The gardens, the most outstanding feature of Tresco, were started by Augustus Smith in the mid-1830s. When he began, the area was a barren hillside, a fact that visitors now find hard to believe.

The gardens are a nature-lover's dream, with more than 5,000 species of plants from 100 different countries. Although some historians date it to A.D. 964, the old abbey or priory, now in ruins, was supposedly founded by Benedictine monks in the 11th century. Of special interest is Valhalla, a collection of nearly 60 figureheads from ships wrecked around the islands; the gaily painted figures have a rather eerie quality, each one a ghost with a different story to tell.

After a visit to the gardens, walk through the fields, along paths, and across dunes thick with heather. Flowers, birds, shells, and fish are abundant. Birds are so unafraid that they land within a foot or so of you and feed happily.

Tresco Abbey Gardens, Tresco Estate. ✆ **01720/422849.** Admission £8.50 ($14) adults, free for children 16 and under. Daily 10am–4pm.

WHERE TO STAY & DINE: WORTH A SPLURGE

The New Inn ✶ Composed of an interconnected row of 19th-century fisher-men's cottages and shops, the New Inn is situated at Tresco's center, beside its unnamed main road. The medium-size nonsmoking rooms are tastefully decorated in modern blue and creamy yellow hues. They feature matching twin or double beds and well-maintained bathrooms with a tub and shower. The more expensive units offer sea views. The place is known for its pub; the pictures in the bar show many of the ships that sank or foundered around the islands in the past, as well as some of the gigs used in pilotage, rescue, smuggling, and pillage.

Tresco, Isles of Scilly, Cornwall TR24 0QQ. ✆ **01720/422844.** Fax 01720/423200. www.tresco.co.uk/holidays/new_inn.asp. 15 units. £87–£115 ($139–$184) per person. Rates include half board. MC, V. **Amenities:** Restaurant; bar; pool; tennis court; laundry. *In room:* TV, coffeemaker, hair dryer.

ST. MARY'S

To get around St. Mary's, cars are available but hardly necessary. The **Island Bus Service** charges £2 ($3.20) from one island point to another; children ride for half fare.

Bicycles are one of the most practical means of transport. **Buccabu Bicycle Rentals,** The Strand, St. Mary's (✆ and fax **01720/422289**), is the only bike-rental outfit. They stock "shopper's cycles" with 3 speeds, "hybrid" bikes with 6 to 12 speeds, and 18-speed mountain bikes. All are available at prices ranging from £4 to £6 ($6–$10) daily. A £10 ($16) deposit is required.

Isles of Scilly Museum, on Church Street in St. Mary's (✆ **01720/422337**), illustrates the history of the Scillies from 2500 B.C., with drawings, artifacts from wrecked ships, and assorted relics discovered on the islands. A locally themed exhibit changes annually. It's open Monday through Saturday from 10am to noon and 1:30 to 4:30pm from Easter to October, with additional evening hours (7:30–9pm) June through September. Off season (Nov–Apr), it's open only on Wednesday, from 2 to 4pm. Admission is £1 ($1.60) for adults and 50p (80¢) for children.

WHERE TO STAY

Anjeric Close to beaches, shops, and the quay, this centrally located B&B is a haven for nonsmokers. A two-story hotel, it rents plainly furnished but comfortable bedrooms, with a view of the town beach or of offshore islands. The setting is friendly and relaxed; the food served here is hearty and wholesome, with an emphasis on seafood dishes.

The Strand, Hugh Town, St. Mary's, Isles of Scilly TR2 0PS. ✆ and fax **01720/422700.** 8 units, 7 with bathroom. £34.50 ($55) per person without bathroom; £36 ($58) per person with bathroom. Rates include breakfast. No credit cards. Closed Nov–Mar. **Amenities:** Dining room; lounge. *In room:* Coffeemaker, hair dryer, no phone.

Crebinick House Named after a massive offshore rock that in the 19th century caused a major shipwreck, this house is owned and operated by two refugees from London, Lesley and Phillip Jones. Though originally built (1760) of granite blocks, additions have significantly expanded it in back; as a landmark building, however, its facade is sacrosanct. The house sits in the village center; while there are no sea views, the water is within 45m (150 ft.) in two directions. The small nonsmoking bedrooms are nicely furnished and filled with floral-patterned fabrics. Lesley prepares dinners for residents only.

Church St., Hugh Town, St. Mary's, Isles of Scilly, Cornwall TR21 0JT. $\mathcal{C}$ and fax **01720/422968.** www.crebinick.co.uk. 6 units. £58–£68 ($93–$109) doubles only. Rates include breakfast. No credit cards. Closed Nov–Mar. **Amenities:** Dining room; lounge. *In room:* TV, coffeemaker, hair dryer, no phone.

Evergreen Cottage Guest House ⭐ *(Finds* This is one of the island's oldest cottages (1790s). The Evergreen was first the home of sea captains and later a smithy. Located in the town center, its considerable character is enhanced by maritime artifacts. The modernized nonsmoking guesthouse provides adequate facilities; bedrooms, although small, are tastefully and comfortably appointed, each with a private shower-only bathroom. The proprietors offer breakfast only.

The Parade, Hugh Town, St. Mary's, Isles of Scilly, Cornwall TR21 0LP. $\mathcal{C}$ **01720/422711.** 5 units. £35–£55 ($56–$88) per person. Rates include English breakfast. No credit cards. **Amenities:** Breakfast room; lounge. *In room:* Coffeemaker, hair dryer, iron, no phone.

Mincarlo Guest House Run by the Duncan family since the 1950s, this lovely house lies only a 5-minute walk from the harbor. Colin and Jill Duncan offer a range of small to midsize accommodations, comfortably arranged and well furnished, with adequate hallway facilities. Many rooms overlook the harbor. Colin prepares and cooks the evening meal, featuring local produce, fish, and shellfish.

The Strand, Hugh Town, St. Mary's, Isles of Scilly, Cornwall TR21 0PT. $\mathcal{C}$ **01720/422513.** 12 units, 4 with bathroom. £23 ($37) single without bathroom; £46–£50 ($74–$80) double without bathroom; £65 ($104) double with bathroom. Rates include English breakfast. No credit cards. Closed Nov–Feb. **Amenities:** Dining room; lounge. *In room:* No phone.

WHERE TO DINE

Chez Michel FRENCH The finest dining outside the hotels is found at this warm and cozy 24-seat restaurant. The cooks emphasize fresh ingredients, whatever the season. In the heart of town, the restaurant is licensed to sell beer and wine. Lunches are fairly light, including such standards as a Cornish crab sandwich or a fresh lobster salad made from seafood harvested right off the shores. At night the fare is more elaborate. Count on such delights as Cornish beef filet with a white mushroom sauce or baked and crusted fresh sea bass. The breast of duckling with cranberry sauce is another tasty treat.

Parade, Hugh Town, St. Mary's. $\mathcal{C}$ **01720/422871.** Reservations required for dinner. Lunch £4–£7 ($6–$11); dinner £10–£15 ($16–$24). No credit cards. Easter–Sept daily 9am–1:30pm and 6:30–10pm. Off season daily 9am–1:30pm; Sat only 6:30–10pm. Closed 3 weeks late Oct to early Nov.

ST. AGNES

St. Agnes lies farther southwest than any other community in Britain and, luckily, remains relatively undiscovered. Much of the area is preserved by the Nature Conservancy Council. As the main industries are flower farming and fishing, there is little pollution; visitors can enjoy crystal-clear waters ideal for snorkeling and diving. Little traffic moves on the single-track lanes crossing the island. The curving sandbar between St. Agnes and its neighbor, Gugh, is one of the best beaches in the archipelago. The coastline is diverse and a walker's paradise. A trail leads to any number of sandy coves, granite outcroppings, flower-studded heaths and meadows, even a freshwater pool. The unfailingly romantic sunsets are followed by a brilliant showcase of stars. This is a truly soothing place of endless natural wonderment.

A boat departs from the quay at St. Mary's every day at 10:15am, 12:15pm, and 2pm, requiring a 15- to 20-minute transfer to St. Agnes, for a round-trip charge of about £5.80 ($9). Boats return on a schedule determined by the tides, usually at 2:15 and again at 4:45pm. The day's transportation schedule is chalked onto a blackboard on the quay at St. Mary's daily. Schedules usually allow you to visit St. Agnes for the day. The boats are operated by two family-run companies: Briar Boat Services (© **01720/422886**) and Hicks Boating (© **01720/422541**).

WHERE TO STAY

Coastguards 🏆   Danny and Wendy Hick's home opens onto excellent sea views from its location near St. Warna's Cove. Charles, Prince of Wales (and Duke of Cornwall) is the landlord; he makes regular visits to Scilly, which he considers a jewel in the duchy's crown. Accommodations, in two adjacent and roomy cottages, are furnished simply and pleasantly. One of the doubles has two beds. The non-smoking rooms have a shower stall; housekeeping is excellent. There's no choice on the daily menu, but special diets are catered to if advance notice is given.

St. Agnes, Isles of Scilly, Cornwall TR22 0PL. © or fax **01720/422373**. 3 units. £37.50–£40 ($60–$64) per person. Rates include breakfast and dinner. No credit cards. Closed Nov–Mar. **Amenities:** Dining room. *In room:* Coffeemaker, iron, no phone.

Covean Cottage   Built 200 years ago for a local fisher, the home of Heather and Peter Sewell is constructed of solid blocks of local granite; its slate roof shuts out the hardiest of gales. Despite a slight drabness, especially in winter, this is the first bed-and-breakfast you'll see when heading into town after your arrival at the pier. There's a garden that wraps itself around its walls; the sweeping views extend out over the sea. Like a typical cottage, each nonsmoking room is unique and blessed with character; dimensions are a bit cramped, however. Evening meals are served in a tidy dining room.

St. Agnes, Isles of Scilly, Cornwall TR22 0PL. © **01720/422620**. 4 units, 2 with bathroom. £27–£30 ($43–$48) single without bathroom; £54 ($86) double without bathroom; £65 ($104) double with bathroom. Rates include breakfast. AE, MC, V. **Amenities:** Breakfast room; pre-arranged dinner. *In room:* TV, coffeemaker, hair dryer, no phone.

WHERE TO DINE

The Turks Head ENGLISH   In a solid-looking building that was constructed in the 1890s as a boathouse, this is the only pub on the island. Prominently located a few steps from the pier, it's run by John and Pauline Dart, who serve pub snacks and solid fare, including steaks and platters of local fish. The pub is the second building after the arrival point of the ferryboats from St. Mary's. Also

---

Finds **An Idyllic, Remote Escape**

One of the loveliest beauty spots in the west of England is **St. Just in Roseland** 🏆🏆, a tiny hamlet of stone cottage terraces and a church dating from the 1200s. It's as if time stood still here. Locals call it their Garden of Eden because of its subtropical foliage including rhododendrons and magnolias. There are even palm trees. St. Just lies 14km (9 miles) south of Truro. To visit it, drive to Trelissick, 10km (6 miles) north of Falmouth on B3289. Here you can take a chain-drawn car ferry, King Harry Ferry (© **01872/862312**), making several trips daily over to the isolated Roseland Peninsula and St. Just. The cost is £3.50 ($6) per car or 20p (30¢) per foot passenger.

here is a twin-bedded room with shower and tub, costing £29 ($46) per person including breakfast.

St. Agnes, Isles of Scilly, Cornwall TR22 0PL. ⓒ **01720/422434**. Main courses £3.75–£10.95 ($6–$18). AE, MC, V. Daily noon–2:30pm and 6–9pm. Pub daily 10:30am–4:30pm and 6:30–11pm.

5 Newlyn ⟨*⟩, Mousehole ⟨*⟩ & Land's End ⟨*⟩

Newlyn: 1½km (1 mile) S of Penzance; Mousehole: 5km (3 miles) S of Penzance, 3km (2 miles) S of Newlyn; Land's End: 15km (9 miles) W of Penzance

At the western tip of some of Cornwall's most beautiful countryside, Land's End is literally the end of Britain. While the natural grandeur of the place has been marred by theme-park-type amusements, the view of sea crashing against rocks remains uncompromised. If you stay in the area, you'll find accommodations in Newlyn or Mousehole, two lovely Cornish fishing villages. If you visit in July and August, you'll need reservations far in advance, as neither village has enough bedrooms to house the summer hordes.

ESSENTIALS

GETTING THERE   From London, journey first to Penzance (see earlier in this chapter), then take a local bus for the rest of the journey (bus A to Mousehole and bus no. 1 to Land's End; a bus also runs from Penzance to the old fishing cottages and crooked lanes of Newlyn). There is frequent service throughout the day.

If you're driving from Penzance, take the B3315 south.

NEWLYN

From Penzance, a promenade leads to Newlyn, another fishing village of infinite charm on Mount's Bay. Its much-painted harbor seems to have more fishing craft than Penzance's. Painter Alexander Stanhope Forbes founded an art school in Newlyn; in the past few years the village has achieved a growing reputation for its artists' colony, attracting both serious painters and Sunday sketchers. Forbes' work is now in demand, as is that of his wife, Elizabeth Adela Forbes, and other artists from the "Newlyn school."

WHERE TO STAY & DINE

Carn Du Hotel   Twin bay windows gaze over the top of the village onto the harbor with its bobbing fishing vessels. The hotel's rooms (all doubles or twins) offer much comfort. Five rooms were recently redecorated. Most units have a shower stall, although two come with a tub-and-shower combination. The owners will arrange sporting options for active vacationers, but won't mind if you prefer to sit and relax.

Raginnis Hill, Mousehole, Cornwall TR19 6SS. ⓒ and fax **01736/731233**. 7 units. £28 ($45) single; £56–£76 ($90–$122) double. Rates include English breakfast. AE, MC, V. Take B3315 from Newlyn past the village of Sheffield (2.4km/1½ miles) and bear left toward Castallack; after a few hundred meters, turn left to Mousehole, which is signposted; coming down the hill, the Carn Du is on the left facing the sea. **Amenities:** Dining room; bar; lounge. *In room:* TV, coffeemaker, hair dryer.

MOUSEHOLE

Located in a sheltered cove of Mount's Bay, the fishing village of Mousehole (*Mou*-sel) attracts hordes of tourists who fortunately haven't changed it much. Cottages still sit close to the harbor wall, fishers bring in the day's catch, salts sit around smoking tobacco and talking about the good old days, and the lanes are as narrow as ever. The most exciting thing ever to happen here was the

Fun Fact **Cornwall's Geodesic Domed Eden**

At first you think some space ship filled with aliens has invaded sleepy old Cornwall. A second look reveals one of England's newest and most dramatic attractions, the **Eden Project**, Bodelva, St. Austell (© **01726/ 811911**; www.edenproject.com), a 48km (30-mile) drive west of Plymouth. This sprawling attraction presents plants from the world over on 50 hectares (125 acres) of a former clay quarry. One of the two conservatories is nearly 2 hectares (4 acres) in dimension, reaching 54m (180 ft.) high, housing tropical plants from some of the world's rain forests, including the Amazon. The smaller dome, covering 1 hectare (1½ acres), grows plants from everywhere from California to South Africa. A roofless biome houses plants that thrive in the Cornish climate, including species from everywhere from India to Chile. The site takes in a small lake and offers a 2,300-seat amphitheater where special shows are staged. Within this biome is also a giant global garden planted in a crater. The crater is totally hidden from view until you walk through the visitor center, which is on the lip of the pit.

Open from late March to late October, daily from 10am to 6pm, and from November to late March, daily from 10am to 4:30pm. Admission is £9.80 ($16) for adults, £7.50 ($12) for seniors, £5 ($8) for students, £4 ($6) for children 5 to 15, or £23 ($37) for a family ticket. The project lies 9.5km (6 miles) from the St. Austell train station, to which it is linked by frequent buses.

arrival in the late 16th century of Spanish galleons, whose sailors sacked and burned the village. Today Mousehole has become the nucleus of an artists' colony.

WHERE TO STAY

Lamorna Cove Hotel ⭐ Near one of the most perfect coves in Cornwall, the Lamorna sits 8km (5 miles) south of Penzance on a winding, narrow road. This 19th-century private home was skillfully terraced into a series of rocky ledges that drop down to the sea. Its rocky garden clings to the cliff sides and surrounds a small swimming pool and sun terrace overlooking the sea. A lift is available. The small to medium-size rooms, all with sea views, are constantly being upgraded; each is furnished in a lovely old-fashioned way with a compact private bathroom with tub and shower. Smoking is not permitted. The dining room is in the old chapel; a public lounge is furnished with comfortable chairs, centered around a wintertime log fire, with pictures and antiques.

Lamorna Cove, Penzance, Cornwall TR19 6XH. © **01736/731411**. www.lamornacove.com. 12 units. £80 ($128) per person. MC, V. Closed Nov–Feb. Take a taxi from Penzance. Children not permitted. **Amenities:** Restaurant; bar; sun terrace; room service; laundry. *In room:* TV, dataport, coffeemaker, hair dryer, trouser press.

Renovelle At the edge of the village, just past the large parking area, is a pretty blue-and-white villa on a cliff beside the sea. Mrs. Edwina Reynolds, the owner, has made the nonsmoking inn so inviting that guests keep returning. Each small bedroom is comfortable, with good views of the sea; all are equipped with a private shower-only bathroom. It's a pleasure to have breakfast set before you in the sunny little dining room.

6 The Parade, Mousehole, Cornwall TR19 6PN. ☎ 01736/731258. 3 units. £17 ($27) per person. Rates include English breakfast. No credit cards. **Amenities:** Breakfast room; TV; lounge. *In room:* Coffeemaker, hair dryer, no phone.

The Ship Inn   This charming pub is located on the harbor. Its stone facade and interior have retained much of the original rustic charm with black beams and paneling, granite floors, built-in wall benches, and, of course, a nautical motif decorating the bars. The smallish but comfortable rooms, each a double, have window seats and offer views of the harbor and the bay. The nonsmoking rooms are simply furnished with floral chintz fabrics and have compact bathrooms with a shower stall.

S. Cliff, Mousehole, Penzance, Cornwall TR19 6QX. ☎ 01736/731234. 3 units. £27.50 ($44) single; £55 ($88) double. Rates include English breakfast. AE, MC, V. **Amenities:** Restaurant; 2 bars. *In room:* TV, coffeemaker, hair dryer, no phone.

WHERE TO DINE

Pam's Pantry SEAFOOD   This small and cheerful cafe on the main road features fish caught locally. You can order crab salad (a summer favorite) or smoked mackerel. To complete a meal, a homemade apple pie with clotted cream is served. You can also order sandwiches to go and pizzas. Come here more for convenience than for subtle flavors or spicing.

3 Mill Lane. ☎ 01736/731532. Main courses £4.25–£8.50 ($7–$14). No credit cards. Daily 9am–6:30pm.

LAND'S END

Craggy Land's End is where England runs out of ground. America's coast is 5,296km (3,291 miles) west of the rugged rocks that tumble into the sea here. Some enjoyable cliff walks and panoramic views are available.

WHERE TO STAY

The Old Success Inn   This 17th-century fisherman's inn faces the sea and wide sandy beaches. Waves roll in from the Atlantic almost to the foot of the seawall beneath it. The inn has been extended and modernized, and now offers bright, small clean rooms mainly with private, shower-only bathrooms. There are 12 regular rooms, 11 of them with private bathroom, plus three self-catering apartments (these are booked by Brits for longer stays). A comfortable lounge with a color TV has panoramic views of the Atlantic.

Sennen Cove, Land's End, Cornwall TR19 7DG. ☎ 01736/871232. Fax 01736/871457. www.oldsuccess.com. 15 units, 14 with bathroom. £42 ($67) per person. Rates include English breakfast. AE, DC, MC, V. Bus: 1. Turn right and follow the road down to Sennen Cove just before you reach Land's End. The inn is at the bottom. **Amenities:** Restaurant; bar; lounge. *In room:* TV, dataport, coffeemaker, hair dryer.

Fun Fact **The End of the Earth**

To ancient Cornish mariners, it was known as *Pen an Wlas* or "the end of the earth," a reference to what is today **Land's End,** the most westerly point on the British mainland. It is at the very tip of the granite peninsula of Penwith, one of the ancient kingdoms of Cornwall. The nearest town to Land's End is Penzance, 16km (10 miles) away. The A30 ends its run at Land's Inn, which is 1,407km (874 miles) from John O'Groats, which is the most northerly point of Britain, lying in Scotland.

> **Tips** **When to Visit St. Ives**
>
> St. Ives becomes virtually impossible to visit in August, when you're likely to be trampled underfoot by busloads of tourists, mostly the English themselves. However, in spring and early fall the pace is much more relaxed, and a visitor can truly experience the art colony.

Super-Cheap Sleeps: A Youth Hostel

Land's End Youth Hostel This inviting youth hostel, one of the most remote but dramatically situated in southwest England, lies outside the town of St. Just, 8km (5 miles) from Land's End. In the old Cornish style, it's reached by going down a rock-strewn road through meadowland with grazing cows. Although a bit country-crude, it's welcoming. Young people from the world over meet in the public areas—gathering around the fireplace on a windy and rain-swept night, or retreating to the conservatory with views of the often turbulent Atlantic. The very basic and modest bedrooms are well kept. There's a self-catering kitchen, although good homemade meals are also served. There's more of the warmth of a cozy B&B or a small inn here than in your typical impersonal youth hostel.

Letcha Vean, Cot Valley, St. Just, Penzance, Cornwall TR19 7NT. ✆ 01736/788437. Fax 01736/787337. 43 beds. £12.50 ($20) adults, £9 ($14) 18 or under. MC, V. Closed Nov to mid-Feb. **Amenities:** Dining room. *In room:* No phone.

WHERE TO DINE

The King's Arm ENGLISH The oldest pub in St. Just stands in the center of town. It's the best place for low-cost food in the Land's End area. A pub has stood on this site since 1700; some recipes haven't changed much since. Begin with a glass of a local cask ale pumped directly "from the wood," as they say here. You can get steaks, roast, and perhaps fresh crab sandwiches in summer. The kitchen is proud of their Cornish pasties. To go really local at lunch, order the ploughman's lunch with smoked mackerel.

5 Market Sq., St. Just. ✆ 01736/788545. Main courses £4–£10 ($6–$16). No credit cards. Daily 11am–11pm.

6 The Artists' Colony of St. Ives ⓕ

510km (319 miles) SW of London; 34km (21 miles) NE of Land's End; 16km (10 miles) NE of Penzance

This north-coast fishing village, with its sandy beaches, narrow streets, and well-kept cottages, is England's most famous artists' colony. The artists settled in many years ago and have integrated with the fishers and their families. St. Ives artists live and create their art at studios or cottages throughout the town.

Artists here have developed several schools or "splits," and they almost never overlap—except in a pub where artists hang out or when classes are held. The old battle continues between advocates of representational and abstract art, with each group recruiting young artists all the time. There are also potters, weavers, and other craftspeople who work, exhibit, and sell in this area.

ESSENTIALS

GETTING THERE There is frequent service throughout the day between London's Paddington Station and the rail terminal at St. Ives. The trip takes 8 hours and 20 minutes. Call ✆ 0845/7484950 for schedules and information.

Several coaches a day run from London's Victoria Coach Station to St. Ives. The trip takes 7 hours. Call ℂ **0870/5808080** for schedules and information.

If you're driving, take the A30 across Cornwall, heading northwest at the junction with the B3306, heading to St. Ives on the coast. During the summer, many streets in the center of town are closed to vehicles. You may want to leave your car in the Lelant Saltings Car Park, 5km (3 miles) from St. Ives on the A3074, and take the regular train service into town, an 11-minute journey. Departures are every half-hour. It's free to all car passengers and drivers, and the parking charge is £8 to £10.50 ($13–$17) per day. You can also use the large Trenwith Car Park, close to the town center, for £1.50 ($2.40), and then walk down to the shops and harbor or take a bus that costs 40p (65¢) per person.

VISITOR INFORMATION   The **Tourist Information Centre** is at the Guildhall, Street-an-Pol (ℂ **01736/796297**). From January to mid-May and from September to December, hours are Monday to Friday from 9am to 5pm, and Saturday from 10am to 4pm. From mid-May to August, hours are Monday through Saturday from 9am to 6pm and Sunday from 10am to 4pm.

SEEING THE SIGHTS

Tate Gallery St. Ives ★★   This branch of London's famous gallery boasts a spectacular site overlooking Porthmear Beach, close to the home of Alfred Wallis and to studios used by other St. Ives artists. The gallery exhibits changing groups of about 100 works from the Tate's preeminent collection of St. Ives painting and sculpture from about 1925 to 1975. The gallery is administered jointly with the Barbara Hepworth Museum (see below). The collection includes works by Wallis, Hepworth, Ben Nicholson, Naum Gabo, Peter Lanyon, Terry Frost, Patrick Heron, and Roger Hilton. All the artists on exhibit here had a decisive effect on the development of painting in the United Kingdom in the second half of the 20th century.

Porthmear Beach. ℂ **01736/796226.** www.tate.org.uk. Admission £4.25 ($7) adults, £2.50 ($4) students, free for seniors and children under 18. Mar–Oct daily 10am–5:30pm; Nov–Feb Tues–Sun 10am–4:30pm. Closes occasionally to change displays; call for dates.

Barbara Hepworth Museum and Garden ★   Dame Barbara Hepworth lived at Trewyn Studio from 1949 until her death in 1975 at age 72. In her will she asked that her home be turned into a museum. The museum and garden are virtually just as she left them. On display are about 47 sculptures and drawings, covering her work from 1928 to 1974, as well as photographs, documents, and other Hepworth memorabilia. You can visit her workshops, housing a selection of tools and unfinished carvings. The gallery is administered jointly with the Tate Gallery St. Ives (see above).

Barnoon Hill. ℂ **01736/796226.** Admission £4 ($6) adults, £2 ($3.20) students, free for seniors and children under 18. Mar–Oct daily 10am–5:30pm; Nov–Feb Tues–Sun 10am–4:30pm.

WHERE TO STAY

Hobblers House   This black-and-white building is right on the harborside, next to a surf shop. The house was built in the 17th century as a pilot's house. Renting rooms seems a secondary objective here; most of the attention focuses on operating the profitable restaurant below. Bedrooms—all doubles—are small but quite adequate; each is well maintained and simply furnished. It's tough to get a room here in high season, and one downside of this place is that you'll have to find a parking spot in St. Ives, which can sometimes be difficult. See our review of the restaurant under "Where to Dine," below.

Wharf Rd., St. Ives, Cornwall TR26 1LR. ☎ **01736/796439.** www.hobblers.co.uk. 3 units, none with bathroom. £45 ($72) double. Rates include English breakfast. AE, DC, MC, V. Closed Jan to 2 weeks before Easter. **Amenities:** Restaurant; bar. *In room:* TV, no phone.

Hollies Hotel Only a 5-minute walk from Porthminster Beach, the house is built of gray granite with a slate roof, in a row of about a dozen similar semidetached homes constructed a century ago. Much of this hotel's charm comes from its Anglo-American owners, John and Beverly Dowland, who seem to enjoy what they're doing. Many of the midsize bedrooms open onto views of the water; several are large enough to shelter families comfortably. In a pine-paneled dining room, guests enjoy a freshly cooked breakfast.

4 Talland Rd., St. Ives, Cornwall TR26 2DF. ☎ and fax **01736/796605.** www.hollieshotel.freeserve.co.uk. 10 units. £20–£29 ($32–$46) per person. Rates include English breakfast. MC, V. **Amenities:** Breakfast room; bar; lounge. *In room:* TV, coffeemaker, no phone.

The Old Vicarage Hotel ★ This Victorian house is .75km (½ mile) from the heart of the resort area off St. Ives/Land's End Road, away from the bustling tourist activity at the harbor. This is one of the most desirable of the area's B&Bs, offering nonsmoking rooms, all doubles, in a variety of sizes, substantially furnished in Victorian mode and equipped with private shower-only bathrooms for the most part. Guests meet for drinks in the bar or enjoy one of the books from the library/lounge.

Parc-an-Creet, St. Ives, Cornwall TR26 2ES. ☎ **01736/796124.** Fax 01736/796343. www.oldvicaragehotel.com. 8 units. £28 ($45) per person. Rates include English breakfast. MC, V. Closed Oct–Easter. **Amenities:** Breakfast room; bar; lounge. *In room:* TV, coffeemaker, hair dryer, no phone.

The Pondarosa *Value* This nonsmoking Edwardian house offers good value for the money. It sits in a prominent location near the harbor and Porthminster Beach; two private parking areas adjoin the house. The functionally furnished small rooms have recently been upgraded; they have private shower-only bathrooms. Patricia Tyldesley, the owner, will prepare an evening meal of good quality if notified.

10 Porthminster Terrace, St. Ives, Cornwall TR26 2DQ. ☎ **01736/795875.** Fax 01736/797811. 11 units. £25–£32 ($40–$51) single; £52–£64 ($83–$102) double. Rates include English breakfast. MC, V. **Amenities:** Breakfast room; bar; lounge. *In room:* TV, coffeemaker, hair dryer, no phone.

Primrose Valley Hotel This is one of the first hotels to be built in the region a century ago. Half of it burned down in the 1960s. Today, much repaired, it enjoys a sunny and relatively isolated position in a verdant valley, a 10-minute walk north of the town center, near Porthminster Beach and a putting green. The traditionally furnished and good-size nonsmoking bedrooms are comfortable, each with a private, shower-only bathroom. Cream teas are served in clement weather on a wide patio. The place is more solid and reliable than exciting. Children are welcome.

Primrose Valley Hill, St. Ives, Cornwall TR26 2ED. ☎ **01736/794939.** www.primroseonline.co.uk. 10 units. £35–£60 ($56–$96) single; £50–£86 ($80–$138) double. Rates include English breakfast. AE, MC, V. Closed Dec–Jan (but open Christmas Day and New Year's Day). Approach the hotel from A3074 and turn right down Primrose Valley Hill. **Amenities:** Restaurant; bar. *In room:* TV, coffeemaker, hair dryer, no phone.

WHERE TO DINE

Hobblers Restaurant SEAFOOD This previously recommended guesthouse is located on the harbor, a 5-minute walk from the Tate Gallery. The paneled rooms are decorated with pictures of ships and seascapes; it's cramped, nautical, and intimate. You can order old-style English sea-resort cookery, everything seemingly accompanied by chips and frozen peas. Dishes include scallops, halibut, scampi, and plaice, with mussels and lobster bisque as starters. You might order the chicken Kiev or a filet steak as an alternative.

The Wharf. ✆ **01736/796439**. Main courses £8–£13.50 ($13–$22). AE, DC, MC, V. Daily 6–10:30pm. Closed Jan–Mar.

The Sloop Inn ENGLISH/INTERNATIONAL   Proud of its long history (it dates back to at least 1312), this stone-and-slate building contains one of the busiest and most visible pubs in St. Ives, located on the harborfront in the town center. Most clients come to drink at one of the three different bar areas amid comfortably battered furnishings. If you're hungry, however, place your order at one of the bars and someone will bring your food to your table. Menu items include ploughman's lunches, platters of roast chicken or ham, sandwiches, chili, fish and chips, bangers and mash, and lasagna. The aim seems more to fill you up rather than tantalize your palate.

The Wharf. ✆ **01736/796584**. Bar meals £3.50–£7.95 ($6–$13). DC, MC, V. Daily noon–3pm and 5–9pm. Pub: Mon–Sat 11am–11pm; Sun noon–10:30pm.

Woodcote Hotel *(Finds* VEGETARIAN   Located 5km (3 miles) from St. Ives at the edge of a bird sanctuary and saltwater estuary, the Woodcote, Britain's first veg-etarian hotel, accepts fill-in bookings from nonresidents if space is available. Typi-cal dishes include lentil-and-cumin soup, eggplant goulash with chickpeas and wild rice, and treacle and ginger tart for dessert. The kitchen uses eggs but no fish.

The Saltings, Lelant. ✆ **01736/753147**. Reservations required. Main courses £6–£9.50 ($10–$15); fixed-price 5-course dinner £16.50 ($26). No credit cards. Dinner served around 6:30–7pm for hotel guests; nonguests welcome according to availability. Closed Nov to mid-Mar. The Hoppa bus makes frequent trips from St. Ives, or take the local scenic rail line.

7 Port Isaac ⭐

436km (266 miles) SW of London; 22km (14 miles) SW of Tintagel; 15km (9 miles) N of Wadebridge

Port Isaac is the most unspoiled fishing village on the north Cornish coastline, in spite of many summer visitors. By all means, wander through its winding, nar-row lanes, gazing at the whitewashed fishing cottages with their rainbow trims.

ESSENTIALS
GETTING THERE   Bodmin is the nearest railway station. It lies on the main line from London (Paddington Station) to Penzance (about a 4–4½ hr. trip). Call ✆ **0845/7484950**. Many hotels will send a car to pick you up at the Bod-min station, or you can take a taxi. If you take a bus from Bodmin, you'll have to change buses at Wadebridge, and connections are not good. Driving time from Bodmin to Port Isaac is 40 minutes.

A bus to Wadebridge goes to Port Isaac about six times a day. It's maintained by the Prout Brothers Bus Co. Wadebridge is a local bus junction to many other places in the rest of England.

If you're driving from London, take M4 west, then drive south on M5. Head west again at the junction with A39, continuing to the junction with B3267, which you follow until you reach the signposted cutoff for Port Isaac.

WHERE TO STAY
Castle Rock Hotel ⭐   The most desirable accommodation in Port Isaac, this lovingly cared-for, cream-colored house is adjacent to the town's main parking area, a short walk northwest of the center. Built in the 1920s, it has a panoramic

view of the Cornish coast up to Tintagel. The nonsmoking bedrooms come in various sizes and shapes, each with a private, shower-only or shower-and-tub combination bathroom. The good food served here is part of the Castle Rock's attraction.

4 New Rd., Port Isaac, Cornwall PL29 3SB. ℃ **01208/880300.** Fax 01208/880219. www.castlerockhotel.co.uk. 17 units. £30–£40 ($48–$64) per person. Rates include English breakfast. AE, MC, V. **Amenities:** Restaurant; bar; lounge; laundry. *In room:* TV, dataport, coffeemaker, hair dryer.

The Slipway Hotel ★ *(Kids)*   Originally built in 1527, with major additions made in the early 1700s, this waterside building has seen more uses than any other structure in town, serving as everything from fishing cottages to the headquarters of the first bank here. The building was once a lifeboat station for rescuing sailors stranded on stormy seas. The bedrooms—all doubles—are cozy, with comfortable beds and compact bathrooms with shower stalls or tubs. The Lifeboat Suite above the boathouse is ideal for a family, as it has two bedrooms, a separate bathroom, and a large lounge overlooking the quay.

The Harbour Front, Port Isaac, Cornwall PL29 3RH. ℃ **01208/880264.** www.portisaac.com. 12 units, 10 with bathroom. £56 ($90) double without bathroom; £90 ($144) double with bathroom; £120 ($192) suite. Rates include English breakfast. AE, MC, V. Closed Jan to mid-Feb. **Amenities:** Restaurant; bar; guest lounge. *In room:* TV, coffeemaker, hair dryer.

WHERE TO DINE

Golden Lion ENGLISH/SEAFOOD/INTERNATIONAL   Close to the harbor's edge, this structure is from the 17th century when it first opened as a eating house and pub. Behind thick stone walls you'll find a street-level bar, with windows opening out over the water, and a basement-level bistro. You can order chili, lasagna, or sandwiches at the bar, or head to the bistro for more formal meals including steaks, shellfish, and fresh crab in butter sauce. The mostly standard fare resembles a Cornish family's evening meal.

Fore St. ℃ **01208/880336.** Reservations recommended for the bistro. Main courses £5.75–£12 ($9–$19); pub snacks £1.75–£6 ($2.80–$10). AE, MC, V. Mon–Sat noon–2:30pm and 6:30–9:30pm; Sun noon–2:30pm and 6:30–9pm. Pub hours: Mon–Sat 11:30am–11pm; Sun noon–10:30pm.

8 Tintagel Castle ★★: King Arthur's Legendary Lair

422km (264 miles) SW of London; 78km (49 miles) NW of Plymouth

On a wild stretch of the Atlantic coast, Tintagel is forever linked with the legends of King Arthur, Lancelot, and Merlin. So compelling was this legend that medieval writers treated it as a tale of chivalry, even though any historical Arthur would have lived around the time of the Roman or Saxon invasions. Further speculations: Arthur might have been a warlord, not a king; his reign might have lasted 3 decades; he may have led native Britons in fighting off the Saxons. (The legend gained considerable credibility in Aug 1998 when a stone bearing a Latin inscription referring to King Arthur was uncovered at the ancient ruined castle in Tintagel, where he was supposedly born. The piece of slate, 14-in.-by-10-in., was found in a drain. For Arthur fans this is the find of a lifetime, sufficient to verify the existence of the king.)

Despite the Arthurian legend's universal adoption throughout Europe, it initially developed in Wales and southern England. The story was polished and given a literary form by Geoffrey of Monmouth around 1135. Borrowing and combining Celtic myth and Christian and classical symbolism, Geoffrey forged a fictional history of Britain whose form, shape, and elevated values were centered around the mythical king. Dozens of other storytellers subsequently embellished written and oral versions of the tale.

The Arthurian legend has captured the imagination of the British people like no other. Arthur supposedly lies sleeping at the ruined castle at Tintagel, ready to arise and save Britain in its greatest need. Sir Thomas Mallory's retelling has become the classic, but there have been others: Edmund Spenser in the Tudor period; John Milton in the 17th century; Tennyson, William Morris, and Swinburne in the Victorian age; and T. H. White and C. S. Lewis in the 20th century (not to mention numerous film treatments).

The 13th-century ruins of the castle that stand here—built on the foundations of a Celtic monastery from the 6th century—are popularly known as King Arthur's Castle. They stand 90m (300 ft.) above the sea on a rocky promontory, and to get to them you must take a long, steep, tortuous walk from the parking lot. In summer, many visitors make the ascent to Arthur's Lair, up 100 rock-cut steps. You can also visit Merlin's Cave at low tide.

The castle is 1km (½ mile) northwest of Tintagel. It's open April through October daily from 10am to 6pm (mid-July to mid-Aug until 7pm); November through March daily from 10am to 4pm. Admission is £3.20 ($5) for adults, £2.40 ($3.85) for students and seniors, and £1.60 ($2.55) for children. For information, call © **01840/770328;** www.english-heritage.org.uk.

ESSENTIALS

GETTING THERE   The nearest railway station is in Bodmin, which lies on the main rail line from London to Penzance. From Bodmin, you'll have to drive or take a taxi for 30 minutes to get to Tintagel (there's no bus service from Bodmin to Tintagel). For railway inquiries, call © **0845/7484950.**

By bus, you'll travel from London to Plymouth. One bus a day travels from Plymouth to Tintagel, at 4:20pm, but it takes twice the time (2 hr.) required for a private car, because the bus stops at dozens of small hamlets along the way. For bus schedule information, call © **01209/719988.**

If you're driving, from Exeter, head across Cornwall on the A30, continuing west at the junction with the A395. From this highway, various secondary roads lead to Tintagel.

VISITOR INFORMATION   In Truro, the **Municipal Building,** Boscawen Street (© **01872/274555**), has tourist information and is open from Easter to November, Monday through Friday from 9am to 5:30pm, and Saturday from 9am to 5pm; from November to Easter, it's Monday through Friday from 9am to 5pm.

WHERE TO STAY & DINE IN & AROUND TINTAGEL

Manor Farm   This farmhouse, owned by Mr. and Mrs. Knight, is recorded in the Domesday Book. The present structure may date back to the 12th century; most of it is from the 16th century. On 12 hectares (30 acres), this stone edifice sports a slate roof with wooden beams scattered throughout the interior. Bedrooms are country comfortable, each with a private, shower-only bathroom. Although the house is centrally heated, fires are lit during the winter on exceptionally cold days. Meals are communal. This is a nonsmoking facility.

Crackington Haven, near Bude, Cornwall EX23 0JW. © **01840/230304.** 5 units. £40 ($64) single; £70 ($112) double. Rates include English breakfast. No credit cards. **Amenities:** Dining room; bar; lounge. *In room:* No phone.

Old Borough House   Run by the Dale family, this house is made of thick stone walls, small windows, low ceiling beams, and has an illustrious history dating to 1558. Most of what still stands was completed by the late 1600s, when it served as home for the mayor of Bossiney, who Sir Francis Drake briefly represented in Parliament. The nonsmoking bedrooms are cozy, low ceilinged, antique, and very comfortable; many have been recently refurbished and upgraded. One room is available for those with limited mobility. Bathrooms are tidily kept and compact. If you request in advance, affordable evening meals are available.

Bossiney, Tintagel, Cornwall PL34 0AY. © **01840/770475.** Fax 01840/779000. theoldboroughhouse@hotmail. com. 4 units. £40 ($64) single; £65 ($104) double. Rates include English breakfast. MC, V. Walk north from the ruins of Tintagel Castle for 10 min. **Amenities:** Dining room; bar; lounge. *In room:* TV, coffeemaker, hair dryer, no phone.

Trevigue Farm ★ *Finds*   Owned by the National Trust, this working dairy farm, whose tenants are Ken and Janet Crocker, is located cliff-side, offering access to a beach called The Strangles, where swimming is best experienced during a rising tide. The nonsmoking hotel is housed in two stone buildings: two bedrooms in the 16th-century farmhouse and two in a separate house with views of a wooded valley. Accommodations are cozy and tidy, each with a private shower bathroom or tub. Although only two bedrooms contain TVs, there is a cozy sitting room with television for all guests to enjoy, a log fire, and a wealth of books. Meals feature English fare with international touches.

Crackington Haven, Bude, Cornwall EX23 0LQ. ©/fax **01840/230418.** www.trevigue.co.uk. 3 units. £60–£68 ($96–$109) double. Rates include English breakfast. MC, V. Closed Dec 25. No children under 10. **Amenities:** Restaurant; lounge. *In room:* TV, coffeemaker, no phone.

11

The Cotswolds

Lying between Oxford and the River Severn, 2 hours west of London by car, the pastoral Cotswolds occupy a stretch of grassy limestone hills, deep ravines, and barren plateaus known as wolds, Old English for "God's high open land." Ancient villages with names like Stow-on-the-Wold, Wotton-under-Edge, and Moreton-in-Marsh dot this bucolic area; most of it is in Gloucestershire, with portions in Oxfordshire, Wiltshire, and Worcestershire.

Made rich by wool from their sheep, Cotswold landowners invested in some of the finest domestic architecture in Europe, distinctively built of honey-brown Cotswold stone. The gentry didn't neglect their spiritual duties, either; some of the simplest hamlets have churches that, in style and architectural detail, seem far beyond their means.

Thatched cottages in the Cotswolds, fiercely protected by local bylaws, are endlessly impractical because of their need for frequent repair, maintenance, and replacement. (Their fire insurance costs a fortune!) More common are the Cotswolds roof shingles fashioned from split slabs of stone, requiring massive buttressing as a means of supporting the roof's weight. Buildings erected since the 1700s, however, usually have slate roofs.

You'll really want to rent a car and drive through the Cotswolds at your own pace. This way, you can spend hours viewing the land of winding goat paths, rolling hills, and sleepy hamlets. Another reason to visit the Cotswolds is to take advantage of its natural beauty. Play a round of golf on a scenic course, go fishing, or, better yet, take a ramble across a meadow where sheep graze or alongside a fast-flowing stream.

Mobbed by tourists, the town of Broadway, with its 16th-century stone houses and cottages, is the most popular base for touring this area, but we suggest you also head for Bibury, Painswick, or other small villages to capture the true charm of the Cotswolds. Cheltenham, once a very fashionable spa, boasts a wealth of Regency architecture; you'll find the widest range of hotels and facilities here. In Birdland, in Bourton-on-the-Water, you can see 1,200 birds of 361 different species.

BIKING & HIKING THROUGH THE COTSWOLDS

Biking the country roads of the Cotswolds is one of the best ways to experience the quiet beauty of the area. **Country Lanes,** 9 Shaftesbury St., Fordingbridge, Hampshire SP6 1JF (© **01425/655022**), offers visitors that opportunity.

The company rents 21-speed bicycles fully equipped with mudguards, a water bottle, lock and key, a rear carrier rack, and safety helmets.

Their recommended day trips are self-guided, so you can ride at your own pace. You'll get an easy-to-follow route sheet. As you explore, you'll pass manor farms and pretty cottages of honey-colored stone. Several villages are also on the path, and the Hidcote Manor Garden is a perfect spot to relax if your legs tire of pedaling. The 16km, 32km, or 45km (10-, 20-, or 28-mile) trips end at the Café Dijon, where you're served afternoon tea in the garden. The £25 ($40)

Value   Cheap Thrills: What to See & Do for Free (or Almost) in the Cotswolds

Motor through the Cotswolds. Few experiences in England are as intriguing as wandering leisurely along the hilly country lanes of the old honey-colored villages of the Cotswolds, once England's premier wool district. "Motoring" in Britain means "driving without a specific target." You can deliberately get lost making your way from village green to village green, from Bourton-on-the-Water to Upper Slaughter.

Share a pint at the Lygon Arms. In the enchanting Cotswold town of Broadway, there is no finer place for a drink than at the pub of the 16th-century ivy-covered Lygon Arms on High Street (☎ 01386/852255). Drop in for a beer, as did both Charles I and Oliver Cromwell before you.

Go antiquing in the "Wolds." One of the pleasures of the Cotswolds is to drive down the back roads and stop in to browse the little antiques shops often hidden away. Stroll, search, and munch an ice-cream cone as you look over the bric-a-brac in villages and market towns such as Burford.

"Take the Waters" at Cheltenham. Many have come here to partake of the only potable alkaline water in Britain. The crazed George III took the waters in 1788. The duke of Wellington tasted, and later claimed they cured his "disordered liver." Give them a try even if nothing ails you; their diuretic and laxative effects have been widely hailed. Head for the Town Hall Monday to Friday 9am to 1pm and 2:15 to 5pm. Tasting is free.

Spend a morning at Chipping Campden. If your time is limited, and you want to see a perfect example of a honey-colored stone village, make it pristine Chipping Campden. The town's 15th-century Church of St. James is one of the finest in the Cotswolds. To top your morning, climb Dover's Hill overlooking the town; this is the finest view over the Vale of Evesham.

Walk the Cotswolds. Except perhaps for the Lake District, the gentle country lanes of the Cotswolds are the best in England for walks. Every tourist center has information and maps regarding the finest walks. Some of the most rewarding are along riverside towpaths; many of the stone villages were built along these rivers, and the paths are scenically interesting and easy to follow. See also "Hiking the Cotswold Way," below.

price includes everything listed above. Advanced booking by credit card is essential; call ☎ 01608/650065.

This is also one of the most famous regions of England for hiking. With such a large area in which to ramble, it's a good idea to know where you are (and aren't) welcome. The **Cotswold Voluntary Wardens Service,** Shire Hall, Gloucester (☎ 01451/862000), offers free brochures highlighting trails and paths.

If you'd like to walk and explore on your own without a guide, you can get data from the **Cheltenham Tourist Information Centre** (☎ 01242/522878). The center sells a Cotswold Way map.

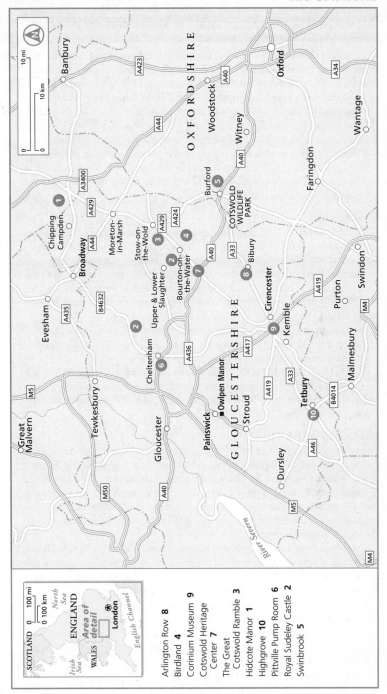

The Cotswolds

Arlington Row **8**
Birdland **4**
Corinium Museum **9**
Cotswold Heritage
Center **7**
The Great
Cotswold Ramble **3**
Hidcote Manor **1**
Highgrove **10**
Pittville Pump Room **6**
Royal Sudeley Castle **2**
Swinbrook **5**

1 Tetbury

181km (113 miles) W of London; 43km (27 miles) NE of Bristol

In the rolling Cotswolds, Tetbury was out of the tourist mainstream until the heir to the British throne and his beautiful bride took up residence at the Macmillan Place, a Georgian building on nearly 140 hectares (350 acres) nearby. Then, crowds came here to catch a glimpse of Prince Charles riding horses and Princess Di shopping. (Today, folks keep an eye out for Charles and Camilla Parker-Bowles, who are occasionally spotted driving by en route to their homes.) Though it can't be seen from the road, the nine-bedroom Windsor mansion, **Highgrove,** is 2.5km (1½ miles) southwest of Tetbury on the way to Westonbirt Arboretum.

Tetbury itself has a 17th-century market hall and a number of antiques shops and boutiques. The town's inns weren't cheap before royalty moved in, and the prices certainly have not dropped since then.

ESSENTIALS

GETTING THERE   Frequent daily trains run from London's Paddington Station to Kemble, 11km (7 miles) east of Tetbury. For more information and schedules, call ✆ **0845/7484950.** You can then take a bus from there to Tetbury.

National Express buses leave London's Victoria Coach Station with direct service to Cirencester, 16km (10 miles) northeast of Tetbury. For information, call ✆ **020/7529-2000;** www.gobycoach.com. Several buses a day connect Cirencester to Tetbury.

If you're driving from London, take the M40 northwest to Oxford, continuing along the A40 to the junction with the A429. Drive south to Cirencester, where you connect with the A433 southwest into Tetbury.

VISITOR INFORMATION   The **Tourist Information Centre,** 33 Church St. (✆ **01666/503552**), is open March through October, Monday through Saturday from 9:30am to 4:30pm, and November through February, Monday through Saturday from 10am to 1pm.

EXPLORING THE TOWN

Everything in Tetbury is located in the village's center; spend a morning wandering in and out of the many antiques shops and gazing up at the old houses.

The **Parish Church of St. Mary the Virgin,** built between 1777 and 1781, is considered the best Georgian Gothic church in England; the spire is among the country's tallest. Extensive restoration work has returned the interior to its original look. For more information, call ✆ **01666/502333;** it's quite possible the vicar himself will answer.

One of the finest Cotswold-pillared market houses is the **1655 Market House of Tetbury.** Still in use, it hosts one of the region's most interesting markets in the antiques stalls of its oak-beamed meeting hall. Try to schedule a Wednesday visit here; you never know where some of that bric-a-brac may be from.

After the market, head for **Chipping Steps.** The Chipping (market) was for centuries the site of "mop fairs," where farmhands and domestic staff offered themselves for employment. Many of the surrounding buildings have medieval origins; in the northeast corner, steep cobbled steps and weavers' cottages retain a delightful atmosphere.

Another place to explore is **Gumstoll Hill,** one of Tetbury's most ancient streets and famous for its annual Woolsack Races. Legend has it that at the bottom of the hill, there was a pool where scolding wives and other miscreants were tied to a ducking stool and plunged underwater for punishment.

The **Police Bygones Museum,** Old Court House, 63 Long St., situated in the former police station and magistrates court, is worth a peek. The old cells house a collection of relics from centuries of Cotswold law enforcement. The location and hours are the same as the Tourist Information Centre (see above).

Chavenage House   Aside from its fine Cromwell-era tapestries, furniture, and artifacts, this Elizabethan country house is worth a visit for its history and legends. Col. Nathaniel Stephens, who owned the house during the English Civil War, was persuaded by Cromwell, a relative by marriage, to vote for the impeachment of Charles I. This so angered Stephens's daughter that she cursed him. Soon after, Stephens died; it is said that his ghostly form was seen being driven away from Chavenage by a headless coachman wearing royal vestments. The house has been featured in several BBC television productions, including *Agatha Christie's Hercule Poirot* and *Grace and Favour.*

3km (2 miles) northwest of Tetbury. © 01666/502329. www.chavenage.com. Admission £5 ($8) adults, £2.50 ($4) children. May–Sept Thurs and Sun 2–5pm; also open on Easter and bank holiday Mon.

ANTIQUES SHOPS & GALLERIES

As in many English villages, Tetbury's shopping centers around antiques and collectibles. **Day Antiques,** 5 New Church St. (© **01666/502413**), specializes in oak and country furniture as well as early pottery and metalware. Most of the other antiques dealers are located in the town center, including several shops specializing in furniture. **Breakspeare Antiques,** 36 Long St. (© **01666/503122**), carries mahogany pieces from the 18th and early 19th centuries and walnut pieces from the 17th century and later. Country Homes, 30 Long St. (© **01666/5 02342**), sells restored pine furniture from England, Ireland, and Europe. **Gales Antiques,** 52 Long St. (© **01666/502686**), features English and French provincial furnishings. For good quality porcelain, try **Dolphin Antiques,** 48 Long St. (© **01666/504242**). **The Antiques Emporium,** at the Old Chape, Long Street (© **01666/505281**), gathers stock from 40 dealers in 163 sq. m (1,750 sq. ft.) of showrooms; you're almost guaranteed to find something. There are several art galleries in Tetbury. **The Connoisseurs Gallery,** 2 Chipping Court Shopping Mall (© **01666/503155**), has prints, sculpture, blown glass, and other works created exclusively by artists-in-residence; **Natural Wood Framing,** Eight Bells Gallery, 14 Church St. (© **01666/505070**), specializes in sporting art; **Tetbury Gallery,** 18 Market Place (© **01666/503412**), carries Victorian watercolors and oils and limited-edition prints.

WHERE TO STAY & DINE

The Crown Inn ⭐ *Value*   One of the best bargains in this expensive town is a three-gabled stone building, built in 1693 as a coaching inn. The inn's pub-type accommodations are on the third floor, under the sloping eaves, reached by climbing a Jacobean staircase. The small and cozy rooms, usually with exposed beams, have private shower-only bathrooms. Most of the Crown's income derives from its busy pub, where food is ordered over the bar, and then carried to your seat in either the pub or in a glassed-in conservatory in back. Two of the rooms are nonsmoking.

Gumstool Hill off Market Place, Tetbury, Gloucestershire GL8 8DG. © 01666/502469. 3 units. £70 ($112) double; £80 ($128) family room. Rates include English breakfast. MC, V. **Amenities:** Restaurant; 2 bars; lounge. *In room:* TV, coffeemaker, iron, trouser press, no phone.

WORTH A SPLURGE

The Hare & Hounds Hotel ⭐⭐   Originally a 19th-century farmhouse, the Hare & Hounds was turned into an inn; the lounge and country bars remain

> ## *Tips* Hiking the Cotswold Way
>
> One of the less-known pleasures of a Cotswolds sojourn is to take an overland pedestrian ramble, the Cotswold Way, intended for the hardy. The idea of establishing a walking trail originated in the 1950s, but formal rights-of-way to connect the 167km (104-mile) path weren't finalized until 1968. The number of hikers using the path has increased annually since then.
>
> The path begins at Chipping Campden, in the northern Cotswolds, and ends at Bath; the meandering route with rolling hills is clearly signposted with bright yellow signs at almost every intersection. Local statisticians say taking the northbound route (Bath to Chipping Campden), you'll ascend 4,053m (13,300 ft.); along the southbound route (Chipping Campden to Bath), you'll ascend 3,931m (12,900 ft.).
>
> We recommend the much less-traveled southbound route; you won't find yourself in "traffic jams" caused by hikers traveling at speeds different from your own. Whatever direction you choose, don't underestimate the effort to make the trip. Tourist officials in Chipping Campden report that most participants take between 7 and 8 days to walk the entire path, and many hikers finish looking like Stanley and Livingston emerging from the African jungle—blistered, sunburned, rain-drenched, and exhausted. At tour's end, many rush off for either a quick return to home comforts or a detour to London for a night or two of pub-crawls and urban decadence.
>
> Despite its discomforts, the allure of the path is potent, the panoramas spectacular, and the sense of medieval England appealing. The planners who laid out the walk made every effort to avoid road

from those days. The substantial main building (1928) was constructed so faithfully in the original stone that it looks much older. Often favored as a conference site, the hotel is run by the Price brothers, who entertain their guests well, making it a worthy choice. It has stone-mullioned windows and gables and sits on 4 hectares (10 acres) of private grounds. The exceedingly comfortable rooms come in various shapes and sizes, each with a small private bathroom with shower-and-tub combination. Fourteen rooms are for nonsmoking guests, and there are six rooms available for those with limited mobility. Under a hammer-beam ceiling, the restaurant serves a combination of British and continental dishes.

Westonbirt, Tetbury, Gloucestershire GL8 8QL. ✆ **01666/880233.** Fax 01666/880241. www.hareandhounds hotel.com. 31 units. £80 ($128) single; £99 ($158) double. AE, MC, V. Take A433 4km (2½ miles) southwest of Tetbury. **Amenities:** Restaurant; bar; tennis court; squash court. *In room:* TV, dataport, coffeemaker, hair dryer.

2 Cirencester ★

142km (89 miles) W of London; 26km (16 miles) S of Cheltenham; 27km (17 miles) SE of Gloucester; 57km (36 miles) W of Oxford

Cirencester, unofficial capital of the Cotswolds, is a throwback to the Middle Ages; known then as Corinium, it flourished as the center of the great Cotswold wool industry. Five roads converged here during the Roman occupation. In size, it ranked second only to London. Today it is a market town and a good base for verges, although for a small portion of the route you will be funneled to the shoulder of roads and highways. (Be aware that in England, for safety reasons, pedestrians are instructed to walk on the right side of the road, facing oncoming traffic.) Most of the route, however, avoids traffic arteries, guiding you through forests, fields, rocky escarpments with views of medieval wool villages, and along the periphery of historic villages.

Whether you opt to detour the quarter mile or so into any of the historic villages en route depends on your level of interest, time, and energy. Along the southbound route, you'll pass through or near Broadway, Hailes, Winchcombe, Cleeve Hill, Seven Springs Crossroads, Crickley Hill, Painswick, Dursley, Wotton-under-Edge, Hawkesbury Upton, and Tormarton, finishing a short distance outside of Bath.

Specific recommendations for stopovers and sights along the way are well documented. Any Cotswold village's tourist office contains shelves groaning under the weight of the ordinance maps and specialized walking tour guides that cover all aspects of the Cotswold Way. One of the best is *The Cotswold Way Handbook and Accommodations List,* published by the English Ramblers' Association, which sells for £2 ($3.20) at dozens of shops en route. You can pre-order the guide by writing to the English Ramblers' Association, Tudor Cottage, Berrow, Malvern, Worcestershire WR136JJ, England. Additional information can be obtained from the tourist offices of Chipping Campden, Bath, or Broadway, or by calling the **Cotswold Voluntary Warden Service** at C 01451/882000. Bring a raincoat, sturdy shoes, and a sense of humor.

touring. (As for pronunciation, there's disagreement even among the English. Say Siren-cess-ter and you won't be too far off.)

ESSENTIALS

GETTING THERE   Cirencester has no railway station, but trains depart several times a day from London's Paddington Station for the 80-minute trip to Kemble, which is 6.5km (4 miles) southwest of Cirencester. You may have to transfer trains at Swindon. For schedules and information, call C **0845/7484950.** From Kemble, a bus travels to Cirencester four to five times a day.

National Express buses leave London's Victoria Coach Station with direct service to Cirencester. For schedules and information, call C **020/7529-2000.**

If driving from London, take the M40 northwest to Oxford, continuing along the A40 to the junction with the A429, which you'll take south to Cirencester.

VISITOR INFORMATION   The **Tourist Information Centre** is at Corn Hall, Market Place (C **01285/654180**). It's open April through October, Monday from 9:45am to 5pm and Tuesday through Saturday from 9:30am to 5:30pm. From November to March it closes at 5pm.

EXPLORING CIRENCESTER

Cirencester has some of the greatest walks and scenic views in the Cotswolds—and you don't have to go miles out of town to enjoy them. They are easily reached from the town center at Market Place. On the grounds of the Cirencester Parish Church (see below), trees and shrubs provide a well-manicured landscape. Swans and wild fowl gather on the River Churn and the lake. You can still see remnants of the Roman walls. For a great stroll, take the riverside walk alongside the Churn from Barton Lane to the Abbey Grounds; for more, head west from Market Place until you reach Cirencester Park, 1,200 hectares (3,000 acres) of parkland with woodland walks. The park opens daily for horseback riding and walking; pedestrian access is from Cecily Hill (no vehicles allowed).

Brewery Arts Centre   The living heart of this arts complex is the workshop area of 15 resident crafts workers who produce everything from baskets to chandeliers. Other components include three galleries with exhibitions of crafts and fine art, a theater, education classes, a shop selling the best in British craftswork, a cafe-bar, and a coffeehouse.

Brewery Ct. (*C*) 01285/657181. Free admission. Year-round Mon–Sat 10am–5pm.

Corinium Museum *★★*   The museum houses one of the finest collections of archaeological remains from the Roman occupation, found in and around Cirencester. Mosaic pavements excavated on Dyer Street in 1849 and other mosaics are the most important exhibits. Provincial Roman sculptures of Minerva and Mercury, pottery, and artifacts salvaged from long-decayed buildings create a link to a remote civilization that once flourished here. The Corinium has been completely modernized; it now shows full-scale reconstructions and special exhibitions on local history and conservation.

Park St. (*C*) 01285/655611. www.cotswold.gov.uk. Admission £2.50 ($4) adults, £2 ($3.20) seniors, £1 ($1.60) students and children, £5 ($8) family ticket. Mon–Sat 10am–5pm; Sun 2–5pm.

Cirencester Parish Church   While a Saxon church may have stood on this spot, the present building dates from Norman times and Henry I. More cathedral than parish church in size, the construction uses a variety of styles, mostly Perpendicular (as in the early-15th-c. tower). Among the treasures inside are a 15th-century "wineglass" pulpit and a silver-gilt cup given to Anne Boleyn 2 years before her execution. In the Trinity Chapel, you can rub some great 15th-century brasses.

Market Place. (*C*) 01285/659317. Free admission; donations invited. Mon–Fri 10am–5pm; Sun 2:30–5:30pm.

SHOPPING

For antiques in Cirencester, try **William H. Stokes,** The Cloisters, 6–8 Dollar St. ((*C*) **01285/653907**), specializing in 16th- and 17th-century furniture, tapestries, and other items. **Rankine Taylor Antiques,** 34 Dollar St. ((*C*) **01285/652529**), sells items from the 17th to early 19th centuries, including silver, glass, and furniture. The **Brewery Arts Centre,** Brewery Court ((*C*) **01285/657181**), has 15 independent workshops of area craftspeople ranging from jewelers to weavers. There is a crafts shop recognized by the Crafts Council that sells many of the artists' wares.

WHERE TO STAY

Old Court *★*   This mansion from the 18th century, known for years as "Cripps House," lies right in the medieval core of the old town within a short walk of the Parish church. The owners, Anna and Stephen Langton, have restored this handsome property and furnished it well, each room comfortably appointed with a private bathroom with shower. All the nonsmoking rooms are doubles, and the best one comes with a four-poster. An English breakfast is taken either in a wood-paneled dining room, or, if the weather is fair, in a summer garden.

Croxwell St., Cirencester, Gloucestershire GL7 2BQ. © **01285/653164.** Fax 01285/642803. www.old-court. co.uk. 4 units. £65–£75 ($104–$120) double. Rates include breakfast. V. **Amenities:** Breakfast room. *In room:* TV, coffeemaker, hair dryer, no phone.

Raydon House Hotel   This Victorian mansion is only 5 minutes from the town center in a peaceful residential area; parking is available. The small but comfortable rooms have private shower-only bathrooms and furnishings complementary to the building's style.

3 The Avenue, Cirencester, Gloucestershire GL7 1EH. © and fax **01285/653485.** 10 units. £30–£39 ($48–$62) single; £50–£60 ($80–$96) double; £60–£75 ($96–$120) family unit. Rates include English breakfast. AE, MC, V. From Market Place, drive along Cricklade St. and Watermoor Rd., and turn left on The Avenue. **Amenities:** Dining room; bar. *In room:* TV, coffeemaker, hair dryer, no phone.

WHERE TO DINE

Cottage of Content *Finds* ENGLISH/INTERNATIONAL   This delightful little restaurant near the parish church is owned by Mr. and Mrs. Pugh, who cook, serve, and do the washing up. They serve a variety of succulent steaks, all with fresh vegetables, salads in season, and dessert. They've added some international dishes to the menu to liven it up.

117 Cricklade St. © **01285/654967.** Reservations recommended. Main courses £6–£13 ($10–$21). No credit cards. Tues–Sat 7:30–10:30pm. Closed bank holidays.

The Crown ENGLISH   This is the most popular pub in town. A coaching inn since the 14th century, it stands opposite the parish church. Many original architectural features have been preserved; the ambience comes from log fires, country chairs, cushioned pews, and plain stonework, with a flower- and vine-ringed beer garden in back. Daily specials on a chalkboard may include home-made eggplant casserole, grilled sausages, or baked ham.

17 W. Market Place. © **01285/653206.** Main courses £5–£10 ($8–$16). MC, V. Mon–Sat noon–11:30pm; Sun noon–midnight. Pub: Mon–Sat 11:30am–11pm; Sun noon–midnight.

Harry Hare's Restaurant and Brasserie ENGLISH   Near the town center in a 15th-century barn, this lighthearted brasserie is popular on weekends. It serves full meals, afternoon teas, and snacks. The hurried staff offers a changing array of such specialties as rack of lamb in red-currant and port wine sauce, fish cakes in hollandaise sauce, lamb's liver with shallots and smoked bacon, and cassoulet pie filled with duck confit, pork sausage, and haricot beans. The food is above the ordinary, and many dishes have real flavor.

3 Gosditch St. © **01285/652375.** Reservations recommended. Main courses £8–£16 ($13–$26). AE, MC, V. Daily 10:30am–10:30pm.

3 Painswick ⭐

6km (4 miles) N of Stroud; 171km (107 miles) W of London; 16km (10 miles) SW of Cheltenham; 24km (15 miles) NW of Cirencester

This sleepy stone-built Cotswold wool town vies with Bibury to be the most beautiful in the Cotswolds. Painswick is a dream of England of long ago, the perfect escape from a string of dull market towns. Its mellow gray stone houses and inns date from the 14th century onward, including some Georgian buildings. Painswick blends in perfect harmony because former builders, regardless of the century, used the same stone.

A visit to Painswick at any time would be idyllic, notwithstanding day-trippers and tourist buses, but there are two truly special occasions. One is the town's Victorian Market Day in early July; you can contact the Tourist Information Centre (see below) for the exact day, announced in late spring. The other is the Clipping Feast (see "Special Events," below).

ESSENTIALS

GETTING THERE   Trains depart London's Paddington Station several times a day for Stroud, the nearest railway station, 5km (3 miles) away. The trip takes from 1½ to 2 hours, and you may have to change trains at Swindon. For rail information, call ✆ **0845/7484950.** From Stroud, buses run to Painswick, some as frequently as every hour. Many taxis also wait at the Stroud railway station.

Buses depart from Bath heading toward Cheltenham on Wednesday and Saturday, stopping in Painswick (and many other small towns) along the way. For schedules, call ✆ **020/7529-2000.**

If you're driving from Cirencester, continue west along the A419 to Stroud, then head north on the A46 to Cheltenham and Painswick.

VISITOR INFORMATION   The Painswick **Tourist Information Centre** is at the Painswick Library, Stroud Road (✆ **01452/813552**), and is open April through September, Monday through Saturday from 10am to 6pm. These hours are true at least in theory, but the staff volunteers manning the office don't always show up. In that case, you can visit the more reliably open tourist office at Stroud, located in Subscription Rooms, George Street (✆ **01453/760960**). Hours are Monday through Saturday from 10am to 5pm.

SPECIAL EVENTS   The **Clipping Feast** of Painswick, also known as the Clipping Ceremony, is an unusual, early medieval ceremony that anthropologists think may have begun in the dim Celtic prehistory of Britain. Every September, a month that coincides with the harvest ceremonies of pagans, adults and as many children as can be mustered hold hands in a circle around St. Mary's Anglican Church. The circle moves first one way, then the other, and the participants sing hymns and pray out loud in a celebration of thanksgiving. Participants and observers come from all over the region to take part in this important rite.

EXPLORING THE TOWN

The charm of this town comes from its mellow, stone-built Cotswold buildings. Funded by wealthy farmers and merchants when wool was called "white gold," the houses of Painswick represent a peak in English domestic architecture. They are best seen by walking around the village center on New Street, one of England's most misnamed roads—it dates from 1450.

You can wander into a pocket of charm by visiting the gardens of **Painswick House,** Gloucester Street, Route B4073, Painswick Stroud (✆ **01452/813204**), about 1km (½ mile) west of the town center. Built by Charles Hyett in 1734 and enlarged in 1830, this mansion had been home to eight generations of the same family until Lord and Lady Dickinson departed in 1999. The new owners may not allow visitors to wander through their home (check locally), and their rococo gardens are not the biggest, but they are among the most cozily charming in the Cotswolds. You're allowed to visit January to October, daily from 10am to 5pm. Admission is £3.60 ($6) for adults, £1.80 ($2.90) for children, and £3.30 ($5) for seniors and students. A family ticket is sold for £9.50 ($15).

St. Mary's Church, Painswick's centerpiece, was built between 1377 and 1399, and reconstructed into its present form in 1480. Its churchyard contains 99 massive yew trees, each at least 200 years old. Local legend claims that, no matter how hard well-meaning gardeners try, they've never been able to grow more than 99 yews here.

If you wish to shop, stop by **Dennis French** on New Street (© **01452/814195**) for woodcrafts influenced by William Morris designs.

WHERE TO STAY & DINE

Hambutts Mynd ⭐ *Finds*   Set in a half acre of gardens about 2 blocks southwest from the town center, this nonsmoking hotel occupies a 17th-century windmill. Since the 1970s it has been the home and B&B hotel of sprightly Elizabeth Warland. Behind a somber, severely dignified stone facade, the hotel is filled with an idiosyncratic and highly pleasing collection of furniture, with everything from William and Mary chests to 1930s kitsch. Windows in all bedrooms offer sweeping views over nearby hills and fields. Rooms range from small to spacious in size, are exceedingly comfortable, and have private bathrooms with shower.

Edge Rd., Painswick, Gloucestershire GL6 6UP. © **01452/812352**. Ewarland@aol.com. 3 units. £30 ($48) single; £55–£60 ($88–$96) double. Rates include English breakfast. No credit cards. Closed Jan 15–Feb 15. **Amenities:** Breakfast room. *In room:* TV, coffeemaker, hair dryer, iron, no phone.

Painswick Hotel ⭐⭐ ENGLISH/FRENCH   Located behind St. Mary's, this hotel is the most prestigious place to stay in this delightful village; nevertheless, it offers one of the finest and most reasonably priced lunches in the area. Lunch is served one flight above street level; the more formal, somewhat pricier dinner is served in the elegant street-level oak-paneled dining room. Typical menu items include terrine of chicken and lobster with a French bean-and-tomato salad, poached filets of lemon sole with a spinach mousse, and a pastry tartlet of veal kidneys on a bed of spinach with a grain-mustard sauce. Staying here might tug at your budget, but if you do, you'll find an elegantly decorated series of rooms, with stunning fabrics, antiques, and period engravings. The more standard rooms, rather than the lavishly adorned units with four-poster beds, begin at £125 ($200) per night in a double.

Kemps Lane, Painswick, Gloucestershire GL6 6YB. © **01452/812160**. www.painswickhotel.com. Reservations recommended. Main courses £21.50–£23 ($34–$37). Fixed-price dinner £28–£31 ($45–$50); fixed-price lunch £14–£17 ($22–$27). AE, MC, V. Daily noon–2pm and 7–9:30pm.

OWLPEN MANOR: A JOURNEY TO BRIGADOON

As beautiful as Painswick is, there is a place even more so: the hamlet of **Owlpen Manor** ⭐ near Dursley, immediately south of Painswick off the beaten track. "Owlpen in Gloucestershire" has been called the English Shangri-la; Vita Sackville-West rhapsodized, "Ah, what a dream is there"; Prince Charles, who lives nearby at Highgrove, has called it "the epitome of an English village."

This fairy-tale hamlet (population 35 lucky souls) is anchored by a medieval church, an Elizabethan manor, and a collection of stone-built, honey-colored cottages. Stroll through the gardens of the triple-gabled manor, constructed between 1450 and 1720. Even England's greatest gardener, Gertrude Jekyll, came to see what all the fuss was about. The manor is open daily April through October 2 to 5pm. Admission is £4.80 ($8) to see inside the antiques-filled house, or just £2.80 ($4.50) to stroll through the beautifully kept grounds. There's also a restaurant, the Cyder House, serving typically English food.

Owlpen is overseen by Nicholas Mander, a descendant of Sir Geoffrey Chaucer, and Karin Mander, fabled Pre-Raphaelite art patrons. For information about visits to the manor and its grounds, the village itself, or cottage rentals, call © **01453/860261** or fax 01453/860819. In the United States you can call The **London Connection** at © **801/393-9120** for more data. From Painswick, go south on A45—signposted Stroud—until you come to the junction on A419. At that point turn south on B4066 in the direction of Uley and follow the signposts to Owlpen Manor.

4 Cheltenham ⭐

158km (99 miles) NW of London; 15km (9 miles) NE of Gloucester; 69km (43 miles) W of Oxford

Legend has it that the Cheltenham villagers discovered a mineral spring when they noticed pigeons drinking from a spring and observed how healthy they were (a pigeon has been incorporated into the town's crest). George III arrived in 1788 and launched the town's career as a spa. The duke of Wellington came to ease his liver disorder; Lord Byron came this way to propose marriage to Miss Millbanke.

Cheltenham remains one of England's most fashionable spas, and visitors come just to see its gardens from spring to autumn. The architecture is mainly Regency, with lots of ironwork, balconies, and verandas. Attractive parks and open spaces of greenery make the town especially inviting. The main street, the Promenade, has been called Britain's most beautiful thoroughfare. Similar streets include Lansdowne Place and Montpellier Parade; with caryatids separating its stores, Montpellier Walk is one of England's most interesting shopping centers.

ESSENTIALS

GETTING THERE   Twenty-one trains depart daily from London's Paddington Station for the 2¼-hour trip. You may have to change trains at Bristol or Swindon. For information, call ℂ **0845/7484950.** Trains between Cheltenham and Bristol take an hour, with continuing service to Bath.

National Express offers nine buses daily from London's Victoria Coach Station to Cheltenham. The ride takes about 2½ hours. For schedules and information, call ℂ **020/7529-2000.**

If you're driving from London, head northwest on the M40 to Oxford, continuing along the A40 to Cheltenham.

VISITOR INFORMATION   The **Tourist Information Centre,** 77 Promenade (ℂ **01242/522878**), is open September through June, Monday through Saturday from 9:30am to 5:15pm and Saturday from 9:30am to 5:15pm.

SPECIAL EVENTS   The **International Festival of Music** and the **Festival of Literature** take place each year in July and October, respectively, and attract internationally acclaimed performers and orchestras. A smaller, weekend-long Festival of Literature takes place in early April.

EXPLORING THE TOWN

Pittville Pump Room   Cheltenham waters are the only natural, consumable alkaline waters in Great Britain and are still taken at one of the spa's finest Regency buildings. The room is open Sundays from late May through September for a host of activities, including lunch, afternoon cream teas, live classical music, landau carriage rides around the city, and brass bands playing in Pittville Park—authentic traditional England.

East Approach Dr., Pittville Park. ℂ 01242/523852. Free admission. Wed–Mon 11am–4pm. From the town center, take Portland St. and Evesham Rd.

Cheltenham Art Gallery & Museum   Located near Royal Crescent and the Coach Station, this gallery houses one of the best collections of the Arts and Crafts movement, notably the fine furniture of William Morris and his followers. One section is devoted to Cheltenham's own, Edward Wilson, who died with Captain Scott in the Antarctic in 1912.

Clarence St. ✆ **01242/237431**. Free admission. Mon–Sat 10am–5:20pm; Sun 2–4:30pm. Closed bank holidays.

Everyman Theatre   Cheltenham is the cultural center of the Cotswolds, a role reinforced by the Everyman Theatre. Designed in the 1890s as an opera house by Frank Matcham, Victorian England's leading theater architect, it retains its ornate cornices, sculpted ceilings, and plush velvets, despite extensive renovations to its stage and lighting facilities. The theater now attracts some of England's top dramatic companies. Shakespeare, musicals, comedies, and other genres are performed in the small (658 seats) and charming hall. Recent productions have included *The Adventures of Robin Hood, Don Giovanni, Antony and Cleopatra,* and performances by noted musical groups.

Regent St. ✆ 01242/572573. Admission £5–£25 ($8–$40). Box office: Mon–Sat 9:30am–8:30pm; Sun open 2 hr. before performance time.

SHOPPING
The different quarters that make up Cheltenham's shopping district turn shopping into an unusually organized event. Start in the Montpellier quarter for a host of individual boutiques and crafts and specialty shops. Continue to the nearby Suffolk quarter to find most of the town's antiques stores. An enjoyable short stroll to the Promenade reveals stores featuring attractive women's and men's clothing and shoes, as well as bookstores. From there, take Regent Street to the mostly pedestrian-only High Street, where you'll find brand-name department stores.

The Courtyard, on Montpellier Street in the heart of the quarter, is an award-winning shopping mall with a fun blend of quality shops specializing in unique fashion, furniture, and gift items. A good mix of restaurants, cafes, and wine bars rounds out the Courtyard.

Cavendish House, the Promenade (✆ **01242/521300**), a long-established shopping landmark, houses two restaurants, a hair and beauty salon, an immense cosmetic and jewelry hall, and departments devoted to fine fashion, housewares, and furniture.

On High Street, you'll find the **Beechwood Shopping Centre.** This mall is touted as Cheltenham's premier shopping center and has restaurants, a car park, and such institutions as Debenhams, C&A, and the Disney Store.

The **weekly market** is in the Henrietta Street car park on Thursday and in Coronation Square on Friday. Weather permitting, markets open around 9am and close toward 4pm.

WHERE TO STAY
If you don't mind roughing it a bit, here is a cheap sleep option. The **YMCA,** 6 Vittoria Walk, Cheltenham (✆ **01242/524024;** fax 01242/232635; www.cheltenhamymca.org), has 47 single rooms and three doubles, but no private bathrooms. Rates are £18 ($29) per person, and breakfast is included. Laundry facilities are available. Call first, though, because students rent most of the rooms, and they can be hard to come by.

Beaumont House Hotel   Minutes from the town center, this tranquil 1850s building with gardens is tastefully converted to receive paying guests. All the bright, airy, color-coordinated nonsmoking bedrooms have private bathrooms or showers. The licensed house serves good British fare.

Shurdington Rd., Cheltenham, Gloucestershire GL53 0JE. ✆ **01242/245986.** Fax 01242/520044. www.beaumonthousehotel.co.uk. 16 units. £56 ($90) single; £78 ($125) standard double; £119 ($190) 4-poster unit. Rates include English breakfast. AE, MC, V. Bus: "Metro." **Amenities:** Breakfast room; lounge. *In room:* TV, dataport, coffeemaker, hair dryer, iron.

Central Hotel   Within easy reach of Cheltenham's attractions, this white-fronted hotel consists of a pair of stone houses built in the 1700s and later combined. Strictly protected from exterior changes by local building codes, it's a family-run hotel with a street-level public house. The small nonsmoking bedrooms are conservatively modern. The private shower bathrooms are compact, and the public bathrooms are adequately maintained (plus, you rarely have to wait in line).

7–9 Portland St., Cheltenham, Gloucestershire GL52 2NZ. ℂ 01242/582172. 14 units, 8 with bathroom. £30 ($48) single without bathroom, £40 ($64) single with bathroom; £50 ($80) double without bathroom; £65 ($104) double with shower only. Rates include English breakfast. MC, V. **Amenities:** Breakfast room; bar. *In room:* TV, dataport, coffeemaker.

Lawn Hotel   Built in 1830 with a stucco exterior, this elegant landmark house lies just inside the iron gates leading to Pittville Park and the Pump Room, about a 10-minute walk to the town center and its Promenade. It's one of 300 town houses built in an area landscaped in the early 19th century by Joseph Pitt. It offers pleasantly decorated, midsize rooms, each comfortably furnished. The Millier family especially welcomes vegetarians, as they are themselves.

5 Pittville Lawn, Cheltenham, Gloucestershire GL52 2BE. ℂ 01242/526638. 9 units, 4 with bathroom. £25 ($40) per person. Rates include continental breakfast. No credit cards. Bus: no. 1A, 2A, or 3A. **Amenities:** Breakfast room; dinner by arrangement. *In room:* TV, coffeemaker.

WHERE TO DINE

Montpellier Wine Bar ⋆ BRITISH   Housed in a distinctive Regency building, this four-story restaurant is so bowed that its front is really a semicircle with sweeping windows. The light and airy upstairs dining room and the outdoor patio are favorite places to eat in warm weather. The downstairs dining room is cozy but modern, with a large stone fireplace balanced by original contemporary paintings and polished wooden floors and tables. A daily menu of seasonal dishes with fish, steak, pork, chicken, British game, and vegetarian items rotate into a list of creative, well-prepared choices. The bottom two floors house a wine bar and a full bar, with a generous listing of vintages.

Bayshill Lodge, Montpellier St. ℂ 01242/527774. Reservations recommended. Dinner main courses £8.50–£16 ($14–$26); lunch main courses £4.50–£8.50 ($7–$14). AE, MC, V. Mon–Sat 11am–11pm; Sun noon–10:30pm.

Moran's Eating House and Wine Bar CONTINENTAL   A lively and popular place (especially on Fri and Sat nights), this establishment inhabits two connected mid-19th-century homes, one a comfortable wine bar with wicker and padded leopard-skin furniture, the other an unassuming dining room with polished wood floors and pine furniture. The halves are unified by a lush garden, popular in warm weather. Main courses include fresh seafood pie with crunchy cheese topping, beef bourguignon, and large mushrooms stuffed with pasta and ratatouille; the wine list has something to go with everything.

123–129 Bath Rd. ℂ 01242/581411. Reservations recommended on Fri–Sat. Main courses £8–£15 ($13–$24). MC, V. 10am–2:30pm and 6–11pm.

Pepper's Café Bar BRITISH   This European-style cafe is a great place to relax and have a snack or a meal. Split into a cafe-pub and a 300-seat dining room, its comfortable atmosphere is created through low-level lighting and music combined with polished wooden floors, raised carpeted sitting areas, and comfortable chairs and settees. There's an outdoor terrace for warm weather drinking and dining. The cafe has snacks, pies, fish and chips, pasta dishes, and a variety of draft and bottled beer. The restaurant serves an array of specialty breads to accompany an extensive selection of steaks, traditional English dishes like steak-and-ale pie, and Italian fare.

Regent St. near the Playhouse. (C) **01242/573488**. Main courses £3.95–£11.95 ($6–$19). AE, MC, V. Cafe-pub: Daily 9am–11pm.

The Retreat *(Finds)* INTERNATIONAL/VEGETARIAN The Retreat is a 5-minute walk south of the village center; in a redbrick building at least a century old, this is the most popular pub/wine bar in town. Its most distinctive feature is a plant-filled courtyard, packed with diners during fine weather. Only lunch is served—the rest of the day is devoted to imbibing. Meals (ordered at a food counter) tend to include an array of fresh salads, with health-conscious ingredients blended into imaginative combinations.

10–11 Suffolk Parade. (C) **01242/235436**. Reservations recommended. Main courses £4.95–£15.95 ($8–$26). AE, DC, MC, V. Mon–Sat noon–2:15pm. Pub: Mon–Sat noon–11pm.

CHELTENHAM AFTER DARK

The major venue for entertainment is the **Everyman Theatre** (see above), Cheltenham's premier sightseeing attraction. But there's a lot more theater at the **Playhouse,** Bath Road ((C) **01242/522852**), with local amateur productions of drama, comedy, dance, and opera staged anew at a dizzying biweekly pace. Tickets are £5 to £10 ($8–$16).

Dancers flock to **Fez Club,** Bath Road ((C) **01242/252925**), which attracts a mixed crowd: Against a backdrop of some vague Moroccan decor, the night heats up with atomic fusion, acid jazz, big beat, or "disko-joose." The best DJs in town appear here, spinning a heady mix of '70s disco, "old skool" funk, garage, and house. As one local, Adam Davis, put it, "The best bit is the giant vibrating bed, although sitting on this will result in falling asleep or being squashed by some ugly couple shagging!" Cover charges range from £3 to £8 ($4.80–$13). The club is open Wednesday to Sunday 9am to 2am.

Choose your groove at **Chemistry,** St. James Square ((C) **01242/527700**); open on Monday, Thursday, Friday, and Saturday nights from 9pm to 2am. Cover ranges from £2 to £5 ($3.20–$8) after 10pm, depending on the night.

A SIDE TRIP TO ROYAL SUDELEY CASTLE

Royal Sudeley Castle *(★)* Sudeley Castle is one of England's finer stately homes. Located in Winchcombe, the former capital of the Mercian Saxon kings (7th–9th c.), it was built by Ethelred II (the Unready) as a wedding present to his daughter Goda. It became the property of the duke of Gloucester, later Richard III. Later, Catherine Parr, the sixth wife of Henry VIII, lived and died here; her tomb is in a chapel on the grounds. Destroyed by Cromwell's troops, Sudeley was restored during the 19th century. The castle is now renowned for its formal gardens, laid out in the Victorian era. Since the 1980s, the Queen's Garden, originally planted with double yew hedges, has sustained a spectacular collection of old-world roses. In the gardens, you're sure to see the waterfowl and flamboyant peacocks that call Sudeley home.

For the past 30 years, Lady Ashcombe, American by birth, has owned Sudeley and welcomed visitors. The castle houses artworks by Constable, Turner, Rubens, and Van Dyck, and has permanent exhibitions, magnificent furniture and glass, and artifacts from the castle's past. In the area to the right of the castle keep, workshops feature talented local artisans using traditional techniques to produce stained glass, textiles, wood and leather articles, and marbled paper.

In the village of Winchcombe (9.5km/6 miles northeast of Cheltenham). ℂ **01242/602308**. www.sudeley
castle.co.uk. Admission £6.70 ($11) adults, £5.50 ($9) seniors, £3.70 ($6) children 5–15, £18.50 ($30) family
ticket. Apr–Oct daily 10:30am–4:30pm. From Cheltenham, take the regular bus to Winchcombe and get off
at Abbey Terrace. Then, walk the short distance along the road to the castle. If you're driving, take B4632 north
out of Cheltenham, through Prestbury, and up Cleve Hill to Abbey Terrace, where you can drive right up to the
castle.

5 Bibury ⟨★⟩

183km (86 miles) W of London; 48km (30 miles) W of Oxford; 42km (26 miles) E of Gloucester

On the road from Burford to Cirencester, Bibury is one of the loveliest spots in
the Cotswolds; William Morris considered it England's most beautiful village. In
the Cotswolds, it is matched only by Painswick for its scenic village beauty and
purity; both remain unspoiled by modern invasions.

GETTING THERE

About five trains per day depart London's Paddington Station for the 1-hour-10-
minute trip to Kemble, the nearest station, 21km (13 miles) south of Bibury.
Some will require an easy change of train in Swindon (the connecting train waits
across the tracks). For information, call ℂ **0845/7484950.** No buses run from
Kemble to Bibury, but most hotels will arrange transportation if you ask in
advance.

Five buses leave London's Victoria Coach Station daily for Cirencester, 11km
(7 miles) from Bibury. For information, call ℂ **0870/5808080.** There are no
connecting buses into Bibury; local hotels will send a car, and taxis are available.

If driving from London, take the M4 to Exit 15, head toward Cirencester, then
follow the A33 (on some maps this is still designated as the B4425) to Bibury.

EXPLORING THE TOWN

On the banks of the tiny River Coln, Bibury is noted for **Arlington Row** ⟨★⟩, a
group of 17th-century gabled cottages protected by the National Trust. First built
for weavers, they are the town's biggest and most-photographed attraction—but
it's rude to peer into the windows, as people still live here.

To see something a bit out of the ordinary for the Cotswolds, check out **St.
Mary's Parish Church.** As the story goes, the area's powerful wealthy merchants
were rebuilding its churches; but they did not finish the work on St. Mary's. As
a result, much of the original Roman-style architecture has been left intact; even
the 14th-century decorated-styled windows have survived. This treasure is often
overlooked.

The once-prosperous mill has been silenced and converted into the **Cotswold
Country Museum** (ℂ **01451/860715**), where visitors are treated to a host of
antiquated wagons and machines once used in the area, and a variety of display
rooms that illustrate the way people used to handle day-to-day existence. It was
recently combined with the Cotswold Countryside Collection (see below) to
form the Cotswold Heritage Center. Open April through November, Monday
to Saturday from 10am to 5pm. Admission to the heritage center is £3 ($4.80)
for adults, £2.50 ($4) for seniors, £1.50 ($2.40) for students, £1 ($1.60) for
children 5 to 16, and free for ages 4 and under. A family ticket covering two
adults and two children is £6.50 ($10).

WHERE TO STAY & DINE

Catherine Wheel Guest House   The main building of the Catherine Wheel
contains Bibury's only pub. Hearty platters of food are served from any of four

bar areas within its historically evocative, richly beamed and paneled premises (Mon–Sat noon–10pm; Sun noon–2:30pm and 7–10pm). As many as three fireplaces blaze away almost constantly between October and March, illuminating the predictable roster of bangers and mash and steak-and-kidney pie as well as more esoteric choices like swordfish, calamari, ham pie, and lobster casserole. Platters cost £4 to£16 ($6–$26).

The rooms are the equal of any three-star British hotel, but are located in the annex of a rustically timbered house built during the 1400s. The nonsmoking bedrooms contain touches of half-timbering and functional but comfortable furnishings, and lie a short walk from the noise and activities of the pub.

Arlington, near Bibury, Gloucestershire GL7 5ND. ℭ **01285/740250.** Fax 01285/740779. 4 units. £50–£69 ($80–$110) single, double, or triple. AE, DC, MC, V. **Amenities:** Restaurant; bar. *In room:* TV, dataport, coffeemaker, hair dryer.

6 Burford ★

122km (76 miles) NW of London; 32km (20 miles) W of Oxford

Gateway to the area and built of Cotswold stone, the unspoiled medieval town of Burford is largely famous for its Norman church (ca. 1116) and its High Street lined with coaching inns. Cromwell passed this way, as did Charles II and his mistress, Nell Gwynne. Burford was one of the last great wool centers, the industry breathing its last as late as the Victorian age. Be sure to photograph the bridge across the River Windrush where Elizabeth I once stood.

The Windrush, flanked by willows as it passes through Burford's meadows, passes beneath an ancient packhorse bridge, goes around the church, and disappears through more meadows. Strolling along its banks is one of the most delightful experiences in the Cotswolds.

ESSENTIALS

GETTING THERE   Many trains depart from London's Paddington Station to Oxford, a 45-minute trip. For information, call ℭ **0845/7484950.** From Oxford, passengers walk a short distance to the entrance of the Taylor Institute, from which about three or four buses per day make the 30-minute run to Burford.

A **National Express** bus runs from London's Victoria Coach Station to Burford several times a day, with many stops along the way. It's a 2-hour ride. For schedules and information, call ℭ **020/7529-2000.**

If you're driving from Oxford, head west on the A40 to Burford.

VISITOR INFORMATION   The **Tourist Information Centre** is at the Old Brewery on Sheep Street (ℭ **01993/823558**) and is open November through February, Monday through Saturday from 10am to 4:30pm; and March and April and in October, Monday through Saturday from 9:30am to 5:30pm; May to September Sunday 10:30am to 3pm.

SEEING THE SIGHTS

Approaching Burford from the south, you'll experience one of the finest views of any ancient market town in the country. The High Street sweeps down to the Windrush, past an extraordinary collection of houses of different styles and ages. The packhorse bridge is still doing duty at the bottom of the hill. The hills opposite provide a frame of fields, trees, and, with luck, panoramic skies.

Although the wool trade has vanished, most of Burford remains unchanged, with its old houses, great and small, in the High Street and nearby side streets. Nearly all are built of local stone. Burford has a Sheep Street (as do many

Cotswold towns) with fine stone-built houses covered with roofs of Stonesfield slate. Burford Church (ca. 1175) is almost cathedral-like in proportion; it was enlarged throughout succeeding centuries until the wool trade's decline. In sum, little has changed here since about 1500.

Traders and vendors still set up their stalls on Fridays under the Tolsey, at the corner of Sheep Street. Here the guild collected tolls from anyone wishing to trade in Burford, beginning in the 12th century. On the upper floor is the minor Tolsey Museum, where you can see a medieval seal bearing Burford's insignia, the "rampant cat."

Three kilometers (2 miles) south of Burford on the A361 lies the **Cotswold Wildlife Park** (© 01993/823006). The 48 hectares (120 acres) of gardens and forests around this Victorian manor house have been transformed into a jungle of sorts, with a Noah's Ark consortium of animals ranging from voracious ants to rare Asiatic lions. Children can romp around the farmyard and the adventure playground. A narrow-gauge railway runs from April to October, and there are extensive picnic areas plus a cafeteria. Hours are Easter through September daily from 10am to 7pm; off season daily from 10am to 5pm. Admission is £7.50 ($12) for adults, £5 ($8) for seniors and children 3 to 16, and free for children 2 and under.

And before you leave Burford, we suggest a slight detour to **Swinbrook,** a pretty village by the River Windrush immediately to the east. It's best known as the one-time home of the fabled Mitford sisters. Visit the local parish church to see the grave of writer Nancy Mitford and the impressive tiered monuments to the Fettiplace family.

On High Street in Burford, you'll find several antiques shops, including **Manfred Schotten Antiques,** The Crypt, 109 High St. (© 01993/822302). Sporting antiques and collectibles, they also carry library and club furniture. **Jonathan Fyson Antiques,** 50–52 High St. (© 01993/823204), carries English and continental furniture and porcelain, glass, and brass items. On Cheltenham Road, **Gateway Antiques** (© 01993/823678) has a variety of items displayed in large showrooms. English pottery, metalware, and furniture dominate the inventory. Unique arts and crafts items and interesting decorative objects are fun to browse through, even if you don't buy.

TEATIME

After you've browsed through the antiques, head for your cuppa to **Burford House,** High Street (© 01993/823151), an old Cotswold house long known as the Andrews Hotel. Retaining a mellow charm, it serves tea Tuesday to Saturday 9am to 5pm. Freshly prepared goods—flans, scones, cakes, and muffins—are here to tempt. The English tea comes with a pot of tea, clotted cream, scones, jam, flan, and fruit. The queen's tea is more modest: a cup of tea with scones and jams. Is the queen on a diet? Teas cost £1.95 to £5.95 ($3.10–$10).

WHERE TO STAY & DINE

The Bull ★   This government-rated three-star hotel on the main street is the oldest hotel in Burford, dating from at least 1475. Once a priory, it was given by Henry VIII to his barber-surgeon in 1544 after the Dissolution. The Bull itself can be traced from 1603, when John Silvester became inn holder. The place has hosted Charles I's troops in battle with Cromwell's Parliament Dragoons, Cromwell himself, and Charles II and Nell Gwynne. The building's brick-and-stone front dates from 1658, when additions increased its size. Today Old-World charm blends with modern comfort in the small to midsize nonsmoking bedrooms, each with a private, shower-only bathroom.

105 High St., Burford, Oxfordshire OX18 4RG. © **01993/822220.** 121 units. £85 ($136) single; £105 ($168) double; £125 ($200) family or 4-poster unit. Rates include English breakfast. AE, MC, V. **Amenities:** Restaurant; pub; bar. *In room:* TV, dataport, coffeemaker, hair dryer.

BURFORD AFTER DARK

The bar at the elegant and expensive 15th-century **Lamb Inn,** Sheep Street (© **01993/823155**), attracts many from all walks of life who appreciate its mellow atmosphere and charm. Guinness, cider, and a collection of ales, including a local brew (Wadworth), are on tap. Bar meals are served Monday to Saturday, 11am to 2pm; an English/French menu is available Monday to Friday, 7 to 9pm. On Sunday a traditional English roast is served noon to 2pm.

7 Bourton-on-the-Water ★

136km (85 miles) NW of London; 58km (36 miles) NW of Oxford

Fans call it the quintessential Cotswold village, with a history going back to the Celts. Residents fiercely protect its 15th- and 16th-century architecture, even though their town is a goal of practically every bus tour rolling through the Cotswolds. Populated in Anglo-Saxon times, Bourton-on-the-Water developed into a strategic outpost along the already ancient Roman road, Fosse Way, that traversed Britain from the North Sea to St. George's Channel. In the Middle Ages, its prosperity came from wool, shipped all over Europe. During the Industrial Revolution, profits shifted to finished textiles; Bourton-on-the-Water became a backwater by sticking with raw wool. But the happy result for us was that it never "caught up," and its traditional appearance was preserved.

You'll feel like Gulliver voyaging to Lilliput as you arrive in this scenic village on the banks of the Windrush. Its mellow stone houses, village greens on the banks of the water, and bridges have earned it the title of "Venice of the Cotswolds." (No gondoliers, though.) This is a good stopover, if not for the night, at least to enjoy a lunch and a rest along the riverbanks. You can peek inside St. Lawrence's Church in the village center; built on the site of a Roman temple, it has a crypt from 1120 and a tower from 1784.

ESSENTIALS

Trains go from London's Paddington Station to nearby Moreton-in-Marsh, a trip of 2 hours. For information, call © **0845/7484950.** From here, take a Pulhams Bus Company coach 9.5km (6 miles) to Bourton-on-the-Water. Trains also run from London to Cheltenham and Kingham; while somewhat more distant than Moreton-in-Marsh, both have bus connections to Bourton-on-the-Water.

National Express buses run from Victoria Coach Station in London to both Cheltenham and Stow-on-the-Wold. For schedules and information, call © **020/7529-2000.** Pulhams Bus Company operates about four buses per day from both towns to Bourton-on-the-Water.

If you're driving from Oxford, head west on the A40 to the junction with the A429 (Fosse Way). Take it northeast to Bourton-on-the-Water.

A TINY VILLAGE, THE BIRDS, VINTAGE CARS & MORE

Within the town are a handful of minor museums, each of which was established from idiosyncratic collections amassed over the years by local residents. They include the **Bourton Model Railway Exhibition and Toy Shop** (© **01451/820686**) and **Birdland,** described below.

After you've seen them, stop by the quaint little tearoom called **Small Talk,** on High Street (© **01451/821596**). It's full of dainty lace and fine china and appetizing scones and pastries. Sit at a table overlooking the water and enjoy a pot of tea and some good conversation.

Birdland   This handsomely designed attraction is set on 3.4 hectares (8½ acres) of field and forests on the banks of the Windrush, about 1.5km (1 mile) east of Bourton-on-the-Water. It houses about 1,200 birds representing 361 species. Here is the largest and most varied collection of penguins in any zoo, with glass-walled tanks that allow you to watch them swim. There's an enviable collection of hummingbirds. Birdland has a picnic area and a children's playground.

Rissington Rd. ✆ 01451/820480. Admission £4.60 ($7) adults, £3.60 ($5) seniors, £2.60 ($4.15) children 4–14, £13 ($21) family ticket, free for children under 4. Apr–Oct daily 10am–6pm; Nov–Mar daily 10am–4pm.

Cotswold Motoring Museum   This museum has fun displays of cars, bikes, 1920s caravans, toys, and Europe's largest collection of advertising signs. There are also village shops from the past. The museum occupies a historic water mill from the 1700s; the British TV program *Brum* was filmed here.

The Old Mill. ✆ 01451/821255. Admission £2.50 ($4) adults, £1.75 ($2.80) children. Feb–Nov daily 10am–6pm.

Cotswold Perfumery   This permanent exhibition details the history of the perfume industry while focusing on its production. There's an audiovisual show in a "smelly vision" theater, a perfume quiz, a garden of plants grown exclusively for their fragrance, and a genealogy chart used by visitors to select their own personal perfume. Perfumes are made on the premises and sold in the shop.

Victoria St. ✆ 01451/820698. Admission £2 ($3.20) adults, £1.75 ($2.80) children and seniors. Mon–Sat 9:30am–5pm; Sun 10:30am–5pm. Closed Dec 25–26.

The Model Village at the Old New Inn   Beginning in the 1930s, a local hotelier, Mr. Morris, whiled away the Great Depression by constructing a scale model (1:9) of Bourton-on-the-Water as testimony to its architectural charms. No tiny, cramped display behind glass here—you can actually walk through this nearly perfect, most realistic model village.

High St. ✆ 01451/820467. Admission £2.75 ($4.40) adults, £2.50 ($4) seniors, £2 ($3.20) children. Daily 9am–6pm or dusk in summer; daily 10am–4pm in winter.

Cotswold Countryside Collection   This museum of rural life is actually located off the A40 between Burford and Cheltenham. It was recently combined with the Cotswold Country Museum to form the Cotswold Heritage Center. You can see the Lloyd-Baker collection of agricultural history, including wagons, horse-drawn implements, and tools. A Cotswold gallery records the social history of the area. "Below Stairs" is an exhibition of laundry, dairy, and kitchen implements. The museum was once a house of correction, and its history is displayed in the reconstructed cellblock and courtroom.

Fosse Way, Northleach (Cotswold District Council). ✆ 01451/860715. Admission to Cotswold Heritage Center £3 ($4.80) adults, £2.50 ($4) seniors, £1.50 ($2.40) students, £1 ($1.60) children 5–16, free for children 4 and under, £7 ($11) family ticket. Apr–Oct Mon–Sat 10am 5pm, Sun 2–5pm; Nov–Dec Sat 10am–4pm.

THE GREAT COTSWOLD RAMBLE

A walking tour between the villages of Upper and Lower Slaughter, with an optional extension to Bourton-on-the-Water, is one of the most memorable in England. It's a mile each way between the Slaughters, and 4km (2½ miles) between Upper Slaughter and Bourton-on-the-Water. The walk can take between 2 and 4 hours.

The architecture of Upper and Lower Slaughter is so unusual that you're likely to remember this easy hike for many years; the honey-colored stone cottages represent a peak in English domestic design. By striking out on foot, you avoid some of the traffic that taxes the nerves and goodwill of local residents during peak season. En route, you're likely to glimpse the waterfowl that inhabit the rivers, streams, and millponds that crisscross this region.

A well-worn footpath known as Warden's Way meanders alongside the swift-moving River Eye. From its well-marked beginning in Upper Slaughter's central car park, the path passes grazing sheep, antique houses of honey-colored local stone, stately trees arching over ancient millponds, and footbridges that have endured centuries of foot traffic and rain. The river powers a historic mill on the northwestern edge of Lower Slaughter. In quiet eddies, you'll see waterfowl and birds, including wild ducks, gray wagtails, mute swans, coots, and Canada geese.

Most visitors turn around at Lower Slaughter, but Warden's Way continues another 2.5km (1½ miles) to Bourton-on-the-Water via the ancient Roman Fosse Way. The path leaves the riverside and strikes out across cattle pastures in a southerly direction. Most of this portion of the path is covered by tarmac; closed to cars, it's ideal for walking or biking. You're legally required to close every gate that stretches across the footpath.

Warden's Way brings you to Bourton-on-the-Water through the hamlet's northern edges. The first landmark you'll see is the tower of St. Lawrence's Anglican Church. From the base of the church, walk south along The Avenue (one of the hamlet's main streets) and end your Cotswold ramble on the Village Green, directly in front of the War Memorial.

You can take this route in reverse, but parking is more plentiful in Upper Slaughter than in Lower Slaughter.

WHERE TO STAY

Broadlands Guest House   One of the more distinctive B&Bs in the area sits in a pleasantly isolated spot, removed from the congestion of the village but only 5 minutes away. (Overflow guests are housed at Landsdowne Villa, at Landsdowne, Bourton-on-the-Water.) The renovated Victorian building retains many of its original features, including a glassed-in conservatory. The nonsmoking rooms, all doubles, have showers and bathtubs. Two of the bedrooms contain a four-poster bed. Dinner can be ordered if prior arrangements are made.

Clapton Row, Bourton-on-the-Water, Cheltenham, Gloucestershire GL54 2DN. ℂ 01451/822002. 11 units. £46–£65 ($74–$104) double. Rates include English breakfast. No credit cards. **Amenities:** Breakfast room; pre-arranged dinners. *In room:* TV, coffeemaker, hair dryer, no phone.

Farncombe ✰ *Finds*   Farncombe lies 4km (2½ miles) from Bourton-on-the-Water. This little hamlet of 20 houses is known only to the discerning English, who stay here when the more popular and famous village is overrun with visitors. Opening onto views of the Windrush Valley, this nonsmoking house makes a good base for touring the Cotswolds. The simply furnished rooms are all doubles.

Clapton on the Hill, Bourton-on-the-Water, Cheltenham, Gloucestershire GL54 2LG. ℂ and fax 01451/820120. 3 units, 1 with bathroom (2 with shower only). £22 ($35) single; £44 ($70) double. Rates include English breakfast. No credit cards. Take A429 toward Cirencester, then the 1st left after Bourton. **Amenities:** Breakfast room. *In room:* Coffeemaker, hair dryer, no phone.

WHERE TO DINE

Old New Inn ✰ ENGLISH   With its popular wine garden, this is one of the best places to eat in Bourton-on-the-Water and is now only open for dinner. There are good, fresh, and reasonably priced bar snacks (easily turned into a full meal). You can also have a more formal dinner in the evening, enjoying good if plain English cookery.

High St. ℂ **01451/820467.** Fixed-price meals 2 courses £15 ($24), 3 courses £18 ($29); bar snacks £3–£8 ($4.80–$13). MC, V. Daily 12:30–1:45pm and 7:30–8:45pm.

8 Stow-on-the-Wold ⟨★

15km (9 miles) SE of Broadway; 16km (10 miles) S of Chipping Campden; 6km (4 miles) S of Moreton-in-Marsh; 34km (21 miles) S of Stratford-upon-Avon

As you pass through Shakespeare's "high wild hills and rough uneven ways," you arrive at Stow-on-the-Wold, its very name evoking the elusive spirit of the Cotswolds, one of the greatest sheep-rearing districts of England. Lying 240m (800 ft.) above sea level, it stands on a plateau where "the cold winds blow," or so goes the old saying. This town prospered when Cotswold wool was demanded the world over. Stow-on-the-Wold may not be the cognoscenti's favorite—Chipping Campden takes that honor—but it's even more delightful as it has a real Cotswold town atmosphere.

The town lies smack in the middle of the Fosse Way, one of the Roman trunk roads that cut a swath through Britain. Kings have passed through here, including Edward VI, son of Henry VIII, and they've bestowed their approval on the town. Stagecoaches stopped off here for the night on their way to Cheltenham.

A 14th-century cross stands in the large Market Square, where you can still see the stocks where "offenders" in the past were jeered at and punished by the townspeople who threw rotten eggs at them. The final battle between the Roundheads and the Royalists took place outside Stow-on-the-Wold, and mean old Cromwell incarcerated 1,500 Royalist troops in St. Edward's Market Square.

The square today teems with pubs and outdoor cafes. But leave the square at some point and wander at leisure along some of the narrowest alleyways in Britain. When the summer crowds get you down, head in almost any direction from Stow to surrounding villages that look like sets from a Merchant/Ivory film.

ESSENTIALS

GETTING THERE Several trains run daily from London's Paddington Station to Moreton-in-Marsh (see below). For schedules and information, call ℂ **0845/ 7484950.** From Moreton-in-Marsh, Pulhams Bus Company makes the 10-minute ride to Stow-on-the-Wold.

National Express buses also run daily from London's Victoria Coach Station to Moreton-in-Marsh, where you can catch a Pulhams Bus Company coach to Stow-on-the-Wold. For schedules and information, call ℂ **08705/808080.** Several Pulhams coaches also run daily to Stow-on-the-Wold from Cheltenham.

If driving from Oxford, take the A40 west to the junction with the A424, near Burford. Head northwest along the A424 to Stow-on-the-Wold.

VISITOR INFORMATION The **Tourist Information Centre** is at Hollis House, The Square (ℂ **01451/831082**). It's open Easter through October, Monday through Saturday from 9:30am to 5:30pm, Sunday from 9am to 5pm; from November to mid-February, Monday through Saturday from 9:30am to 4:30pm; and from mid-February to Easter, Monday through Saturday from 9:30am to 5pm.

ANTIQUES HEAVEN

Don't be fooled by the town's sleepy, bucolic country setting: Stow-on-the-Wold has developed over the last 20 years into an antiques buyer's mecca, with at least 60 merchandisers scattered throughout the town and its environs. **Anthony**

Preston Antiques, Ltd., The Square (✆ **01451/831586**), with four showrooms inside an 18th-century building, specializes in English and French furniture, including large pieces, such as bookcases, and decorative objects, including paperweights, lamps, paintings on silk, and other objects to add a glossy accent to interior decors. **Baggott Church Street, Ltd.** (✆ **01451/830370**), on Church Street, is the smaller of two shops founded and maintained by a well-regarded local merchant, Duncan ("Jack") Baggott, frequently seen at estate sales throughout Britain. The shop's four showrooms show furniture and paintings from the 17th to the 19th century. Baggott's second shop, **Woolcomber House,** on Sheep Street (✆ **01451/830662**), is more eclectic and wide-ranging. Among the largest retail outlets in the Cotswolds, its 17 rooms once constituted a coaching inn; now each is lavishly decorated according to a particular era of English decorative history. **Huntington's Antiques Ltd.,** Church Street (✆ **01451/830842**), covers about half a block in the heart of town. It contains one of the largest stocks of quality antiques in England. Wander through 10 ground-floor rooms, then climb to the second floor where a long gallery and four additional showrooms bulge with refectory tables, unusual cupboards, and other finds.

WHERE TO STAY

Cross Keys Cottage   A minute's drive east of Stow-on-the-Wold's center, this most charming B&B began as a brewery in 1640. The narrow cottage visible from the road is only part of it; there are three interconnected stone cottages, with numbers 2 and 3 built in 1660 and 1950, respectively, and a walled-in cottage garden. The cottage's charming owners, Margaret and Roger Welton, gained their managerial expertise by directing a sports program at a Cypriot resort hotel. All rooms are doubles and comfortably appointed, three with a private, shower-only bathroom and one with shower-and-tub combination. The comfortable interior includes a log-burning fireplace, and the breakfasts are of good quality.

Park St., Stow-on-the-Wold, Gloucestershire GL54 1AQ. ✆ **01451/831128.** www.broadway-cotswolds. co.uk. 4 units. £55–£65 ($88–$104) double. Rates include breakfast. No credit cards. **Amenities:** Breakfast room; 2 lounges. *In room:* TV, coffeemaker, hair dryer, no phone.

The Limes Guest House   This Victorian building sits along A424 (Evesham Rd.), a 4-minute walk from the heart of the town. It has a lovely garden, and in chilly weather, log fires make the house warm and inviting. The small non-smoking bedrooms are rather plain, but one has a four-poster bed. The attentive owners, Mr. and Mrs. Keyte, will cater to vegetarians.

Evesham Rd., Stow-on-the-Wold, Gloucestershire GL54 1EJ. ✆ **01451/830034.** Fax 01451/830034. the limes@zoom.co.uk. 5 units. £45 ($72) double. Rates include English breakfast. No credit cards. Free parking. **Amenities:** Breakfast room. *In room:* TV, coffeemaker, hair dryer, no phone.

The Royalist Hotel ★★   Dating from A.D. 947 (no mistake), The Royalist is listed in the Guinness Book of World Records as the oldest inn in England. A number of clues to its long history still remain: Ask the proprietors, Alan and Georgina Thompson, to tell you about the ancient tunnels leading to the church and Maugersbury Manor, or of young John Shellard, who died in 1638 but remains a frequent visitor to the hotel's bar. The charm and character of the non-smoking inn survived the addition of 20th-century comforts. Each small room now has a private bathroom, and independently controlled heating. Rooms in an annex (ca. 1950) lack the intrigue of those in the original building.

Digbeth St., Stow-on-the-Wold, Gloucestershire GL54 1BN. ✆ **01451/830670.** www.theroyalisthotel.co.uk. 12 units. Fri–Sat £130 ($208) double. Sun–Thurs £60 ($96) single; £90 ($144) double. Rates include English breakfast. AE, DC, MC, V. **Amenities:** 2 restaurants; 2 bars; room service (7am–midnight); dry cleaning. *In room:* TV, dataport, coffeemaker, hair dryer.

WHERE TO DINE

The Old Stocks Hotel BRITISH   This restaurant's woodsy, dark-stained setting fills most of the ground floor of the town's most visible and cost-conscious hotel, a stone-fronted building facing the stocks. The food served is straightforward, old-fashioned, and British. At lunchtime, you place your food order at the battered bar, and someone carries the finished product to your table. At night, the place is more formal and somewhat more expensive, with staff members replicating some of the ambience of an unpretentious Edwardian eatery. Don't expect fancy sauces or garnishes here—you'll find steak-and-kidney pie, grilled or pan-fried trout served with lemon juice, plain grilled Dover sole with seasonal vegetables, chicken supreme, and grilled steaks with potatoes and vegetables. As for the hotel, there are 18 units, most of them nonsmoking, with rates of £80 to £90 ($128–$144) double.

The Square, Stow-on-the-Wold. ✆ 01451/830666. Lunch platters in bar £2.50–£7.50 ($4–$12); fixed-price dinners £13.50–£19.95 ($22–$32). MC, V. Daily noon–2pm; Sun–Thurs 7–9pm; Fri–Sat 7–9:30pm.

9 Moreton-in-Marsh ✦

133 km (83 miles) NW of London; 6km (4 miles) N of Stow-on-the-Wold; 12km (7 miles) S of Chipping Campden; 28km (17 miles) S of Stratford-upon-Avon

Despite the name, this is no swampland; "marsh" derives from an old word meaning "border." Moreton-in-Marsh is a real Cotswold market town, at its most bustling on Tuesday morning, when farmers and craftspeople who live in the area flood the town to sell their wares and produce. Some of the scenes there evoke the hit film and classic musical, *Brigadoon.*

Moreton-in-Marsh has one of the widest High Streets in the Cotswolds. It was an important stopover for Roman legions trudging along the old Fosse Way centuries ago. In later years it provided a layover for stagecoach passengers. Today, visitors and antiques shops abound.

Charles I spent a night here (at the White Hart); you can do the same, for it's a convenient point for touring all the Cotswolds. The town is filled with remnants of its past, including a Market Hall on High Street (built 1887 in Victorian Tudor style) and Curfew Tower on Oxford Street, dating from the 17th century, whose bell was rung daily until the late 19th century.

ESSENTIALS

Trains run from London's Paddington Station to Moreton-in-Marsh, a nearly 2-hour trip. For schedules and information, call ✆ **0845/7484950.**

National Express buses run from London's Victoria Coach Station to Moreton-in-Marsh daily. For schedules and information, call ✆ **020/7529-2000.**

If you're driving from Stow-on-the-Wold (see above), take the A429 north.

SEEING THE SIGHTS

For a fascinating lesson on birds of prey, stop by the **Cotswold Falconry Centre,** Batsford Park (✆ **01386/701043**). These great birds are flown daily by experienced falconers for visitors to see firsthand the remarkable speed and agility of eagles, hawks, owls, and falcons. It's open daily February 15 to November 30 from 10:30am to 5pm. Flying displays are daily at 11:30am, 1:30, 3, and 4:30pm. Admission is £4 ($6) for adults and £2.50 ($4) for children 4 to 14 (free for children 3 and under).

WHERE TO STAY

Blue Cedar House Named after an enormous tree in its front yard, this brown brick house was built in 1952, on the edge of the village center along A429, a 10-minute walk from the rail station. It stands on a half-acre of land with a fishpond. The house is owned and operated by Sandra and Graham Billinger, who offer comfortable midsize nonsmoking bedrooms. There is a TV lounge with hot beverage facilities.

Stow Rd., Moreton-in-Marsh, Gloucestershire GL56 0DW. © 01608/650299. 4 units, 2 with bathroom. £23 ($37) single; £46 ($74) double. Rates include English breakfast. No credit cards. Closed Dec–Jan. **Amenities:** Breakfast room; babysitting. *In room:* TV, coffeemaker, hair dryer, no phone.

Mill Dene ★★ *Finds* A former Cotswold stone water mill, this handsomely converted property lies right outside Moreton-in Marsh in the hamlet of Blockley. Set in 2 acres of award-winning gardens, it's a cliché of English country charm, with paths from the mill pool, stream, and grotto leading up a rose walk. Bask yourself in old English here in a property that dates in the main from the 1600s with parts even going back to around the time of the Norman conquest. Each nonsmoking bedroom, a double, is well furnished and comes with a combination tub and shower for the most part. Barry and Wendy Dare and their Birman cats extend a hearty welcome.

Blockley, near Moreton-in-Marsh Gloucestershire GI56 9HU. © 01386/700457. Fax 01386/700526. www. smoothhound.co.uk/hotels/milldene.html. 3 units. £65–£80 ($104–$128) double per person. Rates include breakfast. No credit cards. Lies 5km/3 miles west of Moreton-in-Marsh. **Amenities:** Breakfast room; outdoor heated pool. *In room:* TV, coffeemaker, hair dryer, no phone.

New Farm Located a mile north of Moreton-in-Marsh, just off A429, this is a dairy farmhouse built in the 1790s. Catherine Righton is the hostess. All the nonsmoking rooms are spacious; one has a private bathroom, and many units contain antiques. New Farm has a large and impressive fireplace in the dining room, where breakfast comes with hot crispy bread.

Dorn, Moreton-in-Marsh, Gloucestershire GL56 9NS. © and fax 01608/650782. 3 units, 1 with bathroom. £25 ($40) single with or without bathroom; £42 ($67) double with or without bathroom. Rates include English breakfast. No credit cards. **Amenities:** Breakfast room. *In room:* TV, hair dryer (on request), iron (on request), no phone.

Treetops Guest House Located a 5-minute stroll from the heart of town, this hostelry's driveway is identified with a sign visible from the main A44 highway. Treetops dates from 1983, when Brian and Elizabeth Dean realized their dream of designing and building their own house. Their home stands amid fir and beech trees in almost an acre of garden. Each midsize double room contains a private bathroom with shower. A sunroom was added in 1998.

London Rd., Moreton-in-Marsh, Gloucestershire GL56 0HE. © and fax 01608/651036. treetops1@talk21.com. 6 units. £50–£55 ($80–$88) double. Rates include English breakfast. MC, V. **Amenities:** Breakfast room; lounge. *In room:* TV, coffeemaker, hair dryer, no phone.

WHERE TO DINE

The Black Bear ★ BRITISH It's not the oldest pub in town (that honor goes to the White Hart, a few steps away), but its regulars claim that it serves the best food and is, at its best, the most fun. The 17th-century setting includes exposed stone, heavy beams, and paneling that reveal the patina of many generations. At lunch, place your food order at the bar; at dinner, someone waits on you. The menu includes the usual lasagna, steak-and-kidney pie, and ploughman's lunches, although there are usually a few dishes that raise the cuisine beyond the pub grub level, such as duck breast in orange and brandy sauce, or peppercorn-encrusted steaks. There's a roster of lagers and stouts on tap, including a local bitter (Donnington).

High St., Moreton-in-Marsh. © **01608/650705.** Main courses £4.95–£12.95 ($8–$21). DC, MC, V. Daily noon–2pm and 6:30–9pm. Pub: daily 11am–11pm.

Inn on the Marsh *Value* BRITISH/INTERNATIONAL   The last pub on A492 heading southward, about 1km (½ mile) from the center, this inn is the most substantial and well rounded of local cost-conscious restaurants. Recent significant improvements come courtesy of its new owners, Wayne and Kim Branagh. The setting is a chronological hodgepodge, including an Elizabethan bar area, lined with turn-of-the-century photos of the nearby marshes before they were drained, and a faux Edwardian conservatory (added 1991), where most sit-down meals are served. Menu items include chicken-and-mushroom pie, deep-fried scampi or plaice, charbroiled chicken, lamb with mint sauce, pork with applesauce, and an 8-ounce rump steak. Everything is served with chips or roasted potatoes and vegetables. No one will mind if you preface or follow your meal with a round of drinks at the pub.

Stow Rd. (Hwy. A492), Moreton-in-Marsh. © **01608/650709.** Main courses £6.95–£9.95 ($11–$16); lunch £1.85–£6.95 ($2.95–$11). MC, V. Daily noon–2pm; Tues–Sun 7–9pm.

Market House ENGLISH   Market House is on the town's main street, a few paces from the Town Hall. Set behind a prominent bow window and a Cotswold stone facade, this 1590s building provides a tearoom-style setting ideal for morning coffee, a flavorful lunch, or a reasonably priced early supper. Choose from relatively simple fare like prawn cocktails or soups, steak-and-kidney pudding, chicken Kiev, and fried plaice, haddock, or cod, followed by a piece of moist cake or other dessert. Sandwiches and fresh salads are also served. In fair weather, a patio is opened.

4 High St., Moreton-in-Marsh. © **01608/650767.** Reservations recommended for large parties. Main courses £3.95–£6.95 ($6–$11). No credit cards. Mon–Fri 9am–5pm; Sat 10am–5pm; Sun 11am–5pm.

10 Broadway ⟨★ ★

23km (15 miles) SW of Stratford-upon-Avon; 149km (93 miles) NW of London; 23km (15 miles) NE of Cheltenham

This is the showcase village of the Cotswolds, overlooking the lovely Vale of Evesham. If you don't mind dealing with the omnipresent coach tours in summer, this is the most attractive spot to rest for the night. Follow in the footsteps of either Charles I or Cromwell by finding a cozy place by the fire at the historic Lygon Arms (see below). Many prime attractions of the Cotswolds, including Shakespeare country, are close at hand. Flanked by honey-colored stone buildings, its High Street is a gem, remarkable for its harmonious style and design.

Don't come here for museums and attractions, however: Show-stopping Broadway is its own magnet. When you see wisteria and cordoned fruit trees covering 17th-century cottages, fronted by immaculately maintained gardens, you'll understand why Henry James found it "delicious to be in Broadway." William Morris was first to write of its charms; in time, a host of British greats followed in his footsteps, including Ralph Vaughan Williams, Edward Elgar, and J. M. Barrie.

As you walk along High Street, you'll be overwhelmed by dozens of tea parlors, antiques galore, and quaint boutiques.

ESSENTIALS

GETTING THERE Rail connections are possible from London's Paddington Station via Oxford. The nearest railway stations are at Moreton-in-Marsh (11km/ 7 miles away) or at Evesham (8km/5 miles away). For schedules and information, call ✆ **0845/7484950.** Frequent buses arrive from Evesham, but you have to take a taxi from Moreton.

One **National Express** coach departs daily from London's Victoria Coach Station to Broadway, a 2½-hour ride. For schedules and information, call ✆ **08705/808080.**

If you're driving from Oxford, head west on the A40, then take the A434 to Woodstock, Chipping Norton, and Moreton-in-Marsh.

VISITOR INFORMATION The **Tourist Information Centre** is at 1 Cotswold Ct. (✆ **01386/852937**), open February through December, Monday through Saturday from 10am to 1pm and 2 to 5pm.

EXPLORING BROADWAY

Broadway's **High Street** ✸✸✸ is perhaps the most beautiful of its kind in England. Many of the street's most striking facades date from 1620 or the 18th and 19th centuries. Its most famous facade belongs to the **Lygon Arms,** High Street (✆ **01386/852255**), a venerable old inn. Standing on 1 hectare (3 acres) of formal gardens, it's been serving wayfarers since 1532. Even if you don't stay here, you might want to visit for a meal or drink.

You might seek out **St. Eadurgha's Church,** a site of Christian worship for more than 1,000 years. It's located just outside Broadway on Snowshill Road, and is open most days, though with no set visiting hours. If it's closed when you visit, a note on the porch door tells you what house to go to for the key. There are occasional Sunday services here.

Also along the street you can visit the **Broadway Magic Experience,** 76 High St. (✆ **01386/858323**), a showcase shop for teddy bear and doll artisans. The site is also the setting for a unique museum displaying hundreds of antique and collectors' teddy bears, toys, and dolls. This 18th-century stone shop offers a historical look at the world of teddy bears, ranging from Steiff to Pooh. Hours are Tuesday through Sunday from 10am to 5pm. Admission is £2.50 ($4) for adults, and £1.75 ($2.80) for children under 14 and seniors, £7 ($11) for a family ticket.

On the outskirts of Broadway stands the **Broadway Tower Country Park** on Broadway Hill (✆ **01386/852390**), a "folly" created by the fanciful mind of the sixth Earl of Coventry. Today, you can climb this tower on a clear day for a panoramic vista of 12 shires. It's the most sweeping view in the Cotswolds. The tower is open from early April to late October daily from 10:30am to 5pm. Admission is £4 ($6) for adults and £3 ($4.80) for children. You can also bring the makings for a picnic here and spread it out for your lunch in designated areas.

South of Broadway is **Snowshill Manor,** at Snowshill (✆ **01386/852410**), a house that dates mainly from the 17th century. It was once owned by Charles Paget Wade, who collected virtually everything he could between 1900 and 1951. Queen Mary once remarked that Wade himself was the most remarkable artifact among his entire flea market. You'll find a little bit of everything here: Flemish tapestries, toys, lacquer cabinets, narwhal tusks, mousetraps, and cuckoo clocks—a glorious mess, like a giant attic of the 20th century. The property, owned by the National Trust, is open April through October, Wednesday through Sunday from noon to 5pm, and Monday in July and August. Admission is £6.40 ($10) per person or £16 ($26) for a family ticket.

TEATIME

The best place in Broadway for a cup of tea is **Tisanes,** The Green (℃ **01386/ 852112**). The shop offers perfectly blended teas with a variety of lighter foods, such as sandwiches and salads. Sweets include fruit tarts, baked cheesecake, and several types of cake. Basic teas are priced from £3.75 ($6). Tisanes also sells teapots, china, and a wide variety of specialty teas.

WHERE TO STAY

The Crown and Trumpet Inn Located just behind the town's village green and set behind a facade of honey-colored Cotswold stone, this 16th-century inn is known locally as a public house more than as a hotel. It does offer a handful of simple upstairs double bedrooms to travelers, each with a private shower.

Church St., Broadway, Worcestershire WR12 7AE. ℃ **01386/853202**. www.cotswoldholidays.co.uk. 5 units. £58–£70 ($93–$112) double. Rates include English breakfast. MC, V. **Amenities:** Breakfast room; pub. *In room:* TV, coffeemaker, hair dryer, no phone.

Old Station House *(Value)* The 19th-century stone house where Pam and David Trueman receive B&B guests is a bargain for Broadway, located in a tranquil location off A44, a 10-minute walk from the village center. There's unlimited parking on the grounds of the house and on the approach drive. The nonsmoking house is centrally heated; a log fire blazes in the guest lounge during cooler weather. Bedrooms are small and neatly kept, each with a private bathroom or shower.

Station Dr., Broadway, Hereford and Worcestershire WR12 7DF. ℃ **01386/852659**. Fax 01386/852891. www. broadway-cotswolds.co.uk/oldstationhouse.html. 6 units. £35 ($56) single; £49–£60 ($78–$96) double. MC, V. **Amenities:** Breakfast room; lounge. *In room:* TV, coffeemaker, minifridge, hair dryer, no phone.

Olive Branch Guest House *(★)* *(Value)* In the heart of an expensive town, this is a terrific bargain. The 1592 house retains its old Cotswold architectural features. Behind the house is a large walled English garden and parking area. Furnishings are basic and comfortable; the nonsmoking rooms are tiny. There is one room available for those with limited mobility. Guests receive a discount for purchases at the owners' attached antiques shop.

78 High St., Broadway, Worcestershire WR12 7AJ. ℃ **01386/853440**. Fax 01386/859070. www.theolive branch-broadway.com. 8 units, 7 with tub or shower. £40 ($64) single without bathroom, £45 ($72) single with bathroom; £60–£75 ($96–$120) double with tub or shower. Rates include English breakfast. MC, V. **Amenities:** Breakfast room; lounge; babysitting; laundry. *In room:* TV, coffeemaker, hair dryer, no phone.

Pathlow House This hostelry comprises the house, built in 1720, and a small cottage in the courtyard. The rates are quite reasonable, considering the location in the heart of the village. Each small nonsmoking unit is a double and is plainly furnished. The house, run by Adrian Green, is centrally heated.

82 High St., Broadway, Worcestershire WR12 7AJ. ℃ and fax **01386/853444**. www.pathlowguesthouse.co. uk. 7 units, 5 with bathroom, 1 family cottage. £50–£55 ($80–$88) double; £110 ($176) cottage. Rates include English breakfast. No credit cards. **Amenities:** Breakfast room; pre-arranged dinner. *In room:* TV, coffeemaker, hair dryer, no phone.

Whiteacres *(★)* One of the best B&Bs in this high-priced town, Whiteacres occupies an unpretentious but charming late Victorian house on the southern extension of High Street, a 5-minute walk from the center. Owned and operated by the Buchan family, its nonsmoking bedrooms, all doubles, are pretty, comfortable and have private shower-only bathrooms. Three rooms contain four-poster beds.

Station Rd., Broadway, Worcestershire WR12 7DE. ℃ **01386/852320**. www.whiteacres-cotswolds.co.uk. 4 units. £35 ($56) single; £50 ($80) double. Rates include English breakfast. No credit cards. **Amenities:** Breakfast room; lounge. *In room:* TV, coffeemaker, hair dryer, no phone.

WHERE TO DINE

Broadway Hotel *Value* ENGLISH/INTERNATIONAL   Formerly used by the abbots of Pershore, this centrally located hotel combines the half-timbered look of the Vale of Evesham with Cotswolds stone. Even the locals agree that its bar is the best low-cost lunch stop in town. Lunches are served at the bar, where you can order one of that day's platters. Dinner, however, is served in the more formal dining room, right on the village green. Traditional English food is featured, including fresh fish, duckling, and (in season) venison. The ingredients are generally good, and most dishes seem to satisfy.

The Green. © **01386/852401.** Fixed-price lunch £10.95–£12.50 ($18–$20); fixed-price dinner £19.50–£21.95 ($31–$35). AE, DC, MC, V. Daily noon–2pm and 7–9pm.

Oliver's ENGLISH/INTERNATIONAL   Set adjacent to the historic Lygon Arms (see "Exploring Broadway," above), this 17th-century building is built of Cotswold stone and filled with antiques. The brasserie-style menu includes such good-tasting dishes as Caesar salad with smoked chicken and Parmesan curls, goat cheese ravioli with a fondue of wild mushrooms, and roasted filets of mullet with saffron-flavored fennel and shellfish-based bouillabaisse. The seasonally changing menu is marked on a chalkboard. An ever-popular dessert is orange and pecan-flavored sponge pudding with Bailey's-flavored custard.

Adjacent to the Lygon Arms Hotel, High St. © **01386/854418.** Reservations recommended. Main courses £9.95–£13.95 ($16–$22). AE, DC, MC, V. Mon–Fri noon–2pm and 7–9pm; Sat–Sun noon–9pm.

11 Chipping Campden ★ ★

58km (36 miles) NW of Oxford; 20km (12 miles) S of Stratford-upon-Avon; 149km (93 miles) NW of London

In the 17th century, Chipping Campden was one of the richest wool towns of England. The wool merchants have long departed, but the architectural legacy of honey-colored stone cottages—financed by "white gold"—remains to delight the visitor. The Campden Trust, a determined group of dedicated conservationists, has preserved the town as it should be.

On the northern edge of the Cotswolds, Chipping Campden opens onto the dreamy Vale of Evesham, which you've seen depicted in a thousand postcards. Except for the heavy summer traffic, the High Street still looks as it did centuries ago—the noted British historian G. M. Trevelyan called it "the most beautiful village street now left in the island." And so it remains.

Arriving through seductively beautiful landscapes, you come upon this country town, whose landmark is the soaring tower of the 15th-century Church of St. James, visible for miles around. Constructed in the Perpendicular style, it is one of the finest churches in the Cotswolds.

The town's long High Street is curved like Oxford's and lined with stone houses dating from the 16th century. Nearby on Church Street you encounter the Gravel House; across the way from it stands the 14th-century Woolstapler's Hall, where the merchants traded. The Market Hall at Market Street, built in 1627, is another graceful structure, composed of 14 stone arches. Sir Baptiste Hycks erected this gabled building "for the sale of local produce."

Of special interest is the Silk Mill, Sheep Street, open Monday to Saturday 9am to 5pm. Poet, artist, and craftsman William Morris (1834–96) called the Cotswold countryside home for most of his life. The worldwide Arts and Crafts movement he led in the 19th century continued to inspire local artists and craftspeople after his death.

The Guild of Handicrafts was established at the Silk Mill in 1902, practicing such skills as bookbinding and cabinetmaking. It folded in 1920 but has been revived today with a series of crafts workshops.

Try to add a stopover here as you rush from Oxford to Stratford-upon-Avon; or visit here the same day that you go to Broadway, 6.5km (4 miles) to the west.

ESSENTIALS

GETTING THERE   Trains depart from London's Paddington Station for Moreton-in-Marsh, a 1½ to 2-hour trip. For schedules and information, call © **0845/7484950.** A bus operated by Castleway's travels the 11km (7 miles) from Moreton-in-Marsh to Chipping Campden five times a day. Many visitors opt for a taxi from Moreton-in-Marsh to Chipping Campden.

The largest and most important nearby bus depot is Cheltenham, which receives service several times a day from London's Victoria Coach Station. For schedules and information, call © **08705/808080.** From Cheltenham, Barry's Coaches are infrequent and uncertain, departing three times per week at most. Call Gloucester Coach Station (© **01452/527516**) for details.

If you're driving from Oxford, take A40 west to the junction with A424. Follow it northwest, passing by Stow-on-the-Wold. The route becomes A44 until you reach the junction with B4081, which you take northeast to Chipping Campden.

VISITOR INFORMATION   The **Tourist Information Centre** is at Noel Court, High Street (© **01386/841206**), open daily 10am to 6pm.

HIDCOTE MANOR

In 1907 the American horticulturist Maj. Lawrence Johnstone created Hidcote Manor Garden, 6.5km (4 miles) northeast of Chipping Campden and 14km (9 miles) south of Stratford-upon-Avon (© **01386/438333**). Set on 4 hectares (10 acres), this masterpiece contains small gardens separated by a variety of hedges, old roses, rare shrubs, trees, and herbaceous borders. *Tip:* In summer, Shakespeare is performed on the **Theatre Lawn** ★★; there is no more memorable experience in the Cotswolds than watching *A Midsummer's Night Dream* performed here on a balmy July evening.

Admission is £5.90 ($9) for adults, £2.90 ($4.65) for children, £14.50 ($23) for a family ticket. Open April through October, Monday, Wednesday, Thursday, Saturday, and Sunday 11am to 6pm; June through July, Tuesday 11am to 7pm also. Last admission 6pm or 1 hour before sunset.

SHOPPING

At the studio of **D. T. Hart Silversmiths, The Guild,** The Silk Mill, Sheep Street (© **01386/841100**), silver is expertly worked by descendants of George Hart (an original member of the Guild of Handicrafts) in the original Ashbee workshop. In the **Robert Welch Studio Shop,** Lower High Street (© **01386/840522**), Mr. Welch has been crafting silverware, stainless steel, and cutlery for more than 40 years. **Martin Gotrel,** The Square (© **01386/841360**), designs and makes fine contemporary and traditional jewelry. **Campden Needlecraft Centre,** High Street (© **01386/840583**), is considered one of the leading specialist embroidery shops in England, with an interesting selection of embroidery, canvas work, fabrics, and threads. If antiques and antiques hunting are your passion, visit **School House Antiques,** High Street (© **01386/841474**). For new, secondhand, and antiquarian books, look up **Campden Bookshop,** High Street (© **01386/840944**), or Draycott Books, 1 Sheep St. (© **01386/841392**).

WHERE TO STAY

Marnic House   This house, in the agrarian hamlet of Broad Campden, about three-quarters of a mile north of Chipping Campden's center, is built of Cotswold stone dating from 1913. It's set on a country lane alongside similar houses, with views over fields and grazing sheep in front and back. The house is surrounded by a rock garden and outdoor terrace, good places to sit in warm weather. Owners Janet and Roy Rawlings named their place after their children, Mark and Nicola. The small nonsmoking bedrooms are comfortable and have private, shower-only bathrooms. No meals other than breakfast are served; the village pub, a short walk away, serves well-prepared food.

Broad Campden, Chipping Campden, Gloucestershire GL55 6UR. ℭ **01386/840014.** Fax 01386/840441. marnic@zoom.co.uk. 3 units. £55 ($88) double. Rates include English breakfast. No credit cards. **Amenities:** Breakfast room; lounge. *In room:* TV, coffeemaker, hair dryer, no phone.

WHERE TO DINE

The Bantam Tea Room ENGLISH   Opposite the historic market hall is a bow-windowed, 17th-century stone house where old-fashioned English after-noon teas are served. Tea might be just a pot and a tea cake, or you can indulge in homemade scones, crumpets, sandwiches, pastries, and cakes. Lunches are served, with a selection of local ham, chicken pie, pâtés, omelets, and salads.

High St. ℭ **01386/840386.** Main courses £3.50–£6.50 ($6–$10); cream tea £4–£5.25 ($6–$8). No credit cards. Tea Mon–Sat 9:30am–5:15pm, Sun 3–5pm; lunch daily noon–2pm. Closed Mon late Oct to early July.

Hicks Brasserie ENGLISH   You can eat a whole day's meals here. Ian and Christa Taylor, owners of Chipping Campden's most elegant hostelry, oversee a staff serving seasonal dishes. Starters include a salad of roasted peppers in olive oil with green beans, herbs, and Parmesan cheese, or the "Forbes Cotswold Cup"—button mushrooms and cubes of blue cheese and bacon pieces under a puff pastry top. These can be followed by a selection of pasta, fish, and meat dishes, including the mixed game and vegetable casserole or freshly made basil and garlic tagliatelle with smoked chicken and mushrooms in an herbed cream sauce. A popular dessert is the homemade ice cream.

In the Cotswold House Hotel, The Square. ℭ **01386/840330.** Main courses £10–£15 ($16–$24). AE, DC, MC, V. Daily 9:30am–9pm.

Kings Arms ENGLISH/CONTINENTAL   The Kings Arms, one of the town's leading inns (with rooms beyond our budget), offers a full restaurant and pub within it. Try to visit for the best bar snacks in town. You'll be tempted by arti-chokes and Stilton dressing, baked eggs, crab with Gruyère cheese and cream, fresh filet of mackerel in mustard-cream sauce, or more prosaic soups and pâtés. Entrees include roast duck in piquant orange sauce, beef stroganoff, and filet of pork Cal-vados. The kitchen does its best to add zest and flavor to the food.

The Square. ℭ **01386/840256.** Reservations recommended. Main courses £9–£12 ($14–$19). AE, MC, V. Daily noon–2:30pm and 6:30–9:30pm; pub: 11:30am–11:30pm.

The Vinery Restaurant ⭐ ENGLISH/CONTINENTAL   The Vinery serves homemade pasta dishes and other delectable items. The chef's specialty is filetto al piatto, thin layers of Scottish beef cooked on an extremely hot plate with olive oil, rosemary, and garlic. Fresh seasonal vegetables accompany main courses. For dessert, sample the crème brûlée. At the Malt House Bar, the hotel's other din-ing spot, you can order simple lunches served daily 11am to 2pm.

In the Seymour House Hotel & Restaurant, High St. ℭ **01386/840429.** Reservations recommended. Main courses £12–£16.50 ($19–$26); 2-course lunch £10.95 ($18). AE, MC, V. Daily noon–2pm and 7–10pm.

12

Shakespeare Country
& the Heart of England

After London, Shakespeare Country is the most popular destination in England for North Americans. Those who don't recognize the county name, Warwickshire, know its foremost tourist town, **Stratford-upon-Avon,** Shakespeare's birthplace and one of the great meccas for writers, readers, and playgoers from around the world.

Shakespeare's hometown is the best center for touring this area. You can take in the theater while in Stratford and branch out for day trips—notably to **Warwick Castle, Kenilworth Castle,** and **Coventry Cathedral.**

You'll also have the heart of England at your doorstep. Begin in nearby **Birmingham,** England's second-largest city. Although abandoned warehouses and bleak factories remain, this industrial city has been spruced up extensively. From here, branch out to any number of lovely old market towns and bucolic spots. There's the scenic **Malverns,** the historic town of **Shrewsbury** (where Ellis Peters's Brother Cadfael mysteries are set), and **Worcester,** of Royal Worcester Porcelain fame. Those who are truly passionate about porcelain flock to the fabled Potteries to visit towns like **Stoke-on-Trent,** where factory and outlet shops sell Wedgwood, Portmeirion, and other fine English tableware at a discount.

1 Stratford-upon-Avon ⟨*⟩

146km (91 miles) NW of London; 64km (40 miles) NW of Oxford; 13km (8 miles) S of Warwick

Crowds overrun this market town on the River Avon during the summer. No wonder: Stratford aggressively hustles its Shakespeare connection, and everyone seems to want to make a buck off the Bard. Will Shakespeare is no doubt turning over in his grave thinking of the average tourist buying a Bard T-shirt and a china model of Anne Hathaway's cottage before sampling a Big Mac. The throngs dwindle in winter, however, and you can at least walk on the streets and seek out places of genuine historic interest.

Along with the sites, the major draw for visitors is the **Royal Shakespeare Theatre,** where Britain's foremost actors perform during a long season. Other than theater, Stratford is rather devoid of rich cultural life, and you may want to return to London after you've done the literary pilgrimage and seen a production of *Hamlet.* But Stratford-upon-Avon is a good base for trips to Warwick, Kenilworth, and Coventry, discussed later in this chapter.

ESSENTIALS
GETTING THERE From London's Paddington Station to Stratford-upon-Avon, the journey takes about 2 hours and a round-trip ticket costs £23.20 ($37). For schedules and information, call ℂ **0845/7484950.** The train station

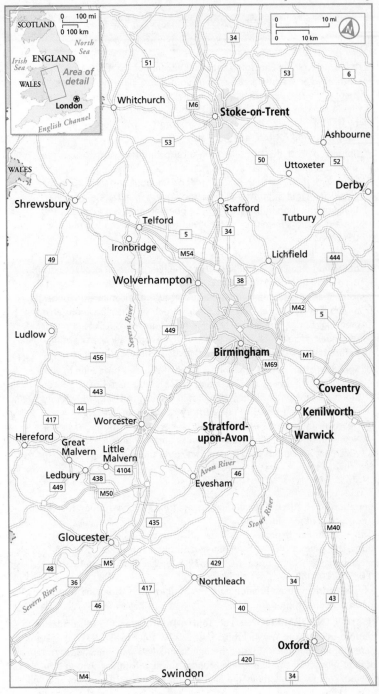

Value Cheap Thrills: What to See & Do for Free (or Almost) in the Land of the Bard

Have a picnic in Bancroft Gardens. Descendants of the swans that enthralled Shakespeare at Stratford-upon-Avon glide by as you picnic among the flower gardens and expanses of lawn in this spot between the Royal Shakespeare Theatre and Clopton Bridge. After, take a stroll by the 1888 Gower Memorial statue, decorated with bronze figures of Lady Macbeth, Falstaff, and Hamlet.

Share a pint at the Dirty Duck. In Stratford-upon-Avon you can see some of England's finest actors upon the stage, but to meet, walk, or drink with them, go to their favorite local hangout, the Dirty Duck, the unofficial name of Stratford's best known pub (p. 452). On a fair day, take your libation in the little terrace opening onto the Avon and the theaters. Actors from Garrick to Olivier have patronized this pub over the centuries.

Visit the secret villages along the Avon. When the crowds in Stratford get to you, head for the villages along the riverbanks, all known to the Bard himself. In Bidford-on-Avon, 11km (7 miles) southwest of Stratford, Shakespeare is said to have patronized the Falcon Inn, no longer a pub but still visible on the main street (in fact, an eight-arch medieval bridge still stands here). Welford-on-Avon, 6.5km (4 miles) southwest of Stratford, sits on a loop of the Avon. Walk across a bridge before taking in the whitewashed, thatched cottages along Boat Lane.

Spend an afternoon in the Stour villages. If you only have time to visit one of the charming villages along the winding banks of the River Stour, make it Alderminster, 8km (5 miles) south of Stratford, with its old stone cottages and a 13th-century church with a Norman nave. Nearby is unspoiled Preston-on-Stour, followed by Clifford Chamners, Newbold-on-Stour, Shipston-on-Stour, and delightful Honington, which has an old five-arch bridge that spans the river.

at Stratford is on Alcester Road. On Sundays from October to May, it is closed, so you'll have to rely on the bus.

Eight **National Express** buses a day leave from London's Victoria Station, with a trip time of 3¼ hours. A single-day round-trip ticket costs £13 ($21) except Friday when the price is £20 ($32). For schedules and information, call © **08705/808080.**

If you're driving from London, take the M40 toward Oxford and continue to Stratford-upon-Avon on the A34.

VISITOR INFORMATION   The **Tourist Information Centre,** Bridgefoot, Stratford-upon-Avon, Warwickshire, CV37 6GW (© **01789/293127**), is open March through October Monday through Saturday 9am to 6pm, Sunday 11am to 5pm; November through Easter Monday through Saturday 9am to 5pm. It provides copious detail about the Shakespeare houses and properties and will assist in booking rooms (see "Where to Stay," later in this chapter). Call and ask

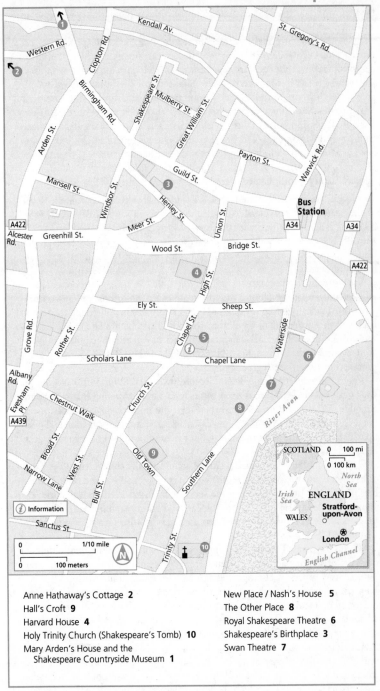

Kendall Av.
St. Gregory's Rd.
Western Rd.
Clopton Rd.
Shakespeare St.
Mulberry St.
Great William St.
Payton St.
Warwick Rd.
Arden St.
Birmingham Rd.
Mansell St.
Windsor St.
Guild St.
Henley St.
Meer St.
Union St.
Bus Station
A34
A34
A422
Alcester Rd.
Greenhill St.
Wood St.
Bridge St.
A422
High St.
Ely St.
Sheep St.
Grove Rd.
Rother St.
Chapel St.
Waterside
Scholars Lane
Chapel Lane
Albany Rd.
Evesham Pl.
A439
Chestnut Walk
Church St.
River Avon
Broad St.
West St.
Bull St.
Old Town
Southern Lane
Narrow Lane
Information
Sanctus St.
Trinity St.

0   1/10 mile
N
0   100 meters

SCOTLAND 0   100 mi
          0 100 km
North Sea
Irish Sea   ENGLAND
WALES   Stratford-upon-Avon
            London
English Channel

Anne Hathaway's Cottage **2**
Hall's Croft **9**
Harvard House **4**
Holy Trinity Church (Shakespeare's Tomb) **10**
Mary Arden's House and the
  Shakespeare Countryside Museum **1**

New Place / Nash's House **5**
The Other Place **8**
Royal Shakespeare Theatre **6**
Shakespeare's Birthplace **3**
Swan Theatre **7**

for a copy of their free "Shakespeare Country Holiday" guide. They also operate an American Express currency exchange office.

Built next door to Shakespeare's Birthplace, **The Shakespeare Centre,** on Henley Street (© **01789/204016;** www.shakespeare.org.uk), is the best place to get information about the Bard and about the attractions associated with him. The center is the headquarters of **The Shakespeare Birthplace Trust,** which administers the properties. Built to commemorate the 400th anniversary of Shakespeare's birth, the center is also a library and study center devoted to the Bard. An extension houses a visitor's center that acts as a reception area for those coming to the birthplace. The Shakespeare Centre is open March 20 to October 19, Monday to Saturday from 9am to 5pm, Sunday 9:30am to 5pm. From October 20 to March 19, it's open Monday to Saturday from 9:30am to 4pm, Sunday 10am to 4pm. Closed December 23 to December 26.

The Royal Shakespeare Theatre ★★★   On the banks of the Avon, the Royal Shakespeare Theatre, Waterside, Stratford-upon-Avon CV37 6BB (© **01789/ 295623**), is a major showcase for the Royal Shakespeare Company and seats 1,500 patrons. The theater's season runs from November until September and typically features five Shakespearean plays. The company has some of the finest actors on the British stage.

You'll usually need ticket reservations. There are two successive booking periods, each one opening about 2 months in advance. You can pick these up from a North American or English travel agent. A small number of tickets are always held for sale on the day of a performance, but it may be too late to get a good seat if you wait until you arrive in Stratford. Tickets can be booked through New York agent **Keith Prowse** (© **800/669-8687** or 212/398-1430; www.keith prowse.com). A service charge is added.

You can also call the theater box office directly (© **01789/403403**) and charge your tickets. The box office is open Monday to Saturday from 9:30am to 8pm, although it closes at 6pm on days when there are no performances. Seat prices range from £8 to £50 ($13–$80). You can make a credit-card reservation and pick up your tickets on the performance day, but you must cancel at least two full weeks in advance to get a refund.

Opened in 1986, the **Swan Theatre** is architecturally connected to the back of its older counterpart and shares the same box office, address, and phone number. It seats 430 on three sides of the stage, as in an Elizabethan playhouse, an appropriate design for plays by Shakespeare and his contemporaries. The Swan presents a repertory of about five plays each season, with tickets ranging from £10 to £30 ($16–$48).

Within the **Swan Theatre** is a painting gallery, which has a basic collection of portraits of famous actors and scenes from Shakespeare's plays by 18th- and 19th-century artists. It also operates as a base for guided tours with lively running commentary through the world-famous theaters. Guided tours are conducted at 1:30 and 5:30pm, and four times every Sunday afternoon, production schedules permitting. Tours cost £4 ($6) for adults and £3 ($4.80) for seniors, students, or children. Call ahead for tour scheduling, which is subject to change.

An addition to the Royal Shakespeare complex is **The Other Place,** a small, starkly minimalist theater located on Southern Lane, 274m (900 ft.) from its counterparts. It was redesigned in 1996 as an experimental workshop theater without a permanent stage; seats can be radically repositioned (or removed completely) throughout the theater. A recent example was a "promenade production" of *Julius Caesar,* in which the actors spent the whole play moving freely among a stand-up audience. Tickets are sold at the complex's main box office and generally range from £13 to £24 ($21–$38) each, but prices are subject to change.

SEEING THE SIGHTS

Besides the attractions on the periphery of Stratford, many Elizabethan and Jacobean buildings are in town, many of them administered by the **Shakespeare Birthplace Trust** (✆ **01789/204016**). One ticket—costing £13 ($21) adults, £12 ($19) for seniors and students, and £6 ($10) for children—lets you visit the five most important sights. You can also buy a family ticket to all five sights (good for two adults and three children) for £29 ($46)—a good deal. Pick up the ticket if you're planning to do much sightseeing (obtainable at your first stopover at any one of the Trust properties).

Guided tours of Stratford-upon-Avon leave from near the **Guide Friday Tourism Centre,** Civic Hall, Rother Street (✆ **01789/294466**). In summer, open-top double-decker buses depart every 15 minutes daily from 10am to 6pm. You can take a 1-hour ride without stops, or you can get off at any or all of the town's five Shakespeare properties. Though the bus stops are clearly marked along the historic route, the most logical starting point is the sidewalk in front of the Pen & Parchment Pub, at the bottom of Bridge Street. Tour tickets are valid all day so you can hop on and off the buses as many times as you want. The tours cost £8.50 ($14) for adults, £7 ($11) for seniors or students, and £3 ($4.80) for children under 12. A family ticket sells for £18 ($29), and children under 5 go free.

Anne Hathaway's Cottage ★   Before she married Shakespeare, Anne Hathaway lived in this thatched, wattle-and-daub cottage in the hamlet of Shottery, 1.5km (1 mile) from Stratford-upon-Avon. It's the most interesting and the most photographed of the Trust properties.

The Hathaways were yeoman farmers, and the cottage provides a rare insight into the life of a family in Shakespearean times. The Bard was only 18 when he married Anne, who was much older. Many of the original furnishings, including the courting settle and utensils, are preserved inside the house, which was occupied by descendants of Anne's family until 1892. After visiting the house, you'll want to linger in the garden and orchard.

Cottage Lane, Shottery. ✆ **01789/292100**. Admission £5 ($8) adults, £4 ($6) children, £29 ($46) family ticket (2 adults, 3 children) for all 5 Shakespeare-related houses. Nov–Mar daily 10am–4pm; Apr–May Mon– Sat 9:30am–5pm, Sun 10am–5pm; June–Aug Mon–Sat 9am–5pm, Sun 9:30am–5pm; Sept–Oct Mon–Sat 9:30am–5pm, Sun 10am–5pm. Closed Dec 23–26. Take a bus from Bridge St. or walk via a marked pathway from Evesham Place in Stratford across the meadow to Shottery.

Hall's Croft   It was here that Shakespeare's daughter Susanna probably lived with her husband, Dr. John Hall. Hall's Croft is an outstanding Tudor house with a beautiful walled garden, furnished in the style of a middle-class home of the time. Dr. Hall was widely respected, and he built up a large medical practice in the area. Exhibits illustrating the theory and practice of medicine in Dr. Hall's time are on view. Visitors to the house are welcome to use the adjoining Hall's Croft Club, which serves morning coffee, lunch, and afternoon tea.

Old Town (near Holy Trinity Church). ✆ **01789/292107**. Admission £3.50 ($6) adults, £1.70 ($2.70) children, £29 ($46) family ticket (2 adults, 3 children) for all 5 Shakespeare-related houses. Nov–Mar daily 11am–4pm; Apr–May daily 11am–5pm; June–Aug Mon–Sat 9:30am–5pm, Sun 10am–5pm; Sept–Oct daily 11am–5pm. Closed Dec 23–26. To reach Hall's Croft, walk west from High St., which becomes Chapel St. and Church St. At the intersection with Old Town, go left.

Harvard House   The most ornate home in Stratford, Harvard House is a fine example of an Elizabethan town house. Rebuilt in 1596, it was once the home of

Katherine Rogers, mother of John Harvard, founder of Harvard University. In 1909, the house was purchased by a Chicago millionaire, Edward Morris, who presented it as a gift to the famous American university. Today, following a restoration, it has reopened as a Museum of British Pewter. The museum displays trace the use of pewter from the Roman era until modern times. Pewter, as you learn, used to be the most common choice for household items. Even kiddie toys were made from pewter. Highlights include a tankard engraved with the images of William and Mary, a teapot inspired by the Portland Vase, and a rare bell-based Elizabethan candlestick. Two "hands-on" activities allow children to examine original items.

High St. © **01789/204507.** £1.50 ($2.40) adults, 50p (80¢) children. May–Nov Tues–Sat and bank holiday Mon 11:30am–4:30pm, Sun 10:30am–4:30pm.

Holy Trinity Church (Shakespeare's Tomb)   In an attractive setting near the Avon River is the parish church where Shakespeare is buried ("and curst be he who moves my bones"). The Parish Register records his baptism in 1564 and burial in 1616 (copies of the original documents are on display). The church is one of the most beautiful parish churches in England.

Shakespeare's tomb lies in the chancel, a privilege bestowed upon him when he became a lay rector in 1605. Alongside his grave are those of his widow, Anne, and other members of his family. You can also see the graves of Susanna, his daughter, and those of Thomas Nash and Dr. John Hall. Nearby on the north wall is a bust of Shakespeare that was erected approximately 7 years after his death—within the lifetime of his widow and many of his friends.

Old Town. © **01789/266316.** Free admission to church; admission to Shakespeare's tomb donation £1 ($1.60) adults, 50p (80¢) students. Apr–Oct Mon–Sat 8:30am–6pm, Sun 12:30–5pm; Mar Mon–Sat 9am–5pm, Sun 12:30–5pm; winter Mon–Sat 9am–4pm, Sun 12:30–5pm. Walk 4 min. past the Royal Shakespeare Theatre with the river on your left.

Mary Arden's House & the Shakespeare Countryside Museum ⭐   So what if millions of visitors over the years have been tricked into thinking this timber-framed farmhouse was the girlhood home of Shakespeare's mother, Mary Arden? It's still one of the most intriguing sights outside Stratford, even if local historian Dr. Nat Alcock discovered in 2000 that the actual childhood home of Arden was the dull-looking brick farmhouse, Glebe Farm, next door. (An 18th-c. tour guide, John Jordan, decided Glebe Farm was too unimpressive to be the home of the Bard's mother, so he told tourists it was this farmstead instead.) Visit it anyway to see the country furniture and domestic utensils. In the barns, stable, cowshed, and farmyard you'll find an extensive collection of farming implements illustrating life and work in the local countryside from Shakespeare's time to the present.

Wilmcote. © **01789/204016.** Admission £5.50 ($9) adults, £5 ($8) students and seniors, £2.50 ($4) children, £29 ($46) family ticket (2 adults, 3 children) for all 5 Shakespeare-related houses. Nov–Mar Mon–Sat 10am–4pm, Sun 10:30am–4pm; Apr–May Mon–Sat 10am–5pm, Sun 10:30am–5pm; June–Aug Mon–Sat 9:30am–5pm, Sun 10am–5pm; Sept–Oct Mon–Sat 10am–5pm, Sun 10:30am–5pm. Closed Dec 23–26. Take A3400 (Birmingham) for 5.5km (3½ miles).

New Place/Nash's House   Shakespeare retired to New Place in 1610 (a prosperous man by the standards of his day) and died here 6 years later. Regrettably, the house was torn down, so only the garden remains today. A mulberry tree planted by the Bard was so popular with latter-day visitors to Stratford that the garden's owner chopped it down. The mulberry tree that grows here today is rumored to be from a cutting of the original tree.

You enter the gardens through Nash's House (Thomas Nash married Elizabeth Hall, a granddaughter of the poet). Nash's House has 16th-century period rooms and an exhibition illustrating the history of Stratford. The popular Knott Garden adjoins the site and represents the style of a fashionable Elizabethan garden.

Chapel St. ℂ **01789/204016.** Admission £3.50 ($6) adults, £3 ($4.80) seniors and students, £1.70 ($2.70) children, £29 ($46) family ticket (2 adults, 3 children) for all 5 Shakespeare-related houses. Nov–Mar daily 11am–4pm; Apr–May daily 11am–5pm; June–Aug Mon–Sat 9:30am–5pm, Sun 10am–5pm; Sept–Oct daily 11am–5pm. Closed Dec 23–26. Walk west down High St.; Chapel St. is a continuation of High St.

The Royal Shakespeare Theatre Summer House   This is a brass-rubbing center, where medieval and Tudor brasses illustrate the knights and ladies, scholars, merchants, and priests of a bygone era. The Stratford collection includes a large assortment of exact replicas of brasses. Entrance is free, but visitors are charged depending on which brass they choose to rub. According to size, the cost ranges from £1 ($1.60) to make a rubbing of a small brass, to a maximum of £19 ($30) for a rubbing of the largest.

Avonbank Gardens. ℂ **01789/297671.** Free admission. May–Oct daily 10am–6pm; Nov–Feb Sat–Sun 11am–4pm; Mar–Apr daily 10am–5pm.

Shakespeare's Birthplace ⭐   The son of a glover and whittawer (leather worker), the Bard was born on St. George's day, April 23, 1564, and died on the same date 52 years later. Filled with Shakespeare memorabilia, including a portrait and furnishings of the writer's time, the Trust property is a half-timbered structure, dating from the early 16th century. The house was bought by public donors in 1847 and preserved as a national shrine. You can visit the living room, a bedroom, a fully equipped kitchen of the period (look for the "babyminder"), and a Shakespeare Museum, illustrating his life and times. Later, you can walk through the garden. About 660,000 visitors pass through the house annually.

Built next door to commemorate the 400th anniversary of the Bard's birth, the modern Shakespeare Centre serves both as the administrative headquarters of the Birthplace Trust and as a library and study center. An extension houses a visitor center that acts as a reception area for all those coming to the birthplace.

Henley St. (in the town center near the post office, close to Union St.). ℂ **01789/204016.** Admission £6.50 ($10) adults, £5.50 ($9) students and seniors, £2.50 ($4) children, £29 ($46) family ticket (2 adults, 3 children) for all 5 Shakespeare-related houses. Nov–Mar Mon–Sat 10am–4pm, Sun 10:30am–4pm; Apr–May Mon–Sat 10am–4pm, Sun 10:30am–5pm; June–Aug Mon–Sat 9am–5pm, Sun 9:30am–5pm; Sept–Oct Mon–Sat 10am–5pm, Sun 10:30am–5pm. Closed Dec 23–26.

SHOPPING

Among the many tacky tourist traps are some quality shops, including the ones described below.

Set within an antique house with ceiling beams, **The Shakespeare Bookshop,** 39 Henley St., across from the Shakespeare Birthplace Centre (ℂ **01789/ 292176**), is the region's premier source for textbooks and academic treatises on the Bard and his works. It specializes in books for every level of expertise on Shakespearean studies, from picture books for junior high school students to weighty tomes geared to anyone pursuing a Ph.D. in literature.

The largest shop of its kind in the Midlands, **Arbour Antiques, Ltd.,** Poets Arbour, off Sheep Street (ℂ **01789/293453**), sells antique weapons from Britain, Europe, and India. If you've always hankered after a full suit of armor, this place can sell you one.

Everything in the **Pickwick Gallery,** 32 Henley St. (ℂ **01789/294861**), is a well-crafted work of art produced by copper or steel engraving plates, or printed

---

Impressions

*We love him [Shakespeare]. It's not even Oedipal anymore, or, let me say
as a woman, Electral, for he's ceased being a father figure and has
become the very source of our literary culture and language, at least if
we are English-speaking. Love means we want him to be with us, and so
we have to renew him, out of joy, pleasure and desire, every time we
feel him slipping away.*

—Jane Smiley (1996)

---

by means of a carved wooden block. Hundreds of botanical prints, landscapes,
and renderings of artfully arranged ruins, each suitable for framing, can be purchased. Topographical maps of regions of the United Kingdom are also available
if you're planning on doing any serious hiking.

At **The National Trust Shop,** 45 Wood St. (© **01789/262197**), you'll find
textbooks and guidebooks describing esoteric places in the environs of Stratford,
descriptions of National Trust properties throughout England, stationery, books,
china, pewter, and toiletries.

A SIDE TRIP TO RAGLEY HALL ✪

Ragley Hall   A magnificent 115-room Palladian country house built in 1680,
Ragley Hall is the home of the earl and countess of Yarmouth. The house has
been restored and appears much as it did during the early 1700s. Great pains
have been taken to duplicate colors and, in some cases, the original wallpaper
patterns. The pictures, furniture, and works of art that fill the vast and spacious
rooms represent 10 generations of collecting by the Seymour family. Ragley Hall
may be a private home, but it has a museum-like quality, and many of its artifacts have great historical importance. The most spectacular attraction is the lavishly painted south staircase hall. Muralist Graham Rust painted a modern
trompe l'oeil work depicting the Temptation. A new mural in the tearoom
depicts a Victorian kitchen and the characters that inhabit it.

Near Alcester (14km/9 miles from Stratford-upon-Avon). © **01789/762090.** Admission to the house, garden, and park £6 ($10) adults, £5 ($8) seniors, £4.50 ($7) children, £22 ($35) family. Apr–Sept Thurs–Fri and
Sun 10am–6pm, Sat 11am–3:30pm (gardens 10am–6pm). You must drive or go by taxi, because there's no
good bus service. Ragley Hall is located off A435 or A46 to Evesham, about 2.5km (1½ miles) southwest of
the town of Alcester. There is easy access from the main highway network, including M40 from London.

TEATIME

After visiting Shakespeare's birthplace, cross the street for tea at **Mistress Quickly,**
Henley Street (© **01789/295261**). This airy tearoom is tremendously popular,
but the very attentive staff more than compensates for its throngs of patrons.
Choose from an array of tea blends, cream teas, and various gateaux, pastries, and
tea cakes—all freshly baked in their own kitchen.

Hathaway Tea Rooms, 19 High St. (© **01789/292404**), housed in a building from the 1590s, is as timbered and rickety as its across-the-street neighbor,
Harvard House; it's also near the landmark Holy Trinity Church. You pass
through a bakery shop and climb to the second floor, into a forest of oaken
beams. Order wholesome food such as a vegetarian dish of the day, Welsh
rarebit, quiches and salads, and the traditional steak-and-kidney pie; a steaming
fruit pie can round things off. Your meal costs £4.80 to £6.50 ($8–$10). High
tea or cream tea is also served for £4 to £6.95 ($6–$11).

Cottage Tea Garden, Cottage Lane, Shottery (© **01789/293122**), is set in a rose garden a few paces from Anne Hathaway's Cottage, on a country lane 2.5km (1½ miles) from Stratford-upon-Avon. Stratford's "blue minibus" passes nearby every 10 minutes throughout the day. The tearoom offers a verdant and refreshing place for respite from the whirlwind of sightseeing. Most visitors prefer a chair on the outdoor patio; a glassed-in conservatory offers seating for 25. Available throughout the day are at least five kinds of "countryman platters": salads, raw vegetables, and cheese (ploughman's lunch); ham (huntsman); tuna (fisher); cold roast beef (cowman); and pasties (Cornishman). Plates cost £6 to £10 ($10–$16).

WHERE TO STAY

During the theater season, you'll need reservations way in advance. The Tourist Information Centre (see "Essentials," earlier in this section) will help find an accommodation in the price range you're seeking. The fee for room reservations is a 10% deposit toward your first night's stay, which is then deducted from the final bill.

IN TOWN

Aidan Guest House ★ *Kids* This 1897 Victorian family house, owned by Lily and John Thompson, sits close to the town center, a 5-minute walk from the theater and railway station. The midsize and impeccably clean nonsmoking rooms (all doubles) have private, shower-only bathrooms. The place is particularly recommended for those with small children; babysitting can be arranged, and cribs are available.

11 Evesham Place, Stratford-upon-Avon, Warwickshire CV37 6HT. © **01789/292824.** Fax 01789/269072. www.aidanhouse.co.uk. 6 units. £45–£55 ($72–$88) double. Rates include English breakfast. AE, MC, V. From the center at the police station on Rother St., walk west. Bus: 16 or 18. **Amenities:** Breakfast room; babysitting. *In room:* TV, coffeemaker, hair dryer, iron.

Church Farmhouse This 17th-century nonsmoking farmstead in a secluded garden is 9.5km (6 miles) from Stratford. The owner, Mrs. Wiggy Taylor, enjoys meeting people from everywhere and welcomes children (she can provide babysitting services). She is continually updating the decor in the large double bedrooms, which come with private shower.

Long Marston, Stratford-upon-Avon, Warwickshire CV37 8RH. © and fax **01789/720275.** www.church farmhouse.co.uk. 2 units. £30 ($48) single; £50 ($80) double. Rates include English breakfast. No credit cards. From Stratford, take A3400 south, forking right onto B4632; go for about 6.5km (4 miles) and, after passing an airfield on your right, turn right (signposted LONG MARSTON); at the T-junction, turn right again into the village and Church Farm is on your left. Bus: 215 from Stratford. **Amenities:** Breakfast room; lounge; babysitting. *In room:* TV, coffeemaker, hair dryer, no phone.

Courtland Hotel The Courtland is a minute from the bus station, a 5-minute walk from the rail station, and 3 minutes from the theater. The hotel is in a large Georgian house with antique furniture. The small, comfortably appointed rooms are well furnished and tidy. The owner, Diana Moore, attends to them personally; she will also pick up guests from the station. The preserves served with breakfast are homemade, and special diets are catered to upon request.

12 Guild St., Stratford-upon-Avon, Warwickshire CV37 6RE. © and fax **01789/292401.** www.courtland hotel.co.uk. 6 units. £35 ($56) single; £55–£65 ($88–$104) double; £80 ($128) family unit. Rates include English and continental breakfast. AE, DC, MC, V. **Amenities:** Breakfast room; babysitting. *In room:* TV, coffeemaker, no phone.

Craig Cleeve House Hotel This nonsmoking hotel sits within a 5-minute walk of Stratford's center, on the far side of the Clopton Bridge, off the A3400 road leading to Oxford. It began in 1906 as two separate redbrick residences. Later they functioned as independently operated guesthouses, the Craig and the Cleeve; in the late 1980s they were combined. The Beese family, the congenial owners, paved over most of the garden to create much-needed parking space, but there's still a pretty landscaped garden in the rear. The small to midsize rooms have been totally refurbished and are individually decorated.

67–69 Shipston Rd., Stratford-upon-Avon, Warwickshire CV37 7LW. © **01789/296573.** Fax 01789/299452. www.craigcleeve.com. 14 units, all with shower. £35–£54 ($56–$86) single; £62 ($99) double. Rates include English breakfast. MC, V. Free parking. **Amenities:** Breakfast room; residents' bar; lounge. *In room:* TV, coffeemaker, iron, no phone.

The Croft Guest House The long-established Croft stands on A3400 only 5 minutes from the town center and the Royal Shakespeare Theatre. It is a late Victorian town house constructed by a local builder in 1881. Kevin Hallworth runs this traditional yet fully modernized guesthouse. Gardens lead to the Avon. This establishment has five nonsmoking rooms.

49 Shipston Rd., Stratford-upon-Avon, Warwickshire CV37 7LN. © **01789/293419.** Fax 01789/552986. www.thecroftguesthouse.activehotels.com. 9 units, 7 with bathroom. £30 ($48) single without bathroom; £52 ($83) double without bathroom, £62–£70 ($99–$112) double with bathroom. Family rates available for 3 to 5 people. Rates include English breakfast. AE, DC, MC, V. **Amenities:** Breakfast room; outdoor heated pool. *In room:* TV, coffeemaker, hair dryer, no phone.

The Hollies Guest House This guesthouse is a renovated three-story building built in 1875 as a school, although it looks like a stately old home. A mother and daughter, Mrs. Mavis Morgan and Mrs. L. Dempster, run it. The non-smoking bedrooms are large with plenty of wardrobe space, and are well furnished. The place serves a good, plentiful breakfast in a sunny dining room.

16 Evesham Place, Stratford-upon-Avon, Warwickshire CV37 6HQ. © and fax **01789/266857.** 6 units, 3 with bathroom. £25 ($40) single without bathroom; £40 ($64) double without bathroom, £50 ($80) double with bathroom. Rates include English breakfast. No credit cards. From the center at the police station on Rother St., walk west for about 3 min. Bus: 16 or 18. **Amenities:** Breakfast room. *In room:* TV, coffeemaker, no phone.

The Hunters Moon Lying 2.5km (1½ miles) north of Stratford on the A422 Stratford-Worcester road, in a half-acre garden near Anne Hathaway's Cottage, this guesthouse is owned and operated by Rosemary and David Austin. Built of brick in the early 1900s and enlarged many times since, the house has been completely refurbished. The rooms are midsize and come with private shower-only bathrooms.

150 Alcester Rd., Stratford-upon-Avon, Warwickshire CV37 9DR. © **01789/292888.** Fax 01789/204101. www.huntersmoonguesthouse.com. 7 units. £28–£32 ($45–$51) single; £52–£60 ($83–$96) double. Rates include English breakfast. V. From town center, take the bus marked W. Green Dr. **Amenities:** Breakfast room. *In room:* TV, coffeemaker, hair dryer, no phone.

Kawartha House Set on a street lined with other B&B hotels, this solid house lies a 5-minute walk from the Royal Shakespeare Theatre. It was built in the late 1800s in mock-Tudor style; its unusual name derives from a spot the original owners had found particularly beautiful during a trip to North America, Canada's Kawartha Lakes. An inn since the early 1970s, it has been tastefully renovated. It offers a well-kept garden in front, and very pretty, pastel-colored, midsize bedrooms upstairs, some overlooking a park.

39 Grove Rd., Stratford-upon-Avon, Warwickshire CV37 6PB. © **01789/204469.** Fax 01789/292837. 6 units, 4 with bathroom. £20–£25 ($32–$40) single without bathroom; £44–£56 ($70–$90) double with bathroom. Rates include English breakfast. MC, V. **Amenities:** Breakfast room. *In room:* TV, coffeemaker, no phone.

Lemarquand   This inn is located close to the theater and town center; its proprietor, Anne Cross, gives good service. The small nonsmoking bedrooms (all
doubles) are comfortably appointed and well maintained. There are other more
glamorous Evesham Road properties, but you'll likely pay more for them.

186 Evesham Rd., Stratford-upon-Avon, Warwickshire CV37 9BS. ℂ **01789/204164.** annecross@ntlworld.com.
2 units. £48–£50 ($77–$80) double. Rates include English breakfast. No credit cards. From the center at the police
station on Rother St., walk west. Bus: 28S. **Amenities:** Breakfast room. *In room:* Coffeemaker, no phone.

The Marlyn Hotel ★★   The Marlyn is situated near Hall's Croft, just a 5-
minute walk from the town center and the Royal Shakespeare Theatre. This Victorian house has welcomed guests since 1870; the Evans family, who have owned
and managed it since 1994, endeavor to make their guests comfortable.

The hotel's good-size bedrooms contain comfortable furnishings. Like Gideon's
Bible, a copy of the Bard's complete works is in every bedroom. There's also a small
lounge with a TV.

3 Chestnut Walk, Stratford-upon-Avon, Warwickshire CV37 6HG. ℂ and fax **01789/293752.** www.marlyn
hotel.co.uk. 8 units, 5 with shower only. £23 ($37) single without bathroom; £40 ($64) single with bathroom;
£52 ($83) double with shower only; £66 ($106) family unit (triple) with shower only. Rates include English
breakfast. MC, V. Free parking. **Amenities:** Breakfast room; massage; babysitting; laundry. *In room:* TV, coffeemaker, hair dryer, iron.

Moonraker Guest House ★ *(Finds)*   Privately owned and personally managed
by Phil and Gill Leonard, this is a delightful choice and a discovery, lying midway between Anne Hathaway's House Cottage and Shakespeare's birthplace.
Each nonsmoking bedroom is comfortably and attractively furnished, six with
showers and the others with combination tub and shower. A luxury suite is available with a bedroom, lounge, and kitchenette, plus two more suites, each with
two rooms. Among the amenities are four-poster beds, a nonsmoking lounge
area, and garden patios. There are five rooms available for those with limited
mobility. A hearty English breakfast is followed by toast and homemade marmalade and jams, all served and prepared by the Leonards.

40 Alcester Rd., Stratford-upon-Avon, Warwickshire CV37 9DB. ℂ **01789/267115.** Fax 01789/295504.
www.moonrakerhouse.com. 10 units. £40 ($64) single; £55–£85 ($88–$136) double. Rates include English
breakfast. MC, V. The Moonraker is 2 min. by car from the heart of town on A422. **Amenities:** Breakfast room;
nonsmoking lounge; garden patio. *In room:* TV, coffeemaker, hair dryer.

Parkfield Guest House   This Victorian house is just off B439 (Evesham
Rd.), a 5-minute walk from the Royal Shakespeare Theatre. Jo Pettitt, recipient
of many reader recommendations, runs this nonsmoking place with her husband, Roger. The small rooms have private, shower-only bathrooms. Breakfast
is superb, and vegetarian diets are catered to. If possible, the owner will help
guests obtain theater tickets.

3 Broad Walk, Stratford-upon-Avon, Warwickshire CV37 6HS. ℂ and fax **01789/293313.** parkfield@
btinternet.com. 7 units. £26–£28 ($42–$45) single; £46–£48 ($74–$77) double. Rates include English breakfast. MC, V. Free parking. **Amenities:** Breakfast room. *In room:* TV, coffeemaker, hair dryer, iron, no phone.

Salamander Guest House   This 1906 Edwardian house is a 5-minute walk
from the town center just off B439 (Evesham Rd.). One of the better guesthouses in the area, the homelike Salamander fronts a woodsy park. The owners
rent comfortable, attractive rooms, including one for families.

40 Grove Rd., Stratford-upon-Avon, Warwickshire CV37 6PB. ℂ and fax **01789/205728.** www.salamander
guesthouse.co.uk. 7 units, all with shower only. £18–£30 ($29–$48) per person. Rates include English breakfast. MC, V. Bus: X16. **Amenities:** Breakfast room; babysitting. *In room:* TV, coffeemaker, hair dryer (on
request), iron (on request), no phone.

Twelfth Night ⭐   This nonsmoking Victorian villa is aptly named—it once accommodated actors from the Royal Shakespeare Theatre, who appeared in productions of that well-loved play. Today, this privately owned Victorian house is rated one of the finest guesthouses in Stratford. The midsize bedrooms (all doubles) are cozily and comfortably furnished.

Evesham Place, Stratford-upon-Avon, Warwickshire CV37 6HT. © **01789/414595**. 6 units, all with shower. £54–£62 ($86–$99) double. Rates include English breakfast. AE, MC, V. From the center at the police station on Rother St., head west for 180m (600 ft.). **Amenities:** Breakfast room; lounge. *In room:* TV, coffeemaker, hair dryer, no phone.

NEARBY

Loxley Farm ⭐ *(Finds)*   The village of Loxley, just 6.5km (4 miles) from Stratford-upon-Avon and 11km (7 miles) from Warwick, is an ancient community, boasting one of England's oldest Saxon churches, St. Nicholas. Claimed by some to be Robin Hood's original home, Loxley is a quiet place with a delightful old pub. At historic Loxley Arm, Roderick and Anne Horton live in a thatched cottage with windows peeping out and creeper climbing up the old walls. The garden is full of apple blossoms, roses, and sweet-scented flowers. A stone path leads across the grass and into the flagstone hall, with nice old rugs and a roaring fire. Nonsmoking accommodations are in the Shieling; this 17th-century, one-story, thatched and half-timbered house stands in the garden of Loxley Farmhouse. Its good-size doubles come with a private bathroom, sitting room, and small kitchen. (Sometimes there is a room suite available in the Arm.) Breakfast is served in the house.

Loxley, Warwickshire CV35 9JV. © **01789/840265**. Fax 01789/840645. 2 suites. £64 ($102) double. Rates include English breakfast. No credit cards. Bus: From Stratford take either the "Kineton" or "Wellesbourne" bus. **Amenities:** Breakfast room. *In room:* TV, kitchen, unstocked fridge, coffeemaker, hair dryer, no phone.

Moss Cottage   An ideal base for touring the Cotswolds, the Moss is within walking distance of town, theaters, and places of interest. Pauline and Jim Rush go to great lengths to assure your comfort at this charming cottage, built in 1922. The spacious nonsmoking double rooms include private bathrooms with shower. Guests can relax in the pretty garden.

61 Evesham Rd., Stratford-upon-Avon, Warwickshire CV37 9BA. © and fax **01789/294770**. 2 units. £44 ($70) double. Rates include English breakfast. No credit cards. **Amenities:** Breakfast room; room service (7am–9pm); babysitting. *In room:* TV, coffeemaker, hair dryer, no phone.

Pear Tree Cottage ⭐⭐ *(Finds)*   This late-16th-century former farmhouse is 5.5km (3½ miles) northwest of Stratford-upon-Avon toward Wilmcote, the home village of Shakespeare's mother, Mary Arden (1.5km/1 mile off A3400 to Birmingham). Exposed beams and antique furniture give the house a period charm, but modern plumbing and central heating add modern comfort. Recent investigations into the Arden Estates show that Pear Tree Cottage once belonged to William Shakespeare's parents, Mary (nee Arden) and John Shakespeare, who inherited it from Robert Arden—Mary's father. They mortgaged the property in 1578 and forfeited it, by order of the Chancery Court in 1597, for failure to repay the loan. The nonsmoking cottage stands in nearly an acre of lawn and gardens. Mr. and Mrs. Mander can accommodate up to 15 guests. Three of the bedrooms are in the original buildings, the others in a modern wing "with an old feel" added on in 1987. Two ground floor rooms are available for those with limited mobility. Mary Arden's birthplace is visible across the field from the house.

Church Rd., Wilmcote, Stratford-upon-Avon, Warwickshire CV37 9UX. © **01789/205889**. Fax 01789/262862. www.peartreecot.co.uk. 7 units. £38 ($61) single; £56 ($90) double. Rates include English breakfast. No credit cards. **Amenities:** Breakfast room; lounge. *In room:* TV, coffeemaker, hair dryer, no phone.

Winton House ✦ This enchanting house, a Victorian farmhouse from 1856, is located on the border of the Cotswolds near Warwick Castle. The nonsmoking double rooms are pleasantly decorated with high ceilings and homelike touches. Mrs. Lyon, the owner, goes out of her way to make her guests comfortable, and her breakfasts are a delight. Many footpaths surround the house, and bicycles are for hire.

The Green, Upper Quinton, Stratford-upon-Avon, Warwickshire CV37 8SX. ℭ 01789/720500. www.winton house.com. 3 units. £70 ($112) double. Rates include English breakfast. No credit cards. **Amenities:** Breakfast room; bike rentals; babysitting. *In room:* Coffeemaker, hair dryer, iron, no phone.

SUPER-CHEAP SLEEPS: A YOUTH HOSTEL

Stratford-upon-Avon International YHA Centre This remodeled 200-year-old Georgian mansion is popular with students, backpackers, and families wanting cheap accommodations, so call in advance for reservations, as they are often booked up. Besides the dormitory bunk beds, there are standard doubles, double suites, and family rooms; six feature private bathrooms.

Hemmingford House, Alveston, Warwickshire CV37 7RG. ℭ **01789/297093.** Fax 01789/205513. www.yha. org.uk. 29 units, 132 beds. £16.50 ($26) adults; £12 ($19) youths. Rates include breakfast. AE, MC, V. Bus: 18 or 77. **Amenities:** Dining room; TV room; smoking lounge; game room; laundry. *In private rooms:* TV, unstocked fridge, coffeemaker, iron, safe, no phone.

WHERE TO DINE

Lambs ENGLISH/CONTINENTAL A stone's throw from the Royal Shakespeare Theatre, this cafe-bistro is housed in a building dating back to 1547. For a quick light meal or pre-theater dinner, it's ideal. The menu changes monthly. Begin with a tomato-and-mozzarella salad, perhaps Scottish smoked salmon or pasta, then follow with pan-fried filet of beef with roasted shallots or grilled filet of monkfish with an avocado-and-tomato salsa. The chef takes chances (no doubt inspired by trips to the Continent), and it's a nice departure from the bland tearoom food served for decades in Stratford.

12 Sheep St. ℭ **01789/292554.** Reservations required Sat night. Main courses £8.50–£15.95 ($14–$26); fixed-price menu £11.50 ($18) for 2 courses, £14.50 ($23) for 3. MC, V. Mon–Sat noon–2pm and 5–10:30pm; Sun 6–10pm.

Marlowe's Restaurant ENGLISH Marlowe's is made up of the Elizabethan Room, a 16th-century oak-paneled dining room, and Georgies, once the ancient house's hayloft. There is a garden patio, where you may have a drink or even an alfresco meal. Hours are timed so that you can make the opening curtain at the theater. A traditional Sunday lunch features prime ribs of beef and Yorkshire pudding. The Elizabethan Room serves such dishes as chateaubriand with Yorkshire pudding and béarnaise sauce, or drunken duck marinated in red wine, gin, crushed peppercorns, lemon juice, and juniper berries. Georgies, across the patio from the Elizabethan Room, serves bistrolike lunches and dinners from £9 ($14); it keeps the same dinner hours as the dining room. Try rib of beef, rack of lamb with mint and rosemary sauce, or fresh filet of bream in a white-wine sauce. Theatergoers are welcome for dessert and coffee after the show during regular hours.

Marlowe's Alley, 17–18 High St. ℭ **01789/204999.** Main courses £10–£15 ($16–$24); 3-course fixed-price dinner £23 ($37). AE, DC, MC, V. Mon–Fri noon–2:30pm and 5:45–10pm; Sat noon–2:30pm and 5:45–11pm; Sun noon–2:30pm and 7–9:30pm.

Margaux ENGLISH/SEAFOOD This eatery is near Slug & Lettuce, north of Bridge Street in the town center. Its informal mood and bright, breezy atmosphere give the feel of a French bistro. The chef specializes in typically British food. An interesting range of starters include such exotic treats as pot-roast belly pork with basmati and guava on a macadamia nut coulis or else a mosaic of game with apple jelly. Main courses that stir interest are Gressingham duck breast with wilted greens and water chestnuts or roasted loin of rabbit on a cumin-infused sweet corn broth. Try also the baked cod with sweet spices, served with a lobster and truffle brandade.

6 Union St. ℂ **01789/269106.** Reservations recommended, especially Fri–Sat nights and for pre-theater. Main courses £10–£17.50 ($16–$28). AE, MC, V. Mon–Sat noon–2pm and 5:30–10:30pm.

The Quarto's Restaurant ✪ FRENCH/ITALIAN/ENGLISH   This restaurant enjoys the best location in town—in the theater itself, with glass walls providing an unobstructed view of swans on the Avon. You can purchase an intermission snack feast of smoked salmon and champagne, or dine by flickering candlelight after the performance. Many dishes, such as apple-and-parsnip soup, are definitely old English; others reflect a Continental touch, such as fried polenta with filets of pigeon and bacon. For your main course, you may select Dover sole, pheasant supreme, or roast loin of pork. Homemade crème brûlée is an old-time favorite. The theater lobby has a special phone for reservations.

In the Royal Shakespeare Theatre, Waterside. ℂ **01789/403415.** Reservations required. Matinee lunch £16 ($26); dinner £14–£20 ($22–$32). AE, MC, V. Thurs and Sat noon–2:30pm; Mon–Sat 5:30pm–midnight.

Russons INTERNATIONAL   This is a great place for a pre-theater meal; the Royal Shakespeare is a short stroll away. The restaurant is housed in a 400-year-old building. The two simply furnished dining rooms, one with hardwood floor, the other with flagstones, feature inglenook fireplaces. The seasonal menu changes regularly, and fresh seafood is their specialty. The chalkboard specials include rack of lamb, guinea fowl, and vegetarian dishes. Finish with a simple but delicious homemade dessert.

8 Church St. ℂ **01789/268822.** Reservations required. Lunch main courses £7.50–£15.75 ($12–$25); dinner main courses £8.50–£15.75 ($14–$25). AE, MC, V. Tues–Sat 11:30am–1:30pm and 5:15–9:30pm.

Vintner Wine Bar EUROPEAN   Around the corner from the Shakespeare Hotel and a short walk from the Royal Shakespeare, the Vintner demonstrates why wine-bar dining is all the rage in England. Its Elizabethan decor fits in with the town's history; its name is in reference to a famous local vintner and wine merchant, John Smith, who operated on these premises in 1600. This popular drink-and-dine spot has daily specials. Many guests prefer one of the tempting cold plates at lunch. You can also order a vegetable dish of the day, vegetarian soup, an oven baked tuna steak, or spicy meatballs in rich tomato sauce with spaghetti. While the cookery may lack verve at times, it is straightforward and filling, making the locals happy. Food is available more or less continuously.

5 Sheep St. ℂ **01789/297259.** Reservations recommended. Lunch main courses: £5.50–£7.95 ($9–$13); dinner main courses £9–£15 ($14–$24). AE, MC, V. Daily 10am–11pm. Bus: X16 or X18.

BEST PLACES FOR A PINT

The Black Swan ("The Dirty Duck") ✪✪ ENGLISH   This has been a popular hangout for Stratford players since the 18th century. The wall is lined with autographed photos of its many famous patrons. The front lounge and bar crackles with intense conversation. In the spring and fall, an open fire blazes. Typical English grills are featured in the Dirty Duck Grill Room, although no one has ever accused it of serving Stratford's best food. Choose from a dozen appetizers, most of which would make a meal in themselves. In fair weather, take your drinks in the front garden and watch the swans glide by on the Avon.

Waterside. ℂ **01789/297312**. Reservations required for dining. Main courses £8–£15 ($13–$24); bar snacks £5–£7.25 ($8–$12). AE, DC, MC, V (in the restaurant only). Daily 11am–11pm.

The Garrick Inn ENGLISH   Near Harvard House, this black-and-white timbered Elizabethan pub (1595) is imbued with an unpretentious charm. The front bar offers tapestry-covered settles, an old oak refectory table, and an open fireplace that serves as a people-magnet. The back bar has a circular fireplace with a copper hood and mementos of the English stage. The specialty is homemade pies such as steak-and-kidney or chicken-and-mushroom.

25 High St. ℂ **01789/292186**. Main courses £6.25–£12.50 ($10–$20). MC, V. Meals daily noon–9pm. Pub Mon–Sat 11am–11pm, Sun noon–10:30pm.

The White Swan ✫ ENGLISH   In the town's oldest building you'll find this atmospheric pub, with cushioned leather armchairs, oak paneling, and fireplaces. You and amiable fellow drinkers revel in a setting once enjoyed by Will Shakespeare himself when it was called the Kings Head. At lunch you can choose from the day's hot dishes along with fresh salads and sandwiches.

In The White Swan hotel, Rother St. ℂ **01789/297022**. Dinner reservations recommended. Bar snacks £5.75–£6.95 ($9–$11); fixed-price 3-course Sun lunch £19.95 ($32). AE, DC, MC, V. Morning coffee daily 10am–noon; self-service bar snacks daily 12:30–3pm; afternoon tea daily 2–5:30pm; dinner Mon–Thurs 5:30–8:30pm, Fri–Sun 6–9pm.

2 Warwick: England's Finest Medieval Castle ✫✫✫

147km (92 miles) NW of London; 13km (8 miles) NE of Stratford-upon-Avon

Most visitors come here just to see Warwick Castle, England's finest medieval castle; some combine it with a visit to Kenilworth Castle (see section 3 later in this chapter). But the historic center of ancient Warwick has a lot more to offer.

Warwick cites Ethelfleda, daughter of Alfred the Great, as its founder. But most of its history is associated with the earls of Warwick, a title created by William II (Rufus) in 1088. The story of those earls makes for an exciting episode in English history.

A devastating fire swept through the heart of Warwick in 1694, but a number of Elizabethan and medieval buildings still stand, along with fine Georgian structures from a later date.

ESSENTIALS

GETTING THERE   Trains run frequently between Stratford-upon-Avon and Warwick. Call ℂ **0845/7484950** for schedules and information.

One **Stagecoach** bus per hour departs Stratford-upon-Avon during the day. The trip takes 15 to 20 minutes. Call the tourist office (ℂ **01789/293127**) for schedules.

Take A46 if you're driving from Stratford-upon-Avon.

VISITOR INFORMATION   The **Tourist Information Centre** is at The Court House, Jury Street (ℂ **01926/492212**), open daily 9:30am to 4:30pm; closed December 24 through December 26 and January 1.

SEEING THE SIGHTS

Lord Leycester Hospital   The great fire also spared this group of half-timbered almshouses at the West Gate. The buildings were erected around 1400; Robert Dudley, Earl of Leicester, founded the hospital in 1571 as a home for old soldiers. It's still used by ex-service personnel and their spouses. On top of the West Gate is the attractive little chapel of St. James, built in the 12th century but renovated many times since. The back gardens, closed to the public since 1903, were recently reopened. The restoration was based on Nathaniel Hawthorne's descriptions of his visits to the gardens in 1855 and 1857. The queen herself along with Prince Philip made a well-publicized visit in 1996.

High St. ✆ **01926/491422**. Admission £3.20 ($5) adults, £2.70 ($4.30) students and seniors, £2.20 ($3.50) children. Easter–Oct Tues–Sun 10am–5pm; Nov–Easter Tues–Sun 10am–4pm.

St. John's House Museum   At Coten End, not far from the castle gates, this early-17th-century house has exhibits on Victorian domestic life. A schoolroom is furnished with original 19th-century furniture and equipment. During the school term, Warwickshire children dress in period costumes and learn Victorian-style lessons. Groups of children also use the Victorian parlor and the kitchen. It's impossible to display more than a few items at a time, so a study room is provided where you can see objects from the reserve collections. The costume collection is particularly fine, and visitors can study the drawings and photos that make up the costume catalog. (These facilities are available by appointment only.) Upstairs, a military museum traces the history of the Royal Warwickshire Regiment from 1674 to the present.

St. John's, at the crossroads of the main Warwick–Leamington Rd. (A425/A429) and the Coventry Rd. (A429). ✆ **01926/412021**. Free admission. Tues–Sat (and bank holidays) 10am–5:30pm; Easter–Sept Sun 2:30–5pm.

St. Mary's Church   Partly destroyed by the 1694 fire, this church, with its rebuilt battlemented tower and nave, is among the finest examples of late-17th- and early-18th-century architecture. The Beauchamp Chapel, spared by the fire, encases the Purbeck marble tomb of Richard Beauchamp, a powerful earl of Warwick who died in 1439 and is commemorated by a gilded bronze effigy. This tomb is one of the finest remaining examples of Perpendicular-Gothic style from the mid–15th century. The tomb of Robert Dudley, Earl of Leicester, a favorite of Elizabeth I, is against the north wall. The Perpendicular-Gothic choir dates from the 14th century, and the Norman crypt and the chapter house are from the 11th century.

Church St. ✆ **01926/403940**. www.saintmaryschurch.co.uk. Free admission; donations accepted. Apr–Sept daily 10am–6pm; Oct–Mar daily 10am–4pm. All buses to Warwick stop at Old Sq.

Warwick Castle   Perched on a rocky cliff above the River Avon in the town center, a stately early-17th-century mansion is surrounded by a magnificent 14th-century fortress. Surrounded by gardens, lawns, and woodland, where peacocks roam freely, and skirted by the Avon, Warwick Castle was described by Sir Walter Scott in 1828 as "that fairest monument of ancient and chivalrous splendor which yet remains uninjured by time."

Ethelfleda, daughter of Alfred the Great, built the first significant fortifications here in 914. William the Conqueror ordered the construction of a motte and bailey castle in 1068. The mound is all that remains today of the Norman castle, which was sacked by Simon de Montfort in the Barons' War of 1264. The Beauchamp family, most illustrious of the medieval earls of Warwick, are responsible for the appearance of the castle today; much of the external structure remains unchanged from the mid–14th century. When the castle was granted to Sir Fulke Greville by James I in 1604, he spent £20,000 (then an enormous sum) converting the existing buildings into a luxurious mansion.

The staterooms and Great Hall house fine collections of paintings, furniture, arms, and armor. The armory, dungeon, torture chamber, ghost tower, clock tower, and Guy's tower create a vivid picture of the castle's turbulent past and its important role in the history of England.

The private apartments of Lord Brooke and his family, who recently sold the castle to Tussaud's Group, are open to visitors. They house a display of a carefully reconstructed Royal Weekend House Party of 1898. The major rooms contain wax portraits of important figures of the time, including a young Winston Churchill. In the Kenilworth bedroom, the Prince of Wales, who would become King Edward VII, reads a letter. The Duchess of Marlborough prepares for her bath in the red bedroom. Among the most lifelike figures is a little uniformed maid bending over to test the temperature of the water running into a bathtub.

You can also see the Victorian rose garden, a re-creation of an 1868 design by Robert Marnock. Near the rose garden is a Victorian alpine rockery and water garden. You should plan to spend at least 3 hours at the castle.

(C) **0870/442-2000.** www.warwick-castle.co.uk. Admission £12.50 ($20) adults, £7.50 ($12) children 4–16, £9 ($14) seniors, free for children 4 and under, £32 ($51) family ticket. Apr–Sept daily 10am–6pm; Oct–Mar 10am–5pm. Closed Christmas Day.

Warwick Doll Museum One of the most charming Elizabethan buildings in Warwick houses this doll museum near St. Mary's Church. Founded in 1955, its seven rooms display an extensive collection of dolls in wood, wax, porcelain, and fabric.

Oken's House, Castle St. (off Jury St. in the town center). (C) **01926/495546.** Admission £1 ($1.60) adults, 70p ($1.10) children. Easter–Oct Mon–Sat 10am–5pm, Sun 11:30am–5pm; Nov–Easter Sat 10am–4pm.

Warwickshire Museum This museum was established in 1836 to house a collection of geological remains, fossils, and an exhibit of amphibians from the Triassic period. There are also displays illustrating the history, archaeology, and natural history of the county, including the famous Sheldon tapestry map.

Market Hall, The Market Place. (C) **01926/412500.** www.warwickshire.gov.uk. Free admission. Tues–Sat 10am–5pm; Sun May–Sept 11:30am–5pm. From Jury St. in the town center, take a right onto Swan St., which leads to the museum.

WHERE TO STAY

Many people stay in Warwick and commute to Stratford-upon-Avon, although the accommodations here are inferior to those at Stratford.

Agincourt Lodge This hotel lies a 5-minute walk from the castle toward Leamington Spa Road. Built in 1844 as a family home, it was designed to coexist with the enormous copper beech in the front yard. Today, the Black-Band family receives guests, and the beech is bigger than ever. The comfortable bedrooms vary slightly in size and contain private bathrooms with showers; three feature a four-poster bed. There's a long and narrow garden in back; visitors can walk in nearby St. Nicholas Park.

36 Coten End, Warwick, Warwickshire CV34 4NP. (C) and fax **01926/499399.** www.agincourtlodge.co.uk. 6 units. £40–£50 ($64–$80) single; £50–£75 ($80–$120) double. Rates include English breakfast. AE, MC, V. **Amenities:** Breakfast room; lounge; bar. *In room:* Coffeemaker, hair dryer.

The Old Rectory ⭐ This 17th-century farmhouse is just off A46 between Warwick and Stratford-upon-Avon, less than 5km (3 miles) southwest of Warwick and just under 1km (½ mile) from M40 (Junction 15). It has been restored and decorated with antiques. The owners, Sandra and David Payne, maintain a delightful old place, with a wealth of beams, inglenook fireplaces, and flagstone and elmwood floors. The landmark rectory stands in a half-acre of lovely walled gardens. First called the White Horse Inn, it later housed the canon of St. Mary's Church in Warwick. There are rooms in the main house and a converted carriage house suitable for a family. The nonsmoking rooms vary from large to average and several bedrooms have antique brass beds; all have private bathrooms with shower.

Vicarage Lane, Stratford Rd., Sherbourne, near Warwick, Warwickshire CV35 8AB. ℂ **01926/624562.** Fax 01926/624995. www.warwickoldrectory.co.uk. 7 units. £75 ($120) single; £85 ($136) double. Rates include English breakfast. MC, V. Free parking. **Amenities:** Restaurant; bar; walled garden. *In room:* TV, dataport, coffeemaker, hair dryer.

Tudor House Inn & Restaurant ⭐ *Finds* At the edge of town, on the main road from Stratford-upon-Avon to Warwick Castle, is a black-and-white-timbered inn built in 1472; it escaped the fire that destroyed High Street in 1694. Off the central hall are two large very Elizabethan rooms. The simply furnished bedrooms have washbasins; two contain doors only 4 feet high. Two rooms have four-poster beds. The double rooms are small to medium in size.

90–92 West St. (opposite the main Warwick Castle car park, 1km/½ mile south of town on A429), Warwick, Warwickshire CV34 6AW. ℂ **01926/495447.** Fax 01926/492948. 10 units, 7 with bathroom or shower. £35 ($56) single without bathroom; £65–£75 ($104–$120) double with bathroom. Rates include English breakfast. DC, MC, V. **Amenities:** Restaurant; bar; lounge. *In room:* TV, coffeemaker, hair dryer.

Warwick Lodge Guest House Located about 1km (½ mile) from Warwick, this informal place is close enough to Stratford-upon-Avon to be a base for touring Shakespeare Country. The rather basic rooms have hot and cold running water, but no private bathrooms; the shared hallway bathrooms are adequate.

82 Emscote Rd., Warwick, Warwickshire CV34 5QJ. ℂ **01926/492927.** 7 units, none with bathroom. £22 ($35) single; £42 ($67) double. Rates include English breakfast. MC, V. From St. John's, continue along Coten End leading to Emscote Rd. toward Leamington Spa. Bus: X16 or X18. **Amenities:** Breakfast room. *In room:* TV, coffeemaker, no phone.

Westham Guest House The guesthouse lies on A445 to Leamington Spa; from London, come in from M1, then follow the signs for Coventry onto A46, leading into Warwick. It's about a 5-minute walk from the center of Warwick. In a residential section of town along a busy road, the Donald McIlwrath family manages this canopied building with a garden. The nonsmoking bedrooms, ranging from quite large to small, are utterly plain but reasonably comfortable and clean—hard to beat for the price.

76 Emscote Rd., Warwick, Warwickshire CV34 5QG. ℂ and fax **01926/491756.** 6 units, 1 with bathroom. £25 ($40) single; £40–£48 ($64–$77) double. Rates include English breakfast. No credit cards. From St. John's, continue along Coten End leading to Emscote Rd. toward Leamington Spa. Bus: X16 or X18. **Amenities:** Breakfast room. *In room:* TV, coffeemaker, hair dryer, no phone.

WHERE TO DINE

There's nothing like the ancient ambience of tea at **Brethren's Kitchen,** Lord Leycester Hospital (ℂ **01926/491422**), open March through January Tuesday to Sunday and bank holidays. It has cool stone floors and wonderful exposed oak beams. Indian, Chinese, and herbal teas are all available, as well as scones with fresh cream, sponge cake, and fruit cake.

Fanshaw's Restaurant BRITISH/FRENCH In the heart of Warwick, at the edge of the city's commercial center, this restaurant occupies a late Victorian building enlivened by flowered window boxes.

Inside, there are only 32 seats within a well-maintained, rather flouncy dining room lined with mirrors. A well-trained staff serves food from a menu that changes every 2 months, and that usually includes sirloin steak; filet of beef

Wellington-style, with a red wine and shallot sauce; and breast of pheasant with a shiitake and oyster mushroom brandy sauce. Especially elegant, usually offered during game season, is a brace of quail with a hazelnut-and-apricot stuffing.

22 Market Place. © 01926/410590. Reservations recommended. Fixed-price menus £19 ($30). AE, MC, V. Mon–Sat 6:30–10pm.

Findon's Restaurant BRITISH   The building is authentically Georgian, constructed in 1700. You'll dine surrounded by original stone floors and cupboards, within a setting for only 43 diners to dine in snug comfort. Michael Findon, owner and sometime chef, works hard at orchestrating a blend of traditional and modern British cuisine. The fixed menus include such dishes as a sauté of pigeon breast with red wine and celery, followed by a suprême of cod with lemon and prawn butter and deep-fried parsley. A la carte meals might include pave of beef with basil crust and game jus, or filet of sea bass with a fumet of lime. Consider a lunchtime visit to this place, when a two-course "plat du jour" includes a soup of the day followed by such platters as venison sausages with a mustard sauce and fresh vegetables (or a suitable vegetarian substitute), all for only £5 ($8), a great deal considering that's about what you'd pay for a mediocre lunch in a local pub.

7 Old Sq. Warwick © 01926/411755. Reservations recommended. Main courses £10.95–£18.95 ($18–$30); fixed-price lunch £9.95 ($16). AE, DC, MC, V. Mon–Fri noon–2pm; Mon–Sat 7–9:30pm.

Piccolino's ITALIAN/INTERNATIONAL   This Italian restaurant is informal and fun, serving a wide selection of pizzas, including a "red hot Mama" with a zesty chile flavor. You can also get such filling pasta dishes as tortellini alla crema and tagliatelle carbonara. Many dishes taste as if prepared from recipes handed down by mama mia. Italian wine may be ordered by the glass.

31 Smith St., between Jury St. and Cotten End. © 01926/491020. Main courses £6–£12.50 ($10–$20). MC, V. Mon–Thurs noon–2:30pm and 5:30–11pm; Fri noon–2:30pm and 5:30–11:30pm; Sat noon–11:30pm; Sun noon–2:30pm and 5:30–10:30pm.

Vanilla 🏷️Value BRITISH   It's the Castle that draws you to Warwick, not the cuisine, but this bistro is notable for serving affordable food that is both good tasting and prepared with fresh ingredients. Launch your repast with a freshly made soup of the day or else something classic such as Parma ham and melon with a honey-and-mustard dressing. We recently dined very well on Gressingham duck breast, served with a fricassee of haricot vert and mushrooms. Our dinner companions preferred the roast cod, which came with buttery leeks, and the grilled Scottish rib-eye steak with wild mushrooms, roasted garlic, and a Claret jus. Save room for one of the old-fashioned desserts such as a vanilla crème brûlée with walnut shortbread or the warm dark chocolate tart with clotted cream.

6 Jury St. © 01926/498930. Reservations recommended. Main courses £10.50–£15 ($17–$24); 2-course lunch £10.50 ($17), 3-course lunch £14 ($22); Sun 2-course lunch £14.95 ($24), 3-course lunch £17 ($27); Sun 2-course dinner £18.50 ($30), 3-course dinner £22.50 ($36). AE, MC, V. Tues–Sat 11am–2pm and 6:30–10pm; Sun 11:30am–6pm.

3 Kenilworth Castle 🌟🌟

163km (102 miles) NW of London; 9km (5 miles) N of Warwick; 21km (13 miles) N of Stratford-upon-Avon

The big attraction in the village of Kenilworth, an otherwise dull English market town, is its castle—which is reason enough to stop here.

ESSENTIALS

GETTING THERE **InterCity** train lines make frequent and fast connections from London's Paddington and Euston stations to either Coventry or Stratford-upon-Avon. For information, call ℭ **0845/7484950.** Midland Red Line buses make regular connections from both towns to Kenilworth.

If you're driving from Warwick, take the A46 toward Coventry.

VISITOR INFORMATION The **Tourist Information Centre** is in the village at the Kenilworth Library, 11 Smalley Place (ℭ **01926/852595**). It's open Monday, Tuesday, and Thursday from 9:30am to 7pm, Friday from 10am to 7pm, and Saturday from 9:30am to 4pm.

THE MAGNIFICENT RUINS OF KENILWORTH CASTLE

Kenilworth Castle The castle was built by Geoffrey de Clinton, a lieutenant of Henry I. At one time, its walls enclosed an area of 3 hectares (7 acres), but it is now in magnificent ruins. Caesar's Tower, with its 5m (16-ft.) thick walls, is all that remains of the original structure.

Edward II was forced to abdicate at Kenilworth in 1327 before being carried off to Berkeley Castle in Gloucestershire, where he was undoubtedly murdered. In 1563, Elizabeth I gave the castle to her favorite, Robert Dudley, earl of Leicester. He built the gatehouse, which the queen visited on several occasions. After the civil war, the Roundheads were responsible for breaching the outer walls and towers and blowing up the north wall of the keep. This was the only damage inflicted following the earl of Monmouth's plea that it be "Slighted with as little spoil to the dwelling house as might be."

The castle is the subject of Sir Walter Scott's romance, *Kenilworth.* In 1957, Lord Kenilworth presented the decaying castle to England, and limited restoration has since been carried out.

ℭ **01926/852078.** Admission £4.40 ($7) adults, £3.30 ($5) seniors, £2.20 ($3.50) children 5–16, £11 ($18) family, free for children under 5. Good Friday–Oct daily 10am–6pm; other months daily 10am–4pm. Closed Jan 1 and Dec 24–26.

WHERE TO STAY

Abbey Guest House Jane and Warren Edward's home is imbued with a certain old-fashioned quality; built in 1900, it has Victorian charm and an inviting atmosphere, although all modern amenities have been installed. Many guests here are returning visitors. Nonsmoking bedrooms are midsize and well furnished, with private, shower-only bathrooms. Occupants of one bedroom have a private bathroom outside their door. In the residents' lounge, guests gather and enjoy the house's license to serve drinks.

41 Station Rd., Kenilworth, Warwickshire CV8 1JD. ℭ **01926/512707.** Fax 01926/859148. www.abbeyguest house.com. 7 units. £30 ($48) single; £50 ($80) double. Rates include English breakfast. MC, V. Bus: X16 or X17. **Amenities:** Breakfast room; lounge; bar. *In room:* TV, coffeemaker, hair dryer, no phone.

WHERE TO DINE

Ana's Bistro ⭐ *Finds* FRENCH Located south of town toward Warwick, this bistro sits underneath the Restaurant Diment (one of the finest in Kenilworth for those able to spend extra cash). Ana's offers well-prepared seasonal food. Try grilled whole plaice (or other fish), homemade lasagna, or sirloin steak in redwine sauce.

121–123 Warwick Rd. ℭ **01926/853763.** Reservations recommended Tues–Thurs, required Fri–Sat. Main courses £9.70–£11 ($16–$18); fixed-price lunch £14.95 ($24) weekdays, £15.95 ($26) Sun. AE, DC, MC, V. Tues–Sat 7–10:30pm; Sun noon–2:30pm. Closed Aug 1–21 and 1 week at Easter.

4 Coventry

160km (100 miles) NW of London; 32km (20 miles) NE of Stratford-upon-Avon; 29km (18 miles) SE of Birmingham; 83km (52 miles) SW of Nottingham

Coventry has long been known as the ancient market town through which Lady Godiva took her famous ride in the buff. The veracity of the story is hard to pin down; it's been suggested that she never appeared nude in town, but was the victim of scandalmongers. Coventry today is a Midlands industrial city; it was partially destroyed during the Blitz, but the restoration is miraculous.

ESSENTIALS

GETTING THERE   Trains run every half-hour from London's Euston Station to Coventry (trip time: 1¼ hr.). For schedules and information, call © **0845/7484950.**

From London's Victoria Coach Station, buses depart every hour throughout the day for the 2-hour trip. From Stratford, **bus no. X-16** runs from the town's bus station every hour for Coventry's bus station at Pool Meadow, Fairfax Street. This bus takes 60 to 90 minutes, and stops at Kenilworth and Warwick en route. For schedules and information, call © **0870/5808080.**

VISITOR INFORMATION   The **Coventry Tourist Office,** Bayley Lane (© **02476/227264**), is open Easter through mid-October Monday through Friday 9:30am to 5pm, Sunday 10am to 4:30pm; mid-October through Easter Monday through Friday 9:30am to 4:30pm, Saturday through Sunday 10am to 4:30pm.

TOURING THE CATHEDRAL

Coventry Cathedral ★★★   Consecrated in 1962, Sir Basil Spence's controversial Coventry Cathedral is the city's main attraction. The cathedral is on the same site as its 14th-century Perpendicular predecessor; you can visit the original tower. Perhaps the structure is more appreciated by the foreign visitor because Brits are more attached to traditional cathedral design. Some visitors consider the restored site one of the world's most poignant and religiously evocative modern churches.

Outside is Sir Jacob Epstein's bronze masterpiece, St. Michael Slaying the Devil. Inside, the outstanding feature is the 21m (70-ft.) tall altar tapestry by Graham Sutherland, said to be the largest in the world. The floor-to-ceiling abstract stained-glass windows are the work of the Royal College of Art. The West Screen (an entire wall of stained glass installed during the 1950s) depicts rows of stylized saints and prophets with angels flying around among them.

In the undercroft of the cathedral is a visitor center, where a 20-minute documentary is shown more or less continually. Also there is the Walkway of Holograms, whose plain walls are accented with three-dimensional images of the Stations of the Cross. One of the most moving objects is a charred cross wired together by local workmen from burning timbers that crashed to the cathedral's floor during the Nazi bombing. As an audiovisual exhibit on the city and church points out, 450 aircraft dropped 40,000 firebombs on the city in one day.

Priory Row. © 024/76227597. Suggested donation of £3 ($4.80) to cathedral. Admission to tower £1.50 ($2.40) adults, 75p ($1.20) children; to visitor center £1.75 ($2.80) adults, £1.25 ($2) children 6–16, free for children under 6. Cathedral: Easter–Sept daily 8:30am–6pm; Oct–Easter daily 9:30am–5pm. Visitor center: Easter–Oct Mon–Sat 10am–4pm.

5 Birmingham ⟨★⟩

192km (120 miles) NW of London; 40km (25 miles) N of Stratford-upon-Avon

England's second-largest city may fairly lay claim to the title "Birthplace of the Industrial Revolution." It was here that James Watt first used the steam engine to mine the Black Country. Watt and other famous members of the Lunar Society (Joseph Priestly, Charles Darwin, and Josiah Wedgwood) regularly met under a full moon in the nearby Soho mansion of manufacturer Matthew Boulton. Together, the "lunatics," as they cheerfully called themselves, launched the revolution that thrust England and the world into the modern era.

Today, this brawny, unpretentious metropolis still bears some of the scars of industrial excess and the devastation of the Blitz. But there's been an energetic building boom in recent years, and "Brummies" have remade Birmingham into a convention city that hosts 80% of all trade exhibitions in the United Kingdom.

Birmingham has worked diligently in recent decades to overcome the blight of over-industrialization and poor urban planning. New areas of green space and the city's cultivation of a first-rate symphony and ballet company, as well as art galleries and museums, have all made Birmingham more appealing.

Although not an obvious tourist highlight, Birmingham serves as a gateway to England's north. With more than one million inhabitants, Birmingham serves up a vibrant nightlife and restaurant scene. Its three universities, 2,428 hectares (6,000 acres) of parks and nearby pastoral sanctuaries, and restored canal walkways offer welcome quiet places.

ESSENTIALS

GETTING THERE By Plane Three major international carriers fly transatlantic flights directly to **Birmingham International Airport (BHX)** from four North American gateways. **British Airways** (© 800/AIRWAYS in the U.S. and Canada) has daily direct flights from Toronto and New York's JFK airport. **American Airlines** (© 800/882-8880) flies nonstop 7 days a week from Chicago's O'Hare Airport to Birmingham. **Continental Airlines** (© 800/525-0280) flies every evening from Newark to Birmingham.

Details on Birmingham flights and schedules are available through the airport (© 0121/767-5511; brochure hot line 0845/330-6600), or the website at www.bhx.co.uk.

Direct air service between Birmingham and London is almost nonexistent. Many air carriers, however, maintain a virtual air-shuttle service between London airports and nearby Manchester, which is a 1½-hour trip to Birmingham via ground transport. For example, British Airways (BA) operates 28 daily flights from London's Heathrow to Manchester, 17 daily flights from London's Gatwick, and 6 daily flights from Stansted to Manchester. BA runs even more return flights daily from Manchester to London.

Birmingham's airport lies about 13km (8 miles) southeast of the Birmingham City Centre and is easily accessible by public transportation. **AirRail Link** offers a free shuttle bus service every 10 minutes from the airport to the Birmingham International Rail Station and National Exhibition Centre (NEC). **InterCity** train services operate a shuttle from the airport to New Street Station in the City Centre, just a 10-minute trip.

By Train InterCity offers half-hourly train service (Mon–Fri) between London's Euston Station and Birmingham, a 90-minute rail trip. Regular train service is also available from London's Euston Station. Trains depart every 2 hours

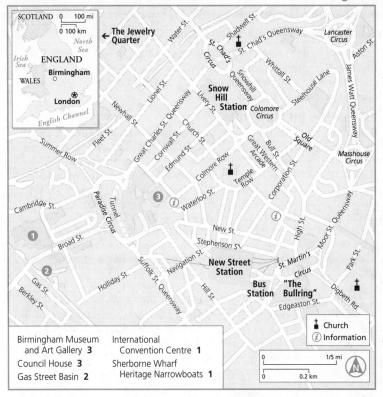

Birmingham Museum
and Art Gallery **3**

International
Convention Centre **1**

Council House **3**

Sherborne Wharf
Heritage Narrowboats **1**

Gas Street Basin **2**

✝ Church
ⓘ Information

for Birmingham. Birmingham's New Street Station in the City Centre and the airport's International Station link the city to the national rail network.

Trains leave Manchester's Piccadilly Station nearly every hour for Birmingham. The trip takes 90 minutes. Call ℂ **0845/7484950** for train schedules and current fares.

By Bus National Express (ℂ **020/7529-2000**) and **Flightlink** (ℂ **08705/808080**) provide regular bus service between Birmingham and London, Manchester, and regional towns.

By Car From London, the best route is via the M40, which leads onto the M42, the motorway that circles south and east of Birmingham. Once on the M42, any of the roads from junctions 4 to 6 will lead into the center of Birmingham.

The drive takes about 2 to 2½ hours from London, depending on traffic conditions. Parking is available at various city locations. Contact **National Car Parks** (ℂ **01217/677861**) for parking lot locations.

VISITOR INFORMATION The **Birmingham Convention & Visitor Bureau (BCVB),** 2 City Arcade, near New Street in the City Centre (ℂ **01216/432514**), is open Monday through Saturday from 9:30am to 5:30pm.

GETTING AROUND Birmingham's City Centre hosts a number of attractions within easy walking distance. **Centro** (ℂ **01212/002700**) provides information on all local bus and rail services within Birmingham and the West

Midlands area. A **Day Saver Pass** costs £2.50 ($4) and is an economical way to use the Centro bus and local train system. A weekly **Centro Card** costs £19.50 ($31). Exact change is required on one-way local bus and train trips.

Centro (✆ **01212/002700**) links Birmingham and surrounding Midland towns with regular bus service. Taxis queue at various spots in City Centre, rail stations, and the National Exhibition Centre. Travelers can also call a radio-cab operator like **BB's** (✆ **01216/933333**).

EXPLORING BIRMINGHAM

Stephenson Place, at the intersection of New and Corporation streets, is a good starting point for sampling the attractions of City Centre. A 5-minute stroll along New Street leads to Victoria Square, where **Council House,** Colmore Row (✆ **01213/032040**), the city's most impressive Victorian building, anchors the piazza. Built in 1879, it is still the meeting place for the Birmingham City Council and an impressive example of the Italian Renaissance style.

Along Broad Street is the **Gas Street Basin** (✆ **01212/369811**). Operated by Second City Canal Cruises, it forms the hub of the 3,220km (2,000-mile) canal network that runs in all directions from Birmingham to Liverpool, London, Nottingham, and Gloucester. From the Basin, you can take a cruise along the canals, or just walk by the towpaths.

Just a 10-minute walk from City Centre is the **Jewelry Quarter** at 75–79 Vyse St. (✆ **01215/543598**). This complex includes more than 100 jewelry shops. The skill of the jeweler's craft can be viewed at the Discovery Centre's restored Smith and Pepper factory displays or by visiting shop workbenches that still produce most of the jewelry made in Britain. A unique time capsule of the ancient craft of jewelry making and working with precious metals, the quarter offers bargain-hunters the opportunity to arrange repairs, design a custom piece, or just browse. Admission to the Museum of the Jewelry Quarter is £3 ($4.80), seniors £2 ($3.20), and £7 ($11) for a family ticket. It is open Monday through Friday from 10am to 4pm and Saturday from 11am to 5pm.

Sherborne Wharf Heritage Narrowboats (✆ **0121/455-6163**) depart from the International Convention Centre Quayside, taking you on 1-hour tours where you can see Birmingham from the water. You cruise along quiet stretches of the canal that first brought commercial life to the city at the start of the Industrial Revolution. Departures are daily from Easter to October at 11:30am, 1pm, 2:30pm, and 4pm, costing £4.25 ($7). Call off season as tours are conducted only Saturday and Sunday if weather permits.

Blakesley Hall, Blakesley Rd., Yardley (✆ **0121/464-2193**), which opened in 2002, is a restored Tudor farmhouse from 1590. The half-timbered structure is typical of buildings once common in the West Midlands. Its original architectural features, including a herringbone floor, are still intact. The Great and Little Parlours on the ground floor have been restored. Oak furnishings include carved, panel-back armchairs, long refectory tables, and other period pieces. Many artifacts from the era are on display, including pewter goblets and candlesticks. In the painted Bedchamber, paintings on the walls from 1590 were uncovered after having been hidden for centuries. Admission is free, and the museum is open daily from Easter until the end of October Tuesday to Friday 1 to 4pm and Saturday and Sunday noon to 4pm.

Thinktank at Millennium Point, Curzon St. (✆ **0121/202-2222**), combines science and history in 10 galleries where you can get active with the exhibits spread over four floors. The place is for both learning and for fun. Kids can do everything from grab a handful of polar bear blubber to take control of a digger. Various sections deal with such subjects as "Medicine Matters," exploring surgical instruments and health in general. Nature is uncovered in the "wild Life" section, as you learn how scientists study the wild world and how animals adapt to change. "Futures" gives you a look into a living tomorrow. In addition to many hands-on scientific exhibitions, there is also an IMAX Theatre, where you can see great animated adventures. Open Saturday to Thursday from 10am to 5pm; admission is £6.50 ($10) or £10.50 ($17) with one IMAX film.

Birmingham Museum and Art Gallery ★   Known chiefly for its collection of pre-Raphaelite paintings (including works by Ford Maddox Brown, Dante Gabriel Rossetti, Edward Burne-Jones, and Holman Hunt), the gallery also houses exceptional paintings by English watercolor masters from the 18th century. The BMAG is instantly recognized by its "Big Brum" clock tower.

Chamberlain Sq. ℂ 01213/032834. Free admission. Special exhibition charge. Mon–Thurs and Sat 10am–5pm; Fri 10:30am–5pm; Sun 12:30–5pm.

Barber Institute of Fine Arts ★★   Don't be put off by the stark, stone-and-brick building that houses the Barber Institute collection; some consider it the finest small art museum in England and the equal of any museum outside London. The choice selection of paintings includes works by Bellini, Botticelli, Brueghel, Canaletto, Delacroix, Gainsborough, Gauguin, Guardi, Murillo, Renoir, Rubens, Turner, van Gogh, and Whistler.

University of Birmingham (just off Edgbaston Park Rd., near the University's East Gate, 4km/2½ miles south of City Centre). ℂ 01214/147333. Free admission. Mon–Sat 10am–5pm; Sun noon–5pm. Bus: 61, 62, or 63 from City Centre.

The Black Country Museum   Much of the area around Birmingham is called the "Black Country" for the black smoke that billowed over the city during the iron-working era. That period is best preserved at this museum in Dudley, a town about 10 miles northwest of Birmingham. The museum occupies a sprawling landscape in the South Staffordshire coalfields, an early forge of the Industrial Revolution, and it re-creates work and life in the Black Country of the 1850s. A tramway takes visitors to a thick underground coal seam; trolleys move through a reconstructed industrial village with a schoolhouse, anchor forge, rolling mill, working replica of a 1712 steam engine, and trade shops.

Tipton Rd., Dudley (5km/3 miles north of Junction 2 exit on M5). ℂ 01215/579643. Admission £8.25 ($13) adults, £7.25 ($12) seniors, £4.75 ($8) children, £22.50 ($36) family ticket. Mar–Oct daily 10am–5pm; Nov–Feb Wed–Sun 10am–4pm.

WHERE TO STAY

The cheapest living in Birmingham is provided by the "Ys," all of which accommodate long-term guests. Call ahead to make sure a room is available. There's a **YWCA** at the Alexandra Residential Centre, 27 Norfolk Rd., Birmingham B15 EPY (ℂ 0121/454-8134), that accepts men and women over 18; rates start at £10 ($15) per night. No meals are available here, and a key deposit of £15 ($23) is imposed. Take bus no. 9 or 19 from Colmore Row. The **YWCA** at Stone Road, Birmingham B15 2HH (ℂ 0121/440-2924), admits men and women 16 years and older. The charge is £10.50 ($16) per night and a £10 ($15) key deposit. No meals are served, but there is a communal kitchen. This is not the safest area of Birmingham and guests should be particularly wary at night. Take bus no. 61, 62, or 63 to the McDonald's on Bristol Road. The Y is next door.

Ashdale House Hotel ★ This spacious Victorian terrace house is one of Birmingham's best B&Bs. The cozy rooms range from small- to midsize. Rooms with a bathroom contain a shower stall and adequate shelf space; for those without, corridor bathrooms are well maintained. Organic produce is offered at breakfast along with some vegetarian choices. Your host Margaret Read invites you to use the library with television. This nonsmoking B&B is an inviting, homelike place for an affordable stay in Birmingham. There is one room available for those with limited mobility.

39 Broad Rd., Acock's Green B27 7UX. ℂ 01217/063598. Fax 0121/7072324. www.ashdalehouse.co.uk. 9 units, 5 with bathroom. £42 ($67) double without bathroom, £48 ($77) double with bathroom. Rates include English breakfast. AE, MC, V. *In room:* TV, coffeemaker.

Awentsbury Hotel University and Pebble Mill Studio visitors will find this lodging convenient and comfortable. The place is kept spick-and-span, and the small- to midsize nonsmoking rooms, while not stylish, are reasonably comfortable and well furnished. Two rooms are large enough for families. Bathrooms are extremely small with a shower stall; there are enough corridor bathrooms so that waiting is rare.

21 Serpentine Rd., Selly Park B29 7HU. ℂ and fax **01214/721258.** www.awentsbury.com. 16 units, 11 with bathroom. £38 ($61) single without bathroom, £42 ($67) single with bathroom; £52 ($83) double without bathroom, £60 ($96) double with bathroom. Rates include English breakfast. AE, DC, MC, V. Take A38 from City Centre for about 3km (2 miles), turn left at Bournebrook Rd., then take the 1st right onto Serpentine Rd. *In room:* TV, coffeemaker.

Copperfield House Hotel The Copperfield is reached via the M5, Junction 4 to the A38 to City Centre. Turn left at Priory Road, then right at first light (A441) and right again at Upland Road. This redbrick Victorian Gothic house rests on a steep slope along a residential street. Rooms vary remarkably in spaciousness and quality. Room nos. 3, 4, and 10 are among the most desirable, thanks to garden views and particularly large and well-outfitted bathrooms. Room nos. 18 and 16 are the most recently renovated, and consequently very much in demand, too. There are two rooms available for those with limited mobility.

60 Upland Rd., Selly Park, Birmingham B29 7JS. ℂ **0121/472-8344.** Fax 0121/415-4655. www.copperfield househotel.fsnet.co.uk. 17 units. Single £63–£73 ($101–$117) Mon–Thurs, £50–£60 ($80–$96) Fri–Sun; double £75–£90 ($120–$144) Mon–Thurs, £65–£75 ($104–$120) Fri–Sun. Rates include English breakfast. AE, V. **Amenities:** Restaurant; bar; lounge. *In room:* TV, coffeemaker, hair dryer.

Lyndhurst Hotel Nine miles from the airport, this stone-exterior Victorian hotel in the northern suburbs is convenient to the Convention and City Centres and Aston University. Although the house is Victorian, furnishings are contemporary. The nonsmoking, comfortable rooms are a bit small but well organized. Bathrooms are also small; three have a tub-and-shower combination, the others shower

---

Moments **"Bucket Dining" Kashmiri Style**

A growing phenomenon, which we can only call the **Birmingham Balti Experience,** may interest those who love spicy food. *Balti* literally means bucket, but it refers to a Kashmiri style of cooking over a fast, hot flame. With the city's large Kashmiri population, there are now many *baltihouses* in Birmingham. Most of these restaurants are bare-bones, BYOB affairs. One of the better ones is **Celebrity Balti,** 44 Broad St. (ℂ **01216/326074**), close to the Convention Centre, open daily from 6pm to midnight.

only. Those who have trouble with steep steps may prefer the ground-floor rooms. The garden-view restaurant serves standard but affordable dishes.

135 Kingsbury Rd., Erdington B24 8QT. (℃ **01213/735695.** Fax 01213/735697. 14 units. £47–£58 ($75–$93) double. Rates include English breakfast. AE, DC, MC, V. From junction 6 of M6, follow A5127, take the right signposted Minworth onto Kingsbury Rd. The hotel is on the right. **Amenities:** Bar. *In room:* TV, coffeemaker, hair dryer, no phone.

WHERE TO DINE

Chung Ying CHINESE   There are more than 400 flavor-filled items on this predominantly Cantonese menu (40 dim sum items alone). Samples include pan-cooked Shanghai dumplings, stuffed crispy duck packed with crabmeat, steamed eel in bean sauce, and a variety of tasty casseroles. If you want to go really authentic and sample some of the dishes the local Chinese community likes, try fried frogs' legs with bitter melon, steamed pork pie with dried or fresh squid, or fish cakes. The **Chung Ying Garden,** another restaurant owned by the same proprietor, is at 17 Thorpe St. (℃ **0121/6666622**).

16 Wrottesley St., City Centre. (℃ **01216/225669.** Meals around £20 ($32) per person. AE, DC, MC, V. Daily noon–11:30pm (Sun until 11:30pm).

Maharaja INDIAN   Set a few doors down from the Birmingham Hippo-drome, this rather good restaurant specializes in Mughlai and North Indian dishes. Dining is on two floors, with framed fragments of Indian printed cloth on the walls. The menu features such dishes as lamb dhansak (cubes of lamb in thick lentil sauce), chicken patalia (chicken cooked in spices, herbs, and fruit), and prawn madras. The kitchen's balanced use of spices, herbs, and other fla-vorings lends most dishes an aromatic but delicate taste.

23 Hurst St., near the Hippodrome. (℃ **0121/6222641.** Main courses £7.20–£8.65 ($12–$14). AE, DC, MC, V. Mon–Sat noon–2pm and 6–11pm.

Shimla Pinks INDIAN   A carefully selected menu featuring mostly Indian and Sri Lankan dishes is served by a very courteous staff in this relaxed, elegant restau-rant. Try the achari chicken from Uttar Pradesh, or sample the Karachi dishes from the north. Special buffets complement the main menu on Sunday and Monday nights. Parking is available on Tennent Street behind the restaurant.

Another Shimla Pinks is located at 44 Station Rd., Solihull (℃ **0121/7040344**).

215 Broad St., City Centre. (℃ **01216/330366.** Main courses £6.25–£13 ($10–$21). AE, MC, V. Mon–Fri noon–2:30pm; daily 6–11pm.

BIRMINGHAM AFTER DARK
THE PERFORMING ARTS

Connected to the Convention Centre, **Symphony Hall,** at Broad Street (℃ **01217/803333**), has been hailed as an acoustical gem since its completion in 1990. Home to the **City of Birmingham Symphony Orchestra,** it also hosts special classical music events.

The **National Indoor Arena,** King Edward's Road (℃ **01212/002202**), seats 13,000 and is a favorite site for jazz, pop, and rock concerts; sporting events; and conventions.

The **Birmingham Repertory Theatre** on Broad Street at Centenary Square (℃ **01212/364455**), houses one of the top companies in England. Some of the world's greatest actors have performed with the repertory company over the years, including Lord Olivier, Albert Finney, Paul Scofield, Dame Edith Evans, and Kenneth Branagh. The widely known "Rep" comprises the **Main**

House, which seats 900 theatergoers, and **The Door,** a more intimate 140-seat venue that often stages new and innovative works. The box office is open from 9:30am to 8pm Monday through Saturday. Tickets cost £8 to £22 ($13–$35).

Midlands Arts Centre (MAC) in Cannon Hill Park (© **01214/403838**) is close to the Edgbaston Cricket Ground and reached by car or bus (route no. 1, 35, 42, or 45). The MAC houses three performance areas and stages a lively range of drama, dance, and musical performances, as well as films. The box office is open daily from 9am to 8:45pm.

The **Alexandra Theatre,** Station Street (© **08706/077533**), hosts national touring companies, including productions from London's West End. Tickets for all theaters are available through Birmingham visitor offices. The theater serves as a temporary home to many of England's touring companies. Contact the box office for show details.

The restored **Birmingham Hippodrome,** Hurst Street (© **0870/7301234** or 0870/7304321), is home to the **Birmingham Royal Ballet** and visiting companies from around the world. It hosts a variety of events from the Welsh National Opera and musicals to dance. The box office is open Monday through Saturday from 10am to 5pm.

CLUBS & PUBS

Bobby Brown's The Club, 48 Gas St., along the City Centre canal (© **01216/432573**), is a converted warehouse with several small bars and a disco. **Ronnie Scott's,** 258 Broad St. (© **01216/434525**), lets guests unwind with live jazz in a casual setting. **Liberty's,** 184 Hagley Rd. (© **01214/544444**), is a large, fashionable club featuring French cuisine in the Piano Bar restaurant, champagne, cocktails, and other smaller bars.

The **Old Varsity Tavern Public House,** 561 Bristol Rd. (© **01214/723186**), the third-largest pub in England, is popular with university students. One local fan says it's "good for dodgy music." Another laments that while it is "generally a good pub, there are vast numbers of wasted students."

---

6 Worcester ⟨★⟩

198km (124 miles) NW of London; 42km (26 miles) SW of Birmingham; 102km (61 miles) N of Bristol

Awash with some of the most magnificent and lush river scenery in all of Europe, the River Wye Valley contains some of the most charming small villages in west-central England. Where wool used to be the main industry in this area, most of the locals today make their living by fruit growing, dairy farming, and, increasingly, tourism.

Worcestershire has become a household name around the world, thanks to the famous sauce used to accent myriad dishes and perk up any respectable Bloody Mary. One of the quaintest of the Midland counties, it covers portions of the rich valleys of the Severn and Avon. Between the two cathedral cities of Hereford and Worcester, the ridge of the Malverns rises from the Severn Plain.

The River Severn flows through the heart of Worcester, a world-famous porcelain center. In medieval times, the river—close to the bustling High Street—was the hub of the city's commercial life. Today, it plays host to more leisurely activities like boat trips, fishing, and rowing. The river's bridge also affords the city's best views of 900-year-old Worcester Cathedral, with its 60m (200-ft.) high tower.

ESSENTIALS

GETTING THERE   Regular trains depart London's Paddington Station for Worcester, arriving about 2¼ hours later. For schedules and information, call © **0845/7484950.**

National Express buses leave throughout the day from London's Victoria Coach Station. For schedules and information, call © **08705/808080.**

Driving from London, take the M5 to Junction 7 toward Worcester. Give yourself about 3 hours. From Hereford, it's a short drive to Worcester. Just take the A449 42km (26 miles) west.

VISITOR INFORMATION   The **Worcester Tourist Information Centre,** in Queen Anne's Guildhall on High Street (© **01905/726311**), is open from 9:30am to 5:30pm Monday through Saturday.

SPECIAL EVENTS   The **Three Choirs Festival** was founded in 1715 by the cathedral choirs of Worcester, Gloucester, and Hereford. The cathedrals rotate every year as hosts, with the other two choirs as guests. Ticket prices range from £4 to £32 ($6–$51).

SEEING THE SIGHTS

Bickerline River Trips, 98 Christine Ave., Rushwick (© **01905/831639;** www. riverboattrips.co.uk), lets you see Worcester from the river aboard the 88-passenger *Marianne.* These 45-minute trips set sail daily on the hour from 11am to 5pm from March to October. Light refreshments are served and party bookings are available.

If you're interested in shopping, you might want to take a stroll down the architecturally important **Friar Street,** taking in the eclectic collection of individual timber-framed and brick shops. **G. R. Pratley & Sons,** Shambles (© **01905/ 22678** or 01905/28642), offers a smorgasbord of glass, china, and earthenware; it's an agent for Royal Worcester, Royal Doulton, Wedgwood, Spode, Duchess Fine Bone China, and Wood & Sons Ltd. You can also find finely woven Oriental rugs and carpets and top-quality furniture here.

Bygones of Worcester, 55 Sidbury and Cathedral Square (© **01905/23132** or 01905/25388), is actually two shops packed with an intriguing collection of antiques and odds and ends. Wander through this store to find furnishings for your home that range from the bizarre to the decorative and fanciful—all from cottages and castles in England.

Worcester Cathedral ★★   Historically speaking, the most significant part of Worcester Cathedral is its crypt, a classic example of Norman architecture from 1084. Still used today, it contains the tombs of King John and Prince Arthur, elder brother of Henry VII. Both tombs lie near the high altar. The 12th-century chapter house is one of England's finest; it and the cloisters evoke the cathedral's rich monastic past. The cathedral is also known for a distinguished history of fine choral music, and it takes part in Europe's oldest choral festival, the Three Choirs Festival.

College Yard at High St. © 01905/611002. Free admission, but adults asked for a £3 ($4.80) donation. Daily 7:30am–6pm.

Royal Worcester Porcelain Factory ★   This factory has been creating "ware of a form so precise as to be easily distinguished from other English porcelain" ever since its founding in 1751. It produces a unique range of fine china and porcelain that remains unsurpassed throughout the world. Behind-the-scenes tours last about 45 minutes. *Note:* These tours do not accept children under 11, very elderly visitors, or persons with disabilities, because of safety regulations. The Retail and Seconds Shops at the factory are open to all, and offer a unique chance to buy beautiful Royal Worcester at bargain prices. Many of the pieces are marked as seconds, but most of the time you won't be able to tell why. The Dyson Perrins Museum is also located at the factory and houses the world's largest collection of Worcester porcelain.

Severn St. ℂ **01905/746000.** www.royal-worcester.co.uk. Factory tours available Mon–Fri beginning at 10:30am; cost is £5 ($8). Call ahead to reserve (for a same-day tour, phone before 10am). Museum admission £3 ($4.80) adults, £2.25 ($3.60) seniors and children. Ticket for tour and museum £8 ($13) adults, £6.75 ($11) children. Museum Mon–Sat 9am–5:30pm, Sun 11am–5pm.

The Commandery   A 3-minute walk from Worcester Cathedral, the 11th-century Hospital of St. Wulstan was gradually transformed into a sprawling 15th-century, timber-framed building, the country home of the Wylde family. This was the headquarters of Charles II during the Battle of Worcester in 1651, the last battle in the Civil War. The Great Hall has a hammer-beam roof and a minstrels' gallery. England's premier Civil War Centre is now situated here. This exciting, interactive, and hands-on museum incorporates life-size figures, sound systems, and videos to take you through the bloody, turbulent years of the mid–17th century. You can try on helmets, handle weapons, and pick up cannon balls. The Commandery also has canal-side tearooms, a picnic area, and a Garden of Fragrance.

Sidbury. ℂ **01905/361821.** Admission £4 ($6) adults, £2.80 ($4.50) children and seniors, £10 ($16) family ticket. Mon–Sat 10am–5pm; Sun 1:30–5pm. The Commandery is a 3-min. walk from Worcester Cathedral.

Worcester Guildhall   The guildhall was built between 1721 and 1723. Here you'll find statues dutifully erected by the Royalists honoring Charles I and Charles II, as well as one of the most beautifully decorated Queen Anne rooms in England. The tourist office is located here.

High St. ℂ **01905/723471.** Free admission. Mon–Sat 8:30am–4:30pm.

Sir Edward Elgar's Birthplace Museum   This charming and inviting red brick country cottage, stable, and coach house are set on well-tended grounds. Elgar, perhaps England's greatest composer, was born in this early-19th-century house on June 2, 1857. Today, the cottage houses a unique collection of manuscripts and musical scores, photographs, and other personal memorabilia.

Crown East Lane, Lower Broadheath. ℂ **01905/333224.** Admission £4.50 ($7) adults, £4 ($6) seniors, £2 ($3.20) children, £11 ($18) family ticket. Year-round daily 11am–5pm. Drive out of Worcester on A44 toward Leominster. After 3km (2 miles), turn off to the right at the sign. The house is 1km (½ mile) on the right.

WHERE TO STAY

Burgage House   Within a stone's throw of the cathedral, this brick-sided Georgian-style house was originally two separate structures built in 1750; they were combined in 1858. The place has country-cottage look of soft chintzes. You'll find clusters of old, sometimes-antique furnishings in the public rooms. Nonsmoking bedrooms come in various sizes, all exceedingly well kept, with private bathrooms, mostly with shower. There is one room for those with limited mobility.

4 College Precincts, Worcester, Hereford and Worcestershire WR1 2LG. ℂ and fax **01905/25396.** www.burgagehouse.co.uk. 4 units. £30 ($48) single; £55 ($88) double. No credit cards. **Amenities:** Breakfast room. *In room:* TV, coffeemaker, hair dryer, no phone.

Osborne House   A family-run house, this well-maintained choice lies only a 5-minute walk from the center of town. It's a narrow building with the feel of a private home, which it more or less is. Once you check in, you're given your own key to come and go as you please. Bedrooms are old fashioned and comfortable, with neat, organized bathrooms with shower. Breakfast is generous.

17 Chestnut Walker, Worcester, Worcestershire WR1 1PR. ℂ and fax **01905/22296.** www.osborne-house. freeserve.co.uk. 4 units. £25 ($40) single; £45 ($72) double; £60 ($96) triple; £45 ($72) family unit. **Amenities:** Breakfast room. *In room:* TV, coffeemaker, hair dryer (on request), iron, no phone.

WHERE TO DINE

Across from the cathedral, **The Pub at Ye Old Talbot Hotel,** Friar Street (ℂ **01905/23573**), contains lots of Victorian nostalgia and old-fashioned wood paneling that has been darkened by generations of cigarette smoke and spilled beer. It offers predictable pub grub that's a bit better than expected, especially when it's accompanied with a pint of the house's half-dozen ales on tap.

One of Worcester's most whimsical pubs is the **Little Sauce Factory,** London Road (ℂ **01905/350159**). The entire place is a takeoff on Worcester's famous sauce, with posters advertising food flavorings, all the accessories of an old-fashioned kitchen, and an enormous ceiling map of Britain in ceramic tiles.

Farriers Arms BRITISH   This is the most historic and evocative drinking and dining haven in Worcester. It's in the second-oldest building in town, a 15th-century half-timbered affair exceeded in age only by the Cardinal's House. Don't expect grand cuisine; the viands are ham-fisted, very British, and without a shred of Continental artistry. Food is served here as a foil for any of the quintet of ales and lagers (including Courage Directors Bitter) that keep flowing from taps. Rib-sticking platters usually include steak-and-ale pie, fisherman's pie, and fried plaice with tartar sauce.

9 Fish St. ℂ **01905/27569.** Sandwiches £3–£4.25 ($4.80–$7); main courses £4–£7 ($6–$11). No credit cards. Food: daily noon–3pm. Pub: Mon–Sat 11am–11pm, Sun noon–10:30pm.

Pasha Indian Cuisine INDIAN   This is the best, most authentic Indian restaurant in town, purveying a spicy, slow-cooked cuisine across the Severn from the cathedral. Within an ambience dotted with the handcrafts and lore of India, enjoy such dishes as chicken with yogurt, lamb with coriander and cumin, and a particularly succulent version of *tandoori shahi masala* (king prawns slow-cooked in a tandoori oven).

56 St. Johns. ℂ **01905/426327.** Main courses £4.95–£9.95 ($8–$16). AE, MC, V. Daily noon–2pm and 5:30pm–midnight.

7 Ledbury

190km (119 miles) NW of London; 22km (14 miles) W of Hereford; 26km (16 miles) SW of Worcester

A thriving market town since 1120, Ledbury has a wealth of historic black-and-white, half-timbered buildings set against a rustic backdrop, especially when springtime bluebells and wild daffodils abound and apple-blossom scent fills the air. The poet Elizabeth Barrett Browning spent her childhood in nearby Wellington at Hope End (now a hotel); renowned poet laureate John Mansfield was born and reared in Ledbury.

ESSENTIALS

GETTING THERE   Six trains depart London's Paddington Station for Ledbury daily (a 2½-hr. ride). For information, call ℂ **0845/7484950.**

Two **National Express** buses leave daily from London's Victoria Coach Station for the 3-hour or so trip to Ledbury. For schedules and information, call ℂ **08705/808080.**

If you're driving from London, take the M50 south toward Wales. Then, take exit NW on the A417 toward Ledbury.

VISITOR INFORMATION The **Ledbury Tourist Information Centre** is located at 3 The Homend (✆ **01531/636147**) and is open from 10am to 4pm daily year-round; closed Sunday in winter.

SEEING THE SIGHTS

Within easy walking distance of the Tourist Information Centre is the delightfully cobbled **Church Lane,** which is so well preserved it's often used as a movie set. *Little Lord Fauntleroy* and *By the Sword Divided* are two films in which you'll be able to spy Church Lane.

The Painted Room (✆ **01531/632306**), located in the Old Council Offices in Church Lane, features a series of 16th-century frescoes found during a 1991 renovation of the building. It's open Friday through Wednesday from 11am to 2pm if a staff member is available, or a tour can be arranged by phoning ahead.

Eastnor Castle This castle transports you back to a more romantic time. Built in 1812 by a local aristocrat, Eastnor has undergone a virtual renaissance thanks to the hard work of the Hervey-Bathursts, descendants of the original owner. The many rooms are spectacularly appointed and overflow with early Italian fine art, 17th-century Venetian furniture, and Flemish tapestries, plus medieval armor and paintings by Van Dyck, Reynolds, Romney, and Watts. Lunches and teas are also available.

4km (2½ miles) east of Ledbury on A438. ✆ 01531/633160. Admission £6 ($10) adults, £3 ($4.80) children, £15.50 ($25) family ticket. Easter–Oct Sun and bank holiday Mon 11am–5pm; July–Aug Sun–Fri 11am–5pm. Closed Oct–Easter.

Hellen's Much Marcle Begun in 1292, Much Marcle was the boyhood home of an original Knight of the Garter, a knighthood bestowed only upon those who have accomplished something extraordinarily courageous or exceptional for Great Britain. This haunting ancient manor still houses the great fireplace at which Queen Isabella of England waited for the Great Seal and abdication of King Edward II in 1326 and the bedroom prepared for Bloody Mary in 1554.

6.5km (4 miles) southwest of Ledbury in Much Marcle. ✆ 01531/660504. Admission £5 ($8) adults, £2.50 ($4) children, £10 ($16) family ticket. Guided tours on the hour 2–5pm Wed, Sat, and Sun from Good Friday to beginning of Oct.

Westons Cider Mill Situated in the middle of apple and pear orchards, this cider mill was established in 1880. Although the tour is long (2½ hr.), it's a real treat, including a tasting of ciders and perries (fermented pear juices) in the Visitors Centre and Shop. Tours need to be booked in advance. If your time is limited, skip the tour, but drop into the shop for a free cider tasting. A restaurant, Scrumpy's House, serves sandwiches and salads for lunch Monday through Saturday and a traditional British menu Thursday through Saturday evenings.

The Bounds, Much Marcle. ✆ 01531/660233. Tours £3 ($4.80). Mill open year-round Mon–Fri 9:30am–4:30pm, Sat 9:30am–noon. Tours Mon, Wed, and Fri at 2:30pm.

WHERE TO STAY

The Barn House ⭐ *Finds* In the heart of Ledbury, this charming nonsmoking B&B occupies what was built around 1600 as a farmhouse and barn; during the late Victorian age, it served as corporate headquarters of a local mineral water bottling plant. Most of the improvements that made the place livable were added in the 1920s, and oaken panels and fine woodwork were inserted to add an

Edwardian flavor to an otherwise 17th-century design. Bedrooms—all doubles—are homelike and uncomplicated, like private, tasteful but unflashy homes throughout England. Your hosts are Richard and Judy Holland, whose family had lived in the house for at least 30 years before they began accepting overnight guests.

New St., Ledbury, Herefordshire HR8 2DX. ℂ **01531/632825.** 3 units, 1 with bathroom. £60 ($96) double without bathroom, £70 ($112) double with bathroom. Rates include breakfast. MC, V. **Amenities:** Breakfast. In room: TV, no phone.

The Talbot ⭐ *Finds*   Among centrally located Ledbury restaurants and pubs, the Elizabethan authenticity of this place is matched only by the half-timbering of The Feathers, which in some ways this place closely resembles. The main allure of the Talbot derives from its restaurant and pub (see "Where to Dine," below). The nonsmoking bedrooms, all doubles, are evocative, but a bit battered, with floors that are a bit squeaky and crooked. Room nos. 1 and 2, in the oldest section, are good examples of sleeping arrangements in "Olde England." Most often requested are room nos. 6 and 7, the largest and most appealing.

New St., Ledbury, Herefordshire HR8 2DX. ℂ **01531/632963.** Fax 01531/633796. www.talbotledbury.co.uk. 7 units. Sun–Thurs only £40 ($64) single; £55 ($88) double. MC, V. **Amenities:** Restaurant; pub. In room: TV, coffeemaker, hair dryer, no phone.

Wall Hills Country Guesthouse ⭐⭐   This guesthouse lies 2.5km (1½ miles) west of Ledbury, beside the A438 highway. During its construction in 1750, the manor's builders positioned the brick house to profit from sweeping views leading downhill through cider apple orchards and fields of hops. In the late 1980s, it was bought and refurbished by David and Jennifer Slaughter, devoted hosts and chefs, who accurately maintain that the highlight of a visit to Wall Hills is one of their fixed-price evening meals (available only with a few hours' notice). David, a master chef who grows some of the produce that goes into his food, carefully crafts the menu items. Especially succulent are Blue Nile perch prepared with vermouth and fresh fennel, salmon with a saffron cream sauce, and breast of pigeon with elderberry port. The nonsmoking accommodations are large, high ceilinged, comfortable, and refreshingly free of trendiness. Rooms evoke the Georgian era, the style prevailing during the original construction, and they open onto panoramic views over the rural Herefordshire countryside. Unlike the building's original design, private bathrooms have been added, with tub and shower. The place's 2.5 hectares (6 acres) contain architectural oddities from the 15th century (an A-framed cruck barn and an oast house). Even more impressive, the somber-looking ruin of an Iron Age fort lies in a field atop a nearby hill.

Hereford Rd., Ledbury, Herefordshire HR8 2PR. ℂ **01531/632833.** www.wallhills.com. 3 units. £48–£58 ($77–$93) single; £60–£70 ($96–$112) double. Discounts offered for stays of 3 nights or more. Rates include full English breakfast. MC, V. **Amenities:** Restaurant; bar. In room: TV, coffeemaker, hair dryer, iron.

WHERE TO DINE

Wall Hills Country Guesthouse and its restaurant are described in "Where to Stay," above.

The Talbot Hotel Restaurant BRITISH   This place, one of the most evocative pubs in town, has seen thousands of pints of beer quaffed or spilled by clients, who at one time or another have included virtually every local resident. If you tipple longer than you planned, a room upstairs can shelter you for the night (see "Where to Stay," above). You can even dine on simple, rib-sticking dishes marked on a chalkboard. Examples include bangers and mash, steak-and-ale pies, turkey scaloppine, halibut steak with tartar sauce, and pork tenderloin.

Place your food order at the bar; a staff member transports the finished product to your table.

New St. ℂ **01531/632963.** Main courses £5–£13 ($8–$21). AE, MC, V. Daily noon–2pm and 6:30–9pm.

8 Hereford ⭐

213km (133 miles) NW of London; 82km (51 miles) SW of Birmingham

Situated on the Wye, the city of Hereford is one of the most colorful towns in England. The red sandstone Hereford Cathedral contains an eclectic mix of architectural styles from Norman to Perpendicular.

It was the birthplace of David Garrick—actor, producer, and dramatist who breathed life back into London theater in the mid–18th century—and Nell Gwynne, an actress who was the mistress of Charles II. Surrounded by pristine countryside, orchards, and lush pasturelands, Hereford is home to the world-famous, white-faced Hereford cattle and some of the finest cider around, best sampled in one of the city's traditional and atmospheric pubs.

ESSENTIALS

GETTING THERE   By train from London's Paddington Station, Hereford is a 3-hour trip. For schedules and information, call ℂ **0845/7484950.**

To make the 4-hour-plus trip by bus from London, you'll need to catch a **National Express** bus from Victoria Coach Station. For schedules and information, call ℂ **08705/808080.**

The trip to Hereford makes a scenic 3-hour drive from London. Take the M5 to either Ledbury or Romp-on-Wye, then turn onto the A49 toward Hereford.

VISITOR INFORMATION   Hereford's **Tourist Information Centre** (ℂ **01432/268430**) is located at 1 King St. and is open Monday through Saturday from 9am to 5pm and on Sunday from 10am to 4pm in summer, and Monday through Saturday from 9am to 5pm off season.

EXPLORING THE TOWN

Interesting shopping can be had within a labyrinth of historic buildings known collectively as **High Town.** Limited only to pedestrians, it's enhanced with street performers and visiting entertainers. Principal shopping streets include Widemarsh Street, Commercial Road, St. Owen's Street, and perhaps the most charming and artfully old-fashioned of them all, Church Street.

Also near the town center is **Hereford Market,** evoking West Country street fairs of old with its cornucopia of collectibles and junk displayed in an open-air setting. It's conducted throughout the year, every Wednesday and Saturday from 8am to 3:30pm. The area pulsates with life as vendors sell items ranging from sweatshirts and saucepans to paintings and pet food.

Andrew Lamputt, The Silver Shop, 28 St. Owen St. (ℂ **01432/274961**), is the place to pick up the perfect silver gift. It boasts an extensive array of quality silverware and fine gold jewelry, and maintains a stable of skilled craftspeople who restore old pieces.

Hereford Cathedral ⭐⭐   This is one of the oldest cathedrals in England (its cornerstone was laid in 1080). It is primarily Norman, with a Lady Chapel erected in 1220, as well as a majestic "Father" Willis organ, one of the finest in the world. Exhibited together in the new library building at the west end of the cathedral are two unique and priceless treasures: the Mappa Mundi of 1290, portraying the world oriented around Jerusalem, and a 1,600-volume library of chained books, some dating from the 8th century. The cathedral also contains the Diocesan Treasury and the St. Thomas à Becket Reliquary.

Hereford city center. ✆ **01432/374202.** Cathedral open year-round with free admission. Guided tours £3.50 ($6) per person. Admission for exhibitions at Mappa Mundi and Chained Library exhibition £4.50 ($7) adults, £3.50 ($6) children and seniors, free for children under 5, £10 ($16) family ticket (2 adults and 3 children). Mon–Sat 10am–4:15pm, Sun 11am–3:15pm in summer; Mon–Sat 11am–3pm off season.

The Cider Museum and King Offa Cider Brandy Distillery This museum tells the story of traditional cider making from its heyday in the 17th century right through to modern factory methods. The King Offa Distillery has been granted the first new license to distill cider in the United Kingdom in more than 250 years, and visitors can see it being produced from beautiful copper stills from Normandy. The museum shop sells cider, cider brandy, cider brandy liqueur, and Royal Cider, the "real wine" of old England, plus various gifts and souvenirs.

Pomona Place, Whitecross Rd. (a 5-min. walk from the city center and .5km/¼ mile from the city ring road on A438 to Brecon). ✆ **01432/354207.** www.cidermuseum.co.uk. Admission £2.70 ($4.30) adults; £2.20 ($3.50) children, seniors, and students. Museum Apr–Oct daily 10am–5:30pm; Nov–Mar Tues–Sun 11am–3pm.

The Old House This half-timbered building from 1621, with 17th-century furnishings on three floors, was painstakingly restored; it includes a kitchen, hall, and rooms with four-poster beds.

High Town. ✆ **01432/260694.** Free admission. Apr–Sept Tues–Sun 10am–4pm; Oct–Mar Tues–Sat 10am–4pm.

WHERE TO STAY

Charades ★★ The inn's name derives from a comment made by its Scottish-born owner, Mrs. Betty Mullen, referring to the slow pace of her hotel's renovation (five men working for a full year) as "a charade." Since the work's completion, however, this charming B&B has emerged as one of the most likable and appealing in Hereford. Mrs. Cullen passed away in 2002, and the inn is now run by her daughter, Mrs. Yvonne Proffer. It sits on 1 hectare (1½ acres) within an 8-minute walk south of the town center, and is composed of mirror-image brick-sided houses, both from the 1830s, that were joined together in the 1980s. The non-smoking bedrooms are high ceilinged and outfitted with built-in furnishings, and have views stretching out over the Black Mountains.

34 Southbank Rd., Hereford, Herefordshire HR1 2TJ. ✆ **01432/269444.** 7 units, 4 with bathroom. £25 ($40) single without bathroom, £30 ($48) single with bathroom; £40 ($64) double without bathroom, £50 ($80) double with bathroom. Rates include breakfast. No credit cards. **Amenities:** Breakfast room. *In room:* TV, no phone.

The Merton Hotel This choice is closer to the railway station than any of its competitors. It was built in the 1790s for the overseer of the local prison, which at the time was located across the street. All vestiges of a punitive function here have disappeared in favor of a fairly straightforward hotel, with clean if slightly cramped bedrooms and conservatively modern furnishings. Rooms contain private, shower-only bathrooms. There are rooms on the ground floor for those with limited mobility.

28 Commercial Rd., Hereford, Hereford and Worcester HR1 2BD. ✆ **01432/265925.** Fax 01432/354983. www.mertonhotel.co.uk. 19 units. £45 ($72) single; £60 ($96) double. Rates include breakfast. AE, MC, V. **Amenities:** Restaurant; bar; gym. *In room:* TV, dataport, coffeemaker, hair dryer.

The Somerville This imposing guesthouse, a 15-minute walk northeast of the cathedral, was built of red brick around 1900. It functioned briefly as a retirement home before its conversion into this efficiently decorated hotel in the early 1980s. Bedrooms are spacious with high ceilings, functional, old-fashioned furnishings, and private, shower-only bathrooms. The front garden is now a parking lot, but the back garden retains some original plantings and can be seen from the large, much-renovated breakfast room. Five rooms are available for nonsmoking guests.

Bodenham Rd., Hereford, Hereford and Worcester HR1 2TS. (©) **01432/273991.** Fax 01432/268719. www. smoothhound.co.uk. 9 units. £30 ($48) single; £48–£53 ($77–$85) double; £60–£70 ($96–$112) family unit. Rates include breakfast. AE, MC, V. **Amenities:** Breakfast room; lounge. *In room:* TV, coffeemaker, hair dryer (on request), no phone.

WHERE TO DINE

Shires Restaurant ENGLISH/FRENCH   Set on the ground floor of Hereford's most historic and prestigious hotel, this restaurant is sheathed with paneling from the 17th century and later, all carved from Herefordshire oak. Everyone here considers it the stateliest restaurant in town, suitable for formal family celebrations. Lunchtime main courses are selected from an all-English carvery table, where a uniformed attendant carves from roasted joints of beef, turkey, or ham, garnished with traditional fixings. Dinners are more French in their flavor, conducted with some fanfare. The menu includes pâté of duck meat and wild mushrooms served with juniper chutney; filet of beef with red-wine-and-mushroom sauce; and pan-fried filet of salmon with avocado.

In The Green Dragon Hotel, Broad St. (©) **01432/272506.** Main dinner courses £10.95–£15.95 ($18–$26); 4-course dinner £20 ($32). AE, DC, MC, V. Daily 7–9:45pm.

A FAVORITE LOCAL PUB

One of the most popular pubs is the **Orange Tree,** 16 King St. ((©) **01432/ 267698**), attracting beer lovers and tipplers from across the county. There's nothing particularly unusual about this woodsy place—you come to soak up local color—but its beers on tap include Buddington's and a changing roster of ales and lagers sent on spec from local breweries.

9 Shrewsbury ⟨★⟩

262km (164 miles) NW of London; 62km (39 miles) SW of Stoke-on-Trent; 77km (48 miles) NW of Birmingham

The finest Tudor town in England, Shrewsbury is noted for its black-and-white buildings of timber and plaster, including Abbot's House (dating from 1450) and the tall gabled Ireland's Mansion (ca. 1575) on High Street. These houses were built by powerful and prosperous wool traders, or drapers. Dickens wrote of his stay in Shrewsbury's Lion Hotel, "I am lodged in the strangest little rooms, the ceilings of which I can touch with my hands. From the windows I can look all downhill and slantwise at the crookedest black-and-white houses, all of many shapes except straight shapes." The town has a number of Georgian and Regency mansions, some old bridges, and handsome churches, including the Abbey Church of Saint Peter and St. Mary's Church.

ESSENTIALS

GETTING THERE   Shrewsbury-bound trains depart London's Euston Station daily every half-hour. You change trains in Birmingham before you arrive in Shrewsbury 3 hours later. For information, call (©) **0845/7484950.**

Three **National Express** buses depart daily from London's Victoria Coach Station for the 5-hour trip. For information, call (©) **08705/808080.**

By car from London, the drive is 2½ hours; take the M1 to the M6 to the M54 to reach the A5, which will take you directly to Shrewsbury.

VISITOR INFORMATION   From May 26 to September 30, the **Shrewsbury Tourist Information Centre,** The Square ((©) **01743/281200**), is open from

10am to 6pm Monday through Saturday and from 10am to 4pm Sunday. From October to Easter, its hours are from 10am to 5pm Monday through Saturday.

SEEING THE SIGHTS

Many tales and stories are locked within Shrewsbury's winding narrow streets and black-and-white buildings. The best way to learn this local lore is to take one of the many walking or coach tours hosted by official Shrewsbury guides. Special themed walking tours such as Ghosts, Brother Cadfael, and the Civil War are also available. A typical tour starts in the town center and lasts 1½ hours. Tickets can be purchased from the Tourist Information Centre (see above).

Shrewsbury Castle   Built in 1083 by a Norman earl, Roger de Montgomery, this castle was designed as a powerful fortress to secure the border with Wales. The Great Hall and walls were constructed while Edward I reigned, but 200 years ago, Thomas Telford extensively remodeled the castle. Today, it houses the Shropshire Regimental Museum, which includes the collections of the King's Shropshire Light Infantry, the Shropshire Yeomanry, and the Shropshire Royal Horse Artillery. These collections represent more than 300 years of regimental service; you'll see a lock of Napoleon's hair and an American flag captured during the seizure and burning of the White House during the War of 1812.

Castle St. © **01743/358516.** Free admission. Feb 4–Mar 15 Wed–Sat 10am–4pm; Mar 18–Dec 19 Tues–Sat 10am–5pm, Sun–Mon 10am–4pm; Easter–Sept 26 10am–4:30pm; closed Dec 20–Feb 3.

Rowley's House Museum   This museum is housed in a fine 16th-century timber-frame warehouse and an adjoining 17th-century brick-and-stone mansion dating from 1618. The museum includes displays on art, local history, Roman and prehistoric archaeology, geology, costumes, and natural history. The great treasures include the Hadrianic forum inscription and silver mirror, both from the nearby Roman city of Viroconium (Wroxeter).

Barker St. © **01743/361196.** Free admission. Easter–Sept Tues–Sat 10am–5pm, Sun 10am–4pm; Oct–Easter Tues–Sat 10am–4pm.

Attingham Park   This elegant classical house set on 250 acres of woodlands and landscaped deer park is graced with superbly decorated state rooms, including a red dining room and blue drawing room. House treasures include Regency silver used at 19th-century ambassadorial receptions and elegant Italian furniture. A tearoom and gift shop on the grounds make a pleasant stop before or after your tour.

Shrewsbury. © **01743/709203.** House admission £4.60 ($7) adults, £2.30 ($3.70) children, £12 ($19) families. Park and grounds £2.20 ($3.50) adults. House, tearoom, and shop Mar 23–Nov 3 Fri–Tues 1:30–4:30pm (the tearoom opens an hour earlier for lunch); park and grounds open daily 8am–5pm (until 9pm in summer).

Shrewsbury Abbey ✪   Founded in 1083, Shrewsbury Abbey became one of England's most powerful Benedictine monasteries. It's the setting of the Brother Cadfael tales, a series of mysteries written by Ellis Peters recently adapted for television. The church remains in use to this day; visitors can see displays devoted to the abbey's history as well as the remains of the 14th-century shrine of St. Winefride.

Abbey Foregate. © **01743/232723.** Free admission, but donations requested for the Abbey Fund. Easter–Oct daily 9:30am–5:30pm; Nov–Easter daily 10:30am–3pm.

SHOPPING

The narrow, cobbled streets of Shrewsbury host wonderful, small shops in Tudor-fronted buildings, selling everything from secondhand books and Art Deco bric-a-brac to geological specimens, musical instruments, and antiques.

The staff at **Mansers Antiques,** Coleham Head (© **01743/351120**), is always ready to dispense free advice—and one of the largest comprehensive stocks of antiques in the United Kingdom. Items include furniture of all periods, silver, china, glass, clocks, metal goods, jewelry, linen, paintings, and Oriental items. The shop has a restoration department, and they will ship purchases. For prints, the **Victorian Gallery** at 40 St. John's Hill (© **01743/356351**) is the place to go.

WHERE TO STAY

Sydney House Hotel Built around 1900, the Sydney lies only .5km (¼ mile) from the railway station, and a 10-minute walk north of the town center. This is a whimsical-looking Edwardian house, combining brick walls with vague aspects of a Teutonic chalet. Inside you'll find a comfortably upholstered if not lavish set of public areas and bedrooms, each sunny, bright, and very clean, but without antique references. The street level is devoted to a restaurant that's open Monday through Saturday. Four rooms are for nonsmoking guests.

Coton Crescent, Coton Hill, Shrewsbury, Shropshire SY1 2LJ. © and fax **01743/354681.** www.sydney housishotel.co.uk. 7 units. £25–£30 ($40–$48) single; £50–£55 ($80–$88) double. AE, MC, V. **Amenities:** Breakfast room; bar. *In room:* TV, coffeemaker, hair dryer, no phone.

WHERE TO DINE

Country Friends MODERN BRITISH Built in 1673 as a private home, this pleasant restaurant today boasts a much-restored Tudor facade amid attractive gardens. Inside, a hardworking kitchen concocts modern reinventions of such old-fashioned dishes as lamb noisettes roasted in mustard crust with mint hollandaise and filet of steak with a leek and horseradish topping and red-wine sauce. Some aspects of the menu change almost every week. They also feature one bedroom at a rate of £130 ($208) double occupancy, including dinner and breakfast.

Dorrington (9.5km/6 miles south of Shrewsbury via A49), Shropshire S45 7JD. © **01743/718707.** Light luncheon platters £3.90–£10 ($6–$16); 2-course fixed-price menus £28.50 ($46); 3-course fixed-price menus £31.30 ($50). MC, V. Wed–Sat noon–2pm and 7–9pm.

The Peach Tree ★ *Finds* BRITISH/EUROPEAN Its name derives from the hundreds of ripe peaches, peach trees, and peach boughs that someone laboriously stenciled onto the walls. The setting dates from the 15th century, when this was a weaver's cottage adjacent to the abbey. The food is based on solid, time-tested recipes made with fresh ingredients and loads of European savoir-faire. It's some of the best in town. Main courses include medallions of venison over caramelized red-onion mash with a robust gingerbread sauce and such vegetarian dishes as ragout of woodland mushrooms with phyllo pastry and a basil and crème fraîche. The dessert that keeps everyone coming back for more is homemade meringue with ice cream, traditional butterscotch sauce, and roasted coconut shreds. Although the upstairs restaurant is more fancy, you can have any of the platters informally in the street-level bar if you're alone or in a hurry.

21 Abbey Foregate. © **01743/355055.** Reservations recommended on weekends. Main courses £7.95–£15.95 ($13–$26). AE, DC, MC, V. Mon–Sat 9am–midnight; Sun 9am–11pm.

SHREWSBURY AFTER DARK

Quench your thirst or have a bite to eat at the **Lion & Pheasant Hotel** bar, 49–50 Wyle Cop (© **01743/236288**), where in colder months, an inviting firelight ambience presides. Or check out the **Boat House Pub,** New Street (© **01743/ 231658**), located beside a beautiful old park on the River Severn. In summer, they open up the terrace overlooking the river, and it becomes a popular date place.

Couples enjoy a healthy selection of beers and ales, along with a tasty pub grub that ranges from soup and sandwiches to pies.

The **Buttermarket Nightclub** (© **01743/241455**), set in the old butter market on Howard Street, caters to the over-25 crowd. It has two theme nights: Saturday (disco) and Thursday (world music). Other clubs include the **Liquid Diva,** Ravens Meadows (© **0173/289022**).

The **Music Hall,** The Square (© **01743/281281**), hosts musicals, plays, and concerts year-round. Tickets range from £5 to £18 ($8–$29).

10 Ironbridge

216km (135 miles) NW of London; 58km (36 miles) NW of Birmingham; 29km (18 miles) SE of Shrewsbury

Ironbridge, located in the Ironbridge Gorge, is famous for its role in the early stages of the Industrial Revolution. Indeed, this part of the Severn River valley has been an important industrial area since the Middle Ages because of its iron and limestone deposits. But the event that clinched this area's importance came in 1709, when the Quaker ironmaster, Abraham Darby I, discovered a method for smelting iron by using coke as a fuel instead of charcoal. This paved the way for the first iron rails, boats, wheels, aqueducts, and bridge, cast in Coalbrookdale in 1779. So momentous was this accomplishment that this area was renamed Ironbridge; new transportation and engineering innovations soon followed.

Today, you'll find an intriguing complex of museums that documents the rich history of Ironbridge Gorge. Gift shops and other stores in town have plenty of unusual souvenirs to help you remember your visit.

ESSENTIALS

GETTING THERE   Seven days a week, trains leave London's Euston Station hourly for Telford Central Station in Telford. From here, take a bus or taxi into Ironbridge. The entire journey takes about 3 hours. For schedules and information, call © **0845/7484950.**

Three buses daily depart London's Victoria Coach Station, arriving in Telford about 5 hours later. Call © **08705/808080** for information. Local buses that leave Telford for the 20-minute ride to Ironbridge include nos. 6, 8, 9, and 99.

If you're driving a car from London, take the M1 to the M6 to the M54, which leads directly to Ironbridge.

VISITOR INFORMATION   The **Ironbridge Gorge Tourist Information Centre,** 4 The Wharfage (© **01952/432166**), is open Monday through Friday from 9am to 5pm and Saturday and Sunday from 10am to 5pm.

EXPLORING THE AREA

The Ironbridge Valley plays host to seven main museums and several smaller ones, collectively called the **Ironbridge Gorge Museums** ★★, Ironbridge, Telford (© **01952/433522** on weekdays and 01952/432166 on Sat and Sun). Museums include the **Coalbrookdale Museum,** with its Darby Furnace of Iron and sound-and-light display, as well as restored 19th-century homes of the Quaker ironmasters; the **Iron Bridge,** with its original tollhouse; the **Jackfield Tile Museum,** where you can see demonstrations of tile-pressing, decorating, and firing; the **Blists Hill Open Air Museum,** with its re-creation of a 19th-century town; and the **Coalport China Museum.** A passport ticket to all museums in Ironbridge Gorge is £12.50 ($20) for adults, £11.25 ($18) for seniors, £8.25 ($13) for students and children, and £40 ($64) for a family of two adults and up to five children. The sites are open from Easter to November daily from

10am to 5pm. The Iron Bridge Tollhouse and Rosehill House are closed from November to March.

You can also find some good shopping. You can buy Coalport china at the **Coalport China Museum** and decorative tiles at the **Jackfield Tile Museum.** Another place worth visiting is just beyond the Jackfield Museum: **Maws Craft Center (℃ 01952/883923)** is the site of 20 workshops situated in an old Victorian tile works beside the River Severn. Here, you can browse for porcelain dolls, glass sculptures, dollhouses, original and Celtic art, pictures with frames made while you wait, jewelry, stained glass, and children's clothes. There's also a tearoom on site that's open for lunch and afternoon tea.

WHERE TO STAY

Bridge House Set 2.5km (1½ miles) west of Ironbridge, on the outskirts of the hamlet of Buildwas, this ivy-draped, half-timbered coaching inn is from 1620. Resident proprietor Janet Hedges will tell you unusual stories about the house, such as the 365 nails (one for every day of the year) that hold together the planks of the front door, or the fact that the building's front porch was removed from the nearby abbey. Rooms are genteel and comfortable, sometimes with touches of Edwardian drama (lavishly draped beds, in some cases). Others have exposed beams, and all have creaking floors and uneven walls that testify to the age of the building. Rooms are small but snug, and each is individually decorated. The compact bathrooms are efficiently organized, each with shower.

Buildwas, Telford, Shropshire TF8 7BN. ℃ **01952/432105.** Fax 01952/432105. 4 units. £60–£70 ($96–$112) double; £85 ($136) family unit. Rates include breakfast. No credit cards. Closed for 2 weeks at Christmas. *In room:* TV, coffeemaker, hair dryer, no phone.

Severn Lodge ★ This elegant Georgian house with terraced gardens overlooks the river and Ironbridge. The Severn was built in 1832 by Sir Buckworth Soames as a wedding gift for his daughter, who married a local doctor. Built on impressive sandstone foundations, it remained a medical office until 1975, when it was made into a B&B hotel. Bedrooms are outfitted, a la Laura Ashley, in an appropriate 19th-century style, each with private bathroom.

New Rd., Ironbridge, Telford, Shropshire TF8 7AS. ℃ **01952/432147.** Fax 01952/432062. 3 units. £48 ($77) single; £62 ($99) double. Rates include English breakfast. No credit cards. **Amenities:** Breakfast room. *In room:* Coffeemaker, no phone.

WHERE TO DINE

Restaurant Chez Maw BRITISH   The name refers to Arthur Maw, long-ago owner of the house and founder of a nearby factory that produced decorative tiles during the 19th century. Prized examples of his ceramic creations line the reception area and the monumental staircase. Outfitted with crisp linens, Windsor-style chairs, and a high ceiling, the restaurant serves such updated British food as tortellini laced with cream, herbs, and slices of Parma ham; platters of smoked tuna and marinated salmon; and filets of pork and beef drizzled with sauce made from Shropshire blue cheese.

In The Valley House Hotel. ℃ **01952/432247.** Reservations recommended. Main courses £13.50 ($22); fixed-price menu £24.50 ($39). AE, DC, MC, V. Sun–Fri noon–2pm and 7–9:30pm.

A FAVORITE LOCAL PUB

A rebuilt Victorian pub, complete with a chicken coop in the backyard? Yes, it's the **New Inn,** in the Blists Hill Museum complex (℃ **01952/586063**). It has atmosphere galore, with its gas lamps, sawdust floors, and knowledgeable and friendly staff sporting vintage Victorian garb. You'll find a good selection of ales; hearty, rib-sticking, home-cooked meals; and plenty of pub games.

11 Stoke-on-Trent: The Potteries

259km (162 miles) NW of London; 77km (46 miles) N of Birmingham; 99km (59 miles) NW of Leicester; 66km (41 miles) S of Manchester

Situated halfway between the Irish and the North Seas, Staffordshire is a county of peaceful countryside, rugged moorlands, and Cheshire plains. Pottery is Staffordshire's real claim to fame; although it's been made in the area since 2000 B.C., it wasn't until the Romans rolled through in A.D. 46 that the first pottery kiln was set up at Trent Vale. Now it's Stoke-on-Trent, a loose confederation of six towns (Tunstall, Burslem, Stoke, Fenton, Longton, and Hanley, the most important) covering an 11km (7-mile) area, that's the real center of the trade. During the Industrial Revolution, Stoke-on-Trent became the world's leading producer of pottery; today it's a tourist attraction.

ESSENTIALS

GETTING THERE   It's a direct train ride of 2 hours to Stoke-on-Trent from London's Euston Station. Trains make hourly departures daily. For schedules and information, call © **0845/7484950.**

Six **National Express** buses leave London's Victoria Coach Station daily for the 4- to 5-hour trip to Stoke. For information, call © **08705/808080.**

By car from London, drive along the M1 to the M6 to the A500 at Junction 15. It will take you 2 to 3 hours by car.

VISITOR INFORMATION   The **Stoke-on-Trent Tourist Information Centre,** Quadrant Road, Hanley, Stoke-on-Trent (© **01782/236000**), is open Monday through Saturday from 9:15am to 5:15pm. You can pick up a China Experience visitor map, noting most potteries, shops, and museums in the area.

HISTORY FIRST: TWO WORTHWHILE MUSEUMS

The Potteries Museum and Art Gallery ★   Start here for an overview of Stoke-on-Trent. It houses departments of fine arts, decorative arts, natural history, archaeology, and social history. It has one of the largest and finest collections of ceramics in the world. And it's a great place for training your eyes before exploring the factories and shops of Stoke-on-Trent.

Bethesda St., Hanley. © 01782/232323. Free admission. Nov–Feb Mon–Sat 10am–5pm, Sun 2–5pm; Mar–Oct Mon–Sat 10am–5pm, Sun 2–5pm.

The Gladstone Pottery Museum ★   The only Victorian pottery factory restored as a museum, the Gladstone offers craftspeople who provide daily demonstrations in original workshops. Galleries depict the rise of the Staffordshire pottery industry—and check out the toilets of all shapes, sizes, colors, and decoration! Make use of great hands-on opportunities for plate painting, pot throwing, and ornamental flower making.

Uttoxeter Rd. at Longton. © 01782/319232. Admission £4.95 ($8) adults, £3.95 ($6) seniors and students, £3.50 ($6) children, £14 ($22) family ticket. Daily 10am–5pm; last admission at 4pm.

TAXES & SHIPPING

Each of the factories we discuss here offers shipping and can help you with your value-added tax (VAT) refund. Expect your purchases to be delivered within 1 to 3 months.

TOURING & SHOPPING THE POTTERIES

With more than 40 factories in Stoke-on-Trent, you'll need to get in shape for this adventure. All have on-site gift shops; some have several shops, selling everything from fine china dinner services to hand-painted tiles. Seconds are always a great bargain; they're high-quality pieces with imperfections that only a professional eye can detect. But don't expect bargains on top-of-the-line pieces; most of the time, prices for first-quality items are the same as they are in London, elsewhere in England, or in America. During the big January sales in London, many department stores, including Harrods, truck in seconds from Stoke factories.

Wedgwood Visitor Centre ⭐ The visitor center includes a demonstration hall to watch clay pots being formed on the potter's wheel, and witness plates being turned and fired, then painted. Highly skilled potters and decorators are happy to answer your questions. An art gallery and gift shop showcase samples of factory-made items that also can be purchased. (Note that the prices at this shop are the same as those found elsewhere.) Tours must be booked in advance.

Also located at the Wedgwood Centre, the **Wedgwood Museum** covers 3 centuries of design and features living displays including Josiah Wedgwood's Etruria factory and his Victorian showroom. Other room settings can also be seen at the museum. The Josiah Wedgwood Restaurant is the perfect place to relax with a cup of coffee or a full meal.

Wedgwood seconds, which are available at reduced prices, are not sold at the center, but are available at the **Wedgwood Group Factory Shop,** King Street, Fenton (© **01782/316161**).

Barlaston. © **01782/204218.** Admission £7.25–£8.95 ($12–$14) adults; £5.25–£6.95 ($8–$11) seniors, students, and children; £23.95–£29.95 ($38–$48) family ticket (up to 2 adults and 3 children). Factory tours Mon–Thurs at 10am and 2pm; they last 2 hr. and must be booked in advance. Centre open Mon–Fri 9am–5pm; Sat–Sun 10am–5pm. A taxi from the Stoke-on-Trent train station will cost around £7.75 ($12). If you're driving from London, head north along M1 until you reach M6. Continue north to Junction 14, which becomes A34. Follow A34 to Barlaston and follow the signs to Wedgwood.

Royal Doulton Pottery Factory ⭐ Wear comfortable shoes if you take the tour here—you'll walk nearly a mile and tackle upwards of 250 steps—but you will see exactly how plates, cups, and figures are made from start to finish. Live demonstrations of how figures are assembled from a mold and decorated are given at the Visitor Centre, which possesses the world's largest collection of Royal Doulton figures. Next door to the Visitor Centre is the Minton Fine Art Studio, where plates and pillboxes are hand-painted and richly decorated with gold before your eyes. The Gallery Restaurant serves cakes and coffee, light lunches, and afternoon tea—on the finest bone china. The gift shop is stocked with a range of Royal Doulton figures and tableware, and a selection of bargains.

Nile St. Burslem, near Stoke-on-Trent. © **01782/292434.** Admission for both tour and Visitor Centre £6.50 ($10) adults; £5 ($8) children 10–16, students, and seniors; £17 ($27) family tickets. Admission to just Visitor Centre £3 ($4.80) adults; £2.25 ($3.60) children 5–9; £2.25 ($3.60) children 10–16, students, and seniors; £7 ($11) family tickets. Tours offered Mon–Fri 10:30am–2pm; they must be booked in advance. Visitor Centre open Mon–Sat 9:30am–5pm, Sun 10:30am–4:30pm; shop open Mon–Sat 9am–5:30pm, Sun 10:30am–4:30pm. A taxi from the Stoke-on-Trent train station will cost about £5 ($8). If you're driving from London, follow M1 north until you reach M6. Take it to Junction 15, which becomes A500. Follow A500 to its junction with A527, then follow the brown signs to the factory.

John Beswick Studios of Royal Doulton This studio has been building a reputation for fine ceramic sculpture since 1896. Most renowned for authentic studies of horses, birds, and animals, the studio also makes the famed Character and Toby Jugs of Royal Doulton. You may even see Peter Rabbit and other

Beatrix Potter figures in the making during a visit. The 1½-hour tour ends in the factory shop.

Gold St., Longton, near Stoke-on-Trent. ⓒ **01782/319232.** Factory tours Mon–Thurs at 1:30pm. Tours need to be booked in advance by calling 01782/319232; tour price is £4.90 ($8) adults, £3.95 ($6) seniors and children 10 and older, free for children under 10. Shop Mon–Fri 10am–5pm. The easiest way to get here from the Stoke-on-Trent train station is by taxi, which will run you about £5 ($8). If you're driving from London, follow M1 north until you reach M6. Take it to Junction 15 to join A500, turn off onto A50 (signposted DERBY) and take the second exit (signposted LONGTON). Go straight on at the island, then turn on the 2nd left for the car park.

Spode   The oldest English pottery company still operating on the same site (since 1770) and the birthplace of fine bone china, Spode offers factory tours lasting approximately 1½ hours and connoisseur tours lasting 2½ hours. In the Craft Centre, visitors can also see demonstrations of engraving, lithography, hand painting, printing, and clay casting. An unrivaled collection of Spode's ceramic masterpieces is displayed in the Spode Museum. The Blue Italian Restaurant cooks up refreshments and lunch—served on Spode's classic Blue Italian tableware. The Factory Shop sells seconds at reduced prices.

Church St., Stoke-on-Trent. ⓒ **01782/744011.** Basic factory tour £4.50 ($7) adults, £4 ($6) children 12 years and older, students, and seniors. Connoisseur factory tour £7.50 ($12) adults, £6.50 ($10) children 12 years and older, students, and seniors. Tours Mon–Thurs 10am and 11am, Fri 10am. Tours must be booked in advance. Free admission for Spode Visitor Centre and Museum. Visitor Centre open Mon–Sat 9am–5pm, Sun 10am–4pm. Spode is a 10-min. walk from the Stoke-on-Trent train station. If you're driving from London, follow M1 north until you reach M6. Take it north to Junction 15, which becomes A500. Follow the signs.

Moorcroft Pottery   Moorcroft, a welcome change from the world-famous names above, was founded in 1898 by William Moorcroft, who produced a unique brand of pottery and was his own exclusive designer until his death in 1945. Today, the firm is in the hands of William's son, John, who carries on the family traditions, creating floral designs in bright, clear colors (think of it as the Art Nouveau of the pottery world). Decoration is part of the first firing here, giving it a higher quality of color and brilliance than, say, Spode. Someone is always around to explain the processes and to show you the museum, with its collections of early Moorcroft. The factory seconds shop has an excellent selection.

West Moorcroft, Sandbach Rd., Burslem, Stoke-on-Trent. ⓒ **01782/207943.** Factory tours £2.50 ($4) adults, £1.50 ($2.40) seniors and children under 16; must be booked in advance. Tours Mon, Wed, and Thurs 11am and 2pm, Fri 11am. Museum and shop open Mon–Fri 10am–5pm, Sat 9:30am–4:30pm. A taxi from the Stoke-on-Trent train station will run about £6 ($10). If you're driving from London, follow M1 north to M6. Take it north to Junction 15, which becomes A500. Follow the signs.

WHERE TO STAY

Corrie Guest House   This brick-fronted and substantial house is composed of a pair of late Victorian terraced houses that a previous owner interconnected and set in a beautiful city garden. The owners live at this straightforward and competent inn. The small nonsmoking bedrooms are conservatively outfitted in traditional ways and are comfortable and neat, with adequate hallway bathrooms. The location is on a quiet cul-de-sac.

13 Newton St., Basford, Stoke-on-Trent, Staffordshire ST4 6JN. ⓒ **01782/614838.** www.thecorrie.co.uk. 8 units, 4 with bathroom. £22 ($35) single without bathroom, £31 ($50) single with bathroom; £38 ($61) double without bathroom, £44 ($70) double with bathroom. No credit cards. **Amenities:** Breakfast room. *In room:* TV, coffeemaker, no phone.

Haydon House Hotel   This imposing late Victorian dark-brick house is the home of the Machin family. You'll find many of the original Victorian fittings (paneling, elaborate cove moldings, bay windows, a dignified staircase), an unusual collection of clocks, and many amenities to make your stay comfortable. They've added built-in mahogany furniture to the roomy bedrooms, most with a tub-and-shower combination. Half of the rooms are for nonsmoking guests. Ground floor rooms are available for those with limited mobility.

1–9 Haydon St., Basford, Stoke-on-Trent, Staffordshire ST4 6JD. © **01782/711311**. Fax 01782/717470. www. haydon-house-hotel.co.uk. 31 units. Mon–Thurs £60 ($96) single, £85 ($136) double, £120 ($192) suite; Fri–Sun £40–£50 ($64–$80) single, £60 ($96) double, £100 ($160) suite. DC, MC, V. **Amenities:** Restaurant; bar; room service (7am–11:30pm); laundry service. *In room:* TV, dataport, coffeemaker, hair dryer, trouser press.

WHERE TO DINE

George Hotel ✪ BRITISH/INTERNATIONAL   Although no one enforces this, the restaurant at the George is the kind of place where it might be better if men wore a jacket and necktie. It's in the town's most visible hotel, a redbrick from 1929. The restaurant, one of the best in town, is a long narrow room with a tactful, well-trained staff. The dishes served have a touch of flair but appeal nonetheless to conventional palates. Examples include sirloin steak garni, Devon-style pork (inspired by Normandy in its use of apples, Calvados, and cream), and grilled halibut with a tomato-and-onion enhanced white-wine sauce.

Swan Sq., Burslem. © **01782/577544**. Reservations recommended. Fixed-price lunch £11.50 ($18); 2-course fixed-price dinner £13.50 ($22); 3-course fixed-price dinner £16.50 ($26); main courses £8–16.50 ($13–$26). AE, DC, MC, V. Daily noon–2pm and 7–9:30pm.

Jeremiah Johnson's *Value* TEX-MEX   This Spanish tapas and Tex-Mex bar is one of the best value places to eat in Hartshill, and it also serves some of the tastiest food. For lunch try the wrap-and-roll special for £2.95 to £4.95 ($4.70–$8) where you choose the type of tortilla you want and then just add the fillings of your choice. For dinner sample Cajun-style tuna steak, or the ever-popular fajitas. Tapas food is also available, such as *gambas al ajillo* (prawns in garlic) or *tortilla española* (traditional Spanish potato-and-onion omelet). They also offer a reasonable selection of Spanish and South American wines.

325 Hartshill Rd., Hartshill. © **01782/634925**. Main courses £8.50–£12.50 ($14–$20). AE, DC, MC, V. Daily noon–midnight.

12 Stafford

227km (142 miles) NW of London; 42km (26 miles) N of Birmingham; 27km (17 miles) S of Stoke-on-Trent

The county seat of Staffordshire was the birthplace of Izaak Walton, the British writer and celebrated fisherman. Long famous as a boot-making center, it contains many historic buildings, notably St. Chad's, the town's oldest church; St. Mary's, with its unusual octagonal tower; and the Ancient High House, the largest timber-frame town house in England.

ESSENTIALS

GETTING THERE   To get here from London, take a train from Euston Station for the approximately 2-hour trip. For schedules and information, call © **0845/7484950**.

National Express buses depart London's Victoria Coach Station, arriving about 5 hours later. For schedules and information, call © **08705/808080**.

For a 3-hour car trip, take the M40 to the M6, which leads directly to Stafford.

VISITOR INFORMATION   Visitor information is available from the **Stafford Tourist Information Centre,** located in the Ancient High House, Greengate Street (© **01785/619136**). It is open Monday through Friday from 9am to 5pm and Saturday from 10am to 5pm.

EXPLORING THE TOWN

The **Shire Hall Gallery,** Market Square (© **01785/278345**), housed in the richly restored historic courthouse (1798), is an important visual-arts complex offering a lively program of exhibitions and a crafts shop that stocks a wide range of contemporary ceramics, textiles, jewelry, and glass objects. All are of high quality and displayed in original surroundings.

Ancient High House Reputedly the tallest timber-frame town house in England, the Ancient High House (1595) housed Charles I and his nephew Prince Rupert at the start of the Civil War in 1642. A year later, the house became a prison for Royalist officers. Many of the rooms throughout the house have been restored, and each corresponds with an important period in the house's history.

Greengate St. © **01785/619131.** Free admission. Year-round Mon–Fri 9am–5pm; Apr–Oct Sat 10am–4pm; Nov–Mar Sat 10am–3pm.

Stafford Castle Built on an easily defensible promontory, Stafford Castle began as a timber fortress in 1100, a scant 40 years after the Norman invasion. Its long history peaked in 1444 when the owner, Humphrey Stafford, became the duke of Buckinghamshire. During the Civil War, the castle was defended by Lady Isabel but was eventually abandoned and almost entirely destroyed. In 1813, the ruins of the castle were reconstructed in the Gothic Revival style but once again fell into disarray by the middle of the 20th century. The Visitor Centre has the floor plan of a 12th-century Norman guardhouse; its collection of artifacts from on-site excavations is designed to bring to life the tumultuous history of the castle. Programs, events, and reenactments are scheduled throughout the year (during winter, torchlight tours of the castle are arranged for organized groups). The castle also has a 16-bed herb garden and a host of arms and armor that visitors can try on.

Newport Rd. © **01785/257698.** Free admission. Apr–Sept Tues–Sun 10am–5pm; Oct–Mar Tues–Sun 10am–4pm.

Izaak Walton Cottage In 1654, after publishing *The Compleat Angler,* Izaak Walton bought a 16th-century, typical mid-Staffordshire cottage now open to visitors. To this day, Walton's work is recognized as one of the greatest books on fishing ever written. After a difficult history, including two fires in the 20th-century alone, the cottage has been rethatched and restored to its original condition. A cottage garden and an angling museum can be found on the grounds.

Worston Lane. © **01785/760278.** Free Admission. Apr–Oct Tues–Sun and bank holiday Mon 11am–4:30pm.

WHERE TO STAY

Abbey Hotel About 2.5km (1½ miles) south of Stafford's historic core, this hotel comprises five early-20th-century brick houses that were interconnected either by breaking down interior walls or by covering over alleyways with a glass canopy. Painted in contrasting shades of black and white, the houses provide comfortable and unpretentious, if blandly contemporary accommodations, each in a monochromatic color scheme. All bedrooms in the main building have private bathrooms and, except for one under the eaves, lie one flight above street level; there's no elevator. Those without bathrooms are in the annex.

65–68 Lichfield Rd. Stafford, Staffordshire ST17 4LW. © **01785/258531.** Fax 01785/246875. www.abbey hotelstafford.co.uk. 31 units, 25 with bathroom. £25 ($40) single without bathroom; £45 ($72) single with bathroom; £45 ($72) double without bathroom; £60 ($96) double with bathroom. Rates include breakfast. AE, MC, V. Closed Dec 22–Jan 7. **Amenities:** Restaurant; bar. *In room:* TV, coffeemaker.

The Vine Hotel Built around the half-timbered core of a greatly expanded 15th-century inn, this is a reliable, slightly dowdy hotel that retains its old-world allure, despite alterations that have connected it with the former mew houses and stables in back. Although three of them retain vestiges of half-timbering, most bedrooms are modernized and uncomplicated; despite the layer of wall-to-wall carpeting that sheaths their floors, they retain such eccentricities as squeaking floors and slightly uneven walls.

Salter St., Stafford, Staffordshire ST16 2JU. ℂ **01785/244112.** Fax 01785/246612. 27 units. £56 ($90) single; £65 ($104) double; £85 ($136) family unit. Rates include English breakfast. AE, MC, V. **Amenities:** Restaurant; bar. *In room:* TV, coffeemaker, iron.

WHERE TO DINE

Spaggos ⭐ ITALIAN This is one of the best restaurants in town, providing Mediterranean flair from a sand-colored Victorian cottage adjacent to central Stafford's only cinema. The twin dining rooms are outfitted in soft tones of green and gold, evoking the Italian harvest. Menu items include pappardelle cacciatore (wide noodles with chicken, mushrooms, onions, bacon, and mozzarella); avocados stuffed with Gorgonzola and bacon and drizzled with cheese sauce; and crepes stuffed with mushrooms in green sauce. Steaks, prepared with Gorgonzola, pizzaiola, or red wine and pesto, are grilled in the Tuscan style and are usually tender and flavorful.

13 Bailey St., Woodlings Yard. ℂ **01785/246265.** Reservations recommended. Fixed-price 3-course menu £12.95 ($21). MC, V. Mon–Sat 12:30–2:30pm and 6:30–10:30pm; Sun 12:30–4:30pm.

PUBS

The Stafford Arms, 43 Railway St. (ℂ **01785/253313**), is a happening, fun, and friendly place, drawing patrons from all walks of life. The staff is outgoing, serving a fine array of ales, ever-changing microbrewery specials, and good inexpensive grub. **The Malt & Hops,** 135 Lichfield Rd. (ℂ **01785/258555**), is more laid-back, though it attracts an energetic young crowd on weekend nights. It also has a wide choice of ales and good food.

13 Lichfield

205km (128 miles) NW of London; 26km (16 miles) N of Birmingham; 48km (30 miles) SE of Stoke-on-Trent

Set near the heartland of the Midlands, Lichfield, dating from the 8th century, has escaped excessive industrialization. Visitors can reflect on the past as they stroll down the medieval streets, replete with a mix of Georgian, Tudor, and Victorian architecture. Fans of Samuel Johnson make pilgrimages to see where the author of the first important English dictionary was born in 1709. The city is noted for its cathedral, with three spires known as the "Ladies of the Vale." The half-timbered houses in the vicar's close and the 17th-century bishop's palace have survived innumerable sieges down through the years.

ESSENTIALS

GETTING THERE A few direct trains leave daily out of London's Euston Station in the early morning and evening. The trip takes about 2½ hours. For schedules and information, call ℂ **0845/7484950.**

To travel here by bus, take the **National Express** from London's Victoria Coach Station to Birmingham, then change to local bus no. 912 to reach Lichfield. Plan on about 4 hours for the bus trip, depending on your connection in Birmingham. (The Birmingham-Lichfield leg takes approximately 1 hr.) For schedules and information, call ℂ **08705/808080.**

If you plan on making the 3-hour drive from London yourself, take the M1 to the M42 to the A38.

VISITOR INFORMATION   The **Lichfield Tourist Information Centre,** Donegal House, Bore Street, Lichfield (✆ **01543/308209;** www.Lichfield-tourist. co.uk), provides visitor information Monday through Friday between 9am and 4:45pm and Saturday between 9am and 2pm from September to May; and Monday through Friday from 9am to 5pm and Saturday from 9am to 4:30pm during the summer months.

SPECIAL EVENTS   In summer, Lichfield District is home to many small but fun events. June brings a jazz-and-blues festival, a real-ale festival with more than 50 different brews to sample, and a folk festival. The Lichfield Festival plus Fringe occurs in July and is a music, arts, and drama extravaganza. Contact the Tourist Information Centre for exact dates.

SEEING THE SIGHTS

The Samuel Johnson Birthplace Museum   Dedicated to one of England's most gifted writers, this museum occupies the restored house where Dr. Johnson was born in 1709. He wrote poetry, essays, biographies, and, of course, the first important English dictionary. The museum contains tableaux rooms showing the house's appearance in the early 18th century, four floors of exhibits illustrating Johnson's life and work, a bookshop, a reading room, and displays of his manuscripts and other personal effects.

Breadmarket St. ✆ 01543/264972. Admission £2.20 ($3.50) adults, £1.30 ($2.10) children and seniors, £5.80 ($9) family ticket (up to 2 adults, 4 children). Apr–Sept Mon–Sun 10:30am–4:30pm; Oct–Nov Mon–Sat noon–4:30pm. Last admission at 4pm.

Lichfield Heritage Centre   This former parish church, which maintains the Dyott Chapel for worship, has been transformed into a treasury and exhibition room with a coffee shop and gift shop. The best panoramic views of the town can be seen from the 40m (131-ft.) viewing platforms in the spire of St. Mary's Centre.

In St. Mary's Centre, Breadmarket St. in Market Sq. ✆ 01543/256611. Across the street from Dr. Johnson's Birthplace Museum stands the Heritage Centre and Treasury. Admission £3.50 ($6) adults, £2.60 ($4.15) seniors and students, £1 ($1.60) children 4–14, £8 ($13) family ticket. Viewing platform admission £1 ($1.50) adults; 80p ($1.20) children over 10, students, and seniors. Daily 10am–5pm (last admission at 4:15pm).

Guildhall Cells   Just behind the Heritage Centre is the Victorian Gothic Guildhall. Rebuilt in 1846, this former city council meeting place was constructed over the medieval city dungeons where, it is reported, a man was imprisoned for 12 years for counterfeiting a sixpence. Many of its prisoners were burned at the stake in Market Square.

Bore St. ✆ 01543/250011. Admission 40p (65¢) adults, 30p (50¢) seniors and children. Dungeons open May–Sept Sat 10am–4pm; Oct–Apr Sat 10am–4pm.

Lichfield Cathedral ✸✸   The west front end of Lichfield Cathedral was built around 1280. The entire cathedral received heavy damage during the Civil War but was restored first in the 1660s and then in the 1800s. Its three spires, known as the "Ladies of the Vale," can be seen from miles around, with its tallest spire rising more than 76m (250 ft.). The cathedral's many treasures include the illuminated "Lichfield Gospels"; Sir Francis Chantrey's famous sculpture *The Sleeping Children;* 16th-century Flemish glass in the Lady Chapel; and a High Victorian pulpit and chancel screen by Gilbert Scott and Francis Skidmore.

The Old Registry, The Close. ℂ **01543/306240.** www.lichfield-cathedral.org.uk. Free admission. Suggested donation £3 ($4.80). Cathedral daily 7:30am–5:30pm (7:30pm in summer); Visitors Study Centre May–Sept daily 9am–5pm.

WHERE TO STAY

Little Barrow Hotel   The best of the town's modest inns, this place has been enlarged and improved so many times during its lifetime that the exterior today includes everything from half-timbering to relatively modern stucco. This is the largest hotel in Lichfield, and its interior seems like a personalized version of a modern, upscale chain hotel run by a well-trained staff. Bedrooms are warm, clean, and cozy. The modernized rooms, mostly small- to midsize, have recently been refurbished. Baths are small but tidy, with a shower stall.

Beacon St., Lichfield, Staffordshire WS13 7AR. ℂ **01543/414500.** Fax 01543/415734. www.tlbh.co.uk. 24 units. £80 ($128) double; £90 ($144) family room. Rates include breakfast. AE, MC, V. **Amenities:** Restaurant; bar; limited room service. *In room:* TV, coffeemaker, hair dryer, trouser press.

WHERE TO DINE

Little Barrow Restaurant BRITISH   This respectable, highly competent restaurant offers the genteel decor you would expect in a country-club dining room, plus tactful service from a well-trained staff. Most business lunches are conducted over the reasonably priced fixed menu; evening meals are a la carte, more leisurely, and more elaborate. Menu items include prime filet of scotch sirloin with a cream, brandy, and black-pepper sauce; whole breast of chicken with shallots, almond slivers, cream, and diced ham; and rack of lamb coated with honey and herbs, served atop a port-and-red-currant jus. Less formal, less-expensive meals ranging from sandwiches to steaks are served in the bar.

Beacon St. ℂ **01543/414500.** Reservations recommended. Bar: platters £3.50–£9 ($6–$14). Restaurant: fixed-price lunch £10–£16 ($16–$26); fixed-price dinner £18.50–£21 ($30–$34). AE, MC, V. Bar meals daily noon–2pm, Sun–Fri 6:30–9pm; restaurant daily noon–2pm and 7–9:30pm.

Pig & Truffle Bar & Bistro FARM-STYLE BRITISH/INTERNATIONAL   No other inexpensive joint in Lichfield matches the level of service and whimsical charm of this very popular pub-bistro. It occupies a stone, stucco, and faux-timbered facade resting on 17th-century foundations, in the heart of town. Diners and drinkers congregate at the same tables; the staff maneuvers around what sometimes becomes a mob of locals who use the place as rendezvous and gossip exchange. (Be warned that because of the crush, no dinners are served on weekends.) No one minds if you drop in just for a drink, but if your intention involves sustenance, know that every menu item here derives its inspiration from barnyard nomenclature. Your barbequed sandwich is a "Pigsty Baguette," your burger (in any of a half-dozen variations) is a "Bullyburger," and your stuffed baked potato is a "Percy (the pig's) boot."

Tamworth St. ℂ **01543/262312.** Main courses £5.45–£7.95 ($9–$13). Mon–Thurs set-price 2-course meal £5.95 ($10) all day. AE, MC, V. Daily noon–9pm.

PUBS

The King's Head, Bird Street (ℂ **01543/256822**), saw quite a bit of action during the Civil War and has no problem attracting a noisy, animated, and frenetic crowd. In a 15th-century coaching inn decorated with military memorabilia, the town's under-25 crowd enjoys live music, reasonable ales, good food, and a disco (Fri–Sun).

13

Cambridge & East Anglia

The bucolic counties of East Anglia (Essex, Suffolk, Norfolk, and Cambridgeshire) were ancient Anglo-Saxon kingdoms dominated by the Danes. It's a land of heaths, fens, marshes, and inland lagoons known as "broads." Old villages and market towns abound, and bird-watchers, anglers, walkers, and cyclists are all drawn to the area.

Cambridgeshire is in large part an agricultural region, with distinctive features such as the black peat soil of the Fens, a district crisscrossed by dikes and drainage ditches. **Cambridge,** in the shire's center, is the most visited city in East Anglia, with its university the most famous (but not sole) attraction.

Even though Essex is close to London and is industrialized in places, this land of rolling fields has rural areas and villages, many on the seaside. Stretching east to the English Channel, its major city, **Colchester,** is known for oysters and roses. Colchester was the first Roman city in Britain and is the oldest recorded town in the kingdom. Since Colchester is not on most visitors' itinerary, we focus instead on tiny villages in western Essex, such as **Thaxted,** just south of Cambridge and easily explored on your way there from London.

The easternmost county of England, Suffolk is a refuge for artists, as it was when its famous native sons, Constable and Gainsborough, preserved its landscapes on canvas. Although a fast train can whisk you from London to East Suffolk in 1½ hours, its fishing villages, historic homes, and national monuments remain off the beaten track. To capture Suffolk's true charm, explore its little market towns and villages. Beginning at the Essex border, we head eastward toward the North Sea, highlighting such scenic villages as **Long Melford** and **Lavenham.**

Seat of the dukes of Norfolk, **Norwich** is less popular, but those who venture to it are rewarded with some of England's most beautiful scenery. An occasional dike or windmill makes you think you're in the Netherlands. From here you can branch out and visit the "Broads" or travel to **Sandringham,** the country home of four generations of British monarchs.

1 Cambridge ✦✦✦: Town & Gown

88km (55 miles) N of London; 128km (80 miles) NE of Oxford

The university town of Cambridge is a collage of images: the Bridge of Sighs; spires and turrets; drooping willows; dusty secondhand bookshops; carol-singing in King's College Chapel; dancing until sunrise at the May balls; the sound of Elizabethan madrigals; narrow lanes where Darwin, Newton, and Cromwell once walked; the "Backs," where the college lawns sweep down to the River Cam; the tattered black robe of a hurrying upperclassman flying in the wind.

Along with Oxford, Cambridge is one of England's ancient seats of learning. In many ways their stories are similar, particularly the age-old conflict between town and gown. As far as the locals are concerned, alumni such as Isaac Newton, John Milton, and Virginia Woolf aren't "of the past." Cambridge continues to graduate many famous scientists such as physicist Stephen Hawking, author of *A Brief History of Time*. More and more high-tech ventures are installing themselves here to produce new software—thousands of start-up companies producing £2 billion ($3 billion) a year in revenues. Even Bill Gates, in 1997, decided to finance a £50 million ($80 million) research center here, claiming that Cambridge was becoming a "world center of advanced technology."

ESSENTIALS

GETTING THERE   Trains depart frequently from London's Liverpool Street and King's Cross stations, arriving an hour later. For inquiries, call © **08457/ 48-49-50.** An off-peak, same-day, round-trip ticket is £15.60 ($25). A peak-time, same-day, round-trip ticket is £18.10 ($29). An off-peak, longer stay round-trip ticket (up to 5-day period) is £24.60 ($39).

National Express buses leave hourly from London's Victoria Coach Station for the 2-hour trip to Drummer Street Station in Cambridge. A one-way or same-day round-trip costs £8 ($13). To return in a day or two, the cost is £14 ($22). For schedules and information, call © **020/7529-2000.**

If you're driving from London, head north on the M11.

VISITOR INFORMATION   The **Cambridge Tourist Information Centre,** Wheeler Street (© **01223/322640;** www.cambridge.gov.uk), is in back of the Guildhall. The center has a wide range of information, including data on public transportation in the area and on different sightseeing attractions. From April to October, hours are Monday to Saturday 10am to 6pm and Sunday (Easter–Dec only) 11am to 4pm. In July and August, the office is open daily 10am to 7pm. From November to March, hours are Monday to Saturday 10am to 6pm.

Guide Friday Ltd. (© **01223/362444**) operates a tourist reception center for Cambridge and Cambridgeshire at Cambridge Railway Station. The center, on the concourse of the railway station, sells brochures and maps. Also available is a full range of tourist services, including accommodations booking. Open in summer daily from 9:30am to 6pm (closes at 3pm off season). Guided tours of Cambridge leave the center daily between 9:30am and 5:45pm; the frequency of the tours depends on demand.

GETTING AROUND   The center of Cambridge is made for pedestrians, so leave your car at one of the many parking lots (they get more expensive as you approach the city center) and stroll to some of the colleges spread throughout the city. Follow the courtyards through to the "Backs" (the college lawns) and walk through to Trinity (where Prince Charles studied) and St. John's College, including the Bridge of Sighs.

Another popular way of getting around is bicycling. **City Cycle Hire** (© **01223/293030**), has bicycles for rent for £6 ($10) for 3 hours, £6 ($10) per day, or £13 ($21) per week. A deposit of £25 ($40) is required. Call their number to reserve a bike. At that time you'll be told the address at which to pick up the cycle. Open daily in summer from 9am to 6pm; off season Monday through Saturday from 9am to 5:30pm.

Stagecoach Cambus, 100 Cowley Rd. (© **0870/6082608**), services the Cambridge area with a network of buses, with fares ranging in price from 60p to £1.80 (95¢–$2.90). The local tourist office has bus schedules.

SPECIAL EVENTS   Cambridge's artistic bent peaks from the end of June to the end of July during **Camfest** (© **01223/359547**), a visual and performing arts festival. Event tickets are generally between £5 and £12 ($8–$19).

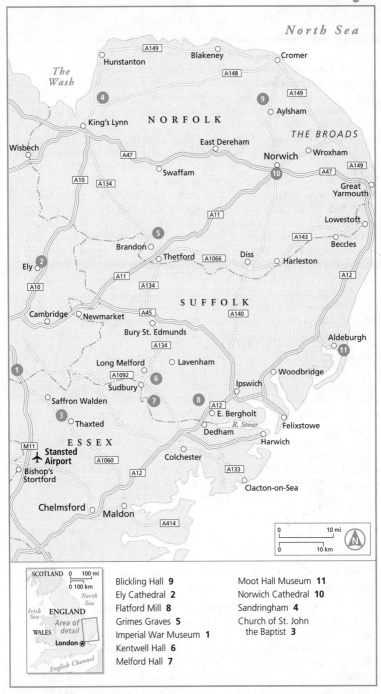

North Sea

A149

Hunstanton   Blakeney   Cromer

The Wash   A148

④   ⑨   A149

King's Lynn   N O R F O L K   Aylsham

THE BROADS

Wisbech   East Dereham   Wroxham

A47   Norwich

Swaffam   ⑩   A47   A149

A10   A134   Great Yarmouth

A11   Lowestoft

Ely ②   ⑤   A143   Beccles

A10   Brandon   Thetford   A1066   Diss   Harleston

A11   A134   A12

S U F F O L K

Cambridge   Newmarket   A45   A140

Bury St. Edmunds   Aldeburgh

A134   ⑪

Long Melford   Lavenham   Woodbridge

① A1092   ⑥

Sudbury   Ipswich

Saffron Walden   ⑦   ⑧   A12

③ Thaxted   E. Bergholt   Felixstowe

R. Stour

E S S E X   Dedham   Harwich

M11   Stansted Airport   Colchester

Bishop's Stortford   A1060   A12   A133

Chelmsford   Maldon   Clacton-on-Sea

A414

| 0 | | 10 mi |
| 0 | | 10 km |

N

ORGANIZED TOURS

For an informative spin on Cambridge, join a **Guided Walking Tour** given by a Cambridge Blue Badge Guide (© **01223/322640**). Two-hour tours leave the Tourist Information Centre (see above) and wind through the streets of historic Cambridge, visiting at least one college and the famous "Backs." From mid-June to August, drama tours are conducted, during which participants may see various costumed characters walk in and out of the tour. Henry VIII, Queen Elizabeth I, Isaac Newton, and others help to breathe life into the history of Cambridge during these tours. Regular tours are from April to mid-June, daily at 11:30am and 1:30pm; from mid-June to September, daily at 11:30am, 1:30pm, and 2:30pm; October through March, daily at 1:30pm and Saturday at 11:30am. Drama tours are July and August on Tuesday at 6:30pm. Admission for regular tours is £7.85 ($13) per person, £4.50 ($7) per person for drama tours.

In addition to its visitor information services (see "Essentials," above), **Guide Friday Ltd.,** on the concourse of Cambridge Railway Station (© **01223/362444**), offers daily guided tours of Cambridge via open-top, double-decker buses. In summer, they depart every 15 minutes from 9:30am to 4pm. Departures are curtailed off-season depending on demand. The tour can be a 1-hour ride, or you can get off at any of the many stops and rejoin the tour whenever you wish. Tickets are valid all day. The fare is £7.50 ($12) for adults, £5.50 ($9) for seniors and students, £3 ($4.80) for children 6 to 12, and free for kids 5 and under. A family ticket for £18 ($29) covers two adults and up to three children. Office hours are daily from 8:45am to 7pm in summer and from 9:30am to 5pm during off season.

EXPLORING THE UNIVERSITY

Oxford University (see chapter 5) predates Cambridge, but by the early 13th century, scholars began coming here, too. Eventually, Cambridge won partial recognition from Henry III, and its destiny was tied to the approval (or disapproval) of subsequent English monarchs. Cambridge now consists of 31 colleges for both men and women. Colleges are closed for exams from mid-April until the end of June.

The following is only a sample of some of the more interesting colleges. If you're planning to be in Cambridge awhile, you might also want to visit **Magdalene College,** on Magdalene Street, founded in 1542; **Pembroke College,** on Trumpington Street, founded in 1347; **Christ's College,** on St. Andrew's Street, founded in 1505; and **Corpus Christi College,** on Trumpington Street, which dates from 1352.

KING'S COLLEGE ★★ The adolescent Henry VI founded King's College on King's Parade (© **01223/331212;** www.kings.cam.ac.uk) in 1441. Most of

---

Tips **Caution: Students at Work**

Because of the disturbances caused by the influx of tourists, Cambridge has had to limit visitors, or even exclude them altogether, from various parts of the university. In some cases, a small entry fee will be charged. Small groups of up to six people are generally admitted with no problem, and you can inquire with the local tourist office about visiting hours (see above). All colleges are closed during exams and graduation, on Easter and all bank holidays, and at other times without notice; check with the guard posted at the gate of the campus you want to visit.

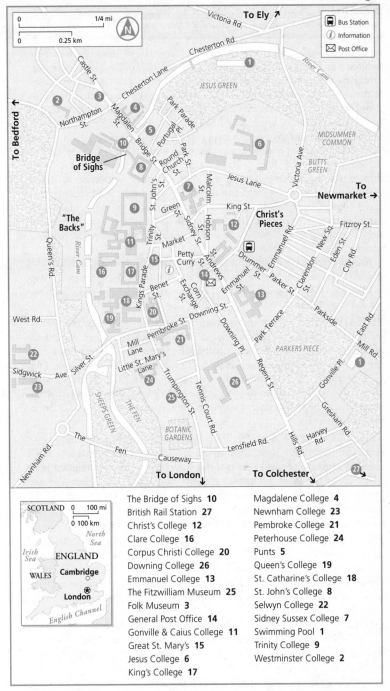

Cambridge

To Ely ↗

To Bedford ←

To Newmarket →

To London ↓

To Colchester ↓

- 🚌 Bus Station
- ⓘ Information
- ✉ Post Office

Victoria Rd.
Chesterton Rd.
Chesterton Lane
Castle St.
Northampton St.
Magdalen St.
Bridge St.
Park Parade
Portugal Pl.
Park St.
Round Church St.
JESUS GREEN
River Cam
MIDSUMMER COMMON
BUTTS GREEN
Victoria Ave.
Jesus Lane
Malcolm St.
King St.
Christ's Pieces
Green St.
Trinity St.
St. John's St.
Sidney St.
Hobson St.
Market
Petty Curry
Benet St.
Kings Parade
Corn Exchange St.
St. Andrews St.
Emmanuel St.
Drummer St.
Emmanuel Rd.
Parker St.
Clarendon St.
New Sq.
Eden St.
City Rd.
Fitzroy St.
Pembroke St.
Downing St.
Downing Pl.
Park Terrace
Parkside
East Rd.
Mill Rd.
Gonville Pl.
PARKERS PIECE
Regent St.
Tennis Court Rd.
Trumpington St.
Little St. Mary's Lane
Mill Lane
Silver St.
West Rd.
Queen's Rd.
Sidgwick Ave.
SHEEPS GREEN
THE FEN
BOTANIC GARDENS
The Fen Causeway
Newnham Rd.
Lensfield Rd.
Hills Rd.
Harvey Rd.
Gresham Rd.
Bridge of Sighs
"The Backs"
River Cam

The Bridge of Sighs **10**
British Rail Station **27**
Christ's College **12**
Clare College **16**
Corpus Christi College **20**
Downing College **26**
Emmanuel College **13**
The Fitzwilliam Museum **25**
Folk Museum **3**
General Post Office **14**
Gonville & Caius College **11**
Great St. Mary's **15**
Jesus College **6**
King's College **17**

Magdalene College **4**
Newnham College **23**
Pembroke College **21**
Peterhouse College **24**
Punts **5**
Queen's College **19**
St. Catharine's College **18**
St. John's College **8**
Selwyn College **22**
Sidney Sussex College **7**
Swimming Pool **1**
Trinity College **9**
Westminster College **2**

SCOTLAND
North Sea
Irish Sea
ENGLAND
WALES
Cambridge
London
English Channel
0   100 mi
0   100 km

its buildings today are from the 19th century, but its crowning glory, the **Perpendicular King's College Chapel** ★★★, dates from the Middle Ages and is one of England's architectural gems. Its most characteristic features are the magnificent fan vaulting, all of stone, and the great windows, most of which were fashioned by Flemish artisans between 1517 and 1531. The stained glass portrays biblical scenes, in hues of red, blue, and amber. The chapel also houses Rubens's *The Adoration of the Magi*. The rood screen is from the early 16th century. *Insider's tip:* For a classic view of chapel, you can admire the architectural complex from the rear, which would be ideal for a picnic along the river. E. M. Forster came here to contemplate scenes for his novel, *Maurice*.

The chapel is open during vacation time, Monday to Friday from 9:30am to 3:30pm, on Saturday from 9:30am to 3:15pm, and Sunday from 1:15 to 2:15pm and 5 to 5:30pm. During the term, the public is welcome to attend choral services Monday through Saturday at 5:30pm and on Sunday at 10:30am and 3:30pm. During school vacations, the chapel is open to visitors Monday to Saturday from 9:30am to 4:30pm and on Sunday 10am to 5pm; it is closed from December 23 to January 1. It may be closed at other times for recording sessions, broadcasts, and concerts.

An exhibition in the seven northern side chapels shows why and how the chapel was built. Admission to the college and chapel, including the exhibition, is £3.50 ($6) for adults, £2.50 ($4) for students and children 12 to 17, and free for children under 12.

PETERHOUSE   This college, on Trumpington Street (✆ **01223/338200**), is the oldest Cambridge college, founded in 1284 by Hugh de Balsham, the bishop of Ely. Of the original buildings, only the hall remains, but this was restored in the 19th century and now boasts stained-glass windows by William Morris. Old Court, constructed in the 15th century, was renovated in 1754; the chapel dates from 1632. Ask permission to enter at the porter's lodge. The often-neglected Little Church of St. Mary's next door was the college chapel until 1632. Pay it the honor of a visit.

TRINITY COLLEGE ★★   On Trinity Street, Trinity College (not to be confused with Trinity Hall) is the largest college in Cambridge. Henry VIII, who consolidated a number of smaller colleges that had existed on the site, founded it in 1546. The courtyard is the most spacious in Cambridge, built when Thomas Nevile was master. Sir Christopher Wren designed the library. For entry to the college, apply at the Great Gate, or call ✆ **01223/338400** (www.trin.cam.ac.uk) for information. There is a charge of £2 ($3.20) from March to November.

EMMANUEL COLLEGE   On St. Andrew's Street, Emmanuel (✆ **01223/334274;** www.emma.cam.ac.uk) was founded in 1584 by Sir Walter Mildmay, a chancellor of the exchequer to Elizabeth I. John Harvard, patron of Harvard University, studied here. You can take a nice stroll around its attractive gardens and visit the chapel designed by Sir Christopher Wren and consecrated in 1677. Both the chapel and college are open daily from 9am to 6pm (closed during exam time). *Insider's tip:* Harvard men and women, and those who love them, can look for a memorial window in Wren's chapel dedicated to John Harvard, an alumnus of Emmanuel who lent his name to that other university in Cambridge, Massachusetts.

QUEENS' COLLEGE ★   On Queens' Lane, Queens' College (✆ **01223/335511;** www.quns.cam.ac.uk) is the loveliest of Cambridge's colleges. Dating from 1448, it was founded by two English queens, one the wife of Henry VI, the

> **Moments Cambridge's Most Bucolic Spot**
>
> The Grove at Queen's College fronts the west bank of the River Cam on the north side of the bridge. It's a riot of blossoms in spring. The walk along the riverbank reveals the best view of King's College but ends at a small branch channel in the river. Beyond the lawn on the other side of the river, the high stone wall dividing the two colleges is the last fragment of a Carmelite monastery dissolved in 1538. Here's your best chance to relax a bit from a hectic day of sightseeing. From Queen's College wide green lawns lead down to "the Backs," where you may go punting. Take in Mathematical Bridge, which is best viewed from the Silver Street road bridge, dating from 1902. Right by this bridge, stop off at the old pub, the Anchor.

other the wife of Edward IV. Its second cloister is the most interesting, flanked by the early-16th-century President's Lodge. Admission is £1.50 ($2.40); free for children under 12 accompanied by parents. A printed guide is issued. Visiting hours vary according to school terms and holidays; call the number above or visit the website for details. Entry and exit is by the old porter's lodge in Queens' Lane only. The old hall and chapel are usually open to the public when not in use.

ST. JOHN'S COLLEGE On St. John's Street, this college (© **01223/ 338600;** www.joh.cam.ac.uk) was founded in 1511 by Lady Margaret Beaufort, mother of Henry VII. A few years earlier she had founded Christ's College. Before her intervention, an old hospital had stood on the site of St. John's. The impressive gateway bears the Tudor coat of arms, and Second Court is a fine example of late Tudor brickwork. Its best-known feature is the Bridge of Sighs crossing the Cam, built in the 19th century and patterned after the bridge in Venice. It connects the older part of the college with New Court, a Gothic Revival on the opposite bank with an outstanding view of the famous Backs. The Bridge of Sighs is closed to visitors but can be seen from the neighboring Kitchen Bridge. The college is open from Easter to early November weekdays from 10am to 5pm, Saturday and Sunday from 9:30am to 5pm. Admission is £1.75 ($2.80) for adults and £1 ($1.60) for children. Visitors are welcome to attend choral services in the chapel. *Insider's tip:* The Bridge of Sighs links the old college with an architectural "folly" of the 19th century, the elaborate New Court, which is a crenellated neo-Gothic fantasy. It's adorned with a "riot" of pinnacles and a main cupola. Students call it "the wedding cake."

CAMBRIDGE'S OTHER ATTRACTIONS

The Fitzwilliam Museum One of the finest museums in Britain is worth the trip here, assuming renovations are completed by the time you get here (see the note below). Although it features temporary exhibitions, its permanent collections are noted for their antiquities from ancient Egypt, Greece, and Rome. The Applied Arts section features English and European pottery and glass, along with furniture, clocks, fans, and armor, Chinese jades and ceramics from Japan and Korea, plus rugs and samplers. The museum is also noted for its rare-coin collection. Many rare printed books and illuminated manuscripts, both literary and musical, are also on display.

The paintings are the main attraction, however, and include masterpieces by Simone Martini, Domenico Veneziano, Titian, Veronese, Rubens, Van Dyck, Canaletto, Hogarth, Gainsborough, Constable, Monet, Degas, Renoir, Cézanne, and Picasso. There's also a fine collection of other 20th-century art, miniatures, drawings, watercolors, and prints.

Note: At press time, the museum was announcing it would be closed from December 22, 2003, to May 31, 2004, for a renovation of its courtyard area. We recommend contacting the museum to verify the reopening date if you plan to visit in the spring of 2004.

Trumpington St., near Peterhouse. (𝒞 01223/332900. www.fitzmuseum.cam.ac.uk. Free admission, donations appreciated. Tues–Sat 10am–5pm; Sun 2:15–5pm. Guided tours £3 ($4.80) per person, Sun 2:45pm. Closed Jan 1, Good Friday, May Day, and Dec 24–31.

Great St. Mary's Cambridge's central church was built on the site of an 11th-century church, but the present building dates largely from 1478. It was closely associated with events of the Reformation. The cloth that covered the hearse of King Henry VII is on display in the church. There is a fine view of Cambridge from the top of the tower.

King's Parade. (𝒞 01223/741716. Admission to tower £2 ($3.20) adults, children £1 ($1.60). Tower summer Mon–Sat 10am–5pm, Sun noon–4:30pm; church daily 9am–6pm.

SHOPPING

You'll find plenty of shops lining St. John's Street, Trinity Street, King's Parade, and Trumpington Street.

Check out **English Teddy Bear Company,** 1 King's Parade (𝒞 01223/300908), which sells teddy bears handmade in cottages all over the United Kingdom—a real British souvenir.

Primavera, 10 King's Parade (𝒞 01223/357708), is a showplace of British crafts, featuring pottery, glass, ceramics, jewelry, ironwork, and fabric crafts ranging from ties to wall hangings. Be sure to explore their basement exhibition of paintings and crafts items.

Another well-defined shopping district is comprised of Bridge Street, Sidney Street, St. Andrew's Street, and Regent Street. Particularly worth noting in this area is **James Pringle Weavers,** 11 Bridge St. (𝒞 01223/361534), a Scottish haven. You'll find a mind-boggling array of Scottish tartans, kilts, tweeds, fine knitwear, Scottish food, and, of course, postcards.

A posh area of extremely chic, small, and exclusive shops runs between Market Square and Trinity Street and is called **Rose Crescent.** Here, you can buy leather goods, smart women's clothing, fine hats, as well as jewelry and a host of very expensive gift items.

Cambridge's pedestrian shopping district runs between Market Square and St. Andrew's Street and is known as the Lion Yard. **Culpepper the Herbalists,** 25 Lion Yard (𝒞 01223/367370), carries a complete herbal line that includes everything from extracts of plants to jellies, honeys, teas, cosmetics, bath products, pillows, and potpourri.

If you're a book lover, Cambridge's bookstores will truly delight you. **Heffers of Cambridge** is a huge book, stationery, and music store with six branches, all of which can be contacted through their central phone number (𝒞 01223/568568). The main store, at 20 Trinity St., carries academic books; the children's book shop is at 30 Trinity St.; the stationery store can be found at 19 Sydney St.; Heffers's paperback and video shop is at 31 St. Andrews St.;

⌒Moments Punting on the Cam

Punting on the River Cam in a wood-built, flat-bottomed boat (which looks somewhat like a Venetian gondola) is a traditional pursuit of students and visitors to Cambridge. Downstream, you pass along the ivy-covered "Backs" of the colleges, their lush gardens sweeping down to the Cam.

People sprawl along the banks of the Cam on a summer day to judge and tease you as you maneuver your punt with a pole about 4.5m (15 ft.) long. The river's floor is muddy, and many a student has lost his pole in the riverbed shaded by the willows. If your pole gets stuck, it's better to leave it sticking in the mud instead of risking a plunge into the river.

About 3km (2 miles) upriver lies Grantchester, immortalized by Rupert Brooke. Literary types flock here by punting or by taking the path following the River Granta for less than an hour to Grantchester Meadows (the town lies about a mile from the meadows). When the town clock stopped for repairs in 1985, its hands were left frozen "for all time" at 10 minutes to 3, in honor of Brooke's famed sonnet "The Soldier."

After so much activity, you're bound to get hungry or thirsty, so head to **The Green Man,** 59 High St. (✆ **01223/841178**), a 400-year-old inn named in honor of Robin Hood, where a crackling fire warms you in cold weather and summer features a back beer garden, leading off toward the river, where your punt is waiting to take you back to Cambridge.

Scudamore's Boatyards, Granta Place (✆ **01223/359750**), by the Anchor Pub, has been in business since 1910. Punts and rowboats rent for £12–£14 ($19–$22) per hour. A £60 ($96) cash or credit card deposit is required (MasterCard and Visa accepted). There is a maximum of six persons per punt. They are open from March to late October daily from 9am until dusk, and from November to February on weekends only from 10am to dusk, depending on the weather and number of clients. You may prefer a chauffeur, in which case there is a minimum cost of £35 to £40 ($56–$64) for two people and £8 ($13) per person after that.

We recommend **The Scudamore's Punt Company,** working out of **The Anchor Pub,** Silver Street, beside the Silver Street Bridge (✆ **01223/359750**; see below), for its 45-minute punt tours. A guide (usually a Cambridge student) dressed in a straw boater hat will both punt and give running commentary to groups of between 1 and 12 persons. Tours cost a minimum of £50 to £60 ($80–$96) for two and £8 ($13) per each extra adult, and £6 ($10) for children 5 to 12; kids 4 and under ride free. The Anchor Pub's service staff can call a guide over to your table. If you want to row yourself along the Cam, "unchauffeured" boats rent for £12 to £14 ($19–$22) per hour. The company is open daily from 9am to dusk, although everyone packs up if it rains or if the winds get too high.

their art-and-graphics shop has an address of 15–21 King St.; and the music store at 19 Trinity St. features classical and popular cassettes, CDs, and choral college music.

G. David, 16 St. Edward's Passage (© **01223/354619**), hawks secondhand books, publishers' overruns at reduced prices, and antiquarian books. **Dillons,** 22 Sydney St. (© **01223/351688**), deals exclusively in new books on a variety of subjects. **The Haunted Bookshop,** 9 St. Edward's Passage (© **01223/312913**), specializes in out-of-print children's books and first editions.

WHERE TO STAY

Ashley Hotel   One of the most popular B&Bs in Cambridge, the Ashley is a gray stone Edwardian building built as a private home. Less than 1km (½ mile) north of the center near the Cam and Jesus Green, it offers spacious bedrooms. There's a rose garden in back. Only breakfast is served, but guests are welcome to use the dining and drinking facilities of the Ashley's companion hotel, the Arundel House Hotel, at 53 Chesterton Rd. The hotel has 12 nonsmoking rooms for guests, and three rooms are available on the ground floor for those with limited mobility.

74 Chesterton Rd., Cambridge, Cambridgeshire CB4 1ER. © 01223/350059. Fax 01223/350900. www.arundelhousehotels.co.uk. 14 units. £59.50 ($95) single or double; £67.50–£79.50 ($108–$127) family room. Rates include English breakfast. MC, V. Bus: 3 or 3A. **Amenities:** Breakfast room; lounge. *In room:* TV, dataport, coffeemaker, hair dryer.

Avimore Guest House   This nonsmoking guesthouse is about 3km (2 miles) from the heart of Cambridge, near Addenbrookes Hospital. Parking is available, but you can depend on reliable public transportation or walk (about 20 min. to the city center). Now well established, the Avimore offers a good standard of B&B accommodations; the bedrooms are somewhat bland but all contain hot and cold running water. Rooms vary greatly in size, so call ahead to reserve a larger room. Three rooms are available for those with limited mobility.

308–310 Cherryhinton Rd., Cambridge, Cambridgeshire CB1 4AU. © and fax 01223/410956. Reservations recommended. 11 units, 8 with bathroom. £30 ($48) single without bathroom, £42 ($67) single with bathroom; £54 ($86) double with bathroom. Rates include English breakfast. MC, V. Bus: 4 or 5. **Amenities:** Dining room; lounge. *In room:* TV, coffeemaker, no phone.

Bridge Guest House   About 1.5km (1 mile) south of the city center, this hotel is a pair of interconnected houses built shortly after World War II. An extension, constructed around 1987, contains some of the simple, well-kept accommodations. The rooms vary in size, but even the smallest is more spacious than the average B&B. Each comes with a private, shower-only bathroom. Two rooms are available for those with limited mobility. Your hosts, Mr. and Mrs. Petrou, are a good source of local information.

151 Hills Rd., Cambridge, Cambridgeshire CB2 2RJ. © 01223/247942. Fax 01223/416585. www.bridge guesthouse.co.uk. 12 units. £35 ($56) single; £55 ($88) double. Rates include English breakfast. AE, MC, V. Bus: 5 or 10. **Amenities:** Dining room; lounge. *In room:* TV, dataport, coffeemaker, hair dryer.

Dresden Villa Guest House   The Dresden Villa is about 2km (1¼ miles) south of the Market Place in Cambridge. It has an Edwardian-era painted facade with four sunny bay windows. The owners, the Ruggiero family, came originally from a village near Sorrento, Italy. The recently redecorated place is tidy. Single rooms are a bit small, but doubles are a good size, and each comes with a small, shower-only bathroom.

34 Cherryhinton Rd., Cambridge, Cambridgeshire CB1 7AA. © 01223/247539. Fax 01223/410640. 13 units. £32–£35 ($51–$56) single; £50–£55 ($80–$88) double; £75 ($120) family unit for 3; £80 ($128) family unit for 4. Rates include English breakfast. No credit cards. Bus: 1, 2, 4, 5, or 44. **Amenities:** Breakfast room. *In room:* TV, coffeemaker, hair dryer, no phone.

Hamilton Hotel *Value*   One of the better and more reasonably priced of the small hotels of Cambridge, this redbrick establishment lies about 1.5km (1 mile) northeast of the city center, close to the River Cam. A well-run, modestly accessorized hotel, it stands on a busy highway, but there's a parking area out back. The well-furnished bedrooms contain reasonably comfortable twins or double beds. Bathrooms are compact with shower stalls. The hotel has a small, traditionally styled licensed bar, offering standard pub food and snacks.

156 Chesterton Rd., Cambridge, Cambridgeshire CB4 1DA. *©* **01223/365664.** Fax 01223/314866. www.hamiltonhotelcambridge.co.uk. 26 units, 22 with bathroom. £28 ($45) single without bathroom, £45 ($72) single with bathroom; £50 ($80) double without bathroom, £59–£65 ($94–$104) double with bathroom. Rates include English breakfast. AE, DC, MC, V. Bus: 3 or 3A. **Amenities:** Breakfast room; bar; lounge. *In room:* TV, dataport, coffeemaker, hair dryer.

Helen Hotel   This yellow-fronted Victorian hotel, about 1.5km (1 mile) south of the center, is a Mediterranean-inspired refuge maintained by Stella and Andrew Papson. The reasonably sized rooms have been recently refurbished with new furniture and other comforts, such as private, shower-only or shower-tub bathrooms. The hotel has 18 nonsmoking rooms for guests. This hostelry is much bigger than others in this section, and benefits from gardens laid out with boxwood in a symmetrical and formal Italian style.

167–169 Hills Rd., Cambridge, Cambridgeshire CB2 2RJ. *©* **01223/246465.** Fax 01223/214406. www.helenhotel.co.uk. 22 units. £55 ($88) single; £75 ($120) double; £85 ($136) family unit. Rates include English breakfast. AE, DC, MC, V. Bus: 5 or 6. **Amenities:** Breakfast room; bar; lounge. *In room:* TV, dataport, coffeemaker, hair dryer.

Regency Guest House   In a desirable location near the town center, overlooking the verdant city park known as Parker's Piece, this hotel dates from 1850. Set behind a stone facade, and similar in design to many of its neighbors, it offers bedrooms with 1950s-style retro furniture. The nonsmoking rooms are painted about every six months and have a bright, fresh look. Most of the rooms are small, and the beds are reasonably comfortable. The compact bathrooms have adequate shelf space and a shower.

7 Regent Terrace, Cambridge, Cambridgeshire CB2 1AA. *©* **01223/329626.** Fax 01223/301567. www.regencyguesthouse.co.uk. 8 units, 2 with bathroom. £48 ($77) single without bathroom; £68 ($109) double without bathroom, £78 ($125) double with bathroom. Rates include continental breakfast. No credit cards. Bus: 5. **Amenities:** Breakfast room. *In room:* TV, coffeemaker, no phone.

SUPER-CHEAP SLEEPS: A YOUTH HOSTEL

Cambridge Youth Hostel   This converted Victorian town house with added wings is popular for its location—only 10 minutes from the center of Cambridge and about 3 minutes from the train station—as well as for its conveniences: free storage lockers, bicycle and baggage storage, currency exchange, laundry facilities, a shop selling postcards, stamps, laundry soap, and other necessities—and no curfew. There is a self-catering kitchen; meals are also provided in the cafeteria-style dining room. Yet another bonus is the hotel's table license, allowing beer and wine with meals only. The staff, professional and friendly, can answer your questions, suggest things to do, and point you to a bicycle rental shop up the block. Call ahead to reserve a room, because many backpackers end up staying over for an extra day or two. If you're driving, the one big drawback is a lack of parking; you'll have to scramble around for 2-hour metered spaces.

97 Tension Rd., Cambridge, Cambridgeshire CB1 2DN. *©* **01223/354601.** Fax 01223/312780. 25 units, 100 beds. £16 ($26) adults; £12 ($19) 18 and under. MC, V. **Amenities:** Dining room; lounge; laundry; currency exchange.

WHERE TO DINE

Drop down into the cozy **Rainbow Vegetarian Bistro,** King's Parade, across from King's College (© **01223/321551**), for coffee, a slice of fresh-baked cake, or a meal from their selection of whole-food and vegetarian offerings. Open Monday to Saturday from 11am to 10:30pm. The cafe lies at the end of a lily-lined path. The **Clown's Café,** 54 King St. (© **01223/355711**), a popular student hangout, is named for the clown art on its walls, remnants of an annual competition. The cafe offers sandwiches, salads, quiches, lasagna, and daily specials. The Clown serves daily 9am to midnight. The **Cambridge Curry Centre,** 45–47 Castle St. (© **01223/302687**), is a two-story eatery offering traditional curry and tandoori dishes, along with flavor-filled chicken jalfrazi. Open daily noon to 2:30pm and 6pm to midnight. **Cambridge Health Food,** 5 Bridge St. (© **01223/350433**), offers a variety of whole-food supplies and supplements plus a carryout section of items such as pastas, quiche, and pizza. Open Monday to Saturday 9am to 5:30pm.

The Anchor ENGLISH Set a few steps from the River Cam, beside the Silver Street Bridge, this is a verdant and time-tested establishment that opened in the 1970s in a former grain and flour warehouse. It has an outdoor terrace where punters will agree to row up to four visitors up and down the river while giving running commentary. In 1994 the Anchor was refurbished and returned to an old-world ambience with lots of exposed wood and a choice of real ales on tap. There's dining and drinking on two levels. Food is simple, tasty, and well prepared. A homemade soup of the day is always featured, as are stuffed baked potatoes and freshly made salads. Daily specials appear on the chalkboard menu—perhaps steak pies, lamb and mushroom curry, and only on Sunday, roast beef and Yorkshire pudding.

15 Silver St. © 01223/353554. Bar snacks and platters £2–£7.50 ($3.20–$12). MC, V. Mon–Fri noon–7pm; Sat noon–3pm; Sun noon–2pm. Pub Mon–Sat 11am–11pm; Sun noon–11pm.

Arundel House Restaurant ✦ FRENCH/BRITISH/VEGETARIAN One of the best and most acclaimed restaurants in Cambridge is in a hotel overlooking the River Cam and Jesus Green, a short walk from the city center. Winner of many awards, it's noted not only for its excellence and use of fresh produce, but also for its good value. The decor is warmly inviting with Sanderson curtains, Louis XV-upholstered chairs, and spacious tables. The menu changes frequently, and you may dine a la carte or from the fixed menu. Perhaps you'll begin with a homemade golden-pea-and-ham soup or a white-rum-and-passion-fruit cocktail. Fish choices include plaice or salmon; try the pork-and-pigeon casserole, or the Japanese-style braised lamb.

53 Chesterton Rd. © 01223/367701. Reservations required. Main courses £10–£16 ($16–$26); fixed-price lunch £17.95 ($29); fixed-price dinner £19 ($30). AE, DC, MC, V. Daily 12:30–2pm and 6:30–9:30pm. Bus: 3 or 5.

Browns ✦ *Value* ENGLISH/CONTINENTAL With a neoclassical colonnade in front, Browns has all the grandeur of the Edwardian era, but inside, it's the most lighthearted restaurant in the city, with wicker chairs, high ceilings, pre–World War I woodwork, and a long bar covered with bottles of wine. The extensive bill of continually varied fare includes pasta, scores of fresh salads, several selections of meat and fish (from charcoal-grilled leg of lamb with rosemary to fresh fish in season), hot sandwiches, and the chef's daily specials posted on a chalkboard. If you drop by in the afternoon, you can also order thick milk shakes or natural fruit juices. In fair weather, there's outdoor seating.

23 Trumpington St. (5 min. from King's College and opposite the Fitzwilliam Museum). ✆ **01223/461655.** Main courses £8–£15 ($13–$24). AE, MC, V. Mon–Sat noon–11:30pm; Sun noon–10:30pm. Bus: 2.

Free Press ENGLISH   This crowded and convivial place is named after a radical local newspaper that went bankrupt in the 1830s partly due to its fervent editorials against the dangers of alcohol. In 1840 the matriarch-founder of this pub gleefully attached its name to her new watering hole, ensuring an endless round of local jokes that continue to this day. Owners Chris Lloyd and his American-born wife, Debbie, claim their nonsmoking establishment to be the only British pub never visited by royalty. Its decorative theme includes rowing and punting memorabilia. Food includes freshly made soups, meat pies, moussaka, vegetarian platters, and hot chef's specials of the day. Curiously enough, the more lager you have, the better the food tastes. There are a small number of outdoor tables, much in demand during warm weather.

7–9 Prospect Row. ✆ **01223/368337.** Bar snacks £2.85–£7.95 ($4.55–$13). AE, MC, V. Mon–Fri noon–2pm and 6–9pm; Sat noon–2:30pm and 6–9pm; Sun noon–2pm. Pub: Mon–Fri noon–2:30pm and 6–11pm, Sat noon–3pm and 6–11pm, Sun noon–3pm and 7–10:30pm.

Live & Let Live ENGLISH   It's a bit of a "backwater" in Cambridge, but many hip students flock here to this tranquil and cozy pub with some gas lighting and one of the town's most intriguing selection of beers along with local cider. There's also a good choice of traditional food. Order a beer, Everard's Tiger, if you can, to appear in the know. The decor is of timbered brickwork and varnished pine tables and chairs. In winter a kettle of soup is kept bubbling, and you can partake of such dishes as spicy prawns with asparagus, scampi and chips, sweet and sour pork, savory chili, and chicken in Marsala. On Sunday the special is roast beef with Yorkshire pudding. On Sunday evening there's live music.

40 Mawson Rd., ✆ **01223/460261.** Lunch £2.25–£6 ($3.60–$10); dinner £5–£10 ($8–$16). MC, V. Mon–Sat 11:30am–2:30pm; Mon–Fri 5:30–11pm; Sat 6–11pm; Sun noon–2:30pm and 7–10:30pm.

Martin's Coffee House TEA/SANDWICHES/PASTRIES   Near the Fitzwilliam Museum is a small, simple, and modern coffeehouse of high standards. It offers pleasing sandwiches and pastries along with English breakfasts. Wholemeal rolls are filled with turkey, ham, beef, salad, cheese, and eggs. Homemade cakes, scones, and doughnuts are sold to accompany the endless pots of tea that emerge, steaming, from a modern samovar. This is the kind of food you'd get at an English church supper.

4 Trumpington St. ✆ **01223/361757.** Sandwiches £1.40–£3.50 ($2.25–$6); pastries £1–£2.50 ($1.60–$4); English breakfast £5–£5.70 ($8–$9). No credit cards. Daily 7am–5pm. Bus: 4 or 5.

Varsity Restaurant GREEK/CONTINENTAL   One of the oldest and best-established restaurants in Cambridge, the Varsity lies in a building dating from 1650. In a bare, whitewashed room with black beams and pictures of boats and islands on the walls, you dine on such Greek specialties as stuffed vine leaves; kebabs are served with rice and salad, and there are some Continental dishes for less adventurous palates. The recipes from the old country have lost a little in translation, but students come here for a "good tuck-in" nevertheless.

35 St. Andrew's St., between Sidney and Regent sts. ✆ **01223/356060.** Main courses £7–£14 ($11–$22). AE, DC, MC, V. Daily noon–2:30pm and 5:30–10:45pm.

CAMBRIDGE AFTER DARK

You can take in a production where Emma Thompson and other well-known thespians got their start at **The Amateur Dramatic Club,** Park Street near Jesus

Lane (© **01223/359547;** box office © **01223/503333**). It presents two student productions nightly, Tuesday through Saturday, with the main show tending toward classic and modern drama or opera, and the late show being of a comic or experimental nature. The theater is open 40 weeks a year, closing in August and September, and tickets run from £4 to £8 ($6–$13).

Then there's the most popular Cambridgian activity: the **pub-crawl.** There are too many pubs in the city to list them all here, but you might as well start at Cambridge's oldest pub, the **Pickerel,** on Bridge Street (© **01223/355068**), which dates from 1432. English pubs don't get more traditional than this. If the ceiling beams or floorboards groan occasionally—well, they've certainly earned the right over the years. Real ales on tap include Bulmer's Traditional Cider, Old Speckled Hen, or Theakston's 6X, Old Peculiar, and Best Bitter. **The Maypole,** Portugal Place at Park Street (© **01223/352999**), is the local hangout for actors when they're not in the nearby ADC Theatre. It's known for cocktails instead of ales, but you can get a Tetley's 6X or Castle Eden anyway.

The Eagle, Benet Street off King's Parade (© **01223/505020**), will be forever famous as the place where Nobel Laureates Watson and Crick first announced their discovery of the DNA double helix. Real ales include Icebreaker and local brewery Greene King's Abbott, so make your order and raise a pint to the wonders of modern science.

To meet up with current Cambridge students, join the locals at the **Anchor,** Silver Street (© **01223/353554**), or **Tap and Spiel (The Mill),** Mill Lane, off Silver Street Bridge (© **01223/357026**), for a pint of Greene King's IPA or Abbott. The crowd at the Anchor spills out onto the bridge in fair weather, whereas the Tap and Spiel's clientele lay claim to the entire riverside park.

There's also musical entertainment to be had, and you can find out who's playing by checking out flyers posted around town, or reading the *Varsity.* **The Corn Exchange,** Wheeler Street and Corn Exchange (© **01223/357851**), hosts everything from classical concerts to bigger-name rock shows.

Entertainment in some form can be found nightly at **The Junction,** Clifton Road, near the train station (© **01223/511511**), where an eclectic mix of acts take to the stage weeknights to perform all genres of music, comedy, and theater, and DJs take over on the weekend. Cover charges vary from £7 to £13 ($11–$21), depending on the event.

5th Avenue, Lion Yard (© **01223/364222**), a second-story club, has a huge dance floor and plays everything from house to the latest pop hits, Monday through Saturday from 9pm until 2am. Sometimes they even DJ the old-fashioned way, by taking requests. The cover charge ranges from £2 to £8 ($3.20–$13), depending on what night you're here.

SIDE TRIPS FROM CAMBRIDGE
A GLIMPSE OF WARTIME BRITAIN

Imperial War Museum ⭐   In this former Battle of Britain station and U.S. Eighth Air Force base in World War II, you'll find a huge collection of historic civil and military aircraft from both world wars, including the only B-29 Superfortress in Europe. Other exhibits include midget submarines, tanks, and a variety of field artillery pieces, as well as a display on the U.S. Eighth Air Force.

In the summer of 1997, Elizabeth II opened the American Air Museum here as part of the larger complex. It houses Europe's finest collection of historic American combat aircraft and is the largest pre-cast concrete structure in Europe.

Aircraft on show range from a World War I biplane to the giant B-52 jet bomber. A number are dramatically suspended from the ceiling as if in flight.

Duxford, on A505, at Junction 10 of M11. ℂ **01223/835000**. Admission £8.50 ($14) adults, £6.50 ($10) seniors, £4.50 ($7) children over 16 and students, free for children under 16. Mar–Oct daily 10am–6pm; Nov to mid-Mar daily 10am–4pm. Closed Dec 24–26. Bus: Cambus no. 103 from Drummer St. Station in Cambridge. By car, take M11 to Junction 10, 13km (8 miles) south of Cambridge.

THAXTED ✸

The nearby village of Thaxted is famous for its well-preserved Elizabethan houses and for hosting the famous Morris Ring, the first weekend after Spring Bank Holiday, a processional street dance that attracts more than 300 dancers and culminates with a haunting horn dance as dusk falls.

Thaxted is 8km (5 miles) south of Saffron Walden. To get here from Saffron Walden, drive along B184 (the Thaxted Rd.), following signs to Thaxted and Great Dunmow. A bus follows this route Monday to Saturday five to six times a day.

Thaxted has the most beautiful small church in England, the **Church of St. John the Baptist, Our Lady and St. Lawrence** (ℂ **01371/830221**); its graceful spire can be seen for miles around. Its belfry has special chimes that call parishioners to church services. Dating from 1340, the church is a nearly perfect example of religious architecture.

Other sights include the **Thaxted Guildhall** (ℂ **01371/831339**), located next to the church and the site of a medieval marketplace. It is a fine example of a medieval Guildhall, few of which now remain. It was believed to have been built by the Cutlers Guild between 1393 and 1420. Open April through September, Saturday to Monday, and bank holidays, from 2 to 6pm.

SAFFRON WALDEN

In the northern corner of Essex, 24km (15 miles) southeast of Cambridge, is the ancient market town of Saffron Walden, named for the crop of *Crocus sativus* grown here for centuries as a spice and an additive in medicine and dye. Despite its proximity to London, it isn't disturbed by heavy tourist traffic; residents of Cambridge use it as a quiet weekend escape.

Trains leave London's Liverpool Street Station in the direction of Cambridge several times a day. Two or three stations before Cambridge, passengers should get off in the hamlet of Audley End, 13km (8 miles) north of Thaxted and 1.5km (1 mile) from Saffron Walden. There is a bus from Audley End, but it meanders around so much that most visitors prefer to take a taxi instead. For schedules and information, call ℂ **0845/7484950.**

Cambus no. 102 leaves Cambridge Monday to Saturday and runs several trips to Saffron Walden between 7am to 5pm. Cambus no. 9 departs Sunday only every 1½ hours 10am to 6pm; the last bus back on Sunday departs Saffron Walden at 7:10pm. Call ℂ **01223/423554** for information and schedules. National Express buses leave London's Victoria Coach Station several times a day and stop at Saffron Walden, 10km (6 miles) north of Thaxted. For schedules and information, call ℂ **08705/808080.** From here, about three (at most) buses head on to Thaxted. Most visitors find it easier to take a taxi.

If you're driving from Cambridge, take A1301 southeast, connecting with B184 (also southeast) into Saffron Walden and the adjoining village of Thaxted.

Saffron Walden's **Tourist Information Centre** is at 1 Market Sq. (ℂ **01799/ 510444**), open November to March, Monday to Saturday 10am to 5pm; April to October, Monday to Saturday 9:30am to 5:30pm. This office also handles inquiries for Thaxted.

Seeing the Sights

Audley End House ★ (© 01799/522842) is one of East Anglia's finest mansions. It's located 2km/1¼ miles (a 20-min. walk) from Audley End Station (where trains arrive from Cambridge) on B1383, a country road 1.5km (1 mile) west of Saffron Walden. Begun by Thomas Howard, the royal treasurer, in 1605, this house was built on the foundation of a monastery. The house has an impressive Great Hall with an early-17th-century ornamental screen at the north end, one of the most beautiful in England. The rooms decorated by Robert Adam feature fine furniture and works of art. Among the attractions are a "Gothick" chapel and a charming Victorian ladies' sitting room. Landscaped by Capability Brown, the park surrounding the house has a lovely rose garden, a river and cascade, and a picnic area. The house and grounds are open April to September Wednesday to Sunday and bank holidays noon to 6pm. Admission to the house and grounds is £8 ($13) for adults and £4 ($6) for children 5 to 16. The grounds only are open Wednesday to Sunday 11am to 6pm and cost £4 ($6) for adults and £2 ($3.20) for children.

Where to Stay

The Cross Keys Hotel   The Cross Keys sits opposite the post office, at the northern end of the main street. As famous for its pub as it is for its rooms, this hotel was built in 1449 and retains its black-and-white half-timbered facade. The midsize bedrooms are cozily arranged beside crooked upstairs hallways; all have comfortable furnishings. Even if you don't stay here, drop into the pub for a pint of ale beside the huge inglenook fireplace where fleeing clerics used to hide in the priest's hole.

32 High St., Saffron Walden, Essex CB10 1AX. © 01799/522207. Fax 01799/526550. www.thecrosskeys hotel.com. 5 units, 3 with bathroom. £35 ($56) single with or without bathroom; £55 ($88) double with or without bathroom; £65 ($104) suite. Rates include English breakfast. AE, DC, MC, V. **Amenities:** Restaurant; bar; laundry service. *In room:* TV, dataport, coffeemaker, hair dryer.

Queen's Head Inn   In the environs, the Queen's Head is on B1383, 5 minutes by car from Junction 9 (M11) if you're coming from the south, or Junction 10 if you're coming from the north; it's minutes from the heart of Saffron Walden by car. This 16th-century inn rents comfortably furnished if somewhat dowdy bedrooms, each with a private, shower-only bathroom. Two of the rooms are larger, so call ahead to request one of these. The nonsmoking inn provides a large parking area, a large garden, and a good restaurant that serves English and classic French food unpretentiously rather than grandly.

High St., Littlebury, near Saffron Walden, Essex CB11 4TD. © and fax 01799/522251. 6 units. £45 ($72) single; £60–£65 ($96–$104) double. Rates include English breakfast. MC, V. **Amenities:** Restaurant; bar; lounge; garden. *In room:* TV, coffeemaker, no phone.

Where to Dine

Eight Bells INTERNATIONAL   The Eight Bells lies beside the main road leading to Cambridge, a 5-minute walk from the center. Behind an Elizabethan black-and-white half-timbered facade sits the most popular pub in town, favored by students from Cambridge. Depending on business, a formal dining room, the Tudor Barn, may or may not be open when you arrive. This timbered hall, with oaken beams and furniture, serves menus with a choice of meat, vegetables, and fish. The cookery doesn't aspire to greatness; the aim is to feed you. When business is less brisk, meals are served in a warmly traditional dining room located a few steps from the busy pub, in what the staff calls "The Top Bar."

18 Bridge St. © 01799/522790. Reservations recommended on weekends only. Main courses £5.50–£9.95 ($9–$16); bar menu £2.50–£5.25 ($4–$8). AE, MC, V. Daily noon–2:30pm and 6–9:30pm. Bar daily 11am–11pm.

2 Ely

112km (70 miles) NE of London; 26km (16 miles) N of Cambridge

Ely Cathedral is the top attraction in the Fens, outside of Cambridge. After seeing the cathedral, you can be on your way, as Ely is a sleepy market town that can't compete with the life and bustle of Cambridge.

ESSENTIALS

GETTING THERE   Ely is a major railway junction served by express trains to Cambridge. Service is frequent from London's Liverpool Street Station. For **schedules and information,** call (?) **0845/7489950.**

Campus buses run frequently between Cambridge and Ely. Call (?) **01223/ 423554** for schedules and information.

If you're driving from Cambridge, take A10 north.

VISITOR INFORMATION   The **Tourist Information Centre** is at Oliver Cromwell's House, 29 St. Mary's St. ((?) **01353/662062**); open April through September daily from 10am to 6pm; October through March, Monday to Saturday from 10am to 5pm.

SEEING THE SIGHTS

Ely Cathedral ★★   The near-legendary founder of this cathedral was Etheldreda, the wife of a Northumbrian king who established a monastery on the spot in 673. The present structure dates from 1081. Visible for miles around, the landmark octagonal lantern is the crowning glory of the cathedral. Erected in 1322 following the collapse of the old tower, it represents a remarkable engineering achievement. Four hundred tons of lead and wood hang in space, held there by timbers reaching to the eight pillars.

You enter the cathedral through the Galilee West Door, a good example of the early English style of architecture. The lantern tower and the Octagon are the most notable features inside, but visit the Lady Chapel, too. Although its decor has deteriorated over the centuries, it's still a handsome example of the Perpendicular style, having been completed in the mid–14th century. The entry fee goes to help preserve the cathedral. Monday to Saturday, guided tours gather at 11:15am and 2:15pm; in the summer, tours occur throughout the day.

There's also a Brass Rubbing Centre, where a large selection of replica brass is available for you to rub. These can produce remarkable results for wall hangings or special gifts. The center is open year-round in the North Aisle, outside the Cathedral Shop.

(?) **01353/667735.** Admission £4.80 ($8) adults, £4.20 ($7) seniors and students, free for children under 16. Apr–Oct daily 7am–7pm; Nov–Mar Mon–Sat 7:30am–6pm, Sun 7:30am–5pm.

Ely Museum   A gallery presents a chronological history of Ely and the Isle from the Ice Age to the present day. Displays include archaeology, social history, rural life, local industry, and military, as well as a tableau of the debtor's cell and condemned cell, which are also on view.

The Old Gaol, Market St. (?) **01353/666655.** Admission £3 ($4.80) adults; £2 ($3.20) children, students, and seniors; free for children 6 and under. Daily 10:30am–4:30pm. Closed Dec 20–Jan 2.

Oliver Cromwell's House   This recently restored house was owned by the Puritan Oliver Cromwell, a name hardly beloved by the royals, even today. He rose to fame as a military and political leader during the English Civil War of 1642 to 1649. These wars led to the execution of Charles I, and the replacement of the monarchy by the Commonwealth. In 1653, Cromwell was declared lord protector, and the local farmer became the most powerful man in the land until his death in 1658. Exhibitions, displays, and period rooms offer insight into Cromwell's character and 17th-century domestic life. The tourist center is also located here.

29 St. Mary's St. (next to St. Mary's Church). © 01353/662062. Admission £3.50 ($6) adults; £3 ($4.80) children, seniors, and students; £8.50 ($14) family ticket. Apr–Oct daily 10am–5pm; off season Mon–Sat 10am–5pm, Sun 11:15am–4pm.

Grimes Graves This is the largest and best-preserved group of Neolithic flint mines in Britain; it produced the cutting edges of spears, arrows, and knives for prehistoric tribes throughout the region. Because of its isolated location within sparsely populated, fir-wooded countryside, it's easy to imagine yourself transported back through the millennia.

A guardian will meet you near the well-signposted parking lot. After determining that you are not physically impaired, he or she will open one or several of the mineshafts, each of which requires a descent down an almost-vertical 30-foot ladder (a visit here is not recommended for very young children, elderly travelers, or those with disabilities). Since the tunnel and shaft have been restored and reinforced, it's now possible to see where work took place during Neolithic times. Although it's not essential, many archaeologists, professional and amateur, bring their own flashlights with them. The mines, incidentally, are situated close to the military bases that housed thousands of American Air Force personnel during World War II.

On B1107, 4km (2¾ miles) northeast of Brandon, Norfolkshire. © 01842/810656. Admission £2.30 ($3.70) adults, £1.90 ($3.05) students and seniors, £1.30 ($2.10) children 5–15, free for children 4 and under. Apr–Oct daily 10am–1pm and 2–6pm; Nov–Mar Wed–Sun 10am–1pm and 2–4pm. Take A134 for 11km (7 miles) northwest of Thetford, then transfer to B1107.

WHERE TO STAY

Cathedral House ★ This Georgian house is from the mid-1800s and has been lovingly restored by Jenny and Robin Farndale. It sits, with its walled garden, in the shadow of the cathedral and is close to Cromwell's House. The owners have retained the original features and added new decor and furnishings to public and private rooms. The well-appointed nonsmoking bedrooms are generous in size, with garden views and private bathrooms with shower and tub. Children over 10 years old are welcome.

17 St. Mary's St., Ely, Cambridgeshire CB7 4ER. © and fax 01353/662124. www.cathedralhouse.co.uk. 3 units, 2 suites. £40 ($64) single; £70–£80 ($112–$128) double and suites. No credit cards. Free parking. Closed Dec 25 and Jan 1. **Amenities:** Breakfast room; lounge. *In room:* TV, coffeemaker, hair dryer, no phone.

The Nyton In a quiet residential section of Ely, Barton Road is accessible from the cathedral and railway station, lying on the A142 Ely-Newmarket road off the A10 Ely-Cambridge road. This licensed family-run hotel is surrounded by a .8-hectare (2-acre) flower garden with lawns and trees and right next to an 18-hole golf course. You'll have views of the fens and the cathedral. Each standard-size bedroom is clean and comfortable, eight come with a private, shower-only bathroom and two have shower-tub bathrooms. Two rooms are available for those with limited mobility.

7 Barton Rd., Ely, Cambridgeshire CB7 4HZ. © 01353/662459. Fax 01353/666214. 10 units. £45 ($72) single; £70 ($112) double. Rates include English breakfast. AE, DC, MC, V. **Amenities:** Restaurant; bar; lounge; nearby golf course. *In room:* TV, dataport, coffeemaker, hair dryer, iron.

WHERE TO DINE

Around the corner from St. Mary's Church is **Steeplegate,** 16–18 High St. (© **01353/664731**), a tearoom and crafts shop with wooden tables and ancient windows. There are tea selections plus light lunch items, scones, and creamy gâteaux. After tea, venture downstairs to the crafts shop and have a look at the variety of handmade pottery, glass, and baskets.

An unusual choice is **The Almonry Restaurant & Tea Rooms in The College,** Ely Cathedral (© **01353/666360**). Housed in the medieval college buildings on the north side of the Cathedral, this is a comfortable tearoom with table service in a beautiful 12th-century undercroft licensed to sell drinks. You can take your tea out to a garden seat in good weather. It is open for late morning coffee, lunches, and afternoon teas. Meals start at £5.50 ($9).

The Old Fire Engine House ★★ ENGLISH   It's worth making a special trip to this converted fire station in a walled garden, within a building complex that includes an art gallery. Soups are served in huge bowls, accompanied by coarse-grained crusty bread. Main dishes include lamb noisettes in pastry with tomato and basil, jugged hare, casseroled pheasant, and rabbit with mustard and parsley. In summer, you can dine outside in the garden and even order a cream tea.

25 St. Mary's St. (opposite St. Mary's Church). © 01353/662582. Reservations required. Main courses £10–£15 ($16–$24). MC, V. Mon–Sat 12:15–2:15pm and 7:15–9:15pm; Sun 12:15–2:15pm. Bus: 109.

3 Bury St. Edmunds

126km (79 miles) NE of London; 43km (27 miles) E of Cambridge; 20km (12 miles) N of Lavenham

Bury St. Edmunds is "a handsome little town, of thriving and cleanly appearance." That's how Dickens described it in *Pickwick Papers,* and that's how it is today. Founded around the powerful Benedictine Abbey in 1020, the town takes its name from St. Edmund, Martyr, king of the East Angles in the 9th century. It was in the Abbey Church that the barons of England united in 1214, eventually forcing John to sign the Magna Carta. Buildings were given face-lifts in the 17th and 18th centuries; you have to step inside them to realize that Bury is filled with medieval buildings. During the 18th century, this market town was prosperous with a thriving cloth-making industry. The many fine Georgian buildings bear testament to the wealth of that time.

When the Vikings came to this area, they dubbed it "The Summer Country." The summer, when the town bursts into bloom, is the best time to visit. Most historic sites and gardens open for the season on Easter.

ESSENTIALS

GETTING THERE   Trains leave regularly from either Liverpool Street Station or King's Cross Station in London; however, none are direct. Leaving from Liverpool Street, you will change at Ipswich. And from King's Cross Station, you'll have to switch trains at Cambridge. The trip takes approximately 1½ hours. For schedules and information, call © **08457/48-49-50.**

National Express runs several direct buses every day from London's Victoria Coach Station, which reach Bury in 2 hours. For schedules and information, call © **08705/808080.**

By car, take the M11 north out of London. As you near Cambridge, get on the A45 and continue on to Bury. The drive takes about 1½ hours.

It's also possible to get here by train or bus from Cambridge. Regular trains leave from the Cambridge Rail Station and arrive about 45 minutes later in Bury

St. Edmunds. **Cambus Bus Company** runs five buses a day to Bury from the Drummer Street Bus Station in Cambridge; it's a 1-hour ride. Call ✆ **01223/ 423554** for information and schedules. By car, simply take the A45 directly from Cambridge. It's a 45-minute drive.

VISITOR INFORMATION The **Bury St. Edmunds Tourist Information Centre,** 6 Angel Hill (✆ **01284/764667**), is open from November to Easter, Monday through Friday from 10am to 4pm and Saturday from 10am to 1pm; from Easter to October, Monday through Saturday from 9:30am to 5:30pm and Sunday from 9:30am to 5:30pm.

SPECIAL EVENTS The **Bury St. Edmunds Festival** (✆ **01284/757099**) is held annually in May. The 17-day festival includes performances from leading ensembles and soloists ranging from classical to contemporary. Exhibitions, talks, walks, films, plays, and a fireworks display are integral parts of this internationally renowned festival.

EXPLORING THE TOWN

For a bit of easy and always interesting sightseeing, take one of the hour-long **guided walks** around Bury St. Edmunds. Choices include a Blue Badge Guided Tour and theme tours with Bury's historical monk, Brother Jocelin, or gravedigger William Hunter. Tours leave from the Tourist Information Centre (see above) where tickets can also be purchased.

The normally quiet town center is a hub of hustle and bustle on Wednesday and Saturday mornings when the market arrives. Weather permitting, hours are approximately from 9am to 4pm. You'll find a pleasing mix of family-run businesses and High Street names for shopping in and around town and its pedestrian zones.

Bury St. Edmunds Art Gallery, Market Cross, Cornhill (✆ **01284/762081**), hosts eight fine art and crafts exhibitions each year and serves as a venue for local craftspeople and artists. A crafts shop located in the gallery sells ceramics, prints, books, glassware, and jewelry. **The Parsley Pot,** 17 Abbeygate St. (✆ **01284/ 760289**), sells an assortment of gift items, including china and porcelain.

Several parks are located just outside of town. Eleven kilometers (7 miles) north of Bury is the 125-acre **West Stow Country Park** with heathland, woodland, and a large lake bordered by the River Lark. This diverse area is perfect for the proverbial "walk in the park" with a rustic twist. **The West Stow Anglo-Saxon Village** (✆ **01284/728718**) is part of West Stow Country Park. This reconstructed village is built on the excavated site of an ancient Anglo-Saxon village, and period re-enactments take place throughout the year. The park is open October through March daily from 9am to 5pm and April through October daily from 8am to 8pm. Admission is free. The village is open year-round from 10am to 5pm. Admission is £5 ($8) for adults and £4 ($6) for children. Family tickets are also available for £14 ($22).

Nowton Park (✆ **01284/763666**) is 2.5km (1½ miles) outside of Bury on 200 acres of Suffolk countryside. Landscaped a century ago, the park is typically Victorian and has many country-estate features. In the springtime, walk the avenue of lime trees with its masses of bright yellow daffodils. Marked walking paths snake through the park. Depending on the path, walks take between 20 and 75 minutes. It's open daily from 8:30am to dusk; free admission.

The Abbey The Visitor Centre is a good starting point for a visit to the entire Abbey precinct. (The Abbey itself is in ruins today and sits in the middle of the

Abbey Gardens.) The Visitor Centre is housed in the west front of the Abbey of St. Edmunds's remains and uses a clever series of displays to give the visitor an idea of what life was like in this powerful abbey from its beginnings in 1020 to its dissolution in 1539.

Moving on to the formal Abbey Gardens with its flowerbeds and well-kept lawns, you'll see the ruins of the abbey. When the long shadows cast themselves across the weathered ruins, the landscape becomes surreal and looks much like a Dalí masterpiece. In reality, the abandoned abbey was used as a quarry for the townspeople down through the ages, and that is the reason for the extremely worn condition and melted character of the ruins. Medieval monk Brother Jocelin leads a rather interesting tour of the Abbey Gardens, bookable through the **Tourist Information Centre** at ✆ **01284/764667.**

Samson's Tower. ✆ **01284/757490** for Visitor Centre. Free admission. Visitor Centre Easter–Oct daily 10am–5pm. Abbey Gardens and ruins year-round Mon–Sat 7:30am to half-hour before dusk; Sun 9am–half-hour before dusk.

The Cathedral Church of St. James This 16th-century church has a magnificent font, beautiful stained-glass windows, and a display of 1,000 embroidered kneelers.

Angel Hill. ✆ **01284/754933.** Free admission. Daily 8:30am–dusk.

Ickworth House This National Trust property was built in 1795 and contains an impressive rotunda, state rooms, and art collections of silver and paintings. An Italian garden surrounds the house, and all is set in a peaceful, landscaped park.

5km (3 miles) south of Bury at Horringer. ✆ **01284/735270.** Admission £6.10 ($10) adults, £2.75 ($4.40) children. Easter–Oct Fri–Wed 1–5pm.

Moyse's Hall Museum Located in one of England's last surviving Norman stone houses, this museum has nationally important archaeological collections and local artifacts.

Cornhill. ✆ **01284/706183.** Admission £2.50 ($4) adults, £2 ($3.20) seniors and children. Mon–Sat 10:30am–4:30pm; Sun 11am–4pm.

Manor House Museum Housed in a restored Georgian mansion, this museum uses touch-screen computers to help interpret its displays of fine and decorative art.

Honey Hill. ✆ **01284/757076.** Admission £2.50 ($4) adults, £2 ($3.20) seniors and children, £8 ($13) family ticket. Wed–Mon 11am–4pm.

St. Mary's Church St. Mary's was built on the site of a Norman church in 1427. Note its impressive roof and nave. It is also where Henry VIII's sister, Mary Rose, is buried.

Crown St. ✆ **01284/754680.** Free admission. Call the church to arrange a tour.

WHERE TO STAY

Butterfly Hotel This standard, rather ordinary hotel, built relatively recently, is located 10 minutes from Bury on the A14 motorway. The grassy grounds are landscaped, and there is a sunny patio for dining alfresco. All the rooms are decorated in the same bland style, with landscape pictures and an armchair or two, along with an accompanying desk. Because of the hotel's proximity to the motorway, the windows are double paned to reduce traffic noise and to help guests get a better night's rest. Often midsize, the rooms are well laid out, each containing a king-size or twin-size bed. Twenty rooms are rented to nonsmokers. The compact bathrooms are clean and well maintained. One room is available for those with limited mobility.

Symonds Rd., Bury St. Edmunds, Suffolk IP32 7BW. © 01284/760884. Fax 01284/755476. www.butterfly hotels.co.uk. 66 units. Mon–Thurs £89–£98 ($142–$157) double; Fri–Sun £54–£73 ($86–$117) double. AE, DC, MC, V. **Amenities:** Restaurant; bar. *In room:* TV, dataport, coffeemaker, hair dryer.

WHERE TO DINE

Maison Bleve at Mortimer's 🦐 SEAFOOD   This restaurant is the town's best. The open and airy dining room has a nautical theme, in keeping with the fresh seafood that's served here. The same menu is available for both lunch and dinner and changes regularly with the season. Favorites include filet of sea bass in a fennel sauce; boneless wing of skate with bacon, onion, and mushrooms; and lobster in a cream-and-brandy sauce.

31 Churchgate St. © 01284/760623. Dinner reservations recommended. Main courses £8.95–£25.50 ($14–$41); fixed-price lunch £7.95 ($13); 3-course fixed-price dinner £19.95 ($32). AE, MC, V. Tues–Sat noon–2:30pm and 7–9:30pm (open until 10pm Fri–Sat).

BURY ST. EDMUNDS AFTER DARK

Throughout the centuries, Bury has enjoyed a well-deserved reputation as a small center of arts and entertainment. The **Theatre Royal,** Westgate Street, is the oldest purpose-built theater in England. Its Georgian building has been lovingly and richly restored to its original grandeur. Programs include opera, dance, music, and drama from the best touring companies. Tickets are £5 to £15 ($8–$24) and can be purchased at the **box office** (© 01284/769505).

Stop by the 17th-century pub **Dog and Partridge,** 29 Crown St. (© 01284/764792), and see where the bar scenes from the BBC hit series *Lovejoy* were filmed while you sample one of the region's Greene King Ales. Also try wiggling your way into the **Nutshell,** corner of The Traverse and Abbeygate Street (© 01284/764867). This pub has been notoriously dubbed the smallest pub in all of England and is a favorite tourist stop. **The Masons Arms,** 14 Whiting St. (© 01284/753955), features more of a family atmosphere and welcomes children. Home-cooked food is served along with a standard selection of ales. There's a patio garden in use in summer.

A SIDE TRIP TO SUDBURY

Thirty-two kilometers (20 miles) south of Bury St. Edmunds along the A134 is Sudbury, a town that has prospered through the ages thanks to its sheep (the wool industry) and prime location along the banks of the River Stour. A handful of medieval half-timbered buildings and Georgian homes attest to the town's ripe old age. Its most famous native son is Thomas Gainsborough, who was born in 1727 and went on to become one of England's most well-liked painters.

His birthplace, **Gainsborough's House,** 46 Gainsborough St. (© 01787/372958), is a museum and arts center that has many of his works of art on display. Visitors will notice that several different architectural styles make up the house, and there is a walled garden in back worth seeing. It's open from mid-April to October, Tuesday through Saturday from 10am to 5pm and Sunday from 2 to 5pm; from November to mid-April, Tuesday through Saturday from 10am to 4pm and Sunday from 2 to 4pm. Admission is £3 ($4.80) adults, £2.80 ($4.50) seniors, £1.50 ($2.40) children and students during the year, but it is free during the month of December.

WHERE TO STAY

The Mill Hotel ⭐ *Finds*   As its name implies, this hotel is located in the shell of an old mill. In fact, the River Stour, which runs under the hotel, still turns the mill's 5m (16-ft.) water wheel. Rooms vary in size; some have heavy oak beams and massive columns, but all are outfitted with comfortable furnishings, including good king-size or twin-size beds. Bathrooms are compact but have generous shelf space. You may even be able to watch the local cows occasionally pass by the water's edge, as many of the rooms have a river or millpond view. The restaurant and bar areas are welcoming with their polished hardwood floors, Oriental carpets, and antiques.

Walnuttree Lane, Sudbury CO10 1BD. © **01787/375544.** Fax 01787/373027. www.millhotelsuffolk.co.uk. 56 units. £59 ($94) single; £79 ($126) double. AE, DC, MC, V. **Amenities:** Restaurant; bar. *In room:* TV, dataport, coffeemaker, hair dryer.

WHERE TO DINE

Brasserie 47 INTERNATIONAL   Right next door to the Gainsborough House, this friendly brasserie, full of pine furnishings and lots of earthy terra-cotta and navy accents, is ideal for lunch or dinner. In fact, the same menu is used for both, along with a host of specials that change daily. Popular main dishes include the pan-fried salmon with saffron and a white-wine sauce; grilled rib-eye steak with tarragon sauce; and lamb steak in rosemary sauce served with couscous and a leafy salad. Homemade ice creams and exotic sorbets, such as orange caramel and toasted poppy seed, highlight the dessert selection. But the hot-syrup sponge cake with vanilla custard sauce is hands-down the most popular dessert.

47 Gainsborough St. © **01787/374298.** Reservations recommended for dinner. 2-course fixed-price menu £13.50 ($22), 3-course fixed-price menu £16.50 ($26). AE, DC, MC, V. Tues–Sat noon–2pm and 7–10pm. Closed 5 days during Christmas.

4 Lavenham

106km (66 miles) NE of London; 56km (35 miles) SE of Cambridge

Once a great wool center, Lavenham is a classic Suffolk village, beautifully preserved today. It features half-timbered Tudor houses washed in the characteristic Suffolk pink. The town's wool-trading profits are seen in its guildhall, on the triangular main "square." The guildhall has exhibits on Lavenham's textile industry, showing how yarn was spun, then "dyed in the wool" with *woad* (a plant used by the Picts to dye themselves blue), following on to the weaving process. Another display shows how half-timbered houses were constructed.

   The Church of St. Peter and St. Paul, at the edge of Lavenham, has interesting carvings on the misericords and chancel screen, as well as ornate tombs. This is one of the area's "wool churches," built by pious merchants in the Perpendicular style with a landmark tower.

ESSENTIALS

GETTING THERE   Trains depart London's North Street Station at least once an hour, sometimes more often, for Colchester, where they connect quickly to the town of Sudbury. For information, call © **08457/48-49-50.** From Sudbury, **Beeston's Coaches, Ltd.,** has about nine daily buses making the short run to Lavenham. The trip from London takes between 2 and 2½ hours.

   National Express buses depart from London's Victoria Coach Station, carrying passengers to the town of Bury St. Edmunds, some 14km (9 miles) from Lavenham. For information, call © **08705/808080.** From Bury St. Edmunds, you can take another bus onto Lavenham. The trip takes about 2½ hours.

If you're driving from Bury St. Edmunds, continue south on the A134 toward Long Melford, but cut southeast to Lavenham at the junction with the A1141.

VISITOR INFORMATION The **Tourist Information Centre** is on Lady Street (© **01787/248207**) and is open Monday through Friday from 9am to 5pm, Saturday 10am to 3pm; April to September Saturday 10am to 5pm.

SHOPPING & TEATIME

Shoppers from all over East Anglia flock to **Timbers,** 6 High St. (© **01787/ 247218**), a center housing 24 dealers specializing in antiques and collectibles, including books, toys, military artifacts, glass, porcelain, and much more. It's open daily.

After strolling the medieval streets of Lavenham, stop by **Tickle Manor Tea Rooms,** 17 High St. (© **01787/248438**). This two-story timber-frame home was built by the son of a priest in 1530 and provides an ample dose of history for patrons to absorb while sipping any one of a selection of teas that are served with English breakfast, sandwiches, or a piece of cake.

WHERE TO STAY

The Angel Hotel ✦ The best B&B in town, first licensed in 1420, this family-run inn stands in the village center overlooking the marketplace and the guild-hall. It's a good restaurant, a popular pub for the locals, and a comfortable place to spend the night. All bedrooms are well kept and a cot is available on request. Each unit comes with a private, shower-only bathroom. The bar contains a double inglenook Tudor fireplace and a rare Tudor shuttered shop-window front. The restaurant features home-cookery and a new menu daily. If you're on a budget, avoid checking in here on Saturday night when the prices skyrocket. Dinner is included, but even so the tariffs are of the break-the-bank type.

Market Place, Lavenham, Suffolk, C010 9QZ. © **01787/247388.** Fax 01787/248344. www.lavenham.co.uk/ angel. 8 units. Sun–Thurs £50 ($80) single; £75 ($120) double; £100 ($160) family unit. Fri–Sat £150 ($240) single; £230 ($368) double; £280 ($448) family unit. Rates include English breakfast. Sat rates include dinner. AE, MC, V. Bus: 17 or 27. **Amenities:** Restaurant; bar; limited room service; laundry service. *In room:* TV, dataport, coffeemaker, hair dryer, iron.

WHERE TO DINE

The Bell Inn ✦ *Finds* TRADITIONAL ENGLISH Off the A1141/B1115 road from Lavenham to Hadleigh, 15 minutes from the main A12 trunk road, the Bell Inn lies in what has been called "the most photographed village in the world," with a *watersplash* (a river that runs across a road) in the middle of the main street. This 13th-century inn has a blazing fireplace and ceiling beams. The Bell offers good snacks in a timbered bar with glinting horse brasses. In the Pink Room, the main restaurant, lunches and dinners include the finest lamb, duck, sole, and fish dishes, even vegetarian specialties—typical English "soul food."

The Street, Kersey, near Ipswich, Suffolk IP7 6DY. © and fax **01473/823229.** Reservations recommended. Restaurant/bar menu main courses £6–£12 ($10–$19). MC, V. Daily 11am–3pm and 6–9pm. Pub 11am–11pm.

---

5 Two Stately Homes in Long Melford

98km (61 miles) NE of London; 54km (34 miles) SE of Cambridge

Long Melford has been famous since the days of the early cloth makers. Like Lavenham, it attained prestige and importance during the Middle Ages. Of the old buildings remaining, the village church is often called "one of the glories of the shire." Along its 5km (3-mile) long High Street—said to boast the highest concentration of antiques shops in Europe—are many private homes erected by wealthy wool merchants of yore. Of special interest are Long Melford's two stately homes, Melford Hall and Kentwell Hall.

ESSENTIALS

GETTING THERE   Trains run from London's Liverpool Street Station toward Ipswich and on to Marks Tey. Call 𝄐 **08457/48-49-50** for information. Here, you can take a shuttle train going back and forth between that junction and Sudbury. From the town of Sudbury, it's a 5km (3-mile) taxi ride to Long Melford.

From Cambridge, take a Cambus Bus Company coach to Bury St. Edmunds, then change for the final ride into Long Melford. These buses run about once an hour throughout the day and early evening.

If driving from Newmarket, continue east on the A45 to Bury St. Edmunds, but cut south on the A134 (toward Sudbury) to Long Melford.

VISITOR INFORMATION   There is a **Tourist Information Office** in the Town Hall, Sudbury (𝄐 **01787/881320**), that's open Monday through Friday from 9am to 5pm and Saturday from 10am to 4:45pm during summer, and Monday through Friday from 9am to 5pm and Saturday from 10am to 2:45pm during winter.

BEATRIX POTTER'S ANCESTRAL HOME & A TUDOR MANSION

Melford Hall   This is the ancestral home of Beatrix Potter, who often visited. Jemima PuddleDuck still occupies a chair in one of the bedrooms upstairs, and some of Potter's other figures are on display. The house, built between 1554 and 1578, has paintings, fine furniture, and Chinese porcelain. The gardens alone make a visit here worthwhile.

Long Melford, Sudbury, Suffolk. 𝄐 **01787/880286.** Admission £4.60 ($7) adults, £2.25 ($3.60) children. May–Sept Wed–Sun and bank holiday Mon 2–5:30pm; Apr and Oct Sat–Sun and bank holiday Mon 2–5:30pm.

Kentwell Hall   At the end of an avenue of linden trees, the redbrick Tudor mansion called Kentwell Hall, surrounded by a broad moat, has been restored by its owners, Mr. and Mrs. Patrick Phillips. A 15th-century moat house, interconnecting gardens, a brick-paved maze, and a costume display are of interest. There are also rare-breed farm animals here. Two gatehouses are constructed in 16th-century style. The hall hosts regular re-creations of Tudor domestic life, including the well-known annual events for the weeks of June 16 to July 7 when admission prices tend to escalate slightly.

On A134 between Sudbury and Bury St. Edmunds. 𝄐 **01787/310207.** Open Mar–Oct. Times and admission costs vary according to the event. It's advisable to call first. The entrance is north of the green in Long Melford on the west side of A134, about 1km (½ mile) north of Melford Hall.

WHERE TO STAY

The Black Lion Hotel and Restaurant   Since the 1100s an inn has stood on this spot, and 14th-century documents make it the spot where drinks were dispensed to participants during one of the Peasants' Revolts. The present building dates from the early 1800s; its owners have richly restored it. The Black Lion overlooks one of the loveliest village greens in Suffolk. Each individually decorated nonsmoking bedroom is comfortable and well appointed, with a private, shower-only bathroom. Rooms are priced according to size at this splurge choice. An added bonus is the hotel's well-patronized restaurant (see "Where to Dine," below).

The Green, Long Melford, Suffolk CO10 9DN. © 01787/312356. Fax 01787/374557. www.blacklionhotel. net. 10 units. £85–£106 ($136–$170) single; £109.50–£146 ($175–$234) double. Rates include English breakfast. AE, MC, V. **Amenities:** Restaurant; bar; room service; babysitting; laundry service. *In room:* TV, data-port, coffeemaker, hair dryer, iron, safe.

WHERE TO DINE

The Black Lion Restaurant TRADITIONAL ENGLISH   This restaurant operates out of a fully restored 17th-century coaching inn (see "Where to Stay," above) overlooking one of Suffolk's loveliest village greens near Holy Trinity Church. At lunch, your only options are relatively simple platters. At dinner, you can opt for the bistro or for a more elaborate meal in the restaurant, with its candlelit ambience and views over the Victorian walled garden. Restaurant choices may include a delicate poached filet of sole, roasted rack of English lamb with rosemary-and-mint sauce, sirloin steak with piquant sauce, freshwater cray-fish Newburg style, or deep-fried whitebait. Roast prime English beef is a Sunday feature. Flavor, taste, and imagination emerge from the kitchen here.

In the Black Lion Hotel and Restaurant, The Green. © 01787/312356. Reservations recommended. In restaurant, fixed-price meals £26.95–£30.95 ($43–$50). In bistro, main courses £5–£10 ($8–$16). MC, V. Lunch in bistro Tues–Sun noon–2pm. Dinner in restaurant and bistro Tues–Sat 7–10pm.

Bull Hotel ⭐ ENGLISH/CONTINENTAL   If you're passing through, try to visit one of the oldest (1540) inns of East Anglia. Built by a wool merchant, it's Long Melford's finest and best-preserved building. Within are a medieval weavers' gallery and an open hearth with Elizabethan brickwork. The dining room is the Bull's outstanding feature, with high-beamed ceilings, trestle tables, settles, hand-made chairs, and a huge fireplace. Menu items include a timbale of prawns and avocados; chicken liver and chorizo salad; seared salmon and bean sprouts; and breast of chicken with mozzarella and Parma ham. Desserts such as sticky toffee pudding or a chocolate and hazelnut-meringue roulade will tempt you.

Hall St. © 01787/378494. Reservations recommended. Main courses £9.95–£23.95 ($16–$38). 2-course fixed price lunch £10.95 ($18); 3-course fixed-price dinner £23.95 ($38). AE, DC, MC, V. Daily 12:30–2pm and 7–9:30pm.

6 Dedham

100km (63 miles) NE of London; 13km (8 miles) NE of Colchester

Remember Constable's *Vale of Dedham?* That very valley lies between the towns of Colchester and Ipswich through which runs the River Stour, the boundary between Essex and Suffolk. It's not only the Constable link that makes this vale so popular: It's one of the most beautiful, unspoiled areas left in southeast England. The little Essex village of Dedham, with its Tudor, Georgian, and Regency houses, is set in the midst of the Stour's water meadows. Constable painted its church and tower. Flatford Mill is only a mile farther down the river. Dedham makes a good center for exploring both North Essex and the Suffolk border country.

ESSENTIALS

Trains depart every 20 minutes from London's Liverpool Street Station for the 50-minute ride to Colchester. For schedules and information, call © 08457/ 48-49-50. From Colchester, it's possible to take a taxi from the railway station to the bus station, then board a bus run by the Eastern National Bus Company for the 8km (5-mile) trip to Dedham. (Buses leave about once an hour.) Most people take a taxi from Colchester directly to Dedham.

National Express buses depart from London's Victoria Coach Station for Colchester, where you have the choice of taking either another bus or a taxi to Dedham. For schedules and information, call © **08705/808080.**

If you're driving from the London ring road, travel northeast on the A12 to Colchester, turning off at East Bergholt onto a small secondary road leading east to Dedham.

VISITING THE PAINTERS' HOMES

Less than a mile from the village center is **The Sir Alfred Munnings Art Museum,** East Lane (© **01206/322127**), home of Sir Alfred Munnings, president of the Royal Academy from 1944 to 1949, and painter extraordinaire of race-horses and other animals. The house and studio, which have sketches and other works, are open from early April to early October, on Sunday, Wednesday, and bank holidays (plus Thurs and Sat during Aug) from 2 to 5pm. Admission is £3 ($4.80) for adults, £2 ($3.20) students and seniors, and 50p (80¢) for children.

The English landscape painter John Constable (1776–1837) was born at East Bergholt, north of Dedham. Near the village is **Flatford Mill,** East Bergholt (© **01206/298283**), subject of one of his most renowned works. The mill was given to the National Trust in 1943, and has since been leased to the Field Studies Council for use as a residential center. The center offers more than 170 short courses each year in all aspects of art and the environment. Fees are from £125 ($200) for a weekend and from £350 ($560) for a full week. The fee includes accommodations, meals, and tuition. Write to Field Studies Council, Flatford Mill Field Centre, East Bergholt, Colchester CO7 6UL.

WHERE TO STAY

Rooms can also be rented at the Marlborough Head Hotel (see "Where to Dine," below).

Dedham Hall/Fountain House Restaurant ★ *Finds*   A 3-minute walk east of the center of town, this is a well-managed hotel that has flourished since its adoption by Jim and Wendy Sarton in 1991. Set on 2 hectares (5 acres) of grazing land whose centerpiece is a pond favored by geese and wild swans, it consists of a 400-year-old brick-sided cottage linked to a 200-year-old home of stately proportions. The older section is reserved for the breakfast room, a bar, and a sitting room for residents of the six second-floor bedrooms. Each cozy room comes with a compact bathroom. A cluster of three converted barns provides accommodations for many artists who congregate here several times throughout the year for painting seminars and art workshops. There are two nonsmoking rooms available, and the ground floor has rooms available for those with limited mobility.

In the restaurant there's a wide selection of dishes with all-fresh ingredients and an abundance of natural flavors.

Brook St., Dedham CO7 6AD. © **01206/323027.** Fax 01206/323293. www.dedhamhall.demon.co.uk. 16 units. £50 ($80) single; £80 ($128) double. Rates include English breakfast. MC, V. **Amenities:** Restaurant; bar; room service. *In room:* TV, minibar, coffeemaker, hair dryer, iron, safe.

WHERE TO DINE

The Marlborough Head Hotel *Kids* ENGLISH   The most historic and popular pub in the area, the Marlborough Head also rents four bedrooms upstairs. Set opposite Constable's old school, and known for its stone-and-frame construction, it contains sections dating from the 1400s. Place your food order at the bar and an employee will bring it to you. Food includes an array of pâtés, quiches, beef, fish, poultry, and offal (such as kidney-and-liver) dishes, each prepared in solidly conservative English ways. During warm weather, the crowd moves onto an outdoor patio near a small garden. Children are welcome; you're likely to see a few families dining here.

The inn's four simple but adequate bedrooms have plaster walls and wooden floors engagingly skewed and sloped because of their age. All have a shower and toilet. For B&B, rates are £50 ($80) for a single and £60 to £70 ($96–$112) for a double.

Mill Lane, Dedham, Essex C07 6DH. ☎ **01206/323250.** Main courses £6–£11 ($10–$18); sandwiches £3.75–£4.95 ($6–$8). MC, V. Daily noon–2:30pm and 6:30–9pm.

7 Woodbridge & Aldeburgh

Woodbridge: 130km (81 miles) NE of London; 75km (47 miles) S of Norwich. Aldeburgh: 155km (97 miles) NE of London; 66km (41 miles) SE of Norwich

On the Deben River, the market town of Woodbridge is a yachting center. Its best-known, most famous resident was Edward FitzGerald, Victorian poet and translator of the "Rubaiyat of Omar Khayyam." Woodbridge is a good base for exploring the East Suffolk coastline, particularly the small resort of Aldeburgh, noted for its Moot Hall.

On the North Sea, 24km (15 miles) from Woodbridge, Aldeburgh is an exclusive resort, and it attracts many Dutch visitors, who make the sea-crossing via Harwich and Felixstowe, both major entry ports for traffic from the Continent. Aldeburgh dates from Roman times and has long been known as a small port for North Sea fisheries. The Aldeburgh Festival, held every June, is the most important arts festival in East Anglia, and one of the best attended in England.

ESSENTIALS

GETTING THERE   Woodbridge is on the rail line to Lowestoft from either Victoria Station or Liverpool Street Station in London. Get off two stops after Ipswich. For schedules and information, call ☎ **08457/48-49-50.** The nearest rail station to Aldeburgh is on the same line, at Saxmundham, six stops after Ipswich. From Saxmundham, you can take a taxi or one of six buses that run the 9.5km (6 miles) to Aldeburgh during the day.

One National Express bus a day passes through Aldeburgh and Woodbridge on the way from London's Victoria Coach Station to Great Yarmouth. It stops at every country town and narrow lane along the way, so the trip to Aldeburgh takes a woeful 4½ hours. For information, call ☎ **08705/808080.** Many visitors reach both towns by Eastern County Bus Company's service from Ipswich. That company's no. 80/81 buses run frequently between Woodbridge and Aldeburgh.

If driving from London's ring road, take the A12 northeast to Ipswich, then continue northeast on the A12 to Woodbridge. To get to Aldeburgh, stay on the A12 until you reach the junction with the A1094, then head east to the North Sea.

VISITOR INFORMATION   The **Tourist Information Centre** is at the Cinema, 152 High St., Aldeburgh (☎ **01728/453637**), and is open daily year-round from 9am to 5pm.

SPECIAL EVENTS   Aldeburgh was the home of Benjamin Britten (1913–76), renowned composer of the operas *Peter Grimes* and *Billy Budd,* as well as many orchestral works. Many of his compositions were first performed at the **Aldeburgh Festival,** which he founded in 1946. The festival takes place in June, featuring internationally known performers. There are other concerts and events throughout the year. Write or call the tourist office for details. The Snape Maltings

Concert Hall (© **01728/687100**) nearby is one of the more successful among the smaller British concert halls; it also houses the Britten-Pears School of Advanced Musical Studies, established in 1973.

SEEING THE SIGHTS IN ALDEBURGH

There are two local golf courses, one at Aldeburgh and another at Thorpeness, 3km (2 miles) away. A yacht club is situated on the River Alde, 14km (9 miles) from the river's mouth. There are also two bird sanctuaries nearby, **Minsmere** and **Havergate Island.** Managed by the Royal Society for the Protection of Birds, they are famous for their waterfowl.

Insider's tip: Seek out Crag Path, running along Aldeburgh's wild shore. It is unusually attractive, with its two lookout towers built early in the 19th century to keep watch for vessels putting down or needing pilots.

Constructed on a shelf of land at the sea level, the High Street runs parallel to the often-turbulent waterfront. A cliff face rises some 89m (55 ft.) above the main street. A major attraction is the 16th-century **Moot Hall Museum,** Market Cross Place, Aldeburgh (© **01728/453295**). The hall dates from the time of Henry VIII, but its tall twin chimneys are later additions. The timber-frame structure displays old maps, prints, and Anglo-Saxon burial urns, as well as other items of historical interest. It is open July and August daily from 10:30am to 12:30pm and 2:30 to 5pm. It is also open from Easter to May, Saturday and Sunday from 2:30 to 5pm, and in June, September, and October daily from 2:30 to 5pm. Admission is £1 ($1.60) for adults and free for children.

Aldeburgh is also the site of the nation's northernmost Martello tower, erected to protect the coast from a feared invasion by Napoleon.

WHERE TO STAY
NEAR WOODBRIDGE

The King's Head Inn ✦   In Orford, an ancient town known for the ruins of its 12th-century castle, this 13th-century inn, reported to have a smuggling history, lies in the shadow of St. Bartholomew's Church. The nonsmoking spacious bedrooms are comfortably furnished; each has an immaculately kept private bathroom with shower unit. A wealth of old beams and a candlelit dining room add to the ambience of the inn. Tasty meals use fresh fish and locally caught game. Lunchtime bar snacks are available.

Front St., Orford, near Woodbridge, Suffolk IP12 2LW. © 01394/450271. www.kingshead-orford-suffolk. co.uk. 3 units. £60 ($96) single or double. Rates include English breakfast. MC, V. Take B1084 for about 16km (10 miles) east of Woodbridge, following the signs to Orford. **Amenities:** Restaurant; bar. *In room:* TV, coffeemaker.

IN ALDEBURGH

Uplands Hotel ✦   Opposite the parish church on the main road into town, this is a privately owned and family-run hotel that was once the residence of Elizabeth Garrett Anderson, the first woman doctor in England. Set in lovingly cultivated, award-winning gardens, the hotel offers a warm atmosphere and comfortable accommodations. All rooms are doubles, each with a private, shower-only bathroom. Some of the larger rooms can fit up to two additional beds. The breakfast room with its sculpted Italian ceiling overlooks the garden. The menu features English cooking, using fresh local produce.

Victoria Rd., Aldeburgh, Suffolk IP15 5DX. © 01728/452420. Fax 01728/454872. 10 units. £65 ($104) single; £87.50 ($140) double. Rates include English breakfast. MC, V. **Amenities:** Breakfast room; bar; sitting room. *In room:* TV, coffeemaker, hair dryer (on request).

WHERE TO DINE
IN WOODBRIDGE

Captain's Table SEAFOOD/MODERN BRITISH   This is a good choice for intimate dining near the railway station. The exact age of the building is unknown; estimates put it at 600 years. The atmosphere near the wharf is colorful. The restaurant's outside is sheathed in a layer of plaster or stucco, and the interior is filled with old timbers and wooden tables. The licensed restaurant serves well-prepared specialties, including Dover sole and scallops cooked in butter with bacon and garlic. The desserts are rich and good tasting. The day's chalkboard specials might include oysters, sea salmon, or turbot in lobster sauce.

3 Quay St. ✆ **01394/383145.** Reservations recommended. Main courses £6–£12.50 ($10–$20). MC, V. Tues–Sun noon–2pm (Sun until 3pm) and 6:30–9:30pm (Fri–Sat until 10pm).

The Spice Bar CONTINENTAL/MALAYSIAN/MEDITERRANEAN   Built as an alehouse in the 1640s, this popular dining spot in the village center offers reasonably priced food and drink. Many guests drop in for a glass of wine (25 labels, plus 3 house wines by the glass), a draft beer, or spirits. The home-cooked meals are based on seasonal produce; many dishes have flair and flavor. Main courses include beef strips with chiles and Chinese greens or King Prawn Sanbal. The desserts are sumptuous, including the crème brûlée.

17 Thoro'fare. ✆ **01394/382557.** Reservations recommended. Main courses £6.75–£12 ($11–$19). AE, MC, V. Mon–Sat noon–2pm and 7–10pm. Closed Jan 1–6.

IN ALDEBURGH

Aldeburgh Fish and Chip Shop ✦ FISH AND CHIPS   Despite a humble appearance and limited seating, this is one of the region's most famous fish and chips emporiums. Set on the main street, it sells only one version of either plaice or cod. The product is wrapped in paper, doused Victorian-style in malt vinegar, and consumed by enthusiasts, usually on the open-air seawall. The greasy-but-flaky products have been enjoyed here since around 1900 by clients who have included Benjamin Britten and his longtime companion, tenor Peter Pears, who used to take visitors for walks along the oceanfront followed by fish and chips.

226 High St. ✆ **01728/452250.** Main courses £3.50–£6 ($6–$10). No credit cards. Daily 11:45am–2pm and 6–9pm. Closed Sun–Mon late Oct to early Apr.

Ye Old Cross Keys ENGLISH/SEAFOOD   A few paces from the sea in the town center, this is a genuine 16th-century pub with the feel of a real Suffolk local. In summer, drinkers take their mugs of real English ale or lager out and sit on the seawall to watch the pounding waves, always within sight of the flowering baskets that hang from the building's eaves. Artists, who during cooler months sit beside an old brick fireplace and eat smoked salmon, seafood platters, seafood pie, and lasagna, favor the pub. Place your food order at the special counter and someone will call your number when it's ready. Don't expect too much in the way of cuisine here.

Crabbe St. ✆ **01728/452637.** Main courses £5–£8.75 ($8–$14). No credit cards. Daily noon–2pm and 7–9pm. Pub: Daily 11am–3pm and 5–11:30pm.

8 Norwich ✦✦

174km (109 miles) NE of London; 32km (20 miles) W of the North Sea

Norwich still claims to be the capital of East Anglia. Despite partial industrialization, it's a charming and historic city. In addition to its cathedral, it has more than 30 medieval parish churches built of flint. It's the most important shopping center in East Anglia and has lots in the way of entertainment and interesting hotels, many of them in its narrow streets and alleyways. There's also a big open-air market every weekday, where fruit, flowers, vegetables, and other goods are sold from stalls with colored canvas roofs.

ESSENTIALS

GETTING THERE   Hourly train service from London's Liverpool Street Station takes nearly 2 hours. For information, call ✆ **08457/48-49-50.**

National Express buses depart London's Victoria Coach Station once each hour for the 3-hour ride. For schedules and information, call ✆ **08705/808080.**

If driving from London's ring road, head north toward Cambridge on the M11. Turn northeast at the junction with the A11, which takes you to Norwich.

GETTING AROUND   For information about buses serving the area, go to the **Norfolk Bus Information Centre** at Castle Meadow (✆ **0870/608-2608**). The office there can answer your transportation questions; open Monday through Saturday from 8:30am to 5pm.

VISITOR INFORMATION   The Tourist Information Centre is located in the **Millennium Plane,** Norwich, near the marketplace in the center of town (✆ **01603/727927**). It's open April through October Monday through Saturday from 10am to 6pm and Sunday from 10:30am to 4:30pm; November through March Monday through Saturday from 10am to 5:30pm.

SEEING THE SIGHTS

Norwich Cathedral ★★   Dating from 1096, and principally of Norman design, Norwich Cathedral is noted primarily for its long nave with lofty columns. Built in the late Perpendicular style, the spire rises 96m (315 ft.); together with the keep of the castle, it forms a significant landmark on the Norwich skyline. More than 300 *bosses* (knoblike ornamental projections) on the ceiling depict biblical scenes. The impressive choir stalls with handsome misericords date from the 15th century. Edith Cavell, an English nurse executed by the Germans during World War I, is buried on the cathedral's Life's Green. The quadrangular cloisters, which date from the 13th century, are the largest monastic cloisters in England.

The cathedral visitor center includes a refreshment area and exhibition and film room with tape/slide shows about the cathedral. Inquire at the information desk about guided tours from June through September. A short walk from the cathedral will take you to Tombland, one of the most interesting old squares in Norwich.

62 The Close. ✆ **01603/218321.** Free admission, but £3 ($4.80) donation suggested. Oct–May daily 7:30am–6pm; June–Sept daily 7:30am–7pm.

Sainsbury Centre for Visual Arts ★   The center was the gift of Sir Robert and Lady Sainsbury, who, in 1973, contributed their private collection to the University of East Anglia, 5km (3 miles) west of Norwich on Earlham Road. Together with their son David, they gave an endowment to provide a building to house the collection. Designed by Foster Associates, the center was opened in 1978 and has since won many national and international awards. Features of the structure are its flexibility, allowing solid and glass areas to be interchanged, and the superb quality of light, which permits optimum viewing of works of art. Special exhibitions are often presented in the 1991 Crescent Wing extension. The Sainsbury Collection is one of the foremost in the country, including modern, ancient, classical, and ethnographic art. Its most prominent works are those by Francis Bacon, Alberto Giacometti, and Henry Moore.

University of East Anglia, Earlham Rd. ℂ 01603/456060. Admission £2 ($3.20) adults, £1 ($1.60) children and students. Tues–Sun 11am–5pm. Bus: 25, 26, 27, or 76 from Castle Meadow.

The Mustard Shop Museum   The Victorian-style Mustard Shop displays a wealth of mahogany and shining brass. The standard of service and pace of life reflect the personality and courtesy of a bygone age. The Mustard Museum features exhibits on the history of the Colman Company and the making of mustard, including its properties and origins. There are old advertisements, as well as packages and "tins." You can browse in the shop, selecting whichever mustards you prefer, including the really hot English type. The shop also sells aprons, tea towels, pottery mustard pots, and mugs.

15 Royal Arcade. ℂ 01603/627889. Free admission. Mon–Sat 9:30am–5pm. Closed bank holidays.

Second Air Division Memorial Library   A memorial room honoring the Second Air Division of the Eighth U.S. Army Air Force is part of the central library. The library staff will assist veterans who wish to visit their old air bases in East Anglia. At the library, you can find pertinent books, audiovisual materials, and records of the various bomber groups.

The Forum, Millennium Plain. ℂ 01603/774747. Free admission. Mon–Sat 9am–5pm.

Blickling Hall ★★   Massive yew hedges bordering a long drive frame your first view of Blickling Hall, a great Jacobean house built in the early 17th century, one of the finest examples of such architecture in the country. The long gallery has an elaborate 17th-century ceiling, and the Peter the Great Room, decorated later, has a fine tapestry on the wall. The house is set in ornamental parkland with a formal garden and an orangery. It's a good idea to call ahead before visiting to confirm opening hours.

Blickling, near Aylsham. ℂ 01263/733084. House and gardens, Tues–Sat £6.90 ($11) adults, £3.45 ($6) children. Gardens only, Tues–Sat £3.90 ($6) adults, £1.95 ($3.10) children. Open late Mar to Oct Wed–Sun and bank holiday Mon 1–4:15pm. (Garden, shop, restaurant, and Plant Centre open Thurs–Sun and bank holiday Mon 10:15am–5:15pm.) Blickling Hall lies 23km (14 miles) north of the city of Norwich, 2.5km (1½ miles) west of Aylsham on B1354; take A140 toward Cromer and follow the signs. Telephone before visiting to confirm opening arrangements.

EXPLORING THE BROADS ★

Wroxham, 11km (7 miles) northeast of Norwich, is the best center for exploring the Broads, mostly shallow lagoons connected by streams. These are fun to explore by boat, of course, but some folks prefer to ride their bikes along the Broads.

To get to Wroxham from Norwich, take bus no. 51. The 30-minute ride costs £2 ($3.20) for a return ticket. Information about touring the Broads is provided by the **Hoveton Tourist Office,** Station Road (ℂ 01603/782281), open from Easter to October daily from 9am to 1pm and 2 to 5pm. At this office you can get a list of boat-rental facilities. During the winter months contact the office of the Broads Authority (ℂ 01603/610734) in Norwich for information around town.

If you don't want to handle your own boat, you can take an organized tour. The best ones are offered by **Broads Tours,** near the Wroxham bridge (ℂ 01603/782207). Their cruises last 1½ to 3½ hours. In summer, most departures are at either 11:30am or 2:30pm. The cost ranges from £5.50 to £6.30 ($9–$10) for adults, and from £3.70 to £4.90 ($6–$8) for children 5 to 15 years.

The Royal Residence of Sandringham

Some 177km (110 miles) northeast of London, 7,000-acre **Sandringham** ★ has been the country home of four generations of British monarchs; Queen Victoria's son, the Prince of Wales (later King Edward VII), purchased it in 1861. He and his Danish wife, Princess Alexandra, rebuilt the house, which became a popular meeting place for British society. The red-brick-and-stone Victorian-Tudor mansion has more than 200 rooms, some of which are open to the public, including two drawing rooms, the ballroom, and a dining room. The atmosphere of a well-loved family home is a contrast to the formal splendor of Buckingham Palace. Guests can also view a loft salon with a minstrel's gallery used as a sitting room by the royal family and full of photographs and mementos.

A Land Train designed and built on the estate makes it easy for visitors to reach Sandringham House, which sits at the heart of 24 hectares (60 acres) of beautiful grounds. The train's covered carriages have room for wheelchairs.

The Sandringham Museum holds a wealth of rare items relating to the history of the royal family's time here and displays tell the story of the monarchs who have owned the estate since 1862. Visitors can see the big-game trophies in settings that include a safari trail.

Sandringham is some 80km (50 miles) west of Norwich and 13km (8 miles) northeast of King's Lynn (off the A149). King's Lynn is the end of the main train route from London's Liverpool Street Station that goes via Cambridge and Ely. Trains from London arrive at King's Lynn every 2 hours; the trip takes 2½ hours. From Cambridge, the train ride takes only 1 hour. Buses from both Cambridge and Norwich run to King's Lynn, where you can catch bus no. 411 to take you the rest of the way to Sandringham.

The grounds and museum of Sandringham (© **01553/772675**) are open from April 19 to July 18 and from July 26 to October 26 daily from 11am to 4:45pm (in Oct, the house closes at 3pm). Admission to the house, grounds, and museum is £6.50 ($10) for adults, £5 ($8) for seniors, and £4 ($6) for children. Admission to the grounds and museum only is £5.50 ($9) for adults, £4.50 ($7) for seniors, and £3.50 ($6) for children 5 to 15 years.

SHOPPING

For the best in antiques, books, and crafts, shoppers can search out the historic lanes and alleys of the town center.

Norwich Antiques Centre, 14 Tombland (© **01603/619129**), is a three-floor house opposite the cathedral where 60-plus dealers set up shop. The selection is wide and varied and includes everything from small collectibles to antique furniture. There's also a small coffee shop in the house.

Right next to the Antiques Centre, **James and Ann Tillett,** 12–13 Tombland (© **01603/624914**), have a marvelous shop specializing in antique silver, barometers, and jewelry old and new.

If you're into dolls, don't miss the **Elm Hill Craft Shop,** 2 Elm Hill (✆ **01603/621076**), with its custom-made doll houses and furnishings, plus traditional children's toys, books, and children's jewelry.

WHERE TO STAY

Norwich is better equipped than most East Anglian cities to handle guests who arrive without reservations. The **Norwich City Tourist Information Centre** maintains an office at the Guildhall, Gaol Hill, opposite the market (✆ **01603/ 666071**). Each year a new listing of accommodations is drawn up, including licensed and unlicensed hotels, B&B houses, and even living arrangements on the outskirts.

The Beeches Hotel & Victorian Gardens This nonsmoking hotel is composed of two of Edwardian houses, both on the same side of Earlham Road and within a minute's walk from each other. The Beeches's centerpiece, housing the reception desk, bar, and restaurant, is at no. 6; but no matter which building you occupy, you'll get a sense of the Edwardian era in the public areas. The midsize bedrooms have been modernized, each outfitted in tones of pink, beige, or blue, and each with a private, shower-only bathroom. There is one room available for those with limited mobility. The restaurant is open only for dinner.

2–6 Earlham Rd., Norwich, Norfolk NR2 3DB. ✆ **01603/621167.** Fax 01603/620151. www.beeches.co.uk. 36 units. £69 ($110) single; £87–£99 ($139–$158) double. Rates include English breakfast. AE, DC, MC, V. **Amenities:** Restaurant; bar; 24-hr. room service. *In room:* TV, dataport, coffeemaker, hair dryer, minibar (in superior rooms).

Marlborough House Hotel This hotel is centrally situated close to the railway station, Riverside Walk, the cathedral, and the central library. It has a small parking area on its grounds, and there is adequate off-street parking as well. This centrally heated hotel offers pristine small bedrooms. All the doubles contain a private bathroom with shower. There are 5 rooms available for nonsmoking guests. There's a comfortable TV lounge. Evening meals with home-style cooking are served.

22 Stracey Rd., Norwich, Norfolk NR1 1EZ. ✆ and fax **01603/628005.** 11 units, 6 with bathroom. £28 ($45) single without bathroom; £38 ($61) single with bathroom; £55 ($88) double with bathroom; £80 ($128) family unit with bathroom. Rates include English breakfast. No credit cards. **Amenities:** Dining room; bar; TV lounge. *In room:* TV, coffeemaker, hair dryer, no phone.

Pearl Continental Hotel This building dates from the 18th century when it was the private home of the Lord Mayor. The refurbished bedrooms are situated in the main building, as well as in two semidetached cottages. The cottages have bay windows and wooden beams, as well as a private garden. Most bedrooms are midsize, each with a comfortable bed, plus a bathroom with a shower stall.

The reception area's chandeliers light the way to the restaurant, where fixed-price lunches and dinners are served.

116 Thorpe Rd., Norwich, Norfolk NR1 1RU. ✆ **01603/620302.** Fax 01603/761706. www.pc-hotels.co.uk. 37 units. Mon–Thurs £75 ($120) double; Fri–Sun £74 ($118) per person double. Weekend rates include English breakfast. AE, MC, V. Take Thorpe Rd. 1km (½ mile) east of city center. **Amenities:** Restaurant; bar; room service (7:30am–9pm); laundry/dry-cleaning service. *In room:* TV, coffeemaker, hair dryer.

Wedgewood House A large, rambling, Edwardian-era house (1902), this pleasant guesthouse is painted white with Wedgwood-blue trim. It is popular with repeat visitors because of its convenient parking and location a 5-minute walk south of the city center. The nonsmoking house is clean, cozy, and run with a lighthearted sense of irreverent fun. Bedrooms come in a range of sizes, but all of them are well appointed.

42–44 St. Stephens Rd., Norwich, Norfolk NR1 3RE. ⓒ **01603/625730.** Fax 01603/615035. www.wedgewood house.co.uk. 12 units, 9 with bathroom. £29.50 ($47) single without bathroom; £39 ($62) single with bathroom; £44 ($70) double without bathroom, £50–£55 ($80–$88) double with bathroom. Rates include English breakfast. MC, V. **Amenities:** Breakfast room. *In room:* TV, coffeemaker, hair dryer, no phone.

SUPER-CHEAP SLEEPS: CAMPING, YOUTH HOSTELS & MORE

From camping to youth hostels to student housing, Norwich has the cheapest accommodations in all of East Anglia.

A most economical way to spend time in Norwich is to pitch a tent at **Lakenham Camp Site,** Martineau Lane, located 1.5km (1 mile) from the center of town (ⓒ **01603/620060**). Facilities include clean toilets and showers. Gates close at 11pm, so if you're in a car, get here before then. But if you're traveling by foot, you can still get in after 11pm. Call ahead for availability of sites. Rates are July to August £5 ($8) for adults and £1.65 ($2.65) for children; September through June £3.35 ($5) for adults and free for children. Non-members pay an additional £4.50 ($7) pitch fee.

Reduced-rate campus housing rooms for bona fide, card-carrying university students are available through **Student Housing,** University of East Anglia, Accommodations & Conference Office, Norwich, Norfolk NR4 7TJ (ⓒ **01603/ 593271**). Non-students are still welcome, but are only eligible for the more expensive rooms. The small rooms for students are typical of student housing—bed, wardrobe, desk, and chair. There is laundry service available. Book rooms ahead through the Conference Office. Reduced student housing rates are only available late June to mid-September: £25 ($40) single without bathroom, £43 ($69) single with bathroom with breakfast included. These rooms are comparable to standard B&B accommodation and contain TVs and beverage-making facilities.

WHERE TO DINE

Briton Arms Coffee House *(Value* TRADITIONAL BRITISH/CONTINENTAL In the heart of the old city near the train station, the Briton Arms is a good place to stop after you tour the cathedral, only a block away. It overlooks the most beautiful cobblestone street in town. Its history can be traced back to the days of Edward III. It's one of the least expensive eating-places in town, as well as one of the most intimate and informal, with old beamed ceilings and Tudor benches. The coffeehouse has several rooms, including one in back with an inglenook. Go to the little counter, purchase your lunch, and bring it to the table of your choice. Everything we've tried was homemade and well prepared. Try Norfolk turkey thyme-and-onion pie with mixed greens. A different kind of soup is offered daily.

Elm Hill. ⓒ **01603/623367.** Main courses £5.50–£5.75 ($9). No credit cards. Mon–Sat 9:30am–5pm (lunch 12:15–2:30pm).

Pinocchio's ITALIAN/MEDITERRANEAN/VEGETARIAN This restaurant brings a touch of the Mediterranean to the Norwich dining landscape. The cookery is competent and often filled with flavor; occasionally, a dish could stand more Italian flair. The menu changes every 4 to 6 weeks and always features at least six pasta and six vegetarian dishes. It may include smoked goose salad, tagliatelle carbonara, eggplant stuffed with chestnut-and-spinach risotto, or haunch of venison with a red-wine sauce. Italian wines are featured here, with wine tastings held every 6 weeks. If you want to splurge, the wine tasting costs £24.50 ($39) and includes a three-course dinner, a glass of wine with each course, and a talk conducted by a representative of the winery whose products are featured. On Monday and Thursday evenings you can enjoy live jazz, beginning at around 8pm.

11 St. Benedict St. (℃ **01603/613318**. Reservations recommended. Main courses £7–£12 ($11–$19). AE, DC, MC, V. Tues–Sat noon–2pm; Mon–Sat 5–11pm.

NORWICH AFTER DARK

From fine art to pop art, there's quite a lot happening around Norwich at night. Information on almost all of it can be found at the box office of the Theatre Royal, Theatre Street (℃ **01603/630000**), where you can also pick up tickets to just about any event.

The Theatre Royal hosts touring companies performing drama, opera, ballet, and modern dance. The Royal Shakespeare Company and London's Royal National troupe are among the regular visitors. Ticket prices run from £16 to £30 ($26–$48), with senior and student discounts usually available for Wednesday, Thursday, and Saturday matinees. The box office is open Monday through Saturday from 9:30am to 8pm on performance days, closing at 6pm on nonperformance days.

Hosting productions of classic drama on most evenings, the **Norwich Playhouse,** Gun Wharf, 42–58 St. George's St. (℃ **01603/598598**), offers tickets ranging from £8 to £14 ($13–$22). The box office is open daily from 9:30am until 8pm.

An Elizabethan-style theater, the **Maddermarket Theatre,** 1 St. John's Alley (℃ **01603/620917**), is home to the amateur Norwich Players' productions of classical and contemporary drama. Tickets, ranging from £7 to £12.50 ($11–$20), and schedules are available at the box office Monday through Saturday from 10am to 9pm and from 10am to 5pm on nonperformance days.

The city's **Theatre in the Parks** (℃ **01603/212137**) includes about 40 outdoor performances every summer in various outdoor venues.

Located in a converted medieval church, **Norwich Puppet Theatre,** St. James, Whitefriars (℃ **01603/629921**), offers original puppet shows most afternoons and some mornings in an octagonal studio that holds about 50 people. Tickets are £5.50 ($9) for adults, £4 ($6) students and seniors, and £3.75 ($6) for children 16 and under, and are available at the box office Monday through Friday from 9:30am to 5pm, and on Saturday on days of performances.

The most versatile entertainment complex in town, the **Norwich Arts Centre,** Reeves Yard, St. Benedict's Street (℃ **01603/660352**), hosts performances of ballet, comedy, poetry, and an emphasis on ethnic music. Tickets are £2 to £15 ($3.20–$24), and the box office is open Monday through Friday from 9:30am to 5pm, and Saturday from 11am to 4pm. On days of performances, the box office is open until 9pm.

Before or after your cultural event, check out the local culture at **Adam and Eve,** 17 Bishopgate (℃ **01603/667423**), the oldest pub in Norwich, founded in 1249, which serves a well-kept John Smith's or Old Peculiar. **The Gardener's Arms,** 2–4 Timberhill (℃ **01603/621447**), pours Boddington's and London Pride to a lively crowd of locals and students. A good place to wait for the next film, **Take 5,** St. Andrew's Street (℃ **01603/763099**), a cafe-bar located next door to Cinema City, is the hangout for the local arts crowd.

The East Midlands

This area mixes dreary industrial sections with incredible scenery, particularly in the Peak District National Park in Derbyshire. You'll also find the tulip land of Lincolnshire, the 18th-century spa of Buxton in Derbyshire, and the remains of Sherwood Forest. If you have Pilgrims in your past, you can trace your roots here.

Except for **Sulgrave Manor** and **Althorp House,** childhood home of Princess Diana, Northamptonshire is off the tourist circuit. If you do stop here, the best place to stay is **Northampton,** the capital. In Leicestershire, use the industrialized county town of **Leicester** as a base to explore many countryside sights, including Belvoir Castle, setting for the movie *Young Sherlock Holmes,* and Bosworth Battlefield, site of one of England's most important battles.

Derbyshire is noted for the **Peak District National Park;** Byron felt that the Peak District landscapes rivaled those of Switzerland and Greece. There are also some historic homes—notably **Chatsworth,** home of the 11th duke of Devonshire. The best places to base yourself here are **Buxton, Bakewell,** and **Ashbourne.** In Nottinghamshire, the capital city of **Nottingham** is a good base for exploring what's left of **Sherwood Forest,** Robin Hood's legendary stamping grounds. If you're headed for Lincolnshire, visit the capital and cathedral city of **Lincoln,** with a stopover at the old seaport of **Boston,** after which the famous American city was named.

1 Northamptonshire

In the heart of the Midlands, Northamptonshire has been inhabited since Paleolithic times. Traces have been found of Beaker and other Bronze Age people, and remains of several Iron Age hill-forts are still visible. Two Roman roads—now Watling and Ermine streets—ran through the county; relics of Roman settlements have been discovered at Towcester, Whilton, Irchester, and Castor. West Saxons and Anglicans invaded in the 7th century. In 655, the first abbey was established at Medehamstede, now Peterborough. In the Middle Ages, castles and manor houses dotted a county rich in cattle, sheep farms, and leather artisans. American visitors mostly come here to see Sulgrave Manor, George Washington's ancestral home.

NORTHAMPTON

110km (69 miles) NW of London; 66km (41 miles) NE of Oxford

Fortified after 1066 by Simon de Senlis (St. Liz), Northamptonshire's administrative and political center was a favorite meeting place of Norman and Plantagenet kings. The barons whose demand for policy changes led to the Magna Carta besieged King John here. During the War of the Roses, Henry VI was defeated and taken prisoner. Northampton supported Parliament and Cromwell in the Civil War.

Value Cheap Thrills: What to See & Do for Free (or Almost) in East Midlands

Spend a morning at Stamford. After you've seen Lincoln Cathedral, head south for 80km (50 miles) to the old town of Stamford, called "a museum piece predating the Industrial Revolution." Located on the River Welland, this Georgian town reflects the region's prosperity in the 1600s and 1700s. The 500 buildings of landmark status are worth the trip here—you'll recognize them from the BBC miniseries, *Middlemarch.*

Visit Cotswold-like villages. Stamford lies 80km (50 miles) from Lincoln, and can be used as a base to explore some lovely little villages in Northamptonshire that rival any in the Cotswolds. Take the A43 route out of Stamford, signposted Kettering, and head for Easton-on-the-Hill, Colleyweston, King's Cliffe, Woodnewton, and Fortheringhay, where in 1587 Mary Queen of Scots was beheaded. (The castle in which she died is now nothing but a mound.) Pass along the village High streets with their stone cottages and old churches.

Explore the Peak District National Park. The Edale in the Noe River Valley is home to many quaint villages and hamlets. The Pennine Way, Britain's first and best-known National Trail, has its southern terminus here, as it begins its long passage to Scotland. Pick up a copy of a pamphlet, "Eight Walks Around Edale," at national park information centers for only £1.20 ($1.90). It details the best dramatic walks here, including a 5.5km (3½-mile) trek from Edale to Castleton.

Make a day of it in Sherwood Forest. Errol Flynn in green tights is just a memory; the legendary forest is largely gone, but there's enough lore, legend, and trees left to draw visitors to Sherwood Forest (p. 548), 29km (18 miles) north of Nottingham. Home of Robin Hood and His Merry Men, the forest is riddled with walks and footpaths.

Discover the Dukeries. A medieval holdover, these gigantic country estates take up much of what remains of Sherwood Forest (p. 548). The highlight is the 3,800-acre Clumber Park, a National Trust woodland that is ideal for strolls or a family picnic.

Before 1675, Northampton was a fascinating city architecturally; Defoe once called it "the handsomest and best town in this part of England." But a fire destroyed the old city. Nothing of the castle (ca. 1100) where Thomas à Becket stood trial in 1164 is left standing. Today's city was created essentially after the railway came in the mid–19th century. For ancient architecture, you'll find Lincoln more interesting.

Located on the River Nene, Northampton has long been an important center for the making of boots, shoes, and other leatherwork, pursuits traced through the centuries in two of the city's museums.

ESSENTIALS
GETTING THERE   Trains depart from London's Euston Station every 30 minutes throughout the day for the 1-hour trip to Northampton. For information in Northampton and the rest of the Midlands, call ✆ **08457/48-49-50.**

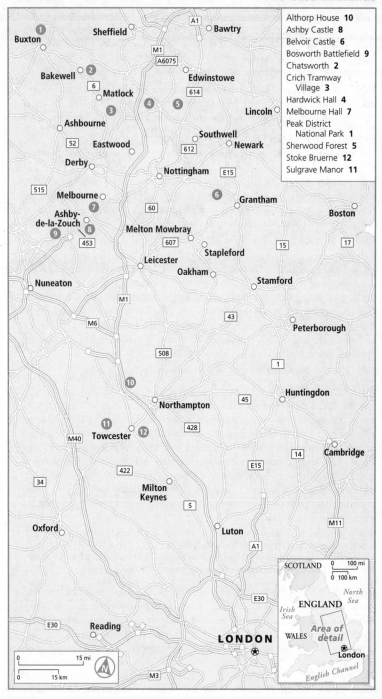

The East Midlands

Althorp House **10**
Ashby Castle **8**
Belvoir Castle **6**
Bosworth Battlefield **9**
Chatsworth **2**
Crich Tramway
   Village **3**
Hardwick Hall **4**
Melbourne Hall **7**
Peak District
   National Park **1**
Sherwood Forest **5**
Stoke Bruerne **12**
Sulgrave Manor **11**

Buxton

Sheffield

Bawtry

A1

M1

A6075

Bakewell

Edwinstowe

6

Matlock

614

Ashbourne

Lincoln

52

Eastwood

Southwell

Derby

612

Newark

Nottingham

E15

515

Melbourne

6

Grantham

Ashby-
de-la-Zouch

Boston

8

60

453

9

Melton Mowbray

15

17

607

Stapleford

Leicester

Oakham

Nuneaton

Stamford

M1

Peterborough

M6

43

508

1

Northampton

45

Huntingdon

Towcester

11

12

428

M40

14

Cambridge

422

34

Milton
Keynes

E15

5

Oxford

Luton

M11

A1

SCOTLAND

0   100 mi

0   100 km

E30

North
Sea

ENGLAND

Irish
Sea

E30

Reading

WALES

*Area of
detail*

London

LONDON

0   15 mi

0   15 km

M3

English Channel

Between three and five motor coaches depart every day from London's Victoria Coach Station, requiring about 2 hours for the ride to Northampton, with many annoying stops in between. For information, call © **08705/808080.**

If driving from London, follow the M1 due north to junction 15, then follow the signs into Northampton. Depending on traffic, the trek takes about an hour.

VISITOR INFORMATION   The **Northampton Visitor Centre** is at the Central Museum and Art Gallery, Guildhall Road (© **01604/238-548**). It's open Monday through Saturday from 10am to 5pm and Sunday from 2 to 5pm.

SEEING THE SIGHTS

The **Church of the Holy Sepulchre,** on Sheep Street, is one of five Norman round churches in England. Simon de Senlis, a famous veteran of the First Crusade, founded it. You can see its circular ambulatory and round nave. Victorian Gothic architecture swept Northampton after the coming of the railway, and the **Guidehall** on St. Giles Square best exemplifies the style. It was built by Edward Godwin in the 1860s, an architect then only in his 20s.

Central Museum & Art Gallery *(Finds)*   One of Britain's most unusual provincial museums and Northampton's key attraction celebrates Northampton's rich cultural and industrial traditions. Proud of the city's status as the boot- and shoe-making capital of Britain, it devotes much of its gallery space to exhibitions of the largest collection of antique shoes in the world, spanning centuries of footwear, with emphasis on the Victorian era. Also on display are artworks from Italy spanning the 15th to the 18th centuries, a wide spectrum from the history of British art, and objects uncovered from nearby archaeological sites dating from the Stone Age.

Guildhall Rd. © **01604/238548**. Free admission. Mon–Sat 10am–5pm; Sun 2–5pm.

WHERE TO STAY

The Poplars Hotel ★ *(Finds)*   This renovated 17th-century farmhouse, with its oak beams and dark wood panels, is now a charming hotel in this small country village, just 6.5km (4 miles) from the city center. Personal attention is lavished upon guests from the moment they check in from owners Bernard and Mary Lawes. The average-size bedrooms have country-style furnishings in keeping with the ambience. Units also contain a private, shower-only or shower-and-tub bathroom. Guests may have a fixed-price dinner Monday to Thursday. Nonsmoking areas include all bedrooms, but smoking is permitted in the dining room, and one of the two lounges.

Cross St., Moulton, Northampton, Northamptonshire NN3 7RZ. © **01604/643983**. Fax 01604/790233. www.thepoplarshotel.co.uk. 18 units. £44.50–£49.50 ($71–$79) single; £57.50–£69.50 ($92–$111) double; family rooms (double plus 2 children) £72.50 ($116). Rates include English breakfast. AE, MC, V. Closed Christmas week. **Amenities:** Dining room; lounge. *In room:* TV, dataport, coffeemaker, hair dryer.

Quinton Green ★   On a gentle slope overlooking 1,200 acres of beautiful green pastures and wheat fields, this 17th-century farmhouse is made of heavy slabs of local stone. The house welcomes guests with a warmth and charm attributable largely to the owners, the Turneys, having lived here since 1919. Just beyond the front door, there is a romantic walled garden. The large upstairs nonsmoking bedrooms have oak and pine furnishings, including wardrobes and comfy armchairs. The standard- to large-size rooms have the kind of rolling countryside views that make you fling the windows open, lean out, and drink in the fresh air and brilliant sunshine. Each comes with a private bathroom with shower. The ground floor, with its wood and brick fireplaces, has a sitting room.

Quinton, Northamptonshire NN7 2EG. ⓒ **01604/863685.** Fax 01604/862230. 3 units. £30 ($48) single; £55 ($88) double. Rates include English breakfast. No credit cards. Closed Dec 25. **Amenities:** Dining room; billiard room; sitting room with piano. *In room:* TV, coffeemaker, no phone.

WHERE TO DINE

Buddies AMERICAN   Americans will feel right at home here, where walls are plastered with stateside memorabilia donated by clients over the past 15 years. This lively and loud bistro-cafe, housed in a 200-year-old church mission school, has a 400-item (!) lunch and dinner menu. Fixed-price lunches include nachos, salads, and burgers. Dinners range from "New York meats"—a hearty duo of ribs and chicken—to fish and vegetarian dishes. Salad and spuds accompany all dinners. Beer lovers can sample some of the twenty beers on tap.

The Old Mission School, Dye Church Lane. ⓒ **01604/620039.** Fixed-price lunch £5.95 ($10); main courses £5–£12 ($8–$19). AE, DC, MC, V. Daily noon–10:30pm.

Luigi's ITALIAN   The pride of Angelo and Giuseppina Miracco, this restaurant overflows with authentic Mediterranean ambience, as candlelight sets the mood. Popular dishes include a cooked-to-order steak Luigi in a sauce of mushrooms, onions, red wine, cilantro, and cream; and baked chicken with a white-wine and cream sauce. All dishes include a vegetable of the day or salad. The must-try dessert is the heavenly espresso-soaked tiramisu.

50 Wellingborough Rd. ⓒ **01604/628621.** Reservations recommended. Main courses £6–£12 ($10–$19). AE, DC, MC, V. Mon–Sat 7–10:30pm.

SULGRAVE MANOR: GEORGE WASHINGTON'S ANCESTRAL HOME ⓖ

Sulgrave Manor   American visitors will be especially interested in this small mid-16th-century Tudor manor, the ancestral home of George Washington. As part of a plan to dissolve the monasteries, Henry VIII sold the priory-owned manor in 1539 to Lawrence Washington, who had been mayor of Northampton. The Washington family occupied Sulgrave for more than a century, but in 1656, Col. John Washington left for the New World. Born in Virginia, George Washington was a direct descendant of Lawrence (seven generations removed).

A group of English people bought the manor in 1914 in honor of the friendship between Britain and the United States. Beginning with a large donation in 1927, the Colonial Dames have been largely responsible for raising the money for a major restoration to return it as much as possible to its original state. Appropriate furnishings and portraits, including a Gilbert Stuart original of the first president, have been donated on both sides of the Atlantic. The Washington family coat of arms on the main doorway—two bars and a trio of mullets—is believed to have been the inspiration for the Stars and Stripes.

Manor Rd. ⓒ **01295/760205.** Admission £5 ($8) adults, £2.50 ($4) children ages 5–16, free for children under 5. Apr–Oct Tues–Thurs and Sat–Sun from 2–5:30pm. Nov–Dec Sat–Sun 2–5:30pm. Jan–Mar no official opening hour, only a roster of special events, parties, private functions, on a very limited basis, usually for schools and pre-booked groups. From Northampton, drive 29km (18 miles) southwest on A43, then B4525 to Sulgrave. From Stratford-upon-Avon, take A422 via Banbury and continue to Brackley; 9.5km (6 miles) from Brackley, leave A422 and join B4525, which goes to the tiny village of Sulgrave. Signs will lead you to Sulgrave Manor.

ALTHORP: THE GIRLHOOD HOME & FINAL RESTING PLACE OF PRINCESS DIANA

Althorp ⓖ   Originally built in 1508 by Sir John Spencer, Althorp has brought a sometimes unwelcome dose of fame to the surrounding rural area because it was the girlhood home of Princess Diana. Raine Spencer, Diana's stepmother, glamorously revived it. At least part of the beauty and historical authenticity of this frequently renovated site is the result of her efforts.

Since the death of Lord Spencer, Diana's father, the house has been under the jurisdiction of Charles Spencer, Diana's older brother, who emigrated to South Africa. The house collection includes paintings by Van Dyck, Reynolds, Gainsborough, and Rubens, as well as an assortment of rare French and English furniture, and porcelain by Sèvres, Bow, and Chelsea.

To visit, *I strongly recommend that you book ahead.* Following the tragic death of Princess Diana in August 1997, a ticket to Althorp House became extremely difficult to obtain. More than 200 24-hour telephone lines handle orders for tickets. Althorp is open to the public only from July 1, Diana's birthday, to August 30, the day before the anniversary of her death.

Diana was buried on an island in an artificial lake on the property. Visitors do not have access to the island, but have a clear view of it across the lake. A museum celebrating Diana's life, complete with schoolgirl letters, her stunning silk wedding dress, and some of her haute-couture clothes, also opened here in the summer of 1998.

The museum also shows poignant films of her as a carefree child dancing in the gardens and later as a mother riding with her sons, William and Harry, plus videos that include the footage of her funeral. It's interesting to note that the museum has chosen to largely ignore or excise entirely any mention of the men in Diana's life—including Dodi Fayed, who died with her in the Paris car crash; James Hewitt, her one-time lover; and even Prince Charles, her estranged husband.

Facilities on-site include a restaurant and a shop selling a range of souvenirs associated with Diana. The estate states that these souvenirs "do not cheapen her memory in any way." We leave that for you to decide.

9.5km (6 miles) northwest of Northampton on A428 in Althorp, near Harlestone. ℭ 08701/679000 or 01804/770107. www.althorp.com. Admission £10.50 ($17) adults, £8.50 ($14) seniors, £5.50 ($8) children 5–17, free for children under 5, £26.50 ($42) family ticket. July 1–Sept 30 daily 1am–5pm.

STOKE BRUERNE: HEART OF THE CANAL NETWORKS

Stoke Bruerne is the center of the East Midland canal networks, the waterway equivalent of a modern motorway junction. The canal reached Stoke Bruerne in 1800, and it has played a central role in the canal system ever since. Today, you can visit the Canal Museum and take a cruise on the waterways.

Stoke Bruerne is 14km (9 miles) southwest of Northampton near Towcester, just south of the Blisworth Tunnel (take the A508 from the M1 junction 15 or the A5).

SEEING THE SIGHTS

A ride along the grand Union Canal complements a visit to the Canal Museum. The most convenient operator is **Indian Chief Cruises** (ℭ **01604/862428**), at the pub of The Boat Inn (see "Where to Dine," below). Two competitors are **Stoke Bruerne Boating Company** (ℭ **01604/862107**), which lies directly across from the canal, and **Blisworth Tunnel Boats** (ℭ **01604/858868**), which operates from the village of Blisworth, 5km (3 miles) to the north.

Any of the three can arrange daylong rentals of 9m (30-ft.) "narrows" boats—long, shallow-bottomed motorboats suitable for up to 12 occupants. The companies offer the same loosely scheduled services, hauling groups of passengers up and down the canal for rides that last between 25 minutes and 6 hours depending on the cruise selected. There are no timetables, and the prices vary depending on the company and on the length of the cruise. Indian Chief Cruises and Stoke Bruerne charge £3 ($4.80) for adults and £2 ($3.20) for children for a 25-minute cruise and as much as £14.50 ($23) for adults and £9 ($14) for children for a 6-hour cruise with a pub stop for a meal. Blisworth Tunnel Boats rents boats that hold 8 to 12 people for £90 to £110 ($144–$176) for the day. Rentals require a refundable deposit of £40 ($64) and are always accompanied with instruction on how to operate and navigate them. Be warned that the operations are extremely fluid and depend a lot on the season and the weather.

Canal Museum Set within a restored corn mill beside the banks of the Grant Union Canal, this museum celebrates 200 years of traditions that developed around the inland canals and waterways of the Midlands. Its exhibits include videos, a collection of horse-drawn barges and motorized vessels from the earliest years of the Industrial Revolution, memorabilia, tools and artifacts, period costumes, and a museum shop that sells posters, postcards, books, and more.

Rte. A508, Stoke Bruerne. (C) **01604/862229**. Admission £3.50 ($6) adults, £3 ($4.80) children under 16 and seniors, £10.25 ($16) family ticket. Apr–Oct daily 10am–5pm; off season Tues–Sun 10am–4pm.

WHERE TO DINE

The Boat Inn BRITISH/FRENCH This is the largest and most popular restaurant in Stoke Bruerne, a canal-side complex that manages to incorporate bars, cocktail lounges, and dining rooms into an interconnected row of 17th-century cottages. Most of the original character resides in the street-level bars, which boast a thatched roof, limestone walls, stone floors, and open fireplaces. You can order platters of simple food along with your beer (which includes lagers and eight kinds of bitter).

More formal meals, with more elaborate service, are offered upstairs in the restaurant, a barn-style extension with lots of exposed wood and a view over the canal. Menu items change with the season but include venison with red-wine sauce, guinea fowl, lobster thermidor, salmon, trout, and chicken.

Stoke Bruerne. (C) **01604/862428**. Reservations recommended for upstairs restaurant, not accepted in street-level bars and bistros. Restaurant: fixed-price menus £19–£24 ($30–$38). Bistro and pubs: main courses £5.50–£12 ($9–$19), tea with pastries or sandwiches £5.50 ($9). MC, V. Restaurant Tues–Sun noon–2pm and daily 7–9:15pm. Street-level bars daily 11am–3pm and 6–11pm.

Bruerne's Lock Restaurant *(Finds* CONTINENTAL/MODERN ENGLISH This is the most sophisticated and, at least in terms of cuisine, elegant restaurant in Northamptonshire, a destination sought out by gastronomes as far away as Birmingham and Manchester. Its present allure dates from 1989, when a trio of Franco-British entrepreneurs took over a thick-walled Georgian building whose foundations were built in the 17th century. Past functions of the building, which is situated near the uppermost of the town's seven canal locks, have included roles as a post office, a surgeon's office, and a nursery.

Within a warm and formal setting you can enjoy the most creative and imaginative cuisine in the region. Examples might include baked goat's cheese served with herb mousse or breast of wood pigeon in puff pastry served with a flap mushroom sauce. Desserts are equally imaginative and include such treats as poached rhubarb and custard tart flavored with orange and ginger, and sticky toffee pudding laced with a butterscotch sauce.

5 The Canalside. (C) **01604/863654**. Reservations recommended. Fixed-price lunch and dinner £18.50 ($30); dinner main courses £17–£34 ($27–$54). AE, MC, V. Tues–Fri and Sun 12:15–2pm; Tues–Sat 7:30–10pm.

2 Leicester

172km (107 miles) NW of London; 69km (43 miles) NE of Birmingham; 39km (24 miles) NE of Coventry; 42km (26 miles) S of Nottingham

Hang on to your hats, because this county town is definitely no Sleepy Hollow. Leicester, pronounced "*Les*-ter," one of the 10 largest cities in England, overflows with hustle and bustle and is by far the most cosmopolitan city in the East Midlands. This city of firsts—Beethoven's music was first performed here, the BBC's first local radio station was BBC Radio Leicester—thrives on the spirit of discovery and adventure. More recently, it gave birth to genetic fingerprinting.

Although it has some historic attractions, think of Leicester as a base for exploring the surrounding countryside. Its real lure with locals and tourists alike is its shopping, art scene, and nightlife.

ESSENTIALS

GETTING THERE   Trains depart from London's St. Pancras Station every 30 minutes throughout the day for Leicester, a trip of about 90 minutes. The fare is £38 ($61) each way on the day of your trip. For schedules and information, call ✆ **0870/48-49-50.**

About eight buses a day leave London's Victoria Coach Station for Leicester. They call at several secondary stops en route and take 2 hours and 45 minutes each way. The round-trip fare is £18.50 ($30) if you stay overnight but only £13.50 ($22) if you return the same day. For information, call ✆ **08705/808080.**

If you're driving from London, follow the M1 north to junction 21 toward Leicester. The drive takes 2 hours.

VISITOR INFORMATION   The main tourist information office is at 7–9 Every St., Town Hall Square (✆ **0906/2941113**). It's open Monday through Wednesday and Friday from 9am to 5:30pm, Thursday from 10am to 5:30pm, and Saturday from 9am to 5pm. They'll supply a useful map. Blue Badge guided walks can be booked by calling ✆ **01162/862252.**

SPECIAL EVENTS   The **Leicester Early Music Festival** (✆ **01162/709984**) takes place in May and June. Tickets for the whole series cost £20 to £25 ($32–$40). Also in June, the **Leicester International Music Festival** (✆ **01162/709984**) attracts some of the biggest names in classical music. Ticket prices vary, but average £5 to £15 ($8–$24).

EXPLORING THE TOWN

Leicester is worth a look if you have an afternoon to spare. In addition to the sights mentioned below, the town has a boating lake, riverside walks, and ornamental gardens.

An exciting wave of new shops has opened in Leicester. In addition to Victorian-style **Shires Shopping Centre,** with its designer and collectible stores, wide walkways, fountains, and sunny skylights, there's **St. Martins Square** in the city center, which has given new life to old restored buildings, with new retailers, cafes, and tea shops. A wealth of specialty shops—out a quarter mile on either side of the railway station—and several antiques stores line Oxford Street and Western Boulevard.

Venture out from the center of town to Belgrave Road and you'll discover the **"Golden Mile."** This neighborhood is home to the largest sari shop outside of India, and the store windows along Belgrave Road overflow with fine Indian silks, organzas, and cottons. Sari shops also generally carry a variety of accessories including bags, jewelry, shoes, and shawls.

Jewry Wall and Archeology Museum   Set near the excavation of an ancient Roman bath, this museum has nothing at all to do with Jewish history. Its name derives from a corruption of the Norman French "Jurad," which referred to the governing magistrates of an early medieval town, who used to gather in the shadow of this wall for their municipal decisions. More than 12m (40 ft.) high, the wall is higher than any other piece of ancient Roman architecture in Britain. Exhibits within the museum include a pair of ancient Roman mosaics, the Peacock Pavement and the Blackfriars Mosaic, which are the finest of their kind in the British Midlands. Each was laboriously sliced from the masonry of ancient villas within the district and set into new masonry beds here.

St. Nicholas Circle (about .5km/¼ mile from the town center, adjacent to the Holiday Inn). ✆ 01162/473021. Free admission. Daily dawn–dusk during summer. Winter Mon–Sat 10am–4pm, Sun 1–4pm.

Leicester Abbey   Set within a verdant public park that's favored by joggers and picnickers, a little over 1km (½ mile) north of Leicester's historic core, these evocative, poetically shattered remains are all that's left of the richest Augustinian monastery in England, built in 1132. In 1530, Cardinal Wolsey came here to die, demoralized and broken after his political and religious conflicts with Henry VIII. The abbey was torn down during the Reformation and stones were used in the construction of Cavendish House next door.

Abbey Park, Abbey Park Rd. ✆ 0116/2221000. Free admission. Daily dawn–dusk during summer. Winter daily 8am–4pm.

Leicester Guildhall   Built in stages between the 14th and 16th centuries, the city's most prominent public building was Leicester's first town hall and contains one of the oldest libraries in Britain. Plaques commemorate its role as a die-hard last bastion of the Parliamentarians during the Civil War. On its ground floor, you'll see a 19th-century police station with a pair of original prison cells, whose mournful effigies afford a powerful testimony to the horrors of the Victorian penal system. Shakespeare's troupe is said to have appeared here.

Guildhall Lane. ✆ 01162/532569. Free admission. Winter Mon–Sat 10am–4pm; Sun 1–4pm; Summer Mon–Sat 10am–5pm, Sun 1–5pm.

Leicestershire Museum and Art Gallery   This multipurpose museum has two distinct features. The street level contains exhibits of archaeology and natural history: a dinosaur bone found in a field near Leicester; a collection of Egyptian mummies and artifacts brought back to the Midlands by Thomas Cook, the 19th-century travel mogul; and geological exhibits. One floor above street level is a collection of paintings by British and European artists (including some by Gainsborough) from the 18th through 20th centuries. The collection of early-20th-century canvasses by German expressionists is one of the largest in Europe.

53 New Walk. ✆ 01162/554100. Free admission but donations accepted. Oct–Mar Mon–Sat 10am–4pm, Sun 1–4pm; Apr–Sept Mon–Sat 10am–5pm, Sun 1–5pm. Closed Dec 24–26 and Jan 1.

St. Martin's Cathedral   It may not have the soaring grandeur of the cathedrals of York or Lincoln, but this is the most venerated and historic church in Leicester. In 1086, it was one of the region's parish churches, and it was enlarged during the 1300s and the 1500s. In 1927, it was designated as the cathedral of Leicester, a nomenclature that adds considerably to its pomp and circumstance. The oak vaulting beneath the building's north porch is one of the most unusual treatments of its kind in England. For walking tours, contact the tourist office (see "Visitor Information," above).

1 St. Martin's E. ✆ 0116/2625294. Free admission. Daily 7:30am–4:30pm.

WHERE TO STAY

Red Cow Hotel Accommodations here are in a two-story, redbrick annex, built in the early 1990s to enlarge one of the region's most famous pubs (see "Where to Dine," below). The decor is functional; the nonsmoking rooms are reasonably sized with private bathrooms. There is one room available for those with limited mobility. Go for at least a drink or bar-side platter at the inn—it's as authentic and cozy as you're likely to find within the neighborhood.

Hinckley Rd., Leicester Forest East, Leicester, Leicestershire LE3 3PG. ℂ **0116/2387878.** Fax 0116/238-6539. 31 units. Sun–Thurs £49.95 ($80) single or double; Fri–Sat £39.95 ($64) single or double. AE, MC, V. **Amenities:** Restaurant; bar. *In room:* TV, dataport, coffeemaker, hair dryer, trouser press.

Scotia Hotel *(Value)* This Victorian building is imbued with ecclesiastic roots. It once belonged to the Church of England and was used to house clerics and others who came in town on church business. The hotel retains much of its original character and architectural features, including cupboards and fireplaces. The rooms vary in size (the larger ones are at the front) and have been redecorated, complete with freestanding wardrobes, to mesh with the house's Victorian flavor. One room is set aside for those with limited mobility.

10 Westcotes Dr., Leicester, Leicestershire LE3 0QR. ℂ and fax **0116/254-9200.** www.scotiahotel.com. 10 units, 4 with bathroom. £23 ($37) single without bathroom, £30 ($48) single with bathroom; £40 ($64) double without bathroom, £45 ($72) double with bathroom. Rates include English breakfast. AE, MC, V. **Amenities:** Breakfast room. *In room:* TV, coffeemaker, hair dryer (on request), iron (on request).

Spindle Lodge Hotel ✮ *(Value)* Constructed in 1876 on West Walk, a fabled Victorian promenade, this B&B lies on a tree-lined street in the center of a largely Dutch-style architectural sector. For more than two centuries, the area has been traffic free. The original Victorian features of the building have been respected, but modern comforts have been installed as well. Bedrooms are mid-size and attractively furnished, mainly with private, shower-only bathrooms. All the bedrooms are on the second and third floors (in England called 1st and 2nd floors), and there is no elevator. The second-floor rooms are all nonsmoking.

2 West Walk, Leicester, Leicestershire LE1 7NA. ℂ **0116/233-8801.** Fax 0116/233-8804. 13 units, 8 with bathroom. £30–£35 ($48–$56) single without bathroom, £42–£47.50 ($67–$76) single with bathroom; £50–£55 ($80–$88) double without bathroom, £60–£65 ($96–$104) double with bathroom; £70–£75 ($112–$120) family unit. MC, V. **Amenities:** Restaurant; bar. *In room:* TV, dataport, coffeemaker.

Stoneycroft Hotel This three-story hotel sits on a quiet residential street, a 15-minute walk from the city center of town. It started at the turn of the 20th century as two separate rooming establishments; these were later connected. The nonsmoking rooms vary in size from small to spacious and are similarly decorated with built-in furnishings. Six rooms are available for those with limited mobility. The restaurant, with a nonsmoking dining room, opens for dinner if there are enough guests.

5–7 Elmfield Ave., Leicester, Leicestershire LE2 1RB. ℂ **0116/270-7605.** Fax 0116/2706067. www.stoneycroft hotel.co.uk. 50 units. £42 ($67) single; £49 ($78) double. Rates include English breakfast. AE, DC, MC, V. **Amenities:** Restaurant; bar; lounge; game room. *In room:* TV, dataport, coffeemaker, hair dryer.

WHERE TO DINE

Friends Tandoori Restaurant INDIAN This spacious two-story restaurant lies along the famous Belgrave Road where you can also shop for a sari; it specializes in the Punjabi cuisine of northern India. Upstairs is a bar and lounge where smoking is allowed; you can relax, have a drink, and place your order here. Downstairs is the nonsmoking dining room and another bar. Plants and

Indian artwork sets the mood for your meal. Menu items can be seasoned according to taste and include offerings of chicken and lamb tikka, vegetable dishes, and a selection of prestigious curries and a wide range of vegetarian and meat starters to complement main courses.

41–43 Belgrave Rd. *C* **0116/266-8809**. Main courses £4–£12 ($6–$19). AE, MC, V. Mon–Sat noon–2pm and 6–11:30pm.

The Red Cow Pub and Restaurant ★ *Finds* ENGLISH   About 8km (5 miles) north of the city center, this historic inn prides itself on a 200-year-old tradition of providing food and drink to travelers and on being the only Leicestershire pub with a real thatched roof. Amid low ceilings, dark paneling, and antique accessories of brass and leather, order simple, wholesome platters in the bar (ploughman's lunches, fish and chips, shepherd's pie), or more substantial fare in the cozy restaurant. Menu items include various preparations of chicken, fish, beef, and vegetarian fare. The food is traditional English fare, and it comes in ample portions. Beers on tap include Carling, LaBatt's, and the Belgian staple lager Stella Artois.

Hinckley Rd., Leicester Forest East. *C* **0116/238-7878**. Reservations recommended for restaurant. Bar platters £4–£11.95 ($6–$19). Restaurant main courses £6–£12 ($10–$19). AE, MC, V. Mon–Sat 11am–11pm; Sun noon–10:30pm.

Rise of the Raj NORTH INDIAN   This restaurant occupies the first two floors of a three-story terrace house and serves northern Indian Punjabi dishes. The menu, same for lunch and dinner, offers chicken, prawns, and lamb served with sauces ranging from mild to hot. The most popular menu item is a *thali,* essentially a taste of just about everything accompanied by basmati rice and naan, a thin, warm, unleavened pitalike bread.

6 Evington Rd. *C* **0116/255-3885**. Main courses £5–£11.95 ($8–$19). AE, DC, MC, V. Tues–Sun 5:30pm–midnight.

LEICESTER AFTER DARK

Phoenix Arts Centre, Newarke Street (*C* **01162/554854**), hosts dance, music, and theatrical productions from around the world; local dancers, musicians, and actors also perform on its stage, and there's even an occasional film screening.

On weekends, the area around the **Clock Tower** in the center of town is alive with bustling crowds headed out to the clubs and bars on Church Gate, Silver Street, and High Street. **Creations,** 97 Church Gate (*C* **01162/629720**), is a popular club pumping out dance music until the wee hours. Open Thursday to Saturday and Monday and Tuesday only. Free before 10pm; after that the cover ranges from £5 to £6 ($8–$10).

As you may expect of a university town, Leicester has a variety of pubs, but the most favored by locals is the **Pump and Tap,** Duns Lane (*C* **01162/540324**). Stop by to sample ales by Leicestershire's two home brewers: Everards and Hoskins.

HISTORIC SIGHTS NEAR LEICESTER

Bosworth Battlefield Visitor Centre and Country Park   This site commemorates the 1485 battle that ended one of England's most important conflicts. The Battle of Bosworth ended the War of the Roses between the houses of York and Lancaster. When the fighting subsided, King Richard III, last of the Yorkists, lay dead, and Henry Tudor, a Welsh nobleman who had been banished to France to thwart his royal ambition, was proclaimed the victor. Henry thus became King Henry VII, and the Tudor dynasty was born.

Today, the appropriate standards fly where the opponents had their positions. You can see the whole scene by taking a 2km (1¼-mile) walk along the marked battle trails. In the center are exhibitions, models, book and gift shops, a cafeteria, and a theater where an audiovisual introduction with an excerpt from the Lord Laurence Olivier film version of Shakespeare's *Richard III* is presented.

29km (18 miles) southwest of Leicester between M1 and M6 (near the town of Nuneaton). *©* **01455/290429.** Admission £3 ($4.80) adults, £2 ($3.20) children under 16 and seniors, £8.50 ($14) family ticket. Visitor center Apr–Oct Mon–Sat 11am–5pm, Sun and bank holidays 11am–6pm; Nov–Dec and Mar Sun only 11am–5pm.

Ashby Castle   If you've read Sir Walter Scott's *Ivanhoe,* you will remember Ashby-de-la-Zouch, a town that retains a pleasant country atmosphere. The main attraction here is the ruined Norman manor house, Ashby Castle, where Mary Queen of Scots was imprisoned. The building was already an antique in 1464 when its thick walls were converted into a fortress.

Ashby-de-la-Zouch (29km/18 miles northwest of Leicester). *©* **01530/413343.** Admission £3.20 ($5) adults, £2.50 ($4) students and seniors, £1.60 ($2.55) children under 16. Apr–Oct daily 10am–6pm; off season Wed–Sun 10am–4pm.

Melbourne Hall   Originally built by the bishops of Carlisle in 1133, Melbourne Hall stands in one of the most famous formal gardens in Britain. The ecclesiastical structure was restored in the 1600s by one of the cabinet ministers of Charles I and enlarged by Queen Anne's vice chamberlain. It was the home of Lord Melbourne, who was prime minister when Victoria ascended to the throne. Lady Palmerston later inherited the house, which contains an important collection of antique furniture and artwork. A special feature is the beautifully restored wrought-iron pergola by Robert Bakewell, noted 18th-century ironsmith.

24km (15 miles) southwest of Leicester on A50, on Church Sq. *©* **01332/862502.** Admission to house and garden £5 ($8) adults, £4 ($6) students and seniors, £3 ($4.80) children 6–15, free for children 5 and under. House only £3 ($4.80) adults, £2.50 ($4) students and seniors, £1.50 ($2.40) children 5–15. Gardens only £3 ($4.80) adults, £2 ($3.20) students, children 5–15, and seniors. House open Aug only, Tues–Sun 2–5pm. Gardens Apr–Sept Wed, Sat–Sun, and bank holidays 1:30–5:30pm.

Belvoir Castle   On the northern border of Leicestershire overlooking the Vale of Belvoir (pronounced *Beaver*), Belvoir Castle has been the seat of the dukes of Rutland since the time of Henry VII. Rebuilt by Wyatt in 1816, the castle contains paintings by Holbein, Reynolds, and Gainsborough, as well as tapestries in its magnificent staterooms. The castle was the location for the movies *Little Lord Fauntleroy* and *Young Sherlock Holmes.* In summer, it's the site of medieval jousting tournaments.

11km (7 miles) southwest of Grantham, between A607 to Melton Mowbray and A52 to Nottingham. *©* **01476/870262.** Admission £7.25 ($12) adults, £6.75 ($11) students and seniors, £4.50 ($7) children 5–16, £19 ($30) family ticket (2 adults, 2 children). May–Sept daily 11am–5pm; Oct only Sun 11am–5pm.

3 Derbyshire & Peak District National Park

The most magnificent scenery in the Midlands is found in Derbyshire, between Nottinghamshire and Staffordshire. Some travelers avoid this part of the country because it's ringed by the industrial sprawl of Manchester, Leeds, Sheffield, and Derby. But missing this area is a pity, for Derbyshire has actually been less defaced by industry than its neighbors.

The north of the county, containing the Peak District National Park, contains waterfalls, hills, moors, green valleys, and dales. In the south, the land is more level and you'll find pastoral meadows. Dovedale, Chee Dale, and Millers Dale are worth a detour.

EXPLORING PEAK DISTRICT NATIONAL PARK ★★

Peak District National Park covers some 1404 sq. km (542 sq. miles), most of it in Derbyshire, with some spilling over into South Yorkshire and Staffordshire. It stretches from Holmfirth in the north to Ashbourne in the south, and from Sheffield in the east to Macclesfield in the west. The best central place to stay overnight is Buxton (see below).

The peak in the name is a bit misleading, because there is no actual peak—the highest point is just 630m (2,100 ft.). The park has some 4,000 walking trails that cover some of the most beautiful hill country in England.

The southern portion of the park, called **White Peak,** is filled with limestone hills, tiny villages, old stone walls, and hidden valleys. August and September are the best and most beautiful times to hike these rolling hills.

In the north, called **Dark Peak,** the scenery changes to rugged moors and deep gullies. This area is best visited in the spring when the purple heather, so beloved by Emily Brontë, comes into bloom.

Many come to the park not for its natural beauty but for the **"well dressings."** A unique park tradition held between May and August, this festival with pagan origins is best viewed in the villages of Eyam, Youlgrave, Monyash, and Worksworth, which lie within the park's parameters. Local tourist offices will supply details. The dressings began as pagan offerings to local "water spirits," but later became part of Christian ceremonies. Dressings of the wells take place from early May to August of every year. Designs are pricked on large boards covered in clay. The board is then decorated with grasses, lichens, bark, seeds, and flowers and placed by the spring or well and blessed.

If you're planning an extensive visit to the park, write for details to the **Peak Park Joint Planning Board,** National Park Office, Aldern House, Bakewell, Derbyshire DE45 1AE (✆ **01629/816200**). A list of publications will be sent to you, and you can order according to your wishes.

GETTING TO THE PARK   You can reach Buxton (see below) by train from Manchester. It's also possible to travel by bus, the Transpeak, which takes 3½ hours from Manchester to Nottingham, with stops at such major centers as Buxton, Bakewell, Matlock, and Matlock Bath. If you're planning to use public transportation, consider the **Derbyshire Wayfarer,** sold at various rail and bus stations; for £7.25 ($12) for adults or £3.65 ($6) for students and children, you can ride all the bus and rail lines within the peak district for a day.

If you're driving, the main route is the A515 north from Birmingham, with Buxton as the gateway. From Manchester, Route 6 heads southeast to Buxton.

GETTING AROUND THE PARK   Many visitors prefer to walk from one village to another. If you're not so hearty, you can take local buses, which connect various villages. Instead of the usual Sunday slowdown in bus service, more buses run on that day than on weekdays because of increased demand, especially in summer. Call ✆ **01298/23098** between 7am and 8pm for bus information.

Another popular way to explore the park is by bicycle. Park authorities operate six **Cycle Hire Centres,** renting bikes for £12.50 ($20) a day for adults and £7.50 ($12) for children 15 and under, with a £25 ($40) deposit, helmet included. Centers are at Mapleton Lane in Ashbourne (✆ **01335/343156**); near the Fairholmes Information Centre at Derwent (✆ **01433/651261**); near New Mills on Station Road in the Sett Valley at Hayfield (✆ **01663/746222**); near Matlock on the High Peak Trail at Middleton Top (✆ **01629/823204**); at the junction of Tissington and High Peak Trails at Parsley Hay (✆ **01298/84493**); and between

Ashbourne and Leek on the A523 near the southern tip of the Manifold Trail at Waterhouses (© **01538/308609**).

BUXTON: A LOVELY BASE FOR EXPLORING THE PARK

277km (172 miles) NW of London; 61km (38 miles) NW of Derby; 40km (25 miles) SE of Manchester

One of the loveliest towns in Britain, Buxton rivaled the spa at Bath in the 18th century. Its waters were known to the Romans, whose settlement here was called *Aquae Arnemetiae*. The thermal waters were pretty much forgotten from Roman times until the reign of Queen Elizabeth I, when the baths were reactivated. Mary Queen of Scots took the waters here, brought by her caretaker, the Earl of Shrewsbury.

Buxton today is mostly the result of 18th-century development directed by the duke of Devonshire. Its spa days have come and gone, but it's still the best center for exploring the peak district. The climate is amazingly mild, considering that at 300m (1,000 ft.) altitude, Buxton is the second-highest town in England.

ESSENTIALS

GETTING THERE   Trains depart from Manchester (see chapter 16) at least every hour during the day. It's a 50-minute trip.

About half a dozen buses also run between Manchester and Sheffield, stopping in Buxton en route, after a 70-minute ride.

To arrive by car, take the A6 from Manchester, heading southeast into Buxton.

VISITOR INFORMATION   The **Tourist Office** is at The Crescent (© **01298/ 25106**) and is open between March and October daily from 9:30am to 5pm; off season daily from 10am to 4pm. For 50p (80¢), the tourist office will sell you a pamphlet entitled "Buxton Town Trail," that provides a map and detailed instructions for a walking tour, lasting between 75 and 90 minutes, from the town center. It will also sell you for 60p (95¢) a pamphlet entitled "Eight Walks around Buxton," outlining pedestrian rambles in the outlying region that require from 90 minutes to 4 hours to complete.

SPECIAL EVENTS   The town hosts a well-known **opera festival** during a 2½-week period in July, followed by a 2½-week **Gilbert and Sullivan festival.** The tourist office can supply details.

SEEING THE SIGHTS

Water from the thermal wells is available for spa treatment only in the hydrotherapy pool at the 23-acre **Pavilion Gardens** (which are open at all times; admission is free). You can purchase a drink of spa waters at the tourist information center or help yourself at the public fountain across the street.

Another sight, **Poole's Cavern,** Buxton Country Park, Green Lane (© **01298/ 26978**), is a cave that was inhabited by Stone Age people, who may have been the first to marvel at the natural vaulted roof bedecked with stalactites. Explorers can walk through the spacious galleries, viewing the incredible horizontal cave, which is electrically lighted. It is open daily March through October from 10am to 5pm. Admission is £5.40 ($9) for adults, £4.40 ($7) for seniors, £3 ($4.80) for children 5 to 16, and free for kids 4 and under. A family ticket costs £14 ($22).

Set about 2km (1¼ miles) south of Buxton's town center is one of the oddest pieces of public Victorian architecture in the Midlands, **Solomon's Temple,** whose circular design may remind you of a straight castellated Tower of Pisa as interpreted by the neo-Gothic designers of Victorian England. Conceived as a folly in 1895 and donated to the city by a prominent building contractor, Solomon

Mycock, it sits atop a tumulus (burial mound) from Neolithic times. Climb a small spiral staircase inside the temple for impressive views over Buxton and the surrounding countryside. It's open all the time, day and night; admission is free.

WHERE TO STAY

Buxton Wheelhouse Hotel   This family-run establishment is in a quiet area a short 8-minute walk from the center of town. A Victorian house needn't be drab and tattered, as proved by this recently renovated, turn-of-the-century B&B. Upon entering this nonsmoking hotel, guests can't help but notice the big, bright sun lounge with its soft couches. Large, airy guest rooms have modern comfortable furnishings including sofas, tables and desks, plus private, shower-and-tub bathrooms. Guests breakfast in the dining room, which has a small bar area.

19 College Rd., Buxton, Derbyshire SK17 9DZ. *C* and fax **01298/24869**. www.buxton-wheelhouse.co.uk. 9 units. £40–£56 ($64–$90) single; £64–£74 ($102–$118) double. Rates include English breakfast. MC, V. **Amenities:** Dining room; bar; lounge. *In room:* TV, coffeemaker, hair dryer.

The Grosvenor House ★   This rather grandiose Victorian house sits on a quiet street in town, a stone's throw from the Pavilion Gardens and the Opera House. Built of stone with a gray slate roof in the 1850s, it has an elegant interior and atmosphere often described by guests as being "home away from home"—a lovely place that is too formal. The exclusively nonsmoking guestrooms range in size from small standard rooms (with shower) to spacious deluxe rooms (with bathroom) and all have period antique furniture. The deluxe rooms have more antiques and the best views of the gardens and the River Wye. Public areas include an inviting lounge with bar and a dining room where guests breakfast and eat an optional three-course dinner (pre-opera dinners have become a tradition). An adjacent coffee shop, Cornerways, open May to late summer Tuesday to Sunday and all year on weekends and bank holidays, serves all comers.

1 Broad Walk, Buxton, Derbyshire SK17 6JE. *C* and fax **01298/72439**. www.grosvenorbuxton.co.uk. 8 units. £45–£50 ($72–$80) single; £50–£75 ($80–$120) double. Rates include breakfast. AE, MC, V. **Amenities:** Dining room; lounge. *In room:* TV, coffeemaker.

Lakenham   A 5-minute walk from the center of town leads you to a quiet, residential area of large stately houses where you'll find this B&B. This fine Edwardian house lies in nearly an acre of lavish lawns and gardens. The entire house is appointed with Victorian antiques. The guestrooms vary in size from average to large, have hospitality trays, and offer views of the gardens. Five rooms contain a private, shower-only bathroom and one room has a shower-and-tub combination bathroom. There is a dining room with private tables where guests can take breakfast.

11 Burlington Rd., Buxton, Derbyshire SK17 9AL. *C* **01298/79209**. www.lakenhambuxton.co.uk. 6 units. £65 ($104) single or double. Rates include English breakfast. No credit cards. **Amenities:** Dining room. *In room:* TV, minibar, fridge, coffeemaker.

An Inexpensive Place to Stay: Camping Barns

Hikers and bikers won't find cheaper accommodations than the region's 11 National Park–operated camping barns, which provide a rudimentary raised sleeping platform, water faucet, and toilet for £9 to £13 ($14–$21) a night per person. Advance booking and payment is mandatory. Contact **Conway Youth Hostel**, Larkhill, Sychnant Pass Rd., Conway LL328AJ (*C* **0870/77061113**), to make reservations or obtain further information.

WHERE TO DINE

The George BRITISH   In a town not known for its cuisine, this pub is a good bet. Situated in a building even older than the Royal Crescent, it serves the least expensive food in Buxton. Bar snacks, sandwiches, and a ploughman's lunch are available throughout the day. The clientele is a mixture of visitors and locals.

The Square. ✆ **01298/24711.** £6.50–£12.50 ($10–$20). V. Daily 10am–9pm.

Hydro Café Tea Rooms BRITISH   These are typically English tearooms, serving visitors for years. Walls are decorated with pictures depicting the development of the town tied to the harnessing of waterpower. All the food is homemade and prepared fresh daily; portions are generous and prices among the most reasonable in town. There is a wide selection of well-stuffed sandwiches and a good steak-and-kidney pie daily. Locals often make an entire meal out of baked potatoes covered with various toppings. In addition, freshly made salads, quiches, pastas, and vegetarian dishes are featured.

75 Spring Gardens. ✆ **01298/79065.** Main courses £4–£7 ($6–$11). No credit cards. Mon–Sat 9:30am–5pm; Sun 10:30am–4:30pm.

ASHBOURNE: HISTORIC MARKET TOWN

235km (146 miles) NW of London; 77km (48 miles) SE of Manchester; 53km (33 miles) NW of Nottingham

Another center for exploring the Peak District, this historic market town has a 13th-century church, a 16th-century grammar school, ancient almshouses, a population that doesn't exceed 5,000, and no fewer than 13 pubs, more than virtually any town its size in the district. The River Dove, which runs nearby, is known for outstanding trout fishing.

ESSENTIALS

GETTING THERE   There's no train service to Ashbourne; the rail lines that used to run into the village have been reconfigured into a walking trail.

The bus connecting Manchester with Derby stops in Ashbourne en route. It runs once a day, and takes about 1¼ hours.

From Nottingham, you can take the train to Derby, then transfer to the Trent bus no. 440, which takes about an hour and runs once a day, Monday through Saturday. For more bus information in and around Ashbourne call ✆ **0870/ 608-2608.**

If you're driving from London, take the M1 motorway north, getting off at Junction 24. Continue east along the A50 for the next 16km (10 miles), turning onto the A515 north into Ashbourne. From Manchester, take the A6 south as far as Buxton, continuing south along the A515 into Ashbourne.

VISITOR INFORMATION   The town's **Information Centre,** 13 Market Place (✆ **01335/343666**), is open from early March to June and from September to October, Monday through Saturday from 9:30am to 5pm; July and August daily from 9:30am to 5pm; off season Monday through Saturday from 10am to 4pm.

WHERE TO STAY

Greenman Royal Hotel   Originally a 17th-century coaching inn, this hotel is ideally located in the town center, close to shops, cafes, and restaurants. Its unusual sign actually crosses over the road and has become somewhat of a local landmark. This establishment's owners have completely renovated the place and added nine new guest rooms. The rooms vary in size from small to quite large, but are smartly decorated with freestanding furniture and private, shower-only bathrooms. Guests can enjoy two bars and a lounge; the larger, oak-paneled bar with two fireplaces, the Boswell, serves breakfast.

St. John's St., Ashbourne, Derbyshire DE6 1GH. ℂ 01335/345783. Fax 01335/346613. 18 units. £40 ($64) single; £60 ($96) double; £85 ($136) suite. Rates include English breakfast. AE, DC, MC, V. **Amenities:** Restaurant; 2 bars; lounge. *In room:* TV, dataport, coffeemaker.

Omnia Somnia ✦ This first-class bed-and-breakfast, built in the 19th century as a coach house and then converted into a school and private home, is set in the town center but nestles quietly in the seclusion of trees planted when it was built. It has been fully renovated to its former glory. The hotel walls are decorated with William Morris wallpaper. The nonsmoking bedrooms in the former stables are decorated with authentic Victorian furniture and fittings. All are quite large and have private bathrooms. Each has its own distinctive character: One is wood-paneled with a four-poster bed, another has a double bathroom, and the third is a duplex with a sitting room on one floor and its own stairs leading up to the bedroom. All of the hotel's rooms provide access for those with limited mobility.

The Firs, Ashbourne, Derbyshire DE6 1HF. ℂ 01335/300145. Fax 01335/300958. 3 units. £50 ($75) single; £70 ($105) double. Rates include English breakfast. MC, V. **Amenities:** Dining room; bar; nearby golf course. *In room:* TV, coffeemaker, hair dryer.

Super-Cheap Sleeps: A Youth Hostel

Ilam Hall Youth Hostel A fine and stately Gothic English mansion, set in the middle of an estate of green lawns, gardens, and thick forest, is now one of England's most extraordinary hostels. Paths behind the house lead down to the Dove, and an old church and stables share the property. The interior with its dark wood, massive pieces of art, and wallpaper still looks and feels part of a private home. The rooms range in size from two to nine beds; most of the larger rooms are in the Brewhouse Wing, with private bathrooms. Public areas include a classroom and game room. During the British academic year the hotel caters to school or university groups on weekdays and is open to the general public on weekends.

Ilam, Ashbourne, Derbyshire DE6 2AZ. ℂ 01335/350212. Fax 01335/350350. www.yha.org.uk. 23 units, 135 beds. £8.25–£18.75 ($13–$30) per person; £45.50–£63 ($73–$101) 4–6 bed family unit. Rates include breakfast. MC, V. **Amenities:** Dining room; game room. *In room:* No phone.

WHERE TO DINE

For the best pot of tea around, try **The Old Post Office Tea Room,** Alstonefield, near Ashbourne (ℂ **01335/310201**). Ernie and Jean Allen, owners and tea aficionados, offer a set tea menu and prepare an assortment of goodies such as baked quiche, soup, and cold roasted meats—all perfect for a light lunch.

Ashbourne Gingerbread Shop ENGLISH This nearly 200-year-old bakery can be found in a 400-year-old building that began as the Roebuck Inn. Before walking into this delightful shop, prepare yourself for the sweet, spicy aroma of freshly baked gingerbread. You can buy a burger or sandwich here, but this place is famous for its gingerbread. It comes in all shapes and sizes, including men, boys, animals, slab cakes, and buns; they also sell Thornton's chocolates.

26 St. John St. ℂ 01335/346753. Snack meals £1.75–£5.25 ($2.80–$8). No credit cards. Year-round Mon–Wed 8:30am–5pm; Thurs–Fri 8:30am–5:30pm; Sat 8:30am–5pm.

The Horns Inn ENGLISH This bustling, cozy restaurant opens its doors in the warm summer weather and fills the sidewalk with tables and chairs to meet the demand from its constant flow of patrons. The simple food is good at this mainly lunchtime gathering place. The menu offers a standard fare of soup, homemade pies like steak-and-kidney or chicken-and-mushroom, burgers, and a few specials.

13–15 Victoria Sq. ⓒ **01335/300737.** Lunch £4.95 ($8); main courses £6.95–£9.95 ($11–$16). MC, V. Mon–Fri 10am–11pm; Sat–Sun 10am–10:30pm. Food served Mon–Fri 10am–4:30pm; Sat–Sun 10am–4:30pm. Dinner in summer Mon–Fri 5:30–8:30pm.

Smiths Tavern *Value* ENGLISH   A series of three rooms in a tall, narrow stone building make up this "proper old-fashioned pub," as proudly described by owner Paul Mellor. Supported by antique wood beams adorned with an assortment of pots and horse brasses, the middle room, which gives way to the dining room, dates back to 1300. Guests sit on well-aged settles and timeworn chairs at plain, sturdy tables. Snacks, homemade hot dishes, and desserts make up the menu. Main courses include steak-and-kidney pie, fresh fish, steak, and sides of fresh vegetables. Children are welcome in the dining room if they are with their parents.

36 St. John's St. ⓒ **01335/342264.** Main courses £4.95–£9.95 ($8–$16). MC, V. Mon–Sat 11am–11pm; Sun noon–10:30pm. Meals and snacks daily noon–3pm and 6–9:30pm.

BAKEWELL
256km (160 miles) NW of London; 42km (26 miles) N of Derby; 59km (37 miles) SE of Manchester; 53km (33 miles) NW of Nottingham

Lying 19km (12 miles) southeast of Buxton, Bakewell is yet another possible base for exploring the southern Peak District, especially the beautiful valleys of Ashwood Dale, Monsal Dale, and Wyedale. On the River Wey, Bakewell is just a market town, but its old houses constructed from gray-brown stone and its narrow streets give it a picture-postcard look. Its most spectacular feature is a medieval bridge across the river with five graceful arches.

Still served in local tearooms is the famous Bakewell Pudding, which was supposedly created by accident. One day, a chef didn't put the proper proportions of ingredients into her almond sponge-cake batter, and it remained gelatinous and runny. Served apologetically, as a mistake, everyone said it was wonderful, and the tradition has remained ever since. The pudding, made as it is with a rich puff pastry that lies at the bottom of the pudding, and covered with a layer first of jam and then the gelatinous version of the almond sponge cake, is richer than the tarts, and relatively difficult to find outside of Bakewell.

The best time to be here is on Monday, **market day,** when local farmers come in to sell their produce. Entrepreneurs from throughout the Midlands also set up flea market stands in the town's main square, The Market Place. Sales are conducted from 8:30am until 5:30pm in winter and until 7:30pm in summer.

ESSENTIALS
GETTING THERE   To reach Bakewell from Derby, take the A6 north to Matlock, passing by the town and continuing on the A6 north toward Rowsley. Just past Rowsley, you'll come to a bridge. Follow the signpost across the bridge into Bakewell.

From London, take the M1 motorway north to Junction 28. Then follow the A38 for 5km (3 miles), connecting with the A615 signposted to Matlock. Once you're at Matlock, follow the A6 into Bakewell.

VISITOR INFORMATION   The **Bakewell Information Centre,** Old Market Hall, Bridge Street (ⓒ **01629/813227**), is open from Easter to October daily from 9am to 5:30pm; from November to Easter daily from 10am to 5pm.

WHERE TO STAY
The **Castle Inn** (see below) also rents rooms.

Tannery House   Hidden in the very center of Bakewell, this hotel is just off the main shopping street, through an arch and down an alley; it is constructed with local stone and is surrounded by a large, attractive garden. Somewhat architecturally hybrid, its origins lie in the 18th century but it has been constantly added on to ever since; the latest addition is the hotel wing (1994). The modern handmade furniture is comfortable. The good-size nonsmoking bedrooms have French doors opening onto the garden. Two of the rooms have double beds and the other has twin beds, but all contain private, shower-and-tub bathrooms. One room on the ground floor is available for those with limited mobility.

Matlock St., Bakewell, Derbyshire DE45 1EE. (C) **01629/815011.** Fax 01629/815327. www.tanneryhouse.co.uk. 3 units. £34–£36 ($54–$58) single; £54 ($86) smaller double for first 2 nights, £48 ($77) thereafter; £58 ($93) large double for first 2 nights, £54 ($86) thereafter. Rates include full English breakfast. No credit cards. **Amenities:** Breakfast room; outdoor heated pool; nearby golf course and fitness center. *In room:* TV, coffeemaker, hair dryer.

Worth a Splurge

The Ashford Arms Hotel & Restaurant ★★   This stone-and-timber building dates from the 1780s; it served as a coaching inn where coach horses, hot and exhausted from a full-day's ride, were exchanged for fresh steeds. It is now a very public place, with a pub and restaurant on the ground floor open to all. The hotel's interior is graced with old beams and two huge stone fireplaces. The upstairs guest rooms (all nonsmoking) range in size from small to large and are furnished with a variety of pieces including four-poster beds. Each comes with a private shower bathroom. The pub serves bar snacks and meals at lunch. There are restaurant meals in the conservatory after 6pm.

Church St., Ashford-in-the-Water, Derbyshire DE45 1QI. (C) **01629/812725.** Fax 01629/814749. 8 units. £55–£75 ($88–$120). Single; £65–£85 ($104–$136) double. Rates include English breakfast. AE, MC, V. **Amenities:** Restaurant; bar. *In room:* TV, dataport, coffeemaker.

WHERE TO DINE

For a look at a working 19th-century flour mill, stop in at **Caudwell's Mill,** Bakewell Road ((C) **01629/734374**). Here, you can have afternoon tea with freshly baked cakes, breads, and pastries made right here at the mill, and then stroll through a variety of shops, including a handcrafted furniture store, glass blowing studio, jewelry shop, and art gallery.

Carriage House Restaurant ENGLISH   If you visit Chatsworth (see "Historic Homes Near Bakewell," below), eat at this restaurant. And if you eat at this restaurant, visit Chatsworth. Located at the top of a hill about 91m (300 ft.) from Chatsworth, the restaurant is indeed a converted 17th-century carriage house, and is quite grand. This self-service buffet is an elegant one; the 16-item lunch changes daily depending on the market. Typical main courses include poached salmon, meat-and-potato pie, and charcoal-grilled chicken. Fresh vegetables and salads plus a nice selection of fluffy desserts and rich cakes round out the buffet.

Chatsworth, near Bakewell. (C) **01246/565377.** Lunch £3.25–£12.50 ($5–$20). MC V. Mid-Mar to Oct daily 10:15am–5pm.

Castle Inn ENGLISH   This ivy-covered stone building is ideally located in the town center on the banks of the Wye and has been a pub for 400 years. The interior is dark with lots of wood and beams along with two huge open fireplaces. The lunch and dinner menus are the same; food ranges from bar snacks to hot and hearty meals, including chicken curry, prawn and cod bake, Yorkshire pudding, and meat-and-potato pie. Daily specials are also posted. Ales on draft are Boddingtons, Castle Eden, Murphy's, and Stella.

A newer feature of the Castle Inn is its four clean, bright double rooms, about 5 years old. They are of modest size and furnishings and include bathroom, TV, and coffeemaker. Rooms are £50 ($80) per room.

Bridge St., Bakewell. ℂ **01629/812103.** Main courses £5.25–£10 ($8–$16). MC, V. Mon–Sat noon–2pm and 6–8pm; Sun noon–3pm.

Renaissance Restaurant ★★ CLASSIC ENGLISH/FRENCH Top-quality cuisine is served in this tastefully converted barn that is a special delight in summer with its walled garden. Chef Eric Piedaniel firmly believes in working with fresh ingredients and taking no short cuts in the kitchen. Fixed-price menus are a feature, and they're cheaper and better value mid-week (see below). Launch your repast with a crayfish salad or a casserole of asparagus and artichokes. Main courses often feature superb venison and such delights as pan-fried filet of sea bass. The lamb shank, braised to tender perfection and flavor in wine, is also a dish worth the trek across town. Desserts are a special highlight, especially the chocolate caramelized cake in a smooth white-chocolate sauce.

Bath St. ℂ **01629/812687.** Reservations required. Tues–Thurs 3-course fixed-price lunch or dinner £14.95 ($24). Otherwise £23.95 ($38) 3-course set menu. MC, V. Tues–Sun noon–1:30pm; Tues–Sat 7–9:30pm. Closed 1st 2 weeks Aug and Dec 25 to 3rd week Jan.

HISTORIC HOMES NEAR BAKEWELL

The tourist office in Bakewell (see above) will provide you with a map outlining the best routes to take to reach each of the attractions below.

Chatsworth ★★★ Here stands one of the great country houses of England, the home of the 11th duke of Devonshire and his duchess, the former Deborah Mitford. With its lavishly decorated interior and a wealth of art treasures, it has 175 rooms, the most spectacular of which are open to the public.

Dating from 1686, the present building stands on a spot where the eccentric Bess of Hardwick built the house in which Mary Queen of Scots was held prisoner upon orders of Queen Elizabeth I. Capability Brown (who seems to have been everywhere) worked on the landscaping of the present house. But it was Joseph Paxton, the gardener to the sixth duke, who turned the garden into one of the most celebrated in Europe. Queen Victoria and Prince Albert were lavishly entertained here in 1843. The house contains a great library and such paintings as the *Adoration of the Magi* by Veronese and *King Uzziah* by Rembrandt. On the grounds you can see spectacular fountains, and there is a playground for children in the farmyard.

6.5km (4 miles) east of Bakewell, beside the A6 (16km/10 miles north of Matlock). ℂ **01246/582204.** Admission £8.50 ($14) adults, £6.50 ($10) students and seniors, £3 ($4.80) children 4–15, free for children 3 and under. Mar 21–Oct 28 daily 11am–4:30pm.

Hardwick Hall Hardwick Hall was built in 1597 for Bess of Hardwick, a woman who acquired an estate from each of her four husbands. It is noted for its "more glass than wall" architecture. The high great chamber and long gallery crown an unparalleled series of late-16th-century interiors, including an important collection of tapestries, needlework, and furniture. The house is surrounded by a 120-hectare (300-acre) park featuring walled gardens, orchards, and an herb garden.

Doe Lea, 15km (9½ miles) east of Chesterfield. ℂ **01246/850430.** Admission £6.40 ($10) adults, £3.20 ($5) children, £16 ($26) family ticket. House Mar–Oct Wed–Sun 12:30–5pm. Grounds open daily year-round; gardens open April–Oct Wed–Sun 11am–5:30pm. Take junction 29 from M1.

MORE ATTRACTIONS AROUND THE REGION

Crich Tramway Village   The Crich Tramway Village is a paradise of vintage trams—electric, steam, and horse-drawn—from England and overseas, including New York. Your admission ticket allows you unlimited rides on the trams, which make the 3km (2-mile) round-trip to Glory Mine with scenic views over the Derwent Valley via Wakeridge, where a stop is made to visit the Peak District Mines Historical Society display of lead mining. It also includes admission to various tramway exhibitions.

At Crich, near Matlock. ℭ **01773/852565.** Admission £7 ($11) adults, £6 ($10) seniors, £3.50 ($6) children 5–15, £19 ($30) family ticket (2 adults, 3 children). Apr–Oct daily 10am–5:30pm; Nov–Mar daily 10:30am–4pm (except for Nov 4–Dec 22 when it's only open Sat–Mon 10:30am–4pm).

Peak District Mining Museum   This museum traces 2,000 years of Derbyshire lead mining. Its centerpiece is a giant water-pressure engine that used to pump water from a lead mine 108m (360 ft.) underground in the early 19th century. You can crawl through a simulated mine tunnel and climbing shaft.

At the Pavilion, Matlock Bath. ℭ **01629/583834.** Admission £2.75 ($4.40) adults, £1.75 ($2.80) seniors and children 5–15, £7 ($11) family ticket. Apr–Oct daily 10am–5pm; off season daily 11am–3pm.

The Royal Crown Derby Visitor Centre   This is the only pottery factory allowed to use both the words *royal* and *crown* in its name, a double honor granted by George III and Queen Victoria. At the end of a 90-minute tour, you can treat yourself to a bargain in the gift shop and visit the Royal Crown Derby Museum.

194 Osmaston Rd., Derby. ℭ **01332/7128000.** Tours £4.95 ($8) adult, £4.75 ($8) seniors and children; museum £2.95 ($4.70) adults, £2.75 ($4.40) seniors and children. Tours Mon–Fri 10, 11am, 1:15, and 2:15pm; visitor center and museum Mon–Sat 10am–4pm, Sun 10am–4pm.

4 Nottinghamshire: Robin Hood Country

"Notts," as Nottinghamshire is known, lies in the heart of the East Midlands. Its towns are rich in folklore or have bustling markets. Many famous people have come from Nottingham, notably those 13th-century outlaws from Sherwood Forest, Robin Hood and his Merry Men. It also was home to the romantic poet Lord Byron; you can visit his ancestral home at Newstead Abbey. D. H. Lawrence, author of *Sons and Lovers* and *Lady Chatterley's Lover,* was born in a tiny miner's cottage in Eastwood, which he later immortalized in his writings.

NOTTINGHAM

195km (121 miles) N of London; 116km (72 miles) SE of Manchester

Although it's an industrial center, Nottingham is still a good base for exploring Sherwood Forest and the rest of the shire. Nottingham is known to literary buffs for its association with author D. H. Lawrence and its medieval sheriff, who played an important role in the Robin Hood story.

It was an important pre-Norman settlement guarding the River Trent, the gateway to the north of England. Followers of William the Conqueror arrived in 1068 to erect a fort here. In a later reincarnation, the fort saw supporters of Prince John surrender to Richard the Lionheart in 1194. Many other exploits occurred here—notably Edward III's capture of Roger Mortimer and Queen Isabella, the assassins of Edward II. From Nottingham, Richard III marched out with his men to face defeat and his own death at Bosworth Field in 1485.

With the arrival of the spinning jenny in 1768, Nottingham was launched into the forefront of the Industrial Revolution. It's still a center of industry and home base to many well-known British firms, turning out such products as John Player cigarettes, Boots pharmaceuticals, and Raleigh cycles.

Nottingham doesn't have many attractions, but it's a young and vital city, and very student-oriented. Its Hockley neighborhood is as hip as anything this side of Manchester or London. A look at one of the alternative newspapers or magazines freely distributed around town can connect you with the city's constantly changing nightlife scene.

ESSENTIALS

GETTING THERE The best rail connection is via Lincoln, from which 28 trains arrive Monday through Saturday and about eight trains on Sunday. The trip takes about 45 minutes. Trains also leave from London's St. Pancras Station; the trip takes about 2½ hours. For information, call © **08457/48-49-50.**

Buses from London arrive at the rate of about seven per day. For schedules and information, call © **08705/808080.**

If you're driving from London, the M1 motorway runs to a few miles west of Nottingham. Feeder roads, including the A453, are well marked for the short distance into town. The drive takes about 3 to 3½ hours.

VISITOR INFORMATION Information is available at the **City Information Centre,** 1–4 Smithy Row (© 01159/155330). It's open Monday through Friday from 9am to 5:30pm and Saturday from 9am to 5pm.

SPECIAL EVENTS Nottingham still gets a lot of reflected glory from its association with Robin Hood and his gang. The **Robin Hood Festival** is a family-friendly, mock-medieval festival scheduled for the first week in August every year. Diversions include food and souvenir stands, jousting and falconry exhibitions, Maypole dances, crowd-pleasing jesters juggling their way through the throngs, and lots of medieval costume. For information, call © **01623/823202.**

EXPLORING THE AREA

Put on your most comfortable shoes and prepare to tackle the more than 800 shops in and around town—Nottingham boasts some of England's best shopping. Start in the city center, with its maze of pedestrian streets, and work your way out toward the two grand indoor shopping malls, the Victoria and the Broad Marsh, located to the north and to the south of the center of town. Then, head over to Derby Road for your fill of antiques.

Fine Nottingham lace can be found in the **Lace Centre,** Castle Road, across the street from Nottingham Castle (© 01159/413539), or in the shops around the area known as the **Lace Market** along High Pavement.

Then, to catch up on the hippest and latest in fashion and furnishing trends, explore the many boutiques in the Hockley area, the Exchange Arcade, and the Flying Horse Mall, all in the city center.

Patchings Farm Art Centre, Oxton Road, near Calverton (© 01159/653479), is a 24-hectare (60-acre) art haven. Restored farm buildings house three galleries, working art and pottery studios, a gift shop, and art and framing shops.

And long known as Britain's first real crafts center, **Longdale Craft Centre,** Longdale Lane, Ravenshead (© 01623/794858), is a labyrinth of re-created Victorian streets where professional craftspeople work on a whole range of craft items, including jewelry, pottery, and prints.

Nottingham Castle Museum and Art Gallery ★ Overlooking the city, Nottingham Castle was built in 1679 by the duke of Newcastle on the site of an old Norman fortress. After restoration in 1878, it was opened as a provincial museum surrounded by a charmingly arranged garden. Of particular interest is the History of Nottingham Gallery, re-creating the legends associated with the city, plus a rare collection of ceramics and a unique exhibition of medieval alabaster carvings, which were executed between 1350 and 1530. These delicately detailed scenes illustrate the life of Christ, the Virgin Mother, and various saints. Paintings cover several periods but are strong on 16th-century Italian, 17th-century French and Dutch, and the richest English paintings of the past 2 centuries.

The only surviving element of the original Norman castle is a subterranean passage called Mortimer's Hole. The passage leads to **Ye Olde Trip to Jerusalem,** 1 Brewhouse Yard at Castle Road (*C* **0115/9473171**), dating from 1189 and said to be the oldest inn in England. King Edward III is said to have led a band of noblemen through these secret passages, surprising Roger Mortimer and his queen, killing Mortimer and putting his lady in prison. A statue of Robin Hood stands at the base of the castle.

Castle Rd. *C* **01159/153700**. Admission Sat–Sun £2 ($3.20) adults, £1 ($1.60) children; free Mon–Fri. Mar–Oct daily 10am–5pm; Nov–Feb Sat–Thurs 10am–5pm.

Brewhouse Yard Museum   This museum consists of five 17th-century cottages at the foot of Castle Rock, presenting a panorama of Nottingham life in a series of furnished rooms and shops. Some of them, open from cellar to attic, display much local history, and visitors are encouraged to handle the exhibits. The most interesting features are in a series of cellars cut into the rock of the castle instead of below the houses, plus an exhibition of a Nottingham shopping street from around 1919 to 1939. This is not a typical folk museum, but attempts to be as lively as possible, involving both visitors and the Nottingham community in expanding displays and altering exhibitions on a bimonthly basis.

Brewhouse Yard, Castle Blvd. *C* **01159/153640**. Admission Sat–Sun and bank holidays £1.50 ($2.40) adults, 80p ($1.30) children, £3.80 ($6) family ticket; free Mon–Fri. Daily 10am–4pm. Closed Christmas Day, Boxing Day (Dec 26), and New Year's Day.

Museum of Costume & Textiles   This is one of the half dozen or so best collections of period costumes in Britain, with exhibitions ranging from the 17th century to the Carnaby Street era of the 1960s. Many garments date from the 1700s, and include exhibitions of *"fallals and fripperies"* (gewgaws and accessories as designated by the disapproving Puritans), as well as lace, weavings, and embroideries, each of them a celebration of the textile industry that dominated part of Nottingham's economy for many generations. Look for the Eyre Map Tapestries, woven in 1632 and depicting the geography of the region.

51 Castle Gate. *C* **01159/153500**. Free admission. Wed–Sun and bank holidays Mon 10am–4pm.

HISTORIC HOMES NEAR NOTTINGHAM

Newstead Abbey *⭑*   Lord Byron once made his home at Newstead Abbey, one of eight museums administered by the city of Nottingham. Some of the original Augustinian priory, purchased by Sir John Byron in 1540, still survives. In the 19th century, the mansion was given a neo-Gothic restoration. Mementos, including first editions and manuscripts, are displayed inside. You can explore the 120-hectare (300-acre) parkland, which contains waterfalls, rose gardens, and a Japanese water garden.

On A60 (Mansfield Rd.), 19km (12 miles) north of Nottingham center in Ravenshead. *C* **01623/455900**. Admission to house and grounds £4 ($6) adults, £2 ($3.20) students and seniors, £1.50 ($2.40) children. Gardens only £2 ($3.20) adults, £1.50 ($2.40) children. House Apr–Oct daily noon–5pm; gardens open year-round daily 9:30am–dusk.

Finds The Search for Pilgrim Roots

Many North Americans who trace their ancestry to the Pilgrims come to this part of England to see where it all started.

The Separatist Movement had its origin in a small area north of Nottingham and south of York called Bassettlaw. Hamlets that were the strongholds of the Separatist membership are clustered into a relatively small area interconnected to Nottingham via the A60 and the A614 highways, between 48km and 56km (30 miles–35 miles) north of Nottingham's center. In the order you'll reach them from Nottingham, they include Babworth, Blyth, Scrooby, and Austerfield Bawtry (you'll see it on maps simply as Bawtry).

Blyth is the most beautiful of the villages. It's no surprise that it looks like a New England town, with a green surrounded by well-kept old houses. The parish church was developed from the 11th-century nave of a Benedictine priory church. On the green is a 12th-century stone building, which was once the Hospital of St. John.

Scrooby is a tiny village of some 160 inhabitants where the Pilgrim leader William Brewster was born in 1566. His father was bailiff of the manor, so the infant Brewster first saw the light of day in the manor house. The original house dated from the 12th century, and the present manor farm, built on the site in the 18th century, has little except its historical association to offer. Brewster Cottage, with its pinfold where stray animals were impounded, lies beside the village church of St. Wilfred, but it's uncertain whether Brewster ever lived in it.

A turnpike ran through Scrooby in the 18th century, and there are many stories of highwaymen, robberies, and murders. The remains of one John Spencer dangled here for more than 60 years as a reminder of the penalties of wrongdoing. He had attempted to dispose of the bodies of the keeper of the Scrooby toll bar and his mother in the river.

The tourist office at Nottingham can offer advice on exploring these villages.

Wollaton Hall This well-preserved Elizabethan mansion, finished in 1588, is the most ornate in England. Today, it houses a natural-history museum with lots of insects, invertebrates, British mammals, birds, reptiles, amphibians, and fish. The hall is surrounded by a deer park and garden. See the camellia house with the world's earliest cast-iron front dating from 1823. The bird dioramas here are among the best in Britain.

In Wollaton Park, 5km (3 miles) southwest from Nottingham center. 01159/153900. Admission on Sat–Sun and bank holiday Mon £1.50 ($2.40) adults, 80p ($1.30) children; free other days. Apr–Oct daily 11am–5pm; Nov–Mar daily 11am–4pm. Drive southwest along A609 (Ilkeston Rd.), which will become Wollaton Rd.

WHERE TO STAY

Balmoral Hotel The Balmoral, comprising two brick houses from the 1880s that are now connected, is 2km (1¼ mile) from the center of town. If you're into sports, you may want to stay here: This hotel is within a stone's throw of Trent Bridge Cricket Ground, where the International Test Matches are played; the English football (soccer) grounds for two of the Nottingham teams; and the

National Water Sports Center. Rooms are on the small side here, with built-in modern furnishings and private shower bathrooms. Public areas include a dining room (where breakfast is served), lounge, and billiards room. Six rooms on the ground floor are available for those with limited mobility.

55–57 Loughborough Rd., West Bridgford, Nottingham, Nottinghamshire NG2 7LA. © 0115/945-5020. Fax 0115/955-2991. www.smoothhound.co.uk/a06758.html. 47 units. £45 ($72) single; £55 ($88) double. Rates include breakfast. AE, MC, V. **Amenities:** Dining room; bar; lounge; billiards room. *In room:* TV, dataport, coffeemaker.

Claremont Hotel *Value*   This is a red brick Victorian that was built as a private house in the 1870s. It sits in a quiet residential street lined with other Victorian homes about a mile from the city center. The ground floor has typically extravagant architectural features, including marbled pillars, stone carvings, and gold-leaf cornices. The average-size nonsmoking bedrooms are basic in design, style, and furnishings, with private showers. The dining room has big windows with which to admire the small garden while eating breakfast.

2 Hamilton Rd., Sherwood Rise, Nottingham, Nottinghamshire NG5 1AU. © and fax **0115/960-8587**. 12 units. £34–£40 ($54–$64) single; £45–£60 ($72–$96) double. Rates include English breakfast. MC, V. Closed Dec 23–Jan 2. **Amenities:** Dining room. *In room:* TV, coffeemaker, no phone.

The Stage 👍   Opposite Forest Park, this reasonably priced hotel lies off the main Mansfield Road or A60, a mile from the heart of the city. Often filled with business people, it is also ideal for visitors with its spacious lounge bar and generous public areas. Bedrooms come in a range of styles and sizes, but each is well furnished, handsomely maintained and, all come with private, shower-only bathrooms. Nonsmoking rooms are available. Five rooms are large enough for occupancy by families.

1–5 Gregory Blvd., Nottingham, Nottinghamshire NG71 6LB. © **0115/9603261**. Fax 0115/9691040. 52 units. £44.50 ($71) single; £54.50 ($87) double. Rates include English breakfast. AE, MC, V. **Amenities:** Restaurant; bar. *In room:* TV, dataport, coffeemaker, hair dryer, trouser press.

WHERE TO DINE

Pinchinello's INTERNATIONAL   Across the street from the Theatre Royal, this fun establishment is housed in a row of three 13th-century brick cottages. The old oak-beam ceilings, terra-cotta tile floor, and sturdy tables combine with two large open fireplaces to create a vibrant atmosphere. The place has become a tradition with theatergoers. Pasta and vegetable dishes are the most popular lunch items; dinner features homemade carrot and French-onion soups served with crusty bread, pasta with prawns and tomatoes, vegetarian lasagna, and Mexican chicken with baked rice.

35 Forman St. © **0115/941-1965**. Lunch £2.95–£6.50 ($4.70–$10); main courses £9.95–£14.50 ($16–$23). AE, MC, V. Mon–Sat noon–10:30pm.

Saagar 👍 INDIAN/KASHMIRI   Owner Mohammed Khizer and chef Mohammed Addiq operate one of the best restaurants in the area. Lunch and dinner use the same a la carte menu, with selections of chicken, lamb, and prawns prepared in traditional recipes from India's Madras area. Don't worry about the heat in your food here; most sauces are mild, such as the cream-and-coconut sauce used in Kurma chicken. Main courses are quite large and include rice. The fixed-price dinner for two includes starters, entrees, rice, vegetables, bread, and dessert.

473 Mansfield Rd., Sherwood. © **0115/962-2014**. Main courses £9.95–£14.20 ($16–$23). AE, MC, V. Mon–Sat noon–2pm; Mon–Sun 5:30pm–midnight. Closed Christmas.

Ye Olde Trip to Jerusalem ENGLISH   Reputedly this is one of the oldest inns in England (built 1189). It was a resting spot for righteous knights and fools on the long road to the Holy Land during the Crusades. The inn was built into the rock base of Nottingham Castle; a natural fault next to the fireplace served as a secret passage to the castle. There are a maze of passages and tunnels hidden behind the inn, each leading somehow to the castle; apparently many a secret assassination took place in these passages. In the inn's gallery, the model of a galleon is said to cause death within a year to anyone who touches it. During a recent renovation, the galleon needed to be moved; a psychic was called to the inn to supervise the operation. There have been no deaths to date because of the move; however, to be safe, the galleon is safely back on display under a glass case. The renovations include a new paint job, reupholstered settles, and new wood tables and chairs. In warmer weather, there's outdoor eating on both front and back patios. Typical pub food—meat pies and sandwiches—is served every day; on Sunday, patrons may enjoy roast beef and Yorkshire pudding. Ales on draft include Kimberley Classic, Best Mild, and Marston's Pedigree.

1 Castle Rd. © **0115/947-3171.** Bar snacks £2.99–£5.99 ($4.80–$10); main courses £5–£7 ($8–$11). MC, V. Mon–Sat 11am–11pm; Sun noon–10:30pm.

SHERWOOD FOREST ⭐

Second only to Germany's Schwarzwald in European lore and legend, **Sherwood Forest** comprises 180 hectares (450 acres) of oak and silver-birch trees owned and strictly protected by a local entity, the Thoresby Estate, and maintained by the county of Nottinghamshire. Actually, very little of this area was forest even when it provided cover for Robin Hood, Friar Tuck, and Little John.

Robin Hood, the folk hero of tale and ballad, fired the imagination of a hard-working, impoverished English people, who particularly liked his adopted slogan: "Take from the rich and give to the poor."

Celebrating their freedom in verdant Sherwood Forest, Robin Hood's eternally youthful band rejoiced in "hearing the twang of the bow of yew and in watching the gray goose shaft as it cleaves the glistening willow wand or brings down the king's proud buck." Life was one long picnic beneath the splendid oaks of a primeval forest, with plenty of ale and flavorful venison poached from the forests of an oppressive king. The clever rebellion Robin Hood waged against authority (represented by the haughty, despotic, and overfed sheriff of Nottingham) was full of heroic exploits and a desire to win justice for victims of oppression.

Now, as then, the forest consists of woodland glades, farm fields, villages, and hamlets. But the surroundings are so built up that Robin Hood wouldn't recognize them today.

Sherwood Forest Visitor Centre (© **01623/823202**) is in Sherwood Forest Country Park at Edwinstowe, 29km (22 miles) north of Nottingham off the A614, or 13km (8 miles) east of Mansfield on the B6034. It stands near the Major Oak, popularly known as Robin Hood's tree, although analysis of its bark reveals that it wasn't around in the 13th century. Many marked walks and footpaths lead from the visitor center through the woodland. There's an exhibition of life-size models of Robin and the other well-known outlaws, as well as a shop with books, gifts, and souvenirs. The center provides as much information as is known about the Merry Men and Maid Marian, whom Robin Hood is believed to have married at Edwinstowe Church near the visitor center. Little John's grave is at Hathersage 58km (36 miles away), and Will Scarlet's grave is at Blidworth (15km/9½ miles away).

The center also has a visitor information facility and the **Forest Table,** with cafeteria service and meals emphasizing traditional English country recipes.

Opening times for the country park are from dawn to dusk, and for the visitor center, April through October daily from 10:30am to 5pm and November through March from 10:30am to 4:30pm. Entrance to the center is free, and "Robin Hood's Sherwood" exhibition is also free. A year-round program of events is presented, mainly on weekends and during national and school holiday periods. Parking costs £1.50 ($2.40) per car per day from April to October.

An odd and somewhat archaic holdover from medieval times are **The Dukeries,** large country estates that contain privately owned remnants of whatever trees and vales remain of Sherwood Forest. Most lie on the edge of heavily industrialized towns and may or may not have privately owned houses of historic merit. Very few can actually be visited without special invitations from their owners. On the other hand, **Clumber Park,** a 3,800-acre tract of park and woodland maintained by National Trust authorities, is favored by local families for picnics and strolls. It contains an 80-acre lake at its center, a monumental promenade flanked with venerable lime (linden) trees, and the Gothic revival **Clumber Chapel.** Built between 1886 and 1889 as a site of worship for the private use of the seventh duke of Newcastle, it's open from early March to mid-January, daily from 10am to 4pm.

The park itself is open year-round during daylight hours, though its allure and services are at their lowest ebb during November and December. The gift shop and tearoom are open daily January through March from 10:30am to 4pm, and from April to late October from 10am to 6pm. Admission to the park, including the chapel, ranges from £3 to £14 ($4.80–$22), depending on your vehicle (a typical compact rental car would cost £3.60/$5.75).

If you're specifically interested in the botany and plant life, head for the park's **Conservation Centre,** a walled garden with extensive greenhouses, open from April 1 to late September on Saturday, Sunday, and bank holiday Mondays from 1 to 4pm. For information about the park and its features, contact the **Clumber Park Estate Office,** Worksop, Nottingham SKO 3AZ (℃ **01909/476592**).

SOUTHWELL
217km (135 miles) NW of London; 39km (24 miles) SW of Lincoln; 23km (14 miles) NE of Nottingham

If you don't want to stay in Nottingham, the ancient market town of Southwell, England's smallest cathedral town, a 27km (17-mile) drive from Lord Byron's Newstead Abbey, is a good center for exploring Robin Hood country. From Nottingham's center, drive northeast along the B686 (the Southwell Rd.), then transfer onto the A612 for the remaining distance into Southwell.

ONE OF ENGLAND'S MOST BEAUTIFUL CHURCHES
Southwell Minster ⭐⭐   The old twin-spired cathedral is an unexpected gem in this part of England. James I found that it held up with "any other kirk in Christendom." The Minster is the only cathedral in England to boast three Norman towers. The west front is pierced by a Perpendicular, seven-light window. Interior architectural highlights include a screen built in the mid-1300s and depicting 286 images of gods, men, and devils. Look also for a stunning early English choir and chapter house from 1288, the first single-span, stone-vaulted chapter house in the Christian world. The chapter house is noted for its "Leaves of Southwell," stone foliage so realistic you can distinguish oak from hawthorn, buttercup from ivy.

Bishops Dr. Admission free but a donation is suggested. Daily 8am–dusk.

WHERE TO STAY

Saracen's Head Other than Southwell Minster, this is the town's most famous and historic building. Built during the Elizabethan age, it retains its original Tudor-style, black-and-white, half-timbered facade. Both Charles I and James I dined here, and Charles I was imprisoned here before the Scots handed him over to the Parliamentarians. After he was beheaded, the name of the inn was changed from the King's Arms to the Saracen's Head. Byron frequently stopped here as well. Today, you'll find cozy bedrooms strewn with nostalgic reminders of old England. That doesn't mean that modern comforts haven't been installed—they have. Nonsmoking bedrooms come in various shapes and styles, although all are comfortable. Each compact bathroom has adequate shelf space and a shower.

Market Place, Southwell, Nottinghamshire NG25 0HE. ℂ 01636/812701. Fax 01636/815408. www.greenekinginns.co.uk/nottinghamshire/inn_01/index.htm. 27 units. £75 ($120) single; £85 ($136) double; £130 ($208) suite. Rates include breakfast. MC, V. **Amenities:** Restaurant; bar; limited room service; limited laundry service/dry cleaning. *In room:* TV, dataport, coffeemaker, hair dryer, trouser press.

WHERE TO DINE

Muscrofts Café Restaurant MODERN/BRITISH If you don't dine at Saracen's Head (see above), this new addition is the other fine choice in town. The atmosphere is rustic, with wooden plank floors and low ceilings with beams. The chef offers fairly traditional British fare with a twist, which generally comes in the form of his creative and imaginative sauces. Try the grilled sirloin steak with a tomato-and-chestnut sauce, topped with almonds; Stilton cheese and sweet corn crepes with a parsley sauce; or Barbary duck served with a brandy, cream, and walnut sauce.

12 King St. ℂ 01636/816573. Reservations recommended. 3-course traditional roast lunch £9.95 ($16); dinner main courses £6–£13.95 ($10–$22). MC, V. Tues–Sat 11am–4pm and 7–9:30pm; Sun 11am–3pm.

A SIDE TRIP TO NEWARK CASTLE

While based at Southwell, you can easily visit the ancient riverside market town of **Newark-on-Trent,** 11km (7 miles) to the east on the A612 and the A617, which is on the Roman Fosse Way.

King John died in **Newark Castle** in 1216. Constructed between the 12th and 15th centuries, the castle survived three sieges by Cromwell's troops, finally falling in 1646. Now in ruins, all that remains are a series of two watchtowers, a gate, and a stretch of wall.

Though the ruins are unsafe to walk on or about, Newark has transformed a nearby building, conceived in the 1880s as a public library, into **The Gilstrap Centre,** Castlegate (ℂ **01636/78962**), an exhibition center and tourist information office. Commemorating the castle's role in English history, its main allure is an exhibit, *The Newark Castle Story and Crossroads,* and three videos available for viewing. The center is open daily from April to September from 9am to 6pm. Off-season hours are daily from 9am to 5pm. Admission is free.

The castle gardens are open during the day. Technically, however, open hours are daily from 9am to dusk. Admission is free.

Parish Church of Mary Magdalene ✮, Church Street (ℂ **01636/706473**), the town's delicately detailed parish church, is among the finest such structures in the country. Its 76m (252-ft.) spire overshadows the Market Place. In the interior, seek out its vast transept windows. A stunning wall painting, *Dance of Death,* in the south chantry chapel, dates from around 1520 (exact year of its origin unknown). Open daily from 8:30am to noon and 1 to 4pm. Admission is free, but there is a donation box.

The Millgate Museum of Social and Folk Life, 48 Millgate (© 01636/ 679403), is housed in a 19th-century oil-seed mill. Today, it contains portrayals of social and industrial life in the area from around 1750 until the dawn of World War II. Agricultural, malting, and printing artifacts are displayed, and a series of rooms depict domestic life in bygone times. The museum is open Monday through Friday from 10am to 5pm and Saturday, Sunday, and bank holidays from 1 to 5pm. Admission is free.

EASTWOOD: A STOP FOR D. H. LAWRENCE FANS

161km (100 miles) N of London; 12km (7½ miles) NW of Nottingham

D. H. Lawrence was born in the Nottinghamshire village of Eastwood on September 11, 1885, son of a coal miner who labored in the nearby mines at Brimsley. The site is commemorated with the **D. H. Lawrence Birthplace Museum,** 8A Victoria St. (© 01773/763312). The memorabilia and furnishings authentically replicate what you might have found in a miner's home in 1885, with an audiovisual presentation that pays tribute to the conditions of the working class during Victorian times. Admission is £2.50 ($4) for adults, £1.75 ($2.80) for seniors and children 5 to 15, free for kids 4 and under. Family ticket £8.50 ($14). The museum is open from April to October daily from 10am to 5pm; from November to March daily from 10am to 4pm.

Just down the road from the birthplace museum is the **D. H. Lawrence Heritage Centre,** Mansfield Road (© 01773/717353), a restored Victorian mansion commemorating the life of the author. There is a gift shop and a coffee shop as well as a restaurant serving light meals. Admission times and costs are the same as the museum. However there is a combined ticket for £3.50 ($6) adults and £1.75 ($2.80) seniors and children, for both venues.

If your interest in Lawrence is still piqued, you might want to stop into **Eastwood's Public Library,** Nottingham Road (© 01773/712209), which devotes a room to folios, manuscripts, and memorabilia associated with the town's famous and iconoclastic writer. It's open Monday, Tuesday, and Thursday from 9:30am to 7pm, Friday from 9:30am to 6pm, and Saturday from 9:30am to 1pm. Admission is free.

Either the museum or the public library can provide a free pamphlet for the town's self-guided "Blue Line Tour." A badly scuffed but still visible blue line will lead you along the village's sites that played a role in Lawrence's life. The museum staff will describe for you a sojourn to the nearby coal mines at Brimsley, where Lawrence's father labored, and an excursion to Cossall, a nearby hamlet that was the home of Lawrence's fiancée and provided the setting for scenes in his novel *The Rainbow.*

To reach Eastwood from Nottingham, go to Victoria Station and board either bus no. 231 or R11. Or you can drive for 12km (7½ miles) northwest along the A610.

5 Lincoln ★★

225km (140 miles) N of London; 151km (94 miles) NW of Cambridge; 132km (82 miles) SE of York

The ancient city of Lincoln was the site of a Bronze Age settlement, and later, in the 3rd century, was one of the four provincial capitals of Roman Britain. In the Middle Ages it was the center of Lindsey, a famous Anglo-Saxon kingdom.

After the Norman Conquest, it grew increasingly important and was known throughout the land for its cathedral and castle. Its merchants grew rich by shipping wool directly to Flanders.

Much of the past remains in Lincoln today to delight visitors who wander past half-timbered Tudor houses, the Norman castle, and the towering Lincoln Cathedral. Medieval streets climbing the hillsides and cobblestones re-create the past. Lincoln, unlike other East Midlands towns such as Nottingham and Leicester, maintains somewhat of a country-town atmosphere. But it also extends welcoming arms to tourists, the mainstay of its economy.

ESSENTIALS

GETTING THERE   Trains arrive every hour during the day from London's King's Cross Station, a 2-hour trip usually requiring a change of trains at Newark. Trains also arrive from Cambridge, again requiring a change at Newark. For schedules and information, call ✆ **0870/48-49-50.**

National Express buses from London's Victoria Coach Station service Lincoln, a 4-hour ride. For schedules and information, call ✆ **020/7529-2000.** Once in Lincoln, local and regional buses service the county from the City Bus Station, off St. Mary's Street opposite the train station.

If you're driving from London, take the M1 north to the junction with the A57, then head east to Lincoln.

VISITOR INFORMATION   Lincoln has two separate tourist information offices. The larger of the two is at 9 Castle Hill (✆ **01522/873213**). The other is at 21 The Cornhill (✆ **01522/873256**). Both of them are open Monday through Thursday from 9:30am to 5:30pm and Friday from 9:30am to 5pm. The office on Castle Hill (but not the one at The Cornhill) is also open Saturday and Sunday from 10am to 5pm.

EXPLORING THE CITY

The best lanes for strolling are those tumbling down the appropriately named Steep Hill to the Witham River.

The cathedral is a good starting point for your shopping tour of Lincoln, as the streets leading down the hill (you won't be working against gravity this way) are lined with a mélange of interesting stores. Wander in and out of these historic lanes, down Steep Hill, along Bailgate, around the Stonebow gateway and Guildhall, and then down High Street. Following this route, you'll find all sorts of clothing, books, antiques, arts and crafts, and gift items.

While walking down Steep Hill, stop in the **Harding House Gallery,** 53 Steep Hill (✆ **01522/523537**), to see some of the best local crafts: ceramics, teddy bears, textiles, wood, metal sculptures, and jewelry. You can peek down St. Paul's Lane, just off Bailgate, to investigate **Cobb Hall Centre,** St. Paul's Lane (✆ **01522/527317**), a small cluster of specialty shops selling outdoor gear, candies and gift items, German figures, and antiques.

Lincoln Cathedral ✮✮✮   No other English cathedral dominates its surroundings as does Lincoln's. Visible from up to 48km (30 miles) away, the central tower is 83m (271 ft.) high, which makes it the second-tallest in England. The central tower once carried a huge spire, which, before heavy gale damage in 1549, made it the tallest in the world at 160m (525 ft.).

Construction on the original Norman cathedral was begun in 1072, and it was consecrated 20 years later. It sustained a major fire and, in 1185, an earthquake.

Only the central portion of the West Front and lower halves of the western towers survive from this period.

The present cathedral is Gothic in style, particularly the early English and decorated periods. The nave is 13th century, but the black font of Tournai marble originates from the 12th century. In the Great North Transept is a rose medallion window known as the Dean's Eye. Opposite it, in the Great South Transept, is its cousin, the Bishop's Eye. East of the high altar is the Angel Choir, consecrated in 1280, and so called after the sculpted angels high on the walls. The exquisite wood carving in St. Hugh's Choir dates from the 14th century. Lincoln's roof bosses, dating from the 13th and 14th centuries, are handsome, and a mirror trolley assists visitors in their appreciation of these features, which are some 70 feet above the floor. Oak bosses are in the cloister.

In the **Seamen's Chapel** (Great North Transept) is a window commemorating Lincolnshire-born Capt. John Smith, one of the pioneers of early settlement in America and the first governor of Virginia. The library and north walk of the cloister were built in 1674 to designs by Sir Christopher Wren. In the Treasury is fine silver plate from the churches of the diocese.

℘ 01522/544544. Admission £3.50 ($6) adults, £3 ($4.80) seniors, students, and children. June–Aug Mon–Sat 7:15am–8pm, Sun 7:15am–6pm; Sept–May Mon–Sat 7:15am–6pm, Sun 7:15am–5pm.

Museum of Lincolnshire Life This is the largest museum of social history in the Midlands. Housed in what was originally built as an army barracks in 1857, it's a short walk north of the city center. Displays here range from a Victorian schoolroom to a collection of locally built steam engines.

Burton Rd. ℘ 01522/528448. Admission £2.50 ($4) adults, £1 ($1.60) children. Mon–Sat 10am–5:30pm; Sun 2–5:30pm (opens at 10am May–Sept). Closed Good Friday, Dec 24–27, and New Year's Day.

WHERE TO STAY

Carline Guest House ⭐ Among the finest B&Bs in this city, the Carline is a charming double-fronted Edwardian house only a 6-minute stroll from the city center. Since the nonsmoking house's opening in 1977, it has gained a reputation for excellence, competitive pricing, and a warm, welcoming atmosphere. The reasonably sized bedrooms are traditionally furnished. The upstairs rooms have full bathrooms; those downstairs have a shower and toilet. There is a sitting room in which you can browse through stacks of tourist literature and information to ensure you get the most from your Lincoln visit. The proprietors will happily recommend eating establishments for your lunch or dinner.

1–3 Carline Rd., Lincoln, Lincolnshire LN1 1HN. ℘ and fax **01522/530422.** 8 units. £30–£35 ($48–$56) single; £46 ($74) double. Rates include English breakfast. No credit cards. **Amenities:** Sitting room. *In room:* TV, coffeemaker, hair dryer, iron.

Castle Hotel ⭐ This redbrick, three-story, traditional English hotel is sited in old Lincoln. It has been carefully converted from what was the North District National School, dating from 1858. It boasts splendid views of the castle and cathedral, which is just a 3-minute walk away. The bedrooms have been individually decorated, and one is large enough to rent to families. All rooms have private baths; most have a tub-and-shower combination, the rest have shower units. Children under ten are not permitted.

Westgate, Lincoln, Lincolnshire LN1 3AS. ℘ 01522/538801. Fax 01522/575457. www.castlehotel.net. 20 units. £88 ($141) double. Rates include English breakfast and newspaper. AE, DC, MC, V. **Amenities:** Restaurant; bar; room service; laundry service. *In room:* TV, coffeemaker, hair dryer.

Duke William Hotel   This hostelry, in the heart of the city near the Roman arch, is within walking distance of the cathedral. Although the structure, built in 1791, has undergone many architectural changes, care has been taken to preserve the atmosphere of an 18th-century inn; many bedrooms have their original heavy timbers. The rooms are of average size, each with a private bathroom with shower. The hotel features a good restaurant and a cozy bar.

44 Bailgate, Lincoln, Lincolnshire LN1 3AP. ℂ **01522/533351.** Fax 01522/531169. 11 units. £50 ($80) single; £60–£70 ($96–$112) double; £70–£80 ($112–$128) family room. Rates include English breakfast. No credit cards. **Amenities:** Restaurant; bar. *In room:* TV, coffeemaker.

Hillcrest Hotel 🐾 *Value*   This is a fine redbrick house built in 1871 as the private home of a local vicar. Although it has been converted into a comfortable, small, licensed hotel, it retains many of its original features. The Hillcrest offers a cozy atmosphere and tries to accommodate personal requests. It's on a quiet, tree-lined road overlooking 10 hectares (26 acres) of parkland, in the old high town and within easy walking distance of Lincoln Cathedral and the Roman remains. All bedrooms are well furnished and kept in shape. Rooms range in size and shape, but each has comfortable twin or double beds; some rooms have a four-poster and nearly all of the rooms open onto a view. The compact bathrooms have shower stalls.

15 Lindum Terrace, Lincoln, Lincolnshire LN2 5RT. ℂ and fax **01522/510182.** www.hillcrest-hotel.com. 14 units. £81 ($130) double. Rates include English breakfast. AE, DC, MC, V. From Wragby Rd., connect with Upper Lindum St.; continue to the bottom of this street, make a left onto Lindum Terrace, and the hotel is 180m (600 ft.) along on the right. **Amenities:** Restaurant; bar; room service; babysitting; laundry service. *In room:* TV, coffeemaker.

Hollies Hotel   Built around 1840 and now owned by the Powell family, this cream-fronted nonsmoking hotel sits in a commercial district less than 1km (½ mile) west of the cathedral. This elegant Victorian residence has many of its original features remaining, including the original quarry-tiled floor and pitched pine staircase of the entrance hall. Resident proprietors Mike and Shirley Powell ensure that your stay is pleasant and comfortable. Each of the midsize bedrooms has a private bathroom with shower unit. There are some ground-floor rooms available. The dining room has a licensed bar for residents; your three-course dinner is chosen from a fixed-price menu (including vegetarian meals).

65 Carholme Rd., Lincoln, Lincolnshire LN1 1RT. ℂ and fax **01522/522419.** www.hotellincoln.co.uk. 8 units. £35 ($56) single; £45 ($72) double. Rates include English breakfast. MC, V. **Amenities:** Dining room; bar. *In room:* TV, coffeemaker, hair dryer.

Tennyson Hotel   Lying 2.5km (1½ miles) from the cathedral precincts at the edge of South Park, near the A15 and A1434 Junction, the Tennyson makes a good base for exploring the area, especially if you have a car. It is run by Kim and Jeff Longmuir. The comfortable hotel has nicely sized bedrooms, each with a private bathroom with shower. A fortifying English breakfast (or other kind) is served in the dining room. A well-appointed lounge contains original features including a fine old fireplace; relax here at day's end and have a quiet drink.

7 S. Park Ave., Lincoln, Lincolnshire LN5 8EM. ℂ and fax **01522/521624.** www.tennysonhotel.com. 8 units. £33–£37 ($53–$59) single; £45–£47 ($72–$75) double. Rates include English breakfast. MC, V. **Amenities:** Dining room; lounge. *In room:* TV, dataport, coffeemaker, hair dryer, trouser press.

WHERE TO DINE

Brown's Pie Shop ENGLISH   This restaurant is housed in a building from 1527 that was once a hotel that sheltered Lawrence of Arabia many times. Near the cathedral, it is a beamed and rustic English dining room. As the name suggests, it specializes in pies, including fish, vegetarian, steak-and-kidney, chicken-and-chestnut, and more. Don't like pies? Try Cumberland sausage or honey-glazed pork tenderloins. This good, wholesome cooking fills you up.

33 Steep Hill. ✆ 01522/527330. Reservations recommended. Lunch main courses £2.50–£14 ($4–$22); 2-course fixed lunch £6.50 ($10); dinner main courses £7–£15 ($11–$24). Sat–Sun full English breakfast £4.95 ($8). AE, MC, V. Daily noon–3pm and 5:30–11pm.

Crust INTERNATIONAL/VEGETARIAN   This bistro-style restaurant in a 1790s building is in a pedestrian zone; the cathedral is a 10-minute walk up one of the town's most historic streets. There are ample parking facilities. *Note:* The restaurant is on the second floor and is not wheelchair accessible.

The chef and patron, Malta-born Victor Vella, has won many awards. His talent shines in dishes such as steak Diane, coq au vin, and traditional roast beef with Yorkshire pudding; he also specializes in fish. More imagination in the kitchen is shown here than at most Lincoln eateries. Vegetarian meals are also served.

252 Upper High St. ✆ 01522/540322. Reservations recommended. Main courses £5.50–£14 ($9–$22); lunch main courses £4.85–£6.90 ($8–$11); 3-course fixed-price meals £4.50 ($7) at lunch, £12 ($19) at dinner. AE, DC, MC, V. Daily 11:30am–3pm; Tues–Sat 7–11pm.

Lion and Snake TRADITIONAL BRITISH   This is the oldest pub in Lincoln, and still has its original windows. Once a stable, the place is reputedly haunted; ghosts have been spotted in the basement and upstairs. It has great views of Lincoln's sights, including the cathedral. Enjoy a traditional steak-and-kidney pie, fish and chips, roast beef, or a three-course meal, and a restorative pint. A particularly good bet is the fisherman's selection, with filet of cod, breaded haddock, and salmon steak.

79 Bailgate. ✆ 01522/523770. Main courses £2.99–£5.99 ($4.80–$10); pub snacks from £1 ($1.60); 3-course Sun lunch £6.95 ($11). MC, V. Restaurant: Mon–Sat 11am–11pm; Sun noon–3pm and 7:30–10:30pm.

Lord Tennyson BRITISH   This busy old pub is located just off Yarborough Road at the top of the hill near the cathedral. You can enjoy excellent traditional British food at reasonable prices. A lunch special costs only £3 ($4.80). A huge steak dinner and a bottle of wine for two goes for £13.99 ($22).

72 Rasen Lane. ✆ 01522/889262. Main courses £4.95–£7 ($8–$11). No credit cards. Daily 11:30am–9pm.

Stokes High Bridge Café BRITISH   This busy tearoom is located in a 16th-century half-timbered style house built on a medieval high bridge (ca. 1160) over the Witham. Morning tea is served 9am to 11:30am; you can get anything from scones, jam, and tea cakes to a fried egg over toast. Lunch is from 11:45am to 2pm. Afternoon tea, similar to morning tea, is served 2 to 4:30pm. For a truly relaxing experience, sip your tea while watching the swans float by.

207 High St. ✆ 01522/513825. Morning and afternoon teas £1.15–£5.25 ($1.85–$8); lunches from £4.50–£6 ($7–$10). No credit cards. Mon–Sat 9am–4:30pm.

Wig & Mitre ★★ INTERNATIONAL   This is not only the best pub in old Lincoln, but it serves fine food, too. Sitting on the aptly named Steep Hill near the cathedral, and loaded with an Old English atmosphere, it operates somewhat like a cafe-brasserie. The main restaurant, behind the bar on the second floor, has oak timbers, Victorian armchairs, and settees. This 14th-century pub has been substantially restored over the years. If the restaurant is full, you can dine in the bar downstairs. Starters are always intriguing, ranging from a salad of smoked mackerel to deep fried salmon, crab, and spring-onion fish cakes. The menu is constantly kept up-to-date, like in a trendy London wine bar.

30 Steep Hill. $\textcircled{C}$ 01522/535190. Reservations recommended. Main courses £9.75–£17 ($16–$27); sandwiches £5.75–£6.75 ($9–$11). AE, DC, MC, V. Daily 8am–11pm. Bus: 8.

FAVORITE LOCAL PUBS

Drop by the **Adam & Eve Tavern,** Lindum Hill ($\textcircled{C}$ **01522/537108**), the oldest pub in Lincoln, dating from 1701. Here you can knock back a Magnet, Old Speckled Hen, or Theakston's Best Bitter in a homey, cottage atmosphere complete with gas fires and a large front garden for warm-weather drinking.

The **Jolly Brewer,** 27 Broadgate ($\textcircled{C}$ **01522/528583**), dates from 1850, and it's a basic wooden floorboards place where you'll be welcomed into a mixed straight and gay crowd. If you're hungry, there's pub grub at lunchtime only, and draft ales include Tiger Bitter and Robinson's, as well as rotating guests.

A SIDE TRIP TO BOSTON

196km (122 miles) N of London; 56km (35 miles) SE of Lincoln; 89km (55 miles) E of Nottingham

New Englanders like to visit this old seaport, which gave its name to the more famous Massachusetts city. But it's ironic that the Pilgrims chose to name their seaport after this English town, for they suffered a great deal here.

In 1607, about a dozen years before their eventual transit to the New World on the *Mayflower,* some Pilgrims arranged for a ship to carry them to new lives in Holland via The Wash and the sea lanes of the North Sea. The captain of the ship betrayed them and absconded with their money; as a result, the group was imprisoned in Boston's guildhall for a month for attempting to emigrate from England without the king's permission. The cells they occupied can still be visited within Boston's Guildhall. Also at Scotia Creek, on a riverbank near town, is a memorial to those early Pilgrims.

GETTING THERE

From Lincoln, there are about half a dozen trains a day, each of which requires a transfer in the town of Sleaford. The trip takes about an hour. From London, about 10 trains a day depart from King's Cross Station for the 2½-hour trip. For schedules and information, call $\textcircled{C}$ **0845/7484950.**

There's no bus service from Lincoln, and perhaps one or two buses a day depart from London's Victoria Coach Station to Boston. For schedules and information, call $\textcircled{C}$ **08705/808080.**

If you're driving from Lincoln, take A17 southeast for 56km (35 miles); the trip takes about 45 minutes. From London, take the A1 motorway north to Peterborough, then follow the signs to Boston. It's about a 3½-hour drive.

SEEING THE SIGHTS

The center of Boston is closed to cars, so you will have to walk to visit attractions such as the **Boston Stump,** the lantern tower of the Church of St. Botolph with a view for miles around of the all-encircling fens. As it stands, the tower was finished in 1460. In the 1930s, the people of Boston, Massachusetts, paid for the restoration of the tower, known officially as St. Botolph's Tower. The stairs aren't in good shape, so we don't recommend that you climb the tower. The city officials were going to add a spire, making it the tallest in England, but because of the wind and the weight, they feared the tower would collapse. Therefore, it became known as "the Boston Stump."

The 1700s **Fydell House** (© **01205/351520**) is an adult-education center but has a room set aside to welcome visitors not only from Boston, Massachusetts, but also from the rest of the United States. It is open Monday to Thursday from 9:30am to 12:30pm and 1:30 to 4:30pm, and Friday from 9am to 4pm. Admission is free.

PUBS WHERE YOU CAN EAT, DRINK & STAY

Admiral Nelson Pub   Eight kilometers (5 miles) north of Boston, it isn't plush or luxurious; you might surmise that these accommodations are intended for those too drunk to drive home after an alcoholic binge. But if you're not too fussy and want an insight into an English village's pub life, this establishment maintains a pair of battered, average-size but clean accommodations upstairs. Don't overlook the charms of the antique pub, where log-burning fireplaces add a glow to the old-fashioned panels and much-used bar area. Platters of pub grub cost £2.25 to £8.50 ($3.60–$14) and tend to go well with the roster of Bateman's Ales, Carlsberg, Murphy's, and Caffreys.

Main Rd., Bennington, near Boston, Lincolnshire. © **01205/760460**. 2 units, none with bathroom. £25–£35 ($40–$56) per person, single or double. Rates include English breakfast. No credit cards. **Amenities:** Restaurant; bar. *In room:* TV, coffeemaker.

Castle Inn   The Castle, a traditional pub with brick facade and old-timey aura, lies about 2.5km (1½ miles) from the center of Boston, beside the A52 highway. (Follow the signs to Skegness.) The upstairs bedrooms are as basic as anything we're willing to recommend, but for cost-conscious travelers who want easy access to the sociability and warmth of a busy pub, they're a worthy choice. The average-size bedrooms have twin beds and congenially battered, strictly utilitarian furniture; none have sinks. All rooms have access for those with limited mobility.

Haltoft End, Freiston, Boston, Lincolnshire PE22 0MY. © **01205/760393**. 4 units, none with bathroom. £20 ($32) per person. MC, V. **Amenities:** Restaurant; bar. *In room:* Coffeemaker.

Kings Arms Inn ★ *Finds* ENGLISH   The neighborhood's most charming pub, built of softly weathered red brick, lies less than 1km (½ mile) west of the town center, across from the Mard Foster Canal, near what was once a windmill. It was built in the 1830s to serve the men who operated the longboats carrying grain up and down the canal. (The 5th-generation publican-owners, the Cooper family, remember when downing 8 pints of beer in a sitting was considered normal for most of their clients.) Today, the pub retains its antique aura, but with a more temperate attitude toward food and drink. Bateman's Real Ale, brewed fewer than 29km (18 miles) away, is the beverage of choice, along with Bass Ale and whatever promotional brew is being marketed at the time. The food is flavorful and comes in very generous portions—especially the English-style mixed grill, which is hands down the most popular platter. As an alternative, consider a curry, ham steak, any chicken dish, or a sandwich. There are seven cozy bedrooms on the second floor, each with a shower and sink; all share a communal toilet off the hallway. A "proper English breakfast" is included in the price of £20 ($32) per person.

13 Horncastle Rd., Boston, Lincolnshire PE21 9BU. © and fax **01205/364296**. Platters £4.95–£7.50 ($8–$12). No credit cards. Mon–Sat 11:30am–11pm; Sun 11am–3pm and 5–11pm. **Amenities:** Restaurant; bar. *In room:* TV, coffeemaker, no phone.

15

The Northwest

The great industrial shadow of the 19th century cast such a pall over England's Northwest that the region is still avoided by some visitors. Most Americans rush through, heading for the Lake District and Scotland. But in spite of its overgrown industrial and commercial areas, the Northwest still has much to offer, including some beautiful, unspoiled countryside.

We will concentrate on three of its more important cities—**Manchester, Liverpool,** and **Chester**—with a side trip to **Blackpool,** a huge Coney Island–style resort, which you may want to visit less for its beaches than for its kitschy, old-world appeal.

1 Manchester ✈: Gateway to the North

323km (202 miles) NW of London; 137km (86 miles) N of Birmingham; 56km (35 miles) E of Liverpool

The second-largest city in England, Manchester has become increasingly important; major airlines now fly here from North America, making it a gateway to northern England. Recently, Manchester has made great strides toward shaking its image as an industrial wasteland. Chimneys still spike the skyline, but they no longer turn the metropolitan sky into an ash-filled canopy. Abandoned warehouses have become sleek new loft apartments for yuppies. Rustic factory equipment turns up in museums rather than in salvage yards. Aging Victorian architecture has been given a facelift. The overall effect is a gritty kind of charm.

Manchester's roots date from A.D. 79, when the Romans settled here; it remained under Roman occupation until A.D. 411, when the empire began its storied fall. The ancient west gate has been reconstructed on its original site. Little is known of Manchester's Middle Ages.

But in the mid–17th century, Manchester began capitalizing on the opportunities that the burgeoning textile industry offered. The city became the Dickensian paradigm of the urban-industrial complex and the resulting blight. The railways helped catapult the city to the forefront of the industrial movement; England found it convenient as a terminus and as a refinement center for raw goods to become viable exports. It is apt that the Museum of Science and Technology resides here.

Many of the factory laborers were immigrants who flocked to Manchester for the promise of work; the atrocity of their conditions is well documented. But these immigrants had a profound effect on the city's culture. Today's nearly 20,000 descendants of Chinese immigrants give Manchester England's highest Chinese population outside London. These residents have adapted their surroundings to fit their heritage. The murals, gardens, and decor that pay homage to a once-displaced working force enliven Falkner Street, particularly the monumental Imperial Chinese Archway.

The most recent stars of Manchester have been Oasis, best known stateside for the album *(What's the Story) Morning Glory.* These rock stars haven't exactly

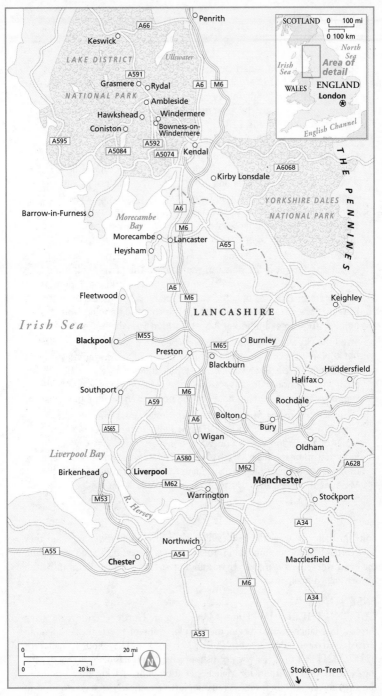

done for their city what the Beatles did to put Liverpool on the map, but they have certainly made an impression. Manchester is increasingly cited as hip, and the band whose *Definitely Maybe* was the fastest-selling debut album in British history helped make it so.

ESSENTIALS

GETTING THERE   By Plane   More and more North Americans are flying directly to Manchester to begin their explorations of the United Kingdom. **British Airways (BA; ✆ 800/247-9297** in the U.S. and Canada, or 08457/222111 in the UK; www.british-airways.co.uk) has daily flights departing New York's JFK airport for Manchester at 6:30pm, arriving after 7 hours in the air. You can also fly from BA's many North American gateways nonstop to London, and from here take the almost shuttle-like service from either Gatwick or Heathrow airports to Manchester, a 50-minute flight.

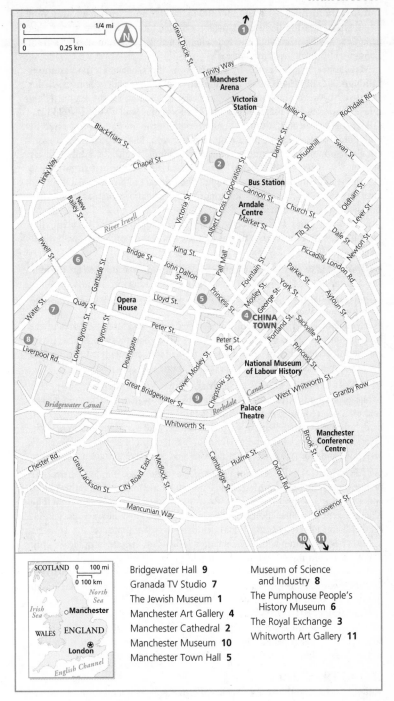

0 1/4 mi
0 0.25 km

Great Ducie St.

Trinity Way

Manchester Arena

Victoria Station

Miller St.

Rochdale Rd.

Blackfriars St.

Trinity Way

Chapel St.

Dantzic St.

Shudehill

Swan St.

New Bailey St.

River Irwell

Victoria St.

Albert Cross Corporation St.

Cannon St.

Bus Station

Church St.

Oldham St.

Lever St.

Arndale Centre

Market St.

Trib. St.

Dale St.

Newton St.

Irwell St.

Gartside St.

Bridge St.

King St.

John Dalton St.

Pall Mall

Fountain St.

Piccadilly London Rd.

6

Quay St.

Lower Byrom St.

Byrom St.

Opera House

Lloyd St.

Princess St.

Mosley St.

York St.

George St.

Parker St.

Ayroun St.

7

Water St.

5

4 **CHINA TOWN**

Portland St.

Sackville St.

8

Liverpool Rd.

Deansgate

Peter St.

Peter St. Sq.

National Museum of Labour History

Princess St.

Great Bridgewater St.

Lower Mosley St.

Chepstow St.

Rochdale Canal

West Whitworth St.

Granby Row

9

Palace Theatre

Bridgewater Canal

Whitworth St.

Manchester Conference Centre

Chester Rd.

Great Jackson St.

City Road East

Medlock St.

Cambridge St.

Hulme St.

Oxford Rd.

Brook St.

Grosvenor St.

Mancunian Way

10

11

American Airlines (© 800/433-7300 in the U.S. and Canada; www.aa.com) offers a daily nonstop flight to Manchester from Chicago's O'Hare Airport that departs at 6:40pm, arriving the following morning. American also flies from London's Heathrow back to Chicago.

Manchester is also served by flights from the Continent. For example, **Lufthansa** (© 800/645-3880; www.lufthansa.com) has frequent nonstop flights each week between Frankfurt and Manchester, depending on the season. Flight time is 1 hour and 45 minutes. For airport information, call © 01614/993322.

Manchester's airport, 24km (15 miles) south of the town center, is served by both public transportation and a motorway network. The **Airport Link,** a modern aboveground train, connects the airport terminal to the Piccadilly Railway Station downtown in Manchester. Trains leave every 15 minutes from 5:15 to 10:10pm, sometimes through the night. The ride takes 25 minutes. Direct rail lines link the airport to surrounding northern destinations such as Edinburgh, Liverpool, and Windermere.

Buses no. 44 and 105 run between the airport and Piccadilly Gardens Bus Station every 15 minutes (hourly during the evenings and on Sun). The bus ride takes 55 minutes.

By Train, Bus & Car   Trains from London's Euston Station travel directly to Manchester (© 0845/7484950). The trip takes 2½ hours to 3 hours.

National Express (© 08705/808080) buses serve the Manchester region from London's Victoria Coach Station.

If you're driving from London to Manchester, go north on the M1 and the M6. At junction 21A, go east on the M62, which becomes the M602 as you enter Manchester. The trip from London to Manchester usually takes from 3 to 3½ hours, but it could be longer because of traffic and construction.

VISITOR INFORMATION   The **Manchester Visitor Centre,** Town Hall Extension, Lloyd Street (© 01612/343157; www.manchester.gov.uk/visitor centre), is open Monday through Saturday from 10am to 5:30pm and Sunday and bank holidays from 10:30am to 4pm. To reach it, take the Metrolink tram to St. Peter's Square. Especially useful is a series of four free pamphlets with information on accommodations, dining, city attractions, and cultural/entertainment options.

GETTING AROUND   It's not a good idea to try to hoof it in Manchester. It's better to take the bus and Metrolink. Timetables, bus routes, fare information, and a copy of a helpful leaflet, the "Passenger's Guide," are available from **The Kiosk,** a general information booth within the Piccadilly Gardens Bus Station, Market Street (© 01612/287811), open daily from 8am to 8pm.

Buses begin running within Manchester at 6am and operate in full force until 11pm, then continue with limited routes until 3am. Tickets are sold at a kiosk at Piccadilly Gardens Bus Station. A day pass, the **Wayfarer** (© 01612/287811), costs £3.30 ($5) and is valid for a complete day of public bus travel. Another source of bus information is **Stagecoach** (© 01612/733377).

Metrolink (© 01612/052000) streetcars connect the bus stations and provide a useful north-south conduit. Self-service ticket machines dispense zone-based fares. The streetcars operate Monday through Saturday from 6am to 11:30pm, and on Sunday from 7am to 10:30pm. They are wheelchair accessible.

SEEING THE SIGHTS

Manchester Art Gallery ★★   Following an extensive expansion and rejuvenation, this gallery today is the proud owner of one of the best and most prestigious art collections in the north of England. Literally doubled in size, the new gallery displays works that are wide-ranging—from the pre-Raphaelites to old Dutch masters, from the land- and seascapes of Turner to Lowry's industrial panoramas.

Designed by Sir Charles Barry, this gallery has been a landmark since 1882. Today's fine collection is also noted for its paintings by Ford Madox Brown, Holman Hunt, and its bevy of 18th- and early-19th-century art, including High Victorian, Edwardian, and British modern. A highlight for us is the magnificent collection of Turner watercolors.

The gallery's decorative art collection is one of the finest outside London, especially in its 17th- and 18th-century pieces, its metalwork, and porcelain. The silver, in particular the Assheton Bennett collection, is especially distinguished.

If you're here between Easter and September, consider a visit to **Heaton Hall** (✆ **0161/7731231**), the museum's annex, 6.5km (4 miles) to the east. It's the centerpiece of 260 hectares (650 acres) of rolling parkland, and accessible via the Metrolink tram (get off at Heaton Park). Built of York stone in 1772, and filled with furniture and decorative art of the 18th and 19th centuries, it is open only between Easter and September. Opening hours may vary, however they are generally Thursday through Sunday from 10am to 5:30pm. Call the Visitor Centre to confirm. Admission is free.

Mosley St. ✆ **0161/235-8888**. www.cityartgalleries.org.uk. Free admission. Daily 10am–5pm.

Manchester Town Hall ✮
Alfred Waterhouse designed this neo-Gothic structure that first opened in 1877, and extensions were added just before World War II. The tower rises nearly 91m (300 ft.) above the town. The Great Hall and its signature hammer-beam roof houses 12 pre-Raphaelite murals by Ford Madox Brown, commissioned between 1852 and 1856. The paintings chronicle the town's storied past, from the 1st century Roman occupation to the Industrial Revolution of the 19th century.

Albert Sq. ✆ **01612/343157**. Free admission. Mon–Fri 8am–5pm; Sun 8am–5pm. Closed Dec 25–26 and New Year's Day. Guided tours 2nd and 4th Wed and Sat at 2pm.

Manchester Cathedral ✮
Originally just a medieval parish in 1421, Manchester achieved cathedral status in 1847 with the creation of the new diocese. The cathedral's nave, the widest of its kind in Britain, is formed by six bays, as is the choir. The choir stall features unique 16th-century misericord seats—caricatures of medieval life. The choir screen is a wood carving from the same era. Carel Weight provides her 20th-century canvas rendition of the beatitudes and there's also a sculpture by typographer Eric Gill.

Victoria St. ✆ **0161/8332220**. Daily 8am–6pm.

The Jewish Museum
The premises here were originally built in the Moorish revival style in 1874 as a Sephardic synagogue. It's one of only two such museums in Britain (the other is in London). It traces the culture and history of Manchester's Jewish community, estimated today at around 27,000. Part of the emphasis is on the experiences of immigrants, many from Eastern Europe, whose recorded voices describe the experience of life in Manchester's Jewish quarter in the years before World War II.

Cheetham Hill Rd. ✆ **01618/349879**. www.manchesterjewishmuseum.com. Admission £3.75 ($6) adults; £2.75 ($4.40) children, students, and seniors; £8.95 ($14) family. Mon–Thurs 10:30am–4pm; Sun 10:30am–5pm. Closed Jewish holidays. Bus: 21, 56, 59, 89, 134, 135, or 167.

People's History Museum
Few other museums in Europe catalog and commemorate the social history of the working class as carefully and with as much objectivity as this one. The museum began to take shape in 1990 when this was

designated the archive of Britain's Communist party. Despite the fact that every exhibit is carefully couched in apolitical terms, it remains the most controversial museum in the Midlands. Of special note are exhibitions that describe the 1819 Peterloo Massacre of trade union activists by government forces, and the ongoing struggles of the coal miners of Yorkshire in their fight for higher wages and better working conditions.

Left Bank, Bridge St. 🕐 **01618/396061**. www.nmlhweb.org. Admission £1 ($1.60) adults Sat–Thurs, free Fri; free for students, seniors, and children. Tues–Sun 11am–4:30pm. Tram: Metrolink to St. Peter's Sq.

Manchester Museum This venerable museum showcases an eclectic and sometimes eccentric collection of the spoils brought back by local industrialists from their adventurous forays outside of England; there are archaeological finds from all over the world, including England's largest collection of ancient Egyptian mummies outside the British Museum in London. The museum is undergoing major refurbishment over the next 2 years, which may, at certain times, affect some of its exhibits. Call ahead to check.

University of Manchester, Oxford Rd., near Booth St. 🕐 **01612/752634**. http://museum.man.ac.uk. Free admission. Mon–Sat 10am–5pm; Sun 11am–4pm. Metrolink tram to St. Peter's Sq., then bus 11, 16, 41, 42, or 45.

Salford Art Gallery ⭐ At the newly restored docklands area, called the Lowry, the industrial city landscapes of artist L. S. Lowry (1887–1976) are showcased as never before. Before it disappeared forever, Lowry depicted the grimness and horror of the industrial north of England. The smokestacks and viaducts in his paintings dwarf his matchstick people. Lowry's paintings, as seen here, imposed a vision on a grim and gloomy urban sprawl. Lowry found a cohesion and lyric beauty in these industrial landscapes.

The Lowry. 🕐 **0161/8762000**. Free admission. Mon–Wed 11am–5pm; Thurs and Sat–Sun 11am–8pm; Fri 11am–10pm. Bus: no. 51, 52, 71, 73, or M11.

EXPLORING CASTLEFIELD ⭐

Manchester had its origins in **Castlefield,** the city's historic core; recently, local authorities have designated it an "urban heritage park." It comprises the densely populated neighborhood that housed as many as 2,000 civilians beginning in A.D. 79, when Manchester was Mancestra, a fortified Roman camp strategically positioned between Chester and Carlisle, two other Roman outposts. After the Romans abandoned the nearby fortress in A.D. 411, the settlement stood alone throughout the Dark Ages.

Castlefield's next major development was the Bridgewater Canal, which transferred coal from Worsley. Warehouses arose around the wharves, their names suggesting their wares (for example, Potato Wharf). Later, Liverpool Road housed the world's first passenger railway station, today home to the Museum of Science and Technology.

Although the city atrophied for decades after its reign as industrial capital of the world, an interest in urban renewal emerged in the 1970s. Many of the grand canals and warehouses have been restored, and Castlefield is once again a thriving, vibrant area full of attractions.

Museum of Science and Industry Set within five separate antique buildings, this complex was built in 1830 as the first railway station in the world. Its many exhibits celebrate the Industrial Revolution and its myriad developments, such as printing, the railroad, electricity, textile manufacturing, and industrial machinery, plus the history of flight and aerospace exploration.

Liverpool Rd. (1.5km/1 mile north of Manchester's center), Castlefield. ℂ **01618/832-2244**. www.msim.org. uk. Free admission. Daily 10am–5pm. Closed Dec 24–26. Parking £4 ($6). Bus: 33.

Whitworth Art Gallery   Whitworth was originally established in 1889 with a bequest to the city from a wealthy industrialist. The gallery was opened to the public in 1908. Behind the magnificent redbrick facade lies a light and spacious interior. The gallery is one of the richest research sources in England for antique patterns of wallpaper and textiles and the weaving techniques that produced them. There's a superb collection of 18th- and 19th-century watercolors on display, including many by Turner.

At the University of Manchester, on Oxford Rd., near the corner of Denmark Rd. ℂ **01612/757450**. www.whitworth.man.ac.uk. Free admission. Mon–Sat 10am–5pm; Sun 2–5pm. Metrolink to St. Peter's Sq., then bus 41, 42, or 45.

SHOPPING

Not only does Manchester offer a vast number and variety of boutiques, shops, galleries, and crafts centers, but it's one of the best hunting grounds for bargains in all of England.

Most of the larger shopping areas in the city are pedestrian-only. These include **King Street** and **St. Ann's Square,** full of exclusive boutiques and designer stores; **Market Street,** with its many major chain and department stores; **Arndale Centre,** Manchester's largest covered shopping center; and the recently revitalized **Piccadilly** and **Oldham streets,** for fashion, music, and plenty of bargains. **Deansgate Street** is not pedestrian-only but does have a lot of adventure-sports shops.

For the young at heart, interested in everything from World War II RAF bomber pilot gear to outrageous club wear, it's one-stop shopping at **Affleck Palace** (no relation to Ben), 52 Church St. This complex provides 50 of the most widely varied shops in the city divided among 4 floors.

ANTIQUES & FINE ART   Those who like rooting through dusty stacks of stuff in search of treasures will find Manchester and the greater Manchester area prime hunting grounds.

More pricey antiques can be found along Bury New Road in Prestwich village, just outside of Manchester.

ART GALLERIES   If you're into contemporary art, stop by the artist-run **Castlefield Gallery,** Liverpool Road (ℂ **01618/328034**). **The Gallery Manchester's Art House,** 131 Portland St. (ℂ **01612/373551**), focuses on artists whose work can be classified as from the Northern School.

ARTS & CRAFTS   You can really rack up a lot of one-of-a-kind items while exploring the many shops devoted to craftspeople and their art. For ceramics, glass, textiles, jewelry, toys, dollhouses, and the like, visit the exquisite Victorian building that houses **Manchester Craft Centre,** 17 Oak St. (ℂ **01618/324274**), and **St. George's Craft Centre,** St. George's Road, Bolton (ℂ **01204/398071**).

FASHION   Most of the fashion stores are centered around St. Ann's Square and King Street.

Men's and women's avant-garde clothing can be found at **Flannels,** St. Anne's Place (ℂ **01618/325536**).

MARKETS   Here in the north, markets are a tradition and offer you a chance to jump in and barter with the locals. Tourists tend to steer clear of them, so this is a great chance for a really authentic experience.

Though markets tend to sell everyday items and foodstuff, some stalls are devoted to flea-market goods and "antiques." Market days vary throughout the city, but you're bound to find at least one in full swing each day of the workweek.

The major ones include Arndale Market and Market Hall in Manchester Arndale Centre, Grey Mare Lane Market and Beswick District Shopping Centre in Beswick, and Moss Side Market and Moss Lane East in Moss Side.

MILL SHOPS   Manchester is an industrial stronghold with lots of textile mills. Most mills used to have a store, or mill shop, on-site where customers could come to buy mill goods. Today, more and more of the mills are setting up shop in towns across the country.

Bury New Road in Cheetham Hill, near Boddington's Brewery, has a great selection of factory shops, discount stores, warehouses, cash-and-carry outlets, and street stalls on Sunday mornings. Some of the stores along this road do not sell to the general public and others require a minimum purchase.

A. Sanderson & Sons, 2 Pollard St., Ancoats (© **01612/728501**), is one of England's most famous brands. The shop is right outside the heart of downtown and easy to get to. It's clean, modern, and fun to shop for fabrics by the yard, gift items made of Sanderson fabrics, as well as bed linen and draperies.

MUSIC   Audiophiles take note: More than live Britpop can be found in Manchester. The largest secondhand album and CD shop in all of England is the city's **Vinyl Exchange Used Record & CD Shop,** 18 Oldham St. (© **01612/281122**), with recordings from all musical genres split between vinyl on the first floor and CDs upstairs. With more than 25,000 selections in stock, it's worth setting aside some browsing time. You may just walk out with that single you've been trying to track down for the past few years.

Also check out the secondhand music stalls found near Piccadilly Station along Church Street.

For newer music, go to the **Virgin Megastore,** 52–56 Market St. (© **01618/ 331111**).

WHERE TO STAY

The Highbury Hotel   This is a well-run and winning choice with a high standard of comfort in its well-furnished accommodations, each coming with a private bath or shower. Both commercial clients and holiday makers are attracted to this guesthouse with its inviting atmosphere. Nonsmoking rooms are available. After a good night's sleep, guests are rewarded with a first-rate breakfast and a goodly selection of menu choices. Residents can also enjoy a drink in the licensed lounge at night.

113 Monton Rd., Monton, Manchester M30 9HQ. © **0161/7878545.** Fax 0161/7879023. 16 units. Mon–Thurs £38 ($61) single; £42–£49.50 ($67–$79) double. Fri–Sun £35 ($56) single; £46 ($74) double. AE, MC, V. **Amenities:** Breakfast room; lounge; bar. *In room:* TV, dataport, coffeemaker, hair dryer, trouser press.

Kempton House Hotel   A large Victorian house located 4km (2½ miles) south of the city center, this hotel offers basic, centrally located accommodations at a reasonable rate. You don't get much in the way of grand comfort in the rather smallish rooms here, but you do get a good bed for the night at a reasonable rate. Rooms that contain private plumbing will have a shower stall. There are two nonsmoking rooms. Several buses go by the hotel on a regular basis.

400 Wilbraham Rd., Chorlton-Cum-Hardy M21 0UH. © and fax **01618/818766.** www.thekempton.co.uk. 9 units. £35 ($56) single; £55 ($88) double. Rates include English breakfast. AE, DC, MC, V. **Amenities:** Breakfast room. *In room:* TV, coffeemaker, hair dryer, no phone.

New Central Hotel Located just off the A665 Cheetham Hill Road, 2.5km (1½ miles) from Victoria Station, this hotel offers simple but comfortable accommodations. Rooms are smallish but decently maintained with comfortable beds. You stay here for the price, not any grand luxury. Be sure to specify your needs when booking a room, because two rooms share all bathroom facilities, and none has private toilet facilities. Some rooms have a shower unit.

144–146 Heywood St., Cheetham, M8 0PD. ✆ and fax **01612/052169.** 10 units, 8 with shower. £25 ($40) single without bathroom, £30 ($48) single with bathroom; £50 ($80) double with shower. Rates include English breakfast. MC, V. **Amenities:** Breakfast room; lounge. *In room:* TV, coffeemaker, hair dryer.

Thistlewood Hotel This large Victorian house is located 6.5km (4 miles) from the city center, close to junction 7 of the M63; several buses stop outside the hotel. The midsize rooms contain bathing facilities and are well maintained. There's a comfortable lounge; a dining room looks out over a stepped garden. In the evening, a variety of hot and cold snacks and light meals can be arranged.

203 Urmston Lane, Stretford M32 9EF. ✆ **0161/8653611.** Fax 0161/8668133. 9 units. £32 ($51) single; £46 ($74) double. Rates include English breakfast. AE, DC, MC, V. **Amenities:** Dining room; bar; lounge. *In room:* TV, coffeemaker, hair dryer, trouser press.

SUPER-CHEAP SLEEPS: A YOUTH HOSTEL

YHA Manchester Situated in a newly constructed £2 million ($3.2 million) waterfront building in the middle of the Castlefield urban renewal project, this is billed as England's premiere YHA hostel; guests say that it's the nicest hostel in the world. Each nonsmoking four-bed suite has its own shower, toilet, and wash basin. Doubles and premium suites have their own television and beverage makers; private or family rooms are available as well. Besides a self-catering kitchen, the facility offers full catering. There are two rooms available (eight beds) for those with limited mobility. Meals can be purchased individually or as part of bed-and-breakfast, half-board, or full-board accommodations, ranging from economy to premium in all categories. The hostel is open year-round; it sets neither curfew nor daytime lockout.

Potato Wharf, Liverpool Rd., Castlefield, Manchester M3 4NB. ✆ **0161/8399960.** Fax 0161/8352054. www. yha.org.uk. 144 beds in 36 units. £19 ($30) adult; £14 ($22) youth under 18 years of age, for occupancy of rooms with 4 beds; £42 ($67) double, £68 ($109) premium suite for four. Rates include breakfast. AE, MC, V. **Amenities:** Dining room; TV lounge; game room; laundry; storage lockers. *In room:* No phone, TV (in 2nd-floor rooms).

WHERE TO DINE

Al-Faisal Tandoori *(Value)* PAKISTANI One of many nondescript Subcontinental eateries in the area, this is primarily a carryout kitchen, although a few tables are available. What is remarkable about this place is its inexpensive menu; a chicken or lamb tikka goes for £3.60 ($6), a large spicy vegetable curry for £3.30 ($5). These prices keep students and budget travelers coming back.

58 Thomas St. ✆ 0161/8343266. Main courses £4–£5 ($6–$8). No credit cards. Mon–Sat 11am–7pm; Sun 11am–4pm.

Atlas Bar ITALIAN/ENGLISH This cafe-bar, located in the renovated Knott Mill complex, runs through a two-story shop front and the undercroft of a railway arch, then spills out in back over a landscaped terrace. The front is composed of glazed glass screens, creating an atmosphere in which street traffic and cafe patrons are mutually exposed. Birch, pitch pine, York stone, and Kirkstone slate combine to create a warm, modern interior. The menu includes homemade soups, salads, pasta dishes such as tortellini with sun-dried tomato pesto or pappardelle with roast peppers, goat cheese, and pine nuts, and specials such as smoked salmon tart or roast vegetables with couscous and harissa dressing.

376 Deansgate. (C) **0161/8342124.** Lunch specials £6.45 ($10); main courses £3.95–£12.95 ($6–$21). MC, V. Food service: daily noon–8pm (limited menu only 3–5pm); breakfast served Sun 11am–5pm. Bar hours: Mon–Sat 11am–11pm; Sun 11am–10:30pm.

Bella Pasta ITALIAN   This rustic trattoria serves up an assortment of traditional "mamma mia dishes" that are filled with flavor. A local Manchester student described the food here as "good, cheap eats." The pizzas arrive piping hot and full of aroma and flavor from the Dante's Inferno ovens. The pasta dishes come with homemade sauces, and there is a wide selection of other dishes as well, including fresh seafood.

Deansgate and St. Mary's St. (C) **0161/8324332.** Reservations recommended. Main courses £5–£8 ($8–$13). AE, MC, V. Daily 11am–11pm (Sun open at noon).

Duke 92 BRITISH   This pub sits in the middle of what was an old industrial area, but the neighborhood is in the midst of urban renewal and has become quite trendy, full of hidden-away places like this one. Built out of converted canal horse stables, the spacious interior mixes black wrought iron and whitewashed plaster walls with a handsome marble bar and Edwardian furniture. A beautiful spiral staircase leads up to an upper room and balcony. It's rather elegant for a place in which to find a bargain meal; nonetheless, this sibling to the Mark Addy in Salford (see below) offers a simple ploughman's lunch featuring a huge portion of two cheeses, two pâtés, or one of each with fresh granary bread; cheese choices include obscurities like a black currant Lancashire. The bar sells Boddingtons on tap as well as the Belgian white wheat beer Hoegaarden. When the weather's pleasant, go out and sit alongside the canal.

Castle St., below the bottom end of Deansgate. (C) **0161/8398646.** Ploughman's lunch £4 ($6). MC, V. Mon–Thurs 11:30am–11pm; Fri–Sat 11:30am–midnight; Sun noon–10:30pm.

Lass O'Gowrie Brewhouse BRITISH   This Victorian pub is popular with office workers (lunch) and students (evening). Its long bar is illuminated by gaslights. You can watch beer being made in the cellar microbrewery through a central glass cage. Its malty Lass Ale is quite popular, as are the inexpensive lunches, such as *baps* (large bread rolls filled with meats and vegetables), ploughman's lunches (available on request), sausages, and pies.

36 Charles St. (C) **0161/2736932.** Main courses £2.75–£4.95 ($4.40–$8). AE, MC, V. Mon–Sat 11am–11pm; Sun noon–10:30pm.

Mark Addy BRITISH   This pub, named after a 19th-century hero who rescued more than 50 drowning people from the River Irwell outside, is one of Manchester's great "cheese pubs." The ploughman's lunch comes with a choice of two cheeses, two pâtés, or one of each, plus fresh-baked granary bread and a pickle. There are more than 50 English and European cheeses to choose from; servings are so large that a doggy bag automatically comes with your order. Order a pint of Boddingtons or Timothy Taylors Landlord to wash it down. You may linger here if you settle into one of the private and comfortable barrel-vaulted red sandstone bays. In warm weather there's a courtyard bursting with color from the blossom of flowers.

Stanley St., Salford. (C) **0161/8324080.** Ploughman's lunch £3.80 ($6). MC, V. Mon–Sat 11:30am–11pm; Sun noon–10:30pm.

Pearl City CANTONESE   This fast-paced eatery dishes up some of the finest Cantonese food in Manchester, all at a reasonable price. Don't expect polished service, however. Manchester's growing array of Asian citizens have staked this one out for its authentic, unusual dishes, based whenever possible on the freshest of ingredients. Dig into their roast duckling aromatically flavored with herbs and spices or a huge assortment of other good eats.

33 George St. ✆ 0161/2287683. Reservations recommended. Main courses £8–£15.50 ($13–$25). AE, MC, V. Mon–Thurs noon–2am; Fri–Sat noon–4am; Sun noon–midnight.

Royal Oak BRITISH   This old worn room is another "cheese pub." Order a ploughman's lunch with your pint of Batemans Mild or Marstons Bitter or Pedigree, choosing two cheeses, a bread, and a pâté, or two pâtés to go with a big hunk of bread. It's the 50-plus cheeses that keep patrons returning; even rare cheeses are plopped down in front of you by the pound, so expect to ask for a doggy bag—it's a request the friendly staff hears all the time.

729 Wilmslow Rd., Didsbury. ✆ 0161/4344788. Ploughman's lunch £3.95 ($6). MC, V. Pub daily 11am–11pm; food Mon–Fri 11am–2:15pm.

Royal Orchid Thai Restaurant ✦ THAI   Located close to the city center, this popular restaurant offers authentic Thai cuisine. Seafood, pork, chicken, and beef are available with a variety of sauces, vegetables, and noodles. Menu items include dim sum, crab claws fixed six different ways, mild Thai chicken or beef Muslim curry, garlic-fried beef, pork, or chicken, and steamed fish with preserved plums. There's a respectable wine list; house wines are available by the glass. Dine on the last Friday of the month and you may be entertained by traditional Thai dancing.

36 Charlotte St. ✆ 0161/2365183. Main courses £7–£12.50 ($11–$20). AE, DC, MC, V. Mon–Fri 11:30am–2:30pm and 5:30–11pm; Sat 1–11:30pm; Sun 1–11pm.

MANCHESTER AFTER DARK
THE CLUB & MUSIC SCENE

Above all else, Manchester is known for its recent contributions to pop music. From The Smiths and New Order to Oasis and the Stone Roses, the "Manchester sound" has been known throughout the world for over a decade. Yet surprisingly enough, live music went by the wayside in the early 1990s, and clubs were in short supply until they started making a comeback in the last couple of years.

Bar 38, 10 Canal St. (✆ 01612/366005), is known for its design, with artwork displayed on the bright orange glow of the walls. On weekends DJs play house and disco for the young crowd of all sexual persuasions. Sometimes a live funk band provides the hottest show in town. The club lies a 2-minute walk west of the town center, and the bar serves tasty tapas.

The Attic, 50 New Wakefield (✆ 01612/366071), just southwest of the town center, offers the best of both worlds. Downstairs is a relaxing pub aptly named Thirsty Scholar, with a lot of gorgeous guys and dolls. Upstairs you descend into the funk/soul chaos of a club, The Attic, drawing a hip young crowd to dance and drink.

South, 4A King St. (✆ 01618/317756), is a small industrial-style club. A 10-minute walk north of Piccadilly Gardens, this club has a sophisticated young aura, with '60s and '70s music on Friday and a hot house DJ on Saturday.

Dry Bar, 28–30 Old Oldham St. (✆ 01612/369840), was launched by the band New Order and Factory Records. A lot of young, hip media people are drawn to this "stretch" bar with its ultra-modern industrial steel look. A 5-minute walk north of the town center, the bar features live music every weekend and on some weekdays, ranging from hip-hop to acid jazz. Surprisingly, the food dished out here is inspired by Jamaica, including authentic jerk chicken.

The Roadhouse, Newton Street (© **01612/281789**), the hottest small venue in Manchester, hosts bands up to 7 nights a week. Monday through Saturday check out **Band on the Wall,** 25 Swan St. at Oak Street (© **01618/326625**), where live rock, blues, jazz, and reggae can be heard. For edgier music, check the stage at **Star & Garter,** Farefield Street (© **01612/736726**), on Wednesday through Friday, when harder rock and hard-core acts take the stage.

Dance clubs here are still going strong. Just stroll through the Castlefield district on a weekend night and check out all the bars featuring a DJ. Located in the old three-story headquarters of Factory Records, **Industry,** 112–116 Princess St. (© **01612/735422**), offers up techno and disco to a mainly gay crowd.

A PUB-CRAWL

Peveril of the Peak, Great Bridgewater Street (© **01612/366364**), is easy enough to find—just look for a 380-year-old triangular building covered in tile from top to bottom. No one seems to know why it was designed or built that way, but you can step inside and enjoy a pint of Wilson's Original, Theakston's Best Bitter, Yorkshire Terrier, or Webster's Best Bitter while you puzzle over it.

Manto, 46 Canal St., behind Chorlton Street Coach Station (© **01612/ 362667**), is more than a gay pub; it's a major scene and serves as a sort of clearinghouse of information on the hottest happenings in the gay community. Read the flyers posted around the interior and strike up a conversation with an employee or regular to find out what's what if you're out and about.

A late Victorian drinking house renowned for its environment as well as its ales, the **Marble Arch,** 73 Rochdale Rd., Ancoats, at the corner of Gould Street just east of Victoria Station (© **01618/325914**), has high barrel-vaulted ceilings, extensive marble and tile surfaces, a mosaic barroom floor, a carved wooden mantelpiece, and glazed brick walls. It's a great place to linger over a pint of Hopwood Bitter, Oak Wobbly Bob, or Titanic Captain Smith. For fans of slapstick, the Laurel and Hardy Preservation Society shows old movies here on the third Wednesday of the month. Recent improvements include the opening of their own microbrewery featuring four of their homemade suds.

THE PERFORMING ARTS

Everyone knows about the rock scene in Manchester, but the fine arts thrive as well.

For drama with an unobstructed view, go to the nation's largest theater-in-the-round, **The Royal Exchange,** St. Ann's Square (© **01618/339833**), which is housed in a futuristic glass-and-steel structure built within the Great Hall of Manchester's former Cotton Exchange and offers 48 weeks of in-house dramaturgy every year.

Home of the renowned **Halle Orchestra, The Bridgewater Hall,** Lower Mosley Street (© **01619/079000**), is a state-of-the-art, 2,400-seat concert hall. In addition to the orchestra's season, it also presents other classical performances as well as some pop and comedy, too.

The University of Manchester's Department of Music, Dunmark Road (© **01612/754982**), is home to one of the nation's most distinctive classical string quartets, the **Lindsay String Quartet,** which performs a series of eight evening concerts in the department's auditorium during the year. For a real bargain, check on its luncheon recital series, which is free.

The internationally acclaimed **BBC Philharmonic** performs Friday and Saturday evening concerts 12 times a year at Bridgewater Hall (box office ℭ **01619/ 079000**).

2 Liverpool ⟨★

353km (219 miles) NW of London; 221km (103 miles) NW of Birmingham; 56km (35 miles) W of Manchester

Liverpool, with its famous waterfront on the River Mersey, is a great shipping port and industrial center. King John launched it on its road to glory when he granted it a charter in 1207. Before that, it had been a tiny 12th-century fishing village, but it quickly became a port for shipping men and materials to Ireland. In the 18th century, it grew to prominence because of the sugar, spice, and tobacco trade with the Americans. By the time Victoria came to the throne, Liverpool had become Britain's biggest commercial seaport.

Recent refurbishing of the Albert Dock, the establishment of a Maritime Museum, and the conversion of warehouses into little stores similar to those in Ghirardelli Square in San Francisco have made this an up-and-coming area once again, with many attractions for visitors. Liverpudlians are proud of their city, with its new hotels, two cathedrals, shopping and entertainment complexes, and parks. And of course, whether they're fans of the Fab Four or not, most visitors to Liverpool want to see where Beatlemania began.

ESSENTIALS

GETTING THERE Liverpool has its own airport (ℭ **01512/884000**), which has frequent daily flights from many parts of the United Kingdom, including London, the Isle of Man, and Ireland.

Frequent express trains depart London's Euston Station for Liverpool, a 2¾-hour trip. For schedules and information, call **0845/7484950.** There is also frequent service from Manchester, a 45-minute ride away.

National Express buses depart London's Victoria Coach Station every 3 hours for the 4¼-hour trip to Liverpool. Buses also arrive every hour from Manchester, a 1-hour ride away. For schedules and information, call ℭ **020/7529- 2000.**

If you're driving from London, head north on the M1, then northwest on the M6 to the junction with the M62, which heads west to Liverpool.

VISITOR INFORMATION The **Tourist Information Centre** is at the Atlantic Pavilion, Albert Dock (ℭ **01517/088854**), and is open daily from 10am to 5:30pm. Another Tourist Information Centre in the City Centre, **Queen's Square Centre,** Roe Street (ℭ **01517/093285**), is open Monday to Saturday from 9am to 5:30pm, and Sunday from 10am to 4:30pm.

SPECIAL EVENTS At the end of August and running into the first couple of days of September, the annual **International Beatles Week** attracts about 100,000 fans to Liverpool for a 7-day celebration highlighted by concerts from bands from Argentina to Sweden (with names such as Lenny Pane, Wings Over Liverpool, and The Beats). You can hear the news today at the Sgt. Pepper concert, and take in many other Beatles tributes, auctions, and tours. **Cavern City Tours,** a local company, offers hotel and festival packages that include accommodations and tickets to tours and events, starting around £99 ($158) for 2 nights. For information, contact Cavern City Tours at ℭ **01512/369091** (www.cavern-liverpool.co.uk) or the Tourist Information Centre in Liverpool at ℭ **01517/088854.**

SEEING THE SIGHTS

If you'd like a Beatles-related bus tour, **Cavern City Tours** (© **01512/369091**) presents a daily 2-hour Magical Mystery Tour, departing from Albert Dock at 2:20pm and from Roe Street at 2:30pm. This bus tour covers the most famous attractions associated with the Beatles. Tickets cost from £10.95 ($18) and are sold at the Tourist Information Centre at the Atlantic Pavilion on Albert Dock or at the Queen's Square Centre on Roe Street. For more information about tickets, call either © **01517/098111** or 01517/088574.

In the Britannia Pavilion at Albert Dock, you can visit **"The Beatles Story"** (© **01517/091963**), a museum housing memorabilia of the famous group, including a yellow submarine with live fish swimming past the portholes. It's open Monday through Friday from 10am to 5pm, and Saturday and Sunday from 10am to 6pm. From Easter to September, it's open daily from 10am to 6pm. Admission is £7.95 ($13) for adults and £5.45 ($9) for children and students, and a family ticket is £19 ($30).

Everyone's curious about **Penny Lane** and **Strawberry Field.** Actually, the Beatles' song about Penny Lane didn't refer to the small lane itself but to the area at the top of the lane called Smithdown Place. Today, this is a bustling thoroughfare for taxis and buses—hardly a place for nostalgic memories.

John Lennon lived nearby and attended school in the area. When he studied at Art College, he passed here almost every day. To reach Penny Lane and the area referred to, head north of Sefton Park. From the park, Green Bank Lane leads into Penny Lane itself, and at the junction of Allerton Road and Smithdown Road stands the Penny Lane Tramsheds. This is John Lennon country—or what's left of it.

Only the most diehard fans will want to make the journey to **Strawberry Field** along Beaconsfield Road, which is reached by taking Menlove Avenue east of the center. Today, you can stand at the iron gates and look in at a children's home run by the Salvation Army. As a child, John played on the grounds, and in 1970 he donated a large sum of money to the home. A garden party held every summer here was attended by John. His son, Sean, and Yoko Ono made two visits here in 1984. The first was a media circus, but the second was conducted in secrecy. Yoko spent many hours talking to the children and bringing them gifts, along with $80,000 to help run their home.

Because these sights are hard to reach by public transport and lie outside the center, you may want to take one of the Cavern City Tours (see above) that feature both Strawberry Field and Penny Lane.

A fun thing to do is to take the famous **Mersey Ferry** that travels from the Pier Head to both Woodside and Seacombe. Service operates daily from early morning to early evening throughout the year. Special cruises run throughout the summer including trips along the Manchester Ship Canal. For more information, contact **Mersey Ferries,** Victoria Place, Seacombe, Wallasey (© **01516/301030**).

Albert Dock 🅐   Built of brick, stone, and cast iron, this showpiece development on Liverpool's waterfront opened in 1846, saw a long period of decline, and has now been extensively renovated and refurbished. The dockland warehouses now house shops, restaurants, cafes, an English pub, and a cellar wine bar. One pavilion encompasses the main building of the Merseyside Maritime Museum (see below) and another is the home of the Tate Liverpool, the National Collection of modern art in the north of England (see below). Parking is available.

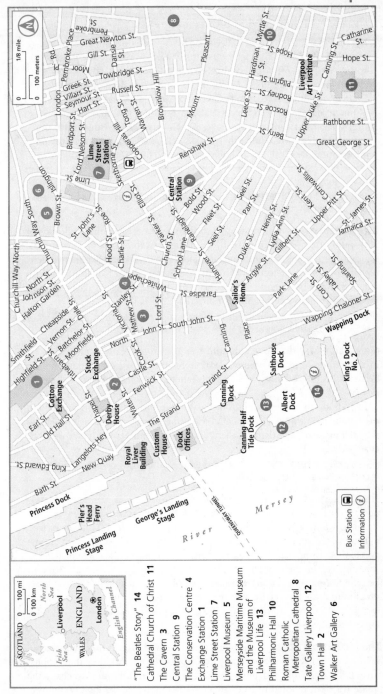

Liverpool

Great Newton St.
Pembroke Place
Gill St.
Dansie St.
Moor St.
London Rd.
Pembroke Pl.
Greek St.
Villars St.
Seymour St.
Towbridge St.
Russell St.
Birdport St.
Hart St.
Lord Nelson St.
Lime St.
Coppers Hill
Tong St.
Warren St.
Brownlow Hill
Mount
Renshaw St.
Pleasant
Myrtle St.
Hope St.
Catharine St.
Canning St.
Hope St.

Liverpool Art Institute

Rathbone St.
Great George St.

Leece St.
Roscoe St.
Rodney St.
Hardman St.
Pilgrim St.
Upper Duke St.
Berry St.
Leece St.

Lime Street Station 7

i

Central Station 9

Skethorne St.
Lime St.
Elliot St.
Bold St.
Wood St.
Fleet St.
Seel St.
Seel St.
Parr St.
Duke St.
Henry St.
Argyle St.
Lydia Ann St.
Gilbert St.
Cornwallis St.
Kent St.
Upper Pitt St.
St. James St.
Jamaica St.
Upper Pitt St.

Roe St.
St. John's Lane
Hood St.
Charle St.
Church St.
Ranelagh St.
Parker St.
Whitechapel
School Lane
Hanover St.
Paradise St.
Park Lane
Con St.
Tabley St.
Spalling St.
Wapping

Sailor's Home

Victoria St.
Stanley St.
Mathew St.
Lord St.
John St.
South John St.
Canning
Canning
Place
Strand St.
The Strand
Wapping Chaloner St.

Wapping Dock

Churchill Way North
Churchill Way South
Islington
Brown St.
North St.
Johnson St.
Halton Garden
Cheapside St.
Vernon St.
Batchelor St.
Dale St.
Moorfields
North
Cook St.
Castle St.
Fenwick St.
Smithfield St.
Highfield St.
Titheban St.
Chapel St.

Stock Exchange 2

Cotton Exchange 1

Earl St.
Old Hall St.
Derby House
Water St.
King Edward St.
Langelots Hey
New Quay
Bath St.

Royal Liver Building

Custom House

Dock Offices

Salthouse Dock

Canning Dock

Canning Half Tide Dock 12

Albert Dock 13

14

King's Dock No. 2

i

Princess Dock

Pier's Head Ferry

George's Landing Stage

Princess Landing Stage

River   *M e r s e y*

QUEENSWAY TUNNEL

Bus Station
Information i

N
1/8 mile
100 meters
0

SCOTLAND
North Sea
Irish Sea
ENGLAND
WALES
Liverpool
London
English Channel
100 mi
100 km

> ⟨*Value* **A Money-Saving Sightseeing Pass**
>
> The National Museums and Galleries on Merseyside (NMGM) sells the economical **Eight Pass,** which lets you visit some of Liverpool's best museums and galleries as often as you like over a 12-month period for only £3 ($4.50) for adults, £1.50 ($2.25) for seniors and students. Free for children 5 and under. The pass covers the Liverpool Museum, Merseyside Maritime Museum, HM Customs and Excise National Museum, Museum of Liverpool Life, Walker Art Gallery, Lady Lever Art Gallery, Sudley House, and the Conservation Centre. For further details call ℰ **0151/2070001,** or for an information pack, call the 24-hour hot line at ℰ **0151/4784747.**

Albert Dock Co. Ltd. ℰ **01517/087334.** Free admission. Shops daily 10am–6pm. Bars and restaurants daily 11am–11pm. Smart Bus from city center.

Tate Liverpool ⚐ This museum displays much of the National Collection of 20th-century art, complemented by changing art exhibitions of international standing. Three- and 4-month special exhibitions are frequently mounted here, perhaps the prints of Joan Miró or the sculptures of the iconoclastic British sculptress Rachel Whiteread. The tourist office has full details of all special exhibitions, or you can call the museum directly.

Albert Dock. ℰ **01517/027400.** www.tate.org.uk/liverpool. Free admission except special exhibitions. Tues–Sun 10am–5:50pm. Bus: "Albert Dock Shuttle" from city center.

Merseyside Maritime Museum and the Museum of Liverpool Life ⚐ Set in the historic heart of Liverpool's waterfront, this museum provides a unique blend of floating exhibits, craft demonstrations, working displays, and special events.

In addition to restored waterfront buildings, exhibitions present the story of mass emigration through Liverpool in the last century, shipbuilding on Merseyside, the Battle of the Atlantic Gallery, and Transatlantic Slavery. There is wheelchair access.

Albert Dock. ℰ **0151/478-4499.** www.liverpoolmuseums.org.uk. Free admission. Daily 10am–5pm. Bus: "Albert Dock Shuttle" from city center.

The Conservation Centre The Conservation Centre, in the heart of Liverpool, is the first of its kind in Europe. The Caught in Time exhibition uncovers the secret world of museum conservation and reveals how the 1.2 million artifacts in national museums and galleries on Merseyside collections are kept from the ravages of time. Using state-of-the-art hand-held audio guides, video linkups, demonstrations, behind-the-scenes tours, and interactive displays, visitors can see how everything from fine art and a Beatles gold disc to a mummified crocodile are saved from decay by expert conservators using the most up-to-date techniques.

Whitechapel, Liverpool. ℰ **01514/784999.** www.liverpoolmuseums.org.uk/conservation. Free admission. Mon–Sat 10am–5pm; Sun noon–5pm. Closed Dec 23–26 and Jan 1.

The McCartney House The house where the McCartneys lived in Liverpool before Paul's meteoric rise to superstardom has been purchased by the National Trust. Working from old photographs taken by Paul's brother Michael, the house has been restored to its original 1950s appearance. Its look is complete with the patterned brown sofa and armchair with the white linen antimacassars where Paul and John scribbled out their first songs; and the Chinese willow print wallpaper that doesn't reach the corners because the family was too poor to buy enough. It's hardly Graceland, but it does give an insight into the humble beginnings of one of the world's most famous and influential entertainers. The house is only open to the public through tours organized by the National Trust. Six tours a day depart from Speak Hall, The Walk. Groups are limited to 14 people at any one time. Book well in advance.

20 Forthlin Rd., Allerton 16. (☎) **01517/088574** booking office; 08709/000256 information line. www.spekehall. org.uk/beatles.htm. Admission £5.50 ($9) adults, £2.80 ($4.50) children. Late Mar to late Oct Wed–Sat; early Nov to early Dec Sat only 10:50, 11:40am, and 12:30pm (Albert Dock), 2:30, 3:10 and 4pm (Speke Hall).

John Lennon Home   This is the second childhood home of a Beatle to be restored and can be seen by the public on a National Trust tour. Yoko Ono purchased the house, called Mendips, and donated it to the National Trust. Constructed in 1933, Mendips is a semi-detached house in Woolton, a suburb of Liverpool. It has been returned to its look from 1945 to 1963 when Lennon lived here, and the original features such as stained-glass windows and fireplaces are intact. In Lennon's tiny bedroom you can see such memorabilia as pictures of Elvis, Rita Hayworth, and Brigitte Bardot. Lennon slept in this bedroom from ages 5 to 23 when he lived with his aunt and uncle, Mimi and George Smith, after his parents broke up.

251 Menlove Ave. Minibus tours run from Albert Dock to Mendips 4 times a day Wed–Sun. (☎) **0151/ 708-8574** for morning tours, or (☎) 0151/427-7231 for afternoon tours. Tours cost £10 ($16).

Walker Art Gallery ☆☆   One of Europe's finest art galleries offers an outstanding collection of European art from 1300 to the present day. The gallery is especially rich in European old masters, Victorian and pre-Raphaelite works, and contemporary British art. It also has an award-winning sculpture gallery, featuring works from the 18th and 19th centuries. Seek out, in particular, Simone Martini's *Jesus Discovered in the Temple* and Salvator Rosa's *Landscape with Hermit.* Rembrandt is on show, as is an enticing *Nymph of the Fountain* by Cranach. The work of British artists is strongest here, ranging from *Horse Frightened by a Lion* by Stubbs to *Snowdon from Llan Nantlle* by Richard Wilson. Among the pre-Raphaelites are Ford Madox Brown and W. R. Yeames. French Impressionists include the works of Monet, Seurat, and Degas, among others. Modern British paintings include works by Lucian Freud and Stanley Spencer. The admission charged is good for 1 year into any and all of the eight museums and galleries on Merseyside.

William Brown St. (☎) **01514/784199.** www.liverpoolmuseums.org.uk/walker. Free admission. Mon–Sat 10am–5pm; Sun noon–5pm. Closed Dec 23–26 and Jan 1.

Liverpool Museum ☆   One of Britain's finest museums features collections from all over the world—from the earliest beginnings with giant dinosaurs through centuries of great art and inventions.

At the Natural History Centre you can use microscopes and video cameras to learn about the natural world. Living displays from the vivarium and aquarium form a large part of the collections, and a planetarium features daily programs covering modern space exploration—an armchair tour toward the beginning of the universe and the far-flung reaches of the cosmos. There is a small charge for the planetarium and temporary exhibitions.

William Brown St. (☎) **01514/784399.** www.liverpoolmuseum.org.uk. Free admission. Mon–Sat 10am–5pm; Sun noon–5pm.

Cathedral Church of Christ ★★ The great new Anglican edifice overlooking the River Mersey was begun in 1904 and was largely completed 74 years later; it was the last Gothic-style cathedral to be built worldwide. Dedicated in the presence of Queen Elizabeth II in 1978, it is the largest church in England and the fifth-largest in the world. Its vaulting under the tower is 53m (175 ft.) high, the highest in the world, and its length, 186m (619 ft.), makes it one of the longest cathedrals in the world. The organ has nearly 10,000 pipes, the most found in any church. The tower houses the highest (66m/219 ft.) and the heaviest (31 tons) bells in the world, and the Gothic arches are the highest ever built. From the tower, you can see to North Wales.

A Visitor Centre and Refectory features an aerial sculpture of 12 huge sails, with a ship's bell, clock, and light that changes color on an hourly basis. You can enjoy full meals in the charming refectory.

St. James Mt. ✆ **01517/096271.** Admission to cathedral free; tower and embroidery gallery £2 ($3.20) adults, £1 ($1.60) children. Cathedral daily 8am–6pm. Tower closed during winter; open daily Mar–Oct 11am–3pm.

Roman Catholic Metropolitan Cathedral of Christ the King ★★ Less than 1km (½ mile) away from the Anglican cathedral stands the Roman Catholic cathedral—the two are joined by a road called Hope Street. The construction of the cathedral, designed by Sir Edwin Lutyens, was started in 1930, but when World War II interrupted in 1939, not even the granite and brick vaulting of the crypt was complete. At the end of the war it was estimated that the cost of completing the structure as Lutyens had designed it would be some £27 million. Architects throughout the world were invited to compete to design a more realistic project to cost about £1 million and to be completed in 5 years. Sir Frederick Gibberd won the competition and was commissioned to oversee the construction of the circular cathedral in concrete and glass, pitched like a tent at one end of the piazza that covered all of the original site, crypt included.

Construction was completed between 1962 and 1967, and today the cathedral provides seating for more than 2,000, all within 15m (50 ft.) of the central altar. Above the altar rises a multicolored glass lantern weighing 2,000 tons and rising to a height of 87m (290 ft.). Called a space-age cathedral, it has a bookshop, a tearoom, and tour guides.

Albert Dock. ✆ **0151/7099222.** www.liverpool-rc-cathedral.org.uk. Free admission. Daily 8am–6pm (until 5pm in winter). Bus: "Albert Dock Shuttle" from city center.

WALKING TOUR	IN THE FOOTSTEPS OF THE FAB FOUR

Start:	Town Hall
Finish:	St. Silas School
Time:	2½ leisurely hours
Best Times:	Daily 9:30am to 4:30pm to avoid rush-hour traffic.

Liverpudlians feel a deep pride and love for "their" four boys who changed musical history—in fact, upon the recent death of George Harrison, the Union Jack was flown half-mast at the Liverpool town hall. Wherever you turn today, somebody is hawking a Beatles tour. But if you'd like to set your own pace, put on a pair of walking shoes and head out on your own trail with a little help from your friends (us).

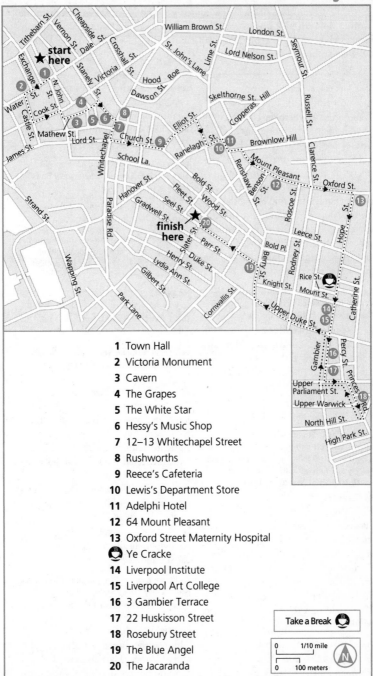

1 Town Hall
2 Victoria Monument
3 Cavern
4 The Grapes
5 The White Star
6 Hessy's Music Shop
7 12–13 Whitechapel Street
8 Rushworths
9 Reece's Cafeteria
10 Lewis's Department Store
11 Adelphi Hotel
12 64 Mount Pleasant
13 Oxford Street Maternity Hospital
Ye Cracke
14 Liverpool Institute
15 Liverpool Art College
16 3 Gambier Terrace
17 22 Huskisson Street
18 Rosebury Street
19 The Blue Angel
20 The Jacaranda

Take a Break

0   1/10 mile
0   100 meters

N

At The Cavern (see below), now touted as "The Most Famous Club in the World," you can pick up a Cavern City Tour map to find locations in the city center. More in-depth exploration will require the "Liverpool A to Zed" map, available at most newsstands.

Start your tour at:
❶ Town Hall

Water Street is where the city of Liverpool held a civic reception for The Beatles on July 10, 1964, while they were in town for the northern premiere of their first feature film, *A Hard Day's Night.* Nearly a quarter of a million fans turned out, lining the way from Liverpool Airport into the city center, and there was an explosion of cheering when John, Paul, George, and Ringo finally appeared on the Town Hall's balcony.

Near the intersection of Water and Castle streets, John Lennon first wooed girlfriend Thelma Pickles in 1958 on the steps of:
❷ Victoria Monument

A fellow art-school student also abandoned by her father, she is best remembered for helping John come to terms with his mother's tragic death. Thelma was hit by a car and killed while walking on July 15, 1958.

Walk up Castle Street (which starts at Water Street), turn left onto Cook Street, and take a right on North John Street. Almost immediately, you'll turn left onto Mathew Street. At no. 10 Mathew St. stands the legendary:
❸ Cavern

The Beatles played 292 gigs here between 1961 and 1963. The first show was on March 21, 1961, for which they were paid the rather less-than-princely sum of £5 ($8). Manager Brian Epstein first saw them here on November 9, 1961. By December 10, he had signed a contract with the band.

Cross Mathew Street and enter:
❹ The Grapes pub

Through much of its heyday, the Cavern had no alcohol license, so the Beatles and other bands would come here for a quick drink. Occasionally, however, the boys were barred from The Grapes for rowdy or drunken behavior. They would then find it necessary to venture elsewhere.

Continue up the street and hang a right onto Rainford Gardens, where you'll find:
❺ The White Star

This pub always stood ready to haul out the pints for the lads.

Head back to Mathew Street, continue away from The Cavern, and you'll dead-end on Stanley Street. Turn right, and just around the corner stands:
❻ Hessy's Music Shop

It was here where Aunt Mimi bought John his first guitar for £17 ($27) in 1957.

Continue up Stanley Street and you'll come to Whitechapel. Take a right to find, on your left:
❼ 12–13 Whitechapel St.

Now an appliance store called Rumbelows, this was the home of NEMS (Northern End Music Stores), Brian Epstein's family-owned record shop, where repeated requests for the Beatles's record (actually the single "My Bonnie" by fellow Hamburg nightclub performer Tony Sheridan, on which The Beatles appeared as "The Beat Brothers") made him curious enough to head to The Cavern and catch a show.

Backtrack now, walking past the intersection with Stanley Street again. Also located on the east side of Whitechapel, you'll find Hessy's competitor:
❽ Rushworths

This was the shop that upgraded John and George Harrison to Gibson acoustic guitars in 1962—their prize for being named Liverpool's best band in a Mersey Beat poll.

Now turn around, backtrack a bit on Whitechapel, and make a left onto Church Street. After about 3 blocks, you'll come to:

⑨ Reece's Cafeteria

John Lennon and Cynthia Powell held their wedding reception here on August 23, 1962. Brian Epstein escorted them to lunch after their ceremony, with witnesses George Harrison and Paul McCartney in tow. Brian not only picked up the bill, but also announced that he was giving them his comfortable apartment at 36 Falkner St. as a wedding present (his real motive was actually to protect John's sexy single image by hiding away the pregnant Cynthia).

Backtrack along Elliot Street, and turn right on Great Charlotte Street. Keep going and turn left on Ranelagh Street. To your right will be:

⑩ Lewis's Department Store

Upon returning to home life after the excitement of Hamburg, Paul was told by his father to quit moping around the house, so he found short-lived employment here as a delivery-van assistant during the 1960 Christmas season. The doorway of this store is also where John and Cynthia met to start many an evening on the town when they were dating.

Just across Renshaw Street, between Copperas Hill and Brownlow Hill, sits the:

⑪ Adelphi Hotel

The Adelphi Hotel, on Ranelagh Place, is where John's father, Freddie Lennon, worked in his youth. This is also where John the art student, dressed as a vicar, persuaded the staff to lend him a mop and bucket. He proceeded to mop the pedestrian crosswalk out front while singing at the top of his lungs. Later, in the mid-1960s, the hotel housed not only the Beatles, but also other pop luminaries, including Bob Dylan, when they passed through town.

Head to the intersection of Renshaw Street and Brownlow Hill. Take Brownlow for 1 block, then veer off to your right onto Mount Pleasant. After two and a half blocks, you'll come to:

⑫ 64 Mount Pleasant

This is the site of the former Register Office where John and Cynthia were married on August 23, 1962, with Brian, George, and Paul in attendance.

Continue along Mount Pleasant until it becomes Oxford Street. Just past the intersection of Hope Street is the:

⑬ Oxford Street Maternity Hospital

John was born at this hospital, on Cambridge Street, during a 7am air raid on October 9, 1940.

TAKE A BREAK Located on Rice Street close to the Liverpool Art College (take Hope Street from the Oxford Street hospital several blocks to Rice), **Ye Cracke** was a hangout frequented by John and Stuart Sutcliffe in their art-school days. It was here that John brought future wife Cynthia, plying her with alcohol until she agreed to return with him to Stuart's flat at 3 Gambier Terrace, Hope Street, where he seduced her for the first time. (*Note:* Regulars here are sick of talking to tourists about John's drinking days in the pub. Just absorb the atmosphere and move on.)

From Ye Cracke, backtrack to Hope Street, where you'll turn right. The next intersection on your right is with Mount Street. Sitting at the corner, on Mount Street, is the:

⑭ Liverpool Institute

Both George and Paul attended high school here.

Adjacent to it on Hope Street is the old:

⑮ Liverpool Art College

Now Liverpool John Moores University, this is where John enrolled in 1958, as a lettering major. It was here that John met Cynthia, Stuart, and Bill Harry, his art-school friend. Owing to the proximity of their schools, Paul and George often took their guitars to school and met John at the art college, holding impromptu jam sessions in the canteen or in room no. 21.

Keep heading down Hope Street; it will change names and become Gambier Terrace. Stuart's former apartment is on the left, at:

⑯ 3 Gambier Terrace

This is the Liverpool apartment shared by John and Stuart in early 1960. An unknown John appears sprawled on the floor of this apartment in a photo accompanying a derogatory article about beatniks in a July 1960 article from *The People*. It's also where John first seduced Cynthia; he used to sleep in a satin-lined coffin because he claimed it was comfortable.

Continue south on Gambier Terrace, and turn left on Huskisson Street, where, situated on your right, you'll find a large, 4-story Victorian house at:

⑰ 22 Huskisson St.

Here is the childhood home of John's mother Julia, Aunt Mimi, and his other three aunts.

Backtrack to Gambier Terrace, turn left, take a left on Upper Parliament Street, then go right on Princess Road. To your left you'll find:

⑱ Rosebury Street

A block party held here, to celebrate the 750th anniversary of Liverpool receiving its first royal charter, is touted as "The Quarry Men's" first professional gig, on June 22, 1957, on the back of a coal lorry. A picture from this gig of John playing and singing in a checkered shirt is famous today as the first photo of the future superstar at work. The gig was so successful that The Quarry Men had to wait inside a friend's home for a police escort, as some local toughs,

noticing the amount of female attention they were receiving, threatened them with bodily harm.

Now backtrack to Gambier Terrace and head back up. Make a left on Upper Duke Street, continuing for a few blocks until you reach Berry Street. Turn right onto Berry. Walk up well past Knight Street and on your left, at 108 Seel St., will be a club called:

⑲ The Blue Angel

In May 1960, when it was the "Wyvern Social Club," the band auditioned here as the Silver Beatles for British promoter Larry Parnes (the United Kingdom's answer to Col. Tom Parker). The band was chosen to accompany Parnes's crooner, Johnny Gentle, on a nine-stop tour of Scotland—their first professional gig as the Beatles. In August that year, desperately needing a drummer to accept their infamous Hamburg gig, they auditioned Pete Best on this stage. It actually opened as the Blue Angel on March 22, 1961, and was later the site of the first meeting between Ringo Starr and Brian.

Keep going on Seel Street for a couple of blocks until you reach the intersection of Seel and Slater. At 23 Slater St. you'll find:

⑳ The Jacaranda

Allan Williams' wine cellar is now a music club with a dance floor. Although he claimed to have never liked their music, Williams acted as the quartet's first manager and occasionally booked them here in 1960. It is from this location that Williams drove them to the ferry on their way to Hamburg in August 1960. John and Stuart supposedly painted murals still visible on the walls when the club was preparing to open.

SHOPPING

Pedestrian shopping areas with boutiques, specialty shops, and department stores include Church Street, Lord Street, Bold Street, Whitechapel, and Paradise Street. Right on the river, Albert Dock also houses a collection of small shops.

For shopping centers, go to **Cavern Walks** on Mathew Street, the heart of Beatleland (℗ **01512/369082**), or **Quiggins Centre,** 12–16 School Lane (℗ **01517/092462**).

If you want to buy that special piece of Beatles memorabilia, wander through the **Beatles Shop,** 31 Mathew St. (✆ 01512/368066), or the **Heritage Shop,** 1 The Colonnades, Albert Dock (✆ 01517/097474).

For a huge selection of British crafts, visit **Bluecoat Display Centre,** College Lane (✆ 01517/094014), with its gallery of metal, ceramics, glass, jewelry, and wood pieces by some 350 British craftspeople.

Frank Green's, 97 Oakfield Rd., Anfield (✆ 01512/603241), is where you'll find prints by this famous local artist who has been capturing the Liverpool scene on canvas since the 1960s. His work includes city secular buildings, churches, and street life.

Two of Liverpool's best bookshops include **Waterstone's,** 14–16 Bold St. (✆ 01517/086861), and **Gallery Shop,** Tate Gallery, Albert Dock (✆ 01517/027575). Because the Gallery Shop is located in Tate Gallery, it also carries gallery-related merchandise.

A couple of other specialty shops that warrant a visit include **Sewill Marine,** Unit 19, Setton Lane Industrial Estate, Maghull (✆ 08707/522444), which has been making nautical instruments longer than anyone in the known world; and **Thornton's,** 16 Whitechapel (✆ 01517/086849), where you can choose from a dizzying selection of continental and traditional English chocolates, toffees, and mints.

WHERE TO STAY

Aachen Hotel   Five minutes from the city center near the Roman Catholic cathedral, this well-run, good-value establishment is a landmark building in a conservation district. The modernized bedrooms are comfortable, though a bit drab; hallway bathrooms are adequate.

89–91 Mt. Pleasant, Liverpool, Merseyside L3 5TB. ✆ 0151/7093477. Fax 0151/7091126. www.aachen hotel.co.uk. 18 units, 12 with bathroom. £32 ($51) single without bathroom, £40 ($64) single with bathroom; £50 ($80) double without bathroom, £60 ($96) double with bathroom. Rates include English breakfast. AE, DC, MC, V. Parking £6.50 ($10). **Amenities:** Breakfast room; bar. *In room:* TV, coffeemaker, hair dryer, trouser press, safe.

Aplin House Hotel   This hotel is off A561, close to the Garston Railway Station; it's 10 minutes by train from the city center, 3km (2 miles) from the Liverpool airport, and 20 minutes by car from the Irish ferries. A well-kept residence facing the park, it was built in 1901, the year of Victoria's death. It's run by Mr. and Mrs. Atherton. The standard-size rooms are comfortable, each with private facilities. Mrs. Atherton makes breakfast "as you like it." The Aplin is located within a mile of where the Beatles lived and went to school; Mrs. Atherton will happily arrange a private tour through "Beatles Country."

35 Clarendon Rd., Garston, Liverpool, Merseyside L19 6PJ. ✆ 0151/4275047. 4 units. £26–£30 ($42–$48) single; £38–£55 ($61–$88) double. No credit cards. Northern Line train to Garston. Bus: no. 80 or 86. **Amenities:** Breakfast room. *In room:* TV, coffeemaker, hair dryer (on request).

Feathers Hotel   This brick-fronted hotel is composed of four separate Georgian-style town houses. It sits in the heart of the city, adjacent to the modern Metropolitan Cathedral. The bedrooms are comfortable, with simple traditional furniture, but don't expect much charm. Each is well maintained nonetheless and offers old-fashioned comfort. Some 40 units come with both tub and shower.

119–125 Mt. Pleasant, Liverpool, Merseyside L3 5TF. ✆ 01517/099655. Fax 01517/093838. www.feathers. uk.com. 70 units. £79–£89.95 ($126–$144) double. Rates include buffet breakfast. AE, DC, MC, V. Bus: 80 (the airport bus). **Amenities:** Restaurant; bar; room service; dry cleaning. *In room:* TV, coffeemaker, hair dryer, iron, trouser press.

WHERE TO DINE

Bar Italia/Ristorante Italiano ITALIAN   In the city's commercial heartland, this restaurant, established in June 1999, attracts crowds to its satisfying Italian food at reasonable prices. Polished wood floors, an attentive waitstaff, and excellent and moderately priced French and Italian wines make this place a sure-fire bet to stick around for a while. The day's specials are seasonally based. Choose an excellent seafood risotto or else have vegetarian dishes or pepper steak. The chef does an excellent filet of chicken with brandy, cream, and mushrooms. The widest array of pastas in Liverpool is available here.

48A Castle St. (*C*) **01512/363375.** Reservations recommended. Main courses £11.95–£16.95 ($19–$27); pastas £6.95–£7.95 ($11–$13). MC, V. Mon–Fri 11:30am–3pm; Tues–Sat 5:30–10:30pm.

Casa Italia ITALIAN   For your Italian fix, head here. You get fresh food at affordable prices. The pasta dishes are especially recommendable as are several versions of tasty pizza. We enjoyed both while taking in the sight of a young man who looked like a dead ringer for John Lennon (obviously by design).

40 Stanley St. (*C*) **0151/2275774.** Reservations recommended. Main courses £4.95–£6.95 ($8–$11). MC, V. Mon–Sat noon–10pm.

Don Pepe Restaurant and Tapas Bar ⭐ SPANISH   This emporium is inside the imposing stone walls of one of the city's most architecturally distinguished buildings. Built a century ago as the headquarters of a local shipping company, the Union House had degenerated into a derelict fruit warehouse until its restoration. Inside, a group of local investors has created one of England's most vividly evocative Spanish decors, with hand-painted tile murals and Iberian fountains. No meal here would be complete without a pre-dinner trip to the marble-topped tapas bar, where choices include portions of fried calamari, chorizo, salty but savory slices of Serrano ham, and well-seasoned croquettes of potatoes. Many visitors move on to eat in the adjacent dining room. *Merluza a la romana* (hake in a light batter), *zarzuela de pescado* (seasoned fish stew), escallops of pork fried in breadcrumbs, and an array of lamb dishes (especially *cordero de la casa*) are highly recommended. Service is the job of a well-trained battalion of Spanish waiters.

19–21 Victoria St. (Union House). (*C*) **0151/2311909.** Reservations recommended. Main courses £6.95–£12.50 ($11–$20). In tapas bar: beer and wine from £2.40 ($3.85); tapas £1.10–£6.75 ($1.75–$11). AE, MC, V. Mon–Sat noon–3pm and 5:30–10:30pm.

Everyman Bistro INTERNATIONAL   Part of the Everyman Theatre complex, this bistro is informal, crowded on weekends, fun, and reasonably priced. After 23 years on the street that connects the Roman Catholic and Anglican cathedrals, the Everyman is considered a local institution. A buffet offers a wide range of pâtés, quiches, pizzas, soups, meat and vegetarian entrees, seasonal salads, cheeses, desserts, and pastries. The menu, changed twice daily, is seasonal and uses only fresh produce. A typical full meal consists of carrot soup with French bread, chicken pie with new potatoes and green salad, strawberries in white wine with cream, and coffee. These simple heart-warming dishes won't wow but are varied and plentiful.

5–9 Hope St. (*C*) **0151/7089545.** Main courses £4.30–£7.50 ($7–$12). MC, V. Mon–Wed noon–midnight; Thurs noon–1am; Fri–Sat 11am–2am.

Signals Restaurant (*Value*) ENGLISH   In the premises of a busy modern commercial hotel, this is one of the city's best food values. A uniformed server helps you carve portions of honey-baked ham, turkey, beef, leg of lamb, or pork; you serve yourself from steaming dishes of vegetables and seasonal specialties. There is a vegetarian special available daily. These dishes qualify as soul food to the English, or "heady realism," in the words of one diner.

In St. George's Hotel, St. John's Precinct, Lime St. ℂ **0151/7097090.** Reservations recommended. £9 ($14) main course; 2-course carvery dinner £9.50 ($15), 3-course carvery dinner £9.95–£18 ($16–$29). AE, DC, MC, V. Daily 6–9:30pm. Bus: no. 12 or 13.

Valparaiso ⭐ *Finds* SOUTH AMERICAN/INTERNATIONAL This is more upmarket than most of our low-budget eateries in Liverpool. Lying in a convenient location "between the cathedrals," it is a handy choice for spicier fare than you usually encounter in the city. The decor takes you "South of the Border," and there's an exotic Latin touch to the place. Many international specialties are offered, with a focus on South American dishes, including those of Chile. The menu is based on fresh produce.

4 Hardman St. ℂ **0151/7086036.** Reservations recommended. Main courses £8.80–£16.50 ($14–$26). AE, MC, V. Tues–Sat 4–11pm.

LIVERPOOL AFTER DARK

Liverpool's nightlife is nothing if not diverse. Several publications and places will help you get a handle on the entertainment options around town. The evening *Liverpool Echo* is a good source of daily information about larger and fine-arts events; the youth-oriented *L: Scene* magazine will provide you with a thorough calendar of club dates and gigs; and the free *City X Blag,* available in most clubs and pubs, will do the same. Available free in gay clubs and pubs, *Pulse* lists gay activities and events throughout the region.

The **Student Entertainment Office** (ℂ **01517/944143**) at the University of Liverpool can tell you about the range of activities sponsored by the school, or you can stop by the student union on Mount Pleasant and check out the bulletin board. Two other good places for finding out about the underground scene are **The Palace,** Slater Street (ℂ **01517/088515**), and **Quiggins Centre,** School Lane (ℂ **01517/092462**). Each is overflowing with flyers advertising local events.

Open year-round, the **Liverpool Empire,** Lime Street (ℂ **08706/063541**), hosts visiting stage productions ranging from dramas and comedies to ballets and tributes. The box office is open Monday through Saturday from 10am until 6pm.

Philharmonic Hall, Hope Street (ℂ **01512/102895**), is home to **The Royal Philharmonic Orchestra,** one of the best orchestras outside of London, which usually performs twice weekly. When the orchestra is not on, there are often concerts by touring musicians, and films are sometimes shown as well.

Open Monday through Saturday nights, **Lomax,** 11–13 Hotham St. (ℂ **01517/079977**), is a good place to catch local and touring indie bands.

At the **Zanzibar Club,** 43 Seel St. (ℂ **01517/070633**), DJs spin drum and bass and hip-hop Monday through Saturday nights, with the occasional rock or pop booking thrown in for good measure.

Beatles fans flock to the **Cavern Club,** 8–10 Mathew St. (ℂ **0871/222-1957**), thinking that this is where the Fab Four appeared. Demolished years ago, the old Cavern Club has faded into history. However, locals still go to this new version to hear live bands (regrettably, not as good as the dear, departed ones). There's no cover until 10pm; after that you pay a £2 ($3.20) door charge. For a more nostalgic evening, head for the **Cavern Pub,** also on Mathew St. (ℂ **0151/236-1957**). This is where many groups in England got their start before going on to greater glory. The names of the groups who appeared here from 1957 to 1973 are recorded.

A cafe by day, **Baa Bar,** 43–45 Fleet St. (✆ **01517/070610**), serves an eclectic menu, and free dancing to a DJ brings in a lot of the evening's business.

A pub with a Fab Four spin, **Ye Cracke,** Rice Street (✆ **01517/094171**), was a favorite watering hole of John Lennon in pre- and early Beatles days (but expect regulars to suggest you quit living in the past if you ask about it). Better just soak up the little-changed atmosphere over a pint of Oak Wobbly Bob, Cains, or Pedigree.

THE GAY NIGHTLIFE SCENE

You won't find as frenetic or as varied a nightlife scene in Liverpool as you will in, say, Manchester or Leeds. But something about the rough-and-tumble streets of this monument to the Industrial Revolution makes for hard-party times at some of the city's gay bars. At **Masquerade,** 10 Cumberland St. (✆ **01512/ 367786**), a gay version of a Victorian pub, the scene is the most consistently crowded and animated of the several gay bars in its neighborhood near the Moorfields Railway Station, off Dale Street. Come to the street-level bar to drink, talk, and watch the occasional cabaret *artiste,* whose acts are presented after 8pm every Friday and Saturday. Head for the basement-level dance floor for a bit of boogieing with the 'Pudlians. At **G-Bar,** Eberle Street (✆ **01512/ 2364416**), the street level is a pseudo-Gothic piece of kitsch that only a rave party could fully appreciate. The cellar has a floor where crowds of gay and sexually neutral fans dance, dance, dance. There's even a "love lounge" where you may catch up on a bit of dialogue, or whatever, in circumstances that are highly relaxing. Cover is between £3 and £5 ($4.80 and $8), depending on the night of the week.

The Lisbon, 35 Victoria St. (✆ **01512/316831**), is set close to Moorfield railway station. This is the quietest and calmest of the four pubs listed in this section, alluring a nicer blend of men than at some of the seedier gay dives nearby.

3 The Walled City of Chester ★★

333km (207 miles) NW of London; 31km (19 miles) S of Liverpool; 147km (91 miles) NW of Birmingham

A Roman legion founded Chester on the Dee River in the 1st century A.D. It reached its pinnacle as a bustling port in the 13th and 14th centuries but declined following the gradual silting up of the river. While other walls of medieval cities of England were either torn down or badly fragmented, Chester still has 3km (2 miles) of fortified city walls intact. The main entrance into Chester is Eastgate, which dates only from the 18th century. Within the walls are half-timbered houses and shops, though not all of them date from Tudor days. Chester is unusual in that some of its builders used black-and-white timbered facades even during the Georgian and Victorian eras.

Chester today has aged gracefully and is a lovely old place to visit, if you don't mind the summer crowds who overrun the place. It has far more charm and intimacy then either Liverpool or Manchester and is one of the most interesting medieval cities in England.

ESSENTIALS

GETTING THERE   About 21 trains depart London's Euston Station every hour daily for the 2½-hour trip to Chester. Trains also run every hour between Liverpool and Chester, a 45-minute ride. For schedules and information, call ✆ **0845/7484950.**

Chester

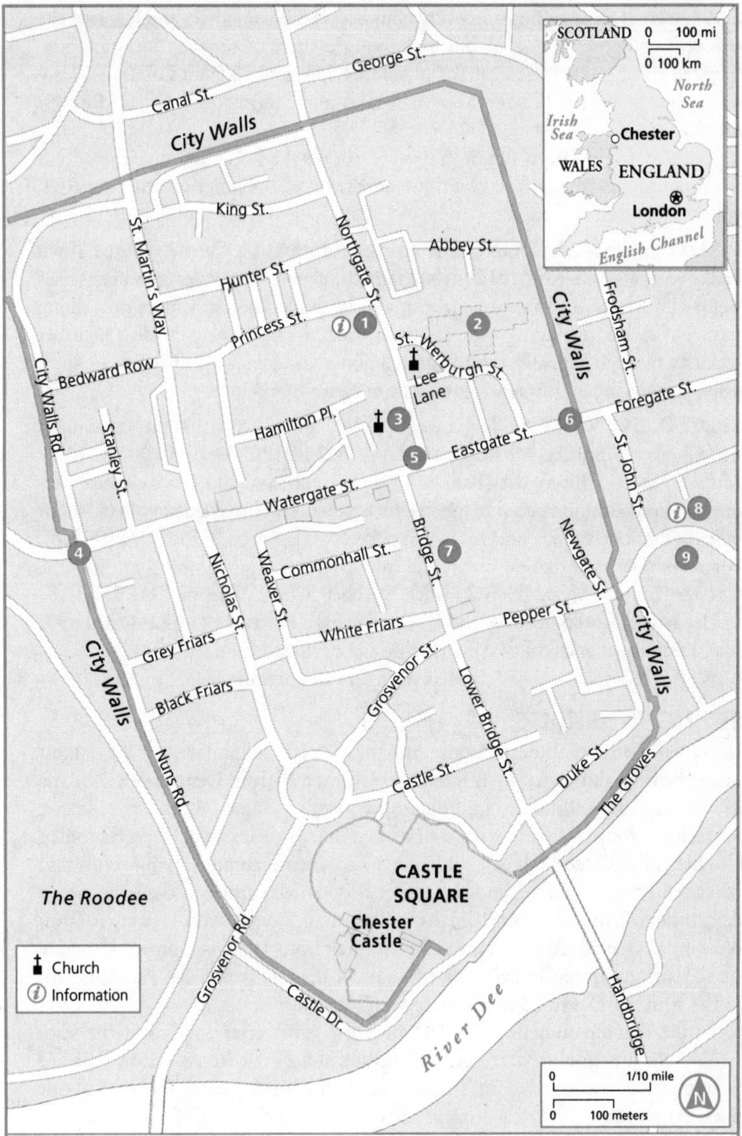
SCOTLAND
0 100 mi
0 100 km
North Sea
Irish Sea
Chester
WALES
ENGLAND
London
English Channel
George St.
Canal St.
City Walls
King St.
St. Martin's Way
Northgate St.
Abbey St.
Hunter St.
Princess St.
St. Werburgh St.
Lee Lane
Frodsham St.
Bedward Row
City Walls Rd.
Stanley St.
Hamilton Pl.
Foregate St.
Eastgate St.
St. John St.
Watergate St.
Newgate St.
Bridge St.
Commonhall St.
Weaver St.
Nicholas St.
Pepper St.
White Friars
Grey Friars
Black Friars
Grosvenor St.
Lower Bridge St.
Duke St.
The Groves
Castle St.
Nuns Rd.
CASTLE SQUARE
Chester Castle
The Roodee
Grosvenor Rd.
Castle Dr.
River Dee
Handbridge
Church
Information
0 1/10 mile
0 100 meters
N
1
2
3
4
5
6
7
8
9

Chester Cathedral **2**
Chester Visitor Centre **8**
The City Cross **5**
Eastgate **6**
Roman Amphitheater **9**
The Rows **7**
St. Peter's Church **3**
Town Hall **1**
Watergate **4**

A **National Express** bus runs every hour between Birmingham and Chester; the trip takes 2 hours. The same bus line also offers service between Liverpool and Chester. It's also possible to catch a National Express coach from London's Victoria Coach Station to Chester. For schedules and information, call © **08705/ 808080.**

If you're driving from London, head north on the M1, then take the M6 at the junction near Coventry. Continue northwest to the junction with the A54, which leads west to Chester.

VISITOR INFORMATION The **Tourist Information Centre** is at the Town Hall, Northgate Street (© **01244/402385**). It offers a hotel-reservation service as well as information. Arrangements can also be made for coach tours or walking tours of Chester (including a ghost-hunter tour). It's open May through October Monday through Saturday from 9am to 5:30pm and Sunday from 10am to 4pm; off season, Monday through Saturday from 10am to 5:30pm.

SPECIAL EVENTS The last 2 weeks of July are an active time in Chester, as the **Chester Summer Music Festival** (© 01244/320700 or 01244/341200; Mon–Fri 9am–5:30pm, Sat 10am–4pm) hosts orchestras and other classical performers from around Britain in lunch concerts, with tickets averaging £6 ($10); or in small indoor evening concerts, where tickets cost between £6 to £30 ($10–$48). For additional information about the music festival, you can also write to the Chester Summer Music Festival Office, 8 Abbey Square, Chester CH1 2HU.

Occurring simultaneously, the **Chester Fringe Festival** (© **01244/321497**) focuses on other musical genres, offering Latin, rock, Cajun, folk, and jazz concerts. Ticket prices vary widely, depending on the performer.

SEEING THE SIGHTS

In a big Victorian building opposite the Roman amphitheater, the largest uncovered amphitheater in Britain, the **Chester Visitor Centre,** Vicars Lane (© **01244/351609**), offers a number of services to visitors. A visit to a life-size Victorian street, complete with sounds and smells, helps your appreciation of Chester. The center has a gift shop and a licensed restaurant serving meals and snacks. Admission is free, and the center is open May through October, Monday through Saturday from 9am to 6:30pm and Sunday from 10am to 4pm; November through April, Monday to Saturday from 10am to 5pm and Sunday from 10am to 4pm. Guided walking tours of the city depart daily at 10:30am in the winter and at 10:30am and 2pm in the summer.

To the accompaniment of a hand bell, the **town crier** appears at the City Cross—the junction of Watergate, Northgate, and Bridge streets—from April to September at noon and 3pm Tuesday through Saturday to shout news about sales, exhibitions, and attractions in the city.

In the center of town, you'll see the much-photographed **Eastgate clock.** Climb the nearby stairs and walk along the top of the **city wall** for a view down on Chester. Passing through centuries of English history, you'll go by a cricket field, see the River Dee, formerly a major trade artery, and get a look at many 18th-century buildings. The wall also goes past some Roman ruins, and it's possible to leave the walkway to explore them. The walk is charming and free.

Eastgate Street is now a pedestrian way, and musicians often perform for your pleasure beside St. Peter's Church and the Town Cross.

The Rows ★★ are double-decker layers of shops, one tier on the street level, the others stacked on top and connected by a footway. The upper tier is like a continuous galleried balcony—walking in the rain is never a problem here.

Chester Cathedral ⭐   The present building, founded in 1092 as a Benedictine abbey, was made an Anglican cathedral church in 1541. Many architectural restorations were carried out in the 19th century, but older parts have been preserved. Notable features include the fine range of monastic buildings, particularly the cloisters and refectory, the chapter house, and the superb medieval wood carving in the choir (especially for misericords). Also worth seeing are the long south transept with its various chapels, the consistory court, and the medieval roof bosses in the Lady Chapel.

St. Werburgh St. ⓒ **01244/324756.** www.chestercathedral.org.uk. £3 ($4.80) donation suggested. Daily 9am–5pm.

Chester Zoo ⭐ *Kids*   The Chester Zoo is the largest repository of animals in the north of England. It is also the site of some of the most carefully manicured gardens in the region—44 hectares (110 acres) that feature unusual shrubs, rare trees, and warm-weather displays of carpet bedding with as many as 160,000 plants timed to bloom simultaneously.

Many rare and endangered animal species breed freely here; the zoo is particularly renowned for the most successful colonies of chimpanzees and orangutans in Europe. The water bus, a popular observation aid that operates exclusively in summer, allows you to observe hundreds of water birds that make their home on the park's lake. There's also a monorail, which stops at the extreme eastern and western ends of the zoo, making visits less tiring. Youngsters love the Monkey's Island exhibit.

Off A41, Upton-by-Chester, 3km (2 miles) north of the town center. ⓒ 01244/380280. www.chesterzoo.org. Admission £10.50 ($17) adults, £8.50 ($14) seniors and children 3–15, £36 ($58) family ticket. Monorail £1.80 ($2.90) adults, £1.40 ($2.25) children. Free for kids under 3. Opens daily 10am; closing times vary, call for details. Closed Dec 25. From Chester's center, head north along Liverpool Rd.

SHOPPING

Chester has three main shopping areas. The **Grosvenor Precinct** is filled with classy, expensive shops and boutiques that sell a lot of trendy fashion and art items. This area is bordered on three sides by Eastgate Street, Bridge Street, and Pepper Street.

For stores with more character and lower prices, explore **the Rows,** a network of double-layered streets and sidewalks with an assortment of shops. The Rows runs along Bridge Street, Watergate Street, Eastgate Street, and Northgate Street. Shopping upstairs is much more adventurous than down on the street. Thriving stores operate in this traffic-free paradise: tobacco shops, restaurants, department stores, china shops, jewelers, and antiques dealers. For the best look, take a walk on arcaded Watergate Street.

Another shopping area to check out is **Cheshire Oaks,** a huge retail village of 60 shops, mainly clothing, perfume, and shoe outlet stores. Cheshire Oaks is located about 13km (8 miles) north of Chester on the M53.

Chester has a large concentration of antiques and crafts shops. Some better ones include **Lowe & Sons,** 11 Bridge St. Row (ⓒ **01244/325850**), with antique silver and estate jewelry; **The Antique Shop,** 40 Watergate St. (ⓒ **01244/ 316286**), specializing in brass, copper, and pewter items; **Adam's Antiques,** 65 Watergate Row (ⓒ **01244/319421**), focusing on 18th- and 19th-century antiques; and **City Road Emporium,** 32 City Rd. (ⓒ **01244/329959**), a cluster of eight antiques dealers in a three-story 18th-century grain-storage building.

Weekly antiques shows and auctions are held on Thursday at the Guildhall in Chester. Call the **Tourist Information Board** in Chester at ⓒ **01244/402111.**

One of the better shops for jewelry is **Boodle and Dunthorne,** 52 Eastgate St. (© **01244/326666**). Since the days of George III, **Brown's of Chester,** 34–40 Eastgate Rd. (© **01244/350001**), has carried women's fashions, perfumes, menswear, and children's clothes.

For a good selection of cheeses, chutneys, olives, pastas, and English fruit wines, seek out **The Cheese Shop,** 116 Northgate St. (© **01244/346240**).

WHERE TO STAY

Cavendish Hotel ⭐   In one of Chester's most prestigious neighborhoods, this hotel lies beside A5104, on a tree-lined street about a mile west of the city center. Two semidetached houses built around 1840 were connected and transformed into a hotel in the 1980s. Completely renovated, the comfortable nonsmoking bedrooms have lots of cozy charm and private, shower-only bathrooms. The rooms' variation in size is reflected in the price.

42–44 Hough Green, Chester, Cheshire CH4 8JQ. © 01244/675100. Fax 01244/678844. 19 units. £45 ($72) single; £60–£70 ($96–$112) double. Rates include English breakfast. AE, DC, MC, V. Bus: no. 28. **Amenities:** Restaurant; bar; limited room service; laundry service. *In room:* TV, dataport, coffeemaker, hair dryer.

Derry Raghan Lodge   This Victorian guesthouse lies a 1.5km (1 mile) from the city center and 5km (3 miles) from the zoo. Meryl and Peter Bold welcome guests to a cozy stopover for the night. Their rooms are pleasantly furnished. The ground- and second-floor bedrooms are spacious and tastefully decorated, all with private, shower-only bathrooms. In the morning a wide variety breakfast selections is served in the breakfast room.

54 Hoole Rd., Chester, Cheshire CH2 3NL. © 01244/318740. www.derryraghanlodge.co.uk. 8 units. £30–£32 ($48–$51) single; £55 ($88) double. Rates include English breakfast. MC, V. Take A56 north from the city center. Bus: no. 53. **Amenities:** Breakfast room. *In room:* TV, coffeemaker, hair dryer, no phone.

Green Gables   Set about 1km (½ mile) north of the city's historic core, this guesthouse under the supervision of the Perruzza family occupies a sprawling, red brick house (ca. 1904) built by a local merchant as a showplace home. Inside, five cream-colored bedrooms, all with high ceilings and floral-pattern curtains and upholsteries, are available, each with hints of the original Edwardian decor.

11 Eversley Park, Chester CH2 2AJ. © 01244/372243. Fax 01244/376352. 4 units. £30 ($48) single; £44 ($70) double. Rate includes English breakfast. No credit cards. Bus: no. 2, 3, 4, or 4A. **Amenities:** Breakfast room. *In room:* TV, coffeemaker.

Redland Hotel ⭐⭐   Many have rated this the finest small hotel in Chester. Open year-round, it lies a mile from the city center opposite the Chester Golf Course in the direction of the Welsh border; some guests use it as a base for exploring northern Wales. It's a Victorian town house of character and charm, with oak paneling and stained glass windows. Rooms vary in size, but all contain private, shower-only bathrooms and antique Victorian fittings and furnishings. The hotel has a residential license to serve alcohol.

64 Hough Green, Chester, Cheshire CH4 8JY. © 01244/671024. Fax 01244/681309. 13 units. £49 ($78) single; £70 ($112) double; £85–£95 ($136–$152) honeymoon suite. Rates include English breakfast. MC, V. Bus: no. 28. **Amenities:** Breakfast room; honor bar; sauna; solarium. *In room:* TV, coffeemaker, hair dryer.

Ye Olde King's Head Hotel ⭐   A 5-minute walk from the bus station, this place is a 16th-century museum piece of black-and-white architecture. From 1598 to 1707, the well-known Randle Holme family, noted heraldic painters and genealogists (some of their manuscripts have made it to the British Museum) occupied it. Since 1717, the King's Head has been a licensed inn. Many of the walls and ceilings are sloped and highly pitched, with exposed beams. The host rents standard-size bedrooms with private, shower-only bathrooms, although they're nowhere near the equal of the public rooms for charm and character.

48–50 Lower Bridge St., Chester, Cheshire CH1 1RS. ⓒ **01244/324855.** Fax 01244/315693. 8 units. £27.95 ($45) single; £57.90 ($93) double; £77.95 ($125) family rooms. AE, DC, MC, V. **Amenities:** Restaurant; bar. *In room:* TV, coffeemaker, hair dryer, trouser press.

WHERE TO DINE

The Falcon ⚑ BRITISH This is the most famous and appreciated pub in town, thanks to good food, stiff drinks, an 800-year-old history, and a half-timbered setting that screams Merrie Olde England. Savory platters are dispensed at lunchtime from a food bar, where you place and retrieve your order. The Falcon specializes in small-batch brews from the Yorkshire town of Tadcaster; most visible of these is Old Brewery Bitter. If you ask, and if the pub isn't hysterically busy, someone will lead you down into the cellar for a Plexiglas-covered, "camera friendly" view of an ancient Roman wall and a Gothic-era archway. Food prepared by the jovial staff includes beef simmered in Old Brewery Bitter; chicken-and-mushroom pie; spicy blackened Cajun chicken; deep-fried battered cod; and chicken tikka masala.

Lower Bridge St. ⓒ **01244/342060.** Bar platters £3.95–£6.95 ($6–$11). No credit cards. Bar service Mon–Sat 11am–11pm, Sun noon–10:30pm. Food service daily noon–2:30pm.

Francs Restaurant ⚑⚑ FRENCH This restaurant serves some of the finest food for the price in Chester. It's adjacent to the police station just off the main North Wales circular road. Within the city walls, it's housed in a building constructed with oak beams in the 1600s. The cuisine is country French. You can order homemade sausages, a good cassoulet, or the plats du jour, perhaps your best bet. The wine list is reasonably priced, the atmosphere formal but convivial.

14 Cuppin St. ⓒ **01244/317952.** Reservations required. Main courses £7.95–£13.90 ($13–$22); fixed-price 3-course meal £14.95 ($24); Sun lunch £10.85 ($17). Separate children's menu. AE, MC, V. Daily 11am–11pm. Take any bus heading into the city center.

Old Harkers Arms ⚑ ENGLISH Seemingly rarely visited by tourists, this Victorian canal-side warehouse lies at the edge of town en route to the train station. A spacious and old-fashioned pub, with wooden floors, bare walls, and a ceiling lined with old port crates, it attracts everyone from office workers to the Lord Mayor. It has our favorite selection of beers, including Manchester's Boddingtons. The kitchen turns out superior pub grub as well. At lunch you can fill up on homemade soups, sandwiches, and the like. But more complicated and sophisticated dishes are offered as well, from stir-fried pork in black-bean sauce to a wild mushroom and spinach crepe. They also do a mean rib-eye steak.

1 Russell St. ⓒ **01244/344525.** Main courses £3.95–£12.95 ($6–$21). AE, DC, MC, V. Daily 11:30am–11:30pm; Sun noon–10:30pm.

Ye Olde Boot Inn ENGLISH This is one of Chester's most atmospheric pubs, established in 1643 on a street near the Anglican cathedral. In 1986, it expanded into a covered alleyway and row of shops; it has retained low ceilings, stone or wood floors, most of the ceiling beams, and an old oak bar in back. In front, the Eastgate Room provides the only view from any pub in the city of the Eastgate clock. Most visitors come here to drink, but at lunchtime the place is crowded because of its food values. These include ploughman's lunches, a "giant's Yorkshire pudding" in which a leaf of "pud" imitates a crepe and gets filled with steak-and-kidney stew, Boozy Boot (lean chunks of steak marinated in old brewery cask bitter, mixed with fresh vegetables), lasagna, or scampi. The most enduring food item has changed little since the inn's founding: the "hot boot sandwich," containing oversized beef slices with gravy nestled between two sides of a thick granary roll is still a favorite.

9 Eastgate Row. ✆ **01244/314540.** Bar snacks £1.95–£5.95 ($3.10–$10). MC, V. Daily noon–2:30pm. Pub: Mon–Sat 11am–11pm, Sun noon–10:30pm. Bus: no. 10 or 18.

CHESTER AFTER DARK

If you want to relax in a pub, grab a pint of Marston's at the **Olde Custom House,** Watergate Street (✆ **01244/324435**), a 17th-century customhouse with many original features still intact. The **Pied Bull,** Northgate Street (✆ **01244/325829**), is an 18th-century coaching inn where you can still eat, drink, or rent a room. Real ales on tap include Flowers, and Greenall's Bitter and Traditional. At **Ye Olde King's Head,** Lower Bridge Street (✆ **01244/324855**), ales are not the only spirits you may encounter. This B&B pub, built in 1622, is said to be haunted by three ghosts; a crying woman and baby in room no. 6, and the ghostly initials "ST" that appear in steam on the bathroom mirror of room no. 4. If you prefer your spirits in a glass, stick to the pub, where you can sip on a Boddington's Bitter, or Greenall's Original or Local.

Live Irish music and atmosphere can be sampled at **The Red Lion,** 59 Northgate St. (✆ **01244/321750**), where you can hear traditional music on Wednesday and Sunday nights for the price of a pint of Guinness. **Alexandre's,** Rufus Court off Northgate Street (✆ **01244/340005**), offers more varied entertainment.

4 Blackpool: Playground of the Midlands

396km (246 miles) NW of London; 142km (88 miles) W of Leeds; 90km (56 miles) N of Liverpool; 82km (51 miles) NW of Manchester

This once-antiquated Midlands resort is struggling to make a comeback by marketing itself to a new generation of vacationers. The result may remind you of Atlantic City or even Las Vegas (with a weird Victorian twist). The city has a midwinter population of 125,000 that swells to three or four times that in midsummer.

The country's largest resort makes its living from conferences, tour groups, families, and couples looking for an affordable getaway. Its 11km (7 miles) of beaches, 9.5km (6 miles) of colored lights, and dozens of Disney-like attractions and rides make Blackpool one of the most entertaining (and least apologetic) pieces of razzle-dazzle in England.

Disadvantages include unpredictable weather that brews over the nearby Irish Channel; a sandy, flat-as-a-pancake landscape that's less than inspiring; and a (sometimes undeserved) reputation for dowdiness. But some people love the brisk sea air, the architectural remnants of Britain's greatest Imperial Age, the utter lack of pretentiousness, and the poignant nostalgia that clings to the edges of places like Coney Island, where people look back fondly on the carefree fun they had in a simpler time.

ESSENTIALS

GETTING THERE   Two trains from Manchester pull in every hour (trip time: 1½ hr.), and there's one every hour from Liverpool (trip time: 1½ hr.). For schedules and information, call ✆ **0845/7484950.**

National Express buses arrive from Chester at the rate of three per day (trip time: 4 hr.); from Liverpool at the rate of six per day (trip time: 3½ hr.); from

Manchester, five per day (trip time: 2 hr.); and from London, six per day (trip time: 6½ hr.). For schedules and information, call ℭ **08705/808080.**

If you're driving from Manchester, take the M61 north to the M6 then the M55 toward Blackpool. The trip takes about 1 hour.

VISITOR INFORMATION   The helpful **Tourist Office,** located at 1 Clifton St. (ℭ **01253/478222**), is open November through March Monday through Friday from 9am to 4:45pm, and Saturday from 9am to 4:30pm; April through October, Monday through Saturday from 9am to 5pm and Sunday from 10am to 4pm.

SEEING THE SIGHTS

Blackpool is famous for the **Illuminations,** an extravaganza of electric lights affixed to just about any stationary object along the Promenade. It features hundreds of illuminated figures, including Diamonds Are Forever, Santa's Workshop, Lamp Lighters, and Kitchen Lites. The tradition began in 1879 with just eight electric lights, and has grown with time and technology to include 9.5km (6 miles) of fiber optics, low-voltage neon tubes, and traditional lamps. The illuminations burn bright into the night from the end of August to the beginning of November. Take a tram ride down the Promenade for a great view of the tacky but festive spectacle.

Without a doubt, the most famous landmark in this town is the **Tower** along the Central Promenade (ℭ **01253/622242**). In 1891, during the reign of Queen Victoria, a madcap idea started floating around to construct a 155m (518-ft.) tower that resembled a half-size version of Paris's Eiffel Tower. The idea was first formerly presented to the town leaders of Brighton, who laughed at the idea, thinking it was a joke. But the forward-thinking leaders of Blackpool, when presented the plan, immediately saw the advantages of having such an attraction and quickly approved the tower's construction. You be the judge.

Lit by more than 10,000 bulbs, this landmark has become a tower of fun. It is truly an indoor entertainment complex both day and night and features the Tower Ballroom (one of the great Victorian ballrooms of Britain), the Tower Circus, the Hornpipe Galley, and the Dawn of Time dinosaur ride for kids, as well as the Tower Aquarium. An elevator takes visitors to the top of the Tower for a 97km (60-mile) view. The Tower is open from Easter to May, Saturday and Sunday from 10am to 6pm and June through October daily from 10am to 11pm. The circus has two to three shows daily (except Fri evening). Tower admission is £7 to £11 ($11–$18).

WHERE TO STAY

The Berwyn Hotel   The plot of land the Berwyn sits on isn't any bigger than those of most of the equivalent guesthouses in Blackpool, but you'll feel that you're in a large estate thanks to its overlooking the city's municipal park, Gynn Gardens. There are many windows set into the ground-floor facade of this house (ca. 1910) that flood the interior with sunlight and views. The hotel was transformed in 1942 into the spacious and much-modernized establishment of today. Your hardworking host is Ian Cessford. Bedrooms are simple, even ordinary, but comfortable and restful, each with a private, shower-only bathroom. Rates decrease for stays of two nights or more, and there are senior discounts available. Evening meals, some of the best served within any comparable establishment here, cost a supplement of £6 ($10) per person.

½ Finchley Rd., Gynn Sq., Blackpool FY1 2LP. © **01253/352896**. Fax 01253/594391. www.
heberwyn.freeserve.co.uk. 20 units. £28 ($45) single; £56 ($90) double. Rates include breakfast. AE, DC, MC,
V. **Amenities:** Dining room; bar. *In room:* TV, coffeemaker, hair dryer.

Burlees Hotel　There are many dozens of guesthouses similar to the Burlees
dotting this urban landscape, but it's probably a bit better maintained than the
norm. Presenting a bow-windowed, stucco-sheathed facade to a neighborhood
of equivalent houses, it's run by the Lawrence family. The nonsmoking rooms,
if not grand, are comfortably furnished, each with a private, shower-only bathroom. The garden faces south, a fact prized by those who maintain it. There is
one room available for those with limited mobility.

40 Knowle Ave., North Shore, Blackpool FY2 9TQ. © **01253/354535**. www.burlees-hotel.co.uk. 9 units.
£25 ($40) single; £50 ($80) double. Rates include breakfast. Discounts available for stays of 3 nights or
more. AE, DC, MC, V. Closed Nov–Feb. **Amenities:** Dining room; bar; lounge. *In room:* TV, coffeemaker, hair
dryer, no phone.

Grosvenor View Guesthouse　Built as halves of a brick-fronted house in the
1930s, these premises were merged by a previous owner into the freestanding
guesthouse of today. Public areas are bright thanks to the large bay windows,
whose leaded glass breaks sunlight into geometric shapes. Bedrooms are well
kept and comfortably furnished. A pair of TV lounges (designated respectively
for smokers and nonsmokers) provides places to socialize. The guest rooms are
all nonsmoking. Part of the appeal of this place derives from owners Dave and
Sheila Jackson, whose set-price evening meal, served only to residents, is a genuine bargain. Its only drawback is the hour it's served—5:30pm—which transforms the meal into a high tea rather than a bona fide dinner. Why so early?
Because those who attend then head off to one of Blackpool's many pubs,
nightlife venues, shows, or concerts.

7–9 King Edward Ave., North Shore, Blackpool FY2 9TD. © **01253/352851**. 15 units, 11 with bathroom.
£18–£20 ($29–$32) per person, single or double, without bathroom; £20–£25 ($30–$37.50) per person, single or double, with bathroom. Rates include breakfast. AE, MC, V. Free parking. **Amenities:** Dining room; 2
TV lounges. *In room:* TV, coffeemaker, no phone.

Revill's　Opposite the North Pier, and lying just north of Blackpool Tower,
this is a family-run hotel with a seaside location. It is a more substantial hotel
than many other budget lodgings which are more like a B&B. It has all the elements of a real Midlands-at-the-sea party hotel, including video machines, a
snooker room, and an active bar. Bedrooms are comfortably furnished and come
in a wide range of sizes, from cramped singles to larger family rooms; the best
units, of course, are those fronting the sea. Each comes with a small bathroom
with either tub or shower.

190–194 North Promenade, Blackpool FY1 1RJ. © **01253/625768**. Fax 01253/624736. 47 units. £45–£60
($72–$96) double. Single supplement £5 ($8). Rates include breakfast. MC, V. **Amenities:** Restaurant; bar;
game room. *In room:* TV, coffeemaker, hair dryer.

WHERE TO DINE

Autumn Leaves MODERN ENGLISH　This wood-beamed restaurant
offers an old-world decor and ambience with dining tables set around a central
stage. It is known as a place to get a good steak; traditional chicken and seafood
dishes are also available. We particularly enjoy the breast of duck with wild
strawberries and a brandy glaze.

82 Topping St. © **01253/620730**. Reservations recommended. Main courses £10–£17 ($16–$27); 3-course
early-bird menu £11.95 ($19), until 7:30pm. AE, DC, MC, V. Mon–Fri 5–10pm; Sat 4–11pm; Sun noon–10pm.

Brewer's Fayre CONTINENTAL   This restaurant is in a contemporary building attached to the Yeadon Way Travel Inn. It re-creates the ambience of a traditional brewer's pub with red floral carpets, brick walls and a fireplace, wooden beams and furnishings, and a row of decorative plates, mugs, and bottles set just below the ceiling. The menu is designed to appeal to the widest possible tastes, with the usual English roasts, mixed grills, salads, pasta dishes, fish, and scampi, accompanied by Whitbread's selection of beers. Steaks are perhaps the most popular item here, although the chef occasionally goes exotic with a chicken tandoori.

Yeadon Way. ℂ 01253/341415. Main courses £4.99–£9.50 ($8–$15). AE, MC, V. Mon–Sat 11am–10pm; Sun noon–10pm.

Harry Ramsden's SEAFOOD   This is one of the most appealing of a chain of 60 restaurants whose mission is to export British fish and chips to the world at large. Since being established in Guisley, West Yorkshire, in the early 1920s, its award-winning formula for this staple has been duplicated as far away as Jeddah, Singapore, and Heathrow. The restaurant's allure has resonated deeply in Blackpool, where one of the chain's most opulent restaurants offers a takeout counter, where a portion of haddock and chips, suitable for munching during a promenade on the nearby pier, sells for £6.70 ($11). More appealing is the terra-cotta and wood-paneled restaurant, where the nostalgia of yesteryear is preserved with a uniformed staff, big chandeliers, and reminders of the Art Deco age. In addition to fish and chips, there's a steak-and-kidney pudding "filled with savory goodness," plain salmon with tartar sauce or lemon, meat sausages, and vegetarian selections.

60–63 The Promenade. ℂ 01253/294386. Reservations recommended. Main courses £4.80–£12.35 ($8–$20). Nov–Apr daily 11:30am–7pm; May–July daily 11:30am–8pm; Aug–Oct daily 11:30am–10pm. AE, DC, MC, V.

Peppermill BRITISH   "Come on, ducky, let's go over to the Peppermill" is a curious phrase often heard in Blackpool. This newly refurbished restaurant has what the headwaiter terms a "French Continental decor." No one in the kitchen gets too imaginative, but they turn out the usual array of soups, salads, sandwiches, and pastas, the preferred daytime fare. At night, they get a little fancier, preparing their best seafood and steak dishes. In both upstairs and downstairs, look for varieties of curry, tagliatelle, meatloaf, shepherd's pie, and steak. The place is fully licensed.

15 Barley St. ℂ 01253/622253. Platters in street-level cafe £3–£5 ($4.80–$8); main courses in upstairs restaurant £6–£11.50 ($10–$18). MC, V. Cafe daily 7am–6pm; restaurant daily 11am–2:20pm.

16

The Lake District

The Lake District, one of the most beautiful parts of Great Britain, is actually quite small, measuring about 56km (35 miles) wide. Most of the district is in Cumbria, though it begins in the northern part of Lancashire.

Bordering Scotland, the far-north-western part of the shire is generally divided geographically into three segments: the **Pennines,** dominating the eastern sector (loftiest point at Cross Fell, nearly 900m/3,000 ft. high); the **Valley of Eden;** and the **lakes and secluded valleys of the west,** by far the most interesting.

So beautifully described by the romantic poets, the area enjoys many literary associations with William Wordsworth, Samuel Taylor Coleridge, Charlotte Brontë, Charles Lamb, Percy Bysshe Shelley, John Keats, Alfred Lord Tennyson, and Matthew Arnold. In Queen Victoria's day, the Lake District was one of England's most popular summer retreats.

The largest town is **Carlisle,** up by the Scotland border, which is a possible base for exploring Hadrian's Wall (see chapter 17)—but for now, we will concentrate on the district's lovely lakeside villages. **Windermere** is the best base for exploring the Lake District.

WALKS & RAMBLES

Driving through this scenic shire is fine for a start, but the best way to take in its beauty is by walking—an art best practiced here with a crooked stick. There is much rain and heavy mist, and sunny days are few. Pack good waterproof hiking boots and a lightweight rain jacket; even if you set out on a nice morning, you need to prepare for a wet afternoon. When the mist starts to fall, do as the locals do: head for the nearest inn or pub and drop in to warm yourself beside an open fireplace. You'll find yourself back in the good old days, as many places in Cumbria have valiantly resisted change.

If you want to make hiking in the Lake District a major focus of your vacation, you might want an organized outing. **Countrywide Holidays,** Grove House, Wilmslow Road, Didsbury, Manchester M20 2HU (© **01942/823430**), has offered walking and special-interest vacations for more than 100 years. Experienced guides lead safe and sociable guided walks for all ages and abilities. It's ideal for independent walkers, with boot-drying rooms provided. They have four comfortable, informal, and welcoming guesthouses set in beautiful Lakeland locations.

1 Kendal

432km (270 miles) NW of London; 102km (64 miles) NW of Bradford; 115km (72 miles) NW of Leeds; 15km (9 miles) SE of Windermere

The River Kent winds its way through a rich valley of limestone hills and cliffs, known as the fells, and down through the "auld grey town" of Kendal, named for the large number of gray stone houses found there. Many visitors to the Lake

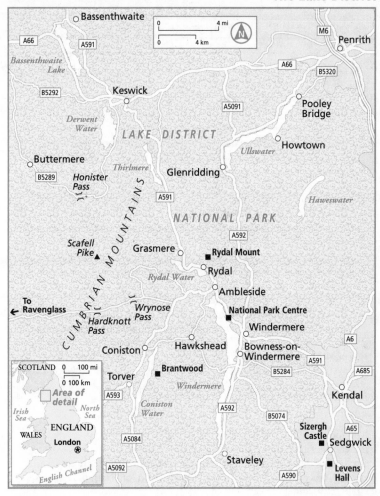

District simply pass through Kendal on their way to more attractive destinations. Kendal is a gateway rather than a true stopping place, and has never depended solely on tourism. This should not deter you, however, from taking a bit of time to discover this market town's more intriguing areas.

Kendal contains the ruins of a castle where Catherine Parr, Henry VIII's last wife, was allegedly born. Recent speculation about her actual birthplace has clouded the historic record; even so, it is still said that she probably lived at the castle at some point. Kendal also has a 13th-century parish church that merits a visit.

Today, Kendal is famous for its mint cake and its surrounding limestone fells, which offer excellent vistas of the area and make for great hikes.

ESSENTIALS

GETTING THERE   Trains from London's Euston Station do not go directly to Kendal; seven daily trains arrive in Oxenholme, about 2.5km (1½ miles) away. From here, you'll be able to take a cab or board one of the local trains that

---

Value Cheap Thrills: What to See & Do for Free (or Almost) in the Lake District

---

Make a literary pilgrimage. In this land of the "Lake Poets," including Wordsworth, Coleridge, and Southey, one reason to visit is to see where they lived and worked. This would include Dove Cottage of Wordsworth fame (p. 608) and Brantwood of John Ruskin fame (p. 611).

Discover the joys of Ullswater. Such lakes as Windermere are overrun in summer by visitors. Ullswater, a lake beginning 26 miles (41km) southeast of Keswick, is less trampled. This 9-mile (14km) expanse of water stretches from Pooley Bridge to Patterdale; it's the second-largest lake in the district. It offers walks and hikes around the shore, rock climbing, mountain biking, canoeing, sailing, and even windsurfing. The summer-only **Tourist Information Centre** at the Main Car Park, Glenridding (*℡* **01768/482414**), can provide complete information.

Spend a day in Borrowdale. One of the most scenic parts of the Lake District, Borrowdale stretches south of Derwentwater to Seathwaite in the heart of the county. It's an excellent center for walking, climbing, and exploring, and is home to Scafell, England's highest mountain. The southernmost settlement of Borrowdale is the village of Seatoller, at 358m (1,176 ft.). It's the site of a **Lake District National Park Information Centre** at Dalehead Base, Seatoller Barn (*℡* **01768/777294**). After leaving Seatoller, you can drive through the dramatic Honister Pass and Buttermere Fell, your route lined with towering boulders.

---

leave approximately every hour to Kendal proper (total trip time: 3½ hr.). For train schedules and information, call *℡* **0845/7484950.**

To Kendal from London by bus, take one of the three daily National Express buses (trip time: 7 hr.). For schedules and information, call **National Express** at *℡* **020/7529-2000.**

If you're driving, follow the M1 out of London, then the M6 to Kendal (trip time: 5 hr.).

VISITOR INFORMATION The **Tourist Information Centre of Kendal,** Town Hall, Highgate (*℡* **01539/725758**), is open September to December and March to June, Monday to Saturday 9am to 5pm and Sunday 10am to 4pm; January and February Monday to Saturday 9am to 5pm; July and August Monday to Saturday 9am to 6pm and Sunday 10am to 5pm.

SEEING THE SIGHTS

Kendal Museum One of England's oldest museums takes visitors on a journey of discovery from Roman times to the present. A natural-history section includes a nature trail from mountaintop to lakeside, on which visitors are brought face to face with many of the inhabitants of the area. The World Wildlife Gallery displays a vast collection of exotic animals. One of the exhibitions introduces visitors to the fell-tops' best-known visitor, Alfred Wainwright, who walked, talked, and wrote with a passion and flair about the region. Wainwright worked diligently until his death in 1991.

Explore the area on two wheels. There is no finer biking country than in the Lake District. Any tourist office will provide a list of rental shops. The 419km (260-mile) Cumbria Cycle Way goes from Carlisle in the north to the Lake District. Even if you ride only part of the trail, you'll encounter some of the most dramatic scenery in northern England along the way. All tourist offices are stocked with an excellent little pamphlet, "The Cumbria Cycle Way," providing maps and detailed information about the route.

Follow in the footsteps of Wordsworth. Grasmere is one of the best centers for walkers in the district. Its most strenuous walk is a 2-hour jaunt up to the top of the little mountain Helm Cragg, which locals call "The Lamb and the Lion." Another adventurous walk, favored by the poet himself, is the 9.5km (6-mile) Wordsworth Walk, which circumnavigates the two lakes of the River Rothay. This route passes Dove Cottage and the poet's grave.

Soak up the scenery in Buttermere. Flee the tourist hordes and head for the placid waters and little hamlet of Buttermere, 9.5km (6 miles) from Rosthwaite. Well-known and written about by the lake poets, the lake at Buttermere was painted by Turner who was greatly impressed by its beauty. Just to the northwest is Crummock Water, the twin lake of Buttermere. Off the north end of Crummock Water is Loweswater, but Buttermere is even more enchanting. Nearby is 38m (125-ft.) Scale Force, one of the most beautiful waterfalls in the area.

Station Rd. ⓒ **01539/721374.** www.kendalmuseum.org.uk. Admission £3.50 ($6) adults, £1.75 ($2.80) children, £9 ($14) family. Mid-Feb to Mar and Nov–Dec 24 Mon–Sat 10:30am–4pm; Apr–Oct Mon–Sat 10:30am–5pm. Closed Dec 24 to mid-Feb.

Museum of Lakeland Life   From the re-creation of a Victorian Kendal street, complete with pharmacy and market, the visitor can discover the lost crafts and trades of the region and the ways of life that accompanied them.

Kirkland. ⓒ **01539/722464.** www.lakelandmuseum.org.uk. Admission £2.75 ($4.40) adults, £1.40 ($2.25) children, £7 ($11) family. Mid-Feb to Mar and Nov–Dec Mon–Sat 10:30am–5pm; Apr–Oct Mon–Sat 10:30am–4pm. Closed Jan to mid-Feb.

Abbot Hall Art Gallery   The Georgian elegance of Kendal's Abbot Hall Art Gallery has created an ideal setting for its display of fine art. Paintings by the town's famous son, 18th-century portrait painter George Romney, fill the walls of rooms furnished by Gillows of Lancaster. A major display of work by 20th-century British artists such as Graham Sutherland, John Piper, and Ben Nicholson are on permanent display. Visitors can see the region through the eyes of the many painters who have been inspired by the landscapes in another of the gallery's permanent exhibitions housed in The Peter Scott Gallery.

Kirkland. ⓒ **01539/722464.** www.abbothall.org.uk. Admission £3.75 ($6) adults, £1.75 ($2.80) children, £9.50 ($15) family ticket. Apr to late Oct Mon–Sat 10:30am–5pm; Mid-Feb to Mar and Nov to late Dec Mon–Sat 10:30am–4pm. Closed late Dec to mid-Feb.

Sizergh Castle   This castle has a fortified tower that dates from the 14th century. Inside, visitors can see a collection of Elizabethan carvings and paneling, fine furniture, and portraits. The complete garden, largely from the 18th century, incorporates a rock garden and a famous planting of hardy ferns and dwarf conifers. The castle is surrounded by a show of fiery colors in autumn.

5.5km (3½ miles) south of Kendal (northwest of interchange A590/591). ✆ **01539/560070.** Admission £5 ($8) adults, £2.50 ($4) children, £12.50 ($20) family ticket (2 adults and 2 children). Late Apr to Oct Sun–Thurs 1:30–5:30pm (last admission 5pm). The shop and gardens open at 12:30pm.

Levens Hall and Gardens   This Elizabethan mansion was constructed in the 1500s by James Bellingham. Today, the house is filled with Jacobean furniture and a working model of steam collection. The estate also has a topiary garden dating from 1692, with a host of yews and box hedges clipped into a variety of intriguing shapes.

Levens Park, Levens (6.5km/4 miles south of Kendal). ✆ **01539/560321.** www.levenshall.co.uk. Admission £7 ($11) for house and gardens; £5.50 ($9) for gardens only. Apr–Oct 14 Sun–Thurs noon–5pm (gardens open at 10am).

WHERE TO STAY

Garden House Hotel & Restaurant   Built in 1812, this is an inviting Georgian country house. It was once a convent for local nuns, and has been a hotel for the past 30 years or so. It's nestled in 1 hectare (2 acres) of walled garden and green pastureland, and is perfectly serene. The guest rooms are decorated in pastels with lots of lace and contemporary furnishings; some have fireplaces and four-poster beds. Each tiled bathroom, quite compact, comes with a tub-and-shower combination. The public areas include a somewhat formal sitting room, an informal lounge bar with lots of seating, an elegant breakfast room with a dark mahogany fireplace, and a restaurant conservatory.

Fowling Lane, Kendal, Cumbria LA9 6PH. ✆ **01539/731131.** Fax 01539/740064. www.gardenhousehotel.co. uk. 11 units. £79 ($126) double; £85 ($136) for 4-poster bed; £5 ($8) extra bed. Rates include English breakfast. MC, V. **Amenities:** Restaurant; bar; putting green; croquet lawn; limited room service; limited laundry service. *In room:* TV, coffeemaker, hair dryer, trouser press.

WHERE TO DINE

Latino's ITALIAN/MEXICAN   You've got to look a little for this one, but it's well worth it. Go down a little alley off Finkle Street, then up a flight of stairs to the first floor. Inside, you'll find a happy marriage of a large sitting area with a cozy feel—a romantic candlelit ambience. Lunch dishes are chosen from a menu or specials board with such items as pizza or bow-tie pasta with lobster sauce. Dinner includes tagliatelle with leeks and scampi in a rich cream sauce; a house lasagna of layers of egg, ham, and pepperoni in a Bolognese sauce; and baked chicken stuffed with salami and cheese in a mushroom-and-Napoli sauce. The wine list constantly changes and favors robust reds. The restaurant also has an extensive choice of Mexican food.

24 Finkle St. ✆ **01539/720547.** Reservations recommended. Lunch £3–£8 ($4.80–$13); dinner main courses £4.50–£8.50 ($7.20–$14). AE, DC, MC, V. Mon–Sat noon–2pm and 5:30–10pm.

Moon INTERNATIONAL   This bistro cooks up the best food in Kendal. Set in a building that's more than 250 years old, and was once a grocery store, the dining room offers patrons a close, friendly, and informal environment. The food is interesting without being gimmicky. The owners take pride in offering market-fresh ingredients when available. Main courses include lamb shank with either a mustard and Soya sauce, or a cream, leek, and white-wine sauce; or for vegetarians, goat's cheese, red pepper, and mango wrapped in phyllo pastry with an apple, gooseberry, and honey sauce.

129 Highgate. © **01539/729254.** Main courses £8.75–£13.75 ($14–$22). MC, V. Tues–Sun 6–10pm. Winter Wed–Sun 6–10pm.

2 Windermere & Bowness-on-Windermere ✮✮

438km (274 miles) NW of London; 16km (10 miles) NW of Kendal; 88km (55 miles) N of Liverpool

The largest lake in England is Windermere, whose eastern shore washes up on the town of Bowness (or Bowness-on-Windermere), with the town of Windermere 2.5km (1½ miles) away. From either town, you can climb **Orrest Head** in less than an hour for a panoramic view of the Lakeland. From that vantage point, you can even view **Scafell Pike,** rising to a height of 963m (3,210 ft.)—it's the tallest peak in all of England.

ESSENTIALS

GETTING THERE   Trains to Windermere meet the main line at Oxenholme for connections to both Scotland and London. Information about rail services in the area can be obtained by calling the railway information line at © **0845/7484950.** Frequent connections are possible throughout the day. To get to Bowness and its ferry pier from Windermere, turn left from the rail terminal and cross the center of Windermere until you reach New Road, which eventually changes its name to Lake Road before it approaches the outskirts of Bowness. It's about a 20-minute walk downhill. The CMS Lakeland Experience bus also runs from the Windermere Station to Bowness every 20 minutes.

The **National Express** bus link, originating at London's Victoria Coach Station, serves Windermere, with good connections also to Preston, Manchester, and Birmingham. For schedules and information, call © **020/7529-2000.** Local buses operated mainly by **Stagecoach** (© **08706/082608**) go to Kendal, Ambleside, Grasmere, and Keswick. Call for information on various routings within the Lake District.

If you're driving from London, head north on the M1 and the M6 past Liverpool until you reach the A685 junction heading west to Kendal. From Kendal, the A591 continues west to Windermere.

VISITOR INFORMATION   The **Tourist Information Centre** at Windermere is on Victoria Street (© **01539/446499**). From November to March daily 9am to 5pm and April to October daily 9am to 6pm.

EXPLORING THE AREA

There is regular **steamer service** around Windermere, the largest of the lakes (about 17km/11 miles long). It's also possible to take a steamer on Coniston Water, a small lake that Wordsworth called "a broken spoke sticking in the rim." Coniston Water is a smaller and less heavily traveled lake than Windermere.

Launch and steamer cruises operated by **Windermere Lake Cruises Ltd.** (© **01539/443360;** www.windermere-lakecruises.co.uk) depart from Bowness daily throughout the year. Service is available from Bowness to Ambleside and to Lakeside at rates ranging from £5.80 to £10 ($9–$16) for adults and £2.90 to £5 ($4.65–$8)for children. There is a 45-minute Island Cruise for £4.50 ($7) for adults and £2.25 ($3.60) for children.

At Lakeside, you can ride a steam train to Haverthwaite. A combination boat/train ticket is £4.50 ($7) for adults and £2 ($3.20) for children. An attraction at Lakeside, near Newby Bridge, is the **Aquarium of the Lakes** (© **01539/530153;**

www.aquariumofthelakes.co.uk), with an exhibit of fish and wildlife. The aquarium is open daily from 9am to 4pm November through March, and 9am to 5pm April through October. Combination boat/admission tickets are £14.25 ($23) for adults, £8.15 ($13) for children, and £42.95 ($69) for a family ticket from Ambleside; and £10.75 ($17) for adults, £6 ($10) for children, and £33.45 ($54) for a family ticket from Bowness. Aquarium-only admission is £5.75 ($9) for adults, £3.75 ($6) for children, and £16.95 ($27) for a family ticket (two adults and two children).

Directly south of Windermere, **Bowness** is an attractive old lakeside town with lots of interesting architecture, much of it dating from Queen Victoria's day. This has been an important center for boating and fishing for a long time, and you can rent boats of all descriptions to explore the lake.

Windermere Steamboats & Museum   This museum houses the finest collection of steamboats in the world. Important examples of these elegant Victorian and Edwardian vessels have been preserved in working order. The steamboats are exhibited in a unique wet dock where they are moored in their natural lakeside setting. The fine display of touring and racing motorboats in the dry dock links the heyday of steam with some of the most famous names of powerboat racing and the record-breaking attempts on Windermere, including Sir Henry Segrave's world water-speed record set in 1930.

All the boats have intriguing stories, including the veteran SL *Dolly*, built around 1850 and probably the oldest mechanically driven boat in the world. The vessel was raised from the lake bed of Ullswater in 1962 and, following restoration, ran for 10 years with its original boiler. The *Dolly* is still steamed on special occasions.

The SL *Swallow* (1911) is steamed most days; visitors can make a 50-minute trip on the lake at a cost of £5 ($8) for adults and £2.50 ($4) for children, with the crew serving tea or coffee made using the Windermere steam kettle.

Rayrigg Rd. (*C*) **01539/445565.** www.steamboat.co.uk. Admission £3.50 ($6) adults, £2 ($3.20) children, £8.50 ($14) family ticket. Daily 10am–5pm. Closed Nov to mid-Mar.

The World of Beatrix Potter   This exhibit uses the latest technology to tell the story of Beatrix Potter's fascinating life. A video wall and special film describe how her tales came to be written and how she became a pioneering Lakeland farmer and conservationist. There is also a shop with a wealth of top-quality Beatrix Potter merchandise, from Wedgwood ceramics to soft toys. It's mobbed on summer weekends; try to come at any other time.

The Old Laundry, Bowness-on-Windermere. (*C*) **01539/488444.** www.hop-skip-jump.com. Admission £3.75 ($6) adults, £2.50 ($4) children. Easter–Oct daily 10am–5:30pm; rest of year daily 10am–4:30pm. Take A591 to Lake Rd. and follow the signs.

WHERE TO STAY

The Queens Head and the Punch Bowl (see "Where to Dine," below) also rent rooms.

Beaumont Hotel   This stone-sided Lakeland villa, originally built in the 1850s, is on a quiet residential street about a minute's walk from Windermere's commercial center. Mr. and Mrs. James C. Casey massively upgraded what had been a rather dowdy interior. Each of the bedrooms is named after one of the characters in the Beatrix Potter sagas (our favorite is Jemima PuddleDuck) and contains either some kind of elaborate canopy or a four-poster bed, fitted with a quality mattress. All the accommodations have recently been refurbished, with

Lake District National Park

Despite the reverence with which the English treat the Lake District, it required an act of Parliament in 1951 to protect its natural beauty. Sprawling over 2,292 sq. km (885 sq. miles) of hills, eroded mountains, forests, and lakes, the **Lake District National Park** is the largest and one of the most popular national parks in the United Kingdom, with 14 million visitors a year. Lured by descriptions from the romantic lake poets, visitors arrive to take in the mountains, wildlife, flora, fauna, and secluded waterfalls. Much of the area is privately owned, but landowners work with national park officers to preserve the landscape and its 2,898km (1,800 miles) of footpaths.

Alas, the park's popularity is now one of its major drawbacks. Hordes of weekend tourists descend, especially in summertime and on bank holiday weekends. But despite the crowds, great efforts are made to maintain the trails that radiate in a network throughout the district preserving the purity of a landscape that includes more than 100 lakes and countless numbers of grazing sheep.

Before setting out to explore the lakes, stop in at the **National Park Visitor Centre** (✆ **01539/446601**), located on the lakeshore at Brock-hole, on the A591 between Windermere and Ambleside. It can be reached by bus or by one of the lake launches from Windermere. Here, you can pick up useful information and explore 30 acres of landscaped gardens and parklands; lake cruises, exhibitions, and film shows are also offered. Lunches and teas are served in Gaddums tearooms. Normally, admission is free, except for special events staged here. Parking costs £4 ($6) for a full day.

When setting out anywhere in the Lake District, it's wise to take adequate precautions. Weather conditions can change rapidly in this area, and in the high fells it can be substantially different from that found at lower levels. A **weather** line (✆ **01768/775757**) provides the latest conditions.

Tourist information offices within the park are richly stocked with maps and suggestions for several dozen bracing rambles. Regardless of the itinerary you select, you'll spot frequent green-and-white signs, or their older equivalents in varnished pine with Adirondack-style routed letters, announcing FOOTPATH TO . . . .

Be aware before you go that the Lake District receives more rainfall than any other district of England, and sturdy walking shoes and rain gear are essential. Hiking after dark is not recommended under any circumstances.

Any tourist information office within the park can provide leaflets describing treks through the park. The **Windermere Tourist Information Centre,** Victoria Street, Windermere, Cumbria LA23 1AD (✆ **01539/446499**), is especially helpful.

See also section 5 of this chapter, "Coniston & Hawkshead," for details about boating in the national park.

new showers, carpets, and curtains. No meals are served other than breakfast, so the owners keep local restaurant menus on hand for their guests to consult.

Holly Rd., Windermere, Cumbria LA23 2AF. ℂ and fax **01539/447075.** www.lakesbeaumont.co.uk. 10 units. £60–£100 ($96–$160) double. Rates include English breakfast. MC, V. *In room:* TV, coffeemaker, hair dryer.

Brendan Chase *Kids* Mr. and Mrs. Graham welcome guests to their long-established, centrally located Edwardian home, 137m (450 ft.) off A591 leading into town. The guesthouse is a tranquil location yet convenient to the attractions. Each large, well-furnished room is clean and comfortable, four with a private-shower bathroom. Families are welcomed and quoted special rates.

College Rd., Windermere, Cumbria LA23 1BU. ℂ and fax **015394/45638.** 8 units. £15–£25 ($24–$40) with or without bathroom. Rates include English breakfast. No credit cards. Free parking. **Amenities:** Breakfast room; laundry service. *In room:* TV, coffeemaker, hair dryer.

Fir Trees ★ *Value* This is one of the finest guesthouses in Windermere. It's very well run, essentially providing hotel-like amenities at B&B prices. Opposite St. John's Church, halfway between the villages of Bowness and Windermere, Fir Trees is a Victorian house furnished with antiques. The proprietors offer a warm welcome and rent well-furnished bedrooms. The tiled bathrooms are beautifully maintained, each with a shower. Some units are large enough for families. The owners can provide their guests with detailed information on restaurants, country pubs, or where to go and what to see.

Lake Rd., Windermere, Cumbria LA23 2EQ. ℂ and fax **01539/442272.** www.fir-trees.com. 9 units. £56–£64 ($90–$102) double. Rates include English breakfast. MC, V. No smoking. **Amenities:** Free use of nearby health club. *In room:* TV, coffeemaker, hair dryer.

Kenilworth Guest House *Value* Located near Broad Street in the town center, this year-round house is known for cleanliness, comfort, and good value. Christopher and Christine Busby offer pleasant bedrooms of varying size, all with hot and cold running water. Bedroom furnishings are modern, but there is period furniture in the TV room and throughout the house. An informal atmosphere prevails.

Holly Rd., Windermere, Cumbria LA23 2AF. ℂ **015394/44004.** Fax 015394/46554. busby@kenilworth-lake-district.co.uk. 6 units, 3 with bathroom. £20 ($32) single without bathroom; £38 ($61) double without bathroom; £44 ($70) double with bathroom; £55–£65 ($88–$104) family unit with bathroom. Rates include English breakfast. AE, MC, V. Limited free parking. **Amenities:** TV room; breakfast room. *In room:* TV, coffeemaker, hair dryer.

Rockside Guest House ★ *Kids* Rockside is only a 2-minute walk from the bus, train, or village of Windermere, near the train station. This guesthouse is one of the best B&Bs in the area. Standard rooms have hot and cold running water basins; "top choice" rooms contain private showers and toilets. Each bed, often a twin or double, is fitted with fine linen, and the breakfast menu offers a wide choice. Family suites are rented out with an interconnecting door leading to a set of bunk beds.

Ambleside Rd., Windermere, Cumbria LA23 1AQ. ℂ and fax **015394/45343.** www.rockside-guesthouse.co.uk. 10 units. £40–£45 ($64–$72) double; £54–£60 ($86–$96) family room. Rates include English breakfast. MC, V. Limited parking. **Amenities:** Breakfast room. *In room:* TV, coffeemaker, hair dryer.

WHERE TO DINE

Miller Howe Café ★★ INTERNATIONAL This restaurant is run by former actor John Tovey, the celebrated owner of the Miller Howe Hotel. Now owned by his former head chef, Ian Dutton, this charming little cafe lies at the back of a shop that is known as one of the largest retailers of "creative kitchenware" in Britain. Amid a very modern decor, clients place their food orders at a countertop, then wait until waitresses bring the dishes to their tables. The cuisine draws upon culinary traditions from around the world, and includes such dishes as diced and curried beef in a spicy sauce, filet of salmon with a fresh garden-herb sauce, macaroni baked with heavy cream and red Cheddar cheese, and breast of chicken served in a red-wine gravy. The restaurant is adjacent to the town's railway station.

Lakeland Limited, Station Precinct. ℰ **01539/446732**. Main courses £6.95–£8.95 ($11–$14). MC, V. Mon–Fri 9am–6pm; Sat 9am–5pm; Sun 10:30am–4pm.

Punch Bowl ✩ CONTINENTAL Since chef Stephen Doherty took over this 16th-century inn, it's been known for more than beds and a pint. Doherty, who studied under the brothers Roux, has brought a flare to the dining room so appealing that there's no guarantee you'll get a table if you don't call first. The restaurant/pub service area is very spacious, with a large main room with high-beamed ceiling and upper minstrel galleries plus four additional rooms off a hallway a few steps down from the main room. Choose Cumbrian goat's cheese salad with Italian-style marinated and grilled vegetables, or filet of salmon antiboise with fresh spinach and a tomato-based sauce with basil, black olives, and anchovies, served with potatoes and fresh vegetables. Starters include deliciously simple pea-and-ham soup and a chicken and foie gras pâté with homemade chutney. Besides the a la carte menu, there are daily chalkboard specials, and the menu changes semiannually to reflect seasonal changes. There are three comfortable sleeping rooms available, all with double beds; the rate is £50 ($80) for bed-and-breakfast and £105 ($168) for dinner plus bed-and-breakfast.

Crosthwaite, Windermere, Cumbria LA8 8HR. ℰ **015395/68237**. Reservations recommended. Main courses £8.95–£15 ($14–$24). MC, V. Tues–Sat noon–2pm and 6–9pm; Sun noon–2pm.

Queens Head ✩ MODERN ENGLISH Once voted Cumbria Dining Pub of the Year, and still as good, this unusual and popular 17th-century coaching inn uses a huge Elizabethan four-poster bed as its serving counter and has other eclectic antiques among its traditional wooden bar furniture. The menu, which changes every 6 weeks, also combines common items in unusual ways, making traditional dishes more exotic. Recent main courses included chicken rolled in garlic and herbs, served on a bed of creamed leeks with beetroot sauce; and roasted breast of duck served on creamed cabbage bordered with plum sauce. Finish with one of their lovely puddings, perhaps an orange-and-chocolate tart with a Grand Marnier zabaglione. There's a full bar and a good wine selection, or you can quaff a pint of Mitchells Lancaster Bomber, Tetley's, or Boddington's. Looking for a place to stay? The Queens Head has nine well-furnished rooms with a double going for £85 ($136).

A592 north of Windermere, Cumbria LA23 1TW. ℰ **015394/32174**. Reservations recommended. Main courses £7.95–£15.50 ($13–$25). MC, V. Daily noon–2pm and 6:30–9pm.

FAVORITE LOCAL PUBS

Drive a short distance south of Windermere to Cartmel Fell, situated between the A592 and the A5074, and you'll find a pub-lover's dream. The **Mason Arms,** Strawberry Bank (ℰ **01539/568486**), is a Jacobean pub with original oak paneling and flagstone floors. Sturdy, comfortable wooden furniture is spread through a series of five rooms in which you can wander or settle. The outside garden, attractive in its own right, offers a dramatic view of the Winster Valley beyond. The pub offers so many beers that they have a 24-page catalog to help you order, plus a creative, reasonable menu that includes several tasty vegetarian options. Beer prices start at £2 ($3.20).

Southeast of the village, off the A5074 in Crosthwaithe, the **Punch Bowl** (© **01539/568237**) is a 16th-century pub; the central room features a high-beamed ceiling with upper minstrel galleries on two sides. Outdoors, a stepped terrace on the hillside offers a tranquil retreat. Theakston's Best Bitter, Jennings Cumberland, and Cocker Hoop are available on tap.

A popular 17th-century pub, **The Queens Head,** on the A592 north of Windermere (© **01539/432174**), uses a gigantic Elizabethan four-poster bed as its serving counter, and has an eclectic mix of antiques strewn in with basic bar furnishings. There are 14 rooms in which you can settle with a pint of Mitchell's Lancaster Bomber, Tetley's, or Boddington's.

Established in 1612, the **Hole in t' Wall,** Lowside (© **01539/443488**), is the oldest pub in Bowness, a real treasure for its character and friendliness. The barroom is decorated with a hodgepodge of antiquated farming tools, and there's a large slate fireplace lending warmth on winter days plus a good selection of real ales on tap. The menu is determined daily, and there's real ingenuity illustrated in an eclectic mix of vegetarian, seafood, and local game dishes. A small flagstoned terrace in the front offers lingering on warmer days and evenings.

A SIDE TRIP TO BOWNESS-ON-WINDERMERE

Directly south of Windermere, Bowness-on-Windermere is an attractive old lakeside town with lots of interesting, largely Victorian architecture. This has long been an important center for boating and fishing, and you can rent boats of all kinds to explore the lake.

WHERE TO STAY

Belsfield House   Built in the 1830s by a wealthy Midlands industrialist, this oft-renovated house is in the heart of town. It has walls of Lakeland slate, a facade covered with white stucco and layers of white paint, and, at the back, a view out over the Windermere. This guesthouse is owned by the Harbison family. The spacious bedrooms are modernized and cozy, each with a neat, shower-only bathroom. There is one nonsmoking room and one room available for those with limited mobility. Breakfast is the only meal served.

4 Belsfield Terrace, Kendal Rd., Bowness-on-Windermere, Cumbria LA23 3EQ. © **015394/45823**. www. belsfieldhouse.co.uk. 9 units. £32.50 ($52) single; £28–£35 ($45–$56) double. Rates include English breakfast. MC, V. Free parking. **Amenities:** Breakfast room. *In room:* TV, coffeemaker, hair dryer (on request).

The Fairfield   This 2-century-old Lakeland home lies in a tranquil garden setting, a short walk from the center of the village of Bowness. Friendly and welcoming, it is a country house of some charm. Wander through the half-acre secluded garden with its scent of camellia and wisteria before enjoying a night's rest in one of the well-furnished bedrooms. These rooms were once occupied by Annie Garnet, a famous figure in the Lake District known for her designing and watercolors. The artist converted the stables of the original house into a workshop, which was later converted into sleeping cottages. In cooler weather guests gather in the lounge, enjoying the roaring log fire.

Brantfell Rd., Bowness-on-Windermere, Cumbria LA23 3AE. © **015394/46565**. www.the-fairfield.co.uk. 9 units. £29–£34 ($46–$54) per person. Rates include breakfast. AE, MC, V. **Amenities:** Bar; breakfast room. *In room:* TV, coffeemaker, hair dryer.

WHERE TO DINE

Porthole Eating House FRENCH/ITALIAN/ENGLISH   In a white-painted Lakeland house near the center of town, this restaurant, owned and operated by Gianni and Judy Barten for the last quarter of a century, serves French, English, and Italian cuisine inspired by Italian-born Gianni. Amid a decor enhanced by rows of wine and liqueur bottles and nautical accessories, you can enjoy well-flavored specialties that change with the seasons. Examples include lobster-and-crab bisque; vegetarian lasagna made with mixed vegetables, fresh herbs, and a fresh tomato coulis and basil sauce; and filet of beef lightly grilled and served with a reduction of butter, fresh herbs, and a touch of white wine.

3 Ash St. (C) 01539/442793. Reservations recommended. Main courses £11–£17 ($18–$27). AE, DC, MC, V. Sun and Thurs–Fri noon–2pm; Wed–Mon 6:30–10pm.

3 Ambleside & Rydal

445km (278 miles) NW of London; 22km (14 miles) NW of Kendal; 6km (4 miles) N of Windermere

An idyllic retreat, Ambleside is just a small village, but it's one of the major places to stay in the Lake District, attracting pony trekkers, hikers, and rock climbers. It's wonderful in warm weather and even through late autumn, when it's fashionable to sport a raincoat. Ambleside is perched at the north end of Lake Windermere.

Between Ambleside and Wordsworth's former retreat at Grasmere is Rydal, a small village on one of the smallest lakes, Rydal Water. The village is noted for its sheep-dog trials at the end of summer. It's 2.5km (1½ miles) north of Ambleside on the A591.

ESSENTIALS
GETTING THERE　Take a train to Windermere (see earlier in this chapter), then continue the rest of the way by bus.

Stagecoach Cumberland ((C) **08706/082608**) has hourly bus service from Grasmere and Keswick (see below) and from Windermere. All the buses into Ambleside are labeled either no. 555 or 557.

If you're driving from Windermere, continue northwest on the A591.

VISITOR INFORMATION　The **Tourist Information Centre** is at Market Cross Central Building, in Ambleside ((C) **01539/432582**), and is open daily from 9am to 5pm.

EXPLORING THE AREA
Lakeland Safari Tours, 23 Fisherbeck Park, Ambleside ((C) **01539/433904;** www.lakesafari.co.uk), helps you discover the Lakeland's hidden beauty, heritage, and traditions. The owner, a qualified Blue Badge Guide, provides an exciting selection of full-day and half-day safaris in his luxury six-seat vehicle. A half-day safari is £22 ($35) per person; a daylong trek is £33 ($53) per person.

Rydal Mount ✦　This was the home of William Wordsworth from 1813 until his death in 1850. Part of the house was built as a farmer's lake cottage around 1575. A descendant of Wordsworth now owns the property, which displays numerous portraits, furniture, and family possessions, as well as mementos and the poet's books. The 2-hectare (4½-acre) garden, landscaped by Wordsworth, is filled with rare trees, shrubs, and other features of interest.

Off A591, 2.5km (1½ miles) north of Ambleside. (C) 01539/433002. Admission house and garden £4 ($6) adults, £3.25 ($5) seniors and students, £1.50 ($2.40) children 5–16, free for kids 4 and under. Mar–Oct daily 9:30am–5pm; Nov–Feb Wed–Mon 10am–4pm.

WHERE TO STAY
IN AMBLESIDE
Crow How Hotel　This small hotel lies along a private drive off A591 north of Ambleside and a few minutes' walk from Rydal Water. The Crow How was

originally a large Victorian 1880 farmhouse of Lakeland stone. The proprietors are Pat and Jim Redman. The bedrooms are plainly furnished and have beverage makers, controllable heaters and private-shower bathrooms. The hotel has a lounge and 1 hectare (2 acres) of gardens. Dinner is optional.

Rydal Rd., Ambleside, Cumbria LA22 9PN. *C* **015394/32193.** Fax 015394/31170. www.crowhowhotel.co.uk. 9 units. £47–£52 ($75–$83) single; £64–£75 ($102–$120) double. Rates include English breakfast. AE, MC, V. Free parking. **Amenities:** Dining room; bar; guest lounge. *In room:* TV, coffeemaker, hair dryer.

Queens Hotel   In the heart of this area is the Queens, an old-fashioned family-run hotel where guests are housed and fed well. It began as a private home in the Victorian era, and was later transformed into a hotel, with some restoration completed in 1992. Bedrooms are a bit smallish but reasonably comfortable, and the small baths have shower stalls.

Market Place, Ambleside, Cumbria LA22 9BU. *C* **01539/432206.** Fax 01539/432721. 26 units. Sun–Thurs £60–£70 ($96–$112) double; Fri–Sat £62–£72 ($99–$115) double (or 2-night minimum stay). AE, MC, V. **Amenities:** 2 restaurants; 2 bars. *In room:* TV, coffeemaker, hair dryer.

Rothay Garth Hotel ★★   On the southern edge of Ambleside, along A591 from Kendal, an elegant, century-old country house is set in beautiful gardens. The bedrooms vary in size and are tastefully decorated, warm, and comfortable each with a private, shower-only bathroom. The Loughrigg Restaurant serves a table d'hôte menu. Guests can enjoy a sunny garden room or the cozy lounge with its seasonal log fires. Yachts, canoes, and sailboards may be rented.

Rothay Bridge, Ambleside, Cumbria LA22 0EE. *C* **01539/32217.** Fax 01539/434400. www.rothay-garth.co.uk. 16 units. £44 ($70) single; £88 ($141) double; £96–£136 ($154–$218) suite. Rates include English breakfast. AE, DC, MC, V. Take A593 1km (½ mile) south of Ambleside. **Amenities:** Restaurant; bar; nearby tennis courts and golf course; limited room service; laundry/dry cleaning. *In room:* TV, coffeemaker, hair dryer, iron.

IN RYDAL

Foxghyll ★ *Value*   You may need good directions to find Foxghyll (a 1.5km/1-mile walk north of town), but if you succeed you'll have found one of the best-value small B&Bs in the region. You're welcomed by Marjorie Mann, who happily shares this handsomely restored house once occupied by the writer Thomas De Quincey *(Confessions of an English Opium Eater)*. The house has a Victorian decorative overlay, but parts of the building are said to date from the 1600s. Each good-size room contains a comfortable chair or settee for reading. One room has a Jacuzzi-style tub, another a four-poster bed. Foxghyll can only house about six guests a night, so reservations are important. Please note that children under 5 cannot be accommodated. The house stands on extensive grounds, which you can explore at leisure.

Under Loughrigg, Rydal, near Ambleside, Cumbria LA22 9LL. *C* **015394/33292.** www.foxghyll.co.uk. 3 units. £49–£56 ($78–$90) single or double. Rates include English breakfast. No credit cards. Free parking. **Amenities:** Breakfast room. *In room:* TV, hair dryer, iron.

IN ELTERWATER

The Britannia Inn   Just off B5343 6.5km (4 miles) west of Ambleside is a 1690s traditional village inn (with a recently added annex) adjoining the green in this unspoiled village. Views from the inn look over the meadows to the three tarns (lakes) making up Elterwater ("lake of the swan") and the fells beyond. David Fry, the innkeeper, rents snug though well-appointed double bedrooms. Bar meals are served in the cozy bar where a log fire blazes in cool weather.

Elterwater, Ambleside, Cumbria LA22 9HP. *C* **015394/37210.** Fax 015394/37311. www.britinn.co.uk. 9 units, 8 with shower only. £72–£80 ($115–$128) double without bathroom, £80–£88 ($128–$141) double with bathroom. Rates include English breakfast. AE, MC, V. Free parking. Closed Christmas. Take A593 from Ambleside to Coniston for 4km (2½) miles, then turn right onto B5343 to Elterwater. Bus: no. 516 from Ambleside. **Amenities:** Restaurant; bar. *In room:* TV, coffeemaker, hair dryer.

WHERE TO DINE
IN AMBLESIDE

Sheila's Cottage Country Restaurant and Tea Room MODERN ENGLISH/INTERNATIONAL Established long ago by a since-departed woman named Sheila, this restaurant is in a 1740s stone-sided Lake District cottage in the town center. The restaurant has traditional decor with oak tables and modern Lakeland prints on the walls. The relatively informal meals feature an impressive array of mouth-watering dishes. Start with a smoked chicken salad, then continue with roasted peppers and Gruyère cheese with pine nuts and pesto. Changing specials include kingfish with roasted peppers, couscous and balsamic sauce, or duck breast stuffed with prunes. Sheila's is well known for desserts; apart from those traditional English puddings so perfect for cold wintry days, there are exotic concoctions such as chocolate fondant and sautéed strawberries or pineapple with black-pepper caramel.

The Slack, Ambleside. © 015394/33079. Reservations recommended for dinner. Main courses £7.95–£14.95 ($13–$24); fixed-price afternoon cream tea £4.95 ($8). MC, V. Daily 11am–9pm (close Sat at 9:30pm).

Zeffirellis WHOLE-FOOD VEGETARIAN In the town's only movie theater, this restaurant is tucked away into simply decorated corners. Some diners make a visit here part of an evening on the town, incorporating a movie into their dinner schedule. The theater is an old-fashioned small-scale structure with a Japanese-inspired Art Deco theme. The food includes pastas, pizzas, salads, and platters of fresh vegetables covered, perhaps, in a Stilton sauce. You won't encounter exciting taste sensations; all the dishes taste, well, wholesome. Wine and beer are available. Films are shown twice daily.

Compston Rd. © 015394/33845. Main courses £6.95–£8.45 ($11–$14). MC, V. Garden Room Café: daily 10am–5pm. Pizzeria and restaurant: Mon–Fri 6–9:45pm; Sat–Sun 5–9:45pm. Movie and 3-course, fixed-price meal £16.50 ($26) for second showing. Bus: no. 555.

FAVORITE LOCAL PUBS

The friendliest pub in Ambleside is the **Golden Rule,** Smithy Brow (© **01539/433363**), named for the brass yardstick mounted over the bar. The barroom has a country hunt theme that features comfortable leather furniture and cast-iron tables. You can step into one side room and throw darts, or go into the other for a quiet, contemplative pint. Behind the bar, a small but colorful garden provides a serene setting in warm weather. There's inexpensive pub grub if you get hungry.

Located 5km (3 miles) west of town, off the A593 in Little Langdale, **Three Shires** (© **01539/437215**), a stone-built pub with a stripped timber-and-flagstone interior, offers stunning views of the valley and wooded hills. You can get good pub grub here, as well as a pint of Black Sheep Bitter, Ruddles County, or Webster's Yorkshire. Malt whiskeys are well represented.

4 Grasmere

451km (282 miles) NW of London; 29km (18 miles) NW of Kendal; 69km (43 miles) S of Carlisle

On a lake of the same name, Grasmere was the home of Wordsworth from 1799 to 1808. He called this area "the loveliest spot that man hath ever known."

ESSENTIALS

GETTING THERE Take a train to Windermere (see above) and continue the rest of the way by bus.

Cumberland Motor Services (© **08706/082608**) runs hourly bus service to Grasmere from Keswick (see below) and Windermere (see above). Buses running in either direction are marked no. 555 or 557.

If you're driving from Windermere (see above), continue northwest along the A591.

VISITOR INFORMATION The summer-only **Tourist Information Centre** is on Red Bank Road (© **01539/435245**) and is open April through October daily from 9:30am to 5:30pm, and November through March Friday, Saturday, and Sunday only from 10am to 3:30pm.

A LITERARY LANDMARK

Dove Cottage/The Wordsworth Museum ⚑ Wordsworth lived with his writer-diarist sister, Dorothy, at Dove Cottage, now part of the Wordsworth Museum and administered by the Wordsworth Trust. Wordsworth, the poet laureate, died in spring 1850 and was buried in the graveyard of Grasmere's village church. Thomas De Quincey was another tenant of Dove Cottage. The Wordsworth Museum houses manuscripts, paintings, and memorabilia. Several paintings are by Percy Horton, who was director of the Royal Academy of Fine Arts during World War II and was responsible for evacuating many British masterpieces out of London during the Blitz. There are special exhibitions throughout the year that explore the art and literature of English Romanticism.

Afternoon tea is served in the **Dove Cottage Tearoom and Restaurant** (© **01539/435268**). A good selection of open sandwiches, scones, cake, and tea breads is offered along with Darjeeling, Assam, Earl Grey, and herbal teas. The tearoom is open daily from 10am to 5pm and the restaurant from 6:30 to 9pm Wednesday through Sunday.

On A591, south of the village of Grasmere on the road to Kendal. © 01539/435544. www.wordsworth.org.uk. Admission to both Dove Cottage and the adjoining museum £5.80 ($9) adults, £2.60 ($4.15) children. Daily 9:30am–5:30pm. Closed Dec 24–26 and Jan 6–Feb 2.

WHERE TO STAY

How Foot Lodge ⚑ This 1843 Victorian house, which once belonged to friends of Wordsworth's, lies directly south along A591, the road from Dove Cottage and Rydal Mount. The nonsmoking lodge is owned by the Wordsworth Trust. The high-ceilinged, large bedrooms are elegantly furnished with reproduction pieces and modern beds. All of them have shower-only bathrooms.

Town End, Grasmere, Cumbria LA22 9SQ. © 015394/35366. Fax 015394/35268. www.howfoot.co.uk. 6 units. £26–£28 ($42–$45) per person per night for 1–2 nights. Discounts for longer stays. Rates include English breakfast. MC, V. Free parking. **Amenities:** Breakfast room. *In room:* TV, coffeemaker, hair dryer (on request)

Moss Grove Hotel This centrally located old Lakeland house is just past the village church. A hotel since 1894, it is warm and well furnished. The nonsmoking rooms vary in size but most are spacious enough. Some units have four-poster beds. There are two lounges, one with a small bar. Dinner is well cooked, usually a roast joint or poultry with fresh vegetables. There are also cottages available for weekly rental. Call for details.

Grasmere, Cumbria LA22 9SW. © 015394/35251. Fax 015394/35691. www.mossgrove.co.uk. 13 units. £44 ($70) single; £82–£100 ($131–$160) double. Rates include English breakfast. MC, V. Closed Dec–Jan. Free parking. Bus: no. 555. **Amenities:** Breakfast room; bar; nearby pool; sauna. *In room:* TV, coffeemaker, hair dryer.

Oak Bank Hotel ★ *(Finds*   The poets and artists of the Lake District, were they alive today, might gravitate to this cliché of Lakeland charm. The River Rothay flows by, and log fires burn in the lounge bar on chilly nights, which is generally the case around here. A good center for touring the district, this nonsmoking B&B is a welcoming oasis, with handsomely decorated bedrooms. Bedrooms contain immaculately kept private bathrooms with shower.

Broadgate, Grasmere, Cumbria LA22 9TA. ⓒ **01539/435217.** Fax 01539/435685. www.lakedistricthotel.co.uk. 15 units. £55–£65 ($88–$104) single; £90–£120 ($144–$192) double. Rates include breakfast. MC, V. **Amenities:** Restaurant; bar. *In room:* TV, coffeemaker, hair dryer, iron.

Riversdale Guest House *(Value*   This lovely old house, built in 1830 of traditional Lakeland stone, is situated on the outskirts of the village of Grasmere along the banks of the River Rothay. The nonsmoking bedrooms are tastefully decorated and offer every comfort, including hospitality trays, as well as views of the surrounding fells. Bedrooms, most often midsize, have quality furnishings. Each unit has a small bathroom, most with a tub-and-shower combination. Mariea Cook is a wealth of information on day trips, whether by car or hiking. Her breakfasts, which are a delight, are served in a dining room overlooking Silver How and the fells beyond Easdale Tarn. This establishment does not accommodate children.

Riversdale, White Bridge, Grasmere, Cumbria LA22 9RQ. ⓒ **01539/435619.** www.riversdalegrasmere.co.uk. 3 units. £40 ($64) single; £50–£65 ($80–$104) double. Rates include English breakfast. No credit cards. Drive 16km (10 miles) north of Windermere along A591 (signposted to Keswick), then turn left by the Swan Hotel. In 360m (1,200 ft.), you'll find the inn on the left side of the road facing the river. *In room:* Coffeemaker, hair dryer, no phone.

Woodland Crag   The home of Geraldine and Bob Hamilton, this Victorian Lakeland stone-built house dates from 1852. It's set on an acre of wooded gardens, lying near Dove Cottage, the former home of William Wordsworth. The walk to the center of Grasmere village takes only 5 minutes. Vegetarians receive a special welcome, and packed lunches are available year-round. Each bedroom is tastefully decorated and comfortable, opening onto views of lake, fell, or garden. Two singles share a neat and tidy bathroom.

How Head Lane, Town End, Grasmere, Cumbria LA22 9SG. ⓒ **01539/435351.** Fax 01539/435351. www. smoothhound.co.uk/a09531.html. 5 units. £28–£35 ($45–$56) single; £56–£70 ($90–$112) double. Rates include breakfast. MC, V. **Amenities:** Breakfast room. *In room:* TV, coffeemaker, hair dryer, iron.

SUPER-CHEAP SLEEPS: A YOUTH HOSTEL

Grasmere Youth Hostel (Butterlip How) *(Value*   The immediate area in front of this stone-and-slate Victorian farmhouse is known as Butterlip How and has historical significance. A Viking stronghold, it later served as a repository for the remains of King Bothar's soldiers who fell in battle, according to archaeologists. Five rooms sleep two persons each; 10 family rooms sleep four each, two rooms handle six each, one sleeps eight, another 10. Most of the hostel is nonsmoking. Reception is open 7 to 10:30pm; the curfew is enforced.

Easedale Rd., Grasmere, Cumbria LA22 9QG. ⓒ **015394/35316.** Fax 015394/35798. www.yha.org.uk. 88 beds. £13 ($21) adults; £9 ($14) children under 18. MC, V. Curfew: 11pm. Open Jan–Oct (subject to change). Limited free parking. **Amenities:** Dining room; drying room for clothes; game room. *In room:* No phone.

5 Coniston & Hawkshead

421km (263 miles) NW of London; 83km (52 miles) S of Carlisle; 30km (19 miles) NW of Kendal

At Coniston, you can visit the village famously associated with John Ruskin. It's also a good place for hiking and rock climbing. The Coniston "Old Man" towers in the background, at 790m (2,633 ft.), giving mountain climbers one of the finest views of the Lake District.

Just 6.5km (4 miles) east of Coniston sits the village of Hawkshead, with its 15th-century grammar school where Wordsworth studied for 8 years (he carved his name on a desk that is still there). Nearby, in the vicinity of Esthwaite Water, is the 17th-century Hill Top Farm, former home of author Beatrix Potter.

ESSENTIALS

GETTING THERE   Take a train to Windermere (see earlier in this chapter) and proceed the rest of the way by bus.

From April to September, eight buses per day make the trip to Hawkshead; the service is run by **Mountain Goat** (© 01539/45164).

By car from Windermere, proceed north on the A591 to Ambleside, cutting southwest on the B5285 to Hawkshead.

Windermere Lake Cruises Ltd. (© 01539/443360; www.windermere-lake cruises.co.uk) operates a ferry service in summer from Bowness, directly south of Windermere, to Hawkshead. It reduces driving time considerably (see "Windermere & Bowness-on-Windermere," earlier in this chapter).

VISITOR INFORMATION   The **Tourist Information Centre** (© 01539/ 436525) is at Hawkshead in the Main Car Park and is open daily from 9:30am to 5:30pm during high season, and Friday through Sunday from 10am to 3:30pm during winter.

EXPLORING THE AREA

Of the many places to go boating in the Lake District, Coniston Water in the Lake District National Park may be the best. Coniston Water lies in a tranquil wooded valley between Grisedale Forest and the high fells of Coniston Old Man and Wetherlam. The **Coniston Boating Centre,** Lake Road, Coniston LA21 (© 01539/441366), occupies a sheltered bay at the northern end of the lake. The center provides launching facilities, boat storage, and parking. You can rent rowboats that carry from two to six people, sailing dinghies carrying up to six passengers, or Canadian canoes that transport two. There is a picnic area and access to the lakeshore. From the gravel beach, you may be able to spot the varied water birds and plants that make Coniston Water a valuable but fragile habitat for wildlife.

You can also cruise the lake in an original Victorian steam-powered yacht, the *Gondola.* Launched in 1859, and in regular service until 1937, this unique boat was rescued and completely restored by the National Trust. Since 1980 it has become a familiar sight on Coniston Water, and sailings to Park-a-Moor and Brantwood run throughout the summer. Service is subject to weather conditions, of course. Trips are possible from April to October costing £4.80 ($8) round-trip for adults or £2.80 ($4.50) for children. For more information, call © 01539/36216.

Coniston Launch (© 01539/436216; www.conistonlaunch.co.uk) is a traditional timber boat that calls at Coniston, Monk Coniston, Torver, and Brantwood. (Discounts are offered in combination with admission to Brantwood house; see below.) This exceptional boating outfitter offers special cruises in summer.

Summitreks operates from the lakeside at Coniston Boating Centre, offering qualified instruction in canoeing and windsurfing. A wide range of equipment can be rented from the nearby office at Lake Road (© 01539/441212; www. summitreks.co.uk).

In Hawkshead, the **Beatrix Potter Gallery** (✆ **01539/436355**) has an annually changing exhibition of Beatrix Potter's original illustrations from her children's storybooks. The building was once the office of her husband, solicitor William Heelis, and the interior remains largely unaltered since his day. To get here, take bus no. 505 from Ambleside and Coniston to the square in Hawkshead.

Brantwood ✮   John Ruskin, poet, artist, and critic, was one of the great figures of the Victorian age and a prophet of social reform, inspiring such diverse men as Proust, Frank Lloyd Wright, and Gandhi. He moved to his home, Brantwood, on the east side of Coniston Water, in 1872 and lived here until his death in 1900. The house today is open for visitors to see his memorabilia, including some 200 of his pictures.

Part of the 100-hectare (250-acre) estate is open as a nature trail. The Brantwood stables, designed by Ruskin, have been converted into a tearoom and restaurant, the Jumping Jenny. Also in the stable building is the Coach House Craft Gallery, which follows the Ruskin tradition of encouraging contemporary craftwork of the finest quality.

Literary fans may want to pay a pilgrimage to the graveyard of the village church, where Ruskin was buried; his family turned down the invitation to have him interred at Westminster Abbey.

Coniston. ✆ **01539/441396**. www.brantwood.org.uk. Admission £4.75 ($8) adults, £3.50 ($60) students, £1 ($1.60) children 5–16, £10 ($16) family ticket (2 adults, 3 children). Garden walk £2 ($3). Mid-Mar to mid-Nov daily 11am–5:30pm; mid-Nov to mid-Mar Wed–Sun 11am–4:30pm. Closed Christmas Day and Boxing Day.

Ruskin Museum   At this institute, in the center of the village, you can see Ruskin's personal possessions and mementos, pictures by him and his friends, letters, and his collection of mineral rocks.

Yewdale Rd., Coniston. ✆ **01539/441164**. www.ruskinmuseum.com. Admission £3.50 ($6) adults, £1.75 ($2.80) children, £9 ($14) family ticket (2 adults, 2–3 children). Mar–Nov daily 10am–5:30pm; Nov–Mar Wed–Sun 10:30am–3:30pm.

WHERE TO STAY

In addition to the following listings, the **Queen's Head** (see "Where to Dine," below) also has sleeping accommodations.

The Kings Arms Hotel   This is an old coaching inn in the Hawkshead village center near the police station, with leaded windows and sloping roofs. Inside, low beams, whitewashed walls, and a friendly bar patronized by locals complete the picture. The midsize bedrooms are routine pub style, clean and decent, occasionally a little noisy. There's also a restaurant offering grills and steaks.

The Square, Hawkshead, near Ambleside, Cumbria LA22 0NZ. ✆ **015394/36372**. Fax 015394/36006. www. kingsarmshawkshead.co.uk. 9 units, 8 with shower. £32–£36 ($51–$58) single without bathroom; £74–£82 ($118–$131) double with bathroom. Rates include English breakfast. MC, V. Free parking. **Amenities:** Restaurant; bar. *In room:* TV, coffeemaker, hair dryer (on request).

The Sun Hotel   This is the most popular, traditional, and attractive pub, restaurant, and hotel in Coniston. It's a country-house hotel of much character, dating from 1902, though the inn attached to it is from the 16th century. Situated on beautiful grounds above the village, 135m (450 ft.) from the town center, it lies at the foot of the Coniston "Old Man." Each nonsmoking bedroom is decorated with style and flair, and one of them has a four-poster bed. Rooms range from small to midsize, each with a comfortable bed. Eight of the rooms contain a tub-and-shower combination.

Brow Hill, Coniston, Cumbria LA21 8HQ. ℂ **01539/441248.** Fax 01539/441219. www.thesunconiston.com. 11 units. £35 ($56) single; £80 ($128) double. Rate includes English breakfast. MC, V. **Amenities:** Restaurant; bar; room service (10am–10pm); laundry service. *In room:* TV, coffeemaker, hair dryer.

IN FAR SAWREY

Sawrey Hotel ★ *Finds*   This hotel, 1.5km (1 mile) west of the Windermere car-ferry beside B5285, is in the village where Beatrix Potter lived the happiest years of her life. It was built of stone and "pebble-dash" (a form of stucco) as a coaching inn in the early 1700s. James Brayshaw and his family are the hosts, offering comfortable accommodations in three sections of the hotel: the oldest rooms with thick plaster walls; plainer rooms above the pub, renovated during the 1970s; or a new wing of rooms built in the mid-1990s. The stone-sided pub, converted from a very old stable, serves bar meals. Popular with the locals, it retains its antique hayracks and stall dividers.

Far Sawrey, near Ambleside, Cumbria LA22 0LQ. ℂ and fax **015394/43425.** www.smoothhound.co.uk/hotels/ sawreyho.html. 18 units. £31.50 ($50) single; £63 ($101) double. Rates include breakfast. MC, V. **Amenities:** Restaurant; 2 bars. *In room:* TV, coffeemaker, hair dryer (on request).

WHERE TO DINE

Queens Head Hotel ENGLISH/INTERNATIONAL   This is the most famous pub in town. Behind a mock black-and-white timber facade, it's a 17th-century structure of character. It serves a special brew, Robinson's Stockport, from old-fashioned wooden kegs. Try a sizzling sirloin steak, local Cumberland sausages, grilled rainbow trout, or pheasant in casserole. There is more exotic cuisine ranging from Thai curry to Moroccan chicken. Vegetarians are catered for with several dishes. The Queen's Head may be more inn than pub; it rents 13 bedrooms with private bathroom, TV, and phone. The comfortably old-fashioned bedrooms rent for £65 to £85 ($98–$128) double (two with four-poster beds). English breakfast is included.

Main St., Hawkshead. ℂ **01539/436271.** Fax 01539/436722. www.queensheadhotel.co.uk. Reservations recommended. Main courses £11–£15 ($18–$24). Daily noon–2:30pm and 6:45–8:45pm.

FAVORITE LOCAL PUBS

A display case of fishing lures is the first tip-off, then there's the pond itself—yes, it's true, you can fish while you drink at the **Drunken Duck,** Barnsgate (ℂ **01539/436347**). Or you can just sit on the front porch and gaze at Lake Windermere in the distance. Inside, you can choose from an assortment of cushioned settees, old pews, and tub or ladder-back chairs, then order a beef filet in red-wine sauce or minted lamb casserole to go with a pint of Mitchell's Lancaster Bomber, Yates Bitter, or Yates Drunken Duck Bitter, brewed especially for the pub. If you want stronger spirits, there are more than a dozen malt whiskeys to choose from.

Overlooking the central square of the village, the **Kings Arms** (ℂ **01539/ 436372**) offers a pleasant front terrace or lots of plush leather-covered seating inside the cozy barroom. Traditional pub grub is supplemented with a few pasta dishes, burgers, and steaks, and ales include Greenall's Original, Tetley's, and Theakston's XB. Malt whiskeys are also well represented.

6 Keswick

35km (22 miles) NW of Windermere; 470km (294 miles) NW of London; 50km (31 miles) NW of Kendal

Keswick opens onto Derwentwater, one of the loveliest lakes in the region, and the town makes a good base for exploring the northern half of Lake District

National Park. Keswick has two landscaped parks, and above the small town is an historic stone circle thought to be some 4,000 years old.

St. Kentigern's Church dates from A.D. 553, and a weekly market held in the center of Keswick can be traced from a charter granted in the 13th century. It's a short walk to Friar's Crag, the classic viewing point on Derwentwater. The walk will also take you past boat landings with launches that operate regular tours around the lake.

Around Derwentwater are many places with literary associations that evoke memories of Wordsworth, Robert Southey, Coleridge, and Hugh Walpole. Several of Beatrix Potter's stories were based at Keswick. The town also has a professional repertory theater that schedules performances in the summer, a swimming pool complex, and an 18-hole golf course at the foot of the mountains 6.5km (4 miles) away.

ESSENTIALS

GETTING THERE   Take a train to Windermere (see earlier in this chapter) and proceed the rest of the way by bus.

   Stagecoach Cumberland (✆ **08706/082608**) has a regular bus service from Windermere and Grasmere (bus no. 555).

   From Windermere, drive northwest on the A591.

VISITOR INFORMATION   The **Tourist Information Centre,** at Moot Hall, Market Square (✆ **01768/772645**), is open daily April through September from 9:30am to 5:30pm, and October through March daily from 9:30am to 4:30pm. It's closed Christmas and New Year's days.

SEEING THE SIGHTS

The Teapottery, off Heads Road at the central car park entrance (✆ **017687/73983**), is internationally known for its unique handmade teapots. It now has a Keswick branch where visitors may watch the craftspeople at work. You experience the history of tea and see the whole range of wild and wonderful teapots in this shop.

Mirehouse   Mirehouse is a tranquil Cumbrian family home that has been passed on by inheritance since 1688; it has wide-ranging literary and artistic connections. Classical music is played on the piano when guests stop by. The park around it stretches to Bassenthwaite Lake, and has extensive gardens, plus woodland adventure playgrounds. It is in easy reach of the ancient lakeside church and the Old Sawmill Tearoom, known for its generous Cumbrian cooking.

On A591, 5.5km (3½ miles) north of Keswick. ✆ 01768/772287. Admission to house and gardens plus a lakeside walk £4.40 ($7) adults, £2.20 ($3.50) children and seniors, £12.50 ($20) family ticket (2 adults plus 4 kids ages 5–16). Gardens alone £2 ($3.20) adults, £1 ($1.60) children. House open Apr–Oct Sun and Wed (also Fri in Aug) 2–4:30pm. Tearoom and grounds Apr–Oct daily 10am–5:30pm.

WHERE TO STAY

Allerdale House   Close to the town center, this large 1877 Victorian home can be an ideal base near Derwentwater; you get real Lakeland warmth and hospitality. The spacious nonsmoking doubles are comfortably furnished and well maintained, each with a private-shower bathroom. Guests are accepted year-round; they can arrange to have a home-cooked dinner.

1 Eskin St., Keswick, Cumbria CA12 4DH. ✆ 017687/73891. Fax 017087/74068. www.smoothhound.co.uk/hotels/allerdale.html. 6 units. £27.50 ($44) single; £50–£55 ($80–$88) double. Rates include English breakfast. No credit cards. Free parking. **Amenities:** Breakfast room. *In room:* TV, coffeemaker, hair dryer.

Cumbria House *(Value)* You get a warm Lakeland welcome here at this stone-built, traditional house. Most accommodations open onto panoramic views of the fells, which you can explore armed with the advice of the hotel's owners, Barry and Katherine Colam, both experienced hill walkers. Known for its excellent home cooking, this guesthouse gives good value for money. Some guests prefer the top floor with its single, double, and twin units, with one shower and toilet. This can be rented as a whole family unit or else individually. At breakfast you can order a meal of your choice, everything from Cumbrian sausage to Linda McCartney's vegetarian sausage.

1 Derwentwater Place, Ambleside Rd., Keswick, Cumbria CA12 4DR. © **017687/73171.** www.cumbria house.co.uk. 8 units, 4 with bathroom. £20–£22 ($32–$35) single without bathroom; £25–£27 ($40–$43) per person double with bathroom. **Amenities:** Breakfast room. *In room:* TV, coffeemaker, hair dryer.

George Hotel *(★)* Its fame dates from 1590 when it was a coaching inn called the George & Dragon. In time Wordsworth, Southey, and Coleridge dropped in frequently for a pint. Painted an easy-to-spot black and white, it lies on the upper part of the town's main street, near the Market Square. The nonsmoking bedrooms are comfortable and recently refurbished, with many of their original ceiling beams intact. The rooms vary in character and size. There is an old-world bar and a restaurant.

4 St. John St., Keswick, Cumbria CA12 5AZ. © **017687/72076.** Fax 017687/75968. 13 units. £30–£50 ($48–$80) per person; £45 ($72) single. Rates include English breakfast. AE, DC, MC, V. **Amenities:** Restaurant; bar. *In room:* TV, coffeemaker, hair dryer (on request).

WHERE TO DINE

Dog & Gun *(★)* ENGLISH The most famous pub in Keswick, this joint evokes hunting sports and has a warm character that fills the tavern rooms. Dating from 1690, the Dog & Gun offers low beams, slate floors, brass bric-a-brac, and open fires in winter. Patrons can have anything from bar snacks to full meals. Main courses are hearty and may include an authentically spicy Hungarian goulash (a favorite with local climbers), roast chicken, or baked local Borrowdale trout.

2 Lake Rd. © **017687/73463.** Main courses £5.95–£7.25 ($10–$12). AE, DC, MC, V. Mon–Sat noon–11pm; Sun noon–10:30pm.

The Langstrath Inn ENGLISH This bar-restaurant offers plenty of lively atmosphere against a backdrop of pine and oak woodwork, beams, and tables. The place features a selection of healthy foods all made with fresh local products. Lunch offerings tend toward hearty homemade soups like French onion or carrot; a fell-walkers lunch of cheeses, ham, and crusty bread; and open-face sandwiches with prawns, ham, or bacon, lettuce, and tomato. The larger regional dinner menu includes stir-fried duckling, fresh steak-and-kidney pie, Scottish salmon, Cumberland sausage, and a cornucopia of vegetarian dishes.

Stonethwaite, near Borrowdale. © **017687/77239.** Main courses £7.50–£13 ($12–$21). MC, V. Mon–Sat noon–2pm, 3–5pm (afternoon tea), and 6–8:30pm; Sun 6–10:30pm. Bar: Mon–Sat 11:30am–11pm; Sun 6–10:30pm.

AN EXCURSION TO BORROWDALE & SCAFELL PIKE

One of the most scenic parts of the Lake District, Borrowdale stretches south of Derwentwater to Seathwaite in the heart of the county. The valley is an excellent center for exploring, walking, and climbing. Many use it as a center for exploring **Scafell,** England's highest mountain, at 963m (3,210 ft.).

This resort is in the Borrowdale Valley, the southernmost settlement of which is Seatoller. The village of Seatoller, at 353m (1,176 ft.), is the terminus for buses to and from Keswick. It's also the center for a **Lake District National Park Information Centre** at Dalehead Base, Seatoller Barn (℃ **01768/777294**).

After leaving Seatoller, the B5289 takes you west through the Honister Pass and Buttermere Fell, one of the most dramatic drives in the Lake District. The road is lined with towering boulders. The lake village of Buttermere also merits a stopover (see the box "Cheap Thrills: What to See & Do for Free [or Almost] in the Lake District," earlier in this chapter).

7 Penrith

464km (290 miles) NW of London; 50km (31 miles) NE of Kendal

This former capital of Cumbria, in the old Kingdom of Scotland and Strathclyde, may take its name from the Celts who called it "Ford by the Hill." Its namesake hill is marked today by a red-sandstone beacon and tower. Because of Penrith's central location right above the northern Lake District and beside the Pennines, this thriving market center was important to Scotland and England from the beginning, prompting England to take it over in 1070.

The characteristically red-sandstone town has been home to many famous and legendary figures through the ages, including Richard, Duke of Gloucester; William Cookson, grandfather of William and Dorothy Wordsworth; and the giant Ewan Caesarius, slayer of monsters, men, and beasts. Caesarius's grave allegedly rests in St. Andrew's Churchyard. Penrith remains best known as a lively market town.

ESSENTIALS

GETTING THERE   Trains from London's Euston Station arrive in Penrith four times a day. The trip takes 4 hours. For train schedules and information, call ℃ **0845/7484950.**

To take a bus from London to Penrith, hop on one of the two daily National Express buses to Carlisle and then take a Stagecoach Cumberland bus to Penrith, a total journey of 8 hours. The Stage Coach Cumberland buses leave every hour. For schedules and information, call **National Express** at ℃ **020/7529-2000** and **Stagecoach Cumberland** at ℃ **08706/082608.**

To drive, take the M1 out of London, getting on the M6 to Penrith. The trip should take no more than 6 hours.

VISITOR INFORMATION   The **Tourist Information Centre,** Robinson's School, Middlegate, Penrith (℃ **01768/867466**), is open from November to Easter, Monday to Friday from 10am to 4pm, Saturday 10:30am to 4pm; from Easter to May and the month of October, Monday through Saturday from 9:30am to 4:45pm and Sunday from 1 to 5pm; June through September, Monday through Saturday from 9:30am to 5pm and Sunday from 1 to 4:45pm.

EXPLORING THE AREA

Penrith is a small town, but it has lots of shops to explore. Major shopping areas include the covered **Devonshire Arcade** with its name-brand stores and boutiques, the pedestrian-only **Angel Lane** and **Little Dockray,** with an abundance of specialty shops, and **Angel Square** just south of Angel Lane.

For handmade earthenware and stoneware from the only remaining steam-powered pottery in Britain, stop by **Wetheriggs Country Pottery,** Clifton Dykes, 3km (2 miles) south of Penrith on the A6 (℃ **01768/892733**).

In the 130-year-old **Briggs & Shoe Mines,** Southend Road (℃ **01768/899001**), you'll have a shoe-shopping extravaganza. It is the largest independent shoe shop in the Lakelands, carrying famous names and offering great bargains, including sportswear, walking boots, clothing, and accessories.

Penrith Museum For perspective on Penrith and its environs, a visit here isn't a bad idea. Built in the 1500s, the building was turned into a poor-girls school in 1670. Today, the museum offers a survey of the archaeology and geology of Penrith and the Eden Valley, a desert millions of years ago.

Robinson's School, Middlegate. © **01768/212228**. Free admission. June–Sept Mon–Sat 10am–5pm, Sun 1:30–4pm; Oct–May Mon–Sat 10am–4pm.

Penrith Castle This park contains the massive ruins of the castle, whose construction began in 1399, ordered by William Strickland, the bishop of Canterbury. For the next 70 years, the castle grew in size and strength until it became the royal castle and residence for Richard, duke of Gloucester.

Just across from the train station along Ullswater Rd. No phone. Free admission. Always accessible.

Acorn Bank Garden ⚘ *Finds* A stroll in this English garden reveals a varied landscape of blooming bulbs, plants, and walled spaces. Its claim to fame is its extensive herb garden, perhaps the best in northern England. The Acorn Bank Garden is part of an estate from 1228, now owned by the National Trust. Buildings include a partially restored water mill, parts of which are also 13th-century, and a red-sandstone, primarily Tudor house, not open to the public.

Temple Sowerby, 9.5km (6 miles) east of Penrith on A6. © **017683/61893**. Admission £2.60 ($4.15) adults, £1.30 ($2.10) children, £6.50 ($10) family ticket (2 adults, 2 children). Wed–Mon 10am–5pm (last admission at 4:30pm). Closed Nov–Good Friday.

WHERE TO STAY

Norcroft Guesthouse "More room than needed to swing a cat"—that's how the owner describes this huge red-sandstone Victorian B&B and its guest rooms. Built in 1854, this house sits in a quiet residential area very near the town center. The nonsmoking guest rooms, located on three floors, are grand, awash with good pictures, dark wood, and an original English staircase that leads up to a huge first-floor landing. All rooms are decorated with antiques, excellent carpets, and (in some cases) English hunt or flower prints. The front rooms look out onto Victorian churchyards—a favorite wandering place for guests. Units come with small, shower-only bathrooms. Guests go to the dining room, with its Victorian features and fireplace, to meet, socialize, and have breakfast as well as dinner, if they wish. Two rooms are available for those with limited mobility.

Graham St., Penrith, Cumbria CA11 9LQ. © and fax **01768/862365**. www.norcroft-guesthouse.co.uk. 9 units. £25.50 ($41) per person. Rates include English breakfast. AE, DC, MC, V. Free parking. **Amenities:** Dining room. *In room:* TV, coffeemaker, hair dryer.

Yorkshire & Northumbria

Yorkshire, known to readers of *Wuthering Heights* and *All Creatures Great and Small,* embraces both the moors of North Yorkshire and the dales. Across this vast region came the Romans, Anglo-Saxons, Vikings, monks of the Middle Ages, English kings, lords of the manor, craftspeople, hill farmers, and wool growers, all leaving their mark. You can still see Roman roads and pavements, great abbeys and castles, stately homes, open-air museums, and crafts centers, along with parish churches, old villages, and cathedrals.

Some cities and towns still carry the taint of the Industrial Revolution, but there's also wild, remote beauty to be found—limestone crags, caverns along the Pennines, rolling hills, heather-covered moorlands, broad vales, and tumbling streams. Yorkshire also has 160km (100 miles) of shoreline, with cliffs, sandy bays, sheltered coves, fishing villages, bird sanctuaries, former smugglers' dens, and yachting havens. And in summer, the moors in **North York Moors National Park** bloom with purple heather. You can hike along the 177km (110-mile) Cleveland Way National Trail, encircling the park.

Yorkshire's most visited city is the walled city of **York.** York Minster is noted for its 100 stained-glass windows. The literary shrine of

Haworth, home of the Brontës, is in West Yorkshire.

On the way north to **Hadrian's Wall,** spend the night in the ancient cathedral city of **Durham.** This great medieval city is among the most dramatically sited and most interesting in the north.

Northumbria is made up of the counties of Northumberland, Cleveland, and Durham. The Saxons carved out this kingdom in the 7th century; at that time it stretched from the Firth of Forth in Scotland to the banks of the Humber in Yorkshire. Again, this slice of England has more than its share of industrial towns, but you should explore the wild hills and open spaces and cross the dales of the eastern Pennines.

Northumbria evokes ancient battles and bloody border raids. We don't have the space to cover this area in great detail. The hurried North American visitor often overlooks it, but you should at least visit Hadrian's Wall, a Roman structure and one of the great achievements of the ancient Western world. The finest stretch of the wall lies within the **Northumberland National Park,** between the stony North Tyne River and the county boundary at Gilsland. Some 64km (40 miles) of the 241km (150-mile) Pennine Way, one of Britain's most challenging hiking paths, meander through the park.

1 York ✭✭✭

325km (203 miles) N of London; 42km (26 miles) NE of Leeds; 141km (88 miles) N of Nottingham

Few English cities have as rich a history as York. It's still encircled by 13th- and 14th-century city walls, about 4km (2½ miles) long, with four gates; one of

Value Cheap Thrills : What to See & Do for Free (or Almost) in Yorkshire & Northumbria

Find a "perch" along the North Yorkshire Coast. Bridlington is a good starting point for a seaside journey. A fishing port with an ancient harbor, its wide beach and busy seafront markets draw crowds. Flamborough Head juts out into the North Sea, with a 25m (85-ft.) lighthouse standing atop a chalk cliff 51m (170 ft.) above the sea. A path up the cliffs ends at Bempton, site of one of the coast's finest bird sanctuaries.

Spend a day in Whitby. This old whaling port and resort town is at the mouth of the River Esk. Captain James Cook set out from here to circumnavigate the globe. Herman Melville paid tribute to William Scoresby, captain of some of the first ships to sail to Greenland and inventor of the crow's nest, in *Moby-Dick;* Bram Stoker found inspiration for *Dracula* in Whitby's quaint streets. The ruins of 12th-century **Whitby Abbey,** Green Lane (© **01947/603568**), lie high on the East Cliff, visible from almost everywhere in town. In the uniquely designed Church of St. Mary, the stairway of 199 steps leading to the church begins at Church Street.

Walk the Cleveland Way. The little town of Helmsley is your best bet for walking part of this horseshoe-shaped footpath, which runs for 177km (110 miles) around the North York Moors National Park. The most exciting walk is 5km (3 miles) northwest of Helmsley to the ruins of Rievaulx Abbey, reached via a signposted footpath.

Stroll the medieval walls around York. The best way to get acquainted with this ancient cathedral city is to make the 5.5km (2½-mile) walk along its medieval walls. Make this grand promenade early in the morning before the tourist hordes descend. A free map called "Historic Attractions of York," available at the tourist office, guides you on your way.

Pay a visit to Holy Island. Six miles east of A1, north of Bamburgh, lies Lindisfarne (Holy Island), cradle of northern England's Christianity. The site, connected to the mainland by a long causeway, is accessible only 10 hours a day, when high tides are not covering the causeway. Lindisfarne Castle was built about 1550 as a fort to protect the harbor; in 1903, Sir Edwin Luytens converted the castle into a private home open to the public.

these, Micklegate, once grimly greeted visitors from the south with the heads of traitors. You can still walk on the footpath of the walls.

The crowning achievement of York is its minster, or cathedral, making the city an ecclesiastical center the equal of Canterbury. You can stop to see it while driving to Edinburgh; or, after visiting Cambridge, make a swing through the great cathedral cities of Ely, Lincoln, York, and Ripon.

There was a Roman York, then a Saxon York, a Danish York, a Norman York (William the Conqueror slept here), a medieval York, a Georgian York, and a Victorian York (the center of a flourishing rail business). Today, much of 18th-century York remains, including Richard Boyle's restored Assembly Rooms.

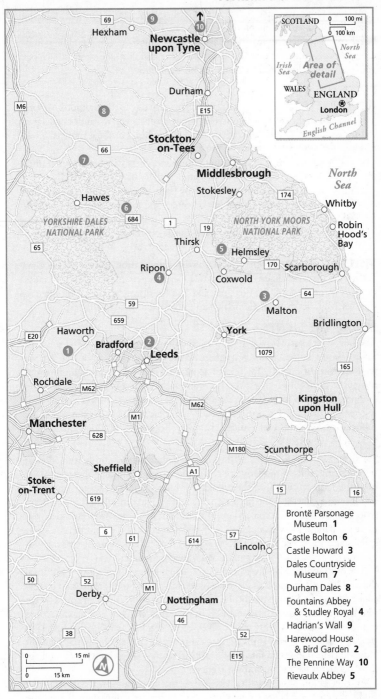

Yorkshire & Northumbria

SCOTLAND

0 ___ 100 mi
0 ___ 100 km

North Sea

Irish Sea

Area of detail

WALES

ENGLAND

⊛ London

English Channel

69

Hexham

9

↑ **10**

Newcastle upon Tyne

Durham

M6

E15

8

66

Stockton-on-Tees

7

Middlesbrough

Stokesley

174

Hawes

6

684

1

19

YORKSHIRE DALES NATIONAL PARK

NORTH YORK MOORS NATIONAL PARK

Whitby

Robin Hood's Bay

Thirsk

5 Helmsley

170

Scarborough

65

Ripon

4

Coxwold

59

3

64

659

Malton

Bridlington

Haworth

E20

1

Bradford

2

Leeds

York

1079

165

Rochdale

M62

M62

Kingston upon Hull

Manchester

M1

628

M180

Scunthorpe

Sheffield

A1

Stoke-on-Trent

619

15

16

6

61

614

57

Lincoln

50

52

M1

Derby

Nottingham

46

38

52

E15

0 ___ 15 mi
0 ___ 15 km

North Sea

Brontë Parsonage Museum **1**

Castle Bolton **6**

Castle Howard **3**

Dales Countryside Museum **7**

Durham Dales **8**

Fountains Abbey & Studley Royal **4**

Hadrian's Wall **9**

Harewood House & Bird Garden **2**

The Pennine Way **10**

Rievaulx Abbey **5**

At some point, you may want to visit the Shambles, once the meat-butchering center here; it predates the Norman Conquest. The messy business is gone now, but the ancient street survives, filled with jewelry stores, cafes, and buildings huddling so closely together that you can stand in the middle of the street, stretch out your arms, and almost touch the houses on both sides.

ESSENTIALS

GETTING THERE British Midland flights arrive at Leeds/Bradford Airport, a 50-minute flight from London's Heathrow Airport. For schedules and fares, call the airline at ℭ **0870/6070555.** Connecting buses at the airport take you east and the rest of the distance to York.

From London's King's Cross Station, York-bound trains leave every 30 minutes. The trip takes 2 hours. For information, call ℭ **0845/7484950.**

Four **National Express** buses depart daily from London's Victoria Coach Station for the 4½-hour trip to York. For schedules and information, call ℭ **0870/5808080.**

If you're driving from London, head north on the M1, cutting northeast below Leeds at the junction with the A64, heading east to York.

VISITOR INFORMATION The **Tourist Information Centre** at De Grey Rooms, Exhibition Square (ℭ **01904/621756**), is open in winter from Monday through Saturday from 9am to 5pm and Sunday from 10am to 4pm; open in summer Monday through Saturday 9am to 6pm and Sunday 10am to 5pm.

SEEING THE SIGHTS

The best way to see York is to go to Exhibition Square (opposite the Tourist Information Centre), where a volunteer guide will take you on a **free 2-hour walking tour** of the city. You'll learn about history and lore through numerous intriguing stories. Tours are given April through October, daily at 10:15am and 2:15pm, plus 7pm from June to August; from November to March, a daily tour is given at 10:15am. Groups can book by prior arrangement by contacting the **Association of Volunteer Guides,** De Grey Rooms, Exhibition Square, York YO1 2HB (ℭ **01904/640780**).

York Minster ★★★ One of the great cathedrals of the world, York Minster traces its origins from the early 7th century; the present building, however, dates from the 13th century. Like the cathedral at Lincoln, York Minster is characterized by three towers built in the 15th century. The central tower is lantern-shaped in the Perpendicular style, and from the top of the tower on a clear day there are panoramic views of York and the Vale of York. The climb up a stone spiral staircase is steep and not recommended for very elderly or very young visitors, or anyone with a heart condition or breathing difficulties.

The outstanding characteristic of the cathedral is its **stained glass** ★★★ from the Middle Ages, in glorious Angelico blues, ruby reds, forest greens, and honey-colored ambers. See especially the Great East Window, the work of a 15th-century Coventry-based glass painter. In the north transept is an architectural gem of the mid–13th century: the Five Sisters Window, with its five lancets in grisaille glass. The late-15th-century choir screen in its Octagonal Chapter House has an impressive lineup of historical figures—everybody from William the Conqueror to the overthrown Henry VI.

At a reception desk near the entrance to the minster, groups can arrange a guide, if one is available. Conducted tours are free, but donations toward the upkeep of the cathedral are requested.

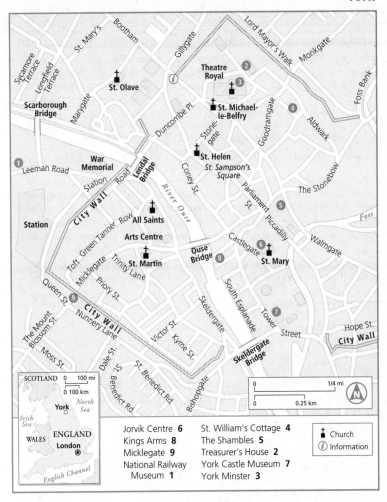

Jorvik Centre 6
Kings Arms 8
Micklegate 9
National Railway Museum 1

St. William's Cottage 4
The Shambles 5
Treasurer's House 2
York Castle Museum 7
York Minster 3

✝ Church
ⓘ Information

At the converging point of Deangate, Duncombe Place, Minster Yard, and Petergate. ☎ 01904/557216. www. yorkminster.org. Admission to Chapter House is free (a £3.50/$6 donation is suggested); crypt, foundations, and treasury £3.80 ($6) adults, £1.50 ($2.40) children. Chapter House, undercroft, and tower Mon–Sat 10am–6:30pm, Sun 1–6pm (closing time in winter 4:30pm). Call ahead to verify times, as they are subject to change.

Jorvik Centre ★ This Viking city, discovered many feet below present ground level, was reconstructed as it stood in 948, and underwent major refurbishment in 2001. In a "time car," you travel back through the ages to 1067, when Normans sacked the city, and then you ride slowly through the street market peopled by faithfully modeled Vikings. You also go through a house where a family lived and down to the river to see the ship chandlers at work and a Norwegian cargo ship unloading. At the end of the ride, you pass through the Finds Hut, where thousands of artifacts are displayed. The time car departs at regular intervals.

Coppergate. ☎ 01904/643211. www.jorvik-viking-centre.co.uk. Admission £6.95 ($11) adults, £5.10 ($8) children 5–15 years, £6.10 ($10) seniors and students, £21.95 ($35) family ticket. Rates may change depending on the event. Apr–Oct daily 10am–5pm; Nov–Mar daily 10am–4:30pm.

National Railway Museum ★★★ This was the first national museum to be built outside London, and it has attracted millions of train buffs. Adapted from an original steam-locomotive depot, the museum gives visitors a chance to see how Queen Victoria traveled in luxury, and to look under and inside steam locomotives. In addition, there's a collection of railway memorabilia, including an early-19th-century clock and penny machine for purchasing tickets on the railway platform. More than 40 locomotives are on display. One, the *Agenoria,* dates from 1829 and is a contemporary of Stephenson's well-known *Rocket.* Of several royal coaches, the most interesting is Queen Victoria's *Royal Saloon;* it's like a small hotel, with polished wood, silk, brocade, and silver accessories.

Leeman York Rd. ℂ 01904/621261. www.nrm.org.uk. Free admission. Daily 10am–6pm. Closed Dec 24–26.

Treasurer's House The Treasurer's House lies on a site where a continuous succession of buildings has stood since Roman times. The home was built in 1620, but Frank Green, a Yorkshire industrialist, refurbished the main part of the house at the turn of the 20th century; he used this elegant town house to display his collection of 17th- and 18th-century furniture, glass, and china. An audiovisual program and exhibit explain the work of the medieval treasures and the subsequent fascinating history of the house. It has an attractive small garden in the shadow of York Minster.

Minster Yard. ℂ 01904/624247. Admission £3.80 ($6) adults, £2 ($3.20) children, £9.50 ($15) family ticket. Sat–Thurs 11am–4:30pm. Closed Nov–Mar.

York Castle Museum ★ On the site of York's Castle, this is one of the finest folk museums in the country. Its unique feature is a re-creation of a Victorian cobbled street, Kirkgate, named for the museum's founder, Dr. John Kirk. He acquired his large collection while visiting his patients in rural Yorkshire at the beginning of this century. The period rooms range from a neoclassical Georgian dining room to an overstuffed and heavily adorned Victorian parlor to the 1953 sitting room with a brand-new television set purchased to watch the coronation of Elizabeth II. In the Debtors' Prison, former prison cells display crafts workshops. There is also a superb collection of arms and armor. In the Costume Gallery, displays are changed regularly to reflect the collection's variety. Half Moon Court is an Edwardian street, with a gypsy caravan and a pub (sorry, the bar's closed!). During the summer, you can visit a water mill on the bank of the River Foss. Allow at least 2 hours for your museum visit.

The Eye of York off Tower St. ℂ 01904/653611. Admission £6 ($10) adults, £3.50 ($6) children. Daily 9:30am–5pm.

SHOPPING

Several of the main areas to explore include **Gillygate** for antiques dealers, **St. Mary's Square** and its **Coppergate** pedestrian mall for name brands and chain stores, and **Newgate Marketplace** for local vendors selling a variety of wares Monday through Saturday.

Several specialty shops that have ideal gift items include **Maxwell and Kennedy,** 79 Low Petergate (ℂ **01904/610034**), a candy store specializing in both Belgian chocolate and Cambridge Wells dark, milk, and white chocolate; **Mulberry Hall,** 17 Stonegate (ℂ **01904/620736**), housed in a medieval house from 1436, with 16 showrooms on three floors devoted to the best in British and European porcelain, fine china, crystal, and some antiques; and **Wooden Horse,** 9 Goodramgate (ℂ **01904/626012**), featuring an eclectic mixture of

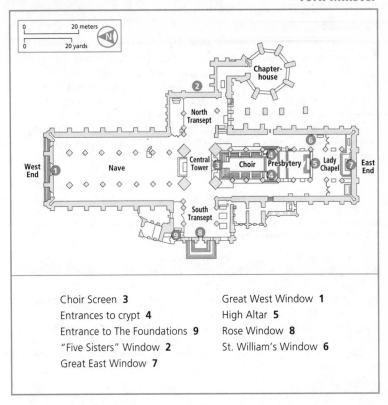

Choir Screen **3**	Great West Window **1**
Entrances to crypt **4**	High Altar **5**
Entrance to The Foundations **9**	Rose Window **8**
"Five Sisters" Window **2**	St. William's Window **6**
Great East Window **7**	

ethnic items such as shirts, tops, jewelry, cushions, rugs, and throws from Africa, India, China, and Mexico.

WHERE TO STAY

Arnot House *(Value)*   Grosvenor Terrace is a 15- to 20-minute walk from the train station, off Bootham (A19), just outside the city walls at Bootham Bar. Like other houses on the terrace, Arnot House has views over Bootham Park, toward the minster. This 1870 Victorian house contains its original fireplaces, cornices, and a fine old staircase. The atmosphere is warm and comfortable, and it's good value for the area. The nonsmoking spacious bedrooms are all furnished in Victorian style; some have brass beds, and each comes with a shower-only bathroom.

17 Grosvenor Terrace, Bootham, York, North Yorkshire Y03 7AG. *(C)* and fax **01904/641966**. www.arnothouse york.co.uk. 4 units. £60 ($96) single or double. Rates include English breakfast. MC, V. Bus: 8. **Amenities:** Breakfast room. *In room:* TV, coffeemaker, hair dryer.

The Avenue Guest House   Appealing and cheerful, this brick-sided guesthouse (built around 1900) is a 10-minute walk north of York's center and a few steps from the edge of the River Ouse. It is across the road from St. Peters, a venerable private school whose graduates include Guy Fawkes. Owned by Adèle and Clive Allen, the nonsmoking hotel boasts two rare laburnum trees in the front garden and a delightful interior. The bedrooms contain Laura Ashley–styled flowered fabrics and accessories.

Moments Haunted York

York has been witness to more beheadings, medieval tortures, and human anguish than any other British city except London. Psychics and mystics insist that dozens of lost souls wander the city's historic core, reliving their earthly traumas. Several outfits conduct ghost walks every evening, but the most charming one, **The Original Ghost Walk of York,** leaves at 7:30pm every night from The Shambles. The 1-hour tour costs £3 ($4.80) for adults and £2 ($3.20) for children. Be prepared for lively commentary and more ghoulishness than you may expect. Call ✆ **01904/608700** (www.ghosthunt. co.uk) for more information.

6 The Avenue, Clifton, York YO3 6AS. ✆ **01904/620575.** www.avenuegh.fsnet.co.uk. 8 units, 4 with bathroom. £20 ($32) single without bathroom; £24 ($38) double without bathroom, £42 ($67) double with bathroom. Rates include English breakfast. No credit cards. Take A19 north of the city. **Amenities:** Breakfast room. *In room:* TV, coffeemaker, hair dryer (on request).

Beechwood Close Hotel   Beechwood is a large house surrounded by trees, a garden with a putting green, and a parking area. Mr. and Mrs. Blythe run the small hotel, which offers comfortable bedrooms with tasteful furnishings. Each small bathroom is well maintained; most have a tub-and-shower combination. The hotel is a 15-minute walk to the minster, either by road or along the river.

19 Shipton Rd. (on A19 north of the city), Clifton, York, N. Yorkshire YO30 5RE. ✆ **01904/658378.** Fax 01904/647124. www.beechwood-close.co.uk. 14 units. £80 ($128) double. Rates include English breakfast. AE, DC, MC, V. **Amenities:** Restaurant; bar; room service; laundry service. *In room:* TV, coffeemaker, hair dryer, iron/ironing board.

City Guest House   Jeff and Sue Robinson offer warm, friendly service in this small Victorian B&B (built 1860) close to the city center. The nonsmoking rooms are fairly basic but above average in size. Though all rooms have private bathrooms, guests staying in the cheapest room (which can be reserved as a single or double) use a private toilet across the hall. The "family unit" is a double room that contains an extra bed. The large breakfast will fill even the hungriest guest. The Robinsons are happy to help guests make sightseeing plans and find nearby restaurants or pubs.

68 Monkgate, York YO3 7PF. ✆ **01904/622483.** www.cityguesthouse.co.uk. 7 units. £35–£38 ($56–$61) single; £60–£66 ($96–$106) double; £75–£80 ($120–$128) family unit. Rates include English, continental, or vegetarian breakfast. MC, V. **Amenities:** Breakfast room. *In room:* TV, coffeemaker, hair dryer, trouser press.

Cottage Hotel *Value*   About a 10-minute walk north of York Minster, this hotel comprises two refurbished and extended Victorian houses overlooking the village green of Clifton. The hotel offers cozy, small bedrooms with simple furnishings. Each comes with a well-maintained bathroom with a shower stall. Some 400-year-old timbers rescued from the demolition of a medieval building in one of the city's historic streets (Micklegate) grace the restaurant and bar, which does a thriving business. The hotel provides secured parking for its guests.

3 Clifton Green, York, N. Yorkshire YO3 6LH. ✆ **01904/643711.** Fax 01904/611230. 25 units. £70–£80 ($112–$128) double. Rates include English breakfast. MC, V. Free parking. **Amenities:** Restaurant; bar. *In room:* TV, coffeemaker, hair dryer.

Dairy Guest House   This lovely Victorian town house lies just south of the medieval city walls, within easy access of car parking. Architectural charm is found in the stained- and etched-glass windows, pitch-pine doors and staircase, cast-iron fire grates, and wonderfully ornate ceiling roses and cornices. It's decorated throughout in the Habitat–Sanderson–Laura Ashley style. Each non-smoking bedroom sports unusual amenities such as maps, books, and games. Breakfast choices range from traditional English to whole-food vegetarian.

3 Scarcroft Rd., York, North Yorkshire YO2 1ND. ⓒ 01904/639367. www.dairyguesthouse.co.uk. 5 units, 4 with bathroom. £32 ($51) single without bathroom; £42 ($67) single with bathroom; £45 ($72) double without bathroom, £55 ($88) double with bathroom. Rates include English breakfast. AE, MC, V. **Amenities:** Breakfast room. *In room:* TV, coffeemaker, hair dryer.

Feversham Lodge

This lodge is a 19th-century Methodist manse converted to receive guests in 1981. The proprietors maintain neatly kept nonsmoking bedrooms, all with private shower bathrooms. Some rooms open onto views of the minster. The lodge retains its lofty dining room, and there's a TV lounge.

1–3 Feversham Crescent, York, North Yorkshire YO31 8HQ. ⓒ and fax 01904/623882. www.fevershamlodge guesthouseyork.co.uk. 5 units. £35 ($56) single; £52–£70 ($83–$112) double. Rates include English breakfast. MC, V. From Bootham Bar, proceed north along Gillygate; Feversham Crescent is a left turn. **Amenities:** Breakfast room. *In room:* TV, coffeemaker.

Heworth Court

Just a 10- to 15-minute walk east of the city center is this three-story redbrick Victorian structure (many of its bedrooms are located in a modern extension added during the 1980s). The rooms are agreeably furnished, and some open onto the courtyard. Each comes with a comfortable bed, plus a compact bathroom with a shower stall (some have tubs).

76 Heworth Green, York, N. Yorkshire YO3 7TQ. ⓒ 01904/425156. Fax 01904/415290. www.heworth.co.uk. 28 units. £96–£111 ($154–$178) double. Rates include English breakfast. Free parking. AE, DC, MC, V. Take the A1036 to the east side of the city. **Amenities:** Restaurant; bar; laundry service. *In room:* TV, coffeemaker, hair dryer.

Holme Lea Manor

In a cul-de-sac in one of the choice sectors of the city, this is a well-maintained nonsmoking Victorian house filled with charm and character. From the English breakfast served in the old-fashioned dining room to the comfortable drawing room, the house caters well to its guests. Bedrooms are midsize to spacious, each tastefully decorated, often with four-poster beds. Bedrooms come with neatly kept private bathrooms with shower.

18 St. Peters Grove, Clifton, York, North Yorkshire YO30 6AQ. ⓒ 01904/623529. www.holmelea.co.uk. 10 units. £50 ($80) single; £60–£80 ($96–$128) double; £70–£80 ($112–$128) triple. Rates include breakfast. MC, V. **Amenities:** Breakfast room. *In room:* TV, coffeemaker, hair dryer.

Nunmill House ✧

Fronted by a small garden, this brick-with-stone-trim late Victorian house sits in a residential neighborhood a 20-minute walk southeast of the minster. This cozy and much-restored B&B hotel offers comfortable bedrooms aspiring to elegance, with an occasional four-poster or half-tester bed. Each nonsmoking room contains a private, shower-only bathroom. Only breakfast is served.

85 Bishopthorpe Rd., York, North Yorkshire YO2 1NX. ⓒ 01904/634047. Fax 01904/655879. www.nunmill. co.uk. 8 units. £50–£60 ($80–$96) single; £55–£65 ($88–$104) double. 50% discount for children under 12 in parent's room. Rates include English or continental breakfast. No credit cards. Closed Dec–Jan. **Amenities:** Breakfast room. *In room:* TV, coffeemaker, hair dryer.

Sycamore Guest House ✧

The Sycamore is close to the city center off A19 to Thirsk, 10 minutes by foot to the minster, 15 minutes to the rail station; it's on a quiet cul-de-sac. Built as a home in 1902, this house has been carefully converted to a family-owned hotel that offers a high level of accommodations while maintaining much of its original splendor. The well-kept, good-size nonsmoking rooms have comfortable furnishings.

19 Sycamore Place, Bootham, York, North Yorkshire YO30 7DW. ℂ and fax **01904/624712**. www.the sycamore.co.uk. 6 units, 3 with bathroom. £46 ($74) double without bathroom, £60 ($96) double with bathroom. Rates include English breakfast. No credit cards. **Amenities:** Breakfast room. *In room:* TV, coffeemaker, hair dryer.

Tree's Hotel   A 10-minute walk north of Bootham Bar, the north gate of old York, this small, immaculate hotel is nestled amid similar late Victorian redbrick houses. Set in front of a village green ringed with a white picket fence, it evokes the rural side of York, despite the urban location. The nonsmoking bedrooms, rented by Mr. and Mrs. Tree, are carpeted and have hot- and cold-water basins, wardrobes, and dressing tables. *Note:* The hotel also operates the **Inglewood Guest House,** next door at 7 Clifton Green (ℂ **01904/653523**), which charges the same tariffs.

8 Clifton Green, Clifton, York, North Yorkshire YO3 6LH. ℂ **01904/623597**. www.homestead.com/treeshotel/ index.html. 8 units, 3 with bathroom. £25 ($40) single without bathroom, £30 ($48) single with bathroom; £45 ($72) double without bathroom, £60–£100 ($96–$160) double with bathroom. Rates include English breakfast. No credit cards. Take the A19 toward Thirsk. **Amenities:** Breakfast room. *In room:* TV, coffeemaker, hair dryer.

WHERE TO DINE

Betty's Cafe Tea Rooms ⚝ *(Kids)* ENGLISH   Established in 1919 and now one of Yorkshire's most visible tearoom chains, Betty's interior retains much of its original paneling and Edwardian-era stained-glass windows. English breakfasts, genteel afternoon teas with scones, and fish-and-chips high teas are favorites. Healthy salads and whole-food quiches are also available. Betty's is famous for its cream cakes. The wide variety of light suppers and cooked and cold meals makes this a good place to stop in the evening; order a fine Alsatian wine to complement your meal. Every evening there is music (often a pianist), usually at 6pm and 9pm. Families with children are especially welcome.

6–8 St. Helen's Sq. ℂ **01904/659142**. Main courses £6.75–£8.95 ($11–$14); tea from £2.20 ($3.50); pastries from £2.30 ($3.70). MC, V. Daily 9am–9pm.

Blake Head Vegetarian Café *(Finds)* VEGETARIAN/VEGAN   Located in the back of a bookstore, this inviting place is a sort of counter-cultural center and a favorite rendezvous spot for the students of York. The canopy roof lets in light to give a bright and cheerful atmosphere; you can dine on the patio in fair weather. Salads are serious business here. The fixed lunch menu, served daily noon to 3pm, is one of the city's best food values; it changes daily. You can browse the store for a book and enjoy one of their homemade cakes, desserts, and a good cuppa.

104 Micklegate. ℂ **01904/623767**. Main courses £5.75 ($9); 2-course lunch £7.50 ($12). MC, V. Mon–Sat 9:30am–5pm; Sun 10am–5pm.

Oscar's Wine Bar and Bistro INTERNATIONAL   This lively and bustling restaurant, located in a historic building, offers good, affordable, hearty fare in big portions. It serves a variety of burgers from vegetarian to Cajun to Mexican, along with lasagna, chili, Yorkshire sausage, and sizzling sirloin steaks. When weather permits, you can dine in the courtyard. Music plays a role here. On special occasions, there may be live jazz or blues. The popular happy hour is Sunday to Monday 4pm to close, Tuesday to Thursday 5pm to 7pm.

8 Little Stonegate, Off Stonegate. ℂ **01904/652002**. Main courses £3.25–£9.50 ($5–$15) at lunch, £5.95–£10.95 ($10–$18) at dinner. MC, V. Mon–Sat 11am–11pm, Sun noon–10:30pm.

Rubicon VEGETARIAN/VEGAN   This nonsmoking restaurant offers vegan and gluten-free food in a very tidy, warm, relaxed, and intimate atmosphere with candlelight. Bring your own wine at no extra charge and enjoy starters such as Stilton or baked eggplant, followed by delicious vegetarian moussaka or lasagna verde.

5 Little Stonegate, off Stonegate. ℂ **01904/676076.** Main courses £9 ($14). MC, V. Daily 11:30am–10pm.

Russells Stonegate ⍟ ENGLISH   This restaurant sits on York's most ancient street, a 1-minute walk from the minster; there's another branch at 26 Coppergate (ℂ **01904/644330**). Russells restaurants are, according to one observer, "probably the only true British restaurants in York." Although this point may be argued, Russells does offer fresh food of a high standard. Many of its recipes are "just like mother used to make." The place works like a carvery, where the waitstaff brings appetizers, desserts, and drinks to your table while you carry your plate up for roast joints and main courses. The fare includes roast beef with Yorkshire pudding, along with roast potatoes and seasonal vegetables. A good range of appetizers is offered, and the desserts are very English and very fattening, especially bread-and-butter pudding. Wine is available by the glass or bottle, and the kitchen always has a good selection of English cheese.

34 Stonegate. ℂ **01904/641432.** Reservations recommended. Snacks £4–£8 ($6–$13); main courses £8–£10 ($13–$16) at lunch, £10.50–£12.50 ($17–$20) at dinner. MC, V. Daily noon–2:30pm and 5:30–9:30pm.

Tandoori Night *(Value)* INDIAN   Once inside this exotically decorated restaurant, you'll feel as if you're in India. Some of the best, most affordable Indian meals in town may be found here; select from a variety of chicken, lamb, or rice dishes, ranging from very mild to very hot. They also serve special Malaysian dishes with fruit, rice, and coconut (chicken Malaya is recommended).

23 Bootham. ℂ **01904/613366.** Main courses £3.50–£7.50 ($6–$12); 5-course lunch £4.95 ($7). AE, MC, V. Daily noon–2:30pm and 6pm–midnight.

A YORK PUB-CRAWL

One of the city's oldest inns, **The Black Swan,** Peaseholme Green (ℂ **01904/ 686911**), is a fine, timber-framed house that was once the home of the lord mayor of York in 1417; the mother of General James Wolfe of Quebec also lived here. In front of a log fire in a brick inglenook, you can enjoy pub meals such as fish and chips, burgers, and steaks. This is one of York's "musical pubs," featuring live folk music on Monday and Thursday and jazz on Wednesday and Sunday, with a small cover charge starting at £4 ($6).

⟮*Tips* **A Regal Banquet**

Check out **St. William's Restaurant** at the front of St. William's Cottage (ℂ **01904/634830**), close to the east end of the minster. This splendid timbered building provides a setting daily for coffee, an affordable lunch, or tea. Here you can get tasty quiches, homemade soups, and luscious desserts. Not only that, if you can arrange for a party of 35 or more, you can have a medieval banquet staged on your behalf, complete with minstrels, jesters, and jugglers. One way to do this is to post a notice at your hotel and get people to sign up and invite their newly made acquaintances. In one day our party swelled to nearly 50, and we were regally fed and entertained.

Situated at the base of the Ouse Bridge, a few steps from the edge of the river, the 16th-century **Kings Arms Public House,** King's Staith (© **01904/659435**), is boisterous and fun. An historic monument in its own right, it's filled with charm and character and has the ceiling beams, paneling, and weathered brickwork you'd expect. Because of its location by the river, the pub can flood if rain is heavy enough. Expect a virtually indestructible decor, the kind that can (and often does) sit under water for days at a time. In summer, rows of outdoor tables are placed beside the river. Your hosts serve a full range of draft and bottled beers, the most popular of which (Samuel Smith's) is still brewed in Tadcaster, only 16km (10 miles) away.

On a pedestrian street in Old York, **Ye Olde Starre Inne,** 40 Stonegate (© **01904/623063**), dates from 1644 and is York's oldest licensed pub. An inn (of one kind or another) has stood on this spot since 900. In a pub said to be haunted by an old woman, a little girl, and a cat, you enter into an atmosphere of cast-iron tables, open fireplace, oak Victorian settles, and time-blackened beams. Recently, the owners have added a year-round glassed-in garden. In all types of weather, guests can enjoy the plants and view of the minster from their tables.

2 Leeds

326km (204 miles) NW of London; 120km (75 miles) NE of Liverpool; 69km (43 miles) NE of Manchester; 118km (74 miles) N of Nottingham

The foundations for a permanent community were laid nearly 2,000 years ago when the Romans set up a small camp called Cambodunum, but the next step toward Leeds didn't come until the 7th century, when King Edwin of Northumbria built a residence. Kirkstall Abbey was founded in 1152. In 1207, Leeds finally obtained its charter and laid out the grid pattern still evident today.

During the Middle Ages, Leeds took the Golden Fleece as its coat of arms, symbolizing its growth and importance as a wool town; it eventually became the region's greatest center for the cloth trade. Industrial advancements played a great role in the city's development; the introduction of steam power led to the development of the coalfields to the south. Other innovations spurred continued growth of its textile industry as well as the rapid development of such upstart industries as printing, tailoring, and engineering.

After languishing for years and being dismissed for its industrial blight, the city is progressing once again. There's been some economic growth. Many of the great Victorian buildings in its bustling central core have been renovated: the **Corn Exchange,** the **Grand Theatre,** and the **Victoria Quarter.** Add the recently passed "24-Hour City Initiative," making it the only U.K. location to allow, indeed *encourage* around-the-clock work and entertainment options, and you've got an up-and-coming city with lots of new energy.

ESSENTIALS

GETTING THERE   Leeds-Bradford International Airport (© **01132/509696**) about 14km (9 miles) north of town has daily flights to and from London, with air transport taking less than an hour. There is also a 24-hour direct rail link between Manchester airport and Leeds.

Trains from London's King's Cross Station arrive hourly during the day, with the trip taking about 2 hours. For information, call © **0845/7484950.**

Leeds is also serviced daily by **National Express** buses from London. For schedules and information, call © **08705/808080.**

Leeds lies at the crossroads of the north-south M1 and the east-west M62 routes, making it easily accessible by car from anywhere in England or Scotland.

VISITOR INFORMATION The **Gateway Yorkshire Regional Travel & Tourist Information Centre,** The Arcade, City Station (✆ **01132/425242**), is open Monday through Saturday from 9am to 5:30pm and Sunday from 10am to 4pm. Leeds also has a website (www.leeds.gov.uk) with information on transportation, lodging, dining, shopping, and entertainment in the city.

Information on local bus and train routes and times is available by calling **Metroline** at ✆ 01132/457676.

SPECIAL EVENTS In July, more than 40,000 opera lovers turn out at **Temple Newsam,** Temple Newsam Road, off Selby Road (✆ **01132/425242**), for the single performance of Opera in the Park, the largest free outdoor opera concert in the United Kingdom. The gargantuan **Party in the Park** (✆ **01132/ 478222**), also held at Temple Newsam, is one of the largest free pop and rock concerts in the United Kingdom. It's usually held the day following Opera in the Park and features some of the hottest acts in rock music.

Film buffs turn out in droves for the annual **Leeds International Film Festival** (✆ **01132/478308;** www.leedsfilm.com). Screened the first two weeks in October at cinemas throughout Leeds, it's the only theme-based film festival in the United Kingdom. It regularly features British as well as world-premiere films and hosts film-related lectures, seminars, and workshops.

EXPLORING LEEDS

Despite its longtime reputation as a grimy northern industrial city, Leeds will surprise you with the beauty and diversity of its **city center,** where £400 million ($640 million) has been invested in both new construction and renovation of warehouses and landmark Victorian structures into homes, lodging, shops, and restaurants along The Waterfront and in the central shopping district.

The Henry Moore Institute ⭐ Located next door to the City Art Gallery, this is the largest sculpture gallery in Europe, as well as the first devoted to the display, study, and research of sculpture from all periods and cultures. The institute is named after the greatest British sculptor of the 20th century, Henry Moore (1898–1986), who was a Yorkshireman. This center shows the range of his accomplishments, from his early *Reclining Figure* (1929) to his most powerful postwar statements like *Meat Porters.* The works of many of Moore's contemporaries are also displayed. Lectures throughout the year supplement the institute's exhibitions.

74 The Headrow. © 01132/467467. www.henry-moore-fdn.co.uk. £3 ($4.80) adults, free for visitors 18 and under. Mon–Tues and Thurs–Sun 10am–5:30pm; Wed 10am–9pm.

Leeds City Art Gallery ⭐ Spread over three floors, this gallery, founded in 1888, houses England's best collection of 20th-century art outside of London, including collections of French post-Impressionist paintings, contemporary British sculpture, prints, watercolors, and drawings. Throughout the year it also hosts visiting exhibits, enhanced by workshops, talks, and other related events.

Located within the gallery, the **Craft Centre and Design Gallery** (© **01132/478241**) showcases contemporary ceramics, jewelry, prints, textiles, and applied arts from around the world. It also hosts openings and exhibits by local and regional artists working within these mediums.

74 The Headrow. © 01132/478248. www.leeds.gov.uk/artgallery. Free admission. Mon–Tues and Thurs–Sat 10am–5pm; Wed 10am–8pm; Sun 1–5pm.

Royal Armouries Museum ⭐⭐ A notable construction along The Waterfront, this £42 million ($67 million) facility is the home of London Tower's Royal Armouries, England's oldest museum, dating from the working arsenal of the medieval kings. It is designed to exhibit the many pieces that have been in perpetual storage because of inadequate facilities in London. The museum illustrates the development and use of arms and armor for war, sport, hunting, self-defense, and fashion.

Armouries Dr. © 01132/201999. www.armouries.org.uk. Free admission. Daily 10am–5pm. Closed Dec 24–25.

WHERE TO STAY

If you'd like advice on local lodging, or if you'd just like to tell someone your price range and requirements and let them book you a room, contact the **Gateway Yorkshire Accommodation Booking Line** (© **0800/808050** or 01132/425242). For a £3 ($4.80) handling fee and a refundable deposit of 10% of your first night's stay, they'll find you a bed for the night.

Aragon Hotel Located only 3km (2 miles) north from City Centre, this small family-run hotel is set well back from the road on an acre of gardens. The surrounding properties stretch out in open fields and woods. Accommodations, while not luxurious, are neat and comfortable. Bedrooms range from small to midsize, each with a small bathroom with a shower stall. A pleasant lounge for residents features a large marble fireplace as well as a full bar, both of which look out over the gardens. The hotel is completely nonsmoking.

250 Stainbeck Lane, Leeds LS7 2PS. © 01132/759306. Fax 01132/757166. www.aragonhotel.co.uk. 12 units. £49.90 ($80) single; £59.90 ($96) double; £69.90 ($112) family room. Rates include English breakfast. AE, DC, MC, V. From Leeds, follow A61 Harrogate signs out of the city. This becomes Scott Hall Rd. (A61). Take the 2nd roundabout, turning left onto Stainbeck Lane, and follow it down one hill and up another. The hotel is on the right. It is also conveniently located about 180m (600 ft.) from a bus stop with routes to Leeds and the surrounding area. **Amenities:** Dining room; lounge; bar. *In room:* TV, dataport, coffeemaker, hair dryer, trouser press.

WHERE TO DINE

Haley's Restaurant BRITISH   This hotel restaurant, in a beautifully restored Victorian mansion, is so popular among locals that even the guests have to reserve long in advance. Chef John Vennell changes his menu monthly to take advantage of the freshest and best market ingredients. Starters might feature a tantalizing "tasting" of quail with an autumn plum chutney, or a terrine of chicken, ham, and rabbit. We've found that some of the best main courses include char-grilled breast of Gressingham duck leg with braised cabbage and shallots, and a pan-seared sea bass with eggplant "caviar" and a tomato confit. You might finish off with a chocolate and Grand Marnier cake. The wine cellar has interesting offerings from around the world.

In Haley's Hotel, Shire Oak Rd., Headingley. © 01132/784446. Reservations required well in advance. Main courses £12.50–£18.95 ($20–$30); fixed price Sun lunch £15.50 ($25) for 3 courses; fixed price dinner £27.50 ($44) for 3 courses. AE, DC, MC, V. Mon–Sat 7:15–9:30pm; Sun 12:15–1:45pm. Closed Dec 26–30.

Leodis Brasserie BRITISH   Another fine choice in the revitalized canal district, Leodis is housed in an artfully renovated paint mill (ca. 1853). You dine in a comfortable space created from the mill's original cast-iron columns and new glass screens. The menu here changes weekly. At lunch, you have four three-course set meals to choose from, plus several a la carte options. Dishes are simple, yet incredibly well prepared. Starters may include fish cakes in tomato-lime salsa, followed by a main course of roast salmon with spinach and rösti or an old-fashioned steak pudding. There's a full bar and a lengthy wine list as well.

Victoria Mill, Sovereign St. © 01132/421010. Reservations recommended. Main courses £9–£16 ($14–$26); fixed-price lunch £15.95 ($26). AE, DC, MC, V. Mon–Fri noon–2pm and 6–10pm; Sat 6–11pm.

LEEDS AFTER DARK

Thanks to a recently passed city initiative aimed at relaxing licensing restrictions and increasing late-night entertainment options, it's safe to say that Leeds now rocks around the clock. It was already humming with classical concerts, opera, jazz, dance, theater, cinema, rock and dance clubs, cafes, and pubs.

THE CLUB & MUSIC SCENE   Leeds has a thriving rock scene, with recent bands like Sisters of Mercy and The Mission rising out of the music scene at **The Warehouse** (see below). Today's up-and-coming music scene is, not surprisingly, very influenced by the Manchester scene (see chapter 15), but innovative bands like Black Star Liner, Bedlam A Go Go, and Embrace show that Leeds still has a musical voice all its own.

The **Cockpit/The Rocket,** Bridge House, Swinegate (© 01132/441573), can host about 600 fans who turn out to hear the latest indie bands in a converted railway arch setting. Usually open Monday through Saturday night with a cover charge ranging from £3 to £10 ($4.80–$16).

When you feel like grooving to the beat, you can head to a vast array of dance clubs around town. Leeds' dance music scene is thriving, as is evident by the presence of such internationally acclaimed clubs as **The Warehouse,** Somers

Street (© **01132/468287**), on Tuesday through Saturday (depending on the night), with admission ranging from £3 to £10 ($4.80–$16).

You'll find the jazz you're looking for at **Arts Café**, 42 Call Lane (© **01132/ 438243**), a European-style cafe bar that offers tapas, bottled beers, and coffees.

Considering its size, there is a substantial gay scene in Leeds. The most popular club at the moment is **Queens Court**, Lower Briggate (© **01132/459449**). Downstairs is a restaurant and bar which is open daily from noon to 7pm; after which, head upstairs for the disco which is open daily from 11pm to 2am with a cover charge ranging from £2 to £4 ($3.20–$6). Another hot spot for gay men at the moment is **The Bridge Inn,** 1–5 Bridge Inn (© **01132/444734**), which has a friendly local pub atmosphere and becomes increasingly clubby as the night progresses. Cover is £3 ($4.80) on Friday and Saturday.

PUBS   Stop by **Whitelocks,** Turks Head Yard (© **01132/453950**), in the alley of Briggate, next to Marks and Spencers. There's a copper-topped bar with a handmade ceramic-tile front, a marble sandwich bar, old advertising mirrors, and stained-glass windows. Locals keep the conversation flowing in a thick, northern accent. If you get hungry, there's cheap traditional pub grub. Tap selections are varied and quite good, including McEwan's 80, Younger's IPA, and Theakston's Old Peculiar.

Hearkening back to Leeds' glory days, **Victoria,** Great George Street (© **01132/451386**), is every bit as Victorian as its name suggests, with ornate globe lamps, etched mirrors, and a well-adorned bar. Politicians and lawyers frequent the place. Join in the conversation or sit back and listen while you enjoy a pint of Tetley's Mild and maybe a bar snack or two.

THE PERFORMING ARTS   **Leeds Town Hall,** The Headrow (© **01132/ 477985,** or box office 01132/476962), hosts orchestras from around the globe as part of the city's annual **International Concert Season,** and is also home to the world-famous **Leeds International Pianoforte Competition,** held every 3 years, with the next scheduled competition in 2003. Opera North offers three to four productions during its season from October to April at the **Leeds Grand Theatre and Opera House,** New Briggate (© **01132/226222**), featuring a well-renovated 1,500-seat auditorium behind its original 1878 Victorian facade.

Theatergoers are much impressed by the facilities at the £12 million **West Yorkshire Playhouse,** Playhouse Square, Quarry Hill (© **01132/137700**), home to the "national theatre of the north." Playhouse artistic director Jude Kelly started out strong in the early inaugural seasons, with 17 productions, including eight British or world premieres. There has been no slowing down since then, and you can find a dramatic offering at most any time in either The Playhouse's Quarry Auditorium, which seats 750, or The Courtyard, which seats 350. The Playhouse, which is the cornerstone of a proposed £70 million Quarry Hill arts complex, also hosts other events throughout the year, including the annual Jazz at the Playhouse series.

The **Yorkshire Dance Centre,** St. Peters Building, York Street (© **01132/ 439867**), houses the internationally renowned **Phoenix Dance Troupe.**

3 Bradford

339km (212 miles) N of London; 51km (32 miles) NE of Manchester; 14km (9 miles) W of Leeds

This city of nearly half a million souls retains a rich ethnic heritage from the succession of immigrants who came to work its mills, beginning in the mid–19th century. Generations of Irish, German, Italian, Eastern European and, later, Asian and African Caribbean immigrants, today give this West Yorkshire city an international flavor.

Bradford boosters say the city is one of the best-kept secrets in the United Kingdom. High-tech firms, galleries, and museums have displaced many of the textile factories. Centrally located between the Yorkshire Dales and the Pennines, Bradford provides a nice diversion and is convenient to a historic countryside where the Brontës once dwelled and armor-covered soldiers clashed in the Wars of the Roses.

ESSENTIALS

GETTING THERE   Bradford is reached by car via the M62 and the M606.

Most rail links go through nearby Leeds (see section 2, above), but at least one direct train each day connects London's Kings Cross Station with Bradford (a 3-hr. trip). Train travel from Manchester takes about 1 hour; it's 3 hours from Birmingham.

Leeds/Bradford Airport (℗ **01132/509696**) is located about 16km (10 miles) from Bradford, and a number of scheduled flights connect to London's Heathrow and Gatwick airports and most major regional U.K. airports. A taxi from the airport to town costs about £10 ($16).

VISITOR INFORMATION   Call the **Bradford Tourist Information Centre,** City Hall, Centenary Square (℗ **01274/433678**). The center assists visitors in selecting accommodations and provides public transit timetables and city guides. Hours are Monday through Saturday from 9:30am to 5pm in winter, and until 5:30pm in summer.

EXPLORING BRADFORD

Bradford's museums, mill shops, and restaurants provide the main attractions for tourists. The city also boasts Bradford University, one of the better regional universities in the United Kingdom.

The Industrial Museum and Horse at Work, Moorside Mills, Moorside Road (℗ **01274/435900**), depicts mill life for worker and owner in the 1870s and offers Shire horse rides for kids and adults. The **Saltaire,** Salt's Mill, is the restored model factory-community developed in the mid–19th century by mill owner and philanthropist Titus Salt. The **1853 Gallery** at Saltaire (℗ **01274/ 531163**) exhibits more than 400 works of local artist David Hockney, among other works.

Visitors can travel by steam-driven train on the **Keighley & Worth Valley Railway** (℗ **01535/645214**) for a tour of Brontë Country in Haworth, through Oakworth's Edwardian station, and Damen's Station, billed as Britain's smallest rail station. It operates daily in summer and weekends in the winter.

National Museum of Photography, Film, and Television, Little Horton Lane (℗ **01274/202030;** www.nmpft.org.uk), captures the history of photography, film, and television in audiovisual presentations that span 150 years. The five-story-high IMAX screen, the largest in England, explores a dazzling variety of cinematic images in a series of new and continuing exhibitions. Admission to the museum is free; the IMAX movie costs £5.80 ($9) for adults, £4 ($6) for children, £16.60 ($27) family ticket (two adults and two children), and advance booking is recommended. Open Tuesday through Sunday from 10am to 6pm.

Bradford's textile industry is still represented in dozens of area mill shops where bargain hunters may find a great variety of mohair, pure-wool yarns, fabrics, sportswear, and other clothing and accessories. Some mill shops provide tours of factory spinning, weaving, and textile finishing.

Suit Length & Fabric Centre, Wakefield Road, Dudley Hill (© 01274/ 729103), will customize suits and garments for the individual tastes and fit of shoppers. **British Mohair Spinners,** Louler Holme Mills, Shipley (© 01274/ 583111), showcases the art of spinning hair and cotton into the heavy, shiny mohair fabric.

WHERE TO STAY

The Best Western Guide Post Hotel *Kids* Catering to both business and leisure travelers, this is a winning little choice. You get a warm welcome as you're shown to your spacious, well-furnished room, equipped with a compact bathroom with shower. The more expensive executive rooms have a spacious lounge area. Ten rooms are reserved for nonsmoking guests. The reasonable price combined with the size of the rooms makes this a good choice for families as well.

Common Rd. (5km/3 miles from Junction 26 of M62), Low Moor, Bradford, W. Yorkshire BD12 OST. © 01274/ 607866. Fax 01274/671085. www.guideposthotel.net. 43 units. Sun–Thurs £70 ($112) single, £80 ($128) double; Fri–Sat £45 ($72) single, £55 ($88) double. Rates include breakfast. AE, DC, MC, V. **Amenities:** Restaurant; bar; lounge; room service (7am–9:15pm); laundry service. *In room:* TV, dataport, coffeemaker, hair dryer, trouser press, iron/board.

WHERE TO DINE

Bradford is called "the curry capital of the U.K.," boasting a vast array of Asian restaurants featuring dishes from Kashmir, Gujerat, the Punjab, and beyond.

Vic and Bert's ★★ CONTINENTAL/ASIAN This elegant brasserie offers wood-grill cooking with an Oriental flavor. The clever chefs here have managed to lighten and modernize many dishes, though still showing a respect for traditional favorites. Their eclectic menu may include filet of steak slathered in mushrooms or any other number of courses such as beef bourguignon and confit of duck.

In the Victoria Hotel, Bridge St. © 01274/728706. Reservations recommended. Main courses £11.50–£16.50 ($18–$26). AE, DC, MC, V. Daily noon–2pm and 6–9:30pm.

BRADFORD AFTER DARK

Alhambra Theatre, Morley Street (© 01274/752000), offers a variety of presentations ranging from amateur to professional. At certain times of the year, leading actors of the English stage and screen may appear here. You can also see children's theater, ballet, and musicals. Ticket prices vary depending upon the type of performance. The theater is closed for a few weeks in August.

But perhaps you're just looking for a local pub. In the city center, the **Shoulder of Mutton,** 28 Kirkgate (© 01274/726038), has a beer garden that comes complete with flowerbeds and hanging baskets. The oldest brewery in Yorkshire, it was originally Samuel Smith's Old Brewery. Lunch is available, and they also sell real ale here. As many as 200 drinkers can crowd in here on a summer night.

As an alternative choice, try the **Fighting Cock,** 21–23 Preston St. (© 01274/726907), an old-fashioned alehouse with bare floors and 12 different bitters. The best ales are Exmoor Gold, Timothy Taylor's, Black Sheep, and Green King Abbott, but they also sell foreign-bottled beers and farm ciders. On nippy nights, coal fires keep the atmosphere mellow. Bar snacks are among the most reasonable in town; the house specialty is chili (the chef guards the recipe).

4 Haworth: Home of the Brontës

72km (45 miles) SW of York; 34km (21 miles) W of Leeds

Haworth, a village on the high moor of the Pennines, is famous as the home of the Brontës, the most visited literary shrine in England after Stratford-upon-Avon.

ESSENTIALS

GETTING THERE   To reach Haworth by rail, take the Arriva Train from Leeds City Station to Keighley (it leaves approximately every 30 min.). Change trains at Keighley and take the Keighley and Worth Valley Railway to Haworth and Oxenhope. Train services operate every weekend year-round, with 7 to 12 departures. From late June to September, trains also run four times a day Monday through Friday. For general inquiries, call ✆ **01535/645214;** for a 24-hour timetable, dial the tourist office ✆ **01535/642329.**

Keighley & District Bus Co. offers bus service between Keighley and Haworth. Bus nos. 663, 664, and 665 will get you there. For information, call ✆ **01535/642329.**

If you're driving from York, head west toward Leeds on the A64 approaching the A6120 Ring Road to Shipley; then take the A650 to Keighley, to the A629 to Halifax, and finally link up with the B6142 south to Haworth.

VISITOR INFORMATION   The **Tourist Information Centre** is at 2–4 West Lane in Haworth (✆ **01535/642329**). It's open April through October daily from 9:30am to 5:30pm; November through March daily from 9:30am to 5pm (closed Dec 24–26).

LITERARY LANDMARKS

Anne Brontë wrote two novels, *The Tenant of Wildfell Hall* and *Agnes Grey;* Charlotte wrote two masterpieces, *Jane Eyre* and *Villette,* which depicted her experiences as a teacher, as well as several other novels; and Emily is the author of *Wuthering Heights,* a novel of passion and haunting melancholy. Charlotte and Emily are buried in the family vault under the **Church of St. Michael.**

While in Haworth, you'll want to visit the **Brontë Weaving Shed,** Townend Mill (✆ **01535/646217**). The shop is not far from the Brontë Parsonage, and features the famous Brontë tweed, which combines browns, greens, and oranges to evoke the look of the local countryside.

Brontë Parsonage Museum ✦   The parsonage where the Brontë family lived has been preserved as this museum, which houses their furniture, personal treasures, pictures, books, and manuscripts. The stone-sided parsonage, originally built near the top of the village in 1777, was assigned for the course of his lifetime as the residence of the Brontës' father, Patrick, the Perpetual Curator of the Church of St. Michael and All Angel's Church. Regrettably, the church tended by the Brontës was demolished in 1870; it was rebuilt in its present form the same year. The parsonage contains a walled garden very similar to the one cultivated by the Brontës, five bedrooms, and a collection of family furniture (some bought with proceeds from Charlotte's literary success), as well as personal effects, pictures and paintings, and original manuscripts. It also contains the largest archive of Brontë family correspondence in the world.

The museum is maintained by a professional staff selected by the Brontë Society, an organization established in 1893 to perpetuate the memory and legacy of Britain's most famous literary family. Contributions to the society are welcomed. The museum tends to be extremely crowded in July and August.

Church St. ℃ 01535/642323. www.bronte.org.uk. Admission £4.80 ($8) adults, £3.50 ($6) seniors and students, £1.50 ($2.40) children 5–16, free for children under 5, £10.50 ($17) family ticket (2 adults and 3 children). Oct–Mar daily 10am–5:30pm; Apr–Sept daily 11am–5:30pm. Closed mid-Jan to early Feb and at Christmastime.

WHERE TO STAY IN & AROUND HAWORTH

Weaver's Restaurant (see "Where to Dine," below) also rents rooms.

Ferncliffe ★ Located about a mile east of Haworth, on the outskirts of the neighboring town of Keighley, Ferncliffe offers one of the area's most outstanding accommodations. Built after World War II and converted into a hotel with enlargements in the early 1980s, this modern hotel and its dining room open onto views of the surrounding *Wuthering Heights* countryside. A rock garden in front, maintained by the affable owners, Elizabeth Corboy and Tom Martin, contains a wide spectrum of alpine plants. The cozily decorated nonsmoking bedrooms are well maintained. The fixed-price dinners feature good Yorkshire cooking.

Hebden Rd., Haworth, Keighley, West Yorkshire BD22 8RS. ℃ 01535/643405. 6 units, all with shower only. £44 ($70) double. Rates include English breakfast. V. Closed Dec 26–30. **Amenities:** Restaurant. *In room:* TV, coffeemaker, hair dryer, no phone.

Moorfield Guest House This nonsmoking guesthouse is located between Haworth and the moors, a 3-minute walk to the village center and the Brontë Parsonage Museum, with unrestricted views of the moors. The owners rent well-furnished and comfortable nonsmoking bedrooms, with private, shower-only bathrooms. Evening meals are available with prior arrangement.

80 West Lane, Haworth, Keighley, West Yorkshire BD22 8EN. ℃ and fax 01535/643689. www.moorfield gh.demon.co.uk. 5 units. £23–£28 ($37–$45) single; £46 ($74) double. Rates include English breakfast. MC, V. Closed Dec 25 and Jan. **Amenities:** Dining room; bar; guest lounge. *In room:* TV, coffeemaker, hair dryer.

Ponden House About 5km (3 miles) from Haworth, this 16th-century barn lies .5km (⅓ mile) from the main road between Ponden Reservoir and the moors. The building has its original stonework and roofing but has been completely renovated with its transformation into a modern B&B. The standard-size nonsmoking rooms offer scenic views of the reservoir and moorland. The owner has created a warm, hospitable environment and is an excellent source of information on local history.

Stanbury, near Keighley, West Yorkshire BD22 0HR. ℃ 01535/644154. www.pondenhouse.co.uk. 3 units, 2 with bathroom. £32 ($51) single; £48 ($77) double. Rate includes English breakfast. No credit cards. **Amenities:** Breakfast room. *In room:* TV, coffeemaker, hair dryer.

SUPER-CHEAP SLEEPS: A YOUTH HOSTEL

Haworth Youth Hostel Built by a local mill owner in 1884, this hostel retains many characteristics of its English country heritage—leaded painted-glass windows, lots of wood paneling, and a wide, sweeping staircase doubling back on itself as it leads to a first-floor balcony. Most rooms are quite large, containing ornate fireplaces, and sleep anywhere from 2 to 16 people. No smoking is allowed inside. Reception is open 7:30am to 10pm.

Longlands Hall, Longlands Dr., Haworth, West Yorkshire BD22 8RT. ℃ 01535/642234. Fax 01535/643023. www.yha.org.uk. 92 beds. £10.25 ($16) adults; £7 ($11) children under 18. MC, V. Curfew: 11pm. Closed Jan. **Amenities:** Restaurant; dining room; game room. *In room:* No phone.

WHERE TO DINE

The Black Bull Hotel ENGLISH This is a 350-year-old stone building which has been a regular watering hole for many—most notably Bramwell Brontë (Anne, Charlotte, and Emily's brother), who came here whenever he was having a gray day, sat in his favorite chair, and partook of some local ale to try to pick himself up. Today, his chair has become a shrine for Brontë devotees; some say that his spirit still mopes around. The bar and restaurant have lots of dark wood panels, tables, and doors. The same menu serves lunch and dinner and offers strictly standard fare—sandwiches, roast beef or lamb, Yorkshire pudding, and traditional English pies.

119 Main St. ℭ **01535/642249.** Main courses £3.50–£8 ($6–$13). V. Mon–Sat 11am–8pm; Sun noon–8pm. Bar: Mon–Sat 11am–11pm; Sun noon–10:30pm.

The Cobbled Way Tea Room ENGLISH   Look up when seeking out this tearoom. It sits at the top of a steep street in a row of similarly constructed houses, yet stands out by way of its large rooftop sign. This small cafe—with its airy, even coquettish atmosphere of fine lace and frills—serves a fixed-price menu with a starter, a main course such as roast beef, pork, turkey, or lamb, and a sweet. Main dishes include vegetarian pastas and hearty lasagnas. Its license lets it serve wine with meals only. Afternoon teas and cream teas with homemade cakes and scones are specialties.

60 Main St. ℭ **01535/642735.** Main courses £2.75–£4.50 ($4.40–$7); fixed-price meal £7.25 ($12); tea with sandwich and scone £3.25 ($5). No credit cards. Apr–Sept daily 10:30am–7pm; Oct–Mar daily 10:30am–6pm.

Weaver's Restaurant ★ MODERN BRITISH   The best restaurant in Haworth, this spot is British to the core. It has an inviting, informal atmosphere and serves excellent food made with fresh ingredients. Jane and Colin Rushworth are quite talented in the kitchen. Dinners include such classics as slow-cooked Yorkshire lamb. If it's available, try a Gressingham duck, widely praised in the United Kingdom. For dessert, select a British cheese or a homemade delicacy. The restaurant usually closes for vacation at some point during the summer, so call in advance. They also rent four bedrooms of high caliber that cost £75 ($120) for a double.

15 West Lane. ℭ **01535/643822.** Reservations recommended. Main courses £9.50–£16.50 ($15–$26); 3-course fixed-price dinner £12 ($19). AE, DC, MC, V. Tues–Sat 6:30–9:30pm.

5 Yorkshire's Country Houses, Castles & More ★★

Yorkshire's battle-scarred castles, Gothic abbeys, and great country-manor houses (from all periods) are unrivaled in Britain. Here are some of the highlights.

IN NORTH YORKSHIRE

Castle Howard ★★   In its dramatic setting of lakes, fountains, and extensive gardens, Castle Howard, the 18th-century palace designed by Sir John Vanbrugh, is undoubtedly the finest private residence in Yorkshire. The principal location for the TV miniseries *Brideshead Revisited,* this was the first major achievement of the architect who later created the lavish Blenheim Palace near Oxford. The Yorkshire palace was begun in 1699 for the third earl of Carlisle, Charles Howard.

The striking facade is topped by a painted and gilded dome, which reaches more than 24m (80 ft.) into the air. The interior boasts a 58m- (192-ft.-) long gallery, as well as a chapel with magnificent stained-glass windows by the 19th-century artist Sir Edward Burne-Jones. Besides the collections of antique furniture, porcelains, and sculpture, the castle has many important paintings, including a portrait of Henry VIII by Holbein and works by Rubens, Reynolds, and Gainsborough.

The seemingly endless grounds around the palace also offer the visitor some memorable sights, including the domed *Temple of the Four Winds,* by Vanbrugh, and the richly designed family mausoleum, by Hawksmoor. There are two rose gardens, one with old-fashioned roses and the other featuring modern creations.

Malton (24km/15 miles northeast of York, 5km/3 miles off A64). © **01653/648333**. www.castlehoward. co.uk. Admission £9 ($14) adults, £8 ($13) seniors and students, £6 ($10) children 4–16. Feb to late Nov, grounds daily 10am–5pm, house daily 11am–4:30pm (during winter, call to verify times).

Fountains Abbey & Studley Royal Water Garden ✸✸✸ On the banks of the Silver Skell, this abbey was founded by Cistercian monks in 1132 and is the largest monastic ruin in Britain. In 1987, it was awarded World Heritage status. The ruins provide the focal point of the 18th-century landscape garden at Studley Royal, one of the few surviving examples of a Georgian green garden. A lake and 160 hectares (400 acres) of deer park bound the garden at its northern edge. The Fountains Hall and Elizabethan Mansion are undergoing restoration. The easiest way to get here is by car, although it can be reached from York by public transportation.

At Fountains, 6.5km (4 miles) southwest of Ripon off B6265. © **01765/608888**. www.fountainsabbey.org.uk. Admission £4.80 ($8) adults, £2.50 ($4) children, £12 ($19) family. Oct–Mar daily 10am–4pm; Apr–Sept daily 10am–6pm. Closed Dec 24–25, Fri in Nov–Jan. It's best to drive, though it can be reached from York by public transportation. From York, take bus no. 143 leaving from the York Hall Station to Ripon, 37km (23 miles) to the northwest (A59, A1, and B6265 lead to Ripon). From Ripon, it will be necessary to take a taxi 6.5km (4 miles) to the southwest, though some prefer to take the scenic walk.

IN WEST YORKSHIRE

Harewood House & Bird Garden ✸✸ (Kids) Thirty-five kilometers (22 miles) west of York, the home of the earl and countess of Harewood is one of England's great 18th-century houses. It has always been owned by the Lascelles family. The fine Adam interior has superb ceilings and plasterwork and furniture made especially for Harewood by Thomas Chippendale. There are also important collections of English and Italian paintings and Sèvres and Chinese porcelain.

The gardens, designed by Capability Brown, include terraces, lakeside and woodland walks, and a 2-hectare (4½-acre) bird garden with exotic species from all over the world, including penguins, macaws, flamingos, and snowy owls. Other facilities include an art gallery, shops, a restaurant, and cafeteria. Parking is free, and there is a picnic area, plus an adventure playground for the children.

At the junction of A61 and A659, midway between Leeds and Harrogate, at Harewood Village. © **01132/ 886331**. www.harewood.org. House, grounds, bird garden, and the terrace gallery £9.50 ($15) adults, £7.75 ($12) seniors, £5.25 ($8) children, £32 ($51) family ticket. Grounds only £6.75 ($11) adults, £5.75 ($9) seniors, £4.25 ($7) children 15 and under, £21 ($34) family ticket. House, bird garden, and adventure playground Mar–Oct daily 11am–4:30pm. Terrace gallery 11am–5pm; Nov–Dec garden and grounds 10am–4pm, bird garden 10am–3pm. From York, head west along B1224 toward Wetherby and follow the signs to Harewood from there.

6 Yorkshire Dales National Park ✸

The national park consists of some 1,812 sq. km (700 sq. miles) of water-carved country. In the dales you'll find dramatic white limestone crags, roads and fields bordered by dry-stone walls, fast-running rivers, isolated sheep farms, and clusters of sandstone cottages.

Malhamdale receives more visitors annually than any dale in Yorkshire. Two of the most interesting historic attractions are the 12th-century ruins of Bolton Priory and the 14th-century Castle Bolton, to the north in Wensleydale.

Richmond, the most frequently copied town name in the world, stands at the head of the dales and, like Hawes (see below), is a good center for touring the surrounding countryside.

EXPLORING THE DALES

For orientation purposes, head first for **Grassington,** 16km (10 miles) north of Skipton and 40km (25 miles) west of Ripon. Constructed around a cobbled marketplace, this stone-built village is ideal for exploring Upper Wharfedale, one of the most scenic parts of the Dales. In fact, the Dales Way footpath passes right through the heart of the village.

Drop in to the **National Park Centre,** Colvend, Hebdon Road (© **01756/ 752774**), which is open April through October daily from 9:30am to 5:15pm. From November to March, hours are Monday from 11am to 1pm, Wednesday and Friday from 11am to 4pm, and Saturday and Sunday from 10am to 4pm. Maps, bus schedules through the dales, and a choice of guidebooks are available here to help you navigate your way. If you'd like a more in-depth look than what you can do on your own, you can arrange for a qualified guide who knows the most beautiful places and can point out the most interesting geological and botanical features of the wilderness.

Sixteen kilometers (10 miles) west of Grassington (reached along the B6265), **Malham** is a great place to set out on a hike in summer. Branching out from here, you can set out to explore some of the most remarkable limestone formations in Britain. First, it's best to stop in for maps and information at the **National Park Centre** (© **01729/830363**), which is open from Easter to October daily from 9:30am to 5pm; off season, only Saturday and Sunday from 10am to 4pm. Amazingly, this village of 200 or so souls receives a half-million visitors annually. May or September are the times to come; the hordes descend from June to August.

The scenery in this area has been extolled by no less an authority than Wordsworth, and it has been painted by Turner. A trio of scenic destinations, **Malham Cove, Malham Tarn,** and **Gordale Scar,** can be explored on a circular walk of 13km (8 miles) that takes most hikers 5 hours. If your time (and your stamina) is more limited, you can take a circular walk from the heart of the village to Malham Cove and Gordale Scar in about 2 hours. At least try to walk 1.5km (1 mile) north of the village to Malham Cove, a large natural rock amphitheater. Gordale Scar is a deep natural chasm between overhanging limestone cliffs, and Malham Tarn is a lake in a desolate location.

Kettlewell lies 13km (8 miles) northwest of Malham and 9.5km (6 miles) north of Grassington. This is the main village in the Upper Wharfedale and is a good base for hiking through the local hills and valleys, which look straight out of *Wuthering Heights.* Narrow pack bridges and riverside walks characterize the region, and signs point the way to **The Dales Way** hiking path.

After Kettlewell, you can drive for 6.5km (4 miles) on B6160 to the hamlet of **Buckden,** the last village in the Upper Wharfedale. Once here, follow the sign to **Kidstone Pass,** still staying on B6160. At **Aysgarth,** the river plummets over a series of waterfalls, one of the dramatic scenic highlights of the Yorkshire Dales.

HAWES: A BASE FOR EXPLORING YORKSHIRE DALES NATIONAL PARK

About 105km (65 miles) northwest of York, on the A684, Hawes is the natural center of Yorkshire Dales National Park and a good place to stay. On the Pennine

Way, it's England's highest market town and the capital of Wensleydale, which is famous for its cheese. Trains from York take you to Garsdale, which is 8km (5 miles) from Hawes. From Garsdale, bus connections will take you into Hawes.

While you're there, you may want to check out the **Dales Countryside Museum,** Station Yard (the old train station; ✆ **01969/667494**), which traces folk life in the Dales, a story of 10,000 years of human history. Peat cutting and cheese making, among other occupations, are depicted. The museum is open April through October daily from 10am to 5pm. Winter opening hours vary; you'll have to check locally. Admission is £3.50 ($6) for adults and £2.50 ($4) for children, students, and seniors.

WHERE TO STAY

The Crown pub (see "Where to Dine," below) also has quaint rooms for rent.

Cockett's Hotel & Restaurant ✦ This is an atmospheric choice, with reminders of its age. This 1668 building has the date of its construction carved into one of its lintels. Set in the center of town, it's a two-story, slate-roofed, stone cottage whose front yard is almost entirely covered with flagstones. Accommodations are done in an old-world style with exposed wooden beams; they're cozy, each with a good mattress and a small shower-only or shower-and-tub bathroom. All rooms are nonsmoking.

Market Place, Hawes, North Yorkshire DL8 3RD. ✆ **01969/667312.** Fax 01969/667162. www.cocketts.co.uk. 8 units. £45 ($72) single; £59–£69 ($94–$110) double. Rates include English breakfast. AE, MC, V. **Amenities:** Restaurant; lounge; bar. *In room:* TV, dataport, coffeemaker, hair dryer, trouser press.

Super-Cheap Sleeps: A Youth Hostel

Hawes Youth Hostel This two-story nonsmoking hostel, built in 1972, lies a 10-minute walk from the town center. The owners have taken care, however, to create a very homelike environment, with matching duvets and curtains, nice carpeting, flowers on tables, fresh wallpaper, and even van Gogh prints. There are 12 bedrooms, 10 upstairs and 2 downstairs, with two to eight beds apiece. The 11:30pm curfew is taken seriously. Reception is open from 8 to 10am and from 5 to 10pm.

Lancaster Terrace, Hawes, North Yorkshire DL8 3LQ ✆ **01969/667368.** www.yha.org.uk. 54 beds. £10.25 ($16) adults, £7 ($11) children under 18. Open mid-Feb to early Jan. Closed Sun May–June. Curfew: 11:30pm. AE, MC, V. **Amenities:** Dining room; lounge; game room. *In room:* No phone

WHERE TO DINE

The Crown BRITISH/CONTINENTAL In an old stone building, this is a local favorite. The Crown has been a pub since the early 1900s, and is the most reasonable place to eat in Hawes. Main courses include roast chicken or duck served with new potatoes, hearty lasagna, and paella, a house specialty. Good ales, like Theakston's Old Peculiar and John Smith, are available. In warmer months, patrons sit on the outdoor terrace with its spectacular views of the hills, known as the Butter Tubs. The Crown also has three rooms available to rent at £25 ($40) per person, including either an English or continental breakfast.

Market Place ✆ **01969/667212.** Main courses £4.50–£10 ($7–$16). MC, V. Mon–Sat noon–2:30pm and 6:30–9pm; Sun noon–2:30pm and 7–9pm.

7 North York Moors National Park ✦

The moors, on the other side of the Vale of York, have a wild beauty all their own, quite different from that of the dales. This rather barren moorland blossoms in summer with purple heather. Bounded on the east by the North Sea, it embraces a 1,434-sq.-km (554-sq.-mile) area, which has been preserved as a national park.

If you're looking for a hot, sunny beach vacation where the warm water beckons, the North Yorkshire Coast isn't for you—the climate here is cool because of the brisk waters of the North Sea. Even the summer months aren't extremely hot. Many Britons do visit North Yorkshire for beach vacations, however, so you will find a beach town atmosphere along the coast. Brightly colored stalls line the seafront, and the people seem to be a bit more relaxed than their inland counterparts.

The beauty and history of the area are the real reasons to visit North Yorkshire. The national park is perfect for solitary strolls and peaceful drives. For remnants of the area's exciting days of smugglers and brave explorers, visitors can follow the Captain Cook Heritage Trail along the coast. The fishing industry is still very much alive in the area, although the whaling ships of yesteryear have been anchored, and the fishmongers now concentrate on smaller trappings.

Because the park sprawls over such a large area, you can access it from five or six different gateways. Most visitors enter it from the side closest to York, by following either the A19 north via the hamlet of **Thirsk,** or by detouring to the northeast along the A64 and entering via **Scarborough.** You can also get in through **Helmsley,** where the park's administrative headquarters are located; just follow the roads from York that are signposted Helmsley. Gateways along the park's northern edges, which are less convenient to York, include the villages of **Whitby** (accessible via A171), and **Stokesley** (accessible via A19).

For information on accommodations and transportation before you go, contact **North York Moors National Park,** The Old Vicarage, Bondgate, Helmsley, York Y062 5BP (© **01439/770173**). Advice, specialized guidebooks, maps, and information can be obtained at the **Sutton Bank Visitor Centre,** Sutton Bank, near Thirsk, North Yorkshire Y07 2EK (© **01845/597426**). Another well-inventoried information source is **The Moors Centre,** Danby Lodge, Lodge Lane, Danby, near Whitby Y021 2NB (© **01439/772737**).

EXPLORING THE MOORS

Bounded by the Cleveland and Hambleton hills, the moors are dotted with early burial grounds and ancient stone crosses. **Pickering** and **Northallerton,** both market towns, serve as gateways to the moors.

The North York Moors will always be associated with doomed trysts between unlucky lovers, and ghosts who wander vengefully across the rugged plateaus of their lonely and windswept surfaces. Although the earth is relatively fertile in the river valleys, the thin, rocky soil of the heather-clad uplands has been scorned by local farmers as suitable only for sheep grazing and healthy (but melancholy) rambles. During the 19th century, moguls of the Industrial Revolution built a handful of manor houses on their lonely promontories. Not until 1953 was the 1,435-sq.-km (554-sq.-mile) district designated the North York Moors National Park.

Encompassing England's largest expanse of moorland, the park is famous for the diversity of heathers, which thrive between the sandstone outcroppings of the uplands. If you visit between October and February, you'll see smoldering fires across the landscape—deliberately controlled attempts by shepherds and farmers to burn the omnipresent heather back to stubs. Repeated in age-old cycles every 15 years, the blazes encourage the heather's renewal with new growth for the uncounted thousands of sheep that thrive in the district.

Although public bridle paths and footpaths take you to all corners of the moors, there are two especially noteworthy, clearly demarcated trails that comprise the most comprehensive moor walks in Europe. The shorter of the two is the **Lyle Wake Walk**, a 64km (40-mile) east-to-west trek that connects the hamlets of Osmotherly and Ravenscar. It traces the rugged path established by 18th-century coffin bearers. The longer trek (the **Cleveland Walk**) is a 117km (110-mile) circumnavigation of the park's perimeter. A good section of it skirts the Yorkshire coastline; other stretches take climbers up and down a series of steep fells in the park's interior.

Don't even consider an ambitious moor trek without good shoes, a compass, an ordinance survey map, and a detailed park guidebook. With descriptions of geologically interesting sites, safety warnings, and listings of inns and farmhouses (haunted or otherwise) offering overnight stays, the guidebooks sell for about £4 ($6) each at any local tourist office.

The isolation and the beauty of the landscape attracted the founders of **three great abbeys:** Rievaulx near Helmsley, Byland Abbey near the village of Wass, and Ampleforth Abbey. Nearby is **Coxwold,** one of the most attractive villages in the moors. The Cistercian Rievaulx and Byland abbeys are in ruins, but the Benedictine Ampleforth still functions as a monastery and well-known Roman Catholic boys' school. Although many of its buildings date from the 19th and 20th centuries, they do contain earlier artifacts.

BASING YOURSELF IN THIRSK

You can drive through the moorland while based in York, but if you'd like to be closer to the moors, there are places to stay in and around the national park.

The old market town of Thirsk, in the Vale of Mowbray, 39km (24 miles) north of York on the A19, is near the western fringe of the park. It has a fine parish church, but what makes it such a popular stopover is its association with the late James Herriot (1916–95), author of *All Creatures Great and Small.* Mr. Herriot used to practice veterinary medicine in Thirsk. You can drop in to a visitor center, **The World of James Herriot,** 23 Kirkgate (© **01845/524234**), which is dedicated to his life and to veterinary science. The Kirkgate surgery where he practiced from 1930 until his death in 1995 and the house next door have been transformed into *The Herriot Experience.* You can view the surgery and see various exhibitions and displays on veterinary science. Open daily from Easter to September from 10am to 5 pm, and from October to Easter from 11am to 4pm. Admission is £4.50 ($7) adults, £3.20 ($5) children 5 to 16.

WHERE TO STAY & DINE IN & AROUND THIRSK

Oswalds Restaurant with Rooms *Value* *Finds* Radically renovated and upgraded since 2002, this establishment focuses most aggressively on its cozy, rustically decorated restaurant, and offers an octet of comfortable bedchambers as a sideline to any traveler who wants one. Operated by Heather Jones (she tends the dining room and the bedrooms) and Graham Raine (he's the chef), it's known locally as the site where the late veterinarian, James Herriot, treated his last horse. The organization operates out of an old stable block and granary, with a street-level dining room that's loaded with "kitchenalia" (their word) that consists of dozens of cooking implements and tools that might remind you of an artfully arranged collection of what you might have found in the attics of historic homes throughout the region. Main courses range in price from £9 to £14 ($14–$22), and might include, among others, fresh monkfish with pancetta-style ham and a tomato-garlic sauce; fresh haddock from nearby Whitby, served with mushy peas; and rack of English lamb with rosemary sauce. Starters might include an excellent version of baked scallops with Gruyère, and a parfait of chicken livers. Bedrooms lie upstairs from the restaurant, and are outfitted in creamy, pale colors, with French-inspired furniture and patterned fabrics showing an idealized version of French country life. The establishment, incidentally, was named after Sowerby's most famous church, a medieval structure honoring St. Oswald.

Front St., Sowerby, near Thirsk. North Yorkshire YO7 1JF. © **01845/523655.** Fax 01845/524720. www.oswalds restaurantwithrooms.co.uk. 8 units. £85 ($136) double. Rates include English breakfast. DC, MC, V. **Amenities:** Restaurant; bar. *In room:* TV, coffeemaker, hair dryer, iron.

EXPLORING THE NORTH YORKSHIRE COAST

Scarborough: 29km (18 miles) NW of Bridlington; 54km (34 miles) NE of York; 405km (253 miles) N of London

Along the eastern boundary of the park, North Yorkshire's 72km (45-mile) coastline shelters such traditional seaside resorts as Filey, Whitby, and Scarborough; the latter claims to be the oldest seaside spa in Britain, located supposedly on the site of a Roman signaling station. The spa was founded in 1622, when mineral springs with medicinal properties were discovered. In the 19th century, its Grand Hotel, a Victorian structure, was considered the best in Europe. The Norman castle on the big cliffs overlooks the twin bays.

It's easy to follow the main road from Bridlington north to Scarborough and on to Robin Hood's Bay and Whitby. As you drive up the coast, you'll see small fishing ports and wide expanses of moorland.

The city of **Scarborough** is divided into two districts by a green headland that holds the remains of Scarborough Castle, from Norman times. South of the headland, the town conforms to its historical image; high cliffs and garden walks are interspersed with early-Victorian residences. The north side is more touristy: Souvenir shops and fast-food stands line the promenade. "Rock" candy (brightly colored hard candy that can be etched with your choice of sayings) and cotton candy ("candy floss" to Britons) should satisfy any sweet tooth.

VISITOR INFORMATION For more information, call or visit the **Tourist Information Centre,** Pavillion House, Valley Bridge Road (© **01723/373333**), open May through September daily 9:30am to 6pm; October through April Monday to Saturday 10am to 4:30pm.

GETTING THERE Trains leave London's Victoria Station approximately every 30 minutes for York, where you transfer to another train. The entire trip takes 2 hours and 10 minutes. For more information on schedules and prices, call © **0845/7484950.** One bus a day leaves London for York, where you pick up another for Scarborough. If you're taking the bus, plan on spending most of the day riding. **National Express** bus service can be reached at © **08705/808080.**

EXPLORING SCARBOROUGH

The ruins of **Scarborough Castle,** Castle Road (© **01723/372451**), stand on the promontory near a former Viking settlement. From the castle, you can look out over the North Bay, the beaches, and the shoreline gardens. In summer, there are fairs and festivals to celebrate ye olden days with mock battles, pageantry, and falconry displays. Open April through September daily 10am to 6pm; October 10am to 5pm; November through March Wednesday to Sunday 10am to 4pm. Admission is £3 ($4.80) for adults, £2.30 ($3.70) for seniors and persons with disabilities, and £1.50 ($2.40) for children 5 to 15. Children under 5 enter free.

Nearby is the medieval **Church of St. Mary,** Castle Road (no phone), where Anne Brontë, the youngest of the three literary sisters, was buried in 1849. She died here after being brought from Haworth in hope that the sea air would restore her health.

Wood End Museum, The Crescent (© **01723/367326**), was once the vacation home of writers Edith, Osbert, and Sacheverell Sitwell. It now houses a library of their works as well as the collections of the **Museum of Natural History.** The house is open from May to September, Tuesday through Sunday from 10am to 5pm. The rest of the year it is open Wednesday, Saturday, and Sunday from 11am to 4pm. Admission is £2 ($3.20) adults, £1.50 ($2.40) seniors and children 5 to 16, £5 ($8) family ticket. Children under 5 enter free. This ticket also allows entry to the Art Gallery and the Rotunda Museum.

Also located at The Crescent is **The Art Gallery** (© **01723/374753**). The gallery's permanent collection features pieces ranging from 17th-century portraits to 20th-century masterworks. Many of the works relate to the Scarborough area. Changing exhibitions by young artists and local craftspeople are also displayed. If you're interested in learning how to create your own works of art, you may want to spend a while at the **Crescent Arts Workshop,** located in the basement of the gallery. Local artists offer courses and demonstrations in their respective mediums. The Art Gallery is open from May to mid-October, Tuesday through Sunday from 10am to 5pm. The rest of the year it is open Thursday through Saturday from 11am to 4pm. Admission is £2 ($3.20) for adults, £1.50 ($2.40) for seniors and children, and £5 ($8) for a family ticket. Children under 5 are admitted free. This ticket also allows entry to the Wood End Museum and the Rotunda Museum. For information about workshop offerings, call © **01723/351461.**

Local history collections and displays of important archaeological finds can be found at the **Rotunda Museum,** Vernon Road, down the street from Wood End (© **01723/374839**). The museum is housed in a circular building, constructed in 1829 for William Smith, the "Father of English Geology," to display his collection; it was one of the first public buildings in England built specifically for use as a museum. The Rotunda is open from May to September, Tuesday through Sunday from 10am to 5pm; from mid-October to April, Tuesday, Saturday, and Sunday from 11am to 4pm. Admission is £2 ($3.20) for adults, £1.50 ($2.40) for seniors and children 5 to 16, and £5 ($8) for a family ticket. Children under 5 are admitted free. Admission is to both the Wood End Museum and the Art Gallery.

More than 70 species of sea creatures are housed at the **Sea Life Centre,** Scalby Mills, North Bay (© **01723/376125**). An acrylic tunnel passes under the watery habitat of rays and sharks and feeding pools; hands-on displays encourage interaction with the animals. A favorite of children and adults alike is the Seal Rescue and Rehabilitation Centre, which takes in and cares for stray pups and provides a haven for resident adult gray seals. The center is open daily from 10am to 6pm in the summer and from 10am to 4pm the rest of the year. Admission is £6.50 ($10) for adults, £3.50 ($6) for seniors and students, and £4.75 ($8) for children.

WHERE TO STAY

Lyncris Manor Hotel   Situated on the North Bay overlooking Peasholm Park, Lyncris Manor is ideal as a base for touring. The proprietors offer a comfortable and friendly environment for their guests and will provide helpful advice about what to see and do during your stay. The nonsmoking rooms are spacious and clean. The large dining room is attractively decorated and offers good home cooking. Vegetarian choices and children's portions are served.

45 Northstead Manor Dr., Scarborough, North Yorkshire YO12 6AF. ℂ **01723/361052.** www.manorhotel. fsnet.co.uk. 6 units, 4 with bathroom. £16 ($26) single without bathroom, £21 ($34) single with bathroom; £32 ($51) double without bathroom, £42 ($67) double with bathroom. Rates include English breakfast. No credit cards. **Amenities:** Dining room. *In room:* TV, coffeemaker.

The Pickwick Inn   A stately building in the town center, the Pickwick is near the beach, promenade, and a variety of pubs and restaurants. The bedrooms are comfortably furnished; the rooms located on the upper floors offer pleasant views of Scarborough. All bedrooms are well appointed; one has a regal four-poster bed and all are equipped with private showers. All rooms have access for those with limited mobility.

Huntriss Row, Scarborough, North Yorkshire YO11 2ED. ℂ **01723/375787.** 11 units. £28 ($45) single; £54 ($86) double. Rates include breakfast. AE, DC, MC, V. **Amenities:** Breakfast room. *In room:* TV, dataport, coffeemaker, hair dryer, trouser press.

The Windmill Hotel *(Finds*   This is an interesting alternative to standard hotel accommodations. The owners have converted an old corn windmill (six sails) and its surrounding courtyard buildings into the main building and guestrooms. The mill now houses the common areas, including a homelike dining room. The guest rooms are fairly large but sparsely decorated, each with a private shower.

Mill St., off Victoria Rd., Scarborough, Yorkshire YO11 1SZ. ℂ **01723/372735.** Fax 01723/377190. www. windmill-hotel.co.uk. 13 units. £45–£70 ($72–$112) per person. Rates include English breakfast. AE, MC, V. **Amenities:** Breakfast room; toy museum. *In room:* TV, coffeemaker, no phone.

WHERE TO DINE

Lanterna ✦ ITALIAN   Small, straightforward, and charming, this is a high-quality Italian restaurant whose owners, the Alessio family, maintain a strict allegiance to the recipes and ingredients (especially truffles) of their original home in Northern Italy. Set in the center of old town, without any view of the sea, it offers places for 340 diners in a room that's ringed with art photographs of Italian wine, food products and, of course, truffles. Menu items include lots of fresh fish (the owners make a trip to the fish market every morning at 7:30am), including whole sea bass roasted "on its bone" with olive oil and herbs. Pastas are made fresh almost every day and may include a succulent version of venison ravioli. A particularly unctuous starter is *tajarin* (strips of flat pasta), served with a relatively bland sauce of mushrooms and cream. The intent of this mild dish involves allowing the nutty, woodsy flavor of the truffles—added tableside at the last minute—to emerge, unencumbered by other, more strident flavors.

33 Queen St. ℂ **01723/363616.** Reservations recommended. Main courses £13–£30 ($21–$48). MC, V. Mon–Sat 7–10pm.

SCARBOROUGH AFTER DARK

Alan Ayckbourn, a popular contemporary playwright, calls Scarborough home. **The Stephen Joseph Theatre,** Westborough, performs many of his plays as well as other favorites. Call the box office at ℂ **01723/370541** for information about shows and prices.

The Hole in the Wall, Vernon Road (ℂ **01723/373746**), is a well-stocked, lively pub where both locals and visitors gather to share drinks. Sheppard Neame's Master Brew, Fuller's ESB, and Durham's Margus are among the ales served at the long bar, and basic meals are served from noon to 3pm and 5 to 8pm.

8 Durham ★★★

403km (250 miles) N of London; 24km (15 miles) S of Newcastle upon Tyne

This medieval city took root in 1090 after the Normans, under William the Conqueror, took over and began construction of Durham's world-renowned cathedral and castle on a peninsula surrounded by the River Wear. The cathedral, "Half Church of God, half Castle 'gainst the Scots," was built as a shrine to protect the remains of St. Cuthbert, while also providing a sturdy fortress against the warring Scots to the north.

The cathedral castle thrust Durham into its role as a protective border post for England. For centuries, Durham Castle was the seat of the prince bishops—kings of the wild northern territories in all but name—and a pilgrimage site for Christians coming to pay tribute to St. Cuthbert, a monk on Lindisfarne. His life of contemplation and prayer led to his consecration as a bishop in 685, and his sainthood after death.

Today, Durham boasts a university (built on the cornerstone of the castle), and is an excellent base for exploring this stretch of the North Sea coast, as well as the unspoiled rolling hills and waterfalls of the Durham Dales in the North Pennines.

ESSENTIALS

GETTING THERE   Trains from London's King's Cross Station arrive hourly during the day, with the trip taking about 3 hours, and trains from York leave every 15 minutes, arriving approximately an hour later. Durham lies on the main London–Edinburgh rail line. For information, call ✆ **0845/7484950.**

Blue Line buses from London arrive twice daily, with the trip taking about 5 hours. For information, call **National Express** at ✆ **08705/808080.**

If you're driving from London, follow the A1(M) north to Durham.

VISITOR INFORMATION   The **Durham Tourist Office** is at Millennium Place (✆ **01913/843720**), and is open year-round Monday through Saturday from 9:30am to 5:30pm, and Sunday from 11am to 4pm.

SPECIAL EVENTS   At the **Durham Folk Festival,** held the last weekend in July, you can sing, clog, or just cavort to music; almost every event is free. The weekend also includes free camping along the River Wear, though you'd better arrive early on Friday if you want to get a choice spot. In early June, crowds swarm along the riverbank to cheer the crew racing the **Durham Regatta.**

SEEING THE SIGHTS

Durham Castle ★   Adjoining the cathedral, the castle was the seat of the prince bishops of Durham for more than 800 years. In 1832, it became the first building of the fledgling local college, now Durham University, and today still houses University College. During university breaks, it offers unique bed-and-breakfast accommodations to the public.

Palace Green. ✆ 01913/343800. Admission £3 ($4.80) adults, £2 ($3.20) children, £6.50 ($10) family ticket. Guided tours Apr–June daily 2–4pm; July–Sept daily 10am–noon and 2–4:30pm; other times of the year Mon, Wed, Sat, and Sun 2–4:30pm. Closed during university Christmas breaks.

Durham Cathedral ★★★   Under construction for more than 40 years, the cathedral was completed in 1133, and today is Britain's largest, best-preserved Norman stronghold and one of its grandest surviving Romanesque palaces. The structure is not only breathtaking to view, it is also architecturally innovative, the first English building to feature ribbed-vault construction. It is also the first stone-roofed cathedral in Europe, an architectural necessity because of its role as a border fortress. The treasury houses such relics as the original 12th-century door knocker, St. Cuthbert's coffin, ancient illuminated manuscripts, and more. You can still attend daily services in the sanctuary.

Palace Green. ℂ **01913/864266**. www.durhamcathedral.co.uk. Free admission to cathedral, donations appreciated; tower £2 ($3.20) adults, £1 ($1.60) children; treasury £2 ($3.20) adults, 50p (80¢) children; Monk's Dormitory 80p ($1.30) adults, 20p (30¢) children, £1.50 ($2.40) family ticket; audiovisual Visitors' Exhibition 80p ($1.30) adults, 20p (30¢) children. Cathedral June–Sept daily 9:30am–8pm; Oct–May Mon–Sat 9:30am–6:15pm, Sun 12:30–5pm. Guided tours July to mid-Sept Mon–Sat at 10:30am and 2pm (also 11:30am during Aug). Donations are appreciated. Treasury Mon–Sat 10am–4:30pm; Sun 2–4:30pm. Monk's Dormitory Apr–Oct Mon–Sat 10am–3:30pm; Sun 12:30–3:15pm. Audiovisual Visitors' Exhibition Mar–Oct Mon–Sat 10am–3pm.

Oriental Museum   This is the nation's only museum devoted entirely to Eastern culture and art. It covers all major periods of art from ancient Egypt through India, as well as relics from Tibet, China, and Japan. The attractions are displayed in a way designed to make them understandable to the nonspecialist.

Elvet Hill off South Rd. ℂ **01913/345694**. Admission £1.50 ($2.40) adults, 75p ($1.20) children 5–16 and seniors, £3.50 ($6) family ticket. Mon–Fri 10am–5pm; Sat–Sun noon–5pm.

GETTING OUTSIDE

Fishing is a good sport all along the Rivers Tees and Wear, and in the several reservoirs and ponds throughout the county. Boating is also available, and **Brown's Boat House,** Elvet Bridge (ℂ **01913/869525**), rents rowboats for pulls up or down the Wear, as well as offering short cruises April through October, at the price of £4.50 ($7) for adults and £2 ($3.20) for children.

Hikers can take the challenge provided by the 435km (270 miles) of trails (64km/40 miles of which are in the county) along the **Pennine Way,** the **Weardale Way**'s 126km (78-mile) course along the River Wear from Monkwearmouth in Sunderland to Cowshill in County Durham, or the **Teesdale Way,** running 145km (90 miles) from Middleton in Teesdale to Teesmouth in Cleveland. Rambles in town along public footpaths have recently been supplemented by more than 80km (50 miles) of former railway. Seven such trails make use of interlinked routes and range from the 7.5km (4.5-mile) **Auckland Walk** to the 17km (10.5-mile) **Derwent Walk.** If you don't feel like going it alone, there are also more than 200 guided walks throughout the county, providing background on the history, culture, and plant and animal life of the surrounding area; contact the tourist office (see "Visitor Information," above).

Cyclists can opt for road biking along quiet country lanes and converted railway routes, or mountain biking in **Hamsterley Forest.** The acclaimed **C2C national cycle route** passes through the Durham Dales and North Durham, on a 225km (140-mile) signposted route. Both road and mountain-bike rentals are available at several locations, including **Cycle Force 2000 Ltd.,** 87 Claypath St. (ℂ **01913/840319**), open Monday through Friday from 9am to 5:30pm, Saturday from 9am to 5pm, and Sunday from 11am to 3pm. A bike rental costs £12 ($19) per day, with a £38 ($61) deposit.

WHERE TO STAY

Bay Horse Inn   Less than 5km (3 miles) from the town center, the 10 stone-built chalets that make up this inn offer some of the best and most affordable bedrooms around. Each room is comfortable and well equipped with a shower, toilet, and phone. Rooms are doubles or twins, with one room suitable for families; singles can occupy a room at the quoted rates. Lunch is available, but most people are out exploring; however, if you arrange it, the owners will prepare a filling and hearty dinner.

Brandon Village, Durham DH7 8ST. ✆ 0191/378-0498. 10 units. £40 ($64) single; £50 ($80) double; £50 ($80) honeymoon suite; £65–£70 ($104–$112) family unit. Rates include English breakfast. AE, DC, MC, V. **Amenities:** Dining room; bar; lounge. *In room:* TV, dataport, coffeemaker, hair dryer.

Castle View Guest House   This 250-year-old Georgian home sits near the river's edge with a great view of the cathedral and castle. Although it's no pacesetter, its nonsmoking rooms are comfortably furnished and well kept, each with a private shower. One triple is suitable for families. The English breakfast is excellent.

4 Crossgate, Durham DH1 4PS. ✆ and fax 0191/386-8852. 6 units. £45 ($72) single; £60 ($96) double. Rates include English breakfast. MC, V. **Amenities:** Breakfast room. *In room:* TV, coffeemaker, hair dryer, no phone.

Georgian Town House 🎯 *Value*   This is the most desirable B&B in Durham, an unusually decorated place lying on a steep cobbled Georgian terrace street, close to everything, including the cathedral. It is a wonder of decoration, especially the reception hallway with its stenciled pillars and leaf patterns. It's almost like entering an arbor in sunny Sicily. In the lounge, "stars" twinkle on the walls. Sofas are placed around the fireplace where guests can mingle. Rooms, except for a cramped single, are tastefully decorated and are light and airy. The small bathrooms include showers. Maintenance is very high here. The house has a panoramic view of the cathedral and castle. The Pancake Café, attached to the main building, serves various sweet and savory pancakes for £3.75 to £5.10 ($6–$8.15) from 10am to 6pm Tuesday to Saturday.

10 Crossgate, Durham DH1 4PS. ✆ and fax 01913/868070. www.thegeorgiantownhouse.co.uk. 8 units. £55 ($88) single; £70–£75 ($112–$120) double; £85 ($136) triple. Rates include breakfast. No credit cards. **Amenities:** Breakfast room; cafe; guest lounge. *In room:* TV, coffeemaker, hair dryer, no phone.

Gilesgate Moor Hotel   Only minutes north from the center of Durham, you can stay at this friendly, family-run pub hotel. For more than a century, it has been welcoming wayfarers and providing them with food and drink. Although an antique, the building has been kept up-to-date and provides modern comforts. The nonsmoking bedrooms are well decorated. There's a cozy pub and a good restaurant serving typically English fare.

Teasdale Terrace, Gilesgate, Durham DH1 2RN. ✆ and fax 0191/386-6453. www.smoothhound.co.uk/hotels/gilesgate.html. 7 units, 3 with bathroom. £20 ($32) single without bathroom; £40 ($64) double without bathroom, £45 ($72) double with bathroom; £60 ($96) family unit without bathroom. MC, V. **Amenities:** Restaurant; pub; breakfast room. *In room:* TV, coffeemaker, no phone.

WHERE TO DINE

Bistro 21 🎯 INTERNATIONAL   A big hit locally, this is a bright, farm-themed bistro. Chef Adrian Watson's cuisine is precise and carefully prepared, with market-fresh ingredients that are allowed to keep their natural essence without being overly sauced or disguised. We especially recommend trying the chalkboard specials. The food is full of flavor and rather forceful, borrowing from all over Europe—certainly the Mediterranean, but also offering traditional British fare at times, such as deep-fried plaice and chips. You can finish with one of the rich desserts, including double chocolate truffle cake. If you want to be terribly old-fashioned and English, ask for the toffee pudding with butterscotch sauce. It's prepared to perfection here.

Aykley Heads House, Aykley Heads. ✆ 01913/844354. Reservations recommended. Main courses £10–£19.50 ($16–$31); fixed-price lunch £12–£14.50 ($19–$23). AE, DC, MC, V. Mon–Fri noon–2pm and 7–10:30pm; Sat noon–2pm and 6–10:30pm.

DURHAM AFTER DARK

Much of Durham's nightlife revolves around its university students. When school is in session, **The Hogs Head,** 58 Saddler St. (© **01913/869550**), is a popular traditional English-style pub. It's open Monday through Saturday from 11am to midnight, and Sunday from noon until 10:30pm. **Coach and Eight,** Bridge House, Framwellgate Bridge (© **01913/860056**), has disco Thursday through Sunday nights and is open Monday through Thursday from 11am to 11pm, Friday through Saturday 11am to 1:30pm, and Sunday from 11am to 10:30pm.

SIDE TRIPS TO THE DURHAM DALES, BARNARD CASTLE & BEAMISH

This densely populated county of northeast England was once pictured as a dismal place, with coalfields, ironworks, mining towns, and shipyards. Yet the **Durham Dales,** occupying the western third of the county, is a popular panorama of rolling hills, valleys of quiet charm, and wild moors. **Teesdale** is particularly notable for its several waterfalls, including **High Force,** the largest waterfall in England, which drops a thundering 21m (70 ft.) to join the River Tees. It is equally known for the rare wildflowers that grow in the sugar limestone–based soil of the region; they have helped it earn protection as a National Nature Reserve.

Also notable is **Weardale,** once the hunting ground of Durham's prince bishops, with its idyllic brown sandstone villages. For more information on the wide range of options the area has to offer, contact the **Durham Dales Centre,** Castle Garden, Stanhope, Bishop Auckland, County Durham DL13 2SJ (© **01388/527650;** fax 01388/527461). Hours are November through March, Monday through Friday from 10am to 4pm and Saturday and Sunday from 11am to 4pm; and April through October daily from 10am to 5pm.

The 12th-century **Barnard Castle** ✸ (© **01833/690909;** www.barnard-castle.co.uk) is an extensive Norman ruin overlooking the River Tees. It is open daily, April through October from 10am to 5:30pm; November through March from 11am to 4pm. Admission is £2.50 ($4) for adults, and £1.30 ($2.10) for students and children under 16.

Barnard Castle is also home to the **Bowes Museum** ✸ (© **01833/690606;** www.bowesmuseum.org.uk), a sprawling French-style château housing one of Britain's most important collections of European art, including paintings from Goya to El Greco, plus tapestries, ceramics, costumes, musical instruments, and French and English furniture. There is also a children's gallery. The museum is open daily from 11am to 5pm. Admission is £5 ($8) for adults; £4 ($6) for children over 16, students, and seniors; and £15 ($24) for a family ticket. Children under 16 enter free. Buses run from Durham several times daily.

Beamish, the North of England Open Air Museum   West of Chester-le-Street, 13km (8 miles) southwest of Newcastle upon Tyne, and 19km (12 miles) northwest of Durham City, this is a vivid re-creation of an early-19th-century village. A costumed staff demonstrates rituals of daily life in shops, houses, pubs, a newspaper office, and garage, as well as a Methodist chapel, village school, home farm, and railway station. An average summer visit takes around 4 hours, and a winter visit, including the town and railway only, takes about 2 hours.

Just off A693 in Beamish. © 0191/370-4000. www.beamishmuseum.com. Admission spring and summer £12 ($19) adults, £7 ($11) children 5–16; winter £4 ($6) for all. Free for children under 5. Spring and summer daily 10am–5pm; off season Sat–Sun and Tues–Thurs 10am–4pm. Closed Dec 13–Jan 4.

9 Hexham, Hadrian's Wall ★★ & the Pennine Way ★★

490km (304 miles) N of London; 60km (37 miles) E of Carlisle; 34km (21 miles) W of Newcastle upon Tyne

Above the Tyne River, the historic old market town of Hexham has narrow streets, an old market square, a fine abbey church, and a moot hall. It makes a good base for exploring Hadrian's Wall and the Roman supply base of Corstopitum at Corbridge-on-Tyne, the ancient capital of Northumberland. The tourist office (see "Visitor Information" below) has lots of information on the wall, whether you're hiking, driving, camping, or picnicking.

ESSENTIALS

GETTING THERE   Take one of the many daily trains from London's King's Cross Station to Newcastle upon Tyne. At Newcastle, change trains and take one in the direction of Carlisle. The fifth stop after Newcastle will be Hexham. For schedules and information, call ℂ **0845/7484950.**

Hexham lies 23km (14 miles) southeast of Hadrian's Wall. If you are primarily interested in the wall (rather than in Hexham), get off the Carlisle-bound train at the third stop (Haltwhistle), which is 4km (2½ miles) from the wall. At either of these hamlets, you can take a taxi to whichever part of the wall you care to visit. Taxis line up readily at the railway station in Hexham but less often at the other villages. If you get off at one of the above-mentioned villages and don't see a taxi, call ℂ **01434/321064** and a local taxi will come to get you. Many visitors ask their taxi drivers to return at a prearranged time (which they gladly do) to pick them up after their excursion on the windy ridges near the wall.

National Express coaches to Newcastle and Carlisle connect with Northumbria bus service no. 685. Trip time to Hexham from Carlisle is about 1½ hours and from Newcastle about 1 hour. For information, call ℂ **020/7529-2000.** Local bus services connect Hexham with North Tynedale and the North Pennines.

If you're driving from Newcastle upon Tyne, head west on the A69 until you see the cutoff south to Hexham.

VISITOR INFORMATION   The **Tourist Information Centre** at Hexham is at the Wentworth Car Park (ℂ **01434/652220**). It's open from Easter to September Monday through Saturday from 9am to 6pm, and Sunday from 10am to 5pm; November through March, Monday through Saturday from 9am to 5pm.

HADRIAN'S WALL & ITS FORTRESSES

Hadrian's Wall ★★, which extends for 118km (73 miles) across the north of England, from the North Sea to the Irish Sea, is particularly interesting for a stretch of 16km (10 miles) west of Housesteads, which lies 4km (2¾ miles) northeast of Bardon Mill on the B6318. Only the lower courses of the wall have been preserved intact; the rest were reconstructed in the 19th century using original stones. From the wall, there are incomparable views north to the Cheviot Hills along the Scottish border and south to the Durham moors.

The wall was built in A.D. 122 after the visit of the emperor Hadrian, who was inspecting far frontiers of the Roman Empire and wanted to construct a dramatic line between the empire and the barbarians. Legionnaires were ordered to build a wall across the width of the island of Britain, stretching 118km (73 miles), beginning at the North Sea and ending at the Irish Sea.

The wall is one of Europe's top Roman ruins. The western end can be reached from Carlisle, which also has an interesting museum of Roman artifacts; the eastern end can be reached from Newcastle upon Tyne (where some remains can be seen on the city outskirts; there's also a nice museum at the university).

You can find more information about Hadrian's Wall at the website www. hadrians-wall.org.

From early May to late September, the Tynedale Council and the Northumberland National Park run a **bus service** that visits every important site along the wall, then turns around in the village of Haltwhistle and returns to Hexham. Buses depart from a point near the railway station in Hexham five times a day. Call ℂ **01434/652220** for more information. The cost is £5 ($8) for adults, £2.50 ($4) for children, and £10 ($16) for a family ticket. Many visitors take one bus out, then return on a subsequent bus 2, 4, or 6 hours later. Every Sunday, a national park warden leads a 2½-hour walking tour of the wall, in connection with the bus service. The Hexham tourist office (see "Visitor Information," above) provides further details.

Housesteads Fort and Museum ★★   Along the wall are several Roman forts, the most important of which was called Vercovicium by the Romans. This substantially excavated fort, on a dramatic site, contains the only visible example of a Roman hospital in Britain.

5km (3 miles) northeast of Bardon Mill on B6318. ℂ **01434/344363**. Admission £3.10 ($4.95) adults, £2.30 ($3.70) seniors and students, £1.60 ($2.55) children 5–16. Apr–Sept daily 10am–6pm; Oct–Nov daily 10am–5pm; Dec–Mar daily 10am–4pm. Closed Dec 25–26 and Jan 1.

Vindolanda   This is another well-preserved fort south of the wall; the last of eight successive forts to be built on this site. There is also an excavated civilian settlement outside the fort with an interesting museum of artifacts of everyday Roman life.

Just west of Housesteads, on a minor road 2km (1¼ miles) southeast of Twice Brewed off B6318. ℂ **01434/ 344277**. www.vindolanda.com. Admission £3.90 ($6) adults, £3.30 ($5) seniors and students, £2.80 ($4.50) children. Jan 25–Nov daily 10am–4pm. Closed Dec–Jan 24.

Roman Army Museum ★   Near Vindolanda at the garrison fort at Carvoran, close to the village of Greenhead, the Roman Army Museum traces the growth and influence of Rome from its early beginnings to the development and expansion of the empire, with special emphasis on the role of the Roman army and the garrisons of Hadrian's Wall. A barracks room depicts basic army living conditions. Realistic life-size figures make this a strikingly visual museum experience. Within easy walking distance of the Roman Army Museum is one of the most high-standing sections of Hadrian's Wall, **Walltown Crags,** impressive for the height of the wall and magnificent views to the north and south.

At the junction of A69 and B6318, 29km (18 miles) west of Hexham. ℂ **01697/747485**. www.vindolanda. com. Admission £3.10 ($4.95) adults, £2.70 ($4.30) seniors and students, £2.10 ($3.35) children. Late Feb and Nov 10am–4pm; Mar and Oct 10am–5pm; Apr and Sept 10am–5:30pm; May and June 10am–6pm; July and Aug 10am–6:30pm.

HIKING THE PENNINE WAY IN NORTHUMBERLAND NATIONAL PARK

Northumberland National Park, established in 1956, encompasses the borderlands that were a buffer zone between the warring English and Scots during the 13th and 14th centuries. Today, the park comprises almost 1,035 sq. km (400 sq. miles) of the least populated area in England and is noted for its rugged landscape and associations with the northern frontier of the ancient Roman Empire.

Touching the border with Scotland, the park covers some of the most tortuous geology in England, the Cheviot Hills, whose surfaces have been wrinkled by volcanic pressures, inundated with sea water, scoured by glaciers, silted over by rivers, and thrust upward in a complicated series of geological events. Much of the heather-sheathed terrain here is used for sheep grazing; woolly balls of fluff adorn hillsides ravaged by high winds and frequent rain.

Northumberland Park includes the remains of Hadrian's Wall, one of the most impressive classical ruins of northern Europe. Footpaths run alongside it, and there are a variety of walks in the country to the north and south of the monument. One of the most challenging hiking paths in Britain, the **Pennine Way** ★★, snakes up the backbone of the park. The 129km (80 miles) of the 403km (250-mile) path that are in the park are clearly marked; one of the most worthwhile (and safest) hikes is between Bellingham and the Hamlet of Riding Wood.

A map of the trails, priced at 50p (80¢), can be purchased for these and other hiking trails at almost any local tourist office in the district. There are **National Park Centres** at Once Brewed (© **01434/344396**), Rothbury (© **01669/ 620414**), and Ingram (© **01665/578248**). The Head Office is at Eastburn, South Park, Hexham, Northumberland NE46 1BS (© **01434/605555;** www. northumberland-national-park.org.uk).

WHERE TO STAY

Beaumont Hotel ★ In the town center overlooking the abbey and a park, the Beaumont offers excellent facilities, including two comfortable bars and a delightful restaurant. Martin and Linda Owens have completely refurbished the bedrooms, which contain private, shower-only bathrooms.

Beaumont St., Hexham, Northumberland NE46 3LT. © **01434/602331.** Fax 01434/606184. www.beaumont-hotel.co.uk. 25 units. £65 ($104) single; £85 ($136) double. AE, DC, MC, V. **Amenities:** Restaurant; 2 bars. *In room:* TV, coffeemaker, hair dryer, trouser press.

Lyndale Guest House In this ancient border town outside Hexham, you'll find good accommodations and home-cooking at this well-run guest house, ideal for touring the Northumbrian countryside, especially Hadrian's Wall (what's left of it). The nonsmoking accommodations are well appointed, containing private, shower-only bathrooms. Dinner can be ordered in a sun lounge opening onto a vista. You're greeted with tea and crackers on the terrace next to a fountain, and you can hang out in the gazebo in the walled garden overlooking River North Tyne and Dunterley Fellside.

Bellingham, Hexham, Northumberland NE48 2AW. © and fax **01434/220361.** www.smoothhound.co.uk/hotels/lyndale.html. 4 units. £30 ($48) single; £50 ($80) double; £75 ($120) family unit. MC, V. **Amenities:** Breakfast room; TV lounge; sun lounge; private fishing rights. *In room:* TV, hair dryer, iron/ironing board, no phone.

West Close House Located in a 1920s house on a private road, West Close House is owned and operated by Patricia Graham-Tomlinson, who greets guests with warm hospitality. The nonsmoking bedrooms are more spacious than those of many competitors and are well equipped. There is a sitting room with a TV.

Hextol Terrace, Hexham, Northumberland NE46 2AD. © **01434/603307.** 4 units, 2 with bathroom. £20–£27 ($32–$43) per person. Rates include English or continental breakfast. No credit cards. **Amenities:** Breakfast room; TV lounge. *In room:* Coffeemaker, hair dryer.

WHERE TO DINE

The Twice Brewed Inn ENGLISH Diners and pubgoers are grateful for this place. The inn was built as a drovers' inn in 1715—Hexham is the midpoint for the sheep drive from Carlisle to Newcastle. The bar and restaurant, in two different rooms, have the same dark-wood-and-beam atmosphere. The bar serves snacks and offers a fireplace and pool table for distraction. The restaurant offers traditional pub meals, including beef pies, scampi, lasagna, and vegetarian dishes.

Military Rd. © 01434/344534. Main courses £3.50–£6.75 ($6–$11). No credit cards. Mon–Sat noon–11pm; Sun noon–3pm and 7–10:30pm.

Appendix A:
England in Depth

England has been both conqueror and conquered. Its history stretches back thousands of years, to a time when Celts, Romans, Saxons, and Normans all successively trod this soil. For a non-Brit, keeping the many monarchs straight seems to require a scorecard (or at least a well-worn almanac). From William of Normandy's successful invasion at Hastings to Henry VIII's many wives (and beheadings) to the Empire's renaissance under Victoria and the contemporary scandals and intrigues that keep the royal family on the front pages of the tabloids, England has a history that rivets and enlightens.

1 History 101

FROM MYSTERIOUS BEGINNINGS TO ROMAN OCCUPATION Britain was probably split off from the continent of Europe some 8 millennia ago by continental drift and other natural forces. The early inhabitants, the Iberians, came to be identified with fairies, brownies, and "little people." Although few facts are known about them, they are believed to have built that great and mysterious monument, Stonehenge. The iron-wielding Celts invaded around 500 B.C., driving the Iberians into the Scottish Highlands and Welsh mountains, where some of their descendants still live.

In 54 B.C. Julius Caesar invaded England, but the Romans did not establish themselves until A.D. 43. They went as far north as Caledonia (now Scotland), where they retreated from "the painted ones," the warring Picts. The wall built by the Emperor Hadrian across the north of England marked the northernmost reaches of the Roman Empire. During almost 4 centuries of occupation, the Romans built roads, villas, towns, walls, and fortresses; they farmed the land, pursued trade, and introduced first their pagan religion, then Christianity to the populace.

Dateline

- 54 B.C. Julius Caesar invades England.
- A.D. 43 Romans conquer England.
- 410 Jutes, Angles, and Saxons form small kingdoms in England.
- 500–1066 Anglo-Saxon kingdoms fight off Viking warriors.
- 1066 William, duke of Normandy, invades England, defeats Harold II at the Battle of Hastings.
- 1154 Henry II, first of the Plantagenets, launches their rule (which lasts until 1399).
- 1215 King John signs the Magna Carta at Runnymede.
- 1337 Hundred Years' War between France and England begins.
- 1485 Battle of Bosworth Field ends the War of the Roses between the Houses of York and Lancaster; Henry VII launches the Tudor dynasty.
- 1534 Henry VIII brings the Reformation to England and dissolves the monasteries.
- 1558 The accession of Elizabeth I ushers in an era of exploration and a renaissance in science and learning.
- 1588 Spanish Armada defeated.
- 1603 James VI of Scotland becomes James I of England, thus uniting the crowns of England and Scotland.
- 1620 Pilgrims sail from Plymouth on the Mayflower to found a colony in the New World.
- 1629 Charles I dissolves Parliament, ruling alone.

FROM ANGLO-SAXON RULE TO THE NORMAN CONQUEST

The Roman legions withdrew around A.D. 410. The country was subject to waves of invasions by Jutes, Angles, and Saxons, who established small kingdoms throughout the former colony. From the 8th through the 11th centuries, the Anglo-Saxons contended with Danish raiders for control. By the mid–11th century, the Saxon kingdoms were united under an elected king, Edward the Confessor. His successor, Harold, was to rule less than a year before the Norman invasion.

The date 1066 marks an epic event—the only successful military invasion of Britain ever, and one of English history's great turning points. Harold, the last Anglo-Saxon king, was defeated at the Battle of Hastings, and William of Normandy was crowned as William I. One of his first acts was to order a survey of the land he had conquered, assessing all property in the nation for tax purposes. The resulting document, called the Domesday Book, was completed around 1086 and remains a fertile sourcebook for British historians to this day.

Norman rule had an enormous impact on English society. Normans held all high offices. The Norman barons, given great grants of lands, built Norman-style castles and strongholds throughout the country. French was the language of the court for centuries—few realize that heroes such as Richard I, Coeur de Lion (Lionheart), probably spoke little or no English.

FROM THE RULE OF HENRY II TO THE MAGNA CARTA

Henry II was the first Plantagenet king (r. 1154–89). A physically powerful, charming yet terrifying man, he ruled a vast empire—most of Britain, Normandy, Anjou, Brittany, and Aquitaine. Henry also reformed the courts and introduced the system of common law, still the foundation of

- 1642–49 Civil War between Royalists and Parliamentarians; the Parliamentarians win.
- 1649 Charles I beheaded, and England becomes a republic.
- 1653 Oliver Cromwell becomes lord protector.
- 1660 Charles II restored to the throne with limited power.
- 1665–66 Great Plague and Great Fire decimate London.
- 1688 James II, a Catholic, is deposed, and William and Mary come to the throne, signing a bill of rights.
- 1727 George I, the first of the Hanoverians, assumes the throne.
- 1756–63 In the Seven Years' War, Britain wins Canada from France.
- 1775–83 Britain loses its American colonies.
- 1795–1815 The Napoleonic Wars lead, finally, to the Battle of Waterloo and the defeat of Napoleon.
- 1837 Queen Victoria begins her reign as Britain reaches the zenith of its empire.
- 1901 Victoria dies, and Edward VII becomes king.
- 1914–18 England enters World War I and emerges victorious on the Allied side.
- 1936 Edward VIII abdicates to marry an American divorcée.
- 1939–45 In World War II, Britain stands alone against Hitler from the fall of France in 1940 until America enters the war in 1941. Dunkirk is evacuated in 1940; bombs rattle London during the Blitz.
- 1945 Germany surrenders. Churchill is defeated; the Labour government introduces the welfare state and begins to dismantle the empire.
- 1952 Queen Elizabeth II ascends to the throne.
- 1973 Britain joins the European Union.
- 1979 Margaret Thatcher becomes Prime Minister.
- 1982 Britain defeats Argentina in the Falklands War.
- 1990 Thatcher is ousted; John Major becomes Prime Minister.
- 1991 Britain fights with Allies to defeat Iraq.

continues

English law and an influence upon the American legal system. But he is best remembered for a dispute that led to the infamous murder of Thomas à Becket, Archbishop of Canterbury. Henry exclaimed, "Who will rid me of this turbulent priest?" His knights overheard, took him at his word, and murdered Thomas at the high altar in Canterbury Cathedral.

Henry's wife, Eleanor of Aquitaine, the most famous woman of her time, was no less colorful. She accompanied her first husband, Louis VII of France, on the Second Crusade, where she allegedly had an affair with the Saracen leader, Saladin. Domestic and political life did not run smoothly, however, and Henry, Eleanor, and their sons were often at odds. The pair has been the subject of many plays and films, including *The Lion in Winter, Becket,* and *Murder in the Cathedral.*

Two of their sons were crowned kings of England. Richard the Lionheart (r. 1189–99) spent most of his life outside England, on crusades or imprisoned in France. The other son, John (r. 1199–1216), was forced by his nobles to sign the Magna Carta at Runnymede, in 1215—another crucial date in English history. The "Great Charter" declared the king to be subservient to the rule of law and gave certain rights to his subjects. These provisions eventually led to the development of modern British parliamentary democracy— another practice that would have enormous influence on the American colonies many years later.

1992 Royals jolted by fire at Windsor Castle and marital troubles of their sons Charles and Andrew. Britain joins the European Single Market. Deep recession signals the end of the booming 1980s.

1994 England is linked to the Continent by rail via the Channel Tunnel or Chunnel. Tony Blair elected Labour party leader.

1996 The IRA breaks a 17-month cease-fire with a truck bomb at the Docklands that claims two lives. Charles and Diana divorce. The government concedes a possible link between "Mad Cow Disease" and a fatal brain ailment afflicting humans; British beef imports face global banishment.

1997 London swings again. The Labour party ends 18 years of Conservative rule with a landslide election victory. The tragic death of Diana, Princess of Wales, prompts worldwide outpouring of grief.

1998 Prime Minister Tony Blair launches "New Britain"—young, stylish, and informal.

1999 England rushes toward the 21st century with the Millennium Dome at Greenwich.

2000 London "presides" over millennium celebration; gays allowed to serve openly in the military; hereditary peers in House of Lords get boot from Blair.

2001 Mad cow disease and foot-and-mouth epidemic affect cattle, pigs, and sheep, and bring devastation to the British economy.

2002 Queen Elizabeth, the Queen Mother, dies at age 101.

2003 Britain joins the U.S. in overthrow of Iraqi dictator.

Although the Magna Carta represents the cornerstone of English liberties, it actually only granted them to the barons. It took the rebellion of Simon de Montfort (1263–65) to introduce the notion that the boroughs and burghers should also have a voice and representation.

THE BLACK DEATH & THE WARS OF THE ROSES In 1348, the Black Death began to ravage England. By the end of the century, the population of Britain had fallen from four million to two million. The country endured the Hundred Years' War, which went on intermittently for even longer than its name suggests. By 1371, England had relinquished control of most of its French holdings. Henry V (r. 1413–22), immortalized by Shakespeare, revived England's claims to France. His victory at Agincourt made obsolete the practice of medieval chivalry and warfare.

After Henry's death, disputes concerning the royal succession resulted in a long period of civil strife between the Yorkists and the Lancastrians that became known as the Wars of the Roses. The last Yorkist king was Richard III, who got bad press from Shakespeare but remains to this day a hero to the city of York. Richard's defeat at Bosworth Field led to the first Tudor king, the shrewd and wily Henry VII.

THE TUDORS TAKE THE THRONE   The Tudors introduced into England a strong central monarchy with far-reaching powers. The system worked well for a century under that strong and capable dynasty. Henry VIII (r. 1509–47) is surely the most notorious Tudor. Imperious and flamboyant, this colossus among English royalty slammed shut the door on the Middle Ages, bringing the Renaissance to England.

Henry is best known, however, for his six wives and the unfortunate fates that befell five of them. His first wife, Catherine of Aragon, gave birth to the future Mary I, but did not produce a male heir. When his mistress, Anne Boleyn, became pregnant, he tried to annul his marriage; the pope refused, and Catherine contested the action. Defying the power of Rome, Henry had his marriage with Catherine declared invalid and secretly married Boleyn in 1533.

The religious controversy that erupted would dominate English politics for the next 4 centuries. Henry broke with the Roman Catholic Church by forming the Church of England, with himself as supreme head. He ordered the dissolution of the monasteries. The confiscation of the church's land and possessions brought untold wealth into the king's coffers; this in turn was distributed to a new aristocracy who supported the monarch. In one sweeping gesture, Henry had destroyed the ecclesiastical culture of the Middle Ages. Civil unrest and much social dislocation followed. Among those executed for refusing to cooperate with Henry was Sir Thomas More, humanist, author of *Utopia,* and subject of *A Man For All Seasons.*

Anne Boleyn bore Henry a daughter, the future Elizabeth I, but did not produce a male heir. Brought to trial on a trumped-up charge of adultery, she was beheaded. In 1536, Henry married Jane Seymour, who died giving birth to the future Edward VI. For his next wife, he chose Anne of Cleves, but she proved disappointing—he called her "The Great Flanders Mare." Henry divorced her that same year and married a young woman from his court, Catherine Howard. She was also beheaded on a charge of adultery, probably with cause. Finally, Henry married an older woman, Catherine Parr, in 1543. She survived him.

Henry's heir, sickly Edward VI (r. 1547–53), died officially of consumption but allegedly of overmedication; succeeded by his sister, Mary I (r. 1553–58), their father's break with Rome came home to roost. Mary restored Roman Catholicism to England; her persecution and execution of Church of England adherents earned her the name "Bloody Mary." She had an unpopular, unhappy marriage to Philip II of Spain, and they produced no heirs. Elizabeth I (r. 1558–1603) ascended to the throne, ushering in an era of peace and prosperity, exploration, and a renaissance in science and learning—the Elizabethan Age. The last great monarch to rule England, her passion and magnetism were said to match her father's. Through her era marched Drake, Raleigh, Frobisher, Grenville, Shakespeare, Spenser, Byrd, and Hilliard. "Good Queen Bess" set the appalling precedent of ordering the execution of a fellow sovereign (Mary was accused in a plot to overthrow Elizabeth).

Building Blocks of History

When it comes to identifying the period in which a building was constructed (or reconstructed), details of architecture and decoration are the most important features to look for. In a country like England, where the age of buildings can span a thousand-year period (a few Anglo-Saxon churches are even older than that), many different styles evolved. The architectural periods are often named for the monarch or royal family reigning at the time. Your enjoyment of England's abundance of historic buildings will be enhanced if you know a few key features of the different styles. The following is a brief primer in English architectural history from Norman to Victorian times.

Norman (1066–1189)   Round arches, barrel vaults, and highly decorated archways characterize the Romanesque style of this period.

Early English Gothic (1189–1272)   The squat, bulky buildings of the Norman period gave way to the taller, lighter buildings constructed in this style.

Decorated Gothic (1272–1377)   Buildings in this style have large windows, tracery (ornamental work with branching lines), and heavily decorated gables and arches.

Perpendicular Gothic (1377–1483)   Large buttresses (exterior side supports) allowed churches to have larger windows than ever before. Tracery was more elaborate than in previous Gothic buildings, the four-centered arch appeared, and fan vaulting (a decorative form of vaulting in which the structural ribs spread upwards and outwards along the ceiling like the rays of a fan) was perfected.

Tudor (1485–1553)   During this period, buildings evolved from Gothic to Renaissance styles. Large houses and palaces were built with a new

---

Her diplomatic skills kept war at bay until 1588, when, at the apogee of her reign, the Spanish Armada of Philip II was defeated.

CIVIL WAR   The Stuarts ascended the English throne in 1603. While the dynasty survived a century of civil war and religious dissension, its kings were less capable than the Tudors at juggling the needs of a strong centralized monarchy with the ever-increasing demands of the people's Parliament.

Charles I (r. 1625–49), inspired by the French idea of the divine right of kings, considered himself above the law, a mistake the Tudors had never made. Reacting to Puritans and other dissenters seeking greater power, he dissolved Parliament, determined to rule without it. The Civil War followed, and the victory went to the Puritan "Roundheads" under Oliver Cromwell. Charles was tried, convicted, and beheaded.

Cromwell, melancholy, unambitious, and a clumsy farmer, became England's virtual dictator. He saw his soldiers as God's faithful servants, promising them rewards in heaven. The English people, however, did not take kindly to this form of government, and after Cromwell's death, Charles II, the dead king's son, returned and was crowned in 1660, but given very limited powers.

building material—brick. England has many half-timbered Tudor and Elizabethan domestic and commercial buildings. This method of construction used brick and plaster between visible wooden timbers.

Elizabethan (1553–1603)   The Renaissance brought a revival of classical features, such as columns, cornices (prominent rooflines with brackets and other details), and pediments (a decorative triangular feature over doorways and windows). The many large houses and palaces of this period were built in an E or H shape and contained long galleries, grand staircases, and carved chimneys.

Jacobean (1603–25)   In England, Inigo Jones used the symmetrical, classically inspired Palladian style that arrived from Italy. Buildings in this style incorporated elements from ancient Greek and Roman buildings.

Stuart (1625–88)   Elegant classical features—such as columns, cornices, and pediments—are typical of this period in which Christopher Wren was the preeminent architect.

Queen Anne (1689–1714)   Buildings from the English baroque period mix heavy ornamentation with classical simplicity.

Georgian and Regency (1714–1830)   During these periods, elegant terraced houses were built; many examples exist in Brighton and Bath. Form and proportion were important elements; interior decoration inspired by Chinese motifs became fashionable.

Victorian (1830–1901)   A whole range of antique styles emerged—everything from Gothic and Greek Revival to pseudo-Egyptian and Elizabethan. Hundreds of English churches were renovated during the Victorian era.

—*Donald Olson*

FROM THE RESTORATION TO THE NAPOLEONIC WARS   The first decade of Charles II's reign saw London decimated by the Great Plague and destroyed by the Great Fire. His successor, James II, attempted to return the country to Catholicism; this so frightened the powers that be that James was deposed in the "Glorious Revolution" of 1688 and succeeded by his daughter Mary II and her husband William (III) of Orange. This secured the Protestant succession that continues to this day. (Catholics were deprived of civil rights for years to come.) William and Mary signed a bill of rights, establishing the principal that the monarch rules not by divine right but by Parliament's will. Mary's sister, Anne (r. 1702–14), was the last Stuart, outliving all her children. Her reign saw the full union of England and Scotland.

After Anne's death, England had to find a Protestant prince to succeed her. They chose George, Elector of Hanover. He took the throne as George I and thus began a 123-year-long dynasty. He spoke only German and spent little time in England; he left the governing to the English politicians and instituted the idea of a prime minister. Under the Hanoverians, the powers of Parliament were extended, and the constitutional monarchy developed into today's system.

Although the American colonies were lost under George III (r. 1760–1820), the British empire grew dramatically. Canada was won from the French in the Seven Years' War, British control over India was affirmed, and Captain Cook claimed Australia and New Zealand for England. The British became embroiled in the Napoleonic Wars (1795–1815), achieving two of their greatest victories and acquiring two of their greatest heroes: Nelson at Trafalgar and Wellington at Waterloo.

THE INDUSTRIAL REVOLUTION & THE REIGN OF VICTORIA

The mid– to late 18th century also saw the beginnings of the Industrial Revolution, which transformed England from a rural, agricultural society into an urban, industrial economy. This development changed the lives of the laboring class, created a wealthy middle class, and made England a world-class financial and military power. Male suffrage was extended; women continued living under a series of civil disabilities for the rest of the century.

When Victoria (r. 1837–1901) ascended the throne, the British monarchy was in ill repute; but her reign, the longest in English history, was an incomparable success. The Victorian era was shaped by the growing power of the bourgeoisie, the queen and her husband's well-publicized moral positions, and the responsibilities of managing a vast empire. During this time, the first trade unions were formed, a state school system developed, and railroads were built. Victoria never recovered from the death of her German husband, Prince Albert, from typhoid fever in 1861; she went into hiding for 3 years, and did not remarry. While she found her many children tiresome, she publicly remained a pillar of family values.

While middle-class values ruled Victorian England, the racy England of the past went underground. Our present-day view of England is still influenced by the "official" attitudes of the Victorian era; we forget that earlier English society was famous for its rowdiness, sexual license, and spicy scandal.

Victoria's son Edward VII (r. 1901–10), who waited too long in the wings, was famous for keeping mistresses and for his love of elaborate dinners. Despite his reign's brevity, it inspired a historical appellation, the Edwardian Age—England was at the height of its imperial power, the motorcar and the telephone radically changed social life, and the women's suffrage movement began.

Prior to World War I, people assumed that peace, progress, prosperity, empire, and social improvement would continue indefinitely. The horrors of the "war to end all wars" and the subsequent social unrest, economic uncertainty, and rise of Nazism and Fascism put an end to such assumptions.

THE WINDS OF WAR

Soon after World War II began (1939), Britain elected a new, inspiring leader, Winston Churchill, who led the nation during its "finest hour." For many months, Britain stood alone against the Axis; the evacuation of Dunkirk, the Blitz of London, and the Battle of Britain were dark hours for the British people. After their American allies joined the British forces, the tide slowly turned, culminating in the D-Day invasion of German-occupied Normandy. These bloody events still fill the British with pride, along with nostalgia for an era when Britain was still a great world power.

The years following World War II brought many changes. Britain began to lose a grip on its empire (India and Pakistan became independent in 1947). The Labour government, in power from 1945, established the welfare state and brought profound social change.

QUEEN ELIZABETH RULES TO THE PRESENT DAY

Upon the death of the beloved "wartime king" George VI, Elizabeth II ascended the throne in

1952. Her reign has seen the erosion of Britain's once-mighty industrial power and more recently, a severe recession.

Political power has seesawed back and forth between the Conservatives (Tories) and Labour. Margaret Thatcher, who became Prime Minister in 1979, seriously undercut the welfare state and was ambivalent toward the European Union. Her popularity soared during the successful Falklands War, when Britain seemed to recover some of its military glory, however briefly.

Although Elizabeth II remained steadfast and punctiliously performed her ceremonial duties, rumors about the royal family abounded. In 1992, a year she described as an "annus horribilis," a devastating fire swept through Windsor Castle, the marriages of several of her children crumbled, and she agreed to pay taxes for the first time. By 1994 and 1995, Britain's economy was improving after several glum years, although Tory Prime Minister John Major was coming under increasing criticism.

The Irish Republican Army (IRA), reportedly enraged at the slow pace of peace talks in Northern Ireland, broke a 17-month cease-fire. In February 1996, a massive bomb in London's Docklands killed two people and injured more than 100. Another bomb went off in Manchester in June.

Headlines about the IRA bombing gave way to another bombshell—the end of the marriage of Princess Diana and Prince Charles. But details of the £42 million ($26 million) divorce settlement didn't satisfy the curious: Scrutiny of Prince Charles's and Princess Diana's personal relationships continued in the tabloid press.

Another shocking revelation, the danger for humans exposed to "Mad Cow Disease," led to panic, caused a reduction in beef sales, and brought about lowered prices. The planned slaughter of Britain's 11 million cows was scrapped because of pressure from beef industry representatives. As scientists predicted, and because of precautions taken by the British government, Mad Cow disease petered out in 2001.

With John Major and the Tories reeling from these and other events, it seemed inevitable that in May 1997 the Labour Party, led by Tony Blair, would end 18 years of Tory rule in a landslide.

Blair's election had many British entrepreneurs ready to take advantage of what they saw as enthusiasm for new ideas and ventures. London, certainly, was being acclaimed by the global press for a renaissance in the realms of art, music, fashion, and dining.

Events turned abruptly horrific in August 1997, when Princess Diana was killed with two others in a high-speed, paparazzi-dodging car crash in Paris. "The People's Princess" remains an iconic and much-loved figure for millions.

Although the royal family doesn't rule Britain anymore, the monarchy's future remains a hot topic of discussion in Britain. Despite wide criticism of the royal family's behavior in the wake of Diana's death, polls label three-quarters of the British populace as in favor of the institution's continuation. Even Prince Charles is making a comeback, appearing in public with his longtime mistress, Camilla Parker-Bowles. At the very least, the monarchy is good for the tourist trade, on which Britain is increasingly dependent. And what would the tabloids do without it?

The true spotlight remains on Tony Blair, who continues to pursue a program of constitutional reform without parallel in this century. Some fear that Blair's devolutionary policies will one day produce a "dis-United Kingdom," with an independent Scotland (it now has its own Parliament) and a self-governing Northern Ireland (as per the 1998 Good Friday accords).

At the dawn of the millennium, major social changes occurred in Britain. No sooner had the year 2000 begun than Britain announced a change of its code of conduct for the military, allowing openly gay men and women to serve in the armed forces. The action followed a European court ruling in the fall of 1999 that forbade Britain to discriminate against homosexuals. This change brings Britain in line with almost all other NATO countries, including France, Canada, and Germany. (The United States remains at variance with the trend, with its "don't ask, don't tell" policy.)

Economic woes dogged Britain as the 21st century dawned. In the wake of mad cow disease flare-ups, the country was swept by a foot-and-mouth disease epidemic that disrupted the country's agriculture. Hundreds of thousands of animals were put to death to stem the spread of the epidemic, and farmers wept on camera over the destruction of their livelihoods. The crisis threatened one of the major sources of British livelihoods, its entrenched tourist industry, which lost billions of pounds in revenue.

Following the terrorist attacks on New York City and Washington, D.C., on September 11, 2001, Tony Blair and his government joined in a show of support for the United States, condemning the aerial bombardments and loss of life. Not only that, British joined in the war in Afghanistan against the dreaded Taliban.

In 2003, Tony Blair once again, in spite of massive opposition at home and on the continent, backed the United States and ordered British forces to Iraq to join American troops in toppling Saddam Hussein, bringing an end to a reign of terror but unleashing new problems domestically as that country struggles to redefine itself.

2 Pies, Pudding & Pints: The Lowdown on British Cuisine

The late British humorist George Mikes wrote that "the Continentals have good food; the English have good table manners." But the British no longer deserve their reputation for soggy cabbage and tasteless dishes. Contemporary London—and the country as a whole—boasts many fine restaurants and sophisticated cuisine.

There's a lot more to British food today than the traditional roast, which has been celebrated since long before the days of Henry VIII. Of course, parsnip soup is still served, but now it's likely to be graced with a dollop of walnut salsa verde. In contemporary England, the modern chef has taken on celebrity status. The creator of breast of Gressingham duck topped with deep-fried seaweed and served with a passion fruit sauce is honored the way rock stars were in the 1970s. Some restaurants are so popular that they are demanding reservations 2 weeks in advance, if not more.

If you want to see what Britain is eating today, just drop in at Harvey Nichol's fifth floor in London's Knightsbridge for its dazzling display of produce from all over the globe.

The new buzzword for British cuisine is *magpie,* meaning borrowing ideas from global travels, taking them home, and improving on the original.

Be aware that many of the trendiest, most innovative restaurants are mind-blowingly expensive, especially in London. We've pointed out some innovative but affordable choices in this book, but if you're really trying to save on dining costs, you'll no doubt find yourself falling back on the traditional pub favorites (or better still, turning to an increasingly good selection of ethnic restaurants).

WHAT YOU'LL FIND ON THE MENU   On any pub menu you're likely to encounter such dishes as the Cornish pasty and shepherd's pie. The first, traditionally made from Sunday-meal leftovers and taken by West Country fishers for Monday lunch, consists of chopped potatoes, carrots, and onions mixed together with seasoning and put into a pastry envelope. The second is a deep dish of chopped cooked lamb mixed with onions and seasoning, covered with a layer of mashed potatoes, and served hot. Another version is cottage pie, which is minced beef covered with potatoes and also served hot. In addition to a pasty, Cornwall also gives us "Stargazy Pie"—a deep-dish fish pie with a crisp crust covering a creamy concoction of freshly caught herring and vegetables.

The most common pub meal, though, is the ploughman's lunch, traditional farmworker's fare, consisting of a good chunk of local cheese, a hunk of home-made crusty white or brown bread, some butter, and a pickled onion or two, washed down with ale. You'll now find such variations as pâté and chutney occasionally replacing the onions and cheese. Or you might find Lancashire hot pot, a stew of mutton, potatoes, kidneys, and onions (sometimes carrots). This concoction was originally put into a deep dish and set on the edge of the stove to cook slowly while the workers spent the day at the local mill.

Among appetizers, called "starters" in England, the most typical are potted shrimp (small buttered shrimp preserved in a jar), prawn cocktail, and smoked salmon. You might also be served pâté or "fish pie," which is a very light fish pâté. Most menus will feature a variety of soups, including cock-a-leekie (chicken soup flavored with leeks), perhaps a game soup that has been doused with sherry, and many others.

Among the best-known traditional English meals is roast beef and Yorkshire pudding (the pudding is made with a flour base and cooked under the roast, allowing the fat from the meat to drop onto it). The beef could easily be a large sirloin (rolled loin), which, so the story goes, was named by James I when he was a guest at Houghton Tower, Lancashire. "Arise, Sir Loin," he cried, as he knighted the leg of beef before him with his dagger. Another dish that makes use of a flour base is toad-in-the-hole, in which sausages are cooked in batter. Game, especially pheasant and grouse, is also a staple on British tables.

On any menu, you'll find fresh seafood: cod, haddock, herring, plaice, and Dover sole, the aristocrat of flatfish. Cod and haddock are used in making British fish and chips (chips are fried potatoes or thick french fries), which the true Briton covers with salt and vinegar. If you like oysters, try some of the famous Colchester variety. On the west coast, you'll find a not-to-be-missed delicacy: Morecambe Bay shrimp. Every region of England has its seafood specialties. In Ely, lying in the marshy fen district of East Anglia, it might be fenland eel pie with a twiggy seaweed as your green vegetable.

The East End of London has quite a few interesting old dishes, among them tripe and onions. In winter, Dr. Johnson's favorite tavern, the Cheshire Cheese on Fleet Street, offers a beefsteak-kidney-mushroom-and-game pudding in a suet case; in summer, there's a pastry case. East Enders can still be seen on Sunday at the Jellied Eel stall by Petticoat Lane, eating eel, cockles (small clams), mussels, whelks, and winkles—all with a touch of vinegar.

The British call desserts "sweets," although some people still refer to any dessert as "pudding." Trifle is the most famous English dessert, consisting of sponge cake soaked in brandy or sherry, coated with fruit or jam, and topped with cream custard. A "fool," such as gooseberry fool, is a light cream dessert whipped up from seasonal fruits. Regional sweets include the northern "flitting"

A Beer Primer: Are You Bitter or Stout?

Most of the pubs in the United Kingdom are tied to a particular brewery and sell only that brewery's beers (an outside sign displays the brewery name). Independent pubs can sell more brands than a tied pub. Either way, you still have to choose from what may seem like a bewildering variety of brews. The colorful names of individual brews don't provide much help—you can only wonder what Pigswell, Dogs Bollocks, Hobgoblin, Old Thumper, or Boondoggle taste like. The taste of any beer, whether on draught or in a bottle, is crafted by the brewery and depends on all sorts of factors: the water, the hops, the fermentation technique, and so on. You can get a few U.S. and international brands, but imports are more expensive than the home-grown products.

When you order beer in a pub, you need to specify the type, the brand, and the amount (pint or half-pint) that you want. Asking the bartender to recommend something based on your taste preferences is perfectly okay. Here are some brief descriptions that may come in handy in a pub:

- **Bitter,** what most locals drink, is a clear, yellowish traditional beer with a strong flavor of hops.

- **Real ale** is a bitter that's still fermenting (alive) when it arrives from the brewery and is pumped and served immediately.

- **Ale** isn't as strong as bitter and has a slightly sweeter taste. You can order light or pale ale in a bottle; export ale is a stronger variety.

- **Lager,** when chilled, is probably closest to an American-style beer. Lager is available in bottles or on draught.

- **Shandy,** equal parts bitter and lemonade (sometimes limeade or ginger beer, a nonalcoholic, very gingery ginger ale), is for those individuals who like a sweet beverage that's only partially beery.

- **Stout** is a dark, rich, creamy version of ale. Guinness is the most popular brand. A black and tan is half lager and half stout.

—Donald Olson

dumpling (dates, walnuts, and syrup mixed with other ingredients and made into a pudding that is easily sliced and carried along when you're "flitting" from place to place). Similarly, hasty pudding, a Newcastle dish, is supposed to have been invented by people in a hurry to avoid the bailiff. It consists of stale bread, to which some dried fruit and milk are added before it is put into the oven.

Cheese is traditionally served after dessert as a savory. There are many regional cheeses, the best known being cheddar, a good, solid, mature cheese. Others are the semi-smooth Caerphilly—from a beautiful part of Wales—and Stilton, a blue-veined crumbly cheese that's often enriched with a glass of port.

ENGLISH BREAKFASTS & AFTERNOON TEA   Britain is famous for its enormous breakfast of bacon, eggs, grilled tomato, and fried bread. Some places have replaced this cholesterol festival with a continental breakfast, but you'll still find the traditional morning meal available.

Kipper, or smoked herring, is also a popular breakfast dish. The finest come from the Isle of Man, Whitby, or Loch Fyne, in Scotland. The herrings are split open, placed over oak chips, and slowly cooked to produce a nice pale-brown smoked fish.

Many people still enjoy afternoon tea. This may consist of a simple cup of tea or a formal tea that starts with tiny crustless sandwiches filled with cucumber or watercress and proceeds through scones, crumpets with jam, or clotted cream, followed by cakes and tarts—all accompanied by a proper pot of tea. The tea at Brown's, in London, is quintessentially English, whereas the Ritz's tea is an elaborate affair, complete with orchestra and dancing.

In the country, tea shops abound, and in Devon, Cornwall, and the West Country, you'll find the best cream teas; they consist of scones spread with jam and thick, clotted Devonshire cream. It's a delicious treat, indeed. People in Britain drink an average of four cups of tea a day, although many younger people prefer coffee.

WHAT TO WASH IT ALL DOWN WITH   English pubs serve a variety of cocktails, but their stock-in-trade is beer (see the box "A Beer Primer: Are You Bitter or Stout?" above). The standard English draft beer is much stronger than American beer and is served "with the chill off," because it doesn't taste good cold. Lager is always chilled, whereas stout can be served either way. Beer is always served straight from the tap, in two sizes: half-pint (8 oz.) and pint (16 oz.).

One of the most significant changes in English drinking habits has been the popularity of wine bars, and you will find many to try, including some that turn into discos late at night. Britain isn't known for its wine, although it does produce some medium-sweet fruity whites. Its cider, though, is famous—and mighty potent in contrast to the American variety.

Whisky (spelled without the *e*) refers to scotch. Canadian and Irish whiskey (spelled with the *e*) are also available, but only the best-stocked bars have American bourbon and rye.

While you're in England, you may want to try the very English drink called Pimm's, a mixture developed by James Pimm, owner of a popular London oyster house in the 1840s. Although it can be consumed on the rocks, it's usually served as a Pimm's Cup—a drink that will have any number and variety of ingredients, depending on which part of the world (or empire) you're in. Here, just for fun, is a typical recipe: Take a very tall glass and fill it with ice. Add a thin slice of lemon (or orange), a cucumber spike (or a curl of cucumber rind), and 2 ounces of Pimm's liquor. Then finish with a splash of either lemon or club soda, 7-Up, or Tom Collins mix.

The English tend to drink everything at a warmer temperature than Americans are used to. So if you like ice in your soda, be sure to ask for lots of it, or you're likely to end up with a measly, quickly melting cube or two.

Appendix B:
Useful Toll-Free Numbers & Websites

AIRLINES

Aer Lingus
✆ 800/474-7424 in the U.S.
✆ 01/886-8888 in Ireland
www.aerlingus.com

Air Canada
✆ 888/247-2262
www.aircanada.ca

Air France
✆ 800/237-2747 in the U.S.
✆ 0820-820-820 in France
www.airfrance.com

Air New Zealand
✆ 800/262-1234 or -2468 in the U.S.
✆ 800/663-5494 in Canada
✆ 0800/737-767 in New Zealand
www.airnewzealand.com

Alitalia
✆ 800/223-5730 in the U.S.
✆ 8488-65641 in Italy
www.alitalia.it

All Nippon Airways
✆ 800/235-9262 in the U.S.
✆ 0120/029-222 in Japan
www.fly-ana.com

American Airlines
✆ 800/433-7300
www.aa.com

Asiana
✆ 800/227-4262 in the U.S.
✆ 1588-8000 in Korea
www.asiana.co.kr

Austrian Airlines
✆ 800/843-0002 in the U.S.
✆ 43/(0)5-1789 in Austria
www.aua.com

BMI
No U.S. number
www.flybmi.com

British Airways
✆ 800/247-9297 in the U.S.
✆ 0345/222-111 or 0845/77-333-77
  in Britain
www.british-airways.com

Cathay Pacific
✆ 800/233-2742 in the U.S.
✆ 10800/852-1888 in China
www.cathaypacific.com

Continental Airlines
✆ 800/525-0280
www.continental.com

Delta Air Lines
✆ 800/221-1212
www.delta.com

Czech Airlines
✆ 800/223-2365 in the U.S.
✆ 420/224-81-04-26 in
  Czech Republic
www.czechairlines.com

easyJet
No U.S. number
www.easyjet.com

Egyptair
© 800/334-6787 in the U.S.;
   212/315-0900 in New York City
© 3903-444 in Egypt
www.egyptair.com.eg

El Al
© 800/223-6700 in the U.S.;
   212/768-9200 in NY, NJ, CT
© 03/9710000 in Israel
www.elal.co.il

Finnair
© 800/950-5000 in the U.S.
© 358/09-818-800 in Finland
www.finnair.com

Iberia
© 800/772-4642 in the U.S.
© 902/400-500 in Spain
www.iberia.com

Icelandair
© 800/223-5500 in the U.S.
© 354/50-50-100 in Iceland
www.icelandair.is

Japan Airlines
© 800/525/3663 in the U.S.
© 0120/25-5971 in Japan
www.jal.co.jp

KLM
© 800/374-7747 in the U.S.
© 020/4-747-747 in Netherlands
www.klm.nl

Lufthansa
© 800/645-3880 in the U.S.
© 49/(0)-180-5-8384267 in Germany
www.lufthansa.com

Malaysia Airlines
© 800/552-9264 in the U.S.
© 1300/88-3000 in Malaysia
www.malaysiaairlines.com.my

Northwest Airlines
© 800/225-2525
www.nwa.com

Olympic Airways
© 800/223-1226 in the U.S.
© 80/111-44444 in Greece
www.olympic-airways.gr

Qantas
© 800/227-4500 in the U.S.
© 612/9691-3636 in Australia
www.qantas.com

Royal Jordanian
© 800/223-0470 in the U.S.;
   212/949-0050 in New York City
© 567-8321 in Jordan
www.rja.com.jo

Ryanair
No U.S. number
www.ryanair.com

Saudi Arabian Airlines
© 800/472-8342 in the U.S.;
   718/551-3020 in NY, NJ, CT
© 01/488-4444 in Saudi Arabia
www.saudiairlines.com

Scandinavian Airlines
© 800/221-2350 in the U.S.
© 0070/727-727 in Sweden
© 70/10-20-00 in Denmark
© 358/(0)20-386-000 in Finland
© 815/200-400 in Norway
www.scandinavian.net

Singapore Airlines
© 800/742-3333 in the U.S.
© 65/6223-8888 in Singapore
www.singaporeair.com

South African Airways
© 800/722-9675 in the U.S.
© 0861-359722 in South Africa
www.flysaa.com

Swiss International Airlines
© 877/359-7947 in the U.S.
© 0848/85-2000 in Switzerland
www.swiss.com

Thai Airways International
© 800/426-5204 in the U.S.
© (66-2)-535-2081-2 in Thailand
www.thaiair.com

Turkish Airlines
© 800/874-8875 in the U.S.;
   212/339-9650 in NY, NJ, CT
© 90-212-663-63-00 in Turkey
www.flyturkish.com

United Airlines
✆ 800/241-6522
www.united.com

US Airways
✆ 800/428-4322
www.usairways.com

Virgin Atlantic Airways
✆ 800/862-8621 in the
continental U.S.
✆ 0293/747-747 in Britain
www.virgin-atlantic.com

CAR-RENTAL AGENCIES

Alamo
✆ 800/327-9633
www.goalamo.com

Auto Europe
✆ 800/223-5555
www.autoeurope.com

Avis
✆ 800/331-1212 in the
continental U.S.
✆ 800/TRY-AVIS in Canada
www.avis.com

Budget
✆ 800/527-0700
www.budget.com

Hertz
✆ 800/654-3131
www.hertz.com

Kemwel Holiday Auto (KHA)
✆ 800/678-0678
www.kemwel.com

National
✆ 800/CAR-RENT
www.nationalcar.com

Sixt
No U.S. number
www.sixt-europe.com

MAJOR HOTEL CHAINS

Best Western International
✆ 800/528-1234
www.bestwestern.com

Hilton Hotels
✆ 800/HILTONS
www.hilton.com

Holiday Inn
✆ 800/HOLIDAY
www.basshotels.com

Hyatt Hotels & Resorts
✆ 800/228-9000
www.hyatt.com

Inter-Continental Hotels & Resorts
✆ 888/567-8725
www.interconti.com

ITT Sheraton
✆ 800/325-3535
www.starwood.com

Marriott Hotels
✆ 800/228-9290
www.marriott.com

Radisson Hotels International
✆ 800/333-3333
www.radisson.com

Renaissance
✆ 800/228-9290
www.renaissancehotels.com

Sheraton Hotels & Resorts
✆ 800/325-3535
www.sheraton.com

Index

Not just 4 anoraks

...but 3 duffel coats
59 gorgeous models
5 Tube simulators
4 dead man's handles
3 mucky miners
and 1 brilliant time had by all.

... be *moved*

London's Transport
Museum
Covent Garden Piazza

kids go
FREE

www.ltmuseum.co.uk

FROMMER'S® MEMORABLE WALKS

Chicago
London

New York
Paris

San Francisco

FROMMER'S® WITH KIDS GUIDES

Chicago
Las Vegas
New York City

Ottawa
San Francisco
Toronto

Vancouver
Washington, D.C.

SUZY GERSHMAN'S BORN TO SHOP GUIDES

Born to Shop: France
Born to Shop: Hong Kong,
  Shanghai & Beijing

Born to Shop: Italy
Born to Shop: London

Born to Shop: New York
Born to Shop: Paris

FROMMER'S® IRREVERENT GUIDES

Amsterdam
Boston
Chicago
Las Vegas
London

Los Angeles
Manhattan
New Orleans
Paris
Rome

San Francisco
Seattle & Portland
Vancouver
Walt Disney World®
Washington, D.C.

FROMMER'S® BEST-LOVED DRIVING TOURS

Britain
California
Florida
France

Germany
Ireland
Italy
New England

Northern Italy
Scotland
Spain
Tuscany & Umbria

HANGING OUT™ GUIDES

Hanging Out in England
Hanging Out in Europe

Hanging Out in France
Hanging Out in Ireland

Hanging Out in Italy
Hanging Out in Spain

THE UNOFFICIAL GUIDES®

Bed & Breakfasts and Country
  Inns in:
  California
  Great Lakes States
  Mid-Atlantic
  New England
  Northwest
  Rockies
  Southeast
  Southwest
Best RV & Tent Campgrounds in:
  California & the West
  Florida & the Southeast
  Great Lakes States
  Mid-Atlantic
  Northeast
  Northwest & Central Plains

  Southwest & South Central
    Plains
  U.S.A.
Beyond Disney
Branson, Missouri
California with Kids
Central Italy
Chicago
Cruises
Disneyland®
Florida with Kids
Golf Vacations in the Eastern U.S.
Great Smoky & Blue Ridge Region
Inside Disney
Hawaii
Las Vegas
London
Maui

Mexio's Best Beach Resorts
Mid-Atlantic with Kids
Mini Las Vegas
Mini-Mickey
New England & New York with
  Kids
New Orleans
New York City
Paris
San Francisco
Skiing & Snowboarding in the West
Southeast with Kids
Walt Disney World®
Walt Disney World® for
  Grown-ups
Walt Disney World® with Kids
Washington, D.C.
World's Best Diving Vacations

SPECIAL-INTEREST TITLES

Frommer's Adventure Guide to Australia &
  New Zealand
Frommer's Adventure Guide to Central America
Frommer's Adventure Guide to India & Pakistan
Frommer's Adventure Guide to South America
Frommer's Adventure Guide to Southeast Asia
Frommer's Adventure Guide to Southern Africa
Frommer's Britain's Best Bed & Breakfasts and
  Country Inns
Frommer's Caribbean Hideaways
Frommer's Exploring America by RV
Frommer's Fly Safe, Fly Smart

Frommer's France's Best Bed & Breakfasts and
  Country Inns
Frommer's Gay & Lesbian Europe
Frommer's Italy's Best Bed & Breakfasts and
  Country Inns
Frommer's Road Atlas Britain
Frommer's Road Atlas Europe
Frommer's Road Atlas France
The New York Times' Guide to Unforgettable
  Weekends
Places Rated Almanac
Retirement Places Rated
Rome Past & Present

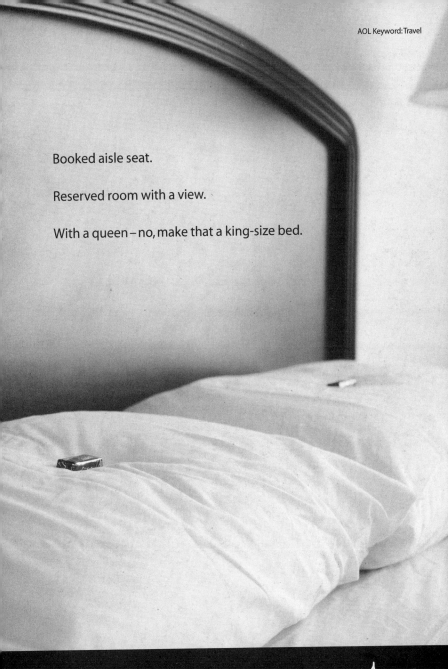

Booked aisle seat.

Reserved room with a view.

With a queen – no, make that a king-size bed.

With Travelocity, you can book your flights and hotels together, so you can get even better deals than if you booked them separately. You'll save time and money without compromising the quality of your trip. Choose your airline seat, search for alternate airports, pick your hotel room type, even choose the neighborhood you'd like to stay in.

Travelocity

Visit www.travelocity.com or call 1-888-TRAVELOCITY

AOL Keyword: Travel

Fly.
Sleep.
Save.

Now you can book your flights and
hotels together, so you can get even better deals
than if you booked them separately.

Travelocity
Visit www.travelocity.com
or call 1-888-TRAVELOCITY